ASCO-SEP®

MEDICAL ONCOLOGY SELF-EVALUATION PROGRAM

SEVENTH EDITION

EDITOR

Benjamin P. Levy, MD

ASSOCIATE EDITORS

Jill Lacy, MD
Tara C. Mitchell, MD
S. Vincent Rajkumar, MD
Scott M. Schuetze, MD, PhD

AUTHORS

Anthony J. Alberg, PhD, MPH
Karla V. Ballman, PhD
Judy C. Boughey, MD
Dean E. Brenner, MD, FASCO
Keith A. Casper, MD
Daniel V. Catenacci, MD
Joseph I. Clark, MD, FACP
Don S. Dizon, MD, FACP, FASCO
David J. Einstein, MD
Marc B. Garnick, MD
Jonathan E. Grim, MD, PhD
Lee P. Hartner, MD
Matthias M. Holdhoff, MD, PhD
Ravindran Kanesvaran, BSc, MD, MRCP, FAMS
Georgia S. Karachaliou MD, MSc
Jonathan L. Kaufman, MD
Jill M. Kolesar, Pharm D, FCCP, BCPS
Amrita Krishnan, MD
Thomas W. LeBlanc, MD
Mark R. Litzow, MD
Stephen V. Liu, MD
Sagar Lonial MD, FACP
Filipa C. Lynce, MD
Michelle L. Mierzwa, MD
Supriya G. Mohile, MD, MS, FASCO
Stergios J. Moschos, MD
Rodrigo Ramella Munhoz, MD
Ariela M. Noy, MD
Maria Raquel Nunes, MD
Blase N. Polite, MD, MPP, FASCO
Eric J. Roeland, MD
Erin Salo-Mullen, MS, GCG
Aditi Shastri, MBBS
Zofia K. Stadler, MD
Francis P. Worden, MD

2318 Mill Road, Suite 800
Alexandria, VA 22314
ISBN Print: 978-1-951909-00-0
ISBN online: 978-1-951909-01-7

Permission requests should be directed to:
Rights and Permissions
American Society of Clinical Oncology
2318 Mill Road, Suite 800
Alexandria, VA 22314
Phone: 571-483-1722
Email: permissions@asco.org

Editorial correspondence should be directed to:
Education, Science, and Professional Development Department—ASCO-SEP®
American Society of Clinical Oncology
2318 Mill Road, Suite 800
Alexandria, VA 22314
Phone: 888-282-2552
Email: elearning@asco.org

Printed in the United States of America.

Cover photograph, **credit to** Getty Images (vitanovski), used with permission.

LETTER FROM THE EDITOR

Dear Colleague:

On behalf of ASCO, I am pleased to present the 7th edition of *ASCO-SEP®: Medical Oncology Self-Evaluation Program.* This self-assessment resource is designed to give a comprehensive overview of the current landscape of medical oncology. In doing so, we hope to achieve several aims including assessing the latest practice changing updates in oncology, assisting in the maintenance of certification (MOC), and providing resources to aid in the everyday care of individual oncology patients. Given the increasing complexity of oncology care, deliberate efforts for this edition have been made to facilitate learning and retention. This includes the addition of more illustrations, tables, algorithms, and limiting references to key manuscripts to prioritize the data reviewed. With this edition, we are launching ASCO eBooks, an eReader app, and online book. The app and online experience will implement the capability to take notes, search capabilities within the book, and bookmark important information, as well as embedded graphics and videos for additional resources for the "on-the-go" learner.

ASCO-SEP® is a comprehensive learning tool that includes 22 chapters, focusing on specific disease sites and oncology topics, as well as over 80 multiple-choice questions that can be used for self-study which will be updated annually. With several new authors joining us for this edition including fellowship training program directors, the chapter content has been updated from the last edition to reflect the changing landscape of the field and redesigned to help learners navigate the complexity of cancer care. Given the need for engagement of providers outside of the US, all chapters include a new global perspective to underscore important differences in oncology care in different regions. Similar to past editions, each chapter has a self-assessment which can be completed to obtain credit to allow assessment of knowledge.

This *ASCO-SEP®* 7th Edition would not have been possible without the efforts of the outstanding Associate Editors, who dedicated substantial time, commitment, and resources to ensure the high quality of the content: Jill Lacy, MD, Tara C. Mitchell, MD, S. Vincent Rajkumar, MD, and Scott Schuetze, MD. The success of this publication was also predicated on the time and dedication of both the chapter authors, question writers, global contributors, and peer reviewers, who graciously shared their expertise. Of course, none of this could have come to fruition without the focus and organization of the ASCO staff who contributed an enormous amount of time, effort, and expertise to the publication.

Thank you for participating in this worthwhile continuing medical education program. If you have comments or suggestions regarding *ASCO-SEP®*, please send an e-mail to elearning@asco.org.

Sincerely,

Benjamin Levy, MD

Benjamin P. Levy, MD
Editor, *ASCO-SEP®* 7th Edition

EDITOR BIOGRAPHIES

Editor in Chief

Benjamin P. Levy, MD, is the Clinical Director of medical oncology for the Johns Hopkins Sidney Kimmel Cancer Center at Sibley Memorial Hospital, as well as an associate professor of oncology for Johns Hopkins University School of Medicine. He serves on the ALLIANCE Respiratory Committee, the IASLC Staging Committee, and the IASLC Career Development & Fellowship Committee.

Associate Editors

Jill Lacy, MD, is Professor of Medicine in the Section of Medical Oncology at Yale School of Medicine. She is actively involved in education as Director of the Medical Oncology-Hematology Fellowship at Yale University and has served on national committees focused on optimizing the education of Medical Oncology trainees and recruiting minority students to careers in Oncology.

Tara C. Mitchell, MD, is an Assistant Professor of Medicine at the University of Pennsylvania's Abramson Cancer Center where she leads the clinical trials program in melanoma and cutaneous malignancies.

S. Vincent Rajkumar, MD, is an Edward W. and Betty Knight Scripps Professor of Medicine and Consultant in the Division of Hematology at the Mayo Clinic, Rochester, Minnesota. He serves as co-chair of the International Myeloma Working Group, and chair of the NCI ECOG-ACRIN myeloma steering committee.

Scott M. Schuetze, MD, PhD, is Clinical Professor of Medicine in the Division of Hematology/Oncology, University of Michigan Comprehensive Cancer Center. He is the Director of the Connective Tissue Oncology Program in the University of Michigan Comprehensive Cancer Center and Medical Co-Director of the Oncology Clinical Trials Support Unit in Michigan Medicine.

CONTRIBUTORS

EDITORIAL BOARD

Benjamin P. Levy, MD – Editor in Chief
Johns Hopkins Sidney Kimmel Cancer Center
Washington, DC

Jill Lacy, MD
Yale Cancer Center
New Haven, CT

S. Vincent Rajkumar, MD
Mayo Clinic
Rochester, MN

Scott M. Schuetze, MD, PhD
University of Michigan
Ann Arbor, MI

Tara C. Mitchell, MD
Perelman School of Medicine, University of Pennsylvania
Philadelphia, PA

CHAPTER 1: EPIDEMIOLOGY AND PREVENTION

Anthony J. Alberg, PhD, MPH
University of South Carolina
Columbia, SC

Dean E. Brenner, MD, FASCO
University of Michigan
Ann Arbor, MI

GLOBAL CONTRIBUTOR:

Surendranath S. Shastri, MBBS, MD, DPh
The University of Texas MD Anderson Cancer Center
Houston, TX

REVIEWERS:

Benjamin Haaland, PhD
Huntsman Cancer Institute, University of Utah
Salt Lake City, UT

Noelle K. LoConte, MD
University of Wisconsin
Madison, WI

Eva Szabo, MD
National Cancer Institute
Bethesda, MD

Adrienne Nedved, PharmD, MPA BCOP
Mayo Clinic
Rochester, MN

Rachael L. Schmidt, APRN-NP
Fred & Pamela Buffett Cancer Center
Omaha, NE

CHAPTER 2: MOLECULAR BIOLOGY

Jonathan E. Grim, MD, PhD
Fred Hutchinson Cancer Research Center
Seattle, WA

GLOBAL CONTRIBUTOR:

Shahin Sayed, MBChB, MMED
Aga Khan University Hospital
Nairobi

REVIEWERS:

Mark E. Burkard, MD, PhD
University of Wisconsin School of Medicine
Madison, WI

Patrick J. Kiel, PharmD, BCBS, BCOP, FHOPA
Indiana University (IU) Simon Cancer Center
Indianapolis, IN

Teresa J. Knoop, MSN, RN, AOCN®
Vanderbilt Ingram Cancer Center
Nashville, TN

Michael L. Maitland, MD, PhD
Inova Schar Cancer Institute
Falls Church, VA

Daniel Shao-Weng Tan, MD
National Cancer Centre Singapore
Singapore

CHAPTER 3: CLINICAL PHARMACOLOGY

Jill M. Kolesar, PharmD, FCCP, BCPS
University of Kentucky
Lexington, KY

GLOBAL CONTRIBUTOR:

Alex Sparreboom, PhD
The Ohio State University Comprehensive Cancer Center
Columbus, OH

Shuiying Hu, PhD
The Ohio State University Comprehensive Cancer Center
Columbus, OH

REVIEWERS:

Eric Chen, PhD, MD
Princess Margaret Cancer Centre
Toronto, Ontario, Canada

Edward Chu, MD
University of Pittsburgh Cancer Institute
Pittsburgh, PA

R. Donald Harvey, PharmD, BCOP, FCCP, FHOPA
Winship Cancer Institute of Emory University
Atlanta, GA

Colleen M. Lewis, NP
Winship Cancer Institute of Emory University
Atlanta, GA

Mary S. Mably, RPh, BCOP
University of Wisconsin
Madison, WI

CHAPTER 4: PRINCIPLES OF IMMUNO-ONCOLOGY AND BIOLOGIC THERAPY

Joseph I. Clark, MD, FACP
Loyola University Medical Center
Chicago, IL

Rodrigo Ramella Munhoz, MD
Hospital Sírio-Libanês
São Paulo, Brazil

GLOBAL CONTRIBUTOR:

Paolo A. Ascierto, MD
Instituto Nazionale Tumori
Naples, Italy

REVIEWERS:

Flávia De Angelis, MD
Université de Sherbrooke
Quebec, Canada

Brianna W. Hoffner, NP, MSN, RN
University of Colorado Hospital
Aurora, CO

Whitney E. Lewis, RPh, PharmD, BCOP
The University of Texas MD Anderson Cancer Center
Houston, TX

Douglas G. McNeel, MD
University of Wisconsin
Madison, WI

Michael A. Postow, MD
Memorial Sloan Kettering Cancer Center
New York, NY

CHAPTER 5: CLINICAL TRIALS AND BIOSTATISTICS

Karla V. Ballman, PhD
Weill Cornell Medical College
New York, NY

Judy C. Boughey, MD
Mayo Clinic
Rochester, MN

GLOBAL CONTRIBUTOR:

Edith A. Perez, MD
Mayo Clinic
Jacksonville, FL

REVIEWERS:

Jonathan S. Bleeker, MD
Sanford Cancer Center
Sioux Falls, SD

Benjamin Haaland, PhD
Huntsman Cancer Institute, University of Utah
Salt Lake City, UT

R. Donald Harvey, PharmD, BCOP, FCCP, FHOPA
Winship Cancer Institute of Emory University
Atlanta, GA

Colleen M. Lewis, NP
Winship Cancer Institute of Emory University
Atlanta, GA

Daniel Zelterman, PhD
Yale Cancer Center
New Haven, CT

CHAPTER 6: GENETIC TESTING FOR HEREDITARY CANCER SYNDROMES

Erin Salo-Mullen, MS, GCG
Memorial Sloan Kettering Cancer Center
New York, NY

Zofia K. Stadler, MD
Memorial Sloan Kettering Cancer Center
New York, NY

GLOBAL CONTRIBUTOR:

Judith Balmaña Gelpi, MD, PhD
Vall d'Hebron University Hospital
Barcelona, Spain

REVIEWERS:

Susan E. Chmael, NP
Yale New Haven Hospital
New Haven, CT

Heather L. Hampel, MS, LGC
The Ohio State University Comprehensive Cancer Center
Columbus, OH

Erin W. Hofstatter, MD
Yale Cancer Center
New Haven, CT

Patrick J. Kiel, PharmD, BCBS, BCOP, FHOPA
Indiana University (IU) Simon Cancer Center
Indianapolis, IN

Joanne Ngeow Yuen Yie, BMedSci, MBBS, FRCP, MPH, FAMS
National Cancer Centre Singapore
Singapore

CHAPTER 7: CANCER IN THE OLDER PATIENT

Ravindran Kanesvaran, BSc, MD, MRCP, FAMS
National Cancer Centre Singapore
Singapore

Supriya Mohile, MD, MS, FASCO
James Wilmot Cancer Institute at the University of Rochester
Rochester, NY

GLOBAL CONTRIBUTOR:

Enrique Soto Perez De Celis, MD, MSc
Instituto Nacional de Ciencias Médicas y Nutrición Salvador Zubirán
Mexico City, Mexico

REVIEWERS:

Alice Kindschuh, DNP, APRN-CNS, GCNS-BC
Nebraska Methodist College
Omaha, NE

Heidi D. Klepin, MD
Wake Forest Baptist Health
Lexington, NC

Adrienne Nedved, PharmD, MPA, BCOP
Mayo Clinic
Rochester, MN

Razvan A. Popescu, MD
Hirslanden Medical Center
Aarau, Switzerland

James Wallace, MD
University of Chicago Medicine Ingalls Memorial
Harvey, IL

CHAPTER 8: PAIN AND SYMPTOM MANAGEMENT

Eric Roeland, MD
Massachusetts General Hospital Cancer Center
Boston, MA

GLOBAL CONTRIBUTOR:

Marie T. Fallon, MD
University of Edinburgh
Edinburgh, United Kingdom

REVIEWERS:

Victoria Caulfield MSN, APRN, FNP-C, AOCNP, CCRN
Northwestern Medicine
Chicago, IL

Dawn L. Hershman, MD, MS, FASCO
Herbert Irving Comprehensive Cancer Center at Columbia University
New York, NY

Razvan A. Popescu, MD
Hirslanden Medical Center
Aarau, Switzerland

Susan G. Urba, MD
University of Michigan
Ann Arbor, MI

Tanya J. Uritsky, PharmD, BCPS
Perelman School of Medicine, University of Pennsylvania
Philadelphia, PA

Michael A. Smith, PharmD, BCPS
University of Michigan
Ann Arbor, MI

CHAPTER 9: PALLIATIVE CARE AND CARE AT THE END OF LIFE

Thomas W. LeBlanc, MD
Duke University School of Medicine
Durham, NC

GLOBAL CONTRIBUTOR:

Camilla Zimmerman, MD
University of Toronto
Toronto, Canada

REVIEWERS:

Toby C. Campbell, MD, MS
University of Wisconsin Carbone Cancer Center
Madison, WI

Kathleen Clifford, NP
St. Luke's Mountain States Tumor Institute
Boise, ID

Razvan A. Popescu, MD
Hirslanden Medical Center
Aarau, Switzerland

Cardinale B. Smith, MD, PhD
Tisch Cancer Institute, Icahn School of Medicine at Mount Sinai
New York, NY

Tanya J. Uritsky, PharmD, BCPS
Perelman School of Medicine, University of Pennsylvania
Philadelphia, PA

CHAPTER 10: BREAST CANCER

Filipa C. Lynce, MD
MedStar Georgetown University Hospital Lombardi Comprehensive Cancer Center
Washington, DC

Maria Raquel Nunes, MD
Sidney Kimmel Comprehensive Cancer Center
Johns Hopkins School of Medicine
Washington, DC

GLOBAL CONTRIBUTOR:

Evangelia D. Razis, MD, PhD
Hygeia Hospital
Athens, Greece

REVIEWERS:

Layth Mula-Hussain, MB ChB, CCI, MSc, JB, EF
Cross Cancer Institute, University of Alberta
Edmonton, Canada

Kate Jeffers, PharmD, MHA, BCOP
University of Colorado Health
Aurora, CO

Catherine E. Klein, MD
Denver Veterans Affairs Medical Center
Aurora, CO

Jacquelyn H. Lauria, NP
Rutgers Cancer Institute of New Jersey
New Brunswick, NJ

Tiffany A. Traina, MD
Memorial Sloan Kettering Cancer Center
New York, NY

CHAPTER 11: LUNG CANCER

Stephen V. Liu, MD
Georgetown University Medical Center
Washington, DC

GLOBAL CONTRIBUTORS:

Herbert H.F. Loong, MD
Prince of Wales Hospital
Hong Kong, China

Tony S. K. Mok, BMSc, MD, FRCP(C), FRCP (Edin.), FHKCP, FHKAM (Medicine), FASCO
The Chinese University of Hong Kong
Hong Kong, China

REVIEWERS:

Joshua M. Bauml, MD
Perelman School of Medicine, University of Pennsylvania
Philadelphia, PA

Lisa Carter-Harris, NP
Memorial Sloan Kettering Cancer Center
New York, NY

Scott N. Gettinger, MD
Yale Cancer Center
New Haven, CT

Ashley E. Glode, PharmD, BCOP
University of Colorado
Aurora, CO

Gilberto de Lima Lopes Jr., MD, MBA, FAMS, FASCO
Sylvester Comprehensive Cancer Center
Miami, FL

CHAPTER 12: HEAD AND NECK CANCER

Francis P. Worden, MD
University of Michigan
Ann Arbor, MI

Keith A. Casper, MD
University of Michigan
Ann Arbor, MI

Michelle L. Mierzwa, MD
University of Michigan
Ann Arbor, MI

GLOBAL CONTRIBUTORS:

Petr Szturz, MD, PhD
Lausanne University Hospital
Lausanne, Switzerland

Jan B. Vermorken, MD
University of Antwerp
Antwerpen, Belgium

REVIEWERS:

Ezra E.W. Cohen, MD, FRCPC, FASCO
University of California San Diego
San Diego, CA

Anil D'Cruz, MD
Tata Memorial Hospital
Mumbai, India

Ashley E. Glode, PharmD, BCOP
University of Colorado
Aurora, CO

Jennifer E. Jacky, MSN, ARNP
Seattle Cancer Care Alliance, University of Washington School of Medicine
Seattle, WA

Ranee M. Mehra, MD
Marlene and Stewart Greenebaum Comprehensive Cancer Center
Baltimore, MD

CHAPTER 13: GASTROINTESTINAL CANCERS

Daniel V. Catenacci, MD
University of Chicago
Chicago, IL

Blase N. Polite, MD, MPP, FASCO
The University of Chicago Medical Center
Chicago, IL

GLOBAL CONTRIBUTORS:

Kohei Shitara, MD
National Cancer Center Hospital East
Chiba, Japan

Hiroya Taniguchi, MD
Aichi Cancer Center Hospital
Nagoya, Japan

REVIEWERS:

Kristina Frinzi Byers, PharmD, BCOP
Winship Cancer Institute of Emory University
Atlanta, GA

Patricia Gambino, MSN, RN
Abramson Cancer Center, University of Pennsylvania
Philadelphia, PA

Layth Mula-Hussain, MB ChB, CCI, MSc, JB, EF
Cross Cancer Institute, University of Alberta
Edmonton, Canada

Charles D. Lopez, MD, PhD
Oregon Health & Science University
Portland, OR

Kim A. Reiss Binder, MD
Perelman School of Medicine, University of Pennsylvania
Philadelphia, PA

CHAPTER 14: GENITOURINARY CANCERS

David J. Einstein, MD
Beth Israel Deaconess Medical Center
Boston, MA

Marc B. Garnick, MD
Beth Israel Deaconess Medical Center
Boston, MA

GLOBAL CONTRIBUTORS:

Cora N. Sternberg, MD
Weill Cornell Medicine
New York, NY

Dario Trapani, MD
European Institute of Oncology
Milan, Italy

Alexandru E. Eniu, MD, PhD
Cancer Institute Ion Chiricuta
Cluj-Napoca, Romania

REVIEWERS:

Christine Cambareri, PharmD, BCPS, BCOP, CSP
Penn Medicine, University of Pennsylvania Health System
Philadelphia, PA

Layth Mula-Hussain, MB ChB, CCI, MSc, JB, EF
Cross Cancer Institute, University of Alberta
Edmonton, Canada

Emily A. Lemke, DNP, AGPCNP-BC, AOCNP
The University of Texas MD Anderson Cancer Center
Houston, TX

Alicia K. Morgans, MD, MPH
Robert H. Lurie Comprehensive Cancer Center
Chicago, IL

Sumanta Kumar Pal, MD
City of Hope Comprehensive Cancer Center
Duarte, CA

CHAPTER 15: GYNECOLOGIC CANCERS

Don S. Dizon, MD, FACP, FASCO
Lifespan Cancer Institute/Rhode Island Hospital
Providence, RI

GLOBAL CONTRIBUTOR:

Angelica Noriega Rodrigues, MD, PhD
Dom Oncologia
Brazil

REVIEWERS:

Flávia De Angelis, MD
Université de Sherbrooke
Quebec, Canada

Katherine L. Byar, APRN-NP
Nebraska Medicine
Omaha, NE

Linda R. Duska, MD, MPH
University of Virginia
Charlottesville, VA

Kate Jeffers, PharmD, MHA, BCOP
University of Colorado Health
Aurora, CO

Erica M. Stringer-Reasor, MD
University of Alabama Birmingham School of Medicine
Birmingham, AL

CHAPTER 16: MELANOMA AND OTHER SKIN CANCERS

Stergios Moschos, MD
UNC Lineberger Comprehensive Cancer Center
Chapel Hill, NC

Georgia S. Karachaliou MD, MSc
UNC Lineberger Comprehensive Cancer Center
Chapel Hill, NC

GLOBAL CONTRIBUTOR:

Jean Rene V. Clemenceau, MD
Hospital Angeles del Pedregal
Mexico City, Mexico

REVIEWERS:

Flávia De Angelis, MD
Université de Sherbrooke
Quebec, Canada

C. Lance Cowey, MD
Texas Oncology-Baylor Charles A. Sammons Cancer Center
Dallas, TX

Douglas B. Johnson, MD, MSCI
Vanderbilt-Ingram Cancer Center
Nashville, TN

Whitney E. Lewis, PharmD, RPh, BCOP
The University of Texas MD Anderson Cancer Center
Houston, TX

Suzanne McGettigan, CRNP
Abramson Cancer Center, University of Pennsylvania
Philadelphia, PA

CHAPTER 17: SARCOMA

Lee P. Hartner, MD
Perelman School of Medicine, University of Pennsylvania
Philadelphia, PA

GLOBAL CONTRIBUTOR:

A.J. Gelderblom, MD
Leiden University Medical Center
Leiden, Netherlands

REVIEWERS:

Leah Clark, NP
H. Lee Moffitt Cancer Center
Tampa, FL

Sandra P. D'Angelo, MD
Memorial Sloan Kettering Cancer Center
New York, NY

Kristina Frinzi Byers, PharmD, BCOP
Winship Cancer Institute of Emory University
Atlanta, GA

Gilberto de Lima Lopes Jr., MD, MBA, FAMS, FASCO
Sylvester Comprehensive Cancer Center
Miami, FL

Breelyn A. Wilky, MD
University of Colorado Anschutz Medical Campus
Aurora, Colorado

CHAPTER 18: CENTRAL NERVOUS SYSTEM TUMORS

Matthias M. Holdhoff, MD, PhD
Johns Hopkins Sidney Kimmel Comprehensive Cancer Center
Baltimore, MD

GLOBAL CONTRIBUTOR:

Lawrence Cher, MBBS, FRACP
Austin Health
Melbourne, Australia

REVIEWERS:

Isabel C. Arrillaga-Romany, MD, PhD
Massachusetts General Hospital Cancer Center
Boston, MA

Monika Laurans, APRN
Yale Cancer Center
New Haven, CT

Adrienne Nedved, PharmD, MPA BCOP
Mayo Clinic
Rochester, MN

Reena P. Thomas, MD PhD
Stanford University Hospital
Stanford, CA

Martin J. Van Den Bent, MD, PhD
Daniel den Hoed Cancer Center
Rotterdam, Netherlands

CHAPTER 19: LEUKEMIAS AND OTHER MYELOID NEOPLASMS

Mark R. Litzow, MD
Mayo Clinic
Rochester, MN

Aditi Shastri, MBBS
Montefiore Medical Center
Bronx, NY

GLOBAL CONTRIBUTOR:

Itaru Matsumura, MD, PhD
Kindai University
Osaka, Japan

REVIEWERS:

Inhye E. Ahn, MD
National Cancer Institute
Bethesda, MD

Harry P. Erba, MD, PhD
Duke University School of Medicine
Durham, NC

Christopher A. Fausel, PharmD, MHA, BCOP
Indiana University School of Medicine
Indianapolis, IN

Phillip Scheinberg, MD
Hospital Sao Jose, Beneficencia Portuguesa de Sao Paolo
Sao Paolo, Brazil

Darci L. Zblewski, APRN, CNP
Mayo Clinic
Rochester, MN

CHAPTER 20: LYMPHOMAS

Ariela Noy, MD
Memorial Sloan Kettering Cancer Center
New York, NY

GLOBAL CONTRIBUTOR:

Kazuhito Yamamoto, MD, PhD
Aichi Cancer Center
Aichi, Japan

REVIEWERS:

Katherine L. Byar, APRN-NP
Nebraska Medicine
Omaha, NE

Joseph M. Connors, MD, FRCPC
BC Cancer Agency
Vancouver, British Columbia

Ajay K. Gopal, MD
Seattle Cancer Care Alliance, University of Washington School of Medicine
Seattle, WA

Kathryn T. Maples, PharmD, BCOP
Memorial Sloan Kettering Cancer Center
New York, NY

Fredrick Chite Asirwa, MD
International Cancer Institute
Eldoret, Kenya

CHAPTER 21: MULTIPLE MYELOMA

Sagar Lonial MD, FACP
Winship Cancer Institute of Emory University
Atlanta, GA

Jonathan L. Kaufman, MD
Winship Cancer Institute of Emory University
Atlanta, GA

GLOBAL CONTRIBUTOR:

María-Victoria Mateos, MD, PhD
University of Salamanca
Salamanca, Spain

REVIEWERS:

David E. Avigan, MD
Beth Israel Deaconess Medical Center
Boston, MA

Kathryn T. Maples, PharmD, BCOP
Memorial Sloan Kettering Cancer Center
New York, NY

Joseph Mikhael, MD, MEd, FRCPC, FACP
Mayo College of Medicine
Phoenix, AZ

Phillip Scheinberg, MD
Hospital Sao Jose, Beneficencia Portuguesa de Sao Paolo
Sao Paolo, Brazil

CHAPTER 22: CELLULAR THERAPIES

Amrita Krishnan, MD
City of Hope Comprehensive Cancer Center
Duarte, CA

GLOBAL CONTRIBUTOR:

Li Mei Michelle Poon, MD
National University Cancer Institute Singapore
Singapore

REVIEWERS:

Kevin Brigle, PhD, ANP
Virginia Commonwealth University Massey Cancer Center
Richmond, VA

Corey S. Cutler, MD, MPH, FRCPC
Dana-Farber Cancer Institute
Boston, MA

Christopher A. Fausel, PharmD, MHA, BCOP
Indiana University School of Medicine
Indianapolis, IN

Sergio A. Giralt, MD
Memorial Sloan Kettering Cancer Center
New York, NY

Phillip Scheinberg, MD
Hospital Sao Jose, Beneficencia Portuguesa de Sao Paolo
Sao Paolo, Brazil

ASCO STAFF

Publisher
Katherine P. Grefe, PhD

Content Development Manager
Stephanie K. Wamsley

Production Manager
Donna Dottellis

Permissions Coordinators
Renisha Jones
Maggie Cool

CONTINUING EDUCATION AND MAINTENANCE OF CERTIFICATION

Please visit https://elearning.asco.org/product-details/asco-sep-7th-edition for more information about:

- Conflict of Interest Disclosures
- Continuing Education Credit
- Available Certificates
- MOC points from the ABIM
- ILNA points from the ONCC
- Submitting Feedback
- Disclaimer and Unlabeled Usage Statement

CONFLICT OF INTEREST DISCLOSURE

As the CE provider for the ASCO-SEP® Medical Oncology Self-Evaluation Program, ASCO is committed to balance, objectivity, and scientific rigor in the management of financial interactions with for-profit health care companies that could create real or perceived conflicts of interest. Participants in the Program have disclosed their financial relationships in accordance with ASCO's Policy for Relationships with Companies; review the policy at asco.org/rwc.

ASCO offers a comprehensive disclosure management system, using one disclosure for all ASCO activities. Members and participants in activities use coi.asco.org to disclose all interactions with companies. Their disclosure is kept on file and can be confirmed or updated with each new activity.

Please email coi@asco.org with specific questions or concerns.

CONTENTS

1

EPIDEMIOLOGY AND PREVENTION

Dean E. Brenner, MD, MD, FASCO, and Anthony J. Alberg, PhD, MPH

RECENT UPDATES

- In the United States, colorectal cancer incidence and mortality rates have been increasing in younger cohorts for reasons that remain unexplained. (Siegel RL, *JAMA* 2017; Siegel RL, *J Natl Cancer Inst* 2017)
- The role of electronic cigarettes (e-cigarettes) as either a cause of cancer or a harm reduction strategy has been controversial, with an epidemic of e-cigarette use among US youth, a UK randomized trial showing efficacy of e-cigarettes for smoking cessation, and an outbreak of vaping-related severe respiratory illness in the United States. (Cullen KA, *MMWR Morb Mortal Wkly Rep* 2018; Layden JE, *N Engl J Med* 2019; Hajek P, *N Engl J Med* 2019)

OVERVIEW

Prevention is intended to reduce cancer incidence and mortality. The cancer prevention paradigm outlines a continuum from basic sciences aimed at discovery of mechanisms of carcinogenesis and cancer etiology to interventions with the goal of reduction of cancer incidence and mortality (Fig 1-1).

EPIDEMIOLOGY

Epidemiology is the study of the distribution of disease (descriptive epidemiology) and the study of disease determinants (analytic epidemiology) in populations. First, we describe the concepts related to the distribution of cancer in populations; we then address key concepts in the approach to studying determinants of cancer.

DISTRIBUTION OF CANCER IN POPULATIONS

Characterizing the distribution of cancer in populations is a critical first step to understanding the scope of the problem posed by cancer. Central to this process is ongoing surveillance activities to systematically and rigorously track the occurrence of cancer in a population according to person, place, and time. Cancer registries are population-based cancer surveillance systems used to ascertain newly diagnosed cases of cancer and deaths resulting from cancer. In the United States, the National Cancer Institute (NCI) sponsors the SEER registries, which cover 35% of the population,[1] and the Centers for Disease Control and Prevention (CDC) sponsors statewide registries in the remaining states. Together, these two surveillance systems are referred to as the National Program of Cancer Registries.

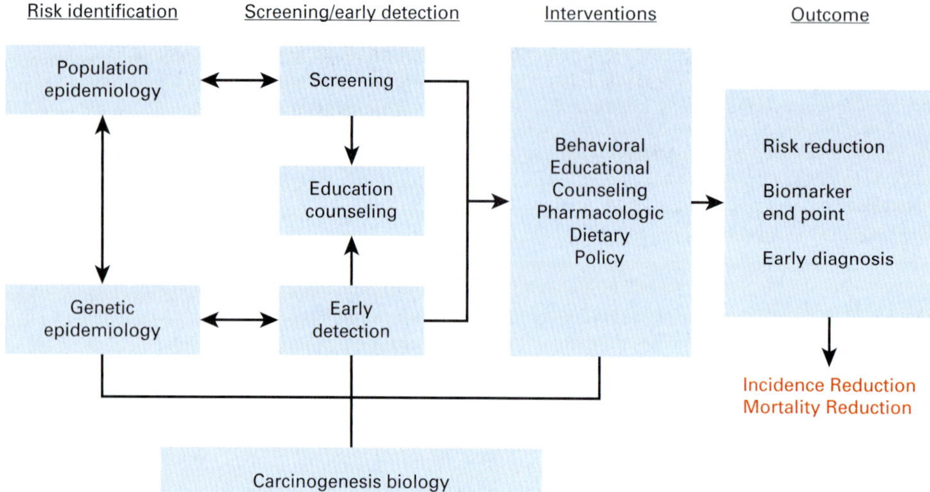

Fig. 1-1 Cancer prevention paradigm. This paradigm is a continuum of basic sciences (population and genetic epidemiology, carcinogenesis biology) that is translated into tools used for populations and individual patients with the goal of reducing cancer incidence and mortality.

Measuring the Distribution of Cancer

Measures of disease occurrence are used to characterize how common cancer is and to assess the burden cancer poses in populations. Population rates are usually expressed in units per 100,000 population. Comparison of rates between different populations or within the same population across time are adjusted for age, because the risk of most cancers increases steeply with age, and age distributions may vary markedly between populations or across time within the same population (eg, the US population is getting progressively older).

Cancer surveillance systems generate the data to enable the calculation of incidence rates, survival rates, and mortality rates:

- Incidence rate is the number of new cases of cancer diagnosed of the total population during a specified time period (usually 1 year).
- Survival rate is the time from diagnosis to death.
- Mortality rate is the number of deaths resulting from cancer of the total population during a specified time period (usually 1 year).

The incidence rate measures the risk of developing cancer. Prevalence refers to the number of existing cancer cases in a population at a point in time. Prevalence is not a measure of cancer risk, because it is a function of both incidence and duration of the disease. Thus, as cancer survivorship has increased (ie, the duration of the disease has increased), the prevalence of cancer has increased, even as cancer incidence rates have decreased. However, by providing a measure of the proportion of the population affected by cancer, prevalence is useful for planning for the provision of cancer control programs and oncology services in a region.

Mortality rate measures the risk of dying as a result of cancer and is a function for both the incidence rate and cancer survival. A commonly used survival rate measure is the proportion of patients alive 5 years postdiagnosis. For cancers that tend to have excellent prognoses, such as breast or prostate cancer, a longer timeframe, such as 10-year survival, may be more meaningful.

Describing the Distribution of Cancer

An initial step to describe the distribution of cancer in populations is to do so according to person, place, and time.

Person. Characteristics of persons measured in cancer registries include age, sex, and race/ethnicity. Cancer incidence and mortality rates increase steeply with age. For example, during the period from 2012 to 2016, the SEER incidence rates for all cancers were 8.8-fold greater in those ≥ 65 compared with those < 65 years of age (1,958.4 *v* 222.6 per 100,000); an even greater 17.9-fold difference was observed for mortality rates (999.3 in those age ≥ 65 years *v* 51.3 in those age < 65 years per 100,000).

Table 1-1 summarizes the rates of all cancer sites combined according to race and sex. The sex-stratified data show cancer rates are higher in men compared with women, by 14% for incidence and by 39% for mortality. The race-stratified data show higher rates in blacks compared with whites, by only 2% for incidence, but by 13% for mortality. These observations identify men, and to a lesser extent blacks, as a high-risk group.

Additional insights are achieved by stratifying by both sex and race together (Table 1-2). Compared with white women, cancer incidence rates were 5% lower for black women, 12% higher for white men, and 23% higher for black men. Even though black women have the lowest risk of developing cancer, they also have the lowest survival rate, 14% lower than white women on average (Table 1-2).[2] The lower survival rates in black women result in cancer mortality rates that are 12% higher for black women than white women. Compared with mortality rates for white women, the mortality rates were 38% higher for white men and 64% higher for black men.

In summary, these findings indicate that in the United States, black women have the lowest risk of developing cancer and

Table 1-1 Age-Adjusted Incidence and Mortality Rates for Period 2012-2016 and 5-Year Relative Survival for Period 2009-2015 for All Cancer Sites Combined, SEER Data

	Stratified by Sex			Stratified by Race		
Rate/Survival	Male	Female	Difference (%)[a]	Black	White	Difference (%)[a]
Incidence rate, per 100,000	469	411	+14	451	444	+2
5-year relative survival, %	69	70	−1	64	70	−9
Mortality rate, per 100,000	186	134	+39	178	158	+13

[a]Percentage difference = ([males − females]/females) × 100 and ([blacks − whites]/whites) × 100.
Data collected from Siegel RL, Miller KD, Jemal A: Cancer statistics, 2018. CA Cancer J Clin 68:7-30, 2018.[3]

black men have the highest risk. With regard to mortality, there is a racial disparity for both women and men, and this disparity is largely driven by black men, who have the highest cancer mortality rates.

A timely application of descriptive epidemiology is the identification of disparities populations (ie, those experiencing a disproportionate share of the cancer burden). One such disparities population is black men. Although black women have a lower risk of developing cancer, because of their poor survival and higher mortality rates, they are also identified as a disparities population. Identification of disparities populations leads to research to determine the root causes of these disparities, so they can be reduced and eventually eliminated. Disparities research entails assessing multilevel factors such as social determinants of health, socioeconomic factors, access to and use of health care, lifestyle and behavioral factors, and biologic factors.

Place. Comparing rates between different places can distinguish high- and low-risk areas. In SEER data for all cancers combined for the period from 2012 to 2016, a 38% difference in incidence is present in the SEER states with the highest and lowest age-adjusted cancer incidence rates (Kentucky, 510.4 and New Mexico, 368.7 per 100,000).[1] For mortality, there is a 56% difference between the SEER states with the highest and lowest age-adjusted cancer mortality rates (Kentucky, 197.9 and Utah, 127.0 per 100,000).

Factors such as the historically high cigarette smoking prevalence in a tobacco-producing state contribute to the high rates in Kentucky. In contrast, in Utah, a state with a high proportion of followers of the Mormon faith, which forbids cigarette smoking and alcohol drinking, low cigarette smoking prevalence contributes to the low mortality rates. Such comparisons show how descriptive epidemiology can be used to provide clues to cancer etiology.

Time. The American Cancer Society publishes time trends of incidence and mortality rates for major cancers in the past 75 years (Figs 1-2 and 1-3).[3] Evaluating cancer rates over time permits assessment of the presence of trends and whether the trends are increasing or decreasing. Inspecting the occurrence of cancer in populations may also lead to the generation of new hypotheses about the etiology of cancer. Increases in incidence may result from

Table 1-2 Age-Adjusted Incidence and Mortality Rates (per 100,000) for Period 2012-2016 and 5-Year Relative Survival for Period 2009-2015 for All Cancer Sites Combined, Stratified by Race-Sex Subgroups, SEER Data

Rate/Survival	White Women	Black Women	White Men	Black Men
Incidence rate (2012-2016), per 100,000	425	402	474	522
Difference, %[a]	0 (referent)	−5	+12	+23
5-year relative survival (2009-2015), %	71	61	70	66
Difference, %[a]	0 (referent)	−14	−1	−7
Mortality rate (2012-2016), per 100,000	135	151	186	222
Difference, %[a]	0 (referent)	+12	+38	+64

[a]Percentage differences were calculated using white females as the comparison group for all comparisons, using the formula: ([other group − white females]/white females) × 100.
Data collected from Siegel RL, Miller KD, Jemal A: Cancer statistics, 2018. CA Cancer J Clin 68:7-30, 2018.[3]

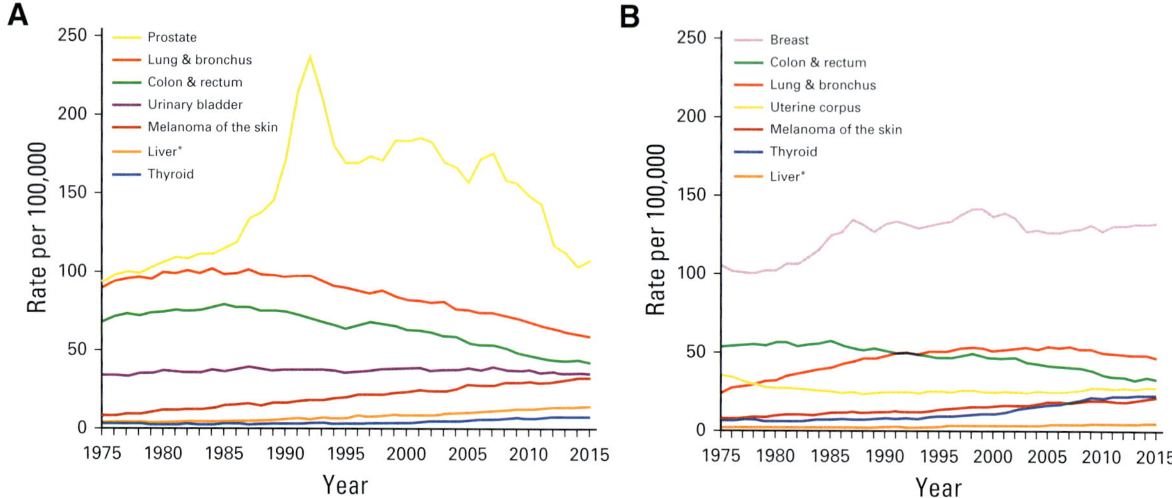

Fig. 1-2 Incidence rates in males (A) and females (B) in the United States for major cancers (1975-2015).

Rates are age adjusted to the 2000 US standard population. Incidence rates also are adjusted for delays in reporting.[3]

*Includes intrahepatic bile duct.

Reprinted by permission from Copyright Clearance Center: Siegel RL, Miller KD, Jemal A: Cancer statistics, 2018. CA Cancer J Clin 68:7-30, 2018.

increases in risk factors, and decreases in incidence may result from primary prevention interventions; decreased mortality rates may result from screening and new treatments.

For example, the rise in prostate cancer incidence after 1985 and subsequent fall are attributed to the widespread use of the prostate-specific antigen (PSA) test for screening (Fig 1-2). The rise in the incidence of cutaneous melanoma in both sexes is primarily a result of increased exposure to ultraviolet radiation (UVR), both from the sun and from indoor tanning devices.[4,5]

Figure 1-3 shows the changes in mortality for selected cancers since 1930. A notable trend is the dramatic rise in lung cancer mortality rates that accompanied the rise in cigarette smoking in the 20th century. The incidence in men peaked approximately in 1985 and then began falling, 20 years after the 1964 Surgeon General's Report that determined cigarette smoking caused lung cancer. As cigarette smoking prevalence decreased, the lung cancer incidence and mortality rates decreased and will continue to fall for the foreseeable future.

Gastric cancer was the leading cause of cancer mortality in the United States before World War II, but then a striking decrease occurred. The reasons for this decrease are not well understood, but the identification of *Helicobacter pylori* as a key cause of gastric cancer raises the possibility that this decrease may have resulted from factors that reduced the prevalence of *H pylori* infections.[6] The initial decreases in the mid 1900s likely resulted from general improved sanitation, but in more recent years, these decreases likely resulted from accelerated by antibiotic use followed by *H pylori* screening.

Among women, a dramatic fall in cervical cancer occurred after World War II because of the widespread implementation of the Papanicolau test for screening. The decline in breast cancer mortality after the mid 1980s has been attributed to a combination of mammographic screening and advances in treatment, such as the use of adjuvant therapy.[7,8]

DETERMINANTS OF CANCER

The goal of research into the determinants of cancer is to find causes of cancer, potentially opening pathways to prevention. In epidemiology, a cause is defined as a factor that increases the relative frequency of disease when present and decreases the relative frequency of disease when absent. In this framework, disease causation is viewed as multifactorial, and causes are relative rather than absolute. Given the multifactorial causes of cancer, the concept of a necessary cause only rarely comes into play; one example is infections with oncogenic strains of human papillomavirus (HPV) as a necessary cause of HPV-caused malignancies, such as cervical cancer.

Causal inference is the synthesis of a body of evidence according to prespecified criteria. Of many causal criteria used in epidemiology, three are central to causal inference:

1. Temporal sequence: refers to establishing that the exposure precedes the disease.
2. Strength of the association (including dose response): premised on the likelihood that the stronger the association between exposure and outcome, the less likely it is to be a result of confounding factors, and under most circumstances, risk would be expected to increase with higher levels of exposure.
3. Consistency of the association: indicates that if an association is truly causal, it would be expected to be repeatedly observed in studies carried out with different study designs, among diverse populations, in different locations, and by different research teams.

Epidemiologists use a spectrum of different study designs to carry out research on determinants of cancer. The hierarchy of evidence rates study designs based on the strength of evidence provided by each (Table 1-3). It is a concise way to

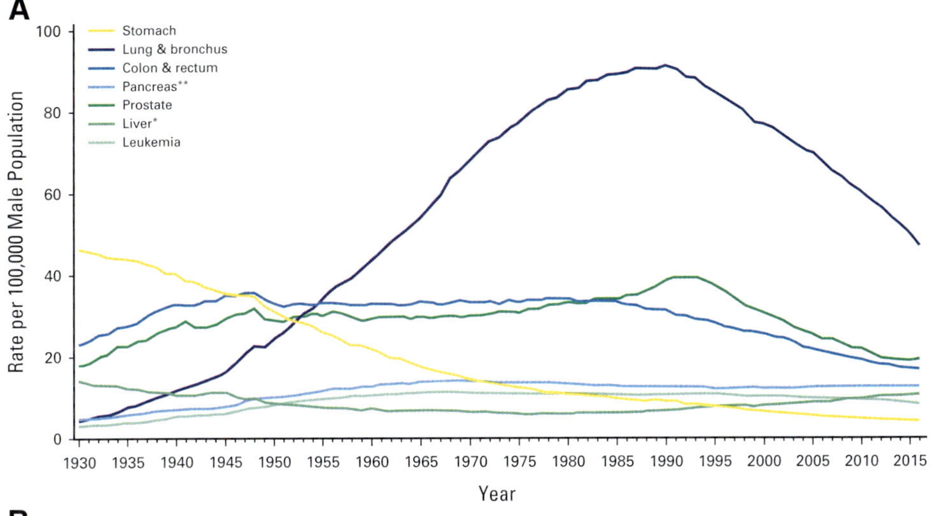

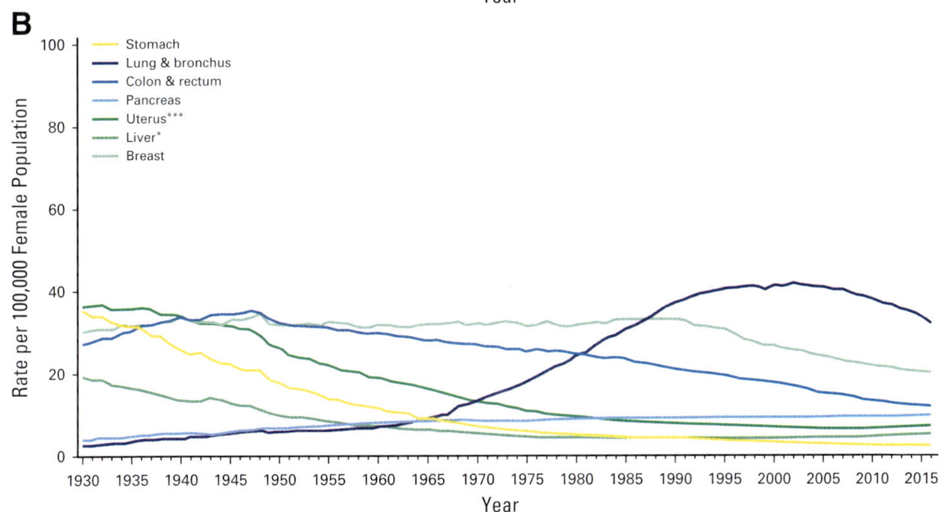

Fig. 1-3 **Trends in United States mortality rates since 1930 for selected cancers among males (A) and females (B).**

Rates are age adjusted to the 2000 United States standard population and adjusted for delays in reporting.

*Includes intrahepatic bile duct.

**Mortality rates for pancreatic and liver cancer are increasing.

***Refers to uterine cervix and uterine corpus combined.

Reprinted by permission from Copyright Clearance Center: Siegel RL, Miller KD, Jemal A: Cancer statistics, 2018. CA Cancer J Clin 68:7-30, 2018.

conceptualize the relative strengths and weaknesses of the different designs and thus holds value both for causal inference as well as for development of evidence-based guidelines.

Randomized trials are at the top of the hierarchy of evidence. The approach taken in these studies is experimental rather than observational (ie, through randomization, the investigator actually controls assignment of the intervention, such as a chemopreventive agent or a new cancer screening test).

The next level in the hierarchy of evidence comprises observational studies (Table 1-3). Because of ethical considerations, the experimental approach of randomized trials can only be taken under circumstances when the intervention being tested is potentially health enhancing. A major focus in advancing knowledge of determinants of disease is to identify harmful exposures. Therefore, the predominant study designs used in epidemiology involve testing for associations when the exposures occur in populations based on factors over which the researchers have no control, but rather are self-selected by the study participants (eg, lifestyle factors) or occur naturally (eg, germline genetic variants). The researchers then rely on measuring associations based on these observations, hence the term observational studies. The specific observational studies from highest to lowest in the hierarchy of evidence are cohort studies, case-control studies, and cross-sectional studies. As summarized in Table 1-4, each of these study designs has strengths and weaknesses that reflect a balance between time and resources and susceptibility to biases.

Other types of studies beneath observational studies in the hierarchy of evidence include ecologic studies and case series studies. Ecologic studies are good for hypothesis generation but are limited because the unit of observation is groups rather than individuals.

KEY POINTS

- Epidemiology is the study of the distribution and determinants of disease in populations.
- Epidemiology focuses on population health, rather than the health of the individual patient, but is still relevant to research and practice in clinical oncology.

- To characterize the distribution of cancer in populations, incidence, mortality, and survival rates are used to make comparisons across person, place, and time. These analyses can identify high-risk populations, as well as cancer disparities.
- Confirming a factor as a cause of human cancer requires establishing a strong body of evidence, including epidemiologic studies, according to criteria such as temporal sequence and strength and consistency of the association. A hierarchy of evidence is helpful for rating the quality of evidence provided by epidemiologic studies.
- The study of cancer determinants largely relies on observational studies, such as cohort studies and case-control studies, to identify risk factors and protective factors for cancer.

EXTRINSIC AND INTRINSIC FACTORS ASSOCIATED WITH CANCER RISK

Extrinsic influences on cancer risk are factors outside the individual's own body, such as environmental exposures, lifestyle factors, infectious agents, and dietary factors. In contrast, intrinsic influences on cancer risk are factors unique to each person, such as genetic predisposition to cancer. Case-control and cohort studies have identified associations between extrinsic factors, which include lifestyle factors and environmental exposures, and cancer. For some extrinsic factors,

Table 1-3 **Hierarchy of Evidence for Different Study Designs**

Study Type	Evidence
Experimental	
Randomized	Highest-quality evidence, but use limited to testing health-enhancing interventions (better treatments, preventive or screening interventions)
Observational	
Cohort	Highest-quality observational evidence because of measurement of exposure and follow-up for occurrence of the outcome
Case control	Useful for studying rare disease such as specific cancer types, but susceptible to information and selection biases because of measurement of exposure after the occurrence of disease and challenges of selecting and recruiting a control group representative of the population from which the cases arose
Cross sectional	Limited by studying only prevalent cases and measurement of exposure and outcome at a point in time
Other	
Ecologic	Unit of observation is group-level data, not individuals, so results are limited, but good for hypothesis generation
Case series	Commonly used clinical design, but lack of a comparison group severely limits inferences

NOTE. Studies higher up in the hierarchy of evidence provide stronger evidence because of higher internal validity (or lower risk of bias).

Table 1-4 **Summary of Characteristics of Observational Study Designs**

	Study Type		
Characteristic	**Prospective Cohort**	**Case Control**	**Cross Sectional**
Cost	More expensive	Less expensive	Less expensive
Duration	Long	Shorter	Shorter
Direction of studying exposure and outcome	Forward, start with exposure and follow-up for occurrence of outcome	Backward, start with outcome and then measure exposure	No directionality, exposure and outcome measured at the same point in time
Establishes temporal sequence	Yes, exposure measured before outcome	No, exposure measured after outcome	No, exposure and outcome measured at the same point in time
Potential for biases	Present	Strong	Present
Good for studying rare diseases	No	Yes	No
Measure of association	Relative risk (risk ratio, rate ratio, hazard ratio)	Odds ratio	Prevalence ratio

clear-cut causal associations have been established. Examples of these include cigarette smoking, alcohol drinking, radiation (including UVR), and infections with specific microorganisms. These are discussed in more detail in Interventions for Preventing Cancer.

Cigarette smoking is causally associated with 12 different malignancies: cancers of the lung, oral cavity, larynx, esophagus, bladder, kidney, pancreas, stomach, cervix, colon and rectum, liver and acute myelogenous leukemia.[9] An estimated 48% of all deaths resulting from cancer in the United States are attributable to cigarette smoking.[9] Exposure to radiation has also been demonstrated to cause cancer. Ionizing radiation is an established cause of leukemia, thyroid cancer, and cancer of the female breast.[9] Exposure to UVR, either from sunlight or from indoor tanning devices, is a major cause of melanoma and nonmelanoma skin cancers.[10] Infectious agents have been estimated to cause 18% of all cancer cases worldwide,[11] with greater importance in lower-income versus upper-income countries. Examples of cancer-causing infectious agents include oncogenic strains of HPV (cancer of the cervix, penis, vagina, anus, and oropharynx), hepatitis B and C viruses (liver cancer), Epstein-Barr virus (EBV; Burkitt lymphoma), and *H pylori* (gastric cancer).

The potential contribution of diet and lifestyle to cancer has also been intensively researched. The World Cancer Research Fund/American Institute for Cancer Research (WCRF/AICR) report assessed the overall evidence of diet in relation to cancer prevention. The evidence for each dietary factor in relation to cancer was evaluated and rated; dietary factors in the strongest evidence classification were rated as convincing, and the next highest evidence ranking was probable.[12,13] Alcohol drinking had strong evidence of being a risk factor in the report; the evidence was rated as convincing for increased risk of cancers of the liver, colorectum (men), breast, oral cavity, and squamous cell esophagus. High amounts of red and processed meat are linked to increased risk of colorectal cancer. For protective factors, fruits and nonstarchy vegetables were rated as associated with probable decreased risk for cancers of the oral cavity, esophagus, and stomach. The WCRF/AICR evidence review also highlighted the importance of energy balance to several malignancies. Decreased physical activity was rated as convincing for colorectal cancer risk and probable for postmenopausal breast and endometrial cancers. Risk associations for obesity were rated as convincing for esophageal adenocarcinoma and pancreatic, colorectal cancer, kidney, endometrial, and postmenopausal breast cancers. (The National Institutes of Health report obesity to increase the risk for up to 13 different types of cancer: endometrial, esophageal, gastric, liver, kidney, pancreatic, colorectal cancer, gallbladder, postmenopausal breast, ovarian, thyroid cancers, multiple myeloma, and meningioma).[14]

In addition to extrinsic factors, factors intrinsic to individuals influence cancer susceptibility. Intrinsic, or host, factors encompass age, sex, race/ethnicity, and family history of cancer, as well as biologic factors. Biologic factors include, for example, markers of inflammation and immune dysregulation, hormones, oxidative stress, and genetic and epigenetic variants that may affect biologic pathways relevant to carcinogenesis.

A simple dichotomy of high-risk mutations and low-risk polymorphisms is useful to show the range of ways that

Table 1-5 Selected Hereditary Neoplastic Syndromes (clinical tests available)

Syndrome	Site of Most Common Cancer	Associated Gene
Hereditary breast and ovarian cancers	Breast, ovary	*BRCA1, BRCA2*
Cowden	Breast, thyroid	*PTEN*
Li-Fraumeni	Brain, breast, adrenal cortex, leukemia, sarcoma	*TP53*
Familial adenomatous polyposis	Large bowel, small bowel, brain (Turcot), skin, bone (Gardner)	*APC*
Hereditary nonpolyposis colorectal cancer	Colorectal and endometrium; also ovary, pancreas, stomach, small bowel	*MSH2, MLH1, PMS1, PMS2, MSH6*
Multiple endocrine neoplasia 1	Pancreatic islet cell, pituitary adenoma, parathyroid adenoma	*MEN1*
Multiple endocrine neoplasia 2	Medullary thyroid, pheochromocytoma	*RET*
Neurofibromatosis type 1	Neurofibrosarcoma, pheochromocytoma	*NF1*
von Hippel-Lindau	Hemangioblastoma, nervous system, renal cell	*VHL*
Retinoblastoma	Eye, bone	*RB1*
Melanoma, hereditary	Skin	*CDKN2/p16, CDK4*
Basal cell	Skin	*PTCH*
Hereditary diffuse gastric cancer	Stomach, lobular breast	*CDH1*

genetic variants can play a role in determining cancer risk (Table 1-5). Markers of genetic susceptibility can be classified by frequency and penetrance into rare, high-penetrant mutations and common, low-penetrant polymorphisms. Rare, high-penetrant genetic variants are associated with major inherited disease susceptibility and are thus a major driver of cancer risk. An example is disease-conferring mutations in *BRCA1* and *BRCA2* genes that lead to significantly increased risk of breast and ovarian cancers and other cancers. Chapter 6 reviews these important syndromes.

By contrast, for genetic polymorphisms with low penetrance but relatively highly frequent occurrence, the contribution to an individual patient's risk may be small, but because of the higher prevalence, the public health impact may be large. One way that polymorphisms may exert influence on carcinogenesis is via gene-environment interactions (ie, by affecting metabolism and host response to environmental carcinogens in ways that affect cancer susceptibility). For example, polymorphisms in genes in the cytochrome P450 enzyme system that metabolizes carcinogens in cigarette smoke can cause variability in susceptibility to the effects of cigarette smoke. Genome-wide association studies across cancer sites have identified many single-nucleotide polymorphisms (SNPs) that are associated with different malignancies. For some of these SNPs, there is evidence of a biologic role, whereas for others, the implications remain to be determined.

INTEGRATING EXTRINSIC AND INTRINSIC FACTORS: MOLECULAR EPIDEMIOLOGY

Exposure to carcinogens via lifestyle behaviors and environmental exposures are important to cancer etiology, but there is also substantial interindividual variability in susceptibility to carcinogens. For example, even as robust a cause of cancer as cigarette smoking only causes lung cancer in a minority of exposed persons, suggesting genetic susceptibility plays a role. Cancer risk thus reflects the combined influence of exposure to carcinogenic agents and individual susceptibility to these carcinogens. This combination of carcinogen exposure and host susceptibility, including genetic predisposition, introduces the notion of gene-environment interactions and hence the approach of molecular epidemiology.

Molecular epidemiology is an approach that merges the population and laboratory tools used to advance understanding of human carcinogenesis, such as susceptibility to environmental carcinogens. There are many models of molecular epidemiology, but common elements across the models are a multistep carcinogenesis pathway and integration of biomarkers to measure the steps in the pathway. Figure 1-4 shows an example of a traditional molecular epidemiologic model, with the steps in the pathway composed of exposure, internal dose, biologically effective dose, preclinical biologic effect, and clinical cancer.[2] Susceptibility factors affect the probability of progression along each step of the pathway; in this case, genetic polymorphisms are the susceptibility factors.

Biomarkers are central to the molecular epidemiologic paradigm. Biomarkers are based on measurements from

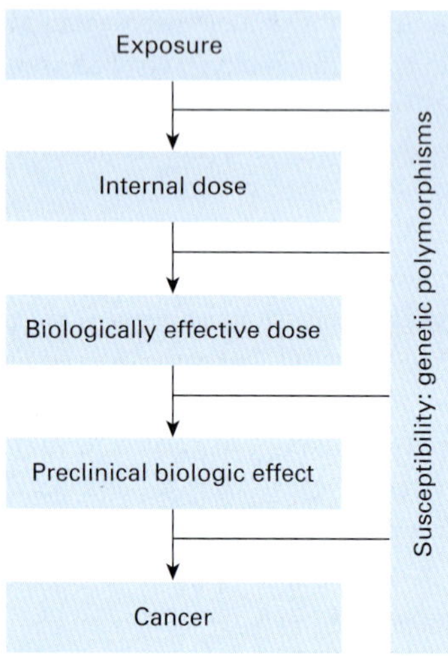

Fig. 1-4 Traditional molecular epidemiologic model.

laboratory assays using biologic materials, such as tissue samples, blood, urine, and saliva. Biomarkers are used to measure status at each stage in the pathway: biomarkers of exposure, internal dose, biologically effective dose, preclinical biologic effect, and clinical disease (eg, biomarker of early detection). Consider the example of cigarette smoking in relation to cancer risk. The measurement of smoking may be via self-report, but measures of internal dose could include assessment of nicotine metabolites, such as serum/plasma cotinine. A DNA adduct is an example of a measure of biologically effective dose. Preclinical biologic effect may be measured as actual DNA damage, including somatic mutations or even functional changes such as oncogene activation or tumor suppressor gene inactivation.

This brief introduction to molecular epidemiology emphasizes genetic variants as susceptibility factors. However, advances in understanding of DNA methylation, histone modification, and other epigenetic phenomena will likely lead to new insights into susceptibility to environmental factors and may suggest new targets for intervention.[15,16]

MOLECULAR EPIDEMIOLOGY AND PRECISION PREVENTION/SCREENING

The integration of the molecular epidemiologic paradigm to investigate determinants of cancer has advanced the understanding of the mechanisms of cancer causation. Molecular epidemiology is also relevant to prevention and screening, for example, to discover biomarkers of early detection. Using the results of molecular epidemiologic studies, the concepts underlying precision medicine can also be applied to cancer screening and prevention. The integration of key extrinsic and intrinsic risk factors can be used to identify the highest risk strata in a population most likely to benefit from screening and prevention, for example, using risk prediction models. A prevention intervention or screening test that is efficacious in average-risk patients is likely to be of even greater value in those at higher risk. The ability to accurately classify those most likely to benefit from prevention or screening interventions is referred to as precision prevention or precision screening.[17]

IS EPIDEMIOLOGY USEFUL IN THE ONCOLOGY SETTING?

In contrast to the provision of clinical care, the focus of epidemiology is on population health. Even so, the epidemiologic approach is relevant to clinical oncology. Epidemiologic evidence provides the foundation for the prevention of cancer (Fig 1-1). Epidemiologic approaches are also used to assess the benefits of intervention programs, such as cancer prevention or screening.

In addition to their relevance in cancer prevention, epidemiologic methods are commonly applied to clinical questions, including the assessment of treatment outcomes, such as survival, and the long-term sequelae of cancer and its treatment. When randomized trials are not feasible, observational studies may be used to investigate questions involving treatment efficacy and risk of adverse events from treatments and assess the cost effectiveness of different treatment regimens.

Furthermore, epidemiologic evidence is integrated into the practice of evidence-based medicine. For example, collection of risk factor information such as tobacco and alcohol use, body mass index (BMI), and family history of cancer is based on evidence from numerous epidemiologic studies. In turn, this information is used to provide advice and guidance to patients (eg, regarding tobacco use cessation), identify high-risk patients, guide early detection and prevention strategies, and assist with cancer diagnosis.

KEY POINTS

- Epidemiology provides evidence that forms the foundation of cancer prevention and screening.
- Extrinsic influences are factors outside the individual's own body, such as environmental exposures, lifestyle factors, infectious agents, and dietary factors.
- Intrinsic influences are factors unique to each person, such as genetics.
- Cancer risk can be increased by both intrinsic and extrinsic influences, and the molecular epidemiologic approach merges the study of intrinsic and extrinsic factors.
- Germline genetic mutations, which confer an increased risk for many cancers, have been identified. Patients who carry a germline (heritable) predisposition to cancer can be identified in the clinical setting through germline testing/genetic screening, clinical manifestations of these syndromes, and family history.

INTERVENTIONS FOR PREVENTING CANCER

Epidemiology and basic science research form the foundation for the development and implementation of interventions aimed to delay or reverse cancer progression. Interventions manipulate genetic, biologic, and environmental factors in carcinogenesis.

Lifestyle interventions include:

- Smoking cessation
- Limiting alcohol intake
- Sun avoidance
- Diet modification
- Maintaining a healthy weight and increased physical activity

Medically based interventions incorporate clinical cancer prevention (historically referred to as chemoprevention) using:

- Medicines (eg, tamoxifen for breast cancer prevention)
- Micronutrients
- Nutritional extracts
- Control of infectious agents (eg, vaccines and antiviral agents)

Screening for precancerous lesions (intraepithelial neoplasia) can reduce mortality in high-incidence cancers (colon, breast, and cervical cancers). Establishing whether a new screening modality actually leads to a reduction in cancer mortality is challenging because the process is susceptible to many biases in data sets, as discussed later in this chapter.[18]

LIFESTYLE INTERVENTIONS

TOBACCO

Impact of Tobacco Use on Health

Cigarette smoking is the leading cause of morbidity and premature mortality in the United States and most upper-income nations. Cigarette smoking is causally associated with 12 different malignancies: cancers of the lung, oral cavity, larynx, esophagus, bladder, kidney, pancreas, stomach, cervix, colon and rectum, liver, and acute myelogenous leukemia.[9] An estimated 48% of all deaths resulting from cancer in the United States are attributable to cigarette smoking. In addition to the substantial adverse health effects from active cigarette smoking, even second-hand smoke is an established cause of lung cancer in nonsmokers, indicating there is no safe level of cigarette smoke exposure.[9]

The risks of cigarette smoking–caused disease and death are dose dependent, with the risk of cancer increasing with the number of years of smoking and the number of cigarettes per day. Compared with persistent smoking, smoking cessation is associated with an immediate decrease in cancer risk. However, former smokers remain at elevated risk of cancer compared with never-smokers, even after decades of cessation. As with cigarette smoking, other forms of combustible tobacco smoking, such as pipes and cigars, are associated with adverse health effects. For example, pipes and cigars are strongly associated with lung cancer risk, but the associations are weaker than those for cigarette smoking, not because pipes and cigars are less harmful but because they tend to be used less frequently and smoke is inhaled less deeply than with cigarettes.[9]

The tobacco marketplace has changed significantly during the past 15 years, with the most prominent shift being an upsurge in the use of e-cigarettes, particularly among youth and young adults.[19] The long-term health effects of e-cigarettes are not yet known, but the constituents of the vapor include carcinogens, making it likely e-cigarette use increases cancer risk.[19] In the United States, there is currently an outbreak of severe respiratory distress associated with the use of vaping devices, but the cause of the outbreak remains to be determined. This outbreak highlights the need for more complete characterization of the potential health effects of e-cigarettes.

Medical Professional Counseling

Most adult US smokers begin smoking before age 18 years. Therefore, smoking prevention interventions directed to the pediatric and adolescent populations are a major public health priority. Studies show that a physician's simple advice to avoid or quit smoking can significantly improve the likelihood of a quit attempt and successful quitting.[20,21] Despite this, a survey found that although > 80% of oncologists assess their patients' smoking behavior, < 20% feel confident enough to intervene in this important area.[22] Because evidence has clearly documented the negative impact of cigarette smoking on the prognosis of patients with cancer,[9] the provision of smoking cessation services in the oncology setting is recognized to be of central importance.[21]

Smoking Cessation Programs

Smoking is an addiction. Evidence shows that smokers are most likely to benefit from a multifaceted cessation program that includes counseling, behavioral strategies, and drug therapy. If drug therapy is needed, the recommended first-line therapies are nicotine replacement therapy, bupropion, and varenicline, with clonidine and nortriptyline as possible second-line therapies. Smoking cessation can be strongly enhanced by even a small amount of encouragement from a health care provider. The smoker who is quitting goes through a process with identifiable stages that include contemplation of quitting, an action phase during which the smoker quits, and a maintenance phase. There now exist numerous effective strategies beyond counseling for advising and assisting the cooperative patient with his or her goal.[20,21,23]

Policy

In addition to tobacco control at the individual level, policy-level interventions have also been shown to reduce smoking prevalence. Examples of important tobacco control policies are tax increases on cigarettes, smoke-free workplace legislation, and increasing the minimum legal age of access to tobacco products.

Comprehensive tobacco control policies have led to progress in reducing smoking prevalence. Current smoker rates in the United States have decreased to almost 15%, which will result in continued downward trends in the smoking-caused burden of cancer.[24] However, cigarette smoking remains a major cancer risk factor globally, especially in Asia, and lung cancer is the leading cause of cancer mortality worldwide. Much concern has been raised about smoking rates in India and China, in particular, and global efforts to reduce smoking rates are being increased.[25]

E-Cigarette Use

The potential role of e-cigarettes in tobacco control is controversial. In the United States, there has been a striking increase in the prevalence of e-cigarette use among youth, and evidence shows that in addition to the direct harmful effects of e-cigarettes both known (eg, nicotine addiction, cough, wheezing) and unknown, e-cigarette use is a robust risk factor for going on to smoke combustible tobacco cigarettes among never-smokers.[19] However, among adult addicted smokers, e-cigarettes have the potential to be another tool to enhance smoking cessation.[19] Even if e-cigarettes are efficacious in smoking cessation, they would never be first-line therapy because of their adverse health effects; the extent of the adverse health effects remains to be fully characterized. In addition to nicotine, e-cigarettes contain numerous toxins, including carcinogens, but these are substantially fewer than those contained in combustible tobacco cigarettes.[19] The current outbreak of severe respiratory distress in the United States serves as a cautionary note about the need for more complete evidence on the health effects of e-cigarettes.[26,27] The CDC has recommended "not using e-cigarette, or vaping, products that contain THC or any e-cigarette, or vaping, products obtained from informal sources. E-cigarette, or vaping, products should never be used by youths, young adults, or pregnant women."[26,27] Because of the recent finding of a relationship between vitamin E acetate and product-associated lung injury, the CDC recommends that vitamin E acetate not be added to e-cigarettes or vaping products.[26,27]

Marijuana

Thirty-three states and the District of Columbia have passed laws legalizing marijuana use in some form. Most of the studies on marijuana use and cancer risk have focused on the upper aerodigestive tract and lung, but at present, there is no clear-cut evidence of an association with marijuana use and these cancers.[28] The only cancer with which marijuana use has been consistently associated is testicular cancer; 3 case-control studies have shown an association, although a biologic explanation for this association has not been established.[29]

KEY POINTS

- Cigarette smoking is the leading cause of disease and premature death in the United States and is the cause of nearly one half of deaths resulting from cancer in the United States.
- Cigarette smoking usually begins during childhood and adolescence, so primary prevention interventions aimed at youth are important for tobacco control.
- Addicted smokers are most likely to benefit from multifaceted strategies that combine counseling with pharmacologic interventions to quit. Even so, even brief provider advice has significant benefits.
- Smoking cessation is important in the oncology setting.

- Policies such as increased cigarette taxes, smoke-free workplace legislation, and increasing the minimum legal age of access to tobacco products are effective tobacco control measures.
- In the absence of better evidence, the use of e-cigarettes for smoking cessation remains controversial. This issue is difficult to consider in isolation from the adverse consequences of e-cigarette use in youth.

ALCOHOL

The International Agency for Research on Cancer[30] has synthesized the epidemiologic and other scientific evidence and judged that alcohol is a cause of cancers of the oral cavity, pharynx, larynx, esophagus, colorectum, liver (hepatocellular carcinoma), and female breast. For esophageal cancer, the association with alcohol drinking is largely specific to squamous cell carcinoma.[30] These associations do not vary substantially according to whether it is beer, wine, or liquor that is ingested.[30] On the basis of these associations, it has been estimated that alcohol drinking is responsible for approximately 6% of all cancer cases and 6% of deaths resulting from cancer globally.[31] The associations between alcohol drinking and cancer are often dose dependent.[31] On the basis of this evidence, the guidelines for alcohol use recommend no more than two drinks per day for men and one drink per day for women, and those who do not drink alcohol are recommended to continue to avoid alcohol use.[31]

For some malignancies that are linked to both cigarette smoking and alcohol drinking, synergistic interactions have been established between these two causes of cancer. This means that the cancer risks in those who are both cigarette smokers and alcohol drinkers are substantially larger than the risks observed for those who only smoke cigarettes or only drink alcohol. For example, a study that pooled data from numerous case-control studies observed that cigarette smoking and alcohol drinking interacted synergistically to elevate the risk of cancers of the oral cavity, pharynx, and larynx.[32] Evidence such as this helps demonstrate why an ASCO statement on alcohol and cancer highlighted the importance of alcohol screening and intervention in the oncology setting.[31]

UVR EXPOSURE

Exposure to UVR, either from sunlight or from indoor tanning devices, is the predominant cause of both melanoma and nonmelanoma skin cancers.[33] The major determinants of the occurrence of skin cancer in populations are cumulative UVR exposure in combination sun-sensitive phenotypes (eg, propensity to sunburn upon UVR exposure, fair skin, freckles). UVR exposure in childhood and adolescence is associated with increased skin cancer risk in adulthood. The use of tanning beds is causally associated with the risk of melanoma,[34] and the associations between tanning bed use and nonmelanoma skin cancer are also consistent with a causal association. Reduction in sun exposure throughout the life course by using protective clothing and sunscreen and avoidance of the most intense and direct sunlight (between 10AM and 4PM) are recommended as ways to lower the risk of skin cancer.[35] Interventions to prevent the use of UVR-emitting tanning devices include educational interventions and policy-level interventions, such as health warnings and increasing the minimum legal age of access.

OBESITY

Obesity is often defined as a BMI > 30 kg/m^2, but this definition has poor validity.[36] Large waist circumference increases health risks even in persons within the normal BMI range of 20 to 24.9 kg/m^2. Obesity and overweight rates are epidemic in the United States. Currently, less than one third of the population is within the normal weight range. Risk associations for obesity were rated as convincing for esophageal adenocarcinoma and pancreatic, colorectal cancer, kidney, endometrial, and postmenopausal breast cancers.[12,13] The NCI extends this list to include gastric, liver, gallbladder, ovarian, thyroid cancers, multiple myeloma, and meningioma. Excess adiposity also increases cancer recurrence rates and cancer-specific mortality and reduces treatment efficacy in multiple cancers.[37]

Excess adiposity drives insulin resistance, cytokine synthesis, and related adipokines, potentially from the adipocyte or from macrophages within the adipose tissue, to establish a proinflammatory state. Humoral products stimulate both cancer and epithelial stem-cell self-renewal.[38] These phenomena are generally observed in conjunction with obesity with an abdominal distribution of adiposity and with physical inactivity, a syndrome known as metabolic syndrome.[39]

A study of approximately 37,000 women in the Women's Health Initiative showed that intentional weight loss among postmenopausal women was associated with a reduced risk of endometrial cancer. During an 11-year follow-up, women who had a > 5% intentional weight loss over a 3-year period had a 29% lower risk for endometrial cancer compared with women with a stable weight (hazard ratio [HR], 0.71; 95% CI, 0.54 to 0.95). Those who gained weight had a higher risk of endometrial cancer.[40]

Diet Modification and Caloric Restriction

Rates of cancers of the breast, colon, endometrium, and prostate are higher in North America and Western Europe than in Asia. Immigrants from Asia and their offspring acquire a higher risk for these cancers after they have been in the United States for some time. These observations, as well as data from animal studies, are the basis for the hypothesis that dietary modification can significantly lower cancer risk for people in the United States.[41]

Diet is a highly complex exposure to many nutrients and chemicals. Low-fat diets, which are usually low in red meat and high in fruits and vegetables, may render some protection through anticarcinogens in vegetables, fruits, legumes, nuts, and grains. Potentially protective substances in foods include polyphenolics, such as curcuminoids, resveratrol, and ginger; sulfur-containing compounds, such as sulforaphane; and flavones.[12,42] Vitamins, minerals, or nutritional supplements in amounts greater than those provided by a balanced diet have not been demonstrated to be of value. Most randomized trials of vitamin supplements have not shown benefit in terms of cancer prevention; in some instances, they have even shown harm.[12]

Weight loss and bariatric surgery reduce risks of multiple cancers.[43] The metabolic effects of bariatric surgery rapidly precede clinical weight loss. These effects include shifting of adipokines and hormonal environment toward a lower level of chronic inflammation, thus reducing the inflammatory state resulting from obesity-associated metabolic syndrome.[44,45] The mechanisms by which these surgical procedures cause such a rapid reversal in chronic metabolic syndrome are of intense research interest.

Despite the epidemiologic associations and biomarker data, the causal relationship between dietary fat and cancer has not been definitively demonstrated. Case-control and cohort epidemiologic studies have yielded conflicting results. No prospective clinical trial to date has demonstrated that cancer can be prevented through lowering dietary fat or increasing fiber intake. For example, a randomized trial in the Women's Health Initiative did not find an effect of low-fat diet on risk of cancer of the breast or colon.[46,47] However, among women with early-stage breast cancer, a low-fat diet seems beneficial. A randomized trial of > 2,400 women with early-stage breast cancer showed that patients assigned to a low-fat diet, in addition to standard adjuvant therapy, had a significantly improved survival compared with women eating a regular diet (HR, 0.76; 95% CI, 0.60 to 0.98).[48]

Physical Activity

Lower levels of physical activity increase colorectal cancer risk and probably increase risk for postmenopausal breast and endometrial cancers.[12] Approximately 25% of the US population is considered sedentary, and this lifestyle is considered to be responsible for up to 5% of cancers.[49]

In addition to the possible role of physical activity in preventing cancer, increases in physical activity may be helpful for cancer survivors. Associations have been observed with decreased recurrence, progression, and improved survival. Among cancer survivors, the strongest benefits of physical activity have been observed for colorectal cancer, breast, and prostate cancer survivors.[50]

INFECTIOUS AGENTS

The bacterium *H pylori* triggers the carcinogenesis cascade, resulting in noncardia gastric carcinomas.[51] Control of viral expansion and integration through vaccination or inhibition of viral replication with antiviral drugs has emerged as a means of primary prevention. This has been achieved for hepatitis B,[52] hepatitis C,[53] and HPV.[54,55] *H pylori* eradication therapy was found to lower the incidence of gastric cancer among those treated for *H pylori* infection, compared with those who were not treated, in a pooled analysis (pooled incidence rate ratio, 0.53; 95% CI, 0.44 to 0.64).[56]

KEY POINTS

- A key prevention strategy is to avoid exposure to carcinogens. Cigarette smoking, alcohol drinking, and UVR exposure are examples of exposures that are causally associated with many different malignancies.
- Obesity is a risk factor for at least 13 cancers, including endometrial, breast, colon cancers, and esophageal adenocarcinoma.
- Vaccination or antiviral drugs can decrease the risk for developing cancer. Examples include HPV vaccination to reduce cervical cancer incidence and mortality, hepatitis B vaccination to reduce hepatocellular carcinoma incidence and mortality, and antiviral therapy (viral protease inhibitors) to reduce hepatitis C–induced hepatocellular carcinoma incidence and mortality.

CLINICAL CANCER PREVENTION

Clinical cancer prevention (chemoprevention) is the use of natural or synthetic chemical agents to reverse, suppress, or prevent carcinogenesis before the development of an invasive malignant process.[57] Although the concept that pharmacologic agents can prevent a cancer is relatively new, the idea that a compound can prevent chronic disease is not. Antihypertensive agents are used to prevent heart disease, kidney disease, and stroke. Lipid-lowering drugs are prescribed to prevent coronary artery disease.

CARCINOGENESIS CONTINUUM

Cancer may be regarded as a continuum of genetic and epigenetic events that ultimately cause an invasive, transformed cellular phenotype (Fig 1-5). The initial genetic changes of carcinogenesis, termed initiation, can be inherited or acquired. Acquired genetic damage is the result of physical, infectious, or chemical carcinogens. The influences that cause the initiated cell to change phenotypically are called promoters. Known promoters include androgens, linked to prostate cancer, and estrogen, linked to breast and endometrial cancers. The distinction between the initiator and the promoter can sometimes blur. For example, some components of cigarette smoke are referred to as complete carcinogens and serve as both initiators and promoters. Cancer can be prevented or controlled through interference with the factors that cause disease initiation, promotion, or progression (Table 1-6).

EFFECTIVE CLINICAL CANCER PREVENTIVE AGENTS

Compounds of interest in clinical cancer prevention include anti-inflammatory agents, antioxidants, differentiating agents, and hormone antagonists. A long-term randomized placebo-controlled clinical trial is generally necessary to establish the efficacy of a clinical preventive agent. Such trials have shown that tamoxifen, raloxifene, and aromatase inhibitors reduce the incidence of breast adenocarcinoma. Nonsteroidal anti-inflammatory drugs (NSAIDs), particularly aspirin, can reduce the occurrence of colorectal adenomas and the incidence of colorectal adenocarcinoma. HPV vaccines reduce the incidence of squamous cell carcinoma of the

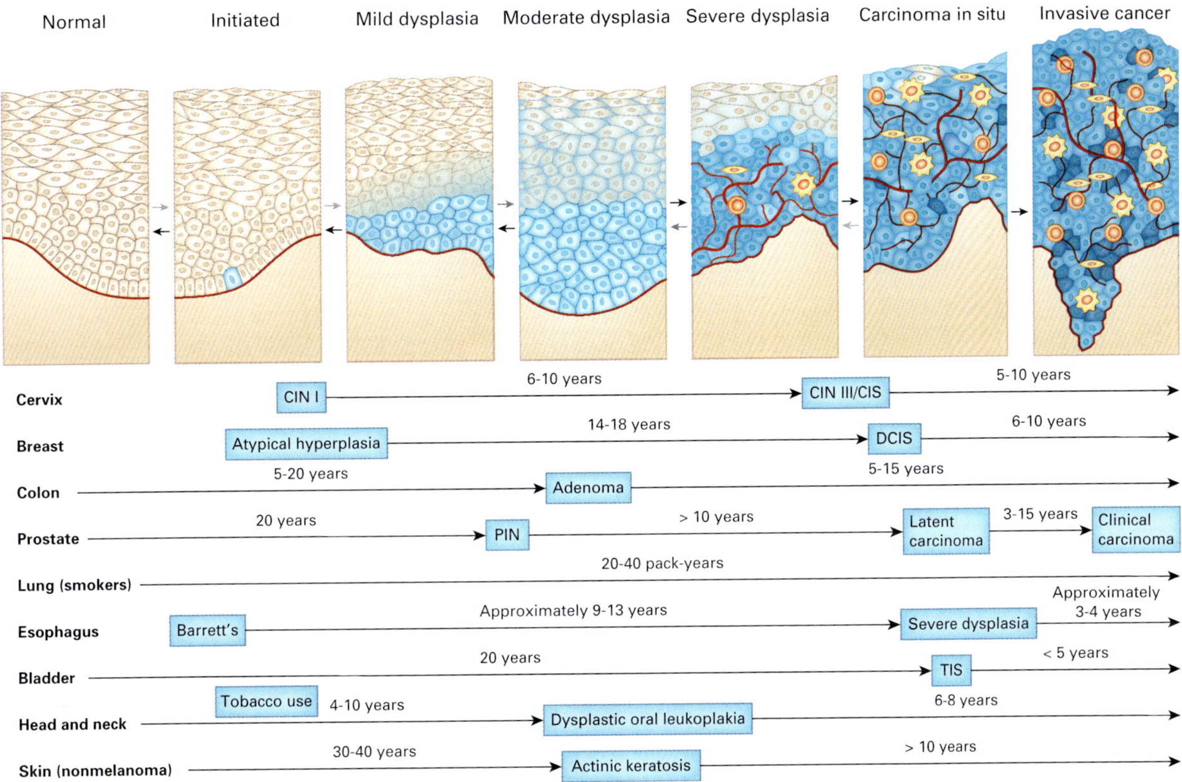

Fig. 1-5 Carcinogenesis in different organs.

While many of the genetic events that drive carcinogenesis are common across multiple organ sites, the order, time of progression, and morphologic changes are both tissue and neoplasm specific. Appropriately targeted interventions should interrupt the cancer-promoting consequences of genetic mutations and/or epigenetic modifications, thereby halting progression through the cancer continuum. Orange cells represent changes to the tumour microenvironment, including the recruitment of immune cells, the induction of angiogenesis and the alterations in the surrounding cells such as fibroblasts.

Abbreviations: CIN, adenocarcinoma in situ; CIS, carcinoma in situ; DCIS, ductal carcinoma in situ; TIS, transitional cell carcinoma in situ.

Reprinted by permission from Nature: Nat Rev Cancer, Umar A, Dunn BK, Greenwald P: Future directions in cancer prevention. Nat Rev Cancer *12:835-848, 2012.*

cervix and head and neck, and *H pylori* eradication reduces the incidence of gastric adenocarcinoma. Table 1-7 lists selected large randomized chemoprevention trials that have been conducted.

CLINICAL CANCER PREVENTION BY ORGAN SITE

Lung, Head and Neck, and Upper Esophageal Carcinomas

Numerous observational studies had previously suggested that diets high in carotenoid-rich fruits and vegetables and beta carotene may be associated with a lower risk of lung cancer. However, two randomized placebo-controlled trials in people at high risk for lung cancer, the Alpha-Tocopherol, Beta-Carotene (ATBC) Cancer Prevention Trial and the Beta-Carotene and Retinol Efficacy Trial, found increased lung cancer incidence and mortality in the beta carotene treatment groups.[58,59]

Retinoids have shown some efficacy as chemopreventive agents for squamous cell cancers of the head and neck, possibly by promoting terminal differentiation.[60] In a randomized study of 103 patients with a first primary squamous cell carcinoma of the head and neck, two patients who received 13-*cis*-retinoic acid developed a second primary head and neck cancer in 3 years, compared with 12 in the placebo group.[61] Two follow-up phase III trials (in curatively treated patients with non–small-cell lung cancer or head and neck cancer) were conducted using lower doses of 13-*cis*-retinoic acid because of its unacceptable toxicity.[62,63] Lower doses were not clinically effective.

Oxidative metabolism of carotenoids may alter retinoid metabolism and signaling pathways. Beta carotene in high concentrations has pro-oxidant activity. Such dual activity may partially explain the seemingly contradictory data of pro-carcinogenesis activity in humans, despite large bodies of preclinical data in vivo suggesting the opposite.[63] Smoking may induce genetic and epigenetic changes in the lung that affect retinoid activity. Smoking may also affect the metabolism of retinoids and carotenoids, perhaps enhancing the pro-oxidant effects of these bifunctional compounds. The adverse effects of supplemental nutrients are not limited to smokers. For example, selenium increases prostate cancer risk among men without baseline selenium deficiency.[65] The data to date suggest that some multifunctional micronutrients may have

Table 1-6 **Initiators and Promoters of Cancer**	
Carcinogen	**Associated Cancer**
Alkylating agents	Acute myelocytic leukemia, bladder
Androgens	Prostate
Aromatic amines (dyes)	Bladder
Arsenic	Lung, skin
Asbestos	Lung, pleura, peritoneum
Benzene	Acute myelocytic leukemia
Chromium	Lung
Diethylstilbestrol (prenatal)	Vaginal (clear cell)
Epstein-Barr virus	Burkitt lymphoma, nasopharynx
Estrogens	Endometrium
Estrogen plus progesterone	Breast
Ethyl alcohol	Liver, esophagus, head and neck
Helicobacter pylori	Gastric
Hepatitis B virus	Liver
Hepatitis C virus	Liver
Human T-cell leukemia-1 virus	Adult T-cell leukemia, lymphoma
Human herpesvirus 8	Kaposi sarcoma
HIV	Non-Hodgkin lymphoma, Kaposi sarcoma, squamous cell carcinoma of cervix
Human papillomavirus	Squamous cell carcinoma of cervix, anogenital area, oropharynx
Immunosuppressive agents (azathioprine, cyclosporine, corticosteroids)	Non-Hodgkin lymphoma
Nitrogen mustard gas	Lung, head and neck, nasal sinuses
Nickel dust	Lung, nasal sinuses
Phenacetin	Renal pelvis, bladder
Polycyclic aromatic hydrocarbons	Lung, skin (especially squamous cell)
Schistosomiasis	Bladder (squamous cell)
Sunlight (UV)	Skin (squamous cell and melanoma)
Tobacco (including smokeless)	Upper aerodigestive tract, bladder, pancreas
Vinyl chloride	Liver (angiosarcoma)

NOTE. Agents listed are thought to act as cancer initiators or promoters for the cancers with which they have been associated.

the capacity to both induce and reduce carcinogenesis. Reducing oxidative stress as a clinical prevention strategy in smokers without a more focused mechanism-based approach is not effective.

Lower Esophageal Neoplasms

Esophageal adenocarcinoma is a growing health problem because of its rapidly rising incidence, substantial morbidity, and high mortality. Barrett's esophagus, a serious complication of gastroesophageal reflux disease involving the reflux of gastric and duodenal contents, is the only known precursor of esophageal adenocarcinoma. Esophageal adenocarcinoma develops in patients with Barrett's esophagus at an annual rate of 0.12%.[66] Despite the high risk for progression from Barrett's metaplasia to dysplasia and invasion, effective strategies for both detection and prevention are lacking. Endoscopic eradication therapies consisting of mucosal resection, radiofrequency ablation, and cryotherapy are now recommended in patients with dysplastic Barrett's.[67] Such therapies fail in 10% of patients with high-grade dysplasia, and 40% of patients develop recurrence of dysplasia or metaplasia.[68] Obesity, especially central adiposity, has emerged as a strong, consistent, and dose-dependent risk factor for lower esophageal carcinogenesis.[69]

Gastric Neoplasms

Before World War II, gastric adenocarcinoma was one of the most common malignancies in the United States. Although gastric adenocarcinoma incidence has been declining in the United States, high incidence and mortality are observed in Latin America and China and in parts of the developing world. Heavy intake of smoked and cured meats and foods, limited consumption of fresh fruits and vegetables, and infection with *H pylori* are associated with an increased risk of gastric cancer.[6] A 2-week course of antibiotic treatment induces regression of nonmetaplastic gastric atrophy and intestinal metaplasia in geographically diverse regions. In a pooled analysis of clinical trials and cohort studies of *H pylori* eradication therapy, eradication reduced incidence of gastric adenocarcinoma compared with untreated groups (pooled incidence rate ratio, 0.53; 95% CI, 0.44 to 0.64).[56] However, eradication of *H pylori* infection is associated with increased risk for esophageal adenocarcinoma and gastric cardia carcinoma.[70]

Colon and Rectal Neoplasms

NSAIDs. The results of prospective intervention trials have shown positive effects of NSAIDs on the prevention of polyps. Meta-analyses of randomized trials of aspirin have demonstrated that these agents prevent colorectal cancer.[71,72] Trials to assess COX-2 inhibitors and other NSAIDs for the prevention of colorectal adenomas have shown preventive benefits; however, these agents are associated with increased cardiovascular risk. The risk of colon cancer can be reduced by doses of aspirin as low as 80 mg daily.[72] The US Preventive Services Task Force (USPSTF) recommends use of a low dose of aspirin (75-100 mg daily) for prevention of colorectal cancer in adults age 50 to 59 years who have a life expectancy of at least 10 years. For adults age 60 to 69 years, the task force recommends that the decision be individualized.[73] Low-dose aspirin use (≤ 100 mg daily or every other day) increases major GI bleeding risk by 58%.[74] Data reporting that NSAIDs reduce neoplastic progression in patients with familial nonpolyposis colon cancer (Lynch syndrome) suggest interventions targeting inflammatory pathways may play a role in high-penetrance genetic syndromes.[75] The use of NSAIDs for patients with familial adenomatous polyposis after colectomy may be reasonable in conjunction with endoscopic screening.

Calcium. Diets high in calcium are associated with a lower risk of colon cancer. Calcium binds bile and fatty acids, reducing intraluminal exposure to compounds that cause hyperproliferation of the colonic epithelium. However, a Women's Health Initiative prospective study of calcium and vitamin D supplementation did not show lower incidence of colorectal cancer in women who received calcium supplements.[76] Prospective randomized studies have shown that calcium supplementation decreases the risk of recurrence of adenomatous polyps by approximately 20%.[77] However, a more recent trial failed to confirm these findings.[78]

Prophylactic Colectomy. Colectomy is used as a preventive measure for individuals at extremely high risk of colorectal cancer as a result of a history of ulcerative colitis or of a genetic predisposition to the disease, such as familial adenomatous polyposis.[79]

Hepatocellular Carcinoma

Chronic hepatitis B infection is prevalent in Asia, Africa, Southern Europe, and Latin America, with a hepatitis B surface antigen–positive rate of 2% to 20%. An estimated 1 million people in the world have chronic hepatitis B infection, causing 1 million deaths yearly. Since the hepatitis B vaccine was introduced in Taiwan in 1984, the risk of hepatocellular carcinoma (the leading cancer in Taiwan) has been reduced by > 70% among those vaccinated.[52]

The hepatitis C virus infects approximately 3% of the population worldwide and 1.3% of the population in the United States. In the United States, after peaking in the 1980s, hepatitis C infections rates have rapidly declined to 16,000 cases per year.[53] The trend of reduced hepatitis C infection in the United States has not been replicated in other parts of the world, particularly in low- and middle-income countries. Hepatitis C viral liver disease progresses slowly and asymptomatically. As populations infected in the 1980s age, incidence and mortality resulting from cirrhosis and hepato-cellular carcinoma are increasing. Antiviral therapy for hepatitis C with direct-acting viral protease inhibitors eradicates the virus and is associated with a 54% reduction in all-cause mortality, including reduced morality resulting from hepatocellular carcinoma.[53]

Breast Neoplasms

Selective Estrogen Receptor Modulators. Tamoxifen acts as an estrogen agonist in the endometrium and bone and as an estrogen antagonist in breast tissue. It also upregulates transforming growth factor β, which decreases breast cell proliferation. Large randomized prospective clinical trials with an invasive breast adenocarcinoma incidence end point are outlined in Table 1-7. Expert guidance from the USPSTF and ASCO recommends both tamoxifen (20 mg per day for 5 years) or raloxifene (60 mg per day for 5 years) to reduce incidence of estrogen receptor–positive invasive breast adenocarcinoma.[80,89] Notably, neither drug reduces estrogen receptor–negative invasive breast adenocarcinoma incidence or breast cancer–specific or all-cause mortality rates. ASCO recommends preventive intervention in "premenopausal women age who are ≥ 35 years with a 5-year projected absolute breast cancer risk > 3% according to the NCI Breast Cancer Risk Assessment Tool (or equivalent measures), or with lobular carcinoma in situ."[81(p2946)]

Aromatase Inhibitors. Aromatase inhibitors lower estrogen levels by stopping an enzyme from changing other hormones into estrogen. However, they cannot stop the ovaries from making estrogen; therefore, these drugs are only ideal for postmenopausal women. Anastrozole, letrozole, and exemestane are used to treat hormone-positive breast cancers but have also been found to lower breast cancer risk in postmenopausal women. These drugs have not been approved by the US Food and Drug Administration (FDA) yet for chemoprevention, but they may be a reasonable option for women who are at higher risk for blood clots, because they have a different clinical toxicity profile than selective estrogen receptor modulators. However, neither of these aromatase inhibitors increases survival compared with placebo. ASCO recommends exemestane (25 mg/day for 5 years) and anastrazole (1 mg/day for 5 years) for breast cancer prevention in postmenopausal women, in addition to tamoxifen and raloxifene.[89]

Hormone Replacement Therapy. The Women's Health Initiative reported an increased risk of breast cancer (odds ratio, 1.24; 95% CI, 1.01 to 1.54) among postmenopausal women taking active hormone replacement estrogens with progestins.[82] A parallel trial of estrogen alone compared with placebo for women with a prior hysterectomy did not show an increased risk of breast cancer among women taking estrogen.[83] There is no benefit of postmenopausal estrogens for women beyond a short-term reduction in perimenopausal symptoms.[84]

Management of Women With High-Penetrance Germinal Mutations (*BRCA*). Prospective trials in which women self-select for mastectomy or close surveillance have found the short-term risk of breast cancer is lower for women with certain *BRCA1* and *BRCA2* mutations who choose prophylactic mastectomy. However, prophylactic bilateral mastectomy to prevent breast cancer has not been assessed in a rigorously randomized trial. Because this surgery leaves some breast tissue behind, a patient's risk is not reduced to zero. When bilateral mastectomy is coupled with prophylactic bilateral salpingo-oophorectomy, ovarian cancer risk is markedly decreased, and there is an added benefit of breast cancer prevention.[85] A Cochrane review concluded that bilateral prophylactic mastectomy for those at very high risk for breast cancer (eg, those with deleterious *BRCA* mutations) was effective in reducing the incidence of and subsequent mortality resulting from breast cancer.[86]

Prostate Cancer

Antiandrogens. Androgens stimulate prostate cell proliferation and drive prostate carcinogenesis. Finasteride and dutasteride deprive the prostate of androgen stimulation by inhibiting 5-α reductase, the enzyme responsible for converting testosterone into the active dihydrotestosterone. Randomized placebo-controlled clinical prevention trials have found that 5-α reductase inhibitors reduce the incidence of prostate cancer by approximately 20% (Table 1-7).[87] An initial finding indicating that men treated with finasteride who experienced progression to invasive prostate cancers developed high Gleason score (7-10) lesions compared with those in the placebo arm[88] was not borne out with longer-term follow-up.[89] With 18 years of follow-up, treatment with a 5-α reductase inhibitor (finasteride) did not change overall survival.[90] Furthermore, sexual function adverse effects (erectile dysfunction, loss of libido, gynecomastia) were more common in the finasteride- or dutasteride-treated groups.

Testosterone Replacement Therapy. Testosterone therapy is increasingly common in the United States. Millions of men are receiving some form of replacement. No cohort study large enough to adequately address the question of whether this low dose of androgen supplementation increases the risk of prostate cancer incidence or mortality has been conducted to date. However, several small studies have shown no evidence of an increase in prostate cancer risk associated with testosterone replacement therapy (TRT). In addition, there has there been no evidence of progression of existing prostate cancer induced by the concomitant use of TRT.[91] TRT may increase the risk of cardiovascular disease.

Micronutrients. Findings from epidemiologic studies indicate a correlation between a high intake of antioxidants, such as selenium and vitamin E, and a lower risk of prostate cancer. The results of a small randomized skin cancer prevention trial of selenium compared with placebo verified the population-based data,[92] as did a secondary analysis of a large clinical prevention trial of selenium and other micronutrients for the prevention of lung cancer (ATBC Cancer Prevention Trial).[93] A prospective randomized placebo-controlled trial, the Selenium and Vitamin E Cancer Prevention Trial, assessed these drugs in 32,400 participants and reported no reduction in prostate cancer incidence (Table 1-7).[94]

Cervical Cancer

HPV Vaccination for Prevention. HPV vaccination using the 9-valent vaccine (Gardasil; Merck, Kenilworth, NJ) effectively reduces the incidence of cervical carcinoma. The CDC recommends a 2-dose schedule, with doses 6 months apart, for girls and boys age 9 to 14 years.[54,55] For girls and boys age 15 to 26 years and for those with a compromised immune system, the CDC recommends a 3-dose schedule, with doses 6 and 12 months apart. ASCO guidelines are similar to CDC guidelines but emphasize vaccination of girls.[95] Most recent HPV vaccination rates for children and adolescents, especially those in the target range of 9 to 13 years, remain low (coverage ≥ 1 dose: girls, 22.4%; boys, 24.2%). The highest coverage rates are in girls age 14 to 19 years (54.9%).[96] Because these same viruses are involved in other cancers, the incidence of anal, vaginal, penile, and oropharyngeal cancers may also decline if a sufficient percentage of the population can be protected from the HPV virus. HPV vaccination was recently approved for men and women up to age 45 years by the FDA. ASCO provides a resource-stratified guideline for primary prevention of cervical cancer globally.[95]

Surgical Ablative Prevention. Conization, loop electrosurgical excision procedure, cryosurgery, electrocauterization, laser ablation, and hysterectomy removing cervical dysplasia or intraepithelial neoplasia (both of which are precursors to invasive cervical cancer) effectively prevent progression to invasive neoplasms. The procedures, although well tolerated and effective, require substantial equipment and infrastructure, making them inaccessible to large populations in low- and middle-income countries and to underserved populations in wealthier developed countries.

Ovarian Cancer

Epidemiologic data indicate that oral contraceptive hormones reduce the risk of ovarian adenocarcinoma; however, no prospective studies have verified these population-based associations.[97] For women at very high risk for ovarian cancer because of a *BRCA* genetic mutation, bilateral salpingo-oophorectomy after completion of childbearing remains the treatment of choice (including fallopian tube removal).[85] Women with Lynch syndrome, associated with large and small bowel polyps and cancers, are at elevated risk for endometrial and ovarian cancers. For these women, prophylactic hysterectomy and bilateral salpingo-oophorectomy may also be recommended.

KEY POINTS

- Most randomized trials of vitamins or nutritional supplements as clinical preventive agents have had negative results.
- Tamoxifen and aromatase inhibitors are established breast cancer preventives.
- Aspirin and other NSAIDs have preventive activity in colorectal neoplastic progression.
- Vaccinations or antiviral therapy for cancer-causing infectious agents, such as hepatitis B and HPV, have led to reduced incidence of and mortality resulting from associated cancers (hepatocellular carcinoma, cervical and other anogenital cancers).

CANCER SCREENING AND EARLY DETECTION

RATIONALE AND CONCEPTS

Cancer screening is an attempt to detect noninvasive or invasive neoplasms in asymptomatic individuals with the goal of intervening and decreasing morbidity and mortality. A screening test is not typically diagnostic for cancer; rather, it determines whether a neoplastic lesion might be present and whether additional testing, such as imaging or biopsy, is necessary. To be of true benefit, screening must lead to earlier treatment that offers a better outcome, usually reduced mortality, compared with treatment that starts at the onset of symptoms. The ideal evaluation of a screening approach is through the assessment of disease-specific and overall mortality in a prospective randomized clinical trial. Early detection of an apparently localized invasive neoplasm does not automatically confer benefit.

POTENTIAL BIASES

The evaluation of the benefits of a screening test is subject to several biases, including lead time, length, and healthy volunteer selection biases. The influences of these biases are reduced in a randomized trial.[98] Lead and length time biases can lead one to believe that there is a benefit to a screening test, when in truth, there is none; there may even be a net harm. Screening, regardless of benefit, will usually increase the number of specific cancers diagnosed. It can also produce a shift toward a greater proportion of cancers being diagnosed at lower stages. This will seem to improve survival statistics without reducing mortality (ie, the number of deaths resulting from a given cancer per number of people at risk for the disease; Fig 1-6). The healthy volunteer effect, a type of selection bias, occurs because volunteers for cancer prevention trials are more health conscious and are likely to have better prognoses or lower mortality rates, regardless of whether they are screened. Overdiagnosis occurs when a slow-growing invasive neoplasm fulfills the histologic criteria for cancer but has a clinically indolent course and is not life threatening (Fig 1-7).[99] Older people may be more likely to die as a result of other causes, such as heart disease, than of an indolent cancer.

POTENTIAL HARMFUL EFFECTS

People can be harmed as a result of screening. A harmful effect can be associated with the test itself, the workup of positive results of screening tests (both true-positive and false-positive results), and adverse events from the treatment of true-positive results. Screening can detect some cancers that would never have caused medical problems; the unnecessary treatment of these cancers can be harmful. In addition to the health adverse effects of screening, there are the financial and emotional costs associated with screening and with all of the additional tests and treatments.

ACCURACY

The results of screening tests can be classified into four categories (Table 1-8). The accuracy of any medical test is usually described by sensitivity and specificity. Positive predictive value and negative predictive value measure test performance. Sensitivity and specificity are relatively independent of the underlying prevalence or risk of the population being screened, but the positive and negative predictive values are highly dependent on prevalence (Table 1-9). In other words, screening is most beneficial, efficient, and economic when targeting a cancer common to the general population or groups with a high prevalence (or high risk) of the specific disease being screened. Sensitivity need not be extremely high. The key criterion for the public health recommendation of a screening test is that it is able to reduce cancer mortality.

A screening test that is not efficacious in reducing mortality in an average-risk population does not become efficacious if used in a high-risk population. Conversely, if a screening test is efficacious in reducing mortality, it is certainly preferable to use this test for higher-risk populations (eg, those with family history). A good example is chest x-ray screening for early detection of lung cancer. Proven not to reduce lung cancer mortality, chest x-ray screening would not work any better in heavy smokers or asbestos workers.

KEY POINTS

- Evaluation of the benefits/efficacy of a cancer screening test is far more complicated than simply performing the test and detecting localized cancers.
- The biases of screening are lead time, length, and healthy volunteer effect. These biases can make a screening test seem beneficial when there is actually no benefit, or the test may even cause harm.
- Overdiagnosis occurs when a screening test identifies indolent cancers that do not pose a mortal threat. The costs of overdiagnosis are high: unnecessary screening

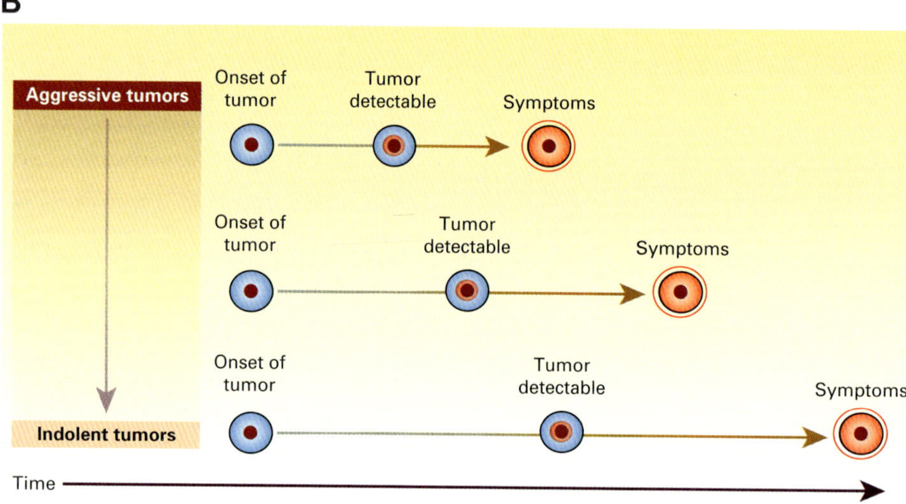

Fig. 1-6 Lead-time and length-time biases.

(A) Lead-time bias occurs when survival (the time from diagnosis to death) is increased, but treatment does not prolong life. Patients do not live longer; they are merely diagnosed at an earlier date. (B) Length-time bias occurs when slow-growing, less aggressive cancers are detected during screening. Cancers diagnosed as the result of the onset of symptoms between scheduled screenings are, on average, more aggressive, and treatment outcomes are not as favorable.

of large populations, unnecessary medical procedures, and emotional and financial harm.

- To offset these biases, a randomized trial is the best way to assess a screening test with the end point of reduction in cancer-related mortality.
- Sensitivity, specificity, and positive predictive value can be important measures of the accuracy of a screening test and the rate of false-positive and false-negative results. However, these metrics are not used to decide whether a screening test should be used on a large scale; the main criterion for this purpose is reduction in mortality.

CURRENT SCREENING AND EARLY DETECTION GUIDELINES BY ORGAN SITE

There is convincing evidence that screening for cervical, colorectal cancer, and breast cancers is beneficial at certain ages for people at average risk. Although increased surveillance of people at high risk for specific cancers, because of family history or genetic risk, may be prudent, few studies have been carried out to assess the true worth of this approach. The USPSTF,[100] Canadian Task Force on Preventive Health Care,[101] and American Cancer Society[102] are among the more prominent organizations publishing screening recommendations after a rigorous review process consisting of a structured evaluation of the literature by screening experts. Current screening recommendations from these three organizations are summarized in Table 1-10 and in following paragraphs.

BREAST CANCER

Breast Self-Examination

The results of the largest randomized controlled study of breast self-examination reported to date showed both an increased rate of biopsy and enhanced detection of benign lesions, but little or no stage shift and no reduction in breast cancer mortality.[103]

Mammography

Screening women age > 50 years who are at average risk using mammography alone or mammography and clinical breast

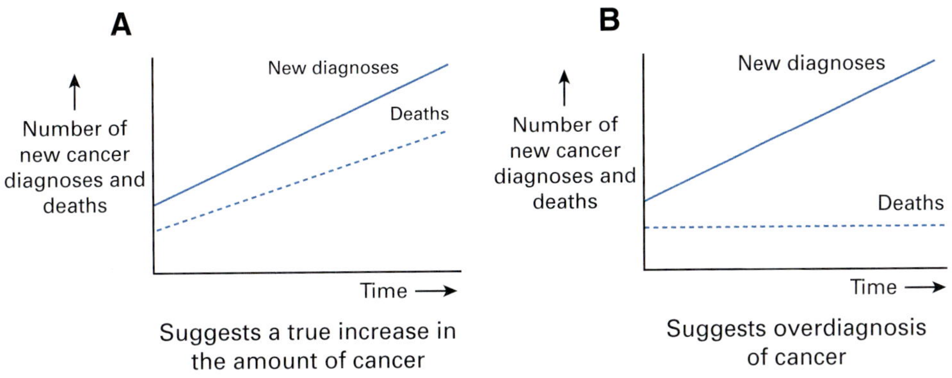

Fig. 1-7 Overdiagnosis.

(A) Assuming no major improvement in treatment outcomes, an increase in new diagnoses of a cancer will parallel an increase in the number of deaths. (B) Overdiagnosis occurs when the number of diagnoses and number of deaths are discordant.

Data collected and adapted from Welch HG, Black WC. Overdiagnosis in cancer. J Natl Cancer Inst. 2010 May 5;102(9):605-13.[99]

examination every 1 to 2 years decreases mortality by 20% to 30%, according to several randomized trials. Each trial has been criticized for a certain aspect of its design, but there is power in the consistency of the observations. The introduction of mammographic screening in the United Kingdom starting in 1991 for women age 49 to 64 years has led to an overall reduction in breast cancer mortality of 21%.[104] Recent consensus publications from the USPSTF and the Canadian Task Force on Preventive Health Care recommend mammographic screening every 2 to 3 years for average-risk women between the ages of 50 and 69 years (Canadian recommendation) or 50 and 74 years (US recommendation).

Mammographic screening for women of average risk between the ages of 40 and 49 years remains controversial. Two recent consensus publications from the USPSTF[105] and the Canadian Task Force on Preventive Health Care[106] find no benefit to screening women age < 50 years. Despite a potential 18% reduction in mortality, the concomitant number of false-positive screens was high enough to negate effective population-based screening. The American Cancer Society amended its longstanding screening guidelines in 2015 to recommend that screening for women at average risk begin at age 45 years.[107]

Magnetic Resonance Imaging for High-Risk Populations

Among women with *BRCA1* or *BRCA2* mutations, magnetic resonance imaging (MRI) has greater sensitivity than mammography or ultrasound. Its high cost and unproven survival benefit make it undesirable for general use, but it can increase yield in a cost-effective fashion for young *BRCA* mutation carriers, as well as for other women at increased risk for breast cancer.[108] The American Cancer Society has developed guidelines[109] for the use of MRI in women who have a lifetime risk of breast cancer that is 20% to ≥ 25%, as determined by the Gail, Claus, or Tirer-Cusik model.[110] Another category of women who are at elevated risk for breast cancer are those

Table 1-8 Indices for Describing the Accuracy of Screening Tests

Term	Definition	Ability of Test	Equation
Sensitivity	Proportion of people with the disease who have a positive result on a screening test	To detect disease when it is present	A/(A + C)
Specificity	Proportion of people who do not have the disease who have a negative result on a screening test	To correctly identify the absence of disease	D/(B + D)
Positive predictive value	Proportion of people with a positive result on a screening test who actually have the disease	To accurately predict the presence of disease	A/(A + B)
Negative predictive value	Proportion of people who have a negative result on a screening test who truly do not have the disease	To accurately predict the absence of disease	D/(C + D)

Abbreviations: A, true-positive result; B, false-positive result; C, false-negative result; D, true-negative result.

Table 1-9 Influence of Prevalence on Predictive Value

Disease Prevalence	PPV	
5 affected individuals per 1,000 population		
Sensitivity	0.8	0.95
Specificity, %		
0.95	7	9
0.999	80	83
1 affected individual per 1,000 population		
Sensitivity	0.8	0.95
Specificity, %		
0.95	0.2	0.2
0.999	7	9

Abbreviation: PPV, positive predictive value.

with dense breasts; recommendations for these women vary, sometimes including ultrasound, MRI, or other tests in addition to mammography. The most recent USPSTF statement issued in 2016 acknowledges enhanced detection with additional imaging procedures, but does not recommend their use for screening women with dense breasts because of increased false positives and wide CIs of end points as a result of sparse data.[111]

CERVICAL CANCER

Papanicolau Test

In developed countries, early detection of cervical neoplasia, either noninvasive or invasive, has for 60 years relied upon cytology (Papanicolaou [Pap] smear), with sensitivity of 78% (range, 30%-87%) and specificity of 62% (range, 61%-94%).[112] Cytologic screening is subject to sampling errors, problems with cellular preservation, and reader subjectivity. Because of the requirement of colposcopy referral only for women with positive cytology examinations, the false-negative rate is not well measured but has been reported to be as high as 50%.[112]

HPV DNA Test

In a meta-analysis of cross-sectional studies, screening with a one-time HPV DNA test has a pooled sensitivity of 90% (95% CI, 88% to 93%) for precancerous lesion cervical intraepithelial neoplasia (CIN) II and 95% (95% CI, 93% to 97%) for CIN III. The test specificity was consistently lower when directly compared with parallel cervical cytology: HPV test specificity of 88.5% (95% CI, 87% to 90%) for CIN II and 89% (95% CI, 87.2% to 88.5%) for CIN III.[113]

For women age 30 to 64 years, the USPSTF recommends screening:

- With cervical cytology (Pap) alone every 3 years OR
- With HPV DNA molecular testing alone every 5 years OR
- With combined cervical cytology and HPV DNA molecular testing every 5 years

In women age < 30 years, transient infection reduces HPV test specificity. The task force recommends cervical cytology screening every 3 years for women age 21 through 29 years.[114] More frequent screening leads to additional procedures and treatment of transient lesions but no incremental benefit. HPV DNA molecular testing has become low cost and accessible in low- and middle-income countries, increasing the number of women screened in environments where cervical cytology tests are difficult to conduct properly. Screening remains recommended in women who have received the vaccine for HPV, because the previously used vaccine does not provide protection against all high-risk HPV types. This recommendation may be amended as the 9-valent vaccine becomes more widely used throughout the world. The ASCO cervical screening guidelines reflect those of the USPSTF.[95]

COLORECTAL CANCER

Fecal Occult Blood Test Screening

Fecal occult blood tests (FOBTs) screen for colorectal neoplasms by detecting traces of blood in the stool. The guaiac-based FOBT was the first screening test to demonstrate reduced colorectal adenocarcinoma incidence and mortality by one third.[115] Randomized controlled trials have shown that annual or biennial FOBTs reduce colorectal cancer mortality by 15% to 33%.[115-117] The reduction is durable over three decades.[118] The guaiac-based FOBT is not specific for human blood, and consequently, it has high false-positive rates. The fecal immunochemical test (FIT) detects human hemoglobin, thus eliminating the false positives caused by nonhuman hemoglobin in the diet.[119] FITs are more sensitive at detecting colorectal cancers CRCs (sensitivity, 61%-91%) and adenomas (sensitivity, 16%-31%) than colorectal cancer, 25%-38%; (advanced adenomas, 16%-31%).[120,121] A meta-analysis of data from 19 prospective randomized trials or cohorts using eight different commercially available FITs reported an overall sensitivity for detection of colorectal adenocarcinoma of 79% and specificity of 94%.[122] A recently marketed stool DNA FIT has high sensitivity for detection of colorectal cancer, but data demonstrating reduced colorectal incidence and mortality are not published. Test performance rapidly degrades for noninvasive neoplasms.[123]

Flexible Sigmoidoscopy, Colonoscopy, and Computed Tomography Colonography

Flexible sigmoidoscopy screening reduces distal colon cancer incidence and mortality by 22% to 26% with long-term effects, but has no benefit for cancers in the proximal colon (which is not imaged with sigmoidoscopy).[124,125] Population-based cohort studies of colonoscopic screening have demonstrated reduced colorectal cancer mortality, primarily in distal but not in the proximal colon.[126-128] This discrepancy has been

Table 1-10 **Screening Recommendations for Asymptomatic Patients With Normal Risk**			
Test or Procedure	**US Preventive Services Task Force**	**Canadian Task Force on Preventive Health Care**	**American Cancer Society**
FOBT for colorectal cancer	Annual FOBT or FIT, starting at age 50 years	FOBT or FIT every 2 years, starting at age 50 years	Annual FOBT or FIT, starting at age 45 years (qualified recommendation); age 50 years (strong recommendation; FIT preferred)
Flexible sigmoidoscopy for colorectal cancer	Flexible sigmoidoscopy every 5 years, starting at age 50 years	Flexible sigmoidoscopy every 10 years, starting at age ≥ 50 years	Flexible sigmoidoscopy every 5 years, starting at age 45 years; consider combining with annual FOBT or FIT
Colonoscopy for colorectal cancer	Every 10 years, starting at age 50 years	Insufficient evidence	Every 10 years, starting at age 50 years
CT colonography for colorectal cancer	Every 5 years, starting at age 50 years	Insufficient evidence	Every 5 years, starting at age 50 years
DRE	No recommendation	Poor evidence to include or exclude for men age > 50 years	Recommend against
PSA	For men age 55-69 years, the decision for PSA screening is an individual one, based on shared discussion between physician and patient; screening offers small potential benefit of reducing chance of death resulting from prostate cancer in some men	Age < 55 years: recommend not screening for PSA Age 55-69 years: recommend not screening, weak recommendation, discussion of risks/benefits with patients who place high value on small amount of mortality reduction Age > 70 years: recommend not screening for PSA	Shared decision between physician and patient; annually, starting at age 50 years in men with life expectancy of ≥ 10 years
Pap cytology, HPV DNA for cervical cancer	Starting at age 21 years, Pap test every 3 years from age 21-65 years; alternatively, Pap test combined with HPV testing every 5 years, starting at age 30 years	Starting at age 25 years, screen every 3 years to age 69 years	Starting at age 21 years, screen every 3 years with conventional Pap test or liquid-based Pap test; at age ≥ 30 years, women with three normal tests in a row may screen every 3 years with cervical cytology alone or every 5 years with HPV DNA test plus cervical cytology; women age ≥ 65 years who have had ≥ three normal Pap tests and no abnormal tests in the past 10 years and women who have had total hysterectomy stop cervical cancer screening
BSE for breast cancer	Recommend against clinicians teaching women how to perform BSE	No longer recommended at any age	Women should also know how their breasts normally look and feel and report any breast changes to health care provider right away
CBE for breast cancer	Insufficient evidence to recommend adding over and above mammography	No longer recommended at any age	No longer recommended at any age

Table 1-10 **continued**

Test or Procedure	US Preventive Services Task Force	Canadian Task Force on Preventive Health Care	American Cancer Society
Mammography for breast cancer	Every 2 years for women age 50-74 years; screening before age 50 years should consider patient context and patient values regarding specific benefits and harms; no benefit to screening before age 50 years	Mammography every 2-3 years for women age 50-69 years; no benefit to screening before age 50 years	Annually starting at age 45 years; women age 40-44 years should have the opportunity to begin mammographic screening; women age ≥ 55 years should transition to biannual screening; clinical breast examination not recommended
LDCT scan for lung cancer	For those age 55-80 years who have 30-pack-year smoking history who currently smoke or have quit within the past 15 years, annual LDCT	For those age 55-74 years with 30-pack-year smoking history who currently smoke or have quit within the past 15 years, annual screening up to three consecutive times	For those age 55-74 years with 30-pack-year smoking history who currently smoke or have quit within the past 15 years, discuss potential benefits and harms of screening and emphasize smoking cessation

NOTE. These recommendations are for the general population (ie, asymptomatic people who have no risk factors, other than age or sex, for the targeted condition).
Abbreviations: BSE, breast self-examination; CBE, clinical breast examination; CT, computed tomography; DRE, digital rectal examination; FIT, fecal immunochemical test; FOBT, Fecal occult blood testing; HPV, human papillomavirus; LDCT, low-dose computed tomography; Pap, Papanicolau; PSA, prostate-specific antigen.

attributed to endoscopic quality issues, the technical difficulties in detecting lesions in the right colon, and the more frequent occurrence of flat and depressed dysplastic lesions in the right colon.[129-132] The reported sensitivity of computed tomography (CT; virtual) colonography for detection of adenomas measuring ≥ 10 mm ranges from 67% to 94%, with specificity ranging from 86% to 98%.[133]

Guidelines

Among the multiple screening tests for colorectal cancer, the USPSTF found no tests demonstrating superiority others.[73] The task force guidelines recommend screening in average-risk individuals with no polyps or precancerous lesions on prior endoscopies from age 50 to 75 years using shared decision making, with patients being offered:

- Annual stool-based screening (annual high-sensitivity standard guaiac-based test [Sensa II; SmithKline Diagnostics, San Jose, CA] or FIT or FIT DNA every 1 to 3 years) OR
- Endoscopic procedure (flexible sigmoidoscopic screening once every 5 years with yearly FIT or colonoscopy every 10 years) OR
- CT colonography

Barium enema as a screening tool is not recommended. Recommendations of the Canadian Task Force on Preventive Health Care differ from the US recommendations by extending the frequency to stool-based screening to every 2 years and flexible sigmoidoscopy to every 10 years and not recommending colonoscopy[134] (Table 1-10). Colonoscopy should be used for patients at high risk, such as those with a genetic predisposition to colorectal cancer, prior colorectal cancer, prior large adenomatous polyps, or inflammatory bowel disease.

Despite reduced incidence and mortality rates of colorectal cancer in the United States over 20 years, SEER data show an alarming increase in younger individuals who now comprise 20% of all colorectal cancer diagnoses and 30% of all rectal cancers.[135] The 2018 guidelines from the American Cancer Society recommend people at average risk start colorectal screening at age 45 years,[102] and in 2017, the US Multi-Society Task Force (a group representing three societies of gastroenterologists) recommended that colorectal screening for African Americans, who have disproportionate mortality and risk of early-onset colorectal cancer, begin at age 45 years.

LUNG CANCER

Screening for lung cancer with chest x-ray and sputum cytologic testing was evaluated in four randomized lung cancer screening trials and a large prospective cohort study. The Prostate, Lung, Colorectal, and Ovarian Screening Trial (PLCO) found no reduction in lung cancer mortality.[136] The National Lung Cancer Screening Trial (NLST) reported that low-dose spiral CT scanning reduces lung cancer mortality by 20%.[137] Spiral CT scans increase the number of lesions diagnosed and thus will increase the number of diagnostic and therapeutic procedures performed. Cost-benefit analyses for spiral CT screening concluded that the benefits for certain subgroups of heavy smokers outweigh the harms of overdiagnosis and false-positive results.[138] Most expert organizations now recommend CT screening for current or former heavy smokers of > 30 pack-years[102,139] (Table 1-10). The American Cancer Society recommends annual lung cancer screening with a low-dose CT scan for people age 55 to 74 years in fairly good health who currently smoke, have quit within the past 15 years, or have at least a 30-pack-year smoking history.

PROSTATE CANCER

The digital rectal examination (DRE) and measurement of serum PSA are commonly used in the United States, although most professional organizations advise caution in the use of such screening tools (Table 1-10). Prostate cancer screening is prone to lead-time bias, length bias, and overdiagnosis. Although screening using PSA levels and DRE clearly detects many asymptomatic cancers, it has a limited ability to reliably distinguish tumors that could be lethal but still curable from those that pose little or no threat to health. Between 20% and 40% of localized prostate cancers diagnosed through screening are indolent and clinically nonsignificant. Treatment of screen-detected cancers may cause morbidity, such as impotence and urinary incontinence, and carries a small risk of death.

Two large prospective prostate cancer screening trials have influenced screening guidelines. First, PLCO found no mortality reduction from prostate cancer screening.[140] Second, the European Randomized Study of Screening for Prostate Cancer (ERSPC) reported a 21% reduction in cancer mortality associated with prostate cancer screening.[140] The high rate of screening in the control group of PLCO (estimated to be 80%) compared with that in ERSPC may be a result of the discrepant findings and subtle differences in end point analysis. PLCO focused on absolute mortality reduction, meaning the likelihood of an individual avoiding death resulting from prostate cancer, whereas ERSPC reported relative mortality reduction, meaning the reduction in risk of dying as a result of prostate cancer relative to death that would have occurred in the absence of screening.

In 2012, the USPSTF concluded that the risk-benefit ratio for prostate cancer screening was insufficient to justify population-based PSA-based screening. In 2018, the USPSTF modified its recommendations, stating "for men aged 55 to 69 years, the decision to undergo periodic PSA-based screening for prostate cancer should be an individual one. Before deciding whether to be screened, men should have an opportunity to discuss the potential benefits and harms of screening with their clinician....Screening offers a small potential benefit of reducing the chance 902of death from prostate cancer in some men."[141(p1902)] This recommendation is consistent with recommendations of other major expert organizations[102,142] (Table 1-10).

An increasingly popular approach to prostate cancer screening with PSA addresses the issue of overdiagnosis. Use of a prostate risk calculator, developed from long-term longitudinal follow-up data from the Prostate Cancer Prevention Trial, enables prediction of low-grade (Gleason score < 7) and high-risk cancers to make biopsy and treatment decisions.[143] Another approach employs risk stratification integrating age-specific PSA levels and other epidemiologic risk factors to identify those men who should be screened frequently and undergo additional diagnostic procedures.[144]

OVARIAN CANCER

Adnexal palpation, transvaginal ultrasound, and measurement of serum CA125 have all been considered for ovarian cancer screening, but none has been shown to be effective. No randomized prospective trial of screening for ovarian cancer has shown a reduction in ovarian cancer mortality. The results of such screening tests could lead to futile invasive diagnostic testing that might include laparotomy. Large randomized trials of screening using CA125 and transvaginal ultrasound in the United States and the United Kingdom have not reported clear-cut benefit to screening.[145]

SKIN CANCERS

Nonmelanoma skin cancers (basal and squamous cell carcinomas), although the most common types of cancer in the United States, rarely cause mortality, whereas melanomas cause substantial mortality. No randomized study has been conducted to assess whether a clinician visual screening program for skin cancer decreases mortality. A population-based screening program in Germany resulted in a reduction of melanoma mortality of one per 100,000. Harms may be considerable, including repeated biopsies and potential overdiagnosis and overtreatment. For these reasons, the updated USPSTF recommendations conclude that the current evidence is insufficient to assess the balance of benefit and harm of visual skin examination by a clinician to screen for skin cancers in adults.[146]

LOWER ESOPHAGEAL ADENOCARCINOMAS

The dramatic rise in the incidence of esophageal adenocarcinoma during the past two decades has raised concerns regarding prevention. The main risk factor for Barrett's esophagus is gastroesophageal reflux disease, a condition that has increased dramatically, perhaps in part because of the epidemic of obesity. Guidelines from the American College of Gastroenterology recommend upper endoscopic screening in high-risk individuals, defined as men with chronic (> 5 years) and/or frequent (≥ weekly) symptoms of gastroesophageal reflux (heartburn or acid regurgitation) and two or more of the following risk factors for Barrett's esophagus or esophageal adenocarcinoma: age > 50 years, white race, presence of central obesity (waist circumference > 102 cm or waist-hip ratio > 0.9), current smoker or history of smoking, and confirmed family history of Barrett's esophagus or esophageal adenocarcinoma (in a first-degree relative).[67] Evidence demonstrating benefit in randomized screening trials or reduced mortality data is not available.

SCREENING FOR OTHER CANCERS GLOBALLY

Although this chapter has focused on cancer screening in the United States, screening for some other cancers may be worthwhile in countries where these cancers are more common. One example is oral cancer, which is the most common cancer among men in India, largely because of the interaction between consumption of tobacco products (via smoking and chewing) and indigenous carcinogenic botanicals, such as the betel nut. A randomized trial has shown that in one region, the use of visual screening of the oral cavity reduced mortality significantly.[147] Screening guidelines specific to India have been recently published.[148]

Radiographic screening for hepatocellular carcinoma (HCC) in East Asia and Africa using ultrasonography or MRI reduces mortality. The Shanghai trial of > 18,000 carriers of hepatitis B, randomly assigned to a serum α fetoprotein test plus ultrasonography every 6 months or no screening found a 37% mortality reduction in the screened group.[149] The combined use of ultrasound and MRI detected most HCCs at an early stage, when they were likely to be resectable.[150]

Recent guidelines on gastric cancer screening from Japan recommend radiographic upper GI imaging or endoscopy. These guidelines are based on observational trials. No randomized trial has been conducted to confirm the efficacy of these tests in reducing mortality.[151] Endoscopic screening for squamous cell cancer of the esophagus in high endemic areas in China seems to reduce mortality by 50%.[152]

Screening for exposure to EBV using a plasma EBV DNA test identifies persistently positive individuals for further screening. Of a cohort of 20,174 plasma screens in Shanghai, China, 5.5% tested positive, of which approximately one quarter were persistently positive. These patients underwent further testing with endoscopy, and 34 were found to have nasopharyngeal carcinoma, mostly early stage. Only one carcinoma developed among those who were EBV negative.[153]

KEY POINTS

- PLCO and NLST have revolutionized our knowledge of and approach to screening for lung, colorectal cancer, prostate, and ovarian cancers:
  - Although chest x-ray is ineffective as lung cancer screening, low-dose CT scan screening is effective.
  - Sigmoidoscopy is effective in reducing mortality resulting from colorectal cancer.
  - CA125 and transvaginal ultrasound screening for ovarian cancer are not effective.
  - Controversial data on PSA screening for prostate cancer remain.
- Mammography screening for breast cancer among women age > 50 years reduces mortality, but screening in women age < 50 years remains controversial.
- Decisions on PSA-based prostate cancer screening should be individualized and include patient-clinician discussion of risks and benefits.
- Low-dose spiral CT screening is an established new approach to reducing lung cancer mortality among heavy smokers.
- The use of HPV DNA molecular testing in conjunction with the Pap test for women age ≥ 30 years can allow the extension of the interval between screenings for cervical cancer to 5 years.
- Both FOBT and sigmoidoscopy are recommended as screening modalities for colorectal cancer. There is now evidence to support the use of colonoscopy for colorectal cancer screening, although the benefits are modest compared with FOBT with FIT ± sigmoidoscopy. Evidence for colonoscopy is not based on head-to-head prospective randomized trials.

Acknowledgment

We thank Alfred I. Neugut, MD, PhD, for his contribution to prior versions of this chapter.

Table 1-7 **Randomized Chemoprevention Trials With Cancer Incidence End point**					
Population	**Drug/Dose**	**No.**	**End point**	**Primary Outcome**	**Reference**
Head and neck					
HNSCC	13-*cis*-retinoic acid 50-100 mg/m^2/day	103	Second primary in HN	Significant reduction in second primary tumors at 32 and 55 months; however, substantial toxicity	61
HNSCC	Etretinate 50, 25 mg/day	316	Second primary in HN	No effect	60
HNSCC	13-*cis*-retinoic acid 30 mg/day	1,190	Second primary in HN	No effect	63
HNSCC	Beta carotene 50 mg/day	264	Second primary in HN	No effect	154
HNSCC	Beta carotene 75 mg/day × 3 months, 1 month off	214	Second primary in HN	No effect	155
HNSCC	Beta carotene 30 mg/day + vitamin E 400 IU/day	540	Second primary in HN	Mortality increased in treatment arm	156
Lung					
Male smokers	Beta carotene 20 mg/day; vitamin E 50 mg/day	29,133	Lung cancer	Lung cancer increased with beta carotene; no effect with vitamin E	93
Smokers and asbestos workers	Carotene 30 mg/day; vitamin A 25,000 IU/day	18,314	Lung cancer	Lung cancer increased with beta carotene and vitamin A	58
Prior HNSCC, prior NSCLC	Vitamin A 300,000/150,000 IU/day; N-acetylcysteine 600 mg/day	2,592	Second primary cancer	No effect	157
Prior NSCLC	13-*cis*-retinoic acid 30 mg/day	1,166	Second primary cancer	No difference; second primary tumors lower in nonsmokers on drug and higher in smokers on drug	62
Prior NSCLC	Selenium 200 mg/day	1,561	Second primary cancer	No effect	158
Skin					
Prior BCC/SCC	13-*cis*-retinoic acid 5-10 mg/day; vitamin A 25,000 IU/day	524	Second skin cancer	No effect	159
Prior BCC/SCC	Beta-carotene 50 mg/day	1,805	Second skin cancer	No effect	160
Prior BCC	13-*cis*-retinoic acid 10 mg/day	981	Second skin cancer	No effect	161
Prior AKs; keratosis	Vitamin A 25,000 IU/day	2,298	Skin cancer incidence	Reduction in SCC but not BCC	162
Renal transplantation patients	Acitretin 30 mg/day	38	Skin cancer incidence	Significant reduction	163
Prior BCC/SCC	Selenium 200 μg/day	1,312	Recurrence	No effect	164

Table 1-7 **continued**					
Population	**Drug/Dose**	**No.**	**End point**	**Primary Outcome**	**Reference**
AKs	Celecoxib 200 mg twice daily	240	New AKs	Reduction of new AKs	165
BCC/SCC	Nicotinamide 500 mg twice daily	386	New BCC/SCC	Reduction of new BCC/SCC	166
BCC/SCC	Difluoromethylornithine 500 mg/m^2/day	291	New BCC/SCC	No effect	167
Breast					
Gail model: 5-year predicted risk of ≥ 1.66%; IEN	Tamoxifen 20 mg/day	13,388	Breast adenocarcinoma	Reduced risk; HR, 0.52; 95% CI, 0.42 to 0.64	168,169
Normal risk	Tamoxifen 20 mg/day	5,408	Breast adenocarcinoma	Reduced risk; HR, 0.67; 95% CI, 0.59 to 0.76	170
Family history	Tamoxifen 20 mg/day	2,471	Breast adenocarcinoma	Reduced risk; HR, 0.87; 95% CI, 0.63 to 1.21	171
Prior breast cancer	Fenretinide 200 mg/day	2,972	Breast adenocarcinoma in contralateral breast	Reduced risk in premenopausal women; HR, 0.62; 95% CI, 0.46 to 0.83	172
Gail model: 5-year predicted risk of ≥ 1.66%; IEN	Raloxifene 60 mg/day *v* tamoxifen 20 mg/day	19,747	Breast adenocarcinoma	Equivalent	173,174
Gail model: 5-year predicted risk of ≥ 1.66%; IEN	Exemestane 25 mg/day	4,560	Breast adenocarcinoma	Reduced risk; HR, 0.35; 95% CI, 0.18 to 0.70	175
High risk, multiple criteria + 10-year risk > 5 years	Anastrozole 1 mg/day	1,920	Breast adenocarcinoma	Reduced risk; HR, 0.47; 95% CI, 0.32 to 0.68	176
Healthy women	Calcium 500 mg twice daily + vitamin D_3 200 IU twice daily *v* placebo	36,282	Breast adenocarcinoma	No effect	177
Colorectal					
Healthy women	Calcium 500 mg twice daily + vitamin D_3 200 IU twice daily *v* placebo	36,282	Colorectal adenocarcinoma	No effect	76
Prostate					
Men age > 55 years	Finasteride 5 mg/day	18,882	Prostate adenocarcinoma	Reduced risk; HR for prostate cancer, 0.70; 95% CI, 0.65 to 0.76	88,90
Age 50-75 years; PSA 2.5-10.0 ng/mL; core biopsy within 6 months	Dutasteride 0.5 mg/day	6,729	Prostate adenocarcinoma	Reduced risk; RR for prostate cancer, 0.77; 95% CI, 0.70 to 0.85	178

Table 1-7 continued

Population	Drug/Dose	No.	End point	Primary Outcome	Reference
Healthy men age > 55 years (African American age > 50 years)	Selenium 200 μg/day; vitamin E 400 IU/day; combined, placebo	35,533	Prostate adenocarcinoma	No effect	94
Esophagus/stomach					
General population in geographic hotspot	Beta carotene 15 mg/day + vitamin E 30 mg/day + selenium 50 μg/day	29,584	Death resulting from gastric adenocarcinoma; death resulting from esophageal SCC	Significant decrease in death resulting from stomach cancer; no effect on death resulting from esophageal at 26-year follow-up	179,180
General population in geographic hotspot	Multivitamin/ multimineral + beta carotene 15 mg/day	3,318	Death resulting from gastric adenocarcinoma; death resulting from esophageal SCC	No effect	181

Abbreviations: AK, actinic keratosis; BCC, basal cell carcinoma; HN, head and neck; HNSCC, head and neck squamous cell carcinoma; HR, hazard ratio; IEN, intraepithelial neoplasia (non-invasive neoplasm); NSCLC, non-small-cell lung cancer; PSA, prostate-specific antigen; RR, relative risk; SCC, squamous cell carcinoma.

EPIDEMIOLOGY AND PREVENTION GLOBAL PERSPECTIVE: ASIA

Surendra Shastri, MBBS, MD, PhD, University of Texas MD Anderson Cancer Center, Houston, TX

INTRODUCTION

Wide variation exists globally in the incidence and mortality rates of recorded cancer types. Contributing factors to this variation include disparities in the availability of screening, diagnosis, treatment, and palliative care services. When interpreting the available data, we must consider the serious limitations in the quality and completeness of data from resource-poor countries. This perspective focuses on the cancer burden in Asia, comparing it with that in the United States wherever relevant.

Asia is the largest landmass and is home to half the world population. A large majority of the Asian countries fall into the low- and middle-income categories. Many of them have been facing internal and external social and economic disruptions over the last three decades. Asian countries are at various stages of epidemiologic transition, creating interesting epidemiologic observational and quasiexperimental situations that could provide important clues about and insights into the causes of cancer.

CANCER BURDEN IN ASIA

Table 1-11 provides a list of the top five cancers among women and men in the four geographically distinct and ethnically and culturally diverse regions of Asia (namely, Western, South Central, South Eastern, and Eastern Asia). Data from the United States have been added for the sake of comparison.

Four of the top five cancers in both sexes in Western and Eastern Asia, which have a number of high-income countries, are the same as those in the United States, suggesting similar etiologic patterns. The predominance of cancer of the lip and oral cavity, in both sexes, in South Central Asia is attributable to widespread smokeless tobacco use (chewing, snuff) observed in the region. The role of human papillomavirus (HPV) in the high incidence of oral cancers in South Central Asia is currently unknown, because adequate information on the prevalence of HPV in oral cancers in the region is lacking. There is a high incidence of cervical cancer among women in South Central and South Eastern Asia; however, this is likely because of the absence of population-based screening programs. Among men in South Eastern and Eastern Asia, cancers of the GI system, including the esophagus, stomach, and liver, predominate and are attributable to the high prevalence of *Helicobacter pylori* and hepatitis B infections.

Table 1-11 Top Five Cancers (all ages) in 2018 in Asia and the United States

Sex	Western Asia	South Central Asia	South Eastern Asia	Eastern Asia	United States
Female					
	Breast	Breast	Breast	Breast	Breast
	Colorectum	Cervix uteri	Cervix uteri	Lung	Lung
	Thyroid	Ovary	Colorectum	Colorectum	Colorectum
	Corpus uteri	Lip and oral cavity	Lung	Thyroid	Thyroid
	Lung	Colorectum	Ovary	Stomach	Corpus uteri
Male					
	Lung	Lip and oral cavity	Lung	Lung	Prostate
	Prostate colorectum	Lung	Liver	Stomach	Lung
	Bladder	Stomach	Colorectum	Colorectum	Colorectum
	Stomach	Esophagus	Prostate	Liver	Bladder
		Colorectum	Stomach	Esophagus	Melanoma of skin

Data adapted.[182]

Remarkable differences can also be noted between the United States and Asia with regard to the overall cancer incidence and mortality rates (Fig. 1-8). The estimated age-standardized incidence rate for all cancers, in both sexes, and all ages in Asia is approximately 47% of that in the United States. The mortality rate in Asia is, however, 11% greater than that in the United States, clearly reflecting the lack of organized prevention, screening, and early detection programs, combined with poor diagnostic and treatment infrastructures in most Asian countries, except for a few high-income countries like Bahrain, Israel, Japan, Kuwait, Qatar, Saudi Arabia, Singapore, South Korea, and the United Arab Emirates.

Although the current cancer incidence in Asia is less than half that in the United States, substantial increases in aging population cohorts, along with rapidly changing lifestyles that affect diet, physical activity, and obesity, increasing alcohol and tobacco use, and extensive use of agricultural fertilizers and pesticides, contribute to the increasing cancer burden in Asia. An estimated 65% increase in the number of incident cancer cases (from 8,750,932 in 2018 to 14,463,671 in 2040) and a 77% increase in the number deaths (from 5,477,064 in 2018 to 9,712,276 in 2040) are projected over the next two decades in Asia.[182] This calls for a drastic review of cancer control policies and investments in the region. Investments in health promotion (eg, healthy diets and physical activity, reduction of tobacco use and alcohol consumption), prevention (eg, HPV, HBV vaccination), and population screening/early detection (eg, screening for cervical, breast, stomach, and colorectal cancers) could pay rich dividends and reverse the projected trends. Increasing specialized workforce and treatment infrastructures should also become a priority.

More than 40% of incident cervical cancers and 54% of annual deaths occurring globally are reported from Asia.[182] The cervical cancer incidence and mortality rates in Asia are on a gradual decline, as a result of unexplained causes not related to screening (few Asian countries have population-based cervical screening). However, the sheer numbers and a high mortality-to-incidence ratio (0.53) continue to cause serious concern.

More than 74% of incident stomach (gastric) cancers and annual deaths occurring globally are reported from Asia.[182] The incidence and mortality rates of stomach cancer are also on a gradual decline in Asia. The alarming mortality-to-incidence ratio (0.76), however, continues to remain a significant public health concern in several Asian countries. Breast cancer incidence and mortality continue to rise exponentially in Asia.

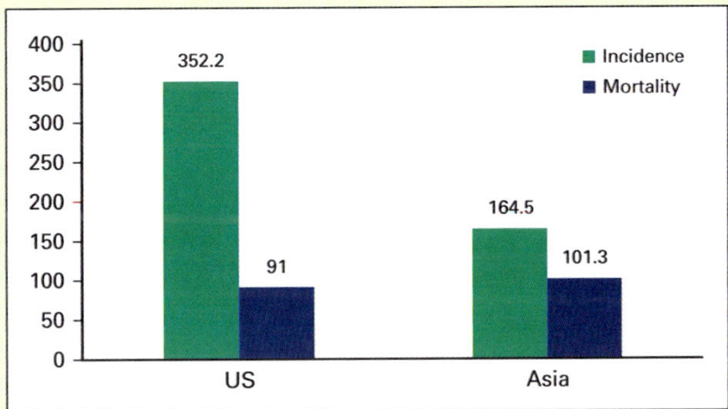

Fig. 1-8 Estimated age-standardized incidence and mortality rates for all cancers, both sexes and all ages per 100,000 in the US and Asia in 2018.

Data collated from IARC-Global Cancer Observatory, accessed on 04/20/2019.

GLOBAL GUIDELINES

ASCO recently published resource-stratified guidelines for primary[95] and secondary prevention[183] and treatment[184] of cervical cancers that provide evidence-based recommendations for different levels of health care resources globally. Using a methodology similar to that of the Breast Health Global Initiative,[185] experts from Asian countries have developed resource-stratified guidelines for prevention, early detection, diagnosis, and management of stomach cancers.[186] The International Agency for Research on Cancer has published breast screening guidelines for different health care situations,[187] and ASCO has published resource-stratified practice guidelines for palliative care in global settings.[188] Asian countries could significantly reduce cervical and stomach cancer incidence and mortality and breast cancer mortality by adopting these guidelines. The quality of end-of-life care could also be significantly improved by following the new ASCO guidelines on palliative care.

2

MOLECULAR BIOLOGY

Jonathan E. Grim, MD, PhD

OVERVIEW

Molecular oncology is rapidly evolving, and our understanding of the genes and processes that drive tumorigenesis is constantly expanding. Older techniques and studies provided fundamental insights into cancer biology, helping to identify a majority of genes and pathways frequently altered in both common and uncommon tumor types. More recent studies have taken advantage of new technologies to provide unprecedented depth and breadth of analysis of individual cancer samples, finding rare but important cancer genes and revealing surprising new cancer pathways. This knowledge has fueled the development of therapeutics that target specific oncogenic processes, both common and rare.

It is now both feasible and rational to perform limited or extensive molecular analyses of a patient's cancer sample in real time, and this increasingly allows clinicians to rationally apply targeted therapies to treat individual cancers. As our therapeutic armamentarium continuously expands to include new molecularly targeted agents to complement older, traditional cytotoxic compounds, it is essential that cancer care providers have at least a basic understanding of the molecular basis of cancer, as well as of established and emerging technologies used to aid in cancer diagnosis, prognosis, and therapy.

BASIC PRINCIPLES OF MOLECULAR BIOLOGY

DNA is a macromolecule comprising nucleotides containing 1 of 4 bases (adenine [A], guanine [G], cytosine [C], or thymine [T]; Fig 2-1) plus a deoxyribose sugar and a phosphate group. Each nucleotide base is connected to a deoxyribose sugar forming a nucleoside, and phosphodiester bonds between the sugar moieties form the DNA strand. The nucleosides of 1 DNA strand form hydrogen bonds with nucleosides on the complementary strand (C pairs with G and A pairs with T) to create a double-stranded DNA helix molecule. When DNA is replicated, the strands separate, and each provides a template for an exact complement to be synthesized, thereby generating 2 identical helixes.

The human genome contains approximately 3 billion nucleotides partitioned among 23 chromosomes. Only 1% of the genome is composed of coding DNA, which contains the gene sequences that encode proteins. The other 99% is considered noncoding DNA, which contains instructions for the formation of specialized RNA molecules (eg, transfer RNA and ribosomal RNA), as well as structural (eg, centromeres, telomeres, and G-quadruplexes), regulatory (eg, promoters, enhancers, and silencers), and other elements (eg, transposons, retrotransposons, and interspersed nuclear elements). Most human cells contain a complete genomic copy of DNA, but there are exceptions. For example, erythrocytes contain no genomic DNA, mature lymphocytes delete fragments of DNA within either immunoglobulin or T-cell receptor genes to generate

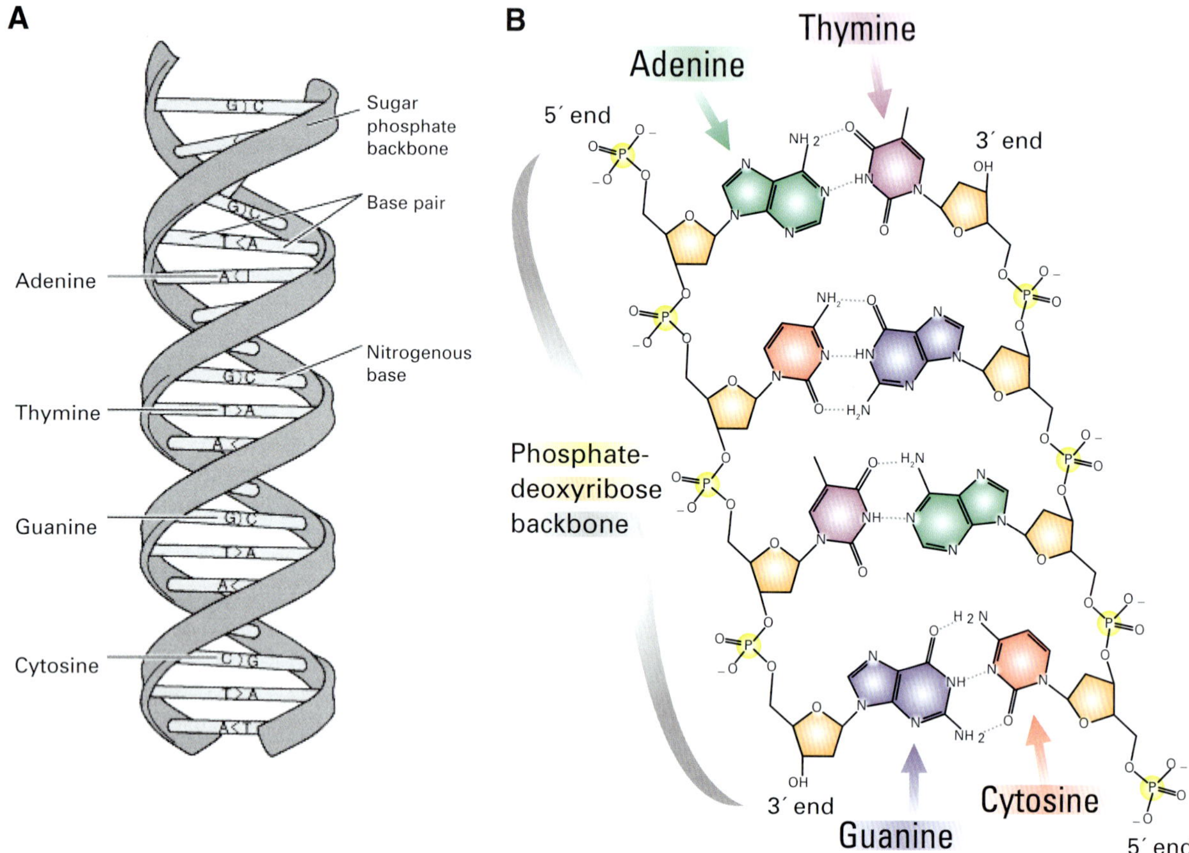

Fig. 2-1 The double-helix structure of DNA includes hydrogen bonding between adenine (A) and thymine (T) bases and between guanine (G) and cytosine (C) bases.

(A) DNA double helix. (B) Close-up of the molecular structure of DNA, showing hydrogen bonds between the 2 pairs of bases and the phosphodiester bonds between sugar molecules.

Reprinted from https://commons.wikimedia.org/wiki/File:DNA-structure-and-bases.png.

antigen-recognition proteins, and megakaryocytes contain extra copies of the genome that result from the process of endoreduplication.

GENES AND GENE EXPRESSION

Although its definition continues to evolve, a gene in its most basic form can be thought of as a DNA sequence that encodes a protein or functional RNA.[1] Gene expression refers to the process by which specific genetic sequences direct the synthesis of functional gene products. This process is highly regulated, and individual cell types express only a subset of the full complement of genes. Specific gene expression programs fundamentally drive many biologic processes, including growth and development, cellular differentiation, and neoplastic transformation.

Although protein-coding genes account for only a small portion of chromosomal DNA, they are regarded as the central determinants of cellular and organismal phenotypes. A majority of clinically relevant DNA mutations occur within such genes, and most targeted cancer therapies are directed against specific genetically encoded protein pathways.

The first step in protein synthesis is transcription of the DNA template into a linear RNA copy. Most protein-coding genes are arranged in segments with coding elements called exons and noncoding elements called introns. These core regions are surrounded by additional noncoding DNA elements that dictate gene expression. These include regulatory elements such as promoters (which direct the site of transcription initiation) and enhancers (which increase transcription; Fig 2-2);[2] the regulatory elements are recognized by proteins, called transcription factors, which establish the timing and tissue-specific characteristics of gene expression. Many transcription factors bind directly to these regulatory elements and recruit additional regulatory proteins into the transcription complex. Proteins that mediate the assembly of active transcription complexes by recruiting factors or facilitating chromatin changes that promote transcription are termed coactivators, and those that inhibit transcription are corepressors.[3]

Gene transcription first results in a messenger RNA (mRNA) that contains both exons and introns, termed a premessenger RNA (premRNA). The introns are subsequently spliced out to

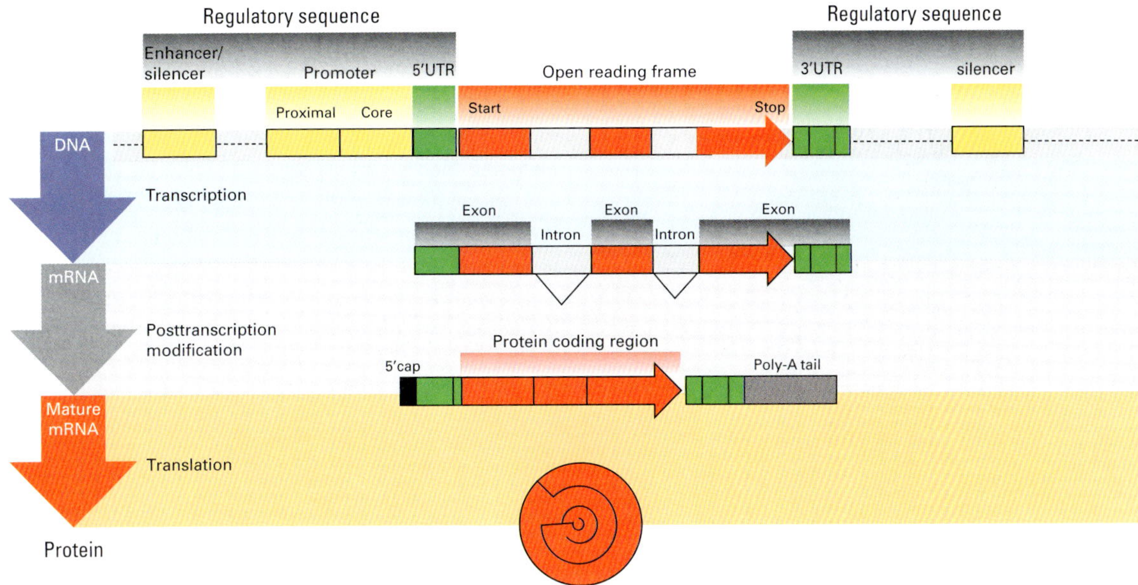

Fig. 2-2 Schematic diagram of an idealized gene, including promoter elements, an enhancer, and the transcribed region of the gene.

Regulatory sequences (yellow) control when and where the protein-coding region (orange) is expressed. Promoter and enhancer regions (yellow) regulate the transcription of the gene into a premessenger RNA, which is modified to add a 5' cap (black) and poly-A tail (gray) and to remove introns. The mRNA 5' and 3' untranslated regions (UTRs; green) regulate translation of the final protein product.

Reprinted from Permission to reuse given by the Creative Common license for Shafee, T; Lowe, R (2017). "Eukaryotic and prokaryotic gene structure". WikiJournal of Medicine 4 (1): 2. doi: 10.15347/wjm/2017.002.

generate a mature mRNA that contains a continuous coding sequence (Fig 2-2). Importantly, alternative splicing of pre-mRNAs can generate distinct mRNA molecules that include or exclude certain exons, effectively allowing a single gene to encode multiple related mRNAs that, in turn, encode multiple protein products, termed isoforms. Another feature of mature mRNAs are the 5′ and 3′ untranslated regions, which extend beyond the coding regions and have regulatory functions, such as determining mRNA stability and translational efficiency.

After a mature mRNA is produced, the process of protein translation uses the mRNA sequence to guide the production of a protein. This process requires ribosomes, which are protein- and RNA-containing structures that bind mRNAs and read nucleotide triplets, termed codons, that specify which amino acids will be incorporated into a nascent polypeptide chain. Once a complete protein is produced, the amino acid sequence can be further modified by posttranslational processes, such as phosphorylation, acetylation, ubiquitination, or methylation. These dynamic and often reversible changes can control protein activity, stability, and cellular localization. They can also dictate the formation of multiprotein complexes.

Although the Human Genome Project was completed in 2003, the exact number of human protein-coding genes remains unclear, because some of these genes inferred from the DNA sequence are not expressed (pseudogenes). Currently, it is estimated that there are 19,000 to 22,000 protein-coding genes. However, the total number of human proteins is considerably greater, because genes can be alternatively spliced into distinct mRNAs to produce multiple protein isoforms, and proteins can undergo posttranslational modification to produce multiple proteoforms. It is estimated that the full set of human proteins, known as the proteome, contains 250,000 to 1,000,000 distinct proteins.

Protein-coding genes are often emphasized; however, there is a second major class of genes termed noncoding RNAs. As their name suggests, these transcriptional units generate RNA sequences that do not code for proteins but nonetheless have important cellular functions. These include microRNAs (miRNAs) and long noncoding RNAs (lncRNAs), both of which are key regulators of gene expression and other cellular processes.

miRNAs are short (approximately 25 nucleotides) RNA molecules encoded within longer primary RNA transcripts that are processed to form mature miRNAs. They decrease expression of specific protein-coding genes through direct interaction with mRNA molecules with similar sequences, which leads to degradation of and/or decreased translation of target mRNAs (Fig 2-3).[4] Individual miRNAs typically target many genes simultaneously (dozens to hundreds), and many human genes are controlled by multiple different miRNAs. More than 2,500 miRNA genes have been identified in humans, where they regulate diverse cellular processes, including differentiation, migration, proliferation, and apoptosis.[5] Aberrant miRNA expression is associated with human neoplasia, and miRNA deregulation causes cancers in mouse models.[6,7] Because specific cancers exhibit characteristic and abnormal patterns of miRNA expression that can be

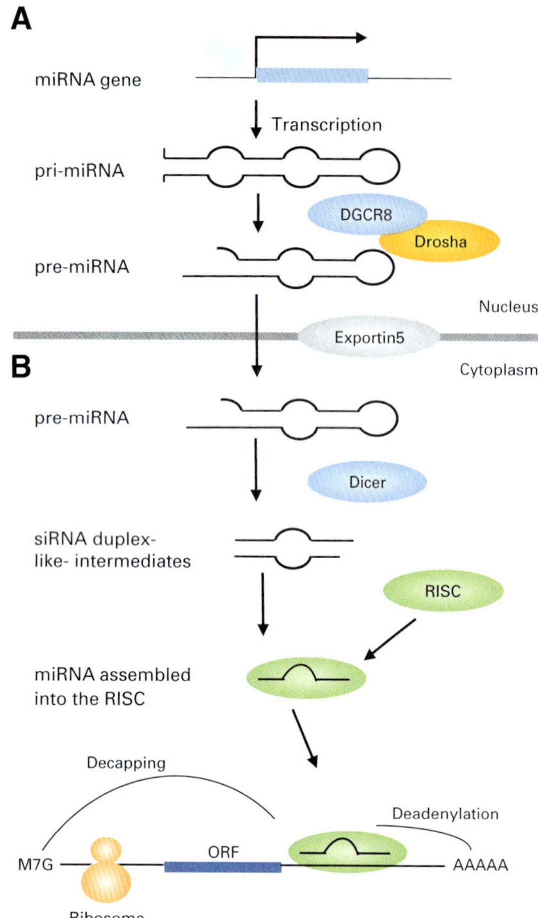

Fig. 2-3 Model of small RNA–guided posttranscriptional regulation of gene expression.

Primary microRNA (pri-miRNA) transcripts are processed to miRNA precursors in the nucleus by the RNase III–like enzyme Drosha. The miRNA precursor (pre-miRNA) is subsequently exported to the cytoplasm by means of the export receptor exportin-5. The pre-miRNA is further processed by Dicer to small interfering RNA (siRNA) duplex–like intermediates. The duplex is unwound while assembling into the miRNA/RNA-induced silencing complex (RISC). Mature miRNAs bind to Ago proteins, which mediate translational repression or cleavage of target mRNAs. Other sources of long double-stranded RNA (dsRNA) in the cytoplasm of a cell are viral RNAs, artificially introduced dsRNAs, dsRNAs generated by RdRPs, and genomic sense and antisense transcripts. Like pre-miRNAs, long dsRNA is processed by the RNase-III enzyme Dicer into 21 to 23 nucleotide dsRNA intermediates. Assisted by the RNA helicase Armitage and R2D2, the single-stranded siRNA-containing RISC is formed. The stability of the dsRNA and its recognition by Dicer can be regulated by specific ADARs and the exonuclease ERI-1.

detected in tumor tissues and blood, miRNA analyses are being developed as important molecular tools in cancer diagnosis and prognosis.[8,9]

lncRNAs are a second group of noncoding RNAs that affect many diverse cellular processes.[10] These RNAs are generally longer than 200 nucleotides, but they can vary in length. lncRNAs have proven difficult to identify and study, so they are less well understood compared with other noncoding RNAs. Although lncRNAs share some features with miRNAs, including the ability to repress gene expression through increased degradation of mRNAs, they have much more varied functions, including silencing transcription, modulating chromatin in time and space, altering mRNA splicing, regulating mRNA translation, and influencing posttranslational modifications of proteins. Several lncRNAs are implicated in carcinogenesis in experimental models, including *NKILA*, which modulates breast cancer phenotypes through altered protein phosphorylation; *MALAT1*, which regulates mRNA splicing and may play a role in multiple cancers; and *TERC*, which influences telomere length to increase cell lifespan and is amplified in multiple cancer types.[11]

EPIGENETIC GENE REGULATION

Epigenetic gene regulation, or epigenetics, refers to heritable processes that profoundly influence gene expression without changing the DNA nucleotide sequence. Epigenetic gene regulation occurs through 2 central processes: DNA methylation and histone modification.[12] DNA methylation occurs when DNA methyltransferases catalyze the addition of methyl groups onto CG dinucleotides in genomic DNA.[13] When CGs lie in gene promoters or other regulatory regions, methylation represses gene transcription. Distinct DNA methylation patterns can be seen in cells at different stages of development or between different cell types, suggesting that DNA methylation controls global gene transcription to define cell identity. Similarly, DNA methylation patterns are altered in various disease states, including cancer, where many tumor suppressor genes are silenced by promoter methylation. Prominent examples include the *MLH1* gene promoter, which is methylated in some intestinal cancers, suppressing expression of this DNA mismatch repair (MMR) enzyme, and the *CDKN2A* gene promoter, which is methylated in many tumor types, leading to decreased expression of the p16 tumor suppressor protein. Although some genes can be inactivated by either mutation or gene silencing, it is now understood that certain cancer-associated genes are inactivated only through genetic mutation, whereas others are inactivated only through epigenetic gene silencing resulting from aberrant methylation. Thus, the study of methylation patterns in human cancer genomes has identified previously unknown tumor suppressor genes.

The second major type of epigenetic regulation results from modifications of histones.[14] Human DNA is packaged and condensed through association with histones and other nuclear proteins to form chromatin. Within a chromatin fiber, DNA is wrapped around innumerable octamers of 8 histone proteins to form a nucleosome (Fig 2-4). This not only compacts DNA sufficiently to allow it to fit within the cell nucleus but also controls which regions of the genome are transcriptionally active or silent at any given time, thus providing an additional mechanism to generate specific gene transcription patterns. Histones are modified covalently (eg, by

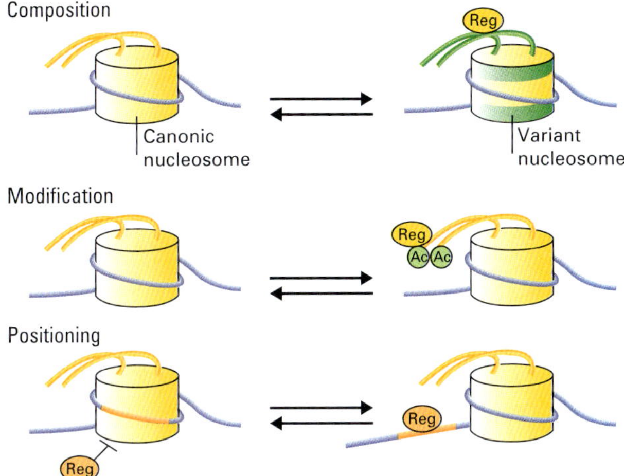

Fig. 2-4 Nucleosome structure and regulation.

Nucleosome regulation. Remodeling complexes can remove the canonic H2A-H2B dimers and replace them with variant histones (indicated in green), forming a variant nucleosome with unique tails that might bind unique regulatory proteins. Nucleosome modification (only acetylation [Ac] is depicted for simplicity) allows the binding of regulatory factors, which have specialized domains that recognize acetylated histone tails. Nucleosome repositioning allows the binding of a regulatory factor to its site on nucleosomal DNA (light blue segment).

Reprinted with permission from Saha A et al: Nat Rev Mol Cell Biol 7:437-447, 2006.

acetylation, methylation, phosphorylation, and ubiquitylation), by changes in subunit composition (eg, replacement of core histones by specialized histones), and by repositioning. Each of these modifications renders DNA either more or less accessible to transcription by RNA polymerase (Fig 2-4). Histone methylase and demethylase enzymes regulate methyl-, dimethyl-, or trimethylation of lysine residues; methylation on some sites facilitates transcription, whereas on others, it represses transcription. Histone acetylation is also regulated by opposing enzymes; acetylation is found in actively transcribed genes, whereas histone deacetylation correlates with repression.

Because of their influence on gene expression, the enzymes that catalyze epigenetic modifications are themselves important targets for cancer therapeutics.[15] The hypomethylating agents 5-azacytidine and 5-aza-2′deoxycytidine (decitabine) inhibit DNA methyltransferase enzymes, which leads to lower methylation of gene promoters. These drugs are used to treat myelodysplastic syndrome (MDS) and other hematologic malignancies and are thought to function in part by reestablishing expression of tumor suppressor genes repressed by methylation.[16] Another example of epigenetic therapies are the histone deacetylase inhibitors, including vorinostat, panobinostat, and belinostat. These drugs have global effects on histone modification and can broadly alter gene expression to inhibit the growth of some cancers, including T-cell lymphoma and multiple myeloma.[17] In addition to these global inhibitors, clinical trials are under way testing compounds that target specific histone methyltransferases, such as EZH2, DOT1L, and KDM1A, which are upregulated in distinct cancer types.[18]

Box 1: Clinical Implications of Basic Research: Aberrant Methylation in the Pathogenesis and Treatment of AML

PATIENT VIGNETTE

A 76-year-old man presents to the clinic with decreasing energy and pallor. A CBC shows pancytopenia. Bone marrow evaluation demonstrates myelodysplasia as well as acute myeloid leukemia (AML) with complex cytogenetics. Chronic medical comorbidities include chronic obstructive pulmonary disease, congestive heart failure, and stroke. He is deemed to be a poor candidate for standard AML induction chemotherapy (eg, idarubicin and cytarabine). He is instead treated with the demethylating agent 5-azacytidine in combination with the B-cell lymphoma 2 (BCL-2) inhibitor venetoclax. He requires blood and platelet transfusions but otherwise tolerates this therapy reasonably well, with no need for hospitalization, minimal decline in performance status, and no dose reductions. This combination leads to sustained partial response before he eventually develops marked cytopenias. Repeat bone marrow evaluation shows progression of AML, and his therapy is discontinued. He dies under hospice care shortly thereafter.

DISCUSSION

Cytosine methylation inhibitors have long been known to have clinical activity in hematologic cancers, including myelodysplastic syndrome (MDS) and AML. Furthermore, large-scale analysis of human MDS and AML samples with methylation arrays showed that abnormal methylation is an important driver of cancer progression, because early, intermediate, and transformed MDSs have increasing levels of methylation. Although abnormal apoptosis was not inferred to be a major driver of AML, preclinical laboratory studies showed that inhibitors of the antiapoptotic protein BCL-2 had clear clinical activity. Given the relatively low toxicity associated with methylation inhibitors and BCL-2 inhibitors, trials combining these 2 approaches were initiated in patients unfit for standard intensive chemotherapy. The dramatic effectiveness of this approach has led to trials evaluating this combination in fit patients as well.[19,20]

KEY POINTS

- Genes are functional units of DNA that provide instructions for the production of RNAs and proteins.
- Cells express only a subset of the genes contained within their genomes. Protein-coding genes are

- transcribed into mRNA, in a process that is controlled by regulatory DNA elements (eg, enhancers and promoters).
- Noncoding RNAs, including miRNAs and lncRNAs, are important regulators of gene expression and are often deregulated in human cancers.
- Gene expression is also regulated by epigenetic modifications of DNA and histones. Chromatin modifications, which include methylations and acetylations, play a major role in determining the timing and extent of gene expression.
- The enzymes that catalyze epigenetic modifications are important targets for cancer therapeutics.

NUCLEIC ACID ANALYSIS AND DETECTION OF CANCER-ASSOCIATED MUTATIONS

DNA

DNA Polymorphisms Facilitate Genetic Analyses of Complex Diseases

Before the development of modern DNA amplification and sequencing techniques, the analysis of cancer genetics on a broad scale was largely limited to familial cancer syndromes. Compared with today's technology, this research was painstaking and imprecise, but it nonetheless resulted in identification of cancer genes in cancer-prone families. This work was facilitated by the study of genetic polymorphisms, which are DNA sequences that exhibit substantial variability in a population that distinguishes between specific alleles (gene variants). Genome-wide maps of polymorphic markers were important tools in analyses of genetic traits. Through linkage analysis of pedigrees in which family members did or did not develop early-onset cancer, the genetic polymorphisms that segregated with the cancer-development phenotype identified many hereditary cancer genes, including those involved in breast cancer (eg, *BRCA1* and *BRCA2*).

Linking polymorphisms to cancer phenotypes continues. DNA sequencing technologies have now cataloged single-base changes throughout the genome, termed single-nucleotide polymorphisms (SNPs). SNPs are the most common polymorphisms and represent approximately 1% of the human genome. Current approaches to identify these variants use microarray-based chips and/or DNA sequencing methods to analyze SNPs on a genome-wide scale.[21] Using this information, geneticists can now apply complex statistical methods of analysis to large populations of people to associate specific SNPs with specific phenotypes, including cancer. Such genome-wide association studies (GWASs) can identify the relationships among specific genes or genetic variants and health traits of interest. In some cases, experimental validation has confirmed hypotheses generated through GWASs. For example, common polymorphisms can affect cellular proliferation, gene transcription and silencing, and sensitivity to specific cancer therapeutics in vitro. Once documented in the laboratory, the relevance of these findings to clinical care can be studied in genetically defined patient cohorts.

Another relatively common type of polymorphism occurs in microsatellites, which are tandem repeats of 2 to 6 nucleotides that occur in thousands of locations in the genome. A common type of microsatellite is composed of CA dinucleotide repeats. These

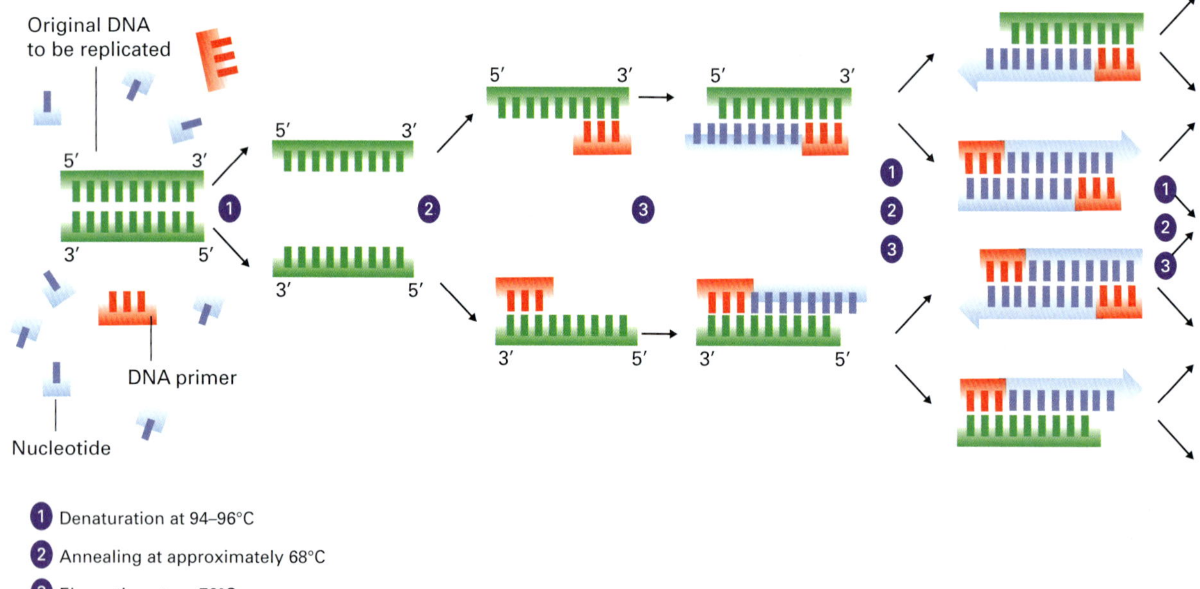

Fig. 2-5 Polymerase chain reaction.

The DNA (target) to be amplified is shown as a double-stranded DNA molecule with complementary segments (in green, far left). Also shown are sequence-specific primers (red) and nucleotides (blue). The temperature changes required for each step are indicated. The DNA is denatured and then allowed to reanneal to the primers. Taq DNA polymerase then extends from the primer using supplied nucleotides, making perfect complementary copies of the segments of DNA (in blue), yielding 2 copies of the target DNA after cycle 1. In subsequent cycles, the DNA is denatured and reannealed, and the steps in cycle 1 are repeated, yielding exponentially increasing copies of target DNA such that with n cycles, the yield of DNA is 2^n.

Source: Wikipedia. Public Domain, https://en.wikipedia.org/wiki/Polymerase_chain_reaction.

regions of the genome are susceptible to imperfect DNA replication, thus leading to a higher mutation rate, creating genetic variation among individuals that allow for facile DNA genotyping. In cancer, microsatellite variation provides a readily detectable sign of DNA MMR defects. MMR enzymes that normally suppress DNA replication errors are mutated in some familial cancers, such as hereditary nonpolyposis colon cancer (HNPCC)/Lynch syndrome. Loss of functional MMR proteins causes increased numbers of altered microsatellite sequences to occur in tumors. This trait, termed microsatellite instability (MSI), serves as a harbinger of widespread tumor-specific point mutations throughout other regions of the genome. Identification of MMR deficiency and MSI is key to diagnosis of common familial cancer syndromes in unaffected and affected individuals, allowing tailored cancer screening, prevention, and, sometimes, therapy. In recent years, it has become apparent that MMR deficiency/MSI predicts response to immune checkpoint inhibitors in diverse cancer types, possibly because the altered protein products encoded by the mutated cancer genome are sufficiently distinct from their normal protein counterparts to permit immune recognition as neoantigens.[22]

Polymerase Chain Reaction

Accurate and high-throughput DNA analysis is generally dependent on error-free amplification of partial or whole genomes. The development of polymerase chain reaction (PCR; Fig 2-5) was a watershed technologic advance because it made synthesis of large quantities of specific DNA sequence fragments from miniscule quantities of template a routine procedure.[23] PCR was essential for producing the draft sequence of the human genome; amplified copies of countless small fragments of the human genome were cloned, sequenced, and aligned to one another. A wide variety of PCR-based techniques have revolutionized virtually all methods used to manipulate, detect, and analyze nucleic acids. In addition, PCR is highly relevant clinically. It is used to identify specific recurrent genomic mutations that have implications for therapy decisions (eg, identification of *RAS* mutations in colorectal cancer that predict resistance to epidermal growth factor receptor (EGFR)–targeted agents).

Next-Generation DNA Sequencing

Next-generation sequencing (NGS) technologies have increased the speed and dramatically reduced the cost of DNA and RNA sequencing (RNA-seq), up to genome scale. NGS methods apply massively parallel sequencing to obtain millions of DNA sequence reads simultaneously.[24,25] Although technology platforms vary, what they have in common is that the length of the sequence read for each DNA molecule is relatively short, typically measuring 100 to 200 base pairs. These technologies rely on sequence analysis methods that use a reference human genome sequence and sophisticated bioinformatics for positioning and alignment of millions of short reads. NGS technologies can also detect structural changes in the genome, such as chromosomal gains and losses and DNA translocations in cancer cells, in addition to other types of mutations (Fig 2-6). The cost and speed of NGS are rapidly improving. For example, in 2008, 2 human genome sequences could be completed in a few months at a cost of approximately $1 million per genome. In 2019, rapid human genome sequencing is available, with costs in the range of $1,000 and timeframes of < 1 day. Rapid and low-cost NGS has enormous implications for understanding cancer biology, prognosis, diagnosis, and treatment, because these techniques enable individualized treatments based on genome-scale sequence data (precision oncology).[26,27]

NGS also allows epigenetic studies on a genome-wide scale. For example, ChIP-Seq is a method that uses antibodies that recognize specific modifications (eg, histone methylation) to isolate fragments of DNA associated with the modified histone, and NGS is then applied to identify all DNA regions that contain the modification.[28,29] This strategy has produced highly detailed maps of the epigenetic marks that regulate gene expression (Fig 2-7). Similar approaches have shown that CpG methylation is a highly dynamic process that changes greatly during cellular differentiation and that distinct CpG methylation patterns can distinguish between normal and cancerous tissues.[30] The Encyclopedia of DNA Elements (ENCODE) project has used NGS approaches to catalog transcription factor binding sites as well as chromatin and histone modifications across the human genome.[31] These technologies are providing an entirely new understanding of how gene expression is regulated in health and disease.

Box 2: Clinical Implications of Basic Research: Hereditary Breast Cancer, *BRCA* Genes, and Targeted Therapies

PATIENT VIGNETTE

A 44-year-old woman presents to her primary care physician after noticing a left breast lump. Mammography confirms a suspicious lesion in the left breast, and a biopsy is performed. This demonstrates invasive ductal carcinoma that is negative for estrogen receptor, progesterone receptor, and human epidermal growth factor receptor 2 (ie, triple-negative breast cancer). Her family history reveals cancer in multiple first-degree relatives, including her paternal aunt and sister (breast cancer) and her father (prostate cancer). Genetic testing reveals a germ line mutation in *BRCA1*. Staging studies reveal no evidence of regional or distant disease, and she is treated with surgery and appropriate adjuvant therapy. Three years later, she presents with weight loss, cough, and headache and is found to have extensive metastatic disease in her lungs, liver, and brain. After brain irradiation, she goes on to receive the poly-ADP ribose polymerase (PARP) inhibitor olaparib, which controls her disease for 24 months.

DISCUSSION

The *BRCA1* gene is likely the best understood cause of familial breast cancers. This gene was discovered as a result of the diligent and long-term work of Mary-Claire King and others. Although analysis of pedigrees suggested an autosomal-dominant cause of a small subset of breast cancers, much more work was required to pinpoint the gene responsible. Using linkage mapping, *BRCA1* was eventually localized to chromosome 17. Tumor sequencing studies have cataloged many different mutations in *BRCA1* that can affect risk of breast and other cancers, including ovarian, prostate, and pancreatic cancers. Importantly, although *BRCA1* was first identified as a cause of familial cancers, some sporadic tumors also harbor mutations in this gene. Extensive laboratory studies show the BRCA1 protein to be a key component of the normal cellular response to DNA damage. The loss of the DNA-damage response results in selective sensitivity to certain drugs, including PARP inhibitors and platinum compounds, and some patients with *BRCA*-mutant cancers show prolonged responses to these agents.

RNA

Reverse-Transcription PCR and Real-Time PCR

PCR-based methods used for RNA analyses use reverse transcription, in which the reverse transcription enzyme and DNA primers first convert mRNA to a DNA copy, called cDNA. This general strategy is termed reverse-transcription PCR (RT-PCR) to reflect both the reverse-transcription and PCR steps. RT-PCR methods are widely used to precisely measure RNA abundance in cells and tissues.

Real-time or quantitative PCR (qPCR) assays use fluorescent dyes to accurately measure the amount of PCR products synthesized in each amplification cycle in real time, as PCR progresses.[32] The advantages of qPCR include extreme sensitivity, technical ease, and the ability to accurately quantitate DNA or RNA over a wide abundance range. qPCR is often the method of choice for analyzing the abundance of specific mRNAs in blood samples from patients with cancer, such as monitoring the expression of the *BCR-ABL* transcript in patients receiving therapy for chronic myeloid leukemia (CML) or detecting minimal residual disease in leukemia and lymphoma.[33-35] qPCR can also simultaneously determine the expression of multiple genes in tumor samples. For example, 1 approved diagnostic test uses qPCR to assess the expression of 21 genes to predict benefit of adjuvant chemotherapy in women with early-stage estrogen receptor (ER)–positive breast cancer.[36]

Microarrays, NGS, and Global Analyses of Transcription

Some RNA analyses measure the expression of thousands of genes simultaneously, and these typically use microarray chips or, more commonly today, NGS. Microarray chips are small slides on which

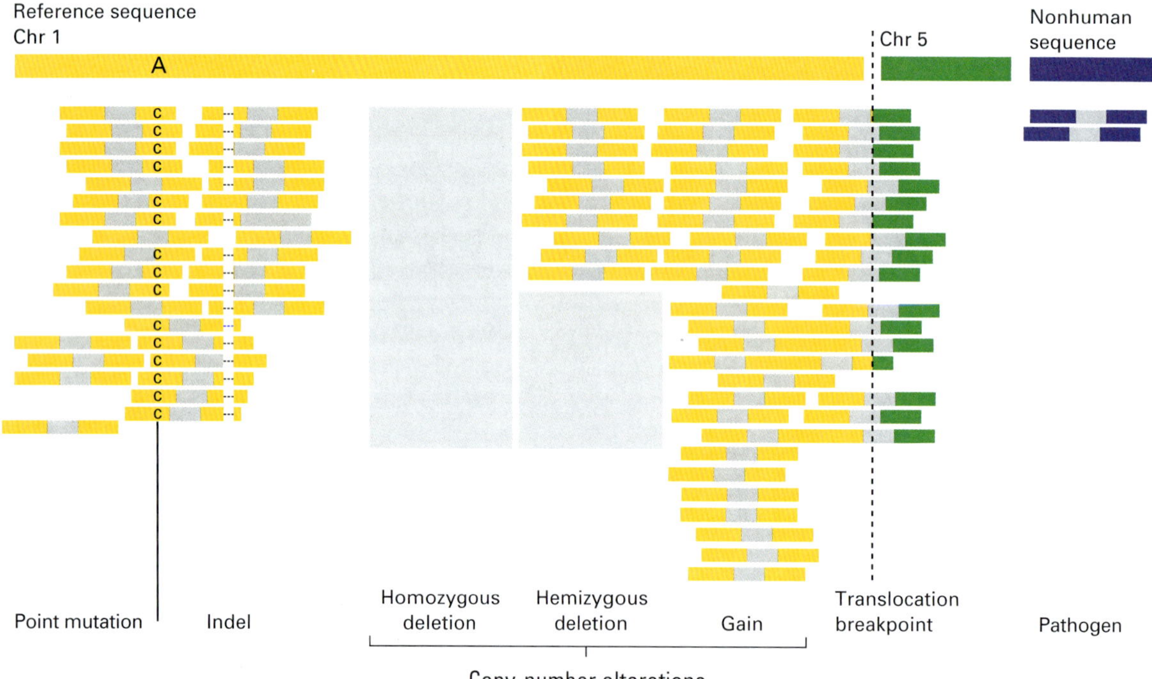

Fig. 2-6 Types of mutations discovered by next-generation genomic sequencing.

Sequenced fragments are depicted as bars, with colored tips representing the sequenced ends and the unsequenced portion of the fragment in gray. Reads are aligned to the reference genome (mostly chromosome 1 [chr 1], in this example). The colors of the sequenced ends show where they align to the target DNA. Different types of genomic alterations can be detected, from left to right: point mutations (in this example, A to C) and small insertions and deletions (indels; in this example, a deletion shown by a dashed line) are detected by identifying multiple reads that show nonreference sequence; changes in sequencing depth (relative to a normal control) are used to identify copy-number changes (shaded boxes represent absent or decreased reads in the tumor sample); paired ends that map to different genomic loci (in this case, chromosome 5) are evidence of rearrangements; and sequences that map to nonhuman sequences are evidence for the potential presence of genomic material from pathogens.

Reprinted by permission from Nature: Meyerson M, Gabriel S, Getz G. Advances in understanding cancer genomes through second-generation sequencing. Nat Rev Genet. *2010 Oct; 11(10):685-96.*[25]

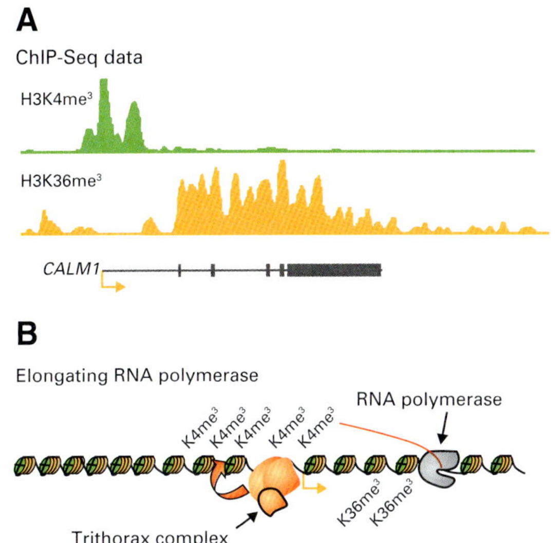

Fig. 2-7 Chromatin state maps reveal a stereotypical pattern at active genes.

(A) In mouse ES cells, the transcription start site for the *CALM1* gene (orange/yellow arrow) is marked by H3K4 trimethylation, a trithorax-associated mark, whereas the remainder of the transcribed region is marked by H3K36 trimethylation. (B) Evidence from model systems supports a central role for initiating and elongating RNA polymerase II in recruiting the relevant histone methyltransferase enzymes.

Reprinted from Current Opinion in Genetics & Development, Vol 18(2), Mendenhall EM and Bernstein BE, Chromatin state maps: new technologies, new insights, Pages No. 109-115, Copyright (2008), with permission from Elsevier.

either oligonucleotides or cDNA probes are spotted in a defined array.[37] By hybridizing cDNA from different conditions onto the oligonucleotides on the chip, each labeled with a different fluorescent dye, it is possible to uncover relative differences in gene expression. If clinical specimens are limited, small amounts of mRNA from the specimen can be first amplified by PCR before hybridization.

At present, NGS has largely supplanted array technologies for gene expression analyses. The quantitative quality of NGS allows for mRNA abundance, and even alternate transcripts, to be identified at the genome scale. The RNA-seq technique, also termed whole-transcriptome shotgun sequencing, overcomes many of the technical limitations of microarrays. Indeed, RNA-seq is now a vital component of cancer diagnosis and treatment.[38]

Microarrays and NGS facilitate global analyses of the set of genes expressed in a tumor sample, termed the transcriptome, and are now commonly used in diagnostic and prognostic applications. Examples include separating large-cell lymphomas into high- and low-risk groups on the basis of their gene expression patterns (which reflect their cell of origin) and predicting outcomes and therapeutic benefits for women with breast cancer.[39]

Research Tools for Modulating Gene Expression and Engineering Genomes: Small Interfering RNAs and CRISPR/Cas9

As discussed, miRNAs are small RNAs that inhibit gene expression epigenetically by binding to cognate mRNA targets. Knowledge of miRNA function enabled the development of simple yet powerful laboratory techniques for inhibition of expression of virtually any gene in the cell. These techniques, termed RNA interference (RNAi), use synthetic double-stranded miRNAs known as small interfering RNAs (siRNAs) to efficiently catalyze the degradation of their cognate mRNAs in vitro. Although genes can be inhibited 1 by 1, RNAi is readily scalable such that genome-wide siRNA screens can be used to dissect complex biologic pathways to ascertain gene function globally and to identify drug targets in cancer cells.[40,41] RNAi is also making its way to the clinic, because siRNAs can serve as drugs to inhibit gene function. The first RNAi-based therapy was US Food and Drug Administration approved in 2018 for complications associated with a rare hereditary disease, transthyretin amyloidosis. Many RNAi-based cancer therapies are currently being tested in clinical trials.[42]

The recent development of simple and robust genome-editing technologies using the CRISPR/Cas9 system has revolutionized science and medicine. CRISPR/Cas9 readily edits or deletes genes, providing a method for complete knockout of the expression of a specific gene and allowing precise study of the effects of cancer-specific mutations on gene function. These techniques are readily adapted to in vitro and *in vivo* applications, and like RNAi, they are readily scalable. CRISPR/Cas9 gene-editing technologies use components of an adaptive immune system from prokaryotes. In this system, short nucleic acids known as guide RNAs (gRNAs) are used to direct an enzyme that cuts double-stranded DNA (the Cas9 endonuclease) to areas of the genome with high degrees of homology with the gRNA. Once the gRNA has targeted Cas9 to a specific site in the genome, Cas9 cuts the DNA. This cut is then repaired by nonhomologous end joining. Because this repair is imprecise, there is generally gain or loss of genomic sequence around the cut site. When this cut-and-repair process occurs within a gene, it frequently results in gene inactivation through introduction of stop codons. This system is exploited in the laboratory and in the clinic to knock out or modify genes of interest. gRNAs targeting a gene of interest are synthesized and then expressed in cells, along with the Cas9 enzyme, guiding Cas9 to cut the gene. Additional components can be added to the system to allow precise gene mutation rather than inactivation. Thus, CRISPR/Cas9 techniques are now complementing or supplanting RNAi in many genetic and drug screening applications.[43-46] CRISPR/Cas9 holds great promise for clinical uses as well.[47] Ongoing clinical trials are using this technology to genetically reprogram T cells to fight cancer, revert disease-causing mutations in specific diseases such as sickle cell anemia and muscular dystrophy, and knock out dominant oncogenes, such as human papillomavirus (HPV) *E6*/*E7* in cervical cancer.

KEY POINTS

- NGS methods use computational analysis of short nucleic acid sequence reads aligned with reference genome sequence information.

- NGS can define entire mutational landscapes of individual tumor samples, including alterations in DNA sequence, as well as structural changes and epigenetic changes.
- Analyses of mRNA by techniques such as RT-PCR or RNA-seq measure the expression of specific genes in tumor samples. This provides insights into cancer biology as well as important diagnostic and prognostic information.
- Whole-genome genetic screens using siRNA or CRISPR/Cas9 technologies can identify genes that promote or suppress cancer or that mediate resistance to chemotherapy.

CHROMOSOME ANALYSIS

Cytogenetics is the study of chromosomal changes in cells and tissues. Cancer cells often exhibit chromosome abnormalities that are pathognomonic for specific diseases. Karyotype analyses examine an individual's entire chromosome complement, and classic analyses identify chromosomes in metaphase spreads based on banding patterns and morphology. Although these techniques are still widely used, particularly to classify hematologic malignancies, they are often augmented with newer techniques that are more sensitive and/or comprehensive. Several cytogenetic methods use fluorescence in situ hybridization (FISH). Fluorescently labeled synthetic, nucleic acid probes of prespecified sequences are incubated with fixed cells in metaphase or interphase. The probes hybridize to their complementary DNA sequences in the cell, which allows visual inspection of the structure of specific genes using a fluorescence microscope. Chromosome- and gene-specific probes are used to determine the copy number of specific oncogenes. For example, significant amplification of the *HER2* gene in breast cancers and gastroesophageal cancers predicts sensitivity to anti–human epidermal growth factor receptor 2 (HER2) therapies. Another common FISH technique uses probes that detect gene fusions and chromosome translocations. For example, the *BCR-ABL* fusion is diagnostic of CML and is sometimes found in acute leukemias (Fig. 2-8). Similarly, the *EML4*–anaplastic lymphoma kinase (*ALK*) translocation defines a subgroup of non–small-cell lung cancers. The identification of these translocations is clinically relevant, because it confers sensitivity to small-molecule tyrosine kinase inhibitors (TKIs). The ability of FISH methods to identify rare cells with abnormal karyotypes makes them useful for detecting residual disease when malignant cells harbor a cytogenetic marker.

KEY POINTS

- Karyotyping reveals gross chromosomal structural anomalies in tumor cells, such as translocations and chromosomal deletions.
- FISH techniques detect structural alterations, such as translocations, deletions, fusions, and copy-number variations, directly inside cancer cells.
- Genome alterations identified by FISH are clinically relevant, because they can predict sensitivity to molecularly targeted therapies and can be used to detect residual disease in hematologic cancers.

PROTEIN ANALYSIS

As noted, despite having approximately 21,000 genes, the human genome encodes > 250,000 distinct proteins, and understanding all aspects of protein production, regulation, and function is integral to understanding cancer. Low- to intermediate-throughput assays for protein detection have been commonly used for decades. Newer methods to study large sets of proteins simultaneously, collectively termed proteomics, are powerful tools to enhance the understanding of cancer and offer the potential for diagnostics that might advance cancer care beyond that achieved with NGS.

ANTIBODY-BASED METHODS

Western Blotting and ELISA

Antibody-based methods are well established low- to intermediate-throughput assays that are routinely used in laboratories to study protein expression and function. A common laboratory technique for protein analysis is called Western blotting. The first step is lysis of cells or tissue samples to solubilize proteins. Proteins in the lysate are then separated by gel electrophoresis and transferred to

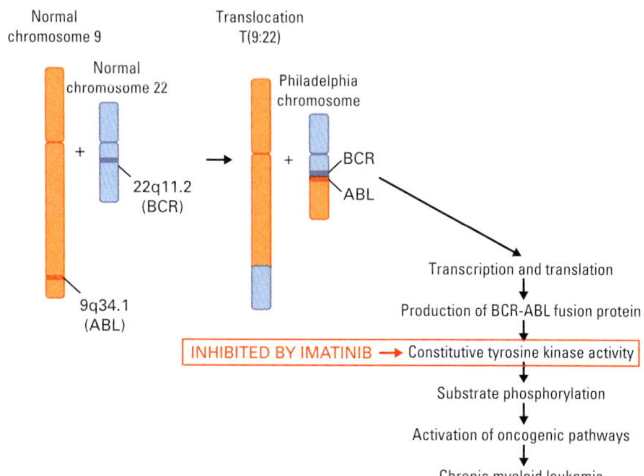

Fig. 2-8 The translocation leading to the Philadelphia (Ph) chromosome and the role of BCR-ABL in the pathogenesis of chronic myeloid leukemia (CML).

The Ph chromosome is a foreshortened chromosome 22 resulting from an exchange between the long arms of chromosomes 9 and 22. This leads to the production of a BCR-ABL fusion protein that has constitutive kinase activity and promotes the development of CML. The tyrosine kinase inhibitor imatinib inhibits this constitutive kinase activity and can lead to long-term control of CML.

Source: Wikipedia. Public Domain, https://en.wikipedia.org/wiki/Philadelphia_chromosome.

membranes, which are then exposed to detection probes, most commonly antibodies specific to the proteins of interest in the sample. Enzyme-linked immunosorbent assay (ELISA) is an analogous technique that allows more precise protein quantification with moderate throughput. In these assays, fixed whole cells or solutions of solubilized proteins from tissue specimens are bound to 96-well plates, then specific proteins are detected with the same detection probes used for Western blotting. A standard curve is generated by plating purified protein at various concentrations, thereby allowing quantification of protein levels within the various samples. Together, these techniques can detect changes in protein size, posttranslational modifications (eg, phosphorylation), and abundance.[48]

Immunohistochemistry

Pathology laboratories routinely use antibody-based immunohistochemistry (IHC) methods to detect the expression of specific proteins in tumor cells. IHC can be used as a diagnostic tool, for example, to define the origins of poorly differentiated cancers or to determine squamous cell carcinoma or adenocarcinoma differentiation in lung cancers. Furthermore, IHC is frequently used to subclassify human tumors to refine prognosis and determine treatment. For example, p16 overexpression is a marker for HPV-associated oropharyngeal cancers, which have a more favorable prognosis compared with non–HPV-associated cancers. Ongoing studies are using HPV status to develop risk-adapted treatment algorithms for this disease. Likewise, HER2 overexpression in a subset of breast, gastroesophageal, and other cancers has both prognostic and therapeutic significance, because these cancers frequently respond to anti-HER2 therapies. Finally, IHC for detection of MMR proteins has long been used to identify cancers associated with Lynch syndrome but has now gained much broader usage as clinical data show MMR deficiency predicts sensitivity to immunotherapy across diverse tumor types.[22]

Flow Cytometry

Another important IHC diagnostic technique, particularly for hematologic cancers, is flow cytometry. This technique detects multiple cell surface markers in complex cell populations, such as bone marrow or peripheral blood. In flow cytometry, living cells are stained with fluorescently labeled antibodies that attach to specific cell surface proteins. As the cells pass through the flow cytometer, the fluorescent dyes are excited by a laser, emitting light at different wavelengths. This process, known as immunophenotyping, can classify leukemias and lymphomas based on their cell surface proteins. Because flow cytometry has high sensitivity and throughput, it can detect small numbers of tumor cells, such as residual leukemia in normal bone marrow. Finally, flow cytometry can determine eligibility for the rapidly expanding array of monoclonal antibody–based therapies and chimeric antigen receptor T cells, including those targeting CD19 and CD20 (for lymphoma and leukemia), CD30 (for Hodgkin and other lymphomas), CD33 (for acute leukemias), and CD38 (for multiple myeloma).

MASS SPECTROMETRY–BASED PROTEOMICS

Antibody-based methodologies for protein analysis are limited by their low throughput. Analogous to the large-scale genomic analyses of DNA sequence or RNA expression, mass spectrometry (MS) is a high-throughput technology that can analyze thousands of proteins simultaneously. MS forms the core of modern proteomics and is used in combination with bioinformatics to quantify and identify the large numbers of proteins present in complex biologic samples.[49,50] These methods are informed by the genome-wide sequencing that allowed construction of the comprehensive databases used to identify the peptides analyzed by MS. In addition, MS can interrogate protein modifications, such as protein phosphorylation and ubiquitylation, on a large scale.

MS is likely to have direct clinical applications in the near future. For example, proof-of-principle preclinical research shows that MS analysis of tumor samples or serum from patients with cancer can be used to generate proteomic signatures that may influence selection of therapy.[51,52] One intense area of proteomic research involves early cancer detection based on defining protein signatures indicative of early-stage cancers in tissues, such as peripheral blood.[51] A related area that is increasing the understanding of cancer biology and treatment is metabolomics, in which MS is used to measure hundreds of cellular metabolites in a clinical sample. These techniques reveal metabolic differences between normal cells and cancer cells that provide clues to how metabolic changes affect cancer development and survival. Results of this work should allow the development of anticancer therapies targeting these differences.[53,54]

KEY POINTS

- Protein analyses reveal protein abundance, as well as functional modifications such as phosphorylation and acetylation.
- Antibody-based protein detection techniques, such as Western blotting, ELISA, IHC, and flow cytometry, are used in a wide variety of clinical tests, including immunophenotyping for cancer diagnosis and classification, detection of minimal residual disease, and selection of therapy.
- MS-based proteomics allows for large-scale analyses of protein expression and modifications in tumor tissues.

ONCOGENES AND TUMOR SUPPRESSORS: ACCELERATORS AND BRAKES ON THE ROAD TO CANCER

Transforming a normal cell into a malignant cell requires a series of mutations in genes, termed oncogenes.[55] To date, several hundred human genes have been implicated as proto-oncogenes, which are genes that have the potential to be converted into oncogenes. Once converted, oncogenes carry dominant gain-of-function mutations (cells with a mutated protein encoded by the oncogene gain a new function, such as evasion of apoptosis), whereas tumor suppressor genes carry recessive mutations that sustain loss of function (tumor suppressor genes cause cancer when they are inactivated by a mutation). Studying oncogene and tumor suppressor functions and the processes they control is integral to understanding cancer biology and, increasingly, cancer therapy.

IDENTIFICATION OF ACTIVATED DOMINANT ONCOGENES

Numerous mechanisms, including gene translocations, amplifications, and point mutations, can activate oncogenes. These different types of alterations lead to distinct functional outcomes and often provide important diagnostic and prognostic information.

Classic Experimental Cancer Models: Retroviral Infections and DNA Transfections

Many oncogenes were first discovered through studies of animal cancers induced by retroviruses, called RNA tumor viruses, which carry viral oncogenes within their genomes. Approximately 30 such viral oncogenes were identified in the 1970s and 1980s. The major breakthrough with respect to human cancer came with the realization that viral oncogenes represent mutated versions of human host proto-oncogenes that have been incorporated into the viral genomes during the retroviral life cycle. Many viral oncogenes are the counterparts of extremely important human oncogenes, and the identification of these human counterparts provided the framework for establishing the role of oncogenes in tumorigenesis.[56] RNA tumor viruses can also cause cancers by insertional mutagenesis, in which the integration of a viral genome into a host chromosome alters expression of a nearby cellular proto-oncogene or tumor suppressor gene. The study of these viruses has revealed important human cancer genes, including *CMYC*.[57] Experimental methods use retroviral or other insertional mutagenesis techniques as genetic tools for the discovery of oncogenes and tumor suppressors.[58]

Another classic strategy used to identify oncogenes is DNA transfection. In this approach, DNA is extracted from tumor cells and introduced into recipient cells, which undergo morphologic and growth alterations (termed transformation) when they incorporate a tumor-derived oncogene. The transfected tumor cell DNA is subsequently isolated and sequenced from the transformed cells, allowing the identification of the transferred oncogene. Some of the earliest such experiments identified the *RAS* family of oncogenes.[59] More recently, related methods identified *EML4-ALK* fusions as important drivers of some human lung cancers.[60] While the search for effective *RAS* inhibitors continues, ALK-targeted therapies are now routine and effective therapies for patients with lung cancer with *EML4-ALK* fusions.[61,62]

Chromosome Translocations and Gene Fusions

Cancers often contain recurrent chromosome translocations; this is particularly true for hematologic malignancies, which are often characterized by chromosome translocations that involve immunoglobulin and T-cell receptor genes.[63] Specific translocations have important diagnostic and prognostic implications, serve as molecular markers for the detection of residual disease, and are increasingly frequent targets of therapy. The regions of DNA commonly involved with translocations are termed breakpoints, and they often contain proto-oncogenes that are activated by the DNA rearrangement. Although some translocations are evident using conventional cytogenetics or FISH, a majority of clinically relevant translocations were discovered using NGS technologies to identify gene fusion events.[64]

Chromosome translocations activate proto-oncogenes in 2 general ways.[65] The most common mechanism involves gene fusions, when the translocation joins 2 genes normally found on separate chromosomes in the same translational reading frame, resulting in production of a novel protein encoded by the 2 fused genes. Fusion proteins often involve transcription factors or tyrosine kinases and have biologic activities that differ from the parental proto-oncogene. Indeed, several translocations are highly relevant to cancer biology and therapy:

- Many hematologic cancers are characterized by pathognomonic chromosomal translocations that produce fusion proteins.[65] The BCR-ABL fusion that results from the reciprocal exchange of DNA between chromosomes 9 and 22, t(9;22), is known as the Philadelphia chromosome (Fig 2-8). This translocation juxtaposes the 5′ end of the *BCR* gene on chromosome 22 and the 3′ end of the *ABL* oncogene on chromosome 9. The resultant novel gene produces a hybrid mRNA that codes for the BCR-ABL oncoprotein, which constitutively activates the tyrosine kinase activity normally associated with the c-ABL protein. This translocation is the key driver of CML and is present in other leukemias as well.
- In Ewing sarcoma (EWS), translocations fuse the *EWS* gene on chromosome 22 to the *FLI1* gene on chromosome 11, and this creates a transcription factor containing a DNA-binding domain derived from FLI1 and a transcriptional activation domain from EWS.[66]
- Alveolar rhabdomyosarcomas also contain pathognomonic translocations, which fuse the *PAX3* or *PAX7* and *FOXO1* transcription factor genes. The presence of these fusions may predict unfavorable clinical outcomes.[67]
- Translocations that join the androgen-responsive *TMPRSS2* gene with 2 *ETS* transcription factor genes, *ETV1* and *ERG*, occur frequently in prostate cancer and result in abnormal ETS expression driven by the androgen-responsive regulatory elements in the *TMPRSS2* gene.[68]
- *NTRK* fusions refer to a highly related group of gene fusions that occur infrequently but can be found across many tumor types. Tumors harboring these fusions are highly responsive to the TRK inhibitors larotrectinib and entrectinib.[69]

Other translocations activate proto-oncogenes by deregulating their expression without affecting the structure of the protein they encode. An example of this type of translocation is found in

Burkitt lymphoma, which is characterized by translocations that cause the *CMYC* oncogene, located on chromosome 8, to be juxtaposed with immunoglobulin genes that are located on chromosomes 14, 2, and 22. In each case, the translocation deregulates *CMYC* expression by placing it under the control of transcriptional elements contained within the immunoglobulin locus. Other examples of proto-oncogenes that are activated by translocations involving immunoglobulin genes include *CCND1*, which encodes the cell cycle driver cyclin D (found in mantle cell lymphoma and multiple myeloma), and *BCL2*, which encodes the antiapoptotic protein BCL-2 (found in various non-Hodgkin lymphomas).

Other genomic rearrangements, such as chromosomal inversions, also create fusion proteins with important therapeutic implications, including the *EML4-ALK* fusion discussed in the previous section.

DNA Amplification

DNA amplification, which results in the increased copy number of a gene, is another mechanism by which cancer cells increase the expression of a gene product.[70] Many human cancers exhibit proto-oncogene amplifications. Gene amplification can be directly detected, using cytogenetic and NGS approaches, or indirectly detected, using protein assays such as IHC to examine protein overexpression. In some cases, the detection of amplified genes provides important prognostic and treatment-related information, as in the cases of *HER2* amplification in breast, gastroesophageal, and other cancers and *NMYC* amplification in neuroblastoma. DNA amplification can also be a mechanism of resistance to targeted therapy. For example, the androgen receptor (AR) gene *AR* is amplified in some castrate-resistant prostate cancers.

Point Mutations

Point mutations (changes in only 1 or a few nucleotides in a gene sequence) can inactivate or impair protein function, and many recurrent point mutations activate dominant oncogenes. Examples of this mechanism of oncogene activation include mutations that alter *KRAS* function in colorectal and other cancers and activating mutations of *EGFR* in lung cancer. Neomorphic mutations change the function of the targeted oncoprotein. For example, isocitrate dehydrogenase 1 (*IDH1*)/*IDH2* mutations in acute myeloid leukemia (AML), glioma, and cholangiocarcinoma result in altered specificity of the enzyme isocitrate dehydrogenase. Because some common oncogenes, such as *KRAS*, are activated by only a few specific point mutations, these mutations were some of the first that were routinely screened for in cancer specimens. However, NGS can now identify most potentially oncogenic point mutations in primary tumor samples and can do so in timeframes that allow genomic-based treatment decisions.[71] One common strategy uses targeted sequencing to interrogate panels of commonly mutated and actionable proto-oncogenes. This approach can provide genomic data in a timeframe and at a cost more concordant with clinical interventions than broader approaches that sequence all protein-coding regions or even whole genomes.

IDENTIFICATION OF TUMOR SUPPRESSOR GENES

Many tumor suppressor genes were first identified by virtue of their association with hereditary cancer syndromes. Importantly, the genes responsible for familial cancers are often the same tumor suppressor genes that are inactivated in sporadic cancers. In most familial cancer syndromes, an individual inherits a mutant copy of a tumor suppressor gene and later in life acquires a mutation or deletion of the other normal allele, leaving him or her without a functional copy of the gene, which can lead to cancer development. Recessive oncogenes, in which disruption of both alleles is associated with cancer formation, are known as 2-step (Knudson) tumor suppressors, named after classic studies of the *Rb* tumor suppressor in retinoblastoma.[72]

Important exceptions to the Knudson model expand our understanding of how tumor suppressor genes are mutated in cancers. One situation in which a tumor suppressor will not conform to the Knudson model is when the tumor suppressor is inactivated by an epigenetic mechanism, such as when the *CDKN2A* cell cycle inhibitor gene is silenced by DNA methylation in cancers. In other cases, loss of a single allele of a tumor suppressor is sufficient to confer cancer susceptibility or contribute to neoplastic progression, even when a normal allele persists. This is termed a haploinsufficient tumor suppressor gene.[73] So-called dominant-negative mutations also result in noncanonic tumor suppressor inactivation, because they inhibit the function of the wild-type protein produced by the normal allele, thereby removing the selective pressure to mutate both alleles. As in the haploinsufficient case, only 1 allele of the tumor suppressor gene will contain a mutation, such as is seen with the *FBXW7* and *SPOP* ubiquitin ligase genes or the *TP53* gene.

Loss of tumor suppressor gene alleles occurs commonly in cancers.[74] In classic studies, delineating a locus involved by allelic loss in a tumor type was often the first step toward identifying a tumor suppressor gene, such as the breast cancer susceptibility gene *BRCA1*.[75] Sites of allelic loss were thus determined by analyzing polymorphic markers, and disease genes were localized to within the smallest common region of allelic loss (see also Box 2). Today, NGS-based technologies are becoming the methods of choice for detecting allelic losses in tumors. NGS approaches also detect numerous other mechanisms that disrupt tumor suppressor gene function, including inactivating point mutations, deletions that lead to premature termination and/or nonfunctional proteins, and promoter methylation.

KEY POINTS

- Proto-oncogenes are normal cellular genes that can be converted into oncogenes by mutations or epigenetic mechanisms, which alter their normal function or expression.
- Dominant oncogenes encode proteins that are activated in tumors by mechanisms such as amplification, point mutation, and translocation.

- Tumor suppressor genes are recessive oncogenes that are inactivated in tumors by mechanisms such as deletion, point mutation, and gene silencing.

CELLULAR FUNCTIONS OF ONCOGENES AND TUMOR SUPPRESSORS

Proto-oncogenes normally function in a remarkably wide array of biologic processes. Many dominant oncogenes are found within the pathways that govern cell division and differentiation in response to specific signals. Oncogene mutations also affect other global cellular pathways and processes, including metabolism, programmed cell death (apoptosis), and protein degradation. Tumor suppressors normally function in these same cellular processes, where they serve to counter the effects of oncogenes. They also have a particularly important role in maintaining the integrity of the genome, by suppressing errors during DNA replication and by coordinating the response and repair mechanisms triggered by DNA damage.

MITOGENIC SIGNAL TRANSDUCTION PATHWAYS

Cell division is triggered by signal transduction pathways that are stimulated when growth factors bind to specific cell surface receptors. These pathways contain proto-oncogenes throughout the signaling chain.[76,77] Most growth factor receptors are anchored in the cell membrane such that an extracellular domain is available for growth factor (ligand) binding and an intracellular domain interacts with downstream signaling molecules. The intracellular portion of a class of growth factor receptors, called receptor tyrosine kinases (RTKs), catalyzes the addition of phosphate to tyrosine residues. Ligand binding causes RTKs to dimerize and autophosphorylate, which recruits signaling proteins that transmit the mitogenic signal down several parallel pathways, including the phosphatidylinositol 3-kinase (PI3K) and mitogen-activated protein kinase (MAPK) pathways (Fig 2-9A). Cytoplasmic tyrosine kinases also transduce these mitogenic signals, including the *ABL* gene product, which is deregulated as a result of fusion with the *BCR* gene in CML. Kinases are often activated in cancer, through dominant mutations, amplifications, and translocations. These genetic alterations lead to overactive signaling, often by nullifying or bypassing negative regulatory processes that would usually attenuate these pathways. Essentially, the checks and balances that are present in normal cells are disrupted in cancer cells, leading to uncontrolled growth.

RAS proteins are membrane-tethered intracellular enzymes that transduce signals for cell division. RAS activity is regulated by binding to guanosine triphosphate (GTP) or guanosine diphosphate (GDP).[78,79] Thus, RAS activity reflects a balance of G nucleotide-exchange factors that activate RAS by replacing bound GDP with a new molecule of GTP and guanosine triphosphatase–activating proteins (GAPs), which hydrolyze RAS-bound GTP to GDP (Fig 2-9B). There are 3 closely related RAS family members (*KRAS*, *NRAS*, and *HRAS*), and all are mutated in human cancer. Oncogenic *RAS* mutations affect amino acids that interface with GAPs at residues 12 and 13, which results in overactivity of proliferative signaling pathways. Furthermore, GAPs themselves can function as recessive oncogenes (eg, the *NF1* gene is a GAP that acquires a loss-of-function mutation in neurofibromatosis).[80]

RAS drives mitogenic signaling via 3 parallel pathways: the MAPK pathway (which activates transcription factors), the RAL/CDC42 pathway (which regulates membrane and cytoskeletal changes), and the PI3K pathway (which affects many cellular functions, including protein synthesis and apoptosis; Fig 2-10). In addition to activation by RAS, the MAPK and PI3K pathways can be activated independently of RAS by mutations of other pathways that also use these signaling components.

- The MAPK pathway is stimulated by the RAF serine/threonine kinase and signals to additional downstream cytoplasmic serine-threonine kinases, which ultimately activate MAPKs and other effectors. Mutations of the *BRAF* gene, specifically V600E mutations, are found in approximately 50% of malignant melanomas. MAPK signaling activates nuclear proto-oncogenes, which are transcription factors, such as FOS, JUN, and MYC. Each of these oncogenic transcription factors promotes carcinogenesis by binding to target genes and affecting their expression.
- The PI3K-AKT pathway phosphorylates various target proteins to stimulate transcriptional and translational responses that affect diverse cellular processes, including cell growth and division, apoptosis, protein synthesis, and cellular metabolism (Fig 2-10). Each of these processes may be abnormal in cancers with *PI3K* mutations, which are among the most common mutations found in cancer cells.[81] AKT is a protein kinase that is downstream of PI3K and is often amplified and/or overexpressed in cancers.[82] Moreover, cancers exhibit elevated AKT activity caused by mutations in genes that regulate AKT. For example, the PTEN tumor suppressor, which is commonly deleted in cancers, opposes PI3K and prevents AKT activation.[83]

Targeting Mitogenic Kinases in Cancer Chemotherapy

The concept of specifically inhibiting mutant oncoproteins in cancer falls under the umbrella term of targeted therapy and has been heavily applied to mitogenic kinases in cancer. In cases where the roles of individual kinases in specific cancers have been recognized for a long time, such as HER2 in breast cancer and BCR-ABL in CML, targeted therapies are already well established. However, the NGS-driven revolution in molecular oncology is now allowing targeted approaches to be directed against a much larger number of cancers that contain sensitizing gene mutations. Although targeted therapies will be discussed in detail in subsequent chapters in the context of specific organ sites and therapies, a general overview of these concepts is provided here.

Several therapeutic strategies that target aberrant RTKs are in clinical use. One approach uses antibodies that bind to and inhibit RTKs. Examples include trastuzumab, which antagonizes

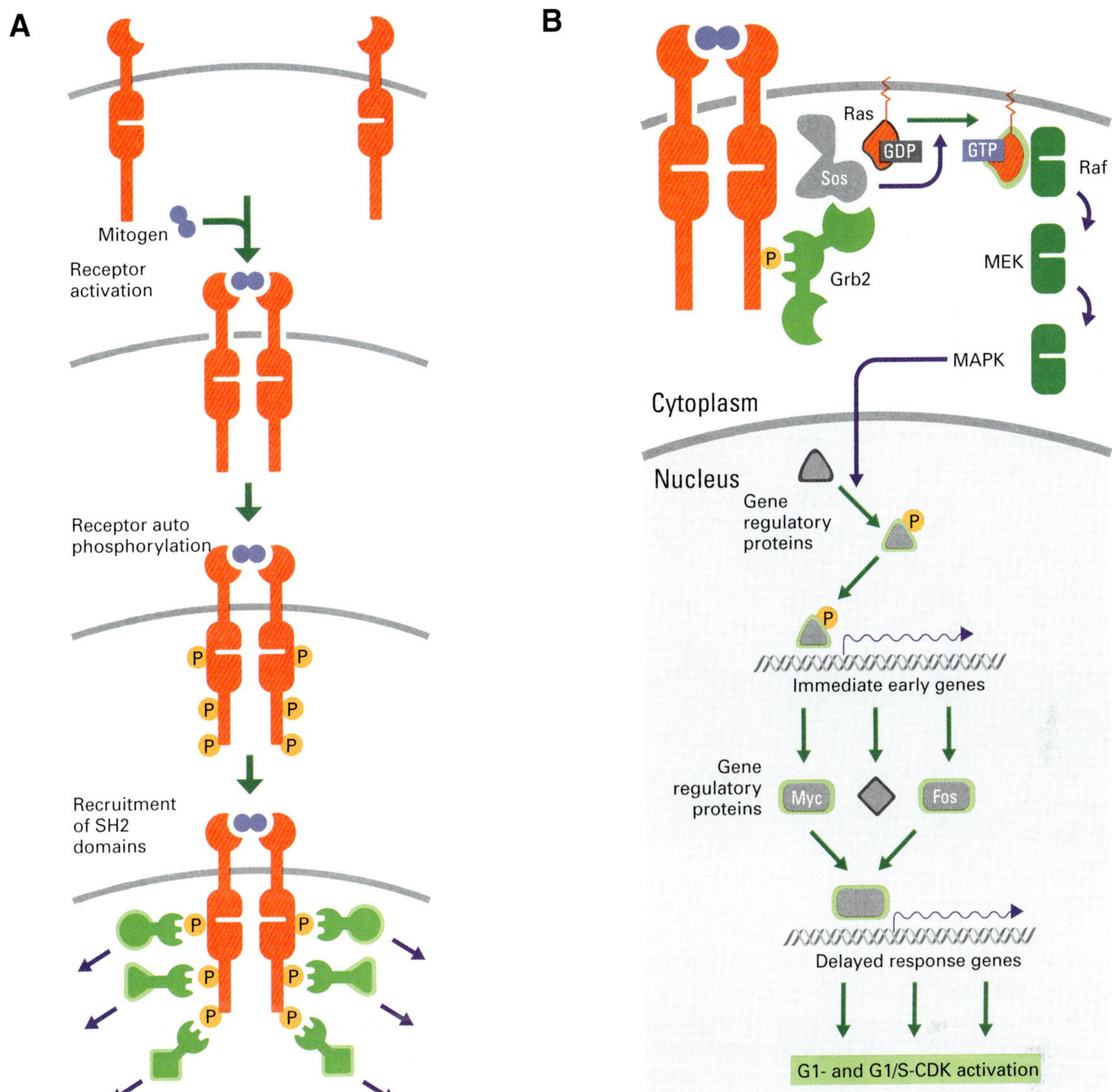

Fig. 2-9 Mitogenic signaling.

(A) Origin of the mitogenic signal at the cell membrane. The binding of growth factors to receptor tyrosine kinases causes receptor dimerization and autophosphorylation. The receptor tyrosine phosphorylation then recruits binding proteins that contain SH2 domains, and these transmit the mitogenic signal. (B) Mitogenic signaling by the RAS pathway. RAS activation stimulates the mitogen-activated protein kinase (MAPK) pathway, which leads to the activation of downstream transcription factors such as JUN and MYC.

David O'Morgan. London: New Science Press; 2006, 297 pp. by permission of Oxford University Press.[76]

HER2 activity and is used in the treatment of breast cancers with *HER2* amplification,[84] and cetuximab, an inhibitory antibody that binds to EGFR and is approved for use in metastatic colon cancer and head and neck cancers.[85,86]

Another important strategy to target RTKs and mitogenic kinases in cancers uses small-molecule inhibitors, such as imatinib, erlotinib, crizotinib, vermurafenib, and larotrectinib, which bind to specific kinases and inhibit their catalytic activity. Most available inhibitors have improved efficacy in tumors that contain mutations within the target kinase. For example, erlotinib and related TKIs are effective against the small fraction of lung cancers with mutations in *EGFR*.[87] Similarly, BRAF inhibitor therapy for melanoma is only effective if tumors have specific *BRAF* mutations.[88] The concept of directing small-molecule inhibitors against tumors with specific gene mutations lies at the crux of precision oncology.

Kinase inhibitors can also be used to treat tumors that depend upon the activity of a kinase pathway but do not have mutations in the kinase itself. Examples of this approach include the treatment of chronic lymphocytic leukemia (CLL) with idelalisib (which inhibits PI3K-δ) and the treatment of mantle cell lymphoma and CLL with ibrutinib (which inhibits Bruton tyrosine kinase).[89]

Resistance to Kinase Inhibitors

Despite the remarkable activity of small-molecule kinase inhibitors, the development of resistance against them limits the durability of clinical responses and may be inevitable in

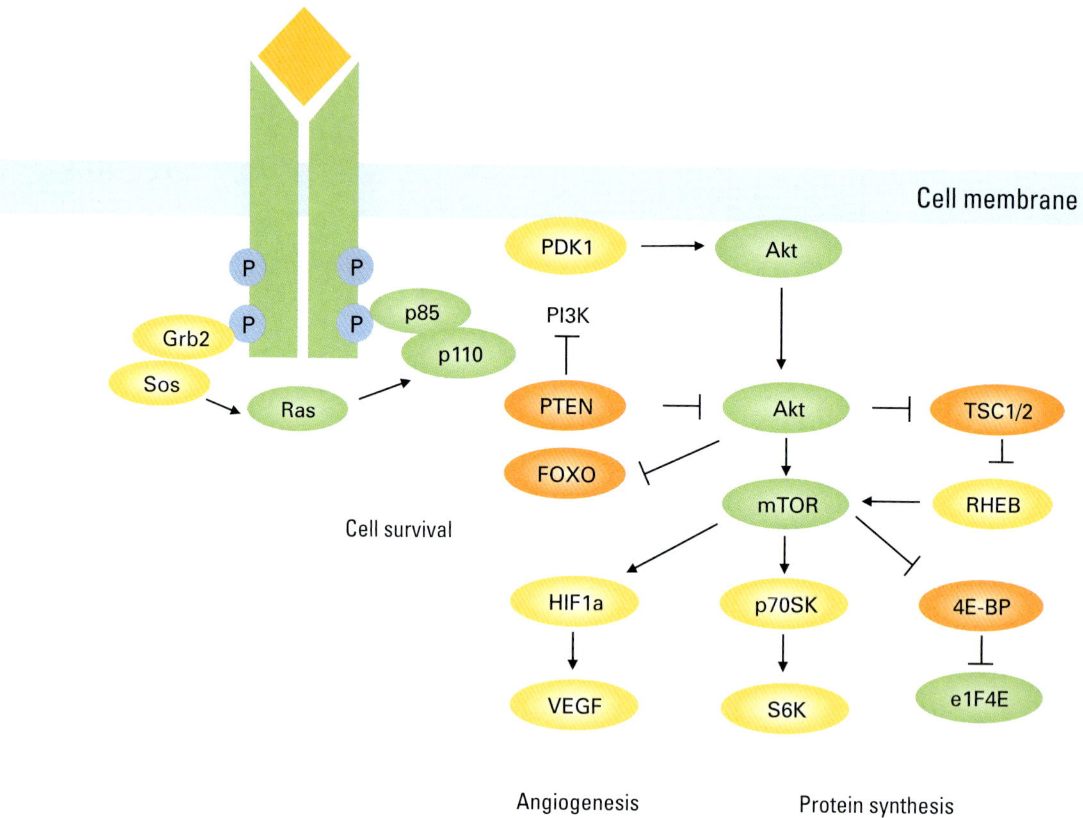

Fig. 2-10 Alterations of the AKT pathway in human cancer.

Activation of growth factor receptors such as the epidermal growth factor receptor, either by ligand stimulation or receptor overexpression/mutation, is 1 of the major mechanisms responsible for upregulation of AKT signaling. Other common mechanisms include activation of oncoproteins and inactivation of tumor suppressors intersecting the AKT signal transduction pathway. Proteins shown in green indicate oncoproteins for which overexpression and/or activating mutations have been implicated in many sporadic human cancers. Proteins in red are tumor suppressors whose loss and/or inactivation have been found to contribute to deregulation of the AKT pathway and tumor formation. FOXO transcription factors have also been implicated as tumor suppressors, although mutations have not been observed in any hereditary cancer syndrome to date. AKT signaling contributes to cancer development by activating multiple processes, including cell survival, angiogenesis, and protein synthesis.

Source: Wikipedia. Public Domain, https://en.wikipedia.org/wiki/Akt/PKB_signaling_pathway.

solid tumors. An exception to this is the use of imatinib and related drugs to inhibit BCR-ABL in CML, where responses are extremely durable, lasting > 10 years on average.[90] In most other cancers, such as the use of BRAF inhibitors in melanoma, impressive initial responses give way to resistant and progressive disease much more quickly, often in ≤ 1 year.[91]

Tumors acquire resistance to kinase inhibitors in several ways[92]:

- New mutations develop in the target kinases, which render the targeted therapy ineffective. In some cases, the mutant kinases can still be effectively inhibited by related small molecules. An example of this mechanism occurs in CML, where the acquisition of *BCR-ABL* mutations leads to the production of proteins that can no longer be inhibited by imatinib, but related agents, such as nilotinib, can continue inhibition. However, some mutations confer resistance to an entire class of kinase inhibitors.
- Bypass pathways develop, where tumor cells rewire their mitogenic signaling to use alternative pathways. In this case, although the target kinase is still sensitive to the pharmacologic inhibitors, the tumors have escaped kinase inhibition through the activation of alternative signaling pathways. An example of this mechanism is the activation of alternative RTKs in lung cancers being treated with EGFR inhibitors. One approach to overcome this type of resistance is the use of additional kinase inhibitors to block the bypass pathway, such as targeting both the BRAF and MAPK pathways in melanoma, although additional mutations also tend to render this approach ineffective over time.

CELL CYCLE CONTROL

Cell cycles are divided into 4 phases that coordinate cell growth, DNA replication, and cell division (Fig. 2-11). G1 phase is a period of growth between mitosis and the onset of DNA synthesis during which cells integrate mitogenic signals and, under certain conditions of mitogenic drive, commit to the onset of DNA replication. S phase is the period of DNA synthesis during which a cell replicates its genomic material. G2 phase follows S phase and is a second period of cell growth. In mitosis or M phase, chromosomes are segregated to daughter cells, and cell division occurs. Under ordinary conditions, cells execute the cell division cycle faithfully, but in cancer, several steps can go awry. In particular, mutations in the genes that regulate the cell cycle through S-phase commitment are among the most common genetic changes in cancer cells.[93]

The cyclin-dependent kinases (CDKs) drive cell cycle transitions by phosphorylating protein substrates with diverse roles in cell division. CDKs are composed of 2 subunits: a catalytic subunit (the CDK) and a regulatory subunit (the cyclin) that activates the CDK. Specific CDK/cyclin pairs are involved in distinct cell cycle transitions. CDK inhibitors counteract CDK activity to prevent cycling. A balance between these 2 opposing activities is central to the control of cell growth and division.

Cyclins and CDKs can act as dominant oncogenes. *CCND1* is rearranged by chromosome inversion in parathyroid adenomas, translocated to the immunoglobulin G heavy chain locus in mantle cell lymphomas, and amplified in 10% to 15% of solid tumors. Similarly, the cyclin E gene (*CCNE1*) was found to be the second most commonly amplified gene in ovarian cancers,[94] and cyclin E is upregulated in cancers by increased transcription or prolonged protein stability.[95] CDKs can also be mutated; an example is the *CDK4* mutation found in familial melanomas that prevents its inhibition by INK4 proteins.[96] Inhibitors of CDK4 and CDK6 are demonstrating great promise in breast and hematologic cancers, as evidenced by the recent approval of palbociclib, ribociclib, and abemaciclib to treat hormone receptor–positive breast cancer. Small molecules that inhibit other cell cycle kinases, such as CDK2 and the Wee1 kinase, which regulates CDK activity, are being tested in clinical trials.[97]

Genes encoding proteins that inhibit CDKs are tumor suppressor genes. INK4 proteins frequently exhibit allelic loss in cancers, such as glioblastoma.[98,99] They can also be epigenetically inactivated in tumors by promoter methylation, most notably in colon and lung cancers.[100] The p27Kip1 CDK inhibitor is a tumor suppressor with prognostic significance in cancers.[101] p27 is an example of a tumor suppressor that is rarely mutated; instead, it is inactivated by mutations in the pathways that regulate its degradation and/or subcellular localization. pRb is the prototype tumor suppressor, and its role in hereditary retinoblastoma provided the basis for the Knudson 2-step model.[72] Importantly, pRb is mutated in many sporadic cancers, including small-cell lung cancer, bladder cancer, and other common tumors.[102]

APOPTOSIS

Cell death can occur via necrosis, which is an unregulated process triggered by various cellular insults, and via apoptosis, an active and highly regulated physiologic process whereby complex biochemical pathways control whether a cell lives or dies. Tumor growth is a consequence of both unrestrained cell division and decreased apoptosis, and the pathways that mediate apoptosis contain proto-oncogenes and tumor suppressor genes that are altered in cancers. There are 2 distinct apoptotic pathways (Fig 2-12):[103]

- The intrinsic or mitochondrial pathway results from a number of stimuli, such as radiotherapy or chemotherapy, and involves changes in the mitochondrial membrane that affect the release of cytochrome C into the

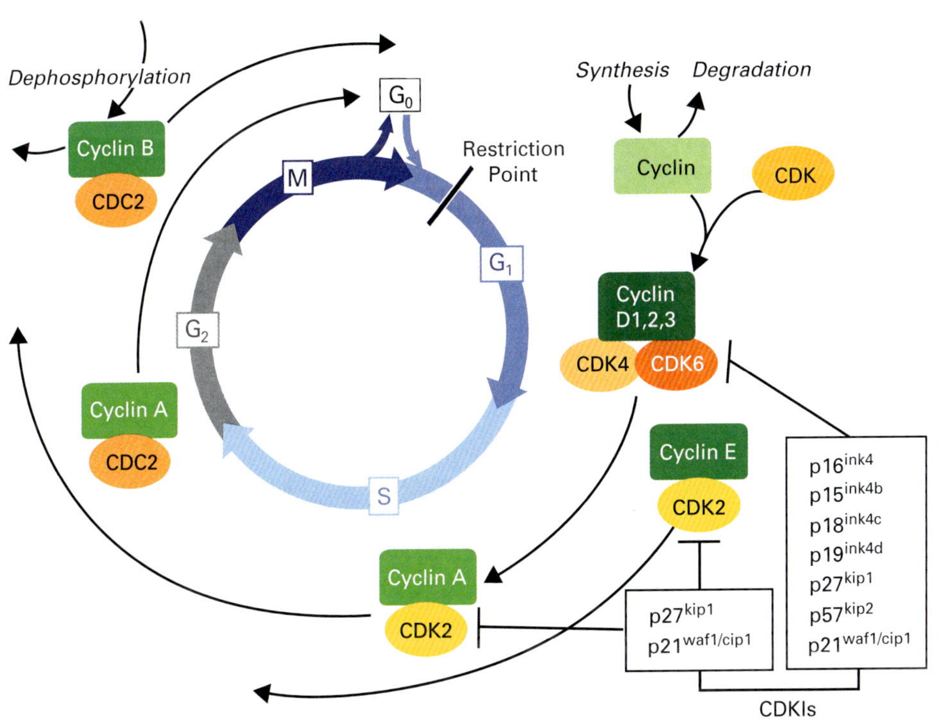

Fig. 2-11 The cell cycle. The cell cycle is divided into 4 phases (G1, S, G2, and M). Progression through the cell cycle is promoted by cyclin-dependent kinases (CDKs), which are regulated positively by cyclins and negatively by CDK inhibitors (CDKIs). The restriction point is the point at which cells progress through the cell cycle independently of external stimuli.

Reproduced with permission from Schwartz G et al: J Clin Oncol 23:9408-9421, 2005.

cytoplasm. The intrinsic pathway also activates a caspase cascade that ultimately leads to DNA fragmentation and cell death.

- The extrinsic pathway is signaled when ligands, such as tumor necrosis factor α (TNFα) and FAS ligand, bind to cell surface death receptors, such as TNF-R1 and FAS. Ligand binding to death receptors initiates a sequence of events leading to activation of proteases, termed caspases, which execute the apoptotic response.

The BCL-2 family comprises proteins that regulate apoptosis that are either proapoptotic (promote cell death) or antiapoptotic (promote cell survival).[104] *BCL2* was first identified as the gene activated by the t(14;18) translocation that is found in follicular lymphomas. The realization that BCL-2 functions to prevent apoptosis was pivotal to understanding the relationship between aberrant apoptosis and cancer biology. The precise mechanisms by which BCL-2 prevents cell death are not fully elucidated, but they involve interactions with proapoptotic family members, as well as alterations in mitochondrial functions. One important consequence of BCL-2 overexpression in tumorigenesis is that it prevents the apoptosis normally triggered by dominant oncogenes, such as *CMYC*, and this likely underlies the aggressive behavior of double-hit lymphomas, which contain activating translocations of both the *CMYC* and *BCL2* genes.[105] Because of their potential to induce apoptosis in tumor cells, drugs that target the BCL-2 protein family are being widely studied in clinical trials, and 1 drug, venetoclax, is now approved for treatment of CLL and AML. (see also Box 1)[19,20,106,107]

Many cancer genes interact with the core apoptotic pathways. The most common mutations that impair apoptosis in tumors involve the *TP53* tumor suppressor gene. Apoptosis is 1 outcome of TP53 activation by cellular stress, and impaired cell death is an important consequence of TP53 loss in cancer. Another signaling pathway that prevents apoptosis is the PI3K-AKT pathway. The interactions of AKT with apoptotic signaling are complex and include direct effects on the mitochondrial membrane, as well as functional interactions with BCL-2 family members, FOXO transcription factors, nuclear factor κ B, and p53.

KEY POINTS

- Mitogenic signaling pathways contain broadly acting proto-oncogenes, and their products are tyrosine kinases. Small-molecule kinase inhibitors and antibody-based therapeutics target many of these proteins.
- The genes that promote or inhibit the normal cell cycle are commonly mutated in cancer cells and are becoming important targets for cancer treatment.
- Many oncogenic mutations disrupt normal apoptotic responses. Inhibitors of proapoptotic proteins constitute another important new class of anticancer drugs.

UBIQUITIN-MEDIATED PROTEIN DEGRADATION

The precise control of protein abundance within a cell is critical to many cellular processes. The rapid degradation of specific proteins is accomplished through the ubiquitin proteasome system. This process first requires site-specific modification, typically phosphorylation, of the protein to be degraded, which serves as a flag that the protein is no longer required in the cell. Next, a multienzyme process catalyzes the transfer of chains of the small protein ubiquitin to the phosphorylated target. Families of enzymes, known as E1s, E2s, and E3s, play specific roles in this ubiquitination step. Finally, this polyubiquitination causes the protein to be recognized and then degraded by a proteolytic organelle called the proteasome (Fig 2-13).[108-110] Additional control of this process is provided by a family of deubiquitinating enzymes, which can remove polyubiquitin chains before degradation takes place. Furthermore, shorter forms of ubiquitin chains can be added to proteins to signal events besides degradation, such as protein-protein interactions and intracellular signaling events.

Given their critical role in the control of protein abundance, enzymes involved in the ubiquitin proteasome pathway are often altered in cancers. E3 ubiquitin ligases, the enzymes that catalyze the final transfer of ubiquitin to substrates targeted for degradation, are particularly important oncogenes and tumor suppressors.

- The E3 ubiquitin ligase *FBXW7* is 1 of the most commonly mutated tumor suppressor genes across cancer types.[111] The Fbxw7 protein targets numerous key oncoproteins for degradation, including cyclin E, c-MYC, Notch, and c-JUN. However, inactivating *FBXW7* mutations prevent degradation of these oncoproteins, promoting tumorigenesis. Some cancer types, such as T-cell acute lymphoblastic leukemia (ALL) and endometrial cancers, exhibit particularly high *FBXW7* mutation rates.
- The *SPOP* ubiquitin ligase gene was recently identified as a tumor suppressor gene. Prostate and endometrial cancers show recurrent mutations in *SPOP* that lead to deregulation of cancer drivers, including AR and ER.[112,113] The SPOP protein also seems to be involved in the DNA repair process, and *SPOP* mutation may predict sensitivity to DNA-damaging agents.[114] Interestingly, *SPOP* may act as an oncogene in clear cell renal cancer and, as such, is an example of a rare gene that can act as both a tumor driver and tumor suppressor, depending on cellular context.[115]
- Inactivating mutations of the von Hippel-Lindau (VHL) E3 ubiquitin ligase are the cause of VHL syndrome, which is associated with susceptibility to renal cell carcinoma (RCC), CNS hemangioblastomas, pheochromocytoma, pancreatic tumors, and other neoplasms. VHL syndrome is diagnosed by the presence of germ line–inactivating VHL mutations. If the second allele is lost in normal tissues, this can lead to cancer. Inactivating VHL mutations are also found in most spontaneous RCCs.[116] One critical VHL target is hypoxia-inducible factor-1α, a transcription factor that regulates genes in response to hypoxia, including an angiogenic transcriptional program that contributes to the highly vascular tumors associated with VHL loss.

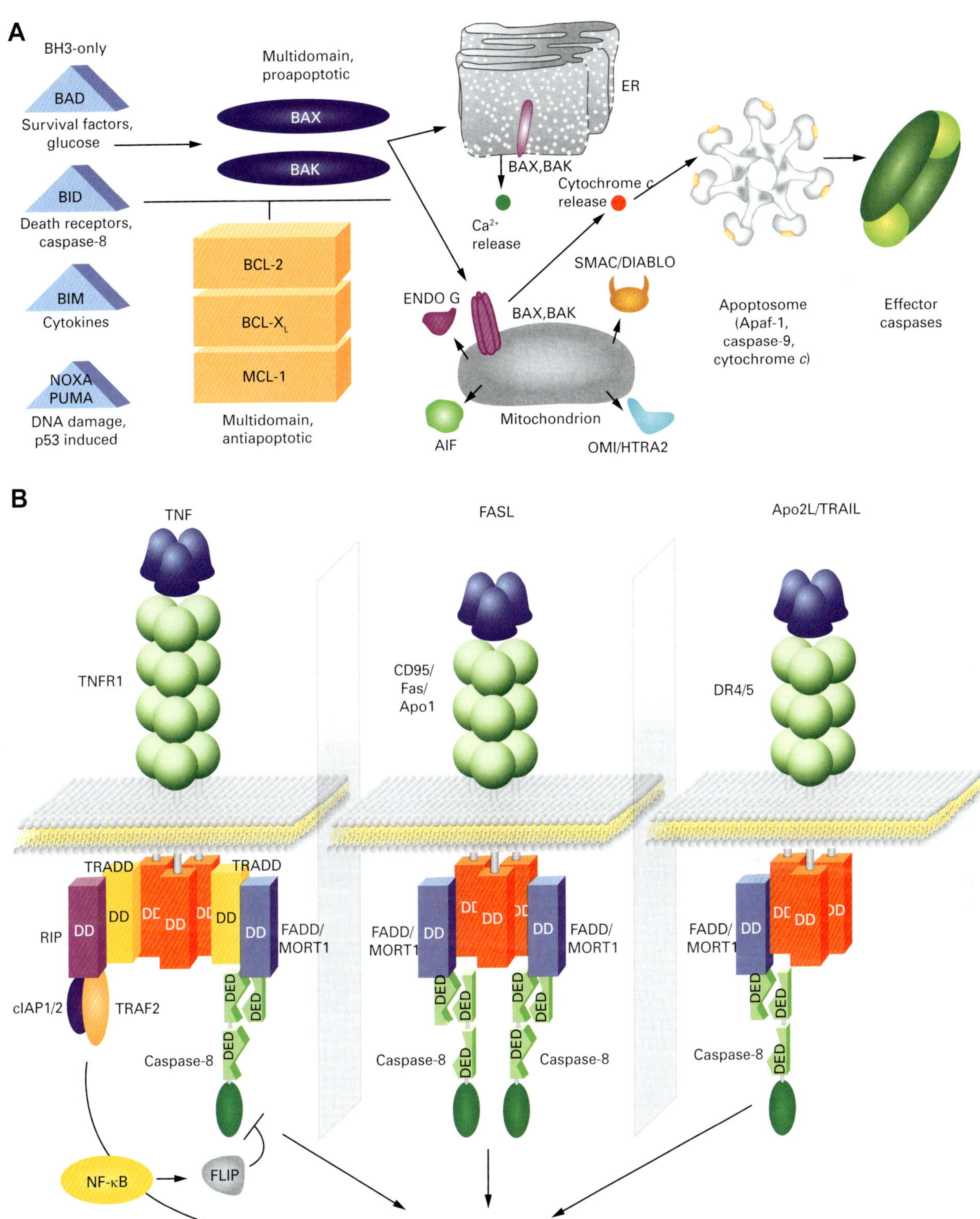

Fig. 2-12 Apoptosis pathways.

(A) The intrinsic apoptosis pathway. (B) Extrinsic death receptor pathways. The distinct composition of the death-inducing signaling complex downstream of the various death receptors TNFR1, CD95, and DR4/5 is illustrated.

Abbreviation: ER, endoplasmic reticulum.

Reprinted from Cell, *Vol. 116(2), Danial NN, Korsmeyer SJ. Cell Death Critical Control Points. Pg. 205-219, Copyright (2004), with permission from Elsevier.*

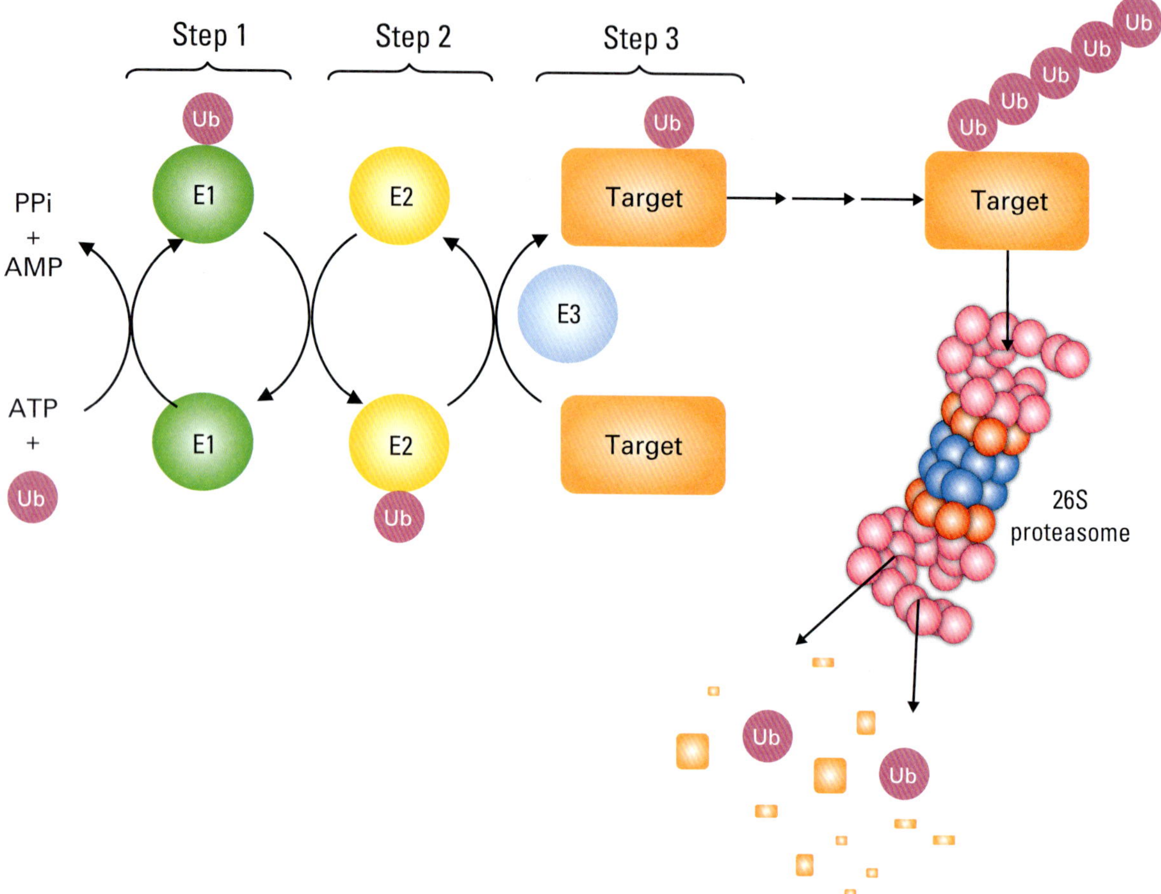

Fig. 2-13 Overview of the ubiquitin (Ub)–proteasome pathway.

The small protein Ub is first transferred to the Ub-activating enzyme E1 in an ATP-dependent manner. This activated Ub is then transferred to the Ub-conjugating enzyme E2. Finally, the Ub is covalently attached to the target protein by an E3 Ub ligase, leading to formation of a polyubiquitin chain. The polyubiquitinated protein is recognized by the 26S proteasome and is destroyed in an ATP-dependent manner.

Adapted from Mani A et al: J Clin Oncol 23:4776-4789, 2005. PMID: 16034054.

- In other cases, E3s are overexpressed and act as dominant oncogenes. One example of this involves MDM2, a ubiquitin ligase that targets the p53 protein for degradation and whose abundance is increased in cancers by mechanisms such as gene amplification.[117]

Proteasome inhibitors, which block protein proteolysis by the proteasome, have emerged as important antineoplastic agents, particularly for the treatment of hematologic cancers.[118,119] Bortezomib, carfilzomib, and ixazomib are useful for the treatment of multiple myeloma and other hematologic malignancies. Other inhibitors of the proteasome or more specific proteasomal pathways are currently being studied in clinical trials. Given that general proteasome inhibitors affect a large number of proteins normally degraded by the proteasome, the mechanisms that account for the therapeutic index associated with these inhibitors remains unclear. In addition to general proteasome inhibitors, activators or inhibitors of specific components of the ubiquitin ligase pathway are of great clinical interest. For example, inhibitors of the SPOP ubiquitin ligase have been developed and show activity in kidney cancer models.[120]

The ubiquitin-proteasome system also plays a role in the actions of other chemotherapeutics. For example, thalidomide and related drugs cause the cereblon E3 ubiquitin ligase to abnormally degrade specific protein substrates, which may explain their efficacy in MDS with chromosome 5q deletions and in multiple myeloma.[121]

CONTROL OF CELLULAR DIFFERENTIATION AND CELL FATE

Most somatic cells are in a terminally differentiated, postmitotic state, which is established by complex transcriptional pathways. Master regulators of cellular differentiation and related processes are often involved in cancer. An important example of this concept is the Wnt/beta-catenin pathway, which has vital roles in development and cellular self-renewal. Indeed, abnormal Wnt signaling is implicated in many cancers.[122] Soluble Wnt proteins bind to membrane-bound receptors, and this prevents the ubiquitin-dependent degradation of beta-catenin by the proteasome. Beta-catenin then translocates to the nucleus, where it stimulates a transcriptional program in concert with the TCF transcription factor. The regulation of this pathway is quite complex, and many proteins augment or restrain Wnt pathway activation. The best-characterized role of Wnt pathway activation in human cancer is in familial adenomatous polyposis (FAP), a hereditary colon cancer syndrome caused by deletion of the APC tumor suppressor (also described in Chapter 13). APC loss upregulates Wnt signaling by increasing beta-catenin stability, leading to inappropriate transcription. Although first described in FAP, *APC* mutations are found in most sporadic colon cancers and are an early step in colorectal cancer progression.[123] Many other cancers also have aberrant Wnt signaling, including uterine cancers, brain cancers, and some leukemias.[102] Inhibitors of the Wnt pathway are being actively studied for cancer therapy.[124] For example, the finding that colorectal cancers require persistent Wnt deregulation for tumor maintenance suggests that Wnt inhibitors may be efficacious in this setting.[125]

OTHER PATHWAYS REGULATING CELLULAR DIFFERENTIATION

Similar to Wnt/beta-catenin, many other proto-oncogenes, often transcription factors and/or coactivators involved in leukemias and lymphomas, affect the pathways that regulate differentiation.[126] For example, retinoic acid receptor α (RARα) is rearranged in several translocations found in acute promyelocytic leukemia (APL), most commonly t(15;17), which produces a PML-RARα fusion protein. This fusion protein acts as a dominant-negative mutant that inhibits expression of RARα target genes and blocks differentiation. The PML-RARα fusion is targeted by all-trans retinoic acid (ATRA), which is used in conjunction with combination chemotherapy to induce remission in patients with APL. ATRA binds to the fusion protein and prevents it from bringing corepressors to RARα target genes, reversing the differentiation block and allowing promyelocytes to proceed down their normal differentiation pathway.[127] Core-binding factor (CBF) is another transcription factor regulating hematopoietic differentiation that is involved in translocations found in acute leukemia. Like PML-RARα, these translocations produce dominant-negative proteins that inhibit CBF target gene expression, which is thought to impair hematopoietic cell differentiation.[128]

The *NOTCH* genes encode transmembrane receptors that influence transcriptional programs involved in cell fate and differentiation. These are frequently altered in human cancers.[129] Signaling is activated by ligand binding, which causes NOTCH proteins to be cleaved, forming intracellular domains that translocate to the nucleus and activate transcription. NOTCH proteins play important roles in lymphoid differentiation and are likely drivers of hematologic cancers. *NOTCH1* was first described as an oncogene involved in the t(7;9) translocation found in a subset of patients with T-cell ALL. Activating *NOTCH1* mutations occur in as many as 50% of patients with this disease.[130] The mechanisms through which NOTCH promotes leukemia are thought to involve impaired differentiation and enhanced self-renewal, and c-MYC is a critical mediator of *NOTCH* gene expression and activity.[131] Interestingly, *NOTCH* may act as a tumor suppressor in some cancers, because 20% of squamous cell carcinomas show inactivating mutations in these genes. How *NOTCH* acts as an oncogene in some clinical situations and as a tumor suppressor in others remains poorly understood.[132] Compounds targeting the NOTCH signaling pathway are being tested as anticancer therapies.

The Hedgehog signaling pathway is another example of a molecular process intricately involved in development and cell fate decisions that is hijacked by cancer cells to promote abnormal growth. In normal cells and organisms, Hedgehog guides development, differentiation, and proliferation through a complex signaling cascade. Hedgehog itself is an extracellular ligand that binds to and activates the Ptch1 cell surface receptor, which in turn allows activation of the Smo cell surface receptor. Smo sends intracellular signals that ultimately lead to the Gli transcription factor activating gene expression programs that drive cellular phenotypes. Mutations or other alterations in Hedgehog signaling components can be found in both hereditary and sporadic tumors and are especially important in basal cell skin cancers and medulloblastomas. Specific inhibitors of components of this pathway, including the Smo inhibitors erismodegib, glasdegib, and vismodegib, are approved for treatment of basal cell cancers and leukemias and are being tested in other disease states. Arsenic trioxide, which is approved for the treatment of APL, is thought to function in part because of inhibition of Gli transcription factors.[133]

DNA REPAIR PATHWAYS

Mammalian cells use 3 major DNA repair pathways to maintain genomic integrity (Fig 2-14). The nucleotide excision-repair (NER) pathway recognizes and repairs UV light–induced nucleotide dimers and other DNA adducts. DNA recombination repair corrects double-stranded DNA breaks induced by ionizing radiation and other agents. Finally, the DNA MMR pathways correct errors during DNA replication by removing the mismatched strand and enabling subsequent repair of the DNA. Mutations that disrupt these pathways cause genetic instability and are associated with inherited diseases characterized by sensitivity to DNA-damaging agents and by cancer predisposition.

NER Pathways

NER pathways correct nucleotide lesions induced by UV light and adducts induced by chemical carcinogens.[134] There are 2 NER pathways: a global repair pathway and a transcription-coupled repair pathway that repairs DNA damage occurring during transcription. Germ line mutations affecting these pathways give rise to sun-sensitive and developmental disorders, including xeroderma pigmentosum, Cockayne syndrome, and trichothiodystrophy. Xeroderma pigmentosum is an autosomal-recessive disorder leading to neurodegeneration, sensitivity to UV light, abnormalities in skin pigmentation, and cancer predisposition. People with this disorder have a risk for skin cancer that is estimated to be

2,000 times higher than that of the general population. Eight genes have been associated with xeroderma pigmentosum; 7 code for excision-repair proteins, and 1 is a DNA polymerase required for accurate replication of damaged DNA. In contrast, Cockayne syndrome is associated with 2 genes, *CSA* and *CSB*, which are involved in transcription-coupled DNA repair. Trichothiodystrophy is caused by mutation of either *ERCC2/XPD* or *ERCC3/XPB*, which encode helicase subunits of the TFIIH transcription complex. Neither Cockayne syndrome nor trichothiodystrophy is associated with an increased cancer risk.

Double-Strand Break Repair

Damage to DNA by radiation, chemicals (eg, chemotherapy), and other insults produces double-strand breaks, which are recognized and repaired by a coordinated response that involves proteins encoded by a wide range of tumor suppressor genes. Germ line mutations of some of these genes cause inherited syndromes with highly variable clinical manifestations. Ataxia telangiectasia is characterized by progressive cerebellar ataxia, telangiectasia, immunodeficiency, and increased tumorigenesis (most commonly hematopoietic neoplasms). The ataxia telangiectasia gene (*ATM*) encodes a large protein kinase with homology to PI3K. ATM is activated by serine phosphorylation in response to DNA breaks and phosphorylates a number of downstream substrates with critical roles in DNA repair and checkpoint pathways, including CHK2, TP53, BRCA1, and NBS1 (Fig 2-15).[135] Cells derived from patients with ataxia telangiectasia exhibit increased DNA damage from radiation, as well as defects in normal cell cycle responses to DNA damage, called checkpoints.

Fanconi anemia (FA) is an autosomal-recessive disease characterized by developmental abnormalities, bone marrow failure, and susceptibility to cancers, particularly AML, squamous cell cancer of the head and neck, gynecologic cancers, and esophageal cancer. Similar to ataxia telangiectasia, cells derived from patients with FA display aberrant responses to DNA-damaging agents. However, FA cells are not hypersensitive to ionizing radiation; rather, they are hypersensitive to DNA cross-linking by agents such as diepoxybutane and mitomycin C. Classic studies defined many FA complementation groups, and 13 FA genes have now been cloned. Remarkably, many of these genes encode proteins that form a complex that catalyzes the monoubiquitination of 2 FA proteins, FANCD2 and FANCI.[136] Monoubiquitinated FANCD2 and FANCI become localized to nuclear repair foci after DNA damage, and these foci also contain FANCD1 (identical with the *BRCA2* breast cancer gene) and other proteins, including BRCA1 and NBS1. The intersection of the BRCA1 and FA pathways underscores the central importance of this DNA-damage sensing and repair mechanism in carcinogenesis.

The NBS1 protein is another component of nuclear repair foci implicated in a chromosome breakage syndrome. Nijmegen breakage syndrome is an autosomal-recessive disease characterized by microcephaly, immunodeficiency, and increased frequency of hematopoietic cancers that is caused by mutations in the *NBS1* gene. NBS1 forms a complex with MRE11 and RAD50, which binds to BRCA1 in nuclear repair foci. Deficiency of the NBS1 protein blocks the formation of the MRE11-NBS1-RAD50 complex, and this impairs the S-phase surveillance responses triggered by ATM. Accordingly, many of the symptoms of this disease are identical to symptoms of ataxia telangiectasia.

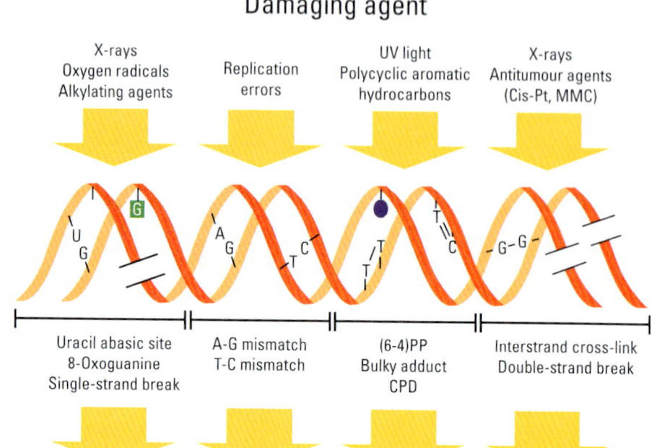

Fig. 2-14 DNA lesions and repair mechanisms.

Common DNA damaging agents (top), examples of lesions that can be introduced by these agents into the DNA double helix (middle), and the most frequently used repair mechanisms for such lesions (bottom). Distinct damaging sources can induce similar types of DNA lesions, and any 1 agent often induces > 1 type of damage. The lesion spectrum of different repair pathways may overlap.

Abbreviations: BER, base excision repair; CPD, cyclobutane pyrimidine dimer; MMC, mitomycin C; NER, nucleotide excision repair.

de Boer J, Hoeijmakers JHJ, Nucleotide excision repair and human syndromes, Oxford University Press, *2000, 21(3), pg. 453-460, by permission of Oxford University Press.*

Mutations in many components of the DNA-damage response (DDR) pathway can be found in both hereditary and sporadic cancers. Identification of these mutations is clinically relevant, because they may predict sensitivity to PARP inhibitors and DNA-damaging agents such as cisplatin. Ongoing studies are testing the efficacy of these agents in various tumor types with mutations in DDR components. Interestingly, tumors associated with germ line DDR mutations may respond much more dramatically than those with somatic DDR mutations, suggesting that timing of the mutation during tumor development is important.

MMR

DNA MMR corrects errors that occur during DNA replication, which are primarily single-base mismatches or short insertions or deletions.[137] A complex of proteins binds to a DNA mismatch, identifies the DNA strand with a mismatch, and then excises and repairs the mismatch. Several of the MMR proteins

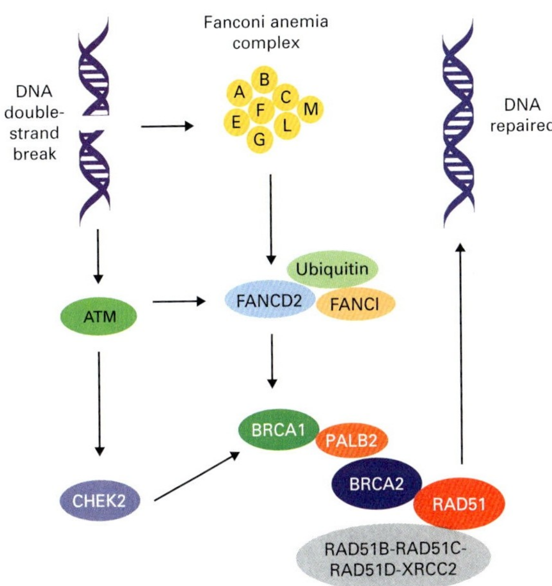

Fig. 2-15 Recombinational repair of DNA double-strand damage.

DNA double-strand breaks recruit protein kinase ATM and also activate the Fanconi anemia core complex (FANCA/B/C/E/F/G/L/M) that monoubiquitinates the downstream targets FANCD2 and FANCI. ATM activates (phosphorylates) CHEK2 and FANCD2 and in turn CHEK2 phosphorylates BRCA1. Ubiquinated FANCD2 complexes with BRCA1 and RAD51. The PALB2 protein then acts as a hub, bringing together BRCA1, BRCA2 and RAD51 at the site of a DNA double-strand break, and also binds to RAD51C, a member of the RAD51 paralog complex RAD51B-RAD51C-RAD51D-XRCC2 (BCDX2). The BCDX2 complex recruits RAD51 or stabilizes the damage sites. RAD51 plays a major role in homologous recombinational repair of DNA during double-strand break repair. In this process, an ATP dependent DNA strand exchange takes place in which a single strand invades base-paired strands of homologous DNA molecules. RAD51 is involved in the search for homology and strand pairing stages of the process.

Source: Wikipedia. Public Domain, https://en.wikipedia.org/wiki/Fanconi_anemia#/media/File:Homologous_recombinational_repair_of_DNA_double-strand_damage.jpg.

are tumor suppressors involved in HNPCC. People with HNPCC/Lynch syndrome are at significantly increased risk of colon and uterine cancers, with less dramatically increased risk of cancers in other organ sites as well.[138] The 2 most commonly mutated MMR genes in Lynch syndrome are *MSH2* and *MLH1*. *MSH2* is involved in the initial recognition of the mismatch, whereas *MLH1* helps determine which DNA strand contains the correct sequence. Mutations in other MMR genes are less commonly associated with HNPCC and include *MSH6*, *PMS1*, and *PMS2*. Patients with HNPCC inherit a nonfunctional MMR gene allele and a subsequent loss of the remaining allele in a somatic cell ultimately gives rise to a tumor. Importantly, impaired MMR causes a hypermutable phenotype, as evidenced by MSI, which is readily detected in tumors by PCR-based assays that reveal novel tumor-specific microsatellite fragments. Although MSI is the hallmark of HNPCC, it is also found in a subset of sporadic colon cancers, but in these cases, *MLH1* is typically silenced by promoter hypermethylation rather than by gene mutation.

As mentioned previously, the detection of MMR deficiency in tumors is of high clinical relevance, because it predicts a high probability of deep and prolonged responses to immune-modulating programmed death-1 (PD-1) inhibitors, including nivolumab and pembrolizumab.[22] Similarly, tumor mutation burden, which quantifies the number of mutations present in a specific cancer specimen and is likely a surrogate marker of defective MMR, may also predict efficacy of immune-modulating agents.[139]

KEY POINTS

- Enzymes that promote protein degradation by the proteasome can function as tumor suppressors.
- Pharmacologic proteasome inhibitors are approved for the treatment of multiple myeloma and other hematologic cancers.
- Genes that regulate cellular differentiation are often mutated in hematologic cancers. Drugs that restore normal differentiation are important treatments for these diseases.
- DNA repair pathways contain many tumor suppressor genes that are mutated in both familial and sporadic cancers. Mutations that disable different elements of DNA repair pathways are associated with specific cancer syndromes.
- Inactivation of DNA damage repair genes may predict response to PARP inhibitors and DNA-damaging agents.
- Inactivation of DNA MMR enzymes predicts response to PD-1 inhibitors.

CHECKPOINTS: CROSSROADS OF DNA REPAIR, CELL CYCLE REGULATION, AND GENETIC INSTABILITY

The fidelity of the enzymes that replicate DNA and segregate chromosomes is largely responsible for the accurate propagation of genetic information. However, these enzymes have an intrinsic error rate, and the frequency of errors is increased by genotoxic insults. Normal cells continually monitor DNA replication and mitosis and stop the cell cycle if these do not occur correctly, allowing the damage to be repaired before proliferation resumes or initiating apoptotic and/or senescent responses to block cell growth. The pathways that link cell cycle progression to the accurate execution of prior cell cycle events are called checkpoints.[140] (Note that this section refers to checkpoints as molecular processes that safeguard the genome from damage; such checkpoints are wholly distinct from the checkpoints present in the immune system that are targeted by immunotherapy approaches.)

Mammalian cells have checkpoints that operate in each phase of the cell cycle and are intricately interwoven with the cell cycle and DNA repair machinery.[141,142] The G1 and G2 checkpoints recognize DNA damage that occurs during these cell cycle phases and initiate responses leading to either cell cycle arrest or cell death. The S-phase checkpoint is also activated by DNA damage, as well as by inhibition of the proper function of the replication machinery (eg, by chemotherapeutics such as hydroxyurea and cytarabine).

Checkpoint pathways are composed of sensors/mediators, signal transducers, and effectors. The sensors and mediators detect DNA damage and form protein complexes that accumulate in DNA repair foci. The DNA damage signal is then transmitted by kinases, first ATM and ATR, and subsequently CHK1 and CHK2, which ultimately activate effectors, such as p53 and Cdc25. The effectors directly affect cell cycle progression, apoptosis, and DNA repair. Small-molecule inhibitors of many of these checkpoint kinases are being evaluated as anticancer therapeutics. Importantly, checkpoint pathways are disrupted in most human cancers, where they are central drivers of genetic instability and tumor progression.

p53 PATHWAY

The p53 protein plays a central role in checkpoint pathways, and its cognate *TP53* gene is the most frequently mutated human tumor suppressor.[143,144] Although *TP53* is mutated in up to half of all spontaneous cancers, its role as a tumor suppressor first came to light in studies of Li-Fraumeni syndrome, a rare autosomal disorder associated with the development of a wide variety of early-onset cancers, including soft tissue and bone sarcomas, as well as breast, brain, and colon cancers. The p53 protein is a transcription factor that, in healthy cells, is activated by many triggers, including DNA damage and replication stress. Activation of p53 can lead to cell cycle arrest, apoptosis, or cellular senescence; these alternative outcomes depend on many factors. p53 accomplishes these outcomes by activating transcription of its target genes and through other activities (Fig 2-16). Tumors most commonly inactivate *TP53* by a combination of loss of 1 gene copy coupled with mutation of the other copy, resulting in expression of a protein with inactivating amino acid changes within critical functional domains.

Another mechanism of suppression of p53 in tumors involves the MDM2 ubiquitin ligase.[117] *MDM2* gene expression is induced by p53, and the MDM2 protein functions in a negative feedback loop to downregulate p53 by ubiquitinating it. The normal MDM2-p53 feedback loop is disrupted in many cancers. MDM2 is overexpressed in a wide spectrum of neoplasms, where it leads to decreased p53 abundance and function. Another gene that affects p53 degradation is the ARF tumor suppressor, which is frequently deleted in cancers.[145] ARF normally binds to MDM2, and this prevents MDM2 from ubiquitinating p53. However, when the *ARF* gene is deleted, MDM2 activity is unrestrained, causing p53 to be degraded. ARF expression is induced by oncogenes such as *MYC* and plays an important role in TP53 activation by oncogenic signaling. Thus, loss of ARF disables an important protective mechanism against oncogenic transformation.

There is enormous interest in developing cancer treatment strategies that target the p53 pathway, because studies in model systems show that restoration of p53 function has potent antitumor activity. Strategies that target the p53 pathway range from peptides that restore p53 protein function in cells with mutant p53 proteins to recombinant adenoviruses that selectively kill cells with *TP53* gene mutations. Some of these strategies are now being tested in clinical trials.[144]

MITOTIC SPINDLE CHECKPOINT

The mitotic spindle assembly checkpoint ensures that chromosomes are equally segregated to daughter cells during mitosis.[146] It is the key safeguard against the gain or loss of whole chromosomes and other changes in chromosome structure, known collectively as chromosomal instability. During mitosis, chromosomes attach to the mitotic spindle through protein structures called kinetochores. In a normal cell, the presence of unattached kinetochores signals that mitosis should not proceed. This signal is activated when spindle checkpoint proteins, including BUB1, BUBR1, MAD1, and MAD2, accumulate at the unattached kinetochores. This, in turn, inhibits the APC ubiquitin ligase and blocks the ubiquitination and turnover of cyclin B and securin, which must be degraded for mitosis to occur. Unlike DNA-damage checkpoint genes, mutations in the genes controlling the mitotic checkpoint are rarely found in human cancers. However, various chemotherapeutic agents (eg, taxanes and vinca alkaloids) target the mitotic spindle and can induce aberrant mitotic divisions or trigger the mitotic checkpoint.

KEY POINTS

- Checkpoints ensure the fidelity of cell division and protect against genomic instability.
- Checkpoint pathways are often dependent on normal tumor suppressor gene and DNA repair protein functions.
- The loss of checkpoint functions causes genomic instability and fosters the accumulation of multiple mutations in cancer cells.
- *TP53* is the most commonly mutated cancer gene, and it participates in diverse checkpoint responses. The p53 protein senses and responds to cellular stress by activating pathways that regulate processes such as cell cycle progression and apoptosis.

MULTISTEP TUMORIGENESIS

The development of fully malignant cancers requires many independent genetic and epigenetic events that dysregulate normal cellular processes sufficiently to transform the cells to a malignant state. Although the specific mutations that cause human cancers vary greatly among cancer types and individuals, the broad consequences of these mutations are abnormal phenotypes that are shared by most cancers. Hanahan and Weinberg[147] originally proposed 6 hallmarks of cancer that

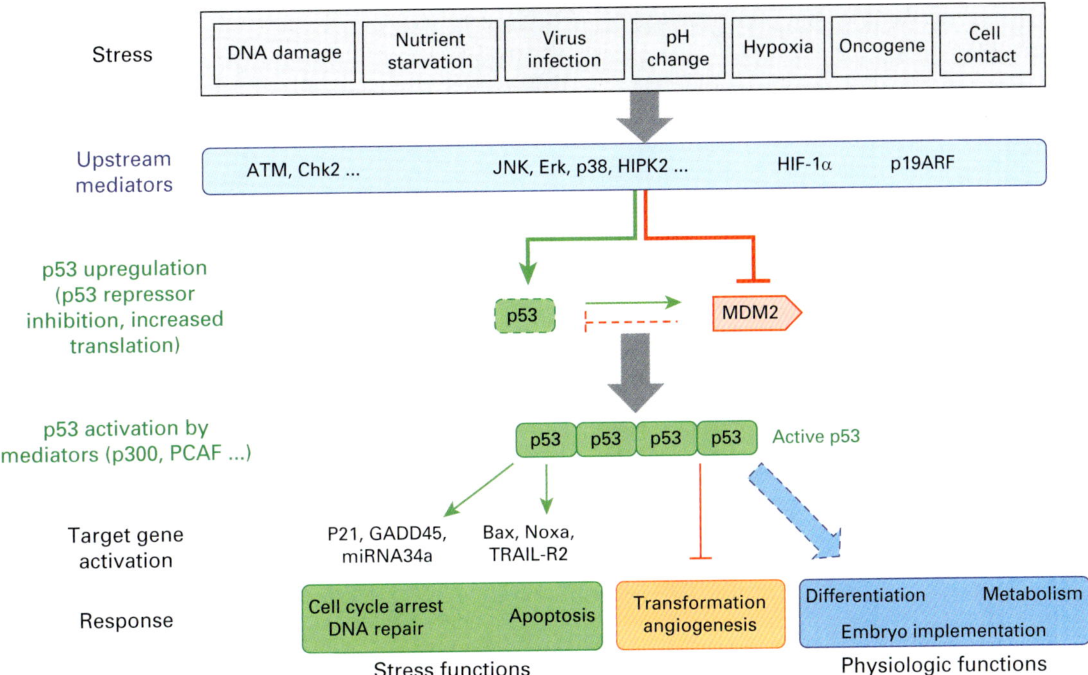

Fig. 2-16 The p53-MDM2-ARF network.

The activation of p53 classically occurs in response to many other cellular stresses that produce DNA damage, including oncogene-induced stress. Depending on the nature of the inducing signal, these DNA-damage responses activate a myriad of upstream mediators that lead to upregulation and activation of p53. This, in turn, results in activation of p53 target genes that serve to counteract the initiating cellular stress and protect the cell from further damage. When p53 is mutated or deleted, as it is in most cancers, these critical safeguards no longer function, and cellular stress continues unabated.

Permission to reuse given by the Creative Common license for Surget S, Khoury MP, Bourdon J. Uncovering the role of p53 splice variants in human malignancy: a clinical perspective. Onco Targets Ther. 2013 Dec 19;7:57-68.

they defined as "distinctive and complementary capabilities that enable tumor growth and metastatic dissemination" (Fig 2-17).[148 (p646)] These include:

1. Sustained proliferative signaling
2. Evading growth suppressors
3. Resisting cell death
4. Enabling replicative immortality
5. Inducing angiogenesis
6. Activating invasion and metastasis

These capabilities can be acquired in different order, and in some cases, a single genetic mutation might provide > 1 capability. This conceptualization provides a framework within which to consider multistep tumorigenesis.

The first 3 of these acquired capabilities involve mutations within the mitogenic signaling, cell cycle, and cell death pathways. The fourth category involves the acquisition of cellular immortality in tumors. Normal cells are limited in the number of times they can divide, even when they are provided with all of the normal mitogenic stimuli required for cell division. In contrast, many cancer cells can divide with apparently limitless potential. One fundamental mechanism that limits human cell division involves repetitive nucleotide sequences, called telomeres, at the ends of chromosomes. Telomeres protect the ends of chromosomes from deterioration. They shorten with each cell division (the length of the telomeres of a cell reflects the number of divisions it has undergone) and eventually are shortened to the point where they can no longer protect the chromosome ends. This leads to a condition termed telomere crisis and, ultimately, to cell death. Unlike normal cells, cancer cells maintain their telomere length during cell division. This usually results from expression of the enzyme telomerase that adds nucleotides back to the telomere. Telomerase activity can be detected in 85% to 90% of cancers, and the remaining tumors maintain their telomeres through a mechanism involving recombination.

The fifth capability of induced angiogenesis reflects the need of a tumor to actively recruit vasculature to grow once it has outgrown its existing blood supply. In normal tissues, the development of new blood vessels is highly regulated by both positive and negative signals. Tumor cells promote angiogenesis by upregulating the pathways that promote blood vessel formation (eg, increased expression of growth factors such as vascular endothelial growth factor [VEGF] and fibroblast growth factor) and by reducing the activity of inhibitory pathways. Some of these pathways involve transcriptional networks under the control of previously discussed genes, such as *VHL* mutations in RCC. The importance of these pathways in tumor cell growth has prompted the development of drugs that target angiogenesis, such as antibody or small-molecule inhibitors of the VEGF pathway.

The sixth hallmark is tissue invasion and metastasis, which accounts for most cancer fatalities. Specific gene products are associated with the ability of tumor cells to metastasize to different organ sites. The composition of the tumor stroma, which is a complex mixture of extracellular matrix components and various cell populations, including fibroblasts, endothelial cells, and immune cells, has a major influence on metastasis as well. Elegant animal models as well as transcriptional profiling of human cancers show that metastasis includes alterations in genes involved in cell adhesion, cell fate, integrin signaling, growth factor and chemokine signaling, and extracellular proteolysis.

Ten years after their initial report on cancer hallmarks,[147] Hanahan and Weinberg[148] expanded on their original work, defining 2 emerging hallmarks and 2 enabling characteristics that make it possible for tumor cells to acquire the 6 core hallmarks. The 2 emerging hallmarks are deregulating cellular energetics and avoiding immune destruction.

The first emerging hallmark, deregulating cellular energetics, is based on growing knowledge that tumors deregulate metabolism to facilitate growth. For example, the concept that tumor cells use glucose differently from normal cells was first noted > 50 years ago. Whereas normal cells tend to use mitochondrial oxidative phosphorylation for energy production, cancer cells use glycolysis even when oxygen is available, a process termed aerobic glycolysis and also known as the Warburg effect. Other metabolic pathways are similarly altered in cancers (Fig 2-17).[54]

The second emerging hallmark reflects the molecular changes in cancer cells that allow them to evade immune destruction. Immunotherapies are a key component of current therapy for cancer in many organ sites and are discussed in other chapters in this book.

The 2 enabling characteristics are properties of cancer cells that facilitate the acquisition of the core hallmarks:

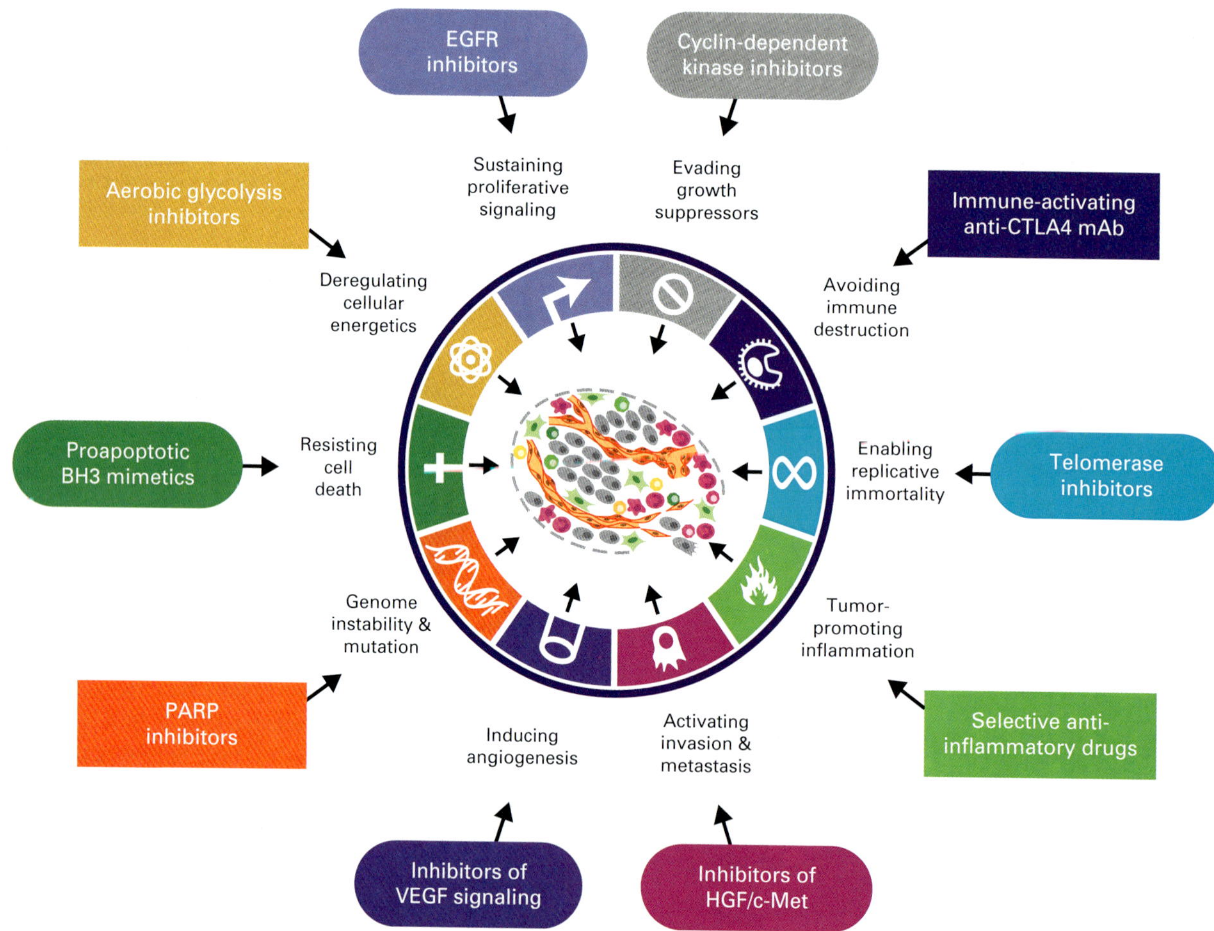

Fig. 2-17 Therapeutic targeting of the hallmarks of cancer.

Drugs that interfere with each of the acquired capabilities necessary for tumor growth and progression have been developed and are in clinical trials or in some cases approved for clinical use in treating certain forms of human cancer. Additionally, investigational drugs are being developed to target each of the enabling characteristics and emerging hallmarks, which also hold promise as cancer therapeutics. The drugs illustrated are examples of the deep pipeline of candidate drugs with different molecular targets and modes of action in the development for most of these hallmarks.

Abbreviations: EGFR, epidermal growth factor receptor; mAb, monoclonal antibody; VEGF, vascular endothelial growth factor.

Reprinted from Cell, Vol 144(5), Hanahan D, Weinberg RA., Hallmarks of Cancer: The Next Generation, Pg. 646-674, Copyright (2011), with permission from Elsevier.[148]

- Genomic instability drives the acquisition of the multiple mutations required for multistep tumorigenesis.
- Tumor-promoting inflammation reflects the rapidly advancing concept that inflammatory responses can facilitate tumor initiation and progression.

One important aspect of the enabling characteristics concept is that it also provides a framework for development of mechanism-based targeted therapies, which target both hallmarks and enabling characteristics. Examples of such therapies include angiogenesis inhibitors and immune checkpoint inhibitors, as discussed here as well as in other chapters of this book.

KEY POINTS

- Tumorigenesis is a multistep process that requires the gain of multiple mutations or characteristics that subvert safeguards preventing normal cells from transforming into cancer cells.
- All tumors share a number of hallmarks that contribute to their malignant phenotypes, but the specific molecular events that produce these phenotypes vary greatly among tumor types and individuals.
- Understanding hallmarks of cancer informs the development of targeted therapies

INFECTIOUS AGENTS AS DRIVERS OF CANCER

Infectious agents contribute to the pathogenesis of approximately 15% of all cancers worldwide, affecting > 2 million people.[149] Most of these cancers are associated with chronic viral infection.

- HPV: squamous cell carcinomas of the cervix, head and neck, and anus
- Epstein-Barr virus (EBV): Burkitt and other types of lymphoma, nasopharyngeal carcinomas, and some stomach cancers
- Hepatitis B and C viruses: hepatocellular carcinoma
- HIV and Kaposi's sarcoma-associated herpesvirus: Kaposi sarcoma
- Merkel cell polyomavirus: Merkel cell carcinoma

Extensive research has elucidated some of the molecular mechanisms infectious agents use to drive carcinogenesis. As noted, retroviruses can cause cancer through insertional mutagenesis. Other cancer-causing viruses express proteins that interfere with critical cancer pathways.

- HPV E6 protein promotes degradation of the tumor suppressor p53, affecting the DDR and DNA-repair response, and HPV E7 promotes degradation of the cell cycle inhibitor Rb, driving cell growth, division, and proliferation.
- Whereas EBV-associated lymphomas are characterized by a translocation involving the *CMYC* oncogene, EBV also promotes B-cell survival and transformation via molecular mimicry, as EBV gene products mimic activated cell surface receptors and antiapoptotic proteins.
- Hepatitis B and C proteins promote expression of genes associated with angiogenesis, enhanced cell motility, invasion, and metastasis.

In fact, many oncogenic viruses produce protein products that affect most of the hallmarks of cancer.[150] Given that virus-associated cancers frequently subvert normal cellular processes, the study of these cancers often yields insights into the biology of sporadic cancers. These insights include the identification of new oncogenes or tumor suppressor genes, as well as more complex aspects of tumor biology (eg, immune surveillance).

Although viruses are most commonly associated with cancer, other pathogens also contribute to carcinogenesis. Chronic infection with the intestinal bacteria *Helicobacter pylori* is associated with stomach cancers and low-grade lymphomas.[151] Similarly, hepatobiliary cancer, which is much more common in Southeast Asian populations, is associated with endemic infection with liver flukes.[152] Although less is known about the molecular mechanisms driving these cancers, chronic inflammation likely plays a major role.

Given the large number of human cancers associated with infections, there is much interest in preventing and/or treating the pathogens that increase cancer risk. Examples include the use of HPV vaccines to prevent squamous cell carcinoma and universal vaccination against hepatitis B virus to decrease the incidence of hepatocellular cancers.[153] Elimination of *H pylori* may prevent gastric cancer and often induces remission of gastric mucosa-associated lymphoid tissue lymphoma.[154,155] As more is learned about the molecular mechanisms driving infection-related cancers, targeted agents that specifically block the functions of viral gene products will likely be developed. Finally, viral proteins expressed on the surface of pathogen-associated cancer cells represent attractive targets for various immunotherapeutics.

KEY POINTS

- Infection-associated cancers are common, affecting > 2 million people per year worldwide, and most of these cancers result from chronic viral infections.
- Infectious agents frequently subvert molecular pathways related to the hallmarks of cancer, including cell cycle checkpoints, proliferation, and apoptosis.
- The study of infection-associated cancers provides insights into the molecular basis of sporadic cancers.

ONCOGENOMICS AND PRECISION ONCOLOGY

Large studies employing NGS to study cancer genetics have radically altered our understanding of the genomic landscape of cancers and demonstrated the immediate effect of targeted gene panels and genome-scale analyses on clinical oncology.

A comprehensive review of the explosion of cancer genomic studies enabled by NGS and other technologies is beyond the scope of this chapter, but some examples follow to highlight the power and importance of these approaches. Two early studies described an integrative approach that included sequencing of protein-coding genes (exome sequencing), analyses of DNA copy number, and RNA-seq to assess gene expression, which led to an in-depth understanding of the genes and pathways mutated in pancreatic cancers and glioblastomas.[156,157] The use of these combined modalities helped distinguish mutations that likely play a causal role in tumorigenesis (driver mutations) from mutations that may be irrelevant (passenger mutations). Importantly, 1 of these studies[157] found that the *IDH* gene, previously unrecognized as an oncogene, was mutated in 12% of glioblastomas. *IDH1* and *IDH2* mutations have subsequently been found in other cancers, including AML, chondrosarcoma, and cholangiocarcinoma. Importantly, *IDH1/IDH2* mutations cause epigenetic dysregulation and DNA hypermethylation,[158] and pharmacologic IDH inhibitors are proving successful in the clinic; ivosidenib and enasidenib were recently approved for use in patients with *IDH*-mutated AML.

Dozens of large-scale cancer genomic studies, many of which have been coordinated by The Cancer Genome Atlas (TCGA; a consortium sponsored by the National Institutes of Health), have identified the molecular features of most common and many uncommon cancers types.[159] The molecular features that have been cataloged include whole-exome sequencing, RNA-seq/RNA expression, copy-number variation, DNA methylation, miRNA expression, and protein analysis. These studies have provided unprecedented insights into cancer biology and revealed many new targets for therapeutic interventions. TCGA initially studied tumors types individually, revealing drivers of specific diseases. For example, the TCGA analysis of adult AMLs revealed that AMLs contain fewer mutations than other adult cancers, with an average of 13 mutations per sample, only 5 of which involve recurrently mutated genes.[160] As these studies of individual tumors were completed, TCGA went on to perform combined cross-cancer analyses across all tumor types, generating the PanCanAtlas. One common theme that has emerged from this work is that although specific organ sites exhibit unique mutational spectra, other pathways are mutated in many, or most, types of cancer.[102,161]

These global approaches set the stage for the use of NGS, at various scales, in real time, to assist with clinical decision making. Indeed, basing treatments on specific mutations present in a patient's unique tumor is a key feature of personalized cancer medicine. Assays can range from small-scale and focused molecular diagnostics with clearly defined therapeutic implications, such as looking for known driver mutations in *EGFR*, *ALK*, and other genes in lung cancers; HER2 overexpression in breast and gastroesophageal cancers; or evaluating *RAS* status in colorectal cancers. In contrast to these focused approaches, individual patient tumor samples can be studied with NGS panels, which analyze hundreds of known and often targetable cancer genes for mutations and other alterations. These panels search for rare driver mutations that suggest treatment with specific targeted agents may be clinically beneficial, even if these agents have not been previously evaluated in the tumor type. This trend toward tumor-agnostic therapies, which are based on molecular mutations rather than tissue of origin, is another key feature of personalized cancer medicine. Larger-scale sequencing, such as whole-exome sequencing or even whole-genome sequencing, is less commonly used to guide therapies for individual patients. The high cost and extended turnaround time required for these approaches were previously prohibitive, but this is no longer the case. The complexity of data analysis remains a barrier. However, it is anticipated that more and more patients with cancer will have their tumors analyzed with these more comprehensive approaches in the near future.

EMERGING CONCEPTS IN TUMOR HETEROGENEITY AND EVOLUTION

Whereas initial studies from TCGA and other consortia were aimed at cataloging gene mutations and other changes in primary tumors from a wide range of organ/tissue types, more recent efforts have included multiple biopsies from the same tumor, concurrent biopsies of primary and matched metastatic lesions, multiple biopsies over time, or single-cell analyses. These data allow comprehensive studies of genetic heterogeneity within a single tumor, as well as the dynamic process of tumor evolution at various stages of disease and its treatment.[162,163] It is now apparent that tumors may exhibit heterogeneous cell populations with distinct genetic changes at their earliest stages and that the idea of a linear progression of tumor evolution is overly simple.[163] In 1 seminal example, analysis of separate regions within a single primary RCC revealed marked genetic heterogeneity.[164] Heterogeneity has important implications for the selection of therapies based on the presence of targetable mutations in a single biopsy specimen, and it also informs our understanding of tumor evolution. For example, inactivation of the tumor suppressor *VHL* was the only genetic lesion present in all samples from a single RCC in the study by Gerlinger et al.[164] In contrast, other frequently mutated genes exhibited multiple and distinct mutations within different areas of the tumor. This suggests a model where the heterogeneous landscape of primary tumors serves as the substrate for subsequent tumor evolution, during which specific clones are enriched or lost as tumors grow, invade, and metastasize.

Molecular comparisons of metastatic lesions with their antecedent primary tumors reveal a similarly complex picture of tumor evolution, including the maintenance and/or enrichment of founder mutations, as well as new mutations unique to the metastatic lesions.[165,166] Indeed, discrete metastases can have markedly different genetic profiles. Together, these types of studies are revealing complex models of tumor evolution, such as parallel evolution, where subclones within a single tumor may evolve independently of one another, and convergent evolution, where unique clonal populations develop molecularly distinct but functionally equivalent alterations in common cancer pathways.[163] It should be noted that many studies of tumor evolution are based on exome or genome sequencing only; thus, other molecular events such as copy-number variation, epigenetic effects, and proteomic changes, are less well understood. Finally, large-scale genetic changes, such as chromosomal instability or chromothripsis (extensive DNA rearrangements that cluster in specific genomic regions), can be seen in both primary and metastatic tumors. Whether these changes are causes or consequences of tumor evolution remains controversial, but there is much interest in targeting these processes in the clinic.[167-169]

Although understanding the heterogeneity and evolution of a patient's tumor could greatly affect therapeutic decisions, serial tumor sampling via invasive biopsy techniques is generally neither feasible nor favored by patients. The emerging field of liquid biopsy, where circulating tumor cells or circulating tumor DNA can be isolated from routine blood draws, allows serial tumor sampling across the cancer continuum, from diagnosis to treatment to surveillance.[170] At diagnosis, liquid biopsies may simplify the identification of targetable mutations, especially when primary biopsy specimens are limited or uninformative. Commercially available genetic panels can be used to look for driver mutations in lung cancer using whole blood. Likewise, larger gene panels can catalog tumor mutations from whole blood in instances where biopsy of other sites is not feasible. Because liquid biopsies allow analysis of tumor evolution in real time, they can also serve as adjuncts to standard assessments of tumor response/progression after therapy has begun. For example, serial sampling of circulating tumor DNA from patients with *KRAS* wild-type colorectal cancer was used to investigate mechanisms of resistance to cetuximab.[171] This analysis showed evidence of *KRAS*-mutated subclones that were enriched after prolonged cetuximab therapy. Notably, cetuximab withdrawal led to resensitization of the tumor to this agent. Similarly, in lung cancer, whole blood can be used to look for secondary resistance mutations in driver genes, such as *EGFR* T790M, that arise after treatment with certain kinase inhibitors. The specific driver mutation can provide clues that influence drug choice in subsequent lines of therapy.

Although there are many unanswered questions and limited clinical data at this early point, liquid biopsy may become routine in the future, because it has the potential to provide new insights into molecular mechanisms of chemotherapy resistance and allow prioritization of targeted therapies based on new or evolving genetic profiles. Finally, liquid biopsy may prove useful for tumor screening in asymptomatic individuals and as surveillance for recurrence after therapy, given its markedly improved sensitivity compared with available methods.[172,173] However, for now, this technique remains investigational.

MOUSE MODELS OF HUMAN CANCER

Genetic techniques developed over the past 2 decades now make it possible to create mouse models that recapitulate sporadic human cancers with increasing fidelity. The first generation of genetically engineered mouse models involved expressing oncogenes from transgenes (genes injected into oocytes) or developing knockout strains in which genes were inactivated by homologous recombination in mouse embryonic stem cells.[174,175] Hundreds of genes have been studied with these techniques, which has led to important advances in understanding gene functions in development and tumorigenesis. In fact, these methods are still in wide use today. However, these strategies affect gene expression early in development and, in the case of knockouts, affect every cell in an organism. These characteristics limit their ability to model human cancers, which sequentially acquire rare mutations in somatic cells.

Moreover, many cancer genes are lethal when disrupted in the mouse germ line or lead to rapidly developing neoplasms in 1 tissue, precluding studies of slower-growing cancers. Various mouse genetic engineering strategies have been developed to circumvent these problems, for example, by restricting mutations to specific cell types or tissues or by temporally controlling gene mutation through the use of molecular switches. These approaches have led to mouse models that much more closely recapitulate human cancers.[176] Furthermore, the use of CRISPR/Cas9 gene editing systems to produce mouse strains with engineered oncogenic mutations is also revolutionizing the development of mouse cancer models, particularly by allowing the rapid development of mice with multiple mutations across different genes in a single step.[177]

Sophisticated xenografting methods, in which human cells are grown in murine hosts, are increasingly used for cancer biology research and may be useful tools to help guide treatment decisions in the future. Patient-derived xenografts (PDXs) are human tumor explants that are directly grown in immunocompetent mice, which is a more physiologic approach than establishing tumor cell lines in petri dishes. PDXs can be readily subjected to sequencing and screening approaches that seek to identify therapeutic vulnerabilities. Moreover, there is the potential to use PDX-bearing avatar mice to determine which chemotherapy drugs may be effective for the patient from whom the PDX was derived.[178] At present, widespread use of PDX models is hampered by high expense, high failure rates, and the prolonged time required to establish and propagate models. Alternative approaches, such as using specialized tissue culture conditions to grow a patient's tumor cells as organoids, may address some of the challenges of PDX models and allow broader use of real-time chemotherapy-sensitivity testing in the future.[179]

KEY POINTS

- NGS offers revealing transformative and comprehensive insights into cancer genomics.
- These technologies may allow personalized and targeted cancer therapy strategies based on specific mutations detected in a patient's tumor cells.
- Serial tumor biopsy reveals marked tumor heterogeneity and provides insights into tumor evolution that affect selection of cancer therapies.

- Gene targeting and transgenic methods are used to create mouse models that mimic the genetic mutations found in human cancers. These models are invaluable for understanding the mechanisms underlying tumorigenesis and are used to determine the role of specific mutations in multistep tumorigenesis.
- Xenografting of patient tumor samples into mice is an additional aspect of personalized cancer medicine; it provides a potential platform to study tumor biology and treatment response in a timeframe that could allow therapeutic decisions to be based on results obtained with animal models.

Acknowledgment

We thank Bruce Clurman, MD, PhD, for his contribution to prior versions of this chapter.

Global Oncology Perspectives: Molecular Biology—Comparison With Northern American Lung, Breast, Cervical, and Prostate Cancer Statistics

Shahin Sayed, MBChB, MMed (Aga Khan University Hospital, Nairobi)

The 2018 Globocan database incorporated 185 countries and 36 cancers to determine estimates of cancers and associated mortality.[180] One of the findings was that estimates of cancer mortality relative to cancer incidence are disproportionately higher in Africa (7.3% mortality rate *v* 5.8% incidence rate) than in Northern America, where the mortality rate is slightly lower than the incidence rate (20.3% *v* 21%).[180]

It has been shown that there is a correlation between cancer survival rates and country income.[181] Approximately 7 million cancer-related deaths occurred worldwide in lower- or middle-income countries (LMICs) in 2018.[182] Lung, breast, prostate, colon, and nonmelanoma skin cancers were estimated to be the most common incident cancers in 2018, and lung cancer remains the most common cause of mortality worldwide.[180] In contrast, cervical cancer is the most common cancer in many sub-Saharan African countries and the leading cause of death resulting from cancer, accounting for 18% of cancer-related mortality worldwide.[183] The situation in LMICs is further exacerbated by the limited availability of screening, diagnostic, and curative services. As an example, in 2017, pathology and treatment services were only available in 26% and 30% of public health facilities in LMICs, respectively, compared with in 90% of such facilities in high-income countries (HICs).[182]

LUNG CANCER

Lung cancer is the most lethal form of cancer, with a 5-year survival rate ranging from 10% to 20%. Approximately 65.5% of lung cancer diagnoses in 2018 occurred in LMICs or developing countries, with a mortality rate approaching 68%.[184] Incidence of lung cancer is heavily linked to tobacco use, with 80% of cases in the West attributable to smoking[185]; bidi smoking in India,[186] exposure to charcoal smoke[187] in China, and water pipe smoking in the Middle Eastern North African countries have also been shown to increase the risk.[188] In Lebanon, outdoor air pollution, specifically that related to polycyclic aromatic hydrocarbons, a carcinogenic byproduct of open-air incineration of solid waste, is also a potential risk factor.[189]

The highest incidence rates of lung cancer in men occurred in Micronesia/Polynesia (age-standardized rate of 52.2 per 100,000 males); China, Japan, and the Republic of Korea (rates > 40 per 100,000 males); and Eastern Europe (highest estimates up to 77.4 per 100,000 males); the lowest rates were found in West Africa (2.4 per 100,000 males) and East Africa (3.4 per 100,000 males).[190] Incidence in Morocco and South Africa was high (31.9 per 100,000 males and 28.2 per 100,000 males, respectively), in contrast to the estimated incidence rate in North America, which was 39.1 per 100,000 males.[180] When analyzed by ethnicity, the highest incidence of lung cancer in the United States was among the African American population, at 76.1 per 100,000 people.[191]

The highest incidence rates in women were observed in North America (30.7 per 100,000 females) and Northern Europe (26.9 per 100,000 females), whereas the lowest rates were found in West Africa (1.2 per 100,000 females) and East Africa (2.2 per 100,000 females).[180] Interestingly, despite the low prevalence of smoking among Chinese women, the incidence rate of 28.2 per 100,000 females was similar to that in some European countries.[180] Estimates for Kenya specifically between 2008 and 2012 show an incidence of 524 lung cancer cases with 423 mortalities within the same time period.[192] However, this is likely to be a gross underestimation of lung cancer cases because of a lack of accurate statistics and limited surveillance data.

Non–small-cell lung cancer (NSCLC) accounts for 85% of all lung cancers, and adenocarcinoma is the most common histologic type, accounting for up to 40% of all cases.[193] Some of the most common molecular targets in lung cancer with important clinical relevance include epidermal growth factor receptor (EGFR) which was found to be overexpressed in 40%–80% of NSCLC but later discovered to be a less important actionable target for therapy than the activating mutations in EGFR which have been reported in 10%–60% of NSCLC.[194] Up to 74% of all lung adenocarcinomas in East Asians are driven by oncogenic mutations in EGFR.[195] In a Shanghai hospital study over a four-year period, 68% of nonsmokers with adenocarcinomas harbored this mutation compared with between 22%–43.5% in Chinese smokers.[195] The activating mutations in EGFR are most often found in tumors of female never-smokers and are susceptible to TKIs such as erlotinib, afatinib, and gefitinib.[196]

Anaplastic lymphoma kinase (ALK) translocations are present in 3% to 7% of lung tumors, particularly in those who have never smoked or are only light smokers, with a frequency of 9% in Chinese nonsmokers.[197] A recent review of East Asian countries reports that the proportion of lung cancers in never-smokers is higher in East Asian women because of the low smoking prevalence in these countries compared with the West (China, 5.2% *v* United States, 94.8%), although this difference is not significant for men (81.5% and 94.4%, respectively).[195] Human epidermal growth factor receptor 2 (HER2) –activating mutations have been reported in approximately 5% of NSCLCs, particularly in women, Asians, never-smokers, and those with adenocarcinoma.[197] Also described but occurring at a much lower frequency are mutations in the *ROS* proto-oncogene, the *RET* proto-oncogene, *NTRK1*, *MET*, *BRAF*, *KRAS*, *NRAS*, *AKT*, and *MAPK2K1*.[198] Notably, the proportion of oncogenic mutations in squamous cell carcinomas of lung, specifically *EGFR*, was significantly higher in Chinese nonsmokers than in Chinese ever-smokers (21% and 11.05%, respectively), raising the possibility that this is a separate subtype of lung cancer.[199]

Lung cancer is associated with a high fatality rate, and survival rates are similar, regardless of world region.[184] Interestingly, African American patients in the United States are 34% less likely to receive timely surgery, chemotherapy, or radiotherapy for stage III lung cancer, thereby contributing to a lower survival rate, which suggests an ethnic or economic component to the statistics.[190]

On the basis of the results of the National Lung Screening Trial, the US Preventive Services Task Force recommends low-dose computed tomography screening for adults age 55 to 80 years who are current smokers and for those who have stopped smoking within the last 15 years as well as those who have a smoking history of 30 packs per year.[200] Despite the evidence that screening has a significant impact on stage at diagnosis and mortality of lung cancer, there are currently no screening guidelines for lung cancer in LMICs.

BREAST CANCER

It has been noted with regard to breast cancer that sub-Saharan African women may have better protective reproductive histories than Western women. The former tend to have late menarche, early menopause, and high parity, with prolonged breastfeeding and fewer ovulatory cycles, lowering their general risk for breast cancer.[201] This protective reproductive history may explain why the incidence of breast cancer in sub-Saharan African women is lower, with an age-standardized incidence rate of 29.9 per 100,000 women compared with 84.8 per 100,000 in North America. A more recent systematic review and meta-analysis of 41 population- and hospital-based registries showed that there are regional differences in the incidence of breast cancer, with a rate of 29.3 per 100,000 women in North Africa versus 22.4 per 100,000 in sub-Saharan Africa.[202] Data from the population-based Nairobi Cancer Registry show that between 2004 and 2008, breast cancer was the most common cancer among women, accounting for 23% of all cases, with an age-standardized incidence rate of 52 per 100,000 women per year.[192] Interestingly, the mean and median age of breast cancer diagnosis in both types of registries ranged from 30.6 to 60.8 years and 50.2 years, respectively, with more than 75% of cases diagnosed between the ages of 30 and 59 years,[202] probably indicative of a high incidence of breast cancer among younger women. A recent population registry report from 11 sub-Saharan African countries[203] found that 66% of 434 patients with breast cancer were diagnosed at stage III or IV. This contributes to the higher breast cancer mortality rate of 15.4 in sub-Saharan Africa, compared with 12.6 in North America.[180] Both Bird et al[204] and Sayed et al[205,206] note that specifically Kenyan breast cancer profiles tend to be shifted toward advanced stages of disease, probably linked to the fact that unlike in the United States, there are no national breast cancer screening programs in Kenya or the East African region as a whole. Interestingly, some valid questions have recently been raised about the effectiveness and efficacy of mammographic screening in reducing breast cancer–specific mortality; it might be more beneficial for LMICs to expend limited financial resources on early detection and treatment of breast cancer.[207]

That being said, limited financial resources for cancer diagnosis and treatment access coupled with sociocultural norms in African patients with breast cancer perhaps also contribute to advanced stage at presentation and poor outcomes.[208] Although advanced stage at presentation,[205] lack of awareness about breast cancer,[209,210] and access to available screening and treatment options may be some of the factors explaining the disparate mortality rates, some issues remain unresolved. After adjusting for age, there are twice as many breast cancers (33% versus 66%) diagnosed in women before the age of 54 years from low income countries compared to high-income countries (Ref 211). Furthermore, in women of African descent despite correcting for risk factor distribution, breast cancers tend to be larger, of higher grade, and more likely to be estrogen receptor (ER) negative,[212] suggesting the interplay of other biologic and genetic differences that remain largely unexplored.

Earlier studies from Kenya reported a low frequency of hormone receptor expression in East African women and therefore fewer hormone-sensitive breast cancers than in Western populations.[204] However, more recent studies from Kenya[205] have shown that, at 20%, the prevalence of triple-negative breast cancers is not too different from that in the West. It is, however, possible that genetic heterogeneity could explain the disparate rates in molecular breast cancer subtypes between East and West Africa. A more concerning situation is that in sub-Saharan Africa, only 16.6% of the 824 patients with breast cancer from 11 cancer registries had testing of tumors for ER and progesterone receptor (PR),[203] an abysmal situation that, it is hoped, will change in the near future as a result of the likely inclusion of these tests in the upcoming Essential Diagnostic List of the WHO.

CERVICAL CANCER

Cervical cancer is the most commonly diagnosed cancer and the leading cause of death resulting from cancer in 42 countries, 28 of which are in sub-Saharan Africa or Southeast Asia.[180] The incidence rate per 100,000 in North America is 6.4, with a mortality rate of 1.9. In contrast, the incidence rate per 100,000 in East Africa is 40.1, with a mortality rate of 30.0. Those in developing countries are most likely more exposed to infectious diseases and less likely to have proper treatment or preventative vaccines. As a result, given that cervical cancer is an infection-associated cancer, LMICs have higher incidence and mortality rates than the

United States. However, a similar disparity is found in underserviced areas of the United States, including the Texas-Mexico border, suggesting access to screening and trained providers is integral to mortality and incidence rates of cervical cancer.[214]

Furthermore, advocacy for screening facilities in LMICs is needed, because up to 89% of patients in LMICs are initially diagnosed at an advanced stage in comparison with those in the United States, where 40% of patients present at an advanced stage.[183] Although countries such as Rwanda have implemented pilot screening programs for cervical cancer using visual inspection of acetic acid and polymerase chain reaction (PCR) for human papillomavirus (HPV), national programs for the screening of cervical cancer are lacking in sub-Saharan Africa,[214] where a skilled workforce shortage is a grim reality. To address some of the gaps, the Extension for Community Healthcare Outcomes project (Project ECHO) is a health worker–targeted telementoring capacity-building program for cervical cancer screening and the management of premalignant lesions that has been initiated in Latin America and sub-Saharan Africa, specifically in Zambia and Mozambique, in partnership with MD Anderson Cancer Center (Houston, TX).[213] Furthermore, the advent of the HPV vaccine has seen governments like Rwanda implement successful national HPV immunizations for adolescents while integrating these with other health interventions.[215]

PROSTATE CANCER

Another leading cause of death resulting from cancer in sub-Saharan Africa is prostate cancer in men. Age-standardized incidence rates per 100,000 show an incidence in North America of 73.7 and a mortality rate of 7.7. East Africa has a lower incidence rate, at 23.9, but the mortality rate is double that of North America, at 14.8.[180] This may be because of a lack of awareness or screening in East Africa, causing African men to be diagnosed later, at an advanced stage and with incurable disease, whereas American men are diagnosed earlier, at a more curable state of the disease.[216] However, rates of prostate cancer are highest among men of African descent in the United States, suggesting an ethnic or genetic predisposition.[217]

A study to determine the cultural factors associated with prostate cancer screening intent among adult Kenyan African men suggested that family was the most significant influence in prostate cancer screening intent and that the low prevalence of prostate cancer screening intent was attributed to fear and fatalistic beliefs.[218] In a study on the clinical presentation of prostate cancer in black South African men, it was reported that black South African men present with higher prostate-specific antigen (PSA) levels and histopathologic tumor grade compared with black Americans, which is further escalated in men from rural localities. The study suggested that lack of PSA testing may be contributing to an aggressive prostate cancer disease phenotype among South African men.[219] Another study showed that making PSA and ultrasound scanning available and affordable contributed to increased awareness and diagnosis of prostate diseases.[220]

Although limited funding and poor access to affordable health care and skilled health personnel are some of the barriers to early diagnosis,[220] these factors are not unique to the African continent, and the underlying genetic, hereditary, and environmental bases of prostate cancer aggressiveness in men of African descent still warrant further research.[221]

PRECISION MEDICINE IN CANCER

Molecular testing is currently driving cancer preventive, diagnostic, and care pathways in HICs.[222] Use of prognostic models based on a combination of comprehensive genomic profiling, clinical data, and machine-learning algorithms has become the norm in many clinical settings.[222] The advent of molecular tumor boards has made precision medicine an exciting reality for patient care, as druggable mutational targets become available in both the clinical trial setting and routine practice. Studies from HICs have provided evidence of ethnic differences in treatment response and toxicity resulting from chemotherapeutic agents because of polymorphisms in metabolizing genes. An example is doxorubicin, where the incidence of cardiotoxicity is higher in African Americans than in their white counterparts.[222] Strategies for implementation of precision medicine around the globe can only succeed with an understanding of these genomic differences among various races and ethnicities.[222]

In LMICs, infection-associated cancers account for 25% of cancers, with *Helicobacter pylori*, HPV, hepatitis B virus, hepatitis C virus, and Epstein-Barr virus as the most common infections associated with gastric cancer, cervical cancer, hepatocellular carcinoma, and lymphomas, respectively.[149] Furthermore, some unique and novel genomic alterations in *BRCA1*/*BRCA2* have been reported in breast and ovarian cancers from studies in Nigeria and India,[223,224,225] which provide increasing evidence of the variation in tumor biology based on ancestry and race. However, there exists a great disparity between HICs and LMICs in access to advanced technologies that can test for these driver mutations, increase our understanding of the biologic and phenotypic differences between ethnic groups in various cancers, and provide evidence for appropriate new molecular targets of therapy. A recent study from India demonstrates how the exorbitant cost of Oncotype DX testing in early breast cancer has shifted oncologist practice toward easily accessible online resources, such as the PREDICT tool, to predict chemotherapy benefit in this group of patients.[228] Point-of-care molecular tests that combine cost effectiveness, rapid turnaround time, and diagnostic accuracy have the potential to leapfrog health system barriers in LMICs.[226] Examples of tests with proven efficacy include careHPV (Qiagen, Germany), which is cheaper and less resource intensive than the standard hybrid capture technology.[226] Field trials are under way in Papua New Guinea after an initial successful pilot study exploring the utility of the Xpert HPVassay

(Cepheid, Sunnyvale, CA) as a mass screening tool for cervical cancer in LMICs using self-collected vaginal specimens with same-day curative cryotherapy or thermocoagulation. In breast cancer, alternative cheaper reverse-transcription PCR–based tests for ER, PR, and HER2 and Ki67 in breast cancers are currently being validated against the gold-standard immunohistochemistry. An example of this is the Xpert Breast Cancer STRAT4 assay, is a cartridge-based test by Cepheid (Sunnyvale CA) that has been optimized for the Gene Xpert platform currently being used in the diagnosis of drug-resistant tuberculosis.

LOOKING TO THE FUTURE

Overall, funding and health disparities research should continue to acknowledge the disproportionately higher cancer mortality rates in Africa compared with the cancer incidence rates, especially when compared with those of Western populations. Further knowledge about how cancer survival rates and country income are correlated would also be extremely beneficial. Avenues to explore include comparisons of treatment guidelines in developed countries with those in developing countries, cost-effectiveness analyses of implementing screening and early detection strategies for various cancers, and comparisons of tumor biology to further understand how potentially biologically different cancers arise in different populations. As Smith et al[227] note, cancer mortality rates in both men and women in the United States continue to decline as a result of reduction in tobacco use, uptake of preventive measures, adoption of early detection methods, and better treatments, many of which are implementable strategies in LMICs for inclusion in universal health coverage.

3

CLINICAL PHARMACOLOGY

Jill M. Kolesar, PharmD, MS

Recent Updates

- ▶ Pembrolizumab was approved for adults and children with cancer that is unresectable or metastatic, microsatellite instability-high (MSI-H), or mismatch repair–deficient, as second-line therapy or where there are no standard therapies. Patients with MSI-H colon cancer should have after treatment with a folinic acid, fluorouracil, and oxaliplatin (FOLFOX)-based regimen. [Yan L, *Cancer Commun (Lond)* 2018]
- ▶ Larotrectinib was approved for adults and children with solid tumors and who have a neurotrophic receptor tyrosine kinase (*NTRK*) gene fusion without a known acquired resistance mutation. There should be no standard therapies or patients' disease should have progressed after standard first-line therapy. [Yan L, *Cancer Commun (Lond)* 2018]

OVERVIEW

Cancer therapy has changed dramatically, and biomarker-driven, targeted therapies and immunotherapy are major recent treatment advances. Despite this, most patients still receive standard cytotoxic chemotherapy, often in combination with immunotherapy or targeted therapies. Many of these drugs exhibit a narrow therapeutic window, meaning the difference between the toxic dose and the therapeutic dose is small. Regardless of the agent, drug dosing requires a balance between the anticancer benefit and the known toxic effects these agents have on normal organs. Thus, managing the adverse effects of immunotherapies has emerged as a major issue. In addition, targeted, oral therapies are administered chronically, making drug interactions and food effects much more relevant issues.

PRINCIPLES OF CHEMOTHERAPY, TARGETED THERAPIES, AND IMMUNOTHERAPIES

Cytotoxic chemotherapy is commonly used for adjuvant, neoadjuvant, as well combined modality therapy, and for the treatment of metastatic disease. Three basic principles underlie the use of cytotoxic chemotherapy:

- The fractional cell-kill hypothesis, which states a constant proportion of cells are euthanized per cycle
- A linear relationship between drugs administered and cell kill
- The Goldie-Coldman hypothesis, suggesting that tumors acquire a spontaneous mutation that confers drug resistance

These principles apply best to rapidly growing cancers, like leukemias and lymphomas, and at least partially explain why cytotoxic chemotherapy is most effective in rapidly growing cells. On the basis of these principles, cytotoxic chemotherapy is typically administered for multiple cycles, at the highest possible dose, and in combination with other agents with different mechanisms of action and nonoverlapping adverse effects.[1] Cytotoxic chemotherapy typically has a narrow therapeutic index, and adverse effects can be severe and sometimes fatal. These agents are administered in the adjuvant, neoadjuvant, and combined modality and metastatic settings and are potentially curative in some malignancies, such as testicular cancer.

Small molecule–targeted therapies are most often based on the presence of an oncogenic somatic mutation. Typically, the mutation is activating an oncogene, and designing a drug to inhibit the abnormal protein is a common and often successful pharmacological strategy.[2-9] In patients with a targetable mutation, head-to-head clinical trials have demonstrated targeted therapies have improved outcomes (ie, response rate and progression-free survival) and reduced incidence of adverse effects; unfortunately, the development of resistance and disease progression frequently occurs. A now-common drug development strategy is to develop second- and third-generation agents that target the same pathway but have improved pharmacological properties compared with the first-generation agents or are able to target known resistance mechanisms. EGFR inhibitors and osimertinib are examples of this: Osimertinib has additional activity in the presence of the known EGFR T790M resistance mutation.[10] Small molecule–targeted therapies are typically oral, administered daily, metabolized by the cytochrome P450 (CYP) system, and drug and food interactions are of clinical importance. Food and other medications can increase or decrease absorption of oral anticancer agents and induce or inhibit metabolism, leading to altered plasma concentrations and either lack of efficacy or increased adverse effects. Table 3-1 lists small molecule–targeted therapies, biomarkers, and drug and food effects. Clinical trials combining small molecule–targeted therapies and cytotoxic chemotherapy have not led to improved outcomes but have resulted in increased incidence of adverse effects; therefore, targeted therapies are typically used as sequential single agents.

Immunotherapy is defined as a therapeutic approach that targets or manipulates the immune system and, ultimately, seeks to harness the host's adaptive and innate immune responses to eliminate cancer cells.[11,12] Immunotherapy can be categorized broadly into passive and active strategies. Passive-mediated immunotherapy includes ex vivo–generated immune elements (eg, antibodies, immune cells) and does not stimulate the host immune response. Monoclonal antibodies are considered passive targeted therapies. For example, bevacizumab is an antibody directed toward soluble vascular endothelial growth factor (VEGF), the ligand for the vascular endothelial growth factor receptor (VEGFR) that drives angiogenesis.[6,13,14] Therefore, inhibition of VEGF by bevacizumab decreases angiogenesis. Active immunotherapy induces the patient's immune response and results in the development of specific immune effectors (ie, antibodies and T cells). The programmed death protein 1 (PD-1) and programmed death ligand 1 (PD-L1) inhibitors are examples of active immunotherapies. PD-L1 expressed on some cancer cells binds to PD-1 on T cells, resulting in T-cell deactivation. The PD-1 and PD-L1 inhibitors (known as immune checkpoint inhibitors) block this receptor-ligand signaling pathway, overcome immune escape mechanisms, and enhance T-cell response, leading to T-cell activation and proliferation.[15] Therefore, PD-1 and PD-L1 inhibitors rely on the host immune system for anticancer effects. PD-L1 expression and microsatellite instability (MSI) status are commonly used clinical biomarkers of checkpoint inhibitor response, and some US Food and Drug Administration (FDA)-approved indications are based on biomarker positivity, although many indications do not require biomarker positivity and patients without these biomarkers often respond to checkpoint inhibitor therapy. Tumor mutation burden is another commonly used biomarker, although there are currently no FDA-approved indications for checkpoint inhibitors based on tumor mutation burden. Several other biomarkers (ie, tumor infiltrating lymphocytes, immune signatures) are actively being investigated.[16,17] PD-1 pathway inhibitors may be combined with cytotoxic T-lymphocyte–associated protein 4 (CTLA4) inhibitors for the treatment of melanoma and renal cell carcinoma and with cytotoxic chemotherapy for some solid tumors; however, they are also commonly used as single agents.

KEY POINTS

- Cytotoxic chemotherapy remains an important component of most cancer therapy regimens in the adjuvant, neoadjuvant, and metastatic settings.
- Small molecule–targeted therapies are effective and reasonably well tolerated in patients with a targetable mutation. Their use is limited by a lack of targetable mutations in some patients and by the development of resistance with chronic therapy in others.
- Checkpoint inhibitors are highly effective across several tumor types, with durable responses observed. They are used predominantly in the advanced and metastatic disease setting for solid tumors. Although PD-L1 expression, MSI status, and tumor mutation burden have been studied as predictive biomarkers of response, many patients without these biomarkers still respond to immunotherapy. Emerging biomarkers are under investigation.

BIOMARKERS FOR DRUG SELECTION OF TARGETED THERAPIES

Cancer is associated with an accumulation of mutations. Most mutations are neutral (passenger mutations), but a few driver mutations give cancer cells a selective advantage. Targeting these mutations with small molecules is an effective treatment strategy and the mutation itself is a predictive biomarker. In 2018 alone, 18 of the 59 new drug approvals were for oncology-related drugs.[18] Of

Table 3-1 **Small Molecule-Targeted Therapies With Biomarker Selection, Drug Interactions, and Food Effects**

Therapy	Sensitive Mutation/ Required Biomarkers	Food Effect	Drug Interactions	FDA Indication	Notes
EGFR inhibitors					
Erlotinib	Exon 19 deletions, exon 21 L858R	Grapefruit, starfruit, Seville oranges, pomelos	Is a CYP3A4 substrate, interactions with CYP3A4 inducers and inhibitors, antacids, H2, PPI	Advanced NSCLC, first line or subsequent, EGFR mutant	Approved before discovery of EGFR biomarker, has maintenance indication in unselected patients
Gefitinib	Exon 19 deletions, exon 21 L858R	Grapefruit, starfruit, Seville oranges, pomelos	Is a CYP3A4 substrate, interactions with CYP3A4 inducers and inhibitors, antacids, H2, PPI	Advanced NSCLC, first line or subsequent, EGFR mutant	Initially approved on basis of phase II data in unselected populations, failed in phase III and was taken off market
Afatinib	Exon 19 deletions, exon 21 L858R, S768I, L861Q, G719X	Empty stomach	Not metabolized by CYP	Advanced NSCLC, first line or subsequent, EGFR mutant	Retains activity in patients with disease resistant to erlotinib or gefitinib. Has maintenance indication in unselected patients
Dacomitinib	Exon 19 deletions, exon 21 L858R	With or without food	Strong CYP2D6 inhibitor, inhibits metabolism of drugs metabolized by CYP2D6, H2, PPI, antacids	Advanced NSCLC, first line or subsequent, EGFR mutant	More effective than gefitinib but has more adverse effects
Osimertinib	Exon 19 deletions, exon 21 L858R, T790M	With or without food	Is a CYP3A4 substrate, interactions with CYP3A4 inducers and inhibitors, potential for QT prolongation	Advanced NSCLC, first line or subsequent, EGFR mutant	Improved PFS in front-line setting compared with gefitinib or erlotinib. Preferred if CNS penetration needed
ALK and ROS1 inhibitors					
Crizotinib	ALK translocation	With or without food	Is a CYP3A4 substrate, interactions with CYP3A4 inducers and inhibitors, potential for QT prolongation	Advanced NSCLC, first line or subsequent, ALK or ROS1 positive	More effective than chemotherapy, but less effective than alectinib. Only ALK inhibitor with ROS1 indication

Table 3-1 **continued**					
Ceritinib	ALK translocation	Grapefruit, starfruit, Seville oranges, pomelos	Is a CYP3A4 substrate, interactions with CYP3A4 inducers and inhibitors	Advanced NSCLC, first line or subsequent, ALK positive	More effective than chemotherapy
Alectinib	ALK translocation	Take with food	Not metabolized by CYP	Advanced NSCLC, first line or subsequent, ALK positive	Improved PFS compared with crizotinib. Preferred if CNS penetration needed
Brigantinib	ALK translocation	With or without food	Is a CYP3A4 substrate, interactions with CYP3A4 inducers and inhibitors	Advanced NSCLC, after crizotinib failure, ALK positive	Improved PFS compared with crizotinib
Lorlantinib	ALK translocation	With or without food	Is a CYP3A4 substrate, interactions with CYP3A4 inducers and inhibitors	Advanced NSCLC, after crizotinib and one other, ALK positive	Often used off label after alectinib
BRAF inhibitors					
Dabrafenib	V600E, V600K	Empty stomach	Is a CYP3A4 and CYP2C8 substrate, interactions with CYP3A4 and CYP2C8 inducers and inhibitors	First-line, adjuvant melanoma, metastatic melanoma, metastatic NSCLC, BRAF mutant	Improved PFS and OS compared with dacarbazine as single agent, used in combination with MEK inhibitor to prevent resistance
Vemurafenib	V600E	With or without food	Is a CYP3A4 substrate, interactions with CYP3A4 inducers and inhibitors	First-line, metastatic melanoma, Erdheim-Chester, BRAF mutant	Improved PFS compared with dacarbazine as single agent, used in combination with MEK inhibitor to prevent resistance
Encorafenib	V600E, V600K	With or without food	Is a CYP3A4 substrate, interactions with CYP3A4 inducers and inhibitors	First-line, metastatic melanoma, BRAF mutant	Improved PFS compared with vemurafenib as single agent, used in combination with MEK inhibitor to prevent resistance
NTRK inhibitor					
Larotrectinib	NTRK fusion	With or without food	Is a CYP3A4 substrate, interactions with CYP3A4 inducers and inhibitors	Solid tumor with known NTRK fusion	First small molecule to receive disease-agnostic approval

Table 3-1 **continued**					
PARP inhibitors					
Olaparib	BRCA1/BRCA2	With or without food	Is a CYP3A4 substrate, interactions with CYP3A4 inducers and inhibitors	Metastatic breast, second line; metastatic ovarian, fourth line; advanced ovarian maintenance, BRCA mutant; recurrent ovarian cancer, maintenance	
Rucaparib	BRCA1/BRCA2	With or without food	Moderate CYP1A2 inhibitor, inhibits metabolism of drugs that metabolized by CYP1A2	Metastatic ovarian, third line; BRCA mutant; recurrent ovarian cancer, maintenance	
Niraparib	Testing not required	With or without food	Not metabolized by CYP	Recurrent ovarian cancer, maintenance	
Talazoparib	BRCA1/BRCA2	With or without food	Not metabolized by CYP	Locally advanced or metastatic breast cancer, BRCA mutant;	
FLT3 inhibitors					
Midostaurin	ITD, point mutations	Take with food	Is a CYP3A4 substrate, interactions with CYP3A4 inducers and inhibitors	Induction therapy in newly diagnosed AML, FLT3 mutant	First-in-class FLT3 inhibitor
Gilitinib	ITD, point mutations	With or without food	Is a CYP3A4 substrate, interactions with CYP3A4 inducers and inhibitors	Relapsed or refractory AML, FLT3 mutant	
IDH1/IDH2 inhibitors					
Enasidenib	IDH2	With or without food	None known drug interactions	Relapsed or refractory AML, IDH2 mutant	First-in-class IDH2 inhibitor
Ivosidenib	IDH1	Avoid high-fat meal (increases AUC by ~25%)	Is a CYP3A4 substrate, interactions with CYP3A4 inducers and inhibitors	Relapsed or refractory AML, IDH1 mutant	First-in-class IDH1 inhibitor

Abbreviations: AML, acute myeloid leukemia; AUC, area under the curve; ITD, internal tandem duplication; NSCLC, non-small-cell lung cancer; OS, overall survival; PFS, progression-free survival; PPI, proton pump inhibitor.

these, there were five first-in-class, new molecular entities including three targeted therapy small molecules: FLT3 inhibitor (giliternib),[9] NTRK inhibitor (larotrectinib),[6,18] IDH1 inhibitor (ivosidenib);[9] one monoclonal antibody (mogamulizumab),[12] and one cytotoxin.[19] Another significant trend in drug development is the approval of next-generation targeted therapies. For example, there are now five EGFR inhibitors available for treating EGFR-mutant non–small-cell lung cancer (NSCLC). New drugs are typically more potent, have better CNS penetration, or have differing adverse-effect or drug-interaction profiles. Variability in pharmacologic properties are used to guide drug selection. In addition, resistance often develops to targeted small molecules after therapy. For example, EGFR inhibitors bind in the tyrosine kinase domain of the EGFR receptor, and when a mutation occurs in the binding pocket, the drug can no longer bind and resistance develops.[10] Next-generation compounds can overcome drug resistance by binding to alternative sites.[20]

BRAF Mutation

BRAF is a downstream signaling mediator of *KRAS* that activates the mitogen-activated protein kinase (MAPK) pathway. Activating *BRAF* mutations are present in 40% to 60% of metastatic melanomas, 10% of colon cancers, and 1% to 3% of NSCLC. *BRAF* mutations most commonly occur at the V600 position of exon 15.

The *BRAF* inhibitors vemurafenib[21] and dabrafenib[22] were initially approved as single agents in *BRAF*-mutated melanoma; however, it was quickly noted that MEK activation was a common resistance mechanism, and MEK inhibitors were added to the regimen. Trametinib is combined with dabrafenib, whereas cobimetinib is combined with vemurafenib.[5] An additional advantage of the MEK inhibitors is a decreased risk of squamous cell carcinomas and keratoacanthomas, which develop in up to 25% of patients treated with a *BRAF* inhibitor alone. Combining a *BRAF* inhibitor and an MEK inhibitor reduces the incidence to approximately 5%, presumably by the MEK inhibitor blocking the paradoxical activation of the MAPK pathway that occurs with *BRAF* inhibition.[23] Encorafenib (a *BRAF* inhibitor) in combination with binimetinib (an MEK inhibitor) was approved in 2018, but the approval was based on a comparison with single-agent vemurafenib, so it is unclear if the regimen has any advantages over current standard-of-care therapy.[24]

The combination of a *BRAF* inhibitor and a MEK inhibitor is effective first-line therapy for both advanced or metastatic melanoma and NSCLC in patients with a *BRAF* mutation in V600E. However, a notable exception is colon cancer, in which *BRAF* inhibition is ineffective, likely due to additional activation and the increased importance of PI3K pathways as driver mutations.[25] Mutations in *BRAF* outside of the V600 position are not sensitive to the current *BRAF* inhibitors; however, clinical trials of alternative agents with activity against mutations outside of V600 are ongoing.

NTRK Fusion

The tropomyosin (Trk) receptor family comprises three transmembrane proteins referred to as TrkA, TrkB, and TrkC receptors, which are encoded by the *NTRK1, NTRK2,* and *NTRK3* genes, respectively. In all reported Trk oncogenic gene fusions, the 3′ region of the *NTRK* gene is joined with a 5′ sequence of a fusion partner gene and functions as an overexpressed kinase. These fusions are uncommon but occur most frequently in appendiceal adenocarcinomas (4%) and NSCLC (1%). Larotrectinib is the first disease-agnostic small-molecule inhibitor approved by the FDA; the approval is for advanced tumors that have an NTRK gene fusion, lack a resistance mutation, and have no satisfactory alternative therapies. Larotrectinib was evaluated in 55 patients (age range, 4 months to 76 years) with various *NTRK* fusion–positive malignancies. Enrolled patients had 17 unique cancer diagnoses, including mammary analog secretory carcinoma of the salivary gland (n = 12 patients), infantile fibrosarcoma (n = 7), thyroid tumor (n = 5), colon tumor (n = 4), lung tumor (n = 4), melanoma (n = 4), GI stromal tumor (n = 3), and other cancers (n = 16). In the entire cohort of 55 patients, the overall response rate by independent review was 75% (13% with a complete response) and responses appeared durable, with 86% of responders still receiving treatment at a median follow-up of 9.4 months. The most common adverse effects were anemia (11%) and elevations in liver function tests (7%).[26]

BRCA1 and *BRCA2* Mutations

Mutations in breast cancer genes 1 and 2 *(BRCA1* and *BRCA2,* respectively) occur in 5% to 10% of breast and ovarian cancers and can be either germline or somatic. PARP enzymes regulate DNA repair, the cell cycle, metabolism, and cell proliferation.[27] There are at least 18 PARP enzymes within the PARP superfamily; however, most cellular PARP activity is through the PARP-1 and PARP-2 enzymes which play substantial roles in single-stranded DNA break repair, nucleotide excision repair, and homologous recombination.[27,28] In cases of severe cellular DNA damage, PARP activation is essential for efficient DNA repair, and the PARP enzyme has been previously identified as a potential drug target. In 2005, two groups[29,30] reported a synthetic, lethal interaction between PARP inhibition and *BRCA1/2* mutation with minimal effects of PARP inhibition on *BRCA* wild-type cells that was suggestive of a new targeted treatment approach. PARP inhibitor indications have less overlap than other targeted therapies and choice of agent is typically based on FDA approved indication. The only indication with three options is maintenance therapy in ovarian cancer, regardless of *BRCA* status, for which olaparib, rucaparib, and niraparib are all approved. Olaparib and rucaparib are also approved for individuals with ovarian cancer and a germline BRCA mutation. Niraparib has more cardiovascular adverse effects, whereas olaparib has more drug interactions—information that can help providers select between agents. Talazoparib was approved in 2018 for *BRCA1/2* mutant metastatic breast cancer.[31]

KEY POINTS

- Proteins with a tyrosine kinase domain (eg, EGFR, FLT3) frequently acquire activating mutations that can be targeted with tyrosine kinase inhibitors.
- Although somatic mutations, occurring only in the tumor, are usually more frequent in one type of cancer, they also occur in other cancers, and targeted therapies are often, but not always, effective in these cancers as well. For example, *BRAF* is mutated in melanoma and lung cancer, and *BRAF* inhibitors have activity in those cancers, although not in colon cancer, where *BRAF* mutations are also reported.
- Resistance usually develops after months to years and is caused by activation of additional oncogenic pathways, amplification of the mutant gene, or new mutations in the gene.
- Targeted therapies are usually taken orally daily and require an increased awareness of food and drug interactions.

PHARMACOKINETICS

Pharmacokinetics (PK), used to describe dose-concentration relationships, is the mathematical relationship describing the time course of absorption, distribution, metabolism, and excretion (ADME) of drugs and metabolites in the body[32-35] and is often described as "what the body does to the drug." The biologic, physiologic, and physicochemical factors that influence the transfer processes of drugs in the body also influence the rate and extent of ADME of those drugs in the body. Typically, PK parameters are determined by measuring plasma or other relevant distribution-site drug concentrations. The ADME properties of a drug determine the amount of drug exposure in the body, including the target site. Table 3-2 provides definitions and uses of basic pharmacokinetic parameters, and Figure 3-1 presents an overview of PK and pharmacodynamics (PD).

The starting point for any drug into the body is the administration. Common routes of administration include oral, intravenous (IV), intramuscular, and subcutaneous. The proportion of the drug that reaches the systemic circulation after administration is the pharmacokinetic parameter bioavailability (abbreviated F in applicable equations and some texts). Historically, almost all anticancer agents were administered IV, and the bioavailability of IV administered agents is defined as 1, or 100%, simplifying pharmacokinetic modeling for these agents. However, small molecule–targeted agents are typically administered orally, making bioavailability an important consideration. Factors that influence oral bioavailability include route of administration, absorption factors, and metabolism factors (Fig 3-2). Absorption is often pH dependent and is discussed in the drug-interaction section of this chapter. In addition, the fraction of drug lost during the process of absorption, or the first pass effect, also reduces drug bioavailability. First-pass metabolism may occur in the liver or in the GI tract, and most anticancer agents with limited bioavailability, have significant first pass effects. Administration by the IV, rectal and sublingual routes, bypass the first-pass effect of either GI or liver metabolism.

The purpose of PK in clinical drug development is to assess relationships between plasma concentrations and clinical outcomes of interest, typically efficacy and adverse effects. Many important pharmacokinetic parameters can be estimated by visual inspection of the plasma-versus-time concentration curve. The maximum concentration (C_{max}) is the highest concentration we can observe. The time that the C_{max} occurs is the T_{max}. C_{max} is useful clinically for predicting acute toxicity, including infusion reactions and EKG changes. T_{max} is useful in predicting when these toxicities are likely to occur.

Measured concentration and time data are used to determine pharmacokinetic parameters, which may be primary or secondary. Primary pharmacokinetic parameters depend on the physiology of the body and the physiochemical properties of the drug, and include clearance, volume of distribution (Vd), and bioavailability. Clearance is the amount of drug eliminated per unit of time, the Vd is a proportionality constant that relates the amount of drug in the body to the concentration of drug that was measured, and bioavailability is the proportion of drug that enters the systemic circulation. Conceptually, the Vd describes the location of the drug in the body. Total body water constitutes 55% to 65% of total body weight and various other fluids make up the total body water. Drugs with a Vd of ≤ 3 L are considered confined to the plasma. If Vd is > 50 L, the drug is considered distributed to all tissues in the body, especially the fatty tissue. The larger the Vd, the more likely the drug is found in the tissues of the body, typically the sites of action.

The primary pharmacokinetic parameter describing excretion is clearance, which is perhaps the most important of all PK parameters because it informs the dose and schedule of drug administration. Clearance is assumed to be constant and is the process by which a drug is removed from the body, either as unchanged drug via renal elimination or by metabolism and subsequent elimination via the urine or feces. Clearance is a proportionality factor that relates the concentration of drug measured in the body to the rate of elimination and is a function of renal or hepatic activity. It is difficult to collect data to directly determine clearance and Vd. For example, to assess the Vd empirically, samples would need to be obtained from all possible body fluids and the volumes of body fluids determined. Therefore, clearance and Vd are modeled from concentration-versus-time data.

Table 3-2 **Basic Pharmacokinetics Definitions**

Parameter Abbreviation	Definition	Equation	Use/Association
C_{max}	Maximal drug concentration	Visual extrapolation	Can be associated with acute adverse effects
T_{max}	Time at which maximum drug concentration is achieved	Visual extrapolation	Time that acute adverse effects occur
t1/2	Time required for the plasma concentration to decrease by half, or half-life	t1/2 = 0.698 × Vd/clearance	Determines how long a drug is measurable in plasma in the body
AUC	Area under the curve	Dose/clearance	Measure of systemic drug exposure
Vd	Volume of distribution	Dose/concentration at time 0 (extrapolated)	Where the drug goes in body
Cl	Clearance	Dose/AUC	How fast the drug is eliminated

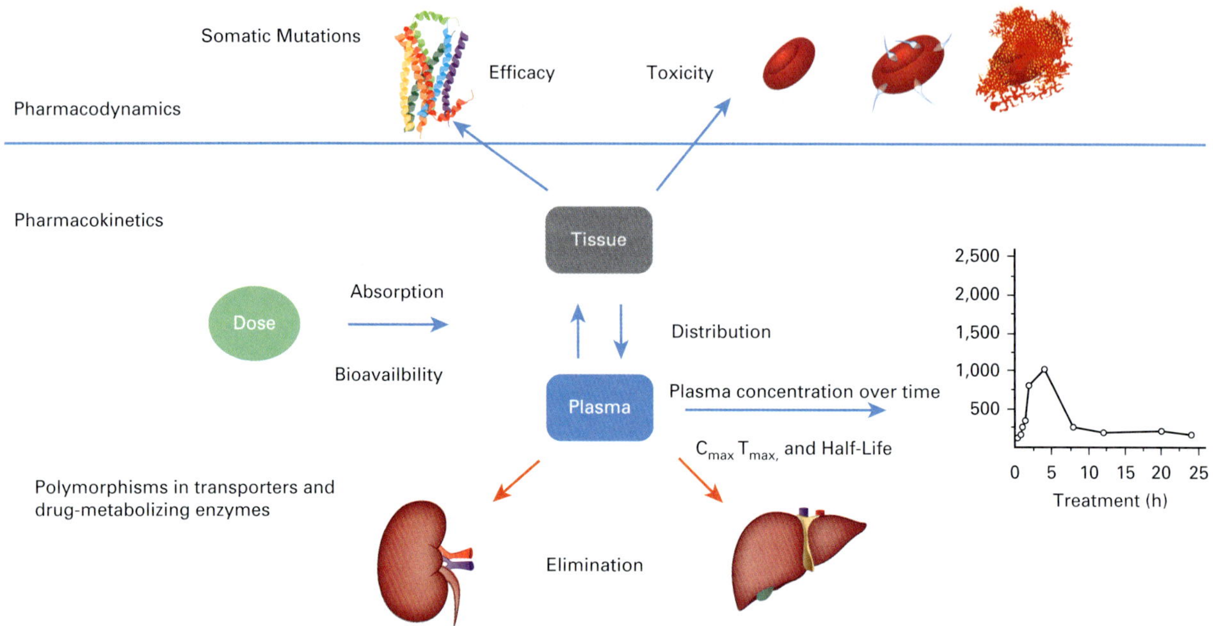

Fig. 3-1 **Overview of pharmacokinetics, pharmacodynamics, and pharmacogenetics.**
C_{max}, maximum concentration; T_{max}, time at which maximum drug concentration is achieved; h, hour.

Half-life and area under the curve (AUC) are secondary pharmacokinetic parameters because they can be calculated from primary parameters (if those are known). They can also be determined from the concentration-versus-time curve. The half-life is the time required for the concentration to decrease by half and is primarily determined by clearance. A drug is considered to be eliminated after five half-lives have elapsed. The half-life is used clinically to determine dosing frequency and washout periods in clinical trials or when starting new medications. For example, erlotinib has a half-life of approximately 36 hours, so in a patient whose disease is progressing with erlotinib therapy and who is switching to osimertinib therapy, typically a week of

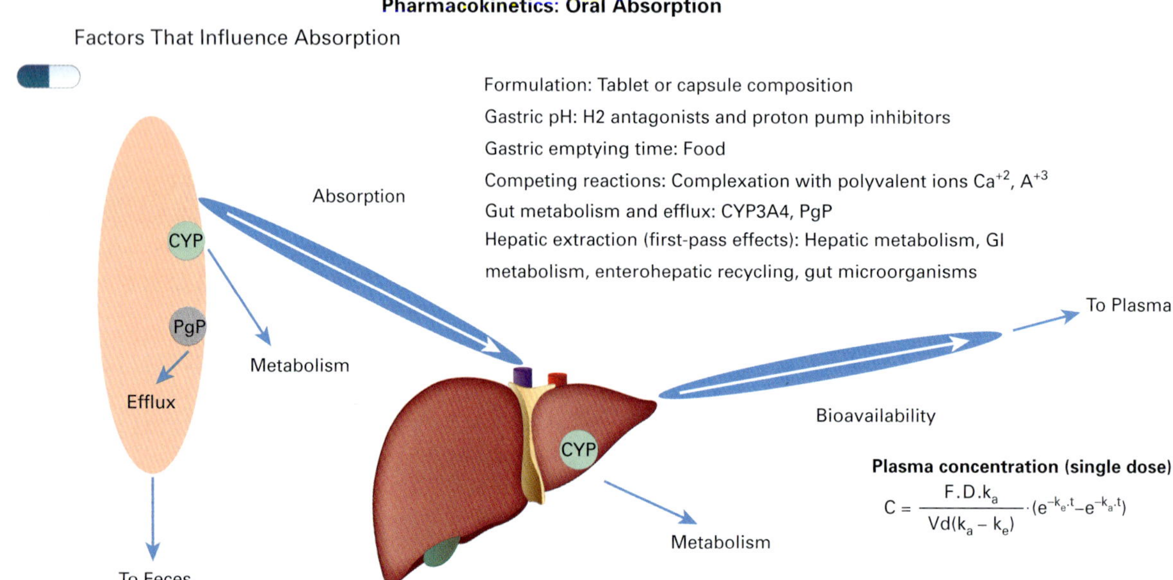

Fig. 3-2 **Factors influencing oral absorption.**
C, concentration; F, bioavailability; PgP, P-glycoprotein; Vd, volume of distribution; H2, histamine 2; Ca, Calcium; A, Aluminum; CYP, Cytochome; GI, gastroinstestinal; D, dose; k, elimination rate constant.

not taking erlotinib should be allowed (180 hours, or approximately 7 days). The AUC represents the total drug exposure over time and can be used to predict response as well as chronic adverse effects. The AUC depends on the drug amount that enters the systemic circulation (ie, dose and bioavailability) and on the ability that the system has to eliminate the drug (ie, clearance).

KEY POINTS

- C_{max}, which occurs at T_{max}, can predict acute toxicity, like EKG changes, infusion reactions, and acute blood pressure elevations.
- AUC can predict response and chronic toxicity.
- Half-life guides the frequency of administration and determines washout periods in clinical trials. Dosing in clinical trials often considers half-life of targeted therapies. For example, patients are often not eligible to initiate dosing of a study agent in a clinical trial until five half-lives of the targeted therapy have elapsed.

PHARMACODYNAMICS

PD is often summarized as the study of "what a drug does to the body."[36,37] Most anticancer drugs are developed to interact with a biologic structure (eg, receptor, enzyme, transporter), with that interaction leading to a pharmacodynamic effect or anticancer effect, although off-target adverse effects also occur. Predicting pharmacodynamic effects is critical to drug development. In some cases, such as the carboplatin AUC predicting thrombocytopenia, plasma PK predicts pharmacodynamic effects. However, assessing anticancer activity in solid tumors is challenging. The difficulty arises from an incomplete understanding of a drug's mechanism of action and from difficulties in measuring drug activity at its target, or in the cancer cell. For example, to measure activity of a tyrosine kinase inhibitor (TKI), a relevant PD study would be to measure tyrosine kinase activity in the cancer cells before and after treatment with the drug. Technical and clinical issues make this type of study difficult because repeated tumor biopsies and real-time enzyme assays would be required. Fortunately, somatic mutations are predictive biomarkers for targeted therapies and can be reliably measured in the tumor (and sometimes in circulating tumor DNA), making these PD biomarkers a clinical reality and active area of ongoing drug development.

In the absence of a measurable PD biomarker, the coupling of PD models with plasma PK data is an effective strategy for the study of exposure to response and clinical trial simulations. A PD model is a mathematic model that describes the effect of a drug as a function of drug concentration. New strategies include the development of physiologic models that recognize blood flow to the cancer varies from plasma blood flow. In addition to pharmacokinetic and pharmacodynamic data, these models incorporate physiologic properties like blood flow and organ volume and drug properties like partition across organs. Incorporation of a predictive preclinical PK/PD model in preclinical studies and early-stage clinical trials can inform the drug development process and reduce the failure rate in later-stage clinical trials.

PHARMACOGENETICS

Pharmacogenetics is the study of variability in drug response due to heredity. In this context, there are germline polymorphisms (occurring in all host cells) in drug-metabolizing pathways or drug targets that are inherited and that can affect individual responses to drugs in terms of therapeutic and adverse effects. Notably, with the exception of UGT1A, which is associated with Gilbert disease, polymorphisms do not typically cause medical conditions. Much of this genetic variation is in the form of single nucleotide polymorphisms (SNPs). SNPs are defined as variants with population frequencies ≥ 1% that can alter the amino acid sequence of the encoded protein or alter RNA splicing, leading to altered kinetics and catalysis of the protein. All drugs with biomarker information (ie, protein targets, germline and tumor mutations) in their product labeling are listed on an FDA webpage (www.fda.gov/drugs/scienceresearch/ucm572698.htm). Evidence-based clinical practice guidelines for using pharmacogenetic information are available from the Clinical Pharmacogenetics Implementation Consortium (cpicgx.org).[38] The Consortium's practice guidelines also include polymorphism frequency by ethnicity (Table 3-3).

Thiopurines

Mercaptopurine and 6-thioguanine are purine antimetabolites used clinically to treat pediatric and adult leukemias. Thiopurines are metabolized in part by *S*-methylation, catalyzed by the enzyme thiopurine *S*-methyltransferase (TPMT) and individuals with reduced activity have substantially increased adverse effects when receiving mercaptorpurine. TPMT activity, measured either by a phenotypic enzyme test or by sequencing for polymorphisms with subsequent dose reductions in patients with intermediate and poor metabolism of the drugs, is routinely performed in clinical practice.[39-43] Polymorphisms in nucleoside diphosphatase (*NUDT15*), which catalyzes the conversion of cytotoxic thioguanine triphosphate metabolites to the less toxic thioguanine monophosphate, are associated with thiopurine adverse effects, have been reported more recently and assessment is moving into clinical practice.[44]

Tamoxifen

Tamoxifen is a prodrug activated by CYP2D6 to its active metabolite, endoxifen. Therefore, a patient with little or no CYP2D6 activity may have a poor response to tamoxifen because of inadequate conversion to the active drug. This relationship is controversial, with conflicting literature reported. The majority of literature discusses the adjuvant treatment of ER+ breast cancer, for where patients with little or no CYP2D6 activity have an increased recurrence risk, but currently there are insufficient data to suggest this affects survival.[45] Current guidelines recommend selecting an alternative therapy in

Table 3-3 **Drugs Commonly Used in Oncology That Have Pharmacogenetic Implications**

Drug	Gene	Variant Genotype	Consequence of Variant Genotype	Recommendation	Strength of Recommendation*
Capecitabine/FU	*DPYD*	IM	Increased toxicity	IM: Reduce starting dose	Strong
		PM		PM: Avoid if possible, or reduce dose by 75%	
Irinotecan	*UGT1A1*	PM	Increased toxicity	Select alternative therapy if possible	Moderate
Mercaptopurine	*TPMT, NUDT15*	IM	Increased toxicity	IM: Reduce dose by 50%	Strong
		PM		PM: Reduce dose 10-fold	
Tamoxifen	*CYP2D6*	PM	Decreased efficacy	Select alternative agent not metabolized by CYP2D6 (eg, aromatase inhibitor if postmenopausal)	Strong

Abbreviations: EM, extensive metabolizer; FU, fluorouracil; IF, intermediate function; IM, intermediate metabolizer; LF, low function; PM, poor metabolizer; RM, rapid metabolizer; UM, ultra-rapid metabolizer,

*Clinical Pharmacogenetics Implementation Consortium evidence level, except irinotecan, the recommendations for which are the author's opinion.

patients who have little or no CYP2D6 activity, which is a reasonable strategy because aromatase inhibitors are preferred for use by postmenopausal women and therapeutic alternatives are available for premenopausal women (eg, ovarian suppression and aromatase inhibitors with or without additional targeted therapies). Like the data on patients with little or no CYP2D6 activity, the literature is also conflicting with regard to concurrent use of CYP2D6 inhibitors and tamoxifen, which is the pharmacologic equivalent of the poor metabolism genotype. Initially, a prospective study reported that plasma endoxifen concentrations were substantially lower in patients receiving concurrent tamoxifen and strong inhibitors of CYP2D6, whereas weak inhibitors had little effect.[46] However, a recently reported population cohort study including > 14,000 women concurrently receiving tamoxifen and selective serotonin reuptake inhibitors (SSRIs) showed no increased risk of death between women taking SSRIs that were weak inhibitors of CYP2D6 compared with those taking strong inhibitors of CYP2D6, although follow-up was short at < 2 years.[47] Given the availability of SSRIs like venlafaxine that are weak CYP2D6 inhibitors, avoiding strong CYP2D6 inhibitors like fluoxetine and paroxetine concurrently with tamoxifen seems prudent.

5-Fluorouracil and Capecitabine

The fluoropyrimidines 5-fluorouracil (FU) and capecitabine are commonly used for treatment of breast and GI cancers. Dihydropyrimidine dehydrogenase (DPD; encoded by *DPYD*) catalyzes the first and rate-limiting step in the conversion of FU to dihydrofluorouracil. Some polymorphisms result in reduced activity of DPD, which subsequently results in reduced clearance and increased half-life of FU, and are associated with adverse effects, including severe myelosuppression, neurotoxicity, and GI toxicity. Capecitabine, a prodrug of FU, is converted to FU and also metabolized by DPD. Therefore, toxic effects are similar in patients with decreased or nonfunctioning *DPYD* variants. Multiple meta-analyses have demonstrated the relationship between these genetic polymorphisms and adverse effects; guidelines recommend dose reductions for patients who do not metabolize these drugs well and alternative dosing strategies are listed on the FDA label.[48] Despite these recommendations, *DPYD* variants are rarely assessed in clinical practice.

Irinotecan

Irinotecan, a prodrug, is metabolized in vivo to 7-ethyl-10-hydroxycamptothecin (SN-38), which is a potent inhibitor of topoisomerase 1. SN-38 is inactivated by glucuronidation to form the glucuronide conjugate, SN-38G, in a reaction catalyzed by the polymorphic hepatic enzyme uridine diphosphate glucuronosyltransferase 1A1 (UGT1A1).[49] A dinucleotide repeat polymorphism in the TATA box in the promoter for *UGT1A1* results in reduced hepatic *UGT1A1* expression and is considered the most common cause of Gilbert syndrome (mild unconjugated hyperbilirubinemia).[50] Patients homozygous for the *UGT1A1*28* polymorphism have substantially lower SN-38 glucuronidation rates and substantially higher rates of grade 4 or 5 neutropenia and severe diarrhea when treated with irinotecan than those who do not carry this genetic variant.[51] Despite an FDA label change, recommending dose reduction for patients who metabolize this drug poorly, irinotecan dose is infrequently adjusted clinically for this polymorphism.

The two most common therapeutic strategies for patients with variant genotypes are dose reduction or use of an alternative agent. However, with the exception of the thioguanines, pharmacogenetic testing is rarely performed in clinical practice for a variety of reasons, including lack of clinical trial evidence supporting appropriate dose reduction, lack of insurance coverage for testing, lack of alternative therapeutic options, physician preference for dose adjustments after toxicity, and the inability to get test results returned in time to affect chemotherapy dosing or drug selection. A recent trend in increased direct-to-consumer pharmacogenetic testing may actually encourage use of pharmacogenetic information in clinical practice.[52]

DRUG INTERACTIONS

Drug interactions are typically pharmacokinetic and result from one drug or effect causing a change in the plasma concentrations of another drug by affecting the drug's absorption (eg, food, pH) or metabolism.

ABSORPTION

The proportion of the drug that reaches the systemic circulation after administration is the pharmacokinetic parameter bioavailability, which is calculated as drug exposure attained relative to that attained with IV administration of the same drug. Changes in absorption often affect bioavailability. Food and pH effects can interfere with drug absorption and are major considerations when developing oral drugs. The FDA typically requires a food effect study for all new agents. Food (in particular, food with high fat content) may increase, decrease, or not affect drug bioavailability, depending on the drug, which is measured by differences in the pharmacokinetic parameters (ie, C_{max} and AUC ratios) between the fed and fasted states.

In addition, acid suppressive therapy, including antacids, H2 antagonists and proton pump inhibitors (PPIs) lower gastric pH and can influence absorption of concurrently administered medications, especially those with pH-dependent solubility.[53] If a drug has reduced solubility above a pH of 6, drug-interaction studies are typically required by the FDA and are of similar design as those described for food effects. The results of drug-interaction studies also inform the product label: If the AUC or C_{max} ratio falls outside of the 90% CI, a significant drug interaction between acid-lowering therapies is determined. Notably, pH-dependent absorption is not always a class effect. For example, bosutinib, dasatinib, and nilotinib have pH-dependent absorption, with reduced absorption at lower pH; however, imatinib has pH-independent absorption.[54] Figure 3-2 and Table 3-1 list the food and pH effects relevant to oral chemotherapy.

Antacids work by binding to and neutralizing stomach acid, resulting in rapid onset and short duration of effect (approximately 2 hours). Histamine H2 receptor antagonists reversibly compete with histamine at the H2 receptors to reduce gastric acid secretion, with effects lasting approximately 12 hours after the dose. PPIs irreversibly bind to the proton pump that secretes gastric acid, resulting in ≥ 24 hours of gastric acid suppression. All therapies can increase gastric pH to above 6. In addition, polyvalent cations found in antacids (eg, Mg^{++}, Ca^{++}) can bind to some drugs forming insoluble chelates that limit drug absorption.[53,55]

METABOLISM

The majority of metabolism occurs in the liver and, to a lesser extent, in the GI tract for orally absorbed drugs. Drugs may be inducers, inhibitors, or substrates of a drug metabolizing enzyme. A complete list of substrates, inhibitors, and inducers of the CYP enzymes can be found on the FDA website (www.fda.gov), although CYP3A4 is most commonly involved in drug interactions involving oral targeted therapies. Observed changes arising from metabolic drug-drug interactions can be substantial—an order of magnitude or more decrease or increase in the plasma concentrations of a drug or metabolite—and can include formation of toxic and/or active metabolites or increased exposure to a toxic parent compound. These large changes in exposure can alter the safety and efficacy profile of a drug and/or its active metabolites in important ways. This is most expected for a drug with a narrow therapeutic range (NTR) but is also possible for non-NTR drugs, as well. From a practical standpoint, drug interactions can be managed either by avoiding the concurrent administration of interacting medications or altering the dose. For many newer medications, dose adjustments are included in the product labeling. For example, erlotinib is metabolized primarily by CYP3A4, and the prescribing information recommends that dose decreases of erlotinib should be considered if it is concurrently administered with strong CYP3A inhibitors.

KEY POINTS

- Drug interactions with oral cancer therapies are common and clinically important.
- Drug interactions affecting drug absorption are usually related to food or pH effects.
- Food effects can be managed by counseling patients when to take their medication (ie, with or without food).
- Absorption effects can be managed by avoiding concurrent administration of pH-lowering agents.
- Drug interactions related to metabolism can be managed by avoiding concurrent administration, if possible, or dose adjustments.

SPECIAL POPULATIONS

RENAL IMPAIRMENT

Most drugs are cleared by elimination of unchanged drug by the kidney and/or by metabolism in the liver. For a drug eliminated primarily via renal excretory mechanisms, impaired renal function may alter its PK and PD.[56] An accurate assessment of renal function is critical to dosing chemotherapy, and both the National Comprehensive Cancer Network and the International Society of Geriatric Oncology recommend assessment of renal function before initiating chemotherapy, although there is currently no consensus on the best method. Creatinine clearance can be measured directly with a 24-hour urine collection, although this is often impractical in terms of time, cost, and convenience. There are also several equations to calculate creatinine clearance; the Cockcroft-Gault (CG)[57] is used commonly, likely on the basis of its incorporation into the FDA guidance for assessing PK in patients with renal dysfunction. The CG was developed in healthy, predominantly white individuals and does not consider body composition, so other methods that attempt to overcome limitations of the CG equation have been developed, including the modification of the Diet in Renal Disease Study equation (MDRD-4 and MDRD-6) and the Chronic Kidney Disease Epidemiology Collaboration equations, although none of these has gained widespread acceptance in oncology.[58] See prescribing information, Chu,[59] or DeVita et al[1] for current dose adjustments for renal impairment.[59] Although the most common type of change arising from renal impairment is a decrease in renal excretion, or possibly renal metabolism, of a drug or its metabolites, renal impairment has also been associated with other changes, such as in absorption, hepatic metabolism, plasma protein binding, and drug distribution.[60] These changes may be more important in patients with severely impaired renal function and have been observed even when the renal route is not the primary route of elimination of a drug.

HEPATIC IMPAIRMENT

The liver is involved in the clearance of many drugs through a variety of oxidative and conjugative metabolic pathways and/or through biliary excretion of unchanged drug or metabolites.[61] Alterations of these excretory and metabolic activities by hepatic impairment can lead to drug accumulation or, less often, failure to form an active metabolite. Hepatic disease can alter the absorption and disposition of drugs (PK) as well as their efficacy and safety (PD). See prescribing information, Chu,[59] or DeVita et al[1] for current dose adjustments for hepatic impairment.

GERIATRICS

Usually, there are no significant differences in PK for cytotoxic agents based on age alone.[62-64] Although a number of age-related changes in drug absorption, distribution, metabolism, and excretion can contribute to differences in treatment tolerance between older and younger patients, these changes are influenced by many other factors and age alone is a poor predictor of drug tolerability.

An important potential issue in elderly patients is renal clearance. Over a lifespan, renal mass decreases by approximately 25% to 30%, and renal blood flow decreases by 1% per year after age 50 years.[65] The decline in glomerular filtration rate with age is estimated at 0.75 mL/min/y after age 40 years; however, approximately one-third of patients have no change in creatinine clearance with age. Because of the physiologic decline in renal function with age, chemotherapy agents primarily excreted renally must be dosed with caution in older patients, although routine dose reductions are not recommended.

Older patients do not appear to have increased adverse outcomes with standard drug doses. Studies with docetaxel likewise did not find clinically relevant changes in PK in the elderly.[65] Therefore, there are few reasons to modify dosing solely on the basis of age, although one exception is with high-dose conditioning chemotherapy regimens used for stem cell transplants,[66] where doses are empirically adjusted in the elderly. In most cases, if an elderly patient has an adequate performance status as well as adequate renal and hepatic function, the dose that would be used in a younger patient should be used.

OBESITY

The ratio of adipose tissue to lean body mass is altered in obesity and can affect the volume of distribution of lipid-soluble medications. Lipid-soluble medications can accumulate in adipose tissue, which serves essentially as a depot, prolonging the duration of drug effect and increasing the total amount of drug in the body. This effect is particularly important for anesthetics;[67] altered dosing regimens are recommended for obese individuals.

The weight used for dosing is another important concern. Typically, chemotherapy dosing is based on body surface area (BSA), which is commonly calculated with the Mosteller formula and is based on actual height and weight. Because of toxicity concerns, clinicians sometime use either ideal body weight, adjusted ideal body weight, or cap the BSA at 2.0 m^2 rather than using the actual body weight to calculate BSA. Observational studies show that ≤40% of obese patients are dosed lower than their actual body weight.[68-70] Treating patients with less than full weight–based dosing of chemotherapy is thought to contribute to the higher mortality rate observed in obese patients. ASCO convened an expert panel to evaluate the literature about obesity and dosing. The panel concluded there was no evidence that actual weight dosing in obese patients resulted in more adverse effects, and the panel recommended that full weight–based chemotherapy doses be used.[71]

DRUG DEVELOPMENT: NOVEL CLINICAL TRIAL DESIGN AND SPECIAL POPULATIONS

Clinical trials are critical to the development of new anticancer therapies and an understanding of novel clinical trial designs for targeted therapies is critical.

KEY POINTS

- Empirical dose reductions are recommended for some drugs in patients with underlying hepatic and/or renal dysfunction.
- With the exception of conditioning regimens used for stem cell transplants, no empirical dose reductions are recommended that are based solely on age.
- Actual body weight and actual BSA should be used for dosing obese patients with drugs that use weight-based dosing.

NOVEL TRIAL DESIGNS

With molecular characterization of cancers becoming routine in clinical practice, treating tumors according to molecular chracteristics rather than histologic classification is becoming more widespread, requiring new study designs. Common designs include the umbrella and basket trials. In umbrella trials, multiple mutations in a single tumor type are targeted by different drugs. An example is a current National Cancer Institute (NCI) clinical trials network study in second-line squamous cell cancer of the lung in which mutations in MET, PI3K, CDK4/6, and others are targeted by different agents.[72,73] Basket trials involve the treatment of different tumor types that have the same mutation with the same therapy. In this fashion, therapy is targeting a specific molecular aberration regardless of the tissue of origin. An example of a basket trial is the NCI-MATCH trial.

KEY POINT

- With the emergence of molecularly targeted agents, novel study designs, including basket and umbrella trials have been introduced.

Acknowledgment

Alex A. Adjei, MD, PhD, FASCO is acknowledged and thanked for his contribution to prior versions of this chapter.

CLINICAL PHARMACOLOGY: A GLOBAL PERSPECTIVE

Alex Sparreboom, PhD; and Shuiying Hu, PhD (The Ohio University, Columbus, OH)

Chemotherapeutic agents are still commonly administered at the maximum dose a patient can tolerate before the onset of unacceptable toxicity. However, the therapeutic window for most anticancer agents is extremely narrow and, in many cases, the selection and dosage of drugs remains largely empirical. Given that the effect of a therapeutic agent is generally a function of its concentration at the site of action, it is usually more meaningful to have knowledge of drug exposure measures rather than of absolute dose only. This is substantiated by the notion that for many oncology drugs, systemic exposure is correlated with clinical outcomes, thereby further highlighting the importance of precision dosing.

There is often a marked variation in the handling of drugs between individual patients, resulting in variability in systemic exposure and pharmacodynamic effects, and there is growing evidence suggesting that ethnicity is an important contributing factor to variability observed with cytotoxic chemotherapy[74] as well as targeted therapies such as TKIs.[75] A combination of intrinsic factors (eg, physiologic variables, genetic characteristics) and extrinsic factors (eg, medicine use, dietary habits, cultural and social norms) can alter the relationship between the administered dose and a drug's plasma concentration–time profile. It is rarely possible to define the optimum dosage to achieve a required measure of drug exposure a priori for an individual patient from measurable intrinsic or extrinsic variables. Instead, the most common strategy for dose selection is to establish a therapeutic dose in phase I, II, or III clinical trials and subsequently, at best, modify it for individual differences in BSA. This is an unsustainable situation because failure to deliver the right dose in routine practice across different world populations may have detrimental implications for efficacy and safety.[76,77]

An important contributor to interindividual pharmacokinetic variability observed with orally administered drugs such as TKIs is associated with their sensitivity to pH-dependent changes in solubility and subsequent absorption patterns.[78] Furthermore, unintentional drug-drug interactions play a significant role in the observed pharmacokinetic variability, and coadministration of certain prescription medications, over-the-counter drugs, herbal medicine,[79] or even food needs to be carefully considered in individual patients as a function of ethnicity. As discussed elsewhere,[80] the influence of food on the pharmacokinetic properties of many orally administered drugs is particularly problematic and unpredictable, and demands that progressive steps be taken early during the drug development process to properly document the drug-interaction potential, as well as to proactively address labeling issues across different world populations associated with this phenomenon. This has become particularly important in light of recent surveys suggesting that the prevalence and nondisclosure of complementary and alternative medicine use in patients with cancer, including the use of herbal products known or suspected to alter the PK of conventional anticancer drugs, depend on ethnicity and racial ancestry.[81]

An integrated approach in which solubility, physiology, and drug absorption and disposition changes are thoroughly characterized is critical in the design of studies addressing interethnic pharmacokinetic variability. A systems pharmacology approach to build our understanding of treatment success and failure in different populations can be used to improve the safety and efficacy of drugs.[82] Indeed, such an approach can simultaneously take into consideration variability in outcome caused by tumor heterogeneity and provide a platform to optimize chemotherapeutic regimens and tailoring of dosage for individual patients regardless of ethnicity. One additional important consideration in connection with interethnic pharmacokinetic variability is the existence of heritable genetic traits that can affect measures of systemic exposure and subsequently affect efficacy and/or toxicity.[83] The use of companion diagnostics and detailed molecular profiling of an individual's tumor has the potential to increase patient benefit.[84] Moreover, availability of such diagnostic tests may ultimately accelerate the drug development process across world populations and also maximize the ability to generate important biologic information about ethnic diversity of human cancers. Although rarely prospectively used with anticancer drugs, another such companion diagnostic is the implementation of therapeutic drug monitoring. Many patients with cancer, depending on their ethnicity,[85] are under- or overdosed, and chronic suboptimal exposure to such agents can lead to acquired resistance or unacceptable adverse effects.[86] Therapeutic drug monitoring, in which drug levels are measured in the blood at timed intervals after an initial dose that can be subsequently modified to maintain constant levels over time, could be particularly useful for agents administered chronically and daily, allowing for instantaneous dose modifications to be implemented.

Studies over the last decade have provided evidence that many commonly used anticancer drugs, such as docetaxel, doxorubicin, FU, gefitinib, and tamoxifen, exhibit interethnic differences in safety and efficacy that are relevant to treating oncologists.[87] Although molecularly targeted agents have revolutionized the field of oncology, the underlying causes of interethnic variability in PK with such drugs and their contribution to treatment outcome remain poorly understood. It is anticipated that incorporation of clinical pharmacologic concepts in the use of oncology drugs ultimately will result in improved tolerability and effectiveness of established and new treatment modalities for multiple malignant diseases.

4

PRINCIPLES OF IMMUNO-ONCOLOGY AND BIOLOGIC THERAPY

Rodrigo Ramella Munhoz, MD, and Joseph I. Clark, MD

OVERVIEW AND GENERAL CONCEPTS OF IMMUNO-ONCOLOGY

Biologic therapy—whether for neoplastic, infectious, immunologic, or other diseases—refers to the use of biologic products or substances that are made by living organisms, such as cytokines, antibodies, bacterial or viral vectors, and cells. For cancer, these substances are administered primarily to generate or restore host immune responses or to mediate nonimmunologic antitumor activities. Since the introduction of interferon (IFN) > 25 years ago, progress in biologic therapy for cancer has been rapid. Several cytokines have been approved by the US Food and Drug Administration (FDA). An increasing number of monoclonal antibodies are being used clinically, because the introduction of immune checkpoint blockade with monoclonal antibodies has had a major impact in the management of a growing number of malignancies and has paved the way for the development of combined approaches, already in clinical use for the treatment of patients. Cellular therapy on the basis of artificially engineered antigen receptors (either chimeric or modified T-cell receptor) produced remarkable results in patients with refractory hematologic malignancies. Also, the possibility of using cell-based vaccine approaches and viral and bacterial vectors, as exemplified by the approval of a recombinant herpesvirus to treat patients with melanoma, are expanding the applicability of cancer immunotherapy, or immuno-oncology. This chapter focuses on the immunology, pharmacology, and toxicology of biologic therapy in clinical use to treat cancer. More detailed review of the clinical application of specific agents is provided in tumor-specific chapters.

The immune system protects against microbial pathogens while simultaneously maintaining tolerance to "self." The innate response forms the first line of defense. Innate immune cells (eg, macrophages, dendritic cells [DCs], and natural killer [NK] cells) express receptors (eg, toll-like receptors [TLRs], C-type lectin receptors, nucleotide-binding oligomerization domain-like receptors and retinoic-acid–inducible gene-I–like receptors) that serve as initial triggers of the immune response. These receptors are involved in the recognition of conserved molecular patterns, which include pathogen-associated molecular patterns, such as unmethylated CpG DNA motifs, found on exogenous organisms, and cell damage–associated molecular patterns (eg, high-mobility group box 1) but not on normal, uninflamed human tissues. Stimulation through these receptors triggers a cascade of events that includes the production of cytokines, activation of cellular cytotoxicity, an increase in nitric oxide synthesis, and activation of the complement system. These events promote the elimination or lysis of microbial pathogens and promote recruitment and activation of other immune cells (Fig 4-1).

Microbial or cellular fragments that result from the destruction produced by the innate immune response are taken up by professional antigen-presenting cells (APCs; eg, macrophages, DCs, B cells), which then process the fragments and present these antigens to generate the

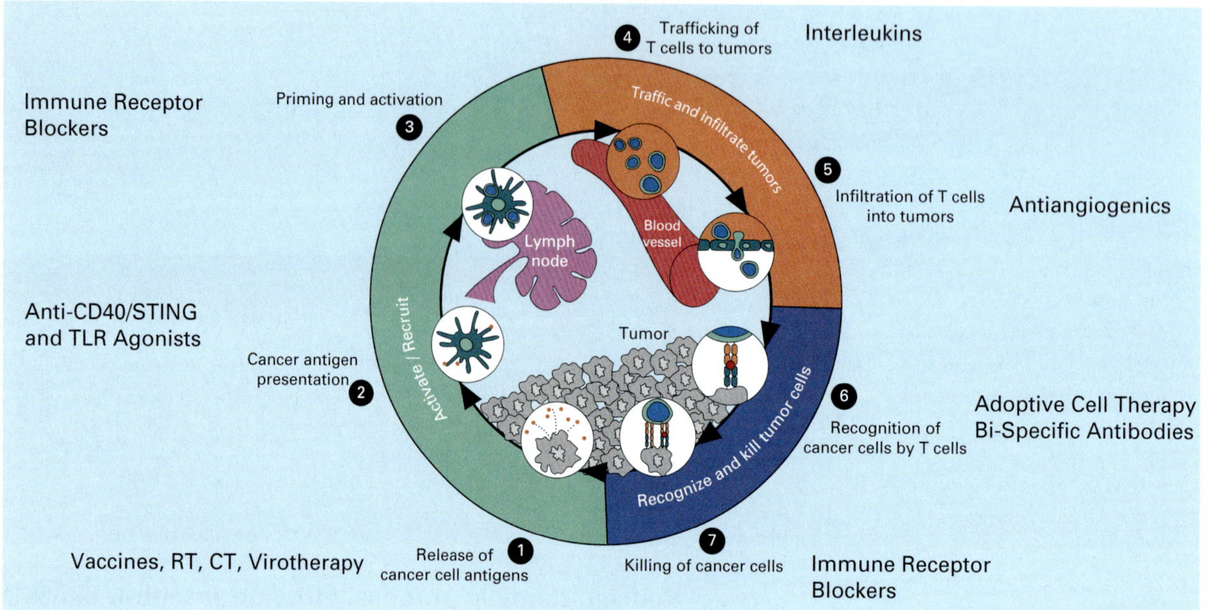

Fig. 4-1 The cancer-immunity cycle.

Abbreviations: CT, cytoxic chemotherapy; RT, radiation therapy; TLR, toll-like receptor.

Adapted and reprinted from Immunity, *Vol 39, Issue 1, Chen DS, Mellman I, Oncology meets immunology: the cancer-immunity cycle, pg. 1-10, Copyright (2013), with permission from Elsevier.*

adaptive response, largely though the activation and mobilization of T cells and antibody-producing B cells. These cells express highly diverse antigen-specific receptors—the T-cell antigen receptors (TCRs) and the B-cell antigen receptors (BCRs)—generated by random rearrangement of the TCR and immunoglobulin (Ig) gene segments, respectively. The adaptive response allows generation of extremely diverse T- and B-cell repertoires that, compared with the innate response, provide a more specific but also broader and more flexible response that includes the capacity for generating "memory."

Immune responses are highly regulated. Many types of cells and molecular factors, including cell-surface molecules, are involved in modulating (either positively or negatively) both the innate and the adaptive responses. A key step in the generation of adaptive immunity is the presentation of antigens by professional APCs to T-helper cells, which promote cellular effectors (eg, cytotoxic T lymphocytes [CTLs]) or humoral effectors (eg, antibodies) through the production of specific cytokines. Regulatory cells and cytokines also suppress the immune response to maintain tolerance to self and limit immune-mediated damage to normal tissues.

KEY POINTS

- Cells of the antigen-nonspecific innate and antigen-specific adaptive responses have been implicated in antitumor immunity.
- Specific immunity to tumors requires uptake of tumor antigens by professional APCs and presentation to T-helper cells, which coordinate the generation of cellular (cytotoxic T cells) and/or humoral (antibody-producing B-cell) responses.
- Immune responses are highly regulated to maintain tolerance to self and limit immune-mediated damage to normal tissues.

IMMUNE CELLS

A wide variety of hematologic and nonhematologic cells are important in innate and adaptive immunity. The following are considered to play prominent roles in antitumor immune responses.

T CELLS AND IMMUNE CHECKPOINTS

T cells are paramount in the adaptive immune responses as effectors and as regulators. The signaling complex of T cells includes the TCR dimer, the accessory molecules (CD4 or CD8), and the CD3 signal transduction module. Unlike antibodies, which can react to intact proteins, T cells, through the TCR, react only to peptide fragments of antigens that are noncovalently complexed with major histocompatibility complex (MHC) molecules, which are integral membrane glycoproteins. There are two types of MHC molecules. Class I MHC (eg, human leukocyte antigens A, B, and C) are expressed on most cell types and serve as the antigen-presenting molecule for CD8+ T cells. Class II MHC (eg, HLA-DR) is recognized by CD4+ T cells and is present primarily on APCs but also can be present on other cells, including tumor cells. Polymorphisms within MHC molecules determine whether a peptide fragment will complex with the MHC molecule and thus whether a T cell from an individual will respond to a specific epitope of an antigen, resulting in the phenomenon referred to as "MHC restriction." Because of this phenomenon, some peptide cancer vaccines are designed to be given only to patients with specific HLA types.

T-cell activation requires not only the presentation of an antigen within the context of an MHC molecule and stimulation through the CD3 module but also "costimulatory" signals. Activation, in turn, is regulated by coinhibitory signals, essential in limiting the magnitude of the immune response and autoimmunity but also exploited as immune evasion mechanisms by tumor cells. The CD28 family of receptors includes the stimulatory receptor CD28 and the inhibitory receptors cytotoxic T-lymphocyte antigen 4 (CTLA-4),and programmed death 1 (PD-1). Receptors of the CD28 family interact with the B7 family of ligands, which include B7-1, B7-2, programmed death ligands 1 (PD-L1, also called B7-^{1}H), and 2 (PD-L2, also called B7-DC). These interactions are referred to as "immune checkpoints." A simplified diagram for the CTLA-4 and PD-1 immune checkpoints is shown in Figure 4-2. Several other receptor-ligand engagements can act as modulators of the immune response, including those mediated by the costimulatory and coinhibitory molecules listed below.

Costimulatory Receptors:

- CD28
- CD137
- CD27
- OX40 (or CD134)
- Inducible T-cell costimulator
- Glucocorticoid-induced tumor necrosis factor receptor–related protein

Coinhibitory Receptors:

- CTLA-4
- PD-1
- B- and T-cell attenuator
- Lymphocyte-activation gene 3
- T-cell immunoglobulin and mucin-domain containing 3
- PD-[1]H (also named VISTA [V-domain Ig suppressor of T-cell activation])
- CD160
- CD244

CYTOLYTIC T LYMPHOCYTES

CTLs are primarily CD8+ T cells and thus, through their unique TCR, recognize antigens presented within the context of MHC class I. Two mechanisms are involved in their cytotoxic effector activity. The predominant mechanism is granule exocytosis and the release of perforin and granzymes. The second mechanism is mediated by the death activator Fas ligand, which is expressed on the cell surface of CTLs. Both mechanisms cause

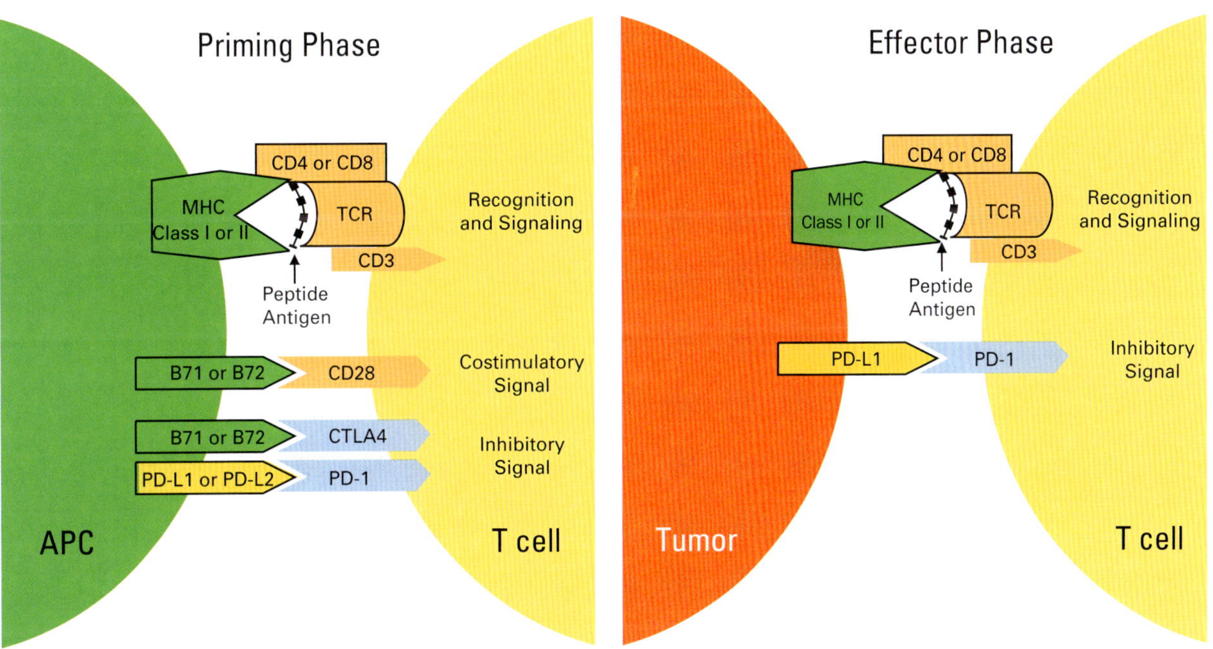

Fig. 4-2 Regulation of T-cell priming and effector function.

During the priming phase of T-cell activation, antigens are presented to the T-cell receptor (TCR) as peptide fragments within major histocompatibility complex (MHC) molecules on antigen-presenting cells (APCs). The primary costimulatory signal is delivered through the CD28 receptor on the T cell after engagement of its ligands, B7-1 or B7-2, on the APC. Fully effective engagement also depends on the interactions among several other molecules, such as adhesion molecules (not shown). Failure of the costimulatory B7/CD28 complex to be engaged results in either a nonactivating T-cell event and/or anergy. Engagement of the cytolytic T-lymphocyte antigen 4 (CTLA-4) receptor (CD152) on the T cell by the same B7-1 or B7-2 ligands results in inhibition of the response. Engagement of the programmed death 1 (PD-1) receptor with one of its two ligands, PD-L1 or PD-L2, on APCs also results in inhibition of the response. PD-L1 is also expressed by tumors. During the effector phase, engagement of PD-1 on the activated T cell by PD-L1 on the tumor results in inhibition of T-cell function.

cells to undergo apoptosis (Fig 4-3). When appropriately activated, these cells also produce cytokines, such as IFN-γ, interleukin-2 (IL-2), and tumor necrosis factor α (TNF-α), that also can mediate or enhance antitumor effects. CTLs can move to another cell and, by reorienting its granules to another region of contact, destroy it. In this manner, CTLs can kill many tumor cells, resulting in a robust and specific "serial killing" response that is considered to play a central role in immune-mediated tumor rejection. Tumor-infiltrating CD8+ lymphocytes can be associated with improved clinical outcome.[1]

T-HELPER CELLS

T-helper cells secrete cytokines that regulate all immune cells. They are essential in generating CTLs, regulating B-cell antibody production, and activating phagocytes. Most T-helper cells express CD4 and thus recognize antigens presented by class II MHC. Depending on the nature of the peptide and the activation status of the APCs, several types of responses can be promoted, including a cellular immune response mediated by CTLs and by macrophages, referred to as T-helper cell type 1 (Th1) response, or a humoral response mediated by antibody, referred to as T-helper cell type 2 (Th2) response (which also includes activation of eosinophils). Predominant cytokines produced in a Th1-associated response are IFN-γ and IL-2. Predominant cytokines produced in a Th2-associated response are IL-4 and IL-5. CD4+ T cells, which are required in an antitumor response largely to help naïve CD8+ T cells, leading to their differentiation and activation into tumor-specific CTLs and the development of antigen-specific memory. Cytokines produced by T-helper cells also may mediate antitumor effects by activating macrophages and NK cells. T-helper cytokines (eg, IFN-γ) may also directly suppress tumor growth.

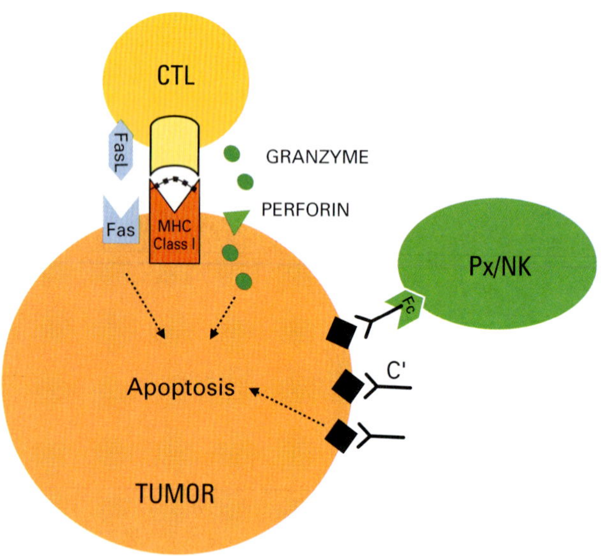

Fig. 4-3 Mechanisms of cell killing by cytolytic T lymphocytes and antibody.

After attaching to the major histocompatibility complex (MHC)-peptide complex, cytolytic T lymphocytes (CTLs) discharge cytoplasmic granules containing perforin and granzymes by exocytosis. Perforin molecules insert themselves into the plasma membrane of target cells, which enables granzymes to enter the cell. Granzymes are serine proteases that, once inside the cell, activate caspases that cause the cells to undergo apoptosis. When CTLs bind to their target, they also upregulate Fas ligand (FasL) on their surface, which binds with the Fas receptor on the surface of the target cell, leading to its death—also by apoptosis. Antibody recognizes antigen in its native conformation. After binding, a complement reactive site on the antibody is activated that sets into motion a cascade of reactions, including the activation of many molecules of the complement system, which, in turn, activate increasing amounts of enzymes resulting in complement-mediated cytotoxicity. A product of the complement cascade also strongly activates phagocytosis by macrophages and neutrophils. These phagocytes (Px) and also natural killer (NK) cells bind their Fc receptor (CD16) to the antibody and destroy the antibody-bound cell (antibody-dependent cellular mechanisms). Antibody-recognizing cell-surface molecules that regulate cell signaling or growth can directly elicit apoptosis.

Abbreviation: C', complement.

REGULATORY T CELLS

Regulatory T cells (Tregs) are subsets of T lymphocytes capable of antigen-specific recognition. In healthy individuals, Tregs maintain tolerance by suppressing expansion of effector cells directed against self-antigen. Tregs that express CD4, CD25, and forkhead box P3 (FOXP3; a forkhead family transcriptional regulator) play a central role in maintaining immune self-tolerance. The mechanism of suppression of self-reactive lymphocytes is not clear but does seem to involve direct cell-to-cell contact or the production of IL-10 or of TGF-β. Given that many tumor-associated antigens are normal self-constituents, CD4+CD25+FOXP3 Treg cells engaged in the maintenance of self-tolerance may impede tumor-reactive T cells. Their role in cancer, however, is not established, and the prognostic significance of intratumoral Treg cells may be context dependent and affected by the tumor type, the other cells in the tumor microenvironment, and soluble molecules that vary with time and treatment. In some cancers, such as breast cancer, data show that intratumoral Treg cells confer a poorer prognosis[2]; however, for other cancers, such as colorectal cancer, there is a better prognosis.[3]

NK Cells

NK cells are a relatively small population (< 10%) of circulating lymphocytes and are distinct from T cells and B cells. They are part of the innate or immediate non–Ag-specific response to pathogens and transformed cells. Although their cytotoxic mechanisms are similar to those of CTLs, NK cells do not require recognition of MHC molecules, and thus killing by NK cells is designated as non–MHC-restricted lysis. In fact, class I MHC molecules send a negative regulatory signal through receptors on the NK cells (killer inhibitory receptors) that inhibit NK cell lytic function. Conversely, loss of class I MHC on tumor cells may result in NK cell killing of cells that could otherwise escape T-cell recognition. Under normal homeostatic conditions, multiple families of NK cell receptors that inhibit their activation exert the predominant effects, whereas inflammation and infection, as well as malignancy, may lead to

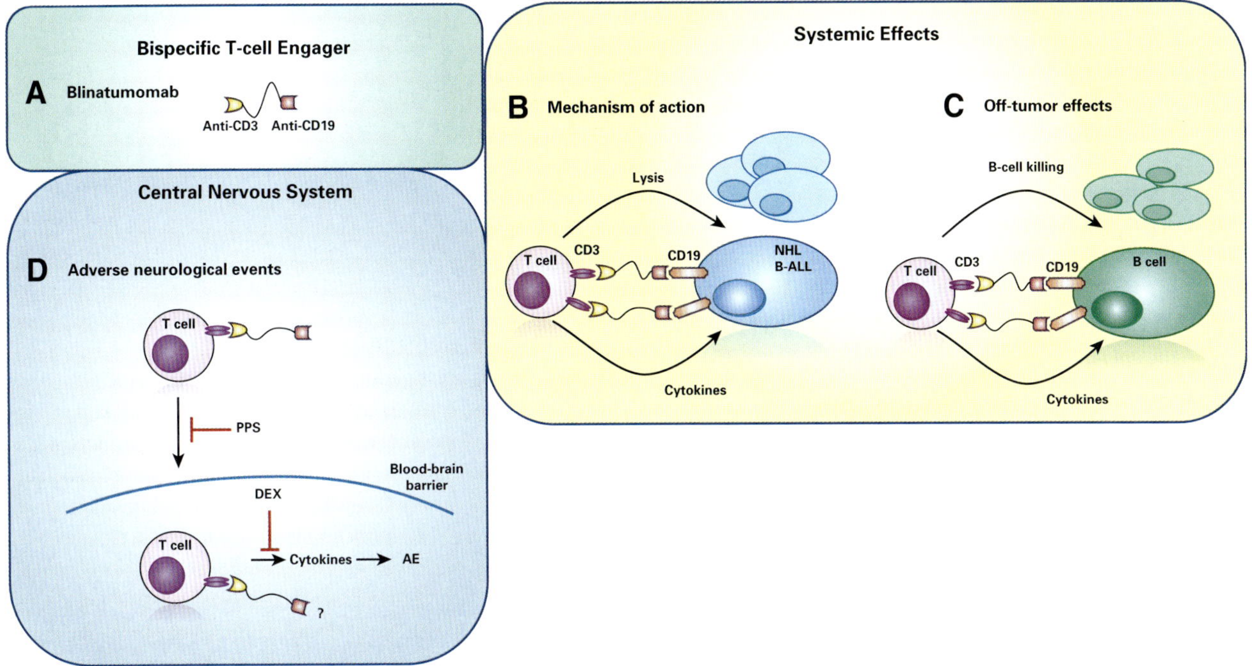

Fig. 4-4 Bispecific T-cell engagers (BiTEs) as treatment of B-cell lymphoma.

Activity of the BiTE blinatumomab. (A) Blinatumomab consists of two single-chain variable fragments, one of which binds to CD3 and the other binds to CD19, with a flexible linker between them. This BiTE protein can connect a T cell and (B) a CD19+ tumor cell or (C) a CD19+ B cell by simultaneously binding CD3 and CD19. When both single-chain variable fragments bind to their target antigens, T-cell activation is triggered, which leads to the release of cytotoxic granules, cytokines (eg, interferon γ, tumor necrosis factor α, interleukin-2), and T-cell proliferation. Lysis of the tumor cell or B cell involves membrane perforation followed by programmed cell death induced by granzymes. BiTEs trigger serial killing by activated T cells. (D) Approaches to limit adverse neurologic events caused by blinatumomab treatment include the blocking of activated T-cell migration into the CNS through pentosan polysulfate (PPS) treatment or the reduction of cytokine activity through the use of corticosteroids, such as dexamethasone (DEX). Which cells blinatumomab may recognize in the CNS (eg, tumor cells) is unknown, but the adverse effects resolve when treatment is discontinued.

Abbreviations: AE, adverse event; B-ALL, B-cell acute lymphoblastic leukemia; NHL, non-Hodgkin lymphoma.

Source: Smits NC, Sentman CL. Bispecific T-Cell Engagers (BiTEs) as Treatment of B-Cell Lymphoma. J Clin Oncol. *2016 Apr 1;34(10):1131-3. PMID: 26884583.*

activation through a number of other activating receptors that recognize soluble and cell-membrane ligands on tumors and infected cells. Also in contrast to CTLs, NK cells express Fc receptors and thus can mediate antibody-dependent cell-mediated cytotoxicity (ADCC). When activated, NK cells also produce IFN-γ. Although NK cells do not require activation for lytic activity, the stimulation of NK cells with IFNs and IL-2 markedly enhances their antitumor activity. In contrast to CTLs, which can kill multiple cells, evidence shows that NK cells must rearm themselves by exposure to IL-2 before they are effective against new targets.[4] Furthermore, for the most part, the NK response has no memory component.

B CELLS

Antibody-producing B cells are involved in adaptive immunity and serve as APCs. The BCR binds soluble antigens, which are then internalized by receptor-mediated endocytosis and processed into peptide fragments that are then displayed at the cell surface within class II MHC. T-helper cells specific for this structure (ie, with a complementary TCR) bind the B cell and secrete cytokines that stimulate the B cell to proliferate into cells with identical BCRs and, ultimately, to differentiate into plasma cells that secrete antibodies (ie, the soluble version of the BCR). In contrast to T cells, which recognize only processed peptide antigen, antibodies produced by B cells recognize the intact protein antigen in its native conformation. Antibodies also can recognize polysaccharides and nucleic acids. Antigen-binding specificity is encoded by three complementarity-determining regions on the fragment-antigen binding (Fab) region, whereas the monomorphic fraction-crystallizable (Fc) region of the antibody is responsible for binding to serum proteins (eg, complement) or to cells such as macrophages and NK cells that express Fc receptors that transmit signals leading to ADCC. Complement-mediated cytotoxicity (CMC) may develop in the case of complement-fixing Fc classes of IgG and multimeric antibodies such as IgM, and subsequent activation for the complement protein cascade. Central to CMC is the ability of the antibody to redistribute the target on the cell membrane into large glycolipoprotein microdomains known as lipid rafts. Antibodies also can directly mediate antitumor effects by interacting with cell-surface receptors that regulate cell growth (Fig 4-3). Although cellular immune responses seem to be central in the generation of effective antitumor immunity, a substantial body of data indicates that antibodies are also important. Furthermore, the antitumor effects of antibodies have been validated by the clinical efficacy of monoclonal antibodies specific for tumor-associated molecules.

DENDRITIC CELLS

DCs are a widely distributed, heterogeneous population of APCs that are derived from bone marrow progenitors and circulate in the blood as immature precursors before migration into peripheral tissues. Within different tissues, DCs differentiate and become active in the uptake and processing of antigens via MHC class I and II molecules, which require distinct intracellular processing pathways, termed the "antigen-processing machinery", generally using class I for endogenous antigens and class II for exogenous antigens, but with substantial overlap. DCs function at the intersection of the innate and adaptive immune responses. Upon stimulation provided by microbes (via TLRs), cytokines, and/or T-cell signals (eg, CD40 ligand), DCs undergo additional maturation and migrate to secondary lymphoid tissues, where they present antigen to T cells. The nature of the immune response elicited depends on a variety of factors, including the mode and duration of activation and the cytokine milieu.

Two distinct DC lineages have been described in humans: myeloid DCs (mDCs) express the receptor for granulocyte–macrophage colony–stimulating factor (GM-CSF) and other myeloid markers. mDCs reside in tissues and are the most efficient APCs, particularly with regard to the primary activation of naïve T cells. They stimulate tumor-reactive CTLs through an IL-12–dependent mechanism. Plasmacytoid dendritic cells lack myeloid cell markers and express the receptor for IL-3 (CD123). They reside in peripheral blood, and after encountering a virus, they secrete large amounts of IFN-α, a cytokine with immunomodulatory as well as antiviral properties. The role of plasmacytoid dendritic cells in antitumor immunity is under investigation.

MACROPHAGES

Macrophages, which derive from peripheral-blood monocytes, are widely dispersed throughout the body and mediate a variety of functions and play a central role in innate and adaptive immunity. Macrophages are specialized phagocytes that function through the enzymatic generation of reactive oxygen and nitrogen species and by proteolytic digestion. Phagocytosis is mediated through surface receptors for complement and other opsonins and through the uptake of particles into phagosomes that then fuse with cytoplasmic lysosomes. Macrophages express Fc receptors for antibodies and can mediate antibody-dependent cellular uptake and cytotoxicity. Similar to DCs, macrophages function at the intersection of the innate and adaptive immune responses, can process antigen via the antigen-processing machinery, and present peptides within MHC molecules to activate specific T- and B-cell effector mechanisms. Macrophages also are potent secretory cells. They are major producers of the proangiogenic vascular endothelial growth factor (VEGF). Distinct activation states of macrophages have been described: M1 macrophages produce high levels of inducible nitric oxide synthase, IL-12, and TNF, whereas M2 macrophages produce arginase, IL-10, TGF-β, and prostaglandin E_2. M1 macrophages are potent effector cells that kill tumors through nitric oxide and TNF, whereas M2 macrophages limit Th1 immune responses and promote angiogenesis, processes that promote tumor growth. Whereas M2 macrophages are associated with a decrease in survival for patients with cancer, M1 macrophages have been associated with an improved survival.[1,2]

MYELOID-DERIVED SUPPRESSOR CELLS

A number of investigations have identified immature myeloid cell populations, referred to as myeloid-derived suppressor cells (MDSCs), present in tumors and lymphoid organs which inhibit T-cell functions and play a role in tumor-associated immune suppression. They have been described in patients with many types of solid tumors.[3,5,6] Human MDSCs are still poorly defined but have been reported to lack the expression of markers of mature myeloid and lymphoid cells (ie, lineage negative) and HLA-DR. MDSCs do express the common myeloid marker CD33. The precise nature of this regulatory cell population and whether they are precursors of granulocytes, macrophages, or DCs seem to depend on the tumor and tumor-derived factors of the host. This highly plastic population suppresses T-cell functions through different molecular pathways, mostly involving arginase metabolism products, inducible nitric oxide synthase, reactive oxygen species, and/or production of soluble inhibitory factors such as TGF-β, IL-10, prostaglandin E_2, and nitric oxide.

KEY POINTS

- T cells recognize antigens presented to the T-cell antigen receptors as peptide fragments within MHC molecules. T-cell activation requires stimulation not only through the T-cell antigen receptor but also through immune costimulatory receptors.
- Interactions with coinhibitory receptors on T cells, referred to as "immune checkpoints," suppress unwanted and harmful self-directed immune activities.
- T-helper cells promote Th1-associated CTLs through the production of cytokines, such as IFN-γ and IL-2, and promote Th2-associated antibodies through production of cytokines, such as IL-4 and IL-5.
- CTLs kill tumors by apoptosis through granule exocytosis and Fas-mediated mechanisms.
- B cells produce antibodies that recognize antigens in their native conformation. Antibodies can react against tumors by complement-mediated and ADCC mechanisms.
- DCs are the most efficient APCs.
- Several lymphoid and myeloid cell populations suppress immune responses, including regulatory T cells and MDSCs.

IMMUNE SURVEILLANCE

Several lines of evidence support the existence of cancer immune surveillance—that the innate or adaptive immune system continually recognizes and removes malignant cells that arise throughout an individual's lifetime. Individuals with suppressed immune systems, such as organ transplant recipients or patients with primary or acquired immunodeficiency disorders, are at increased risk for the development of malignancy. The rare spontaneous regression of cancer and the responses to withdrawal of immunosuppression in some cases, as well as evidences of control of Kaposi sarcoma in patients treated with antiretroviral therapies in the context of HIV/AIDS, are additional evidence in favor of immune surveillance in cancer control. Brisk infiltration by subpopulations of lymphocytes, especially CD8 T cells, in tumor specimens is an independent positive prognostic factor for some cancers, such as melanoma and ovarian cancer.[1,7,8] Likewise, the natural occurrence of a humoral immune response to a tumor-associated antigen is associated with a favorable clinical outcome in cancers such as breast cancer.[9] Human T cells that accumulate within the mass of a tumor can be shown to proliferate, in some instances, in response to autologous tumor cells in vitro. Most importantly, pharmacologic modulation of the immune response with cytokines and with various types of antibodies has produced objective tumor responses in patients.

Effective surveillance requires that the tumor express determinants, capable of being recognized by the immune system (ie, tumor antigens) and that are associated with the tumor immunogenic potential. Numerous tumor-associated antigens, including the differentiation antigens carcinoembryonic antigen, tyrosinase, and prostate-specific antigen, as well as peptides that result from genes overexpressed in tumors (eg, *erbB2*), have been defined with antibodies and applied in diagnosis and in monitoring response to therapy. As outlined previously, antigens that are recognized by the T cells differ substantially from those defined by antibodies. To function as a T-cell rejection antigen, the tumor must express the associated peptide determinant in the context of MHC molecules. Failure of antigen processing or binding to MHC molecules—or inadequate expression of costimulatory or adhesion molecules—may lead to poor immunogenicity. Several targets that can potentially serve as tumor rejection antigens have been identified by a variety of techniques (Table 4-1). Many of these have been targeted in vaccine approaches. Oncofetal, cancer–testis (a group of oncofetal antigens), and differentiation or lineage-specific antigens are expressed by normal adult tissues and, therefore, are not tumor specific. In contrast to those that are overexpressed and not mutated (eg, *erbB2*), oncogenes or tumor suppressors that are mutated can be considered tumor specific and even patient specific (eg, *p53*).

Table 4-1 Potential Immunotherapy Select Shared Targets

Antitumor Antigen	Example	Associated Malignancies
Oncofetal	Carcinoembryocenic antigen	Colorectal, breast, NSCLC
	β-Human chorionic gonadotropin	Colorectal, pancreatic, NSCLC
Cancer-testis	Melanoma antigen	Melanoma, lung, ovary, bladder, liver
	NY-ESO	Melanoma, lung, bladder, liver
Oncogene/tumor suppressor	*HER2*	Breast, gastric
	p53	Multiple
	RAS	Multiple
	WT1	Multiple
	BCR-ABL	Chronic myeloid leukemia
Differentiation/lineage-specific	Prostate-specific antigen	Prostate
	Prostatic acid phosphatase	Prostate
	gp100	Melanoma
	Tyrosinase	Melanoma
	MART/Melan-A	Melanoma
	Ig (idiotype)	B-cell malignancies
Aberrantly glycosylated molecules	MUC1 (mucin)	Pancreatic, breast
	GM2 (ganglioside)	Melanoma, neuroblastoma
	GD2 (ganglioside)	Melanoma, neuroblastoma
Viral	E6, E7 (human papillomavirus)	Cervical cancer
	EBNA (Epstein-Barr virus)	Burkitt lymphoma, nasopharyngeal carcinoma

Abbreviation: NSCLC, non-small-cell lung cancer.

The tumor immunogenicity and response to treatment with monoclonal antibodies targeting immune checkpoints can be also influenced by peptides and antigenic neoepitopes generated from aberrant gene products and increased number of somatic missense mutations, also defined as tumor mutational load.[10-12] As a demonstration of this principle, significant antitumor effect from PD-1 blockade has been demonstrated in patients with mismatch repair (MMR) deficiency-related tumors, marked by genomic instability and a high mutational burden.[13]

Other factors that drive the capacity of mounting an adequate immune response include the expression of proinflammatory chemokines (type I IFNs, CCL2, CCL3, CCL4, CCL5, CXCL9, and CXCL10) and mutations involving pathways that are part of the immune activation cascade, including disruptive mutations or, conversely, amplifications of JAK1 or JAK2 (implicated in IFN-dependent signaling), phosphatase and tensin homolog loss, and activation of the WNT/β-catenin pathway.

The successful detection and eradication of tumor cells mediated by these components of the immune system, also termed elimination phase, may not occur and may be succeeded by two distinct phases, on the basis of the cancer immunoediting concept: the equilibrium phase, in which residual tumor cells are maintained in functional state of dormancy, yet with its overgrowth limited; and the escape phase, in which tumor growth occurs though the avoidance of recognition and destruction by immune cells encircling distinct mechanisms, as discussed in the following section.

KEY POINTS

- Several lines of evidence, including clinical responses with pharmacologic modulation of the immune response, support the role of the immune response in cancer regulation, both in immune surveillance against nascent malignancy and in therapy for established malignancy.
- Recognition of tumor cells by the immune system can be influenced by a variety of factors, including the tumor's intrinsic antigenic potential (eg, mutational burden and neoantigen signature, strength of immunogenicity of tumor antigens), preexisting host immune condition and products of genomic aberrations affecting pathways driving the immune response.
- This continuous interaction between tumor cells and immune cells, not always successful in terms of tumor control (elimination), is characterized as immune surveillance and immunoediting.

IMMUNE ESCAPE

Animal models have demonstrated the existence of immunoediting, in which activation of immune mechanisms initially controls the tumor, but over time leads to the selection of tumor cells that escape the immune pressure, grow progressively and then contribute to the establishment of an immunosuppressive tumor microenvironment.[14] Because most of the tumor antigens identified are nonmutated self-antigens, a high degree of immunologic tolerance exists, limiting the generation of immune effectors. As noted, Treg cells engaged in the maintenance of self-tolerance may impede tumor-reactive T cells. Tumors are heterogeneous, and the repertoire of tumor antigens on the cells of one tumor may be variable, even within the same patient. Downregulation of MHC class I molecules and other components of the antigen-presentation process can occur. Membrane-associated factors expressed by tumor cells that directly inhibit T-cell function have also been identified, and tumors can exploit inhibitory immune checkpoints as evasion mechanisms. Tumor expression of PD-L1 and PD-L2, ligands of the coinhibitory receptor PD-1, is considered a significant mediator of immunosuppression within the tumor microenvironment. However, a large part of the role played by PD-1–expressing T cells may be to secrete IFN-γ upon initial T-cell activation, and this, in turn, upregulates PD-L1 on tumor cells, conferring on the tumor and T-cell interaction a dependence on this ligand-receptor association that can be therapeutically targeted by antibodies. The expression of Fas ligand by some tumor cells may help maintain a state of immune privilege by inducing apoptosis of Fas-sensitive T and NK effector cells—the "Fas counterattack." There also is evidence that a tumor's expression of antiapoptotic molecules, which prevent perforin or death-receptor–dependent cytotoxicity, can result in escape despite expression of the target antigen. In addition, tumor-associated factors, such as underglycosylated tumor-associated mucins, have been shown to reduce binding of antibodies to tumor cell surfaces.

Tumor cells and the surrounding stroma may release a number of suppressive cytokines and other soluble factors, such as prostaglandin E_2, that are not conducive to antitumor immunity. Cancer-associated factors inhibit the production and stimulatory capacity of DCs.[15] The T-helper cell response also may be skewed toward a Th2 phenotype, which inhibits Th1 response and the cellular immunity that is critical in mediating tumor rejection.[16] TGF-β is produced not only by host cells but also by tumors and can inhibit the differentiation of T cells into CTLs and T-helper cells and promote the generation of Treg cells. By producing cytokines (eg, GM-CSF), cancers can promote the infiltration of M2-polarized macrophages and MDSCs that can inhibit T-cell function. Downregulation of the CD3 zeta-chain of the TCR complex and impairment of function have been shown for T cells isolated from patients with cancer.[17]

KEY POINTS

- The ability of cancer to evade the immune response is aided by the fact that most tumor antigens are self-proteins, which impede the generation of immunity via tolerogenic mechanisms, such as the elaboration of Treg cells and the central elimination of autoreactive T cells by thymic selection.

- Although immune checkpoints are necessary to prevent unchecked autoimmunity, tumors can co-opt these mechanisms to escape immune responses.
- Cancer evasion of the immune system results not only from immunosuppressive factors secreted by or expressed on the tumor but also from the ability of the tumor to modulate antigen expression and to be endowed with or later evolve mechanisms of resistance to immune effectors.
- The recognition of evasion mechanisms involved in tumor immune escape can be exploited therapeutically.

IMMUNE SUBVERSION

Although effective antitumor immunity has been demonstrated in experimental systems and in patients, immune responses are abundantly present in tumor-bearing hosts that provide no apparent protection to the host and may contribute to the oncogenic process. Not only can tumors escape immune response, they can also exploit or subvert the immune response to promote their growth, invasion, and metastasis. Local tumor growth within the stroma is promoted by angiogenesis. Immune cells, including macrophages, T cells, and neutrophils, fully participate in tumor angiogenesis by secreting cytokines, such as IL-1, IL-8, and VEGF, that directly affect endothelial cell functions, including proliferation, migration, and activation. In addition to angiogenic factors, macrophages also produce matrix metalloproteinases that degrade the extracellular matrix involved in tumor cell invasion and metastasis. Accumulating data show that many tumor cells express chemokine receptors and respond to chemokine gradients in vitro. Experiments in vivo also have indicated that certain chemokines can serve as tissue-specific attractant molecules for tumor cells, promoting tumor cell migration or metastasis to particular sites. Several cytokines produced by immune cells transmit cell-growth signals in tumor cells and directly promote tumor cell growth. TGF-β, TNF-α, and IL-6 can promote the growth of some tumors while suppressing the growth of others.

KEY POINTS

- The interaction between tumor cells and immune cells is not unidirectional.
- Tumors can subvert the immune response by stimulating the production of immune cell factors that promote angiogenesis, invasion, and metastases.
- Immune cell cytokines also may function as tumor growth factors.

BIOLOGIC AGENTS

Many cytokines, vaccines, modified biologic vectors, monoclonal antibodies, and cell therapies for cancer have been developed and are applied clinically, acting through either immune or nonimmune effector pathways.

The immune response can be activated to mediate tumor destruction through one of several mechanisms. These include increasing immune effectors and modifying tumor cells to increase their susceptibility to immune effectors. A highly effective strategy is to block one or more of the negative immunoregulatory host checkpoints involved in evasion mechanisms. The elimination of cells or cytokines that promote immune escape may permit a more effective and persistent antitumor immune response. This approach cannot be effective without a simultaneous positive immune response to the tumor. This may occur naturally, as is observed among select patients (eg, patients with malignant melanoma with regressed primary lesions). Alternatively, it may have to be induced (eg, by a cancer vaccine).

There are two general immunotherapy approaches. Active immunotherapy attempts to stimulate (in vivo) an intrinsic immune response to the tumor, either nonspecifically with cytokines or specifically with antibody or vaccine approaches. Passive or adoptive immunotherapy involves the preparation of antibodies and cells outside the body (ex vivo), which are then administered to patients.

Biologic agents can also be used to mediate antitumor effects by nonimmune effector mechanisms. Some biologics are administered not to promote antitumor responses but rather to ameliorate the adverse effects (AEs) of therapy and progressing cancer. These include hematopoietic growth factors and immunomodulators used in the context of immune-related adverse events (eg, infliximab, toxicilizumab, vedolizumab) attributed to different forms of immunotherapy. They also include cytokines that are produced by nonimmune cells and that do not directly activate antitumor immune effector mechanisms. For example, human recombinant erythropoietin is used to manage anemia.[18] The human recombinant keratinocyte growth factor palifermin is used to decrease the risk of severe mucositis associated with very high-dose chemoradiotherapy such as in hematopoietic stem-cell transplantation. Denosumab is a fully human monoclonal antibody that targets receptor activator of nuclear factor κ B ligand, a protein that acts as the primary signal to promote bone removal by osteoclasts. It is used for the prevention of skeletal-related events for patients with bone metastases and myeloma as well as in the management of giant-cell tumor of bone.[19,20] Infliximab is an anti–TNF-α monoclonal antibody used to ameliorate certain immune-related toxicities associated with checkpoint inhibitors such as colitis.[21] The anti–IL-6 receptor monoclonal antibody, tocilizumab at times is administered to reverse the cytokine release syndrome associated with anti-CD19 CAR-T cells.[22]

The pharmacokinetics of biologic agents are quite variable. Elimination half-lives for most cytokines are measured in minutes to hours, and for most antibodies, in days to weeks. Infused cells can persist for months. Unlike chemotherapy, which acts directly on the tumor, cancer immunotherapies exert their effects on the immune system and demonstrate kinetics of response that involve generating an antitumor immune response. The approach to assessing and managing response and toxicity can also differ. Immunotherapy may induce patterns of antitumor response not adequately assessed by Response Evaluation Criteria in Solid Tumors (RECIST) or WHO criteria. Patients may have atypical patterns of response, which include an initial apparent worsening of the disease attributable to infiltration of the tumor microenvironment by immune cells (pseudoprogression) or delayed responses after initial tumor progression. Responses can take appreciably longer to become apparent as compared with those for cytotoxic or targeted therapy. Continued disease regression is frequently observed well after immunotherapy is suspended. Furthermore, some patients who do not meet criteria for objective response can have prolonged periods of stable disease that are clinically relevant. New immune-related response criteria designed to more comprehensively capture all response patterns are under investigation.[23] Because the goal of many approaches is to circumvent immune tolerance by the removal of negative immunoregulatory mechanisms, evidence of autoimmunity as an AE of treatment is predicted and has been associated with clinical benefit in some, but not all, studies.

KEY POINTS

- Biologic agents may be used to elicit an antitumor effect through either immune mechanisms or nonimmune pathways or to ameliorate the AEs of anticancer therapies.
- Immunotherapies may stimulate components of an existing tumor-immune interaction ("active immunotherapies"; eg, cytokines, antibodies targeting immune checkpoints) or harness cells or antibodies engineered ex vivo ("passive immunotherapies"; eg, adoptive cell therapies).
- Some biologic agents are administered to ameliorate the AEs of therapy and progressing cancer.

CYTOKINES

Cytokines are a diverse group of small proteins released by immune and nonimmune cells distributed throughout the body. Cytokines play integral roles in innate and adaptive immunity as effector and regulatory molecules. They also play an integral role in a variety of other biologic processes. Cytokines, which are active physiologically at low concentrations, may act locally (autocrine or paracrine) or at a distance (endocrine). They are characterized by pleiotropy (one cytokine, multiple effects), redundancy (multiple cytokines, one effect), and synergy (the sum of the response together is greater than the sum of the individual responses). The administration of a cytokine will initiate a cascade of cytokine production and both stimulatory (amplification) and inhibitory or antagonistic effects. Cytokines act on their target cells by binding specific membrane receptors that contain cytokine-specific and signal-transducing subunits. They can be divided into groups on the basis of function (eg, chemokines are cytokines that are chemoattractants to immune cells) or on cellular source (eg, lymphokines are cytokines produced by lymphocytes). Study of the structure and function of cytokine receptors, however, has led to improved understanding of cytokine action and a more useful classification (Table 4-2). Cytokines can lead to tumor destruction by one of two general mechanisms. They can function indirectly and enhance the activity of antitumor cellular or humoral immune effector mechanisms, or they can interact directly with tumor cells; cytokines, such as TNF-α, IFN-α, IFN-γ, IL-4, and IL-6, have been shown to initiate tumor cell apoptosis or cell cycle arrest. Recombinant cytokines in clinical use are shown in Table 4-3.

CYTOKINES: IFNS AND IL-2

IFNs-α and β (referred to as type I IFNs), produced by many cell types, and IFN-γ (referred to as type II IFN), synthesized primarily by lymphocytes, mediate a wide variety of biological effects, including inducing the transcription of a diverse array of genes, and affect nearly all phases of the innate and adaptive immune responses. IFNs, type I in particular, inhibit virus replication in infected cells. All enhance class I MHC and thereby promote CD8+ CTL responses; IFN-γ is capable of inducing class II MHC. IFNs enhance NK-cell cytotoxicity, upregulate Fc receptors, and promote ADCC mechanisms. They regulate the balance between Th1 and Th2 cells, promoting, for the most part, Th1 responses. In addition to affecting humoral immunity by modulating T-helper cells, IFNs can have direct effects on B cells, including regulating proliferation and antibody production. IFN-γ also plays an important role in macrophage activation.[24] IFNs can directly inhibit the growth of tumor (and normal) cells and produce antiangiogenic effects.

Among the > 20 different, known IFNs, only IFN-α2 has been extensively and clinically evaluated for cancer. Two recombinant IFN-α2 preparations have been approved: IFN-α 2a and IFN-α 2b. The pleiotropic effects of IFNs have led to their evaluation in almost all malignancies, alone or in combinations.[25] However, for the most part, the use of IFN in cancers has been supplanted by more active and potentially less toxic drugs. Toxicities, which are highly diverse, include flu-like symptoms, such as fever, chills, and myalgia, neuropsychiatric AEs (eg, fatigue, depression), liver dysfunction, and myelotoxicity. Novel applications of IFNs are being tested in solid tumors and hematologic malignancies, and interest is growing in the possibility of combining IFN with antibodies against immune checkpoints.

IL-2 is a T-cell growth factor. Antigen binding to the TCR stimulates the secretion of IL-2 and the expression of high-affinity IL-2 receptors (CD25). The interaction between IL-2 and the IL-2 receptor stimulates the growth, differentiation, and survival of antigen-selected T cells. IL-2 is a major activator of CTL and NK cytotoxicity, and is necessary for the development of memory T cells. It also indirectly regulates B cells, hematopoiesis, and the generation and maintenance of Treg cells, which, as noted, has been implicated in abrogating antitumor activity.[26] Furthermore, IL-2 is involved in activation-induced

Table 4-2 **Examples of Cytokines Involved in Immune Regulation**

Group	Function	Receptor	Examples
Hematopoietic	Leukocyte proliferation, differentiation, and activation	Multimers with Trp-Ser-X-Trp-Ser motif	IL-2, IL-3, IL-4, IL-6, IL-7, IL-11, IL-12, G-CSF, GM-CSF
		Signals primarily by receptor-associated JAK and STAT	
Interferon	Inhibit virus replication	Two polypeptide chains with tandem fibronectin domains	IFN-α, IFN-β, IFN-γ
		Signals primarily by JAK-STAT	
TNF	Inflammation and other biological processes	Four extracellular domains activate caspases that mediate apoptosis ("death receptor") or pathways that promote cell survival and inflammation	TNF-α
Chemokine	Attract leukocytes to inflammatory sites	Seven transmembrane helices interact with G proteins	MIP-1α, IL-8
IL-1	Inflammation and hematopoiesis	Extracellular Ig domain and cytosolic toll-IL-1 receptor domain	IL-1 β
		Toll-IL-1 receptor activates signaling pathways	
Growth factor	Growth and differentiation of nonimmune cells	Multimeric complexes with intrinsic tyrosine or serine/threonine kinase activities	TGF-β, VEGF

Abbreviations: G-CSF, granulocyte colony-stimulating factor; GM-CSF, granulocyte-macrophage colony-stimulating factor; IFN, interferon; IL, interleukin; JAK, Janus tyrosine kinase; MIP, macrophage inflammatory protein; STAT, signal transducer and activator of transcription; TGF, transforming growth factor; TNF, tumor necrosis factor; VEGF, vascular endothelial growth factor.

Table 4-3 **Recombinant Cytokines in Clinical Use for Cancer**

Cytokine	Effects	Cancer Indications
Interferon-α; PEG-interferon α	Immune (upregulate MHC, activate NK cells)	Melanoma, hairy cell leukemia, chronic myeloid leukemia, follicular lymphoma, Kaposi sarcoma, renal cell carcinoma
	Antiangiogenesis	
	Direct antiproliferative	
Aldesleukin (IL-2)	Activate cytotoxic T lymphocytes and NK cells	Melanoma, renal cell carcinoma
Sargramostim (GM-CSF)	Stimulates the development and function of neutrophils, monocyte-macrophages, and dendritic cells	Shortens chemotherapy-induced neutropenia in elderly patients with acute myeloid leukemia, promotes myeloid reconstitution after HSCT, mobilizes stem cells
Filgrastim (G-CSF) Pegfilgrastim (G-CSF)	Stimulates the development and function of neutrophils	Shortens chemotherapy-induced neutropenia, promotes myeloid reconstitution after HSCT, mobilizes stem cells; used as a vaccine adjuvant

Abbreviations: G-CSF, granulocyte colony-stimulating factor; GM-CSF, granulocyte-macrophage colony-stimulating factor; HSCT, hematopoietic stem-cell transplantation; MHC, major histocompatibility complex; NK, natural killer; PEG, pegylated.

cell death, a process that leads to the elimination of self-reactive T cells.

Recombinant IL-2, aldesleukin, has been applied in a variety of doses, routes, and schedules.[27-29] Aldesleukin was approved as treatment of patients with metastatic renal cell cancer and melanoma on the basis of experience with the high-dose regimens. Objective responses occur in a minority of patients, approximately 25%, at a cost of significant toxicity. However, in approximately 7% of all treated patients, the response is complete and often prolonged, including in a number of patients with a partial response and even some with stable disease.[30,31] High-dose IL-2 is also used to support the persistence and activity of tumor-infiltrating lymphocyte (TIL) therapies for melanoma and other malignancies. Administration of aldesleukin requires particular expertise, and patients must be treated in an inpatient monitored or intensive care unit setting, because the high dose used is comparable to inducing a controlled state of septic shock with fever, hypotension, decreased renal function, hyperbilirubinemia, rash, and marked malaise.

KEY POINTS

- Cytokines can function indirectly and can enhance the activity of antitumor immune effectors.
- Cytokines, such as the IFNs, also have been shown to directly inhibit tumor cell growth.
- IL-2 was approved and is occasionally used for metastatic renal cell cancer and melanoma on the basis of the experience with a high-dose, intravenous bolus of the agent, a regimen limited by toxicity and low but potentially durable antitumor activity.

ANTIBODIES

Adoptive therapy with monoclonal antibodies, which can mediate antitumor activities by a variety of mechanisms (Fig 4-3), has been one of the major advances in cancer immunotherapy. Most of the approved antibodies in oncology are of the human IgG1 subclass—the subclass that is the most effective at engaging Fc receptors on NK cells and macrophages and mediating CMC and ADCC. Antibody constructs designed not to mediate CMC and ADCC have also been developed, as have antibody-based constructs that target more than one epitope. The monoclonal antibodies used in initial clinical trials were mouse derived and usually generated a vigorous human–anti-mouse antibody (HAMA) response; as such, these antibodies are no longer used. Therapeutic monoclonal antibodies come in the following forms:

- chimeric (ie, mouse variable chain fused to a human constant chain, termed "ximab," and are 65% to 90% human);
- humanized (ie, mouse hypervariable or complementarity-determining regions grafted to human Ig, termed "zumab," and are 95% human);
- fully human (termed "umab").

Most antibodies naturally have long serum half-lives. Limitations, however, have been identified. Triggering of tumor antigen-specific cellular immunity by monoclonal antibody, in conjunction with immune escape mechanisms used by tumor cells, may contribute to differential clinical responses to monoclonal antibody–based immunotherapy.[32] The antigenic heterogeneity of most tumors presents challenges, as does the small fraction of injected antibodies that actually bind to tumors due to the occasional inability of antibodies to penetrate large tumor masses. Furthermore, binding of antibodies to circulating antigens also can limit delivery to the tumor. Although now rare, immune responses to artificial humanized antibodies can still be problematic, causing hypersensitivity reactions or neutralization of the antibody. Whether they target tumor cell membrane determinants, factors involved in tumor progression such as angiogenesis, or immune checkpoints, monoclonal antibodies are mainstays of cancer therapy (Table 4-4).

IMMUNE CHECKPOINT ANTIBODIES

Monoclonal antibodies against immune checkpoints resulted in an initial paradigm shift in the management of melanoma and non–small-cell lung cancer (NSCLC); more recently, approvals have expanded the clinical application of immune checkpoint antibodies to the treatment of patients with squamous cell carcinoma of the head and neck, clear-cell renal cell carcinoma, Hodgkin lymphoma, urothelial carcinoma, small-cell lung cancer, hepatocellular carcinoma, Merkel cell carcinoma, gastric cancer, MMR-deficient advanced colorectal cancer, all microsatellite-high (MSI-H)/MMR-deficient tumors, and cutaneous squamous cell carcinoma, with additional approvals likely.

Increased activation of the immune system and significant (and occasionally, sustained) antitumor effect has been demonstrated in randomized trials investigating the efficacy of monoclonal antibodies targeting CTLA-4, PD-1, and PD-L1. Conceptually, the mechanisms of these immune checkpoints are not redundant: CTLA-4, a CD28 homolog, is induced by exocytosis upon initial activation of naïve T cells, primarily in nodal structures. The PD-1/PD-L1 pathway, however, is implicated in tolerance and evasion mechanisms that involve previously activated T cells with cytotoxic capabilities, acting predominantly, but not exclusively, in the effector phase within the tumor microenvironment in peripheral tissues. Nevertheless, the complete spectrum of activity of these immune checkpoint inhibitors is not understood. As an example, the efficacy of CTLA-4 blockade has been associated with the elimination—via ADCC mediated by the anti-CTLA4 antibody—of Tregs with immunosuppressive effects.[32]

Immune-Related Adverse Events

Despite the unequivocal efficacy of immune checkpoint inhibitors, toxicity can be problematic and results from activation of the immune cells against "self" antigens. These immune-related adverse events (irAEs) include dermatitis, pruritus, colitis or diarrhea, hepatitis, pneumonitis, and endocrinopathies (eg, thyroiditis, hypophysitis, adrenalitis), among others. Virtually any organ or tissue can be targeted by activated immune cells, and cases of Guillain-Barré syndrome, nephritis, pure red-cell aplasia, and myocarditis have been reported. Because of the potentially serious and life-threatening implications of irAEs, including colonic perforation, Stevens-Johnson syndrome, and myocarditis, active surveillance and continuous monitoring are advised, and risk evaluation, mitigation strategies, and algorithms for the management of adverse AEs have been developed.[21,33] In general, toxicities, particularly colitis or diarrhea, fatigue, rash, and hepatitis, are more pronounced with ipilimumab in comparison with monoclonal antibodies targeting PD-1/PD-L1 when used as single agents. Doses are generally withheld for any moderate irAE or for symptomatic endocrinopathy. The management of symptomatic or severe irAEs usually involves the use of systemic corticosteroids (eg, prednisone, methylprednisolone, or equivalent) and, for patients with irAEs that fail to resolve with steroids, additional immunosuppressive agents (eg, infliximab [an anti-TNF monoclonal antibody], mycophenolate mofetil [an inhibitor of purine synthesis]). Permanent treatment discontinuation must be considered in situations of a persistent grade 2 or grade 3 irAE and is usually recommended in the setting of a grade 4 irAE. It is important to highlight that the appropriate management of immune-related AEs with immunosuppressive agents, such as corticosteroids, does not seem to impair an established antitumor response, but steroid therapy before beginning immune checkpoint blockade is not advised.[21] Guidelines encompassing a thorough review of irAEs and detailed management recommendations have been published and are useful tools for the mitigation of risks associated with these agents.[34]

Response Assessment

The unique mechanisms of action of immune checkpoint inhibitors make the assessment of response by conventional criteria difficult, and aberrant patterns of response have been documented. Patients receiving either anti–CTLA-4 or anti-PD-1/PD-L1 agents may experience delayed responses or durable stable disease even after apparent disease progression. Although the immune-related response criteria have been proposed, the applicability and, more importantly, interpretation in clinical practice remain challenging.[23] As a general principle, although infrequent, the possibilities of early or delayed pseudoprogression (ie, initial enlargement of target lesions and/or appearance of new lesions, followed by subsequent response) must be considered, and treatment beyond the first documented radiographic progression may be acceptable in select situations, particularly in the setting of clinical stability or symptomatic improvement.

Anti-CTLA-4 Agents: Ipilimumab

Ipilimumab, the first immune checkpoint inhibitor approved by the FDA, blocks the effects of the negative T-cell regulator CTLA-4 (Fig 4-2), which, in turn, augments T-cell responses to tumor cells. It was the first drug shown to improve overall survival (OS) in metastatic melanoma in randomized clinical trials in both pretreated (as monotherapy) and treatment-naïve (in combination with dacarbazine) patients.[33,35] Objective response rates have been low, on the order of 10% to 15%; nevertheless, long-lasting responses have been demonstrated. In a combined analysis of > 1,800 patients treated with ipilimumab in phase 2 and phase 3 trials, long-term OS rates of approximately 20% were demonstrated, with an apparent plateau in the survival curves beyond 3 years.[36] Ipilimumab is FDA approved for the treatment of melanoma, not only in the metastatic setting but also in the adjuvant setting, where it has been shown to improve relapse-free and OS.[37] Subsequent demonstration of superiority of nivolumab over ipilimumab in the adjuvant setting in a large phase III trial has rendered ipilimumab superfluous in this situation, however.[38]

Ipilimumab is administered intravenously (IV) over 90 minutes every 3 weeks for four doses in the metastatic setting. Nevertheless, the optimal dose recommended for patients with advanced disease remains debatable, in view of a randomized trial that demonstrated an improvement in OS with a higher dose (10 mg/kg) in comparison with the standard, FDA-approved dose (3 mg/kg).[39] The higher dose was accompanied by an increase in treatment-related adverse events, including grade 3 to 5 adverse events (34.3% *v* 18.5%), and its acceptability for treating metastatic disease remains uncertain.

The combination of ipilimumab and nivolumab is approved to treat patients with melanoma, MMR-deficient colorectal cancer, and advanced renal cell carcinoma, and is discussed in more detail in the next section.[40-42]

Anti-PD-1 and Anti-PD-L1 Agents

Distinct monoclonal antibodies targeting PD-1 or PD-L1 have been approved for clinical use, either for patients with advanced disease or, more recently, in the adjuvant setting in specific situations. A comprehensive list of indications is provided in Table 4-4, and it is anticipated that additional approvals will be forthcoming for several cancers.

Pembrolizumab

Pembrolizumab is an IgG4 κ isotype monoclonal antibody against PD-1 that blocks this major immune checkpoint. Pembrolizumab is approved for the treatment of distinct solid tumors and hematologic malignancies (Table 4-4).[7,9,20,23-25,43-52]

The half-life of pembrolizumab is approximately 26 days. The most common toxicities are fatigue, pruritus, rash, diarrhea, and arthralgia. Approximately 10% to 25% of patients experienced grade 3 or 4 toxicity, with significant variability among different indications and trials. Also, immune-related adverse events leading to death have been reported.

Nivolumab

Nivolumab is a fully human IgG4 PD-1 immune checkpoint–inhibitor antibody that selectively blocks the interaction of the PD-1 receptor with its two known programmed death ligands, PD-L1 and PD-L2. Nivolumab is approved for clinical use either as single agent or in combination with ipilimumab (Table 4-4).[2,3,6,53-63]

Nivolumab is administered until disease progression or unacceptable toxicity occurs. Nivolumab's half-life is approximately 27 days. The spectrum of toxicity of nivolumab is comparable to that of pembrolizumab. Again, irAEs are less frequent than with ipilimumab when nivolumab is used as monotherapy; the most serious of these include pneumonitis,

Table 4-4 Unconjugated Monoclonal Antibodies in Clinical Use for Cancer

Antibody	Type	Target	Indication
Immune checkpoint			
Ipilimumab	Human	CTLA-4	Single agent: melanoma. In combination with nivolumab: melanoma, renal cell carcinoma, MMR-deficient colorectal cancer
Cemiplimab	Human	PD-1	Cutaneous squamous cell carcinoma
Pembrolizumab	Human	PD-1	Single agent: melanoma, NSCLC, squamous cell carcinoma of the head and neck, Hodgkin lymphoma, urothelial carcinoma, MMR-deficient solid tumors, gastric/gastroesophageal junction cancer, cervical cancer, mediastinal large C-cell lymphoma, hepatocellular carcinoma, Merkel cell carcinoma, small-cell lung cancer, squamous cell carcinoma of the esophagus
			In combination with carboplatin and pemetrexed or taxanes: NSCLC
			In combination with axitinib: renal cell carcinoma
			In combination with lenvatinib: endometrial carcinoma
Nivolumab	Human	PD-1	Single agent: melanoma, NSCLC, small-cell lung cancer, renal cell carcinoma, Hodgkin lymphoma, squamous cell carcinoma of the head and neck, urothelial carcinoma, MMR-deficient advanced colorectal cancer, hepatocellular carcinoma, small-cell lung cancer
			In combination with ipilimumab: melanoma, renal cell carcinoma, MMR-deficient colorectal cancer
Atezolizumab	Humanized	PD-L1	Single agent: urothelial carcinoma, NSCLC
			In combination with bevacizumab, paclitaxel and carboplatin: NSCLC
			In combination with nab-paclitaxel: triple-negative breast cancer
			In combination with carboplatin and etoposide: small-cell lung cancer
Avelumab	Human	PD-L1	Single agent: Merkel cell carcinoma, urothelial carcinoma
			In combination with axitinib: renal cell carcinoma
Durvalumab	Human	PD-L1	Urothelial carcinoma, NSCLC
Antitumor antibodies			
Rituximab	Chimeric	Binds CD20	Follicular lymphoma, diffuse large B-cell lymphoma, CLL
		CMC/ADCC	
		Direct antiproliferative	CLL
Ofatumumab	Human	Binds CD20	
		CMC/ADCC	CLL, follicular lymphoma
		Direct antiproliferative	
Obinutuzumab	Humanized	Binds CD20	
		Mediates antibody-dependent cellular mechanisms	CLL, follicular lymphoma
		Direct antiproliferative	
Alemtuzumab	Humanized	Binds CD52	
		CMC/ADCC	
Daratumumab	Human	Binds CD38	Multiple myeloma
		CMC/ADCC	
Elotuzumab	Humanized	Targets SLAMF7	Multiple myeloma
		Immunostimulatory effect	

Table 4-4 **continued**			
Antibody	**Type**	**Target**	**Indication**
Antiepidermal growth factor family			
Trastuzumab	Humanized	Binds HER2 CMC/ADCC Direct antiproliferative Antiangiogenesis	Breast cancer, gastroesophageal cancer, gastric cancer
Pertuzumab	Humanized	Binds HER2 and blocks ligand-dependent heterodimerization of HER2 with other HER family members, including EGFR, HER3, and HER4 Direct antiproliferative effects CMC/ADCC Antiangiogenesis	Breast cancer (in combination with trastuzumab and chemotherapy)
Cetuximab	Chimeric	Binds EGFR CMC/ADCC Direct antiproliferative Antiangiogenesis	Colorectal cancer, head and neck cancer
Panitumumab	Human	Binds EGFR CMC/ADCC Direct antiproliferative Antiangiogenesis	Colorectal cancer
Necitumumab	Human	Binds EGFR Direct antiproliferative Antiangiogenesis Direct antiproliferative	Squamous NSCLC
Angiogenic factor			
Bevacizumab	Humanized	Binds VEGF Antiangiogenesis	Colorectal cancer, nonsquamous NSCLC, renal cell carcinoma, glioblastoma, ovarian cancer, cervical cancer
Ramucirumab	Human	Binds VEGF receptor 2 Antiangiogenesis	Gastric or gastroesophageal junction adenocarcinoma, colorectal cancer, NSCLC

Abbreviations: ADCC, antibody-dependent cellular cytotoxicity; CLL, chronic lymphocytic leukemia; CMC, complement-mediated cytotoxicity; CTLA-4, cytotoxic T-lymphocyte antigen 4; EGFR, epidermal growth factor receptor; MMR, mismatch repair; NSCLC, non-small-cell lung cancer; PD-1, programmed death 1; PDGFR, platelet-derived growth factor; PDL-1, programmed death ligand 1; VEGF, vascular endothelial growth factor.

colitis, hepatitis, nephritis and renal dysfunction, and thyroid dysfunction.

Atezolizumab

Atezolizumab is a humanized monoclonal antibody that blocks the PD-L1 protein in the microenvironment, disrupting the PD-1–PD-L1 checkpoint pathway. Atezolizumab is currently approved for the treatment of patients either as single agent or in combination with bevacizumab or carboplatin and etoposide (Table 4-4).[64] The toxicities associated with atezolizumab are largely overlapping with those attributed to anti–PD-1 agents.

Avelumab

Avelumab is a fully human, anti–PD-L1 IgG1 antibody. In 2017, avelumab was granted accelerated approval by the FDA and became the first systemic therapy approved for the treatment of patients with advanced Merkel cell carcinoma.[65] Avelumab has also been approved for the treatment of patients with advanced urothelial carcinoma whose disease progressed while receiving a platinum-based therapy.[66] Patients receiving avelumab should be premedicated with acetaminophen and an antihistamine for the first four infusions and subsequently, as needed, because of the risk of infusion-related reactions, which can manifest in up to 25% of the patients. This is the only immune checkpoint inhibitor with a recommendation for premedication.

Durvalumab

The fully human, anti–PD-L1 human monoclonal antibody durvalumab received accelerated FDA approval for the treatment of patients with chemotherapy-refractory advanced urothelial carcinoma.[67] Durvalumab is also approved for the treatment of advanced NSCLC after definitive treatment with chemoradiation.[68]

Cemiplimab

Cemiplimab is a fully human anti–PD-1 antibody approved for the treatment of patients with metastatic cutaneous squamous cell carcinoma or locally advanced cutaneous squamous cell carcinoma who are not candidates for curative surgery or radiation therapy.[69]

Combinations of Immune Checkpoint Inhibitors

The combination of ipilimumab and nivolumab is approved for clinical use in patients with advanced melanoma, MMR protein-deficient colorectal cancer, and advanced renal cell carcinoma.[39,40,42] This combination also exhibits significant activity in the treatment of melanoma metastatic to the brain.[42,70] In general, however, this combination is associated with a significant increase in the incidence of immune-mediated adverse events compared with either agent alone, requiring experience and close communication among the treating clinician, the patient, and other members of the health care team. Identification of predictors that will allow patients to be selected for single or combined therapy is awaited, and clinical trials are ongoing for immunomodulators that will enhance antitumor activity with less immune-related toxicity. The same combination with different doses and intervals of therapy is being investigated in patients with NSCLC, breast cancer, head and neck carcinoma, and other solid tumors and hematologic malignancies.

Despite the advances achieved with the use of immune-checkpoint blockade, disease progression develops in a significant proportion of patients as a result of mechanisms involved in primary and secondary resistance. Although these mechanisms are yet to be properly characterized, their understanding may pave the way for a rational development of combinations and treatment sequencing in the near future.

KEY POINTS

- Immunologic checkpoint blockade with antibodies against CTLA-4, PD-1, and PD-L1 is an effective method for reversing cancer immunosuppression and promoting immune responses against several cancer types.
- Checkpoint inhibition is associated with a unique spectrum of AEs called irAEs, which include dermatologic, GI, hepatic, endocrine, and other less common inflammatory events.
- The patterns and kinetics of response to immune checkpoint inhibitors can differ from those observed with conventional cytotoxic chemotherapy or targeted therapy.
- The clinical applications of anti–PD-1 and anti–PD-L1 agents, either as single agents or in combinations, continue to expand.
- The combination of immune checkpoint inhibitors (anti–PD-1 in combination with anti–CTLA-4 agents) may result in improved response rates and disease control at a cost of greater toxicities; nevertheless, long-term effects and the impact on survival are still unknown.

MONOCLONAL ANTIBODIES THAT DIRECTLY TARGET THE TUMOR

Rituximab

The first monoclonal antibody to receive FDA approval for therapeutic use was rituximab, a human/mouse chimeric IgG1 directed to CD20, a transmembrane protein expressed on malignant and normal B cells. CD20 is expressed on > 90% of cells in B-cell non-Hodgkin lymphoma and to a lesser degree on chronic lymphocytic leukemia (CLL) cells. CD20 function is not established. The intracellular portion of CD20 contains phosphorylation sites for signaling kinases. It may affect the cell cycle through calcium-channel regulation. The cytotoxic effects of rituximab seem to involve CMC, ADCC, and induction of apoptosis.

Rituximab is approved for the treatment of CD20-positive non-Hodgkin lymphoma (low-grade or follicular B-cell and diffuse large B-cell) and CLL. Dosing of rituximab depends on the clinical setting. Manageable infusion-related reactions occur for most patients, thus premedication with acetaminophen and diphenhydramine is recommended. Mild to moderate flulike symptoms are also common. Severe infusion reactions, such as bronchospasm and hypotension, occur in 10% of patients and are usually reversible with appropriate interventions. Transient hypotension may occur; therefore, withholding antihypertensive drugs 12 hours before infusion should be considered. To address infusion reactions, the initial infusion is administered slowly. If hypersensitivity or infusion-related events do not occur, the infusion rate is increased incrementally. Subsequent infusions also are administered more slowly initially, with incremental rate increases. The incidence of hypersensitivity reactions decreases markedly with subsequent infusions. Rituximab can elicit a tumor lysis syndrome. It also induces B-cell lymphopenia, which lasts for approximately 6 months. Full recovery occurs in 9 to 12 months. CD20 is not expressed on hematopoietic stem cells. Rituximab therapy has been associated with reactivation of hepatitis B and with progressive multifocal leukoencephalopathy as a result of opportunistic viruses, including the JC papovavirus.[71,72] Screening patients for hepatitis B before therapy is recommended. Antiviral therapy and comanagement with infectious disease specialists are recommended for patients with serologic evidence of virus.[73] When used in combination with a variety of chemotherapeutic regimens, rituximab does not add to the toxicity of chemotherapy, with the exception of a slightly higher rate of neutropenia. This does not translate, however, into a higher infection rate.[74] Laboratory assays are being developed to identify patients who are likely to have a response to rituximab, including assays of Fc receptor polymorphisms and tumor apoptotic regulators.[75]

Ofatumumab

Ofatumumab is a human IgG1 monoclonal antibody also directed against the CD20 protein and is currently approved for the treatment of patients with recurrent or progressive CLL. Ofatumumab targets an epitope different from that for rituximab and most other CD20-directed antibodies. Ofatumumab binds to both the small and large loops of the CD20 molecule on B cells. Its location is closer to the membrane, which, in theory, allows for more effective complement deposition and subsequent B-cell killing. Preclinical data suggest improved CMC and ADCC compared with rituximab. Direct effects on B-cell proliferation have also been demonstrated. Ofatumumab can be used in combination with fludarabine and cyclophosphamide for relapsed CLL. Infusion reactions can be problematic, and premedication with an oral or IV antihistamine, oral acetaminophen, and an IV corticosteroid before each dose is recommended. In addition to infusion reactions, which occurred in 44% of patients with the first infusion and 29% with the second infusion, adverse reactions have included infections, neutropenia, and pyrexia. The most serious AE of ofatumumab is an increased risk for infections. Progressive multifocal leukoencephalopathy is a rare but also serious AE. As with rituximab, screening of patients for hepatitis B and comanagement with infectious disease specialists for patients who test positive are recommended.

Obinutuzumab

Obinutuzumab is a humanized, type II CD20 monoclonal antibody that has been glycoengineered to reduce core fucosylation, conferring enhanced affinity for the human FcγRIIIa receptor on effector cells and, hence, enhanced ADCC. As a type II monoclonal antibody, obinutuzumab has lower capacity to relocalize CD20 into lipid rafts upon binding, compared with the type I antibodies rituximab and ofatumumab, and is less potent in inducing CMC. It is, however, more potent in mediating cell adhesion and direct cell death. Obinutuzumab and rituximab bind adjacent and partially overlapping epitopes on CD20 but acquire different orientation upon binding, which most likely contributes to different biological characteristics of type I and II antibodies. In preclinical studies, obinutuzumab showed superior induction of direct cell death and enhanced ADCC with less CMC, compared with rituximab.

Obinutuzumab has been approved for the treatment of patients with rituximab-refractory follicular lymphoma and in combination with chlorambucil for CLL. Premedication with glucocorticoid, acetaminophen, and antihistamine is recommended. The FDA-approved regimen for treatment of CLL is obinutuzumab as outlined above in combination with chlorambucil on days 1 and 15 of each cycle; in patients with refractory non-Hodgkin lymphoma, obinutuzumab is used in combination with bendamustine, followed by obinutuzumab monotherapy.[76] The most common adverse reactions with obinutuzumab in combination with chlorambucil were infusion-related reactions, neutropenia, thrombocytopenia, anemia, pyrexia, cough, and musculoskeletal disorders. As with other CD20-targeted antibodies, hepatitis B virus reactivation and progressive multifocal leukoencephalopathy are also risks that require surveillance and treatment, including screening for hepatitis B, as for the other B-cell–directed antibody therapies.

Alemtuzumab

Alemtuzumab is a humanized IgG1 directed against CD52, a nonmodulating glycoprotein expressed on the surface of normal and malignant B cells, including the malignant B cells of CLL. It is also expressed on T cells, NK cells, monocytes, macrophages, and tissues of the male reproductive system. CD52 function is unknown. The cytotoxic effects of alemtuzumab are presumed to involve ADCC and CMC mechanisms.

Alemtuzumab is approved for the treatment of CLL, cutaneous T-cell lymphoma, and T-cell lymphoma. Alemtuzumab administration can be limited by infusion-related toxicities such as hypotension, rigors, fever, dyspnea, bronchospasm, chills, and/or rash. Premedication with diphenhydramine and acetaminophen before infusion is recommended, as is hydrocortisone if infusion-related events occur. Alemtuzumab induces profound B- and T-cell lymphopenia, and a variety of opportunistic infections have been reported.[77] Severe and prolonged myelosuppression also can occur. Infection prophylaxis, trimethoprim-sulfamethoxazole for *Pneumocystis* prophylaxis, and famciclovir (or its equivalent) for herpetic infections are necessary and must be continued for 2 months after completion of therapy or until CD4 cell counts are > 200, whichever occurs later. Alemtuzumab is also being tested as part of the conditioning regimens for allogeneic hematopoietic stem-cell transplantation (HSCT) to support engraftment.

Daratumumab

Daratumumab is a human IgG1k monoclonal antibody that targets CD38, a protein that is overexpressed in multiple myeloma cells and certain hematopoietic cells, including activated CD8+ T cells.

Daratumumab binds to CD38, resulting in complement-dependent and antibody-dependent cell-mediated cytotoxic effects.

Daratumumab was initially approved as single agent for the treatment of patients with multiple myeloma who have received at least three prior lines of therapy; in 2016, the FDA expanded the indication of daratumumab in combination with lenalidomide or bortezomib and dexamethasone for the treatment of patients with refractory multiple myeloma and at least one prior therapy.[78-80] Most common toxicities include infusion reactions, fatigue, nausea, pyrexia, and respiratory symptoms. Pre- and postinfusion medications (eg, acetaminophen, steroids, antihistamines) are advised to prevent infusion reactions. Daratumumab is associated with anemia, lymphopenia, neutropenia, and thrombocytopenia. Prophylaxis for herpes zoster reactivation is also recommended.

Elotuzumab

Elotuzumab is an immunostimulatory, humanized IgG1k monoclonal antibody targeting the signaling lymphocytic activation molecule F7 (SLAMF7), a cell-surface glycoprotein involved in inhibitory signaling of NK cells. SLAMF7 is expressed on multiple myeloma cells, NK cells, plasma cells, and subsets of cells of hematopoietic lineage. Binding of elotuzumab to the extracellular domain SLAMF7 results in antitumor activity against MM cells through antibody-dependent cellular cytotoxicity and lysis of tumor cells through the activation of NK cells. Elotuzumab is currently approved by the FDA for use in combination with lenalidomide and dexamethasone for the treatment of patients with multiple myeloma in whom prior therapies have failed.[81] The most frequent adverse events include lymphopenia, neutropenia, fatigue, pyrexia, peripheral neuropathy, respiratory symptoms, upper respiratory tract infection, and pneumonia. Infusion reactions and hepatotoxicity may also occur.

Trastuzumab

Trastuzumab is a humanized IgG1 directed against the extracellular domain of HER2, also known as ErbB2, a member of the epidermal growth factor (EGF) family of receptor tyrosine kinases. HER2 may be overexpressed in breast, gastroesophageal, and many other cancers. Overexpression is implicated in the malignant transformation process; is an independent, adverse prognostic factor in breast cancer; and may predict response to chemotherapy and hormonal agents, depending on other characteristics of the tumor cells. Trastuzumab exerts antitumor effects by several mechanisms that are not yet completely understood. Immune effector mechanisms, namely ADCC and CMC, are considered central. Trastuzumab has direct antiproliferative effects, which include cell-cycle arrest and/or induction of apoptosis; it markedly accelerates HER2 endocytosis and degradation. Trastuzumab also can mediate antiangiogenic effects, including the inhibition of VEGF production.

Trastuzumab is approved for use in breast, gastric, and gastroesophageal junction cancers. It is administered IV, with an initial loading dose followed by weekly administration. Other regimens also have been effectively applied. Trastuzumab is generally well tolerated. Infusion reactions do occur, but premedication is usually not required. Cardiac dysfunction may be problematic. It was observed in almost 30% of patients who received an anthracycline and cyclophosphamide; thus, concurrent therapy with anthracyclines is not recommended. Cardiac dysfunction also has been observed in approximately 15% of patients receiving trastuzumab plus paclitaxel and in approximately 5% of patients receiving trastuzumab alone. Patients should undergo monitoring for decreased left ventricular function before trastuzumab treatment and frequently during and after treatment.

Ado-trastuzumab emtansine, an HER-2–targeted antibody-drug conjugate of trastuzumab and mertansine, a microtubule inhibitor, is also approved as a single agent for the treatment of patients with HER2-positive, advanced breast cancer.

Pertuzumab

Pertuzumab targets the extracellular dimerization domain (subdomain II) of HER2 and thereby blocks ligand-dependent heterodimerization of HER2 with other HER family members, including EGF receptor (EGFR), HER3, and HER4, and is used in combination with trastuzumab. Pertuzumab was the first drug approved in the breast cancer neoadjuvant treatment setting. Approval was on the basis of the pathologic complete response rate, defined as the absence of invasive cancer in the breast and lymph nodes, observed in a phase II study involving women with early HER2-positive breast cancer who were randomly assigned to receive to one of four neoadjuvant treatment regimens.[82] The most common adverse reactions observed among patients who received pertuzumab in combination with trastuzumab and docetaxel were diarrhea, alopecia, neutropenia, nausea, fatigue, rash, and peripheral neuropathy. Cardiac dysfunction can occur; however, pertuzumab in combination with trastuzumab and docetaxel was not associated with increases in the incidence of symptomatic left ventricular systolic dysfunction or decreases in left ventricular ejection fraction compared with placebo in combination with trastuzumab and docetaxel. Other significant adverse reactions reported with pertuzumab included infusion-associated reactions, hypersensitivity reactions, and anaphylaxis.

Cetuximab

Cetuximab is a human/mouse chimeric IgG1 to the extracellular domain of the EGFR, also known as ErbB1. It is approved for treatment of colorectal cancer and squamous cell carcinoma of the head and neck. Cetuximab competitively inhibits the binding of EGF and other ligands, such as TGF-α. It blocks activation of receptor-associated kinases, resulting in inhibition of cell growth, apoptosis, and decreased VEGF and matrix metalloproteinase production. EGFR is expressed in many normal epithelial tissues, such as skin. Many different human carcinomas overexpress EGFR, including colorectal and head and neck cancers. EGFR protein overexpression, which can be accompanied by gene amplification, or copy number gains, is associated with a negative prognosis across different cancers. In animal studies, cetuximab inhibited tumor cells that overexpress EGFR as well as increased the activity of chemotherapy and radiation. The presence of mutations in the *KRAS* and *NRAS* oncogenes, which encode a signal transducer that mediates response to stimulation of cell-surface receptors, including EGFR, has been associated with lack of response to cetuximab.[83] *KRAS, NRAS,* and *BRAF* testing is recommended for all patients with metastatic colorectal cancer who are candidates for anti-EGFR antibody therapy, and it is recommended that patients with *KRAS, NRAS,* or *BRAF* mutations should not receive anti-EGFR antibody therapy.[84]

Cetuximab is administered IV; an initial loading dose is administered, followed by weekly infusions. The plasma half-life is approximately 5 days. Every-other-week infusions have also been used. In general, cetuximab has been well tolerated. Infusion reactions do occur and can be severe, particularly with the initial infusions, and premedication with diphenhydramine is recommended. The most common AE has been an acne-like skin rash, which develops in ≤ 75% of patients and which probably represents the biological effects of the blocking EGFR present in the skin. The rash develops rapidly after cetuximab initiation, peaks between weeks 2 and 4, and thereafter tends to steadily abate in severity with continuation. The development of a rash has been associated with greater therapeutic effectiveness.[85] Life-threatening toxicities, such as interstitial lung disease, have been observed rarely.

Panitumumab

Panitumumab is a recombinant, human IgG2 monoclonal antibody that also binds specifically to EGFR with identical target specificity to that of cetuximab. IgG2 is less efficient than IgG1 in mediating ADCC. In contrast to cetuximab, panitumumab is fully human. The theoretical advantage conferred by this agent, compared with its chimeric counterpart, is that there is less potential for an antigenic response against the therapeutic antibody, because panitumumab is fully human. The antitumor effects are considered identical to those of cetuximab. Efficacy has been confined to patients whose tumors do not express *KRAS* and *NRAS* mutations.[86] Panitumumab is administered IV, without a loading dose, every 14 days. As was predicted, the development of human antihuman antibodies has not been detected with treatment. Approximately 1% of patients exposed to panitumumab, however, experienced severe infusion reactions, whereas approximately 3% of patients treated with cetuximab experienced severe infusion reactions. Other toxicities seem to be similar. Skin rash with variable presentation is common. An association between the development of rash and response has also been suggested. Rare but serious adverse events, such as pulmonary fibrosis, have been observed. Anecdotal reports have suggested that patients whose disease is considered intolerant to cetuximab may be safely treated with panitumumab, but their disease is not considered non–cross-resistant, so antitumor activity cannot be rescued with a switch in antibodies. Panitumumab was approved on the basis of a phase III trial in which patients with metastatic colorectal cancer were randomly assigned to receive either panitumumab with best supportive care or best supportive care alone.[87] No patients who had been previously treated with cetuximab were included, and in a randomized comparison trial, panitumumab and cetuximab demonstrated similar antitumor activity and toxicity.

Necitumumab

Necitumumab is a recombinant, fully human IgG1 monoclonal antibody directed against the extracellular region of EGFR that blocks the binding of EGFR to its ligands, also leading to ADCC. In preclinical models, necitumumab resulted in EGFR-binding activity similar to that of cetuximab, both IgG1-class antibodies, and higher than that of panitumumab, an IgG2-class antibody with less pronounced ADCC activity. The FDA granted approval for necitumumab in combination with gemcitabine and cisplatin for first-line treatment of patients with metastatic squamous NSCLC. In a randomized, phase III trial, the addition of necitumumab to chemotherapy resulted in longer OS.[88] The most common adverse events include skin rash and hypomagnesemia. Cardiopulmonary arrest and/or sudden death (3%) and increased risk of venous thromboembolism have been reported in patients receiving necitumumab. Close monitoring of serum electrolytes is recommended.

Mogamulizumab

Mogamulizumab is a monoclonal antibody against the C-C chemokine receptor 4 and has been approved for the treatment of patients with cutaneous T-cell lymphoma. In the phase III MAVORIC trial, 372 patients with mycosis fungoides or Sézary syndrome refractory to at least one prior systemic treatment were randomly assigned to mogamulizumab or vorinostat. Mogamulizumab resulted in superior progression-free survival (PFS; 7.6 *v* 3.1 months) and objective response rate (28% *v* 5%). Mogalizumab 1.0 mg/kg IV is administered weekly for the first 28-day cycle, then on days 1 and 15 of subsequent cycles. Most common adverse events include infusion reaction, rash, nausea, diarrhea, fatigue, pyrexia, upper respiratory tract infection, musculoskeletal pain, skin infection, thrombocytopenia, constipation, anemia, mucositis, cough, and hypertension.[89]

KEY POINTS

- The effectiveness of monoclonal antibodies has been established for hematologic malignancies and solid tumors.
- Targets have included tumor cell membrane determinants and factors involved in tumor progression.
- Monoclonal antibodies can mediate antitumor activity via immune mechanisms (eg, antibody-dependent and complement-mediated cellular mechanisms) and by nonimmunologic mechanisms (eg, direct induction of apoptosis, or interfering with target signaling).

- Although active as single agents in some cases, monoclonal antibodies are most often administered with chemotherapy or radiation therapy.
- Because of infusion reactions, premedication is required for treatment with many monoclonal antibodies, particularly those used to treat hematologic diseases.
- Unique and often severe organ toxicity related to the molecule being targeted can be seen.

ANTIANGIOGENIC ANTIBODIES

Bevacizumab

Bevacizumab is humanized IgG1 directed against VEGF. Often overexpressed by tumor cells as well as by tumor-associated macrophages, VEGF is a pivotal stimulator of endothelial cell development and angiogenesis. Bevacizumab binds the VEGF isoform and prevents the interaction with its receptors (Flt-1 and KDR) on endothelial cells. Bevacizumab inhibits new blood vessel formation in in vitro models and reduces tumor vascularity and progression in in vivo animal tumor models. Bevacizumab has a direct and rapid antivascular effect in the tumors of patients with colorectal cancer.[90] Most of bevacizumab's indications (colorectal cancer, lung cancer, ovarian cancer, cervical cancer) are in combination with chemotherapy. Bevacizumab is also approved in combination with IFN-α for the treatment of patients with metastatic renal cell carcinoma and as a single agent or in combination with irinotecan for the treatment of patients with glioblastoma, although it is rarely used now for either indication because of its toxicity and low antitumor activity.[91] Clinical toxicities include hemorrhagic complications, which are more common among patients with squamous cell histology NSCLC than with adenocarcinoma, which is why it is not indicated in squamous cell NSCLC. Other important toxicities include hypertension, proteinuria, GI perforations, thrombohemorrhagic events, and wound healing complications that make it advisable to avoid bevacizumab for several weeks before any major surgical procedure and to delay its administration until the surgical incisions are fully healed. Administration also should be suspended several weeks before elective surgery. Hypertensive crisis, nephrotic syndrome, and congestive heart failure have been observed. Bevacizumab must be suspended for patients with GI perforation, wound dehiscence, serious bleeding, nephrotic syndrome, or hypertensive crisis. The risk of continuation or temporary suspension for patients with moderate to severe proteinuria is unknown. Infusion reactions are relatively uncommon. Other rare complications, including a reversible posterior leukoencephalopathy syndrome, have been observed among patients treated with bevacizumab.[92]

Ramucirumab

Ramucirumab is a monoclonal antibody that binds to VEGF receptor 2 (VEGFR-2) and blocks the activation and downstream signaling mediated by the receptor. It is the first biologic treatment given as a single drug that has survival benefits for patients with advanced gastric or gastroesophageal junction adenocarcinoma that progressed after first-line chemotherapy.[93] Ramucirumab is also approved for use in combination with paclitaxel for advanced gastroesophageal junction adenocarcinoma after prior fluoropyrimidine- or platinum-containing chemotherapy in combination with folinic acid, fluorouracil, and irinotecan for patients with advanced colorectal cancer whose disease progressed while receiving prior bevacizumab- and oxaliplatin-containing regimens (ie, second-line setting) and in combination with docetaxel for patients with metastatic NSCLC with disease progression after platinum-based chemotherapy.

Premedication with antihistamines is recommended to decrease the risk of infusion-related reactions. Patients who suffer a grade 1 (mild) or 2 (moderate) infusion-related reaction should also be premedicated with acetaminophen and dexamethasone or its equivalent before each infusion, and the infusion rate should be slowed by 50%. The most common adverse reactions of ramucirumab are hypertension and diarrhea. Other important risks include hemorrhage, arterial thrombotic events, infusion-related reactions, GI perforation, impaired wound healing, clinical deterioration among patients with cirrhosis, and reversible posterior leukoencephalopathy.

BISPECIFIC ANTIBODY THERAPY

A bispecific monoclonal antibody is an artificial protein composed of fragments of two different monoclonal antibodies and consequently binds to two different types of antigen. Bispecific monoclonal antibodies have been developed to simultaneously bind to two or more targets on the same cell surface, or to a cytotoxic cell and to a tumor cell to destroy the tumor cell (Fig 4-4).[158]

Blinatumomab

Blinatumomab belongs to a class of constructed antibodies known as bispecific T-cell engagers. It consists of genetically engineered, murine, tandem, single-chain variable fragments (scFvs), which are not actually a fragment of an antibody but instead a fusion protein of the variable regions of the heavy and light chains of immunoglobulins, connected with a short linker. scFvs lack the antibody Fc domains and thus do not mediate CMC or ADCC. One scFv binds T-cell–specific CD3 and the other B-cell–specific CD19. By targeting CTL against the CD-19–expressing B cells, the T cells become activated within minutes and induce perforin-mediated death to the targeted B cells. In contrast to CD20, CD19 is expressed on the earliest B-precursor lymphocytes that undergo malignant transformation in acute lymphocytic leukemia. Blinatumomab is approved by the FDA for the treatment of Philadelphia chromosome–negative relapsed or refractory B-lineage acute lymphocytic leukemia in adult patients, specifically for eradication of minimal residual disease.[94]

Blinatumomab has a short serum half-life of 1 to 2 hours. As a consequence of the short elimination half-life, blinatumomab is administered as a 4-week continuous IV infusion. Shorter infusion times had also been explored but seemed to result in higher incidences of AEs, including neurologic symptoms, such as seizures, and a cytokine-release syndrome—a symptom complex that can be life-threatening and includes fever, nausea, chills, hypotension, tachycardia, headache, rash, and dyspnea that results from the release of cytokines from cells targeted by the antibody as well as immune cells that are recruited.[95] Although blinatumomab was derived from murine sources, HAMA is rare; HAMAs develop in < 1% of patients during therapy. Absence of the Fc region and B-cell depletion resulting from therapy are assumed to be the critical components for this low immunogenicity.

KEY POINTS

- The efficacy of antiangiogenic agents, particularly of monoclonal antibodies against VEGF and VEGFR, has been demonstrated in different solid tumors.
- Bowel perforation, hemorrhagic complications, and thromboembolic events may develop in patients receiving antiangiogenic drugs; treatment suspension is advised in those undergoing surgical procedures.
- Bispecific monoclonal antibodies, such as blinatumomab, have been developed to simultaneously bind to a cytotoxic cell and to a tumor cell to destroy the tumor cell.

IMMUNOTOXINS AND IMMUNOCONJUGATES

Biologic agents have been used to deliver toxins, cytotoxic drugs, or radiation to malignant cells, as opposed to activating host antitumor mechanisms. Denileukin diftitox is a recombinant immunotoxin consisting of IL-2 fused to the enzymatically active domains of diphtheria toxin. It is internalized by endocytosis into cells bearing IL-2–receptor (CD25). Diphtheria toxin activation is controlled by its intracellular cleavage from the bispecific molecule and then inhibits protein synthesis, leading to apoptosis. Denileukin diftitox is indicated for the treatment of patients with persistent or recurrent CD25+ cutaneous T-cell lymphoma.[96] Cytokine release may occur, the result of the killing of T cells, and can result in capillary leak syndrome. Vision loss has also been observed.

Brentuximab vedotin is an antibody-drug conjugate approved to treat anaplastic large-cell lymphoma and Hodgkin lymphoma. The compound consists of the chimeric monoclonal antibody brentuximab, which targets the cell-membrane protein CD30, linked to three to five units of the antimitotic agent monomethyl auristatin E (designated "vedotin"). The antibody portion of the drug attaches to CD30 on the surface of malignant cells, delivering monomethyl auristatin E, which is responsible for the antitumor activity. Brentuximab vedotin is usually well tolerated, with manageable AEs including peripheral sensory neuropathy.[97]

Ado-trastuzumab emtansine, which consists of trastuzumab linked to the cytotoxic agent mertansine, an antitubulin, has demonstrated activity for patients with breast cancer that has not responded to prior treatment with trastuzumab.[98] Although ado-trastuzumab is well tolerated in clinical trials, thrombocytopenia has been reported, and neuropathy and liver and cardiac toxicity can develop. The drug is approved for treatment of advanced breast cancer.

Inotuzumab ozogamicin is an antibody drug conjugate consisting of humanized monoclonal antibody against CD22 combined with the cytotoxic agent ozogamicin (calicheamicin). Inotuzumab ozogamicin has been approved for the treatment of patients with relapsed or refractory, B-cell precursor acute lymphoblastic leukemia (ALL).[99]

Moxetumomab

Moxetumomab pasudotox, a recombinant CD22-targeting immunotoxin, is approved for the treatment of patients with relapsed or refractory hairy cell leukemia, a rare B-cell malignancy with high CD22 expression. Moxetumomab pasudotox is a recombinant immunotoxin composed of an immunoglobulin light-chain variable domain and a heavy-chain variable domain genetically fused to a truncated form of *Pseudomonas* exotoxin PE38. Approval was on the basis of a study that included 80 patients who had received at least two prior systemic therapies, including one purine nucleoside analog. Moxetumomab pasudotox resulted in an 80% hematologic remission rate and a durable complete response rate of 30%. The median time to hematologic remission was 1.1 months. Moxetumomab pasudotox 0.04 mg/kg is administered as an IV infusion over 30 minutes on days 1, 3, and 5 of each 28-day cycle up to six cycles, disease progression, or unacceptable toxicity.[100] Most frequent toxicities were peripheral edema, nausea, fatigue, and headache. Treatment-related serious adverse events included hemolytic uremic syndrome and capillary leak syndrome, and the most common grade 3 or 4 adverse reactions were hypertension, febrile neutropenia, and hemolytic uremic syndrome.[100]

Two mouse monoclonal antibodies to CD20 conjugated to radioisotopes, ^{131}I-tositumomab and ^{90}Y-ibritumomab, have demonstrated clinical effectiveness for patients with lymphoma. Both are indicated for the treatment of relapsed or refractory, low-grade or follicular B-cell non-Hodgkin lymphoma, with or without transformation, including rituximab-refractory disease. Toxicity is typically quite mild. The main AE is reversible myelosuppression, and exposure is limited to a single dose because of the radiation exposure and the high incidence of HAMA development.[101,102]

KEY POINTS

- Biologic agents can be engineered to deliver toxins and radiation to malignant cells, in the form of immunotoxins and radioimmunoconjugates.
- Examples of effective immunotoxins include brentuximab vedotin, approved for the treatment of patients with anaplastic large-cell lymphoma and Hodgkin lymphoma, and ado-trastuzumab, a molecule that incorporates trastuzumab and a cytotoxic agent, used in the treatment of breast cancer.

CELLULAR THERAPY

A distinct immunotherapy approach, termed "adoptive cell therapy," is to infuse immune cells expanded, engineered, or generated ex vivo. A variety of immune effector cells have been explored for adoptive cellular therapy and tested in clinical trials. Early efforts examined the infusion of lymphokine-activated killer cells, which had little activity and required the coadministration of high-dose IL-2 to maintain their activity. Initial studies of patients with advanced melanoma and renal cell carcinoma demonstrated antitumor activity. Comparable results, however, were subsequently seen with IL-2 alone. Methods of generating antitumor CTLs by culturing peripheral blood, lymph node, or TILs with cytokines and tumor antigens ex vivo also have been evaluated clinically. Response rates of ≥ 50% among patients with metastatic melanoma accompanied by long PFS have been observed with the infusion of TIL in nonrandomized studies.[103]

CHIMERIC ANTIGEN RECEPTOR T CELLS

The infusion of T cells that have been genetically modified either with a reprogrammed, recombinant chimeric antigen receptor (CAR) or with an engineered TCR have demonstrated encouraging results in clinical trials. CARs redirect T-cell specificity toward antibody-recognized antigens expressed on the surface of cancer cells and are composed of an extracellular immunoglobulin-derived antigen-recognition domain, a transmembrane domain, and an intracellular T-cell signal domain that includes a CD-3 complex-derived chain. Of note, CARs can recognize a variety of antigens without restriction of their MHC determinants, because the target cell antigen is not processed and presented but is there in its entirety on the malignant cell surface, and costimulatory signals can be incorporated into the intracellular domain to enhance cellular responses. CAR-redirected T cells specific for the B-cell differentiation antigen CD19 have demonstrated significant activity in refractory B-cell malignancies, CLL, and ALL; tisagenlecleucel and axicabtagene ciloleucel are approved for the treatment of patients with refractory childhood ALL and with refractory diffuse large B-cell non-Hodgkin's lymphoma.[22,104] Similarly, CAR-T cells targeting the B-cell maturation antigen seem promising in the treatment of relapsed refractory myeloma. TCR-modified T cells have demonstrated activity in the treatment of selected solid tumors but are structurally dependent on HLA type and antigen expression on MHC molecules of the target cell.[105,106] The toxicities of adoptive T-cell therapies can be severe and differ significantly from those observed with immune-checkpoint blockers; they include B-cell aplasia, cytokine release syndrome (CRS), hypotension, pyrexia, and neurologic adverse events or CAR-T-cell–related encephalopathy syndrome (CRES). CRS is marked by symptoms mimicking a systemic inflammatory response syndrome, ranging from mild constitutional symptoms to life-threatening hypotension, hypoxia, fever, and multiorgan dysfunction. CRS is largely attributed to the secretion of cytokines and chemokines by T cells, monocytes or macrophages, and dendritic cells, including IL-1, IL-2, and IL-6. Patients with bulky disease and comorbidities are at increased risk of CRS development. On the basis of on the underlying mechanisms, IL-6 and IL-6R antagonists (eg tocilizumab, siltuximab) represent the cornerstones in the management of CRS occurring after CAR-T therapy. CRES has a less understood pathogenesis, and may be characterized by confusion, ataxia, aphasia, seizures, and cerebral edema or increased intracranial pressure.[107] Anti–IL-6 agents and steroids are also effective tools in reversing CRES.

Dendritic cells also have been generated ex vivo and are under investigation in vaccine approaches (including sipuleucel-T, detailed later in this chapter), as have monocytes or macrophages as potent APCs.

DONOR LYMPHOCYTE INFUSION

Cells infused in allogeneic HSCT represent an effective adoptive cellular therapy in clinical use. An allogeneic graft-versus-leukemia (GVL) effect, which is a restricted form of graft-versus-host disease (GVHD), has been suggested by the increased relapse rate for recipients of T-cell–depleted allografts, higher relapse rates after either syngeneic or autologous transplantation, and the lower frequency of relapse for patients with more severe GVHD. Given these clinical observations, donor leukocyte infusion (DLI) was tested among patients whose malignancies relapsed after allogeneic transplantation. Numerous reports have documented success of DLI for patients with chronic myeloid leukemia; the majority of these patients achieved durable complete molecular remission.[108] Acute myeloid leukemia has only modest response rates, and ALL rarely responds. DLI also can eradicate Epstein-Barr virus–associated posttransplantation lymphoproliferative disease after allogeneic transplantation. More recent studies have identified potential target antigens among patients responding to DLI. The major drawback of DLI is GVHD, which is a major source of transplantation-related mortality, and methods of promoting GVL over GVHD are under investigation. New investigational approaches aimed at improving the efficacy of DLI include priming of donor lymphocytes to recipient tumor antigens ex vivo and infusions of alloreactive NK cells. The effects of lymphocyte infusions in the setting of myeloablative and nonmyeloablative treatment are also under investigation in solid tumors.[109]

SIPULEUCEL-T

Sipuleucel-T is an autologous cellular immunotherapy designed to stimulate an immune response to prostate cancer. It is approved for the treatment of asymptomatic or minimally symptomatic metastatic castrate-resistant (hormone-refractory) prostate cancer. Sipuleucel-T is manufactured from peripheral blood mononuclear cells (PBMCs) isolated during leukapheresis. PBMCs are cultured ex vivo with PA2024, a fusion protein consisting of prostatic acid phosphatase and GM-CSF for 2 days and then reinfused into the patient. The approach is designed for the GM-CSF portion of the fusion molecule to activate blood monocytes and APCs to present prostatic acid phosphatase as a tumor antigen.[110,111] The final cell product, however, includes a variety of leukocytes, including T and B cells. Median OS was improved for patients treated with sipuleucel-T compared with those receiving similarly prepared autologous dendritic cells not exposed to the antigen–GM-CSF fusion protein.[101,110] Adverse events more commonly reported in the sipuleucel-T group were chills, pyrexia, headache, flulike illness, myalgia, hypertension, hyperhidrosis, and groin pain. These events were generally mild or moderate in severity and usually resolved within 1 to 2 days. Investigations are ongoing to enhance the benefits of sipuleucel-T by the addition of other immunomodulators, and the technology also is being explored in the treatment of other malignancies.

KEY POINTS

- Many cells of the immune system generated and/or modified ex vivo can be administered to an individual to effect an antitumor immune response.
- The use of reprogrammed CAR- and TCR-endowed lymphocytes has produced robust results in hematologic malignancies and promising activity in solid tumors; nevertheless, the applicability of these approaches remains restricted to specialized centers, and toxicities can be limiting.
- Toxicities resulting from CAR-T-cell therapies include CRS and CRES, and may require directed approaches that include the use of anti–IL-6 and anti–IL-6R agents.
- An autologous cell–based vaccine and donor leukocyte infusion after allogeneic hematopoietic cell transplantation are examples of cellular therapies in clinical use and under active investigation.

ONCOLYTIC VIRUSES

Oncolytic viruses are emerging as important agents in cancer treatment. They offer the attractive therapeutic combination of tumor-specific cell lysis together with immune stimulation, thereby acting as potential in situ tumor vaccines. These viruses can be engineered for optimization of tumor selectivity and enhanced immune stimulation and can be readily combined with other agents. Effectiveness in patients depends on activation of host antitumor immune responses. Tumor selectivity in oncolytic virus therapy is driven by several factors:

- Cellular entry via virus-specific, receptor-mediated mechanisms: a specific viral entry receptor is often highly expressed on tumor cells;
- Rapid cell division in tumor cells with high metabolic and replicative activity may support increased viral replication compared with normal quiescent cells;
- Tumor-driven mutations specifically increase the selectivity of virus replication in tumor cells;
- Many tumor cells have deficiencies in antiviral type 1 IFN signaling, therefore supporting selective virus replication.

Viral replication within the tumor microenvironment leads to innate and adaptive immune activation. This activation limits virus spread; in addition, the presence of virus together with cell lysis, with the release of tumor antigens and danger-associated molecular patterns, may overcome immunosuppression in the tumor microenvironment and promote tumor immunity. The success of this approach is influenced by factors including preexisting antiviral and antitumor immunity and incorporation of immune stimulatory transgenes. A wide range of viruses with diverse properties are under investigation, including herpesvirus, adenovirus, measles virus, vaccinia virus, reovirus, poliovirus, coxsackievirus, vesicular stomatitis virus, parvovirus, and retrovirus.[112]

TALIMOGENE LAHERPAREPVEC

Talimogene laherparepvec (T-VEC) is an intralesionally delivered oncolytic immunotherapy comprising a genetically engineered, attenuated herpes simplex virus type 1 of the IS-1 strain. T-VEC invades cancerous and healthy cells but can only replicate in cancer cells, where it secretes GM-CSF in the process. The genes encoding neurovirulence infected cell protein 34.5 (ICP34.5) and the infected cell protein 47 (ICP47) are functionally deleted in the virus, and the gene for human GM-CSF is inserted. ICP34.5 is required for viral replication in normal cells, which is mediated by interaction with proliferating cell nuclear antigen. Whereas cancer cells proliferate independently of ICP34.5 expression, ICP47 is critical for the evasion of HSV-infected cells from cytotoxic T cells by interfering with peptide processing and presentation on MHC-1. Deletion of ICP47 in T-VEC prevents potentially limited viral antigen presentation, which could compromise its function as an in situ vaccine. ICP47 deletion also leads to increased virus replication in cancer cells without decreasing tumor selectivity. GM-CSF is a proinflammatory cytokine that promotes the recruitment and maturation of dendritic cells as well as macrophages into potent APCs, leading to priming of tumor-specific T cells. It has been used successfully as an immune adjuvant in many cancer vaccines. T-VEC has two distinct mechanisms of action, including destruction of the tumor cells directly by the lytic function of the virus and this lysis of cancer cells leads to the release of tumor antigens, virus, and GM-CSF, attracting dendritic cells, thereby creating an in situ vaccine.

T-VEC is approved for the treatment of stage IIIB-IV malignant melanoma on the basis of a phase III trial involving patients with cutaneous or subcutaneous metastases in which patients were randomly assigned 2:1 between T-VEC and GM-CSF, respectively. The results of this trial revealed a statistically significant improvement in the durable response rate, overall response rate, complete response rate, and OS of T-VEC compared with systemic GM-CSF. In general, T-VEC was well tolerated; most AEs included constitutional symptoms and injection-site reactions.[113] Combination studies with checkpoint inhibitors are ongoing and seem promising.[114]

A total of 4 mL of 10^6 pfu/mL T-VEC is injected directly into dermal or subcutaneous lesions, followed 3 weeks later with the same dose, then every 2 weeks until a complete response is achieved, clinically significant progression of disease occurs, or intolerable AEs arise. Different lesions can be treated at each visit. Because the drug is a live, genetically engineered virus that actively replicates in the host, special attention needs to be given with regard to health care provider and patient education, transmission precautions, and environmental safety.

> **KEY POINTS**
>
> - Viruses can be engineered to serve as specific, locally administered anticancer agents that may induce regional and potentially distant tumor responses in the treatment of advanced malignant melanoma.
> - Combination oncolytic virus therapy with other immunotherapeutic agents such as checkpoint inhibitors is undergoing active investigation and holds significant promise for the treatment of a number of malignancies.

SUPPORTIVE CARE BIOLOGIC AGENTS: HEMATOPOIETIC GROWTH FACTORS

Many cytokines affect hematopoiesis either directly or indirectly. Cytokines that serve as hematopoietic growth factors are now in common use for the prophylaxis of febrile neutropenia for patients receiving cytotoxic treatments, and in the setting of HSCT, where they are used to mobilize hematopoietic progenitor cells for transplantation.

GM-CSF

GM-CSF stimulates the development of neutrophils and monocytes or macrophages, and promotes the proliferation and development of early erythroid, megakaryocytic, and eosinophilic progenitor cells. It is produced by endothelial cells and fibroblasts as well as by T cells and monocytes or macrophages. GM-CSF produces a variety of effects on cells of the neutrophil and monocyte and macrophage lineages, including augmentation of monocyte or macrophage MHC class II expression and enhancement of granulocyte and macrophage cellular cytotoxicity and ADCC mechanisms. GM-CSF also is the principal mediator of the proliferation and differentiation of mDCs. It enhances dendritic cell antigen uptake, MHC, and costimulatory molecule expression, as well as the ability of dendritic cells to stimulate T cells.

Recombinant GM-CSF (also called sargramostim) can be used in the prophylaxis of neutropenia. Because of the sensitivity of rapidly dividing myeloid cells, sargramostim is typically initiated 1 to 3 days after completion of chemotherapy and administered daily through postnadir recovery. Sargramostim is generally well tolerated; however, AEs include pain and inflammation at the injection site, bone pain, myalgia, arthralgia, and low-grade fever. Nausea, fluid retention, dyspnea, pericarditis, pleuritis, pulmonary emboli, splenomegaly, and hypersensitivity reactions have been reported but are rare.

The ability of GM-CSF to function as an immunoadjuvant and to stimulate DC and tumor-specific T-cell responses has led to its evaluation in a number of clinical trials as anticancer therapy. Various cancer vaccine approaches that incorporate GM-CSF have been tested clinically, including combination with immune checkpoint inhibition with favorable effects on survival and toxicity in melanoma that are undergoing additional investigation.[115] There also is evidence that administering GM-CSF as monotherapy has antitumor activity for patients with prostate cancer or melanoma in whom increases in DCs have been observed.[116-118] The ability of GM-CSF to promote phagocyte-mediated ADCC is also being tested in clinical trials in which it is being administered with monoclonal antibodies.[119]

GRANULOCYTE COLONY-STIMULATING FACTOR

Granulocyte colony-stimulating factor (G-CSF) is produced by macrophages, lymphocytes, fibroblasts, and endothelial cells. It induces the production and release of neutrophilic granulocytes in the bone marrow and enhances their functional capacity in the periphery. Moreover, G-CSF possesses essential neutrophil-activating functions, such as the oxidative burst, degranulation, phagocytosis, and chemotaxis. G-CSF markedly stimulates neutrophil ADCC mechanisms. As a regulator of neutrophil activity, G-CSF plays a role in innate immune responses. Evidence is growing that G-CSF also exerts immunoregulatory effects in adaptive immunity. G-CSF mediates anti-inflammatory reactions accompanied by Th2 differentiation and promotes tolerogenic APC–T-cell interactions.

Recombinant G-CSF (also called filgrastim) may be used to decrease the risk of febrile neutropenia associated with cytotoxic chemotherapy treatment. It is usually administered subcutaneously daily for up to 2 weeks until postnadir neutrophil recovery is at normal or near-normal neutrophil levels. Because G-CSF stimulates myeloid cells to divide and because dividing cells are sensitive to cytotoxic chemotherapy, G-CSF should be administered no earlier than 24 hours after the administration of cytotoxic chemotherapy and no earlier than 24 hours before the administration of chemotherapy to lessen the risk of aggravating leukopenia. Recently, two biosimilars to G-CSF—filgrastim sndz, and tbo-filgrastim—have been approved for the same indications as those for G-CSF.[120] A pegylated form of recombinant G-CSF, pegfilgrastim, has a variable plasma half-life of 15 to 80 hours, which allows administration once per chemotherapy treatment cycle rather than daily. Pegfilgrastim should not be administered in the period between 14 days before and 24 hours after the administration of cytotoxic chemotherapy. The safety data seem to be similar between filgrastim and pegfilgrastim. The most commonly observed AEs are mild to moderate bone pain after repeated administration and local skin reactions at the site of injection. Fever, diarrhea, edema, dyspnea, skin rash, splenomegaly (with rupture), and hypersensitivity reactions also may occur but are rare. The G-CSF receptor, through which filgrastim and pegfilgrastim act, has been found on tumor cell lines. The possibility that pegfilgrastim acts as a growth factor for any tumor type, including myeloid malignancies and myelodysplasia, diseases for which pegfilgrastim is not approved, cannot be excluded. The immunomodulatory effects of G-CSF, such as the ability to promote ADCC mechanisms and to promote T-cell tolerance in pathologic conditions associated with a Th1-Th2 imbalance are under investigation.

KEY POINTS

- Hematopoietic factors, recombinant G-CSF, and GM-CSF are commonly used for the prophylaxis of febrile neutropenia and in HSCT.
- GM-CSF is used as a vaccine adjuvant.
- The ability of G-CSF and GM-CSF to modulate antitumor immune responses is under investigation, with particular interest in combinations with immune checkpoint inhibitors.

Acknowledgments

The following authors are acknowledged and graciously thanked for their contribution to prior versions of this chapter: Pierre L. Triozzi, MD, and Michael A. Postow, MD.

GLOBAL PERSPECTIVE: PRINCIPLES OF IMMUNO-ONCOLOGY AND BIOLOGIC THERAPY

Paolo A. Ascierto, MD (Istituto Nazionale Tumori IRCCS Fondazione Pascale, Naples, Italy)

The new era of immuno-oncology treatments, especially anti–CTLA-4 and anti–PD-1 checkpoint inhibitors, has resulted in significant global advances in the care of patients with melanoma and other cancers including NSCLC, renal cell carcinoma, bladder cancer, and head and neck cancer. Increasing evidence has shown that immunotherapy can offer long-term benefit to patients with metastatic disease, can be used in combination with other cancer treatments like chemotherapy and radiation therapy, and has a distinct adverse event profile. In addition, research has shown that immunotherapy can be effective in the neoadjuvant and adjuvant settings, and that clinical activity is observed in patients with brain metastases.

LONG-TERM SURVIVAL BENEFIT

A key benefit of immunotherapy is the long-term sustained survival benefit observed in several trials. In the KEYNOTE-006 trial in patients with advanced melanoma, 5-year OS rates were 38.7% in the combined pembrolizumab groups (every 2 or 3 weeks) and 31% with ipilimumab,[121] whereas in KEYNOTE-001, the estimated 5-year OS rate was 34% in all patients and 41% in treatment-naïve patients.[122] For nivolumab plus ipilimumab, the 4-year OS rate was 53% versus 46% with nivolumab alone and 30% with ipilimumab alone in the CheckMate-067 study.[123] However, it should be noted that the combination of ipilimumab and nivolumab is not currently reimbursed in many countries outside of the United States. In Europe, for instance, in countries such as Italy, the combination is not reimbursed by the local health system. Moreover, in low- to medium-income countries, reimbursement of immunotherapies in general may be even more restricted.

Importantly, median PFS or median OS of a checkpoint inhibitor may not be fully indicative of the long-term benefit of treatment.[124] For example, patients receiving targeted agents may have a longer median PFS and a higher response rate, whereas patients treated with immunotherapy have a longer median duration of response (ie, a longer survival curve tail). Because of this, PFS landmark analysis, which incorporates both tumor control and duration of control, may be a more useful end point.

COMBINATION TREATMENT

One particular area of research interest is the combination of immunotherapy with other treatments, especially targeted therapy, chemotherapy, radiation therapy, and surgery. The combination of anti–PD-1/PD-L1 therapy with targeted therapy is not used outside of clinical trials and is still being evaluated in melanoma. Some studies have evaluated a triple combination of BRAF and MEK inhibitors plus a PD-1/PD-L1 inhibitor. In the KEYNOTE-022 study, median PFS was 16.0 months with pembrolizumab plus dabrafenib and trametinib compared with 10.3 months with dabrafenib plus trametinib; this difference (hazard ratio [HR] 0.66; $P = .042870$) was nonsignificant because it did not meet the trial's prespecified significance parameter of an HR ≤ 0.62.[125] However, the pembrolizumab-containing arm had higher rates of adverse events. According to preliminary data from another study (IMPemBra), pembrolizumab plus intermittent dabrafenib plus trametinib seem to be a promising combination in terms of safety and feasibility.[126] The BRAF/MEK inhibitor combination of vemurafenib plus the MEK inhibitor cobimetinib has also been assessed in combination with the PD-L1 inhibitor atezolizumab. Preliminary data suggest this triple combination has a manageable safety profile, with adverse events similar to those observed with atezolizumab plus vemurafenib, and an unconfirmed response rate of 85.3%.[127]

Some studies of combined immunotherapy and targeted therapy have reported disappointing results. The phase III IMspire170 trial that evaluated the combination of cobimetinib and the anti–PDL-1 antibody atezolizumab in 450 treatment-naïve patients with advanced BRAF V600 wild-type melanoma did not meet its primary end point of PFS compared with pembrolizumab in patients with previously untreated, BRAF V600 wild-type advanced melanoma.[128] These data are yet to be fully reported. Similarly, the combination of cobimetinib plus atezolizumab did not achieve its primary end point of improved OS versus regorafenib in the IMblaze370 trial of 363 patients with previously treated metastatic colorectal cancer.[129]

Nivolumab plus erlotinib provided durable responses with manageable tolerability in patients with EGFR-mutant advanced NSCLC.[130] However, the combination of PD-L1 blockade followed by the tyrosine kinase inhibitor osimertinib in patients with EGFR-mutant NSCLC has been shown to be associated with severe immune-related adverse events, including grade 3-4 pneumonitis, colitis, and hepatitis, with these events being most frequent among patients receiving osimertinib within 3 months of prior anti–PD-L1 therapy.[131] In contrast to these findings, the same study reported that no patients receiving erlotinib or afatinib after immune checkpoint blockade developed a severe immune-related adverse event, suggesting this may be an osimertinib-specific concern; although additional investigation is required.

In renal cell carcinoma, pembrolizumab plus the VEGF inhibitor axitinib resulted in significantly improved PFS versus sunitinib as first-line therapy in the KEYNOTE-426 trial setting.[132] Axitinib has also been evaluated in combination with avelumab in the JAVELIN renal 100 trial; researchers reported manageable toxicity and encouraging antitumor activity in preliminary analysis.[133]

Immunotherapy has also been combined with other treatment modalities. In NSCLC, pembrolizumab plus chemotherapy with pemetrexed and a platinum-based drug significantly prolonged OS versus chemotherapy alone in patients with nonsquamous NSCLC.[134] The addition of pembrolizumab to carboplatin plus paclitaxel or nab-paclitaxel also resulted in significantly longer OS and PFS than chemotherapy alone in patients with previously untreated squamous NSCLC.[135]

Immunotherapy may also be used with radiation. Activity and safety of radiotherapy with anti—PD-1 drug therapy has also been shown in patients with metastatic melanoma.[136,137] Several ongoing trials are assessing combined chemoimmunotherapy and radiation in unresectable, locally advanced NSCLC. The PACIFIC-2 trial is evaluating the addition of durvalumab to concurrent chemoradiotherapy, and the KEYNOTE-799 trial is evaluating the safety and efficacy of first-line pembrolizumab plus concurrent chemoradiotherapy. In addition, sequential atezolizumab after standard concurrent chemoradiation is being investigated in the DETERRED trial.

Promising results with immunotherapy and chemoimmunotherapy have also been observed in the neoadjuvant setting. Neoadjuvant chemotherapy and immunotherapy with nivolumab resulted in a high, complete pathologic response rate in the NADIM trial of patients with resectable IIIA NSCLC trial,[138] and the NEOSTAR trial reported a good major pathologic response rate with neoadjuvant nivolumab or nivolumab plus ipilimumab treatment for resectable NSCLC.[139]

Another potential approach is the combination of immunotherapy with surgery. In the phase 2 OpACIN-Neo trial, 86 patients with resectable stage III melanoma involving lymph nodes only were randomly assigned to one of three neoadjuvant dosing schedules: two cycles of ipilimumab 3 mg/kg plus nivolumab 1 mg/kg every 3 weeks, two cycles of ipilimumab 1 mg/kg plus nivolumab 3 mg/kg every 3 weeks, or two cycles of ipilimumab 3 mg/kg once every 3 weeks followed by two cycles of nivolumab 3 mg/kg once every 2 weeks.[140] The ipilimumab 1 mg/kg plus nivolumab 3 mg/kg dosing schedule had the lowest rate of grades 3 and 4 adverse events and induced a pathologic response in a high proportion of patients. A pooled analysis of data from six trials of neoadjuvant immunotherapy and targeted therapy that included patients with RECIST measurable, stage III melanoma who underwent surgery also reported a high, pathologic complete response rate, which was correlated with improved relapse-free survival.[141]

DIFFERENTIAL EFFECTS ON THE BASIS OF BIOLOGY

The combination of nivolumab and ipilimumab has shown superior activity over monotherapy with either nivolumab or ipilimumab in previously untreated patients. A subgroup analysis showed a better impact on the treatment on patients with BRAF mutation compared with those with wild-type BRAF.[123] Ipilimumab 10 mg/kg also resulted in significantly longer OS than lower-dose ipilimumab 3 mg/kg in patients with BRAF mutation,[125] but there were more treatment-related adverse events.[142] Even in such a study, a subgroup analysis showed that a higher dosage of ipilimumab resulted in better outcomes in patients with BRAF mutation than did lower dosage.[125] Previous reports have suggested that immunotherapy might be more effective in NRAS-mutated compared with BRAF-mutated or BRAF/NRAS wild-type melanoma.[143] Patients with BRAF V600K-mutant melanoma seem to benefit less from targeted therapy with a BRAF inhibitor with or without MEK inhibitor than patients with V600E-mutant melanoma, potentially as a result of less reliance on ERK pathway activation and greater use of alternative pathways.[144] In contrast, BRAF V600K melanoma is associated with higher mutational load and better response to immunotherapy.

In patients with NSCLC, EGFR wild-type tumors are associated with improved survival benefit from immunotherapy compared with EGFR mutant tumors.[145] It has been suggested that this could be related to increased expression of the immunosuppressive molecule CD73 in EGFR-mutated NSCLC.[146] A high tumor mutation burden also predicted improved objective response, durable benefit, and PFS in patients with NSCLC treated with nivolumab alone or with ipilimumab.[147] A similar effect was observed in patients with small-cell lung cancer.[148]

In metastatic colorectal cancer, immunotherapy has shown activity in DNA MMR-deficient/MSI-H tumors but no significant clinical activity in the treatment of patients with MMR proficient/non–MSI-H disease has yet been shown.[13,61] Nivolumab is approved in the United States but not in Europe for the treatment of patients with MSI-H or dMMR metastatic colorectal cancer that has progressed after treatment with fluoropyrimidine, oxaliplatin, and irinotecan as a single agent or in combination with ipilimumab.

UNIQUE SAFETY PROFILE

The use of checkpoint inhibitors is associated with a spectrum of characteristic irAEs that are related to the hyperactivation of the immune system. These include a range of mainly dermatologic, GI, endocrine, and hepatic toxicities, as well as several other less frequent inflammatory events. These events have variable times of onset and need careful monitoring, follow-up, and management. With appropriate and timely treatment, these toxicities are generally manageable, but can become severe if not recognized.

Several studies have reported a potential association between the occurrence of irAEs during immunotherapy and treatment efficacy, including in patients with melanoma,[149] NSCLC,[150] and renal cell carcinoma.[151] These findings suggest a possible mechanistic association between irAEs and immunotherapy efficacy, but this remains to be proven.

ADJUVANT SETTING

Prospective, randomized controlled trials provide good evidence that adjuvant immunotherapy is effective. In a phase III trial with patients who had undergone complete resection of stage III melanoma, 5-year recurrence-free survival (RFS) rate was 40.8% with ipilimumab versus 30.3% with placebo (disease recurrence or death HR, 0.76; $P < .001$).[378] The OS rate at 5 years was 65.4% in the ipilimumab group compared with 54.4% in the placebo group (death HR, 0.72; $P = .001$). Although ipilimumab is the only immunotherapy to date to have shown an adjuvant OS benefit, a better RFS benefit has been observed with anti–PD-1 treatment. In a phase III trial of patients who underwent complete resection of stage IIIB-IV melanoma, 1-year RFS rate was 70.5% with nivolumab and 60.8% with ipilimumab (disease recurrence or death HR, 0.65; $P < .001$).[152] Improved RFS has also been observed with adjuvant pembrolizumab with a 1-year RFS rate of 75.4% with pembrolizumab versus 61.0% with placebo (disease recurrence or death HR, 0.57; $P < .001$).[153] These three trials show a consistent benefit of adjuvant immunotherapy.

The benefits of immunotherapy in early disease are also shown by the PACIFIC trial, in which durvalumab, given as maintenance treatment after chemoradiotherapy to patients with NSCLC who did not have disease progression, resulted in significantly increased PFS and OS compared with placebo.[68,154]

DOSING

Across the various checkpoint inhibitors, the most effective dosing regimen may not be known. One factor in this may be that dosing schedules selected for additional development have been largely chosen on the basis of response rate.

In advanced melanoma, ipilimumab at a higher dose of 10 mg/kg resulted in a significantly prolonged OS rate compared with lower dose ipilimumab 3 mg/kg.[142] Most of the key trials of nivolumab involved the first approved dose of 3 mg/kg every 2 weeks. Subsequent to this, a flat-dose of 240 mg every 2 weeks was approved. More recently, a new monotherapy flat-dosing regimen of 480 mg every 4 weeks has been approved in several markets, including the United States and Europe, as an alternative dosing option for several indications. Less frequent dosing offers improved convenience and flexibility for patients and a reduced clinical burden for physicians. Pembrolizumab 2 mg/kg every 3 weeks was selected for development because the same response rate was achieved as with higher dosages with a better safety profile. However, there has been a trend toward superior efficacy with the higher 10 mg/kg every 3 weeks dosage, with a greater improvement in OS versus chemotherapy observed with pembrolizumab 10 mg/kg every 3 weeks compared with 2 mg/kg every 3 weeks, although neither dose resulted in a statistically significant difference.[155]

BRAIN METASTASES

Anti–PD-1/anti–CTLA-4 combination therapy is also being assessed in patients with melanoma metastatic to the brain. In the phase II CheckMate 204 study, nivolumab plus ipilimumab had a high rate of intracranial clinical benefit of 57%, concordant with extracranial activity, with no unexpected neurologic safety signals.[70] Similarly, in a phase II trial in patients with melanoma brain metastases and no previous checkpoint inhibitor treatment, intracranial objective response rate was 53% in patients who were BRAF-inhibitor naïve (*v* 16% in patients who previously were treated with a BRAF inhibitor).[156] Although nivolumab monotherapy also showed clinical activity, patients with symptomatic or leptomeningeal metastases or who had previous local therapy responded poorly to nivolumab alone. Pembrolizumab has also shown intracranial activity with durable responses and an acceptable safety profile in patients with melanoma and those with NSCLC with untreated brain metastases.[157]

5

CLINICAL TRIALS AND BIOSTATISTICS

Karla V. Ballman, PhD, and Judy C. Boughey, MD

OVERVIEW

Variability is ubiquitous across all types of cancer research, from cell-line experiments to human clinical trials. The variability can be attributable to observable as well as unobservable factors. Some variability in outcomes of patients with cancer and responses to cancer treatment arise from differences among cancer types, tumor molecular aberrations, and patient characteristics—all of which can be observed. Although variability can be reduced through a better understanding of factors that give rise to cancer and its response to treatment, the complexity of the underlying biology and differences among patients ensures that random variation and uncertainty will continue to be part of cancer research and treatment. This is due to those factors that remain unobservable.

Statistics is the branch of mathematics that deals with the collection and analysis of data in the face of uncertainty and random variation. "Biostatistics" is a term commonly used to refer to statistical methods and applications related to medical research. The terms biostatistics and statistics are often used interchangeably in clinical research. Statistics plays a significant role in medicine as a whole and in oncology in particular, and statistical concepts and ideas permeate the medical literature relevant to oncologists. This chapter covers topics that an oncologist or oncology provider will encounter and that require a basic understanding to be able to interpret articles in medical journals. The intention for this chapter is not to detail the "how" of statistics (ie, there are no formulas or equations) but rather to elucidate the "what" and "why" of biostatistics in oncology.

It is impossible to summarize in any depth or breadth an entire scientific discipline in a single chapter, even when focused on its application to clinical oncology; as a result, the focus here is on topics commonly encountered or that are frequently misunderstood. In this chapter, we review basic statistical concepts and analytic methods commonly used in clinical research as well as clinical trial design. Clinical trials are an essential part of clinical research and are one way of controlling systematic sources of variation. Properly designed clinical trials isolate the random components of variation that can be quantified using appropriate statistical analysis. In general, proper study design and analysis of the available evidence provide high-level evidence to guide treatment options.

BASIC CONCEPTS

Basic statistical concepts[1-3] commonly used in the analysis of medical data are reviewed in this section. We begin with descriptive statistics for samples and populations and then review inferential statistics, including estimation and hypothesis testing. The section concludes with a brief overview of Bayesian statistics.

SAMPLE AND POPULATION

Most often, it is not feasible to include an entire population in a clinical study. Obtaining measurements on all individuals in the entire population of interest would be too expensive and/or time consuming. A population of interest can be all patients with a specific cancer, such as women with newly diagnosed, early-stage breast cancer. Because it is not possible to obtain the data of interest on all individuals in the identified population, the researcher will obtain data on a sample or subset of individuals from the population. The study sample should be obtained in such a way that individuals included in the sample represent the individuals in the population of interest. The sample data are then used to make inferences about the larger population of interest. The quality of the inferences depends on how well the sample represents the population, which means there are no systematic biases in how the sample of individuals was identified.

A "statistic" is a quantity summarized from a set of data—for example, the mean or median. These are commonly referred to as "descriptive statistics." They may describe quantitative variables, such as age or tumor size; ordinal variables, such as stage of disease; or categorical variables, such as sex or race. Table 5-1 lists definitions of some common descriptive statistics. Most of these terms refer also to characteristics of a population but are considered here as statistics calculated from a sample of data. A common use of a sample statistic is to use it as an estimate of its counterpart in a population. For example, assume that a researcher is interested in the mean body mass index (BMI) of patients at the time of a specific cancer diagnosis. This could be computed by measuring the BMI of all patients at time of diagnosis for the cancer of interest and taking the average. This is called the population mean. It is not feasible to get this information for every patient diagnosed with the specific cancer; therefore, a representative sample is obtained of patients diagnosed with the cancer, which is composed of a small subset of the entire population of patients diagnosed with the cancer. The average BMI for this subset is called the sample mean. The sample mean will be used to estimate the mean BMI of the entire population of patients diagnosed with the specific cancer. Note that the population mean is a fixed value, but one we do not know. The sample mean will vary from sample to sample because each sample will contain a different subset of patients from the population. In summary, a statistic is a value computed from a sample (or subset) taken from a population. The statistic is used to estimate the value for the entire population.

HYPOTHESIS TESTING

The two basic components of inferential statistics are estimation and hypothesis testing.[3] Estimation attempts to ascertain the value of a population parameter or variable. For example, the sample mean is used to estimate the population mean. In contrast, hypothesis testing is used to determine whether there is evidence from the sample to conclude the population mean differs from a particular value or perhaps whether two population means differ from each other. For example, a researcher might be interested in knowing whether the difference in the median survival of patients treated with two different treatments differs from zero. If there is evidence from the sample that the difference in median survival between the groups is not zero, it could be concluded that one treatment is better than the other. Hypothesis testing evaluates the amount of evidence in a sample indicating the medians differ from each other. Many aspects of clinical trial design are framed in terms of hypothesis testing.

A statistical hypothesis test involves three components:

(1) formulation of the null hypothesis and alternative hypothesis,
(2) collection and analysis of data, and
(3) a decision to reject or not reject the null hypothesis. The phrase "not reject" instead of the term "accept," is deliberate.

Table 5-1 Basic Descriptive Statistics

Statistic	Definition and Description
Mean	The average value of the sample.
Median	The value dividing the ordered values of the sample in half; equivalent to the 50th percentile. For an odd sample size, the median is the middle value; for an even sample size, the median is the average of the two middle values.
Percentile	The value below or equal to which a specified percentage of ordered observations fall. Tertiles, quartiles, and quintiles are values dividing an ordered sample into thirds, fourths, and fifths, respectively.
Mode	The most frequent value in the sample. Not often used.
Standard deviation	A measure of the variation of a sample distribution, based on the average squared distance from the sample mean. Most of a sample from a normal distribution is contained within two standard deviations above and below the mean.
Standard error	A measure of variation of the sample mean, or other estimated parameter describing a distribution. It is essentially a measure of the uncertainty in the statistic as an estimate of the population value. Unlike the standard deviation, the standard error gets smaller with larger sample sizes.
Range	The difference between the maximum and minimum values. In practice, the maximum and minimum are usually given, not the difference.

The null hypothesis is a semantic concept that is not the same as a scientific hypothesis. For example, in a trial of a new therapy, the scientific belief or hypothesis is likely that the new therapy will be more efficacious than the currently used standard therapy. However, the null hypothesis would be that the new therapy has the same efficacy as the standard therapy. In the clinical trial setting, the desired scientific outcome is usually to reject the null hypothesis. The amount of evidence against the null hypothesis is determined from the observed sample data. It is done this way because the null hypothesis is very specific and so we can quantify the level of evidence with the *P* value, which is described in the next section. On the other hand, the scientific hypothesis is not specific—it merely states that the new therapy is more efficacious than the standard therapy; it does not state how much better. Given the vagueness, it is not possible to quantify the evidence that supports this hypothesis. Hence, we determine the evidence against the null hypothesis rather than the evidence for the alternative (ie, the scientific) hypothesis.

The hypothesis test allows two outcomes: reject or do not reject the null hypothesis. There are two possible errors that can be made in this scenario (see Table 5-2). One is that the null hypothesis is true and is incorrectly rejected (false positive); the other is that the null hypothesis is false and is incorrectly not rejected (false negative). The first error is called a type I error, and the probability of type I error is called the significance level and is designated as α. The second error is called a type II error, and the probability of a type II error is designated as β. The probability of a type II error requires a precise specification of exactly how the null hypothesis is false, which is referred to as the "alternative hypothesis." What is more commonly of interest is the probability of correctly rejecting the null hypothesis when a particular alternative to the null hypothesis is true, which is called "power" and is equal to $1 - \beta$.

Hypothesis tests require the calculation of a test statistic using data from one or more samples, corresponding to one or more different groups (eg, corresponding to different treatments). The computation of a test statistic and the associated *P* value, discussed in the next section, is done by available statistics software packages. Table 5-3 describes some common statistical tests. These all relate to simple comparisons of a quantitative or categorical characteristic, between groups or within a group. The table includes examples of parametric and nonparametric tests. Parametric tests are derived using a specific assumption about the distribution of the data within the population (eg, normal, binomial, or exponential), whereas nonparametric tests make fewer assumptions. Although the latter feature is desirable, a nonparametric test will generally have somewhat less statistical power than a parametric test that is correctly matched to a specific distribution. Fortunately, these considerations usually become less important with increasing sample size. For large samples, the choice of a parametric or nonparametric test is not critical; for smaller samples a biostatistician should be consulted as to what is the most appropriate test. More complex statistical methods that relate to other types of end points are described later in this chapter.

INTERPRETING *P* VALUES AND CONFIDENCE INTERVALS

One of the most commonly used values in the statistical analysis of medical data, and possibly the most often misunderstood, is the *P* value. The *P* value is calculated from the sample data and it measures the strength of the evidence against the null hypothesis. Essentially, the *P* value is the probability that a result as different from (or more different than) the one observed could be produced by chance alone, assuming the null hypothesis is true. In other words, it calculates the probability of getting the observed data, or data more in favor of the alternative hypothesis, if the null hypothesis is true. If the *P* value is small (close to zero), it means the sample data (or data more different from the null) is not likely to be observed if the null hypothesis is true. This is evidence against the null hypothesis. It is likely that the data are a consequence of some systematic effect. More concretely, it was recently reported that in a trial for men with high-risk, localized prostate cancer, the 4-year overall survival rate was 89% for androgen suppression plus radiation treatment (two-treatment arm) compared with 93% for androgen suppression plus radiation treatment plus docetaxel (three-treatment arm) with a hazard ratio (HR) of 0.69 and a one-sided *P* value of 0.034.[4] Here, the null hypothesis is not explicitly stated, as is often the case. However, it is implied the null hypothesis would be that overall survival is the same between the treatment arms. In this case, the alternative hypothesis is that the three-treatment arm would be better than the two-treatment arm because it has one additional treatment. This is a one-sided alternative hypothesis that will have a one-sided *P* value. Statisticians determine whether there is evidence against the null hypothesis (no difference in overall survival between the two treatment arms). If there is evidence against the null hypothesis, they then reject the null hypothesis in favor of the alternative hypothesis. Typically, as in this example, a level of significance of 0.05 is used to determine if there is sufficient evidence to reject the null hypothesis. The *P* value is then calculated by assuming there is no difference between the

Table 5-2 Hypothesis Test Decisions and Errors

		Truth	
		Null hypothesis is true	Null hypothesis is false
Decision based on data	Reject the null hypothesis	Type I error	Correct decision
	Do not reject the null hypothesis	Correct decision	Type II error

Table 5-3 **Basic Statistical Tests**

Setting	Test	Definition and Description
Comparing means	Two-sample *t*	Used to compare means between two groups for a quantitative variable. Generally robust to small sample size and non-normal distributions, but sensitive to outlying values, which inflate estimates of variability.
	Paired *t*	Used to compare paired quantitative data; for example, a quantitative characteristic measured before and after treatment in each patient. Same sensitivity to outlying values as the two-sample *t* test.
Comparing medians or distributions	Wilcoxon rank-sum (Mann-Whitney)	A nonparametric alternative to the two-sample *t* test. Less sensitive to outlying values than the two-sample *t* test, although somewhat more conservative.
	Wilcoxon signed rank	A nonparametric version of the paired *t* test. Less sensitive to outlying values than the paired *t* test, although somewhat more conservative.
Comparing proportions	χ^2	Used to compare proportions between two or more groups. Fairly robust to small sample sizes, unless there is an imbalance between groups. The continuity correction sometimes applied to the χ^2 test is conservative and generally unnecessary.
	Fisher exact	Used to compare proportions with small sample size. A conservative test compared with the χ^2.
	McNemar	Used to compare paired proportions; for example, a binary characteristic assessed before and after treatment in each patient. It is based only on the discordant pairs (where outcome is different) and is not used to assess concordance.

treatment arms (which would be a HR = 1) and determining how likely it would have been to observe a HR of 0.69 (the value computed from the trial data) or one even less. In this case, an HR of less than 1 favors the three-treatment arm. Because the *P* value is 0.039, meaning that if the HR were equal to 1, the chance of observing a HR of 0.69 or less is 0.039. Because this is less than the level of significance (eg $P = .039$ is less than the level of significance of .05), the conclusion is that the three-treatment arm has superior overall survival outcomes than the two-treatment arm.

What constitutes a small *P* value? This is set by stating a level of significance at the time the study is designed, which is called the level of significance or the significance level. In clinical research, $P < .05$ is commonly used to indicate statistical significance, meaning it is sufficient evidence against the null hypothesis. This number is arbitrary but is as good as any other if one wants only to establish a minimum threshold of evidence against the null hypothesis. In the formal hypothesis testing paradigm, it is equivalent to rejecting the null hypothesis when the type I error rate is set at 5%. There are a couple of common misinterpretations of the *P* value:

- Misinterpretation: the P value is the probability that the null hypothesis is true. Explanation: Because the *P* value is calculated by assuming the null hypothesis is true, it cannot be a statement of the probability that the null hypothesis is true.
- Misinterpretation: when the P value is large or not statistically significant, this means there is no difference. Explanation: When a result is not statistically significant, it only means chance is one possible explanation for the observed data, if the null hypothesis is true. It does not mean it was established or proven that the null hypothesis is true. In other words, absence of evidence against the null hypothesis is not evidence proving the null hypothesis.

What does a large *P* value mean? In the absence of any other information, and assuming the data arise from a properly designed study, the safest and most accurate interpretation is that there is insufficient evidence that the null hypothesis is false. The reality is that the *P* value, whether small or large, actually carries little information. It conveys no information about the direction or magnitude of an effect, no information about the uncertainty in the estimated effect, and no information about the clinical significance of the effect. Even a small *P* value is no guarantee that an effect has clinical significance. In studies with a large sample size, even a modest departure from the null hypothesis can be associated with a high degree of statistical significance, but the departure from the null hypothesis may have little practical meaning. For example, it is possible to obtain a *P* value of less than 0.0001 with an observed difference in median survival between two treatments of only 1 day (which is statistically significant but not clinically meaningful) if the sample sizes are sufficiently large.

It is never sufficient to consider the *P* value alone. What is of most importance is sample estimate of the effect and its CI.[5] The CI represents a range that is likely to contain the true population value. An interval with a 95% CI will be expected to contain the true value of the effect 95% of the time and miss it 5% of the time. Note that for any particular CI, it is unknown whether it contains the true value. The *P* value is only a statement about whether an observed result, or one more extreme, is due to chance, assuming the null hypothesis is true. Figure 5-1 shows a variety of scenarios for the outcome of a statistical analysis and illustrates how CIs relate to the concepts of statistical and clinical significance. A CI for an HR crossing 1 implies there is no difference between the treatments.

When a *P* value is not less than 0.05, the associated null hypothesis value will be contained within the 95% CI. Again, this means that if the null hypothesis is that there is no difference in survival, it can be written as HR = 1. If the *P* value for the tests of hypothesis is greater than the level of significance (0.05), then the 95% CI will contain 1. Similarly, if a 95% CI for an HR does not contain 1, the implication is the result is statistically significant at the 0.05 level of significance (ie there is evidence of a difference in survival). The fallacy of thinking the null hypothesis value is the true value when the *P* value is greater than 0.05 is readily apparent because the null value is only one among a range of possible values that could reasonably have produced the observed data.

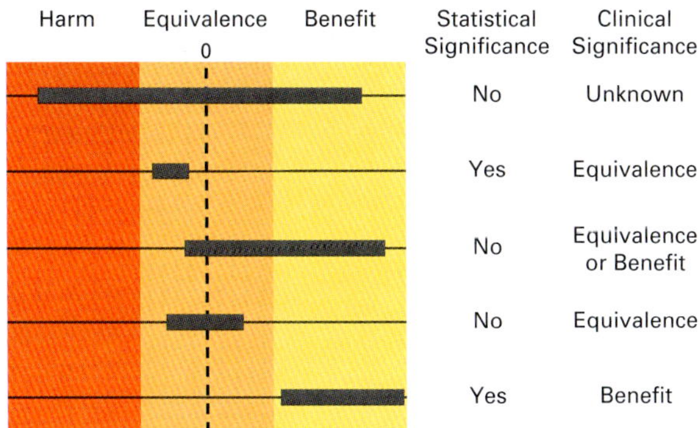

Fig. 5-1 Interpreting CIs with respect to statistical and clinical significance.

Heavy black lines illustrate 95% CIs that could arise from a comparative clinical trial of an experimental therapy compared with standard therapy. The vertical dashed line indicates exact equality between arms, and the light orange area indicates a difference close to equality that is considered clinically insignificant. The yellow area indicates a difference between arms that would be considered a clinically significant benefit for the experimental arm; the dark orange indicates clinically significant harm for the experimental arm. The determination of statistical significance (at the α = 0.05 level) is based only on whether the CI includes 0. The full range of the CI must be examined to determine what conclusions are reasonable with respect to the clinical significance of the study.

KEY POINTS

- Large *P* values are not evidence for a lack of effect; they should generally be regarded as uninformative.
- CIs provide information about statistical and clinical significance.

SAMPLE SIZE AND POWER CALCULATIONS

The calculation of sample size needed for a clinical trial depends on several factors, including the acceptable rate of type I error, the desired power, the value of the null hypothesis, the difference between the null hypothesis and the particular alternative to the null hypothesis (sometimes called the effect size), and the variability of the outcome. In some cases, the latter is determined by the null hypothesis and a specified alternative; in other cases, it can vary independently. These factors influence the sample size in a reasonably intuitive way, as summarized in Table 5-4.

The most common value specified for α (or significance level) is 5 and common values for power are 80% or 90%. However, other values can be used depending on the situation. The factor with the greatest impact on sample size is the particular alternative to the null selected for use in the calculations. The difference between the null hypothesis and the specific alternative hypothesis is often called the effect size. Generally, the effect size is the smallest effect that would be considered clinically or biologically of interest; it is the minimum difference that is considered to be of clinical significance. Depending on the primary end point of the study, the effect size may be expressed as a difference in proportions, a difference in means, or a HR. Care should be taken in understanding the difference between clinical significance and statistical significance. It is possible to have a statistically significant result that is not clinically significant. For example, a clinical trial could show a median improvement of 1 week in overall survival between two treatment arms that is statistically significant (*P* = .001). In this case, the result is statistically significant at the 0.05 level but has little

Table 5-4 Factors Influencing Sample Size in a Comparative Study

Quantity	Effect
Type I error rate	Decreasing error rate increases sample size.
Power	Increasing power increases sample size.
Effect size[a]	Smaller effect size increases sample size.
Variability	Smaller variability decreases sample size.

[a]Difference between null and alternative hypothesis values.

clinical significance, with only a median difference in overall survival of 1 week. On the other hand, it is also possible to have a clinically meaningful difference, say a survival difference of 6 months, that is not statistically significant (P = .15). This latter case may occur when studies are underpowered due a sample size that is too small. Sample size is sensitive to the effect size. In most cases, a halving of the effect size results in approximately a four-fold increase in the sample size requirement, with all other factors unchanged. Conversely, doubling the effect size results in approximately a 75% lower required sample size. Thus, it is critically important to carefully consider what effect size is of clinical importance for a study.

KEY POINTS

- Statistical significance and clinical significance are different concepts.
- Sample size calculations for comparative trials are extremely sensitive to the assumed effect size (difference in outcome between arms); for example, halving the effect size results in a four-fold increase in the total number of patients required for a trial.

BAYESIAN STATISTICS

Most of the familiar statistical concepts and applications encountered in medical research are based on a so-called frequentist view of statistics and probability. In the frequentist perspective, probability is a quantity that reflects the underlying long-term frequency with which an event will occur under repeated observation. This frequency is governed by unknown, but fixed, parameters that define a probability distribution. For example, in a frequentist view, the probability that the flip of a coin will result in heads up is equal to the number of times heads is observed when the coin is flipped a large number of times. If the coin is fair, this probability will be one-half, which will equal the proportion of heads we observe in a large number of flips. The statistical procedures derived from this perspective are all based on relating observed data to the fixed parameters of the probability model that generates the data.

Bayesian statistics also seek to relate observed data to the probability model that generates the data. The term "Bayesian" derives from a basic theorem known as Bayes rule, which was formulated by the Reverend Thomas Bayes in the mid-18th century. The Bayesian formulation allows the incorporation of a more subjective notion of probability—the notion of probability as a measure of the strength of one's belief in a single outcome—for example, the probability that it will rain tomorrow or that the moon is made of green cheese. It also allows the application of this view of probability to unknown parameters governing a probability distribution—for example, the probability that the rate of response to a treatment exceeds a specified value. This is not a meaningful concept in a frequentist framework, because the response rate is viewed as a fixed number.

The Bayesian approach to statistical inference involves three basic steps:

(1) specification of a probability distribution for the unknown parameter (called a prior distribution), based on existing knowledge;
(2) collection of data; and
(3) use of the data to update the prior distribution, resulting in a posterior distribution (or updated probability distribution for the unknown parameter).

A simple example involves an imperfect diagnostic test. For a randomly selected individual, it would be reasonable to assume the probability she has a disease is equal to the prevalence of the disease (the prior distribution). After the test is performed, the result is either positive or negative (the data). This information can be used to recalculate the probability that the person has the disease, which is no longer equal to the disease prevalence (the posterior distribution).

Most clinical trials are designed and analyzed on the basis of a frequentist approach. Basically, there is a null hypothesis and an alternative hypothesis. The null hypothesis would be that there is no difference in outcome between two treatment arms. A two-sided alternative hypothesis would be that there is a difference in outcome between the two-treatment arm. The data are collected, and a P value is computed on the basis of the observed data, which are compared with the level of significance to determine whether the null hypothesis will be rejected. Again, the P value is the probability of observing the data obtained or data more extreme (more in favor of the alternative hypothesis), assuming there is no difference in outcome between the treatment arms. If this value is sufficiently small, less than the level of significance, we conclude there is evidence against the null hypothesis. This means we would reject the hypothesis that the two treatment arms have similar outcomes. The Bayesian approach would be to determine a probability distribution for the difference in outcomes between the two treatment arms; this is called the prior distribution. Often, a noninformative prior is used that essentially assumes all possible differences in outcomes between the two arms are equally likely. Once data are obtained, ta new distribution, the posterior distribution, is generated that combines the information in the prior distribution and the data. This posterior distribution describes the likelihood of each possible difference in outcomes between the two treatment arms. The posterior distribution is then used to decide which treatment arm has better outcomes. For example, using the posterior distribution, the probability that arm A is better than arm B can be computed. If this probability is large, say there is a 90% chance that arm A has better outcomes than arm B, the decision is then that arm A is the better treatment. Frequentist designs evaluate the evidence against the null hypothesis by determining how likely it would have been to get the results observed, or more extreme results, assuming the null hypothesis is true. Small P values mean the result is unlikely if the null hypothesis is true, and so it is taken as evidence against the assumption that the treatments yield the same outcomes. Bayesian designs allow a calculation of the probability that one treatment is better than the other. However, these designs require investigators to state a prior distribution for the possible differences in outcomes between the two treatment arms.

The potential controversy in applying Bayesian methods to medical research lies in the specification of the prior distribution, which is allowed to incorporate subjective judgments about the quantity under investigation. Many statisticians argue that prior beliefs about an unknown quantity represent a form of bias that should be avoided in scientific research; others argue that ignoring prior knowledge is in itself a bias. It is possible to use a Bayesian framework in a way that minimizes the use of information contained in prior beliefs, thereby letting the data speak for themselves. This is done by choosing a prior distribution that is said to be uninformative with respect to the quantity under study (also sometimes called a "flat prior"). Interestingly, statistical procedures conducted using uninformative priors are often similar, or even identical, to those conducted within a frequentist framework, and they produce similar results. They simply use different mathematical machinery and terminology. When Bayesian methods have been used in the design or analysis of a research study, one should always be able to ascertain the nature of the prior distribution. If a subjective or informative prior distribution has been used, its rationale and appropriateness should be carefully considered, and it should be recognized that the choice of a prior distribution can influence the interpretation and conclusions of the study.

KEY POINT

- Frequentist and Bayesian methods provide alternative frameworks for interpreting the evidence in the data.

CLINICAL TRIAL DESIGN

Clinical trials play a fundamental role in cancer research and in the development of treatment, prevention and detection methods.[6-9] Clinical trials have historically been classified according to the general phases of drug development. Although this classification does not account for all clinical trials relevant to oncology, it is a useful starting point for describing the key elements of trial design, which necessarily vary according to the objectives of the trial.

Phase I trials are often the first use of a drug in humans and focus on toxicity, with the goal of determining a dose that would have acceptable toxicity if the drug were effective. Phase II trials are designed to provide a preliminary indication of whether a therapy has anticancer effects. The result is considered preliminary because the study may be uncontrolled, might use a surrogate end point (eg, tumor response instead of survival), or is too small to rule out chance effects. A phase III trial is typically a controlled, randomized trial that is sufficiently large to distinguish chance effects from true treatment effects. There are other trial classifications that are occasionally used, including phase I/II, phase Ib, phase II/III or phase IV. There is no recognized governing body for trial nomenclature and trial sponsors are free to attach whatever labels they wish to a particular study. Sometimes the label selected is motivated by regulatory or insurance considerations: for example, the Food and Drug Administration mandates definitions of trial phases for studies that it regulates, and insurers may decline coverage for patients participating in certain phase trials.

PHASE I TRIALS

The goal of the initial phase of testing a new anticancer agent in humans is finding a dose that yields an acceptable level of toxicity. What is deemed acceptable depends on the disease in question. In diseases like cancer that have significant morbidity and mortality rates, the acceptable level of toxicity may be relatively high. It is often the case with cytotoxic drugs that drug toxicity is a measure of its potential efficacy, meaning that great efficacy is expected with higher doses. However, higher doses mean more toxicity and the goal is to find the highest dose with an acceptable level of toxicity. With newer targeted agents, the presumed relationship of toxicity and efficacy may differ, and the design of appropriate phase I trials for such agents can be challenging. The major objective for a phase I trial is to find an acceptable drug dose to be used in subsequent phase II and higher trials. Phase I trials are not designed to test drug activity or efficacy.

Traditionally, the objective of a phase I trial is to determine the maximum dose of an agent, either alone or in combination with other therapies (including radiation), that yields an acceptable level of adverse events when administered on a specific schedule and by a specific route. This dose is usually referred to as the maximum tolerated dose (MTD) or the recommended phase II dose. For example, a simple definition of acceptable toxicity might be "an adverse event of grade 3 or worse in not more than one out of six patients," where a grade 3 adverse event is defined according to standard criteria. The adverse event criteria used to determine the MTD is said to be dose-limiting toxicity (DLT). Specifically, if a patient has a predefined grade 3 adverse event, this is called a DLT. Once an MTD is established, this dose will often be used in further evaluations of efficacy in phase II trials. However, other factors may be considered that may result in the recommended phase II dose being lower than the MTD.

Phase I End Points and Patient Population

Phase I trials are necessarily small for ethical reasons, because it is not expected that patients enrolled on these trials will obtain benefit. Typically, patients enrolled in phase I trials have received multiple lines of therapy and there are no additional standard treatment options available. The patient population is generally heterogeneous with respect to the type of cancer, but at times may be restricted to specific cancers, depending on the agent being tested and its mechanism of action.

The most important criterion in a phase I trial is the definition of DLT. Although most phase I trials have a similar definition for what constitutes a DLT, the definition can be tailored to reflect adverse events expected on the basis of the mechanism of action of the agent. The most common standard for rating the severity of adverse events is the National Cancer Institute's Common Terminology Criteria for Adverse Events list, which provides specific criteria for grading a wide range of adverse events on a numeric scale: 0 (none), 1 (mild), 2 (moderate), 3 (severe), 4 (life threatening), 5 (fatal). Most definitions of DLT exclude grade 1 or 2 adverse events, and possibly some grade 3 toxicities if these are expected and manageable (eg, neutropenia, nausea/vomiting). A typical definition of a DLT might be "grade 3 or higher nonhematologic adverse event or grade 4 or higher hematologic adverse event that is attributable to the agent being tested." This is the starting definition of a DLT for most trials, and the study team may make a modification on the basis of expected, manageable adverse events yielding, for example, "any grade 3 or higher nonhematologic adverse event other than diarrhea or a grade 4 or higher hematologic adverse event that is attributable." They must also specify the time during which adverse events will be evaluated for purposes of determining a DLT. This is typically a relatively short time and is almost always one treatment cycle; thus, it only reflects acute adverse events. Finally, another important aspect is assigning attribution to the adverse event. DLTs are usually defined as adverse events attributed to the agent being tested (*v* the underlying disease). Adverse events that occur after the specified observation period are not reflected in the determination of the MTD but may influence the choice of the recommended phase II dose or how the agent is used in subsequent phase II trials.

Phase I Design Options

Phase I trials prespecify the starting dose for the treatment being evaluated for the first cohort of patients as well as a sequence of doses to be tested in subsequent cohorts. If the agent in question has not yet been assessed in humans, the initial dose is typically derived from animal experiments. If the agent has been used in humans but with a different route of administration, different schedule, or combined with different treatments (including only as a monotherapy) than what is currently being tested, the starting dose is selected on the basis of all available human experience with the treatment. For trials that are testing the agent for the first time in humans, a common starting dose ranges from one-tenth to one-third of the mouse LD_{10}, the lethal dose for 10% of mice. Subsequent dose levels are determined by increasing the preceding dose by decreasing fractions—for example, 100%, 67%, 50%, 40%, and 33%. This sequence and those with slight variations are called modified Fibonacci dose levels. Starting dose levels for agents that are likely to be well tolerated, such as biologic agents, may be determined by log (ie, 10-fold) or half-log increases of the preceding dose.

There are two important considerations in phase I trial designs: (1) minimize the total number of patients, because of little likelihood that enrolled patients will benefit from participating in the trial, and (2) minimize the number of patients who experience serious adverse events. The most commonly used phase I design is the 3+3 design (Fig 5-2), which was developed in the 1950s. Briefly, cohorts of three patients are entered in the trial at dose levels beginning with the prespecified initial dose level. If there is no observed DLT in all three patients treated at the specified dose, the next cohort of three patients is entered at the next higher dose level. If two of three patients experience DLT at a specified dose, then the adverse event rate associated with that dose is considered unacceptable, and the dose level below it (if any was tested) is considered the MTD. If one of the three patients experiences a DLT, an additional cohort of three patients is entered at the same dose level. If no DLT is seen among the additional three patients, the next cohort of patients will be treated at the next higher dose level; otherwise, the toxicity is considered unacceptable and the dose level below it is considered the MTD.

If the starting dose is too low and/or the spacing of doses is too small relative to the steepness of the dose-response curve, a large number of patients may be enrolled at doses that likely have no therapeutic benefit. In response to this concern, researchers may use an accelerated titration design. In this design, the cohort size for the initial dose level is a single patient. Subsequent patients will be treated at the next higher dose level until a grade 2 or higher drug-related adverse event is observed. Once this happens, a standard 3+3 design is implemented starting at the next lower dose level from that where a grade 2 or higher adverse event was observed. These designs are usually used for treatments for which there is some human experience with the agent and the toxicity profile is known to be manageable.

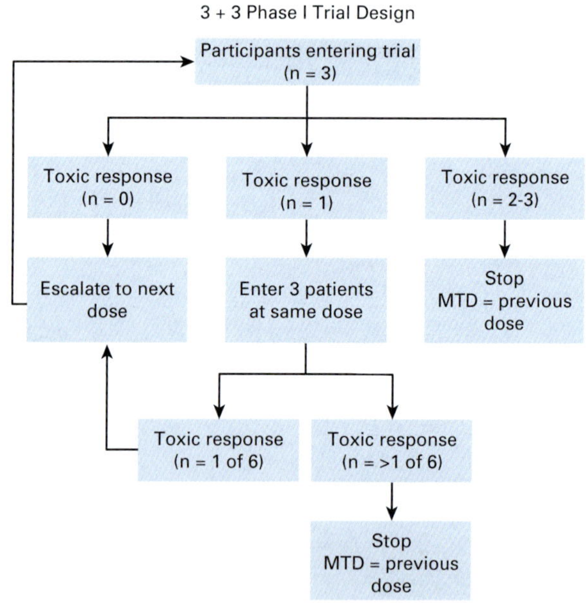

Fig. 5-2 A 3 + 3 phase I trial design. MTD, maximum tolerated dose.

Reproduced with permission from Dr. Colleen Lewis.

Another design option is the continual reassessment method, which uses a Bayesian approach. Although there are many variations of the continual reassessment methods, the basic idea is to specify an acceptable probability of DLT (eg, 20% or 33%), specify a mathematical model for the dose-response curve, and update the mathematical estimate of the dose-response curve after each patient (or cohort of patients) has been treated. The dose level for the next patient (or cohort) that will be treated is the one for which the estimated probability of DLT is closest to the specified target. The advantage of this method is that it produces more accurate estimates of the MTD and minimizes patients who are treated at nontherapeutic levels or too toxic levels. One disadvantage it that it typically requires more patients than a 3+3 design. Another disadvantage of this method is that it is complicated to implement because it requires real-time submission of data by study staff and review by the study statistician to make this work efficiently.

The Bayesian optimal interval design is simple to implement and has superior performance compared with the 3+3 design.[10] This design computes probability intervals defined as underdosing, proper dosing, and overdosing. Bayesian-model–based inference is used to determine the likelihood that a dose adverse event rate will be in each of these intervals. Dose-escalation decisions are easily made on the basis of the three dosing intervals; they can be described using simple tables for ease of application. The Bayesian optimal interval design tends to treat fewer patients at doses greater than the MTD and is more likely than the 3+3 design to identify the true MTD. It is also easy to implement because the tables are generated before the trial starts, so there is no need to perform real-time computation to determine at which dose level to treat the next patient (or cohort).

For some biologic or targeted treatments, toxicity is not expected to be substantial throughout the anticipated therapeutic range of doses. For these trials, the objective of dose finding is to determine the range of biologically active doses. Usually, the end point is not the observation of an adverse event but rather a measure of therapeutic activity. An example of such a trial would be a treatment with a new kinase inhibitor. If it is anticipated that there will be no drug-related adverse events, the goal might be to determine the smallest level that results in sufficient suppression of kinase activity in the tumor. In such a trial, it is only necessary to achieve biologically meaningful suppression and there is no need to escalate beyond this level. The goal of the trial is not to establish an MTD but rather to establish the optimal therapeutic dose. Designs for these types of trials are being developed.

KEY POINTS

- Phase I trials focus on identifying safe doses or combinations of therapies, using small sample sizes to minimize exposure to therapies with unknown adverse event profiles and unknown benefit.
- The dose established in a phase I trial will be used in subsequent phase II trials.

PHASE II TRIALS

Phase II trials encompass a wide array of trial designs. These range from small, single-arm trials with a dozen patients to randomized controlled trials with 200 patients. Nevertheless, there are common features that characterize a phase II trial: The primary end point is related to efficacy or drug activity, the sample size is moderately small, the efficacy end point is short-term and/or not definitive for patient benefit, and the study relies on historical experience as context for judging whether the result is promising enough to carry forward to a phase III trial. This is the type of trial that will be considered phase II for purposes of this discussion.

Phase II End Points and Patient Population

The general objective of a phase II trial is to evaluate the potential efficacy of a drug or regimen in a specific patient population. The patient population is usually somewhat narrowly defined (eg, patients with recurrent glioblastoma). Typically, patients enrolled in phase II trials have experienced treatment failure with at least one or two standard therapies. The idea is to initially test the drug activity in a group of patients for whom there are limited treatment options, rather than in a group of patients for whom potentially curative treatments exist. However, there are scenarios in which a phase II trial is conducted with patients with newly diagnosed disease and who have not yet been treated (eg, in diseases with no effective therapy, or when a new agent is to be added to the standard of care). Finally, a phase II study may be used to evaluate an established treatment in a different patient population (eg, a different type of cancer, or a subtype of cancer defined by a genetic or another biologic marker).

The primary end point of a phase II trial is a measure of potential efficacy or anticancer activity. The specific end point balances the ability to assess it in a relatively short time (ie, weeks or months) and its validity as a measure of long-term benefit. Many trials for solid tumors use tumor response (complete or partial), as assessed by imaging, as the primary end point, which usually can be ascertained within 3 to 6 months from the time a patient started treatment. For neoadjuvant trials, a common end point is pathologic complete response (CR), which is determined by pathologic examination of tissue obtained at time of surgery. There are also trials that use other end points; some examples are 3-month progression-free survival (PFS) rate or 6-month disease-free survival (DFS) rate.

The most common methodology for determining tumor response in solid tumors is RECIST. Most response definitions for solid tumors are based on the change in size of measurable lesions over the course of the trial. Tumor responses are classified as CR, partial response (PR), stable disease (SD), or progressive disease (PD). Determining disease response status on the basis of RECIST depends on targeted and nontargeted lesions. A targeted lesion must be measurable. If there is more than one measurable lesion, a maximum of five lesions are selected. A measure of disease is the sum of the largest diameter of the targeted lesions. All other lesions (either nonmeasurable lesions or measurable lesions not designated as targeted) are called nontargeted. The RECIST criteria depend on the changes in the size of the targeted lesions as well as change in nontargeted lesions. Tables 5-5 and 5-6 list RECIST definitions of CR, PR, SD, and PD.[11] Different criteria are necessary for hematologic malignancies, and these are often tailored to the type of hematologic malignancy. Whatever criteria are used, the trial design must specify how and when response will be assessed. The assessment of the primary end point must be performed the same way for all patients within the trial and should be reasonably comparable to what was used in other trials or how it was assessed in historical controls.

Sometimes a phase II trial may use a tumor biomarker as the primary end point. For example, prostate cancer trials often use increase, progression, or recurrence of prostate-specific antigen levels at a specific time, such as 3 or 6 months, as a phase II end point. A biomarker is a single trait or composition of traits, often called a signature, used to determine the disease status. These traits may include an assessment of tumor genomics, genetic aberration, or a molecular assessment of circulating tumor DNA. There is heightened interest in biomarkers for targeted therapies, which may have specific mechanisms of action that are measured by a variety of assays, possibly from blood or tumor samples that can be obtained quickly and easily. The rationale is that if the mechanism of action is truly understood for a targeted treatment, it should be possible to measure the impact of the treatment on the intended target. There are many different uses for biomarkers in cancer research. In phase II studies, biomarkers are most commonly used as the primary end point as a surrogate of treatment efficacy. Unfortunately, the appropriate use of biomarkers as surrogate end points requires specific criteria that may be difficult to validate. A full discussion of these issues is beyond the scope of this chapter, but in general, one should be cautious when evaluating claims of effectiveness based on biomarkers or other surrogate end points.

Traditional, One-Arm, Phase II Design

A commonly used phase II design is a single-arm trial using historical outcomes as a point of reference for the design and interpretation of the trial. The major analysis is to compare the observed outcome in the single-arm trial and to compare this with the historical control value to determine if there is a statistically significant difference. For example, suppose the primary end point is tumor response and the historical tumor response rate for the standard-of-care regimen is p_0. Furthermore, suppose p_1 is the minimum tumor response rate that would represent meaningful improvement compared with the standard of care. In other words, if there is evidence the new treatment response rate differs from p_0, it would be of interest for further study. In addition, the investigators want reasonable power to reject the null hypothesis if the true treatment response rate were p_1.

The hypothesis-testing paradigm assumes that at the end of the trial, one will either conclude (1) the true response rate for the regimen is greater than p_0 or (2) there is no evidence that the response rate for the regimen differs from p_0. The design parameters must also include a specification of the probability of a type I error (ie, the level of significance, α) and the desired power ($1 - \beta$, or 1 − probability of a type II error). The false-positive error rate is the probability of falsely concluding the true response rate for the regimen is greater than p_0 when, in fact, it is equal to p_0. Power is the probability of correctly concluding that the true response rate for the regimen is greater than p_0 when, in fact, it is greater than p_0. For phase II trial, α is typically is set at 5% or 10%. The power is evaluated at p_1, the target response rate of interest. Power for phase II trials

Table 5-5 **RECIST Definitions of CR, PR, SD, and PD.**

Response	Target Lesions	Nontarget Lesions
CR	Disappearance of all target lesions	Disappearance of all nontarget lesions and normalization of tumor marker level
PR	At least 30% decrease in the sum of diameters of target lesions, taking as reference the baseline sum of diameters	Persistence of one or more nontarget lesion(s) and/or maintenance of tumor marker level above the normal limits
PD	At least 20% increase in the sum of diameters of target lesions, taking as reference the smallest sum in the study. In addition to a relative increase of 20%, the sum must also demonstrate an absolute increase of at least 5 mm.	Unequivocal progression of existing nontarget lesions. The appearance of one or more new lesions is also considered progression
SD	Neither sufficient shrinkage to quality for PR nor sufficient increase to qualify for PD, taking as reference the smallest sum diameters while in study.	N/A

Abbreviations: CR, complete response; N/A, not applicable; NE, not evaluable; PD, progressive disease; PR, partial response; SD, stable disease.

Table 5-6 **Overall Response Evaluation**			
Target lesion	**Nontarget lesion**	**New lesions?**	**Overall response**
CR	CR	No	CR
CR	Non-CR/non-PD	No	PR
CR	Not evaluated	No	PR
PR	Non-PD or not evaluated	No	PR
SD	Non-PD or not evaluated	No	SD
Not all evaluated	Non-PD	No	NE
PD	Any	Yes or no	PD
Any	PD	Yes or no	PD
Any	Any	Yes	PD

Abbreviations: CR, complete response; NE, not evaluable; PD, progressive disease; PR, partial response; SD, stable disease.

typically ranges from 80% to 90%. The possibility of relatively high error rates is accepted because it yields smaller sample sizes and because the results of a phase II trial will be confirmed in a phase III trial. However, differences between p_0 and p_1 have considerably more impact on the sample size than the values for α and power. The larger the difference between p_0 and p_1, the smaller the required sample size. A balance must be struck between the desire for smaller sample sizes and the ability to detect differences between p_0 and p_1 that would be of clinical interest.

Table 5-7 lists sample sizes for single-arm trials under a variety of assumptions about p_0 and p_1 and specified values of α and power. The value r is the minimum number of responses required in a given number of patients (n) to conclude (with the specified type I error rate of, at most, α) the true response rate for the regimen is greater than p_0. A common misconception is that observing r responses allows one to conclude that the true response rate is at least p_1. That this is not the case is obvious from the fact that the observed minimum response rate required (ie, r/n) is less than p_1.

The primary end point for a phase II trial may not be tumor response; rather, it may be based on a time-to-event end point, such as overall survival or PFS. Unfortunately, there are some cancers for which the median time to death or progression is measured in weeks or months. If historical data suggest the median progression-free interval with standard of care is 3 months, this can be recast in a way that parallels testing a tumor response rate. Specifically, a median survival of 3 months is equivalent to specifying that the percentage of patients alive and progression free at 3 months, p_0, is 50%. It is relatively straightforward to convert a hypothetical improvement in the median PFS for the new treatment to a value of p_1 at 3 months, the percentage of patients who are progression-free at 3 months.

As mentioned previously, it would not be good practice in reporting the results of a clinical trial to merely provide the P value for comparing p_1 to p_0, or merely stating that the null hypothesis has been rejected and there is evidence that the new treatment has a higher tumor response rate than the standard-of-care treatment. It is important to also report an estimate of the response rate for the tested treatment as well as its corresponding CI. Knowing the estimate of the tumor response rate of the new treatment allows individuals to place this in context with a host of other factors before deciding whether additional trials are warranted. The estimated response rate is relatively imprecise for phase II trials because of the relatively small sample sizes (Table 5-8) and actually provides only a rough indication of the response rate.

A frequently used alternative to the one-arm, single-stage design is a design that enrolls patients in two stages. The motivation for this alternative is to minimize the number of patients treated with ineffective treatment. For example, consider the first scenario in Table 5-7 that requires a sample size of 55 patients with 10 observed responses to reject the null hypothesis and conclude that the new treatment has a better response rate than the standard of care. Suppose that after 25 patients have been treated, only two responses have been observed. This means eight responses must be observed in the final 30 patients to have sufficient evidence against the null hypothesis, a seemingly unlikely scenario given what has been observed in the initial patients. Two-stage designs formalize the intuitive notion that the trial should be terminated early if the results are poorer than desired and that there is little chance of concluding there is evidence against the null hypothesis. This is accomplished by dividing the enrollment into two stages and specifying the minimum number of responses that must be observed in the first stage before enrolling the second stage. It is the case that there may be a set of two-stage designs that meet a given set of design parameters (eg, α, power, and detectable difference between p_0 and p_1). One commonly used approach for selecting a two-stage design is to minimize the average number of patients that would be enrolled if the true response rate was no better than the historical reference p_0—this is called a Simon optimal design. Table 5-9 shows the optimal Simon two-stage design for the same situations as in Table 5-7. Note that the maximum sample size for these designs is often

Table 5-7 **Examples of Single-Stage Phase II Designs**					
Design Criteria				**Resulting Design**	
p_0	p_1	**A**	**Power**[a]	n	r
0.10	0.25	0.05	0.90	55	10
0.10	0.25	0.05	0.80	40	8
0.10	0.25	0.10	0.90	40	7
0.10	0.25	0.10	0.80	31	6
0.10	0.25	0.05	0.90	33	7
0.10	0.25	0.05	0.80	25	6
0.10	0.25	0.10	0.90	25	5
0.10	0.25	0.10	0.80	18	4
0.50	0.70	0.05	0.90	53	33
0.50	0.70	0.05	0.80	37	24
0.50	0.70	0.10	0.90	39	24
0.50	0.70	0.10	0.80	28	18

Abbreviations: α, type I (false-positive) error rate if $P = p_0$; n, smallest sample size that satisfies design criteria; p_0, response rate under null hypothesis; p_1, response rate under alternative hypothesis; r, minimum number of responses required to reject null hypothesis and conclude that $P > p_0$.
[a]Power refers to the probability of rejecting the null hypothesis if $P = p_1$.

only slightly larger than for a single-stage design, with α and power values satisfying the same specifications. For example, the design for the first scenario uses (at most) 57 patients compared with the 55 patients required with a single-stage design.

The term "optimal" relates to a mathematical criterion, which sometimes leads to a design with an imbalance in the sizes of the stages that seems impractical; for example, by assigning 70% of the enrollment to the first stage. In such cases, there are almost always alternatives that are mathematically not quite optimal but are more appealing in terms of the split between stages while still satisfying the other design parameters. For example, another commonly used approach is to minimize the maximum possible sample size; this is called a minimax design. There is available software and online calculators that will generate a list of possible sample sizes and responses at each of the two stages that meet the desired α, power, and minimum detectable difference.

Additional Phase II Designs

The designs considered so far are single-arm. Increasingly, phase II trials are using randomization to allocate patients to two or more different arms. The reasons motivating randomized phase II designs with multiple therapeutic arms are numerous and may be somewhat controversial. Some studies plan not to compare the arms: Each arm is regarded as an independent trial of regimen. Each treatment arm targets the same patient population, and random assignment is simply a mechanism to ensure the arms enroll patients with somewhat similar characteristics. These are essentially parallel, single-arm phase II trials. Other trials do not perform a formal statistical comparison among the treatments but just pick the winner. Finally,

Table 5-8 **CIs for True Response Rates**					
Observed Rate = 0.10		**95% CI**	**Observed Rate = 0.50**		**95% CI**
n	r		n	r	
10	1	0.3 to 44.5	10	5	18.7 to 81.3
20	2	1.2 to 31.7	20	10	27.2 to 72.8
30	3	2.1 to 31.7	30	15	31.3 to 68.7
40	4	2.8 to 23.7	40	20	33.8 to 66.2
50	5	3.3 to 21.8	50	25	35.5 to 64.5
60	6	4.9 to 17.6	60	30	39.8 to 60.2

Abbreviations: n, sample size; r, observed number of responses.

Table 5-9 **Examples of Two-Stage Phase II Designs (Optimal Simon Design)**

Design Criteria				Resulting Design			
				First Stage		Overall	
p_0	p_1	α	Power[a]	n_1	r_1	N	r
0.10	0.25	0.05	0.90	28	4	57	10
0.10	0.25	0.05	0.80	18	3	43	8
0.10	0.25	0.10	0.90	21	3	50	8
0.10	0.25	0.10	0.80	13	2	34	6
0.10	0.25	0.05	0.90	18	3	35	7
0.10	0.25	0.05	0.80	10	2	29	6
0.10	0.25	0.10	0.90	12	2	35	6
0.10	0.25	0.10	0.80	7	1	18	4
0.50	0.70	0.05	0.90	23	13	57	35
0.50	0.70	0.05	0.80	15	9	43	27
0.50	0.70	0.10	0.90	21	12	45	27
0.50	0.70	0.10	0.80	12	7	32	20

Abbreviations: α, type I (false-positive) error rate if $P = p_0$; n, total sample size after both stages; n_1, sample size for first stage; p_0, response rate under null hypothesis; p_1, response rate under alternative hypothesis; r, total number of responses required to reject null hypothesis and conclude $P > p_0$; r_1, minimum number of responses required in first stage to enroll second stage.

[a]Power refers to the probability of rejecting the null hypothesis if $P = p_1$.

there are trials in which a formal statistical comparison is performed between the arms.

The classic "pick the winner" trial design typically tests two or more variations of the same experimental agent, or two or more closely related experimental agents, and the results are compared to select one for subsequent study or for comparison against standard therapy in a randomized phase III trial. For example, two plausible doses of an agent or a gene vaccine may be carried in three possible vectors. In this case, the stated desire is to compare the arms and pick the best treatment, but because both arms are experimental, there is no need to control the false-positive (type I) error rate. That is, if the true response rate for two experimental arms is equivalent, there is no error in picking one over the other. In a pick-the-winner design, the arm with the highest observed response rate at the end of the trial is selected for further study. The sole design consideration is that if the response rates in the two arms differ by a specified amount, Δ, then the power should be at least $1 - \beta$. Thus, Δ is a difference in response rates that is considered clinically important. If two arms differ by this amount or more, then the sample size should be large enough that the observed response rate in the better arm will be higher than that in the other arm, with probability $1 - \beta$. Table 5-10 provides some examples of design parameters for a randomized phase II trial and the sample size required for each. One advantage of the pick-the-winner design is that the objective of picking the winner requires fairly modest sample sizes, which is often feasible in the phase II setting. However, because of these limited sample sizes, these studies are not powered to do formal statistical hypothesis testing between the arms, and such comparative statistical analyses should not be conducted.

Increasingly, phase II trials are conducted in a biomarker-driven fashion.[12,13] Biomarkers may be prognostic, whereby they affect the risk of the outcome in the absence of treatment, or predictive, whereby they change the outcome in response to a particular targeted treatment. Prognostic biomarkers may be used to identify high-risk patients, so that enriching the patient population for those with the biomarker can make it easier to detect a signal, due to the higher event rate. If the biomarker is predictive for a particular therapy, then a biomarker subgroup would be expected to have a stronger efficacy signal with no or little efficacy in the biomarker-negative group. Basket trials are used to enroll patients with similar tumor molecular characteristics across multiple tumor locations, to treat them with the same biomarker-targeted treatment. In such trials, it may be that there is an arm for each cancer type and the trial is essentially conducting parallel single-arm studies. Umbrella trials are often used to conduct multiple trials under one protocol, sometimes called a master protocol, whereby patients first have their biomarker profile assessed and then are assigned to a particular randomization and biomarker-targeted treatment scheme depending on their biomarker profile.

Another phase II design strategy is the use of adaptive randomization. Trials that use adaptive randomization start by randomly assigning patients in equal proportions to each arm. As outcome data on these patients accumulate, the randomization scheme is altered so it favors the arm(s) in which the strength of the evidence that the response rate is greater than p_0

Table 5-10 **Minimum Sample Size (Per Arm) for Pick-the-Winner Randomized Phase II Designs**

	Two Arms (p_1, p_2)		Three Arms (p_1, p_2, p_3)	
Difference (p_2 − p_1)	**Power[a] = 0.80**	**Power = 0.90**	**Power = 0.80**	**Power = 0.90**
0.10	45	92	78	134
0.15	22	43	37	61
0.20	13	25	22	35

Abbreviations: p_1, lower response rate; p_2, higher response rate.
[a]Power refers to the probability that the arm with highest true response rate has highest observed response rate.

or greater than the control arm is greatest. Conversely, it reduces the likelihood that a patient would be randomly assigned to the arm(s) in which the strength of evidence is weakest, and ultimately may drop arms altogether if the strength of evidence falls too low. Adaptive randomization has been used in biomarker-based designs, such as the I-SPY2 trial[14] in breast cancer, so that patients with certain biomarker profiles who respond more favorably to certain treatments will be randomly assigned more frequently to those agents. Although adaptive randomization seems like a rational way to select among competing experimental regimens, in practice it is often difficult to mount such a trial. The different agents likely have different sponsors and advocates, each of which naturally has a principal interest in their own agent and is reluctant to cede control of its evaluation to an external process. Others have some ethical discomfort with the notion of unequal allocation based on evidence of efficacy, feeling that this violates the principle of clinical equipoise (ie, that one truly is unable to say which treatment is better for the patient population to be enrolled). In addition, it has some disadvantages. The first is that although, theoretically, it would minimize the number of patients randomly assigned to ineffective treatment, the overall sample size for a trial with adaptive randomization is larger than fixed randomization. There are many other issues and there is a split among statisticians regarding whether the benefits of adaptive randomization outweigh the drawbacks.[15,16]

Two more recent designs that have been developed and used are umbrella trials and basket trials (Fig 5-3). An umbrella trial enrolls patients with a single tumor origin or histology and tests many different treatments. Patients are matched to a treatment on the basis of the biomarker their tumor contains. The advantage of an umbrella trial is that it can test many different biomarker-treatment combinations within a single protocol rather than having to have a separate protocol for each different marker-treatment combination. An example of an umbrella trial is Lung-MAP.[17] A basket trial tests a single treatment and single biomarker across different tumor origins or histology. Similarly, an advantage of a basket trial is that it more efficiently tests the treatment-biomarker combination across different tumor types compared with having a separate protocol for each. An example of a basket trial is a trial evaluating vemurafenib in patients with tumors that had a *BRAF* V600 mutation.[18]

Biases in Phase II Trials

Among all the phases of therapeutic development, phase II is the most fraught with the potential for bias. The major source of bias is the absence of contemporaneous, randomized comparison groups. Historical outcomes vary widely for many reasons, and past experience may reflect many factors besides the agents being tested. These can include the eligibility criteria defining the patient population; the definition, timing, and methods used to assess outcome; standards of supportive care that vary by institution and over time; the use of surrogate end points; and, of course, simple random variation. This is more pronounced for end points other than tumor response rates, because tumor response rates are less affected by difference in prognostic factors than end points such as PFS and overall survival. Even in the absence of any systematic bias—an ideal unlikely to be achieved—the random outcomes observed in relatively few patients lead to many false conclusions. The most observable of these are false-positive results—agents that look promising in phase II trials often fail to be proven effective in phase III trials. Less observable, but just as unfortunate, are agents that, in truth, are effective but fail to show positive results in phase II trials. Randomized control arms are sometimes used in phase II trial settings to remove potential sources of bias resulting from historical control comparisons[19]; however, they introduce additional variability in the treatment-effect estimate. As a result, they typically require larger sample sizes and may use a higher type I error rate to maintain sufficient power to identify promising agents in the phase II setting.

KEY POINTS

- The typical sample sizes used in phase II trials provide imprecise estimates of outcome.
- Basket and umbrella trials efficiently evaluate several treatment-marker or treatment-histology combinations.
- Results among phase II trials, especially single-arm trials, are difficult to compare because so many factors can vary from trial to trial.

PHASE III TRIALS

The randomized clinical trial is the gold standard of clinical research, and this is the trial that is most often referred to as a

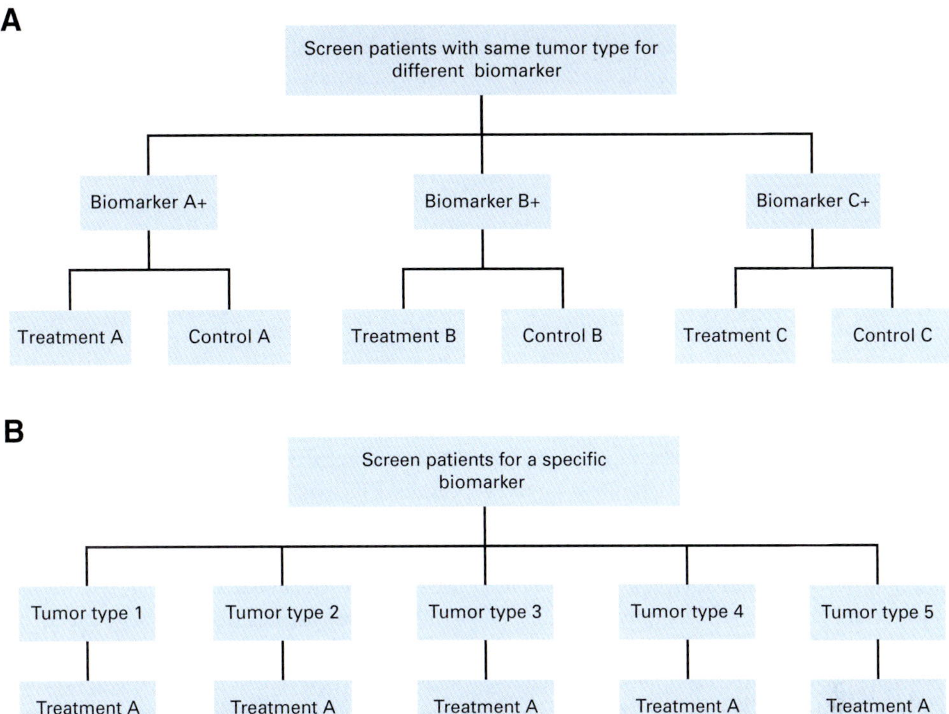

Fig. 5-3 Umbrella and basket trial designs.

(A) An illustration of an umbrella trial design whereby patients with the same tumor type are tested for different biomarkers and then are assigned to a treatment group that targets the biomarker. In this example, patients are randomly assigned to treatment versus to the control arm. An alternative design could be a single-arm design with the patients with a particular biomarker receiving treatment meant to target that biomarker. (B) An illustration of a basket trial design whereby all patients are tested for a particular biomarker and then are entered into a cohort for their tumor type. All patients receive the same targeted treatment that is thought to potentially benefit patients with tumors with the biomarker. This shows each cohort is a single-arm trial, but the cohort could be randomly assigned to treatment and control arms.

"phase III trial." The classic goal for the phase III trial is to compare an experimental treatment with a standard treatment. A common analogy applied to this setting is that of a legal trial. In a clinical trial, one formulates a null hypothesis that the experimental treatment has the same efficacy as the standard treatment. This is similar to the legal trial that assumes the defendant is innocent. A clinical trial is only done where there is some scientific basis to believe the experimental treatment is superior to the standard treatment. In the legal setting, a trial only occurs if the prosecution has evidence. To establish superior efficacy of the new treatment, a clinical trial is conducted that may lead to the rejection of the null hypothesis in a convincing way. In the legal setting, a trial is conducted that presents all the evidence and the jury may conclude the person on trial is guilty beyond a reasonable doubt. Failure to reject the null hypothesis in a clinical trial is not the same as establishing that the two treatments have equivalent efficacy. This is similar to a legal trial, where a finding of not guilty does not establish the innocence of the person on trial. Of course, randomized clinical trials do not always fit the classic paradigm of an experimental therapy compared with standard therapy, but the principles underlying the design and analysis will most likely be equally applicable.

Basic Principles

The primary goal of a phase III trial is to provide a comparison of treatments that is free of the many biases that occur when trying to compare phase II trials conducted at different times, at different institutions, among different patient populations, and so forth. The accepted standard for ensuring freedom from bias is randomization. Randomization is not the only way to create comparable treatment groups, nor does randomization guarantee the results of a particular trial are correct, but it does allow one to control, minimize, and quantify the possibility of error.

The most common randomization strategy is equal allocation among all treatment arms, or 1:1 randomization. From the standpoint of statistical power, this is the most efficient allocation that results in the smallest sample size, and also the one most compatible with the notion of clinical equipoise. A common variation of simple randomization is stratified randomization, which seeks to ensure even greater balance between arms by randomly assigning patients within strata defined by factors that strongly predict outcome. In addition, the randomization may be in blocks, which generally refers to a form of stratification designed to keep the number of patients allocated to each arm balanced over time. Stratification and blocking are most useful in small trials, in which random imbalances large enough to skew the composition of the treatment arms are not impossible. When the trials become larger (several hundred patients), these devices are largely superfluous, because it becomes highly unlikely that the arms will become meaningfully imbalanced by chance.

Departures from equal allocation sometimes occur—for example, a 2:1 allocation between the experimental and control arms. Most commonly, this is justified with the argument that it makes the trial more attractive to potential patients and their physicians, particularly when there is no way to get access to an experimental agent except through participation in the trial. It also allows one to generate more experience with the new agent. However, this argument seems to presume that the experimental therapy is likely to be more effective than standard therapy, which contradicts the principle of equipoise. Furthermore, as mentioned, a 2:1 allocation will require a larger sample size than a 1:1 randomization, with all other trial parameters kept the same.

Other common, but by no means necessary, components of a phase III design include the use of a placebo and the implementation of blinded (to the patient) or double-blinded (to both patient and physician) treatment assignments. Although randomization can help ensure the treatment arms are balanced with respect to patient characteristics at the start of the trial, it cannot remove bias that occurs after the trial starts, when differences arise between arms with respect to the conduct of the trial or the evaluation of trial data. This bias can be entirely unintentional and unconscious, but it reflects behavior by either patients or physicians that compromises the benefits of randomization. The susceptibility of trials to bias can vary considerably depending on the end point in question. For example, placebo effects and ascertainment bias are probably unlikely to affect a trial in which mortality is the primary end point. On the other hand, assessment of tumor response without blinding to treatment assignment could be subject to subtle bias, and studies with self-reported quality-of-life end points are obviously prone to placebo effects.

The use of placebo as the control arm in therapeutic oncology trials is extremely rare because usually some form of therapy is available, even if it has limited efficacy. A placebo control is much more likely to be used in adjuvant trials or in trials of combination therapy in which a new agent is being added to an existing combination. Though one may question the extent to which placebo effects play a role in such settings, if a placebo is feasible, it adds credibility to a trial even if the likelihood of placebo effects is small. In some cases, of course, the nature of the treatments differs so much that neither a placebo nor blinding is feasible.

The most acceptable primary analysis of a phase III trial is the intention-to-treat analysis. This analysis includes all patients enrolled in an arm of a randomized trial, no matter what happens thereafter—for example, if they are unable to receive the full course of treatment, they cross over to another treatment, and so forth. Because any of these contingencies can be related to the treatment itself and to the effectiveness of the treatment, an unbiased analysis must incorporate that information. For example, if a new drug is potentially effective but many patients will not take it because of its adverse effects, then as a practical matter, it may not be as effective as a drug with fewer adverse effects.

Nevertheless, alternative secondary analyses may be undertaken that deviate from the intention-to-treat principle. To emphasize, these are secondary analyses done after the completion of the primary intention-to-treat analysis. Secondary analyses may involve an evaluation of a subset of patients (eg, those who received a minimum amount of therapy) or defining the treatment groups according to the treatment actually received instead of the treatment to which they were randomly assigned. These secondary analyses can be informative but must be interpreted cautiously and are problematic when the results differ markedly from the primary intention-to-treat analysis.

Other subset analyses may be undertaken to evaluate whether the treatment difference, if any, varies according to other factors, such as disease stage, age, or the presence of a biomarker. Even if specified in advance, the results of such subset analyses must be interpreted cautiously. Phase III studies are almost never large enough to have reliable power in subsets of patients; conversely, examining many subsets of patients in a trial with an overall negative result can lead to spurious findings that are caused by only random fluctuation.

Interim Analysis

Randomized phase III trials can be large, expensive, and of several years' duration. For this reason, most phase III trials have a provision for interim analysis at one or more points, with the possibility of terminating the trial early. The indications for early termination can be varied and are generally specified in advance. These may include strong evidence that the experimental therapy is better than the control therapy, strong evidence that it is worse, or a determination that the trial will not be conclusive (futility). Interim analyses are also ethically important because information may be sufficient early to alter trial conduct or even clinical practice.

A number of statistical approaches to interim analysis codify the timing and nature of the analyses and the threshold required to terminate the trial early. If the trial is to be stopped early because of evidence that the experimental therapy is superior, the overall false-positive rate (type I error rate) for the trial needs to be quantified and controlled because multiple analyses of the data without adjustment can lead to inflation of the type I error rate. Because small sample sizes are subject to much random variation, the threshold for stopping a trial early generally involves a high degree of statistical significance, meaning type I error rates that are much lower than a standard 0.05 level of significance (eg, as low as 0.001 or 0.0001). Also, if some of the type I error rate is "spent" during interim analyses, then the significance level for the final analysis will be lower than the stated trial value of α. For example, a decision may be that the overall trial should have a type I error rate of 5% with one planned interim analysis for which the threshold for stopping the trial will be a $P < .01$. Because 0.01 was spent on the interim analysis, the level of evidence required at the end of the study is $P < .04$. This ensures the overall trial will have the desired level of significance of 0.05 (0.01 for the interim analysis plus 0.04 for the final analysis). The threshold significance levels at each of the interim analyses and final analysis constitute the stopping boundaries.

The data at an interim analysis may have little evidence of a difference in outcome between arms or indicate the difference is much smaller than hypothesized when designing the trial. On the basis of the accumulated data and assumptions about the true treatment effect, it is possible to generate estimates of the probability that the trial will prove successful at demonstrating the superiority of the experimental arm. If this probability is too low, the trial may be terminated early to minimize unnecessary time and expense. This is referred to as "stopping for futility." On the other hand, as previously noted, the inability to demonstrate a difference is not the same as demonstrating equivalence. A trial that is terminated early for futility may be inconclusive. Therefore, in some cases, it may be desirable to complete a trial that cannot demonstrate a treatment benefit, if completing the trial might allow one to make firm conclusions regarding the lack of benefit.

The interim analysis plan for a phase III trial should be prespecified and is considered an integral part of the trial design. However, the decision to stop a trial early involves complex and important issues that cannot be summarized in a simple statistical test. Typically, the results of an interim analysis will be reviewed by a data and safety monitoring board. The role of this board is to independently review the results of an interim analysis, consider the results in context with a host of other factors (eg, scientific, ethical, legal, financial), and make a recommendation as to whether to continue the trial.

End Points

Phase III clinical trials intend to establish whether the treatment being investigated provides a direct clinical benefit to patients above the standard of care. The patient population for a phase III trial is composed of people for whom the treatment is intended to be used. Typically, phase III trials have fewer restrictions on which patients are eligible for the trial than do phase I and II trials. In the oncology setting, an improvement in survival is often the gold standard for demonstrating such a benefit. However, other end points are also used to demonstrate clinical benefit while providing efficiencies in trial design.[20] Other end points commonly used include:

- PFS: the time until disease progression or death
- DFS: the time until disease relapse/recurrence or death
- Time to progression (TTP): the time until disease progression
- Event-free survival (EFS): the time until an event of interest, which may include other outcomes in addition to death and disease progression

Advantages of using an outcome other than death is that it can be observed before death and so can speed up trial completion. A disadvantage is that outcomes other than death may contribute to complications with respect to knowing if there is clinical benefit. Superiority in terms of TTP, PFS, or DFS can occur despite a therapy causing more toxic deaths, and superiority of PFS or DFS can occur due to a more favorable safety profile, without any therapeutic effect on the cancer. Often PFS or DFS may not be established surrogate end points for overall survival, meaning it is not known whether an improvement in these end points actually correlates with an improvement in overall survival. This makes it unclear whether an improvement in PFS or DFS really represents a direct clinical benefit to patients, especially in the presence of treatment toxicities. End points may be subject to assessment bias, so additional trial design considerations are important, including patient and physician blinding, independent end point review committees, and regular disease evaluations. Patient-reported outcomes (PROs) use questionnaires to measure how a patient feels and functions; therefore, PROs can also be important for assessing direct clinical benefit of a treatment being evaluated in a clinical trial. These instruments need to undergo rigorous development and testing to ensure they are measuring what is expected and that they are reliable. Several distinct aspects of PROs are important for understanding the benefits and toxicities of treatment, including the burden of disease symptoms, physical functioning and the ability to conduct activities of daily life, and symptomatic adverse events. Blinding in the trial design is important for these outcomes to avoid assessment bias, and completeness of data collection is crucial to minimize the impact of missing PRO data and the biases that this may introduce.

Phase III Design Options

Adaptive trial designs are defined as those that include a provision for changing the future course of the trial using accumulated data. Several features of adaptation in exploratory or early-phase clinical trials have already been described, including continual reassessment methods in phase I trials, and adaptive randomization in phase II trials. Here, adaptations used in the confirmatory clinical trial setting are described.[21] The implications of adaptations are different depending on whether the changes are made blinded or unblinded to the available data on treatment differences; for example, increasing the sample size because of a lower-than-expected overall event rate has minimal impact on the final analysis because it does not actually use the treatment differences. In contrast, unblinded adaptation is subject to greater scrutiny and requires careful attention to statistical methodology and operational procedures to ensure the results are free from bias. Several types of adaptations in late-stage clinical trials have been considered. Seamless phase II/III clinical trials combine the phase II trial (which may involve dose selection from among multiple doses) and the phase III trial (which uses the final selected dose for inference). This can be operationally efficient because it eliminates time between phases II and III, and it can be statistically efficient because the data from the two stages are combined for inference. Sample size re-estimation designs allow for an increase in sample size based on interim assessments of the treatment effect, particularly when the interim treatment effect is in a promising zone in which the study may be underpowered. An adaptive population-enrichment design allows for restricting enrollment to a biomarker-based subgroup at an interim analysis, if it appears the biomarker-positive patients may benefit from treatment and the biomarker-negative patients do not.

Equivalence and noninferiority designs do not attempt to establish that a new treatment is superior to a standard treatment but, instead, aim to establish that the new treatment has equivalent efficacy as a standard treatment or that its efficacy is only a bit worse than that of a standard treatment. Although most phase III trials are undertaken with an underlying goal of demonstrating a difference between treatment arms, there are circumstances in which the goal is merely to demonstrate that one therapy is equivalent, or at least not inferior, to another. For example, a new treatment that is less toxic, less inconvenient, or less expensive than a standard treatment would be preferred if it was nearly equally effective.

It is impossible to design a trial to demonstrate that two therapies are exactly equivalent, and in truth, it is highly unlikely that they are. Instead, one specifies the smallest difference that would be of practical clinical significance—for example, a 5% difference in 10-year survival—and then designs a trial that has high power to reject the null hypothesis (low type II error rate) if such a difference truly existed. A successful trial from the standpoint of equivalence would then fail to reject the null hypothesis. Note that the concepts of a false-positive or a false-negative conclusion are, in a way, reversed from the usual design perspective, and the typical rates of type I and type II error used in such designs might need to be reconsidered. Equivalence studies are notoriously large because the difference in outcome said to define equivalence is typically smaller than the difference hypothesized for a superiority trial, which dramatically affects the sample size. For example, as seen in Table 5-11, a trial with an equivalency threshold set at a 5% difference requires a sample size four times as large as a superiority trial powered to detect a 10% difference.

An alternative to an equivalency design that can require a somewhat smaller sample size is the noninferiority design. In this case, one specifies an acceptable upper limit to inferiority of the new therapy compared with the old—that is, how much worse it could be and still be considered acceptable. The trial is designed by formulating a null hypothesis that the new therapy has that level of inferiority, or worse, and then is powered to reject that null hypothesis for a specified alternative assumption (which might be equivalence, a lesser degree of inferiority, or even superiority). This usually results in a smaller sample size than an equivalence design, partly because it involves a one-sided hypothesis test, but often by claiming a wider limit of acceptability for noninferiority than for equivalence.

KEY POINTS

- Promising results from phase II trials are often not confirmed in phase III trials. Some reasons may be because the phase II and phase III trials have different patient populations or because they use different end points.
- Biomarker-driven trials may improve efficiency by directly targeting patients who are most likely to respond to treatment.
- Phase III trials require careful consideration of study design parameters, including randomization, blinding, and choice of end point, to minimize bias in the assessment of the treatment benefit.

CORRELATIVE STUDIES

Many studies in oncology are focused on evaluating the association between measurable attributes of a patient or the patient's disease at a particular time and subsequent events or outcomes. These attributes may be measured before the start of treatment, possibly with a view toward predicting the therapy most likely to be effective, or after treatment has been initiated, with the intent of predicting whether the treatment is working. Although almost any clinical study is involved with evaluating association in the broad sense, the term "correlative study" most often refers to studies in which the attribute being associated is not clinically apparent but must be assessed through some kind of test procedure, such as imaging, immunohistochemistry, gene expression, or any of a wide range of other procedures. Also bear in mind that a correlative study may or may not involve the analysis of correlation, which is a statistical term for a specific kind of association.

Correlative studies can be conducted during any of the phases of therapeutic development and, in fact, are often explicitly incorporated as ancillary objectives in a therapeutic trial. They can also be conducted completely independently of therapeutic trials. The potential range of correlative studies is

Table 5-11 **Required Sample Size (Per Arm) for Equivalence and Noninferiority Trials with a Binomial End Point (p_0 = 0.50, α = 0.05, and 1 − β = 0.90)**

Allowable Difference ($p_0 - p_1$)	Equivalence Design	Noninferiority Design
0.25	77	69
0.20	124	108
0.15	227	191
0.10	519	429
0.05	2,095	1,713

so broad that it is impossible to summarize succinctly the statistical methods or designs for such studies; this section of this chapter first shows some examples of a basic measure of correlation and illustrates some general pitfalls in the evaluation of correlation. In this section, we also discuss two important issues that can occur under the umbrella of correlative studies: the relationship between correlation and causation and the issue of multiple comparisons.

Examples of Correlation

As noted, correlation is a generic term that might describe almost any trial or analysis of association, but it may be helpful to consider a basic notion of correlation that occurs when both factors being studied are measurable on a continuous scale, exemplified by the *x*–*y* scatterplot and the sample correlation coefficient.[22] The scatterplot is simply a visual representation of how one factor varies as a function of another. The Pearson correlation coefficient, *r*, is a measure of the linear correlation between the two variables: a value of +1 means perfect correlation, a value of 0 means no correlation, and a value of −1 means perfect inverse correlation. The associated value r^2 ranges from 0 to 1 and is interpreted as the fraction of the variation in one variable that is explained by variation in another. For r^2, variation is measured by the sum of squared deviations from the mean, but there are many other measures of variation. The degree of correlation is a function of three factors: (1) the magnitude of the association (ie, whether the change in one variable is associated with a large or small change in the other); (2) the consistency of the relationship (ie, whether the changes are consistent or highly variable); and (3) the linearity of the relationship. The first two factors pertain generally to any measure of correlation; the third is a consideration for the Pearson correlation coefficient.

Figure 5-4 provides several examples of an *x*–*y* scatterplot, along with a fitted line and the value of *r*. The top panels illustrate how both the scatter and steepness of the association affect the degree of correlation. Moving from Figure 5-4A to Figure 5-4B, the data are just as variable, but there is an increase in the rate of change in *y* as a function of the change in *x* (slope), resulting in higher correlation. In Figure 5-4C, the slope stays the same as in Figure 5-4B, but the variability increases, decreasing correlation. The bottom panels illustrate common pitfalls that occur in correlation studies. In Figure 5-4D, the apparent correlation between *x* and *y* is based on a single point that is far away from the majority of data. It is debatable whether this represents a real biologic phenomenon. Conversely, in Figure 5-4E, an outlying observation obscures an apparent correlation in the majority of observations. Finally, in Figure 5-4F, there is a clear relationship between *x* and *y*, but it is not a linear relationship and, therefore, is not reflected in *r*.

Correlation and Causation

One setting in which correlative studies have become common is the development of targeted therapies. These therapies are designed around specific attributes of tumors, which nominally can be quantified by measuring some biologic parameter. It may be possible to establish a clear correlation between this biomarker and prognosis; it may also be possible to establish that a targeted therapy has an effect on the biomarker in a direction that would imply a more favorable prognosis. Taking these two correlations together, it might appear that this is a clear indication that the therapy would be effective for that cancer, but this is not necessarily the case. Figure 5-5 indicates how this seeming contradiction can occur when the biomarker is correlated with the disease process but is not part of the causal pathway related to the ultimate outcomes of interest.

A familiar analogy would be the association of elevated blood pressure and cholesterol levels with various forms of cardiovascular disease. Although there are many drugs that lower blood pressure and cholesterol levels, there is no guarantee these drugs will be effective in lowering the risk for the correlated cardiovascular disease. For this to be true, the elevation of blood pressure or cholesterol levels must be part of the causal pathway to the cardiovascular event, not just a marker or symptom of the severity of the disease process. The same must hold true for the effect of a targeted therapy on a cancer biomarker to be considered an indicator of efficacy; that is, the biomarker must reflect at least part of the direct causal pathway by which growth or spread of the tumor has an effect on the survival of the patient.

Biomarker studies

Many correlative studies are designed to evaluate potential biomarkers. There are two types of biomarkers: a prognostic marker and a predictive marker. A prognostic marker is associated with the outcome, regardless of the type of treatment administered. An example of a prognostic marker would be metastatic status for a survival outcome. In general, patients with metastatic disease have shorter survival then do patients who have localized disease, regardless of the type of treatment they receive. A predictive marker is used to select a specific treatment for a patient. It the patient has the marker she or he will benefit from a particular treatment and if the patient does not have the marker, no or little benefit will result from the treatment. An example of a predictive biomarker is *HER2* status for women with breast cancer. If a woman has *HER2*-positive breast cancer, she obtains benefit (ie, longer survival) if treated with trastuzumab. On the other hand, a woman who has *HER2*-negative breast cancer does not receive benefit from trastuzumab treatment. The goal of a biomarker study is to either identify prognostic or, preferably, predictive markers.

There are two general ways to include a biomarker in a clinical trial. One way is to evaluate the association of the biomarker with patient outcomes, either to discover an association of the biomarker with the outcome or to validate that a previously observed association exists between the biomarker and outcome. These biomarkers are called integrated biomarkers: they are integrated into the study design. Another way a biomarker is integrated into a study design is to make it an integral biomarker. Integral biomarkers are used to make treatment decisions in a clinical trial. One way this might happen is to use the biomarker to screen patients for trial entry. Specifically, if it is thought only

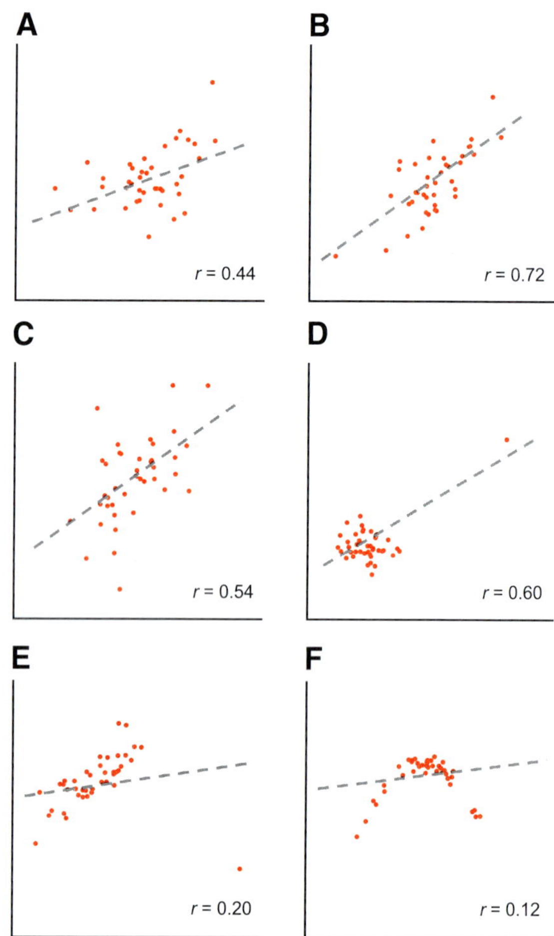

Fig. 5-4 Examples of linear correlation.

The six graphs illustrate possible correlations between two variables, x and y. The dashed line indicates the least-squares line fit to the data, and *r* is the Pearson correlation coefficient. (A) The data have a positive correlation of moderate strength. (B) Compared with the data in A, there is an increased slope in the data and a stronger correlation. (C) The data have the same slope as the data in B but the correlation is weaker (ie, the points have more variability about the best fitting line). (D) The computed correlation is stronger than that in the bulk of the data, due to the influence of one outlier point. If this point were removed, the correlation would be smaller. (E) The correlation with the outlier is weaker than the correlation for the remainder of the data. If the outlier were removed, the correlation would increase. (F) There is a strong nonlinear relationship in the data but the correlation is weak because the correlation measures the strength of linear relationship.

patients with the marker will potentially benefit from the treatment, then patients with the marker will be enrolled and those without the marker will not be enrolled. For example, *HER2* status (positive *v* negative) was used in trastuzumab trials to screen patients who were eligible to enroll. Another example of an integral biomarker is the use of OncoType DX recurrence score to determine treatment cohorts in the TAILORx trial.

Multiple Comparisons

Advances in technology have made it possible to assess hundreds, thousands, or even millions of potential biomarkers within

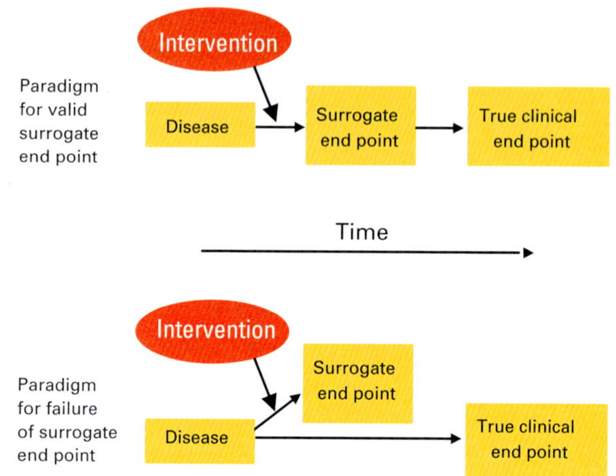

Fig. 5-5 Criteria for surrogate end points are illustrated in this schematic of how a surrogate end point, or biomarker, may or may not be valid as a substitute for the true clinical end point.

At the top, the surrogate end point is in the causal pathway of the disease process. An intervention that affects the surrogate end point should also affect the true clinical end point. At the bottom, the surrogate end point results from an independent causal pathway. It will be correlated with the clinical end point, but an intervention affecting the surrogate end point will have no effect on clinical outcome.

reasonable limits of expense and time. This is particularly true in the field of genomics, in which single chips have the ability to simultaneously quantify the expression of 20,000 genes or to genotype more than 1 million single-nucleotide polymorphisms. Although some sophisticated statistical methodology may underlie the quantification of gene expression or assigning a genotype, the basic methodology for evaluating a correlation with outcome could be based on a simple *t* or χ^2 test that is repeated thousands or hundreds of thousands of times.

From the hypothesis-testing point of view, if each of these tests of association has a positive (type I) error rate set at conventional levels, such as 5%, then the number of false-positive correlations found will be enormous. For example, consider a gene expression study of 20,000 genes that is to be correlated with tumor response in hopes of determining one or more markers that signal a high likelihood of treatment failure. Even if the 20,000 genes have been selected to represent a range of plausible causal pathways, only a small fraction of them are likely to be truly correlated with outcome. As an order-of-magnitude calculation, the number of false-positive correlations that will result from 20,000 hypothesis tests conducted with a 5% type I error rate is 1,000, which is far too many to represent practical progress.

Although it is obvious in this setting that some measure must be taken to decrease the number of false-positive correlations, it is not always clear what specific target to set. For example, if one insists the rate of any false-positive correlation must be 5%, then a simple, though conservative, method is to apply the Bonferroni correction, which divides the nominal single-test error rate by the number of tests. In the example at hand, this would mean conducting each test with a type I error rate of 0.0000025. Although there are methods to make this conservative adjustment more accurate, it is not clear this is even a reasonable goal. For example, it seems unduly conservative to demand that the rate of even a single false-positive result across 20,000 tests be only 5%. Unless the size of the study is increased, a reduction in the false-positive error rate by four orders of magnitude will increase the false-negative error rate, perhaps to the point at which correlations of a plausible magnitude cannot be detected.

Another method of controlling false-positive correlations considers the error rate among the tests that have been declared positive; that is, not among all tests. This is called the false discovery rate (FDR). With this approach, if there were 100 positive tests, an FDR of 5% would mean that, on average, five would be falsely positive. Most researchers would consider such a result highly successful. In fact, 10 positive tests with an FDR of 20% to 30% could be considered an excellent result and would greatly reduce the scale of the subsequent studies required to replicate and validate the findings. The FDR method is generally less conservative than a strict Bonferroni adjustment, though as previously noted, there are ways to calibrate the Bonferroni approach (eg, through permutation) to make it more comparable to the FDR approach.

Although examples have been described previously in which the need to account for multiple tests is obvious, the problem of false-positive correlations remains even when dealing with five to 10 biomarkers. Explicit accounting of the multiple tests is often omitted in such situations, but this does not obviate the need for independent replication and validation of any apparent correlation.

KEY POINTS

- Common measures of correlation assess the linear correlation between variables. Lack of linear correlation does not necessarily mean the variables are not related.
- Measures of correlation may be sensitive to a few outlying observations.
- Correlation, by itself, does not imply causation. Even though a biomarker may be correlated with both treatment and outcome, this is not sufficient to establish the biomarker is a useful surrogate end point.
- Multiple comparisons increase the type I error above the desired level significance level if the *P* values (or significance level) are not adjusted.

STATISTICAL ANALYSIS METHODS

In this section, we discuss some of the more important and advanced statistical methods that are common in oncology studies. Of course, each of these is, itself, the subject of entire books; thus, only the most basic features of these methods can be covered here. The greater part of this section is devoted to the analysis of survival or time-to-event data, which are ubiquitous in the evaluation of clinical research. Some other advanced methods that may be encountered are also covered.

A common feature of the analytic methods discussed here is that they can be extended to incorporate the simultaneous effects of multiple variables on outcome, referred to as "regression analysis." Regression analysis involving multiple variables is frequently referred to as multivariable, in contrast to univariable analysis, which considers only one variable at a time. Many investigators erroneously use the term multivariate analysis rather than multivariable analysis. A multivariate analysis refers to the simultaneous analysis of multiple outcome variables, which is rarely done in medical research. Adjustment for multiple variables is particularly important in comparative studies using retrospective or other nonrandomized data or in developing predictive models to evaluate multiple, possibly correlated factors.

SURVIVAL ANALYSIS

Because of the potentially long temporal course of the disease, a large part of the evaluation of cancer and its treatment involves extended periods of follow-up, often spanning many years. Measures of therapeutic efficacy or prognostic value are frequently defined by the percentage of patients alive at a particular time or alive and free of recurrence at a particular time. Conversely, one might be interested in the median time to death, recurrence, or some other defining event. Often it is not possible to follow all patients until the defining event occurs, or even until they have reached a specified length of follow-up.

The analysis of data related to the duration of time until an event is generically referred to as "time-to-event analysis" or "survival analysis."[23] The methods used in such an analysis must take into account that some patients will not be followed until the time of the event but will provide partial information about the length of that time—that is, the length of time from the start of follow-up until the time of analysis. The discontinuation of follow-up prior to a defining event is called "censoring." The fraction of event times that are censored may range from near zero, in settings where almost all patients die or have recurrent disease, to greater than 90% in settings with excellent survival.

The most common display of censored survival data is the survival curve. This is an estimate of the underlying survival function, $S(t)$, that defines the probability of surviving past time t or, more generally, that the time to a defining event exceeds t. Although this is the way that data are visualized, the statistical analysis of such data are more often based on a related quantity called the "hazard function," $\lambda(t)$, which is the underlying rate at which events occur among the population of patients at risk. This is feasible because there is a well-defined and fundamental mathematical relationship between the survival function and hazard function; intuitively, if the rate of events increases, then the probability of surviving without that event decreases.

The most common methods associated with displaying and analyzing time-to-event data are described later. There are two key assumptions underlying all of these methods. One is that the censoring of event times, if they occur, is not related to the subsequent occurrence of the event—that is, that the reason for censoring is uninformative with respect to what happens afterward. Another fundamental principle of survival analysis, because survival is a predictive quantity, is that only past information can be used in modeling and analyzing future events. An example in which the latter principle is violated would be the division of patients into two groups, depending on whether they had a tumor response, and evaluating time to death from the time of initiation of therapy. Therefore, the groups are defined using future information, and unbiased predictions of survival after the start of therapy cannot use this information.

Kaplan-Meier Curves

The universal standard for providing estimates of survival curves is the Kaplan-Meier estimator (sometimes also called the product-limit estimator). This is typically plotted as a step function, with a step occurring at every unique death time. The calculation involved in the Kaplan-Meier estimator is actually quite simple: The height of each step is the height of the curve at the previous step multiplied by the fraction of patients at risk at the particular death time who survive beyond that time. The number of patients at risk at a particular point is the number of patients who have not died or been censored before that time. For example, suppose the time until death or censoring is measured to the nearest week. If the estimated survival probability just before 14 weeks is 0.6, there are 10 patients who have not died or been censored before 14 weeks, and one patient dies at 14 weeks, then the height of the curve drops at that time from 0.6 to 0.54 [0.6 × (9/10)]. In plots of Kaplan-Meier curves, it is common to indicate points of censor with tick marks or to provide a table indicating the numbers of patients at risk at convenient benchmarks.

Because the Kaplan-Meier estimate is the product of fractions with progressively smaller denominators, the precision of the estimate decreases over time. This is readily apparent if CIs are provided, because the CIs will grow increasingly wide over time. In almost all cases, the CIs provided with a Kaplan-Meier curve are based on pointwise estimates of the variability of the survival estimate; it is usually not correct to infer that the bands contain the entirety of the true survival curve with the stated level of confidence. The step after the last observed time of death is often extended out as far as the last censoring time, although technically, the estimate is undefined after the last death. As previously noted, the steps in the right-hand tail of the estimated curve become steeper as the number of patients at risk decreases. If the last patient under observation dies, then the estimated survival probability drops to zero at that point.

Figure 5-6 illustrates a Kaplan-Meier curve in a relatively small sample of 33 patients, 15 of whom died. Tick marks indicate the points at which surviving patients are last known to be alive. The gray lines indicate pointwise 95% CIs for the survival probability. The green line indicates how median survival is estimated from a Kaplan-Meier curve: this is the time at which the estimated survival probability first drops below 50%.

Although, in the previous discussion, only deaths were referred to, the Kaplan-Meier method readily encompasses the concept of EFS. For example, the estimate of DFS counts both deaths and relapses as events, and the curve steps down whenever either event occurs, using the same calculation. The term overall survival is usually meant to refer to a survival curve that counts only deaths as events. The term actuarial survival is a misnomer—it refers back to a different method of estimating the survival curve (the actuarial or life-table method) that was used before the introduction of the Kaplan-Meier method but is now obsolete in the medical context. The Kaplan-Meier method should not be used when the intent is to estimate the probability of being free of a particular kind of event (eg, a particular cause of death). This is a competing risks problem and requires the use of methods described later in the chapter.

Comparing Kaplan-Meier Curves

The comparison of survival curves can be approached in several ways: (1) by comparing the estimated survival probability at a fixed point in time; (2) by comparing the time at which the estimated survival probability is a fixed value, usually the median; or (3) by comparing the survival curves across the entire period of follow-up. In general, the first two approaches should be avoided unless there is a strong justification for focusing on a particular survival time or percentile. This is because the comparison clearly can vary depending on the point chosen.

The most common way to compare survival curves across time is with the log-rank statistic, as illustrated in Figure 5-6, which compares DFS in a hypothetical clinical trial of an experimental compared with a control treatment. Perhaps somewhat surprisingly, this statistic is not based directly on the calculated survival estimates; rather, it is based on a comparison of the number of events observed in one group with the number of events that would have been expected in that group if the deaths occurred solely in proportion to the numbers of patients at risk. A difference that is too extreme (as reflected in a *P* value) provides evidence that the underlying event rates in the groups are different. The standard log-rank test is most sensitive to situations in which the event rates in the groups differ by the same ratio across time. There are weighted versions of this test that are appropriate if the differences are expected to occur primarily during the early or later periods of follow-up; however, the intent to use a weighted log-rank test should be specified prior to observing where the differences in event rates occur.

The comparison of survival curves is a special case of HR analysis, performed through Cox regression, which is discussed later. In fact, the log-rank test is also a test of the equality of hazard rates in the two groups. The result of the HR analysis is also provided in Figure 5-6, illustrating the notion that better survival is associated with a lower event rate for mortality.

Competing Risks and Cumulative Incidence

As noted previously, when there are multiple types of events that define EFS, or multiple causes of death, then probabilities associated with a specific type of event or a specific cause of death should not be estimated by Kaplan-Meier methods. For example, suppose one is interested in comparing breast cancer

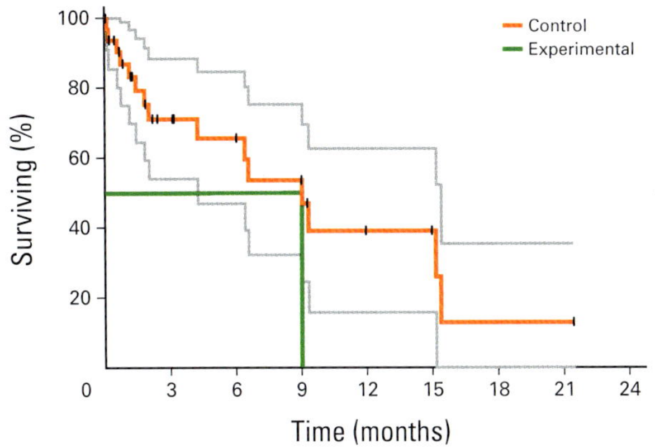

Fig. 5-6 A survival curve and related quantities.

The orange line is an example of a Kaplan-Meier curve for a group of 33 patients. At any point, the curve estimates the probability of surviving at least as long as that time. Gray lines indicate the 95% CIs for the survival probability calculated at each point. Tick marks indicate times at which surviving patients were last known to be alive. The green line indicates how median survival would be calculated: in this curve, the survival probability drops to less than 50% at 9 months.

mortality as opposed to all-cause mortality (the complement of overall survival) between two treatment groups. The relevance of this comparison might be debated because cause-of-death classification can be fairly subjective. A common but incorrect approach to this problem is to censor patients at the time of a non–breast cancer death, and to plot the complement of the resulting Kaplan-Meier curve as a representation of cumulative breast cancer mortality over time. The problem with this approach is that patients who die of other causes are not even hypothetically at risk for future death from breast cancer—the implicit assumption that they are, which is appropriate for the standard types of censoring, results in an overestimation of the probability of breast cancer death.

The correct calculation of cumulative incidence in the competing risks setting must take into account the probability of remaining at risk (or being event free). When this is done, the sum of the cumulative incidence probabilities for each of the types of events is exactly the complement of the EFS probability. For example, at any point in time, (1) the overall survival probability, (2) the probability of breast cancer death, and (3) the probability of non–breast cancer death will sum to 100%.

Although Kaplan-Meier methods are generally inappropriate for generating estimates of cumulative incidence in the presence of competing risks, the comparison of cumulative incidence curves is properly handled using the same previously discussed log-rank statistic, with events other than the type of interest being censored at the time of their occurrence. This seeming contradiction relates to the fact that in neither case is the log-rank statistic based directly on the estimates of the event probabilities themselves. Rather, it is based on the relative numbers of events that occur in each patient group, given the numbers of patients remaining at risk in each group over time. Thus, it is appropriate, for this purpose, to censor patients who experience competing events at the time of the event, because they are no longer at risk for the event of interest.

Figure 5-7 illustrates competing risks analysis derived from the same data shown in Figure 5-6. DFS reflects two competing risks: relapse and death without relapse, which perhaps reflect toxic complications of treatment. Figure 5-6A shows the cumulative incidence of relapse and Figure 5-6B shows the cumulative incidence of treatment-related mortality. The sum of these two incidences, plus the EFS probability from Figure 5-6, will equal 100% at any point in time. The curves and the log-rank analysis clearly suggest the improvement in DFS associated with the experimental arm is based largely on a reduction in treatment-related mortality, with little apparent effect on relapse.

At the risk of making the issue seem overly complicated, it should be noted that in the competing risks setting, the results of statistical analysis may not always appear concordant with the visual interpretation of cumulative incidence curves. This is because incidence is a composite result of (1) the rate at which events occur among those at risk (the hazard rate), and (2) the size of the population at risk. For example, consider a setting in which toxic regimens with potentially fatal complications are used in a setting with high rates of relapse. The events of relapse and nonrelapse death constitute competing risks. Suppose one regimen is much more effective than the other in preventing relapse but has the same underlying toxicity, based on an HR analysis showing equivalent hazard rates for nonrelapse death in the two groups. In this case, the cumulative incidence of nonrelapse death will appear higher in the group receiving the more effective therapy. This is because the effectiveness of the therapy in preventing relapse places more patients at risk for nonrelapse death.

The intent of the previous example is not to imply that the HR analysis is correct or that the cumulative incidence analysis is misleading. The important point is that competing risks should not be evaluated in isolation. Factors that influence one type of event may or may not influence another type, and an informed interpretation of data from a competing-risks setting

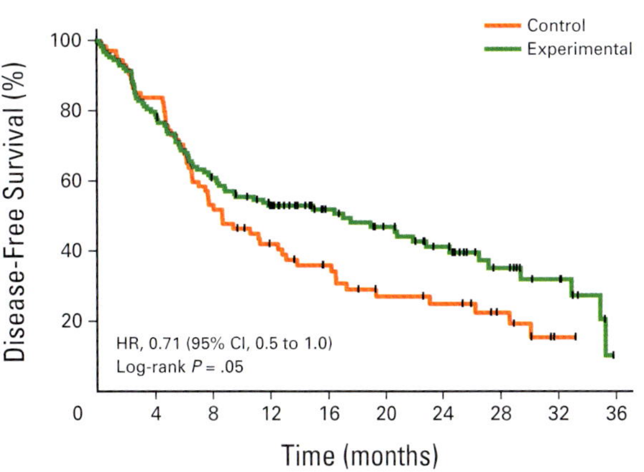

Fig. 5-7 Comparing survival curves.

The two curves represent a hypothetical comparison of disease-free survival for two treatments. The curves drop when a patient experiences relapse or dies without relapse (treatment-related mortality).

should consider each type of event. Furthermore, a complete analysis should evaluate not only the underlying rates of the event types, which may be biologically more meaningful, but also the net outcome reflected in their cumulative incidence, which may bear on clinical interpretation.

KEY POINTS

- Survival analysis techniques are used to analyze outcomes describing the time until an event occurs, which may be subject to censoring or competing risks.
- Although Kaplan-Meier curves are the universal standard for graphically representing time-to-event end points, the statistical analysis of such curves is usually not based on a direct comparison of the curves themselves. Rather, the comparison is based on the underlying hazard rate—the rate of events among patients remaining at risk—using the log-rank test.
- Comparisons of cumulative incidence curves are performed similarly to comparison of survival curves.

BINARY DATA ANALYSIS

In contrast to time-to-event analysis, there are occasions when the outcome of a clinical trial or other exercise may be summarized by the presence or absence of an event, an outcome, or a characteristic. This dichotomization of outcome is said to be binary data. Such data do not necessarily exclude aspects of time: For example, if outcome can be ascertained for all patients, then the occurrence of an event during a defined period can be a binary outcome. This is referred to as risk, but binary outcomes can refer to things other than risk. For instance, two groups of patients with breast cancer might be compared with respect to the percentage of patients with estrogen receptor–positive disease. The same or similar statistical methods may be applied to both scenarios.

χ^2 Analysis

For basic statistical analysis of binary end points, such as comparing one or more groups in terms of the risk of an event or the percentage with a certain characteristic, the most common methodology is based on the χ^2 test (also mentioned in Table 5-1). For small sample sizes, the accuracy of *P* values from the χ^2 analysis may be in doubt, and the Fisher exact test is the most common alternative, although it is generally quite conservative.

Like the log-rank test for survival analysis, the basic methods associated with binary data provide a test of equality but not necessarily a measure of effect. The most straightforward measure of effect is the simple difference in proportions. Other common measures of effect associated with binary outcomes[24] must be used with some caution in typical applications involving clinical data. For example, if p is the risk of an event, then the odds of the event are $p/(1 - p)$. Conversely, if ψ is the odds of an event, then the risk of the event is $\psi/(1 + \psi)$. In certain epidemiologic settings, where p is small, the ratio of the odds of an event between groups (odds ratio [OR]) will be approximately equal to the ratio of the risks (relative risk) and is a standard measure of association or effect. In clinical settings, however, the values of p associated with risk are not necessarily small. Although the same underlying statistical methods may be applicable, the OR in such settings may be nonintuitive or even misleading. For example, consider a patient group with a risk for recurrence of 90% compared with another group with a risk for recurrence of 80%. The OR for risk for recurrence is 2.25, but clearly the risk for recurrence is not nearly doubled. Similar considerations apply when interpreting an HR in survival analysis. If the risk for an event is not too large, then an HR will approximate a risk ratio; however, the divergence between a risk ratio and an HR is not as dramatic as that between a risk ratio and an OR. For example, a risk ratio of 2.0 (0.4/0.2) corresponds to an OR of 2.67 and to an HR of 2.25 (under an exponential assumption).

KEY POINT

- Binary data analysis is used for outcomes with yes/no or binary responses. χ^2 or Fisher exact tests are used to compare proportions between groups. Logistic regression is used to model the odds of a response, where the effect of a covariable is summarized through an OR.

REGRESSION MODELS

Although many clinical trials can be analyzed using only the previous methods, there are many settings in which one wishes to incorporate more information about patient characteristics than just the treatment arm to which the patients were assigned. This is particularly true in nonrandomized comparisons, where patient groups may not be homogeneous with respect to factors known to affect outcome. Although accounting for these imbalances is in no way a substitute for randomization, it is helpful, nevertheless, to evaluate the extent to which patient characteristics influence the difference, or lack of difference, among treatment groups. In other cases, the interest is not in comparing arms of a clinical trial but in determining factors that are predictive of better or worse survival. This information is useful in designing trials, counseling patients about their likely prognosis, or gaining increased biological understanding.

Two commonly used models are Cox regression models and logistic regression models. Like other regression models, the Cox regression model relates patient characteristics, called covariables, to outcome, which is a time-to-event outcome such as survival or PFS. These models can accommodate any number of variables. A Cox model summarizes the association between a variable and the outcome with an HR. The method for incorporating covariate effects on a binary outcome is logistic regression. A logistic model summarizes the association between a variable and the outcome with an OR.

KEY POINTS

- Cox regression is used to model the hazard rate in survival analysis, where the effect of a covariable can be summarized through an HR.
- Logistic regression is used to model the odds of a response, where the effect of a covariable is summarized through an OR.

EVALUATION OF BIOMARKERS

When evaluating a biomarker, the goal is to determine whether it can discriminate among patients. For a prognostic biomarker, an evaluation is performed to determine whether the biomarker can distinguish between patients who have good prognosis and those who have poor prognosis. If the outcome of interest is binary (eg, good prognosis *v* poor prognosis), the discrimination ability is determined using the area under the curve (AUC) of a receiver operator characteristic (ROC) curve. ROC curves apply to biomarkers that have continuous values. The ROC curve plots the true-positive rate (TPR) against the false positive rate (FPR) for various threshold values (eg, values that would determine whether a patient has good prognosis *v* poor prognosis). The TPR is also called the sensitivity, which is the ability of the marker to predict the outcome of interest when that outcome actually occurs (eg, the marker would classify the patient as having good prognosis and they actually did have a good prognosis). The FPR is determined as 1 − specificity. Specificity is the ability of the marker to classify the patient as not having the outcome of interest when the patient does not have the outcome of interest. An example of a ROC curve is presented in Figure 5-8. A biomarker that has perfect discriminatory ability has an AUC equal to 1. This means that it always correctly classifies the patients according to the event of interest. If the event is prognosis, the biomarker can perfectly predict which patient has good prognosis and which patient has poor prognosis. A biomarker that has no discriminatory ability is one with an AUC equal to 0.5. This means that its ability to predict if a patient has the outcome of interest is the same as flipping a fair coin. AUC analysis is used to determine the performance of prognostic biomarkers. In general, for a prognostic biomarker to potentially be useful in clinical practice, it requires an AUC above 0.80.

To determine the potential utility of a biomarker in a clinical trial, it is good to evaluate the strength of the association of the biomarker with the outcome of interest. When the outcome is a time-to-event outcome, the strength of the association will be determined with an HR from a Cox model. To determine whether the marker is prognostic, there needs to be a statistically significant association with the outcome, regardless of treatment. Hence, there would be an association regardless of which treatment the patient received. To determine whether the biomarker is predictive, it is necessary to show there is an association of the biomarker when the patients receive a particular treatment but there is no association when they receive any other type of treatment. To evaluate whether a biomarker is predictive, it is necessary to have four groups of patients: (1) those with the biomarker and receive the treatment of interest, (2) those with the biomarker who do not receive the treatment of interest, (3) those without the biomarker and receive the treatment of interest, and (4) those without the biomarker who do not receive the treatment of interest. To determine whether

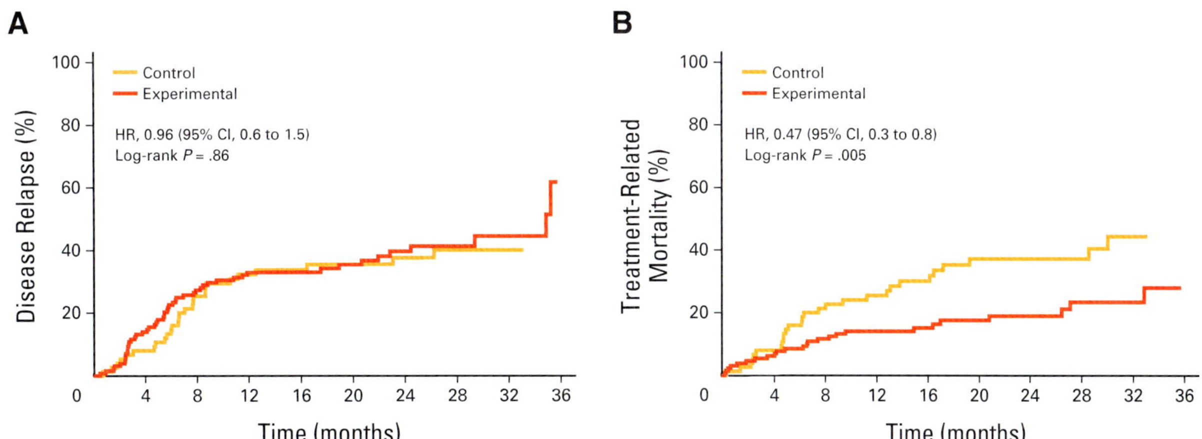

Fig. 5-8 Cumulative incidence curves and competing risks.

The data are decomposed into the two competing risks of (A) relapse and (B) treatment-related mortality. Most of the improvement in disease-free survival in the experimental arm is attributable to a decrease in treatment-related mortality; there is no observed difference in the rate of relapse between arms among those at risk for relapse.

the biomarker is predictive, it is necessary to show there is a statistically significant interaction between the biomarker (present *v* absent) and the treatment of interest (received *v* did not receive) with respect to the outcome of interest.

KEY POINTS

- The discriminatory ability of a prognostic biomarker is measured by computing the AUC for a ROC curve. The closer the AUC is to 1, the better the discriminatory ability.
- To determine whether a biomarker is prognostic, an association between the biomarker and the outcome of interest must be established.
- To determine whether a biomarker is predictive, a statistically significant interaction must be established between the biomarker status (present *v* absent) and the treatment of interest (received *v* did not receive) with respect to the outcome of interest.

LONGITUDINAL DATA ANALYSIS

In many studies, patients may be assessed repeatedly over extended periods. Data that arise from repeated measurement of the same patient over time are called longitudinal data, or sometimes clustered data. Common examples of such data would be quality-of-life assessments or the evaluation of biomarker levels over time. Pharmacokinetic data are a specialized case of longitudinal data; there are specific methods for analysis of these data that are beyond the scope of this chapter.

It is possible to do useful analysis of longitudinal data using basic statistical methods—for example, by comparing groups at a fixed point or by comparing one time to another. However, such methods may not allow one to evaluate the trajectory of the quantity being studied as a whole and do not fully accommodate common features of longitudinal data, such as missing data, variable times of assessment, and risk factors that also change over time. To analyze all the data simultaneously, one must account for the fact that repeated observations from the same patient are likely correlated. For example, one patient may report relatively high quality of life during the entire period of study and another may report low quality of life, although both patients may experience a similar change over time.

Appropriately accounting for this within-patient correlation is not necessarily straightforward, and the methods involved may be quite complex and are beyond what can be presented in detail here. There are two fairly common approaches to handling longitudinal data analysis. Although the nomenclature may vary, one is generally referred to as a linear mixed model approach and the other as a generalized estimating equation approach. The term "mixed" in the former refers to the simultaneous estimation of parameters that model the mean effects (the effects of clinical interest) and parameters that model the within-patient correlation structure of the data. One must make explicit assumptions about the latter, and the results may be sensitive to that assumption. The generalized estimating equation approach makes less explicit assumptions about the correlation structure. This is an advantage, particularly if one has no particular interest in the correlation structure itself, which is often the case when the interest is in comparing outcomes between groups or evaluating the effects of other factors on outcome.

KEY POINT

- Longitudinal data analysis is used to model outcomes that are assessed repeatedly over time. These methods must account for missing data commonly occurring in this setting, as well as correlation between measurements on the same individual.

SUMMARY

Statistical considerations are a key component in the design and the analysis of clinical research studies. Proper study design allows one to control the systematic and random factors that affect patient outcomes in clinical studies, and proper analysis allows one to make the best possible judgment as to which factors are more important. Few oncologists engaged in clinical research have sufficient statistical training or knowledge to do this on their own, which is why statisticians are in high demand in medical research and are considered a vital part of the research endeavor. Statisticians are also frequently engaged in evaluating research proposals for funding purposes and in reviewing research papers for publication in medical journals.

Although most clinical studies published in major medical journals have likely involved a statistician in both the conduct of the study and in the review of the article, it is still essential for the practicing oncologist to have some rudimentary familiarity with common statistical concepts and terminology, which has been the goal for this chapter. Such knowledge will enhance the oncologist's ability to evaluate the medical literature, explain treatment options to patients, and make informed decisions about joining research studies available to the community.

Acknowledgment

The following authors are acknowledged and graciously thanked for their contribution to prior versions of this chapter: Brent R. Logan, PhD; and Barry E. Storer, PhD.

STATISTICS AND CLINICAL TRIALS: GLOBAL PERSPECTIVES

Edith A. Perez, MD, FASCO (Mayo Clinic)

Global oncology, including access to optimized medical care, access to medicines for patients, and understanding how variations in tumor biology affect patient outcome, deserve focused attention. The WHO and many other societies, including the International Agency for Cancer Research (IARC), have worked over the years to aggregate data and assess the impact of cancer as well as generate ideas for areas where improvements could be made. Cancer is the second leading cause of death globally and was responsible for an estimated 9.6 million deaths in 2018 to 2019. Globally, approximately one in six deaths is due to cancer. Approximately 70% of deaths from cancer occur in low- and middle-income countries (LMICs).[25] Moreover, approximately one-third of deaths from cancer are due to the five leading behavioral and dietary risks: high body mass index, low fruit and vegetable intake, lack of physical activity, tobacco use, and alcohol use.

Global trials that address risk factors, prevention, and screening (in addition to therapeutic trials) are critically important for progress. Tobacco use remains the most important risk factor for cancer and is responsible for approximately 22% of cancer deaths.[26] Cancer-causing infections, such as hepatitis and human papillomavirus, are responsible for up to 25% of cancer cases in LMICs,[27] and obesity is an increasing risk.

After cancer is diagnosed, we, as a society, can strive to treat it as soon as possible to minimize morbidity, costs, and deaths. However, late-stage presentation and inaccessible diagnosis and treatment are too common. In 2017, only 26% of low-income countries reported having pathology services generally available in the public sector; whereas more than 90% of high-income countries reported having treatment services available, compared with less than 30% of low-income countries.[28]

Last, but also of importance, the economic impact of cancer is significant and increasing. Although difficult to exactly assess, the total annual economic cost of cancer in 2010 was estimated at approximately $1.16 trillion, which is anticipated to significantly increase in the next decade due to the expected significant increase in the incidence of cancer, as well as costs of newly developed medicines and diagnostic tools.[29] Figures since 2010 have been projected by region, with estimated costs in the United States alone of $80.2 billion in 2015, $110 billion in Europe, and around $46.2 billion in Africa. A critical factor is that the global cost is expected to increase due to increases in the number of cancer cases and the costs of cancer therapies.[30] Initiatives to address cancer as a global challenge include incorporating education, access to current standards, and participation in research. These efforts will lead to discoveries to improve health care and are worthy of full support. The development of guidelines by many professional groups can be an important factor to improve cancer care, although we should do all that is possible to involve people from diverse areas of the world to be part of guideline-developing groups. This strategy will help assure that guidelines are relevant and realistic for the entire global population.

Addressing the full spectrum of cancer care (ie, prevention, screening, treatment, and follow-up), conducting basic research, and clinical trials are areas where we can have a major impact. But conducting clinical trials only in industrialized countries is not enough to improve cancer care globally. Biological differences in individual persons and tumors, access to diagnostics, regulatory and governmental barriers, availability of mentorship for clinical trial conduct, as well as educational initiatives are areas to consider as ways to improve health equity.

A full understanding of potential biologic and pharmacological differences and in metabolism and tolerability in various populations has been impaired by the fact that the majority of clinical trials are performed in the United States and western Europe. The lack of diverse populations prevents a full understanding of geographic variability that may affect patient outcomes. Moreover, according to recent data compiled by the IARC, only approximately 15% of the world population is actually covered by high-quality cancer registries, with even lower registrations in South America (7.5% of the total populations), Asia (6.5%), and Africa (1%).[31,32] However, some hints are available, including increased prevalence of gastric and liver cancers in south Asia compared with the United States, differential rates of *EGFR* alterations and *ALK* mutations by race, younger age at diagnosis of breast cancer in Africa compared with in the United States, and differential tolerability of agents such as capecitabine between patients in Japan compared with white people. Major work is being conducted globally to better unravel genomic differences among various populations.

Considering how science is evolving, and that there is a renewal in global collaboration, the future appears bright for improving global cancer outcomes. Research conducted in a relevant and cost-effective way, supporting the infrastructure of health care systems, clinical trials, education of health care professionals, patients, and governments are keys for success. Evaluating and implementing new diagnostic, screening, prevention, and treatment modalities will help establish new standards of care, which, in turn, improve and prolong lives of patients with cancer, no matter where they were born or live.

6

GENETIC TESTING FOR HEREDITARY CANCER SYNDROMES

Erin E. Salo-Mullen, MS, MPH, and Zsofia K. Stadler, MD

Recent Updates

- In a case-control analysis, the prevalence of pathogenic germline mutations in unselected patients with pancreatic cancer was 5.5%; mutations in six genes (*CDKN2A, TP53, MLH1, BRCA2, ATM, BRCA1*) were statistically increased compared with controls. Odds ratios for pancreatic cancer risk ranged between 2.6 (*BRCA1*) and 12.3 (*CDKN2A*). Given a lack of effective predictors of mutation status based on other personal or family cancer history, the authors recommend that multigene panel germline genetic testing be considered for all patients with pancreatic cancer. (Hu C, *JAMA* 2018)
- Through a long-term surveillance program (Cancer of the Pancreas Screening studies 1 through 4), 354 individuals deemed to be at high risk for pancreatic ductal adenocarcinoma underwent baseline upper endoscopic ultrasound (EUS) and surveillance EUS, magnetic resonance imaging (MRI), and/or computed tomography with a median follow-up time of 5.6 years. Pancreatic lesions with worrisome features or rapid cyst growth were identified in 19%, and neoplastic progression was seen in 7%, including 14 patients with pancreatic ductal adenocarcinoma and 10 with high-grade dysplasia. Of the 10 patients with adenocarcinomas upon surveillance, nine had resectable disease and 85% of those survived 3 years, suggesting support for surveillance with EUS and MRI in high-risk individuals. (Canto MI, *Gastroenterology* 2018)
- In an unselected cohort of patients with advanced renal cell carcinoma (RCC), 16.1% had a germline mutation in one of 17 different cancer-predisposition genes, including 14 mutations in known RCC-associated genes (*FH, BAP1, VHL, MET, SDHA, SDHB*). Patients with non–clear-cell RCC had a higher mutation prevalence, and 35.7% of patients with mutations did not meet criteria for genetic counseling referral, suggesting that especially in non–clear-cell RCC, expansion of guidelines for germline genetic testing should be considered. (Carlo MI, *JAMA Oncol* 2018)
- Among 15,045 patients with cancer, with > 50 cancer types represented in that group, the prevalence of Lynch syndrome was determined according to microsatellite instability (MSI) status. Pathogenic germline mutations in the mismatch repair genes were identified in 16.3%, 1.9%, and 0.3% of patients with MSI-high, MSI-indeterminate, and microsatellite stable tumors, respectively. Many individuals with germline mutations did not have classic Lynch syndrome–associated tumors and did not meet personal or family history criteria for clinical Lynch syndrome evaluation, suggesting that all patients with MSI-high tumors, regardless of cancer type or family cancer history, should undergo germline evaluation for Lynch syndrome. (Latham A, *J Clin Oncol* 2018)

OVERVIEW

During the past two decades, the availability of clinical genetic counseling and testing for hereditary cancer predisposition syndromes has had a major impact on the practice of medical and preventive oncology. The identification and treatment of patients with an inherited predisposition to cancer is now one of the core elements of oncologic care, with statements and guidelines on genetic testing and management provided by ASCO and other organizations.[1-5]

In this chapter, we review the major principles that guide genetic counseling and testing, highlight the differences between testing and counseling for high- versus moderate-penetrance cancer susceptibility genes, and discuss ways of integrating genetic test results into the care of oncology patients. The advent of next-generation sequencing (NGS) technologies has added more complexity to the assessment of the genetic risk of cancer, including implications for tumor and germline analysis, the widespread use of multigene panel testing for inherited cancer susceptibility, and the increased identification of incidental or uncertain genetic findings. Oncologists are encouraged to recognize the importance of pre- and posttest genetic counseling and to build relationships with local genetic counselors and other genetic specialists because they are allies in the challenge of helping patients and their families through a diagnosis of cancer.[6]

Although a detailed description for each of the cancer susceptibility genes and syndromes is outside the scope of this chapter, Figure 6-1 is a concise reference for disease-specific, associated, high- and moderate-penetrance genes. Table 6-1 includes a detailed summary of noteworthy cancer susceptibility genes, including cancer risks, recommended interventions, and syndromic features. In addition, because many of the more common cancer predisposition syndromes are discussed elsewhere, when appropriate, please refer to the specific chapters for additional information on breast cancer, GI cancers, GU cancers, gynecologic cancers, and leukemias (Chapters 10, 13, 14, 15, and 19, respectively).

THE HEREDITARY NATURE OF CANCER

The heritability of cancer has long been recognized, and through the study of cancer-prone families who demonstrate Mendelian modes of inheritance, > 100 high-penetrance, cancer predisposition genes have been identified.[7] However, only a fraction of the familial risks of cancer are explained by the known high-penetrance cancer predisposition syndromes. For example, in the case of familial breast cancer, 10% of diagnoses are related to high-penetrance pathogenic genetic variants (eg, those of *BRCA1* and *BRCA2*), whereas the remainder are due to familial factors (eg, additional shared, but

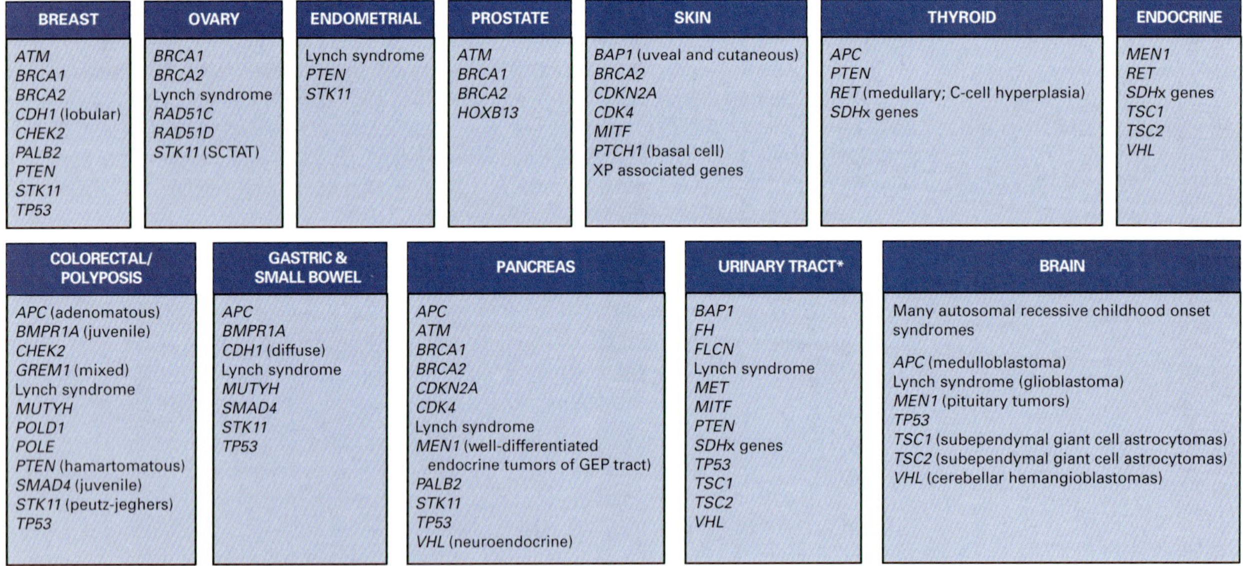

Fig. 6-1 Cancer types and select associated high-penetrance genes.[11,49]

*Urinary tract gene–associated pathologies: *FH*, type 2 papillary, tubule papillary, collecting-duct carcinoma; *FLCN*, oncocytoma, chromophobe, oncocytic hybrid tumor; *MET*, type 1 papillary; Lynch syndrome, ureter and renal pelvis; *TSC1*, *TSC2*, renal cell carcinoma, angiomyolipomas, oncocytoma. Gene-specific pathologies are listed in Table 6-1. GEP, gastro-entero-pancreatic; SCTAT, sex cord tumors with annular tubules; XP, xeroderma pigmentosum.

Table 6-1 **Selected Genes, Syndromes, and Management Considerations**

Gene	Syndrome	Associated Neoplasms	Management Considerations	Other Notes	References
APC	FAP AFAP Variant: Turcot syndrome	Colorectal lesions (adenomatous polyposis and cancer), gastric and duodenal/small bowel lesions (adenomatous polyps and cancer), desmoid tumors, thyroid (particularly cribriform-morula variant of papillary thyroid carcinoma), hepatoblastoma (usually in patients < 5 years old), pancreatic cancer medulloblastoma (Turcot syndrome)	Colonoscopy (beginning as early as 10 years of age) and total colectomy, based on polyp burden. Upper endoscopy, consideration of small-bowel visualization, thyroid examination and consideration of ultrasonography. Consideration of childhood liver palpation, abdominal ultrasound, AFP measurement (investigational)	Genotype-phenotype correlations between classic FAP and AFAP: mutations on the 5′ and 3′ ends of the gene correlate with AFAP. High de novo mutation rate (~20%-25%). Extracolonic features: CHRPE, osteomas, supernumerary teeth, desmoid tumors, epidermoid cysts, gastric fundic gland polyps. Chemoprevention not a replacement for colonoscopy and colectomy	Lynch[45]
*APC**I1307K (c.3920T→A)		Colorectal: moderate penetrance	Colonoscopy, based on family history or similar to risk for first-degree relative	Ashkenazi Jewish founder mutation. Not associated with polyposis	Katona[46] Ma[47] Laken[48]
ATM	Ataxia telangiectasia	Monoallelic carriers: breast Possibly pancreas, ovary, and prostate Biallelic carriers: leukemia, lymphoma	Monoallelic carriers: breast screening with annual mammogram and breast MRI starting at age 40 years or per family history.* Biallelic carriers: AT specialist for multidisciplinary management	Monoallelic carriers: limited evidence for pancreas or prostate cancer. Risk of autosomal recessive AT condition in biallelic offspring of heterozygous carriers. AT: Childhood cerebellar ataxia, telangiectasias of the conjunctivae, immunodeficiency, sensitivity to radiation	Tung[10] Kurian[49] Gatti[50] Suarez[51] Walsh[52]

Table 6-1 **continued**

Gene	Syndrome	Associated Neoplasms	Management Considerations	Other Notes	References
BAP1	*BAP1* tumor predisposition syndrome	Atypical Spitz tumors, uveal melanoma, malignant mesothelioma, cutaneous melanoma, clear-cell renal-cell carcinoma, basal cell carcinoma	Eye examinations, dermatologic examinations, consideration of abdominal ultrasonography and/or MRI of the kidneys	Limited evidence for possible other associated tumors: non–small-cell lung adenocarcinoma, breast cancer, cholangiocarcinoma, meningioma, neuroendocrine carcinoma	Pilarski[53]
BMPR1A and *SMAD4*	Juvenile polyposis syndrome	GI lesions (juvenile/ hamartomatous polyps and cancer [colorectal, stomach, small bowel])	Colonoscopy, based on polyp burden, upper endoscopy. Surgical management based on polyp burden, HHT screening	"Juvenile" refers to polyp histology, not age at onset. *SMAD4* mutations associated with HHT. *SMAD4* mutations associated with massive gastric polyposis. Limited evidence for association with pancreatic cancers	Larsen Haidle[54] Syngal[55]
BRCA1 and *BRCA2*	Hereditary breast and ovarian cancer syndrome	Breast *(BRCA1:* often triple-negative tumor), male breast, ovarian (epithelial; high-grade serous), fallopian tube, primary peritoneal, prostate (high Gleason score), pancreatic (exocrine)	Breast screening with annual mammogram and breast MRI starting at age 25-30 years. Male self-examination and clinical breast examination. Optional risk-reducing mastectomy. Risk-reducing BSO. PSA measurement and digital rectal examination. Consideration of eligibility and pros and cons of chemoprevention with tamoxifen. Consideration of treatment with PARP inhibitors. Investigational pancreas screening.	Founder mutations in certain populations (eg, Ashkenazi Jewish, Icelandic). Risk of autosomal recessive Fanconi anemia with biallelic germline mutations	Chen and Parmigiani[56] Kauff[57] Fong[58] Levy-Lahad[59] Meyer[60] King[61] see Chapter 10 and 15 for HBOC and PARP inhibitors
BRIP1		Ovarian (heterozygous carriers)	Consider risk-reducing BSO at age 50-55 years or per family history	Risk of autosomal recessive Fanconi anemia in biallelic offspring of heterozygous carriers	Tung[10] Ramus[62]

Table 6-1 **continued**

Gene	Syndrome	Associated Neoplasms	Management Considerations	Other Notes	References
CDH1	Hereditary diffuse gastric cancer syndrome	Diffuse gastric cancer, lobular breast cancer	Prophylactic total gastrectomy, breast screening with annual mammography and breast MRI, optional risk-reducing mastectomy	Upper endoscopy not proven to be an effective method of screening for or detecting diffuse gastric cancer. Insufficient evidence for colorectal cancer	van der Post[63]
CDKN2A, CDK4	FAMMM syndrome	Melanoma and dysplastic nevi, pancreas	Dermatologic examination, investigational pancreas screening	Risk of melanoma may be independent of genetic test result. *CDKN2a* (p16) founder mutation in the Netherlands	Goldstein[64] Vasen[65]
CHEK2		Breast: moderate penetrance colon	Breast screening with annual mammography and breast MRI starting at age 40 years, or per family history.* Colonoscopy based on family history or similar to risk for first-degree relative	Genotype-phenotype: different risks for truncating mutations *v* missense mutations. Limited evidence for association with prostate cancer	Tung[10] Katona[46] CHEK2[66]
FH	HLRCC	Cutaneous leiomyomata, uterine leiomyomata, renal tumors (type 2 papillary, tubule-papillary, collecting-duct carcinomas; unilateral, solitary lesions)	Dermatologic and gynecologic examinations; evaluate for changes suggestive of leiomyosarcoma. Medication or resection of leiomyomata, imaging for and surgical management of renal tumors	Fumarate hydratase enzyme assay might be helpful in some situations. Risk for uterine leiomyosarcoma is unclear. Biallelic *FH* mutations cause a recessive disorder known as fumarate hydratase deficiency-metabolic disorder, profound developmental delay, seizures, fumaric aciduria	Pithukpakorn[67] Barrisford[68]

Table 6-1 **continued**

Gene	Syndrome	Associated Neoplasms	Management Considerations	Other Notes	References
FLCN	BHD syndrome	Cutaneous (fibrofolliculomas, trichodiscomas/ angiofibromas, perifollicular fibromas, acrochordons), pulmonary cysts, renal tumors (oncocytoma, chromophobe, oncocytic hybrid tumors)	No consensus at this time. Dermatologic care, imaging for and surgical management (nephron-sparing) of renal tumors	Fibrofolliculomas are specific to BHD. Lung cysts are multiple and bilateral. Spontaneous pneumothorax. Renal tumors are multifocal, bilateral, and slow growing. Other features: parotid lesions, oral papules, thyroid lesions. Unclear data regarding colon cancer. Possible genotype-phenotype correlations	Toro[69]
MEN1	MEN1	GEP tract, well-differentiated endocrine tumors, pituitary tumors (prolactinoma), parathyroid tumors, carcinoid tumors, adrenocortical tumors	Biochemical testing, imaging, surgical management, various medications	Primary hyperparathyroidism, hypercalcemia, oligomenorrhea/amenorrhea, galactorrhea, Zollinger-Ellison syndrome (gastrinoma), insulinoma, glucagonoma, VIP-secreting tumor (VIPomas). Other features: skin (angiofibromas, collagenomas), lipomas, CNS lesions (meningioma, ependymoma), leiomyomas	Giusti[70]
MET (c-Met)	HPRC	Papillary renal cancer (multifocal, bilateral, type 1 papillary)	Imaging, surgical management		Coleman[71]

Table 6-1 **continued**

Gene	Syndrome	Associated Neoplasms	Management Considerations	Other Notes	References
MLH1, MSH2, MSH6, PMS2, and *EPCAM*	Lynch syndrome (formerly HNPCC); variant: Muir-Torre syndrome; variant: Turcot syndrome; variant: constitutional mismatch repair deficiency syndrome (biallelic mutations; recessive inheritance)	Colorectal, endometrial ovarian (epithelial), stomach, small bowel, upper urinary tract (renal pelvis, ureter), pancreas, hepatobiliary tract, sebaceous neoplasms (Muir-Torre syndrome), glioblastoma (Turcot syndrome), prostate	Colonoscopy every 1-2 years starting at age 20-25 years. Consideration of prophylactic colectomy. Hysterectomy, and risk-reducing BSO. Consideration of: upper endoscopy, urinalysis or urine cytology, treatment with checkpoint blockade immunotherapy, and of aspirin for chemoprevention	Tumor analyses with IHC staining, MSI analysis, somatic tumor genetic analysis, BRAF V600E somatic analysis, MLH1 promoter hypermethylation analysis, Amsterdam criteria I and II, revised Bethesda guidelines. Recommendations for universal screening of colorectal and endometrial cancers. Genotype-phenotype correlations emerging but not significant enough to alter management. Limited evidence for moderate risk of breast cancer. Risk of autosomal recessive CMMR-D syndrome (café-au-lait macules, solid tumors, hematologic cancers) in offspring	Lynch[72] Hampel[73] Burn[74] Shia[26] Zhang[23] Vasen[75] Umar[24] Lu[76] Hamilton[77] Le[78] Bakry[116] Raymond[117] see Chapter 13: Gastrointestinal Cancers
MUTYH	MAP	Biallelic mutation carriers: colorectal lesions (adenomatous polyposis and cancer; serrated and hyperplastic polyps also described), stomach, duodenal lesions (adenomatous polyps, cancer)	Colonoscopy and total colectomy, based on polyp burden; upper endoscopy	Phenotypically similar to AFAP. Two northern European founder mutations. Controversy regarding risk in heterozygous carriers (see *MUTYH* monoallelic/ heterozygous carrier)	Al-Tassan[79] Sieber[80]
MUTYH monoallelic/ heterozygous carrier		Controversy regarding risk of colorectal cancer	Colonoscopy, based on family history	Controversy regarding risk	Katona[46] Win[81]

Table 6-1 **continued**

Gene	Syndrome	Associated Neoplasms	Management Considerations	Other Notes	References
NF1	Neurofibromatosis type 1	Cutaneous neurofibromas, plexiform neurofibromas, optic nerve and other CNS gliomas, Malignant peripheral nerve sheath tumors, breast (moderate risk), others: GIST, leukemia	NF1 specialist for management, physical and ophthalmologic examinations; imaging; surgical management; breast screening with annual mammography and breast MRI, per family history*	Café-au-lait macules, axillary and inguinal freckling, iris Lisch nodules, learning disabilities, scoliosis, tibial dysplasia, vasculopathy	Friedman[82] Madinikia[83]
PALB2		Breast Pancreas	Breast screening with annual mammogram and breast MRI starting at age 30 years or per family history.* Optional risk-reducing mastectomy, based on family history. Investigational pancreas screening	Insufficient evidence for ovarian cancer. Risk of autosomal recessive Fanconi anemia in biallelic offspring of heterozygous parents	Antoniu[84] Jones[85] Stadler[86]
PTCH1	Gorlin syndrome/nevoid basal cell carcinoma syndrome	Jaw (odontogenic) keratocysts, basal cell carcinomas, medulloblastoma (PNET-desmoplastic)	Referral to a specialist for management. Physical examination, avoidance of sun exposure and at least annual dermatologic examination, surgical management	Other features: congenital skeletal anomalies, cleft lip/palate, cerebral/falx calcifications, macrocephaly with frontal bossing, polydactyly, intellectual disability, lymphomesenteric or pleural cysts, palmar/plantar pits, cardiac fibromas, ovarian fibromas, ocular abnormalities. Related gene: *SUFU*	Evans and Farndon[87]

Table 6-1 **continued**

Gene	Syndrome	Associated Neoplasms	Management Considerations	Other Notes	References
PTEN	Cowden syndrome/*PTEN* hamartoma tumor syndrome	Breast, thyroid (most often follicular), endometrial, colorectal lesions (hamartomas, ganglioneuromas, cancer), renal cell carcinoma	Breast screening with annual mammography and breast MRI. Optional risk-reducing mastectomy. Thyroid examination and ultrasound, endometrial screening with random biopsy and ultrasonography, optional hysterectomy, colonoscopy, renal imaging	Major and minor criteria (tumors, physical and dermatologic/ mucocutaneous findings, developmental disability). Macrocephaly, Bannanyan-Riley-Ruvalcaba syndrome, *PTEN*-related Proteus syndrome, autism spectrum disorder, Lhermitte-Duclos disease	Eng[88] Tan[89] Pilarski[90]
RB1	Retinoblastoma	Retinoblastoma (trilateral disease: co-occurrence of pinealoblastoma), bone or soft-tissue sarcomas, melanoma, others	Ophthalmologic examination and imaging; care by a multidisciplinary team. Avoidance of radiation	Knudson's two-hit hypothesis. Usually bilateral or multifocal disease. Mosaic forms; therefore, analysis of tumor tissue and blood important. RNA studies may also be recommended. Low-penetrance mutations identified. Parent-of-origin effect in some families	Lohmann[91] Knudson[92] Abramson[93] Abramson[94]
RET	MEN2. Three subtypes: MEN2A (aka, Sipple syndrome); Familial medullary thyroid carcinoma; MEN2B	Medullary thyroid carcinoma (multifocal, bilateral) and primary C-cell hyperplasia, pheochromocytoma (bilateral) (MEN2A and 2B), parathyroid adenoma/ hyperplasia (hyperparathyroidism, hypercalcemia, renal stones; MEN2A)	Prophylactic thyroidectomy (varies from infancy to age ≥ 5 years, depending on specific RET pathogenic mutation; genotype-phenotype correlations). Surgical management of identified disease, serum calcitonin concentration, consideration of eligibility for treatment with kinase inhibitors, biochemical screening and imaging for pheochromocytoma and parathyroid abnormalities	Genotype-phenotype correlations MEN2A: MTC in early adulthood. FMTC: MTC in middle age. MEN2B: MTC in early-childhood, mucosal neuromas (lips, tongue), dysmorphic features (large lips, "marfanoid" body habitus), GI ganglioneuromatosis. *RET* gene also associated with Hirschsprung disease	Marquard and Eng[95] American Thyroid Association[96]

Table 6-1 continued

Gene	Syndrome	Associated Neoplasms	Management Considerations	Other Notes	References
SDHB, SDHC, SDHD, SDHA, and *SDHAF2*	Hereditary paraganglioma-pheochromocytoma syndrome	PGL-sympathetic and parasympathetic PCC GISTs, renal clear-cell carcinoma, papillary thyroid carcinoma (unclear data)	Biochemical screening, physical examination, and imaging. Screening may begin as early as age 10 years. Pharmacologic treatment, surgical management	Secretory and nonsecretory PGL, high blood pressure, headache, anxiety, profuse sweating, palpitations, pallor. *SDHB*: high risk of malignant transformation. *SDHD:* parent-of-origin effect, disease-causing when paternally inherited. *SDHAF2:* possible parent-of-origin effect (paternal inheritance)	Lenders[97] Pai[98] Neumann[99]
STK11 (LKB1)	PJS	GI lesions (PJS-type hamartomatous polyps; colorectal, stomach, small-bowel cancer), breast, pancreas, gynecologic (ovarian, cervix, uterus), testes (Sertoli cell), lung	Colonoscopy, upper endoscopy with small-bowel visualization, breast screening with annual mammography and breast MRI, investigational pancreas screening, gynecologic examination, testicular examination	Mucocutaneous hyperpigmentation of mouth, lips, nose, eyes, genitalia, fingers; may fade after puberty. Females: SCTAT; adenoma malignum of the cervix	Syngal[55] McGarrity[100] Beggs[101] Stoffel[102]
TP53	LFS	Soft-tissue and bone sarcomas, breast, brain, adrenocortical carcinoma, leukemia, others: GI, genitourinary, lung, lymphomas, thyroid, neuroblastoma, skin	Breast screening with annual breast MRI and mammography beginning at ages in the 20s and 30s, respectively. Optional risk-reducing mastectomy. Physical examination, including dermatologic and neurologic examinations. Colonoscopy, whole-body MRI, consideration of radiation avoidance, if clinically appropriate	Classic LFS criteria. Chompret criteria. Consider genetic testing in *BRCA*-negative, isolated, early-onset breast cancer (age < 30 years). Breast cancers more likely to be estrogen-, progesterone-, HER2/ neu-receptor positive	Schneider[103] Li and Fraumeni[104] Li[105] Chompret[106] Villani[107]

Table 6-1 **continued**

Gene	Syndrome	Associated Neoplasms	Management Considerations	Other Notes	References
TSC1 and *TSC2*	TSC	Kidney: renal-cell carcinomas, angiomyolipomas (benign and malignant), epithelial cysts, oncocytoma (benign adenomatous hamartoma)	TSC specialist for management: imaging; dermatologic, dental, ophthalmologic examinations; echocardiography; electrocardiography. Consideration of eligibility for treatment with mTOR inhibitors, surgical management	Skin (hypomelanotic macules, facial angiofibromas, shagreen patches, cephalic plaques, ungual fibromas); brain (cortical dysplasias, subependymal nodules and subependymal giant cell astrocytomas, seizures, intellectual disability/developmental delay, autism spectrum disorder, psychiatric illness); heart (rhabdomyomas, arrhythmias); lungs (lymphangioleiomyomatosis). Genotype-phenotype correlations: higher risk of renal cell carcinoma in *TSC2*. Possible association with neuroendocrine tumors	Northrup[108]
VHL	VHL syndrome	Clear-cell renal-cell carcinoma, pheochromocytoma, paragangliomas, pancreatic neuroendocrine tumors	Neurologic, ophthalmologic, audiologic examinations. Biochemical screening, imaging, surgical management	Hemangioblastomas of the brain, spinal cord, and retina; renal cysts; pancreatic cysts; endolymphatic sac tumors; epididymal and broad ligament cysts. Genotype-phenotype correlations: VHL type 1, type 2A, type 2B, type 2C with different risks of pheochromocytoma or renal cell carcinoma	Frantzen[109] Grubb[110] Corcos[111]

Note: Leukemia/lymphoma predisposition syndromes are not listed; refer to Chapters 19 and 20. The majority of childhood-onset conditions are not listed; refer to Lindor et al.[112]

Abbreviations: AFAP, attenuated familial adenomatous polyposis; AFP, α-fetoprotein; AT, ataxia telangiectasia; BHD, Birt-Hogg-Dube; BSO, bilateral salpingo-oophorectomy; CHRPE, congenital hypertrophy of the retinal pigment epithelium; CMMR-D, constitutional mismatch repair deficiency; FAP, familial adenomatous polyposis; FMTC, familial medullary thyroid carcinoma; GIST, GI stromal tumor; HBOC, hereditary breast and ovarian cancer; HHT, hereditary hemorrhagic telangiectasia; LFS, Li-Fraumeni syndrome; MEN, multiple endocrine neoplasia; MRI, magnetic resonance imaging; MSI, microsatellite instability; mTOR, mechanistic target of rapamycin; NF1, neurofibromatosis type 1; PCC, pheochromocytoma; PGL, paraganglioma; PJS, Peutz-Jeghers syndrome; PSA, prostate-specific antigen; SCTAT, Sex cord tumors with annular tubules; TSC, tuberous sclerosis complex; VHL, von Hippel-Lindau; VIP, vasoactive intestinal peptide.

*Earlier initiation of breast cancer surveillance may be warranted in the presence of a significant family history of breast cancer.

currently undetectable, hereditable factors and/or shared environmental factors).[8]

Outside of the high-penetrance syndromes, shared hereditable factors present in some families may include moderate-penetrance genes and single nucleotide polymorphisms (SNPs)[9,10] (Fig 6-2):

- Dozens of moderate-penetrance genes that generally confer a modest degree of cancer risk with a relative risk of 2 to 5 have been identified. Although genetic testing for such moderate-penetrance genes was not routinely undertaken in the past, with NGS and commercial multigene panel analyses, clinical evaluation of these genes has now become common. However, the value of screening for moderate-penetrance genes remains controversial because neither the clinical validity (ie, the accuracy with which a genetic test predicts the development of cancer) nor the clinical utility (ie, the degree to which the use of the genetic test informs clinical decision-making and leads to improved health outcomes) has been clearly proven.[11]
- Through genome-wide association studies (GWAS), hundreds of additional low-penetrance genetic loci, usually in the form of SNPs, have been identified for nearly all the common malignancies. These low-penetrance loci are often associated with only a slight increase in risk of cancer (relative risk, approximately 1.1 to 1.5).[12] Given the limited clinical validity and utility of SNPs with such small effect sizes, clinical testing for individual risk loci is not routinely performed, although research efforts to incorporate low-penetrance risk alleles into models for risk stratification for public health programs and cancer screening may eventually be feasible.

KEY POINTS

- The high-penetrance cancer-susceptibility genes account for only a small proportion of all cancer diagnoses. Familial risks for cancer exist outside of the high-penetrance cancer susceptibility syndromes related to additional shared hereditable factors and/or shared environmental factors.
- Clinical validity and clinical utility should be taken into account when genetic testing is being considered.
- Genetic testing for moderate-penetrance cancer susceptibility genes associated with a two- to five-fold increased risk of specific cancers has become more commonplace, although the clinical validity and utility of testing for many of these genes is not yet fully defined.

GENETIC COUNSELING

The National Society of Genetic Counselors (NSGC) has defined genetic counseling as the "process of helping people understand and adapt to the medical, psychological, and familial implications of genetic contributions to disease."[13] The traditional model of genetic counseling for hereditary cancer syndromes includes pre- and posttest consultations with a genetic counselor and often a geneticist. Unfortunately, a genetic counselor workforce shortage exists. Thus, expanded models of service delivery are now being used, including telemedicine, telephone-based methods, and genetic counseling provided by other practitioners in the context of coordinated patient care.[1,14] Many oncology patients are now offered genetic testing through NGS analyses of tumor and, sometimes, nontumor

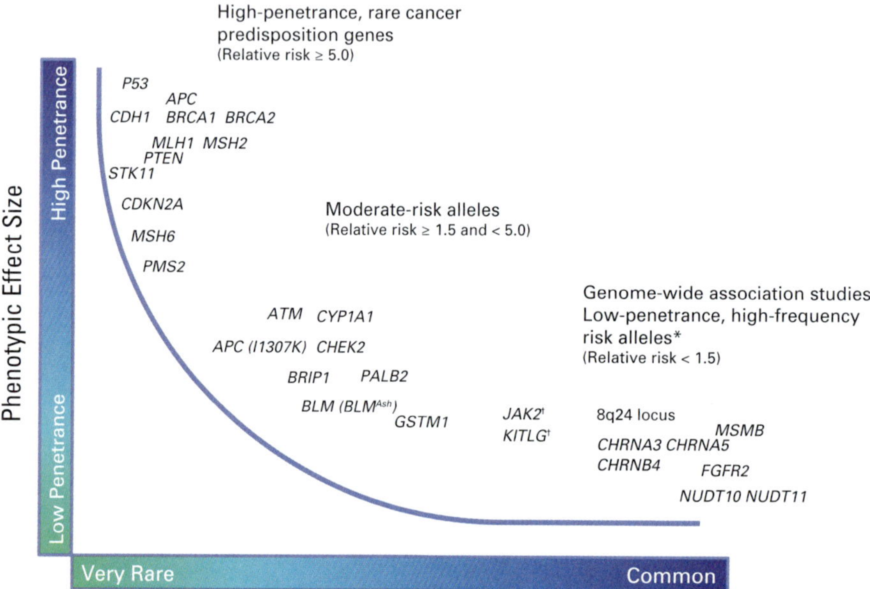

Fig. 6-2 Phenotypic effect size and frequency of occurrence.[129]

*Named genes reflect only the most likely candidate genes to be implicated by the marker single nucleotide polymorphisms (SNPs) identified from the genome-wide association studies. †The marker SNPs mapping to *JAK2* in myeloproliferative neoplasms and *KITLG* in testicular germ cell tumors have odds ratios of approximately 3.0, with allele frequencies ranging from 20% to 40%.

Adapted from Stadler et al.[129]

specimens for the purpose of clinical trial eligibility. Expanding the role of medical oncologists and oncology nurses to include genetic counseling and testing of oncology patients when appropriate is one model to meet patients' needs. Regardless of which clinician provides genetic risk assessment, the principles of genetic counseling should be at the foundation of the patient interaction.

PRETEST GENETIC COUNSELING

Pretest genetic counseling is often considered to be analogous to the informed consent process and is, therefore, a vital step in helping patients and families determine whether genetic testing (and to what extent) is right for them (Table 6-2).[15] Some states require informed consent before genetic testing (eg, New York),[1,16] and genetic counseling is one of the ways to fulfill this requirement. Elements of pretest genetic counseling include:[17]

- Data collection (medical and family histories, pertinent physical examination)
- Data analysis and risk assessment
- Education regarding differential diagnoses and genes
- Evaluation of testing options and possible results
- Selection of appropriate analyses and laboratories
- Discussion of the risks, benefits, and limitations of genetic testing
- Exploration of the medical, psychosocial, familial, and possible financial consequences of testing

The collection of family history is an important part of genetic cancer-risk assessments. Obtaining family history data during an initial patient consultation, as well as periodic reassessment of the dynamic family history during long-term patient follow-up, is an integral part of oncologic care. The recommended key elements for a minimum, adequate cancer family history are highlighted in an ASCO expert statement and should help oncologists identify patients who would benefit from referral to clinical cancer genetics specialists (Table 6-3).[18] The following are of particular note:

- It is standard to evaluate at least three generations of a patient's maternal and paternal lineages.[19]
- Individuals of certain ancestries may have higher risks for specific hereditary syndromes due to the presence of founder mutations;[20] therefore, the knowledge of ancestral background is often critical. Founder mutations have been identified in several populations (historically isolated populations), but the most common example in the field of hereditary cancer is the presence of three founder mutations in the *BRCA1* (c.68_69delT and c.5266dupC) and *BRCA2* (c.5946delT) genes in the Ashkenazi Jewish population, with a prevalence of one in 40 individuals.
- Family structures may be truncated for a variety of reasons, including number of births and miscarriages or terminations, sexes (a paucity of female family members may explain a lack of gynecologic cancers), adoption, divorce, early death from noncancer causes, or estrangement.[21]

POSTTEST GENETIC COUNSELING

Elements of posttest genetic counseling include the following:[17]

- Disclosure and interpretation of test results
- Education about medical risks and management options (screening, risk reduction, therapeutic implications), and appropriate referrals and resources
- Investigation of the psychological reaction and familial repercussions related to the test results
- An opportunity for the clinician to provide emotional support to the patient and family
- Planning for communication of the genetic test results and implications to at-risk family members

Even for patients who have negative or inconclusive results on genetic testing, posttest genetic counseling is still critically important because patients and families may still be considered at increased risk for disease and for negative psychological reactions. Importantly, most family histories of cancer are not explained by pathogenic mutations in the known high-penetrance cancer predisposition genes. As such, many cases of familial breast cancer or familial colorectal cancer remain unexplained, but individuals in these families may still be at increased risk for cancer. Failure to understand the uninformative nature of a negative or inconclusive genetic test result may lead to nonadherence to medical recommendations.[6]

INCORPORATING GENETIC COUNSELING AND TESTING INTO THE CARE OF THE ONCOLOGY PATIENT

Genetic counseling can occur at multiple points in the oncology setting, and it is important for an oncologist to determine, in conjunction with the patient, when genetic counseling and testing are most appropriate (Fig 6-3), including:

- At the time of cancer diagnosis (ie, peridiagnosis, pretreatment): Identification of an inherited cancer predisposition syndrome may affect treatment decisions, including extent of surgery. However, because the peridiagnostic period may be emotional and overwhelming for patients, genetic counseling and testing may be deferred to a later time. Also, many factors, including specific laboratory tests, specific analysis, and insurance authorization, may influence test turnaround time, so obtaining genetic test results within a desired time may not be logistically possible if there is a need for immediate intervention.
- During the treatment period: Genetic testing may allow patients and physicians to make informed decisions about chemotherapy and targeted therapeutic options. This is becoming increasingly important because treatments have been discovered that are effective with certain germline mutations (eg, PARP inhibitors and mutations in the *BRCA* pathway, immunotherapy and microsatellite unstable cancers such as those due to Lynch syndrome).
- During the posttreatment and survivorship follow-up period: Once a patient has completed treatment and is

Table 6-2 **Components of Informed Consent and Pretest Education in Clinical Cancer Genetics**[1]		
Traditional Pretest Counseling for Susceptibility Testing (Purpose of Testing)	**Pretest Counseling for Multigene Panel Testing***	**Pretest Education for Somatic Mutation Profiling with Potential for Incidental Germline Findings (Purpose of Testing)**
Information on specific genetic mutation(s) or genomic variant(s) being tested, including whether range of risk associated with variant will affect medical care.	Discuss specific genes may need to be batched because it may not be feasible to review each gene individually; describe high-penetrance syndromes being evaluated (eg, hereditary breast and ovary, Lynch, hereditary diffuse gastric, Li-Fraumeni); patients should be made aware of possible detection of high-penetrance mutations not suggested by personal or family history; genes of uncertain clinical utility may need to be described more generally.	Discuss the possibility of discovering information relevant to inherited risk and range of possible germline risks that may be identified (differs for targeted sequencing *v* whole-exome or whole-genome sequencing); discuss a mandatory search for secondary findings, and the option to decline to learn results should be provided.
Implications of positive (mutation confirmed to be pathogenic), negative (no identified change in genetic sequence), or uncertain (genetic variant of unknown significance) result.	Emphasize implications of positive results in less well-understood or lesser-penetrance genes and findings of mutations in genes associated with syndromes not suggested by personal or family history.	Discuss criteria that will be used to identify germline variants that would be returned to patient or family.
Possibility test will not be informative.	Emphasize the current high rate of variants of uncertain significance.	Emphasize that purpose of test is not to identify germline risk, germline mutations can be missed, and that dedicated testing directed by personal or family history is available.
Risk that children and/or family members have inherited genetic condition.	Consider potential reproductive implications to family of mutations in genes linked to recessive disorders (eg, *ATM*, Fanconi *[BRCA2, PALB2]*, *NBN*, *BLM*).	Discuss how incidental findings may be relevant to other family members.
Fees involved in testing and counseling; for DTC testing, whether counselor is used by testing company.		
Psychological implications of test results (benefits and risks).		
Risks and protections against genetic discrimination by employers or insurers.		
Confidentiality issues, including DTC testing companies and policies related to privacy and data security.		
Possible use of DNA samples for future research		
Options and limitations of medical surveillance and strategies for prevention after genetic or genomic testing		
Importance of sharing genetic and genomic test results with at-risk relatives so they may benefit from this information.		Consider identifying surrogate who could receive incidental results on behalf of patient in event patient has died or is otherwise unable to receive results.
Plans for disclosing test results and providing follow-up.		

Abbreviation: DTC, direct-to-consumer.

*Same general components as traditional counseling, with special additional considerations as listed.

Table 6-3 Recommended Key Elements for Minimum Adequate Cancer Family History

Element
First-degree relatives: siblings, parents, children
Second-degree relatives: grandparents, aunts, uncles, grandchildren, nieces, nephews, half-siblings
Both maternal and paternal sides
Ethnicity
Consanguineous relationships
For each cancer case in the family, establish:
Age at cancer diagnosis
Type of primary cancer
Results of any cancer predisposition testing in any relative

NOTE. Family history should be taken at diagnosis and updated periodically.
Adapted from Lu et al.[18]

receiving follow-up care, genetic evaluation may assist in making decisions about future cancer surveillance and prevention to help manage the risk for new primary cancers. Also, although genetic evaluation for some individuals might not be indicated at the time of their cancer diagnosis, changes in their dynamic personal or family histories may lead to a referral for genetic testing in the future. Finally, it is important to note that updates in genetic testing (eg, new genes, new methodology) may become available throughout a patient's oncology follow-up period, and it may be reasonable to consider rereferral for updated genetic evaluation. A general guideline may be to consider an update consultation every 5 years.

- Postmortem: If DNA from affected patients can be stored before death, these specimens may be used by family members for appropriate genetic evaluations in the future. Many commercial laboratories now work with patients, families, physicians, and hospice-care providers to have a

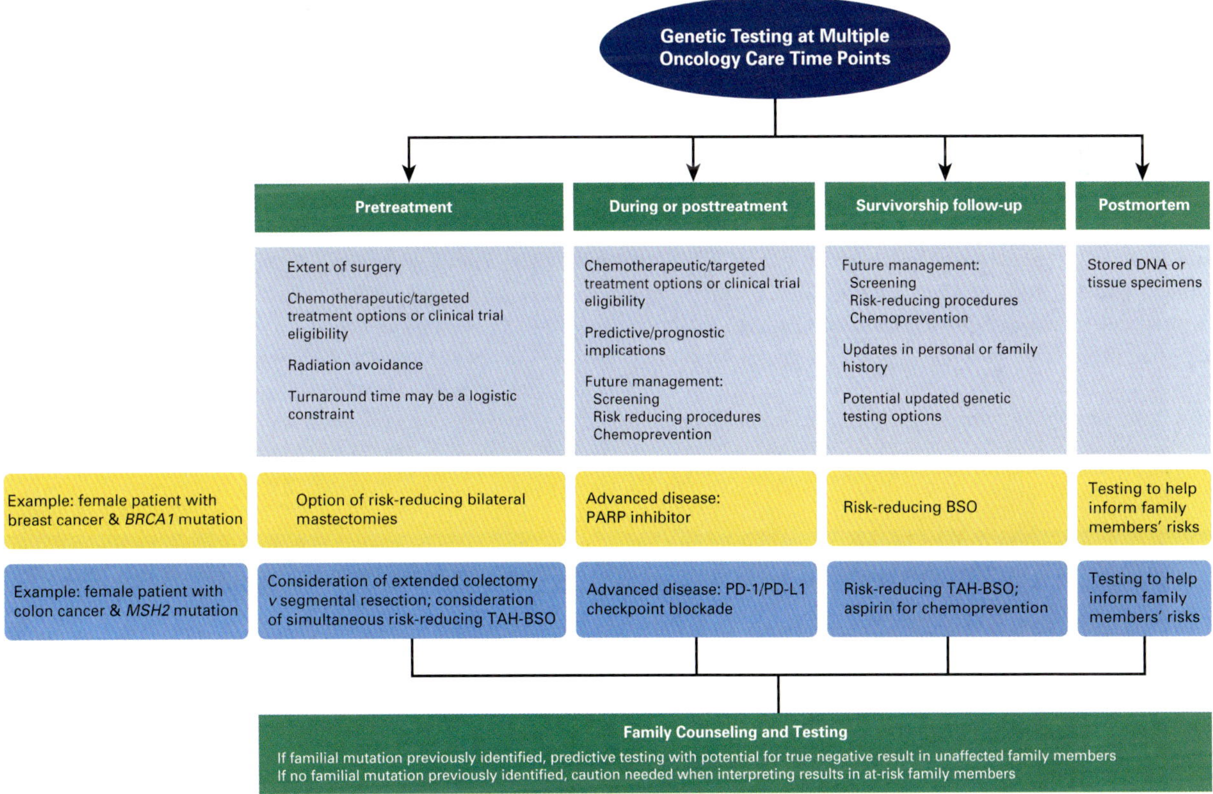

Fig. 6-3 Incorporating genetic counseling and testing into the care of patients with cancer.
BSO, bilateral salpingo-oophorectomy; PD-1/PD-L1, Programmed cell death protein 1 programmed death ligand 1; TAH, total abdominal hysterectomy.

sample of blood (or other tissue) collected before death and stored for use by a designated individual or family member.
- Families: For families identified as harboring a pathogenic, cancer-predisposing genetic mutation, unaffected family members may pursue predictive genetic testing with single amplicon (ie, site-specific) mutation analysis to determine whether they also inherited the familial mutation.

IDENTIFYING APPROPRIATE PATIENTS FOR REFERRAL TO GENETIC COUNSELING AND TESTING

Although most cancers are not due to high-penetrance cancer predisposition syndromes, it is crucial for oncologists to be familiar with common "red flag" indications for referral for genetic counseling (Table 6-4). The National Comprehensive Cancer Network (NCCN) has published criteria for when referrals for genetic counseling and testing should be considered. Also, some third-party payers have established their own criteria for when genetic testing is deemed medically indicated and may not necessarily be congruent with the aforementioned NCCN guidelines.

Although taking a thorough medical and family history is important and will aid the process of identifying possible red flags, it is important for clinicians to realize that not all individuals or families that have a mutation actually fit into the classic syndrome phenotype descriptions. With NGS being performed on patients' tumor and sometimes germline specimens, a substantial number of patients are found to carry germline mutations in genes that would have not been suspected on the basis of their personal or family histories. For example, targeted NGS of matched tumor and germline specimens for 76 known cancer predisposition genes identified that 17.5% of patients with advanced cancer (n = 182 of 1,040) had an actionable germline mutation; 55.5% of these would not have been detected using clinical genetic testing guidelines alone.[22] In fact, over the last few years, authors of several studies focusing on specific cancer types have recommended agnostic germline genetic testing of certain cancer subtypes, including patients with ovarian/fallopian tube/primary peritoneal cancer; metastatic prostate cancer; pancreatic cancer; early-onset colorectal cancer; and non–clear-cell renal cell carcinoma.

The American Society of Breast Surgeons recently recommended that all women with breast cancer be offered germline genetic testing. Given these findings, it is important that genetic counseling models evolve and that clinicians who provide cancer-focused genetic counseling be skilled in discussing the implications of identified germline mutations with patients and families in the absence of a significant history of cancer.

ETHICAL PRINCIPLES AND CHALLENGES IN GENETIC COUNSELING

Although there are multiple principles of ethics that come into play in the field of cancer-focused genetic counseling, autonomy, nonmaleficence, equity, and duty to warn are four key concepts. Table 6-5 provides additional explanation and examples of these four fundamental, guiding principles.

KEY POINTS

- Genetic counseling is a communication process that helps patients understand and adapt to the various implications of having a genetic condition.
- Genetic counseling should include pre- and posttest discussions and can be performed at various times during the care of oncology patients, including the pretreatment and peridiagnostic phase, during treatment and posttreatment, during survivorship follow-up, and even postmortem. There are benefits and limitations associated with performing genetic counseling and testing at each stage.
- Thorough medical and family histories are vital for accurate genetic risk assessments. When assessing a patient's risk to have an inherited cancer predisposition syndrome, red flags such as unusual age at cancer diagnosis, multiple diagnoses in a single individual, similar cancers seen in multiple generations of a kindred, certain neoplastic lesions, and certain ancestries (those with known founder germline mutations) should be considered.
- The field of genetic counseling is guided by multiple ethical principles, including autonomy, nonmaleficence, equity, and duty to warn.

Table 6-4 **"Red Flag" Indications for Referral to Genetic Counseling**
Early or unusual age at cancer diagnosis
Multiple primary cancers (bilateral, synchronous, and/or metachronous diagnoses)
Unique features (See Table 6-6):
Certain types of GI polyps
Certain dermatologic features
Certain neoplastic pathologies
Certain ancestries (ie, those known to have founder mutations)

Table 6-5 **Ethical Principles in Genetic Counseling**

Ethical Principal	Application to Genetic Counseling and Testing	Examples
Autonomy	The right to decide whether to learn what is coded in his or her DNA	Genetic testing of minors: • For inherited predisposition syndromes associated with adult-onset cancer, autonomy of a child is typically maintained with deferral of genetic testing to adulthood[1,15] • For syndromes that involve disease onset or recommended preventive measure in childhood, genetic testing in the context of genetic counseling and with assent from the child (age ~7-17 years) is accepted.[6] • Examples: classic FAP or Li-Fraumeni
Nonmaleficence	"Do no harm," particularly relevant to the process of genetic test result interpretation	Different possible genetic test results with distinct implications: • Understanding of the spectrum of genetic tests results (eg, pathogenic, variant of uncertain significance) • Translation of genetic information into appropriate medical recommendations
		Moderate-penetrance genes and determination of risk: • Understanding the uncertainty associated with moderate-penetrance gene mutations, including lack of evidence-based management recommendations
Equity	Access to genetic counseling services and testing is not uniform	Social and economic barriers: physical access (rural *v* urban); cost; insurance coverage; fear of discrimination and/or social stigma; and mistrust of the medical system.[15]
Duty to warn	The extent of a clinician's responsibility to a patient's family	Previous court rulings have taken different stances on clinicians' duty to warn patients' at-risk family members of inherited risks for cancer.[15]
		Responsibility of the clinician: • Discuss a patient's genetic test result • Inform the patient that family members may be at risk for an inherited cancer syndrome and recommend that family members be made aware of this risk • Clearly document this communication with the patient

TUMOR ANALYSES

A patient's tumor pathology may provide the initial signal of the possibility of an inherited cancer predisposition syndrome. For example, triple-negative (ie, estrogen-, progesterone-, and HER2/neu-negative) breast cancers are associated with an increased incidence of *BRCA1* germline pathogenic variants, and genetic testing is considered medically indicated for all women ≤ 60 years old who have this type of cancer. All patients with medullary thyroid cancer should be referred for genetic testing of the *RET* gene. Table 6-6 lists additional important cancer predisposition syndromes and tumor pathology associations.

TUMOR ANALYSIS INFORMS GERMLINE SUSCEPTIBILITY: THE CASE OF LYNCH SYNDROME

The hallmark feature of tumors associated with Lynch syndrome (previously known as hereditary nonpolyposis colorectal cancer) is the presence of microsatellite instability (MSI) resulting from the accumulation of mismatch mutations in the genome, especially at regions of repetitive DNA known as

Table 6-6 **Genetic Cancer Predisposition Syndromes and Selected Associated Pathologies**

Neoplastic or Preneoplastic Pathologies	Associated Genetic Syndromes and Genes
High-grade or poorly differentiated ductal breast cancer with estrogen-receptor, progesterone-receptor, and HER2-neu negativity	Hereditary breast and ovarian cancer syndrome (*BRCA1*)
Lobular breast cancer	Hereditary diffuse gastric cancer syndrome (*CDH1*)
High-grade serous (papillary serous) ovarian cancer	Hereditary breast and ovarian cancer syndrome (*BRCA1, BRCA2*)
Clear-cell or endometrioid ovarian cancers	Lynch syndrome (*MLH1, MSH2, MSH6, PMS2, EPCAM*)
Ovarian sex cord tumors with annular tubules	Peutz-Jeghers syndrome (*STK11*)
Clear-cell or endometrioid endometrial cancers	Lynch syndrome (*MLH1, MSH2, MSH6, PMS2, EPCAM*)
Uterine leiomyomas	Hereditary leiomyoma renal cell carcinoma syndrome (*FH*)
Adenoma malignum of the cervix	Peutz-Jeghers syndrome (*STK11*)
Colorectal cancer with tumor-infiltrating lymphocytes, Crohn's-like lymphocytic reaction, mucinous/signet-ring cells, medullary growth pattern	Lynch syndrome (*MLH1, MSH2, MSH6, PMS2, EPCAM*)
Lauren's diffuse type/signet ring cell/linitus plastica gastric cancer	Hereditary diffuse gastric cancer syndrome (*CDH1*)
Hamartomatous GI polyps	Peutz-Jeghers syndrome (*STK11*); juvenile polyposis syndrome (*BMPR1A, SMAD4*); Cowden syndrome (*PTEN*)
Pancreatic neuroendocrine tumors	Multiple endocrine neoplasia type 1 (*MEN1*); von Hippel-Lindau (*VHL*)
Renal papillary type I carcinoma	Hereditary papillary renal cancer syndrome (*MET*)
Renal papillary type II, collecting duct, tubulopapillary carcinomas	Hereditary leiomyoma renal cell carcinoma syndrome (FH)
Renal clear-cell carcinoma	von Hippel-Lindau (*VHL*)
Renal oncocytoma	Birt-Hogg-Dube syndrome (*FLCN*); tuberous sclerosis complex (*TSC1, TSC2*)
Renal angiomyolipoma	Tuberous sclerosis complex (*TSC1, TSC2*)
Renal chromophobe	Birt-Hogg-Dube syndrome (*FLCN*)
Sertoli cell tumors of the testes	Peutz-Jeghers syndrome (*STK11*)
Medullary thyroid cancer	Multiple endocrine neoplasia type 2 (*RET*)
Cribriform-morular variant of papillary thyroid carcinoma	Familial adenomatous polyposis (*APC*)
Follicular thyroid cancer	Cowden syndrome (*PTEN*)
Medulloblastoma	Turcot syndrome variant of familial adenomatous polyposis (APC); Gorlin syndrome (*PTCH*)
Glioblastoma	Turcot syndrome variant of Lynch syndrome (*MLH1, MSH2, MSH6, PMS2, EPCAM*)
Basal cell carcinoma	Xeroderma pigmentosum (multiple Xeroderma pigmentosum-associated genes); Gorlin syndrome (*PTCH*)
Sebaceous adenoma, sebaceous carcinoma, keratoacanthoma	Muir-Torre syndrome variant of Lynch syndrome (*MLH1, MSH2, MSH6, PMS2, EPCAM*)
Fibrofolliculomas	Birt-Hogg-Dube syndrome (*FLCN*)
Facial trichilemmomas	Cowden syndrome (*PTEN*)

microsatellites, driven by an underlying defect in the mismatch repair pathway (MMR-D). (Figure 6-4) Identification of MMR-D may either be pursued through a polymerase chain reaction–based technique that assesses MSI at a designated set of markers[23-25] or through immunohistochemical (IHC) staining of the four DNA mismatch-repair proteins (MLH1, MSH2, MSH6, PMS2) to assess for protein loss in one or more of the MMR proteins.[26] MSI and MMR-IHC analyses are highly concordant; however, a benefit of MMR-IHC is that the pattern of protein loss can help inform which of the Lynch syndrome genes may be malfunctioning due to germline or somatic events. Screening of all colorectal and endometrial tumors via MSI or MMR-IHC

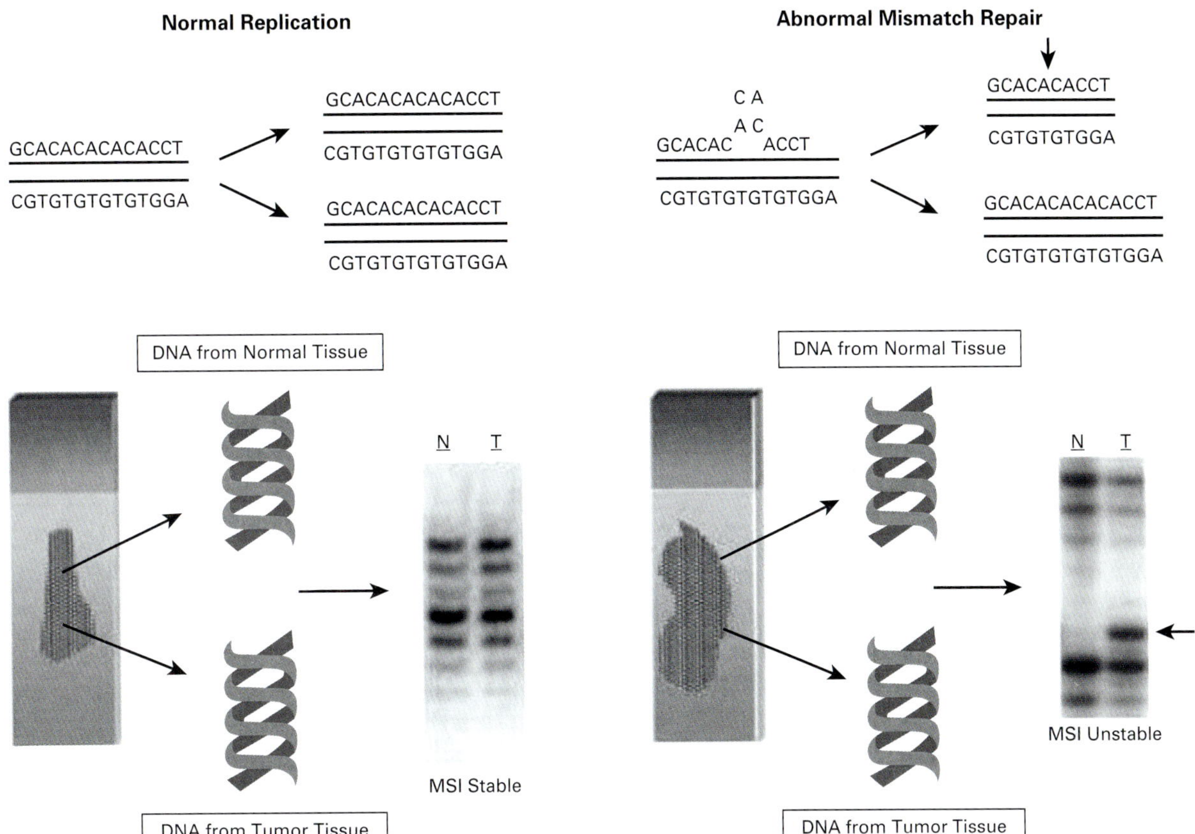

Fig. 6-4 Microsatellite instability.[130]

Republished with permission from The genetics of hereditary non-polyposis colorectal cancer. Gruber SB1, Kohlmann W. 1(1):137-44, 2003; permission conveyed through Copyright Clearance Center, Inc

analysis is now recommended.[27-29] For patients with abnormal screening test results (eg, MSI-high or MMR-D tumor), various algorithms have been developed to help guide subsequent evaluations; these may include germline genetic testing or additional tumor analyses, such as *MLH1* promoter hypermethylation, *BRAF* V600E somatic mutation, and somatic analysis of the MMR genes (Fig 6-5).[27,28,30]

TUMOR NGS: IMPLICATIONS FOR GERMLINE-SUSCEPTIBILITY

NGS of tumors (ie, somatic mutation profiling) to help define therapeutic targets has become increasingly common in the field of medical oncology. Somatic mutation profiling is available via a number of commercial laboratories and academic institutions and generally consists of a multigene panel that incorporates numerous genes previously implicated in carcinogenesis, many of which are also associated with germline cancer predisposition syndromes. Tumor sequencing may be performed with or without a matched normal specimen and could also be performed in the setting of whole-genome/whole-exome platforms. Table 6-7 describes three main types of NGS of tumors and some associated clinical implications.

Somatic mutation profiling may also reveal mutational patterns that predict the presence of a cancer susceptibility syndrome. For example, mutational load on somatic profiling may identify hypermutated tumors, which may result from MMR-D/ MSI-H, a marker of Lynch syndrome.[31] As such, somatic mutation profiling that reveals the presence of a hypermutated endometrial tumor should prompt MMR-IHC or MSI testing and, if appropriate, genetic referral. Bioinformatic tools that predict MSI from somatic mutation profiling have been developed and are being incorporated into the somatic mutation profiling pipelines to help clinicians correctly identify tumors with MMR-D/MSI.[32,33]

KEY POINTS

- Evaluation for Lynch syndrome typically starts with tumor screening for MSI or DNA mismatch-repair deficiency. In the case of an abnormal screening test, subsequent tumor and/or germline evaluation is warranted to make the diagnosis of Lynch syndrome.

- NGS of tumors (ie, somatic mutation profiling) for the identification of therapeutic targets can be performed with or without the inclusion of parallel normal (nontumor) DNA sequencing. To appropriately interpret the results and determine potential hereditary risks for the patient, a clinician ordering tumor somatic mutation profiling must be aware of the testing approach used.
- Genetic evaluation of somatic tumor tissue can potentially reveal germline pathogenic variants that may be of significance for a patient and/or family members.

GERMLINE ANALYSES

SPECIMENS AND LABORATORY STANDARDS

For germline genetic testing, the most commonly used specimen is blood because of its high DNA yield. Some commercial laboratories now offer germline genetic analyses on saliva specimens; however, not all analyses may be validated for such use. For patients who have undergone allogeneic bone marrow or stem cell transplantation or those with a hematologic malignancy, tissue, rather than blood, is necessary for germline analysis, and frequently a skin punch biopsy specimen is obtained for fibroblast culture, which can then be used for germline analysis. Last, when single amplicon analysis or targeted mutation analysis is needed, some laboratories may perform the analysis on paraffin-fixed tissue (tumor or normal).

GERMLINE GENETIC TEST RESULTS

Patients must be prepared for several different types of test results from germline analysis (Fig 6-6):

- Pathogenic or deleterious mutation (variant)
  - Altered gene function/protein product associated with disease risk. Patients should be informed of disease risks, medical management implications, and familial ramifications.
- Suspected pathogenic or deleterious mutation (variant)
  - There is high suspicion but not complete certainty about the pathogenicity; caution must be taken when counseling a patient and family members regarding this result.
  - If presymptomatic/predictive testing for the identified variant is performed for a family member, increased cancer surveillance recommendations may still be indicated on the basis of family history, even in the absence of the variant.
- Genetic variant of uncertain clinical significance (VUS)
  - The laboratory does not have enough data to allow for clinical classification or interpretation of the variant's effect. Patients and family members should be counseled about the ambiguity of the result and the continued need for all family members to consider themselves at-risk.
  - Predictive testing should not be offered to at-risk relatives for VUS results, and cancer surveillance should be based on the family history.
  - With time and access to additional data, many laboratories reclassify these variants; and most variants are reclassified as being benign.[34,35] A general recommendation is that patients and families found to have genetic VUS should check every few years with the health care provider who ordered the genetic test to inquire about updates in variant classification.
- Likely benign variant

  An alteration is detected, but the laboratory has a low suspicion of it being associated with disease.
- Negative/normal result
  - No alterations of clinical or uncertain significance identified.
  - Uniformative negative: Negative results may not be informative and a patient and their family members may still harbor a pathogenic mutation in a different cancer predisposition gene that has not been discovered yet, that the current technology cannot detect, or for which they were not tested.
  - True negative: When an individual is being tested for a previously identified, familial pathogenic variant, a negative result is considered a "true negative result," and for the specific syndrome-associated cancers, the individual is generally presumed to be back at the risk level of the general population. It is important to understand that true negative results were historically described in the setting of families with mutations in high-penetrance genes, such as *BRCA1.* In families with moderate-penetrance genetic mutations, for example, *CHEK2* missense mutations, individuals who do not carry the familial mutation may still be recommended to pursue cancer surveillance on the basis of family history.[10]

APPROACHES TO GERMLINE GENETIC TESTING

When assessing a patient's personal and family histories and deciding what genetic tests should be offered, a few different approaches might be taken. Table 6-8 provides details of how traditional, phenotype-directed genetic testing and genetic testing based on ancestral founder mutations or known familial mutations differ from the now-ubiquitous NGS multigene panels.

Phenotype-Directed Genetic Testing

The field of cancer genetic counseling and testing traditionally has followed a phenotype-based approach for genetic testing wherein the selection of genes to be analyzed is based on the patient's personal or family cancer history. A

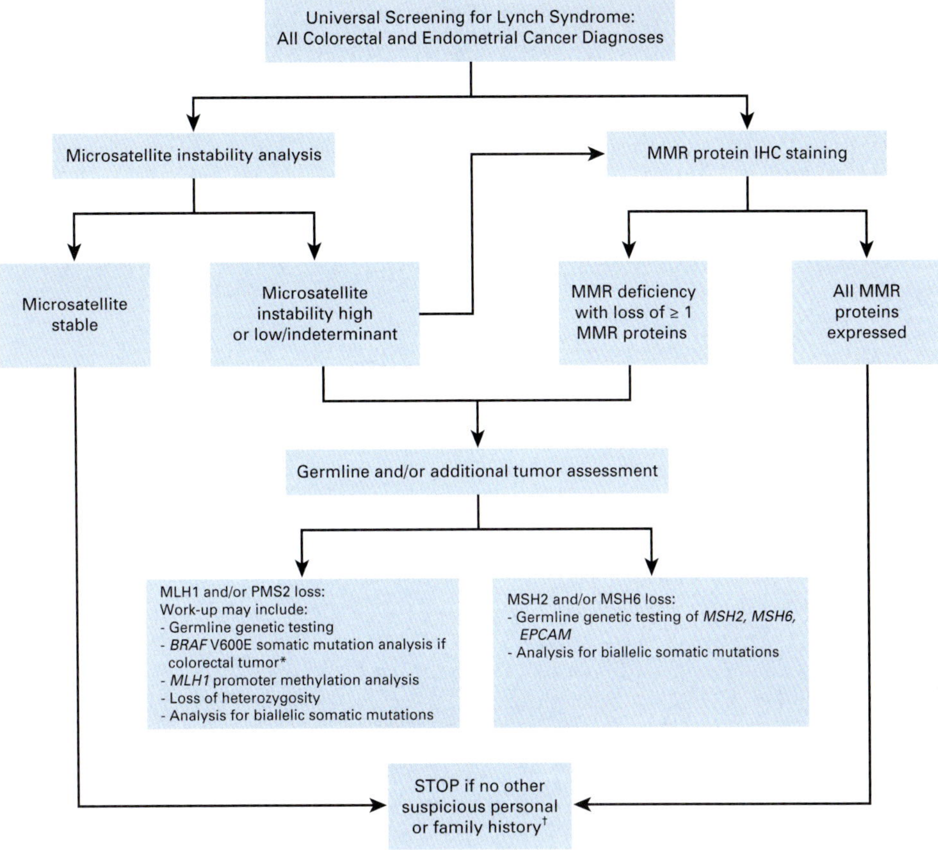

Fig. 6-5 Basic algorithm for Lynch syndrome tumor and germline testing.

*Presence of *BRAF* V600E somatic mutation in colorectal tumor indicates low likelihood for Lynch syndrome. †Exclude polyposis syndromes.

related, second approach is to focus on ancestry-specific founder mutations. Founder mutations are genetic alterations observed with high frequency in a distinct group that is or was geographically or culturally isolated. A third approach pertains to families with a previously identified familial pathogenic variant; in these cases, predictive or presymptomatic testing for the specific familial pathogenic variant can be undertaken.

Genetic Testing Using Multigene Panels

In contrast to phenotype-driven testing, NGS technologies have enabled the use of multigene panels for germline analysis wherein multiple cancer-susceptibility genes are assessed simultaneously. Disease-specific multigene panels for nearly all of the common cancers (ie, breast, ovary, uterine, colon, kidney, advanced prostate) as well as pan-cancer panels are now widely available through commercial laboratories.[11] The ease of use, cost, and time efficiency associated with multigene panel testing for cancer susceptibility have resulted in a dramatic increase in the application of this testing approach over the past several years. It is an especially useful approach when significant genetic heterogeneity exists or multiple genes or syndromes may be implicated on the basis of phenotype or family history.[11]

On the other hand, multigene panels also have some limitations:

- Pretest genetic counseling and informed consent: The in-depth discussion provided for single-gene testing in the traditional model of genetic counseling is not possible for a panel that may include as many as 80 genes (Table 6-2).
- Unexpected results: For panels that include high-penetrance genes such as *TP53* (associated with multiple tumors and childhood cancers) and *CDH1* (associated with risk-reducing total gastrectomy), an unexpected positive result without pretest discussion and preparation may result in distress and anxiety. This is particularly the case when a patient's personal or family history is not in line with the hereditary syndrome identified using the multigene panel. For example, if a *CDH1* pathogenic mutation is unexpectedly identified in a patient who has no personal or family history of diffuse gastric cancer or lobular breast cancer, the patient and physician are left with a clinical conundrum as to whether historical cancer-risk estimates based on ascertainments of familial hereditary diffuse gastric cancer kindreds are applicable and whether to pursue risk-reducing total gastrectomy.

Table 6-7 **Different Forms of Next-Generation Tumor Sequencing**			
Considerations	**Tumor only**	**Tumor + Normal (germline)**	**Whole Genome or Whole Exome**
What might be reported?	Majority of mutations will represent acquired/somatic mutations.	Bioinformatic analysis to "subtract" the germline from the tumor sequence.	Incidental findings: predispositions to nononcologic diseases may be revealed.
What are the limitations?	Germline mutations included, but not distinguished from somatic mutations.	Ability to report only tumor-acquired genetic variants; germline findings are "masked".	Understanding of identified genetic variant and possible phenotype might be limited.
Thoughts for clinical practice	Example: 25-year-old woman with breast cancer. NGS of breast tumor identified a *TP53* mutation. Clinical genetic counseling and testing needed to determine if this is a germline *v* somatic mutation.	Clinical genetic counseling and germline testing needed to reveal inherited findings.	Plan for disclosure of unanticipated test results should be a component of pretest counseling and informed consent. Referral to genetic specialists and confirmatory germline testing is recommended.

Abbreviation: NGS, next-generation sequencing.

- Limited understanding of moderate-penetrance genes: Multigene panels generally include moderate-penetrance genes for which the associated cancer spectrum, lifetime risks, age-associated penetrance, and appropriate management recommendations have not been fully defined. Importantly, the presence or absence of a mutation in a moderate-penetrance gene may not provide clarity with respect to a patient's personal and family history of cancer and their future cancer risk.
- Genetic VUS: Multigene testing results in a higher incidence of VUS, leading to additional difficulties with the interpretation of results.
- Genetic variants associated with reproductive risks: Some genes included on multigene panels may be associated with severe autosomal recessive conditions when biallelic mutations are inherited but associated with no or possibly limited disease risks when in monoallelic form (Table 6-9). It is important that clinicians make the patient and their

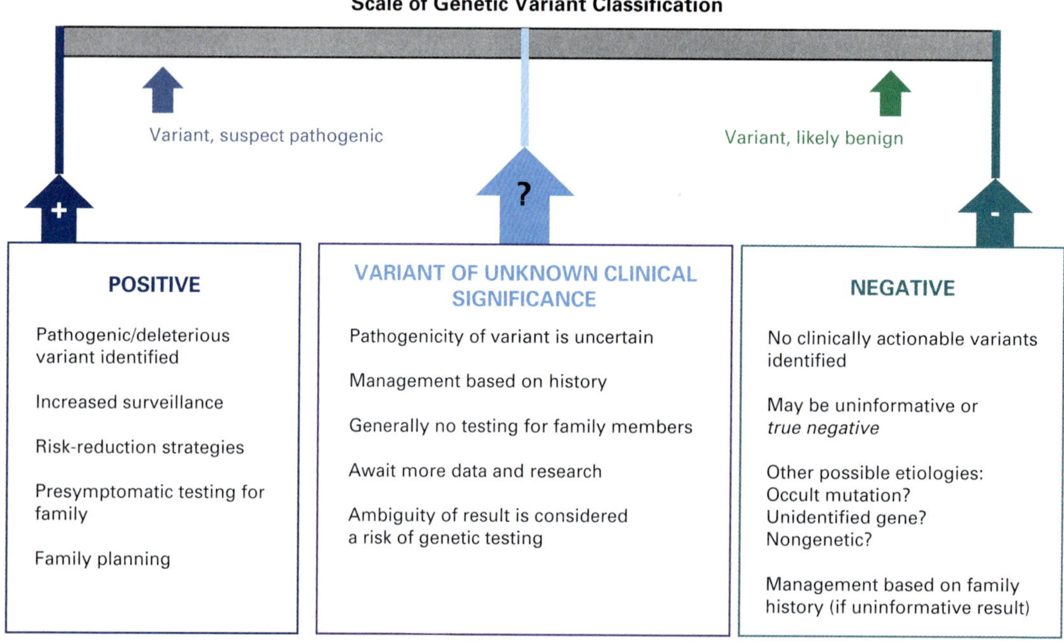

Fig. 6-6 Spectrum of genetic test results.

Table 6-8 Approaches to Genetic Testing

	Phenotype	Ancestry	Predictive/ Presymptomatic	Multigene Panel
Basis	Based on patient's personal and family histories	Geographically or culturally isolated populations with high prevalence for certain genetic mutations	Based on family history of a previously identified pathogenic genetic variant	NGS of multiple genes
Genetic test selection	Phenotype-associated genes	Ancestry-specific founder mutations	Analysis of specific familial variant	Disease-focused panels or pan-cancer predisposition panels
Examples	Personal history of medullary thyroid cancer → RET gene analysis	Diagnosis of breast cancer in setting of Ashkenazi Jewish ancestry → Ashkenazi *BRCA1* and *BRCA2* founder mutation analysis	Unaffected individual with a known family history of a *MSH2* pathogenic variant → Single amplicon analysis for the familial *MSH2* mutation	Diagnosis of early-onset pheochromocytoma → Multigene panel testing allows for simultaneous testing of all PCC-associated genes

Abbreviation: PCC = pheochromocytoma.

family members aware of the reproductive risks so family planning options can be investigated, if desired.

OTHER CONSIDERATIONS RELATED TO GERMLINE GENETIC ANALYSES

Secondary Findings on Genome and Exome Analyses

Through clinical exome and whole-genome sequencing, pathogenic or likely pathogenic variants may be uncovered in genes unrelated to the primary medical reason for testing; these findings have been termed secondary findings.[36] Considerable debate and discussion have been prompted with regard to the extent to which primary data should be analyzed for secondary findings and which, if any, pathogenic variants discovered should be disclosed to patients. In an effort to standardize the reporting of actionable information from clinical genomic sequencing, in 2016, the American College of Medical Genetics and Genomics (ACMG) published a list of 59 medically actionable genes[37,38] in which pathogenic variants are recommended to be reported because of the high likelihood of severe disease that may be preventable if identified before symptoms occur. The ACMG's recommendations provide patients the opportunity to opt out of the analyses of genes unrelated to the indication for testing, with the decision to be made during the process of informed consent before testing. Notably, 24 of the current 59 ACMG reportable genes are associated with cancer predisposition syndromes, highlighting the relevance of these recommendations to the field of medical oncology.

The standardization of variant classification is a significant challenge in the field of germline genetics because, at this time, a particular variant could be classified as pathogenic by one laboratory but as a VUS by another laboratory. Given the current inconsistencies among clinical molecular laboratories and clinical genomic sequencing analyses that have been highlighted,[39] integration of multiple lines of support using standardized methods is necessary to classify genetic alterations into one of five categories: pathogenic, likely pathogenic, uncertain significance, likely benign, and benign. To meet this

Table 6-9 Genes with Autosomal Recessive Disease Risk

Gene	Syndrome
ATM	Ataxia telangiectasia
BLM	Bloom's syndrome
BRCA1, BRCA2, BRIP1, PALB2, RAD51C	Fanconi anemia
MLH1, MSH2, MSH6, PMS2	Constitutional mismatch repair deficiency syndrome
MUTYH	*MUTYH*-associated polyposis
NBN	Nijmegen breakage syndrome
WRN	Werner syndrome
DDB2, ERCC1, ERCC2, ERCC3, ERCC4, ERCC5, POLH, XPA, XPC	Xeroderma pigmentosum

challenge, the National Institutes of Health has supported the formation of ClinGen, an authoritative central resource aimed at defining the clinical relevance of genomic variants for use in precision medicine and research.[40] The cornerstone of ClinGen is ClinVar, a free Web-based archive that is maintained by the National Center for Biotechnology Information and reports on interpretations of clinical significance of variants and allows for deposition and retrieval of variant data and annotations.[41,42]

Direct-to-Consumer Germline Genetic Analyses

Direct-to-consumer (DTC) genetic testing has challenged the traditional practical and ethical frameworks established in the field of clinical genetics. DTC genetic tests are advertised and sold directly to individuals, without supervision by a health care professional. Saliva-collection kits allow consumers to send their specimens directly to commercial laboratories; results generally are returned by mail, e-mail, or phone.

Preimplantation Genetic Diagnosis

Some individuals may consider using genetic test results to help inform reproductive decisions. In vitro fertilization with preimplantation genetic testing of embryos has been used by many families in the setting of multiple inherited cancer predisposition syndromes.[43] The use of donor gametes (ie, eggs or sperm), adoption, or prenatal diagnosis via chorionic villus sampling or amniocentesis are other family planning options that some individuals might consider.

Insurance Coverage and Protections

Most third-party payers include some level of coverage for genetic counseling and testing services. Some payers have established personal and family history criteria that must be met for medical necessity to be established; others may follow suggested testing guidelines that have been published by groups such as the NCCN. Some payers require the involvement of a genetic counselor in the pretest counseling and testing process.

Federal legislation through the Genetic Information Nondiscrimination Act (2008) and, in some cases, additional state legislation, provide protection against genetic discrimination by one's employer and health insurance provider.[44] Unfortunately, protection against discrimination by life, disability, and long-term care insurance providers is not universal in the United States at this time. This lack of protection may be a particular concern for some unaffected individuals who may be pursuing presymptomatic genetic testing.

GENETICS IN MEDICAL ONCOLOGY PRACTICE

The collection of family history data, and the continued, regular updating of this dynamic information are important tasks for medical oncologists that allow for the identification of patients and families who may benefit from genetic counseling and testing. Beyond personal and family cancer history, an increasing number of patients are also being identified and referred for genetic counseling and testing on the basis of tumor-sequencing results. Oncologists are encouraged to recognize the importance of pre- and posttest genetic counseling, the various times during an oncology patient's journey that genetic counseling and testing may be useful, and how different genetic variant classifications may influence a patient's personal medical recommendations and that of their family members. The understanding of cancer risk and the appropriate clinical implementation of cancer prevention recommendations that are specifically tailored to individual patients and/or families are essential components of the care of oncology patients and their families.

Resources to find genetic specialists include NSGC, the American Board of Genetic Counseling, the National Cancer Institute Cancer Genetics Services Directory, and the GeneTests Clinic Directory.[17] Resources to learn more about cancer genetics and risk assessment include the ASCO University Cancer Genetics Program, NSGC, and the National Human Genome Research Institute.[1,9]

KEY POINTS

- Germline genetic test results typically fall into one of five categories of genetic variants: pathogenic, likely pathogenic, uncertain significance, likely benign, and benign. Recommendations for management of cancer risk and predictive testing for family members differ significantly on the basis of the classification of the variant and should be assessed carefully.
- Multigene panel cancer-susceptibility testing is challenging the traditional phenotype-directed approach to genetic testing. When appropriate, multigene panel testing may be a cost- and time-efficient method for genetic testing.
- Multigene panel testing poses challenges for pretest counseling and can result in unexpected pathogenic variants, pathogenic variants in moderate-penetrance genes that do not account for the patient's personal and/or family history of cancer, a higher incidence of genetic VUS, and genetic variants associated with reproductive risks.
- Inconsistencies in genetic variant classification are an important challenge that clinicians must understand. Classification of variants may be discordant among laboratories, and interpretation of variants may change over time with significant potential implications for patients and families.
- The Genetic Information Nondiscrimination Act of 2008 provides protection against genetic discrimination by an individual's employer and health insurance provider.

GLOBAL PERSPECTIVE: GENETIC TESTING FOR HEREDITARY CANCER SYNDROMES

Judith Balmaña, MD, PhD (University Hospital Vall d'Hebron, Barcelona, Spain)

Over the last two decades, NGS has undoubtedly revolutionized the diagnosis of germline susceptibility to cancer. Recent advances in technology have enabled better classification of tumors and driven more-personalized management of disease, as well as an increased understanding of germline susceptibility to different tumor types. So far, > 100 cancer predisposition genes have been identified. Its relevance around the world is heterogeneous, because the prevalence of mutations differs worldwide according to ancestry and the existence of founder mutations. For instance, frequency of *BRCA1/BRCA2* mutations ranges from < 2% in unselected patients with breast cancer from northern Europe to 20% to 30% among patients of Ashkenazi ancestry.[113,114] Similarly, in *CHEK2*, a founder mutation, whose identification is anecdotic, is more frequent in central-northern Europe than in southern Europe.[115,116]

In addition, new moderate-penetrance genes have been discovered for major tumor types, including breast, colon, and ovarian cancer.[117-120] Collectively, they confer a complex architecture to cancer susceptibility added to the individual cancer predisposition, based on SNPs' susceptibility combined with lifestyle and environmental factors. This field is rapidly evolving toward a new paradigm for precision cancer prevention, with the goal of providing accurate cancer-risk estimates to tailor the most adequate cancer prevention and early detection strategies in each individual. For instance, there are ongoing research initiatives in Europe, Canada, Australia and the United States investigating the role of genetic modifiers, such as the polygenic risk score, on the accuracy of cancer-risk estimates among individuals at high risk because of a *BRCA1/BRCA2* mutation to tailor screening surveillance and prophylactic interventions.[121] In contrast, that GWAS have been performed and validated in data sets mainly from European people limits their generalizability to other less represented populations, such as African, Hispanic, or indigenous people.[122] Therefore, well-powered GWAS in diverse populations are needed before this type of data can be applied worldwide.

In addition, a new framework is emerging to accommodate the expanded use of germline testing while preserving genetic counseling processes that respect the individual's autonomy, uphold the principle of nonmaleficence, and promote the duty to advise at-risk family members. As an example, MSI-H has become an agnostic tumor marker for immunotherapy in patients with advanced metastatic disease. The analyses of this molecular marker in > 15,000 tumors from different origins showed that one in six patients with MSI-H carried a germline pathogenic variant in one of the mismatch repair genes associated with Lynch syndrome,[123] the main genetic predisposition to colon and endometrial cancers. Most interestingly, 50% of cancers were not considered to be classic Lynch syndrome–associated tumors, and 45% of these lacked a personal or family history suggestive of Lynch syndrome. Therefore, these patients likely would have remained underdiagnosed without the universal determination of MSI. This reflects a new approach for identification of hereditary cancer syndromes beyond the classic criteria based on family history. Similarly, the increasing use of tumor sequencing or other genetic analysis is pointing to the same conclusion, namely that traditional phenotype-driven germline genetic testing based on personal or family history is not sensitive enough to recognize all individuals with a cancer genetic susceptibility, and new counseling approaches must be sought to accommodate the increased identification of germline susceptibility to cancer.

Current clinical guidelines for the management of hereditary cancer predisposition require continuous updates to incorporate the most recent advances in the prevalence of germline cancer pathogenic variants or the most accurate cancer-risk estimates, which form the basis for cancer screening and prevention recommendations. Differences in clinical guidelines and management of these syndromes are expected globally, depending on the speed at which scientific advances are incorporated into clinical practice (Table 6-10).[124-126] In this regard, one of the global resources currently available to reduce the gap in variant interpretation and improve the sharing of *BRCA1* and *BRCA2* genetic data is the BRCA Exchange Project.[127]

Finally, as germline susceptibility to cancer has also been recognized as an opportunity for targeted therapy, germline genetic testing has become more common in mainstream clinical care. Consequently, new models of germline genetic-testing services need to evolve across the disease continuum. Unfortunately, there is big disparity around the world in the availability and type of models for genetic service delivery. Whereas North America, central and northern Europe, and Australia have implemented many different genetic programs, other regions of the world, such as Central and South America, southern and eastern Europe, Africa, and Asia, lack official models for provision of genetic testing.[128] Consequently, new models of germline genetic-testing services are evolving across the disease continuum.

It is crucial that health care providers promote updated education on the latest advances in this field and follow a multidisciplinary approach to more effectively tackle the complexities of a hereditary cancer syndrome. Such educational initiatives must be embraced, developed, and pursued by all to deliver the best quality of care to our patients with cancer and their families.

Table 6-10 **Comparison of International Guidelines and Recommendations for *BRCA*-Mutated Breast Cancer**

Guideline/ Organization	Country	Type or Recommendation					
		Genetic Counseling	BRCA Genetic Screening	BC Screening	BC Prevention/ RR	BC Treatment	Organization of Care
Asia							
Japanese Breast Cancer Society 2015	Japan	N	N	Y	Y	N	N
Australia							
Cancer Australia 2014	Australia	Y	N	N	Y	Y	N
North America							
Canadian Consensus Guideline 2017	Canada	N	N	N	Y	N	N
NCNN Genetic/ Familial High-High Risk Assessment: Breast and Ovarian, version 3.2019	United States	Y	Y	Y	Y	Y	Y
Europe							
ESMO Prevention and Screening 2016	Europe	Y	N	Y	Y	N	N
ESO-ESMO ABC4 2018	Europe	Y	Y	N	N	Y	N
AGO 2017	Germany	N	Y	Y	Y	Y	N
SEOM 2015	Spain	N	Y	Y	Y	Y	N
NICE (CG14 AND CG41 updates)	United Kingdom	Y	Y	Y	Y	N	Y

Abbreviations: ABC4, 4th International Consensus Guidelines for Advanced Breast Cancer; AGO, Arbeitsgemeinschaft Gynäkologische Onkologie; ESMO, European Society for Medical Oncology; ESO, European School of Oncology; NCCN, National Comprehensive Cancer Network; NICE, National institute for Health and Care excellence; RR, risk reduction; SEOM, Sociedad Española de Oncología Médica.

Adapted from Forbes et al.[126]

7

CANCER IN THE OLDER PATIENT

Ravindran Kanesvaran, MD, and Supriya Mohile, MD, MS, FASCO

Recent Updates

- An ASCO guideline recommends the use of measures from geriatric assessment (GA) for all older patients receiving chemotherapy. (Mohile S, *J Clin Oncol* 2018)
- The ASCO guidelines recommend that for all older patients with cancer considering chemotherapy, the risk of chemotherapy toxicity be calculated using the Cancer and Aging Research Group tool or the Chemotherapy Risk Assessment Scale for High-Age Patients score. (Hurria A, *J Clin Oncol* 2016; Extermann M, *Cancer* 2012)
- Authors of the first phase III, randomized, controlled trial of the use of GA in older patients with advanced non–small-cell lung cancer reported treatment allocation on the basis of GA did not show improvement in treatment failure–free survival or overall survival but did reduce treatment toxicity and the number of treatment failures secondary to toxicity. (Corre R, *J Clin Oncol* 2016)
- A new method to better define frailty in older patients with cancer who receive chemotherapy is based on a deficit-accumulation index. (Cohen HJ, *Cancer* 2016)
- In an updated systematic review of GA evaluation on treatment decisions and outcomes, the majority of studies found that GA and guided geriatric interventions had a positive impact on treatment completion and treatment-related toxicity; however, methods and populations varied, making it difficult to extrapolate the results. (Hamaker ME, *J Geriatr Oncol* 2018)
- A large cluster-randomized study in community oncology clinics in the United States demonstrated that GA with targeted recommendations increased the number of conversations about aging-related concerns and improved patient and caregiver satisfaction. (Mohile SG, *JAMA Oncol*, 2019)

OVERVIEW

Geriatric medicine is a subspecialty that strives to improve care delivery and outcomes of older adults. Although there is no consensus on the specific chronologic age that defines the older patient population, in developed countries, age ≤ 65 years is generally accepted. The International Society of Geriatric Oncology (SIOG) defines a geriatric oncology patient as a patient older than 70 years with cancer. Cancer is a major health concern for older patients and is the second leading cause of death in the United States, after heart disease.[1]

Age is the single most important risk factor for developing cancer with approximately 60% of all newly diagnosed malignant tumors and 70% of all cancer deaths occurring among people ≥ 65 years of age.[2] It has been estimated that by 2030, 20% of the US population (70 million people) will be > 65 years old. The median age range for diagnosis for most major tumors, common to both men and women, is 68 to 74 years, and the median age range at death is 70 to 79 years.[1,2] For most malignancies, the death rate is disproportionately higher in the older population. Possible explanations include more aggressive biology of specific malignancies in older adults, competing comorbidities, decreased physiologic reserve compromising the ability to tolerate therapy, physicians' reluctance to provide aggressive therapy, and barriers to accessing care.[1,3]

Communication between health care providers and older patients may be hampered by deficits in hearing, vision, and cognition.[4] In addition, age-related concerns of patients and caregivers (eg, falls, cognitive impairment, polypharmacy) are not usually addressed by oncology teams, despite influencing unfavorable outcomes for older patients with cancer (Fig 7-1).[5-7] The older patient with cancer often has an older caregiver, and the diagnosis of cancer often affects the health-related quality of life (QOL) of both individuals.[8-10]

These challenges contribute to defining geriatric oncology as a true subspecialty, leading to the development of the National Comprehensive Cancer Network and ASCO guidelines that address special considerations for older adults with cancer.[7,11] Given the increasing numbers of older patients with cancer and the limited workforce of geriatricians, it is imperative that oncologists know how to integrate geriatrics principles into oncology care for older patients with cancer.

LIFE EXPECTANCY

Life expectancy at age 65 years is of substantial relevance when considering the cancer burden in the older population.[7] Over the past four decades, the average life expectancy has increased by 3 years for older men and by 6 years for older women.[12] In addition to this general increase, there exists great variability within age subsets. Recent work has sought to more accurately characterize and predict life expectancy and the difference between chronologic and functional age. Determination of life expectancy is important in decisions regarding cancer screening and treatment planning. In a population-based study of community-dwelling US adults older than 50 years, a prognostic index (namely, the Lee index) was developed using data from 11,701 individuals and validated in 8,009 individuals.[13] Twelve percent of the study population and 11% of the validation cohort had a cancer diagnosis; the 4-year mortality rate was 22%. Data were collected on participants' demographics (ie, age, sex), specific diseases and behaviors (eg, smoking), and difficulties with a series of functional measures. Points were assigned to 12 predictor variables, and the subsequent risk score was strongly associated with 4-year mortality rate in the validation cohort: 0- to 5-point score, ≤ 4% risk of death at 4 years; 6 to 9 points, a 15% risk, 10 to 13 points, a 42% risk, and ≥ 14 points, a 64% risk.

The ASCO guideline in geriatric oncology recommends that clinicians use one of the validated tools (the well-validated Schonberg Index or the Lee Index) listed at ePrognosis (https://eprognosis.ucsf.edu/) to estimate life expectancy without including cancer as a diagnosis to determine if patients have adequate life expectancy to expect benefits from specific cancer interventions, including chemotherapy.[7] The most common domains included in indices developed to predict mortality in community-dwelling older adults are age, sex, health conditions (eg, diabetes, chronic obstructive pulmonary disease), functional status, health behaviors and lifestyle factors (eg, smoking status, body mass index), and self-reported health.[7] The indices have "presence of cancer" as a relevant variable; indicating "no" to the question of cancer presence will allow for noncancer life expectancy, to consider competing risks of mortality (Fig 7-2).[14,15] An estimate of life expectancy outside of a cancer-specific estimate allows the oncologist to thoughtfully assemble a patient's prognosis. Although the exact trajectory of a patient's illness is unknowable, a prognostic estimation can satisfy a patient's wish to understand their prognosis so that it might allow informed decision-making. History tells providers that we routinely overestimate prognosis and that incorporating informative tools in this understanding might influence better-tailored conversations and allow patients to weigh the value of specific cancer-directed therapy.

COST OF CANCER CARE

The costs of cancer care to Medicare are substantial and vary by tumor site, stage at diagnosis, phase of care, and survival. In the 2008 SEER database review, the mean net costs of care were highest in the initial phase and last year of life, and lowest in the continuing phase. Mean 5-year net costs varied widely, from < $20,000 for patients with breast cancer or melanoma of the skin to > $40,000 for patients with CNS, esophageal, gastric, ovarian cancers, or lymphoma. For patients with acute myeloid leukemia (AML), 80% of the costs are related to inpatient hospitalization.[16] However, with the advent of new targeted agents, the cost of anticancer agents has more than doubled in the past decade, from $4,500 to > $10,000/month.[17] Of the anticancer drugs approved by the US Food and Drug Administration since 2016, the majority were immuno-oncology drugs that cost > $12,000/month of therapy. Many targeted agents have been priced between $6,000 and $12,000/month, or approximately $70,000 to $115,000 per patient annually. This high cost may prevent older patients from being able to procure their medications and limit availability of these options for patients in developing countries.[18]

In the United States, cancer care costs equate to > $100 billion annually because of increased health services use, hospital admission, and adverse drug events. The economic impact of cancer survivorship is considerable, remains high years after a cancer diagnosis, and is approximately the same for young and older patients.[19] Older patients who live on limited or fixed incomes and who already have difficulties with costs of basic living needs (eg, food, housing) are particularly vulnerable to financial toxicity (a term used to describe the problems a patient has due to the cost of medical care). Financial toxicity can have varying degrees of severity and can increase if the treatment approach is not adjusted or appropriate supportive measures are not initiated in a timely manner.[20] Some have advocated the inclusion of financial issues when discussing benefits and risks of therapies.

Older adults with cancer are a heterogeneous group, ranging from fit, active, and robust individuals to those who are frail,

Case 1:

Assessment and Management of an Older Patient Considering Adjuvant Chemotherapy

The patient is a 75-year-old man with coronary artery disease who recently has undergone coronary artery bypass surgery; he also has hypertension, hyperlipidemia, and osteoarthritis. He describes his own health as "good." Medications include aspirin, atenolol, and lovastatin. Laboratory examination reveals mild microcytic anemia. Colonoscopy revealed a sigmoid mass. Computed tomography scans are without evidence of metastatic disease. The patient undergoes hemicolectomy. Pathologic examination reveals a T3N2 (four nodes positive) tumor; stage is IIIC. Your assessment of his Eastern Cooperative Oncology Group performance status is 1, and he reports mild fatigue. He lives alone. He has a daughter with him at the visit; she works during the day.

Workflow

In the waiting room, the patient completed a survey that included instrumental activities of daily living (IADLs), one question about falls, and the Geriatric Depression Scale. Additional self-reported questions required for the Cancer and Aging Research Group (CARG) toxicity and ePrognosis tools are also included in the survey. The total time for survey completion by the patient, with assistance from his daughter, took < 10 minutes. When the patient was taken to the examination room, the medical assistant recorded his vital signs and provided the survey results to the oncology nurse. The nurse reviewed comorbidities, weighed the patient, and performed a Mini-Cog in 3 minutes as part of the intake assessment. The nurse (N.B., can also be done by advanced practice provider or the oncologist) completed and calculated the CARG toxicity tool and ePrognosis tool online (3 minutes).

Geriatric Assessment Results

The patient requires assistance with IADls (eg, his daughter fills his pill box each week for him and manages finances, he has difficulty with household chores), has had several recent falls without injury, and has no significant life-limiting comorbidities or medication issues. In addition, his Mini-Cog is abnormal (he is unable to perform a three-word recall), Geriatric Depression Scale score is normal (< 5), and he has had no significant weight loss (body mass index, 29 kg/m^2).

CARG Toxicity Score

The patient's CARG toxicity score is 12, with an 82% risk of grade 3 to 5 toxicity with full-dose monotherapy based on his age (> 72 years), height (180 cm), and weight (80 kg), GI cancer type, full dosage chemotherapy, monotherapy, hemoglobin concentration ≥ 10 g/dL, excellent hearing, one or more falls, requirement for some help with medications, limited a little with walking 1 block, no limitations with social activities, and normal creatinine clearance rate.

Life Expectancy, Noncancer (ePrognosis Calculator for Patients > 65 Years)

The patient's Schonberg Index score is 12, corresponding to a 5-year noncancer mortality of 37% based on age (75 years); sex (male); body mass index (≥ 25 kg/m^2); self-reported health ("good"); no chronic obstructive pulmonary disease, congestive heart failure, or diabetes; and no prior cancer history (to estimate noncancer life expectancy). He has never smoked, has difficulty with walking one-quarter mile without help, has had no hospitalizations in the past 12 months, requires help with handling everyday household chores, has difficulty managing money, has no difficulty with bathing or showering, and has difficulty pushing or pulling large objects.

Shared Treatment Decision Making and Targeted Interventions

Active shared discussion took place with the patient and his daughter (who is the patient's designated health care proxy) about the risks and benefits of adjuvant chemotherapy. The patient's noncancer 5-year mortality risk is estimated by the Schonberg Index to be 37%, and his cancer has a high risk of recurrence, so adjuvant chemotherapy may still be worthwhile in prognostic terms. However, grade 3 to 5 toxicity risk is > 80% according to CARG. In the assessment of decision-making capacity, the patient has mild cognitive impairment, and although he is able to remain independent at home, he requires assistance from his daughter with managing medications, finances, and household chores. He is able to communicate his cancer history, choices for treatment (none v fluorouracil monotherapy), and implications of each treatment choice. He is able to communicate his preferences, stating that he understands there is a high risk of toxicity and that there are limited data for the benefits of adjuvant chemotherapy in patients with cognitive impairment, but he would like to try treatment. It was discussed that having someone stay with him would be important; the daughter decided to arrange time off from work and enlist the help of family to stay with him. Frequent follow-up visits to assess for toxicity and worsening of function and cognition during the first cycle of treatment were arranged.
Because of his fall risk, the patient was prescribed physical therapy to assess balance and the need for an assist device. Home care was arranged for a safety evaluation and medication management assistance.

Case 2:

A Different Patient Who is 85 Years Old Without Any Geriatric Assessment Impairments

A robust 85-year-old patient has a similar cancer history as the patient in case 1 but is without geriatric assessment (GA) impairments, including comorbidities or cognitive issues; is in "excellent" self-reported health; and has no IADL deficits.

CARG Toxicity Score

The patient's CARG toxicity score is 6, with a 44% risk of grade 3 to 5 toxicity with full-dose monotherapy.

Life Expectancy (ePrognosis for Patients > 65 Years)

Schonberg Index score is 7 with an estimated 5-year noncancer mortality risk of 12%.

Treatment Decision-Making and Targeted Interventions

This physically fit, cognitively intact 85-year-old patient is to undergo full-dose monotherapy chemotherapy with no GA-based interventions recommended.

Fig. 7-1 Two case studies: Assessment and management of an older patient considering adjuvant chemotherapy.[7]

have physical and cognitive impairments, and increased risk for disease and therapy-related complications. Knowledge of the biology of aging, impact of comorbidities, the costs of cancer care, use of a geriatric assessment (GA), and a willingness to spend time with the patient and his or her family members are essential to providing care for older patients. In this chapter, we discuss many of the general relationships of oncology and aging. We focus on the epidemiologic, etiologic, and biological relationships between the processes of aging and neoplasia. We also underscore the importance of a GA in treatment decision-making and prediction of chemotherapy toxicity and other outcomes for older adults with cancer. The clinical management of individual malignancies is discussed only as examples of general principles, and the approach to specific malignancies is covered in chapters related to the appropriate organ system.

KEY POINTS

- Cancer is predominantly a disease of older adults.
- For most malignancies, the death rate is disproportionately higher in the older population.
- The cost of cancer care for the older patient population is significant and expected to increase, especially with the advent of new targeted therapies and immuno-oncology agents.

RELATIONSHIP BETWEEN AGING AND CANCER

The molecular, cellular, and physiologic changes that are a part of the aging process also predispose patients to cancer. The landmark paper by Hanahan and Weinberg[21] (please refer to Chapter 2: Molecular Biology) was recently updated to delineate 10 hallmarks of cancer; however, nine hallmarks represent common denominators of aging as well.[22] Carcinogenesis is a multistep process that includes initiation, followed by promotion and progression to disease. The various theories that link aging and cancer include the following:[23-27]

- **Longer duration of carcinogenic exposure:** Aging allows the time necessary for the accumulation of cellular events to result in neoplasm. Somatic mutations are believed to occur at the rate of approximately one in 10 cell divisions, with approximately 10 cell divisions occurring in a human's lifetime.
- **Altered susceptibility of aging cells to carcinogens:** Aging increases susceptibility of normal cells and tissue to transformation into cancerous cells.
- **Decreased ability to repair DNA:** Aging cells are more likely to have impaired ability to repair DNA.
- **Oncogene activation or amplification or decrease in tumor suppressor gene activity:** These processes may be altered in the older host, resulting either in increased action, promotion, or differential clonal evolution.
- **Telomere shortening and genetic instability:** The functions of telomeres and telomerase are intimately involved in senescence and neoplastic processes. Telomeres, the terminal end of all chromosomes, shorten progressively as cells age, beginning at age 30 years, with a loss of approximately 1% per year. This shortening appears to be causally related to controlled cell proliferation. Each time a cell divides, 30 to 200 base pairs are lost from that cell's telomeres. Because the major function of telomeres is to protect the stability of the more internal coding sequences (ie, allow cells to divide without losing genes), this loss may lead to genetic instability, which may promote mutations in oncogenic or tumor-suppressor gene sequences. Without telomeres, chromosome ends could fuse together and degrade the cell's genetic blueprint, making the cell malfunction, become malignant, or, potentially, die.

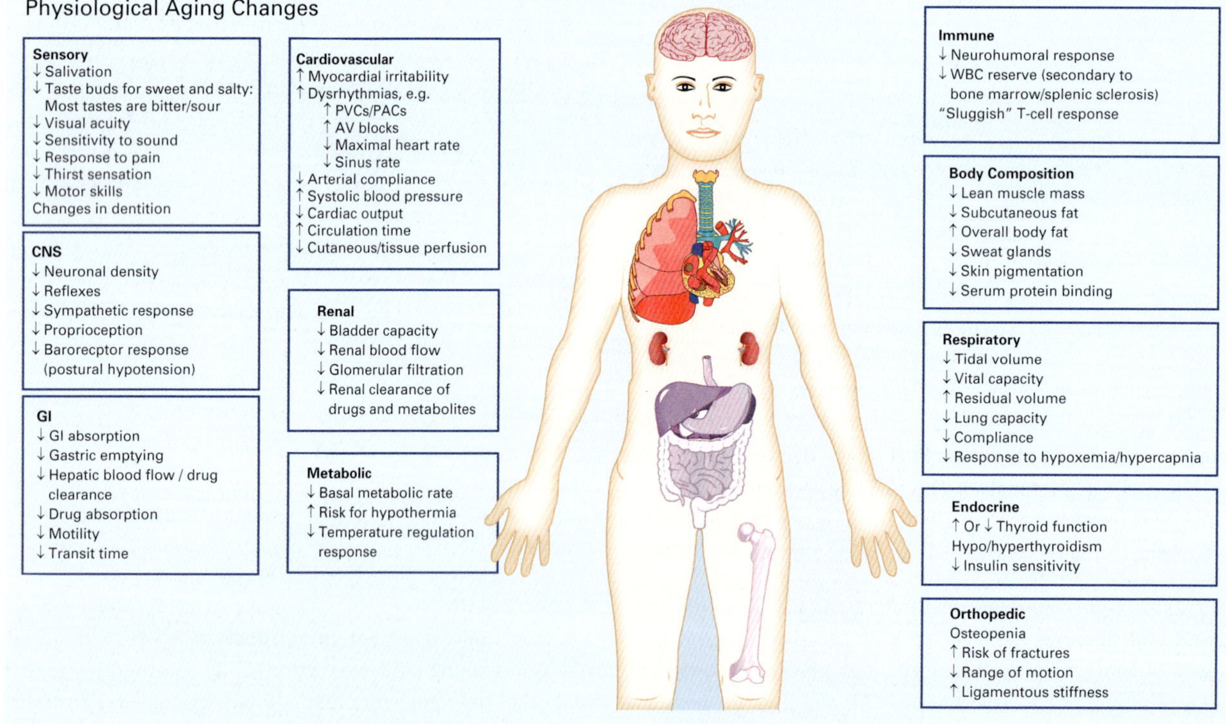

Fig. 7-2 Physiologic aging changes.[132,133]

Abbreviations: A/V, atrioventricular; PAC, premature atrial contraction; PVC, premature ventricular contraction.

Telomere length is a predictor of death in people age ≥ 60 years.[27] Telomerase is responsible for adding back telomeric repeats to the ends of chromosomes (ie, regenerate the telomeres). It is generally not expressed in normal cells, but it is activated in malignant cells. Although telomerase can reverse replicative cell senescence, indiscriminate activity of this enzyme may increase the likelihood of tumor formation.[27]

- **Microenvironment alterations:** Older people accumulate senescent cells and have higher levels of interleukin (IL)-6, the so-called geriatric cytokine, which is one of the causes of frailty. Senescent cells can compromise tissue renewal capacity and secrete multiple factors (eg, IL-1, matrix metalloproteinase 3) that alter tissue homeostasis and create a tissue environment that synergizes with mutation accumulation to facilitate malignant transformation.
- **Decreased immune surveillance:** Loss of tumor-specific immunity occurs with progressive age.

Interactions of these factors—resulting in initiation and cumulative promoting events, including mutations and other alterations in critical genes, which may exceed host resistance factors—occur during the aging process. Cellular senescence suppresses cancer by arresting cells at risk for malignant transformation.[28] However, senescent cells also secrete molecules that can stimulate premalignant cells to proliferate and form tumors. Thus, cellular senescence–induced suppression of malignant transformation, a function important for the organism in early life (through the reproductive period), may be selected for, although such senescence may be deleterious in later life.

AGE-RELATED PHYSIOLOGIC CHANGES

A decline in physiologic functioning begins at age 30 years and continues at a rate of approximately 1% per year. The aging process occurs at a different rate in each person, as does loss of individual organ reserve.[29,30] In most cases, these physiologic changes are clinically imperceptible. However, illness and subsequent medical interventions also affect physiologic processes, which may not return to baseline levels. Changes of aging (Fig 7-2) include thinning skin, increased bruising, decreased cardiac reserve, reduction in cardiac myocytes, increased vascular stiffness, and decreased GI motility and absorption. As blood flow and liver mass decrease, hepatic function declines. Metabolism through the cytochrome P450 microsomal enzyme system also decreases, affecting drug metabolism and elimination.[31] In the kidney, renal blood flow decreases, and both kidney mass and glomeruli are lost and replaced by fat and fibrotic tissue. The kidneys' ability to concentrate urine, excrete water, and eliminate toxins decreases. In view of this, creatinine clearance is a more important measure of kidney function in older adults, compared with just measuring creatinine.

The senescent brain undergoes a number of changes. Brain weight, blood flow, and neurotransmitter production all decline with age. Walking speed and truncal stability correlate with longevity and development of geriatric problems, including depression and dementia.[32,33] With increasing age, gait speed slows, stride length shortens, and individuals increasingly lean forward, perhaps related to a decline in the number of Purkinje cells within the cerebellum.

Neuronal loss may also lead to decreased levels of neuroreceptors, such as the μ and δ receptors, which may be the mechanism for enhanced sensitivity to opioid analgesics in older individuals. This loss also results in a decreased ability to perceive pain and also may contribute to compromised wound healing.

Immunologic dysregulation occurs in older adults. Declines in thymic mass and hormones result in a decrease in naïve lymphocytes and an increase in memory T cells, with maintenance of a normal total lymphocyte count but decreased response to mitogens.[25] Levels of inflammatory cytokines (IL-6 and IL-1β), C-reactive protein (CRP), and transforming growth factor-β increase with age. Elevations of IL-6 and D-dimer levels have been associated with shorter survival and increased functional dependency.[34] IL-2 levels decrease with age, contributing to a loss of lymphocyte proliferation. Although the etiology of increased cytokine levels is uncertain, it has been proposed that inflammatory reactions throughout a lifetime result in accumulation of certain cytokines. These cytokines contribute to a catabolic state and to sarcopenia. Sarcopenia is defined as loss of skeletal muscle mass and strength as a result of aging. Immunoglobulin levels increase, but antibody response decreases.[35] Such immunologic changes result in increased susceptibility to infection and may be responsible for the altered natural history of certain malignant diseases.

In older adults, the CBC count is generally within the normal range, despite an increased fat-to-cell ratio in the bone marrow.[36] The marrow reserve is compromised by illness or oncologic treatment, with greater decline in blood cell counts compared with counts in younger patients.[37] Anemia is more common with age (it is not a physiologic change of aging), occurring in 10% of patients > 65 years old and 20% of patients > 85 years old, according to the National Health and Nutrition Examination Survey.[38]

KEY POINTS

- Physiologic changes of aging begin at age 30 years.
- The rate of physiologic change with aging varies by organ system and individual. These changes need to be considered when deciding on the type and dose of medications for a patient's cancer treatment.
- Immunologic changes from aging result in increased susceptibility to infection and the risk of cancer.
- Marrow reserve is compromised in older patients, leading to greater decline in blood cell counts compared with younger patients.

GERIATRIC ASSESSMENT

Aging is a heterogeneous process that is affected by more than chronologic age. The GA is designed to capture the functional age of older adults to identify those who have diminished life expectancy and/or are at increased risk for hospitalization and functional decline (Tables 7-1 and 7-2).[7] The GA is multidimensional in that it uses validated, patient-reported, and administered measures to capture aging-related domains (eg, function and cognition) known to be associated with morbidity and mortality in community-dwelling older adults.[39,40]

Traditionally in oncology, the Eastern Cooperative Oncology Group performance status (PS) and Karnofsky performance status (KPS) have been used to quantify patient well-being and to determine whether patients can tolerate chemotherapy. However, these measures do not capture age-related domains known to affect morbidity and mortality in older patients with cancer. The GA assesses functional status, comorbidities that may affect cancer therapy, polypharmacy, psychologic and cognitive status, nutritional status, socioeconomic issues, and geriatric syndromes. These GA measures are reliable and valid, and can be obtained in a brief time (< 30 minutes, with the majority of time allocated for patients to complete surveys).

The ASCO guideline in geriatric oncology highlighted the significant and robust evidence demonstrating that GA measures are prognostic for morbidity and mortality in older patients with cancer.[41] Abbreviated screening instruments designed to determine who might need a full assessment and that can be used as stratifiers and predictors are outlined in Table 7-3.[42] Because of the time it takes to do a GA, a paper published by a SIOG task force provided an update on all the GA screening instruments available and the data supporting their use in clinical practice (Table 7-4). These tools are predictive of adverse outcomes such as chemotherapy toxicity and early death in older patients with cancer.[43,44] Geriatric screening instruments can help identify patients who are at high risk of adverse outcome and can be used to identify patients who would most benefit from a full GA (ie, one that assesses all aging-related domains to guide decision-making and interventions).

On the basis of the expert recommendations (which included community oncologists), the ASCO guideline also provides a practical approach to the assessment and management of vulnerabilities in older patients with cancer who are undergoing chemotherapy; after review of the literature, the expert guideline panel suggested a minimum data set of measures that assess the highest priority domains for older patients with cancer (Table 7-4).[7,43]

USES OF GERIATRIC ASSESSMENT IN ONCOLOGY

Various instruments for GA have been used for over a decade to examine multiple end points, including serious toxicity from chemotherapy, early mortality, and functional decline.

CHEMOTHERAPY TOXICITY

In a study by the Cancer and Aging Research Group (CARG) led by Hurria et al,[45] GA variables, sociodemographics, tumor and treatment variables, and laboratory results were incorporated into a model that was predictive for chemotherapy toxicity in 500 older adults. A scoring system in which the median risk score was 7 (range, 0 to 19) was used to risk-stratify patients, with the risk score being the percent incidence of grades 3 to 5 toxicity. This identified older adults at low (0 to 5 points; 30%), intermediate (6 to 9 points; 52%), or high risk (10 to 19 points; 83%) for chemotherapy toxicities (P < .001). This tool was validated in an external cohort of 250 older adults with cancer.[46] In another study of 518 older patients with cancer, led by Extermann et al,[47] 24 parameters, including GA, were incorporated to create the Chemotherapy Risk Assessment Scale for High-Age Patients (CRASH) score to predict grade 4 hematologic or grade 3/4 nonhematologic toxicities. In the CRASH risk categories, patients with low-risk scores had a 7% chance of hematologic and 33% chance of nonhematologic toxicity compared with patients with high-risk scores with corresponding toxicity risks of 100% and 93%, respectively. A limitation of both these studies was the small numbers of patients with hematologic malignancies (who tend to have less bone marrow reserve, making them more vulnerable to hematologic toxicities) and the studies not being designed to predict grade 2 toxicities, which also affect QOL. The ASCO guidelines recommend use of one of these chemotherapy toxicity tools (ie, CARG or CRASH) to evaluate risk of chemotherapy for all older adults aged ≥65 years.[7,47] Both options are available as online calculators. Systematic reviews of geriatric oncology studies confirm the association between GA domains and the risk of chemotherapy toxicity in a majority of studies,[48-51] Luciani et al[52] evaluated the Vulnerable Elders Survey (VES)-13 and found that patients who were vulnerable were at significantly increased risk of hematologic and nonhematologic toxicity.

Age-based reduction of first-cycle chemotherapy doses (primary dose reduction) is not routinely recommended by most guidelines. A CARG study demonstrated that primary dose reductions were more common for older patients receiving chemotherapy with palliative, rather than curative, intent.[53] Increasing age and comorbidities, but not KPS, were independently associated with primary dose reductions.

MORTALITY

Several studies have demonstrated that GA can identify older adults with cancer at increased risk for mortality.[44,54-72] Clough-Gorr et al[54] provided longitudinal evidence that GA domains—sociodemographic, clinical, functional, and psychosocial—are predictive of 7-year mortality in older women with breast cancer. Furthermore, Aaldriks et al[55] found that geriatric variables can help identify elevated risk for mortality in older adults with cancer.

Palumbo et al[44] developed a scoring system based on age, comorbidities, and functional status to identify three categories of fit, intermediate fitness, and frail. The 3-year overall survival (OS) was 84%, 76%, and 57% among older adults with multiple myeloma in the respective three categories. In another study of 74 older patients (median age, 70 years) with acute myelogenous leukemia undergoing induction chemotherapy, OS

Table 7-1 **Domains for Cancer-Specific Geriatric Assessment**

Assessment of the GA Domains Recommended for All Patients Aged ≥ 65 Years	Recommended Tool and Score Signifying Impairment	Evidence to Support Recommendation	Administration Characteristics	Considerations and Other Evaluation Options
Function	IADLs: dependence on any task signifies impairment.	Large prospective studies of older patients with cancer show IADLs predict chemotherapy toxicity, mortality, hospitalizations, and functional decline. Advocated by experts in Delphi consensus panels.	PRO: < 5 minutes	Consider ADLs. Any ADL deficit is used for characterization of frailty. Consider objective measure of physical performance such as SPPB, TUG, or gait speed.
Falls	Single item: "How many falls have you had over the last 6 months (or since the last visit)?" One or more recent falls	Falls are common in older adults with cancer and can lead to serious injury. Falls have been associated with chemotherapy toxicity. Assessment for falls is recommended by geriatric oncology expert panels and the American Geriatrics Society for all older adults.	PRO: < 1 minute	
Comorbidity	Robust review of chronic medical conditions and medications through routine history: three or more chronic health problems or one or more serious health problems	Comorbidity is associated with poorer survival, chemotherapy toxicity, mortality, and hospitalizations.	Part of routine history	Consider validated tools such as CIRS-G or Charlson. History, CIRS-G, and OARS comorbidity recommended by experts.
Cognition	Mini-Cog: an abnormal test result is defined by zero words recalled or one to two words recalled plus an abnormal clock-drawing test. This screening test for cognitive impairment and abnormal scores requires additional follow-up and decision-making capacity assessment. Or BOMC test: a score ≥ 6 identifies patients who have moderate deficits, and a cut point ≥ 11 identifies patients with severe cognitive impairment.	Data show cognitive impairment is associated with poorer survival in older patients with cancer and increased chemotherapy toxicity risk. Mini-Cog has high sensitivity and specificity for identifying cognitive impairment when compared with longer tools. BOMC scale is practical and is included in the cancer-specific GA developed by Hurria et al.[46]	Administered: ≤ 5 minutes	Multiple tools are available for cognitive assessment. The MMSE has more robust data for prediction of outcomes in older patients with cancer and predicts chemotherapy toxicity; it is included in the CRASH tool developed by Extermann et al.[47] The MOCA is also used by geriatricians. Both MMSE and MOCA are considerably longer than Mini-Cog and BOMC.
Depression	GDS 15 item: a score of > 5 suggests depression and requires follow-up.	Depression has been associated with unexpected hospitalizations, treatment tolerance, mortality, and functional decline in older adults with cancer receiving chemotherapy; these studies primarily assessed depression with the GDS.	PRO; ≤ 5 minutes	GDS recommended also by ASCO guidelines for depression. The Patient Health Questionnaire-9 is an alternative and is also recommended by ASCO guidelines for depression. The mental health inventory is an option and has been associated with outcomes in older patients with breast cancer.
Nutrition	Unintentional weight loss; > 10% weight loss from baseline weight); BMI < 21 kg/m^2.	Poor nutrition is associated with mortality in older patients with cancer.	PRO: < 1 minute	Consider G8 and MNA as alternatives; both are associated with mortality in older patients with cancer.

Abbreviations: ADL, activity of daily living; BMI, body mass index; BOMC, Blessed Orientation-Memory-Concentration; CIRS-G, Cumulative Illness Rating Score-Geriatrics; CRASH, Chemotherapy Risk Assessment Scale for High-Age Patients; G8, Geriatric-8; GA, geriatric assessment; GDS, Geriatric Depression Scale; IADL, instrumental activity of daily living; MMSE, Mini-Mental State Examination; MNA, Mini Nutritional Assessment; MOCA, Montreal Cognitive Assessment; OARS, Older Americans Resources and Services; PRO, patient-reported outcome; SPPB, Short Physical Performance Battery; TUG, Timed Up and Go; VES-13, Vulnerable Elders Survey-13.

was significantly shorter in patients whose comprehensive GA (CGA) identified cognitive impairment and impaired physical function.[42] Systematic reviews of geriatric oncology studies have confirmed the association between GA domains and mortality.[48-51]

FUNCTIONAL DECLINE

GA items[73,74] and brief GA-based screening tools[74,75] are predictive of functional decline among older adults receiving chemotherapy. Hoppe et al[73] showed that depression and instrumental activities of daily living (IADLs) are associated with early functional decline during chemotherapy. Owusu et al[75] showed that the VES-13 can identify older women with breast cancer at risk for functional decline. Patients who experienced functional decline were more likely to have had lower baseline activities of daily living (ADL) scores than those who did not functionally decline, have lower IADL scores, to be black (49% *v* 29%; $P = .02$), and have no more than a high school education.[75]

DECISION-MAKING AND MANAGEMENT

Several studies have demonstrated that GA can aid decision-making for cancer treatment and guide nononcologic interventions that address impairments in geriatric domains. In a systematic review by Hamaker et al, the initial cancer treatment plan was modified in 39% of patients on the basis of GA evaluation.[51] Two-thirds of these modifications resulted in less intensive treatment, likely an attempt to adjust treatment in patients who had GA impairments.[48] In the ELCAPA01 study, one of the largest studies evaluating how GA influences decision-making, geriatricians conducted GAs in 375 older patients with cancer to identify factors associated with dose intensification, decrease, or delay of > 2 weeks.[76] In multivariate analysis, functional status as assessed by the ADL score and the presence of malnutrition were independently associated with changes in cancer treatment. In essence, in large cohorts of older patients with cancer who undergo GA, GA influences cancer treatment decisions 20% to 47% of the time, primarily toward less intensive therapy.[7]

GA interventions also are associated with improved chemotherapy tolerance. In a British study, two cohorts of older patients (age ≥ 70 years) receiving cancer chemotherapy were studied.[39] The observational control group received standard oncology care, whereas the high-risk patients in the intervention group received a CGA. Intervention participants undergoing GA received a mean of 6.2 ± 2.6 (range, 0 to 15) GA intervention plans each. They were more likely to complete cancer treatment as planned, with fewer required treatment modifications. A recent prospective phase III trial including older patients with advanced non–small-cell lung cancer (NSCLC) found that GA-based treatment allocation did not improve treatment failure–free survival and OS when compared with standard treatment allocation based on PS and age.[77] However, patients undergoing GA had significantly fewer toxicities of all grades and fewer toxicity-related treatment failures.

A large phase III study has also demonstrated that GA can improve patient- and caregiver-centered outcomes. In this study, community oncology practices were randomly assigned to a GA model of care versus usual care. At the practices enrolled in the intervention, oncologists received GA information and targeted recommendations for aging-related impairments for patients enrolled in the study; patients were aged ≥ 70 years, had at least one GA domain impairment, and were receiving cancer treatment. In the intervention arm, significantly more aging-related concerns were discussed and more interventions were recommended. The intervention also improved patient and caregiver satisfaction but not QOL.

CONCEPT OF FRAILTY

A position statement from the American Medical Association defined the term "frailty" as characterizing "the group of patients that presents the most complex and challenging problems to the physician and all health care professionals," because these are the individuals who have a higher susceptibility to adverse outcomes, such as mortality and institutionalization. Currently, two main models of frailty exist: the phenotype model and the cumulative deficit model.[78]

PHENOTYPE MODEL

The phenotype model was based on a landmark study of 5,210 patients aged ≥ 65 years within the large prospective Cardiovascular Health Study.[79] A frailty phenotype was established with the following five variables: (1) unintentional weight loss, (2) self-reported exhaustion, (3) low energy expenditure, (4) slow gait speed, and (5) weak grip strength. Those patients with three or more of the five factors were judged to be frail, those with one or two factors as prefrail, and those with no factors as robust (or not frail). At 3- and 5-year follow-up, those categorized as frail were reported to have more adverse outcomes in terms of disability and mortality than the other two groups. The mortality rate at 7 years was 12%, 23%, and 43% for the not frail, prefrail, and frail groups, respectively.

CUMULATIVE-DEFICIT MODEL

This frailty index was developed as part of the Canadian Study on Health and Aging, which was a large, 5-year prospective cohort study of 10,263 patients that was designed to investigate the epidemiology and burdens of dementia among older adults in Canada (mean age, 82 years).[80] Frailty was defined using 92 baseline variables of symptoms, signs, abnormal laboratory values, disease states, and disabilities (collectively referred to as deficits). The frailty index was a calculation of the presence or absence of each variable as a proportion of the total (eg, 20 of 92 deficits present gives a frailty index of 20/92 = 0.22). Frailty was defined as the cumulative effect of individual deficits or simply as "the more individuals have wrong with them, the more likely they are to be frail."[80] A recent study using the deficit-accumulation principle demonstrated that a CGA-based deficit accumulation frailty index of 51 items applied to patients with cancer

Table 7-2 Tools Associated with Adverse Outcomes

Tool	Items	Study Population	Administration Characteristics	Considerations and Other Evaluation Options
Tools that can provide estimates of risk for chemotherapy toxicity				
CARG toxicity tool: provides estimates for overall risk of grade 3 to 5 chemotherapy toxicity	Eleven items: prior falls (one or more *v* none), hearing problems (deaf to excellent), limitations in walking 1 block (limited a lot, limited a little, not limited), difficulties with taking medications, interference of social activities by physical health and/or emotional problems (all of the time to none of the time) as well as age, height, weight, sex, cancer type (GI *v* genitourinary *v* other), dosage (standard *v* dose reduced), number of chemotherapy agents (monotherapy *v* polytherapy), hemoglobin level, and creatinine clearance	Patients aged ≥ 65 years with a solid tumor malignancy or lymphoma starting a new chemotherapy regimen (any line)	PRO/administered: 5 minutes. Available online: www.mycarg.org/Chemo_Toxicity_Calculator	Can ask GA variables as part of history or include as part of PRO assessment.
CRASH tool: provides estimates separately for risk of grade 3 hematologic and grade 3 to 4 nonhematologic toxicity	Assessment of risk of hematologic toxicity includes diastolic blood pressure(> 72 mm Hg), IADL score(< 26), and LDH concentration (> 459 U/L). Assessment of risk of nonhematologic toxicity includes ECOG PS, MMSE(< 30), and MNA (< 28). Chemotherapy intensity is assessed with MAX2 index.	Patients aged ≥ 70 years with histologically proven cancer who were starting chemotherapy	PRO/administered: estimated time to completion is on par with full GA (20-30 minutes). Available online: https://moffitt.org/for-healthcare-providers/clinical-programs-and-services/senior-adult-oncology-program/senior-adult-oncology-program-tools	The CRASH scale includes GA measures known also to predict other adverse outcomes, such as mortality, functional decline, and hospitalizations: IADLs, MMSE, and MNA.
Screening tools that have been independently associated with adverse outcomes in older patients with cancer receiving chemotherapy				
G8	Eight items covering appetite, weight loss, neuropsychological problems, mobility, BMI, number of medications, patient self-rated health, and age. Score of ≤ 14 signifies impairment. Derived from the MNA.	Several large studies have been conducted that include patients aged ≥ 70 years and included patients with both solid and hematologic malignancies starting a new chemotherapy agent. G8 is independently associated with mortality (1 year and 3 years), even when controlling for ECOG PS and stage of cancer.	Administered: 5-10 minutes	G8 can also be used as a screening tool to identify older patients who need more comprehensive GA.
VES-13	Thirteen items, including age, self-rated health, common functional tasks, and ability to complete physical activities. Score of ≥ 3 is associated with mortality and chemotherapy toxicity in older patients with cancer. A score of ≥ 7 is associated with functional decline.	VES-13 score is associated with mortality, chemotherapy toxicity, and functional decline.	Administered or PRO (but errors are common with PRO administration): 5-10 minutes	

Abbreviations: CARG, Cancer and Aging Research Group; CRASH, Chemotherapy Risk Assessment Scale for High-Age Patients; ECOG PS, Eastern Cooperative Oncology Group performance status; G8, Geriatric-8; GA, geriatric assessment; IADL, instrumental activity of daily living; LDH, lactate dehydrogenase; MMSE, Mini-Mental State Examination; MNA, Mini Nutritional Assessment; PRO, patient-reported outcome; VES-13, Vulnerable Elders Survey-13.

was predictive of outcomes such as chemotherapy toxicity and hospitalizations.[81]

BIOLOGIC MARKERS OF FRAILTY

Aging is associated with increased levels of circulating cytokines and proinflammatory markers. Aged-related changes in the immune system (eg, immunosenescence, increased secretion of cytokines by adipose tissue) can lead to a state of chronic inflammation or "inflammaging." High levels of IL-6, IL-1, tumor necrosis factor alpha (TNF-α), and CRP in older patients are associated with increased risk of morbidity and mortality.[34] In particular, cohort studies of older adults have indicated that increased TNF-α and IL-6 levels are associated with frailty.[35] These biomarkers of frailty have now been evaluated in patients of all ages with many tumor types (eg, colon cancer, AML, multiple myeloma), with all demonstrating increased levels of proinflammatory cytokines. These frailty cytokines not only have been thought to play a role in carcinogenesis (eg, AML and multiple myeloma) but also are, in fact, responsible for several cancer-related symptom complexes, including cancer cachexia, fatigue, poor PS, and cognitive issues. Factors contributing to the development of frailty are summarized in Figure 7-3.

In a review[82] incorporating biomarkers of aging into cancer research, potential biomarkers were divided into three groups: (1) markers of systemic inflammation (eg, IL-6, CRP, D-dimer); (2) markers of cellular senescence (eg, telomere length); and (3) imaging for sarcopenia. These biomarkers had shown associations with frailty and mortality in numerous studies.[82] It will be important to incorporate biomarkers into oncology clinical trials to assist oncologists in choosing appropriate treatment regiments and supportive care measures.[82]

KEY POINTS

- GA assists in defining physiologic reserve. The 2018 ASCO geriatric oncology guideline suggests oncologists should assess functional status, physical performance and falls, comorbid medical conditions, depression, social activity and support, nutritional status, and cognition as key domains of the GA.
- Aging is associated with an increase in proinflammatory cytokines such as TNF-α and IL-6, which contribute to frailty.
- Frailty is correlated with a severe loss of functional reserve and lack of tolerance to medical intervention.
- Eastern Cooperative Oncology Group or KPS alone may not provide an accurate measure of the functional status of an older patient with cancer.
- GA can be used to predict survival and risk of chemotherapy toxicity in older adults with cancer.
- GA can be used to guide treatment decision-making and interventions for older patients with cancer.

TREATMENT APPROACHES

SURGERY

Surgery and other invasive procedures are frequently part of the care of the older patient with cancer. Concomitant comorbidities, impaired wound healing, and decreased physiologic reserve contribute to prolonged hospital stay and rehabilitation after surgical and other procedures. With regard to wound healing, inflammatory and proliferative responses are decreased, remodeling occurs to a lesser degree, and collagen formation is qualitatively different from that of younger individuals.[83] The normal repair process initiated by inflammation requires intact sensory nerves that stimulate increased blood flow and growth-factor production. Loss of sensory neurons and co-occurring morbidities, such as diabetes and vascular disease, contribute to delayed wound healing.

Complications are more common with emergent surgical procedures. Some procedures may be used as preventive measures, such as hemicolectomy, performed to prevent the need for an emergency operation to treat bowel perforation or obstruction. The American Geriatrics Society Task Force and the American College of Surgeons provide general guidelines for older adults undergoing surgery, which are applicable to older patients with cancer who are undergoing surgery.[84,85]

RADIATION THERAPY

Radiation therapy (RT) may be used with either curative or palliative intent, and as an effective adjunct to surgery and/or chemotherapy. The SIOG Task Force developed the following guidelines for best practices in radiation oncology for older patients with cancer.[86]

- For older patients with breast cancer, shorter courses of hypofractionated whole-breast RT are safe and effective.
- In a study of 636 women (age ≥ 70 years) who had clinical stage I estrogen receptor (ER)-positive breast carcinoma treated by lumpectomy who were randomly assigned to receive either tamoxifen plus RT or tamoxifen alone, there was no difference in OS, disease-free survival, and breast conservation. This highlights the lack of benefit of RT in selected older patients with early-stage breast cancer.[87]
- For patients with NSCLC, conformal RT and involved field techniques without elective nodal irradiation have improved outcomes without increasing toxicity. If comorbidities preclude surgery, stereotactic body radiotherapy (SBRT) is an option for early-stage NSCLC[88] and pancreatic cancer.
- For older patients with intermediate-risk prostate cancer, 4 to 6 months of hormonal therapy combined with external beam radiotherapy (EBRT) is an option.
- Short-course EBRT is an alternative to combined modality therapy for older patients with rectal cancer without significant comorbidities, and endorectal RT may be an option for early disease.
- For primary brain tumors, short courses of postoperative RT after maximal debulking provide comparable survival to longer treatment schedules. SBRT also is alternative to whole-brain RT for patients with limited brain metastases.[89]

Table 7-3 **Comparisons of Geriatric Screening Tools**[43]				
Instrument	**Method**	**Scoring**	**Interpretation**	**Remarks**
G8	Interview with eight questions	Total score: 17	Score 0 to 14: Presence of geriatric risk profile	Takes 2-3 minutes to complete screening
			Score > 14: Absence of geriatric risk profile	
Groningen Frailty Indicator	Conducting screening tests on patient	Total score: 15	Score 0 to 3: Absence of geriatric risk profile	Circle answers and use specific scoring rules set by the test
			Score 4 to 15: Presence of geriatric risk profile	
Vulnerable Elders Survey-13	Self-report and interview	Total score: 10	Score 0 to 2: Absence of vulnerability	Takes < 5 minutes to complete
			Score 3 to 10: Presence of vulnerability	
Senior Adult Oncology Program 2	Self-report and interview	N/A	If one item is positive: respective specialist consulted	Clinic staff administers last page of interview
			If several items impaired: geriatric referral for MDT	
Abbreviated CGA	Interview:		GDS score > 2: complete full 15-item GDS	
	▪ Four questions from the GDS			
	▪ Three questions about ADL		Any impairment of ADL: complete full ADL	
	▪ Four questions about IADL		Any impairment of IADL: complete full IADL	
	▪ Four questions from the MMSE		Cognitive screening score < 6: complete full MMSE	

Abbreviations: ADL, activities of daily living; CGA, comprehensive geriatric assessment; GDS, Geriatric Depression Scale; IADL, instrumental activities of daily living; MDT, multidisciplinary team; MMSE, Mini Mental State Examination; N/A, not applicable.

- Intensity modulated radiotherapy is beneficial in reducing radiation doses to the carotids in head and neck cancer and improves locoregional control in esophageal cancer. Radiation to the oral pharynx and oral cavity can produce a loss of taste, dryness of mucous membranes, and salivary gland involution, which can lead to decreased nutritional intake in frail and older patients with concomitant morbidity.
- Age is associated with a decline in pulmonary reserve, and morbidity may be expected at lower cumulative radiation doses in older patients. However, studies do not show that increasing age as a predictor of pneumonitis in patients who have RT to the thoracic area.[90]
- Depression and cognitive decline are adverse effects of whole-brain RT.

SYSTEMIC THERAPY: CHEMOTHERAPY AND TARGETED AGENTS

Older patients are consistently underrepresented in clinical trials; therefore, much of the treatment data for this population are extrapolated from studies of predominantly younger patients.[91,92] Prospective data are generally lacking[93] for patients > 80 years of age in the majority of malignancies.[94] A notable exception is data supporting a reduced-dose regimen of rituximab and doxorubicin, cyclophosphamide, vincristine, and prednisone chemotherapy, also called *R*-miniCHOP, for patients aged ≥ 80 years with diffuse large B-cell lymphoma. OS is a primary end point in many clinical trials, but in the older patient, survival may be compromised more by comorbidities than the cancer itself.

A SIOG and European Organization for Research and Treatment of Cancer task force has put forth suggestions for clinical trial design and end points in geriatric oncology research, suggesting that oncology trials should be without an upper age limit, include measures of QOL, and note decreases in cancer-related symptoms.[95] One study[94] found that older patients enrolled in phase I clinical trials had similar survival outcomes and toxicity profiles as compared

Table 7-4 Minimum Data Set for Geriatric Assessment Advocated by ASCO Geriatric Oncology Guideline

1.	Predict chemotherapy toxicity (if clinically applicable): CARG or CRASH tools
2.	Estimate (noncancer) life expectancy (if clinically applicable): ePrognosis
3.	Functional assessment: instrumental activities of daily living
4.	Comorbidity assessment: medical record review or validated tool
5.	Screening for falls, question: How many falls have you had in the previous 6 months (or since your last visit)?
6.	Screening for depression: Geriatric Depression Scale or other validated tool
7.	Screening for cognitive impairment: Mini-Cog or Blessed Orientation Memory Concentration Test
8.	Screening for malnutrition: weight loss/body mass index

Abbreviations: CARG, Cancer and Aging Research Group; CRASH, Chemotherapy Risk Assessment Scale for High-Age Patients.

with younger patients.[96] Although older participants had more comorbidities and lower albumin levels at baseline, there was no significant difference in survival (8.8 months *v* 9.9 months; $P = .68$) and clinical benefit rate (69% *v* 56%; $P = .07$) compared with younger patients. Age ($P = .23$) did not affect the frequency of grade 3/4 toxicities.

Chemotherapy

A recent guideline by ASCO provides guidance on practical assessment and treatment of older adults with cancer who are receiving chemotherapy.[7] The SIOG task force has published guidelines for dose modification of chemotherapy agents for older patients with renal insufficiency, as well as those with cancer.[97,98] With oral agents, absorption is adequate despite gastric emptying but may be affected by concomitant medications such as H2 blockers, antacids, and proton pump inhibitors. Polypharmacy, which is common in the elderly, is also associated with higher risk of potential drug interactions which, in turn, is linked to increased chemotherapy toxicity risk.[99] Caution must be used with cytotoxic drugs such as methotrexate, bleomycin, cisplatin, and ifosfamide. Declines in the glomerular filtration rate may contribute to excess toxicity. As lean body mass decreases in the elderly, it is very important to adjust the dose on the basis of a creatinine clearance rate and not merely the creatinine level. Concomitant administration of drugs such as non-steroidal anti-inflammatory drugs may compromise renal function. Acute toxicities such as nausea and vomiting occur less frequently in older patients; however, the lack of functional reserve can readily lead to dehydration and renal insufficiency.[100] Reduced renal function in combination with lower albumin levels may predispose elderly patients to a greater risk of neurotoxicity with high-dose ifosfamide. Neurotoxicity related to taxanes, platinum agents, vinca alkaloids, high-dose cytarabine, and bortezomib; cardiotoxicity from anthracyclines; and mucositis from 5-fluorouracil are all more common and severe in older patients.[97] Whether the risk of myelotoxicity increases with age remains a controversial issue, but studies indicate longer duration of neutropenia in older patients.[97] Pretreatment GA is useful to predict the risk of toxicity for older patients.

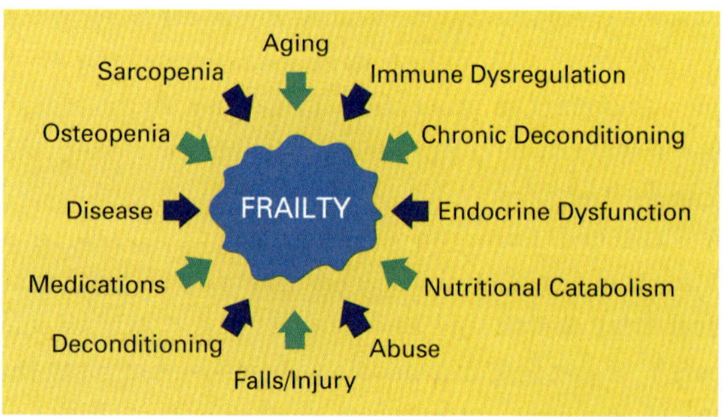

Fig. 7-3 Factors contributing to the development of frailty. Many factors contribute to the development of frailty, which is determined by the clinical assessment of the older patient.

Targeted Agents

Targeted therapeutic agents, including tyrosine kinase inhibitors, mammalian target of rapamycin inhibitors, human epidermal growth factor receptor 2 and *BRAF*-mutation targeted drugs, epidermal growth factor receptor inhibitors, and vascular endothelial growth factor inhibitors have been increasingly used in all patients with cancer in the past decade.[101] As with chemotherapy trials, data for older patients have been extrapolated from trials of predominantly younger patients. A study of older adults with chronic myeloid leukemia found that comorbidities and polypharmacy may affect cytogenetic response. In this study, it was observed that patients with fewer comorbidities who were only receiving tyrosine kinase inhibitors (no polypharmacy) had a better chance of a complete response.[102] In addition, many targeted agents are metabolized by the cytochrome P450 system, increasing the risk for significant drug interactions. In terms of responses to targeted therapies, many studies have shown that older adults benefit from the use of these drugs as much as their younger counterparts.[103] Table 7-5 lists recommendations for the use of targeted therapy in solid tumors in older patients.[101]

Immuno-Oncology Agents

Immune checkpoint inhibitors (ICIs), which affect immune function, are a new class of oncologic agents used in the treatment of a variety of malignancies. Expression of immune checkpoints on T cells increases with age, making immune checkpoint blockade a promising option for older patients

Table 7-5 **Recommendations for Use of Selected Targeted Therapy in Solid Tumors in Elderly Patients**

Drug	Disease Setting	Efficacy Data	Safety Data	Data Source	Specific Considerations in Older Adults
Imatinib	GIST	Limited	Limited	Pivotal adjuvant trials	Potential toxicity concerns: myelosuppression, fluid retention, diarrhea, rash
Gefitinib	Advanced NSCLC	Available; effective	Available; favorable toxicity profile in elderly patients	Elderly-specific data	Well tolerated; monitor for rash and diarrhea
Erlotinib	Advanced NSCLC	Available; effective	Available; increased toxicity	Pivotal trials and elderly-specific data	Extreme caution; close monitoring for toxicity: rash, stomatitis, dehydration, anorexia, and fatigue
Crizotinib	Advanced NSCLC	Limited	Limited	Pivotal trials	Likely reasonable option, although data are limited
Sorafenib	Advanced HCC	Limited; effective	Limited; safe	Elderly-specific data	Monitor for GI and skin toxicity
Everolimus	ER-positive MBC; HER2-positive	Effective	Caution; higher incidence of treatment-related deaths in elderly patients	Elderly-specific data	Close monitoring for stomatitis, diarrhea, and anemia
Palbociclib	ER-positive MBC; HER2-positive	Available; effective	Available; increase myelosuppression in elderly	Elderly specific data	Although myelosuppression was more common in elderly, the incidence of grade 3 myelosuppression is similar across all age groups. Incidence of febrile neutropenia was low among the elderly.
Trastuzumab	Breast cancer; HER2-positive	Limited	Limited	Retrospective data	Use in elderly patients without cardiac risk factors; regular cardiac monitoring
Pertuzumab	MBC; HER2-positive	Available; effective	Limited; increased toxicity in all patients	Pivotal trial	Use in elderly patients without cardiac risk factors
T-DM1	HER2-positive MBC	Limited	Limited	Pivotal trial	Favorable safety profile
Lapatinib	HER2-positive MBC	Limited	Limited	Pivotal trial	Monitor for GI toxicities, arrythmias
Vemurafenib	*BRAF*-mutant advanced melanoma	Limited	Limited	Pivotal trial	Monitor for skin toxicity, fatigue, arthralgia
Dabrafenib	*BRAF*-mutant advanced melanoma	Limited	Limited	Pivotal trial	Monitor for skin toxicity, fever, fatigue, arthralgia

Table 7-5 **continued**

Drug	Disease Setting	Efficacy Data	Safety Data	Data Source	Specific Considerations in Older Adults
Ipilimumab	Advanced melanoma	Available	Available	Pivotal trial; elderly-specific data	Immune-related AEs: dermatologic, endocrine, GI
Sunitinib	mRCC	Available	Available; increased toxicity	Elderly-specific data	Monitor for GI toxicity, HFS, HTN, fatigue; first-line dose modification may be appropriate
Pazopanib	mRCC	Available	Available; favorable toxicity profile in older patients	Pivotal trial	Monitor for GI toxicity, HTN, anorexia
Sorafenib	mRCC	Available	Available	Pivotal trial	Monitor for skin toxicity, diarrhea, fatigue, and rare serious AEs (HTN, cardiac ischemia)
Everolimus	mRCC	Available	Available; well tolerated	Elderly-specific data	Monitor for stomatitis, rash, fatigue
Temsirolimus	mRCC	Available	Available; well tolerated	Pivotal trial	Monitor for rash, fluid retention, hyperlipidemia, hyperglycemia
Axitinib	mRCC	Available	Limited	Pivotal trial	Monitor for HTN, diarrhea, fatigue
Cabozantinib	mRCC	Available	Limited	Pivotal trial	Monitor for HTN, diarrhea, mouth ulcers, HFS
Cetuximab	mCRC	Available; effective	Limited	Pivotal trial	Monitor for rash, GI toxicity
Pantiumumab	mCRC	Available; effective	Limited	Pivotal trial	Well tolerated; monitor for skin toxicity, diarrhea, hypomagnesemia
Bevacizumab	mCRC	Available; effective	Available; increased risk for HTN	Elderly-specific data	Monitor for HTN; screen for vascular risk factors
Aflibercept	mCRC	Available; effective	Available; increased risk of toxicity	Pivotal trial	Cautious use in elderly patients, given toxicity profile
Regorafenib	mCRC	Available; effective; smaller benefit than in younger patients	Available; increased toxicity	Pivotal trial	Cautious use in elderly patients, given toxicity profile and small benefit
Bevacizumab	Advanced ovarian cancer	Available	Limited	Pivotal trials	Monitor for HTN
Trastuzumab	Advanced gastric cancer	Limited	Limited	Pivotal trial	Use in elderly patients without cardiac risk factors
Ramucirumab	Advanced gastric cancer	Limited	Limited	Pivotal trial	Lack of data to support use

Abbreviations: AE, adverse event; ER, estrogen receptor; GIST, GI stromal tumors; HCC, hepatocellular carcinoma; HFS, hand-foot syndrome; HTN, hypertension; MBC, metastatic breast cancer; mCRC, metastatic colorectal cancer; mRCC, metastatic renal cell carcinoma; NSCLC, non-small-cell lung cancer; T-DM1, trastuzumab emtansine.

with cancer.[104] However, the impact of immunosenesence on these agents is not clear. The term age-related immune dysfunction may be used to describe immune-related changes of aging and their potential interaction with immuno-oncology agents.[105] Use in older patients is enhanced by a relatively low toxicity profile as compared with conventional chemotherapy.[106] A recent review of 21 phase II/III clinical trials studying ICI response data showed that older adults enrolled in those studies experienced similar low levels of toxicity as their younger counterparts. The older adults experience immune-related adverse events (like their younger counterparts), which can be managed in a similar manner as well. However, there were differences in the hazard ratios of progression-free survival and OS between the different age groups depending on the type of drug used.[107] In a meta-analysis of nine randomized clinical trials using ICIs comparing the efficacy in younger versus older patients, authors showed a significant benefit in terms of OS and progression-free survival in both groups.[108] ASCO, in collaboration with National Comprehensive Cancer Network, has issued a clinical practice guideline on management of immune-related adverse events in patients treated with ICIs that can be applied to the older adult population.[109] With much more data being learned about the use of this class of agents either as single agents or in combination, much more can be gleaned with regard to its impact on the older adult population.

HEMATOPOIETIC CELL TRANSPLANTATION

Historically, the morbidity and mortality associated with allogeneic hematopoietic cell transplantation (HCT) limited its use to individuals younger than 50 years, unlike autologous transplants, which had been used for older patients. However, in recent times, allogeneic transplants are used for patients up to 70 years old with reasonable success, using reduced-intensity regimens.[110] Because no guidelines are established for using HCT specifically in older adults, patient selection, choice of conditioning regimen, immunosuppression, and cell source are arbitrary and generally based on cardiopulmonary and hepatorenal function. Risk-assessment tools such as CGA and comorbidity measures recently have been applied to delineate potential older candidates for HCT therapy. Reduced-intensity conditioning for allogeneic HCT has led to a more favorable toxicity profile and decreased transplanted-related mortality compared with myeloablative approaches, thus affecting traditional age barriers.[111] Donor selection for older recipients is an additional issue. Older patients may have older human leukocyte antigen–matched siblings, with diminished hematopoietic cell yields and potential health limitations to be donors.

Important geriatric issues such as nutrition, caregiver support, and cognitive assessment have not been extensively evaluated in the setting of HCT. For example, acute delirium occurs in up to 50% of allogeneic HCT recipients and may be more common in older patients.[112] According to the most recent guidelines from the American Society for Blood and Marrow Transplantation, age by itself should not be a contraindication to transplantation in patients who may benefit from this procedure. Selected older patients with limited comorbidities and good functional status can safely receive HCT with a relatively low and acceptable risk of nonrelapse mortality. Instead of chronologic patient age, evaluations such as functional status and the HCT-specific comorbidity index score, European Society for Blood and Marrow Transplantation risk score, and Pretransplantation Assessment of Mortality risk score can assist in determining risks of nonrelapse mortality and transplant candidacy for individual patients.[113] More specific details of HCT are covered in Chapter 22.

SUPPORTIVE CARE MEASURES

Supportive care measures are especially important for older patients because they help improve treatment tolerability and minimize dose reductions and delays in therapy. Many of the specific aspects of supportive care are covered in Chapter 8 and are mentioned here to stress their importance for the management of the elderly patient with cancer. There are established guidelines on the prevention and treatment of mucositis and the use of antiemetics and growth factors.

Neutropenia

Chemotherapy-induced neutropenia is reduced by 60% to 75% with myeloid growth factor use, thus reducing the occurrence of febrile neutropenia and infections. These agents also prevent dose reductions that can compromise the effectiveness of the therapy. The ASCO guideline recommends prophylactic use of colony-stimulating factors (CSFs) to reduce the occurrence of febrile neutropenia when the risk of febrile neutropenia is ≥ 20% and when no other equally effective and safe regimen that does not require CSFs is available.[114] Primary CSF prophylaxis is recommended for patients who are at high risk for febrile neutropenia on the basis of age, medical history, disease characteristics, and myelotoxicity of the treatment regimen. The guideline does not address recommendations for the use of CSFs in AML or myelodysplastic syndromes.[115]

Nausea and Vomiting

Antiemetic prophylaxis with a 5-HT3-receptor antagonist in combination with corticosteroids is recommended for patients receiving moderately to highly emetogenic chemotherapy or radiotherapy.[116] A 2017 ASCO update recommends that all patients receiving highly emetogenic chemotherapy regimens should be given a four-drug combination that includes an NK1 receptor antagonist, a 5-HT3 receptor antagonist, dexamethasone, and olanzapine. Netupitant and palonosetron plus dexamethasone is an additional treatment option in this setting.

Fatigue

Fatigue can affect an older patient's QOL. The etiology of fatigue is multifactorial, ranging from immobility and deconditioning to anemia, depression, pain, poor nutrition, drugs, and metabolic causes. Treatment of fatigue generally requires treatment of the underlying causes (eg, treat anemia with hematinics, iron, vitamin B_{12}, and folate). Exercise programs can have a positive role in the treatment of cancer-related fatigue. Drugs such as methylphenidate and modafinil have been used to treat cancer-related fatigue but have not been well studied in the elderly.[117]

PALLIATIVE CARE AND END-OF-LIFE ISSUES

Many older patients are realistic with regard to nearing the end of life and are open to discussion about their disease and its potential consequences. Patients' individual goals, independence, and physical, emotional, and spiritual health are priorities. In a landmark study of patients age ≥ 60 years who were terminally ill, researchers found that if the outcome was survival but with severe functional impairment or cognitive impairment, 74.4% and 88.8% of participants, respectively, would not choose treatment.[118] Palliative care is an essential component of care throughout the disease process and not just in the terminal stages (these issues are discussed in further detail in Chapter 9: Palliative Care and Care at the End of Life).

An interdisciplinary palliative care team focuses on preventing and relieving suffering, regardless of the disease, stage, or need for other therapies. The goals of palliative care for older patients are the same as those for younger individuals, and accurate identification of all symptoms is particularly useful. Simplified instruments, such as the Edmonton Symptom Assessment Scale, which assesses nine symptoms common among patients with cancer: pain, tiredness, nausea, depression, anxiety, drowsiness, appetite, well-being, and shortness of breath, are useful in providing a profile of symptom severity over time.[119]

KEY POINTS

- In older patients, comorbidities, impaired wound healing, and decreased physiologic reserve contribute to prolonged hospital stay and rehabilitation after surgery.
- Delivery, duration, and dosage of RT must be carefully planned on the basis of organ function, comorbidities, and geriatric evaluation, because adverse effects may be more pronounced in older patients.
- Many chemotherapy toxicities are more common and more severe in older patients. Pretreatment GA is useful to predict the risk of chemotherapy toxicity.
- In older patients, comorbidities and polypharmacy may affect response to targeted therapy, and GA is critical for selection of treatment and dosing.
- Immuno-oncology drugs appear safe for use in older adults and seem to have less toxicity than chemotherapy.

Acknowledgment

The following authors are acknowledged and graciously thanked for their contribution to prior versions of this chapter: Joanne Mortimer, MD, FASCO; Arati Rao, MD; and Harvey J. Cohen, MD.

GLOBAL ONCOLOGY PERSPECTIVE: CANCER IN THE OLDER PATIENT

Enrique Soto-Perez-de-Celis, MD (Instituto Nacional de Ciencias Medicas y Nutricion Salvador Zubiran, Mexico City, Mexico)

An increase in longevity in the United States and other high-income countries (HICs) has been mirrored in developing regions of the world, and most of the projected growth in the population of older adults in the next 30 years will take place in low- and-middle-income countries (LMICs).[120] Currently, of the 650 million people aged ≥ 65 years globally, approximately two-thirds (approximately 436 million) live in LMICs.[121] By 2050, global life expectancy at birth will increase to 74.3 years, the estimated number of people aged ≥ 65 years will be almost 1.5 billion, and one in seven people living in LMICs will be older than 65.3 years. According to GLOBOCAN, > 9 million cancer cases and 5.5 million cancer deaths occurred among people aged ≥ 65 years in 2018.[122] Of these, 50% of cases and > 60% of deaths occurred in LMICs, and this percentage will continue to increase as a consequence of global population aging.[123] The incidence-to-mortality ratio for all cancers among older adults varies greatly by regional income level (Fig 7-4).

There are also significant differences in the incidence of various cancer types among older adults according to world region and income level (Fig 7-5). Although prostate cancer is the most common cancer in people aged ≥ 65 years regardless of income level, the incidence of lung, gastric, esophageal, hepatocellular, and cervical cancers is significantly higher among older adults in

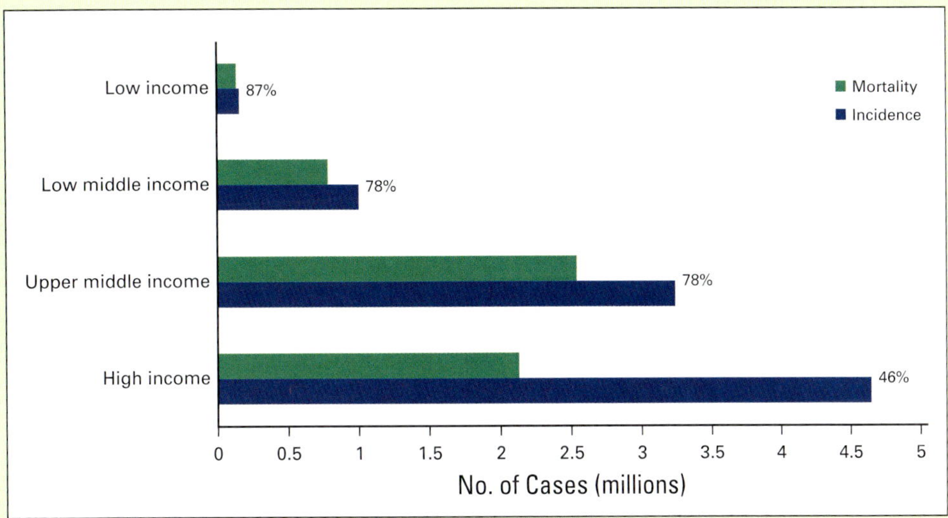

Fig. 7-4 Ratio of incidence to mortality among adults aged ≥ 65 years according to regional income level. Obtained from GLOBOCAN 2018 data.[123]

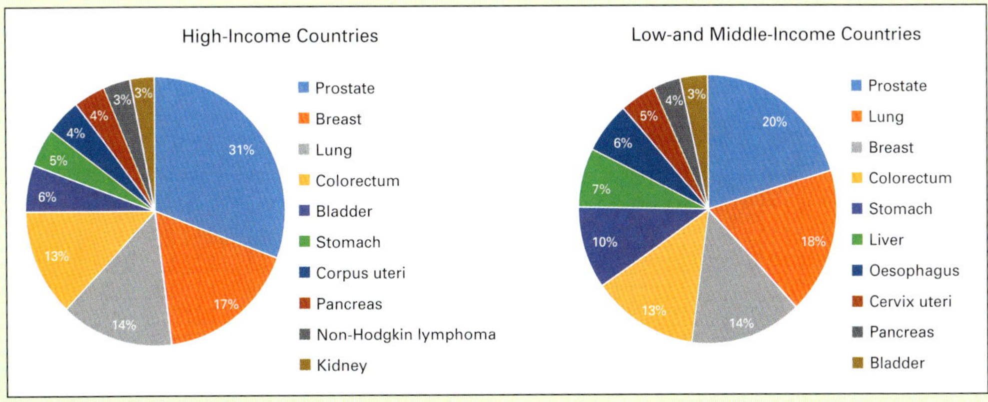

Fig. 7-5 Ten most common cancer types among adults aged ≥ 65 years according to regional income level. Obtained from GLOBOCAN 2018 data.[123]

LMICs than among the same age group in HICs.[123] This difference might be partly related to lifestyle factors and environmental exposures, which differ from those of older adults living in HICs. Smoking rates, for instance, are worryingly high among older adults living in LMICs, and an association between smoking and poverty has been observed.[124,125] The high incidence of infection-related cancers (ie, liver, gastric, cervical) among older adults in LMICs also represents an opportunity for the implementation of prevention initiatives, including population-based vaccination programs and screen-and-treat strategies, particularly starting at younger ages.[126]

In addition, some common cancers can have varying presentations among older adults living in different regions of the world. A recent study conducted in Mexico showed that, in contrast with what is seen in HICs, almost half of older women with breast cancer presented with stage III-IV disease.[127] Although this can be attributed to the lack of screening programs, a more pressing issue may be the existence of barriers for accessing specialized health care promptly, which leads to diagnostic delays and more advanced stage at presentation, as well as a lack of personnel with expertise to provide high-quality care.[128,129]

The availability of health care workers with geriatric expertise is limited in most of the developing world, which not only affects cancer care but also the management of comorbidities among older adults with cancer. In some Latin American countries, such as Brazil or Ecuador, the number of older adults per geriatrician is > 16,000, compared with 6,440 older adults per geriatrician in the United States.[130] Similarly, specialized geriatric oncology clinics, which are increasingly common in HICs like the United States and France, are rare in LMICs.[121] Therefore, novel global strategies are necessary to increase the geriatric competence of the health care workforce in LMICs. In addition, guidelines and tools need to be adapted and tailored to the characteristics of each country's population of older adults, as well as to local needs and availability of resources and personnel. In many regions of the world, for instance, the literacy rates of older adults are < 60%, which means that many of the tools used in everyday clinical practice (eg, self-administered GAs) may not be feasible in those settings.[131] In addition, older adults with cancer treated in LMICs have limited access to clinical trials of new therapeutic strategies and are less likely to receive supportive and palliative care interventions.[129]

The aging of the population should be a priority for health care systems worldwide, but particularly for those of LMICs, which, for the most part, are unprepared to take care of older adults with cancer and other complex, chronic diseases. The development of initiatives aimed at creating innovative solutions to provide tailored care for older patients in settings with varying levels of resources should be a high priority for both the global oncology and the geriatric oncology communities. To this end, the creation of resource-stratified guidelines, the implementation of international educational initiatives, and the design of easy-to-use tools for assessing older adults using readily available and affordable technologies such as mobile health, represent examples of areas for research.

8

PAIN AND SYMPTOM MANAGEMENT

Eric Roeland, MD

Recent Updates

- Symptom monitoring (patient-reported symptoms via tablet computer) versus usual care of patients with cancer consisting of symptom monitoring at the discretion of the clinician demonstrated improved quality of life and survival. (Basch E, *JAMA* 2017; *J Clin Oncol* 2016)
- Universal precautions describes an opioid-prescribing practice referring to a routine clinical approach in which all patients are assessed for history or risk of opioid misuse, regardless of demographic, social, or disease-related variables. (Paice JA, *J Oncol Pract* 2016)
- Carboplatin has been reclassified as highly emetogenic chemotherapy. (Hesketh PJ, *J Clin Oncol* 2017; Berger MJ, *J Natl Compr Canc Netw* 2017; Molassiotis A, *Supportive Care Cancer* 2017)

OVERVIEW

Optimal management of cancer-related symptoms is a critical role of the treating oncology clinician. Poorly controlled symptoms lead to delays and early terminations of cancer-directed therapies. In contrast, optimal palliation improves cancer-related outcomes and quality of life. The following signs and symptoms are discussed in this chapter:

- Cancer-related pain
- Nausea and vomiting
- Cancer-related fatigue
- Anorexia and cachexia
- Delirium
- Diarrhea associated with cancer or cancer therapy
- Oral mucositis
- Chemotherapy-induced peripheral neuropathy
- Dyspnea
- Dermatologic adverse effects
- Management of estrogen-deprivation symptoms
- Management of immune-related adverse effects is discussed in Chapter 4 and additional symptoms are discussed in Chapter 9.

SYMPTOM MONITORING

PATIENT-REPORTED SYMPTOMS

Symptoms are common among patients with cancer who are receiving cancer-directed therapies. Yet, clinicians often under-recognize the magnitude of physical and psychological symptoms that patients with cancer experience.[1] Symptoms such as pain, fatigue, nausea, dyspnea, and peripheral neuropathy lead to poor quality of life (QOL) and psychological distress.[2,3] However, research demonstrates that clinicians often fail to reliably evaluate their patients' symptoms and frequently underestimate the severity of those symptoms.[4,5] Consequently, there is growing interest in incorporating patient-reported outcomes in routine oncology care for symptom monitoring.

In a randomized, single-center study of 766 patients with cancer, outpatient symptom monitoring versus usual care demonstrated improved QOL and survival in the intervention group. Investigators randomly assigned patients receiving routine outpatient chemotherapy for advanced solid tumors to report via weekly e-mail prompts 12 common symptoms or to receive usual care consisting of symptom monitoring at the discretion of clinicians. Treating physicians received symptom printouts at visits and nurses received e-mail alerts when participants reported severe or worsening symptoms. Health-related QOL improved among more participants in the intervention group and were less frequently admitted to the emergency department (34% *v* 41%; *P* = .02) and continued to receive chemotherapy longer (mean, 8.2 *v* 6.3 months; *P* = .002).[6] With a follow-up of 7 years, investigators also found a 5-month improved overall survival in patients with outpatient symptom monitoring versus usual care (hazard ratio, 0.83; 95% CI, 0.70 to 0.99; *P* = .04).[7]

Patient-reported outcomes have also been evaluated in the inpatient setting. In a two-arm, parallel group, cluster randomized trial, investigators evaluated pain outcomes in 19 cancer centers in the United Kingdom and then randomly assigned the centers to either implement clinician-delivered bedside pain assessment or usual care. In 1,921 patients with cancer, patients randomly assigned to the pain assessment arm experienced clinically significant improvement in worst pain without any associated change in distress outcomes or opioid adverse effects.[8] A second study in 150 hospitalized patients with advanced cancer evaluated the feasibility of a global symptom monitoring intervention.[9] Patients assigned to the symptom-monitoring intervention reported their symptoms daily, per the revised Edmonton Symptom Assessment System[10] and Patient Health Questionnaire–4[11] using tablet computers. Patients with advanced cancer who were hospitalized for > 2 days completed symptom assessments that demonstrated, 90% of the time, feasibility of integrating daily symptom monitoring into inpatient oncology care.

KEY POINTS

- Clinicians often do not reliably evaluate their patients' symptoms and they frequently underestimate symptom severity.
- Data demonstrate remote symptom monitoring linked to clinical response improves QOL and overall survival for patients with advanced cancer.
- Daily patient-reported global symptom monitoring is feasible in hospitalized patients with advanced cancer.

CANCER-RELATED PAIN

Pain is a common and distressful symptom with up to 90% of patients with advanced cancer experiencing moderate to severe pain.[12] Optimal pain management is a central role of the treating oncology clinician. The first steps are to assess and identify the etiology of the pain and treat any reversible causes when possible. A pain assessment should include a description of the location, radiation, duration, and quality of the pain, and any factors that alleviate or aggravate the pain. In addition, clinicians should be familiar with the terms used to describe pain (Table 8-1) and know how to effectively assess the temporality and type of cancer-related pain.

TEMPORALITY

Typically, pain temporality is characterized as acute or chronic (Fig 8-1).

Acute Pain

Acute pain occurs over hours up to weeks and is characterized by a well-defined temporal pattern of onset, subjective and objective physical signs, and hyperactivity of the autonomic nervous system. Usually self-limited, acute pain responds to treatment of its precipitating cause in combination with analgesics.

Chronic Pain

In contrast, chronic pain persists for > 3 months, with a less well-defined temporal onset and without the common objective signs to acute pain (eg, tachycardia, facial grimace). Treatment of chronic pain in patients with cancer requires careful assessment of not only the intensity of pain but also its multidimensional aspects, including psychosocial factors. Examples

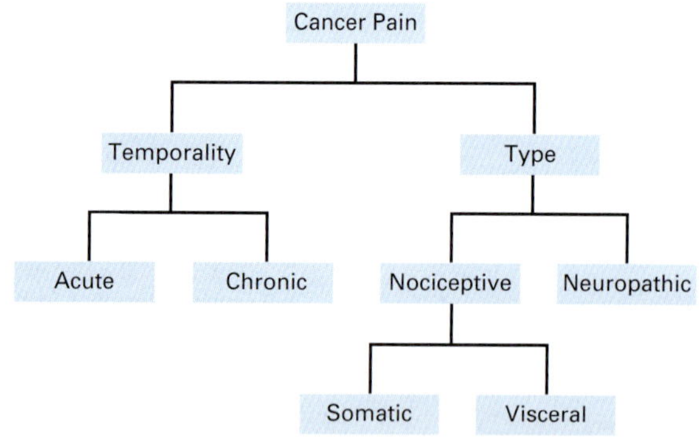

Fig. 8-1 Characterization of pain by temporality and type.

of psychosocial factors may include anxiety, coping poorly with illness, history of misuse of opioids, poor social support, inadequate understanding of illness, or limited access to medications. In addition to pharmacologic approaches, clinicians should consider nonpharmacologic approaches, when appropriate (Table 8-2).

The temporal assessment should also include key features such as onset, duration, and course. Patients will describe temporality in terms of their daily experience with pain (Fig 8-2). Constant pain describes pain experienced for ≥ 12 h/d; breakthrough pain characterizes a transient increase in pain to greater than moderate intensity; and incident pain describes a specific experience of pain associated with an event or movement (eg, wound care).

TYPE

In addition to understanding the pain temporality, it is important to understand the prominent features of the pain. Typically, cancer-related pain can be characterized as nociceptive, neuropathic, visceral, or mixed types.

Table 8-2 Nonpharmacologic Approaches to Treating Cancer Pain[255]

Category	Treatment Type
Alternative, complementary, or integrative strategies	Acupuncture
	Art therapy
	Massage
	Music therapy
	Physical/movement
Interventional	Injection therapies
	Implant therapy
	Neural blockade
	Surgical neuroablation
Rehabilitative	Hydrotherapy
	Occupational therapy
	Physical modalities such as ultrasound
	Therapeutic exercise
	Therapy for specific disorders such as lymphedema
Psychological	Hypnotherapy
	Cognitive-behavioral therapy
	Guided imagery
	Other forms of psychotherapy
	Psychoeducational interventions
	Relaxation therapy
	Stress management
Neurostimulation	Implanted
	Transcranial
	Transcutaneous

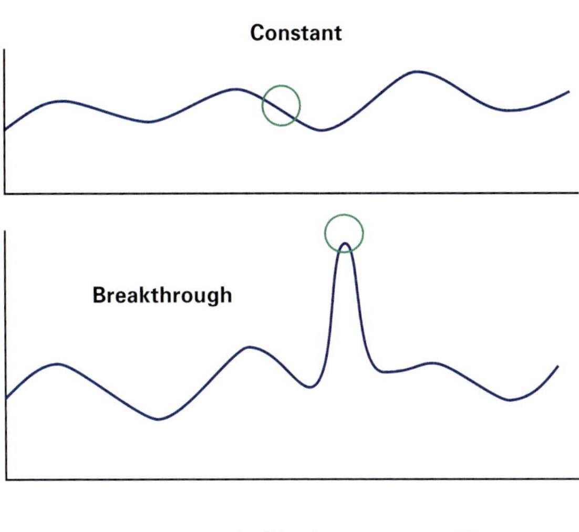

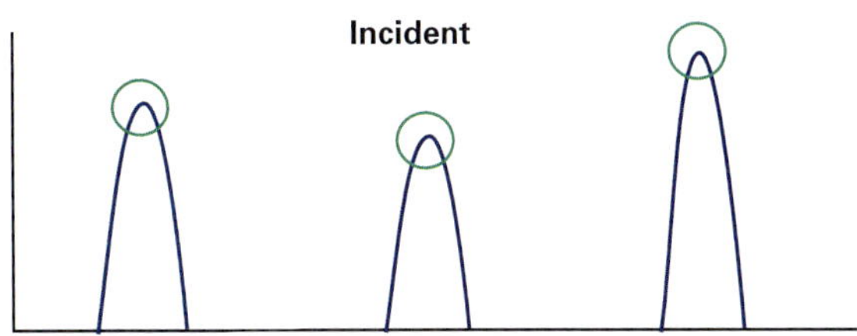

Fig. 8-2 Temporal assessment of cancer pain.
Pain is measured on the *y*-axis and time on the *x*-axis.

Nociceptive Pain

Nociceptive pain may be somatic or visceral and is associated with actual or potential tissue damage caused by ongoing activation of intact nociceptors.

Somatic Pain

Somatic pain is caused by injury to the skin, soft tissue, bones, or joints. Patients with somatic pain can typically localize the pain and describe it as aching, stabbing, or throbbing.

Visceral Pain

Visceral pain results from activation of nociceptors in the viscera by obstruction, infiltration, ischemia, stretching, compression, and/or inflammation. Patients may have a difficult time localizing the pain and frequently experienced referred pain. Patients describe visceral pain as cramping, pressure, gnawing, or squeezing.

Neuropathic Pain

Neuropathic pain results from injury to the peripheral or central nervous systems. Neuropathic pain may share similar descriptors as nociceptive pain but is also described as burning, shooting, tingling, stabbing, scalding, crawling, and painful numbness. It is also common to observe allodynia (pain from light touch or mild pressure) and hyperalgesia (abnormal sensitivity to sensory stimuli) with neuropathic pain. Examples of neuropathic syndromes include postherpetic neuralgia, phantom pain syndrome, and chemotherapy-induced peripheral neuropathy.

TREATMENT

The World Health Organization (WHO) WHO three-step ladder describes a standard approach to treating cancer pain (Fig 8-3). The WHO ladder describes three levels of patient-reported pain, which correspond to selection of analgesic type: nonsteroidal anti-inflammatory drugs and acetaminophen for mild pain, a combination of a weak opioid and acetaminophen or an nonsteroidal anti-inflammatory drug for moderate pain, and strong opioids for severe pain. This ladder also includes adjuvant therapies: nonopioid medications that enhance analgesia and minimize adverse effects. Adjuvant therapies can be used at each level and include anticonvulsants and antidepressants, especially when the patient is experiencing neuropathic pain.[14] The choice of agent depends on the clinician's experience, pharmacokinetics, route of delivery, availability, cost, as well as patient factors, such as age, renal function, comorbidities, and concomitant drugs. Generally, patients experiencing constant pain will receive a scheduled long-acting opioid. Alternatively, in resource-limited settings, a short-acting opioid can be dosed by its half-life (eg, every 4 hours for morphine) and achieve steady-state levels after four to five half-lives. If patients with cancer also experience breakthrough pain, short-acting opioids can be used concomitantly. Breakthrough doses can be safely dosed at a frequency based on the time to maximum concentration (ie, 1 hour for oral morphine; Table 8-3, Fig 8-4). Generally, the breakthrough dose is 10% to 20% of the total daily long-acting dose (except for methadone and short-acting fentanyl products).

RENAL AND HEPATIC CONSIDERATIONS

With careful monitoring and appropriate dosing, opioids are safe and effective in patients with cancer and renal or hepatic dysfunction. For most opioids, half-life of the active drug and its metabolites increase in renal dysfunction (Table 8-3). Therefore, opioid doses should be reduced, a longer interval between doses used, and creatinine clearance closely monitored. For example, morphine is metabolized in the liver to its active metabolites of morphine-3-glucuronide and morphine-6-glucuronide. If not recognized, morphine-6-glucuronide is more likely to accumulate and exacerbate adverse effects in patients with renal dysfunction and induce myoclonus or, rarely, seizures.[15,16] Therefore, in the setting of severe renal dysfunction, avoid morphine and codeine, use hydromorphone or oxycodone with caution and close monitoring, and preferentially use methadone and fentanyl.[17] Clinicians should use opioids cautiously in the setting of severe liver dysfunction, because opioids can contribute to sedation, constipation, and encephalopathy if inappropriately dosed or if responses are not carefully monitored. Because the clearance of opioids in patients with hepatic insufficiency is decreased, consider initial dose reductions and increased dosing intervals.[18] Again, because both fentanyl and methadone lack active metabolites, these drugs are the preferred agents in the setting of severe hepatic dysfunction (Table 8-3). However, if patients with cancer have mild or transient changes in their liver function, most opioids are safe and equally effective.

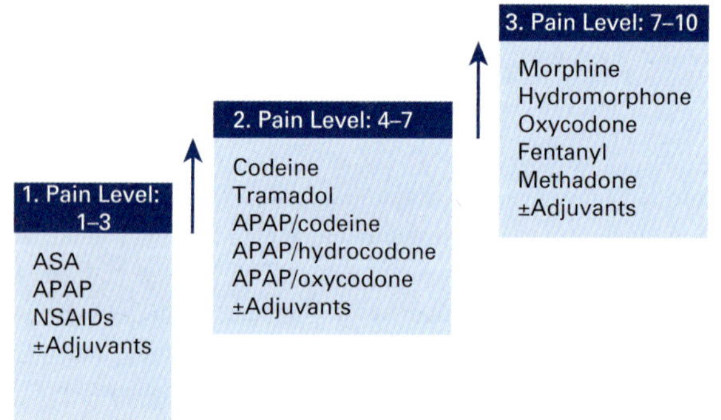

Fig. 8-3 WHO three-step ladder for pain management.[13]
ASA, aspirin; APAP, acetaminophen; NSAIDS, non-steroidal anti-inflammatories.

OPIOID TITRATION AND ROTATION

Unfortunately, the most effective and tolerable opioid for an individual patient cannot currently be predicted a Priority. In clinical practice, opioid selection usually depends on availability, cost, and prior patient experience. If a patient experiences an intolerable adverse effect from one opioid, it may require rotation to another opioid (Table 8-3). Of note, it is important to differentiate anticipated adverse effects from an opioid (eg, transient nausea, pruritus) versus true allergic reactions (eg, hives, shortness of breath). Avoid labeling anticipated adverse effects as true allergies, which occurs commonly, especially with morphine. Despite misconceptions of morphine, it continues to be the most studied, evidence-based, cost-efficient mainstay for the treatment of cancer pain. Equianalgesic tables and dosing charts are available (Table 8-3) to convert routes of administration or rotate opioids. These data were established in single-dose studies in healthy volunteers; consequently, these guidelines should be used with caution because they serve as rough approximations and do not replace clinical judgment.[19] The indications to rotate opioids may include poor analgesic efficacy, intolerable adverse effects, ineffective administration route, drug interactions, development of tolerance, and/or financial constraints. To initiate an opioid rotation, the clinician should convert the daily opioid consumption to an oral morphine equivalent (or morphine equivalent dose) using an equianalgesic table, which should be independently checked by a colleague and documented. Although opioid conversion calculators exist online, they should be used with caution and should never replace clinical judgement. When deciding on opioid rotations, carefully consider the patient's current pain control and account for incomplete cross-tolerance, which may require dose reductions of 30% to 50%. With regard to opioids, cross-tolerance refers to reduced reaction to an opioid with repeated use to a structurally similar drug; in contrast, incomplete cross-tolerance (or incomplete cross-reactivity) refers to a different level of tolerance to an opioid of a different class. During opioid rotations, careful monitoring is required, and liberal breakthrough or immediate-release opioids may be required during the transition. Methadone conversion should be completed with additional care because of its unique pharmacokinetic profile.

Table 8-3 Opioids, Active Metabolites, and Pharmacokinetics[19,22]

Opioid	Active metabolites	Half-Life (hours)	Morphine Equivalent
Morphine	Yes	3-4	1
Oxycodone	Yes	3-6	1-1.5
Hydrocodone	No	4-8	1
Hydromorphone	Yes	3-6	0.2
Fentanyl	No	1-2 (transmucosal) 48-72 (transdermal)	No available conversion 30 mg/d PO morphine → 12 μg/h transdermal fentanyl
Methadone	No	2-3 distribution phase 15-60 h elimination phase	a

NOTE. There is no clear consensus on opioid conversions; these serve as guidelines only.
Abbreviation: PO, by mouth.
[a]No standard conversion ratio exists for converting select opioids to methadone; these conversions should be supervised by a pain expert.

METHADONE

Previously considered as a late-line option for pain management, methadone is increasingly used as second- or even first-line treatment of cancer-related pain.[20] Methadone is a synthetic opioid with a chemical structure unrelated to opium derivatives. It is a unique opioid given its actions as a μ-agonist and *N*-methyl-*d*-aspartate (NMDA) receptor antagonist, making it particularly useful for the treatment of neuropathic cancer pain. Unlike other opioids, another advantage of using methadone is that there are no active metabolites, obviating dose adjustment in renal insufficiency.[21] However, methadone is a complicated drug requiring expert oversight in its prescribing and monitoring.

Methadone's complexity includes oral bioavailability ranging from 41% to 99% and a biphasic elimination—excretion occurring simultaneously with tissue distribution. A rapid and extensive distribution phase occurs at 2 to 3 hours and a slow elimination phase occurs at 15 to 60 hours (Table 8-3). In addition, methadone is extensively metabolized in the liver with major CYP3A4, CYP2B6, CYP2D6, and CYP2C19 interactions causing multiple drug-drug interactions. It is also associated with QTc prolongation, requiring careful monitoring while taking concomitant medications associated with QTc interval prolongation.[23,24] Last, equianalgesic dosing varies dramatically depending on the extent of the patient's previous exposure to opioids.[22] Multiple methods exist to convert other opioids to methadone but should only be considered under the guidance of a pain expert.[22,23,25]

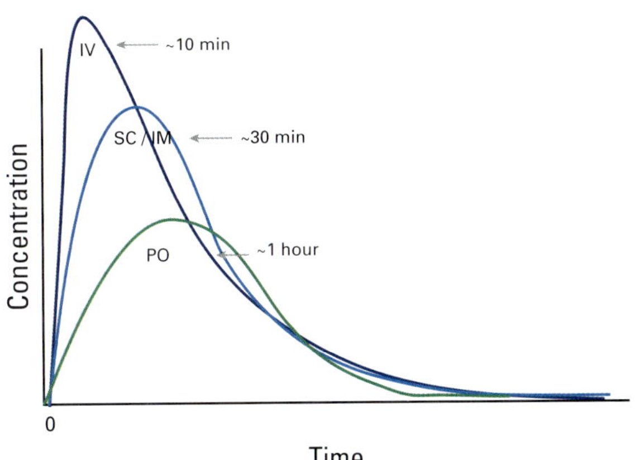

Fig. 8-4 Approximations of time to maximum concentration for short-acting opioids comparing intravenous (IV), subcutaneous (SC)/intramuscular (IM), and oral (PO) routes (does not apply to long-acting preparations or methadone).[250]

TRANSDERMAL OPIOIDS

Transdermal patches offer an alternative long-acting formulation for cancer-related pain control when oral administration of drugs is difficult or undesirable. By maintaining constant plasma drug levels, transdermal systems provide sustained pain relief and reportedly reduce the incidence of adverse effects.[26] Transdermal fentanyl is the most commonly used transdermal product. Given its lipophilicity, fentanyl can be delivered effectively through the skin with preparations lasting up to 72 hours.[27] Once a transdermal patch is applied, a subcutaneous drug reservoir develops over approximately 8 to 12 hours, which may be altered by degree of adiposity.[28] Therefore, dose escalation of transdermal products must be done with caution, and limited data exist regarding opioid rotation and equianalgesic dosing given incomplete cross-tolerance (eg, transdermal fentanyl to morphine).

MANAGING OPIOID ADVERSE EFFECTS

When prescribing opioids to patients with cancer, it is important to anticipate expected adverse effects and provide prophylaxis when appropriate. Common adverse effects include nausea, pruritus, sedation, and constipation (discussed in the next section). Importantly, anticipated adverse effects are not opioid allergies. All adverse effects associated with opioid use are transient except for opioid-induced constipation (OIC). Consequently, clinicians should consider appropriate education and prophylaxis in opioid-naïve patients to prevent attribution of expected adverse effects as allergies preventing their future use.

Opioid-induced nausea is best treated with antiemetics targeting dopaminergic receptors such as prochlorperazine or metoclopramide to avoid the serotonin 5-HT_3-receptor antagonist-associated constipation. Pruritus can be prevented and treated with the use of nonsedating antihistamines (eg, cetirizine). Avoid using diphenhydramine, given its additive sedation when given with opioids, especially in the acutely ill and older patient. Rather, consider a second-generation, nonsedating antihistamine such as cetirizine.

OPIOID-INDUCED CONSTIPATION

OIC is a particularly troublesome adverse effect that can lead to nausea, vomiting, anorexia, and even cessation of opioids. Opioids cause constipation by binding to μ receptors on enteric neurons, disrupting neural coordination necessary for peristalsis, which slows bowel motility. Consequently, the preferred treatment includes stimulant laxatives such as senna (1 to 8 tabs daily) or bisacodyl (5 to 10 mg twice daily). In fact, evidence demonstrates there was no added benefit of a softener with sennosides in the setting of OIC.[29] Prophylaxis should begin at the initiation of an opioid regimen. Constipation prophylaxis (Table 8-4) can be approached in a stepwise, additive fashion. Patients require education that fiber or other bulk-forming laxatives can worsen OIC in patients who are immobile and cannot maintain adequate hydration. The peripheral-acting μ-receptor antagonists (PAMORAs) are the newest class of constipation medications that block the peripheral effects of opioids on the gut. PAMORAs do not cross the blood-brain barrier and consequently do not reduce central analgesic effects. Methylnaltrexone was the first US Food and Drug Administration (FDA)-approved subcutaneous or intravenous injection to treat OIC. Response rates are approximately 48% in patients who had laxation within 4 hours after the first dose, compared with 15% when constipation was treated with placebo.[30] Methylnaltrexone, like other PAMORAs, should be considered a rescue medication after other measures have been ineffective, primarily because of its associated abdominal cramping, diarrhea, and cost. Additional PAMORAs include alvimopan, naloxegol, lubiprostone, and naldemedine but these agents have not been approved in the cancer setting.[31-34] There are no data on long-term, prophylactic use of PAMORAs.

OPIOID-INDUCED HYPERALGESIA

Opioid-induced hyperalgesia is a state of nociceptive sensitization caused by exposure to opioids causing a paradoxical response and exacerbation of pain. The type of pain experienced might be different or the same as the underlying pain. Opioid-induced hyperalgesia appears to be a distinct and definable phenomenon that may explain loss of opioid efficacy in some patients. Mechanisms involving the central glutaminergic system are considered the most likely cause of opioid-induced hyperalgesia, but the precise molecular mechanism is not yet understood. Opioid-induced hyperalgesia more commonly has been observed in patients receiving high opioid doses, rather than low or moderate doses. Clinicians should suspect opioid-induced hyperalgesia when escalating of opioid doses causes increased pain accompanied by tremulousness, confusion, or skin sensitivity in the absence of disease progression. Concerns about opioid-induced hyperalgesia should not be used to justify withholding or limiting opioid therapy. When suspected, it is reasonable to consider dose reduction, opioid rotation, or a nonopioid intervention.

OPIOID RISK MANAGEMENT

Over the past two decades, clinicians have witnessed a growing trend in the aberrant use of opioids. Clinicians should always advocate for ready access to opioids for legitimate medical purposes, especially in the setting of cancer-related pain.[35] However, clinicians must also be aware of the risk for opioid aberrancy by patients and caregivers.

Table 8-4 **Opioid-Induced Constipation Prophylaxis**

Prophylactic Intervention	Examples	Dose Ranges
Stimulant (± stool softener) laxative	Senna	8.6-68.8 mg/d in divided doses 2-3 times daily
	Bisacodyl	5-10 mg PO/PR once to twice daily
	± Docusate	± 100-500 mg/d in divided doses
Osmotic laxative	Polyethylene glycol	17 g in 4-6 oz fluid 1-3 times daily
	Lactulose	15-60 mL 2-3 times daily
	Sorbitol	30-150 mL once daily
	Magnesium hydroxide	15-30 mL 1-3 times daily
Prokinetic laxative	Metoclopramide[a] (preferred)	5-10 mg 3-4 times daily
	Erythromycin	125-250 mg 3-4 times daily

Abbreviations: PO, by mouth; PR, rectally.

[a]Dopamine receptor-2 antagonist with 5-HT_4 agonism causing stimulation of the foregut.

Addiction and Pseudoaddiction

First, clinicians must be very clear about the phenomena and terminology used to describe opioid aberrancy, because these terms continue to evolve and carry strong social meaning (Table 8-5).[36] When discussing these terms with colleagues, patients, or caregivers, it is important to ensure everyone shares the same understanding. Of all these definitions, it is most important for clinicians to consider the difference between addiction and pseudoaddiction. Addiction is a primary, chronic, and neurobiological disease with manifestations influenced by genetic, psychosocial, and environmental factors characterized by behaviors including impaired control over drug use, compulsive use, continued use despite harm, and craving.[36]

The most accepted risk factors for opioid aberrancy include a personal history of alcoholism or drug abuse, a family history of alcoholism or drug abuse, and major psychiatric disorder.[41] The need to prescribe opioids to patients who have a history of drug abuse or other predisposing factors to addiction is relatively common, even in patients with cancer.[37] In contrast, pseudoaddiction is aberrant drug-seeking behavior that occurs in the setting of unrelieved pain. Pseudoaddiction must be considered and/or ruled out when treating a patient with drug-seeking behaviors.[38] Importantly, pseudoaddiction and addiction can coexist, and the possibility of the pseudoaddiction should not undermine the diagnosis and management of addiction.

Universal Precautions

Clinicians also must acknowledge the serious nature of drug abuse and addiction, and the obligation to minimize these outcomes when possible. A balanced approach by prescribing clinicians includes universal precautions. Universal precautions describe an opioid-prescribing practice referring to a routine clinical approach in which all patients are assessed for history or risk of opioid misuse, regardless of demographic, social, or disease-related variables (Table 8-6). Most of the data to support universal precautions in opioid prescribing originate from the noncancer pain literature and in cancer survivorship; nevertheless, this approach has clear applications in the cancer setting.[42,43] Instituting universal precautions in a clinical practice requires outlining opioid-prescribing procedures and obtaining support from institutional leadership and colleagues. Once an opioid-prescribing procedure is outlined, it must be routinely completed at the initiation of opioids for all patients. Consider the following approaches as part of universal precautions: prescription drug–monitoring program (PDMP) reports, electronic prescribing, pain contracts or agreements, opioid-aberrancy risk assessment, urine drug screens, safe storage, and disposal.

Prescription-Drug Monitoring Plans

Nearly all states now provide PDMPs, which digitally store controlled-substance dispensing information and make these data accessible to prescribers and pharmacies. In fact, some states now require that clinicians document that they have reviewed an online PDMP report before prescribing opioids.[44] The PDMP is an important tool to review current opioids, doses, and the number of prescribing clinicians. Electronic prescribing of opioids is now available in many states,

Table 8-5 Opioid Aberrancy Terminology.[36-40,256,257]

Term	Definition
Aberrant	Departing from the accepting standard drug-taking behaviors
Abuse	A maladaptive pattern of a prescription opioid use leading to clinically significant impairment and/or distress
Addiction	A primary, chronic, and neurobiological disease with manifestations influenced by genetic, psychosocial, and environmental factors and characterized by behaviors including impaired control over drug use, compulsive use, continued use despite harm, and craving
Chemical coping	Behaviors focused on obtaining opioids to relieve psychosocial distress rather than pain
Dependence	A state of adaptation indicated by a medication class–specific withdrawal syndrome that can be produced by abrupt cessation, rapid dosage reduction, decreasing blood level of the drug, or administration of an antagonist
Misuse	The inappropriate use of a prescription opioid agent, intentionally or unintentionally, and regardless of motivation
Pseudoaddiction	An iatrogenic syndrome with behaviors that mimic addiction and are driven by unrelieved pain
Substance abuse	Use of a substance in a manner outside of sociocultural conventions
Tolerance	Diminution of one or more drug effects caused by exposure to the drug that may require higher doses for effect
Withdrawal	An uncomfortable but not life-threatening reaction that occurs after the abrupt cessation of opioids and/or use of naloxone; characterized by the presence of one or more of a variable group of symptoms and signs, including tremulousness, anxiety, insomnia, tachycardia, tachypnea, hypertension, nausea and vomiting, diarrhea, piloerection, and sweating

Table 8-6 Universal Precautions in Opioid Prescribing

Universal Precautions in Opioid Prescribing
Prescription Drug Monitoring Program Report
Opioid aberrancy risk assessment
Opioid agreements (or contracts)
Electronic opioid prescribing
Clear documentation in the medical record
Clinically indicated urine drug screens
Pill counts
Consideration of more frequent appointments
Consideration of excess opioid disposal
Consideration of emergency naloxone

avoiding the need to provide a written controlled prescription. Written prescriptions contain the prescribing clinician's state license and drug enforcement agency license number, which can be fraudulently used to obtain opioids. Written prescriptions are also commonly lost or stolen and require patients and/or caregivers to obtain new prescriptions. In patients at high risk for drug aberrancy, electronic prescribing allows clinicians to provide smaller quantities of opioids at more frequent intervals without the obstacle of traveling to obtain written prescriptions. Institutions using electronic prescribing require a two-factor identification authentication (eg, electronic medical record password and text message confirmation) for opioid prescribing. Overall, this provides a convenient, safe, and patient-centered approach to prescribing opioids and has become the new standard in opioid prescribing.[45]

Pain Agreements

Clinicians should also consider the routine use of a pain agreements (or contracts) with patients receiving opioids. The primary aim of opioid agreements is to clearly communicate and document expectations of both prescribing clinicians and patients.[46] Clinician expectations should outline the clinical team members, hours of operation, policies on lost or stolen medication, and clearly state that opioids cannot be prescribed if not used for their intended medical purpose. Patient expectations may include clarity regarding participation at scheduled appointments and referrals, consenting to tests such as pill counts and urine drug screen, abstinence from alcohol and/or other illicit drugs, and opioid consumption limited to the patient. Published guidelines recommend written opioid agreements or contracts for all patients initiating therapy or for patients at higher risk for aberrant drug-related behaviors.[39]

Assessment of Opioid Aberrancy Risk

Assessment of opioid aberrancy risk is also a key strategy. Clinicians may consider risk stratification using validated assessment questionnaires, including the Opioid Risk Tool,[47-49] Screener and Opioid Assessment Measure for Patients with Pain – Revised,[50,51] CAGE Adapted to Include Drugs,[40,52] and Current Opioid Misuse Measure.[50,53,54]

Risk stratification allows clinicians to assess the risk of future aberrant behaviors and tailor clinical practice on the basis of this assessment. Patients are at higher risk of opioid aberrancy if they have a personal history of alcohol or drug abuse, family history of alcohol or drug abuse, and/or major psychiatric disorder. Other factors that suggest increased risk include current heavy smoking, younger age, history of driving automobile accidents, chronic unemployment, limited support system, and/or cancer associated with heavy alcohol use or smoking. On the basis of assessed risk for aberrancy, clinicians can modify opioid quantities, clinic assessment intervals, and the use of urine drug screens. Urine drug screens may be considered at the initiation and periodically throughout opioid therapy to enhance objective data regarding the patient's behaviors. However, before ordering a urine drug screen, it is imperative to understand the methodologic practices of testing (eg, immunoassays, gas chromatography–mass spectrometry) at each institution, including limitations such as false-positive and false-negative rates. Before ordering a drug screen, consider how this will change the clinical management of the patient.[55]

NASAL NALOXONE

There is an increasing number of community-based opioid-overdose prevention programs providing naloxone.[56] For patients at high risk for opioid overdose or with a personal history of overdose, intranasal naloxone is an emergency intervention that can save lives. However, clinicians must educate opioid users and caregivers that intranasal naloxone is effective for only 30 to 90 minutes. When patients have consumed long-acting opioids, a single dose of naloxone will not suffice and the patient requires immediate medical care.

Proper Opioid Storage and Disposal

Last, opioid storage and disposal should be clearly discussed. Patients and caregivers require education regarding the risks of improperly stored opioids leading to diversion or accidental poisoning. Patients and caregivers should remove expired or unused medicines from their home when no longer needed, using periodic opioid take-back events or at permanent collection sites.[57] Opioid disposal is another option, but national agencies have not issued uniform guidelines regarding the safe, effective, convenient, and environmentally friendly disposal of opioids. Clinicians should ask their local institution, pharmacy, and/or government regarding best practices.

In summary, clinicians must ensure access to opioids for patients with cancer while practicing universal precautions to maximize patient and caregiver safety. Consider consultation with a specialist in pain and/or addiction medicine or with a psychologist when necessary, depending on the experience and expertise of the clinician and the complexity of the presenting problem.

KEY POINTS

- Morphine is the most studied, evidence-based, cost-efficient mainstay for the treatment of cancer pain.
- Methadone is a μ-agonist and NMDA receptor antagonist effective at treating neuropathic pain but is a very complex drug requiring expert oversight in its prescribing and monitoring.
- Avoid attributing anticipated and transient opioid-associated adverse effects (eg, nausea, pruritis) as true allergies (eg, hives, shortness of breath).
- When prescribing opioids to patients with cancer, it is important to anticipate expected adverse effects and prophylaxis when appropriate.
- Stimulant laxatives (eg, senna, bisacodyl), not stool softeners, are the most effective preventive and treatment approach to opioid-induced constipation.
- Methadone and fentanyl are the preferred opioids in the setting of renal failure.
- Oncologists must be clear about the phenomena and terminology we use to describe opioid aberrancy.
- Universal precautions describe an opioid-prescribing practice referring to a routine clinical approach in which all patients are assessed for history or risk of opioid misuse, regardless of demographic, social, or disease-related variables.

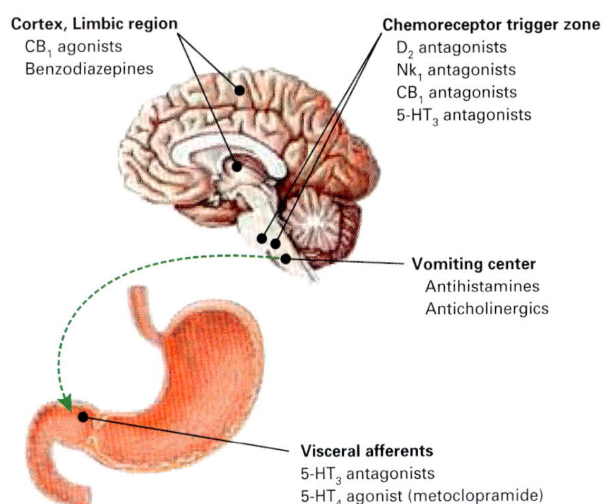

Fig. 8-5 Pathophysiology of nausea and vomiting.[251]

5-HT_3, serotonin receptor 3; 5-HT_4, serotonin receptor 4; CB_1, cannabinoid 1; D_2, dopamine receptor 2; NK-1, neurokinin-1.

Permission to reuse given by Dr. Eric Roeland.

NAUSEA AND VOMITING

Nausea and vomiting are primary concerns for patients undergoing cancer treatment that may greatly reduce a patient's QOL and affect adherence to therapy.[58] Nausea is the unpleasant sensation of the need to vomit, associated with autonomic symptoms, including cold sweats, tachycardia, diarrhea, and pallor. In contrast, vomiting is the involuntary, physical expulsion of stomach contents. Poorly controlled nausea can lead to weight loss and protracted vomiting can lead to dehydration, acute kidney injury, electrolyte imbalances, and even early discontinuation of chemotherapy. The etiology of nausea and vomiting may differ based on the patient's disease and treatment, so an accurate evaluation is crucial for treating the underlying cause. In addition to conducting a thorough history, examination, and review of medications, treating nausea requires an understanding of its pathophysiology.

PATHOPHYSIOLOGY

Two anatomic locations are primarily involved in nausea and vomiting: the brain and the GI tract. The brain has approximately five areas that modulate the perception of nausea: the cortex, fourth ventricle (chemoreceptor trigger zone), brainstem, medulla (vomiting center), and vestibular apparatus.[59] The emetic response can be conceptualized as a brainstem-based reflex arc (Fig 8-5). Identification and blockade of these key neurotransmitter receptors have been the major strategy for the development of effective antiemetic agents (Table 8-7). In cancer, nausea can be caused by increased intracranial pressure in the cortex or the medulla secondary to vascular lesions, neoplasm, inflammation, medications, toxins, electrolyte disturbances, infection, motion, or benign positional vertigo. In the GI tract, obstruction, motility disorders, gastropathy, infection, and constipation may be the cause of nausea. When constipation is the etiology of nausea, aggressive use of laxatives is indicated to relieve both symptoms. In the setting of bowel distension, chemotherapy, or radiation therapy, the enterochromaffin cells of the GI tract stimulate emesis via the release of serotonin and vagus nerve stimulation.

CHEMOTHERAPY-INDUCED NAUSEA AND VOMITING RISK FACTORS

The risk of chemotherapy-induced nausea and vomiting (CINV) is primarily due to the emetic risk of the chemotherapeutic agent. Chemotherapy is divided into four emetic risk categories: highly emetogenic chemotherapy (HEC; > 90% risk), moderate emetogenic chemotherapy (MEC; > 30% to 90% risk), low emetogenic chemotherapy (10% to 30% risk), and minimal emetogenic chemotherapy < 10% risk.

On the basis of risk category, patients should receive evidence-based CINV prophylaxis (Table 8-8). Individual risk factors that also increase the risk for nausea and vomiting include prior CINV, female sex, age < 50 years, low alcohol intake, history of motion sickness, expectation to experience nausea and vomiting, and history of hyperemesis gravidarum.[59-62] Notably, patients who experience CINV during their first cycle of chemotherapy are up to five times more likely to experience nausea in subsequent cycles.[62] When patients have at least one of these risk factors, aggressive antiemetic use, especially before the first cycle of chemotherapy, is indicated.

TABLE 8-7. **Selection of Antiemetics Based on Neurotransmitters Involved**[251]

Anatomic Location	Neurotransmitter Involved	Drug Class	Dose Range
Cortex	Unclear	Dexamethasone	2-8 mg/d in divided doses, morning and early afternoon
		Lorazepam	0.5-1 mg 3-4 times daily
		Cannabinoids	–
Chemoreceptor trigger zone	Dopamine	Haloperidol	0.5-1 mg 2-3 times daily
		Metoclopramide	2.5-10 mg 3-4 times daily
		Prochlorperazine	5-10 mg 3-4 times daily
	Serotonin	Ondansetron	4-8 mg 2-3 times daily
		Oral granisetron	1-2 mg 2-3 times daily
		Transdermal granisetron	1 patch daily
Vomiting center/vestibular apparatus	Histamine	Cetirizine (preferred)	5-10 mg daily (second generation)
		Diphenhydramine	12.5-50 mg 1-2 times daily
		Meclizine	25-50 mg 1-2 times daily
		Hydroxyzine	25-100 mg 1-3 times daily
	Acetylcholine	Scopolamine	1 patch (1 mg) every 3 days

TYPES OF CINV

There are five different types of nausea and vomiting related to chemotherapy: acute, delayed, breakthrough, anticipatory, and chronic (refractory). Acute nausea and vomiting induced by chemotherapy has been defined as that which occurs within the first 24 hours after administration of a chemotherapy agent. Conversely, delayed nausea and vomiting occurs 2 to 5 days after the administration of chemotherapy. This delayed emesis is often of lesser intensity and occurs in fewer patients, but it can last longer than acute emesis. The antiemetic agents that are effective for managing delayed vomiting differ from those that are effective for managing acute vomiting; this suggests that different neurotransmitter mechanisms—if not different physical sites—are involved in these two forms of emesis. Delayed nausea and vomiting remain a challenge to manage even with currently available antiemetics.

Breakthrough nausea and vomiting occur despite receiving guideline-based antiemetic prophylaxis. To treat breakthrough nausea, medications can be used that ideally have unique mechanisms of action compared with the antiemetic prophylaxis (eg, dopamine receptor-2 blocker) (Table 8-7). Anticipatory nausea is a conditioned reflex that can be established rapidly by poor antiemetic protection during an earlier course of chemotherapy. It can be triggered by numerous stimuli associated with chemotherapy and can occur at any time.

Chronic nausea and/or vomiting occurs greater than 120 hours after receiving chemotherapy and is an area of increased research.[63] Nonpharmacologic measures and benzodiazepines are used to treat the subsequent anxiety and can decrease the feeling of nausea.[64]

CINV PROPHYLAXIS

Evidence-based CINV prophylaxis guidelines exist and adherence greatly improves patient-centered outcomes.[60,65,66] One effective method to ensure adherence to antiemetic guidelines is to have guideline-based antiemetics ordering as part of all chemotherapy regimen plans.[67] In 2017, ASCO convened a multidisciplinary panel to update the guidelines for antiemesis.[60] HEC prophylaxis includes a neurokinin-1 receptor antagonist, serotonin-receptor (5-HT_3) antagonist, dexamethasone, and olanzapine.[68] Notably, carboplatin area under the curve ≥ 4 mg/mL/min has been reclassified as HEC per antiemetic guidelines. Patients who receive carboplatin area under the curve ≥ 4 mg/mL/min should also receive an NK-1 recepator antagonoist. MEC requires a serotonin-receptor antagonist and dexamethasone. Low-emetogenic chemotherapy requires a single dose of a serotonin-receptor antagonist or dexamethasone.[60]

OLANZAPINE

Oncologists must be aware of olanzapine, a new, evidence-based medication to prevent and treat nausea and vomiting. Olanzapine is an atypical antipsychotic indicated for the treatment of schizophrenia and bipolar disorder. Adverse effects with longterm use include weight gain, somnolence, dyslipidemia, and hyperglycemia.[69] Low-dose olanzapine has been investigated in the CINV prophylaxis setting, given its association of multiple dopamine and serotonin receptors (ie, D_2, 5-HT_{2A}, 5-HT_{2C}, and 5-HT_3) associated with nausea and vomiting.[68,70,71] In a population of patients with cancer receiving highly emetogenic chemotherapy, 10 mg of olanzapine for 4 days plus standard guideline-based prophylaxis antiemetic medications significantly improved CINV (37% *v* 22%; $P = .002$).[68] Taking olanzapine may cause sedation, but the

Table 8-8 **Abbreviated ASCO Antiemetic Guideline: Antiemetic Dosing for Adults by Chemotherapy Risk Category**[60]	
Emetic Risk Category	**Route and Duration**
High: Cisplatin, carboplatin, and other agents	
NK_1 receptor antagonist	
Aprepitant	PO; 3 days
Fosaprepitant	IV
Netupitant-palonosetron	PO
Rolapitant	PO
$5\text{-}HT_3$-receptor antagonist[a]	
Granisetron	PO, IV, SQ
Ondansetron	PO
Palonosetron	PO, IV
Dolasetron	PO
Dexamethasone	
If aprepitant is used[b]	PO, IV; 4 days
If fosaprepitant is used[b]	PO, IV; 4 days
If netupitant-palonosetron is used[b]	PO, IV; 4 days
If rolapitant is used	PO, IV; 4 days
Olanzapine	PO; 4 days
High: Anthracycline combined with cyclophosphamide[c]	
NK_1 receptor antagonist	
Aprepitant	PO; 3 days
Fosaprepitant	IV
Netupitant-palonosetron	PO
Rolapitant	PO
$5\text{-}HT_3$-receptor antagonist[a]	
Granisetron	PO, IV, SQ
Ondansetron	PO, IV
Palonosetron	PO, IV
Dolasetron	PO
Dexamethasone	
If aprepitant is used[b]	PO, IV
If fosaprepitant is used[b]	PO, IV
If netupitant-palonosetron is used[b]	PO, IV
If rolapitant is used	PO, IV
Olanzapine	PO; 4 days
Moderate[c]	
$5\text{-}HT_3$-receptor antagonist	

Table 8-8 **continued**	
Emetic Risk Category	**Route and Duration**
Granisetron	PO, IV, SQ
Ondansetron	PO twice daily, IV
Palonosetron	PO, IV
Dolasetron	PO
Tropisetron	PO, IV
Dexamethasone	PO, IV; 3 days
Low[d]	
$5\text{-}HT_3$-receptor antagonist	
Granisetron	PO, IV, SQ
Ondansetron	PO, IV
Palonosetron	PO, IV
Dolasetron	PO
Tropisetron	PO, IV
Dexamethasone	PO, IV

NOTE. For patients who receive multiday chemotherapy, clinicians must first determine the emetic risk of the agent(s) included in the regimen. Patients should receive the agent of the highest therapeutic index daily during chemotherapy and for 2 days thereafter. In addition, individual patient risk factors and prior experiences with chemotherapy-induced nausea and vomiting must be considered. Patients can also be offered the granisetron transdermal patch or granisetron extended-release injection, which deliver therapy over multiple days rather than taking a $5\text{-}HT_3$-receptor antagonist daily.

Abbreviations: $5\text{-}HT_3$, 5-hydroxytryptamine-3; IV, intravenous; NK-1, neurokinin 1; PO, by mouth; SQ, subcutaneously.

[a]If netupitant-palonosetron is used, no additional $5\text{-}HT_3$-receptor antagonist is needed.

[b]The dexamethasone dose is for patients who are receiving the recommended four-drug regimen for highly emetic chemotherapy. If patients do not receive an NK-1-receptor antagonist, the dexamethasone dose should be adjusted to 20 mg on day 1 and to 16 mg on days 2-4.

[c]In non-breast cancer populations (eg, non-Hodgkin lymphoma) receiving a combination of an anthracycline and cyclophosphamide with treatment regimens incorporating corticosteroids, the addition of palonosetron without the use of an NK-1-receptor antagonist, and olanzapine is an option.

[d]If carboplatin area under the curve is ≥ 4 mg/mL/min, add an NK-1-receptor antagonist to the $5\text{-}HT_3$-receptor antagonist and dexamethasone. Dexamethasone dosing is day 1 only: 20 mg with rolapitant, and 12 mg with aprepitant, fosaprepitant, or netupitant-palonosetron.

[e]Patients who are treated with low-emetic-risk antineoplastic therapy should be offered a $5\text{-}HT_3$-receptor antagonist or dexamethasone.

Adapted from Hesketh et al.[5]

medication is well tolerated overall.[68] Furthermore, olanzapine has shown improved efficacy over metoclopramide in the treatment of breakthrough nausea and vomiting.[72]

RADIATION-INDUCED NAUSEA AND VOMITING

As with chemotherapy, radiation can cause nausea and vomiting. Determinants of risk include the treatment field, dose of radiation, and pattern of fractionation.[73] Approximately 50% to 80% of patients undergoing radiotherapy will experience nausea and vomiting if no appropriate prophylaxis is applied.[74] Guidelines state that total-body irradiation is associated with the highest risk (> 90%) and radiation to the upper abdomen is associated with moderate risk (30% to 90%) of nausea and vomiting.[66,75] Results of a meta-analysis suggest 5-HT_3–receptor antagonists are the preferred prophylaxis for radiation-induced nausea and vomiting.[76] For those treated with highly emetogenic radiation therapy, a 5-HT_3–receptor antagonist and dexamethasone are recommended. A 5-HT_3–receptor antagonist before each fraction is also recommended before moderately emetogenic radiation therapy, and a 5-day course of dexamethasone is optional. For patients who receive combination chemotherapy and radiotherapy, antiemetic therapy is dictated by the emetogenicity of the chemotherapy, unless the emetic risk of radiation therapy is higher.[60]

KEY POINTS

- Five types of CINV: acute, delayed, breakthrough, anticipatory, and chronic.
- Chemotherapy is classified into four emetic-risk categories: HEC (> 90% risk), MEC (30% to 90% risk), low emetogenic chemotherapy (10% to 30% risk), and minimal.
- Prevention of CINV is key because patients who experience CINV during the first cycle of chemotherapy are up to five times more likely to experience CINV in subsequent cycles.
- Individual risk factors may place patients at higher risk for CINV.
- Olanzapine significantly reduces nausea and emesis in HEC regimens when combined with NK-1 receptor antagonists, 5-HT_3–receptor antagonists, and dexamethasone.
- 5-HT_3–receptor antagonists are the preferred prophylaxis for radiation-induced nausea and vomiting.

CANCER-RELATED FATIGUE

Cancer-related fatigue is a multifactorial symptom defined as a distressing, persistent, subjective sense of physical, emotional, and/or cognitive exhaustion related to cancer or cancer-related treatment.[77] Cancer-related fatigue results in decreased capacity for physical or mental activity and has been reported in up to 80% of patients receiving chemotherapy and/or radiotherapy.[78] Fatigue affects QOL by interfering with a patient's ability to participate in their roles and meaningful activities. The causes of cancer-related fatigue are multifactorial and an in-depth assessment should first focus on identifying possible reversible underlying causes (eg, hypothyroidism, anemia). Contributing factors to fatigue may include adverse effects from medications and treatments, metabolic derangements (eg, hypothyroidism, adrenal insufficiency, hypercalcemia, hypogonadism), poorly managed pain, depression, sleeping disturbances, and deconditioning. Identification and treatment of fatigue might include referral to appropriate specialties such as endocrinology, psychiatry, and/or palliative care.

Nonpharmacologic interventions to treat cancer-related fatigue include energy conservation and cognitive therapies.[79] In addition to treating the underlying contributing factors, nonpharmacologic and pharmacologic interventions have been identified for treating cancer-related fatigue. A meta-analysis demonstrated that nonpharmacologic interventions including exercise and psychological interventions improve fatigue, whereas pharmacologic interventions did not.[80] Cancer-related fatigue is unlikely to respond to increased rest; in contrast, increased measured activity may be of benefit for select patients.[77] Therefore, patients should be encouraged to engage in moderate-level activity as tolerated. In addition, national guidelines recommend educating patients about strategies to promote energy conservation, including prioritizing activities and distraction.[81] Patients are encouraged to set realistic expectations, pace activities, and delegate less essential activities. Behavioral interventions such as cognitive therapy, counseling, relaxation techniques, hypnosis, yoga, and biofeedback also provide benefit, as does social support.[82]

There has been less support for various pharmacologic interventions for cancer-related fatigue. The most widely used pharmacologic management has been psychostimulants (ie, methylphenidate, modafinil), ginseng, and corticosteroids.[83] However, results of the most recent phase III randomized, placebo-controlled trials do not support the use of psychostimulants to treat cancer-related fatigue. Methylphenidate and modafinil demonstrated no benefit over placebo[84,85] except in one study that showed improvement in fatigue with high rate of adverse events leading to discontinuation.[86] In addition, another randomized trial showed mild improvement for patients with severe cancer-related fatigue.[87] American ginseng (*Panax quinquefolius*) has also been evaluated to treat cancer-related fatigue. In a phase III study, 8 weeks of treatment with American ginseng improved fatigue compared with placebo, especially for patients receiving cancer-directed therapies.[88] Last, corticosteroids may show immediate benefit for mood and energy, but the duration of benefit is usually weeks and patients experience well-known associated adverse effects. Furthermore, the use of corticosteroids may be limited in patients receiving immunotherapy.

KEY POINTS

- Cancer fatigue is common and often multifactorial.
- Patients with cancer-related fatigue should be evaluated and treated for coexisting conditions, such as depression, anemia, thyroid dysfunction, and electrolyte disorders.
- In patients with cancer fatigue, exercise during and after therapy appears to improve fatigue.
- Phase III studies do not support the use of psychostimulants to treat cancer-related fatigue.

ANOREXIA AND CACHEXIA

Anorexia describes a loss of appetite and/or an aversion to food. The potential causes of anorexia include constipation, emesis, mucositis, depression, decreased gastric emptying, dysphagia, food aversions, and fat malabsorption. One of the challenges in the clinical assessment of patients with anorexia is to characterize all the different contributors to develop a focused treatment approach. The intensity of symptoms of anorexia varies among patients. The lack of eating is often a bigger problem for the caregivers than for the patient, because the patient may not be bothered by a lack of appetite. When patients abstain from eating, the caregivers lose a chance to nurture their loved ones and this can cause distress. Teaching caregivers to substitute other nurturing activities (eg, help with bathing, massage) may help redirect their concerns about the patient's lack of appetite. A referral to a registered dietitian can also provide key advice and strategies to maximize caloric intake and minimize conflict between patient and caregiver. Clinicians must educate caregivers, given the distress witnessing anorexia, weight loss, weakness, and decreased QOL it causes.

In contrast, cachexia is a multifactorial syndrome of irreversible loss of skeletal muscle mass resulting in functional impairment and poor QOL.[89] According to international guidelines, cachexia can be categorized into three phases: precachexia, cachexia, and refractory cachexia (Fig 8-6).[90] Multiple factors contribute to cachexia including metabolic dysregulation, increased fat and protein breakdown, decreased nutrient intake, and neurohormonal dysregulation of compensatory feeding stimuli. Consequently, these factors result in an energy imbalance and loss of skeletal muscle mass.[90-92] Cancer cachexia is associated with increased toxicity to cancer treatment and predicts poor survival.[93-95] For example, in a large, population-based data set, the degree of weight loss and change in body mass index predicted a limited survival from 20.9 months to 4.3 months.[95]

NONPHARMACOLOGIC APPROACHES

Nonpharmacologic approaches to cancer cachexia include diet and physical activity. However, data evaluating oral nutritional interventions show minimal impact on weight gain, energy or food intake, QOL, or mortality.[96] Enteral nutrition, usually through a gastrostomy or jejunostomy tube, may be considered when food intake is inadequate but the GI tract is functionally intact. This technique often is used for patients with upper aerodigestive tract cancers or for those patients who may have temporary disruption of eating and swallowing while undergoing radiation therapy. The major serious complication associated with enteral nutrition is aspiration, which increases for patients with delayed gastric emptying and advanced age.[97,98] Other adverse effects associated with enteral nutrition include diarrhea, nausea and/or vomiting, abdominal cramping, bloating, and distention.

Conversely, parenteral nutrition is a hyperosmolar, calorie-dense nutrition given via a central catheter. In general, when parenteral nutrition must be used in the preoperative setting of potentially resectable obstructing tumors to periods, it should be limited to < 10 days. Risks of parenteral nutrition are primarily infectious (eg, catheter-associated sepsis, bacteremia) and metabolic (eg, hyperglycemia, electrolyte abnormalities, abnormalities in liver enzymes, essential fatty acid deficiency, hypertriglyceridemia). Overall, studies demonstrate a net harm when providing parenteral nutrition to patients with cancer.[99] Interestingly, evidence also suggests a decreased tumor response to chemotherapy when patients receive parenteral nutrition.[99]

If nutritional support is required, enteral nutrition offers several advantages compared with parenteral nutrition, including fewer risks and complications, delivery of nutrients in a physiologic manner, convenience for home use, and decreased cost. Similarly, limited evidence exists to determine the impact of physical activity on cancer cachexia in adults.[100] Nevertheless, given that there is no evidence of overt harm associated with a well-balanced, high-caloric diet, and physical activity, the inclusion of nutritional and exercise interventions seems appropriate and should be encouraged.[89]

PHARMACOLOGIC APPROACHES

Pharmacologic options evaluated for treating cachexia include megestrol acetate, dronabinol, mirtazapine, cyproheptadine, and dexamethasone. Megestrol acetate and dronabinol are FDA approved for the treatment of anorexia, cachexia, or

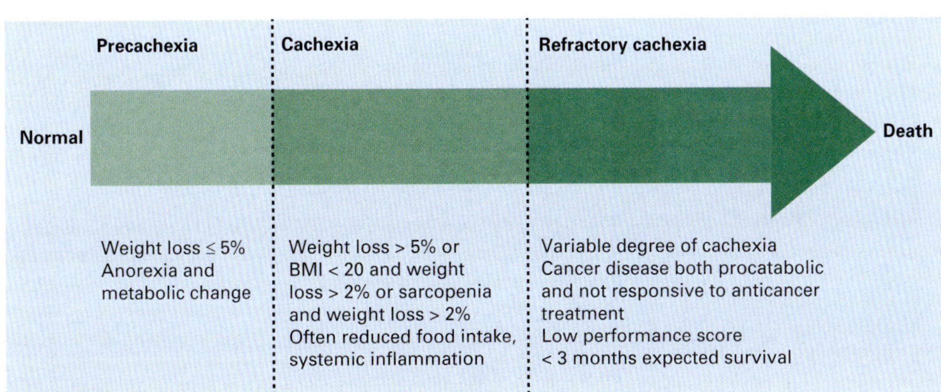

Fig. 8-6 Stages of cachexia: precachexia, cachexia, and refractory cachexia.[90]

Body mass index (BMI) is calculated as kg/m^2.

unexplained weight loss in patients with acquired immunodeficiency syndrome(AIDS)—not cancer. Their use in cancer is off label and frequently requires a prior authorization from insurance. There are also limitations to the use of each of these agents. Megestrol acetate, a synthetic derivative of the naturally occurring steroid hormone progesterone, provides benefits for appetite, caloric intake, and weight gain that appear to plateau at 800 mg.[101, 102] However, the weight gained with the use of megestrol is predominantly adipose tissue, not skeletal muscle. In addition, studies demonstrate that megestrol has no effect on either survival or QOL and can cause diarrhea, rash, edema, thromboembolic events, impotence, and adrenal insufficiency.[103,104] Similarly, dronabinol should be used with caution because it is associated with multiple adverse effects, including drowsiness, dizziness, dysphoria, euphoria, and impaired cognition placing patients with cancer at high risk of falls.[105] Like megestrol acetate, dronabinol primarily increases adipose tissue and/or body fluid and not from lean muscle mass.[106,107]

Other studies include a small, phase II, single-institution study of the antidepressant mirtazapine in treating cancer cachexia, which demonstrated one-quarter of patients experienced weight gain at 4 weeks.[108] In addition, one small study supported the use of olanzapine in combination with megestrol acetate, with results showing increased weight gain at 8 weeks.[109] Yet, the use of mirtazapine and olanzapine to treat cancer cachexia requires additional evaluation in larger, multisite trials.

Cyproheptadine is a serotonin antagonist that has been used as appetite stimulant for patients with cancer. However, in a large, randomized, controlled study of oral cyproheptadine 8 mg three times daily, only a mild increase in appetite and food intake occurred and the regimen had no effect on progressive weight loss.[110] As a result of its adverse effects (notably sedation) and limited efficacy, cyproheptadine is not recommended for patients with cancer-related cachexia.

Last, dexamethasone may transiently improve anorexia, but does not improve skeletal muscle mass. The adverse effects of corticosteroids are many, are associated with duration and cumulative dose, and include Cushing syndrome, hyperglycemia, adrenal insufficiency, myopathy, infection risk, and osteoporosis.[111] Multiple novel agents have been investigated to treat cancer cachexia, but there have been no FDA-approved agents to date.[91]

FAT MALABSORPTION

Fat malabsorption may occur in multiple cancer settings, including pancreatic cancer and exocrine insufficiency, gastric resection, hematopoietic stem cell transplantation, short-bowel syndrome, or chronic radiation enteritis.[112-116] Fat malabsorption is characterized by vague abdominal pain, increased gas, steatorrhea, and increased stool odor.

Exogenous pancreatic enzymes can minimize fat malabsorption. The pancreatic enzymes are enteric-coated to resist destruction or inactivation in gastric acid and to release the enzymes in vivo in the duodenum at pH > 5.5. In the duodenum and proximal small intestine, these exogenous enzymes replace physiologic digestive enzymes secreted by the pancreas, catalyzing the hydrolysis of fats to monoglycerol and fatty acids, protein into peptides and amino acids, and starch into dextrans and short-chain sugars. Pancreatic enzymes should be taken with food, initiated at the lowest recommended dose, and gradually increased on the basis of clinical symptoms, degree of steatorrhea, and fat content of the diet. For adults, initially start at 500 lipase units/kg per meal and titrate to a maximum of 2,500 units/kg per meal. Half of the prescribed dose should be given with snacks between meals.[117]

KEY POINTS

- Categories of cachexia include precachexia, cachexia, and refractory cachexia.
- Cachexia is associated with increased treatment-related toxicity and poor survival.
- Overall, studies demonstrate a net harm when providing parenteral nutrition to patients with cancer.
- There are no FDA-approved pharmacologic treatments for weight loss associated with cancer cachexia.
- The weight gain associated with the use of megestrol acetate, dronabinol, and dexamethasone is primarily adipose tissue and fluid, not skeletal muscle.
- Deep vein thrombosis and adrenal suppression are two notable adverse effects of megestrol acetate.
- Clinicians must educate caregivers regarding cachexia, given the distress it causes caregivers witnessing the patient's anorexia, weight loss, weakness, and decreased QOL.

DELIRIUM

Delirium is a global brain dysfunction presenting with alterations in the state of consciousness and cognition.[118] Symptoms develop acutely over hours or days and may fluctuate over the course of the day, often with deterioration in the night. In contrast to the symptoms of dementia, which develop over months to years, the hallmark diagnostic characteristic of delirium is the rapid onset of symptoms. Primary symptoms include disordered consciousness and reduced ability to focus, shift, or sustain attention. Patients often have difficulties with memory, orientation, and language skills.[119] Delirium is associated with adverse outcomes. One prospective study reported that hospitalized patients with delirium had a two-fold increase of death, an increase in length of stay, and an increased need for long-term care after hospitalization.[120]

Four types of delirium exist: hyperactive, hypoactive, mixed, and terminal delirium (also referred to as terminal agitation).[118,121] Hyperactive delirium is characterized by agitation, vocalizations, emotional lability, and increased movements and is more frequently recognized by caregivers and clinicians than is hypoactive delirium. In contrast, hypoactive delirium is characterized by auditory or visual hallucinations, but patients may remain quiet. Consequently, hypoactive delirium is frequently missed by clinicians unfamiliar with the patient or those who do not adequately assess mental status. Caregivers are frequently the first to recognize hypoactive delirium, given its subtler but equally alarming symptoms. Mixed delirium may have features of both hyperactive and hypoactive delirium. Terminal delirium occurs in the setting of the active dying process, such as decreased urine output, mottling, and inability to control respiratory secretions.[121]

In each case, onset is signaled by an acute change in the patient's level of arousal, which can manifest as disorientation, visual or auditory hallucinations, a change in speech patterns, memory or language alteration, or upset of the sleep/wake cycle. Symptoms typically wax and wane over time.

Whenever possible, a workup should be completed to establish reversible causes of delirium. Possible causes of delirium may include medications, infection, constipation, urinary retention, electrolyte imbalances, undertreated pain, paraneoplastic syndromes, organ failure, and other metabolic derangements. If these potential causes are ruled out, the clinician should discontinue all medications that are not necessary and not associated with an acute withdrawal syndrome.

Nonpharmacologic interventions should be maximized before pharmacologic interventions are used. These include maintaining a quiet, controlled environment, reorientation, sleep hygiene, and optimizing sensory input (eg, glasses, hearing aids).

In hospital settings, nurses can identify patients who are at high risk for developing delirium, minimize precipitating factors, and closely assess the patient for signs of early delirium. When necessary, pharmacologic management can help to calm and improve cognition. For hyperactive and hypoactive delirium, antipsychotics are typically the drugs of choice. The National Comprehensive Cancer Network guidelines recommend haloperidol or one of the atypical antipsychotics (eg, olanzapine, risperidone, or quetiapine).[122] However, data do not suggest that newer antipsychotics are more effective or safer than haloperidol, and they generally are more expensive. Results of one preliminary study suggest patients with advanced cancer and hyperactive or mixed delirium who received both lorazepam and haloperidol compared with haloperidol experienced significantly greater reduction in agitation at 8 hours.[123] However, additional research is required to assess the generalizability of adverse effects of this trial.

To date, the standard of care is to minimize the use of benzodiazepines in patients with hyperactive or hypoactive delirium, because of the potential for paradoxical effects that may worsen agitation. Generally, benzodiazepines should be avoided except to manage agitation that has not responded to antipsychotics. However, terminal delirium is the one type of delirium best treated with benzodiazepines.[122]

KEY POINTS

- The four types of delirium are: hyperactive, hypoactive, mixed, and terminal.
- Despite the distressing symptoms of hypoactive delirium, it is the least recognized type of delirium and requires careful evaluation.
- After assessing and reversing any potential causes, nonpharmacologic approaches are the mainstay in the treatment of delirium.
- Benzodiazepines should be avoided in treating hyperactive and hypoactive delirium; however, terminal delirium is best treated with benzodiazepines.

DIARRHEA

Diarrhea is generally defined as frequent loose or liquid bowel movements. In cancer, diarrhea can result from the cancer itself or its treatment. Examples include the osmotic diarrhea associated with exocrine insufficiency in pancreatic cancer (see the section titled Fat Malabsorption) or the secretory diarrhea associated with medullary thyroid cancer, carcinoid syndrome, and pancreatic islet cell cancers. Cancer treatments such as chemotherapy, radiation therapy to the abdomen, targeted therapy, immunotherapy, and graft-versus-host disease (GVDH) can also cause diarrhea. The incidence of chemotherapy-induced diarrhea is approximately 50% to 80%.[124,125]

A careful history and physical examination are necessary to determine the likely etiology. The history should include onset, frequency, approximate volume, presence or absence of blood, and other stool characteristics. Diarrhea can be classified as acute (< 2 weeks), persistent (2 to 4 weeks), or chronic (> 4 weeks). A complete abdominal examination, digital rectal examination, temperature, and assessment of hydration status are helpful. History and examination will guide potential diagnostic evaluations, which might include stool studies. Blood work may help evaluate hydration status, and evidence of leukocytosis may suggest an infectious etiology. Acute diarrhea is often infectious (ie, viral, bacteria) and, within a population of patients with advanced chronic illness, *Clostridium difficile* should be considered if there is a history of infection, recent hospitalization, and/or or antibiotic use.

CHEMOTHERAPY

In general, diarrhea is most common with chemotherapy regimens including antimetabolites. The most studied of these agents is fluorouracil (FU). The risk of diarrhea from FU increases when leucovorin is given as a modulating agent or with protracted infusions. Like infusions, oral capecitabine provides long-term exposure to FU and has similar toxicities to infusional FU. Consider dihydropyrimidine dehydrogenase testing for severe or uncontrolled diarrhea after 5FU exposure.[126] Other antimetabolites associated with diarrhea include the topoisomerase I inhibitors irinotecan and topotecan. The cholinergic adverse effects of irinotecan cause an acute-onset diarrhea accompanied by abdominal cramping, rhinitis, lacrimation, and salivation. This cholinergic reaction is best treated with the routine use of atropine. After 24 hours, a more severe form of diarrhea occurs, correlating with peak plasma levels of the irinotecan metabolite SN38. The variant of UGT1A1 in approximately 10% of whites leads to poor metabolism of SN-38 and predicts irinotecan toxicity.[127]

Guideline-based recommendations exist in the context of chemotherapy-induced diarrhea.[125] For uncomplicated, noninfectious, mild to moderate diarrhea, management includes opioid-like medications. Of these agents, loperamide and diphenoxylate are the most commonly used for treating acute diarrhea. Oral loperamide 4 mg is given for the first dose, followed by 2 mg every 4 hours (maximum, 16 mg/d) or after an unformed stool. Loperamide decreases intestinal motility and has minimal systemic effects because there is little to no absorption. If diarrhea persists for > 48 hours while receiving loperamide therapy, consider diphenoxylate-atropine or other second-line agents, including deodorized tincture of opium or octreotide. Deodorized tincture of opium is concentrated morphine (10 mg/mL) administered at 10 to 15 drops in water every 4 hours.[125]

For patients with adequate hydration, bulk-forming agents such as psyllium or cholestyramine can be considered. However, in the setting of low-performance status or poor hydration, bulk-forming agents may cause harm. Octreotide is a somatostatin analog that works by decreasing secretion of several GI hormones and prolonging intestinal transit time. The recommended octreotide dose for diarrhea management is 100 to 150 μg three times a day.[128] One study demonstrated improved control of diarrhea with the use of octreotide versus loperamide.[129] Octreotide has also demonstrated efficacy in the secondary prevention of FU- and cisplatin-induced diarrhea.[130,131] However, octreotide must be given subcutaneously, given its short half-life, and it is expensive.

RADIATION

Diarrhea is the most common adverse effect of abdominal and pelvic radiation therapy. Radiation damages the mucosa of the small and large intestines and thereby can produce a secretory diarrhea. The incidence and severity of the diarrhea increase with the addition of FU.[132] Several placebo-controlled clinical trials have tried to identify a drug that can be used to prevent diarrhea induced by pelvic radiation therapy. Randomized clinical trials support the use of probiotics and octreotide. In contrast, sucralfate provided mixed results, glutamine showed no improvement, and sulfasalazine actually exacerbated symptoms.[133-140]

TARGETED AGENTS

Diarrhea is a common adverse effect of many of the new targeted therapies. Studies of small-molecule inhibitors of epidermal growth factor receptor (EGFR; eg, erlotinib, gefitinib, afatinib) report up to 90% incidence of diarrhea, but only 15% of cases are severe.[141] The monoclonal antibodies directed against EGFR (eg, cetuximab, panitumumab) have reported rates of diarrhea in the 20% range, but the incidence of severe diarrhea is minimal.[142,143] Drugs that inhibit the vascular endothelial growth factor pathway (eg, sorafenib, sunitinib, axitinib, pazopanib, cabozantinib, lenvatinib, bevacizumab, regorafenib) have reported incidences of diarrhea ranging from 30% to 80%, with the minority of patients experiencing grade 3 or 4 symptoms.[144-146] The HER-2–directed drugs lapatinib, neratinib, and pertuzumab are both known to cause diarrhea in up to 80% of patients.[147,148] Neratinib, one newly approved HER-2–directed therapy, is associated with a high degree of diarrhea even with loperamide prophylaxis.[149] Treatment of diarrhea is generally supportive, using antimotility agents and withdrawing the offending drug until symptoms resolve.

IMMUNOTHERAPY-INDUCED DIARRHEA

The incidence of diarrhea with immunotherapies such as nivolumab, pembrolizumab, and ipilimumab appears to be dose dependent. Incidence of diarrhea associated with ipilimumab has been reported to be approximately 30%, whereas programmed cell death protein–1 blockade produces diarrhea less frequently.[150,151] Patients receiving immunotherapy need to be educated about the potential life-threatening adverse effect of severe colitis and the need to report symptoms early. Checkpoint inhibitor–induced diarrhea is managed differently than most other types of diarrhea, requiring corticosteroids.[152] Antidiarrheal agents such as loperamide should be used with caution because they can mask the underlying autoimmune pathology. In severe cases, administration of high-dose intravenous corticosteroids and infliximab 5 mg/kg every 2 weeks is recommended.[125,153-156]

GRAFT-VERSUS-HOST DISEASE

For patients who have received a hematopoietic stem cell transplant, diarrhea may result from GVHD and/or from infections related to the use of immunosuppressive therapy. The epithelial damage caused by high-dose chemotherapy can stimulate activation of alloreactive cytotoxic T cells, which release a cascade of inflammatory cytokines that contribute to necrosis of epithelial crypt cells. At the first sign of acute GI symptoms consistent with GVHD, a stool specimen should be evaluated for bacterial, fungal, and viral pathogens. Supportive treatment should be initiated and consultation with a gastroenterologist should be considered. If the findings on stool evaluation are positive for pathologic bacteria, a course of appropriate antibiotics should be started. For patients with a biopsy-proven diagnosis of GVHD, systemic corticosteroids should be initiated and prophylactic immunosuppression optimized. A time-limited trial of octreotide should be considered; if there is no response within 4 days, however, the trial should be discontinued to avoid ileus.[157] If there is no response to octreotide, a second-line therapy such as antithymocyte globulin or infliximab can be considered.

KEY POINTS

- 5FU and the topoisomerase I inhibitors (irinotecan, topotecan) commonly cause diarrhea.
- Irinotecan causes an acute diarrhea due to a cholinergic mechanism and a later, more severe, diarrhea due to its active metabolite SN38.
- In addition to supportive measures, chemotherapy-induced diarrhea is best treated with loperamide. Second-line approaches include diphenoxylate-atropine and/or octreotide.
- In addition to supportive measures, radiation-induced diarrhea is best treated with octreotide.
- Diarrhea is common with the use of targeted therapies and is best treated with antimotility agents and by withdrawing the offending drug.
- Checkpoint inhibitors can cause severe, life-threatening colitis best treated with corticosteroids and, rarely, infliximab.
- GVHD-associated diarrhea should be treated with corticosteroids, optimal immunosuppression, and octreotide.

MUCOSITIS

Oral mucositis and esophagitis are common complications of chemotherapy and radiation therapy. The overall incidence of oral mucositis is approximately 40% for patients who receive standard-dose chemotherapy. The incidence varies with the chemotherapy agents used and increases substantially for patients who receive dose-intensified regimens. Mucositis and esophagitis are common for patients receiving radiation to susceptible areas, and both can be exacerbated by concomitant chemotherapy. Dental evaluation prior to therapy should be encouraged if poor oral hygiene is seen on examination. Mucositis may occur as a result of direct injury from cytotoxic chemotherapy or radiation therapy, secondary infections from treatment-induced myelosuppression, or GVHD.

The severity of mucositis is dose and treatment specific. Mucositis typically starts 5 to 7 days after the initiation of chemotherapy. It often presents first as erythema on the soft palate, the buccal mucosa, the ventral surface of the tongue, and the floor of the mouth. These symptoms may progress to a generalized desquamation. Most ulcerations (> 90%) are localized on nonkeratinized mucosa.

Mucositis that results from chemotherapy can resolve within a few days or last up to 3 weeks; oral mucositis caused by radiation therapy typically lasts an average of 6 weeks. Chemotherapy agents frequently associated with mucositis include the antimetabolites 5FU and methotrexate, and high-dose or prolonged infusions of chemotherapy. In addition, newer targeted agents, including many of the tyrosine kinase inhibitors, such as everolimus, as well as new immune checkpoint inhibitors, can also cause mucositis. Radiation therapy to the oral cavity frequently causes a host of oral complications, including mucositis, xerostomia, dental caries, tissue necrosis, and taste alterations.[158]

PREVENTION OF MUCOSITIS ASSOCIATED WITH CHEMOTHERAPY OR RADIATION-TARGETED THERAPY

Clinical practice guidelines exist for the prevention and treatment of cancer therapy–induced oral and GI mucositis secondary to cancer therapy.[158] In general, a dental evaluation is recommended before the initiation of radiation therapy to the oral cavity. Fluoride carriers can provide fluoride for maintaining tooth integrity and may help prevent radiation scatter from metal dental work if the dental work is worn during radiation.

Numerous agents have been evaluated for the prevention of chemotherapy-induced mucositis, but most are not effective when compared with a placebo, including sucralfate, allopurinol, chamomile tea, glutamine, and vitamin E. One treatment that effectively prevented mucositis in clinical trials is oral cryotherapy; that is, sucking on ice chips during administration of chemotherapy. This treatment produces temporary vasoconstriction and appears to reduce the delivery of bolus-dose 5FU chemotherapy to the oral mucosa. Results from several controlled clinical trials indicate that oral cryotherapy reduces oral mucositis resulting from such treatment by approximately 50%.[159,160] Guidelines also recommend administering the keratinocyte growth factor palifermin to decrease severe mucositis in patients undergoing autologous stem cell transplantation with total-body irradiation–conditioning regimens.[161] Palifermin compared with placebo in the prevention of 5FU-associated mucositis has also demonstrated benefit but has not been widely adopted because of the drug's cost.[162] Last, guidelines recommend the use of low-level laser therapy for the prevention of oral mucositis in adults receiving high-dose chemotherapy in preparation for hematopoietic stem cell transplantation with or without irradiation, but these guidelines only apply to institutions familiar with this treatment.[163] In patients with breast cancer who are receiving everolimus oral-dexamethasone swish-and-spit preparation had markedly decreased mucositis when compared with those receiving placebo.[164]

With regard to radiation-induced esophagitis, data demonstrate no benefit from the use of sucralfate for the prevention of radiation-associated esophagitis.[165] Although evidence suggests amifostine, a cytoprotective adjuvant, can mildly decrease radiation-induced esophagitis, inconvenience and expense limit its widespread use.[166]

MUCOSITIS TREATMENT

Effective management of oral mucositis includes general measures such as oral hygiene, dietary modification, topical local anesthetics, and systemic analgesics. Empirical clinical practices include gently brushing teeth with a soft-bristled toothbrush and fluoride toothpaste two to three times daily. Gentle flossing daily is encouraged to remove food and bacteria buildup. Alcohol mouthwashes should be avoided, but patients can rinse their mouths every 4 hours with a saline and baking soda solution (one-half teaspoon of salt plus one-half teaspoon of baking soda in 1 cup of warm water). Dentures should be removed, particularly at night. Acidic and spicy foods or beverages should be avoided. Adequate relief of pain associated with mucositis may require systemic opioids, including parenteral opioids when patients have severe pain.

Investigators have evaluated multiple mouthwashes in the palliation of mucositis. A mouthwash made of doxepin, a tricyclic antidepressant, has demonstrated improved palliation of radiation therapy–associated oral mucosal pain.[167,168] A randomized study evaluated different mouthwashes consisting of salt and soda, chlorhexidine, and "magic mouthwash" (ie, lidocaine, diphenhydramine, aluminum hydroxide, magnesium hydroxide) and found decreased signs and symptoms of mucositis within 12 days without any significant differences among the three groups. Given the comparable effectiveness of the mouthwashes, the least costly was salt and soda mouthwash.[169]

KEY POINTS

- Evidence-based prevention strategies of mucositis include cryotherapy, palifermin, and low-dose laser therapy.
- Data demonstrate improved prevention of everolimus-induced stomatitis with the use of dexamethasone rinse.
- Doxepin mouthwash improves mucositis-related pain.
- No differences have been observed among mouthwashes consisting of salt and soda, chlorhexidine, and "magic mouthwash."

CHEMOTHERAPY-INDUCED PERIPHERAL NEUROPATHY

Chemotherapy-induced peripheral neuropathy (CIPN) may develop as a consequence of treatment with platinum analogs (ie, cisplatin, oxaliplatin, carboplatin), taxanes (ie, paclitaxel, docetaxel, nab-paclitaxel), vinca alkaloids (ie, vincristine), proteasome inhibitors (ie, bortezomib) and immunomodulators (ie, thalidomide, lenalidomide). The clinical presentation reflects an axonal peripheral neuropathy with glove-and-stocking distribution sensory loss, combined with features suggestive of nerve hyperexcitability, including paresthesia, dysesthesia, and pain. These symptoms may be disabling, adversely affecting activities of daily living and QOL.[170]

The incidence of chemotherapy-induced neurotoxicity appears related to cumulative dose and infusion duration, and individual risk factors may also influence the development and severity of neurotoxicity. Substantial work has evaluated genetic predispositions for CIPN, but no genetic tests have been established for use in clinical practice. Yet, patients who have family members with Charcot-Marie Tooth–associated neuropathies may be predisposed to CIPN from neurotoxic chemotherapy.[171] Data support that CIPN develops more often in patients with obesity, diabetes, and history of alcoholism. Exercise and increased blood to peripheral nerves might mitigate this toxicity.[172-174]

Differences in structural properties between chemotherapies further contribute to variations in clinical presentation. The mechanisms underlying chemotherapy-induced neurotoxicity are diverse and, when used in combination, are additive (Table 8-9). Different chemotherapy classes target different components of the peripheral nervous system, including the dorsal root ganglia neuronal cell bodies, axonal transport pathways, mitochondrial operation, calcium-ion regulation systems, and axonal membrane ion channels (Fig 8-7).[170] In addition, data strongly support that the acute pain syndrome caused by paclitaxel, which classically has been identified as arthralgias and myalgias, is not from an injury to muscles or joints; rather, it appears to be a manifestation of an acute neuropathy.[175,176] ASCO chemotherapy-induced neuropathy guideline reviewed the value of strategies for preventing and treating CIPN.[177] Investigators have evaluated amifostine, amitriptyline, calcium and magnesium, glutathione, and vitamin E for the prevention of CIPN, and none has proven effective. Per this guideline, no agents are recommended for preventing CIPN. However, there is one preventive strategy specific to the administration of bortezomib. Patients with multiple myeloma treated with subcutaneous versus intravenous bortezomib experience less CIPN and similar overall response rates.[178] Consequently, subcutaneous administration of bortezomib to patients with multiple myeloma is now standard of care.

As for the treatment of CIPN, the only agent with proven efficacy for treating established CIPN is duloxetine.[179,180] Limited data do not support the use of acetyl-L-carnitine, tricyclic antidepressants, gabapentin, or topical treatments (ie, baclofen, amitriptyline hydrochloride, and ketamine) in the treatment of CIPN.[177]

KEY POINTS

- There are no established methods for preventing CIPN other than limiting exposure to the offending drugs.
- Patients at higher risk for developing CIPN include those with history of inherited neuropathy, obesity, diabetes, and alcoholism.
- The best-established drug for treating painful CIPN is duloxetine, but its efficacy is limited.

DYSPNEA

Dyspnea is a subjective experience of breathlessness. In patients with advanced cancer, the prevalence ranges from 21% to 79%, with moderate to severe dyspnea occurring in 10% to 63% of patients.[181,182] Dyspnea is a subjectively measured outcome. Objective measurements of compromised respiratory status (eg, respiratory rate, saturation of peripheral oxygen) may or may not correlate with a patient's subjective report.[183] In appropriate patients, consider a short walking test with or without oxygen monitoring to further evaluate dyspnea. Breathing

Table 8-9 **Mechanisms of Chemotherapy-Induced Peripheral Neuropathy**[170]

Chemotherapy	Neurotoxicity	Mechanism of Neurotoxicity	Incidence	Dose	Recovery
Cisplatin	Long-lasting cumulative distal sensory neuropathy	Induces apoptosis in dorsal root ganglia neurons	50%-90% of patients receiving ≥ 500 mg/m^2	Beginning at 300 mg/m^2	Incomplete
Carboplatin	Mild sensorimotor neurotoxicity	Induces apoptosis in dorsal root ganglia neurons	Uncommon; mild in 25% of patients; severe in 5%	More common with high doses: 800-1,600 mg/m^2	Not fully described
Oxaliplatin	Acute cold-associated neurotoxicity and chronic sensory neuropathy	Axonal membrane ion channel dysfunction	Acute symptoms in 95%; severe chronic toxicity in 10%-20% at 750-850 mg/m^2	Acute symptoms at all doses, severe at > 540-700 mg/m^2	May persist for a long time; in 10% of patients at 2 years post treatment
Paclitaxel	Distal sensory neuropathy with pain and motor symptoms at high doses	Microtubule damage and subsequent dysfunction of axonal transport, and mitochondrial dysfunction	Severe dose-dependence in 10%-30% of patients	> 300 mg/m^2 but can occur at lower doses	May persist, although reversibility reported
Docetaxel	Distal sensory neuropathy with pain	Microtubule damage and subsequent dysfunction of axonal transport, and mitochondrial dysfunction	Less severe neurotoxicity than paclitaxel, severe in 6%-10% of patients	> 100 mg/m^2; severe toxicity > 600 mg/m^2	Not fully described
Vincristine	Distal sensorimotor painful neuropathy	Microtubule damage and damage to dorsal root ganglia cell bodies	60% of patients, dose dependent	4-10 mg	≤ 33% of patients report persistent symptoms
Bortezomib	Sensory axonal neuropathy, occasionally demyelinating	Microtubule loss, demyelination and axonal loss, and mitochondrial dysfunction	≥ 35%-50% of patients	1.3 mg/m^2	Resolution in 3 months, may persist
Thalidomide[258]	Sensorimotor painful neuropathy	Peripheral vasculature impairment and distal axonal injury	25% to 75% of patients	At dose ≥ 20 g	Not fully described, symptoms may persist

homeostasis is controlled by the respiratory center located in the medulla oblongata and pons of the brainstem.[184] Chemoreceptors detect blood oxygenation while mechanoreceptors detect stretching and congestion. Alterations in blood pH and/or blood gases increase demand of respiratory signaling by the brain via activation of chemoreceptors and mechanoreceptors resulting in dyspnea.[184] Although there can be many nonrelated cancer etiologies and/or comorbid disease states (eg, chronic obstructive pulmonary disease, asthma, congestive heart failure), in patients with advanced cancer, pleural effusions and pulmonary embolism are common causes.

Limited evidence exists on the effectiveness of nonpharmacologic management of dyspnea in patients with cancer. In the absence of guidelines in the cancer population, guidelines on dyspnea management in advanced lung and/or heart disease may be a reasonable alternative.[185,186] Supplemental oxygen therapy is appropriate in patients who have hypoxia, but not appropriate for treatment of dyspnea without hypoxemia.[187] In a phase III trial of oxygen delivered via nasal cannula compared with room air, oxygen provided no additional symptomatic benefit for relief of refractory dyspnea.[188] Rather, room-air fan therapy positioned at the face of the patient is often effective.[183,189,190] The proposed mechanism of the fan

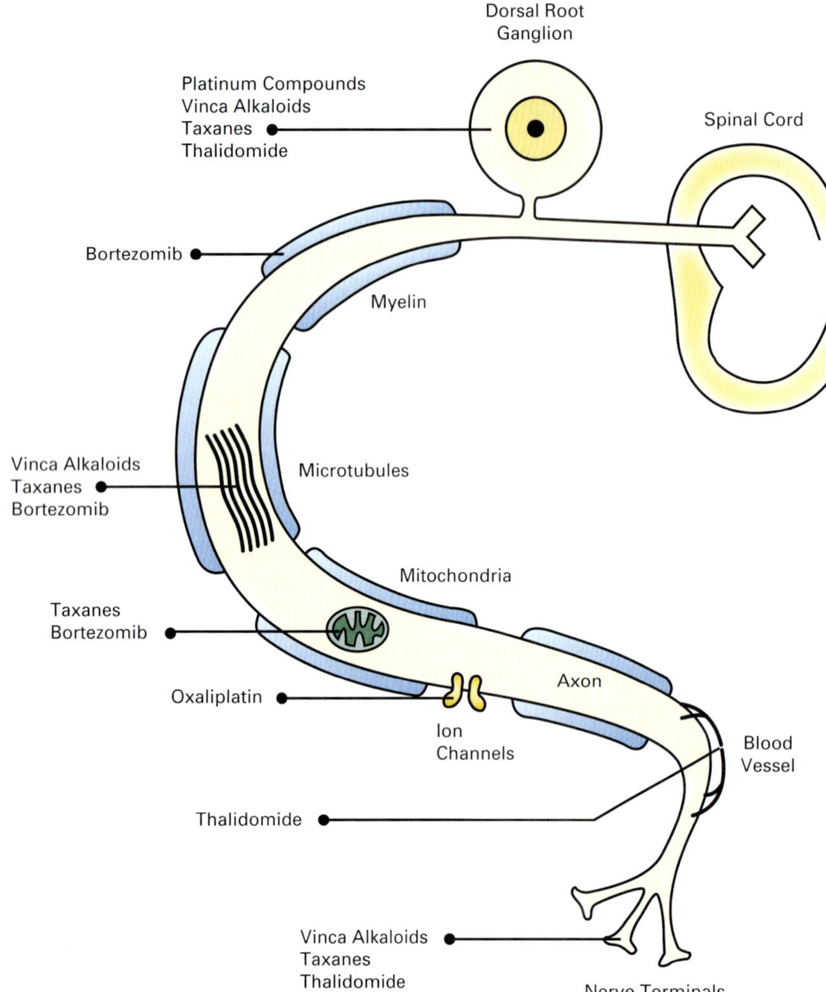

Fig. 8-7 Mechanisms of chemotherapy-induced neurotoxicity. Proposed targets of chemotherapy-induced neurotoxicity in the peripheral nervous system, including damage to dorsal root ganglion neuronal cell bodies (platinum compounds, vinca alkaloids, taxanes, thalidomide), demyelination (bortezomib), microtubule-associated toxicity (vinca alkaloids, taxanes, bortezomib), mitochondrial dysfunction (taxanes, bortezomib), axonal membrane ion channelopathy (oxaliplatin), peripheral vasculature impairment (thalidomide), and distal axonal injury (vinca alkaloids, taxanes, thalidomide).[170]

Adapted from Park SB, Goldstein D, Krishnan AV, et al. Chemotherapy-induced peripheral neurotoxicity: a critical analysis. CA Cancer J Clin. *2013 Nov-Dec; 63(6):419-37.*

intervention is facial cooling of the branches of the trigeminal cranial nerve, resulting in relief.

Practice guidelines, systematic reviews, meta-analyses, and randomized, controlled clinical trials (RCTs) provide sufficient evidence recommending oral or intravenous opioids as first-line agents for dyspnea treatment in patients with cancer.[188,191-195] Opioids, through the same receptors that relieve pain, also relieve dyspnea by reducing ventilation and the central-mediated perception of dyspnea. For opioid-naïve patients, low-dose oral morphine (5 to 10 mg) or intravenous morphine 2 to 5 mg (or equivalent) typically provides relief. Higher doses are likely needed for patients taking opioids chronically.[196] Systematic reviews do not recommend use of nebulized morphine.[193]

KEY POINTS

- Dyspnea is a subjective experience that may or may not correlate with objective findings.
- In the absence of hypoxemia, oxygen provides no additional symptomatic benefit for relief of refractory dyspnea, compared with room air.
- Evidence supports the use of opioids to palliate dyspnea.

DERMATOLOGIC ADVERSE EFFECTS

EPIDERMAL GROWTH FACTOR INHIBITORS

Up to 50% of patients with cancer who receive EGFR inhibitors experience a prominent skin rash.[197] This rash has acne-like characteristics but is not considered acne (Fig 8-8). Other targeted drugs that are associated with a similar rash include inhibitors of mTOR (eg, everolimus and temsirolimus), and multikinase inhibitors (eg, sorafenib and sunitinib). Prophylactic and treatment guidelines exist describing the prevention and treatment of EGFR-inhibitor–associated rashes (Table 8-10).[198] EGFR-inhibitor rash prevention includes topical corticosteroids and moisturizers or oral minocycline or doxycycline. EGFR-inhibitor rash treatment includes topical

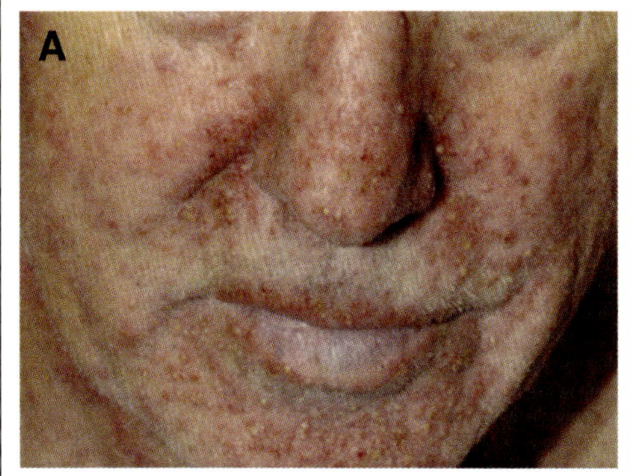

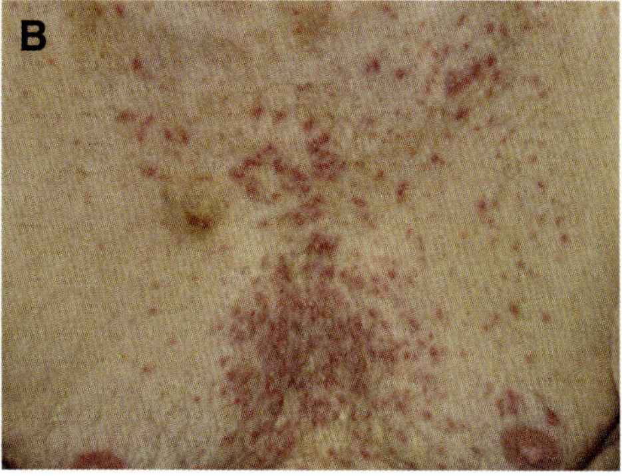

Fig. 8-8 Epidermal growth factor receptor (EGFR)-induced rash involving the (A) face and (B) chest.[259]

corticosteroids or clindamycin, or oral minocycline, doxycycline, or low-dose isotretinoin. Consultation with a dermatologist is recommended for patients with moderate to severe rashes. In addition to the acneiform rash, these drugs can also cause many other dermatologic problems, including periungual disease, photosensitivity, pruritus, xerosis, Stevens-Johnson syndrome, and skin cancers. Of note, data support the development of an EGFR-induced rash as a pharmacodynamic marker of antitumor activity.[156,199-201]

HAND-FOOT SYNDROME

One of capecitabine's dose-limiting toxicities is a prominent rash called palmar–plantar erythrodysesthesia, also known as hand-foot syndrome (Fig 8-9).[202] Symptoms from this problem usually begin with erythema and proceed to pain, swelling, desquamation, and, rarely, ulceration. If the drug is used for too long, this syndrome can lead to substantial morbidity, to the point that patients may be incapacitated and unable to use their hands and feet. Anecdotal experience suggested that vitamin B_6 or urea–lactic acid cream may alleviate hand-foot syndrome, but two large, placebo-controlled studies demonstrated no benefit from either approach. In contrast, in a single-center, randomized trial evaluating the prevention of hand-foot syndrome, celecoxib prevented both moderate to severe and all-grade hand-foot syndrome.[203,204] Other drug-related therapies studied include topical emollients and creams, systemic and topical corticosteroids, nicotine patch, vitamin E, and pyridoxine. However, because of the lack of RCTs with these therapies, the current mainstay of treatment of this toxicity is interruption of therapy and, if necessary, dose reduction.

ALOPECIA

Hair loss is a common concern for patients undergoing cancer-directed therapies. Chemotherapy-induced alopecia is such a feared complication of cancer treatment that nearly 10% of women would consider refusing chemotherapy to avoid alopecia.[205] Two broad mechanisms are felt to be responsible for hair loss: thinning of the hair shaft, leading to breakage; and

TABLE 8-10. Preventive and Treatment Strategies for EGFR-Associated Acneiform Rash Recommendations[198]

Strategy	Recommended	Not Recommended
Preventive		
Topical	Hydrocortisone 1% cream with moisturizer and sunscreen twice daily	Pimecrolimus 1% cream
		Tazarotene 0.05% cream
		Sunscreen as single agent
Systemic	Minocycline, 100 mg daily	Tetracycline 500 mg twice daily
	Doxycycline, 100 mg twice daily	
Treatment		
Topical	Alclometasone 0.05% cream	
	Fluocinonide 0.05% cream, twice daily	
	Clindamycin 1%	
Systemic	Doxycycline, 100 mg twice daily	Photosensitizing agents
	Minocycline, 100 mg daily	
	Low-dose isotretinoin, 20-30 mg daily	

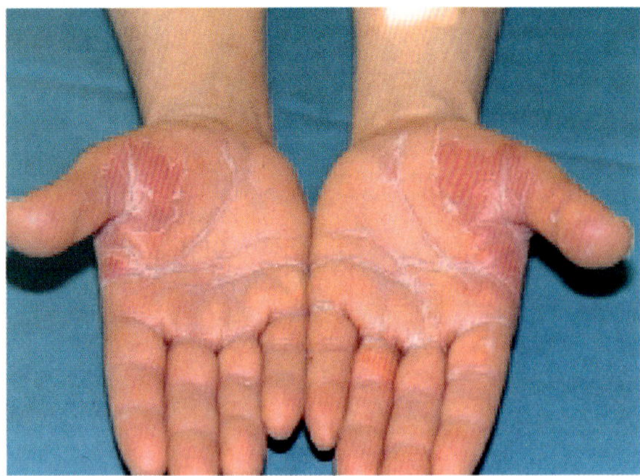

Fig. 8-9 Hand-foot syndrome or palmar-plantar erythrodysesthesia.[252]

inhibition of dividing hair matrix cells resulting in hair separation from the bulb. Risks for alopecia include type of chemotherapy, higher chemotherapy doses, shorter infusion times, certain hair types, female sex, and older age. Hair loss generally occurs 2 to 4 weeks after the initiation of chemotherapy and regrowth occurs 3 to 6 months after cessation of therapy, although irreversible hair loss does rarely occur.[206] Available evidence suggests that regional hypothermia decreases alopecia without an increase in the incidence of scalp metastases in patients with solid tumors.[207-212] In contrast, there are no data to suggest safety in patients with hematologic malignancies, and hypothermia techniques should not be used in this patient population.

KEY POINTS

- Prevention of rash resulting from EGFR-inhibitor treatment includes topical corticosteroids and moisturizers, or oral minocycline or doxycycline.
- Treatment of rash resulting from EGFR-inhibitor therapy includes topical corticosteroids or clindamycin, or oral minocycline, doxycycline, or low-dose isotretinoin.
- No evidence supports the use of vitamin B_6 supplementation or urea–lactic acid cream to prevent or treat hand-foot syndrome associated with capecitabine use.
- Scalp cryotherapy can be effective for select patients with solid tumors, but safety data are lacking for patients with hematologic malignancies.

HORMONE-DEPRIVATION SYMPTOMS

HOT FLASHES

Hot flashes are highly prevalent among patients with breast cancer and in other premenopausal women who undergo ovarian function suppression. In addition, approximately 75% of men undergoing androgen-deprivation therapy will have substantial discomfort due to hot flashes.[213] Estrogens and androgens can alleviate hot flashes for women and men, respectively; however, there is concern about giving exogenous hormones to patients with hormonally driven cancers. Nonetheless, alternative agents are available to control hot flashes for this patient population (Table 8-11).

Evidence supports the use of antidepressants to treat hot flashes. However, clinicians should avoid paroxetine, fluoxetine, and sertraline for patients taking tamoxifen, because these antidepressants can decrease the metabolism of tamoxifen to its active metabolite, endoxifen, by the enzyme CYP2D6. Therefore, it is recommended that these agents should be avoided for patients receiving tamoxifen. Venlafaxine, citalopram, and escitalopram do not alter tamoxifen metabolism as much as some other antidepressants. The results from randomized, placebo-controlled trials indicated clonidine inhibits hot flashes more than placebo, but was limited by anticholinergic adverse effects.[214] Gabapentin is also effective in the control of hot flashes at a dose of 900 mg/d, but not at a dose of 300 mg/d.[215] Last, a placebo-controlled, randomized, double-blinded trial demonstrated that 15 mg of oxybutynin decreased hot flashes to similar degree as antidepressants and gabapentin, with mouth dryness being the most common adverse effect.[214]

Although the findings from a number of pilot studies have suggested that soy products could alleviate hot flashes, the majority of results from large, placebo-controlled clinical trials do not demonstrate any benefit from a phytoestrogen product for breast cancer survivors.[216,217] Likewise, well-conducted studies have not demonstrated any benefit from black cohosh, flaxseed, magnesium oxide, or vitamin E.[218-222] Several nonpharmacologic options to prevent hot flashes have been studied for otherwise healthy postmenopausal women, including electroacupuncture, paced respirations, cognitive behavioral therapy, and hypnosis.[223-225]

VAGINAL DRYNESS, DYSPAREUNIA, AND LOW LIBIDO

More than 60% of people treated for cancer have long-term sexual dysfunction. However, < 25% of those with sexual problems get help from a health professional.[226] Although cancer-related sexual problems usually begin with physiologic damage from cancer treatment, a patient's coping skills and the quality of the sexual relationship are crucial in sexual rehabilitation. Barriers to care for people treated for cancer include a lack of discussion with the oncology team. Vaginal dryness from urogenital atrophy is a major symptom of estrogen depletion for some women. It can contribute to pain with intercourse, as well as itching and irritation. Nonestrogen-containing vaginal lubricants are helpful for alleviating symptoms.[227] Nonetheless, these products appear to be less efficacious than topical estrogen therapy.[228] Clinicians are still concerned about the systemic absorption of topical estrogens and testosterone despite evidence showing rare, persistent estradiol elevation among patients with breast cancer treated

Table 8-11 Nonestrogen Pharmacologic Treatment of Hot Flashes

Treatment	Drug and Dosage
Progesterone analog	Megestrol acetate, 20 to 40 mg/d PO
	Medroxyprogesterone acetate, 400 to 500 mg IM injection (once)
Nonhormonal agents	Venlafaxine, 37.5 mg/d PO for 1 week, then 75 mg/d PO
	Paroxetine, 10 mg/d PO
	Citalopram, 10-20 mg/d PO
	Desvenlafaxine, 50 mg/d PO for 1 week, then 100 mg/d
	Escitalopram, 10-20 mg/d
	Gabapentin, titrate up to 900 mg/d
	Pregabalin, titrate up to 75 mg/d
	Clonidine, 0.1 mg/d
	Oxybutynin, 15 mg/d

Abbreviations: IM, intramuscular; PO, by mouth.

Table 8-12 Approaches to Hormone-Related Symptoms in Patients With Cancer

Symptoms	Evidence Based	Lack of Evidence
Hot flashes	Antidepressants	Phytoestrogen product (soy)
	Clonidine	Black cohosh
	Gabapentin	Flaxseed
	Oxybutynin	Magnesium oxide
	Cognitive behavioral therapy	
	Hypnosis	
Vaginal dryness	Dehydroepiandrosterone	
Dyspareunia	Lidocaine	
Low libido		Transdermal testosterone

with aromatase inhibitors.[229] Patients must be informed of the risks of this therapy, and they should be allowed to balance the desire for controlled symptoms against presumably small potential risks (Table 8-12). There are intriguing data that dehydroepiandrosterone (DHEA) can decrease vaginal dryness and reduce discomfort during sexual activity without leading to increased systemic estrogen levels in women with vaginal dryness who do not have a history of breast cancer.[230,231] In addition, data support that vaginal laser therapy can alleviate vaginal symptoms associated with estrogen depletion (Table 8-12).[232]

For dyspareunia, results of a randomized, double-blind, placebo-controlled clinical trial involving patients with a history of cancer support that DHEA is safe and useful for women with vaginal dryness and/or dyspareunia.[233] Findings of a randomized, placebo-controlled study support the 4% aqueous lidocaine preparation, used topically at the introitus 3 minutes before sexual activity to decrease dyspareunia.[234]

Last, with regard to libido, the results of a randomized, double-blind, placebo-controlled trial of transdermal testosterone in women with cancer did not show any improvement in libido (Table 8-12).[235] A potential explanation for the negative results for patients with cancer is that the women involved in this trial were postmenopausal and did not receive supplemental estrogen. In most of the previous trials in other patient groups, women had been premenopausal and/or had also been receiving estrogen-replacement therapy.

KEY POINTS

- Sexual health concerns are common in patients with cancer, but they are not commonly discussed by oncologists.
- Nonhormonal therapies to decrease hot flashes include the following: selective serotonin reuptake inhibitors, serotonin-norepinephrine reuptake Inhibitor, gabapentin, clonidine, and oxybutynin.
- For patients receiving tamoxifen, avoid paroxetine, fluoxetine, and sertraline, because these medications can decrease CYP2D6 metabolism.
- Hormonal therapy for hot flashes can include the use of progesterone analogs.
- Topical lidocaine applied to the introitus can ease dyspareunia.
- DHEA and vaginal laser therapy can help alleviate vaginal dryness.
- Testosterone, without the addition of estrogen replacement therapy, does not appear to help libido in postmenopausal women with cancer.

Acknowledgment

The following authors are acknowledged and graciously thanked for their contribution to prior versions of this chapter: Charles L. Loprinzi, MD, FASCO; and Timothy Moynihan, MD.

Table 8-1 **Pain Terminology**[253,254]

Term	Definition
Acute pain	Pain occurring over hours up to weeks, characterized by a well-defined temporal pattern of onset with subjective and objective physical signs and hyperactivity of the autonomic nervous system
Baseline pain	Average pain intensity experienced for ≥ 12 hours during a 24-hour period
Breakthrough pain	Transient increase in pain to greater-than-moderate intensity, occurring in addition to baseline pain
Adjuvant	Nonopioid medications used to enhance analgesia and minimize adverse effects, including anticonvulsants and antidepressants
Allodynia	Pain from light touch or mild pressure
Dysesthesia	Unpleasant, abnormal sense of touch
Episodic pain	Transient exacerbation or recurrence of pain
End-of-dose failure	Predictable return of pain before next scheduled dose of medication
Hyperalgesia	Increased pain response to a noxious stimulus
Incident pain	Specific experience of pain associated with an event or movement (eg, wound care)
Incomplete cross tolerance	Different level of tolerance to an opioid of a different class
Narcotic	Agent that produces insensibility or narcosis; historically used to describe opioids; however, because of the negative social association with illegal drugs, it has fallen out of use in medical settings
Nociceptive pain	Somatic or visceral pain associated with actual or potential tissue damage caused by ongoing activation of intact nociceptors
Neuropathic pain	Pain resulting from injury to the peripheral or central nervous systems causing pain described as burning, shooting, tingling, stabbing, scalding, crawling, and painful numbness
Opiates	Natural substances that come from opium, including morphine and codeine
Opioid	Semisynthetic or synthetic products that bind to the same receptors as opiates but do not occur naturally. Used broadly to include both natural or synthetic (or semisynthetic) substances acting on one of the three main opioid receptor systems (μ, κ, δ)

Table 8-1 **continued**

Team	Definition
Paresthesia	Abnormal dermal sensation (eg, a tingling, pricking, chilling, burning, or numb sensation on the skin) with no apparent physical cause
Somatic pain	Localized pain causing activation of the μ-receptors and described as aching, stabbing, or throbbing
Subacute pain	Pain present for between 6 weeks and 3 months
Visceral pain	Poorly localized pain due to activation of nociceptors in the viscera by obstruction, infiltration, ischemia, stretching, compression, and/or inflammation

GLOBAL PERSPECTIVE: PAIN AND SYMPTOM MANAGEMENT

Marie Fallon, MD (University of Edinburgh, Edinburgh, United Kingdom) Mhoira Leng, MD (Makerere University Medical School, Kampala, Uganda) Elizabeth Grant, PhD (University of Edinburgh, Edinburgh, United Kingdom)

THE CHALLENGE

In 2015, > 80% of the 61 million individuals worldwide experiencing serious health-related suffering lived in low- and middle-income countries (LMICs). Before 2003, palliative care was not on the global health agenda and the global inequality of access to pain control and end-of-life care was poorly understood.[236] Palliative care services, when funded, were delivered outside of public health systems because the evidence of why or how to incorporate palliative care into routine services did not exist. Over the last 10 years, a stronger evidence base has been built and there is better understanding of the inequities in care and what can be done about them. A study examining access to palliative care in Scotland and Kenya was one of the first to articulate the differences and their impacts between countries such as the United Kingdom and LMICs (Figs 8-10 and 8-11). This study showed that although patients in Kenya were less isolated and existentially distressed than patients in Scotland, and had stronger community and faith support networks, they died in severe, unalleviated physical pain, with little or no access to morphine.[236]

The demand for palliative care in hospitals in African countries was initially characterized in a study of data from the Ugandan National Referral Hospital.[237] Findings of this study showed almost one-half of the patients there required palliative care.[238] This finding led to the Linked Nurse Scheme to deliver appropriate palliative care, which, in turn, led to a tripling of patients receiving palliative care. The research provided the first evidence that nurse prescribers with the appropriate training can be competent in prescribing oral morphine.

INTEGRATING PALLIATIVE CARE INTO NATIONAL HEALTH SYSTEMS

Clearly, to have any sustainable impact, palliative care has to be integrated into national health systems, and as a model for this, an intervention study in 12 hospital settings (national, provincial, district, urban, rural, semi-urban) in four African countries showed that palliative care can be integrated successfully into national health systems.[238] The number of patients identified for palliative

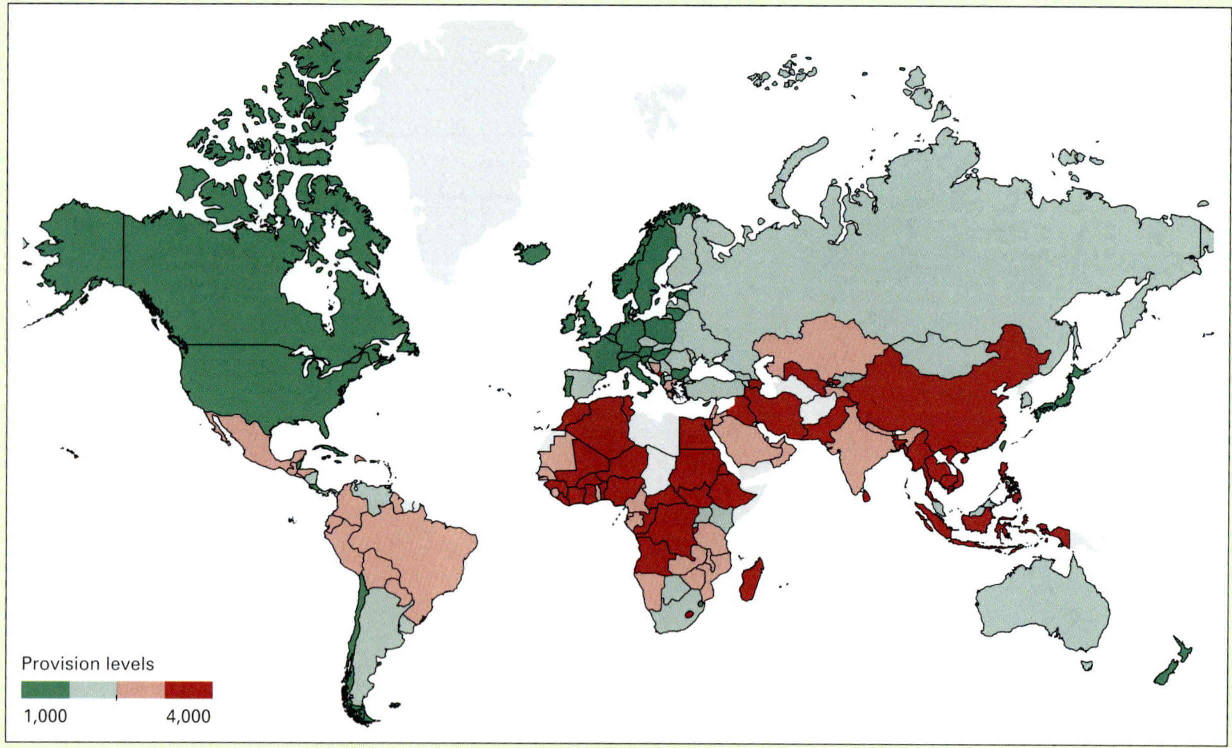

Fig. 8-10 Specialized palliative care services across the world.
Specialized service provision levels of 170 of 234 countries are reported here.[260-265]

care increased by a factor of 2.7 and oral morphine consumption increased by a factor of 2.4 over 2 years. This led to a variety of developments, including the first national plan in Africa, based in Rwanda, for the distribution of oral morphine. The continuing challenge is to ensure the national plan is not compromised by any change in attitude to opioids.

RAISED AWARENESS OF THE COSTS AND NEEDS OF PALLIATIVE CARE IN LMICS

It has been demonstrated that the absence of palliative care services in LMICs results in significant costs being absorbed by the individual, family, and local community. This perpetuates financial losses that entrap families in poverty cycles while stunting local economic growth (eg, children leaving school early to pay for household and hospital bills).[238,239] For patients and families in LMICs, the quest for active cancer treatment will often plunge families into poverty for generations. Although the aforementioned programs are examples of how there can be a significant clinical impact in palliative care and cancer pain control, such systems remain in the vast minority. On the other hand, in North America and much of Europe, pain and symptom control are widely integrated into existing systems of health care. Integration of palliative care, however, does meet with complex challenges in some settings in high-income countries.

PAIN RELIEF

Opioids remain the keystone to cancer pain management worldwide. In the United States, there has been a complex toxic mix of excess availability of opioids; inexpensive street opioids; social and financial pressures; and a health care system vulnerable to a lack of systematic prescribing, monitoring and follow-up, which, along with our societal factors, have contributed to an "opioid crisis." The actual number of opioid-induced deaths is difficult to assess from the available data. The methodology used in the United States involving routine toxicology includes deaths related to any medical event where the patient may have taken a weak opioid for pain at the time of the acute event. Although we need to understand and deal with the opioid crisis, we need to acknowledge that four-fifths of the world population does not have access to opioid medication. We know that one of the main barriers to opioid availability in LMICs is the fear about opioid use. The current reporting of the opioid crisis only exacerbates these fears. There must be truthful, evidence-based, nonsensational reporting of the opioid crisis so we can ensure there are appropriate control systems in place for those who benefit hugely from opioid medication for pain management, remember that the starting point in the rest of the world is striving for adequate access to opioids, and require educational programs to facilitate the safe and appropriate prescribing for patients with cancer pain.

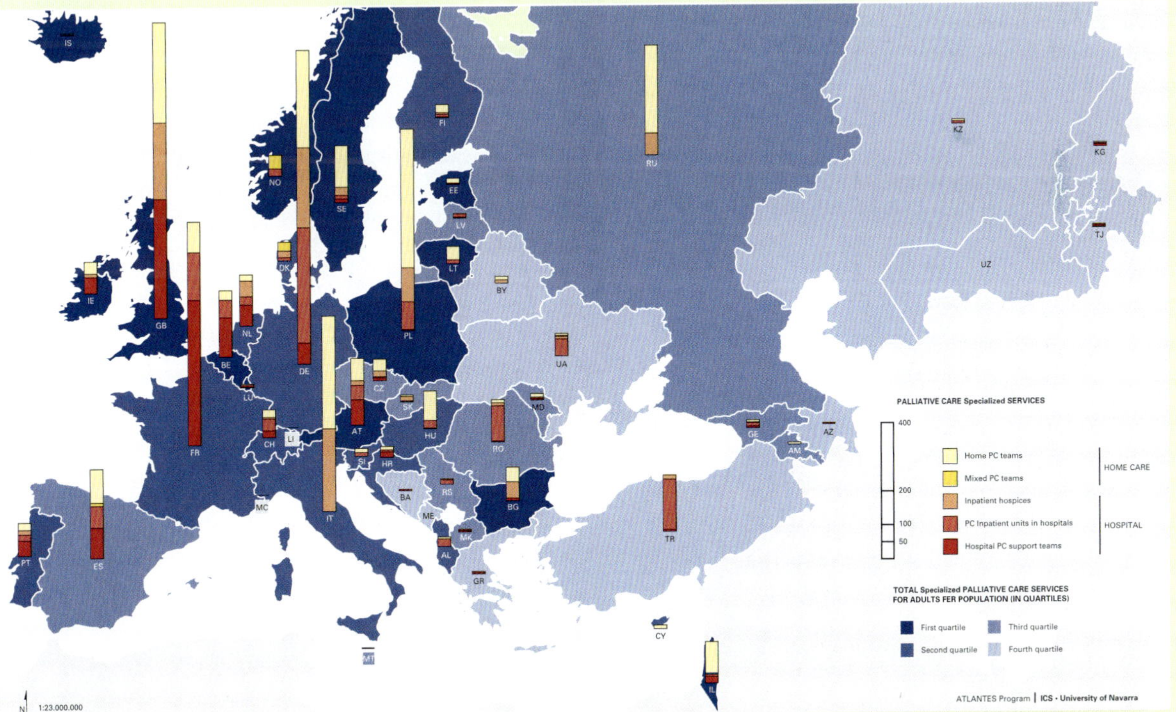

Fig. 8-11 **Number and typology of palliative care services in Europe.**

Abbreviation: PC, palliative care.

Adapted with permission from Arias-Casais et al.[260]

The opioid preparations that should be prioritized are immediate-release oral and injectable morphine for the management of pain and dyspnea.[238] WHO has recognized morphine as an essential medicine.[240] All the essential medicines should be easy to access and cheap.

THE WHO LADDER IN ALL COUNTRIES AND SIMPLIFYING PAIN MANAGEMENT IN LMICS

Pain is the most common and feared symptom in patients with cancer.[241,242] To address this, more than three decades ago, WHO published the analgesic three-step ladder for treatment of cancer pain.[243] Validation studies have shown that the WHO analgesic ladder can provide pain control in up to 80% of patients,[13,243-246] but these studies have not included LMICs, where cost and practical access to opioids need additional consideration. Trial observations from observational studies and small RCTs are encouraging, but it is still not known whether omitting step 2 of the WHO ladder, a weak opioid, results in more effective and sustained pain control without an excess of opioid-related adverse effects.

A multicenter RCT in the United Kingdom, Israel, Uganda, and Mexico aimed to establish whether a two-step approach (omitting the weak opioid second step) to cancer pain relief could achieve stable pain control quicker and without additional adverse effects, compared with the standard three-step approach of the WHO analgesic ladder. Of note, in many LMICs, there is excessive use of expensive weak opioids and little use of inexpensive strong opioids. The trial results demonstrated that in patients with moderate to severe cancer pain, commencing pain treatment with a strong opioid was as effective as using a weak opioid first. Moreover, those patients whose pain management was commenced directly with a strong opioid (negating the weak opioid step, usually, tramadol or codeine) had significantly fewer opioid-related adverse effects.[247,248]

The cost implications are important. Morphine is significantly cheaper than tramadol and codeine preparations, particularly in LMICs, where the difference can be eight-fold. Also, the process of switching from a weak to strong opioid, which is required by 50% of patients in first 10 days after prescription of a weak opioid, means additional travel or visiting and expense. These results are anticipated to influence more efficient and cheaper cancer pain management and, although of global relevance, potentially has more effect in LMICs.

THE SIMPLE ASPECTS OF PAIN AND SYMPTOM CONTROL

It should not be forgotten in LMICs and the rest of the world that we do our patients a disservice by failing to deal with the common problems systematically. Even before considering analgesia or other aspects of symptom control, we need to assess a patient correctly and be prepared to reassess after any treatment prescribed.

It has been demonstrated in a large RCT in the United Kingdom that a simple question about worst pain in last 24 hours, followed up with a few simple questions focusing on the common cancer pains, linked to management algorithms and then reassessment, led to improved pain control, more personalized treatment, less opioid medication, fewer adverse effects, and cost savings.[8] A simple patient-held version of this Edinburgh Pain Assessment Tool approach in rural Kenya also demonstrated an improvement in pain control.[249]

In summary, our greatest challenge globally and particularly in LMICs is to ensure that we can do the basics well for our patients. This will lead to the greatest improvements for the most patients.

9

PALLIATIVE CARE AND CARE AT THE END OF LIFE

Thomas W. LeBlanc, MD, MA, MHS, FAAHPM

Recent Updates

- A 2017 ASCO guideline recommends that patients with advanced cancer across all settings of care receive dedicated palliative care services early in the disease course and concurrent with active treatment. (Ferrell BR, *J Clin Oncol* 2017) A 2018 ASCO guideline on palliative care in the global setting recommends significant expansion, workforce development, and routine implementation of palliative care services, even in resource-poor settings. (Osman H, *J Clin Oncol* 2018)
- The collective evidence via systematic review and meta-analysis of 10 randomized trials demonstrate consistent improvements in patient outcomes with the addition of palliative care to usual oncology care, including symptoms, short-term quality of life, and survival. (Fulton JJ, *Palliat Med* 2018)
- Suggested triggers for specialty palliative care consultation among hospitalized patients with cancer include advanced disease (any cancer stage IV plus stage III pancreas and lung cancer) with at least one unmet palliative care need (eg, pain, advance care planning), and a previous hospitalization. (Adelson K, *J Oncol Pract* 2017)
- ASCO's communication guideline outlines key aspects of high-quality communication in cancer care, including the importance of discussing palliative care when initial cancer therapy begins, especially for those with advanced disease. Per this guideline, clinicians should also establish clear goals with patients, initiate conversations about end-of-life care preferences early in cases of incurable disease and ensure that patients understand their prognosis and treatment options. (Gilligan T, *J Clin Oncol* 2017)

OVERVIEW

In oncology, "palliative care" focuses on the relief of suffering and improvement in quality of life for the patient with cancer and his or her caregivers. Specialist palliative care provides an extra layer of support beyond that provided through standard cancer care and is appropriate at any age, and any stage, for those facing a serious illness. As such, it can be provided even along with curative intent treatments, such as stem cell transplantation. Modern specialist palliative care is provided by an interdisciplinary team, including nurses, chaplains, social workers, pharmacists, advanced practice clinicians, and physicians. Specialist palliative care views the patient and his or her loved ones as the unit of care, emphasizing a focus on understanding the stresses of the patient and the support system around them. As currently conceptualized per the National Consensus Project for Quality Palliative Care,[1] the suffering addressed by palliative care encompasses eight domains:

- Structures and processes of care (eg, the nature of supportive care services available, such as the presence of a truly interdisciplinary team, a bereavement program, and so forth)
- Physical aspects of care (eg, that symptoms are rigorously and regularly assessed and managed appropriately)
- Psychological (emotional) and psychiatric aspects of care (eg, screening and management of mood disorders, symptoms, and grief)
- Social aspects of care (eg, comprehensive interdisciplinary assessment of patient and family social needs, and development of a care plan to address them)
- Spiritual, religious, and existential aspects of care
- Cultural aspects of care
- Care of the imminently dying patient
- Ethical and legal aspects of care (eg, methods to assess values and preferences, and implement goal-concordant care, including but not limited to advance directives)

These areas of focus are the collective responsibility of the entire cancer care team, and they are sometimes complex or time intensive enough to warrant additional consultation with a palliative care specialist.

Although palliative care is relevant across the cancer trajectory and is not synonymous with end-of-life care, this chapter focuses on specialty palliative care services and also on care near the end of life, including hospice. Pain management, a key component of high-quality palliative care, is covered separately in Chapter 8: Pain and Symptom Management. The aims for this chapter are to briefly outline the scope of modern palliative cancer care and to help the cancer care clinician better understand how and when to effectively collaborate with a palliative care specialist.

THE SCOPE OF PALLIATIVE CARE IN ONCOLOGY

The term "palliative care" sometimes creates confusion. In different contexts it may refer to a medical specialty, a philosophy of care, or even a physical location. It also represents a type of care that is provided by many different types of clinicians and individuals, including not only oncologists but also advanced practitioners, nurses, chaplains, social workers, family therapists, and other members of the interdisciplinary team. Alternate terms are sometimes used, such as "supportive care," which also can cause confusion because, to oncology clinicians, this usually refers to the standard interventions we provide to support patients through cancer treatments, including antiemetics and growth factors. To some oncologists, discussions about palliative care can also feel threatening or accusatory (eg, I already provide palliative care to my patients, so why would I need to call someone else now?). A helpful resolution to this issue is to differentiate between different levels and types of palliative care. This concept is outlined in a framework proposed by von Gunten,[2] which separates the basic skills and competencies of providing care supporting quality of life (termed "primary palliative care") from the complex services provided by specialists who have undergone additional training and who offer consultative services (termed "secondary palliative care"). Furthermore, the framework also includes tertiary palliative care services, such as inpatient palliative care units and centers of excellence, where research and education focus on the most complex of cases.

Others draw comparisons between "generalist" and "specialist" palliative care.[3] Oncologists and other cancer care clinicians provide most of the "primary palliative care" for their patients, including assessment and management of symptoms, facilitating discussions about prognosis and goals of care and supporting the patient and caregiver(s) through the difficulties of having a serious illness. Sometimes it is also helpful to add a palliative care specialist to that mix to provide an extra layer of support and additional expertise regarding, for example, refractory symptom management, existential distress, or persistent prognostic misunderstanding, among many possibilities. This is done not at the exclusion of what the primary oncology team is doing but rather in addition to it, akin to the support a cardiologist might render to an oncologist who is treating a patient with refractory heart failure. In this way, specialist palliative care provides an extra layer of support not only to the patient/family but also to the cancer care team.

Remaining agnostic to the team providing the care, it is important to recognize that palliative care begins at diagnosis and extends throughout the course of cancer care. This is consistent with ASCO's position, as memorialized in a 2017 guideline update on the integration of palliative care into standard oncology care. This broader understanding of palliative care includes the care processes that oncology clinicians provide (eg, nausea management during chemotherapy) and also extends beyond the conclusion of active treatment. Most simply stated, palliative care is about helping patients and their loved ones live life to the fullest when faced with the reality of life-threatening illness.

It is important to recognize that specialist palliative care does not duplicate or replace anything done by the cancer care team; instead, it augments that care in areas of persistent patient and caregiver needs. Bickel et al[4] aimed to identify the palliative care processes that fit within the usual scope of oncology practice compared with those that may warrant consultation with a specialist.

Using a Delphi method of achieving consensus opinion, investigators proposed nearly 1,000 care processes to a multidisciplinary panel of experts. Domains with the highest proportion of care processes endorsed by oncologists as fundamental to routine oncology practice included end-of-life care, communication and shared decision-making, and advance care planning. Domains that were least included by oncologists and thus have the most potential for referral to others included spiritual and cultural assessment and psychosocial assessment and management. Delineations between primary and secondary palliative care practices included care that involved pain not responsive to usual opioids, and depression and anxiety requiring more management than standard first-line therapy. These findings mirror those from randomized trials of integrated palliative care in patients with advanced solid tumors, wherein palliative care specialists were noted to focus more on coping and psychosocial care during consultations than do the oncologists seeing those same patients.[5,6]

EVIDENCE SUPPORTING EARLY INTEGRATION OF SPECIALIST PALLIATIVE CARE

Evidence increasingly suggests that specialist palliative care integration improves patient and caregiver outcomes in cancer care. Palliative care can—and should—be delivered simultaneously with antineoplastic treatment whenever the symptom burden is high or the aim of the therapy is not explicitly curative, as recommended by ASCO guidelines;[7] ideally, oncologists and palliative care clinicians should work together daily. This approach is supported by evidence that palliative care improves not only traditional symptom-focused and quality-of-life outcomes but also survival. Results of the several landmark trials in North America of integrated palliative care are summarized in Table 9-1.

More recently, additional evidence from subsequent randomized trials has confirmed several benefits of early integrated palliative care. To date, > 1,000 patients have participated in randomized trials of early palliative care. Resulting benefits shown in these trials include reduced symptom intensity; improved quality of life; reductions in anxiety or depression and posttraumatic stress; improved caregiver outcomes; reductions in caregiver depression; reductions in use and aggressive end-of-life care; improved prognostic understanding, and prolonged overall survival.

A systematic review and meta-analysis of 30 trials involving patients with cancer also concluded that there were consistent and significant improvements in symptoms and quality of life when palliative care is integrated with usual oncology care.[8] A more recent meta-analysis that focused only on trials conducted in the outpatient oncology setting showed consistent effects on symptoms, short-term quality of life, and survival when palliative care is integrated in the care of patients with advanced solid tumors. Most importantly, no study to date has shown any harm by integrating palliative care into oncology care.[9]

On the basis of the rapidly expanding evidence base, ASCO released a provisional clinical opinion in March 2012[10] that was updated and published as a clinical practice guideline update in 2016.[7] The guideline recommended that "inpatients and outpatients with advanced cancer should receive dedicated palliative care services, early in the disease course, concurrent with active treatment." This guideline includes a checklist of items to address when providing high-quality palliative cancer care (Fig 9-1). The authors cited the burgeoning evidence demonstrating significant patient and caregiver benefits conferred by the addition of specialist palliative care services to routine cancer care, including nine randomized clinical trials and five secondary analyses from randomized clinical trials in the 2012 provisional clinical opinion.[10] Furthermore, the rapid expansion of new therapeutics in oncology and our evolving understanding of their adverse effects, the psychosocial and financial implications for patients, and the prognostic uncertainty with great promise at the population level but no guarantees at the individual patient level[11,12] require even more integration between oncology and palliative care. For these reasons, several professional societies now endorse integrated palliative care as a routine practice, including the American College of Surgeons Commission on Cancer,[13] the Oncology Nursing Society,[14] and the National Comprehensive Cancer Network.[15]

KEY POINTS

- Oncologists and their teams provide primary palliative care—the common and foundational services promoting quality of life among patients and families facing cancer—and refer those with more complex needs to specialists who provide palliative care services via consultative interdisciplinary teams.
- A growing body of evidence demonstrates numerous patient and caregiver benefits of integrating palliative care with the usual care of patients with advanced cancer, especially early in the disease course.
- ASCO has released a formal guideline recommending integration of palliative care services concurrent with disease-directed treatment among those patients with advanced cancer and/or significant symptom burden.

WHO PROVIDES SPECIALTY PALLIATIVE CARE?

PALLIATIVE CARE TRAINING AND WORKFORCE

The palliative care workforce is a topic of increasing interest. It is estimated that > 8,000 physicians have been trained and board certified in "hospice and palliative medicine," the official name for this medical specialty. The American Board of Medical Specialties (ABMS) first recognized this specialty in 2006. Since 2013, the ABMS has required candidates to complete a formal fellowship training program (12 months) and pass an examination to become board certified in this specialty.[16] There are > 100 fellowship programs today in the United States, and > 90% of hospitals with at least 300 beds have an available palliative care service.[17] Clinicians from 10 different primary fields can train and certify in hospice and palliative medicine, including family medicine, anesthesiology, pediatrics, obstetrics and gynecology, emergency medicine, surgery, neurology, psychiatry, internal medicine, radiology, physical medicine, and rehabilitation. Some programs specialize in pediatric palliative care; however, at this time there is only one board certification examination, which includes adult and pediatric content. Nonphysician clinicians may also train and certify in palliative care, with various certification programs available through professional societies like the Hospice and Palliative Nurses Association, the National Association of Social Workers, among others.

Fellowship training programs in hospice and palliative medicine emphasize core skills of serious illness care; coordination; and communication, including: symptom assessment and management, prognostic communication, goals-of-care discussion, conflict management and resolution, advance directive completion, psychosocial distress assessment and management, spiritual assessment and support, family and

Table 9-1 **Landmark Trials of Integrated Palliative Care**

First Author; Trial	Trial Design	Results	Conclusions
Bakitas[159]; ENABLE II	Randomized controlled trial of a nurse-led palliative care intervention *v* usual care in people newly diagnosed with advanced cancer	Better quality of life and mood in intervention group Symptom intensity and hospital or ICU visits did not differ between groups.	A nurse-provided palliative care educational intervention can improve quality of life and mood among patients with advanced cancer.
Temel[5]	Randomly assigned patients with newly diagnosed metastatic NSCLC to receive either early palliative care integrated with standard oncologic care or standard oncologic care alone	Better quality of life at 12 weeks in palliative care group *v* standard care group Fewer patients with depression in palliative care group Longer survival in palliative care group	Early palliative care can improve quality of life and mood in patients with metastatic lung cancer, while reducing aggressive end-of-life care and possibly prolonging survival.
Zimmerman[160]	Medical oncology clinics cluster-randomized to early palliative care or standard care for patients with advanced cancer of various solid tumor histologies	Improved quality of life at 3 months (statistically nonsignificant), improved quality of life at the end of life, improved family satisfaction with care Improved symptom intensity, quality of life, and family satisfaction with care at 4 months	Findings suggest benefit of early palliative care in patients with advanced cancer of various types.
Bakitas[161]; ENABLE III	Randomly assigned patients with advanced cancer to early or delayed palliative care	1-year survival rates: 63% in early intervention group 48% in delayed group	Potential survival benefit of integrating palliative care specialist services soon after diagnosis of advanced cancer
Grudzen[162]	Randomly assigned patients with advanced cancer treated at an emergency department to palliative care or usual care	Improved quality of life after 12 weeks with palliative care *v* usual care	Incorporating palliative care services during emergency department visits improves quality of life for patients with advanced cancer.
El-Jawahri[66,163]	Randomly assigned adults with hematologic cancers undergoing stem cell transplant to palliative care or standard transplant care	Palliative care group had smaller decrease in quality of life at 2 weeks, less increase in depression and lower anxiety. Sustained effects on mood and posttraumatic stress at 3 and 6 months.	Use of inpatient palliative care after transplantation can lessen symptom burden and improve quality of life and mood, while reducing posttraumatic stress among transplant survivors.
Temel[164]	Randomly assigned patients with lung cancer or GI cancer to early integrated palliative care and oncology care or usual care	Greater improvement in quality of life at 24 weeks, but not 12 weeks, and less depression in palliative care group *v* usual care group at week 24. Patients with lung cancers appeared to benefit more from integrated palliative care than did patients with GI cancer.	Early palliative care integrated with oncology care improves quality of life for patients newly diagnosed with incurable lung or GI cancers but may have differential effects by cancer type.

Abbreviations: ICU, intensive care unit; NSCLC, non–small-cell lung cancer.

Palliative Care Checklist

- ☐ Assess patient/caregiver medical literacy
- ☐ Assess patient/caregiver willingness to hear prognosis
- ☐ Assess patient/caregiver role preferences
    - o Patient prefers to share the decision with ______________________
    - o Patient prefers to decide him/herself after hearing the views of ______________________
    - o Patient prefers that someone else decides
    - o Patient prefers to decide on his/her own
- ☐ Assess patient/caregiver understanding of diagnosis, illness, and prognosis
- ☐ Offer clarification of treatment goals*
- ☐ Use standardized symptom assessment tools (Edmonton Symptom Assessment Scale or Condensed Memorial Symptom Assessment Scale)**
    - o Pain*
    - o Pulmonary symptoms (cough, dyspnea)*
    - o Fatigue and sleep disturbance*
    - o Mood (depression and anxiety)*
    - o GI (anorexia and weight loss, nausea and vomiting, constipation)*
- ☐ Screen for distress (with tool such as Distress Thermometer)
- ☐ Refer for or conduct psychosocial assessment
- ☐ Take a spiritual history***
- ☐ Refer for psychosocial support
- ☐ Refer to social work for practical issues (e.g. financial, caregiver, home health, transportation)
- ☐ For patients who are earlier in the disease course, consider referral for nutrition, physical and occupational therapy support.
- ☐ Identify care plan for future appointments*
- ☐ Document referrals to other care providers*/information and/or support sources
    - o Document referral to hospice
    - o Advanced Directive
    - o DNR
- ☐ Document new medications prescribed*
- ☐ Document patient/caregivers primary concerns and/or issues

*Adapted from Supplemental Table 1: Ambulatory Palliative Care Guidelines Supplement to: Temel JS, Greer JA, Muzikansky A, et al. Early palliative care for patients with metastatic non-small-cell lung cancer. N Engl J Med 2010;363:733-42.

**Pain and Symptom Management tools – Measure and Evaluation Tools - National Palliative Care Research Center - http://www.npcrc.org/content/25/Measurement-and-Evaluation-Tools.aspx

***FIACA Spiritual History Tool © George Washington University Institute for Spirituality and Health – www.gwish.org

This checklist is derived from recommendations in the ASCO Palliative Care Clinical Practice Guideline Update (2016). This is a practice tool based on an ASCO® guideline and is not intended to substitute for the independent professional judgment of the treating physician. Practice guidelines do not account for individual variation aong patients. This tool does not purport to suggest any particular course of medical treatment. Use of the guideline and this tool are voluntary. The guideline and additional information are available at www.asco.org/palliative-care-guideline.

Fig. 9-1 Palliative care checklist.[7]

DNR, do not resuscitate.

caregiver support, and end-of-life care. Although these topics are often part of what cancer care clinicians do in caring for their patients with advanced disease, palliative care specialists receive advanced training in these areas and thus possess expert, high-level skills in these domains. Given that these topics are of central importance to the practicing oncologist as well, however, they are highlighted briefly in the latter half of this chapter.

Overall, cancer care is facing a looming workforce crisis, with projections forecasting significant shortages of oncologists across the United States in the near future. This problem is also affecting the palliative care workforce, wherein there are simply not enough palliative care specialists to see all the patients who might benefit from their services.[18] As palliative care becomes more mainstream—a key element of high-quality comprehensive cancer care as recommended per ASCO guidelines—workforce issues will only worsen. However, given the limited number of fellowship programs available and the minimal federal funding to support fellowship training programs, there is no clear resolution in sight. And given the scarcity of palliative care specialists, it is important to further identify which cancer populations obtain the most benefit from specialty level palliative care. Some data indicate patients with cancer experience different benefits at varying trajectories of illness. Furthermore, enhancing the primary palliative care skills of primary oncology clinicians will be necessary to ensure all patients with cancer receive timely, high-quality treatment.

CONSULTING PALLIATIVE CARE

Palliative care consultation teams have expanded rapidly into cancer hospitals and clinics, with more than one-third of cancer centers now having access to a palliative care team.[19] Specialty palliative care teams often manage refractory pain or other physical symptoms and complex psychosocial issues (eg, depression, anxiety, grief, and existential distress), address advance care planning, facilitate conflict resolution regarding goals or methods of treatment, and help address cases of perceived nonbeneficial care.

Palliative care consultation teams are intended to complement the role of the oncology team, which provides "primary palliative care," as listed in the section titled The Scope of Palliative Care in Oncology, especially when needs are complex and distress is significant. As mentioned, most patients with cancer do not require a palliative care consultation; rather, the needs of the patient and the capacity for the oncology team to provide those services should dictate when a consultation is requested. Importantly, as the evidence base for palliative care grows, oncologists should incorporate those teams into the multidisciplinary approach, similar to how radiation oncology and surgical oncology are included for certain cancer types and stages.

Criteria or triggers for involving specialty palliative care services are one proposed method of targeting those patients most likely to benefit from consultation, but results have been mixed. Adelson et al[20] have reported the results of a pilot program to automatically consult palliative care when patients with cancer are hospitalized. Consultation criteria include any stage IV solid tumors or stage III lung or pancreas cancer with any of the following: prior hospitalization within 30 days, length of stay longer than 7 days, and at least one uncontrolled symptom. The authors demonstrated high acceptance of the triggers, a decrease in the mortality index, and an almost 50% reduction in the 30-day hospital readmission rate.

Other evidence from a prospective trial of a solid-tumor oncology service points to implementation challenges and unclear impact.[21] As such, triggers for when to include palliative care in the routine care of patients with cancer are still immature and in development. Other initiatives actively involve palliative care specialists as part of the inpatient oncology team, recognizing that being hospitalized as a patient with cancer is often a hallmark of poor outcomes in the near future.[22] Clinicians should assess each patient and their caregivers for potential benefits from seeing a palliative care specialist and keep this option open at all times during the disease course.

KEY POINTS

- Palliative care consultation should be considered for any patient with advanced cancer and/or significant symptoms, per ASCO guideline recommendations.
- In addition to complex or refractory symptom management, palliative care specialists can be helpful with goals of care discussions, advance care planning, and conflict resolution.

ISSUES RELEVANT TO PALLIATIVE CARE

COMMUNICATION AND ILLNESS UNDERSTANDING

Communicating difficult news to patients and families is a critical but challenging aspect of caring for patients who are seriously ill. The provision of accurate information to patients and caregivers can enhance illness understanding and thereby facilitate collaborative decision-making. How the clinician delivers this information can have serious repercussions for the emotional health of patients and their loved ones.[23] Communication skills are like physical examination skills in that they can be taught and then must be practiced and honed over time, lest they atrophy.

Good communication in palliative care should begin with the following:

- assessment of the patient's and family's understanding of the likely course of the disease, the patient's capacity for decision-making or need for a surrogate, and the patient's and family's communication style;
- clarification of how much information the patient would like and how much information should be given to the family; and
- discussion of the patient's and family's preferences for care and quality of life.

This approach, which emphasizes asking permission before embarking on a difficult discussion or addressing an important topic, is an important step in rapport building and keeping communication lines open.[24] It should initiate an ongoing process of clear and consistent discussion with the patient and family regarding treatment, changes of status, prognosis, end of life, and patient and family needs, at diagnosis and at key transition points thereafter (eg, when imaging studies show worsening disease).[25] Timely advance care planning discussions and readdressing planning needs during disease transitions remain major predictors of aggressiveness of end-of-life care and use of hospice, further reinforcing the role of these conversations in optimizing appropriate, patient-centered advanced cancer care.[26] When appropriate, the palliative care team and/or hospice clinicians can assist with these conversations.

Clinician Expectations and Patient Perceptions

Evidence demonstrates that many patients with metastatic cancer incorrectly perceive chemotherapy as being likely to

Table 9-2 **Five Brief Steps for Discussing Prognosis With your Patient: AEGIS**[165]

Strategy	Directive	Example Inquiry
Ask	Ask what the patient knows and what information he or she wants to know.	What have other doctors told you about your prognosis or the future?
		How much have you been thinking about the future?
	Ask the patient whether he or she desires the participation of family members or friends during this discussion.	Would having your family or friend be present during today's discussion be helpful to you?
Explore	Explore what specific information the patient believes would be most helpful.	For some people, prognosis means numbers or statistics about how long they will live. For others, prognosis means reaching a milestone, goal, or a specific date.
	Here, you can frame the discussion to explore whether the patient desires quantitative or qualitative information.	What information would be most helpful to you?
	Expect uncertainty or ambivalence for receiving this information, even if the patient or family inquires.	This must be incredibly challenging for you to talk about. Help me understand the pros and cons of knowing this information for you.
	Negotiating the scope, type, and format of prognostic information is key at this stage.	Some folks prefer a best-case/worst-case scenario. Would that be of benefit to you?
Give	Give information tailored to the patient and sensitive to the patient's needs.	If giving quantitative information:
	Give the information in the form that the patient desires (quantitative or qualitative).	The statistics say that 5-year survival is XX%. That means that about X of 10 people in this situation are expected to still be alive in 5 years.
		The worst-case scenario is [25th percentile], and the best-case scenario is [75th percentile].
	Pause after two sentences or pieces of information to allow the patient to process it cognitively.	If giving qualitative information:
		From my understanding of your case, I think there is a good/slim chance that you will be around for your daughter's wedding.
Invite	Invite inquiry on how much more the patient wants to know. Expect emotion. Name the emotion. Expect silence. Acknowledge the emotional weight that this information carries. Provide empathy.	What information can I clarify for you?
		I know this information can be frightening.
		I see this information is probably not what you were expecting.
		What makes you most worried?
		I can see this information makes you angry.
		I admire how you have been coping with this diagnosis.
Summarize	Check in about the patient's understanding of today's discussion of prognosis.	Do you feel you have all the information on prognosis that you need?
		Might you repeat and summarize what we discussed about the future?
		Tell me, what have you learned from our visit today?
		Do you have all the information you need to make your decisions about the future?
	Summarize that you will revisit prognostic information in the future, especially at important phases of treatment.	We will revisit prognostic information during the course of your treatment, such as at each scan or cycle of treatment.

NOTE. Information is based on the VitalTalk, Comskil, and SPIKES cancer communication programs.
Abbreviation: AEGIS, ask, explore, give, invite, summarize.

cure their disease, reflecting a sizeable gap between clinicians' expectations and patients' perceptions. Underscoring this, Weeks et al[27] demonstrated that > 50% of patients with metastatic colon and lung cancer thought chemotherapy was likely to cure them. Discussing intent and potential benefits of cancer-directed therapies should be considered an integral component of the informed-consent process, alongside the usual conversations about risk and potential adverse effects of antineoplastic therapy. In the era of immunotherapies, prognostication is only becoming more difficult; although exceptional responders to such therapies remain the exception rather than the rule, robust responses are common enough to raise more uncertainty in discussions about the future with patients who previously would be said to have clearly incurable metastatic disease with a life expectancy of weeks to months.[12] Recent evidence shows that prognostic misunderstanding is common among patients with hematologic malignancies, as well.[28,29]

Physicians sometimes unknowingly provide an overly optimistic evaluation of a patient's prognosis[30,31] or, alternatively, provide no prognostic information until the patient nears death.[32,33] In addition, patients often interpret prognostic information in an optimistic way; many patients exhibit a tendency to believe they will be an exception, the one to "beat the odds."[34] Patients' perceptions of prognosis and their choices regarding therapy are demonstrably influenced by the way in which they receive information from their physicians.[35,36] Information presented from a positive perspective (eg, percentage of patients with a given condition who survive to the 5-year point) is perceived to be better than the same information delivered in negative terms (eg, percentage of patients with this same condition who do not survive to 5 years). Patients who harbor falsely optimistic perceptions often opt for aggressive medical therapy, despite evidence that aggressive care, compared with palliative measures only, confers no survival benefit for terminally ill patients.[37] This makes it critically important for clinicians to routinely assess prognostic understanding, to honestly and supportively convey accurate prognostic information to patients and families, and to check back in about their understanding of the information.

Communicating an Accurate Prognosis

Complicating this task is the concern that an accurate prognosis may undermine a patient's hope—a view held by many clinicians.[38,39] The value of hope is rated highly by patients and caregivers, who emphasize that they do not want doctors to lessen hope, even at the end of life.[40,41] In terminal illness, however, physicians can redefine hope—without implying a cure—by helping patients come to a realistic understanding of their prognosis and by setting realistic goals, such as reduction of pain, alleviation of distress, and achievement of closure with family members.[23] Similarly, many people worry that an accurate prognosis will diminish the patient's "fighting spirit," especially when there is coexisting depression. Although it is essential to address any presenting psychiatric illness, little evidence exists to suggest that a fighting spirit improves morbidity or mortality rates.[42] In reality, many patients struggle to cope with news of a poor prognosis; this struggle is often apparent in seemingly contradictory expressions of unrealistic hope for longevity alongside awareness of prognosis (eg, by discussing funeral plans).[43] We also know that patients and families abhor the notion that their oncologist might be withholding or "sugar coating" information about the likely outcome, thus reinforcing the notion that people really do want an honest assessment of prognosis from their oncologist, no matter how difficult the news may be.[38] The challenge, then, is to deliver difficult news with compassion, support, and empathy.

Communication Practices and Techniques

A formal ASCO patient-clinician communication guideline outlines best practices for communication in cancer care, including:

- the importance of communication skills training programs;
- the need for regular discussions of goals of care with patients;
- partnering with patients actively in their care;
- initiating conversations about end-of-life preferences early in serious illness, and often thereafter;
- discussing costs of care; and
- making patients aware of all options for their care, including the early initiation of concurrent palliative care.[45]

Although most guidelines for delivering bad news to patients and families do not have much empirical evidence to support their use,[46] they are based on viable communication principles and consensus expert opinion, and, therefore, have good face validity.[47,48] A formal discussion of bad news might best be preceded by thorough preparation. Clinicians should discuss how patients would like to receive prognostic information (and whether they actually desire it) before starting any conversation involving bad news; consider that patients and families hold different views about who should participate in such discussions, what information should be included, the appropriate setting, and who should convey the information; and ideally endeavor to be prepared with accurate, up-to-date information and to deliver the news themselves.

Recommended frameworks for giving difficult news include the SPIKES method and the REMAP approach, as described in detail elsewhere.[47,49]

Communication techniques that convey compassion and alignment with the patient's feelings of disappointment with bad news should be used. Phrases such as "I wish things were different" and "We are in a different place" are useful ways to express alliance with the patient and a potential need for transition in the goals of care.[5] If possible, the setting should be private and free from distractions, and the oncologist should be seated.[47] Patients and family members must be allowed to speak and ask questions; they perceive more compassion, and that more time was spent with them, when the clinician sits and when they are allowed to talk for a larger proportion of the encounter.[46] On the contrary, the length of a visit is not actually correlated with family satisfaction.[50] (Table 9-2)

To evaluate the patient's and family's levels of understanding and to anticipate their reactions, the clinician should initiate any discussion of bad news by inquiring about what they already know and what they want to know. This enables the patient and family to determine the level of information they seek and how to best convey that information. The physician can then deliver the information but should pause frequently to verify understanding and to allow for questions; a reasonable approach is to provide no more than three items of information before pausing to ensure that the patient and his or her family understand and do not have questions. At the end of the discussion, the clinician should confirm that the patient and family have a sound understanding—for example, by asking them to summarize the information in their own words. This approach is often termed "ask-tell-ask," and is rooted in research and teaching about high-quality communication in serious illness care. Finally, a clear agenda should be established, covering what the patient and family will do, what the physician will do, and when the next contact will occur.[45]

Cultural Competence

Cross-cultural reviews have helped expand the literature related to communication in palliative and end-of-life care; these perspectives are particularly relevant to clinicians treating increasingly heterogeneous populations. An Indian review reported on collusion in palliative care communications resulting in, for example, nearly half of patients with cancer in India being unaware of their diagnosis and treatment.[52] Similar cultural norms with respect to truth telling and withholding of information have been reported in Chinese culture.[53] In both instances, strong family values include a central role for family members in managing the patient's disease, communication, and health care at or near the end of life. Of relevance to the US oncologist, these studies suggest the importance of being aware that patients with a background in other cultures may have different expectations for communication, and explaining and discussing the communication plan with the patient and family members to establish common expectations, before actually communicating bad news. Be sure not to make any assumptions about how much or little a patient wants to know based on his or her cultural background. Inquiry is key. Where available, an interpreter or other cultural liaison may be of help in facilitating effective communication.

ADVANCE DIRECTIVES

Discussion of advance care planning is sometimes a helpful starting point for conversations at or near the end of life and, truly, for any patient with advanced and potentially life-limiting disease. Ideally, these discussions should happen much farther upstream from when the end of life is near. It is important to understand the difference between advance care planning and advance directives.

Advance care planning is a process whereby individuals consider their end-of-life treatment preferences and make them known to loved ones and health care professionals in the event of decisional incapacity. Components of advance care planning, which the patient may or may not have completed in written form, may include advance care directives, health care proxies or powers of attorney, living wills, and do-not-resuscitate orders. When a patient cannot communicate or loses decisional capacity, a selected health care proxy becomes the surrogate decision-maker. Individuals may formally designate a health care proxy and document end-of-life treatment preferences in an advance directive. Completion of an advance care planning process has been associated with a greater likelihood of receiving the care one desires at end of life, and a lower likelihood of dying in the hospital, or otherwise receiving aggressive end-of-life care, and a higher likelihood of using hospice care services.[26] When advance care planning occurs very late in a patient's life, sometimes these discussions are referred to in the framework of "goals of care." Again, advance care planning really should be done in advance—hence the term; very late discussions are not ideal.

An advance directive is a legal document representing a person's preferences regarding their medical care. It may be in the form of a living will, health care proxy, or physician note, which includes the name of the patient's health care proxy. The percentage of individuals with a documented advance directive remains low, even in the setting of serious illness such as advanced cancer, where documentation rates are 20%.[54] When these documents exist, they can be used as the basis of discussion about the patient's values and preferences for end-of-life care. When they have not been completed, the oncologist can enlist the assistance of an appropriate individual (eg, a social worker or member of the palliative care team) to help the family complete forms after he or she has introduced the concept, explained the purpose, and discussed the benefits and process of advance care planning with the patient and any relevant family members or caregivers. In many cases, the patient with very advanced cancer may lose decisional capacity as their illness progresses; here, an assessment should confirm this status and, thereafter, a surrogate should be identified. Options for palliative care, including hospice, should be described at this time. Conversations should elicit the patient's and family's values, feelings, and preferences with respect to decision-making about end-of-life care. There are online advance care planning tools available that are effective at increasing rates of advance directive completion by 25% to 35% and are easily completed via free online resources such as the PREPARE website.[55,56]

KEY POINTS

- Many patients with advanced cancer overestimate their prognosis, expecting they can be cured in cases of incurable disease, or overestimating the likelihood of a good outcome. Assessment and discussion of prognosis are important parts of high-quality communication in cancer care.

- The recent ASCO communication guideline outlines principles of good communication in cancer care, including assessment and discussion of prognosis, elicitation of preferences and values, and discussion about the role of early integrated palliative care.
- Advance care planning should occur at diagnosis of advanced cancer and should include a general discussion of goals, values, and preferences, in addition to the completion of documents to memorialize those thoughts, such as via free web tools.

PSYCHOLOGICAL DISTRESS

Patient

Death is a process fraught with emotion for patients as well as for family members, other informal caregivers, and clinicians, all of whom have a unique relationship to the dying patient. Although psychosocial concerns frequently occur at the end of life, they can be difficult to detect or diagnose. Certain psychological states that may resemble depression are, in fact, normal at the end of life; physical symptoms normally experienced by the patient at the end of life may otherwise constitute somatic diagnostic criteria for psychiatric illnesses. Nevertheless, clinicians must remain vigilant for signs and symptoms of distress, which include concerns about illness, sadness, anger, feelings of loss of control, poor sleep, poor appetite, poor concentration, and preoccupation with thoughts of illness and death. Awareness of psychological concerns takes on greater importance for clinicians treating patients who are terminally ill, for whom psychological distress may increase as death approaches.[57,58]

It is estimated that as many as 82% of patients who are terminally ill experience some form of psychiatric illness,[58,59] including adjustment disorder (10% to 16%),[61,62] depressive disorders (3% to 82%),[61,62] and anxiety disorders (7% to 79%).[59,62] Risk factors for distress in patients with cancer include cognitive impairment, communication barriers (eg, language, literacy), history of psychiatric disorder, history of substance abuse, history of depression or suicidality, psychosocial issues (eg, family conflict, young or dependent children, limited social support, living alone), financial concerns, and uncontrolled symptoms.

Although the end of life is frequently marked by emotional symptoms, physicians often struggle to address these concerns during the medical interview. Many physicians report feeling uncertain about their ability to effectively discuss emotional topics, especially those that accompany bad news.[47,63] Evidence also shows that oncologists frequently miss or ignore opportunities to express empathy when their patients share emotional concerns.[64] Reimbursement restrictions and the typical structure of the medical interview, along with short appointment times, further discourage some clinicians from freely discussing psychosocial issues.[65] Physicians often fear discussions that address emotional content will take too much time or elicit powerful feelings the patient will be unable to manage. The evidence, however, should dispel this concern: research demonstrates that medical encounters are shorter when the physician openly acknowledges the patient's emotional concerns.[66] In addition, emerging data that demonstrate the beneficial effects of specialty-level palliative care suggest this benefit is primarily mediated through improved coping, a critical skill that oncology clinicians can incorporate into everyday practice.[67]

Distress in patients with advanced cancer can be identified using a simple screening tool such as the National Comprehensive Cancer Network Distress Thermometer (Fig 9-2), which asks the patient to rate his or her distress on a 0 to 10 visual scale from "no distress" (0) to "extreme distress" (10). Many other distress assessment instruments exist; one systematic review identified 33 instruments of varying lengths examined in 106 validation studies. In patients receiving palliative care, the Combined Depression Questions performed best of the ultrashort measures (one to four items). Among the short instruments (five to 20 items), the Hospital Anxiety and Depression Scale (HADS) and the Center for Epidemiologic Studies–Depression Scale (CES-D) demonstrated adequate psychometric properties. Long instruments (21 to 50 items) are also available but are often less clinically feasible in the palliative care setting; ones exhibiting robust psychometrics are the Beck Depression Inventory (BDI), General Health Questionnaire–28, Psychosocial Screen for Cancer, Questionnaire on Stress in Cancer Patients–Revised, and the Rotterdam Symptom Checklist.[68] For patients who report significant distress, appropriate referral to psychiatric care, psychotherapy, counseling or social work services, and/or chaplaincy is warranted.

Caregiver/Family

Psychosocial problems are not limited to the patient with a terminal illness. Studies show that 32% to 70% of caregivers (primarily family members, but also including other informal caregivers) of patients with advanced cancer experience a level of distress or depressive symptoms high enough to suggest clinical depression.[69-71] Caregivers often are unprepared for the various commitments—financial, emotional, and physical—that are involved in caring for a dying loved one.[72] Furthermore, many caregivers lack the medical knowledge and skills necessary to anticipate the needs of the patient. Because of the multiple demands of caregiving, family members often are forced to leave their jobs or to work part-time, which adds financial stress at a time that is already emotionally challenging. Moreover, by attending to the needs of their dying loved one, caregivers often neglect their own health and emotional needs.[73]

Certain characteristics of caregivers are associated with negative effects of caregiving. These include age of the caregiver, ethnicity, sex, socioeconomic status, and caregiver health and functional status. Younger, nonwhite, female, and less affluent individuals tend to experience greater negative effects such as distress or depressive symptoms. Other factors associated with

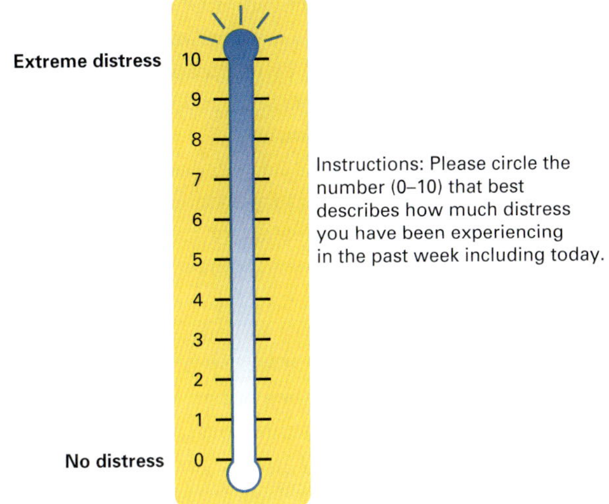
Extreme distress
10
9
8
7
6
5
4
3
2
1
0
No distress
Instructions: Please circle the number (0–10) that best describes how much distress you have been experiencing in the past week including today.

Fig. 9-2 National Comprehensive Cancer Network Distress Thermometer.

Adapted with permission from the NCCN Clinical Practice Guidelines in Oncology (NCCN Guidelines®) for Distress Management V.1.2020. © 2020 National Comprehensive Cancer Network, Inc. All rights reserved. The NCCN Guidelines® and illustrations herein may not be reproduced in any form for any purpose without the express written permission of NCCN. To view the most recent and complete version of the NCCN Guidelines, go online to NCCN.org. The NCCN Guidelines are a work in progress that may be refined as often as new significant data becomes available. NCCN makes no warranties of any kind whatsoever regarding their content, use or application and disclaims any responsibility for their application or use in any way.

negative effects include the duration and intensity of caregiving, mood and physical health of the caregiver, a recurrence of the patient's illness, and the caregiver's subjective sense of burden.[74] Of note, a growing body of evidence suggests that integrated palliative care can yield significant benefits on caregiver well-being, particularly regarding mood.[75,76] This approach is underused.

Providing effective symptom relief is a primary way in which physicians can help caregivers and their patients who are terminally ill.[77] Just as treating depression can improve pain control, control of both pain and nonpain symptoms helps alleviate or prevent depression.[78,79] Patients who have higher levels of symptom distress or depression are more likely to have caregivers with greater depressive symptoms and negative perceptions of their own health.[80-82] When a patient who is terminally ill experiences a reduction in distress, it also can help decrease the caregiving burden and the psychological effects of terminal illness on caregivers. This may explain the caregiver improvements seen in palliative care trials that focus on the patient's well-being.

Support of caregivers has become an important topic within oncology. The latest data report that as many as 40% of all U. adults are now caring for a sick or elderly family member.[83] These caregivers are having important effects on the treatment and outcomes of the patients they care for. For example, one retrospective cohort study of a large cancer registry by Aizer et al[84] showed that patients with spouses were less likely to present with metastatic disease, more likely to receive curative therapy, and less likely to die of cancer after adjusting for demographics, stage, and treatment. Another study demonstrated that the quality and frequency of interactions between patients and caregivers predict hospital readmission—an important measure of care quality.[85] Furthermore, Dionne-Odom et al[76] demonstrated the benefits of caregiver support through palliative care, noting improvements in depression and stress burden when clinicians focus on the caregiver's needs early in the care of patients with advanced cancer. Because many patients with advanced cancer experience an unplanned hospital admission in the last months of life, caregiver support is increasingly recognized as a way oncology teams can further patient-centered, resource-efficient care.

In offering high-quality primary palliative and supportive care at the end of life, the clinician exerts a powerful therapeutic effect simply by being present. By being available, by communicating openly about difficult topics, and by addressing symptoms that are causing distress, the physician can provide significant support. Caregivers particularly value the support and respect of clinicians; those who report that physicians listen to their opinions and concerns are less likely to report depressive symptoms.[86,87] Good communication, which includes anticipatory guidance and clear explanations of what to expect, is an essential therapeutic tool. By providing appropriate referrals to assistance agencies, such as hospice, physicians can greatly support family members.[88] In all cases, effective communication, listening, and availability contribute substantially to alleviating suffering at the end of life.

DEPRESSION

Identifying and differentiating between grief and depression in patients who are dying can be quite difficult, even for seasoned clinicians. In general, depressed patients tend to remain in a persistent state of sadness, to have a poor view of themselves, to sustain a sense of hopelessness, and to derive little pleasure from new situations or from memories of past events.[89,90] By contrast, patients with normal grief reactions typically experience a progression of feelings, are able to maintain a realistic view of themselves, and can modify their health care goals to maintain hope. Diagnosing depression at the end of life is of paramount importance; studies show that untreated depression results in an increase in morbidity and sequelae, including suicide. Depression, as well as hopelessness, loss of meaning in life, and loss of interest in activities, ranks among the risk factors for the desire to hasten death.[23,91] Patients whose psychosocial needs are acknowledged are less likely to persist in their desire for death.[92] When a patient expresses a desire to hasten death, requests should be addressed explicitly and should prompt a reassessment of symptom control, psychosocial issues such as relationship strain or fear of caregiver burden, spiritual or existential suffering, and psychological issues such as depression. The care plan should be clarified with renewed attention to how best to relieve physical, psychological, interpersonal, and spiritual suffering.

Studies in patients with cancer at the end of life report prevalence of general depression and depressive mood ranging from 21% to 37%.[60,93] The median prevalence of major depressive disorder in patients with advanced cancer is reported to be 15%.[94] Several instruments have been created or adapted to help identify depression in the terminally ill. Well-recognized and validated instruments include the BDI-Short Form,[95] HADS,[96] Edmonton Symptom Assessment Scale,[97] Edinburgh Depression Scale, and Brief Edinburgh Depression Scale.[98] Considerable efforts have been devoted to developing simple one-and two-item verbal screens for depression, but a Bayesian meta-analysis found that, although these brief methods perform well at excluding depression in the nondepressed person, they perform poorly at identifying depression; two-item measures are superior to single-item screens, but neither is sufficient for depression assessment.[99] Oncologists may elect to use these brief assessments for convenience and as an initial screen but should not rely exclusively on them. Assessment for symptoms of depression in patients who are terminally ill is a critical component of care and warrants a more thorough assessment using a well-validated instrument. ASCO recommends that all patients with cancer be evaluated for depression and anxiety at various times in their course of illness.[100]

Guidelines established for the general care of psychiatric illness may be applied to the treatment of depression for patients who are terminally ill, but with certain adjustments. Referral should be made to an appropriate clinician, ideally a palliative care expert, psychiatrist, or psychologist with expertise in management of psychological disorders who can tailor care to this stage of illness. Treatments, particularly pharmacologic therapies, must take into account the patient's prognosis. For example, when the patient has a limited life expectancy, selective serotonin reuptake inhibitors may not exert an effect quickly enough; psychostimulants may offer a more realistic treatment strategy.

SPIRITUAL OR EXISTENTIAL SUFFERING

For patients with serious illness, like cancer, the spiritual needs of the patient, family members, and other caregivers typically become heightened. Good spiritual care is essential to high-quality end-of-life care. This involves helping the patient and loved ones address existential issues that may occur, such as "Why me?" "What is the meaning of life?" "Why am I here?" "What have I achieved in my life?" "How do I fit into the universe?" and "What will happen to 'me' after my death?" The clinician should recognize that the spiritual belief systems of all parties concerned, as well as their personal belief systems regarding our spiritual nature, will influence how they react to these broad spiritual questions.

Although physicians typically are not trained to provide spiritual care, patients and families often assume clinicians will be able to adequately introduce and discuss issues surrounding care of the spirit. Many people consider an expected death to be a valuable opportunity to address any outstanding spiritual issues, and they expect that this work will take place in the context of their loved one's medical care. Yet, for many clinicians, the prospect of providing spiritual care to someone at the end of life presents a formidable challenge.

Oncologists may tend to refer to a patient's, family's, or caregiver's belief system (eg, religious affiliation) to evaluate their orientation toward spirituality, life, dying, and death. However, although patients may name a particular belief system, one cannot assume that particular interpretations or beliefs apply, even if they are commonly associated with the declared religion or belief system. Although a religion may provide a broad frame of reference for a person's beliefs, it cannot supply the detail required to understand the ways in which a patient may respond to arising spiritual concerns or to determine how to best support him or her with spiritual care.

Belief systems may help structure broad conversations that occur around life and death; however, clinicians should remember that spirituality and religion are different. A patient need not adhere to any system of belief to successfully resolve existential or spiritual issues. One also must recognize that belief systems may either relieve or worsen anxiety and fear as death approaches. Fear induced by a lack of faith and fear of losing faith in the face of the unknown can exacerbate anxiety. At times, a patient's belief system is tested at the end of life either by the disease (eg, "Only bad people get this disease, and I have been good") or by the mode of death (eg, "No one should suffer like this").

Cancer care at the end of life, perhaps more than in any other phase of the illness, involves multidisciplinary efforts. During spiritual conversations with patients, clinicians should seek to understand the depths and nuances of the patient's orientation toward this potentially complex area of life. This understanding will assist clinicians in identifying needs that other professionals (eg, chaplains, psychotherapists) should address; the oncologist's responsibility is to guide the delivery of compassionate care and to incorporate insights about the patient's spiritual or existential status into clinical decisions to best treat the patient as a whole person.

Many people, especially in developed nations, encounter death infrequently; they may even be well into adulthood before they are first confronted by death. As a person observes the death of a loved one, especially when it is the first time they have witnessed this process, his or her reckoning with mortality can be profound. This personal experience can manifest in a variety of emotions such as anger, fear, or powerlessness. At times, these feelings can be directed toward clinical staff as well as toward family members, the dying person, a deity, or some other construct. As death nears, many patients are forced to confront questions that they might otherwise prefer to ignore. Chief among these are questions concerning the nature and purpose of suffering and the injustice of a painful or premature death.

As patients articulate their beliefs and interpretations about spiritual issues with family members, the emotional rawness of dying and death can become magnified. A family's long-ignored or contentious issues often emerge at this time. When these situations arise, clinicians can help by refocusing family members on the real purpose of spiritual care: to support patients as they explore and express their spirituality at the end of life, to the extent that they wish and in the manner most meaningful and comfortable for them. We often cannot provide answers, but we can always listen and validate emotions while providing support.

Many people value the opportunity to make peace with God, the universe, a deity, or a belief system as death approaches. Those who are dying, their families, and caregivers will appreciate the clinician's efforts to ensure they have the space, quiet, encouragement, and support to explore spiritual issues that are important to them.

DELIRIUM

Characterized by disturbance of consciousness, cognition, and perception, delirium occurs in 28% to 83% of patients as death approaches. It often provokes considerable distress among patients, families, caregivers, and medical providers who are witnessing the patient's transition toward death.[101,102] Delirium is generally an indirect result of various factors associated with the patient's underlying cancer, such as adverse treatment effects, metabolic disorder, nutritional deficiency, or infection; adverse effects of medications seem to be the most common cause of delirium for patients near the end of life.[103]

Four types of delirium are observed in the palliative care population: agitated/hyperactive delirium, hypoactive delirium, mixed, and terminal delirium (also referred to as terminal agitation; see the section titled Management of the Last Days of Life). In contrast to hyperactive delirium, hypoactive delirium is underrecognized, because patients may experience auditory or visual hallucinations but may remain quiet about them. In each case, onset is signaled by an acute change in the patient's level of arousal, which can manifest as disorientation; visual or auditory hallucinations; a change in speech patterns, memory or language alteration; or upset of the sleep/wake cycle. Symptoms typically wax and wane over time.[104]

For clinical diagnosis, delirium is assessed at the bedside using instruments such as the Delirium Rating Scale,[105] Confusion Assessment Method,[106] Delirium Symptom Interview,[107] Memorial Delirium Assessment Scale,[108] or the more general and widely recognized Mini-Mental State Examination (as a method of more formally assessing cognition; this test is not specific for delirium).[109]

To manage delirium, the first step is to screen for and treat any underlying reversible causes; these may include CNS events, bladder outlet or bowel obstruction, hypoxia, metabolic disorder, and medication or substance effects or withdrawal. If these potential causes are ruled out, the clinician typically discontinues all medications (especially psychoactive ones) that are not necessary and not associated with an acute withdrawal syndrome. Reorienting the patient to time and place, ensuring that family and other familiar individuals are available, and restoring normal surroundings and routine can be helpful. Thereafter, the goal of treating delirium is to restore patients to a condition that more closely reflects their baseline mental state, rather than to suppress agitation or to sedate them.[110]

For patients receiving palliative care, intravenous or oral haloperidol is the drug of choice and is titrated upward, as necessary (Fig 9-3). However, data do not suggest these medications are more effective or safer than haloperidol, and they are generally more expensive. Though they may help calm the delirious patient, traditional teaching dictates that

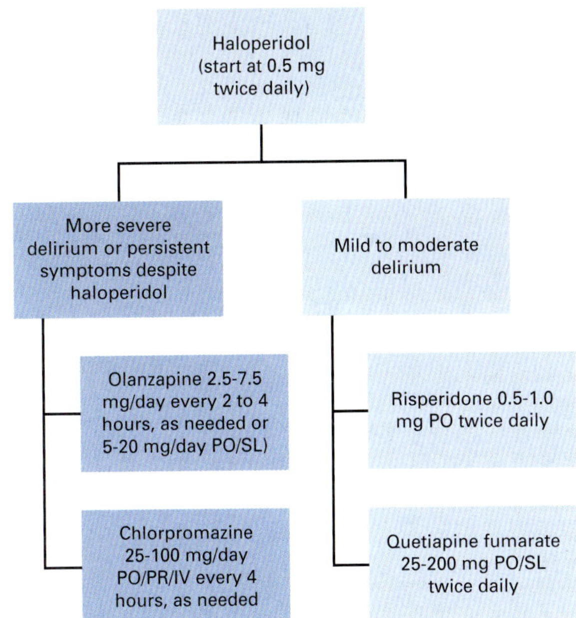

Fig. 9-3 Haloperidol for palliative care.[111]

Abbreviations: IV, intravenously; PO, orally; PR, rectally; SL, sublingual.

benzodiazepines (eg, lorazepam, midazolam) are generally avoided because they can worsen delirium by further sedating and disinhibiting the patient or by causing agitation. Recent evidence has challenged this dogma, however, suggesting that in cases of very agitated delirium, adding lorazepam to haloperidol results in less agitation than haloperidol alone.[111] In cases of agitated and/or refractory delirium, consultation with a palliative care specialist is indicated.[112]

The effectiveness of medical approaches may be enhanced by the presence of family and friends, familiar surroundings, consistent care staff, and a tranquil setting. Satisfactory management of delirium results in adequate control of delirium symptoms, reduction in patient and family distress, regaining a sense of control, relief of caregiver burden, and improved quality of life. Reassessment should be iteratively conducted to ensure ongoing and adequate management of this troubling symptom.

KEY POINTS

- Although psychological distress is normal among patients who are terminally ill, clinicians should remain alert for signals of true psychiatric illness.
- A majority of patients who are dying experience psychological distress. Physicians must be prepared to address related issues using both medical and psychosocial means and to make appropriate referrals.
- Clinicians should be adequately conversant in spiritual matters but should primarily adopt a stance of listening, understanding, and supporting spiritual exploration. Appropriate referrals can be made when the patient is receptive.

- Depression is characterized by a persistent set of emotional symptoms, negative self-analysis, and a lack of pleasure and hope. Identifying and treating depression and its sequelae are important for reducing end-of-life morbidity as well as the desire for hastened death.
- Delirium is frequently a source of great distress for the patient, his or her loved ones, and the care team. The clinician should screen for and treat any underlying reversible causes.

HOSPICE CARE

Hospice is one of the most effective yet underused resources for patients, families, and oncologists as patients approach the end of life with advanced cancer, though use in the United States is, indeed, increasing annually. Regarding efficacy, consistent data demonstrate the benefits of hospice for patients and caregivers, including effects on quality of life, symptoms, and depression. Also, hospice increases quality of care near the end of life and reduces overall health care costs.[113] Additional data highlight a potential survival advantage, with specific cancers like pancreas and lung cancers demonstrating a survival advantage of weeks to months with even 1 day of hospice, versus none.[114] Some data highlight that despite its existence and availability across most counties in the United States for approximately 35 years, referrals to hospice continue to be underused for patients near the end of life; when referrals are made they are often late. For example, data from the National Hospice and Palliative Care Organization (NHPCO) reveal that ≤ 50% of patients have an average length of stay of ≤ 3 days. When looking at average length of stay, which is affected by outliers, the Centers for Medicare and Medicaid Service hospice data from 2009 show numbers in the range of 37 to 59 days. Additional research in this area has demonstrated medians near the 3-week mark.[115]

Late referrals to hospice stem from both patient and oncologist factors. A study of patients with advanced lung cancer revealed that only 53% of patients had discussed hospice with their oncologists 4 to 7 months after diagnosis; predictors of not having the discussion involved patients having overly optimistic assessments of prognosis and lacking moderate to severe pain or dyspnea. In other words, patients with a poor understanding of prognosis who feel well often do not bring up hospice to their oncologists and, likewise, the topic is not broached by their care team, ultimately leading to delayed referrals.

HOSPICE ELIGIBILITY

Quite simply, patients with cancer are eligible for the Medicare hospice benefit if they are thought to have a terminal diagnosis wherein the average life expectancy is ≤ 6 months if the disease runs its usual course. The latter part of this statement is very important, because the "usual course" for any disease is variable. Many times, patients are admitted to hospice for a total of > 6 months; errors in prognostication are not inherently red flags to Medicare nor do they highlight any errors on the part of the admitting physicians as long as proper documentation regarding the expected course is in place. Of note, hospice enrollment also generally entails the cessation of disease-modifying treatments aimed at extending life, in exchange for a focus on comfort, quality of life, and most often, death at home.

Up to 90% of hospice participants elect to use the Medicare hospice benefit, an earned benefit as part of Medicare Part A, to pay for hospice. Patients who use their Part A benefit for other purposes, such as an acute hospitalization or active rehabilitation within a skilled nursing facility, cannot simultaneously be enrolled in hospice. This leads to quandaries when patients are seeking an approach focused on care near the end of life but are reliant on the 24-hour caregiving services or are interested in the intensive physical rehabilitation provided in skilled nursing facilities.

Last, there remains a common misperception regarding the need for patients to have a "do not attempt resuscitation" (DNAR) order in place before referral to hospice. In fact, there is no stipulation of this to participate in residential hospice under Medicare, though some hospice care agencies may strongly discourage enrollment of patients without a DNAR order. In fact, the coercion of patients into a particular resuscitation status can lead to significant penalties for individual clinicians and their organizations. It remains important to speak with patients and their families about decisions for care during times of crisis or near the end of life, but oncology teams must remain agnostic as to the outcome while using a truly shared decision-making approach. That said, performing cardiopulmonary resuscitation on a patient with late-stage terminal disease is highly ineffective and largely incompatible with the philosophy of hospice care, which aims at the promotion and maintenance of comfort and quality of life rather than treatment of disease. As such, it is critical to understand and explore the rationale for maintaining a "full code" status in a patient who elects to receive hospice care, to ensure that the patient and family do not harbor significant misconceptions or unrealistic expectations about the likely outcome.

HOSPICE CARE PROVISION

There are > 6,000 hospices in operation in the United States, covering all 50 states and most territories. Most are independent and free-standing agencies not restricted to serving patients of any particular nursing home, hospital, or home health agency. Hospices are required to provide six foundational services in participating in the Medicare hospice benefit, including a physician medical director, nursing services, social work services, spiritual support, bereavement support, and volunteers. These services are provided along the spectrum of hospice care, often beginning with a comprehensive assessment of needs during the admission process, with frequent reevaluations of needs along the trajectory of care. Integral to this care is the role of the oncology team, who are considered partners in the patient's care. As an example of this, with the right billing and coding approach, oncology practices can still be paid for seeing patients in the clinic who are also receiving hospice care—truly reflecting a concurrent care approach. Often, the primary oncologist serves as the hospice physician of record as well, recognizing that many oncologists view care at the end of life as an important aspect of the primary palliative care that they provide to their patients with cancer.

Many patients with cancer hold an incorrect understanding of hospice as a "place to go," instead of a type of care optimized to patient and family needs near the end of life. Yet, recent data from the NHPCO highlight that ≤ 60% of patients receiving hospice care die in their own residence, including their home or long-term care facility.

LEVELS OF HOSPICE CARE

Hospice is generally provided within one of four levels of care: routine home care, continuous home care, general inpatient care, and inpatient respite care. Most patients (> 90%) receive routine home care, residing in their usual place of residence with a focus on preventing crises and being in familiar surroundings. Within continuous home care, the hospice team comes to the residence to provide brief and continuous crisis-directed care, to make the patient comfortable, and avoid visits to the emergency department or hospital. General inpatient care is used when acute crises, often in the last few weeks of life, cannot be managed at home and require admission to a special hospice facility or through contracted beds in an acute care hospital. Last, inpatient respite care is a time-limited admission to an approved facility to allow caregivers some time away and respite.

MANAGEMENT OF THE LAST DAYS OF LIFE

Clinicians should recognize the process of dying as a result of cancer. The dying process generally manifests in a continued deterioration of a person's overall condition, with increasing lethargy, decreasing levels of consciousness, and at times, increasing confusion, increasing time asleep, less spontaneous movement, decreased urinary output, inability to regulate body temperature, and changes in patterns of respiratory effort (eg, Cheyne-Stokes breathing). For many people, systemic signs can include progressive hypotension, diminishing oxygenation, and progressive loss of peripheral perfusion, causing mottling of the skin. Researchers have identified a "top eight" list of signs of impending death:

1. nonreactive pupils
2. decreased response to verbal stimuli
3. decreased response to visual stimuli
4. inability to close eyelids
5. drooping of the nasolabial fold
6. hyperextension of the neck
7. grunting of vocal cords, and
8. upper GI bleeding[116]

Given the unfamiliarity of caregivers with the signs and symptoms of the dying process, it is critical to share information and educate them so as to minimize fear and anxiety. Frequently, hospice programs will have an informational brochure or handout that can be shared with loved ones who are interested.

In contrast to the usual slow decline described above, the terminal phase of cancer may sometimes be signaled by a sudden change in condition: intracerebral bleeding, a pulmonary embolus, a perforated viscus, or overwhelming sepsis. When this change is superimposed on an already moribund condition, continued symptom control becomes the primary goal. Understanding patients' wishes—often through conversations they have had with their families throughout the course of their illness and during the course of life—will help determine the best course of action. Many people, in the event of a catastrophic change in their condition, may wish to focus on comfort; others may wish to try to achieve functional improvement, however limited at this phase of life.

Whether the end of life approaches as an expected deterioration or as an unexpected catastrophic decline, the issue of comfort is paramount. Clinicians should ensure that all clinical actions contribute to the comfort of the person who is dying.

BEDSIDE CARE AT THE END OF LIFE

Attention to the bedside care of the dying patient is crucial. Regular check of vital signs should be replaced, at this stage, with a regular (eg, every 4 hours) check of symptoms. Good bedside care includes the following:

- Mouth care, to ensure that the dying person's mouth is clean and moist, will aid comfort.
- Eyes can also become dry and painful and may require additional supportive measures such as eye lubricants and/or drops.
- Proper skin care includes regular repositioning of the patient to relieve musculoskeletal pain from inertia and to avoid the excruciating (and difficult to control) pain of skin tears and pressure sores. Use of a pressure-relieving mattress is advised. An air mattress will facilitate shifting of the person's weight.
- The head of the bed can be elevated to help reduce noisy upper respiratory tract secretions.
- Urinary retention and fecal impaction should be evaluated and treated if present.

TERMINAL SECRETIONS

Noisy ventilation (often referred to as "death rattle" or "terminal secretions"), caused by oscillatory movements of accumulated bronchial mucosa and salivary secretions, is common among patients who are dying and are unable to clear secretions by coughing or swallowing.[117] The symptom usually occurs after patients are unconscious, and it may cause considerable distress to families and caregivers. Previous observational studies have estimated that terminal secretions occur in as many as 92% of patients who are unconscious and dying.[118]

Intervention to reduce secretions is often instituted to alleviate the distress of attendant family members, even when the patient seems settled. The primary intervention should be to explain the etiology of this sound to the patient's family or other caregiver(s), with reassurance that it is not associated with any discomfort. Standard nonpharmacologic practices for alleviating terminal secretions include suctioning, positioning (reverse Trendelenburg position), and reducing parenteral and enteral fluids. Suctioning is no longer a recommended intervention, however.[119]

The mainstay of the pharmacologic management of terminal secretions are anticholinergic agents, also known as muscarinic receptor blockers.[120,121] These drugs include scopolamine, hyoscyamine, glycopyrrolate, and atropine. The primary difference in these drugs is whether they are tertiary amines that cross the blood-brain barrier (eg, scopolamine, atropine) or quaternary amines, which are less likely to do so (eg, hyoscyamine, glycopyrrolate). However, all these drugs have the potential for central and peripheral anticholinergic adverse effects, including, but not limited to, delirium and urinary retention, which need to be monitored closely. Atropine, a widely available drug, is frequently used in home care for the treatment of terminal secretions; a common approach is 1% atropine ophthalmic solution, 1 to 2 drops sublingually every 4 hours as needed. Scopolamine (hyoscyamine hydrobromide), a muscarinic receptor antagonist, has been reported to more potently inhibit production of bronchial secretions and cause less tachycardia.[121] Scopolamine and atropine can cause central effects such as sedation, confusion, or paradoxical excitation, especially in elderly patients. Hyoscine butylbromide, a semisynthetic derivative of scopolamine, is effective in treating respiratory tract secretions, has peripheral effects similar to scopolamine, and has no central adverse effects.[122,123]

Some research has been conducted on the relative effectiveness and frequency of adverse effects of atropine, scopolamine, and hyoscine butylbromide for treating terminal secretions in patients who are terminally ill. In an open-label, multisite, prospective, randomized, phase III trial, 333 patients who were terminally ill and had terminal secretions were randomly assigned to receive 0.5 mg of atropine, 20 mg of hyoscine butylbromide, or 0.25 mg of scopolamine, initiated in a subcutaneous bolus followed by continuous administration. In patients across all three study arms, terminal secretions decreased to a nondisturbing intensity or disappeared after 1 hour in 42%, 42%, and 37% of cases, respectively ($P = .72$); effectiveness improved over time without significant differences among the treatment groups.[124] Although, to date, this is the largest randomized, controlled trial of anticholinergics for terminal secretions, it has numerous limitations, including its unblinded design, failure to standardize across sites, and lack of a placebo control.[125] Indeed, although other randomized, controlled trials have been few and have had small sample sizes, they have not established the superiority of one drug (including placebo) compared with another.[126] One might conclude, then, that the anticholinergics are equally ineffective in alleviating terminal secretions.

Given the scant and inconclusive evidence, a 2008 Cochrane review, updated in 2010 to include the previous study, advised that clinicians have an ethical obligation to closely monitor patients for lack of therapeutic benefit and adverse effects and to discontinue ineffective or detrimental treatments. As stated at the forefront of this section, more important than treatment with anticholinergics is discussing terminal secretions with family members to reduce their distress; these conversations should address cause, implications, and caregivers' fears and concerns.[127]

MEDICATIONS

As the patient nears the end of life, the clinician should review all medications and continue only those that contribute to increased comfort. Long-term medications aimed at reducing late effects, such as statins for cardiovascular risk reduction (primary prevention), should be discontinued in most cases, and evidence suggests it is appropriate to do that farther upstream from the very end of life, such as at time of hospice referral. A large, randomized trial points to benefits, and no harms, in following this approach in patients without active cardiac disease.[128] Similarly, implanted defibrillators can be deactivated. Diagnostic tests and functions (eg, transfusions, needle sticks, measurement of intake and output, blood glucose monitoring, oxygen saturation monitoring, suctioning) can be discontinued if deemed unnecessary for symptom control and comfort.

In deciding which medications to discontinue, all medications should be reconsidered for their benefit to the patient, not only those that were introduced for symptom control in the palliative phase of the illness. For example, for type 1 diabetes, insulin is necessary to prevent hyperglycemia to spare the patient unquenchable thirst, and it is common to continue such interventions as comfort measures even at the end of life. Essential medications should be obtained in a form that can be administered to someone who may not predictably be swallowing. Alternative formulations include sublingual, subcutaneous, intravenous, transdermal, intranasal, and rectal. Doses of medications retained for symptom management should be increased as necessary to optimize comfort. It is important to discuss deprescribing as a comfort measure near the end of life and to individualize this approach with each patient and family.

OTHER INTERVENTIONS

Nutrition and Hydration

As patients are actively dying, any nutritional supplements and any parenteral hydration should be reviewed. Almost always, parenteral hydration should be stopped, with appropriate advice to the family, because overhydration will worsen respiratory symptoms and enteral fluids will potentially cause secretions in the gut that may cause vomiting. Evidence suggests that artificial nutrition and hydration do not prolong survival and are not necessarily helpful at achieving comfort.[129] At worst, ongoing hydration can even prolong or worsen difficult symptoms during the dying process, thus worsening the patient and family's discomfort. This requires in-depth conversations with and education of the family and caregivers. Recognize that stopping nutrition and/or hydration can be an emotionally charged issue for loved ones, which may require time to process and extra support from nonmedical colleagues, such as those in social work and chaplaincy, to address emotional and existential-related issues.

Management of Terminal Delirium

Physical agitation can occur in the patient's final days. The clinician should first ensure that this agitation is not a result of pain, urinary retention, or constipation. Terminal delirium (also known as terminal agitation)—delirium that occurs in the setting of the active dying process—requires a different approach from hyperactive and hypoactive delirium. In this case, benzodiazepines are the drug class of choice to palliate symptoms. When symptoms are severe, sedation may be required through the use of continuous infusion of a benzodiazepine or barbiturate (midazolam or pentobarbital are most commonly used).[130,131] Sometimes called palliative sedation, this intervention can be controversial and is associated with significant misconceptions about hastening death. Cases of terminal delirium warrant consultation with a palliative care specialist.

Communication With the Family and/or Caregivers

Communication with the family or other loved ones involved in the last stages of caregiving should be a key focus for health professionals as a patient nears death. What does the family expect? How well do they understand the patient's condition and the dying process? A trusted clinician should clearly, but compassionately, describe the process of dying. Patients and family members should be reassured that, in most cases, the person dying gently slips into a coma and life ebbs away with no dramatic manifestations.[132] The clinician should emphasize that at this important phase, the sole focus of care is the dying person's comfort, and that current medical practice has multiple strategies to optimize comfort.

Management of Care for the Unconscious Patient

Even when a patient is unconscious, clinical staff should carefully assess him or her to ensure comfort. Available tools to assess nonverbal signs of pain include the Assessment of Discomfort and Dementia,[133] Checklist of Nonverbal Pain Indicators,[134] Pain Assessment in Advanced Dementia, Behavioral Pain Scale, and Critical Care Pain Observation Tool.[135] Evaluation cannot be done from the door of the patient's room. An examination is required, with special attention to the face (is it relaxed?), respiration (is it regular, not labored?), and positioning (is the patient positioned comfortably?). The clinician should continue to explain to the patient what is happening in the clinical examination, as if he or she were conscious; it is important for family members to understand that people, even when unconscious, may still recognize their voices and their touch. The clinician should also reassure the family that symptom-control medications will be continued to ensure the patient's comfort even though consciousness has been lost. There is no concern that these medications will hasten death, especially if continued at the same dose.

Many family members have a strong desire to be present at the time of death. This specific time can be difficult to predict, even as the patient's body shuts down. The need to be present varies from family to family, and within families, from one individual to another. If family members have a particular wish to be present at the patient's time of death, the clinician may want to set up a vigil roster to ensure that one member of the family is always present during the patient's last days.

CARE AFTER DEATH

The clinician's role does not end immediately upon the death of the patient. Follow-through with the patient's body, logistical considerations, and attention to family members and other caregivers are crucial last steps in end-of-life care. The clinicians and medical staff involved in the patient's end-of-life care should reflect upon the quality of the patient's death, with a "good death" defined as one that minimized distress and suffering for the patient, family members, and other caregivers; honored the patient's and family's desires; and upheld standards of care clinically, ethically, and culturally.

Immediately after the patient's death, the clinician should allow the family time to spend time with the body, if they so desire. Treatment of the body should be respectful and culturally sensitive. If not addressed previously, plans for eye donation (allowable in many cases of cancer, except some leukemias and eye malignancies) and autopsy are discussed, addressing any family member or caregiver concerns. The clinician files a death certificate, completes any other required forms, and conveys information to the funeral director as needed. In addition, he or she should inform the patient's other health care providers of the death.

Attention should be directed to family members and other caregivers. The normal bereavement process should be described to them; information regarding available bereavement support should be provided, and referral can be made to appropriate services. Palliative care clinicians can help the oncologist identify family members who may be at risk for complicated bereavement, and they can follow through with requisite care. Formal expressions of condolences on the patient's death, such as with a card, phone call, or brief letter, can be immensely meaningful and supportive to family members and caregivers. Amid busy clinical practices, we sometimes forget to pause for a moment to reflect on the profound experience of caring for a patient and their family during the patient's last days. Sharing memories, talking with colleagues and staff about the patient, and reflecting on the experience may be helpful in the prevention of burnout, an issue rising in prevalence among oncologists.

KEY POINTS

- At the very end of life, the patient's comfort should be the primary focus. Unconscious patients should be treated with the same degree of care, concern, and communication as conscious patients.
- Hospice care is the best mechanism for providing high-quality care near the end of life in the United States and greatly enhances the ability of patients to die at home in comfort, surrounded by family and friends. Patients with an expected prognosis of ≤ 6 months are eligible.

- Physical care should address mouth care and musculoskeletal positioning, with attention given to maintaining skin integrity and comfort.
- Terminal secretions can be addressed with the careful administration of anticholinergic agents, as well as with attentive nursing care, positioning, and most importantly, education of family caregivers.
- As the patient nears the end of life, all medications, medical interventions, nutritional supplements, and hydration efforts should be reviewed to continue only those that directly contribute to comfort.
- If agitation occurs, clinicians should determine the source if possible, and address appropriately. Specialist palliative care consultation is recommended in cases of difficult and/or refractory symptoms.
- The wishes of family members with regard to being present at the time of death should be respected and facilitated to the greatest degree possible.

Acknowledgment

The following authors are acknowledged and graciously thanked for their contributions to prior versions of this chapter: Amy P. Abernethy, MD, PhD, FAAHPM; and Arif H. Kamal, MD, MBA, MHS, FAAHPM, FASCO.

GLOBAL PERSPECTIVE IN PALLIATIVE CARE AND CARE AT THE END OF LIFE

Suzanne Ryan, MBChB; and Camilla Zimmermann, MD PhD (University of Toronto, Toronto, Canada)

Of the > 9 million deaths from cancer yearly,[136] > 80% occur in low-and-middle-income countries (LMICs), where patients have little or no access to palliative care.[137] Many patients in LMICs present to medical services with advanced disease, which increases the importance of palliative care. However, of the 234 countries in the world, 32% have no palliative care services, and preliminary or advanced integration of palliative care into health services has been achieved in only 20 countries worldwide (8.6%).[65] In this section, we discuss priorities for improving the delivery of palliative care in LMICs, which include:

- providing access to a coordinated system where palliative care is integrated into oncology and into the health care system as a whole;
- ensuring availability of essential medicines and services;
- educating the public about palliative care and training health care providers in its provision; and
- building and disseminating an evidence base that is applicable to resource-constrained settings.

INTEGRATION OF PALLIATIVE CARE INTO ONCOLOGY CARE AND HEALTH CARE POLICIES

In 2016, ASCO released a clinical practice guideline recommending that patients with advanced cancer "should receive dedicated palliative care services, early in the disease course, concurrent with active treatment."[138] This guideline was based on findings from high-income countries (HICs); a subsequent resource-stratified practice guideline provides recommendations for clinicians and key stakeholders regarding palliative care policy development, service establishment, and delivery in resource-constrained settings.[139]

Regardless of the setting, a coordinated system should be in place where the palliative care needs of patients and their family members are identified systematically and met at all levels.[139] Primary health care providers should be trained in the basics of palliative care; interdisciplinary palliative care teams provide timely care targeted to those with the greatest needs.[140] The European Society of Medical Oncology (ESMO) offers accreditation as an "ESMO Designated Centre of Integrated Oncology and Palliative Care" to cancer centers that provide comprehensive integration with palliative care services.[141] Of the 41 countries with accredited centers, 11 are LMICs.

Integration of palliative care services should be individualized and contextualized to each country, taking into account its health care system, socioeconomic situation, and culture.[142] A roadmap for palliative care development has been developed by the International Palliative Care Initiative, which outlines a range of strategies for countries at varying levels of palliative care development.[143] One successful method of integrating palliative care into health care systems is by initial engagement of key opinion leaders, followed by a country-specific situational analysis of palliative care services, a needs assessment to inform and illustrate requirements, and strategic and business plans that incorporate adequate resources.[144] National interdisciplinary steering committees should involve key stakeholders, including those with international expertise and representatives from ministries of health.[137] For integration to be effective, it must occur at all levels of the health care system, with ownership and support at the community level.[144]

AVAILABILITY OF ESSENTIAL MEDICINES AND SERVICES

An Essential Package of Palliative Care and Pain Relief has been developed and represents a low-cost, high-yield intervention to deliver palliative care in resource-limited settings.[137] This package consists of basic medicines, equipment, and human resources necessary to deliver basic end-of-life care (Table 9-3) and may be supplemented with other medications on the World Health Organization Essential Medicines List.[145] In addition, it must be enhanced by measures to ease social and spiritual distress and should be publicly financed and universally accessible. Despite its low cost, this intervention may have a substantial impact on relief of suffering and improvement in quality of life of patients and their families in LMICs and, therefore, should be prioritized.

Availability of Opioids

Opioids are essential medicines in relieving cancer pain and suffering at the end of life, and there is established evidence for their efficacy.[63] However, 80% of the world's population lacks access to opioids.[65] From 2010 to 2013, HICs had an opioid excess of 233% while LMICs had a deficit of 99.3%.[146] The explanation for this imbalance is multifactorial[147,148] and includes restrictive legislation;[137,148] lack of infrastructure to support distribution and safe storage; limitations on prescribers;[65] insufficient training of health care professionals;[147] and obstructive societal attitudes.[147] Economic factors include insufficient allocation of funding by governments[147] and lack of financial investment to purchase drugs and to adequately fund education and training.[149]

Health care systems should safely provide opioids; the opioid supply must be available continually and opioids should be prescribed and dispensed by trained professionals.[139] The Pain and Policy Studies Group is a global research program at the University of Wisconsin Carbone Cancer Center that has collaborated with United Nations agencies to promote global access to opioids. This group has outlined four steps of addressing regulatory barriers to opioid availability: (1) assessing opioid availability in each country, (2) identifying barriers, (3) developing an action plan, and (4) implementing this action plan with technical assistance.[150] The specific opioid preparations that are immediately required and should be prioritized are immediate-release oral and injectable morphine for the management of pain and dyspnea.[139] The World Health Organization has recognized morphine as an essential medicine.[145]

Excess availability of opioids in some HICs, including the United States, has contributed to an opioid crisis, with escalation in nonmedical opioid use and opioid-related deaths. Although this situation may impart crucial lessons about safe, appropriate opioid prescribing, it should be remembered that in LMICs, the opposite problem exists of overly restrictive policies that prevent access to opioids for those with legitimate needs.[3] Improving availability and accessibility of opioids should commence with the promotion of the central principle of balance.[147] This represents the responsibility of governments to establish a controlled system of opioid availability for medical use while ensuring that adequate safeguards are in place to prevent harms. Improvement of drug availability, importation, and distribution chains, in addition to appropriate prescribing and dispensing practices, are required to improve opioid access. This requires the involvement of multiple stakeholders: policymakers, pharmacists, law enforcement agencies, drug regulators, and prescribers.[143]

Availability of Health Care Services

All health care professionals should be trained in the basics of primary palliative care.[139] In addition, patients with advanced cancer and their families should have access to an interdisciplinary palliative care team,[138] including, but not limited to, a physician, nurse, counselor (and/or social worker, psychologist, psychiatrist, and spiritual care professional, where possible) and pharmacist.[137,139] In resource-constrained settings, available disciplines may need to acquire necessary skills to compensate for a deficiency (eg, nurse or counselor training to deliver spiritual care); in addition, community health

Table 9-3 An Essential Package of Palliative Care and Pain Relief Health Services

Medicines		Medical Equipment	Human Resources
Amitriptyline	Ibuprofen (naproxen, diclofenac, or meloxicam)	Pressure-reducing mattress	Doctors (specialty, general, depending on the level of care)
Bisacodyl (Senna)	Lactulose (sorbitol or polyethylene glycol)	Nasogastric draining or feeding tube	Nurses (specialty and general)
Dexamethasone	Loperamide	Urinary catheters	Social workers and counselors
Diazepam	Metoclopramide	Opioid lockbox	Psychiatrist, psychologist, or counselor, depending on the level of care
Diphenhydramine (chlorpheniramine, cyclizine, or dimenhydrinate)	Metronidazole	Flashlight with a rechargeable battery (if no access to electricity)	Physical therapist
Fluconazole	Morphine (oral immediate release and injectable)	Adult diapers (or cotton or plastic if in extreme poverty)	Pharmacist
Fluoxetine (or other SSRI sertraline, citalopram)	Naloxone parenteral	Oxygen	Community health workers
Furosemide	Omeprazole		Clinical support staff (diagnostic imaging, laboratory technician, nutritionist)
Hyoscine butylbromide	Ondansetron		Nonclinical support staff
Haloperidol	Paracetamol		
	Petroleum jelly		

Abbreviation: SSRI, selective serotonin reuptake inhibitor.
Adapted from Knaul et al.[137]

care workers, volunteers, and clinical officers may be engaged to deliver palliative care.[139] Palliative care should be available in all settings, including in the community, for outpatients, and for inpatients.[138] Distance communication should be instituted to support those providing care in low-resource areas and trained nurses may prescribe medicines, including opioids, where permitted.[139] Ideally, dedicated inpatient palliative care beds should be established in units staffed with health care professionals with expertise in palliative care.

EDUCATION OF THE PUBLIC AND HEALTH CARE PROFESSIONALS

The lack of sufficient training and education is an additional barrier to global palliative care development.[148] This includes education of the public, health professionals, and policymakers. Patients may fear palliative care because of its association with death and because they sustain unrealistic hopes for a cure.[151] Public education is key to improving awareness and understanding of palliative care services and reducing the stigma associated with life-limiting illnesses.[152] Media campaigns have been used successfully to improve public awareness of palliative care in India and Japan.[153,154]

It is important to acknowledge the importance of traditional rituals related to dying and bereavement.[151] Open communication among palliative care teams, cultural leaders, and traditional healers enables coordination of patient care in a culturally sensitive and respectful way.[155] Understanding the patient's and family's perspective is key to developing successful services that are locally acceptable. Trained spiritual care providers should be available, and palliative care providers should respect the religious norms of patients and their families.[139]

The aim of education programs should be to improve palliative care at all levels.[144] Oncologists require training in the basic skills of palliative care, including communication skills and assessment and management of physical, psychosocial, and spiritual needs.[139] Palliative care education should be compulsory in undergraduate and postgraduate medical and nursing curricula.[139] Training should be adapted to the care context and to those available to deliver care. Trained community volunteers working under the supervision of clinicians may play an important part in the palliative care workforce, particularly in resource-limited settings.[139]

There is a wide range of training programs available in LMICs, including 3- to 4-day courses, 2- to 4-week certificate programs, multidisciplinary Master's programs, e-learning modules, and 1-year fellowships.[148] Country-specific palliative care specialty training and development of licensing examinations would further develop the academic base of palliative care internationally,[143] as would standardized global curricula.[137]

BUILDING AND DISSEMINATING AN EVIDENCE BASE

Evidence-based medicine is key to the delivery of high-quality care and must be relevant to the setting in which it is applied. Most of the published evidence in palliative care comes from HICs[138] and may not be applicable to resource-constrained settings.[139] Country-specific research is required to build a relevant body of evidence on which to base clinical guidelines and national policy.[137,139,156] Lack of funding, training, and mentorship are barriers to the progress of palliative care research.[157] International collaborations improve knowledge exchange and provide mentorship. Palliative care researchers may share their expertise by participating in collaborative research, guideline development, and membership in international organizations.

The development of palliative care experts and national champions within LMICs may require training abroad in established academic training programs to develop the necessary skills and expertise to bring home.[143] With this expertise, they may, in turn, develop teaching and training programs in their country, including centers of excellence.[144] It is important for all palliative care experts internationally to invest time in the education of other health care professionals.[144] ASCO's International Development and Educational Award–Palliative Care program supports the development of palliative care physicians in LMICs by pairing them with mentors in countries with integrated palliative care models who remain as contacts for future collaboration.[80]

The success of initiatives to improve the availability and delivery of palliative care will depend on recognition of the importance of palliative care by key stakeholders. Ultimately, solutions need to come from within LMICs, but continued global advocacy for the availability of palliative care as a basic human right[158] and input from well-developed palliative care services internationally support the development of local and national programs.[148] The responsibility lies with us all to deliver palliative care to those who need it.

10

BREAST CANCER

Filipa Lynce, MD, and Maria Raquel Nunes, MD

Recent Updates

MOLECULAR PROGNOSTIC AND PREDICTIVE MARKERS

- Results from prospective evaluation of the 21-gene recurrence score assay (Oncotype DX) provided valuable information regarding the treatment of pre- and postmenopausal women with a recurrence score between 11 and 25. (Sparano JA, *N Engl J Med* 2018)

ADJUVANT SYSTEMIC THERAPY

- In patients with HER2-positive, operable breast cancer, the addition of pertuzumab to trastuzumab significantly improved the rates of invasive disease-free survival (DFS), although the benefit was small. (von Minckwitz G, *N Engl J Med* 2017)
- The addition of ovarian function suppression (OFS) to tamoxifen or to exemestane treatment in premenopausal women with hormone receptor (HR)-positive breast cancer resulted in an improvement in DFS and freedom from distant recurrence compared with tamoxifen alone. The addition of OFS to tamoxifen resulted in a small overall survival (OS) benefit. (Francis PA, *N Engl J Med* 2018)

RESIDUAL DISEASE AFTER COMPLETING NEOADJUVANT SYSTEMIC THERAPY

- Adjuvant capecitabine improved DFS and OS in patients with HER2-negative breast cancer and residual disease after neoadjuvant chemotherapy. Patients with triple-negative breast cancer (TNBC) derived the most benefit. (Masuda et al, *N Engl J Med* 2017)
- In the KATHERINE study, adjuvant ado-trastuzumab emtansine therapy, compared to trastuzumab, improved invasive DFS, including distant recurrence, in patients with residual disease after neoadjuvant chemotherapy and HER2-targeted therapy. (von Minckwitz G, *N Engl J Med* 2019)

RECURRENT OR METASTATIC DISEASE

- In the randomized IMpassion130 trial, the combination of atezolizumab and nab-paclitaxel led to an improvement in progression-free survival (PFS) compared with nab-paclitaxel alone in patients with metastatic TNBC. (Schmid P, *N Engl J Med* 2018)
- In patients with advanced breast cancer and a germline *BRCA1* or *BRCA2* mutation who received talazoparib or standard single-agent therapy of physician's choice, talazoparib led to a significant improvement in PFS. (Litton JK, *N Engl J Med* 2018)

- An update of the MONALESSA 7 trial showed that the addition of ribociclib to endocrine therapy in pre- or perimenopausal women with HR-positive, HER2-negative advanced breast cancer resulted in significantly longer OS than endocrine therapy alone. (Im SA, *N Engl J Med* 2019)
- An update of the MONARCH 2 trial showed that, regardless of menopausal status, in women with HR-positive, HER2-negative advanced breast cancer that progressed after endocrine therapy, abemaciclib plus fulvestrant resulted in a significantly longer OS compared with fulvestrant alone. (Sledge G, *JAMA Oncol* 2019)
- In SOLAR-1, alpelisib and fulvestrant led to an improvement in PFS compared with placebo and fulvestrant in patients with PIK3CA-mutated, HR-positive, HER2-negative advanced breast cancer previously treated with endocrine therapy. (André F, *N Engl J Med* 2019)

OVERVIEW

In the United States, breast cancer is the most common cancer among women. Since 1990 mortality rates have consistently declined, primarily as a result of advances in systemic therapy. For early-stage breast cancer, advances in surgery and radiation oncology have led to the de-escalation of locoregional therapy. There has been substantial progress leading to the approval of new agents for patients with early-stage and metastatic breast cancer. However, better therapeutic options are still needed, as are markers to select patients in whom therapy can be de-escalated. Advances in supportive care have reduced serious complications of breast cancer treatment and improved symptom management and quality of life.

EPIDEMIOLOGY

Breast cancer is the most common malignancy diagnosed among women in the world, with approximately 2.1 million women worldwide diagnosed in 2018, accounting for 24% of all new cancer cases in women.[1] The incidence rates are higher in economically developed regions such as North America, western Europe, and Australia and New Zealand, and lower in economically developing areas such as sub-Saharan Africa and parts of Asia. These differences across countries are likely related to the use of breast cancer screening, reproductive factors, changes in fat intake, body weight, and age at menarche and/or lactation.

In the United States, an estimated 271,270 new cases of invasive breast cancer were expected to be diagnosed in 2019, affecting 2,670 men and 268,600 women.[2] It is also estimated that there will be approximately 62,930 new cases of female breast carcinoma in situ diagnosed in 2019.[3] After a striking 7% decrease in incidence between 2002 and 2003, female breast cancer incidence has slowly increased since 2004 at an average rate of 0.4% per year.[4] This has been attributed, in part, to late childbearing age and increase in obesity. However, there has been no noticeable annual change in the incidence of breast cancer that is metastatic at the time of presentation (6% of patients).

Worldwide, breast cancer is the most common cause of cancer death in females, and it accounted for 626,679 of the total estimated 9.5 million cancer-related deaths in 2018. In the United States, breast cancer continues to be the most common malignancy, and it remains the second most common cause of cancer-related death among women (behind lung cancer), with an estimated 42,260 deaths in women attributed to breast cancer in 2019. Since the 1970s, there has been a decline in breast cancer mortality rate in the United States, which primarily is thought to be due to more effective systemic therapies and improvements in early detection.[3] Death rates fell 1.8% per year on average between 2007 and 2016.[5]

The incidence and mortality rate of breast cancer in the United States differ according to race and ethnicity. The incidence of breast cancer has historically been higher among white women when compared with black women.[6] Some factors that contributed to this difference included more frequent use of postmenopausal hormone replacement therapy and of screening mammography among white women compared with black women. More recently, the incidence of breast cancer in black women has begun to approach the incidence reported in white women. The increasing breast cancer incidence in black women suggests there might be a screening effect from increased use of mammography. At the same time, the decrease in use of postmenopausal hormone replacement therapy, based on findings from the Women's Health Initiative, has led to a decrease in breast cancer incidence in white women.[7]

The breast cancer mortality rate is approximately 40% higher among black women compared with white women; as the incidence in black women has increased, so has this mortality gap.[8] Multiple factors play a role in this observation. Breast cancer is more likely to develop before the age of 40 years in black women than in white women; black women are also more likely to be diagnosed at a more advanced stage of breast cancer and to have high-grade, triple-negative tumors. It is also possible that other nonbiologic factors such as patterns of care and underuse of treatment contribute to the higher mortality rate. Finally, it is possible that more nonsignificant breast cancers—those that would never have caused clinically apparent or life-threatening disease—are diagnosed in white women because of higher rates of screening. Breast cancer–related incidence and death rates are lower among Asian,

Native American, and Hispanic women living in the United States compared with non-Hispanic white women.[9]

KEY POINTS

- The incidence of breast cancer in the United States has been slowly increasing 0.4% each year, on average, since 2004, but the mortality rate has consistently declined, primarily as a result of advances in systemic therapy.
- The incidence of breast cancer is increasing in nonindustrialized countries because of lifestyle changes (namely, obesity and decreased physical activity).
- Compared with non-Hispanic white women in the United States, black women have now a similar incidence of breast cancer but a higher rate of breast cancer–related mortality. The causes behind this significant disparity are not fully understood and likely are multifactorial.

RISK FACTORS

FIXED (NONMODIFIABLE) FACTORS

Age and Sex

In the United States, older age and female sex are the most important risk factors for the development of breast cancer. The lifetime risk for breast cancer among women in the United States is estimated at one in 8 (12%), with multiple risk factors identified (Table 10-1).

Male breast cancer is uncommon, accounting for approximately 1% of all breast cancers.[11] Men are usually diagnosed after age 60 years; the specific risk factors for this disease among men include:[12,13]

- genetic predisposition associated with *BRCA2* or *PALB2* mutations
- Klinefelter syndrome
- testicular alterations that result in testosterone deficiency (e.g., undescended testes or testicular injury)
- syndromes that increase the estrogen-to-testosterone ratio (such as obesity or cirrhosis).

Table 10-1 Established Risk Factors for Breast Cancer: Fixed Factors (Excluding Genetic Mutations)[10]

Factor	Relative Risk
Sex (female *v* male)	100
Age (< 50 *v* > 50 years)	6.7
Endocrine factors	
Age at first birth (> 30 years) or nulliparity	1.2-1.7
Age at menarche (< 12 years) or age at menopause (> 55 years)	1.2-1.3
Benign breast disease	
ADH, LCIS	4.0-5.0
Family history (no known mutation)	
First-degree relatives	1.5-2.0
Ashkenazi Jewish ethnicity	1.4
Therapeutic radiation to the chest < 30 years	7.0-17.0

Abbreviations: ADH, atypical ductal hyperplasia; LCIS, lobular carcinoma in situ.

Familial Risk Factors

A family history of breast and/or ovarian cancer, particularly if onset occurred when the patient was younger than 50 years old, is associated with a higher risk of breast cancer. Approximately 5% to 10% of all breast cancers are associated with highly penetrant gene mutations, such as *BRCA1* and *BRCA2.* An additional 15% to 20% of women diagnosed with breast cancer have a family history of breast and/or ovarian cancer, which may be the result of inheritance of a number of low-penetrance genes or single nucleotide polymorphisms that increase risk, or alternatively, due to shared environmental exposures. In some families, the inheritance of low-penetrance genes and shared environmental factors may operate synergistically. Having first-degree relatives with breast cancer portends a two-fold higher risk of breast cancer.[12] This risk can increase three-to four-fold if a first-degree relative was diagnosed at an age younger than 50 years or when two first-degree relatives are affected.[12,13] Having a previous diagnosis of breast cancer is also associated with a higher risk of contralateral disease developing, which can be compounded when a family history of breast cancer is present.

Genetic Risk Factors

Hereditary breast cancer is characterized by the presence of high- or moderate-penetrance gene mutations associated with distinct syndromes and is associated with other malignancies (Table 10-2). Optimally, the family member to receive genetic testing should be the youngest woman who carries the diagnosis of either ovarian or breast cancer (ie, the proband).

There has been a dramatic shift in the genetic testing landscape over the past several years, due to the development of next-generation sequencing and the Supreme Court decision in 2013 that invalidated a patent restricting *BRCA1/2* testing.[14,24] Multigene-panel testing is now offered to many patients and several multiplex test panels are available that assess high-, moderate-, and low-penetrance genes.[25] The challenges of using these panels include a limited understanding of risk associated with moderately penetrant genes and high likelihood of detecting variants of uncertain significance.[26,27]

Several germline mutations are associated with an increased probability of breast and/or ovarian cancer developing. Depending on the associated risk of breast cancer, these mutations are categorized into high- or moderate-penetrance genes. The most common mutations are localized in the *BRCA1* and *BRCA2* genes; both are highly penetrant mutations

Table 10-2 **Lifetime Cancer Risk for Individuals With High and Moderate Penetrance Mutations in Selected Genes**[15-23]

Gene (Associated Disease)	Cumulative Lifetime Risk of Breast Cancer Development (%)	Other Tumors
High penetrance		
BRCA1	55-70	Ovarian cancer
BRCA2	45-70	Prostate cancer
		Pancreatic cancer
		Malignant melanoma
		Gallbladder and bile duct cancer
		Stomach cancer
TP53 (Li-Fraumeni syndrome)	100	Soft-tissue sarcoma and osteosarcoma
		Brain tumors
		Leukemia
		Adrenocortical cancer
PTEN (Cowden syndrome/PTEN hamartoma tumor syndrome)	85	Follicular thyroid cancer
		Endometrial cancer
		Colon cancer
		Renal cancer
STK11 (Peutz-Jeghers syndrome)	55	Colon cancer
		Pancreatic cancer
		Stomach and small-bowel cancer
CDH1 (Hereditary diffuse gastric cancer)	50-60 (mainly lobular)	Diffuse gastric cancer
PALB2	44	Pancreatic cancer
Moderate penetrance		
ATM	30	
BRIP1	Insufficient evidence	Ovarian cancer
CHEK2 truncating (1100delC)	31.8	Colorectal cancer
CHEK2 missense (I157T)	18.3	
MSH2, MLH1, MSH6, PMS2, EPCAM (Lynch syndrome)	Insufficient evidence	Endometrial cancer, ovarian cancer
NBN	Insufficient evidence	
NF1	18	
RAD51C	Insufficient evidence	
RAD51D	Insufficient evidence	

transmitted in an autosomal-dominant pattern. The protein products of *BRCA1* and *BRCA2* function as tumor suppressors that protect chromosomal stability by enabling homologous recombination after double-stranded DNA breaks. *BRCA2* binds directly to RAD51, an enzyme essential for homologous recombination. *BRCA2* is also the gene related to Fanconi anemia, and it works in concert not only with RAD51 and *BRCA1* but also with PALB2 to facilitate recruitment of these enzymes to sites of DNA damage, resulting in repair. Other high-penetrance genes include *TP53, PTEN, STK11, CDH1,* and *PALB2.*

Characteristics of *BRCA1* and *BRCA2* mutation carriers include the following:

- Among women with *BRCA1* mutations, the risk of breast cancer up to age 70 years ranges from 55% to 70%, and between 45% to 70% in women with *BRCA2* mutations.[28-31]
- The risk of ovarian cancer developing over a lifetime is higher with a *BRCA1* mutation (40% to 45%) than with a *BRCA2* mutation (15% to 20%).[28-31]
- The development of contralateral breast cancer is also increased (*BRCA1* relative risk [RR], 4.5; *BRCA2* RR, 3.4),

although this risk is less pronounced among women older than 50 years (10.8%) than among patients who were diagnosed younger than 30 years (28.2%).[32]

- The risk of male breast cancer before age 80 is approximately 7% among *BRCA2* mutation carriers.[33]
- Approximately 2.5% of people of Ashkenazi Jewish ancestry carry one of three "founder" mutations— 185delAG (also known as 187delAG or c.68_69delAG) in *BRCA1*, 5382insC (also known as 5385insc or c.5266dupC) in *BRCA1*, or 6174delT (c.5946delT) in *BRCA2*. These three mutations account for 12% of breast cancers and 35% of ovarian cancers in this population. An additional 2% to 4% have nonfounder mutations.[34]
- *BRCA1* mutation carriers are more likely to develop triple-negative breast cancer (TNBC) than are *BRCA2* mutation carriers or non-*BRCA* mutation carriers.

Characteristics of other high-penetrance genes include the following:

- The Li-Fraumeni syndrome is associated with pathogenic variants in the tumor suppressor protein p53 gene (*TP53).* It affects one in 5,000 people and is associated with a 90% lifetime risk of a malignancy developing, which includes breast cancer in women younger than 30 years, in addition to other types of malignancies (Table 10-2). HER2-positive breast cancer is more prevalent in women with *TP53* germline mutation compared with women without the *TP53* mutation.[35] In addition, patients with Li-Fraumeni syndrome are at increased risk of secondary malignancies developing in the radiation field.[36]
- Cowden syndrome is a rare autosomal-dominant syndrome; 80% of cases are caused by mutations in the *PTEN* tumor suppressor gene (10q23). In this syndrome, breast cancer can occur in conjunction with other cancers, such as thyroid, endometrial, colon, and renal. Specific physical findings among patients with Cowden syndrome include macrocephaly, hamartomas, autism, and trichilemmomas of the face, hands, and feet.[37]
- Germline pathogenic variants in the cadherin 1 gene (*CDH1*) are associated with increased risk of diffuse gastric cancer and invasive lobular carcinoma.
- *PALB2* (a partner and localizer of *BRCA2)* has emerged as a relevant gene associated with predisposition to breast cancer. Loss-of-function mutations in *PALB2* are observed in 0.6% to 3.9% of families with a history of breast cancer.[15]

The data regarding the cancer risks associated with these genes, as well as the treatment recommendations for mutation carriers are continuously evolving as new findings become available.

Reproductive and Endogenous Hormones

Estrogens clearly play a role in breast cancer risk and development. Increased levels of premenopausal endogenous hormones are associated with an increased risk of disease among postmenopausal women. Terminal differentiation of breast epithelium occurs after a full-term pregnancy. This histologic change in breast parenchyma appears to be protective and associated with a reduction in breast cancer risk when first full-term pregnancy occurs at a younger age (younger than 30 years). Lactation may also convey protection; however, the duration of lactation required for this benefit is not well defined. The use of contemporary hormonal contraceptives has been associated with a higher risk of breast cancer compared with women who had never used hormonal contraceptives; however, the absolute increase in risk is small.[38]

The role of reproductive risk factors is not the same in all breast cancer subtypes. An early onset of menarche, late age of menopause, and nulliparity are all related to extended estrogen exposure and elevated risk of hormone-receptor (HR)-positive disease.[39] In contrast, TNBC is associated with an increasing number of births and is not associated with nulliparity or age at first full-term delivery.[40]

MODIFIABLE FACTORS

Exogenous Hormones

Menopausal hormone therapy in the form of combination estrogen and progesterone is associated with an increased risk of invasive breast cancer developing (hazard ratio, 1.26);[41]however, the risk returns to normal within 2 years after discontinuation of menopausal hormone therapy (Table 10-3).[42] Women taking combination menopausal hormone therapy also have been found to have a more advanced stage of breast cancer at the time of diagnosis.

The global cessation of combination menopausal hormone therapy in 2002 was associated with an 8.6% reduction in the annual incidence of invasive breast cancer, primarily observed in HR-positive disease and in women older than 50 years.

Radiation Exposure

Survivors of Hodgkin lymphoma and other hematologic malignancies who received therapeutic mediastinal or mantle-field radiation have a higher risk of breast cancer developing, which

Table 10-3 **Established Risk Factors for Breast Cancer: Modifiable Factors**

Factor	Relative Risk
Exogenous hormones	
Oral contraceptive pill	0.9-1.0
Estrogen replacement (> 10 years)	1.1
Estrogen and progesterone	1.4-3.0
Postmenopausal obesity (BMI > 30 kg/m^2)	2.5
Exercise (> 3 h/wk)	0.6
Alcohol use	1.1-2.2
Diet	1.0
Extremely dense mammographic tissue	4.0-6.0

Abbreviation: BMI, body mass index.

depends on dose of radiation and the radiation-field volume. The risk is greatest when treatment occurred during active proliferation of breast tissue (ie, between ages 15 and 25 years). The median time to the development of breast cancer after treatment is approximately 18 years; however, increased risk can start as early as 8 years after treatment. Use of lower doses of therapeutic radiation involving smaller volumes has resulted in lower risks of breast cancer.[43-45] For patients with a history of thoracic radiation received between the ages of 10 and 30 years, it is recommended that annual screening mammograms and annual breast magnetic resonance imaging (MRI) start at the age of 25 years.[46]

Mammographic Density

Mammographic density is classified according to the proportion of radiopaque areas on a mammogram, representing epithelial and stromal tissue, relative to radiolucent areas, representing fat. The Breast Imaging Reporting and Data System Atlas issued by the American College of Radiology categorizes breast density composition into four lettered categories based on a visual assessment of the mammogram, as follows:

A. The breasts are almost entirely fatty.
B. The breasts have scattered areas of fibroglandular density.
C. The breasts are heterogeneously dense, which may obscure small masses.
D. The breasts are extremely dense, which lowers the sensitivity of mammography.

Mammograms classified as categories C or D are considered dense. There is a linear trend associated with increasing mammographic density and risk of breast cancer, wherein women with > 75% breast density have a four- to six-fold higher risk of disease.[47] Exogenous hormone use, such as menopausal hormone therapy or oral contraceptives, results in increased mammographic density. Lower mammographic density may be a reflection of involution of the terminal ductal lobular units, a natural aging process of the breast that is associated with a lower breast cancer incidence.[48,49] Mammographic density and mammographic sensitivity are inversely related, primarily because of the masking of cancer by superimposition of overlapping, radiopaque, dense breast tissue. Mammographic density is a principle factor in the failure of mammography to detect cancer, as well as in the presentation of "interval cancers" (ie, cancers presenting during the interval after a normal mammogram).[50]

In the United States, 38 states have legislation requiring that women be notified about breast density after screening mammography, a number that has been increasing steadily for years. However, there is currently no consensus on whether women with dense breasts should be advised to pursue supplemental screening. Supplemental screening modalities, including whole-breast screening ultrasound, digital breast tomosynthesis, molecular breast imaging, and screening breast MRI, increase cancer detection as compared with mammography alone in women with dense breasts, but the impact on breast cancer outcomes is unknown. Insurance coverage for supplemental screening is variable.

Benign Proliferative Breast Disease

Pathologic changes within the breast are independent risk factors for breast cancer. Benign proliferative breast disease with atypia, such as atypical ductal hyperplasia (ADH), atypical lobular hyperplasia (ALH), and lobular carcinoma in situ (LCIS), increase the risk of breast cancer developing in either breast (approximately four-fold for atypical hyperplasia and 10-fold for LCIS).[51] Benign proliferative lesions without atypia seem not to increase breast cancer risk. Flat epithelial atypia is also an atypical proliferation but the associated risk of developing breast cancer is uncertain at this point.

Atypical hyperplasia is associated with approximately a 30% risk of breast cancer developing over 25 years. The magnitude of increase does not seem to be affected by the histologic type of atypical hyperplasia (ie, ductal *v* lobular).[52] After a diagnosis of ADH using core needle biopsy, it is recommended that most individuals undergo an excisional procedure to exclude the possibility of an associated invasive carcinoma. On the other hand, for ALH and LCIS, given the small reported risk of upgrade to ductal carcinoma in situ (DCIS) or invasive carcinoma, incidental radiologic-pathologic concordant cases diagnosed on core needle biopsy no longer require surgical excision.[53]

Behavioral Factors

Consumption of one alcoholic beverage per day is associated with a 12% increased risk of breast cancer and a further 10% increase in risk occurs with every additional 10 g/d of alcohol (or 0.75 to 1.0 alcoholic beverage per day) consumed. The risk is independent of type of alcohol consumed and may be related to an increase in serum hormone levels.[54-56]

Obesity (body mass index [the weight in kilograms divided by the square of the height in meters], > 30) increases the risk of breast cancer in postmenopausal women by > 63% but is inversely correlated with risk in premenopausal women.[57] However, when used as an indicator of body fat distribution, a larger waist circumference is associated with a greater incidence of premenopausal estrogen receptor (ER)-negative breast cancer.[58] Waist circumference and body mass index are markers of visceral adiposity associated with the metabolic syndrome—a condition of hyperglycemia, hyperinsulinemia, and insulin resistance. The association of obesity with increased breast cancer risk and death resulting from breast cancer appears to be due to the effects of obesity on the increased production of estrogen and insulin activation of tyrosine kinase growth receptor pathways.[59,60]

Smoking tobacco is associated with a moderate increase in breast cancer risk, and there is also evidence for a moderate increase in risk with passive smoking.[61] Physical activity appears to be inversely related to breast cancer risk. This topic is developed more in the "Lifestyle Modifications" section.

Isoflavones (ie, phytoestrogens most commonly found in soy), vitamin D, dairy products, and high-fat diets have unclear relationships with the incidence of breast cancer.[62]

RISK-DETERMINATION MODELS

Several models are available to predict the risk of breast cancer on the basis of family history and/or to determine the probability of carrying a *BRCA* mutation (Table 10-4). The Claus model includes first- and second-degree relatives with breast and/or ovarian cancer and incorporates the age at diagnosis. BRCAPRO, the Tyrer-Cuzick model (also called IBIS [International Breast Cancer Intervention Study]), and the BOADICEA model all calculate risk on the basis of the probability of carrying a genetic mutation.[63-66]

The modified Gail model (www.cancer.gov/bcrisktool) is the most widely used risk-assessment tool; it incorporates nongenetic factors such as:

- current age,
- age at menarche and first full-term pregnancy or nulliparity,
- number of breast biopsies and presence of atypical hyperplasia,
- number of first-degree relatives with breast cancer, and
- race.

The original Gail model was modified and validated to incorporate race as a risk factor, specifically assessing breast cancer risk in black women (the Contraceptive and Reproductive Experience [CARE] model).[67]

The modified Gail model is an excellent tool to determine risk on a population basis; however, the 5-year or lifetime risk of disease calculated for an individual woman is not robust.[68] This model will also underestimate risk if there is a significant genetic predisposition. Prevention strategies are often considered when the modified Gail model calculates a 5-year risk > 1.67%; however, this calculation does not take into account factors such as breast density or presence of LCIS, and it may also underestimate the risk associated with atypia.

KEY POINTS

- Although estrogens play a role in breast cancer risk, the role of reproductive risk factors is not the same in all breast cancer subtypes.
- Menopausal hormone therapy in the form of combination estrogen and progesterone is associated with an increased risk of invasive breast cancer development, which increases steadily with duration of use.
- Patients who received therapeutic mediastinal or mantle-field radiation have a higher risk of breast cancer with the risk being the greatest when treatment occurred during active proliferation of breast tissue (ie, between ages 15 and 25 years).
- Atypical hyperplasia and LCIS are associated with a 30% risk of breast cancer development over 25 years.
- *BRCA1* and *BRCA2* mutations are associated with a 50% to 75% lifetime risk of development of breast cancer and a 30% to 40% risk (for those with *BRCA1* mutation) or 10% to 20% risk (for those with *BRCA2* mutation) of development of ovarian or fallopian tube–type cancer.
- Postmenopausal obesity and alcohol use are associated with a higher risk of breast cancer.
- Increased breast density is associated with higher risk of breast cancer.
- Several models are available to predict the risk of breast cancer on the basis of family history and/or to determine the probability of carrying a *BRCA* mutation.

Table 10-4 **Risk Factors Used in Risk Assessment Models**

Model	Risk Factors
Modified Gail model	Age, age at menarche, age at first live birth, number of breast biopsies, history of atypical hyperplasia, number of first-degree relatives with breast cancer, race
Claus model	Age, first-and second-degree relatives with breast cancer, age at onset of breast cancer, ovarian cancer in a relative, paternal family history
BRCAPRO model	Age, first-and second-degree relatives with breast cancer, age at onset of breast cancer in a relative, bilateral breast cancer in a relative, ovarian cancer in a relative, breast cancer in a male relative
IBIS model (Tyrer-Cuzick model)	Age, body mass index, age at menarche, age at first live birth, age at menopause, hormone replacement therapy, number of prior breast biopsies, presence of atypical hyperplasia, lobular carcinoma in situ, number of first-and second-degree relatives with breast cancer, age at onset of breast cancer in a relative, bilateral breast cancer in a relative, ovarian cancer in a relative
BOADICEA	Age, first-, second-, and third-degree relatives with breast cancer, age at onset of breast cancer in a relative, bilateral breast cancer in a relative, ovarian cancer in a relative, breast cancer in a male relative

Abbreviations: BOADICEA, Breast and Ovarian Analysis of Disease Incidence and Carrier Estimation Algorithm; IBIS, International Breast Cancer Intervention Study.

PREVENTION

The goal of breast cancer prevention is to reduce the risk of the development of disease with minimal toxicity. Women with a high-penetrance genetic mutation or a strong family history of breast cancer not associated with a pathogenic mutation in a breast cancer susceptibility gene may consider risk-reducing surgery. Lifestyle and medical risk-reducing strategies can be discussed with women with any degree of breast cancer risk.

RISK-REDUCING SURGERY

Prophylactic surgeries for high-risk patients reduce the risk of breast cancer development and include risk-reducing bilateral salpingo-oophorectomy (RRSO) and bilateral risk-reduction mastectomy (RRM).

Risk-Reducing Bilateral Salpingo-Oophorectomy

Because detecting ovarian or fallopian tube cancer at an early stage is difficult, it is recommended that women with *BRCA1* and *BRCA2* mutations undergo RRSO, typically between ages 35 and 40 years and on completion of childbearing. The National Comprehensive Cancer Network (NCCN) guidelines specifically note it is reasonable to delay RRSO until ages 40 to 45 years in patients with a *BRCA2* mutation, because the median age of onset of ovarian cancer tends to occur 8 to 10 years later than in patients with a *BRCA1* mutation. Bilateral salpingectomy with delayed oophorectomy has been postulated to be an alternative to RRSO for premenopausal women that would allow fertility preservation and avoid early menopause. However, until more evidence is available, this should not be recommended as standard of care.[69]

RRSO has been associated with the following:

- a decrease in the risk of ovarian cancer (which includes primary peritoneal and fallopian tube cancers) by approximately 85% (hazard ratio, 0.14)
- a reduction in the risk of a first diagnosis of breast cancer by 40% and 60% among *BRCA1* and *BRCA2* mutation carriers, respectively (hazard ratios, 0.63 and 0.36, respectively)
- lower breast cancer-specific mortality (hazard ratio, 0.44), lower all-cause mortality (hazard ratio, 0.40), and lower ovarian cancer-specific mortality (hazard ratio, 0.21) rates.[70]

The concern about the adverse effect on mortality from inducing early menopause may be safely mitigated with short-term menopausal hormone therapy given until age 50 years, without an apparent compromise in the overall benefit of RRSO on breast cancer risk reduction.[71]

Bilateral Risk Reducing Mastectomy

Bilateral RRM reduces the risk of breast cancer by > 90% in women with hereditary breast and ovarian cancer syndromes, with most studies focusing on *BRCA* mutation carriers.[72] Prophylactic RRM should be offered to these patients, although the decision should be based on personal preference, given that effective screening is available. Women at high or moderate risk of breast cancer (ie, known genetic linkage or a significant family history without a known genetic predisposition) should also have a discussion with their doctors concerning prevention.

Skin-sparing mastectomy is increasingly being used and appears to be as effective as total mastectomy. Early data indicate nipple-sparing mastectomy may be reasonable in this patient population.[73] Reconstructive surgery after mastectomies does not appear to increase breast cancer risk.

MEDICAL RISK REDUCTION (CHEMOPREVENTION)

Selective Estrogen-Receptor Modulators

The observation that adjuvant tamoxifen used to treat invasive breast cancer led to a significant reduction in the development of breast cancer[74] prompted several randomized trials examining the efficacy of selective estrogen-receptor modulators (SERMs) in reducing the risk of breast cancer among high-risk women. The benefit of tamoxifen for chemoprevention was evaluated in four different trials, which consistently showed a reduction in the risk of invasive breast cancer when compared with placebo (Table 10-5).[78-81] The eligibility requirements of these studies varied, as did the acceptance of concurrent menopausal hormone therapy or bilateral oophorectomy among participants, making cross-study conclusions more difficult. However, a meta-analysis of these four studies led by the US Preventive Services Task Force (USPSTF)[82] concluded that, when compared with placebo, tamoxifen led to:

- a reduction in the incidence of invasive breast cancer by 30%,
- a significant reduction in the incidence of nonvertebral fractures by 34%, and
- no effect on breast cancer–specific or all-cause mortality.

The prevention studies and the studies using tamoxifen for the treatment of breast cancer demonstrated a number of adverse effects attributed to tamoxifen. SERMs such as tamoxifen have either an antiestrogenic activity or an estrogen agonist activity, depending on the tissue. Although its antiestrogenic activity explains its efficacy in breast cancer prevention, some adverse effects may be explained by its estrogen-like activity, as follows:

- increased incidence of endometrial cancers (RR, 3.28), which translated to a 1.6% risk with tamoxifen compared with a baseline 0.7% risk over 7 years.[77] Typically presenting with postmenopausal bleeding, adenocarcinomas are commonly detected at an early stage and affect women older than 50 years. No data support routine screening for endometrial cancer using transvaginal ultrasound or biopsy, unless abnormal vaginal bleeding is present.
- increased incidence of venous thromboembolic events (deep venous thrombosis [DVT] RR, 1.44; pulmonary embolism [PE] RR, 2.15). The risk of stroke was not consistently increased among the tamoxifen studies, and this association is not supported by large population studies. Risks of endometrial cancer and venous thromboembolic events increase with advancing age.
- increased incidence of cataracts, as well as gynecologic (vaginal discharge) and vasomotor symptoms (hot flashes).

Table 10-5 Breast Cancer Medical Prevention Trials

Trial	No. of Patients	Comparison	RR of IBC (95% CI)	RR for HR+ IBC (95% CI)
STAR[78]	19,747	Raloxifene *v* tamoxifen	1.24 (1.065 to 1.47)	NA[a]
MAP.3[75]	4,560	Exemestane *v* placebo	0.35 (0.18 to 0.70)	0.27 (0.12 to 0.60)
IBIS-II[76]	1,920	Anastrozole *v* placebo	0.50 (0.32 to 0.76)	0.42 (0.25 to 0.71)
Italian[79]	5,408	Tamoxifen *v* placebo	0.84 (0.60 to 1.17)	0.61 (0.38 to 0.99)
Royal Marsden[80]	2,471	Tamoxifen *v* placebo	0.78 (0.58 to 1.04)	0.48 (0.29 to 0.79)
IBIS-I[81]	7,145	Tamoxifen *v* placebo	0.73 (0.58 to 0.91)	0.66 (0.50 to 0.87)
BCPT P-1[77]	13,338	Tamoxifen *v* placebo	0.57 (0.46 to 0.70)	0.38 (0.28 to 0.50)

Abbreviations: HR, hormone receptor; IBC, invasive breast cancer; NA, not available; RR, relative risk.
[a]Data not available for most recent evaluation.

- bone loss in premenopausal women.[83] However in the Breast Cancer Prevention Trial P1 trial, a reduction in the incidence of osteoporotic bone fractures (of the hips, spine, or radius) by 29% was seen among women age 50 years or older.[77]

In a recent study, tamoxifen at a dose of 5 mg daily for 3 years, compared with placebo, decreased the risk of disease recurrence by half in women with ADH, LCIS, or DCIS with a favorable toxicity profile,[84] and low-dose tamoxifen may be an alternative in women with intraepithelial neoplasia.

Raloxifene, a second-generation SERM, can also be used for chemoprevention. Raloxifene reduced the incidence of invasive breast cancer by 66% to 72% when investigated as a treatment of osteoporosis in two clinical trials.[85] Raloxifene was not associated with risk of endometrial cancer but increased the risk of DVT/PE. The National Surgical Adjuvant Breast and Bowel Project (NSABP) P-2 Study of Tamoxifen and Raloxifene (STAR) trial compared the efficacy of 5 years of tamoxifen with that of raloxifene.[78] After an extended follow-up of nearly 8 years, raloxifene retained only 76% of the effectiveness of tamoxifen in reducing the risk of invasive cancer.[86] There was no difference in mortality outcome between the two SERMs. Raloxifene use was associated with significantly less toxicity than tamoxifen—specifically, fewer endometrial cancers and thromboembolic events.

A meta-analysis of the individual participant data from all randomized prevention trials involving SERMs (n = 9 trials; n = 83,399 participants) demonstrated a 10-year cumulative incidence of breast cancer that equaled 6.3%, versus 4.2% among patients who received placebo or the SERM, respectively.[87] The reduction in breast cancer was evident during years 0 to 5 (42%) and during years 5 to 10 (25%). The increased risk of endometrial cancer was confined to tamoxifen use during years 0 to 5 (hazard ratio, 1.64), and although the number of venous thromboembolic events was increased overall, there was no effect on incidence of myocardial infarction, stroke, or transient ischemic attacks. SERM use had no effect on the risk of ER-negative breast cancer or on overall mortality.

Aromatase Inhibitors

Similar to SERMs, the observation that adjuvant aromatase inhibitors (AIs) used to treat invasive breast cancer led to a significant reduction in the development of breast cancer prompted the evaluation of AIs in risk reduction of breast cancer among high-risk postmenopausal women. Importantly, AIs are not associated with the risk of endometrial cancer and thromboembolism, although they cause musculoskeletal symptoms and reduce bone density. Two large trials, using eligibility criteria similar to those used in the BCPT and STAR trials, investigated the role of AIs in the prevention of invasive breast cancer among postmenopausal women at high risk:

- The NCIC CTG MAP.3 trial compared exemestane with placebo. At 35-month follow-up, a 65% reduction was demonstrated in the incidence of invasive breast cancer as was a 73% reduction in the incidence of ER-positive invasive breast cancer among women taking exemestane for 5 years, as compared with those taking placebo.[75]
- The IBIS-II trial compared anastrozole with placebo. In this trial, 5 years of anastrozole reduced the risk of HR-positive invasive breast cancer and DCIS by > 50% among postmenopausal women at high risk for the development of breast cancer.[76] As was seen in the prevention studies using SERMs, anastrozole neither conveyed a risk reduction for ER-negative breast cancer nor improved survival.

Few women with *BRCA* mutations have been specifically evaluated in prevention trials; therefore, the role of primary medical prevention in this population is not well understood. However, data suggest tamoxifen can reduce the development of contralateral breast cancers in carriers of *BRCA1* (42% risk reduction) or *BRCA2* (52% risk reduction) mutations after the diagnosis of breast cancer.[88] The use of other medications for breast cancer prevention (eg, metformin, aspirin) remains investigational.

The indications and options for endocrine therapy were recently updated and are summarized in Figure 10-1.

Despite an estimation of > 2 million women in the United States who could benefit from pharmacologic interventions to reduce the risk of breast cancer, the uptake of these measures has been low. There are many factors that may play a role, such as concern for toxicity, concern for lack of benefit, or lack of awareness among women at risk and their providers.

LIFESTYLE MODIFICATIONS

Physical Activity

Studies have linked lifestyle factors and risk of a second primary, contralateral breast cancer or systemic breast cancer recurrence. Moderate exercise (2 to 3 h/wk) has been reported to reduce breast cancer recurrence and all-cause mortality rates by approximately 40% to 67%.[90] Three prospective cohort studies demonstrated that current total or recreational exercise can reduce the incidence of breast cancer by 20% to 30%, primarily among premenopausal women.[91]

Diet and Weight Change

The correlation among alcohol consumption, obesity, and the risk of breast cancer is well established.[92] Good data are lacking as to whether moderate alcohol use after a diagnosis of breast cancer influences mortality risk.[93,94] In terms of diet, most studies have not conclusively supported a reduction in risk with increased consumption of fruits and vegetables. Although a study from the Women's Health Initiative suggested a 9% reduction in risk when women consumed a low-fat diet, prospective studies evaluating dietary changes and their effect on breast cancer risk have not been conclusive.[91,95] Vitamin and mineral supplements, specifically vitamin D and calcium, respectively, have not been shown to date to affect the development of breast cancer.[96] Ongoing studies, such as the BWEL study, are addressing the role of weight loss on breast cancer recurrence. The BWEL study will enroll nearly 3,200 overweight women with early-stage breast cancer to test if weight loss decreases the risk of breast cancer recurrence.[97]

KEY POINTS

- RRSO in *BRCA1/2* carriers is associated with lower breast cancer–specific mortality, lower all-cause mortality, and lower ovarian cancer–specific mortality rates.
- Bilateral RRM reduces the risk of breast cancer by > 90% in *BRCA1/2* carriers.
- Tamoxifen in pre- or postmenopausal women and raloxifene, anastrozole, or exemestane in postmenopausal women are options to reduce the risk of development of ER-positive breast cancer.
- Moderate exercise (2 to 3 h/wk) has been reported to reduce breast cancer recurrence and all-cause mortality by approximately 40% to 67%.
- Alcohol consumption is associated with increased risk of breast cancer and there seems to be a significant dose-response relationship.

SCREENING

AVERAGE RISK

Effective screening for breast cancer detects disease during the preclinical phase (ie, before the development of symptoms). Screening thus has a favorable effect on breast cancer–related mortality, given that earlier-stage disease is associated with a more favorable prognosis. Although published randomized trials have been criticized for variable quality of imaging, flawed study design or execution, insufficient duration of follow-up, and problems regarding lead-time bias (Fig 10-2), additional randomized trials are unlikely to be performed and we are limited to the data at hand.

Benefits and Harms From Screening

A 2002 evaluation of the randomized trials suggested a 22% reduction in breast cancer mortality among women older than 50 years who underwent mammographic screening. An updated evaluation in 2009 demonstrated a 14% reduction in breast cancer mortality among women ages 50 to 59 years, and a 32% reduction among women ages 60 to 69 years.[98] The effect of mammographic screening on breast cancer mortality among women ages 40 to 49 years or older than age 70 years is less robust. In 2014, the International Agency for Research on Cancer evaluated evidence from 20 cohort and 20 case-control studies regarding breast cancer screening and concluded that for women 50 to 69 years of age, there was, on average, a 23% reduction in the risk of breast cancer deaths.[99] The reduction in breast cancer deaths for women ages 40 to 49 years was less pronounced.

Harms from screening include anxiety provoked by false-positive findings, complications from unnecessary biopsies, overdiagnosis, and increased detection of DCIS, which, in many cases, would not proceed to invasive cancer.[100]

Frequency of Screening and Age to Initiate Screening

The optimal frequency for mammographic screening is not known. The advantage of shorter intervals is an increased chance of detecting faster-growing cancer at an earlier stage, but this advantage comes with the disadvantage of a higher false-positive rate. On the basis of six modeling groups that estimated benefits, risks, and use of resources, a biennial screening interval was preferred to annual screening, because it achieved 81% of the benefit with nearly half the number of false-positive results.[100]

The optimal age at which to begin screening remains unclear and is based on personal risk. The USPSTF recommends initiating biennial screening at age 50 years and continuing until age 74 years.[101] The American Cancer Society's (ACS) updated guidelines from 2015 support annual imaging beginning at age

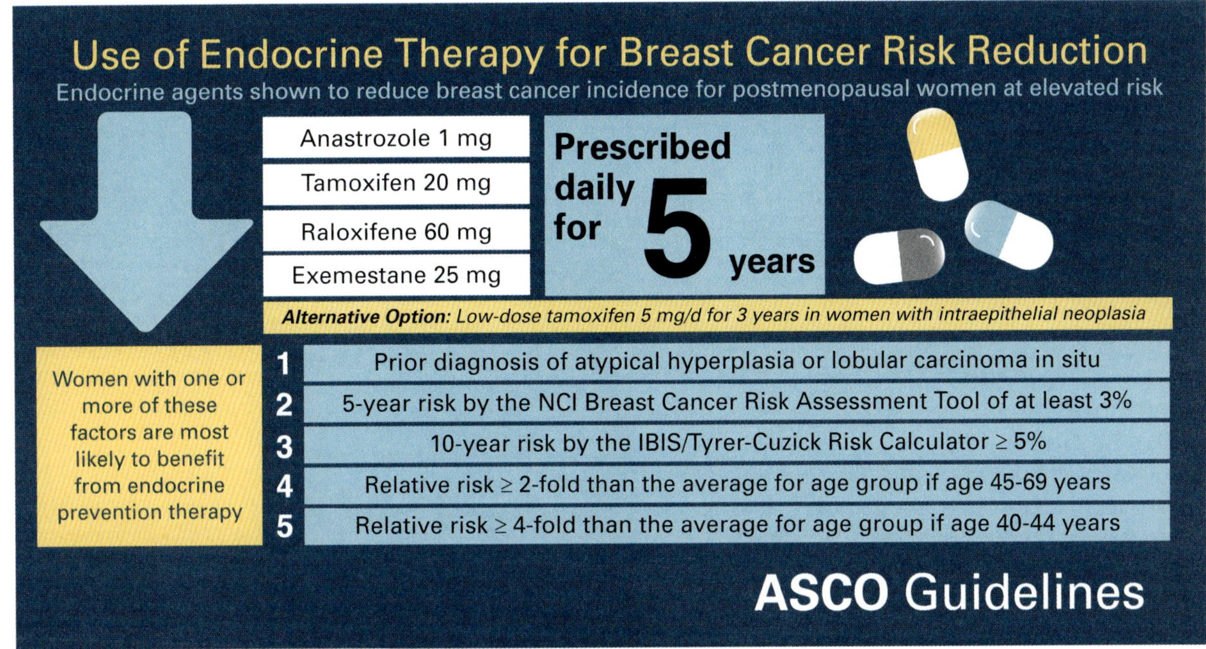

Fig. 10-1 Use of endocrine therapy for breast cancer risk reduction.[89]

Abbreviations: IBIS, International Breast Cancer Intervention Study; NCI, National Cancer Institute

Permission to reuse Visvanathan K, Fabian CJ, Bantug E, et al. Use of Endocrine Therapy for Breast Cancer Risk Reduction: ASCO Clinical Practice Guideline Update. J Clin Oncol. *2019; 37(33):3152-3165. doi:10.1200/JCO.19.01472*

40 years and strongly recommend annual screening from ages 45 to 54 years, followed by a transition to biennial screening, which continues as long as a woman's overall health is good and she has a life expectancy of ≥ 10 years.[102]

Different Screening Modalities

There has been a gradual and now nearly complete conversion to digital from film screen technology in the United States. Although digital imaging provides only a small increase in sensitivity compared with optimally performed film imaging, the move to digital imaging has greatly improved and standardized image quality across all sites.

Digital breast tomosynthesis (DBT) mammography is a newer technology that enables three-dimensional imaging of the breast, similar to computed tomography (CT).[103] DBT results in slightly greater sensitivity and in a significant reduction in recall rates. It is unknown whether DBT leads to a reduction in the number of advanced breast cancers, because of earlier detection. Interpretation times are longer with DBT than with digital imaging, but the amount of radiation exposure is now equivalent to standard mammography when synthesized two-dimensional technology is used.

Breast self-examination (BSE) has not been found to improve the detection of early-stage breast cancer on a population basis. Several studies have shown no difference in the rate of cancer detection, tumor characteristics, or breast cancer–related mortality when BSE was performed after instruction, compared with no BSE.[104,105] Clinical breast examinations also do not appear to have affected breast cancer detection or mortality rates from a population perspective.[106] However, many groups encourage BSE as a method of increasing breast self-awareness to seek medical attention if abnormalities are detected.[101,107,108]

HIGH RISK

The ACS does not recommend routine use of MRI screening for the general population of asymptomatic women, because of

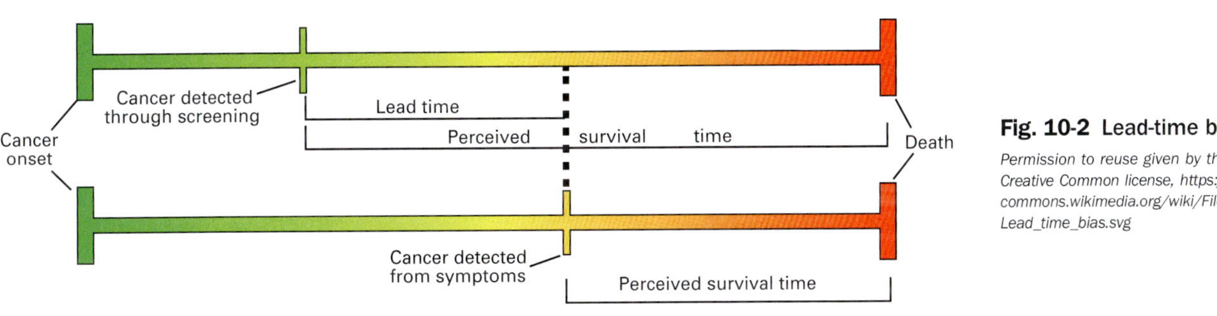

Fig. 10-2 Lead-time bias.

Permission to reuse given by the Creative Common license, https://commons.wikimedia.org/wiki/File:Lead_time_bias.svg

high cost, limited access, and high false-positive rates. Given its substantial sensitivity, the optimal use for this method is in screening a high-risk population. Among patients with *BRCA* mutations, screening mammography can miss > 50% of all breast cancers. Supplementing mammography with MRI improves the sensitivity from 25% to 59% and to 80% to 100% when MRI is added.[109] The specificity of combined mammography and MRI is lower (73% to 93%) than the specificity of mammography alone. Annual MRI screening among *BRCA* carriers detects more interval cancers and earlier-stage cancers (DCIS and stage I: 13.8% with MRI *v* 7.2% without MRI) compared with women not screened with MRI.[110] Adding annual MRI screening to mammography is associated with a 70% reduction in the incidence of lymph node–positive or large invasive breast cancers, although a mortality benefit has not been demonstrated.

Annual breast MRI screening as an adjunct to mammography is usually recommended in the following situations:[102,111]

- *BRCA1/2* mutation carriers;
- first-degree relative of a *BRCA* carrier, who is untested for the presence of a *BRCA* mutation;
- lifetime risk ≥ 20%, as defined by BRCAPRO or other models that largely depend on family history;
- radiation to chest between the ages 10 years and 30 years;
- Li-Fraumeni syndrome and first-degree relatives; and
- Cowden syndrome.

Caution must be used in recommending annual MRI screening for women whose estimated lifetime risk of breast cancer is > 20%. The ACS guidelines specifically state that this risk should be determined using risk models dependent on family history, such as BRCAPRO. The Gail model does not meet these criteria (see the "Risk-Determination Models" section). To date, not enough evidence supports annual MRI screening for women with dense breast tissue or the diagnosis of LCIS, atypical ductal hyperplasia, or DCIS. In addition, data are insufficient to support routine MRI screening for all women whose only risk factor is a history of invasive cancer.

Most data supporting recommendations for breast cancer screening among women at high risk due to hereditary factors stem from studies of *BRCA* carriers. Yet, the recommendations for screening apply to all the aforementioned hereditary breast cancer syndromes. In general, screening for these patients begins at age 25 years and includes annual breast MRI with biannual clinical breast examinations. Annual mammography should begin at age 30 years or be individualized if the earliest onset in the family is in someone younger than 25 years. Given that an estimated 29% of *BRCA*-associated cancers present as interval cancers (ie, cancers presenting during the interval after a normal mammogram), women will often have their breast imaging (mammogram and MRI) alternate every 6 months coincidently with their clinical breast examination, although no data support that this screening schedule is superior to that of concurrent breast imaging.[112]

Women who have received mantle chest-radiation treatment of lymphoma are screened in a similar fashion, beginning approximately 10 years after completing radiation therapy.[113] For women at high risk because of familial (nonhereditary) reasons, initiation of screening should begin approximately 10 years earlier than the age of the youngest woman in the family diagnosed with breast cancer, but not later than age 40 years.

DIAGNOSIS

Algorithms for imaging evaluation of a breast palpable mass are stratified according to the age of the woman. Ultrasonography is usually the first diagnostic procedure performed to evaluate palpable breast masses in women younger than 30 years.[114] Diagnostic mammography is used for this purpose in women older than 30 years. Diagnostic mammography differs from screening mammography in that it adds images to the standard two-view imaging used with screening (ie, craniocaudal and mediolateral oblique). If a suspicious finding is seen on a diagnostic mammogram or if the palpable breast mass is mammographically occult, a targeted ultrasound is used to obtain specific characteristics that will differentiate a suspicious solid mass from a benign cyst.

In a patient with suspicious imaging findings or suspicious palpable breast mass after appropriate imaging work-up, the next step is a biopsy (Fig 10-3). Although a fine-needle aspiration (FNA) biopsy of a palpable breast mass is less invasive than a core-needle biopsy, FNA specimens often yield insufficient tissue for analysis and cannot differentiate invasive from noninvasive carcinoma.[115] FNA of suspicious palpable axillary lymph nodes is often acceptable given the limited variability of tissue present within a lymph node. It is also appropriate to use FNA in the evaluation of a simple cyst detected by ultrasound, because drainage of the cystic fluid without reaccumulation can imply a benign etiology and eliminate the need for additional evaluation.

Core needle biopsy specimens can be obtained via ultrasound guidance or stereotactically when suspicious calcifications are seen on mammography and do not have an associated

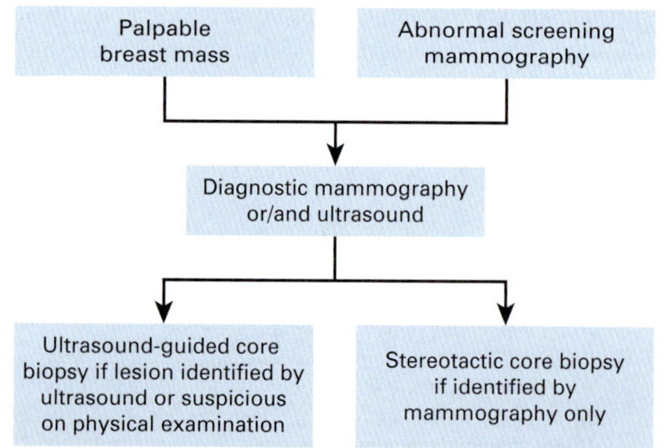

Fig. 10-3 Work-up of palpable breast mass or sreening abnormality.

density. The amount of tissue obtained by core needle biopsy is usually sufficient to characterize the lesion and, when cancer is identified, to perform quantitative immunohistochemical (IHC) analysis of HRs (ER and progesterone receptor [PR]) and HER2 protein status. These results provide sufficient information about the cancer to allow the initiation of neoadjuvant systemic therapy, if needed, without compromising future treatment. The need to identify the site of biopsy is crucial, so a radiolucent clip commonly is placed in the lesion as a locator.

MRI can also be used to evaluate the extent of disease within the breast after the detection of invasive breast cancer. A meta-analysis of 19 studies assessing the role of MRI in revealing multifocal or multicentric disease found a 16% incidence of additional disease within the affected breast.[116] This was associated with an 8.1% conversion from breast conservation to mastectomy and an 11.3% need for additional surgery after wide excision. MRI also can be used to detect multicentric DCIS, but it is not very accurate in assessing noninvasive tumor size. Caution must be used when assessing the contralateral breast with MRI after the diagnosis of breast cancer, because MRI detects an occult contralateral malignancy in approximately 3% of patients. This results in a high rate of biopsies and contralateral mastectomies despite a lack of evidence that these procedures will result in a survival advantage.[117]

KEY POINTS

- Mammographic screening has been shown to result in a 14% to 32% reduction in breast cancer–related mortality among women ages 50 to 70 years. The data on women ages 40 to 49 years or older than 70 years are less robust.
- For women with *BRCA* mutations who have not undergone risk-reducing surgery, annual MRI of the breasts is recommended beginning at age 25 years and annual mammography beginning at age 30 years. For women who have received mantle radiation for the treatment of lymphoma, beginning 10 years after the completion of radiation, annual screening mammography (not before age 30 years) and annual breast MRI (not before age 25) are recommended.
- For breast cancer diagnosis, a core biopsy of a suspicious breast finding is preferable to FNA to accurately assess the histology of the tissue and the status of ER, PR, and HER2.

PROGNOSTIC INDICATORS

TUMOR/NODE/METASTASIS (TNM) STAGING

The eighth edition of the American Joint Committee on Cancer (AJCC) staging[118] for breast cancer includes biologic features, such as tumor grade, HER2, ER, PR, and genomic assays (when appropriate) as elements required to assign stage, in conjunction with the anatomic information provided by the TNM classification. Three stage groups are defined: an anatomic stage, solely based on the T, N, and M categories and intended for use when biomarkers are not available; a clinical prognostic stage; and a pathologic prognostic stage. The clinical prognostic stage is used to assign stage for all patients. It is determined by the clinical T, N, M, and markers including tumor grade, HER2, ER, and PR status. The pathologic prognostic stage is used to assign stage for patients who have surgical resection as the initial treatment of their cancer, before any systemic or radiation therapy. It is based on the pathologic T, N, M, and biomarker information. In the AJCC staging manual, eighth edition, the prognostic stage group is preferred for patient care and should be used for reporting on all patients with breast cancer in the United States.

Multigene panels are not required for staging but may provide additional prognostic and predictive information. On the basis of prospective level I evidence, Oncotype DX score was included in the pathologic prognostic stage group. Patients with a T1N0M0 or T2N0M0 tumor that is HER2 negative and HR positive, with a recurrence score (RS) < 11 are assigned to pathologic prognostic stage IA. Other multigene panels, such as Breast Cancer Index, EndoPredict, MammaPrint, and PAM50, when low risk, place tumors T1-T2, node negative, ER positive, and HER2 negative in the same prognostic category as T1a-T1b N0 ones (level II evidence).

Other important updates in the AJCC staging manual, eighth edition, include the removal of LCIS from TNM staging (LCIS is now treated as a benign entity), and the determination that the presence of cancer within blood, lymph vessels (lymphovascular invasion), or lymph nodes precludes post-treatment classification as a complete pathologic response. It is unclear at this point how the new staging will lead to changes in treatment in tumors that are downstaged or upstaged by the revised classification.

ANATOMIC AND BIOLOGIC PROGNOSTIC INDICATORS

Prognostic features of breast cancer can be divided into two categories: anatomic and biologic. New technologies are leading to an increased understanding of the role of biologic features in determining outcome, and treatment strategies will likely continue to evolve as our knowledge increases.

Anatomic Prognostic Indicators

Lymph Node Involvement. The most important anatomic prognostic indicator for localized breast cancer is the presence of tumor in the axillary lymph nodes. Intramammary lymph nodes are found within the breast parenchyma and are included in the axillary lymph node category when they contain breast cancer metastasis. The clinical detection of ipsilateral internal mammary or supraclavicular lymph node involvement is associated with a greater risk of local recurrence and distant metastasis. Regardless of other characteristics of the breast cancer, having more axillary lymph nodes involved with disease is related to increased risk of systemic recurrence and decreased disease-specific survival.

The size of the metastatic component within the axillary lymph node is also important for prognosis. Lymph nodes with macrometastasis (> 2 mm) or micrometastasis (> 0.2 mm or > 200 cells, but none > 2 mm) are counted as nodal involvement. There is a greater risk for disease recurrence and death with macrometastatic disease as compared with micrometastatic involvement.[119] Isolated tumor cell clusters (clusters of cells or single tumor cells ≤ 0.2 mm, or < 200 cells) found within a sampled axillary lymph node appear to be associated with a prognosis comparable to that of lymph node–negative disease, and the use of IHC to detect these cells is no longer recommended.

Lymphovascular Invasion. The presence of tumor emboli within lymphatic or vascular channels is associated with a less favorable prognosis, mainly because of higher risk of ipsilateral breast recurrence. The presence of lymphovascular invasion does not preclude breast conservation but is often taken in account when the use of radiation is considered.

Tumor Size. Tumor size (which refers to the size of the invasive component) is one of the most important prognostic indicators for breast cancer. The size of associated DCIS does not influence the risk of systemic disease but may contribute to the risk of ipsilateral recurrence after breast conservation. Multifocal (ie, two or more foci of disease within one quadrant of the breast) or multicentric (ie, two or more foci of disease in separate quadrants) disease is associated with a higher frequency of positive lymph nodes and risk of ipsilateral breast recurrence after breast conservation therapy. Tumor staging is based on the size of the largest tumor and does not take into account other smaller foci. The sizes of multiple tumors should not be added. The presence of multiple tumors is noted by adding the (m) modifier to the T category.

Histology. The majority of invasive mammary carcinomas (75%) are of no special type, commonly referred to as infiltrating ductal carcinoma (IDC). Infiltrating lobular carcinoma (ILC) is the second most common type of breast cancer (15%). Compared with IDC, ILC is characterized by the following:

- more difficult mammographic detection,
- increased frequency of multifocality and indistinct borders,
- older age at onset,
- larger tumor size,
- lower grade,
- higher incidence of bilateral involvement at the time of diagnosis, and
- higher likelihood of late recurrence.

Most ILC are ER positive and HER2 negative. ILC frequently displays mutations in the *CDH1* gene and loss of the adhesion molecule E-cadherin, resulting in a more discohesive and infiltrative growth. ILCs tend to have a particular pattern of metastasis, with involvement of serosas, ovary, meninges, and the GI tract.[121]

Rarer subtypes of breast cancer include tubular, mucinous, medullary, micropapillary, and metaplastic tumors. The tubular and mucinous subtypes are associated with a favorable prognosis. On the other hand, metaplastic carcinomas, characterized by epithelial and mesenchymal differentiation, have an unfavorable outcome.[122]

Biologic Prognostic Indicators

Tumor Grade. The histologic grading system for breast cancer is a semiquantitative evaluation of morphologic features consisting of the percentage of tubular formation, degree of nuclear pleomorphism, and mitotic count within a predefined area.[123] On the basis of the scoring of these characteristics, three grades reflect breast cancer differentiation: low, intermediate, and high. The histologic grade is an independent prognostic indicator that has been closely linked to molecular features of breast cancer.[124]

Hormone Receptors: ERs and PRs. The ER functions as a ligand-dependent transcriptional factor that, when activated by estrogen, regulates gene expression and activates oncogenic pathways.[125] The two isoforms of ER are ER-α and ER-β. The precise role of ER-β is currently unclear, and the term ER usually applies to ER-α, a product of the *ESR1* gene.[126] IHC measures ER-α levels and is the method currently used to assess ER expression. ER positivity is predictive of response to endocrine therapy. The PR is a marker of ER-α signaling. The definition of positive HR status remains controversial. The 2010 ASCO/College of American Pathologists (CAP) guideline defines a tumor as ER or PR positive if 1% or more of tumor cell nuclei are immunoreactive.[127] ER-α is expressed in approximately 70% of invasive breast cancers, the majority of which also express PR. Cancers that are ER-positive/PR-negative also respond to endocrine therapy, but they tend to have a less favorable biology. ER-negative/PR-positive cancers are uncommon, and lack of ER expression can often be attributed to a false-negative assay. Patients with these cancers should still receive endocrine therapy.

Hormone receptor expression is frequently associated with older patient age, lower tumor grade and negative lymph nodes. ER-positive/PR-positive disease is associated with a modestly superior disease-free interval, local recurrence rate, and OS compared with ER-negative/PR-negative disease, particularly within the first five to 10 years following diagnosis. However, in HR-positive breast cancer, only half of all relapses occur within the first five years after diagnosis and there is a persistent significant risk of late recurrence (up to 20 years after diagnosis), despite therapy.[120,128]

Approximately 25% of breast cancers are HR negative and 15% of breast cancers are triple negative. Risk of TNBC recurrence is greatest within the first 5 years and significantly declines afterward.[129]

HER2 Overexpression. HER2 is a member of the epidermal growth factor receptor (EGFR) tyrosine kinase family, which includes four transmembrane receptor proteins: EGFR-1, HER2, HER3, and HER4. Receptor activation, either through ligand binding or ligand-independent effects, results in homo- or heterodimerization of the receptor proteins, which stimulates cellular growth, cell survival, migration, and angiogenesis. HER2 is overexpressed or amplified in approximately 20% of all breast cancers. HER2 overexpression is correlated with high proliferation, demonstrated by high-grade histology and lymph node involvement.[130] In the absence of anti-HER2 therapy, HER2-positive disease is associated with a poor prognosis, independently of other prognostic indicators, including size, lymph node involvement, and HR status. HER2 is measured by IHC or in situ hybridization (ISH). HER2 status is defined by the ASCO/CAP guideline, which was updated in 2018 (Fig 10-4).[132]

HER2 overexpression or amplification is a strong predictive factor for response to HER2-directed therapy. The degree of HER2 positivity is not associated with prognosis, and higher levels of HER2 do not predict increased efficacy from HER2-directed therapy.

Proliferation Rate: Ki67. The nuclear antigen Ki67 is currently the most commonly used marker of proliferation rate in breast cancer. Increased proliferation correlates with adverse prognostic indicators such as tumor size, nodal involvement, and histologic grade. Changes in Ki67, particularly after neoadjuvant therapy, have been associated with clinical outcome and incorporated in multiple research studies. The routine use of Ki67 in clinical management has been somewhat limited by the variability of the assay and lack of reproducibility of results among pathologists.[133] Because of these concerns, the ASCO breast cancer biomarkers guideline specifically advises that the Ki67 labeling index by IHC should not be used to guide the choice of adjuvant chemotherapy.[134]

Intrinsic Molecular Subtypes. Gene expression analysis has enabled the classification of breast cancer into distinct groups or intrinsic subtypes,[135] which have specific characteristics and prognosis. The classification according to these intrinsic subtypes is not routinely used for clinical purposes, but the definition of intrinsic subtypes and its applications in research continue to further our understanding of breast cancer biology.

Four main breast cancer intrinsic subtypes have been defined: luminal A, luminal B, basal, and HER2 enriched. The general characteristics of these subtypes are summarized in Table 10-6. There is substantial but not complete overlap between classification according to intrinsic subtypes and with routine immunostains for ER, PR, and HER2.

Gene Expression Signatures. There are several validated tests to assess the risk of breast cancer recurrence, particularly in early-stage, HR-positive breast cancer. MammaPrint is a 70-gene signature that classifies tumors into either high or low risk of recurrence.[136] MammaPrint was prospectively validated in the MINDACT trial.[137] In this phase III study of women with early-stage breast cancer and up to three positive lymph nodes, genomic risk (according to MammaPrint) and clinical risk (according to a modified version of Adjuvant! Online) were determined. Most patients had node-negative and ER-positive tumors. Women at low clinical and genomic risk did not receive adjuvant chemotherapy, and those at high clinical and genomic risk did receive chemotherapy. Patients with discordant clinical and genomic risk results were randomly assigned to either their genomic or clinical risk profile for determination of the use of chemotherapy. Women with high clinical risk but a low genomic risk and who did not receive chemotherapy had a 5-year rate of survival without distant metastases 1.5% lower than with chemotherapy. There was no benefit of chemotherapy in patients with low clinical risk and high genomic risk. ASCO guidelines state the MammaPrint assay could be used to guide decisions on withholding adjuvant systemic chemotherapy in patients with HR-positive, node-negative breast cancer and in select patients with node-positive breast cancer. MammaPrint should only be used in patients with high clinical risk.[138]

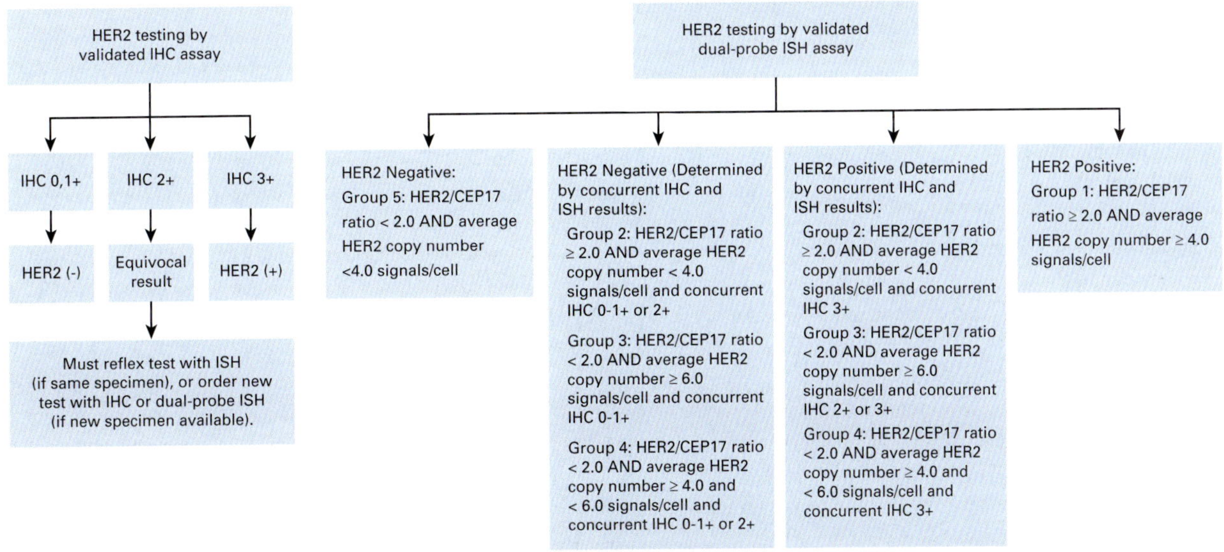

Fig. 10-4 Summary of the ASCO/College of American Pathologists guideline.

Abbreviations: IHC, immunohistochemistry; ISH, in situ hybridization.

Permission to reuse Wolff AC, Hammond MEH, Allison KH, et al. HER2 Testing in Breast Cancer: American Society of Clinical Oncology/College of American Pathologists Clinical Practice Guideline Focused Update Summary. Journal of Oncology Practice *2018 14:7, 437-441.*

Table 10-6 Molecular Subtypes

Subtype	Characteristic
Luminal A	Favorable prognosis
	High ER/PR
	Low proliferation rate
	Grade 1/2
	No sensitivity to chemotherapy
Luminal B	Unfavorable prognosis
	Lower ER and PR
	High proliferation rate
	Grade 2 or 3
	Sensitive to chemotherapy
HER2 enriched	HER2+
	HR+ or −
	High proliferation rate
	Grade 2/3
Basal	ER, PR, and HER2−
	High proliferation rate
	Grade 3

Abbreviations: ER, estrogen receptor; HR, hormone receptor; PR, progesterone receptor.

The 21-gene expression assay known as Oncotype DX[139] is the most widely used prognostic test in the United States. The RS is used as a continuous function to assess the risk of systemic recurrence among women with ER-positive breast cancer treated with tamoxifen for 5 years.[140] The risk of recurrence was initially defined as low (RS < 18), intermediate (RS of 18 to 30), and high (RS ≥ 31), on the basis of prespecified cutoffs. In the initial retrospective validation studies, node-negative tumors with a high recurrence score derived the greatest benefit from chemotherapy.[140] Chemotherapy was not beneficial in women with a low recurrence score, and its role in women with an intermediate-range score was unclear. In addition, postmenopausal women with one to three involved lymph nodes and a low (< 18) RS did not benefit from the addition of chemotherapy to tamoxifen.[141]

The TAILORx trial was designed to clinically validate the prognostic and predictive value of the 21-gene expression assay in HR-positive, HER2-negative, lymph node–negative breast cancer. Patients with a low-risk RS of 0 to 10 received endocrine therapy alone and had a low rate of distant relapse at 5 years.[142] Patients with a recurrence score of 11 to 25 were randomly assigned to either receive adjuvant chemotherapy and endocrine therapy or endocrine therapy alone, whereas patients with a score higher than 25 received chemotherapy in addition to endocrine therapy. In general, there was no benefit with the addition of chemotherapy in patients with a RS of 11 to 25. However, the benefit of chemotherapy varied according to age: women who were 50 years old or younger who received chemotherapy and had an RS of 16 to 20 had a 1.6% lower rate of distant recurrence at 9 years, which increased to 6.5% in women with an RS of 21 to 25. The risk of recurrence and benefit of chemotherapy was further influenced by the tumor size and grade.[143] The ongoing RxPONDER trial is assessing whether women with node-positive breast cancer (one to three nodes) and an RS < 25 can safely avoid chemotherapy.

In the prospective West German Plan B study,[144] women with fewer than three lymph nodes involved and an RS ≤ 11 had a good outcome with endocrine therapy alone, which again supports omitting chemotherapy in women with high clinical risk but favorable biology.

For patients with node-negative disease, the ASCO guidelines recommend addition of chemotherapy for those with an RS > 30. Patients with an RS ≥ 26 or > 16, if younger than 50 years, may also be offered chemotherapy.[138,145]

Other signatures, including PAM50 ROR (a gene signature derived from the original intrinsic subtype classification), EndoPredict, and Breast Cancer Index were retrospectively validated to assess risk of recurrence, including after 5 years of treatment (late recurrence). These currently are used less frequently because of lack of prospective validation.

In summary, gene signatures are now commonly used to inform the use of adjuvant chemotherapy in HR-positive, node-negative breast cancer, in conjunction with other factors. The use of genomic signatures in node-positive breast cancer is more controversial, particularly in premenopausal women. Because patients with node-positive disease overall have a higher risk of recurrence, many still favor chemotherapy in most patients with node-positive disease until more data from prospective trials are available.

KEY POINTS

- Pathologic features associated with favorable prognosis include small tumor size, negative lymph node status, low tumor grade, absence of lymphovascular invasion, and positive HR status.
- ER expression is predictive of response to endocrine therapy.
- A positive HER2 status is predictive of benefit from HER2-directed therapy.
- The 21-gene recurrence score and 70-gene signature have been validated prospectively in large trials and are used to guide the use of adjuvant chemotherapy primarily in HR-positive, HER2-negative, node-negative breast cancer.

INITIAL EVALUATION OF BREAST CANCER

The initial evaluation of patients diagnosed with breast cancer includes a physical examination and breast imaging with diagnostic mammography, with or without ultrasound. Additional diagnostic testing should be individualized, especially the use of breast MRI (see the Diagnosis section earlier in this chapter). Baseline laboratory tests, such as a CBC count and hepatic transaminase, and alkaline phosphatase levels, can be obtained for women who will need chemotherapy and/or for those in whom clinical symptoms or signs are suggestive of metastatic disease. In the absence of symptoms, imaging studies to evaluate for metastases are not recommended for patients with stage I or stage II disease. Patients with stage III disease, however, should have staging with CT imaging of the chest and abdomen (with or without a CT scan of the pelvis) and a bone scan. Positron-emission tomography (PET)/CT imaging is another option, but this has not been shown to be superior to CT and bone scans for staging purposes.[146]

Additional considerations for patients with a new diagnosis of breast cancer include:

- Genetic counseling for patients with a positive family history of cancer or other characteristics that may suggest an inherited predisposition, as outlined in the Risk Factors section of this chapter. The American Society of Breast Surgeons has recommended that genetic testing should be offered to all patients with a personal history of breast cancer. This recommendation has not been widely supported by other oncology societies.
- Premenopausal women who use a hormonal method of contraception should be counseled about nonhormonal alternatives. In such cases, referral to a gynecologist or a women's health specialist is indicated.
- All patients of reproductive age should be counseled regarding the risks of infertility (due to chemotherapy) and/or delayed childbearing (due to adjuvant endocrine therapy). Consultation with a reproductive specialist should be obtained early for those interested in fertility preservation.[147]

Oocyte, sperm, and embryo cryopreservation are established methods of fertility preservation. Several trials have evaluated suppression of ovarian function with gonadotropin-releasing hormone (GnRH) agonists administered concurrently with chemotherapy as a method of fertility preservation. These trials yielded conflicting results. However, in the randomized POEMS study, women with HR-negative breast cancer who received goserelin starting 1 week before initiation of chemotherapy had a higher likelihood of a successful pregnancy.[148] In a meta-analysis including HR-positive and HR-negative breast cancer, the use of GnRH agonists decreased the rate of premature ovarian failure and did not affect breast cancer outcome.[149] ASCO's fertility preservation guideline states that a GnRH agonist may be offered to patients in the hope of reducing the likelihood of chemotherapy-induced ovarian insufficiency. However, GnRH agonists should not be used in place of proven fertility preservation methods.[147]

TREATMENT OF DCIS

DCIS is a neoplastic proliferation of epithelial cells confined to the mammary ductal-lobular system and characterized by subtle to marked cytologic atypia and risk for progression to invasive breast cancer.[150] In the TNM staging, DCIS is designated as Tis/stage 0. Although DCIS occasionally may present as a mass or nipple discharge, 80% to 85% of cases of DCIS are detected by screening mammogram and present without clinical findings. Calcifications are the most common mammographic presentation of DCIS and, because of mammographic screening, DCIS accounts for approximately 20% of all breast cancers in the United States.

DCIS is a heterogeneous entity. Pathologic features used to describe DCIS include:

- nuclear grade (low, intermediate, or high),
- presence of necrosis,
- architectural pattern (comedo, solid, cribiform, micropapillary, and papillary), and
- size or extent of the lesion.

DCIS can be associated with microinvasive tumor (tumor ≤ 1 mm), which is staged as T1mi. An estimated 15% to 50% of DCIS will ultimately progress to invasive disease if left intact, either by direct transformation or by developing in parallel from a single progenitor cell.[151] The exact biologic mechanism is not well understood, nor can we predict which subset of DCIS will progress to invasive breast cancer. ER testing of DCIS is recommended, but there are no current data to support HER2 testing of DCIS.

Although surgical excision (lumpectomy or mastectomy) is a current standard, surgery leads to potential overtreatment in many cases. Recognizing this risk, researchers are conducting several studies to compare surgery with active surveillance in cases of low-risk-DCIS.

The goal of treatment in DCIS is to prevent local recurrence, because approximately half of local recurrences of DCIS are invasive.[152] The risk of local recurrence after a simple mastectomy is 1% to 2%. On the basis of the data on invasive breast cancer, breast-conserving surgery plus radiation (also called breast-conserving therapy [BCT]) was adopted as an appropriate option for treatment of DCIS. BCT or mastectomy provides equivalent long-term, disease-specific survival.[153] The most current guidelines establish 2 mm as the standard for an adequate margin in DCIS treated with radiation.[154] Axillary node dissection or sentinel node biopsy is not routinely done in DCIS. However, sentinel node biopsy should be considered in situations with a higher likelihood of finding invasive cancer in the surgical specimen: (large or palpable lesions) or in patients undergoing mastectomy (because a sentinel lymph node [SLN] biopsy would not be feasible after mastectomy in case invasive tumor is found during surgical pathology evaluation).[155]

RADIATION

After breast-conserving surgery (BCS), women are at risk for recurrence within the breast. The benefit of adding whole-breast irradiation (WBI) to surgical excision for DCIS was evaluated in several randomized trials, which found a decrease in the risk of local recurrence by 35% to 45%. A meta-analysis found adjuvant WBI reduced local recurrences from 28% to 15%.[156] However, in more recent studies, the rate of local recurrence was lower, likely due to the concomitant use of endocrine therapy, along with improvements in imaging and surgical technique. Both conventional (5 to 6 weeks) and hypofractionated (3 to 4 weeks) WBI are appropriate adjuvant radiotherapy options for DCIS.[157] Accelerated partial-breast irradiation (see Invasive Breast Cancer section) is also an available option.[158] Factors associated with increased risk of local recurrence include close (l< 2 mm) or positive surgical margins, high-grade tumor, and presence of necrosis.

Studies have not identified a group of low-risk patients who did not benefit from radiation.[159,160] The Oncotype DX DCIS multigene assay has been validated to predict recurrence risk among patients with DCIS treated with BCS without WBI. However, low-risk patients still had a risk of local recurrence of 12.7%, and the utility of Oncotype DX DCIS in clinical practice has yet to be defined.[161]

ENDOCRINE THERAPY

In the NSABP B24 trial, adjuvant tamoxifen for 5 years after breast-conserving surgery plus WBI for DCIS resulted in a 32% relative reduction in the risk of local recurrence (from 9% to 6.6%) and a 53% relative reduction in the risk of contralateral disease over 15 years.[152] Pre- and postmenopausal women were included. The benefit of tamoxifen was seen only in ER-positive DCIS and has not yet been associated with improved OS.[162] In the NSABP B-35 trial of postmenopausal women who underwent breast conservation therapy for ER-positive DCIS, adjuvant anastrozole was associated with a small improvement in breast cancer–free interval at 10 years compared with tamoxifen (93.5% *v* 89.2%), with benefit mainly limited to women younger than 60 years.[163] Therefore, both adjuvant tamoxifen and anastrozole are appropriate options for postmenopausal women with DCIS, and considerations regarding toxicities should influence treatment choices for individual women. There is no role for endocrine therapy for risk reduction in women who underwent bilateral mastectomy. Women who had a unilateral mastectomy for ER-positive DCIS may consider endocrine therapy for prevention of contralateral breast cancer.

KEY POINTS

- DCIS (stage 0) accounts for approximately 20% of breast cancers in the United States.
- Most cases of DCIS are detected on screening mammogram.
- WBI decreases the risk of local recurrence after breast-conserving surgery.
- DCIS treated by mastectomy or BCT results in equivalent breast cancer–related 5-year survival rates.
- Current guidelines establish 2 mm as an adequate margin of resection in DCIS treated with BCT.
- For women with ER-positive DCIS who elect to undergo BCT, adjuvant endocrine therapy reduces the risk of ipsilateral and contralateral recurrence with no established survival benefit.
- Adjuvant tamoxifen and anastrozole are appropriate options for decreasing subsequent invasive breast cancers in postmenopausal women with ER-positive DCIS treated with BCT.

TREATMENT OF NONMETASTATIC OR EARLY-STAGE INVASIVE BREAST CANCER (STAGES I, II, AND III)

OVERVIEW

Treatment of early-stage invasive breast cancer focuses on reducing the risks of locoregional (breast and regional lymph nodes) and systemic recurrence. The decision to add systemic therapy to the local treatment of breast cancer is based on the risk of development of distant metastasis and the benefit of therapies to reduce that risk. For each patient, a multidisciplinary evaluation should occur at diagnosis to determine the optimal treatment modalities (local and systemic) and its sequencing.

Endocrine therapy and HER2-targeted therapy can safely be given concurrently with radiotherapy; however, chemotherapy is usually completed prior to starting radiation therapy. The choices for both local and systemic therapies are based on the prognostic indicators, and treatment options have been outlined by several organizations to help guide decision-making.

A meta-analysis of data on 4,756 patients with early breast cancer enrolled in clinical trials between 1983 and 2002 showed that preoperative (neoadjuvant) and postoperative (adjuvant) chemotherapy were similarly effective in lowering the risk of distant disease recurrence or breast cancer mortality.[164] Neoadjuvant systemic therapy decreases the size of the tumor, thus allowing a greater proportion of patients to achieve breast conservation, and also allows evaluation of response to systemic therapy.

In recent years, there has been an increase in the use of neoadjuvant therapy, most often given in the form of chemotherapy, although neoadjuvant endocrine therapy can be used in select patients (see Neoadjuvant Endocrine Therapy section).[165]

Achieving a pathologic complete response (pCR) after neoadjuvant systemic therapy is a strong prognostic factor for reduced risk of recurrence, in particular in TNBC and HER2-positive breast cancer.[166] A pCR is defined as absence of invasive carcinoma in the breast and axillary lymph nodes. NSABP B-18 and NSABP B-27 compared neoadjuvant chemotherapy with adjuvant chemotherapy, using chemotherapy regimens of doxorubicin and cyclophosphamide (AC) alone or AC followed by docetaxel.[167] Both studies demonstrated superior DFS and OS among the patients who achieved pCR compared with those who did not, although the pCR rate was only 13% to 26%. A meta-analysis that included 11,955 patients showed that patients who achieve a pCR have improved survival, with greatest benefits in TNBC and HER2-positive breast cancer.[166] Recent studies suggest that patients with TNBC and HER2-positive disease who do not achieve pCR may derive survival advantage from additional adjuvant therapy (discussed later in the chapter).

Stage III disease is often classified as locally advanced disease and can be grouped into two general categories:

1. patients with large tumors or multiple positive lymph nodes who have disease that can be resected, and
2. patients with disease inoperable because of skin involvement, disease attachment to the chest wall, inflammatory carcinoma or extensive nodal involvement that precludes initial surgical resection (eg, matted axillary lymph nodes or supraclavicular lymph node involvement).

Patients with inoperable disease, require neoadjuvant systemic therapy (preoperative or neoadjuvant therapy), followed by surgery and radiation.

KEY POINTS

- The goal of systemic therapy in nonmetastatic disease is to reduce the risk of development of local recurrence and distant metastasis.
- Randomized trials have demonstrated equivalent survival, regardless of whether neoadjuvant or adjuvant chemotherapy is used.
- Patients who present with inoperable disease require neoadjuvant therapy.
- pCR after neoadjuvant systemic therapy is a strong prognostic factor for reduced risk of recurrence, in particular in TNBC and HER2-positive disease.
- Patients with residual disease after completing neoadjuvant systemic therapy may be candidates for additional systemic therapy after surgery.

LOCOREGIONAL TREATMENT

Locoregional treatment includes decisions regarding breast surgery (breast conservation or mastectomy), surgical management of axillary lymph nodes and radiation.

Breast Surgery

The past decades of research regarding breast and axillary surgery have focused on minimizing interventions to lower morbidity while maintaining equivalence in outcomes:

- The NSABP B-04 study established that there is no difference in OS between a Halsted radical mastectomy (ie, removal of the breast, chest wall muscles, and regional lymph nodes) and total (or simple) mastectomy (removal of breast).[168]
- The NSABP B-06 trial established that there are no differences in OS between total mastectomy and lumpectomy either with or without radiation.[168] Patients who received radiation after lumpectomy had fewer local recurrences than those treated with lumpectomy alone, with no difference in local recurrence rates between lumpectomy and radiation compared with mastectomy.

Optimal characteristics for BCT include the ability to resect the entire tumor with negative surgical margins and achieve an acceptable cosmetic outcome. The ability to adequately remove the cancer depends on its size relative to the size of the breast, requiring sometimes the use of preoperative systemic therapy. The current definition of adequate negative surgical margins for invasive breast cancer is no tumor present in the inked margin.[169,170] Patients with invasive cancer with DCIS, including those with an extensive intraductal component (defined as DCIS occupying at least 25% of an invasive carcinoma or a lesion that is predominantly DCIS with one or more foci of invasive disease) should be treated according to the invasive breast cancer guidelines. Individual judgement, however, is important, particularly in patients thought to be at higher risk for residual disease after breast-conserving surgery.

Patients who are not candidates for BCT should undergo a total mastectomy. Contraindications to breast conservation therapy for operable disease include:

- multicentric disease,
- diffuse suspicious calcifications,
- multiple positive margins after initial surgery, and
- pregnancy (a contraindication for radiation).

Prior radiation therapy and connective-tissue diseases involving the skin are considered relative contraindications.[46]

Surgical Management of the Axilla

Surgical management of the axilla is an integral part of the local treatment of breast cancer. The extent of axillary surgery has decreased over time due to the understanding that removal of axillary lymph nodes has more of a prognostic than a therapeutic value. Following are some key findings guiding the current surgical management of the axilla in patients not undergoing neoadjuvant therapy:

- Most women with a clinically negative axilla are candidates for an SLN biopsy at the time of their breast surgery, which results in substantially less morbidity compared with an axillary lymph node dissection (ALND). Routine IHC staining of the SLN for cytokeratins is not recommended, and most therapeutic decisions should be based on assessment of tumor presence in the SLN as determined by hematoxylin and eosin staining. In women with a negative SLN biopsy specimen, the likelihood of additional nodal involvement is small, and no additional surgery is indicated.[171,172]
- A substantial proportion of women with limited axillary nodal involvement no longer require an ALND (complete level I and level II dissection). ACOSOG (American College of Surgeons Oncology Group) Z0011 showed that in patients with clinical T1 or T2 tumors, a clinically negative axilla (N0), and one or two positive SLNs treated with lumpectomy, tangential WBI and adjuvant therapy, SLN dissection was noninferior to ALND.[173] An ALND is still usually performed in patients whose tumors do not fit the

Z11 criteria, who will not receive radiation, or if the SLN is not identified.
- IBCGE 23-01[174,175] showed noninferiority of no axillary dissection when compared with axillary dissection in patients with micrometastatic sentinel nodal disease (with most patients in this study treated with lumpectomy and radiation and a minority treated with a mastectomy).
- In AMAROS (After Mapping of the Axilla: Radiotherapy or Surgery), patients with a T1-T2 tumor and clinically negative axilla but positive SLN were randomly assigned to either axillary surgery or radiation. Most patients had one positive SLN. Both patients treated with lumpectomy (82%) and mastectomy were enrolled. In this study, local control was excellent in both the radiation and surgical arms, but the rate of lymphedema was lower in the radiation arm. Therefore, omission of ALND can be considered if radiation to the axilla is planned (Fig 10-5).[176]

Patients who are candidates for neoadjuvant chemotherapy who present with a clinically negative axilla can undergo SLN surgery after completion of neoadjuvant chemotherapy.[177] If the SLNs are negative, no additional axillary surgery is indicated. If any of the SLNs is positive, complete ALND is recommended.[178]

Patients presenting with a palpable node will need an ALND unless they receive neoadjuvant systemic therapy. The likelihood of downstaging the axilla with neoadjuvant chemotherapy is higher in patients presenting with TNBC or HER2-positive breast cancer, for which approach is particularly favored.[179] Several studies have looked at the feasibility of SLN biopsy after neoadjuvant chemotherapy.[180-182] In ACOSOG 1071, the use of dual-tracer mapping and retrieval of at least three SLNs resulted in clinically acceptable false-negative rates of < 10%, which is similar to the false-negative SLN rate in patients with clinical node-negative disease undergoing upfront SLN biopsy, suggesting that an ALND can be omitted in select cases.

Ongoing clinical trials are also exploring the optimal locoregional management of the axillae after neoadjuvant chemotherapy. Alliance A011202 is randomly assigning patients with a positive SLN after neoadjuvant chemotherapy to axillary dissection or axillary radiation to evaluate which modality provides the best local control and survival. NSABP B-51 is asking whether adjuvant nodal radiation is required in patients who convert from biopsy-proven node-positive disease to pathologically node-negative disease after neoadjuvant chemotherapy, by randomly assigning them to nodal radiation or no radiation.

KEY POINTS

- Treatment of operable breast cancer with mastectomy or BCT results in equivalent survival.
- The definition of adequate margin of resection for invasive breast cancer treated with BCT is no tumor present in the inked margin.
- Contraindications for BCT include inability to remove the tumor with adequate margins and a favorable cosmetic outcome, multicentric disease, and presence of contraindications for radiation.
- Patients presenting with clinically negative axilla should undergo a SLN biopsy.
- Patients with T1-T2 tumors and up to two involved SLN treated with BCT and WBI can avoid ALND.
- Patients presenting with clinically positive lymph nodes require ALND unless neoadjuvant therapy is used, and their approach must be individualized.

Adjuvant Radiation Therapy After BCS

Radiation to the Breast. WBI is recommended for the majority of women treated with breast conservation. This includes women treated with neoadjuvant therapy, regardless of their clinical or pathologic response. A meta-analysis showed that addition of radiotherapy to BCS reduced the rate of locoregional and distant recurrence by about half (from 35.0% to 19.3%) and decreased the absolute risk of breast cancer death by one-sixth (from 25.2% to 21.4%) at 10 and 15 years, respectively. Overall, approximately one breast cancer death was avoided by year 15 for every four recurrences avoided by year 10.[183] Although the proportional benefit was similar in all groups, the absolute benefit of radiation differed according to patient age, tumor grade, ER status, tamoxifen use, and extent of surgery.

Modern systemic therapy has contributed to improved local control after BCT across all tumor types. Recent randomized controlled trials in patients with early-stage breast cancer have reported 10-year local recurrence risks of just 2% to 7%.[184-186]

Hypofractionated WBI, in which the breast receives 40 Gy to 42.5 Gy over 3 weeks (15 to 16 fractions), is now an established option for the majority of women requiring only WBI. This dosing is based on randomized trials demonstrating equivalent local control and favorable toxicity compared with the more traditional approach of 25 fractions over 5 to 6 weeks.[184,186] A boost to the tumor bed is usually recommended after BCS and WBI, except in patients at lower risk of recurrence.[187]

Accelerated partial-breast irradiation (APBI) treats only the tumor bed area and is commonly given over 5 days twice daily. APBI is an option for selected patients. Current guidelines for APBI in invasive cancer, outside of a clinical trial, define suitable candidates as women who are age 50 years or older, have at least 2-mm negative margins, and T1, node-negative tumors.[158]

Older women with favorable tumor characteristics (eg, small, node-negative, ER-positive tumors) who receive endocrine therapy may undergo BCS alone and omit radiation. This approach is based on several studies in women older than 65 or than 70 years showing that although radiation decreased the rate of locoregional failure, this risk was also low in the group assigned to no radiation (approximately 4% to 8%) and survival was similar.[185,188]

Regional Nodal Radiation After BCT. Regional nodal radiation generally includes radiation to the axilla, infra- and supraclavicular nodes, and internal mammary nodes, although the specific approach is individualized depending on the extent of disease and type of axillary surgery. Regional radiation after BCS is indicated for patients with more than three involved lymph nodes and is usually considered in patients with one to three positive nodes. This approach is largely based on the results from two studies, NCIC-CTG MA.20[189] and EORTC (European Organization for Research and Treatment of Cancer) 22922/10925,[190] which compared radiation to the breast with radiation to the breast and nodal fields in women treated with surgery and ALND. In these studies, the addition of nodal radiation led to an improvement in breast cancer recurrence and breast cancer mortality rate at the cost of increased lymphedema and pneumonitis. As discussed previously, studies looking at omitting ALND in women with limited nodal burden who are treated with lumpectomy and WBI have shown an excellent outcome without the addition of regional nodal radiation. Therefore, the decision to add regional radiation in women with a lower nodal burden should be individualized.

Postmastectomy Radiation. In women with positive lymph nodes after mastectomy and ALND, the addition of radiation to the chest wall and regional lymph nodes is associated with improved outcome. The benefit of postmastectomy radiation (PMRT) in node-positive disease was seen in randomized clinical trials, including the Danish Cooperative Radiotherapy Group[191] and the EORTC 22922/10925 trial. An EBCTCG analysis in women who had axillary dissection and one to three positive nodes demonstrated that PMRT reduced the 10-year absolute risk of locoregional and distant recurrence by 11.5% and the 20-year absolute risk of breast cancer mortality by 7.9%. This benefit was higher in women with four or more positive nodes.[192]

PMRT is recommended by the joint ASCO, American Society for Radiation Oncology, and Society of Surgical Oncology guidelines in patients with positive lymph nodes.[193] However, in some patients with one to three axillary lymph nodes and favorable disease, recurrence rates may be low enough that the risks of PMRT outweigh the potential benefits.

In patients with node-negative disease, indications for PMRT include large tumor size (> 5 cm) with unfavorable biologic features, T4 disease, and positive surgical margins. Other high-risk features to consider include lymphovascular involvement, triple-negative tumor status, young age, or close surgical margins (< 1 mm).

In women treated with neoadjuvant chemotherapy outside of a clinical study, recommendations for PMRT are usually based on the characteristics of the disease at presentation.

KEY POINTS

- Hypofractionated radiation is now an established option for the majority of women requiring only WBI.
- APBI is an option for selected patients.
- WBI can be omitted in older women with favorable tumor characteristics.
- Regional nodal radiation after BCS or mastectomy is indicated in patients with more than three positive lymph nodes and can be considered in patients with one to three positive lymph nodes.
- PMRT is also indicated in tumors with positive margins and should be considered in large tumors with poor biology.

SYSTEMIC THERAPY

Stage and biology are used to determine the risk of distant recurrence and guide the choice of adjuvant treatment. Other factors are considered when making treatment decisions. Age is an independent prognostic feature. Women younger than 35 years have a worse 5-year OS compared with women ages 35 to 69 years (74.7% *v* 83.8% to 88.3%),[194,195] therefore the threshold for offering adjuvant therapy is often reduced in younger women.[196] On the other hand, relatively few clinical trials have included a substantial number of women older than 70 years. Patient preferences, treatment toxicity, and comorbidities are also important for treatment considerations.

In general, breast cancers > 0.5 cm and node negative have a high enough risk of systemic recurrence to warrant consideration of adjuvant treatment. Patients with tumors ≤ 0.5 cm and node negative may not gain a clinically significant benefit from systemic chemotherapy or HER2-directed therapy. However, if the cancer is HR positive, adjuvant endocrine therapy is often considered, given its favorable safety profile, to reduce the risk of both systemic and local disease recurrence (Fig 10-6).

The following are general principles regarding adjuvant chemotherapy:

- Administer full-dose chemotherapy based on actual height and weight. The Hematology/Oncology Pharmacy Association (HOPA) recommends that cytotoxic agents be considered independently for dose rounding within 10% of the prescribed dose.
- Combination chemotherapy is used.
- In general, anthracycline- and taxane-containing regimens are appropriate for higher-risk disease, whereas non-anthracycline–containing regimens can be used for node-negative tumors and selected node-positive tumors with more favorable disease biology.
- The benefit of chemotherapy is greater for women with node-positive and/or HR-negative disease.

The choice of regimen depends on the overall risk of disease recurrence and the relative reduction of risk with the administration of chemotherapy, weighed against the toxicity of the regimens, patient comorbidities, and patient preference.

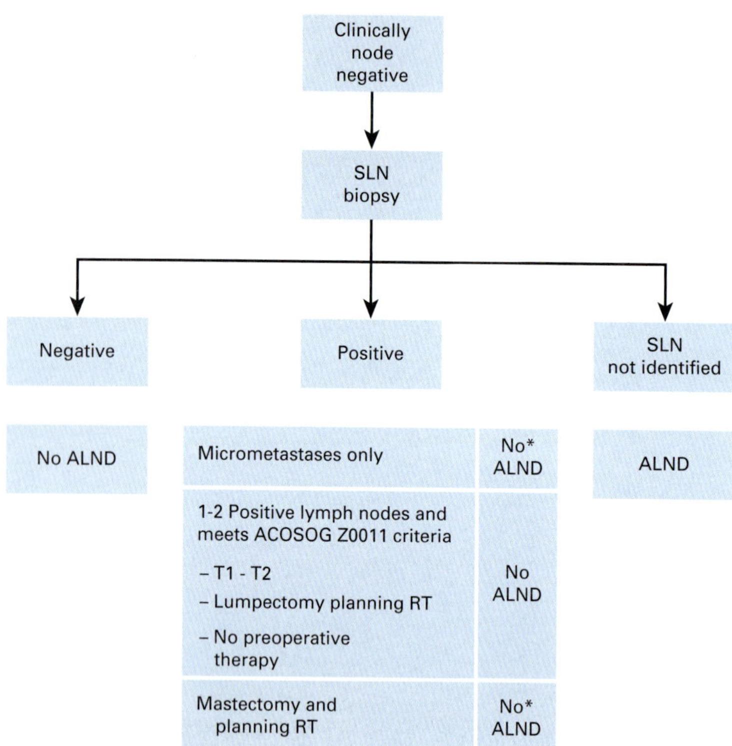

Fig. 10-5 Suggested axillary management for clinically node negative axilla.

Abbreviations: ACOSOG, American College of Surgeons Oncology Group; ALND, axillary lymph node dissection; RT, radiation therapy; SLN, sentinel lymph node.

*Decisions should be individualized.

Triple-Negative Breast Cancer

TNBC accounts for 10% to 15% of all breast cancers. It is more common among young women and/or black women and is more often high grade. Unlike other subtypes of breast cancer, the biology of TNBC is such that its prognosis does not correlate as closely with tumor size or nodal involvement.[197]

Although TNBC is associated with a less favorable overall prognosis, this subtype of breast cancer is more chemosensitive and has a greater propensity of achieving a pCR to neoadjuvant chemotherapy, compared with HR-positive disease. Chemotherapy is the mainstay of adjuvant treatment of TNBC. Adjuvant chemotherapy reduces the risk of relapse early in the disease course (within the first 5 years).

Table 10-7 lists some of the most commonly used chemotherapy-containing regimens for the treatment of nonmetastatic breast cancer. Data supporting the use of current-chemotherapy regimens in HER2-negative breast cancer are discussed in the following sections.

Anthracycline-Based Regimens. In comparison with methotrexate-containing regimens, the use of anthracyclines in adjuvant therapy improved the proportional reduction in risk of breast cancer recurrence by 12% and death by 15%.[74] These data support the use of anthracyclines for adjuvant treatment—the most commonly used combination regimen being doxorubicin and cyclophosphamide (AC) for four cycles. A randomized trial compared four cycles of AC with four cycles of another two-drug regimen, docetaxel and cyclophosphamide (TC), among women with stages I to III breast cancer.[199] After a 7-year follow-up, there was a 6% improvement in DFS and a 5% improvement in OS with the TC regimen.

The question of duration of therapy was addressed by CALGB 40101, which evaluated 3,171 patients with primarily lymph node–negative disease (94%) and randomly assigned them to either four or six cycles of AC or single-agent paclitaxel.[206] Both regimens were administered every 2 weeks, with no difference in outcome (relapse-free survival or OS) between four or six cycles of treatment.

Taxane-Based Regimens. A meta-analysis of 13 randomized trials involving 22,453 women showed that addition of taxanes to anthracycline-containing regimens resulted in a 17% reduction in the relative risk of relapse and an 18% reduction in the relative risk of death at 5 years. This translated in a 5% absolute improvement in DFS and a 3% improvement in OS.[207] This benefit was observed regardless of the type of taxane used (paclitaxel or docetaxel), patient age, or number of lymph nodes involved.

Initial studies using taxanes in the adjuvant setting demonstrated superior DFS and OS when four cycles of paclitaxel were administered after four cycles of AC, compared with four cycles of AC alone (CALGB 9344).[208] NSABP B30 showed a superior DFS and OS with four cycles of AC followed by four cycles of docetaxel compared with four cycles of docetaxel, doxorubicin, and cyclophosphamide (TAC) or four cycles of docetaxel and doxorubicin. This study also showed an association between amenorrhea and improved OS.

A dose-dense chemotherapy schedule, administered every 2 weeks, with growth factor support was associated with improved clinical outcomes compared with chemotherapy

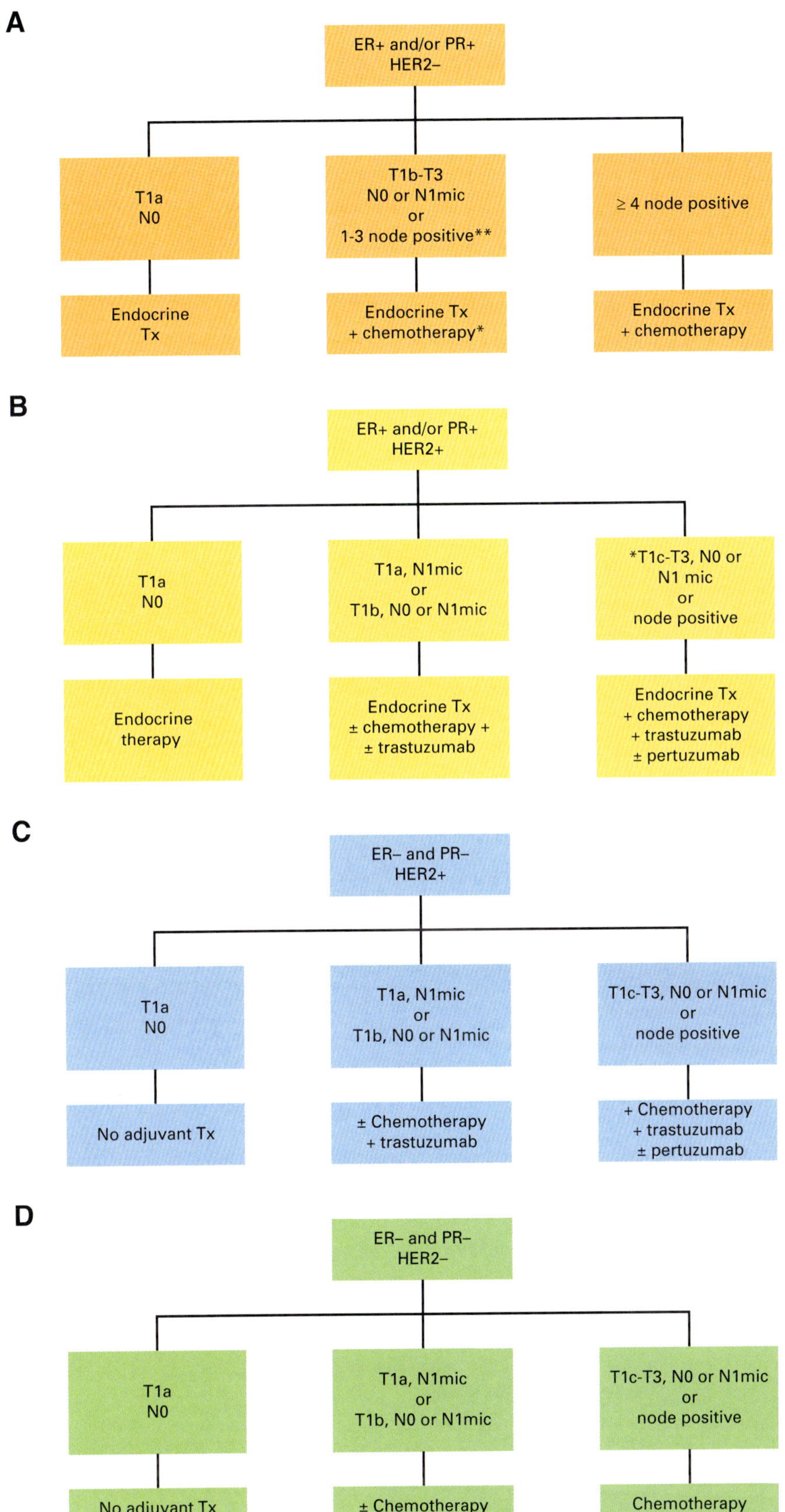

Fig. 10-6 Suggested guidelines for adjuvant systemic therapy for four main breast cancer subtypes.

(A) Hormone receptor (HR)–positive, HER2-negative disease. *Gene signatures may help with decision-making in appropriate patients. **Many oncologists still consider chemotherapy plus endocrine therapy as standard for all node-positive disease.
(B) HR–positive, HER2-positive disease.
(C) HR–negative, HER2-positive disease.
*Clinical trials did not include T1c, N0.
(D) HR–negative, HER2-negative disease.

Abbreviations: ER, estrogen receptor; PR, progesterone receptor; Tx, therapy.

Table 10-7 **Adjuvant or Neoadjuvant Chemotherapy Options According to HER2 Status**

HER2 Status	Chemotherapy Options
HER2 negative	Doxorubicin/cyclophosphamide × 4 cycles[198]
	Docetaxel/cyclophosphamide × 4 cycles[a,199]
	Cyclophosphamide/methotrexate/fluorouracil × 6 cycles[198]
	Dose-dense doxorubicin/cyclophosphamide × 4 cycles followed by dose-dense paclitaxel × 4 cycles[a,200]
	Doxorubicin/cyclophosphamide × 4 cycles followed by 12 weeks of paclitaxel[a,201]
	Docetaxel/doxorubicin/cyclophosphamide × 6 cycles[200]
HER2 positive	Doxorubicin/cyclophosphamide × 4 cycles followed by 12 weeks of paclitaxel and trastuzumab ± pertuzumab followed by trastuzumab ± pertuzumab (over 40 weeks)[a,202]
	Docetaxel/carboplatin/trastuzumab ± pertuzumab × 6 cycles followed by trastuzumab ± pertuzumab (over 34 weeks)[a,203]
	Paclitaxel and trastuzumab weekly × 12 weeks followed by trastuzumab × 40 weeks[204]
	Pertuzumab, trastuzumab, and taxane (either paclitaxel or docetaxel) × 12 weeks total followed by doxorubicin/cyclophosphamide × 4 cycles followed by trastuzumab ± pertuzumab (over 40 weeks)[205]

[a]Preferred regimen, per 2019 National Comprehensive Cancer Network guidelines.[46]

administration on a conventional every-3-week schedule. In CALGB 9741, 2,005 women with lymph node–positive disease were randomly assigned to receive similar doses of AC for four cycles followed by paclitaxel for four cycles, given on a dose-dense or a conventional schedule.[200] The dose-dense regimen (administered every 2 weeks with filgrastim support) resulted in a 26% reduction in relative risk of recurrence and a 31% reduction in relative risk of death. As expected, within the group receiving the superior dose-dense regimen, patients with TNBC had higher reduction in risk of recurrence (32% *v* 19%); however, this was not statistically significant. A meta-analysis of 26 trials with > 37,000 women compared dose-dense with standard dosing and confirmed the CALGB 9741 findings of a 14% relative reduction in risk of recurrence and a 13% relative reduction in risk of dying.[209] TC was associated with less cardiotoxicity and a lower risk of treatment-induced leukemia compared with AC, but both toxicities were relatively rare. This study supports the use of TC as a preferred regimen for breast cancer treatment.

Given the potential for long-term toxicity associated with the use of anthracyclines, identifying who can be safely treated with non-anthracycline–containing regimens is an important question. An analysis of the ABC trials[210] showed that TaxAC (a regimen containing taxanes and anthracyclines) compared with a taxane-only regimen for six cycles improved invasive DFS, although the benefit was seen particularly in patients with TNBC and for those with HR positive breast cancer and a higher number of involved axillary lymph nodes.

Major considerations associated with the most commonly used adjuvant chemotherapy regimens—dose-dense AC followed by paclitaxel and four cycles of cyclophosphamide and docetaxel—include:

Dose-dense AC Followed by Paclitaxel

- AC is considered highly emetogenic (> 90% frequency of emesis).
- Hematopoietic growth factors are required to maintain dose density.
- Anthracyclines are associated with cardiac toxicity; doxorubicin-associated cardiac dysfunction is related to cumulative dose. Risk factors for cardiac toxicity include underlying heart disease, use of anthracyclines concurrently with other cardiotoxic agents or radiation, and previous treatment with mediastinal or chest wall irradiation. A baseline assessment of left ventricular ejection fraction is recommended.
- Paclitaxel can cause severe hypersensitivity reactions and, therefore, requires premedication with steroids and antihistamines.
- Renal impairment: no need for dose adjustment for doxorubicin or paclitaxel. The need for cyclophosphamide dose reduction in renal insufficiency is controversial.
- Hepatic impairment: dose adjustments in doxorubicin, cyclophosphamide, and paclitaxel may be needed. It is recommended to administer 50% of the doxorubicin dose if serum bilirubin is 1.2 to 3 mg/dL, 25% if serum bilirubin is 3.1 to 5 mg/dL. and contraindicated if the bilirubin level is > 5 mg/dL or Child-Pugh class C. It is also advised to avoid cyclophosphamide if the serum bilirubin level is > 5 mg/dL. Paclitaxel dose should be adjusted on the bases of transaminase and bilirubin levels and avoided if transaminase levels ≥ 10 times the upper level of normal (ULN) or bilirubin level is > 5 times ULN.

Four Cycles of TC

- Emesis risk is moderate.
- Steroid pretreatment starting the day before docetaxel administration reduces the incidence of docetaxel-induced fluid retention.
- Renal impairment: no need for dose adjustments for docetaxel. The need for cyclophosphamide dose reduction in renal insufficiency is controversial.

- Hepatic impairment: docetaxel should not be given when serum bilirubin level is higher than ULN; or with transaminase elevations > 1.5 times ULN in conjunction with alkaline phosphatase level > 2.5 times ULN.

Neoadjuvant Chemotherapy. When neoadjuvant chemotherapy is used, the regimen selected should be the same as what would be administered in the adjuvant setting—typically consisting of an anthracycline and a taxane.

Several studies showed that the addition of carboplatin to neoadjuvant chemotherapy in TNBC resulted in an increase in pCR rates, although with added toxicity.[211,212] Recognizing that the platinum agents can be toxic and that these trials lack long-term safety data, as well as the uncertain benefit in the long-term outcome, many experts still consider the use of carboplatin in TNBC investigational and this question is the focus of ongoing clinical studies. Optimal dosing and schedule for carboplatin remain to be determined.

Residual Disease After Completing Neoadjuvant Therapy. Improved treatment options are needed for patients with TNBC who do not have a pCR with neoadjuvant therapy—an area of active research. The CREATE-X[213] trial randomly assigned 910 patients with HER2-negative breast cancer who received neoadjuvant chemotherapy (containing anthracycline, taxane, or both) and had residual disease at time of surgery to receive six to eight cycles of capecitabine or placebo. There was an improvement in OS in the capecitabine group compared with placebo (89.2% *v* 83.6% at 5 years; hazard ratio, 0.59). Patients with TNBC derived the largest benefit, with a DFS at 5 years of 69.8% in the capecitabine group versus 56.1% in the control group (hazard ratio, 0.58), and an OS rate of 78.8% versus 70.3% (death hazard ratio, 0.52; 95% CI, 0.30 to 0.90). The ASCO guideline update from 2018 recommends that patients with early-stage, HER2-negative breast cancer with pathologic, invasive residual disease at surgery after standard anthracycline- and taxane-based preoperative therapy may be offered up to six to eight cycles of adjuvant capecitabine.[214]

Hormone Receptor-Positive Breast Cancer

The adjuvant systemic therapy for patients with HR-positive breast cancer can include chemotherapy and endocrine therapy. Most patients with HR-positive breast cancer will receive endocrine therapy, either tamoxifen or an aromatase inhibitor, with or without ovarian suppression. The decision whether patients should also receive chemotherapy before initiation of endocrine therapy relies on multiple clinical and biologic factors. Factors that prompt the use of chemotherapy are:

- high histologic grade,
- a moderate to large disease burden, and
- a poor prognosis based on a gene signature

Recommendations for the use of gene expression signatures to guide adjuvant chemotherapy decisions in HR-positive disease are discussed in the Gene Expression Signatures section of this chapter. General principles regarding chemotherapy in early-stage breast cancer were addressed in the Triple-Negative Breast Cancer section. When both chemotherapy and endocrine therapy are recommended, chemotherapy is given before endocrine therapy.

Endocrine Therapy. Endocrine therapy reduces the risk of systemic recurrence and death among women with HR-positive (ER and/or PR) breast cancer, regardless of age, menopausal status, nodal involvement, tumor size, HER2 status, or use of chemotherapy. For this reason, adjuvant endocrine therapy should be considered in all women with HR-positive disease.[215,216]

Tamoxifen. Tamoxifen is a SERM that inhibits estrogen binding to ER and is effective in pre- and postmenopausal women. The EBCTCG meta-analysis showed that 5 years of tamoxifen reduced the relative risk of distant recurrence by approximately 41% and the relative risk of dying by 34%.[74] On the basis of multiple studies, the standard duration of adjuvant treatment with tamoxifen has been 5 years. Two large studies now support extending the duration of tamoxifen treatment to 10 years.[217] In the ATLAS trial, extended duration of tamoxifen therapy to 10 years, when compared with 5 years, reduced the rate of recurrence by 3.2% and improved the mortality rate by 2.8%. The difference between the arms of the study did not emerge until year 10, likely due to the carry-over effect after 5 years of tamoxifen from years 5 to 10. Prolonged tamoxifen use was associated with an increased incidence of pulmonary embolism and endometrial cancer, with a 3.1% cumulative risk of endometrial cancer after 5 years of tamoxifen therapy, translating into an absolute increase in endometrial cancer mortality of 0.2%. There was no increase in the risk of stroke or cardiovascular events with prolonged treatment. These results were replicated in the aTTom trial, which had a similar design.[218] Although these data support the efficacy of prolonged use of tamoxifen, longer treatment duration must be weighed against potential adverse outcomes on an individual basis: for patients with early-stage disease (eg, stage I) who are at low risk of disease recurrence, the potential toxicities may outweigh the benefits.

Cytochrome P450 2D6 (CYP2D6) is the primary hepatic enzyme responsible for tamoxifen metabolism to its active metabolite. CYP2D6 polymorphism can result in decreased active metabolite, potentially resulting in decreased efficacy. Currently, the ASCO guidelines do not recommend the use of testing for CYP2D6 polymorphisms to guide selection of adjuvant endocrine therapy.[135] Although this question has been controversial, a recent prospective study did not find differences in outcomes associated with CYP2D6 polymorphisms in women with breast cancer treated with tamoxifen.[219] Caution is still advised in women treated with concomitant medications that are strong inhibitors of CYP2D, such as certain antidepressants like fluoxetine, paroxetine, and bupropion, among others.

Role of Ovarian Function Suppression The SOFT and the TEXT trials evaluated the role of ovarian function suppression (OFS) as adjuvant therapy for HR-positive breast cancer.[220,221] In TEXT, women were randomly assigned to receive 5 years of tamoxifen or exemestane with concurrent OFS. In SOFT, women

Table 10-8 **Summary of SOFT Results**

Absolute difference (%)	Freedom From DR, HR (95 % CI)	OS, HR (95 % CI)
All patients		
Tamoxifen		
Tamoxifen + OFS	1.0, 0.86 (0.66 to 1.13)	1.8, 0.67 (0.48 to 0.92)
Exemestane + OFS	2.8, 0.73 (0.55 to 0.96)	0.6, 0.85 (0.62 to 1.15)
Patients treated with chemotherapy		
Tamoxifen		
Tamoxifen + OFS	2.1, 0.84 (0.64 to 1.12)	4.3, 0.59 (0.42 to 0.84)
Exemestane + OFS	4.5, 0.74 (0.56 to 0.99)	2.1, 0.79 (0.79 to 1.09)

Abbreviations: DFS, disease-free survival; DR, distant recurrence; OFS, ovarian function suppression; OS, overall survival.

who were treated with tamoxifen alone or remained premenopausal within 8 months of completing chemotherapy (based on menses or estradiol level) were randomly assigned to receive 5 years of tamoxifen, tamoxifen plus OFS, or exemestane plus OFS. In both studies, chemotherapy was given per physician's choice. The comparisons of exemestane plus OFS and tamoxifen plus OFS in both trials were analyzed together. After approximately 8 years of follow-up, when compared with tamoxifen alone:

- The addition of OFS to tamoxifen or to exemestane resulted in an improvement in DFS (of 4.3% *v* 7%, respectively) and freedom from distant recurrence (1% *v* 2.8%, respectively).
- The benefit of OFS compared with tamoxifen alone was higher in women who received chemotherapy or were 35 years old or younger.
- Reduction in distant recurrence rate was larger with exemestane than with tamoxifen.
- A small survival benefit has emerged with the addition of OFS to tamoxifen (93.3% *v* 91.5%) Table 10-8 summarizes some of the results of SOFT.

A consistent finding in these studies was that patients with low-risk disease did equally well with tamoxifen alone. Therefore, for women at low risk, tamoxifen alone remains an appropriate choice. This is important, particularly given the added toxicity of OFS and AI therapy, including hot flashes, musculoskeletal symptoms, loss of bone density, and sexual dysfunction.

On the basis of the initial report of the SOFT and TEXT trials, the 2016 ASCO guideline states[215]:

- For women at higher risk for cancer recurrence due to tumor stage (II, III) or biologic features, OFS in addition to adjuvant endocrine therapy is recommended, particularly in women younger than 35 years.
- On the other hand, women with stage I disease for whom chemotherapy is not deemed necessary should not receive OFS.
- OFS and an AI are favored for patients with higher risk and younger women.

Aromatase Inhibitors. Although tamoxifen retains its efficacy in postmenopausal women, AIs (ie, inhibitors of the enzyme that converts androgens to estrogens in peripheral tissues, the primary source of estrogens in postmenopausal women) are usually preferred, based on data from multiple studies comparing both agents in postmenopausal women. AIs are not effective in pre- or perimenopausal women and thus should not be used for adjuvant therapy in this group of patients in the absence of concurrent OFS. It is important to remember that chemotherapy-induced amenorrhea can be transient; therefore, the choice of endocrine therapy should be based on the menopausal status prior to treatment.

There are three third-generation AIs: anastrozole and letrozole (nonsteroidal inhibitors) and exemestane (a steroidal inhibitor). They all appear to have comparable efficacy[222,223] and similar adverse effects, including hot flashes, arthralgias, myalgias, and a reduction in bone density.

Multiple studies addressed the efficacy of AIs in comparison with tamoxifen, either evaluating 5 years of tamoxifen versus an AI, or switching to an AI after 2 to 3 years of tamoxifen, (Table 10-9). Data from a Oxford meta-analysis showed that when compared with 5 years of tamoxifen, the use of an AI in postmenopausal women reduced the 10-year risk of recurrence by approximately 30% and the breast cancer mortality rate by approximately 15%.[224]

Although an AI is generally preferred to tamoxifen in postmenopausal women because of efficacy, the absolute differences in risk reduction associated with an AI are small and multiple studies show poor adherence to the medication because of adverse effects. Therefore, women who are unable to tolerate an AI should be switched to tamoxifen.[225]

Continuation of AI treatment after 5 years of endocrine therapy was also studied. Switching to an AI after 5 years of treatment with tamoxifen demonstrated additional reduction in disease recurrence in postmenopausal women.[226] Several other studies, examined the continuation of an AI after 5 years of treatment that included an AI.[227-230] The optimal duration of extended therapy after year 5 was also evaluated.[231,232] These studies are summarized in Table 10-10. Taken together,

Table 10-9 **Comparison of Tamoxifen and Aromatase Inhibitors in Postmenopausal Women, 5 Years of Therapy**	
Trial, Duration	**Intervention**
ATAC[393]	Tamoxifen
	Anastrozole
	Tamoxifen + anastrozole
BIG 1-98[394]	Letrozole
	Tamoxifen
	Letrozole (2 years), tamoxifen (3 years)
	Tamoxifen (2 years), letrozole (3 years)
ABCSG 8[395]	Tamoxifen
	Tamoxifen (2 years), anastrozole (3 years)
ITA[396]	Tamoxifen after 2-3 years of tamoxifen
	Anastrozole after 2-3 years of tamoxifen
TEAM[397]	Tamoxifen (2.5 years), exemestane (2.5 years)
	Exemestane
IES[398]	Tamoxifen after 2-3 years of tamoxifen
	Exemestane after 2-3 years of tamoxifen

these data showed a modest improvement in DFS in the patients who continued an AI after an AI, largely driven by prevention of contralateral breast cancer. Five years of extended therapy were equivalent to shorter duration. There was no survival benefit with extended AI therapy and there was a higher risk of osteoporosis and fractures. In light of the modest activity of extended AI and added toxicity, patients with higher-risk disease are the most suitable for extended endocrine therapy.

ASCO recommends that postmenopausal women should incorporate an AI during their course of adjuvant endocrine treatment, but the best time to start such therapy remains unclear.[233] Decisions regarding extended duration should be individualized on the basis of cancer stage, risk of late recurrence, and tolerability. Acceptable strategies of extended endocrine therapy duration include:

- AI for 10 years,
- tamoxifen for 2 to 3 years followed by AI for 7 to 8 years,
- tamoxifen for 5 years followed by AI for 5 years, and
- tamoxifen for 10 years.

Neoadjuvant Endocrine Therapy. Neoadjuvant endocrine therapy is an acceptable treatment for postmenopausal women with HR-positive disease, either to achieve breast conservation or to downstage disease that is inoperable at presentation. This approach is particularly valuable in women with tumors with low chemosensitivity or those who are poor candidates for chemotherapy. At least five randomized trials (including patients with stage II disease) have demonstrated superiority with neoadjuvant AI compared with tamoxifen.[234,235] For postmenopausal women, all three third-generation AIs (anastrozole, letrozole, and exemestane) appear to be equally effective in the neoadjuvant setting.[236] Despite low pCR rates associated with neoadjuvant endocrine therapy, surrogate markers of response can offer prognostic information about long-term clinical outcomes,

Table 10-10 **Extended Endocrine Therapy with AI[233]**	
Trial	**Intervention**
Extended adjuvant AI after 5 years of tamoxifen	
MA-17	Letrozole for 5 years or placebo
NSABP B-33	Exemestane for 5 years or placebo
ABCSG 6	Anastrozole for 3 years or placebo
Extended AI after 5 years of therapy that included an AI	
MA 17-R	Letrozole or placebo for 5 years after 5 years of letrozole, (preceded by 5 years of tamoxifen in most patients)
NSABP B-42	Letrozole or placebo for 5 years after 5 years of endocrine therapy with 5 years of an AI or ≤ 3 years of tamoxifen
DATA	Anastrozole for 6 years, 3 years after 2-3 years of tamoxifen
Optimal duration or dosing of AI in years 5 to 10	
IDEAL	Letrozole for 2.5 *v* 5 years after tamoxifen, AI or both for 5 years
ABCSG-18	Anastrozole for 2 *v* 5 years after tamoxifen, AI or both for 4-6 years
SOLE	Letrozole for 5 years or letrozole 9 months on, 3 months off in years 1-4 and continuous year 5, after 4-6 years of adjuvant endocrine therapy

Abbreviation: AI, aromatase inhibitor.

including the expression of Ki67 in residual tumor (low value or decreased compared with baseline is favorable),[237] and prospective validation of these biomarkers is ongoing.

Neoadjuvant endocrine therapy is usually given for no less than 4 to 6 months to allow maximum response prior to surgery. Patients who have a clinical response to neoadjuvant endocrine therapy should continue to receive endocrine therapy after surgery. Those who do not have a clinical response should be considered for adjuvant chemotherapy followed by adjuvant endocrine therapy. Neoadjuvant endocrine therapy in premenopausal women and in men remains investigational.

KEY POINTS

- Tamoxifen is recommended as adjuvant endocrine treatment of pre- and postmenopausal women.
- OFS improves DFS and freedom from recurrence when combined with 5 years of adjuvant tamoxifen or exemestane in premenopausal women with high-risk disease.
- As compared with 5 years, 10 years of adjuvant tamoxifen is associated with a small improvement in DFS and extended-duration tamoxifen is an option in high-risk pre- or postmenopausal patients.
- AIs are the first choice as adjuvant endocrine treatment of postmenopausal women.
- Administering AIs for 5 years results in similar outcomes as initial tamoxifen for 2 to 3 years, followed by an AI for a total of 5 years.
- Extended duration of AI therapy beyond 5 years should be considered in postmenopausal patients with high-risk disease.

HER2-Positive Breast Cancer

Most women diagnosed with early-stage, HER2-positive breast cancer receive HER2-targeted therapy and chemotherapy as adjuvant systemic therapy. Exceptions are those with very small tumors (≤ 0.5 cm, although this should not be considered a strict cutoff and other factors need to be considered) or with significant comorbidities.

Four HER2-targeted therapies are currently used in the adjuvant setting: trastuzumab, pertuzumab, neratinib, and ado-trastuzumab emtansine (T-DM1) (Fig 10-7), as follows:

- Monoclonal antibodies trastuzumab and pertuzumab both target the extracellular domain of HER2; trastuzumab binds to subdomain IV and disrupts ligand-independent downstream signaling, whereas pertuzumab binds to subdomain II, which blocks dimerization of HER2 and subsequent ligand-dependent signaling.
- Neratinib is an oral, irreversible tyrosine kinase inhibitor that blocks signal transduction through the epidermal growth factor receptors (EGFR) family, including HER2.
- T-DM1 is an antibody-drug conjugate that consists of trastuzumab linked to maytansinoid DM1, a potent microtubule-disrupting agent, joined by a nonreducible stable linker.

Trastuzumab-Based Adjuvant Therapy Regimens. Trastuzumab can be given with different chemotherapy regimens. The most commonly used trastuzumab-based regimens in the neoadjuvant or adjuvant setting are:

- combination docetaxel, carboplatin, and trastuzumab (TCH) with or without pertuzumab,
- AC (doxorubicin/cyclophosphamide) followed by paclitaxel plus trastuzumab) with or without pertuzumab, and
- paclitaxel plus trastuzumab.

When added to chemotherapy, trastuzumab substantially improves DFS and OS compared with chemotherapy alone. A meta-analysis of five adjuvant therapy studies demonstrated a 38% reduction in the relative risk of recurrence and a 34% reduction in the relative risk of dying from any cause.[238] The largest individual analysis combined two phase III US studies that compared chemotherapy alone and chemotherapy with trastuzumab (sequential or concurrent): NCCTG N9831 and NSABP B-31. Regardless of patient or tumor characteristics, the addition of trastuzumab to chemotherapy resulted in a 48% relative improvement in DFS and a 39% relative improvement in OS.

Concurrent administration of chemotherapy and trastuzumab may be of greater benefit as compared with sequential treatment. This concept was supported by the NCCTG N9831 study that showed the concurrent administration of trastuzumab with paclitaxel was associated with a 23% reduction in risk of an event as compared with sequential trastuzumab administration. Concomitant administration of trastuzumab is supported by the ASCO clinical practice guidelines. Trastuzumab is continued as a single agent after chemotherapy, commonly given every 3 weeks and concurrently with endocrine therapy for HR-positive disease.[240]

The currently accepted duration of adjuvant trastuzumab is 1 year. The HERA trial evaluated combination chemotherapy followed by observation or 1 or 2 years of adjuvant trastuzumab.[241,242] Trial results showed that 1 year of trastuzumab significantly reduced the risk of a DFS event and death, compared with observation. Two years of adjuvant trastuzumab did not improve DFS outcomes compared with 1 year of therapy[238,242] and was associated with greater cardiac toxicity.[238,242] Other studies examined the question of duration of trastuzumab.[239,243-246] Of these, only the PERSEPHONE trial showed that 6-months of trastuzumab was not inferior to 12-month treatment and was associated with fewer severe adverse events and less cardiac toxicity.[247] Differences in the results of these trials can be explained, at least partially, by the different prespecified statistical analysis plan and patient population of each study. At this point, 12 months of adjuvant therapy continues to be the standard for most patients with HER2-positive disease.

The efficacy of the combination of trastuzumab with a non-anthracycline-containing regimen was evaluated in the BCIRG 006 trial. In this study, patients were randomly assigned to TCH, administered every 3 weeks for six cycles or to four cycles of AC every 3 weeks followed by four cycles of docetaxel with or without trastuzumab (ACT or ACTH). The results of adding trastuzumab to chemotherapy led to improved DSF and OS. There was a nonstatistically significant 3% absolute difference in DFS and a 1% difference in OS at 5 years favoring the AC plus docetaxel and trastuzumab arm over the TCH arm. However, the study was not designed to compare the two trastuzumab-containing arms and any conclusions about the benefits of one regimen over another should be considered exploratory.[248] TCH was associated with less cardiac toxicity and risk of secondary leukemia compared with the ACTH regimen, making it an acceptable treatment alternative. Recently, the US Food and Drug Administration (FDA) approved trastuzumab for subcutaneous use. This was based on two randomized trials, HannaH and SafeHER, that showed comparability between the subcutaneous and intravenous formulations and overall safety and tolerability of this new formulation.[249,250]

In the ExteNET trial, which included 2,840 patients with early-stage, HER2-positive breast cancer who were within 2 years of completing adjuvant trastuzumab therapy, the 2-year invasive DFS rate was 94.2% among those who received adjuvant neratinib for 1 year, compared with a rate of 91.9% in those receiving placebo. The most common adverse events were diarrhea, fatigue, rash, and stomatitis, with 16.8% of patients discontinuing treatment because of diarrhea.[251] These results led to the FDA approval of neratinib for the extended adjuvant treatment of patients with early-stage, HER2-positive breast cancer following adjuvant, trastuzumab-based therapy. Concurrent administration of antidiarrheal prophylaxis is recommended with initiation of neratinib. This is also supported by the ASCO 2018 clinical practices guidelines.

In the phase III APHINITY trial, 4,805 patients with HER2-positive, node-positive breast cancer or high-risk, node-negative breast cancer were randomly assigned to adjuvant chemotherapy with trastuzumab and placebo or pertuzumab.[252] With a median follow-up of 45.4 months, the addition of pertuzumab to chemotherapy and trastuzumab was associated with a modest benefit, resulting in a 3-year invasive DFS rate of 94.1% as compared with the placebo arm rate of 93.2%. Treatment was effective in all subgroups; however, those with node-positive and/or HR-negative disease appeared to derive the most benefit. Diarrhea was increased in the pertuzumab arm, predominantly during chemotherapy and with the TCH regimen. Cardiac toxicity was low and not different between the two arms. The ASCO 2018 guideline states, "Clinicians may add 1 year of adjuvant pertuzumab to trastuzumab-based combination chemotherapy in patients with high-risk, early-stage, HER2-positive breast cancer."[214]

Small Node-Negative Tumors. Retrospective data suggest that small, node-negative, HER2-positive breast cancers have a small but real risk of distant recurrence. However, most patients with these cancers were not eligible for enrollment in the pivotal adjuvant trastuzumab clinical trials. The phase II

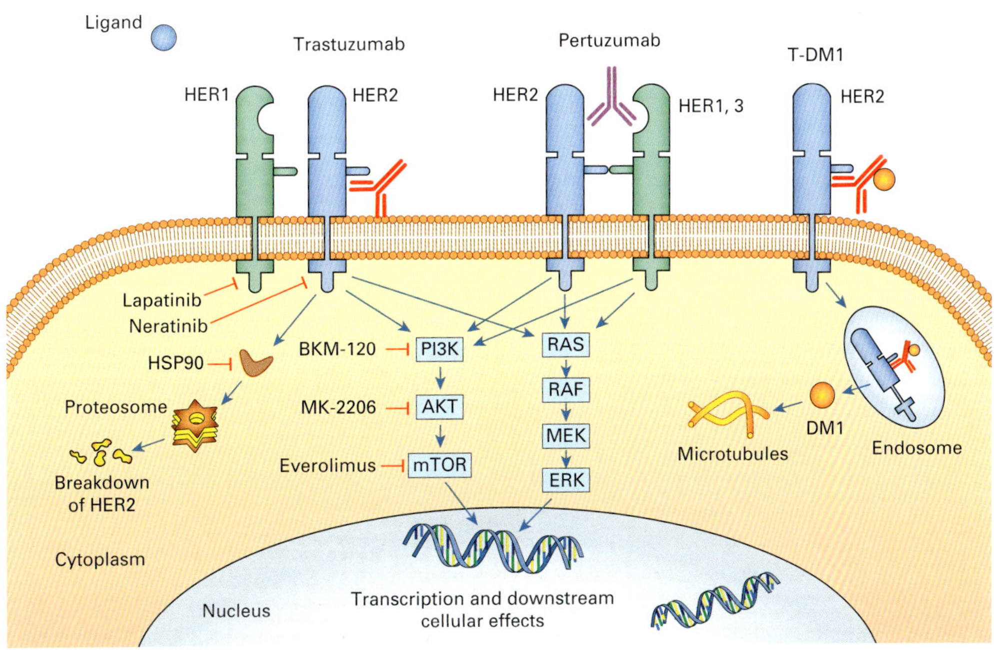

Fig. 10-7 Targets for HER2-targeted therapy.

Abbreviation: T-DM1, ado-trastuzumab emtansine.

Permission to reuse given by the Creative Common license for Singh JC, Jhaveri K, Esteva FJ. HER2-positive advanced breast cancer: optimizing patient outcomes and opportunities for drug development. Br J Cancer. *2014 Nov 11;111(10):1888-98.*

Adjuvant Paclitaxel Trastuzumab (APT) trial sought to explore the efficacy of a trastuzumab-containing adjuvant therapy regimen that included a minimal amount of chemotherapy. The APT trial enrolled 406 patients with node-negative, HER2-positive breast cancers < 3 cm.[204] In this single-arm, study, patients received 12 weeks of paclitaxel (80 mg/m^2) and concurrent trastuzumab, followed by 9 months of single-agent trastuzumab therapy. The 7-year DFS was 93.3% and the 7-year recurrence-free interval was 97.5% at a median follow-up of 6.5 years, with only four DFS events (1%) being distant metastasis. The regimen was well tolerated, with minimal neuropathy and cardiac compromise, and became a common choice in patients with small, node-negative, HER2-positive breast cancer.

Neoadjuvant HER2-Directed Therapy. HER2-positive breast cancer is associated with a high response rate to neoadjuvant chemotherapy, which is increased substantially with the addition of HER2-directed treatment. Two studies evaluated neoadjuvant trastuzumab-containing regimens that administered the trastuzumab with an anthracycline.[253,254] Both studies demonstrated a significant benefit with added trastuzumab in the pCR rate (20% to 40% actual improvement), and a 33% relative reduction in risk of recurrence and death.

Two phase III trials evaluated the role of lapatinib in this setting. GeparQuinto compared four cycles of combined epirubicin and cyclophosphamide followed by four cycles of docetaxel concurrent with either lapatinib or trastuzumab. Among the 620 randomly assigned patients, the pCR rate was significantly higher with trastuzumab compared with lapatinib (30.3% *v* 22.7%, respectively; *P* =.04).[255] Similar findings were found in the NeoALTTO trial, in which 455 patients were randomly assigned to receive 6 weeks of lapatinib alone, trastuzumab alone, or lapatinib combined with trastuzumab before continuing HER2-directed therapy with 12 weeks of paclitaxel (NeoALTTO).[256] Interestingly, combination lapatinib and trastuzumab with paclitaxel resulted in a superior pCR rate of 51.3%.

The benefit seen with dual HER2-directed therapy prompted an evaluation of pertuzumab in the neoadjuvant setting. The NeoSphere trial was an open-label, phase II study that randomly assigned 417 patients to receive four cycles of docetaxel combined with either trastuzumab, pertuzumab, or both agents versus combination pertuzumab and trastuzumab without docetaxel (a nonchemotherapy arm).[205] The combination pertuzumab and trastuzumab with docetaxel achieved the highest pCR rate of 39.3%, compared with the other groups. All patients in the NeoSphere trial also received adjuvant treatment with three cycles of combined 5 -fluorouracil, epirubicin, and cyclophosphamide chemotherapy concomitant with trastuzumab followed by completion of 1 year of trastuzumab therapy.

Residual Disease After Completing Neoadjuvant Therapy. Patients who receive neoadjuvant chemotherapy and HER2 therapy and have residual disease at the time of surgery are at a higher risk of recurrence. In KATHERINE, a study of 1,486 patients who had residual invasive breast cancer after receiving neoadjuvant chemotherapy and HER2 therapy,[257] the use of T-DM1 after surgery was associated with improved DFS and lower risk of distant recurrence compared with trastuzumab. However, there were more serious adverse events with T-DM1 than with trastuzumab (13% *v* 8%, respectively). This regimen has been adopted by many as the treatment of choice for patients with residual disease. If the disease is also HR positive, adjuvant endocrine therapy is administered concurrently with T-DM1.

Major toxicities associated with HER2-targeted therapies include:

- Cardiac toxicity: the addition of trastuzumab in the adjuvant studies resulted in < 4% difference in incidence of congestive heart failure or death between the treatment arms. However, up to 18% of patients experienced asymptomatic decreases in ejection fraction that required discontinuation of trastuzumab.[258] Risk of cardiac compromise was associated with advanced age, hypertension, preexisting cardiac dysfunction, and high body mass index. Cardiac monitoring with echocardiography or multigated acquisition scan is recommended every 3 months during adjuvant trastuzumab treatment. Among patients with asymptomatic low ejection fraction, the decision to use HER2-targeted therapy must be made on an individual basis, assessing the relative risks of cardiac dysfunction from a specific regimen versus disease progression, and in collaboration with a cardiologist.[259]
- Diarrhea: the incidence of all-grade diarrhea across different studies with pertuzumab ranged from 28% to 72%, with grade 3 diarrhea in 0% to 12% of cases.[260] Diarrhea was common, occurred mainly during the first treatment cycle and was manageable with antidiarrheal medications. Diarrhea is an important adverse effect of neratinib (21% of patients in the TBCRC 022 study had grade 3 diarrhea with low-dose loperamide prophylaxis).[261] The use of neratinib mandates prophylactic-intensive loperamide.
- Rash: experienced by 22% of patients overall treated with HER2-targeted therapies,[262] including lapatinib and pertuzumab. Most dermatologic toxicities in patients receiving lapatinib present early and rarely require dose reduction or lead to treatment discontinuation.[263] Rash associated with EGFR inhibitors is typically acneform, accompanied by pruritus and tenderness in 62% of patients, and can be managed with topical hydrocortisone and oral doxycycline or minocycline in most situations. In a meta-analysis with data from 1,726 patients, pertuzumab increased the risk of rash in comparison with controls (relative risk [RR], 1.53).[264]

KEY POINTS

- Anthracycline- and/or taxane-based adjuvant chemotherapy is standard care for women with TNBC. Similar regimens can be used for patients with high-risk, HR-positive disease and in combination with HER2-directed therapy for HER2-positive disease.

- For stage II or III breast cancer, neoadjuvant chemotherapy reduces the need for mastectomy and/or ALND.
- For stage II or III breast cancer, survival is equivalent whether the same chemotherapy regimen is administered in the neoadjuvant or the adjuvant setting.
- Neoadjuvant endocrine therapy is an acceptable treatment approach for postmenopausal women with stage II or III, HR-positive breast cancer. It can result in higher breast-conservation rates, but it infrequently results in pCR.
- For HER2-positive breast cancer:
  - 1 year of adjuvant trastuzumab is recommended, given concurrently for 12 weeks with taxane-based chemotherapy followed by monotherapy to complete1 year.
  - The addition of 1 year of adjuvant pertuzumab to trastuzumab can be considered for high-risk patients because it provides a small absolute reduction in the risk of recurrence of an invasive DFS event.
  - Pertuzumab, when administered concurrently with trastuzumab and taxane-based chemotherapy, is associated with a significantly increased pCR rate.
- Residual disease after neoadjuvant chemotherapy for TNBC and HER2-positive disease is associated with worse DFS compared with those who achieve a pCR.

INFLAMMATORY BREAST CANCER

Inflammatory breast cancer (IBC) accounts for up to 2% of all breast cancers in the United States. IBC (T4d in TNM staging) is a clinical diagnosis in the setting of documented invasive breast cancer and is characterized by a rapid onset of clinical changes in the breast, including skin erythema, warmth, edema (peau d'orange), breast enlargement, and pain. These clinical criteria differentiate IBC from a neglected, locally advanced breast cancer with secondary inflammatory characteristics, which is associated with a more favorable prognosis.

Pathologically, tumor emboli are seen within dermal lymphatics in 75% of cases.[265] The classic physical findings of the breast are due to damage of the dermal lymphatics caused by tumor emboli.[266] Breast imaging with mammography usually finds asymmetrically increased density throughout the affected breast, associated with skin thickening and axillary adenopathy. MRI is more sensitive and specific in finding breast masses and confirming disease response to neoadjuvant chemotherapy, compared with mammography.[267]

Although all subtypes are seen in IBC, HER2-positive or triple-negative subtypes are common. Patients with IBC have as high as a two-fold increased risk of dying of disease as patients diagnosed with noninflammatory, locally advanced breast cancer, with long-term OS rates being consistently < 50%.

IBC is treated with neoadjuvant chemotherapy followed by mastectomy with ALND and PMRT with comprehensive regional nodal irradiation. The approach to nonmetastatic IBC is summarized in the following section.

NEOADJUVANT THERAPY

The optimal neoadjuvant chemotherapy regimen for IBC has not been defined. Results of prospective and retrospective studies support the use of combination anthracycline- and taxane-based regimens. The addition of taxanes to anthracycline regimens has resulted in an improved pCR rate and improved OS.[268] The prognosis of HER2-positive IBC has greatly improved in the era of HER2-directed therapy. HER2-positive IBC should be treated with a dual HER2-targeted neoadjuvant regimen with trastuzumab and pertuzumab, as previously described.

BREAST SURGERY AND RADIATION

Breast conservation is contraindicated, as is SLN biopsy. A total mastectomy with levels I and II ALND improves surgical control, compared with surgeries of lesser extent. Given the high risk of local recurrence, reconstruction of the breast is best deferred to avoid delays in the initiation of radiation therapy. Radiation therapy should follow surgery for all patients, although the optimal radiation dose and sequence are not well established. The chest wall and regional lymph nodes (supraclavicular, infraclavicular, internal mammary) are included in the treatment field.

If a patient is still not operable after completing an initial course of neoadjuvant chemotherapy, additional treatments should be pursued, including additional chemotherapy using different agents or radiation.[269] For patients who present with metastatic disease or who develop metastatic disease during the initial course of therapy, treatment is similar to that for non-IBC.

KEY POINTS

- IBC is treated with neoadjuvant chemotherapy followed by mastectomy with ALND, postmastectomy radiation therapy, and adjuvant endocrine therapy, when indicated.
- Despite optimal multimodality care, DFS is worse with IBC compared with noninflammatory breast cancer, even for patients who achieve a pCR.

TREATMENT OF RECURRENT OR METASTATIC (STAGE IV) DISEASE

LOCOREGIONAL RELAPSE

Locoregional disease relapse can be defined as cancer recurrence in the ipsilateral breast, chest wall, or regional lymph nodes. Isolated locoregional recurrences are treated with curative intent. Those that occur within the first 5 years after diagnosis are associated with a poorer prognosis than later recurrences. Recurrences in the breast that develop after 5 years usually represent de novo second primary tumors and have a more favorable outcome compared with earlier recurrences within the proximity of the original tumor, which usually represent disease that has been resistant to prior radiation and systemic therapy. Nodal recurrence in the contralateral axilla can occur due to aberrant drainage patterns, and breast imaging should be done to exclude a new primary. In the absence of metastatic disease, an isolated, contralateral recurrence should be managed with curative intent. Local recurrence is associated with a high rate of distant metastases and systemic imaging is recommended for these patients.[270]

Ipsilateral breast tumor recurrence (IBTR) after BCT has been associated with a three- to four-fold increase in the risk of developing systemic metastasis. The NSABP reviewed five of its adjuvant studies that involved 2,669 women treated with BCS, radiation therapy, and systemic treatment, and found that patients who experienced an IBTR had a 2.72-fold greater risk of distant disease developing at 5 years and a 2.58-fold greater risk of death, compared with those who did not have disease recurrence.[271] Patients who experienced a chest wall recurrence after mastectomy fared worse, with a 6.68-fold greater risk of distant recurrence at 5 years and a 5.85-fold greater risk of death.

The treatment of locoregional recurrences requires a multidisciplinary approach. The standard treatment of IBTRs that occur after BCT is a total mastectomy, although excision and reirradiation can be considered for select cases.[272] In cases without prior radiation, BCT can be considered. The axilla should be evaluated with physical examination and ultrasound. If clinically negative, SLN surgery can be attempted; however, it has a lower SLN identification rate.[273] ALND should be considered in cases in which SLNs is not identified. In cases with clinically positive nodes or positive SLN(s), an ALND should be performed.

As in IBTR, chest wall recurrences after mastectomy occur most frequently within the first 5 years after treatment and rarely occur after 10 years. The majority of chest wall recurrences develop near the mastectomy incision, whereas fewer recurrences develop in the regional lymph node areas (in order of decreasing frequency: supraclavicular, axillary, internal mammary). The treatment of an isolated chest wall recurrence requires a surgical excision, if feasible, with the goal of obtaining negative margins. The chest wall and supraclavicular lymph nodes should then receive standard radiation therapy, if not given previously.

Systemic therapy is often administered after completion of local treatment of a locoregional recurrence, although the data supporting its use are limited. The international CALOR (BIG 1-02/IBCSG 27-02/NSABP B-37) trial enrolled 162 of a planned 977 patients with invasive breast cancer in whom an isolated local and/or regional ipsilateral recurrence developed after mastectomy or BCT.[274] Patients received radiation therapy, endocrine therapy, as appropriate, and were also randomly assigned to receive chemotherapy or not. Most recurrences occurred after completion of endocrine therapy. The chemotherapy regimen selection and duration of treatment was per physician choice. The 5-year DFS was improved with chemotherapy (69%) compared with no chemotherapy (57%). However, the benefits of chemotherapy appeared to be limited to ER-negative tumors, a finding confirmed after 9 years of follow-up.[275] Although this is a highly underpowered study, it does support consideration of chemotherapy after local or regional disease recurrence in select circumstances.

KEY POINTS

- Locoregional recurrences require a multidisciplinary approach.
- Local recurrence is associated with a high rate of distant metastases, and systemic imaging is recommended for these patients.
- After BCT, the standard treatment of local recurrences involves a total mastectomy.
- The addition of chemotherapy after a surgical management of locoregional recurrence may benefit some patients, especially those with ER-negative disease.

SYSTEMIC THERAPY FOR STAGE IV (METASTATIC) DISEASE

Treatment options depend on disease burden, tumor characteristics, previous treatments, concern for organ failure due to metastatic disease (visceral crisis), and patient's preferences and comorbidities.[276,277]

The incorporation of new therapies over recent decades has resulted in a gradual improvement in OS by 1% to 2% per year.[278] The overall goals of treating metastatic breast cancer are to delay the progression of disease, improve quality of life, and prolong survival while minimizing treatment-associated toxicity. Metastatic breast cancer is a chronic disease; sequential, single-agent therapy is a mainstay of treatment. The benefits of individual regimens are often comparable in first-line or subsequent treatment; therefore, the optimal sequence of therapies has not yet been determined.[279]

Once metastatic disease is diagnosed, its extent should be determined by radiographic imaging. The most common initial sites of metastasis include bone, liver, and lung, which can be imaged by conventional CT and bone scan. PET imaging can complement these studies, especially in the setting of lytic bone metastases, which may be underestimated on bone scan. CNS disease is less likely to be present at the initial appearance of metastatic disease, and MRI of the brain is not necessary in the absence of symptoms. Bone metastases are more common in the HR-positive subtype (68%), whereas TNBC is associated with a high frequency of metastasis to the lungs (40%). HER2-positive disease and TNBC are associated with a higher frequency of brain metastasis compared with the HR-positive subtype.[280]

Discordance of HR and HER2 status between the primary tumor and the metastatic disease can occur in 10% to 15% of patients. A biopsy of metastatic disease at the initial presentation is indicated to determine receptor status and to confirm the presence of metastatic breast cancer rather than another malignancy, either primary or metastatic

Serum markers, such as CA 27.29 or CA15-3, and the carcinoembryonic antigen levels can complement the interpretation of imaging studies in metastatic disease but should not be used alone for monitoring response to treatment.[281] The use of circulating tumor cells or circulating tumor DNA in the interpretation of disease response and management of therapy remains investigational.

ENDOCRINE THERAPY

For HR-positive metastatic breast cancer, endocrine therapy is usually the initial treatment approach, unless chemotherapy is indicated with the aim of a more rapid response in settings of rapidly progressing disease or visceral crisis (ie, impending organ failure). Objective response rates to endocrine therapy are comparable to those of single-agent chemotherapy for first-line treatment; however, the onset of action is slower for endocrine therapy. All patients with metastatic HR-positive breast cancer develop endocrine-resistance and ultimately receive chemotherapy.

The choice of initial endocrine therapy depends on the following:

- menopausal status,
- type of prior endocrine therapy used for adjuvant treatment, and
- duration between adjuvant endocrine therapy and disease recurrence.

There is an association between response to endocrine therapy and level of ER and PR expression.

For premenopausal women with HR-positive metastatic disease, OFS has historically been effective in improving the outcome when added to tamoxifen.[282] Therefore, when tamoxifen is chosen to treat metastatic disease in a premenopausal woman, OFS is usually added.

In postmenopausal women, third-generation AIs (ie, letrozole, anastrozole, and exemestane) are superior to tamoxifen as first-line therapy.[283,284] In addition, switching from a first-line nonsteroidal AI (letrozole or anastrozole) to a steroidal AI (exemestane) can result in a modest disease response as second-line therapy.[285]

Fulvestrant is a selective ER degrader, given as an intramuscular injection. Fulvestrant is active when used both in first-[286] and second-line therapy, after progression while being treated with a nonsteroidal AI.[287] The combination of fulvestrant and anastrozole in first-line[289,289a] therapy led to conflicting results in two studies and was not found beneficial in the second-line setting.[288]

Mammalian Target of Rapamycin (mTOR) Inhibitors

The phosphoinositide-3 kinase (PI3 kinase)-Akt-mTOR pathway is associated with development of endocrine resistance.[290] The addition of mTOR inhibitors to endocrine therapy is thought to reverse endocrine resistance. In the phase III BOLERO-2 trial, 724 postmenopausal women whose disease progressed or recurred while receiving a nonsteroidal AI were randomly assigned to receive the mTOR inhibitor everolimus and exemestane or exemestane alone.[291] The median PFS was improved with combination therapy from 4.1 months to 10.6 months. Everolimus is associated with a relatively common risk of stomatitis and a low, but potentially serious, risk of pneumonitis. Use of a steroidal mouthwash greatly reduces the incidence of stomatitis.[292] Therefore, a combination of everolimus and exemestane is an option for patients with disease progression after a nonsteroidal AI. The combination of everolimus with fulvestrant was also studied in a phase II study involving a population with AI-resistant metastatic breast cancer, resulting in an improvement in PFS from 5.1 months to 10.3 months.[293]

Cyclin-Dependent Kinase 4/6 Inihibitors (CDK 4/6 i)

CDK 4/6 inhibitors interfere with progression from G1 to the S phase of the cell cycle. When CDK4 and CDK6 are activated by D-type cyclins, they phosphorylate the retinoblastoma-associated protein (pRb), releasing pRb's suppression of the E2F transcription factor family. The CDK 4/6 inhibitors prevent progression through this checkpoint, leading to cell cycle arrest.[294]

There are currently three CDK 4/6 inhibitors approved for patients with HR-positive, HER2-negative advanced breast cancer: palbociclib, ribociclib, and abemaciclib. These three were studied as first-line treatment of ER-positive, HER2-negative advanced breast cancer in randomized phase III studies.[295-297] In these trials, patients received either a nonsteroidal AI and placebo or a nonsteroidal AI in combination with a CDK 4/6 inhibitor. In this population with endocrine-sensitive disease (relapse ≥ 12 months after completion of endocrine therapy), the addition of a CDK 4/6 inhibitor consistently resulted in a prolongation of PFS by about 10 months. MONALESSA-3 evaluated the addition of fulvestrant to ribociclib in both first- and second-line therapy.[298] The addition of ribociclib has now shown an improvement in survival, which was 40.0 months with fulvestrant and placebo, and not yet reached in the ribociclib plus fulvestrant arm.[299]

Other studies evaluated the use of CDK 4/6 inhibitors after progression during endocrine therapy. In PALOMA 3, women of any menopausal status and progression of metastatic disease on prior endocrine therapy or recurrence within 12 months of stopping adjuvant endocrine therapy were randomly assigned to receive either palbociclib and fulvestrant or placebo and fulvestrant. Premenopausal women also received goserelin. The median PFS was 9.5 months in the palbociclib group, compared with 4.6 months in the placebo plus fulvestrant group.[300] In the MONARCH-2 trial in which abemaciclib and fulvestrant were compared with placebo and fulvestrant, the median PFS was improved from 9.3 months to 16.9 months, with a significant improvement in the median OS of 9.4 months (from 37.3 months to 46.7 months) with the addition of abemaciclib.[301] Abemaciclib also showed single-agent activity in a single-arm study enrolling heavily pretreated women.[302]

Premenopausal women are commonly offered the same treatment options as those available for postmenopausal women, combined with OFS. MONALESSA-7 compared ribociclib plus endocrine therapy (tamoxifen or a nonsteroidal AI) versus placebo plus endocrine therapy in premenopausal women. All women also received goserelin, and prior endocrine therapy for advanced disease was not allowed. The addition of ribociclib led to an improvement in PFS to 23.8 months compared with 13.0 months in the placebo arm[303,304] and a survival benefit, with 70.2% patients alive at 42 months in the ribociclib group compared with 46.0% in the placebo group.

Despite extensive research, ER expression remains the only known predictive biomarker of response to CDK 4/6 inhibitors. The CDK 4/6 inhibitors as a class are generally well tolerated. The most common adverse effects of these agents include nausea, diarrhea, fatigue, neutropenia, anemia, and thrombocytopenia. Neutropenia is most commonly caused by palbociclib and ribociclib (albeit febrile neutropenia is rare), whereas diarrhea is the most common adverse effect of abemaciclib. Neutropenia is a common reason for dose reduction. Importantly, dose reduction does not seem to decrease the efficacy of palbociclib.[305] Other potential toxicities, including QT prolongation with ribociclib or elevation of aminotransferase levels, can occur and should be monitored in accordance to the agent chosen. The three CDK 4/6 inhibitors are thought to be equivalent in efficacy; therefore, the choice of a particular agent will most often be dictated by differences in toxicity among them. Studies evaluating CDK 4/6 inhibitors are summarized in Table 10-11.

Phosphatidylinositol 3-Kinase (PI3K) Inhibitors

Approximately 40% of HR-positive breast cancers have activating mutations in the *PIK3CA* gene. Alpelisib is an oral, αspecific PI3K inhibitor. In SOLAR-1, a phase III randomized trial, alpelisib and fulvestrant were compared with alpelisib plus placebo in patients with HR-positive, HER2-negative advanced breast cancer who had previously received endocrine therapy.[306] Patients with prior progression on a CDK 4/6 inhibitor were allowed to enroll. Two cohorts were included: those with *PIK3CA* mutation and those with nonmutated *PIK3CA*. At 20 months' follow-up in the cohort of patients with *PIK3CA*-mutated tumors, the PFS was 11.0 months in the alpelisib and fulvestrant arm and 5.7 months in the placebo and fulvestrant arm, but not significantly different in the *PIK3CA*-nonmutated cancer (7.4 months with the addition of alpelisib *v* 5.6 months).

Common adverse events included hyperglycemia (36.6%) and rash (9.9%). On the basis of results from the SOLAR-1 trial, alpelisib was approved by the FDA in 2019 and is an option for patients carrying an activating *PIK3CA* mutation.

Sequencing of Endocrine Therapy

There is little guidance regarding the optimal sequencing of endocrine therapy in metastatic breast cancer. Given its efficacy and favorable toxicity profile, most patients will receive a CDK 4/6 inhibitor for first-line treatment of HR-positive breast cancer. Patients with endocrine-sensitive disease (ie, relapse ≥ 12 months after completion of endocrine therapy) can receive either a nonsteroidal AI or fulvestrant in combination with the CDK 4/6 inhibitor. Patients with endocrine-resistant disease (ie, progression while receiving or within 12 months of receiving an AI) should be treated with a CDK4/6 inhibitor in combination with fulvestrant. There are patients who, because of indolent, low-burden disease or presence of comorbidities, could receive either an AI or fulvestrant alone for first-line treatment. Patients progressing after treatment that includes a CDK 4/6 inhibitor can then be offered everolimus and exemestane before switching to chemotherapy. Alpelisib in combination with fulvestrant or an AI is an option for patients with a *PIK3CA* mutation. Olaparib or talazoparib are options for patients with *BRCA* mutations (Fig 10-8).

Other endocrine therapy options for later lines of treatment include megestrol acetate (progestins), fluoxymesterone (androgens), or estrogen, but these are rarely used, due to a much less favorable efficacy-to-toxicity ratio.

CHEMOTHERAPY

Chemotherapy is the treatment of choice for metastatic HR-negative breast cancer. It is also indicated in HR-positive breast cancer in the setting of rapidly progressing or symptomatic disease, disease associated with visceral crisis, and development of endocrine resistance. Sequential use of single-agent chemotherapy is generally recommended instead of combination chemotherapy regimens (Table 10-12). Although combination chemotherapy is associated with higher chance of response, it is also associated with more toxicity without survival benefit. The exception to this rule is the presence of visceral crisis or rapidly progressive disease that would benefit from prompt cytoreduction.

Table 10-12 summarizes some of the most commonly used chemotherapy agents in metastatic breast cancer. Anthracyclines and taxanes are considered the most active chemotherapies for metastatic breast cancer. Capecitabine, an antimetabolite, is also commonly used in first- or second-line treatment of metastatic disease, given that it is an oral drug and it has a favorable toxicity profile with little alopecia.

The halichondrin B analog eribulin has demonstrated antitumor efficacy in the setting of both anthracycline- and taxane-resistant disease with an improvement in OS compared with physician's choice of chemotherapy (median, 13.1 months *v* 10.6 months).[307]

Other effective single-agent chemotherapies available for patients with prior treatment with anthracyclines and taxanes include gemcitabine (a nucleoside analog) or vinorelbine (a vinca alkaloid) or ixabepilone (epothilone B analog). The platinum salts, such as cisplatin and carboplatin, are DNA-damaging agents that appear to be more effective for the treatment of TNBC, particularly *BRCA*-mutant disease (discussed later in this section).[308]

The duration of treatment must be tailored to each individual patient, considering the toxicity of treatment, control of disease-related symptoms, and patient's goals of treatment and quality of life. Patients whose disease is responding well to chemotherapy without significant toxicity may remain on

Table 10-11 Trials with CDK 4/6 Inhibitors

Treatment	Study	Phase	Description	Median PFS, months (HR, 95% CI)	Median OS, months (HR, 95% CI)
First line	PALOMA-2	III	Palbociclib/letrozole *v* placebo/letrozole	24.8 *v* 14.5s (0.58, 0.46 to 0.72)	Pending
	MONALEESA-2	III	Ribociclib/letrozole *v* placebo/letrozole	25.3 *v* 16.0 (0.56, 0.43 to 0.72)	Pending
	MONALEESA-7	III	Ribociclib/OFS/AI or tamoxifen *v* placebo/ OFS/AI or tamoxifen	23.8 *v* 13.0 (0.55, 0.44 to 0.69)	NR *v* 40.0 (0.71, 0.54 to 0.95)
	MONARCH-3	III	Abemaciclib/AI *v* placebo/AI	NR *v* 14.7 (0.54, 0.41 to 0.72)	Pending
First or second line	MONALEESA-3	III	Ribociclib/fulvestrant *v* Placebo/fulvestrant	20.5 *v* 12.8 (0.59, 0.48-0.73)	40.9 *v* NR (0.72, 0.57-0.92)
Second line	PALOMA-3	III	Palbociclib/fulvestrant *v* placebo/fulvestrant	9.5 *v* 4.6 (0.46, 0.36 to 0.59)	28 *v* 34.9 (0.81, 0.61-1.03)
	MONARCH-2	III	Abemaciclib/fulvestrant *v* placebo/fulvestrant	16.4 *v* 9.3 (0.55, 0.45 to 0.66)	37.3 *v* 46.7 (0.76, 0.61- 0.94)
Later line	MONARCH-1	II	Abemaciclib	6.0	17.7

Abbreviations: AI, aromatase inhibitor; NR, not reached; OFS, ovarian function suppression.

treatment, whereas chemotherapy "holidays" are appropriate for patients who require time to recover from toxicity and whose disease may still be responsive to less toxic targeted therapy, such as endocrine therapy or HER2-directed therapy. Patients with HR-positive or HER2-positive disease who achieve an adequate response can reasonably discontinue chemotherapy and begin or continue a targeted treatment, such as endocrine therapy or HER2-directed therapies, allowing for a break from chemotherapy-related toxicity.

Special considerations regarding the treatment of *BRCA1/2* mutation carriers with metastatic disease include:

- Patients with *BRCA1* and *BRCA2* mutations appear to derive specific benefit from platinum compared with non–*BRCA1/2*-mutation carriers. In the phase III TNT trial,[308] patients with metastatic TNBC were randomly assigned to carboplatin or docetaxel, and carboplatin was not more active than docetaxel in the unselected population. In contrast, in the group of patients with germline *BRCA1* and *BRCA2* mutations, carboplatin had double the objective response rate (ORR) of docetaxel (68% *v* 33%; *P* = .01).
- There are now two PARP inhibitors approved for patients with germline HER2-negative advanced breast cancer with germline *BRCA1* and *BRCA2* mutations: olaparib and talazoparib:

1. The phase III OlympiAD trial evaluated olaparib as monotherapy compared with chemotherapy (physician's choice of capecitabine, eribulin, or vinorelbine) in patients with germline *BRCA*-mutant, HER2-negative advanced breast cancer.[309] Olaparib was associated with an ORR of 60% and a superior median PFS of 7.0 months compared with an ORR of 29% and a median PFS of 4.2 months for patients receiving chemotherapy (hazard ratio, 0.58; *P* = .0009). More low-grade adverse events occurred in those receiving olaparib (primarily nausea and vomiting), whereas there were more high-grade adverse events in those receiving chemotherapy (primarily neutropenia).
2. In the phase III EMBRACA trial,[310] 431 patients with advanced breast cancer and a germline *BRCA1* or *BRCA2* mutation were assigned, in a 2:1 ratio, to receive talazoparib (1 mg once daily) or standard single-agent therapy of the physician's choice. Median PFS was significantly longer in the talazoparib group (8.6 *v* 5.6 months; hazard ratio, 0.54; *P* < .001). Talazoparib caused more grade 3 and 4 anemia than standard chemotherapy (55% *v* 38%), although patient-reported outcomes favored talazoparib.

The role of platinum after progression while being treated with a PARP inhibitor and vice versa is currently unclear, given the concern for similar mechanisms of resistance. It is also unclear what is the optimal sequencing of drugs in the

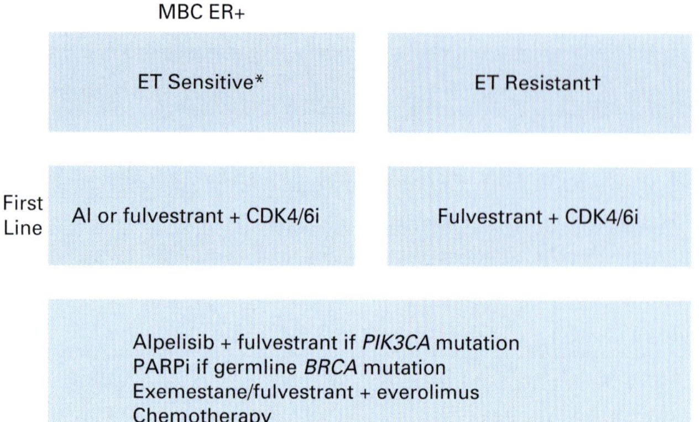

Fig. 10-8 **Suggested treatment sequencing in HR positive metastatic breast cancer.**

BRCA mutation options: olaparib or talazoparib.

*No prior aromatase inhibitor (AI) within 1 year. †Prior AI within 1 year. ET, endocrine therapy; PARPi, PARP inhibitor.

treatment of *BRCA1*- and *BRCA2*- mutation carriers with HER2-negative breast cancer.

HER2-DIRECTED THERAPY

The introduction of HER2 targeted therapy led to an unprecedented survival gain in metastatic disease, compared with the benefit historically reported with chemotherapy alone.

The OS of patients with HER2-positive metastatic breast cancer has increased from 20.3 months reported with chemotherapy alone to the 57.1 months seen with the addition of HER2-targeted therapy (trastuzumab, pertuzumab, and docetaxel in the CLEOPATRA trial).[311-314] Given this survival benefit, most patients with HER2 positive metastatic breast cancer will initiate treatment with chemotherapy in addition to one or more HER2-targeted therapies (Fig 10-9). The following

Table 10-12 Chemotherapy Options for Metastatic Breast Cancer

HER2 Disease Status	Single-Agent or Combination Therapy	Chemotherapy
HER2 negative	Single	Paclitaxel weekly
		Doxorubicin or pegylated liposomal doxorubicin
		Docetaxel, every 21 days
		Nab-paclitaxel, weekly or every 21 days
		Capecitabine
		Gemcitabine
		Vinorelbine
		Eribulin
		Ixabepilone
		Carboplatin
		Cisplatin
	Combination	Ixabepilone/capecitabine
		Gemcitabine/paclitaxel
		Gemcitabine/carboplatin
		Docetaxel/capecitabine
		Metronomic low-dose cyclophosphamide and methotrexate
HER2 positive		Pertuzumab, trastuzumab, and taxane
		Ado-trastuzumab emtansine
		Paclitaxel weekly and trastuzumab
		Vinorelbine and trastuzumab
		Gemcitabine and trastuzumab
		Capecitabine and lapatinib

sections present a summary of the relevant studies in patients with advanced HER2-positive breast cancer (Table 10-13).

First-Line Therapy: Combination of Trastuzumab, Pertuzumab, and a Taxane

The CLEOPATRA trial randomly assigned 808 patients with HER2 positive metastatic breast cancer to receive placebo, trastuzumab and docetaxel or pertuzumab, trastuzumab and docetaxel as first-line treatment. The primary end point was independently assessed PFS. The addition of pertuzumab led to an improvement of 6.1 months (from 12.4 to 18.5 months) in PFS and 16.3 months (from 40.8 to 57.1 months) in OS. The 8-year landmark OS rates were 37% with pertuzumab group and 23% for the control group.[311,316]

Optimal duration of chemotherapy with this regimen is recommended for at least 4 to 6 months or until maximum response, whereas HER2 therapy is continued until disease progression. For patients with HR-positive and HER2-positive disease, endocrine therapy may be added when chemotherapy is discontinued. If a patient completed trastuzumab-based adjuvant treatment in the last 6 months before recurrence (ie, treatment-free interval < 6 months), then second-line therapy should be adopted.

The combination of trastuzumab, pertuzumab, and a taxane is considered optimal first-line therapy per ASCO guidelines.[317-319]

The MARIANNE trial demonstrated that T-DM1 alone or combined with pertuzumab did not result in superior PFS when compared with taxane-based chemotherapy with trastuzumab.[320]

Second-Line Therapy: Trastuzumab Emtansine

The EMILIA study evaluated the effect of T-DM1, an antibody-drug conjugate of trastuzumab and the chemotherapy agent DM1 (T-DM1) Treatment with T-DM1 resulted in a highly significant 3-month improvement in PFS and a 32% reduction in the risk of death compared with lapatinib and capecitabine, with less toxicity. On the basis of the results of the EMILIA study, T-DM1 offers an effective and tolerable option for the treatment of HER2-positive disease that has progressed after trastuzumab and taxane chemotherapy, and it is recommended as a second-line treatment per ASCO guidelines.[318]

Third-Line Therapy and Beyond

The TH3RESA study showed superiority of T-DM1 compared with the treatment of physician's choice, with approximately 30% of the patients enrolled having received more than five prior regimens for recurrent disease.[321]

Lapatinib is effective in the treatment of HER2-positive metastatic breast cancer, when administered either in combination with trastuzumab or in combination with capecitabine.[322,323] The GBG 26/BIG 3-05 study confirmed the benefit of continuing trastuzumab with alternative chemotherapy after disease progression with combination chemotherapy and trastuzumab. On the basis of these data, continuing trastuzumab beyond progression is considered standard of care.[324]

Approximately 45% of HER2-positive breast cancer is also HR-positive, and targeted therapy for both receptors is indicated. Crosstalk exists between HER2 and the ER, resulting in relative resistance to endocrine therapy alone in HER2-positive disease. In clinical trials, the addition of trastuzumab to anastrozole, and lapatinib to letrozole, resulted in a significant but modestly improved PFS and clinical benefit compared with endocrine treatment alone in patients with HR-positive, HER2-positive metastatic disease. However, an OS advantage was not seen, possibly because of the crossover study designs.[325]

IMMUNOTHERAPY

The efficacy of single-agent immune checkpoint inhibitors in TNBC was disappointing.[326,327] In a randomized trial (IMpassion 130), 902 patients with untreated metastatic TNBC were randomly assigned to receive nabpaclitaxel with the PD-L1 antibody atezolizumab or placebo.[328] The median PFS in the overall population was 7.2 months in the atezolizumab group versus 5.5 months in the placebo group, and the median OS was 21.3 months versus 17.6 months, respectively. However, among patients whose tumors expressed PD-L1, the median OS was 25.0 months and 15.5 months, respectively. Grade 3 or higher adverse events were more common in the atezolizumab arm (49% *v* 42%), with neutropenia, peripheral neuropathy, fatigue, and anemia being the most common events. There were three treatment-related deaths among the 451 patients who received atezolizumab (0.7%). On the basis of these results, the FDA granted accelerated approval to atezolizumab in combination with nabpaclitaxel for patients with unresectable locally advanced or metastatic TNBC whose tumors express PD-L1 (Fig 10-10).

BRAIN METASTASES

Although rare in patients with localized disease, brain metastases are diagnosed in approximately 15% of patients with metastatic disease,[329] and have become more common with the improvement in systemic therapies. The risk of brain metastases is greater in patients with TNBC and HER2-positive breast cancer. Recommendations regarding presentation, diagnosis, symptomatic control, and supportive care of brain metastases are discussed in Chapter 18 (Central Nervous System Tumors).

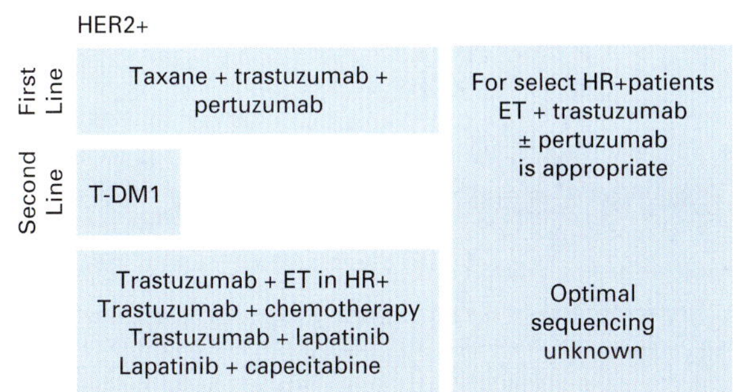

Fig. 10-9 Suggested treatment sequencing in HER2 positive metastatic breast cancer.

Abbreviations: ET, endocrine therapy; HR, hormone receptor; T-DM1, ado-trastuzumab emtansine.

Table 10-13 **Phase III Trials in HER2 Metastatic Breast Cancer**

Trial	Line of Therapy	No. of Patients	Study Arms	Main Results
CLEOPATRA	First	808	Docetaxel and trastuzumab *v* docetaxel and trastuzumab and pertuzumab	PFS: 12.5 *v* 18.5 months (HR, 0.62; *P* < .001) OS: 40.8 *v* 57.1 months (HR, 0.69; 95% CI, 0.58 to 0.82)
MARIANNE	First	1,095	Trastuzumab and taxane *v* T-DM1 *v* T-DM1 and pertuzumab	OS: 50.9 *v* 53.7 *v* 51.8 months Compared with the HT group, HR, 0.93 (97.5% CI, 0.73 to 1.20) for T-DM1 and 0.86 (97.5% CI, 0.67 to 1.11) for T-DM1+pertuzumab
EMILIA	Second	978	T-DM1 *v* capecitabine and lapatinib	PFS: 10 *v* 6 months (HR, 0.65; 95% CI, 0.55 to 0.77) OS: 31 *v* 25 months (HR, 0.68; 95% CI, 0.55 to 0.85)
TH3RESA	≥ Third	602	T-DM1 *v* physician's choice therapy	PFS: 6.2 *v* 3.3 months; HR, 0.53; 95% CI 0.42 to 0.66 OS: 22.7 *v* 15.8 months; HR, 0.68, 95% CI, 0.54 to 0.85
EGF100151[315]	Required previous treatment with an anthracycline, a taxane, and trastuzumab	399	Lapatinib and capecitabine *v* capecitabine	TTP: 8.4 *v* 4.4 months; HR, 0.49; 95% CI, 0.34 to 0.71; *P* < .001 OS: 75.0 *v* 64.7 weeks (HR, 0.87; 95% CI, 0.71-1.08; *P* = .210)

Abbreviations: HR, hazard ratio; OS, overall survival; PFS, progression-free survival; TTP, time to progression.

The approach of brain metastases in breast cancer is determined by the tumor subtype and overall prognosis. Patients with good performance status and controlled systemic disease benefit from aggressive treatment with the goal of optimal local control. Options for local treatment include surgery, stereotactic radiation, and whole-brain radiotherapy (WBRT), with the following recommendations:

- Surgery should be strongly considered in patients presenting with a single metastasis and stable or absent extracranial disease.[330]
- Surgery has a limited role in patients with more than one brain metastasis, except when a large, symptomatic lesion is also present.
- In the presence of multiple lesions, either stereotactic radiosurgery, WBRT, or the combination are usually preferred.

WBRT decreases the risk of intracranial recurrence but does not appear to increase survival, and stereotactic radiosurgery is often preferred to decrease the risk of neurocognitive impairment associated with WBRT.[331] There are no FDA-approved systemic therapies at this time for the treatment of breast cancer brain metastases. Limited data suggest CNS activity of several chemotherapy agents, likely due to disruption of the blood-brain barrier. Responses to tamoxifen and aromatase inhibitors have also been reported.

Brain metastases are common during the course of HER2-positive metastatic breast cancer.[280] They often occur despite optimal systemic control, likely because trastuzumab does not cross an intact blood-brain barrier. Patients with systemic disease that is not progressive at the time of diagnosis of brain metastases should continue to receive the same systemic therapy.[332] In the LANDSCAPE trial, the combination of lapatinib and capecitabine was active in patients with previously untreated metastatic brain disease,[333] but this regimen has not yet been compared with WBRT. In the TBCRC 022 study, the combination of neratinib and capecitabine was associated

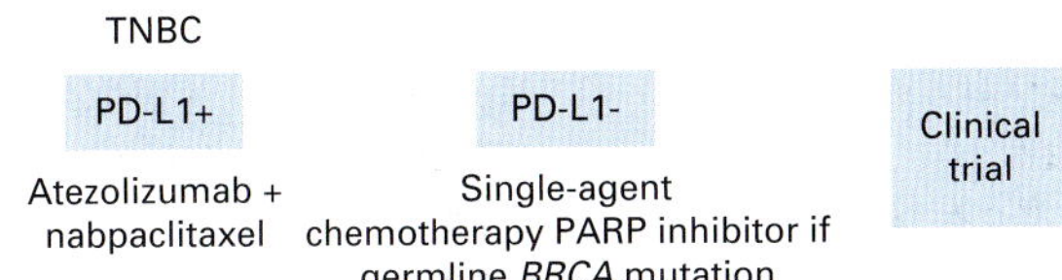

Fig. 10-10 Suggested treatment opinions in triple negative metastatic breast cancer.

with a PFS of 5.5 months in patients with refractory brain metastases and no prior treatment with lapatinib.[261] For patients with brain metastases and poor performance status or uncontrolled systemic disease, the goal of treatment should be optimal palliation.

GENOMIC PROFILING IN METASTATIC BREAST CANCER

The Cancer Genome Atlas led to significant advances in characterizing the genomic diversity of breast cancer. Formerly exclusively a research tool, the use of next-generation sequencing (NGS) to detect somatic mutations is now available through several commercial panels, which test tumor tissue and, more recently, circulating tumor DNA in blood.

Studies evaluating targeted therapy commonly use NGS to select a population more likely to benefit from the therapy tested.

This strategy led to the approval of alpelisib in combination with fulvestrant for HR-positive, HER2-negative metastatic breast cancer with a *PIK3CA* mutation, the most common mutation in HR-positive breast cancer (see the PI3K Inhibitors section). Additional, potentially actionable findings in HR-positive breast cancer include *ESR1* mutations (suggesting resistance to AIs) and *HER2* mutations (predicting possible benefit with HER2-targeted therapy). In TNBC and HR-positive breast cancer, studies with agents targeting AKT1 (ipatasertib and capivasertib) are ongoing.

Although NGS panels are used to detect somatic mutations, occasionally they lead to the finding of germline mutations in patients who had not been previously tested.

With data demonstrating a benefit for mutation-driven therapy (and new drugs being approved as a result), NGS will likely become a routine tool to select treatment options in breast cancer. Many institutions have now molecular tumor boards to provide guidance in interpreting these results, but as of yet, outside of a clinical trial or approved indications, the results of NSG should not be used to determine treatment decisions.

KEY POINTS

- Metastatic breast cancer is incurable; therefore, the goal of treatment is to control disease progression and improve quality of life.
- The choice of systemic therapy is based on the HR and HER2 status, as well as the extent of metastatic disease, effect of disease on quality of life (eg, symptoms, performance status), and pace of metastatic disease.
- Endocrine therapy with a CDK 4/6 inhibitor is the preferred initial treatment of HR-positive, HER2-negative metastatic disease, unless visceral crisis or extensive visceral involvement is present.
- Sequential single-agent chemotherapy is preferable to combination chemotherapy, unless a rapid disease response is required.
- Combined treatment with pertuzumab, trastuzumab, and taxane is the recommended first-line therapy for HER2-positive metastatic disease.
- Atezolizumab is approved for use with nabpaclitaxel in patients with advanced TNBC and PDL1 expression ≥ 1%.
- Patients with brain metastases and good performance status benefit from local control with either surgery, WBRT, or stereotactic radiosurgery.

BONE-MODIFYING AGENTS

Metastatic Treatment

Approximately 65% to 80% of patients with metastatic breast cancer will have bone metastases. Bone metastases most commonly occur among patients with HR-positive cancer. Although bone involvement is associated with a more favorable prognosis than visceral metastases, patients are at higher risk of skeletal-related events (SREs) including pain, pathologic fracture, hypercalcemia, and spinal cord compression. Breast cancer that metastasizes to bone is treated with appropriate systemic therapy. Palliative radiation therapy to specific sites of disease can reduce the morbidity associated with pain and fracture, as well as control disease that may compromise the spinal cord.

Metastases to the bone can produce osteoblastic or osteolytic lesions, both of which are associated with activation of osteoclasts. Breast cancer cells involving the bone can also secrete cytokines that stimulate receptor activator of nuclear factor κ B ligand (RANKL) secretion by osteoblasts, which mediates osteoclast survival. Bisphosphonates are pyrophosphate analogs that are internalized by osteoclasts, which disrupt their function and result in apoptosis. Clinically available bisphosphonates (eg, pamidronate, zoledronate) reduce the incidence of SREs and the time to occurrence of SREs.[334]

In a combined analysis of patients with bone metastases that included 2,046 women with metastatic breast cancer, the RANKL inhibitor denosumab delayed time to first on-study SRE by a median of 8.21 months longer than zoledronic acid and reduced the risk of first SRE by 17% (hazard ratio, 0.83; $P \leq .001$). However, disease progression and OS were similar between both treatments.[335] Zoledronic acid use was associated with renal compromise, whereas hypocalcemia was more common with denosumab. Zoledronic acid is favored over pamidronate because of its ease of infusion.

Calcium and vitamin D supplementation should be used for patients receiving all bone-modifying agents, and renal function should be monitored in patients receiving bisphosphonates. Both drugs are associated with a 2% incidence of osteonecrosis of the jaw; ideally, physicians should avoid administering these agents to patients for an undefined period before or after any invasive dental procedure that involves manipulation of the bone.

Dosing-interval studies were recently reported for zoledronic acid. A randomized trial that evaluated the use of a second year of zoledronic acid, after a year of monthly dosing, demonstrated that dosing zoledronic acid monthly was equivalent to dosing every 3 months.[336] A randomized trial that compared upfront zoledronic acid at monthly versus quarterly intervals for 2 years also demonstrated equivalence.[337] Results from the Swiss REDUSE trial in which denosumab every 12 weeks was compared with every 4 weeks after an induction phase which included four doses given every 4 weeks in patients with metastatic solid tumors are awaited.

According to the ASCO guidelines, bone-modifying agents (ie, bisphosphonates and RANKL inhibitors) are recommended for patients with evidence of bone destruction. Options include the following:[338]

- denosumab, 120 mg subcutaneously, every 4 weeks;
- pamidronate, 90 mg intravenously, every 3 to 4 weeks; and
- zoledronic acid, 4 mg intravenously every 12 weeks or every 3 to 4 weeks.

The optimal duration of treatment with either a bisphosphonate or denosumab is unknown because the therapeutic intervals in published studies vary from 3 months to indefinitely. The ASCO guideline recommends indefinite use of bone-modifying agents until evidence of substantial decline in a patient's general performance status.[338] Two years may also be a reasonable duration for this treatment.[337]

Adjuvant Treatment

Multiple clinical trials have been conducted to determine the role of bisphosphonates in the adjuvant setting to decrease the development of metastatic disease. Data are conflicting, as evident in the following:

- The AZURE trial showed no overall effect of zoledronic acid on invasive DFS among 3,360 patients with stages II and III disease who received chemotherapy. However, zoledronic acid reduced the development of bone metastases and improved invasive DFS in women who were postmenopausal for at least 5 years before enrollment.[339,340]
- In the ABCSG-12 trial, use of zoledronic acid was associated with a 36% reduction in risk of disease recurrence among 1,803 premenopausal women with stages I and II disease who received ovarian suppression and endocrine therapy.[341]
- A meta-analysis of 17 trials with > 21,000 patients demonstrated a 3.5% absolute reduction in the risk of distant relapse, predominantly bone-metastatic relapse, as well as a 2.3% absolute improvement in all-cause mortality (ie, OS) among postmenopausal women who received adjuvant bisphosphonate.[342]

In 2017, Cancer Care Ontario and ASCO published an evidence-based guideline informed by a systematic review of the literature.[343] The guideline recommends that bisphosphonates (ie, zoledronic acid or clodronate) be considered adjuvant therapy for postmenopausal patients (natural or induced menopause) who are deemed candidates for systemic therapy. The guideline also noted that long-term survival data for adjuvant denosumab are still lacking.

KEY POINTS

- Bisphosphonates or denosumab decrease SREs when bone metastases are present.
- Adjuvant bisphosphonates have been associated with a reduction in risk of recurrence and improvement in OS. They should be considered for postmenopausal patients who are candidates for adjuvant systemic therapy.
- Renal function should be monitored with bisphosphonate use.
- Calcium and vitamin D supplementation should be strongly considered for patients receiving bone-modifying agents.

SURVEILLANCE AND SURVIVORSHIP

There are > 3.1 million breast cancer survivors in the United States. The primary goal of surveillance after completion of adjuvant therapy is to detect a new and curable cancer at an early stage. ASCO recommendations for surveillance, detailed in Table 10-14, include:

- A history and physical examination every 3 to 6 months for the first 3 years and then every 6 to 12 months for the next 2 years.
- Mammographic imaging of the affected breast should be done yearly. Patients should wait 6 to 12 months after the completion of radiation therapy to start annual mammogram surveillance.

Additional breast imaging is not usually indicated, with exceptions of women with hereditary breast cancer syndromes or those who had significant medical radiation exposure. The use of other imaging, tumor markers, or laboratory tests among asymptomatic patients has not been found to be beneficial and has been shown to adversely affect quality of life and increase downstream health care use.[344] The surveillance time should also be used to ensure that appropriate referrals for genetic counseling are made. Patients with genetic risks should be screened for second primary cancers, as outlined in the section titled Screening.

Most breast cancer recurrences are often identified between office visits; therefore, it is crucial to focus on patient education concerning signs and symptoms of disease recurrence. Once symptoms occur, appropriate imaging should be performed.

Clinical outcomes are identical when patients continue their post-treatment surveillance with either their oncologist or primary care provider. Understanding potential long-term complications of treatment is important. Chemotherapy-induced amenorrhea or ovarian suppression can result in the onset of menopausal symptoms at an earlier-than-expected age. Hot flashes can often be controlled with venlafaxine or gabapentin. Oxybutynin has also been found to be superior to placebo for management of hot flashes.[345] Intravaginal application of estrogens to improve vaginal dryness and sexual dysfunction can be considered but require a discussion with patients, particularly in patients with HR-positive disease taking AIs, because the safety of intravaginal estrogens' is not clearly established.[346] The use of AIs can adversely affect bone density, which should be closely monitored. Awareness of potential cardiac toxicity from anthracyclines and trastuzumab may require the involvement of cardiologists.[347]

Focusing on healthy activities, such as exercise and maintaining a normal body mass index, appear to favorably affect the risk of disease recurrence or improve well-being. Cognitive dysfunction associated with cancer therapy is a subject of ongoing investigation.[348] The psychosocial ramifications following the diagnosis and treatment of breast cancer cannot be minimized and may require ongoing support and therapy. In 2016, ASCO and the American Cancer Society developed a comprehensive set of recommendations that extend beyond cancer surveillance recommendations to further address symptom management, surveillance and management of late toxicities of cancer therapy, and general wellness (eg, weight management, nutrition, activity) recommendations.[349]

KEY POINTS

- The primary schedule of disease monitoring after the completion of therapy includes an annual mammogram and a complete history and physical examination every 3 to 6 months for the first 3 years and then every 6 to 12 months for the next 2 years.
- Anthracyclines and trastuzumab are associated with a risk of cardiac toxicity.
- Aromatase inhibitors are associated with decreased bone density.
- Chemotherapy and OFS can result in premature amenorrhea, resulting in menopausal symptoms such as hot flashes, vaginal dryness, and sexual dysfunction, and affect bone health.

SPECIAL CIRCUMSTANCES

MALE BREAST CANCER

Male breast cancer is rare, accounting for approximately 1% of all breast cancers.[350] Most cases of breast cancer in men are invasive ductal carcinoma, and other histologic subtypes are rare. Presentation as DCIS is also uncommon. Male breast cancer is almost always ER positive. In a large series of male breast cancer, only 9% of cancers were HER2-positive.[351] Risk factors for male breast cancer are discussed in the Risk Factors section of this chapter.

Most men with breast cancer present with a retroareoalar mass, but nipple changes and axillary adenopathy are also common. Because of the lack of awareness and early detection, men often present with larger tumors and nodal involvement.

The optimal local and systemic treatments of male breast cancer have not been studied in randomized clinical trials. Mastectomy is often performed, although BCT can be offered if standard criteria for BCT are met. In general, recommendations for local disease treatment should be governed by the same criteria outlined for breast cancer in women.

Adjuvant chemotherapy also should be administered using the same criteria used for women. Tamoxifen is the mainstay of endocrine therapy in HR-positive male breast cancer. The efficacy of AIs in men is not well established and may be lower than in women, due to incomplete estradiol suppression.[350] In men with contraindications for tamoxifen, AIs should be combined with gonadotropin-releasing hormone (GnRH) analogs to ensure estradiol suppression.[352] There are limited data on the activity of AIs with or without GnRH agonists and fulvestrant in men with HR-positive metastatic breast cancer. Palbociclib is approved for use in men, primarily based on the results of the PALOMA-2 and PALOMA-3 trials and supported by real-world data.[353]

PREGNANCY-ASSOCIATED BREAST CANCER

Cancer during pregnancy is rare, affecting approximately one in every 1,000 pregnancies. Breast cancer is responsible for approximately 25% of cases.[354] Two recent studies that compared women with breast cancer who received chemotherapy during pregnancy with women who were not pregnant at the time of diagnosis found no negative impact on outcome for women diagnosed during pregnancy.[355,356]

In general, the same treatment recommendations apply as to nonpregnant women, with some exceptions to protect the fetus. The elected strategy should also plan for optimal timing and sequencing of local and systemic therapies to avoid delays in treatment and optimize outcome. The appropriate treatment should be determined in conjunction with an obstetrician who specializes in high-risk cases.

Following is a summary of these recommendations:

- BCS or mastectomy are reasonable options for pregnant women with breast cancer. There is controversy regarding axillary node evaluation.
- If radiation therapy is recommended, it should be administered after delivery.
- Chemotherapy, if indicated, can be safely administered from week 14 and until 3 to 4 weeks before delivery.
- The use of anthracyclines, cyclophosphamide, and taxanes appears feasible and safe during the second and third

Table 10-14 **ASCO Recommendations for Follow-Up Care of Patients With Primary Breast Cancer**[362]

Mode of Surveillance	Summary of Recommendations
Breast cancer surveillance: recommended	
History/physical examination	Every 3 to 6 months for the first 3 years after primary therapy; every 6 to 12 months for years 4 and 5; then annually
Patient education regarding symptoms of recurrence	Physicians should counsel patients about the symptoms of recurrence, including new lumps, bone pain, chest pain, abdominal pain, dyspnea, or persistent headaches; helpful websites for patient education include www.cancer.net and www.cancer.org
Referral for genetic counseling	Criteria include Ashkenazi Jewish heritage; history of ovarian cancer at any age in the patient or any first- or second-degree relatives; any first-degree relative with a history of breast cancer diagnosed before age 50 years; two or more first- or second-degree relatives diagnosed with breast cancer at any age; patient or relative with diagnosis of bilateral breast cancer; and history of breast cancer in a male relative
Breast self-examination	All women should be counseled to perform monthly breast self-examination
Mammography	First post-treatment mammogram 1 year after the initial mammogram that leads to diagnosis but no earlier than 6 months after definitive radiation therapy; subsequent mammograms should be obtained as indicated for surveillance of abnormalities
Coordination of care	Continuity of care is encouraged and should be performed by a physician experienced in the surveillance of patients with cancer and in breast examination, including the examination of irradiated breasts; if follow-up is transferred to a PCP, the PCP and the patient should be informed of the long-term options regarding adjuvant hormone therapy for the particular patient; this may necessitate referral for oncology assessment at an interval consistent with guidelines for adjuvant hormone therapy
Pelvic examination	Regular gynecologic follow-up is recommended for all women; patients who receive tamoxifen should be advised to report any vaginal bleeding to their physicians
Breast cancer surveillance testing: not recommended	
Routine blood tests	CBC counts and liver function tests are not recommended
Breast MRI	Breast MRI is not recommended for routine breast cancer surveillance; MRI may be considered on an individual basis for high-risk women
Systemic imaging studies	Chest radiograph, bone scans, liver ultrasound, CT scans, and FDG-PET scans are not recommended
Tumor markers	CA 15-3, CA 27-29, and carcinoembryonic antigen testing are not recommended

Abbreviations: CT, computed tomography; FDG-PET, fluorodeoxyglucose positron-emission tomography; MRI, magnetic resonance imaging; PCP, primary care physician.

trimesters of pregnancy with minimal maternal, fetal, or neonatal toxicity.[357,358]

- Trastuzumab is contraindicated during pregnancy (category D) and labeling contains a black-box warning about the risk for oligohydramnios and related pulmonary hypoplasia, skeletal abnormalities, and neonatal death
- Neonatal morbidity appears to be mainly related to prematurity; therefore, if possible, delivery should not be induced before 37 weeks.
- Administration of granulocyte colony–stimulating factor during pregnancy seems to be safe, based on retrospective review of limited number of patients.[359]

OLDER PATIENTS

There has been an increase in breast cancer in older adults in the United States. Comorbidities are more common in older adults and are independent predictors of worse survival. However, among healthy older women, chemotherapy regimens given without dose reduction impart the same relative benefit as in younger women.[360] Older women can be more susceptible to some toxicities associated with chemotherapy, including hematologic and cardiac toxicities.[361]

An adequate interpretation of chemotherapy benefit among high-risk older women is difficult to make, given that women older than 65 years make up only 8% of enrollment in clinical trials. The CALGB 49907 trial randomly assigned 633 women older than 65 years to receive adjuvant therapy with capecitabine or the standard AC or cyclophosphamide, methotrexate, and fluorouracil (CMF) regimens.[362] Two-thirds of the women were older than 70 years, and 5% were older than 80 years. The standard regimens of AC and CMF were associated with a 50% lower risk of recurrence or death compared with the less toxic oral capecitabine regimen. These data continue to support the benefit of standard chemotherapy in healthy elderly women who do not have substantial comorbidities.

In order to better understand their overall health status, ASCO recommends performing a geriatric assessment in all older patients with cancer.[363] The geriatric assessment is a multidimensional evaluation which can help unravel the functional, nutritional, psychological, cognitive, and social characteristics of older adults, and identify deficits undetected by usual oncological evaluations.[363] This information can help guide treaments by allowing for an estimation of non cancer-specific life expectancy, as well as of the risk of chemotherapy toxicity.[364,365] Ongoing efforts for the tailoring of treatment for older women with breast cancer include the design of a breast cancer-specific chemotherapy toxicity calculator, which utilizes geriatric assessment variables to predict the risk of Grade 3-4 toxicity.[366]

PHYLLODES TUMOR

Phyllodes tumors of the breast contain both stromal and epithelial components. They are classified as benign, borderline, or malignant. Their prognosis depends largely on the status of surgical margins after resection. The greatest risk of recurrence is local, although metastasis can occur, primarily to the lungs. The primary treatment of a phyllodes tumor is surgical—either with excision or mastectomy—with the intent of obtaining margins > 1 cm.[46] ALND is not indicated; neither is routine adjuvant systemic therapy or radiotherapy. Because this tumor behaves primarily like a stromal malignancy, options for the treatment of metastatic disease can be based on therapies for soft-tissue sarcomas.

KEY POINTS

- The treatment of male breast cancer is extrapolated from information about female breast cancer, with tamoxifen as the preferred agent for adjuvant endocrine therapy.
- There are limited data supporting the use of AIs for the treatment of metastatic disease in men.
- Performance status, comorbidities, and life expectancy, but not age, should be the deciding factors for adjuvant therapy recommendations for breast cancer.
- Breast cancer during pregnancy should be treated with the goal of minimizing fetal harm while ensuring the best oncologic outcomes.

Acknowledgment

The following authors are acknowledged and graciously thanked for their contribution to prior versions of this chapter: Lisa A. Carey, MD, FASCO; Beth Overmoyer, MD; Eric Winer, MD, FASCO; Tufia Haddad, MD; and Charles Loprinzi, MD, FASCO. The authors recognize the contributions of colleagues who have provided thoughtful review and content for this chapter, including Claudine Isaacs, MD; Jean Wright, MD; and Enrique Soto, MD. They also recognize the reviewers for their effort and critical feedback to enhance the chapter.

Global Perspective: Breast Cancer

Evangelia Razis, MD, PhD (Hygeia Hospital, Athens, Greece)

EPIDEMIOLOGY AND SCREENING

Breast cancer is the most common cancer in women worldwide (25.2% of all cancers)[367] and the primary cause of cancer-related deaths in women in Europe, as well as in the Mediterranean basin. Age-standardized breast cancer incidence rates are higher in western Europe than in the United States.[368] Of note, breast cancer mortality rates increased in most European countries until the 1990s, and they have been falling since, but is still estimated to have claimed the lives of > 150,000 women in Europe in 2018.[368] In fact, the incidence of breast cancer is higher in Europe and the Americas than in Asia and Africa, but the incidence of breast cancer is rising globally, with a most rapid increase in low- and middle-income countries (LMICs), and the disease burden is likely to be highest in those countries in the coming decades (Fig 10-11).[369]

There is large variation in screening programs within Europe, ranging from Scandinavian programs that invite all women between a certain age range for regular screening to countries without state-organized screening.[370] Australia, on the other hand, has a well-organized national breast cancer screening program.[371] Meanwhile, breast cancer is increasingly more prevalent in Asia and South America as well as the Middle East, and some countries in these areas are trying to establish formal screening programs, while others are at least setting up opportunistic or targeted screening.[372,373] Finally, sub-Saharan African countries do not have screening programs yet, despite the rapidly increasing incidence of the disease in the area.[374] Unfortunately, women in these regions are not always aware or accepting of the need for screening.[375] Recently, there has been a trend toward less screening, based on studies that showed regular screening may lead to overdiagnosis.[376] Thus, there is a trend toward reduced screening in some European countries that have previously been organized in this regard.

Though the biology of breast cancer is not notably different between the United States and Europe, breast cancer in Africa seems to occur more frequently in premenopausal women and there is an impression that more aggressive types of breast cancer may be more prevalent in sub-Saharan Africa.[369] However, not enough data are available to confirm this observation.

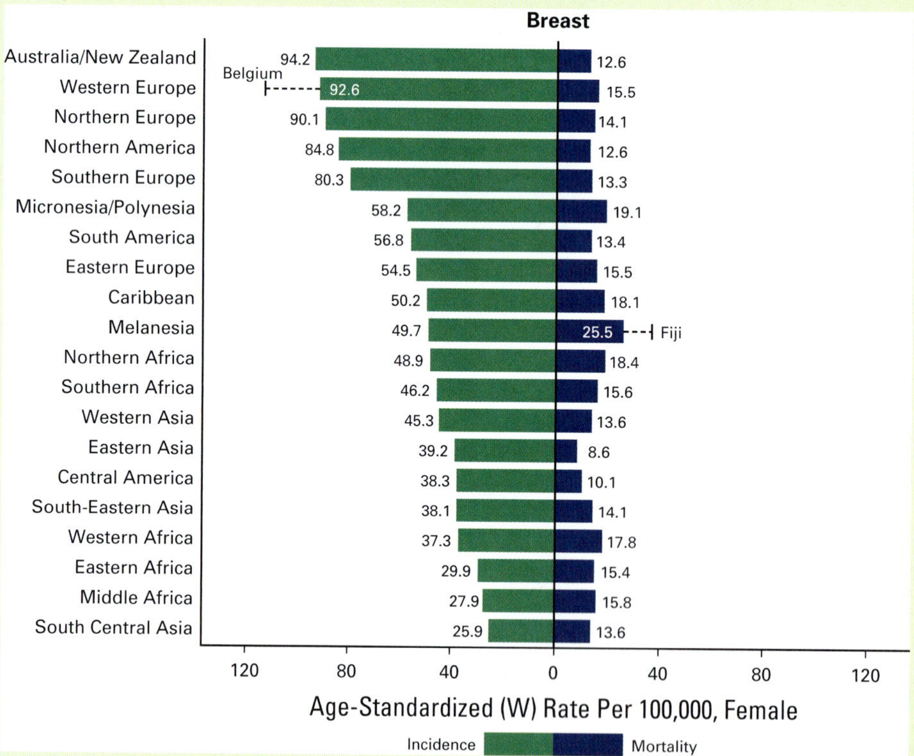

Fig. 10-11 Region-specific incidence and mortality age-standardized rates for cancers of the female breast in 2018. Rates are shown in descending order of the world (W) age-standardized rate; the highest national age-standardized rates for incidence and mortality are superimposed.[1]

Lifestyle, and particularly obesity, may contribute to increasing incidence of postmenopausal breast cancer in high- and upper middle–income countries,[377] although obesity does not appear to affect the incidence of premenopausal breast cancer. Lifestyle changes are thought to affect the incidence of breast cancer in Asian women who move to the West, thus implying that the "westernized" way of life may translate to increased global breast cancer burden with time, especially in countries with previously low breast cancer incidence rates.[378]

Genetic predisposition contributes to a similar extent to the incidence of breast cancer in the United States and in Europe, but the impact of genetic predisposition is unknown in Africa. Regarding stage at diagnosis, overall, there are no major differences between Europe and the United States, but in some Eastern European countries, there is still limited screening and thus more advanced disease stage at diagnosis.[379] This, together with a lower expenditure for health care leading to inferior therapeutic interventions, is thought to lead to lower 5-year survival rates in the Eastern European population, according to a recent study.[379] In this study, trends in breast cancer survival in Europe appeared to be lower than in the United States because of the contribution of Eastern European countries.[379]

BREAST CANCER TREATMENT IN EUROPE AND THE UNITED STATES

Management of breast cancer does not differ significantly between countries in western Europe and the United States, but some differences do exist:

- In early disease, there appears to be a lower rate of contralateral prophylactic mastectomies in Europe and higher use of BCT for breast cancer in Europe compared with the United States, at least until the early years of the 2010s.[380]
- The most recent European Society of Medical Oncology (ESMO) guidelines on radiotherapy in breast cancer, issued in 2019,[381] finally endorse the hypofractionated protocols. More recent scientific data prompted adoption of hypofractionated radiotherapy in the clinic, even before it was incorporated in the guidelines.[382]
- The use of neoadjuvant or adjuvant pertuzumab with trastuzumab for early disease, as well as the use of T-DM1 and neratinib for residual disease after preoperative anti-HER2 therapy, are incorporated in the 2019 ESMO guidelines. The addition of pertuzumab to trastuzumab is recommended for high-risk patients who are HER2 positive (ie, ER negative, node positive) with some reservation, because of the score in the ESMO Magnitude of Clinical Benefit Scale (MCBS), and 18 cycles are recommended without specifying before and/or after surgery.
- The ESMO guidelines loosely recommend the use of multigene predictors of chemotherapy benefit (ie., the guidelines state they "can be used"[381]), since the reporting of data from prospective studies such as TAILORx[383] and MINDACT[137] became available, for "cases of uncertainty" regarding chemotherapy benefit.[381]
- In the field of adjuvant endocrine therapy, the SOFT and TEXT trial[384] data have been adopted by most and are now incorporated in the guidelines; the use of adjuvant bisphosphonates is recommended for postmenopausal women.

No clear trend differences have been identified between Europe and the United States in the adoption of newer approaches to the management of the axilla.

Of great interest is the European use of the ESMO-MCBS.[385,386] Originally published in 2015, this tool enables quantitative assessment of the clinical benefit offered by a new therapy compared with a previous one. This is not exclusive to breast cancer, but it is applied to breast cancer studies as well, and it is used in the composition of guidelines. The most recent ESMO guidelines for advanced breast cancer reflect that change.[387] Of note, ASCO has also published a Value Framework,[388] which includes cost, and the two scales have marked similarity, as shown in a comparator study published in the *Journal of Clinical Oncology* in 2018.[389]

Besides the incorporation of the ESMO MCBS, the recent guidelines regarding advanced breast cancer are characterized by their all-encompassing approach, starting with the psychosocial and palliative care of the patient.[387] Management also includes supportive care recommendations. Though the European guidelines largely overlap with those of the United States, some differences exist:

- There is explicit recommendation for the use of biosimilars for both treatment (trastuzumab) and supportive care (growth factors) in Europe, but not in the United States.
- In advanced breast cancer, bevacizumab is still considered appropriate in some cases in Europe, but it is not used in the United States.
- There is a recommendation for metronomic therapy in the European advanced breast cancer guidelines, whereas in the NCCN guidelines, there is only mention of continuous low-dose regimens.
- The European guidelines explicitly mention complementary medicine approaches that may be useful in advanced breast cancer.

BREAST CANCER IN LIMITED-RESOURCE SETTINGS

In settings of limited resources, there is a lack of screening and delayed diagnosis, leading to increased mortality incidence.[390] In very low-income countries, there is even a lack of breast cancer subtype determination by IHC, and the use of antiestrogens may be recommended without proof of HR positivity.[391] When it comes to therapy, lack of radiotherapy centers or difficulty in accessing the few that are available makes breast conservation impossible. Most advanced medication is not available in these areas or cost renders them inaccessible to most women. Finally, the stigma associated with a cancer diagnosis makes most women avoid seeking care until it is too late. Of note, there are several efforts to create resource-stratified guidelines for screening and therapy.[392]

In summary, breast cancer is a global issue of increasing importance in LMICs. Management in Europe is similar to that in North America, while the rest of the world would greatly benefit from increased awareness and screening for diagnosis at earlier stages.

11

LUNG CANCER

Stephen V. Liu, MD

Recent Updates

- Immunotherapy continues to improve outcomes in non–small-cell lung cancer (NSCLC). The US Food and Drug Administration (FDA) has approved several chemoimmunotherapy combinations (independent of PD-L1 expression) for patients with advanced NSCLC after demonstrating improvement in overall survival compared with chemotherapy alone. The combination of carboplatin, pemetrexed, and pembrolizumab (Gandhi L, *N Engl J Med* 2018) and the four-drug regimen of carboplatin, paclitaxel, bevacizumab, and atezolizumab (Socinski M, *N Engl J Med* 2018) are approved for patients with nonsquamous NSCLC, and carboplatin with paclitaxel or nab-paclitaxel and pembrolizumab is approved for patients with squamous NSCLC. (Paz-Ares L, *N Engl J Med* 2018)
- The addition of the atezolizumab to standard carboplatin plus etoposide for extensive-stage small-cell lung cancer was approved on the basis of an improvement in progression-free survival and overall survival. (Horn L, *N Engl J Med* 2018)
- After definitive chemoradiation for unresectable stage III NSCLC, consolidation therapy with durvalumab led to a significant improvement in overall survival and FDA approval. (Antonia S, *N Engl J Med* 2018)
- Larotrectinib (Drilon A, *N Engl J Med* 2018) and entrectinib (Paz-Ares L, *Ann Oncol* 2019) both received tumor-agnostic FDA approval for the treatment of cancers harboring a fusion in *NTRK1-3*, after demonstrating high response rates across tumor types, including NSCLC.

OVERVIEW

There were an estimated 228,150 new cases of lung cancer in the United States in 2019, making it the second most common cancer in men (behind prostate cancer) and women (behind breast cancer).[1] It is, by far, the most lethal cancer, with approximately 154,000 deaths annually, or approximately 25% of all cancer deaths. More women die of lung cancer each year than of breast, cervical, and uterine cancers combined; more men die annually of lung cancer than of colorectal, prostate, and pancreatic cancers combined. Although there have been important advances in the management of lung cancer, the overall 5-year survival remains only 19% for all stages combined. The incidence of lung cancer has been decreasing for men and women, though there had been an increase in women until 2000. There are notable differences in lung cancer incidence and mortality rate by race.[2] For example, the incidence and mortality rate of lung cancer are higher in black men than white men and lower in black women than white women. Significant geographic variation in lung cancer incidence, mortality rates, and trends also are noted, even within the United States.[3] The patterns and shift in the demographics of lung cancer are related, at least in part, to disparities in risk factors—specifically, smoking.

Two major subtypes of lung cancer are identified: non-small-cell lung cancer (NSCLC), which represents the majority of cases, and small-cell lung cancer (SCLC), which accounts for approximately 14% of cases.[4] Although both are forms of bronchogenic carcinoma, significant differences exist in their underlying biology and overall management. Both subtypes, however, are characterized by diagnosis at a late stage, an important contribution to their high mortality rates. Fortunately, due to recent advances in detection and management, there is a renewed optimism for the future of lung cancer.

KEY POINTS

- Lung cancer is the most common cause of cancer-related death in the United States for men and women.
- Lung cancer includes NSCLC and SCLC; the biology and the management of these diseases is very different.

RISK FACTORS

Although the biology of lung cancer is complex, the link between lung cancer and tobacco use is clear.[3] Numerous epidemiologic and laboratory studies, as well as in vitro data, have tied the present pandemic of lung cancer to the carcinogenic effects of tobacco smoke. It important to recognize, however, that each year in the United States, there are 17,000 to 26,000 lung cancer deaths in never smokers, with an even higher proportion in some geographic areas.[5]

TOBACCO

Cigarette smoking is the most common cause of lung cancer and is associated with approximately 85% of all cases. The risk of lung cancer among cigarette smokers increases with the number of cigarettes smoked and the duration of smoking history; the latter is a stronger risk factor than the number of cigarettes smoked per day. A tripling of the number of cigarettes smoked per day is estimated to triple the risk of lung cancer, whereas a tripling of the duration of smoking is estimated to increase the risk 100-fold.[7] Of note, moderate- to high-intensity smoking (defined as ≥ 10 cigarettes per day) has dramatically declined in the United States since the 1960s.[8] The risk of lung cancer decreases with smoking cessation, and approaches that of the nonsmoking population after 10 to 15 years of abstinence. However, one study among women reported that even after 30 years, the risk was not as low as for the population who had never smoked.[9] It is estimated that approximately half of all lung cancers in the United States occur in former smokers. e-Cigarettes have been explored as a tool to reduce tobacco use, but in other studies, their use led to an increased likelihood of cigarette smoking; the associated risks of developing lung cancer are under investigation.[10-12]

Cigarette smoke contains thousands of constituents, many of which are carcinogenic. Two of the major classes of nicotine-related inhaled carcinogens include the polycyclic aromatic hydrocarbons and *N*-nitrosamines, which are metabolized to nitrosamine ketone and *N'*-nitrosonornicotine. Both compounds are activated by the cytochrome P450 enzyme system and exert carcinogenic effects through the formation of DNA adducts. The distribution of benzo(a)pyrene diol epoxide adducts along the exons of the *TP53* gene occurs preferentially in codons 157, 248, and 273, which are the same mutational hot spots of *TP53*.[13]

ENVIRONMENTAL EXPOSURE

Radon is a naturally occurring, chemically inert gas that is a decay product of uranium. The relative risk of lung cancer is increased for underground miners who are exposed to high levels of radon. For underground miners who smoke, the risk may exceed 10 times the risk for a nonsmoking miner. The relationship between indoor residential radon exposure and lung cancer risk is less well defined, although it is estimated that 2% to 10% of lung cancers may be caused by exposure to residential radon.[14] Exposure to asbestos combined with smoking increases the risk of lung cancer. Other occupational or environmental exposures associated with a risk of lung cancer include arsenic, chromium, nickel, air pollution, and environmental (ie, second-hand) tobacco smoke.[6]

RADIATION THERAPY

High doses of radiation have also been associated with an increased risk of lung cancer. For example, an increased risk has been observed for patients with breast cancer, as well as for long-term survivors of Hodgkin and non-Hodgkin lymphomas, particularly if patients continue to smoke after completing radiation therapy.[15]

FAMILY HISTORY AND GENETIC PREDISPOSITION

Epidemiologic studies have shown that a family history of lung cancer is a predictor of increased risk. Familial aggregation of lung cancer has led to the hypothesis of a genetic susceptibility for lung cancer.[16] This may be related to inherited differences in carcinogen metabolism and activation and also to DNA repair capacity. For example, leukocyte DNA adduct levels have been associated with the risk of lung cancer, with an odds ratio of 1.86 (95% CI, 0.88 to 3.93), particularly for never smokers (odds ratio, 4.04; 95% CI, 1.06 to 15.42).[17] Germline polymorphisms in genes with products that activate (eg, cytochrome P450 1A1 [CYP1A1]) or detoxify (eg, glutathione *S*-transferases M1 [GSTM1] and T1 [GSTT1]) chemical carcinogens found in tobacco smoke have been associated with a risk of lung cancer from environmental tobacco smoke that is substantially greater than the risk for individuals who are heterozygous or homozygous carriers of the wild-type GSTM1 allele.[18] However, some results from these studies are conflicting, suggesting that particular polymorphisms may predict increased risks in specific ethnic populations, limiting generalizability. The EGFR-T790M mutation, most frequently associated with resistance to first- or second-generation EGFR-tyrosine kinase inhibitors (TKIs), can also be present, rarely, de novo and as a germline risk allele for lung cancer.[19] Detection of tumor EGFR-T790M before treatment with EGFR-TKI can be used to screen for familial EGFR-T790M and lead to suitable patients being referred for genetic counseling.[20]

ADDITIONAL RISK FACTORS

Additional factors associated with increased lung cancer risk include previous lung damage, such as chronic obstructive pulmonary disease and fibrotic disorders that restrict lung capacity, such as pneumoconiosis. Diets deficient in vitamins A and C and β-carotene intake also have been associated with increased risk, whereas fruit and vegetable consumption may be weakly protective. Preclinical evidence suggested that higher dietary intake of retinol is associated with a decreased risk of lung cancer, but this was not confirmed in randomized trials. Rather, β-carotene supplementation was associated with an increased risk of lung cancer among high-risk populations of heavy smokers in two of the three trials.[21-23]

KEY POINTS

- Most cases of lung cancer (85%) are caused by carcinogens in tobacco smoke; a small percentage of cases are caused by second-hand smoking or exposure to radon, radiation, or other chemicals.
- Host characteristics, including family history and inherited differences in carcinogen metabolism, may account for different susceptibilities to lung cancer.

PATHOLOGY

More than 95% of lung cancers consist of one of the four major histologic types: squamous, adenocarcinoma, or large-cell (the three subtypes of NSCLC), or small-cell lung cancer (SCLC; Figs 11-1).[24,25] Although the natural history of the subtypes of NSCLC differs somewhat when assessed on a stage-by-stage basis, histologic subtype is not a significant prognostic indicator. Histology does influence treatment selection, based on differences in chemosensitivity and safety profiles in squamous versus nonsquamous tumors. Immunohistochemical staining can help differentiate histologic subtypes.

In the United States, the most common form of lung cancer was squamous cell cancer until approximately 1987, when it was supplanted by adenocarcinoma. SCLC once accounted for approximately 20% of all lung cancers, but its incidence has been declining, as has that of large-cell histology.[26] Other subtypes, which are rare and therefore less well studied, include carcinoid, large-cell cancer with neuroendocrine features, and large-cell neuroendocrine cancer.[25] Extremely rare primary tumors in the lung include sarcomas, cancers with sarcomatoid or sarcomatous elements (eg, giant-cell cancer, carcinosarcoma, pulmonary blastoma), and cancers of the salivary gland type (eg, mucoepidermoid cancer, adenoid cystic cancer).

ATYPICAL ADENOMATOUS HYPERPLASIA

Atypical adenomatous hyperplasia is considered a precursor to adenocarcinoma and is usually identified incidentally, often at the time of resection. The lesions are typically small (a few millimeters) and consist of discrete but ill-defined bronchoalveolar proliferation in which the alveoli are lined by monotonous, slightly atypical, cuboidal to low-columnar epithelial cells. Their prognostic significance is unclear.

ADENOCARCINOMA

Adenocarcinoma is currently the most common histologic subtype in the United States and incidence appears to be increasing, although the reason for this is unknown. It accounts for > 50% of all new lung cancer cases, has been associated with scarring, and is more likely to be peripherally located than squamous cell or SCLC. Lung adenocarcinoma typically stains positive by immunohistochemistry (IHC) for cytokeratin 7 (CK7) and negative for cytokeratin 20 (CK20). The majority of pulmonary adenocarcinomas also stain positive for thyroid transcription factor 1 (TTF-1).[27] Many of the actionable molecular drivers detected in lung cancer, discussed later in this chapter, are more commonly seen in adenocarcinoma.

ADENOCARCINOMA IN SITU

Adenocarcinoma in situ (AIS) is defined as an adenocarcinoma of the lung that grows lepidically, along alveolar septae.[25] In the 1999 World Health Organization/International Association for the Study of Lung Cancer classification, the lack of invasive growth was added as an essential criterion because data suggested that surgical resection might cure disease in such patients. Histologically, pure AIS is rare; more common is adenocarcinoma, mixed subtype, with both AIS features and invasive components.

The tumor typically presents as mucinous or nonmucinous. Mucinous tumors (30% to 40%) tend to be multicentric and TTF-1–negative, and rarely harbor sensitizing EGFR mutations. Nonmucinous tumors (50% to 60%) tend to be solitary and TTF-1–positive, and are enriched for EGFR mutations. This form of lung cancer develops in never smokers more than the other subtypes. Although the prognosis is excellent for patients with small, solitary, nonmucinous tumors, the prognosis for patients with advanced AIS is comparable with prognoses for other lung adenocarcinomas. Of note, small lesions discovered on screening computed tomography (CT) scans, which are commonly found to have a ground-glass appearance, are often AIS. The current staging classification is presented in Table 11-1.[28,29]

SQUAMOUS CELL CANCER

Squamous cell cancers account for approximately 25% of lung cancer. These lesions tend to be located centrally and are more likely to cavitate than other histologic types. Squamous cell cancers, which most often arise in segmental bronchi and involve lobar and mainstem bronchi by extension, are recognized by the histologic features of intercellular bridging, squamous pearl formation, and individual cell keratinization. Squamous cell lung

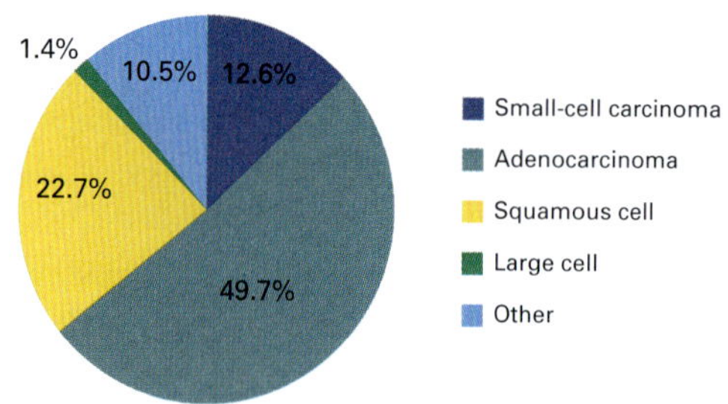

Fig. 11-1 Frequency distribution of different pathological subtypes of lung cancer.

cancer often overexpresses the squamous histology marker p63 and its isoform p40, as well as CK5/6, all detectable by IHC.[30]

LARGE-CELL CANCER

Pure large cell lung cancer accounts for < 5% of new lung cancer cases, but when including other large cell subtypes, including large cell neuroendocrine cancer, the incidence approaches 10%. These tumors are typically poorly differentiated and are composed of large cells with abundant cytoplasm and large nucleoli. With regard to clinical management, including molecular testing and systemic therapy options, large cell cancer is often grouped with adenocarcinoma as "non-squamous" NSCLC.

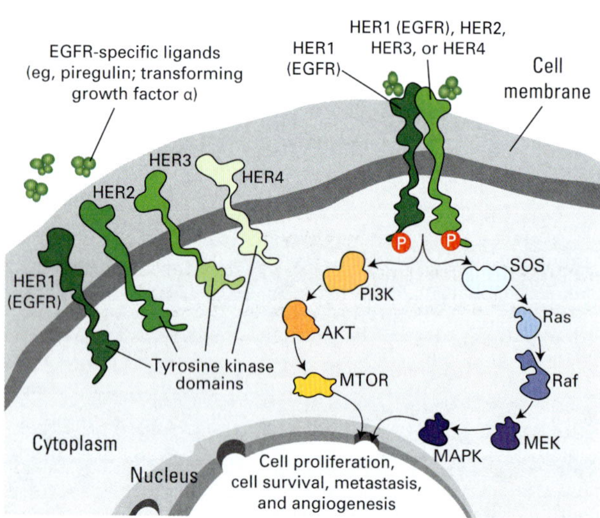

Fig. 11-2 Epidermal growth factor receptor (EGFR) signaling pathways.

Shown in the left portion of the figure are the four members of the ERBB (or HER) family of receptors. All four members of this family have tyrosine kinase domains in the cytoplasmic portion of the receptor. However, the tyrosine kinase domain of HER3 does not have catalytic activity. The right portion of the figure shows that binding of ligands to the HER family of receptors induces either homodimerization or heterodimerization of the receptors. Dimerization results in phosphorylation of the tyrosine residues of the EGFR kinase domain. The activated receptor may then phosphorylate a wide array of intracellular signaling cascades, such as the RAS-RAF-MEK-ERK, and PI3K-AKT pathways, that induce cellular proliferation, angiogenesis, and metastases. EGFR amplification can obviate the requirement for ligand-induced dimerization.

Abbreviations: mTOR, mammalian target of rapamycin; P, phosphorylation; RAS, SOS, son of sevenless.

PULMONARY NEUROENDOCRINE TUMORS

The normal lung contains neuroendocrine cells, although the significance of these cells is unclear. Neuroendocrine lung tumors represent a spectrum of pathologic entities, including typical carcinoid, atypical carcinoid, large-cell neuroendocrine cancer, and SCLC. SCLC and large-cell neuroendocrine cancer are high-grade neuroendocrine tumors, whereas typical carcinoid and atypical carcinoid are low- and intermediate-grade cancers, respectively. Neurosecretory granules, particularly chromogranin A and synaptophysin, often are seen on electron microscopy. The presence of chromogranin, synaptophysin, and CD56 (neural cell adhesion molecule) may be detected by IHC. Approximately 20% to 40% of patients with both typical and atypical carcinoids are nonsmokers, whereas virtually all patients with SCLC and large-cell neuroendocrine cancer have a history of smoking. Five-year survival is 21% for patients with large-cell neuroendocrine cancer, 65% for atypical carcinoid, and 90% for typical carcinoid.[27]

Carcinoid Tumors

Carcinoid tumors are low-grade malignant neoplasms of neuroendocrine cells, which are divided into typical and atypical types, with the latter possessing more malignant histologic and clinical features. Surgery is the primary treatment of typical carcinoid tumors. The prognosis is excellent for patients with typical carcinoids. Compared with typical carcinoids, atypical carcinoids tend to be larger, have more mitoses per high-power field, and are associated with necrosis. Patients also are more likely to have distant metastases at presentation, and survival is significantly reduced.

Large-Cell Neuroendocrine Cancer

Large-cell neuroendocrine cancer is a high-grade, non–small-cell neuroendocrine cancer. These tumors are characterized by histologic features similar to those of small-cell cancer but are formed by larger cells. Large-cell neuroendocrine cancer is defined as a tumor with neuroendocrine morphologic characteristics, including organoid nesting, palisading, a trabecular pattern, and rosette-like structures. A mitotic count of 11 mitoses or more per 2 mm^2 is the main criterion for separating large-cell neuroendocrine cancers and SCLCs from atypical carcinoid tumors. The mitotic rates are usually high for large-cell neuroendocrine cancers and SCLCs, with an average of 70 to 80 mitoses per 2 mm^2. Large-cell neuroendocrine cancers are separated from SCLCs based on histologic characteristics including larger size, more abundant cytoplasm, and less prominent nuclear molding.[31] Large-cell cancers with neuroendocrine morphology are tumors that resemble large-cell neuroendocrine tumors on light microscopy but lack proof of neuroendocrine differentiation on electron microscopy or IHC. The significance of this histology is unknown. The prognosis for patients with large-cell

Table 11-1 **Definitions for Tumor-Node-Metastasis Descriptors**[27,273]

Tumor Type	Description
T (primary tumor)	
TX	Primary tumor cannot be assessed, or tumor proven, by the presence of malignant cells in sputum or bronchial washings but not visualized by imaging or bronchoscopy
T0	No evidence of primary tumor
Tis	Carcinoma in situ
	Squamous cell carcinoma in situ (SCIS)
	Adenocarcinoma in situ (AIS): adenocarcinoma with pure lepidic pattern, ≤ 3 cm in greatest dimension
T1	Tumor ≤ 3 cm in greatest dimension, surrounded by lung or visceral pleura, without bronchoscopic evidence of invasion more proximal than the lobar bronchus (ie, not in the main bronchus)
T1mi	Minimally invasive adenocarcinoma: adenocarcinoma (≤ 3 cm in greatest dimension) with a predominantly lepidic pattern and ≤ 5 mm invasion in greatest dimension
T1a	Tumor ≤ 1 cm in greatest dimension. A superficial, spreading tumor of any size whose invasive component is limited to the bronchial wall and may extend proximal to the main bronchus also is classified as T1a, but these tumors are uncommon.
T1b	Tumor > 1 cm but ≤ 2 cm in greatest dimension
T1c	Tumor > 2 cm but ≤ 3 cm in greatest dimension
T2	Tumor > 3 cm but ≤ 5 cm or having any of the following features:
	▪ Involves the main bronchus regardless of distance to the carina, but without involvement of the carina
	▪ Invades visceral pleura (PL1 or PL2)
	▪ Associated with atelectasis or obstructive pneumonitis that extends to the hilar region, involving part or all of the lung
	T2 tumors with these features are classified as T2a if ≤ 4 cm or if the size cannot be determined, and T2b if > 4 cm but ≤ 5 cm.
T2a	Tumor > 3 cm but ≤ 4 cm in greatest dimension
T2b	Tumor > 4 cm but ≤ 5 cm in greatest dimension
T3	Tumor > 5 cm but ≤ 7 cm in greatest dimension or directly invading any of the following: parietal pleura (PL3), chest wall (including superior salcus tumors), phrenic nerve, parietal pericardium; or separate tumor nodule(s) in the same lobe as the primary
T4	Tumor > 7 cm or tumor of any size invading one or more of the following: diaphragm, mediastinum, heart, great vessels, trachea, recurrent laryngeal nerve, esophagus, vertebral body, or carina; separate tumor nodule(s) in an ipsilateral lobe different from that of the primary
N (regional lymph node)	
NX	Regional lymph nodes cannot be assessed
N0	No regional lymph node metastasis
N1	Metastasis in ipsilateral peribronchial and/or ipsilateral hilar lymph nodes and intrapulmonary nodes, including involvement by direct extension
N2	Metastasis in ipsilateral mediastinal and/or subcarinal lymph node(s)
N3	Metastasis in contralateral mediastinal, contralateral hilar, ipsilateral or contralateral scalene, or supraclavicular lymph node(s)
M (distant metastasis)	
M0	No distant metastasis
M1	Distant metastasis
M1a	Separate tumor nodule(s) in a contralateral lobe; tumor with pleural or pericardial effusion.
	Most pleural (pericardial) effusions with lung cancer are a result of the tumor. In a few patients, however, multiple microscopic examinations of pleural (pericardial) fluid are negative for tumor, and the fluid is nonbloody and not an exudate. If these elements and clinical judgement dictate the effusion is not related to the tumor, the effusion should be excluded as a staging descriptor.
M1b	Single extrathoracic metastasis in a single organ (including involvement of a single nonregional node)
M1c	Multiple extrathoracic metastases in a single organ or in multiple organs

neuroendocrine cancer is worse than that for patients with atypical carcinoid and classic large-cell cancer.

Small-Cell Lung Cancer

Histologically, SCLC is characterized by small cells with scant cytoplasm, finely granular nuclear chromatin, and absent or inconspicuous nucleoli. Nuclear molding and smearing of the nuclear chromatin may be present owing to crush artifact. Mitotic figures are common, and necrosis can be extensive. On electron microscopy, the cells may appear to have neuroendocrine granules. Neuroendocrine markers such as chromogranin and synaptophysin are frequently overexpressed.[25] Clinically, these tumors tend to be centrally located, are often found submucosally, and are more commonly associated with paraneoplastic syndromes. Because of the rapid growth and proliferation of these tumors, the clinical course tends to be more rapid than that of NSCLC. SCLCs are initially more responsive to both chemotherapy and radiation therapy, though responses tend to be transient.

KEY POINTS

- The four most common histologic subtypes of lung cancer are adenocarcinoma, squamous cell carcinoma, large-cell carcinoma (collectively referred to as NSCLC) and SCLC.
- Adenocarcinoma is the most common histologic subtype of lung cancer, followed by squamous cell carcinoma.
- Pulmonary neuroendocrine tumors represent a spectrum of neoplasms, from carcinoid to large-cell neuroendocrine to SCLC, characterized by the presence of neurosecretory granules on electron microscopic evaluation and a distinct immunohistochemical phenotype.

MOLECULAR BIOLOGY

A more sophisticated understanding of the biology of lung cancer has led to further subclassification based on molecular characteristics (Fig 11-2).[32] The presence of specific oncogenic drivers informs the biology and prognosis. Importantly, it also guides systemic therapy. In fact, for patients with advanced, nonsquamous NSCLC, optimal therapy cannot be properly determined without an understanding of the molecular signature of the cancer. As a result, it is imperative to identify these genomic alterations when present. The most common and clinically relevant, molecularly defined subtypes found in nonsquamous NSCLC are described in Fig 11-3.

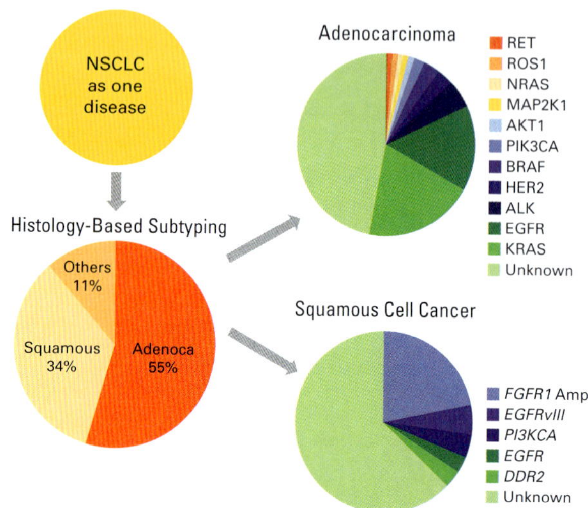

Fig. 11-3 Evolution of non–small-cell lung cancer (NSCLC) subtyping from histologic based to molecular based.

Abbreviations: Adenoca, adenocarcinoma; EGFR, epidermal growth factor receptor; MAP2K1, mitogen-activated protein kinase 1.

Adapted from Li et al.[32]

GENOMIC PROFILING

Actionable genomic alterations in NSCLC are more commonly identified in tumors with nonsquamous histology. Guidelines for molecular testing have been issued by multiple organizations, including the International Association for the Study of Lung Cancer, ASCO, the College of American Pathologists and the National Comprehensive Cancer Network. The current guidelines include testing for *EGFR* mutations, *ALK* translocations, and *ROS1* translocations in all advanced nonsquamous NSCLC, with strong consideration for *BRAF* mutation testing.[53] For each of these alterations, there are targeted agents approved for therapeutic use (described later in this chapter). Molecular testing should also be considered in squamous cell histology, particularly for patients who are never smokers or light smokers, have small biopsy specimens, or have mixed histology, because driver alterations can less frequently be detected in squamous NSCLC.[54] It is also now possible to perform next-generation sequencing of hundreds of genes simultaneously. This broad genomic multiplex profiling offers the opportunity to identify potential oncogenic drivers to treat with US Food and Drug Administration (FDA)-approved drugs or prompt referral to a relevant clinical trial. In the most recent guidelines, for laboratories that perform next-generation sequencing, inclusion of additional genes is recommended to include *NTRK, HER2, MET, BRAF,* and *RET.*[55] These recommendations apply to advanced-stage NSCLC, because their impact on management of earlier stage NSCLC is unclear.

One of the more common genomic events observed in advanced NSCLC is a mutation in *KRAS. KRAS* mutations, which occur primarily in exons 12, 13, and 61, are found mainly among patients with lung adenocarcinomas (approximately 25%) and in smokers. There are no targeted agents currently approved for KRAS-mutant NSCLC, though novel agents are in development.

BLOOD-BASED GENOMIC TESTING

Increasingly, blood-based "liquid biopsy" specimens are being used for molecular analyses of NSCLC.[56,57] Genomic testing can be performed on blood, using various nucleic acid sequencing methods to examine a single gene of interest or a panel of genes. These methods include technology such as droplet digital polymerase chain reaction (PCR), BEAMing (beads, emulsification,

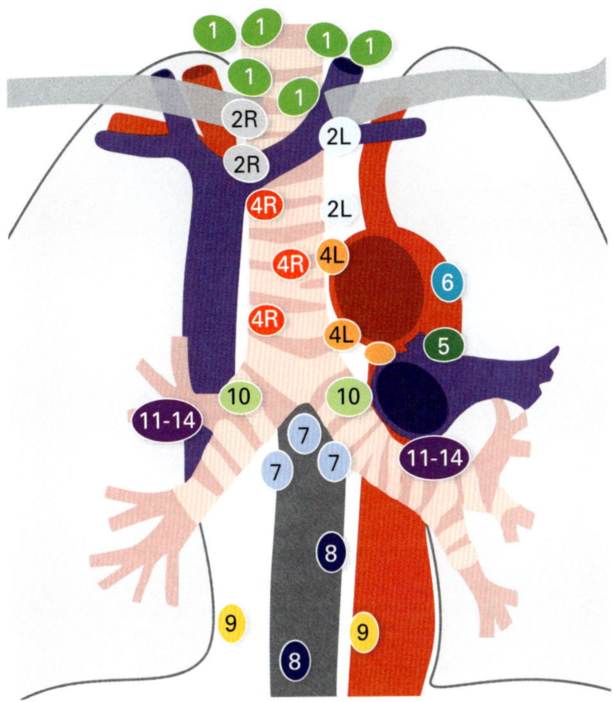

Fig. 11-4 Regional lymph node classification.

Supraclavicular nodes: 1. Low cervical, supraclavicular and sternal notch nodes: From the lower margin of the cricoid to the clavicles and the upper border of the manubrium. The midline of the trachea serves as border between 1R and 1L. Superior mediastinal nodes 2 to 4: 2R, upper paratracheal: From the upper border of manubrium to the intersection of the caudal margin of innominate (left brachiocephalic) vein with the trachea. 2R nodes extend to the left lateral border of the trachea. 2L, upper paratracheal: From the upper border of manubrium to the superior border of aortic arch. 2L nodes are located to the left of the left lateral border of the trachea. 3A, prevascular: Nodes are not adjacent to the trachea, as are the nodes in station 2, but they are anterior to the vessels. 3P, prevertebral: Nodes are not adjacent to the trachea, as are the nodes in station 2, but behind the esophagus, which is prevertebral. 4R, lower paratracheal: From the intersection of the caudal margin of the innominate (left brachiocephalic) vein with the trachea to the lower border of the azygos vein. 4R nodes extend from the right to the left lateral border of the trachea. 4L, lower paratracheal: From the upper margin of the aortic arch to the upper rim of the left main pulmonary artery. Aortic nodes 5 and 6: 5, subaortic: These nodes are located in the aortopulmonary window lateral to the ligamentum arteriosum. These nodes are not located between the aorta and the pulmonary trunk but lateral to these vessels. 6, Paraaortic: These are ascending aorta or phrenic nodes lying anterior and lateral to the ascending aorta and the aortic arch. Inferior mediastinal nodes 7 to 9. 7, Subcarinal. 8, Paraesophageal: Nodes below carina. 9, Pulmonary ligament: Nodes lying within the pulmonary ligaments. Hilar, lobar, and (sub)segmental nodes 10 to 14: These are all N1 nodes. 10, Hilar nodes: These include nodes adjacent to the mainstem bronchus and hilar vessels. On the right, they extend from the lower rim of the azygos vein to the interlobar region; on the left, from the upper rim of the pulmonary artery to the interlobar region.

Reprinted with permission from Robin Smithuis (www.radiologyassistant.nl).

amplification, and magnetics), real-time PCR, or next-generation sequencing. This examination of circulating tumor DNA (ctDNA) differs from examining whole circulating tumor cells because DNA shed in the blood is examined if it is still contained in a tumor cell in the bloodstream.

A real-time PCR test has been approved by the FDA for use in tissue and plasma for the detection of the two most common EGFR-activating mutations, EGFR exon 19 and EGFR L858R, as well as EGFR-T790M (the most common resistance mutation to first- and second-generation EGFR-TKIs). Broader genomic profiling of ctDNA using next-generation sequencing methods that examine multiple genes important in lung cancer (eg, *EGFR, ALK, ROS1, BRAF*) is also appropriate when tissue is insufficient or obtaining a tissue biopsy specimen for molecular testing is not feasible.[57]

A positive blood test is generally specific for the presence of the molecular aberration, and outcomes in EGFR-mutant NSCLCs are similar whether the mutation was detected in tissue or plasma; however, a negative test should be interpreted with caution given the known limits of sensitivity. When possible, negative ctDNA testing should be followed by a tissue biopsy to more conclusively determine the presence or absence of the genomic aberration in question, particularly when approved therapies are available.[58] Some alterations detected in blood, however, may not be reflective of the tumor, particularly in genes mutated in the process of clonal hematopoeisis.[59] When there is concern about clonal hematopoiesis in interpreting ctDNA results, a tissue biopsy may provide useful insight.[60]

LUNG CANCER IMMUNOBIOLOGY

The past several years have seen a tremendous acceleration in our understanding of the immune microenvironment of lung cancer and translation of this understanding to the development of immunotherapy to treat advanced lung cancer. The most promising avenue of investigation has been the development of immune checkpoint inhibitors: monoclonal antibodies that overcome immune inhibition that tumors can exploit to prevent the immune system from attacking the tumor. See Chapter 4: Principles of Immuno-Oncology and Biologic Therapy for mechanistic details regarding the immune system and cancer.

KEY POINTS

- The most readily targeted molecular abnormalities associated with lung cancer include *EGFR* and *BRAF* mutations and *ALK* and *ROS1* translocations.
- Guidelines recommend concurrent testing for *EGFR* mutations and *ALK* and *ROS1* translocations in all advanced, nonsquamous NSCLC and testing should be considered in other appropriate clinical situations.
- Broad genomic profiling through next-generation sequencing to identify molecular aberrations such as mutations in *BRAF*, *MET*, and *HER2* or fusions in *RET* and *NTRK* should also be considered.
- When tissue is not available for proper and indicated genomic testing, blood-based, liquid biopsy specimens can be helpful, though there are limitations to their sensitivity and negative results may need to be confirmed with tissue testing.

Table 11-2 **Symptoms Associated With Lung Cancer**

Frequency	Symptom
Typical	Cough
	Increased production of sputum
	Shortness of breath
Common	Fatigue
	Weight loss
	Anorexia
	Low-grade fever
Less common	Chest pain (usually from a pleural-based lesion)
	Hemoptysis
	Hoarseness (secondary to laryngeal-nerve involvement)
	Bone pain
	Pleural effusion
Infrequent	Signs and symptoms consistent with obstruction of the superior vena cava, superior sulcus, or Pancoast tumors
	Pericardial tamponade
	Paraneoplastic syndromes
	Signs and symptoms consistent with brain metastases

CLINICAL PRESENTATION

Most patients with lung cancer present with symptomatic disease (Table 11-2). The most common symptoms are anorexia, fatigue, weakness, and cough. Patients with AIS may have bronchorrhea (ie, large quantities of foamy sputum) and shortness of breath out of proportion to radiographic findings. Metastatic disease at presentation is common in SCLC (75%) and adenocarcinoma (50%), and many metastatic sites are possible, with the most common being brain, bone, liver, and adrenal gland.[61]

Liver and bone marrow metastases develop in approximately 20% to 30% of patients. Brain metastases occur in > 20% of patients and at much higher rates within specific subsets of lung cancer.[62,63]

PARANEOPLASTIC SYNDROMES

Paraneoplastic syndromes are caused by humoral factors produced by cancer cells that act at a site distant from the primary site and its metastases or by cross-reactivity between host antitumor antibodies and normal tissues.[64,65] For all paraneoplastic syndromes, treatment of the underlying cancer is recommended. In addition, syndrome-specific therapies may be used.

Hypercalcemia and Hypertrophic Pulmonary Osteoarthropathy

Two common paraneoplastic syndromes among patients with NSCLC are hypercalcemia and hypertrophic pulmonary osteoarthropathy. Although hypercalcemia is most often caused by diffuse skeletal metastases, it can be the result of ectopic production of a parathyroid hormone-related peptide or other humoral substances. Humoral-associated hypercalcemia is most commonly related to squamous cell cancers.[66] Manifestations of hypercalcemia depend more on the rate of onset than on the degree of elevation and include mental status changes, polydipsia, GI symptoms, and nephrolithiasis. In addition to treatment of the malignancy, therapy includes intravenous hydration and administration of agents such as bisphosphonates, denosumab, and calcitonin. Use of diuretics, which may exacerbate volume depletion, is discouraged. Hypertrophic pulmonary osteoarthropathy is characterized by clubbing of the digits and, when severe, painful periostitis of the long bones. Hypertrophic pulmonary osteoarthropathy is most common with adenocarcinoma, although it is not pathognomonic for cancer; it may also occur with other pulmonary diseases.

Neurologic Abnormalities

SCLC is strongly associated with paraneoplastic neurologic abnormalities.[67] Central nervous system (CNS) paraneoplastic disorders include (Table 11-3) cerebellar degeneration, dementia, limbic encephalopathy, Lambert-Eaton syndrome, and visual paraneoplastic syndrome with optic neuritis and retinopathy.

Cerebellar degeneration is characterized by progressive cerebellar dysfunction with ataxia, dysarthria, hypotonia, and dementia. This syndrome is associated with four different antineuronal antibodies, the most common being an antibody against Purkinje cell proteins. Limbic encephalopathy is characterized by symptoms such as progressive dementia, hallucinations, depression, agitation, and anxiety. Paraneoplastic

Table 11-3 **Select Neurologic Paraneoplastic Syndromes in Lung Cancer**	
Paraneoplastic Syndrome	**Antibody Target**
Lambert Eaton	Anti-VGCC
Cerebellar degeneration	Anti-Hu, -CV2, -ANNA-3, -PCA-2
Opsoclonus/myoclonus	Anti-Ri
Retinal blindness	Anti-recoverin
Stiff-Person syndrome	Anti-amphiphysin

sensory neuropathy often is associated with the presence of anti-Hu antibody and can lead to subacute distal sensory loss and the absence of deep tendon reflexes with normal muscle strength. Anti-Hu is a circulating polyclonal immunoglobulin G that reacts with CNS neurons as well as the dorsal root and trigeminal ganglia. It can be associated with encephalopathy, autonomic neuropathy, and cerebellar degeneration. Lambert-Eaton syndrome occurs in < 1% of patients. It is caused by onconeural antibodies targeting presynaptic calcium channels and is characterized by proximal muscle weakness. Unlike myasthenia gravis, muscle strength tends to improve with repeated activity.

Hormonal Abnormalities

Excessive production of corticotropin may result in Cushing syndrome with excess cortisol production, resulting in muscle weakness, weight loss, hypertension, hyperglycemia, and profound hypokalemia. This syndrome is most commonly found in SCLC. As a result of the rapid tumor growth, the classic physical stigmata of Cushing syndrome are often absent. The syndrome of inappropriate antidiuretic hormone (SIADH) leads to euvolemic hypo-osmolar hyponatremia. Most cases of SIADH are seen in SCLC, and symptoms are related to the degree and the speed of developing hyponatremia.

KEY POINTS

- Common symptoms of lung cancer include local symptoms, such as cough, pain, and shortness of breath, and constitutional symptoms, such as fatigue, weakness, anorexia, and weight loss.
- The most common sites for metastatic disease in lung cancer are the lungs (ipsilateral and contralateral), adrenal glands, liver, bone, and brain.
- Patients with NSCLC or SCLC may present with a number of paraneoplastic syndromes, including hypercalcemia, neurologic abnormalities, hormonal abnormalities, and SVC syndrome.

Superior Vena Cava Syndrome

Superior vena cava (SVC) syndrome occurs when the SVC becomes obstructed either directly by a tumor, thrombus, or metastases to regional lymph nodes.[68] Common symptoms include distension of the collateral veins over the anterior chest wall and neck; swelling and puffiness of the neck, face, throat, eyes, and arms; headache; and cyanosis.

Although once thought to represent a medical emergency, in almost all cases, the symptoms are mild enough that treatment can be delayed until a histologic diagnosis has been determined. Radiation therapy is used to treat patients with NSCLC or other less chemosensitive tumors (unless an actionable genomic alteration is present), whereas patients with extensive-stage SCLC and mild symptoms often may be treated with chemotherapy alone. Other options include the placement of vascular stents, although the literature regarding their role is relatively sparse.

SCREENING

Most patients with lung cancer present with advanced disease, and prognosis is much worse than at an earlier stage. This has led to great interest in screening to detect lung cancer at an earlier and theoretically more curable stage. Although the role of screening patients at high risk for the development of early-stage disease was debated for many years, CT-based screening has led to a clear reduction in lung cancer mortality.

Low-dose, noncontrast, thin-slice, helical or spiral CT is a scan in which only the pulmonary parenchyma is examined, negating the use of intravenous contrast medium. This type of scan usually can be done quickly (within one breath) and involves low doses of radiation. In a nonrandomized, controlled study from the Early Lung Cancer Action Project, low-dose CT was more sensitive than chest radiograph for detecting lung nodules and lung cancer in early stages.[69]

The National Lung Screening Trial (NLST) was a randomized, multicenter study comparing low-dose, helical CT scans with chest radiographs for the screening of older current and former heavy smokers for early detection of lung cancer. Individuals were enrolled in the study who were between ages 55 and 74 years and who had at least a 30 pack-year smoking history (former smokers needed to have quit within the previous 15 years). More lung cancers were diagnosed in the CT arm (292 cases *v* 190 cases), with the difference most notable in stage IA cancers (132 cases *v* 46 cases).[70] There were 247 deaths from lung cancer per 100,000 person-years in the CT group and 309 deaths per 100,000 person-years in the chest radiograph group, corresponding to a 20% relative reduction

Table 11-4 Points About Lung Cancer Screening to Share with Patients[71,72,254]

Results from observational studies of CT screening among patients at high risk (ie, those with a history of heavy smoking) indicate a high rate of diagnosis of lung cancer in stage I (a relatively curable stage).
CT screening reveals many noncalcified nodules, only a small fraction of which will be lung cancer. The patient must be prepared to live with this uncertainty and must be able to commit to frequent follow-up scans.
Costly invasive procedures that are associated with serious risks may be required to evaluate some nodules.
Despite these considerations, the National Lung Screening Trial, which randomly assigned approximately 50,000 high-risk individuals to annual chest x-ray or low-dose spiral CT scan for 3 years, demonstrated a 20% reduction in lung cancer mortality with CT-based screening.
A diagnostic work-up should be done by physicians who are experienced in such evaluation.
The selection of a facility with physicians who are experienced and credentialed in multidisciplinary fields (including thoracic surgery, pathology, and pulmonology) is critical to an optimal outcome.
Patients who are currently smoking should be reminded that the most effective way them to improve their health is to stop smoking.

Abbreviation: CT, computed tomography.

in lung cancer mortality (P = .004).[71] CT scanning was also associated with a 6.7% reduction in all-cause mortality. On the basis of these data from the NLST trial, the US Preventive Services Task Force issued recommendations for annual lung cancer screening with low-dose CT for adults ages 55 to 80 years who have a smoking history of 30 pack-years or more and who are currently smoking or had quit within the past 15 years. Although the NLST showed for the first time that CT-based screening reduced incidence of lung cancer mortality, numerous questions regarding implementation, cost, associated biomarkers to identify patients with high-risk disease, and management of false-positive test results remain and will be important topics for future studies (Table 11-4). Similar results were seen from the large, randomized NELSON trial.[72] With 10 years of follow-up, use of CT screening led to a 26% reduction in lung cancer mortality; the benefit was seen in men and women and cancers detected by screening were primarily early stage (69% were stage I cancers).

KEY POINT

- On the basis of findings from the NLST trial, screening with low-dose CT is recommended for patients ages 55 to 80 years who had a smoking habit of 30 pack-years or more and who are currently smoking or had quit within the past 15 years.

NSCLC MANAGEMENT

EPIDEMIOLOGY

NSCLC accounts for approximately 86% of new lung cancer diagnoses in the United States.[4] The most common histologic subtype in the United States is adenocarcinoma, followed by squamous cell carcinoma. Although most patients have some exposure to tobacco use, never smokers with lung cancer comprise sizable subsets of NSCLC incidence and associated mortality. Many cases of nonsquamous NSCLC will harbor an activating genomic alteration, though the specific incidence of each alteration can vary significantly by geographic region.

ESTABLISHING A DIAGNOSIS

The diagnosis of lung cancer requires a tissue biopsy. Although blood-based testing (ie, liquid biopsy) can be helpful in the molecular classification of NSCLC, it is not diagnostic for lung cancer on its own. Although lung cancer may be discovered on s chest radiograph, CT scanning of the chest and upper abdomen is necessary to evaluate the extent of the primary disease, mediastinal extension, or lymphadenopathy, as well as the presence or absence of other parenchymal nodules in patients for whom surgical resection is a consideration. Positron emission tomography (PET) scans are helpful primarily in detecting distant metastases, although they also assist in defining N2 stations appropriate for subsequent pathologic confirmation of cancer involvement. If a PET scan is done as part of the staging work-up, a bone scan does not need to be performed. CT or magnetic resonance imaging (MRI) of the brain is recommended for patients with metastatic disease and should also be considered for patients with early-stage and locally advanced NSCLC before undergoing curative therapy.

STAGING

The current (8th edition) tumor-node-metastasis (TNM) staging system of the American Joint Committee on Cancer (AJCC) is based on an analysis of > 94,000 cases of lung cancer internationally (Tables 11-1 and 11-5). Key changes from the 7th edition include several modifications to T and M descriptors, including changes to tumor size cutoffs and additional designations for metastatic spread (ie, M1a if there are contralateral lung and effusions; M1b if there are single extrathoracic metastases; and M1c if there are

Table 11-5 **Staging Groups by TNM Elements**[28,273]

Stage Group	Descriptors			Clinical Stage, 5-Year Survival (%)	Pathologic Stage, 5-Year Survival (%)
	T	N	M		
Occult	X	N0	M0		
Carcinoma					
0	Tis	N0	M0		
IA1	T1mi, T1a	N0	M0	92	90
IA2	T1b	N0	M0	83	85
IA3	T1c	N0	M0	77	80
IB	T2a	N0	M0		73
IIA	T2b	N0	M0	60	65
IIB	T1a,T1b,T1c, T2a, T2b	N1	M0		
IIB	TC3	N0			
IIIA	T1a,T1b,T1c, T2a, T2b	N2	M0		
IIIA	T4	N0, N1	M0		
IIIB	T1a,T1b,T1c, T2a, T2b	N3	M0		
IIIB	T3, T4	N2	M0		
IIIC	T3, T4	N3	M0	13	12
IVA	Any T	Any N	Any M1a		
IVA	Any T	Any N	Any M1b		
IVB	Any	Any	M1c	0	
IIB IIB IIIA IIIB IVA	68 53 36 26 10	IIB IIIA IIIB	56% 41 24		

multiple extrathoracic metastases in more than one organ). Certain stage groupings have also changed, reflecting the importance of size of the primary tumor to prognosis. It should be noted that a great majority of cases analyzed were surgical, regardless of stage, and that some stage changes reflect a selected database.[77]

POSITRON EMISSION TOMOGRAPHY

PET, a metabolic imaging scan using fluorodeoxyglucose, is more sensitive, specific, and accurate than CT and prevents unnecessary invasive procedures for patients whose disease has been subsequently proven to be at a more advanced stage.[78] PET has higher sensitivity and specificity than CT (Table 11-6).[74] However, the limitations of PET include the cost, availability, inability to detect lesions smaller than 8 mm, and lack of specificity, particularly for patients with inflammatory or granulomatous disease.

Despite these problems, preoperative PET (in addition to a conventional work-up) reduces the number of "futile" thoracotomies, as defined by benign disease, exploratory thoracotomy, pathologic stage IIIA (N2) or IIIB disease, postoperative relapse, or death within 12 months.[79] PET also has been used to detect distant metastases; indeed, it is in this area that some investigators believe PET may have its primary role in staging.[78] Negative results on PET for patients without symptomatic disease obviates the need for bone imaging in most patients.[80] PET also may be useful for judging response to therapy, depending on the clinical context; PET scans done early after treatment have been demonstrated to be better predictors of survival than CT, although these data need to be confirmed in larger trials.[81]

Table 11-6 Comparison of Sensitivity and Specificity of PET and CT

Mediastinal Metastases	Sensitivity (%)	Specificity (%)	Accuracy (%)
Detection[73]			
PET*	91	86	NA
CT	75	66	NA
Staging[74]			
PET	96	93	94
CT	68	65	66

Abbreviations: CT, computed tomography; NA, not applicable; PET, positron emission tomography.
*The sensitivity and specificity of PET for detecting distant metastases were 82% and 93%, respectively.

Although PET is a helpful tool, in light of its limitations, PET does not replace invasive mediastinal staging in patients with potentially resectable lung cancer and is not a substitute for dedicated brain imaging.

KEY POINTS

- Mediastinal lymph node sampling, with mediastinoscopy and/or EBUS, should be performed for all patients with enlarged or abnormal nodes detected on either CT or PET imaging who are being considered for definitive therapy.
- PET is useful to guide lymph node biopsy and to evaluate for metastatic disease.
- Although PET is more sensitive and specific than CT for staging disease in the mediastinum, it does not replace invasive mediastinal staging with EBUS or mediastinoscopy, because of the incidence of false-positive and false-negative results.

INVASIVE MEDIASTINAL STAGING

Accurate staging of the mediastinum is critical for patients with NSCLC to guide optimal therapy and determine tumor resectability (Table 11-1; Fig 11-4).[73,74] Although imaging has become increasingly advanced, clinical staging can differ markedly from pathologic staging at the time of resection.[75] Mediastinoscopy had long been considered the gold standard for mediastinal staging. When compared with transthoracic, transbronchial, and endobronchial ultrasound (EBUS)-guided needle aspirations or biopsy specimens, mediastinoscopy has a higher negative predictive value but does not provide access to station 5 and 6 lymph nodes (ie, aortopulmonary nodes), which provide lymphatic drainage for the left lung; assessment of these nodes generally requires a Chamberlain procedure (ie, anterior mediastinotomy). In recent years, EBUS has emerged as an alternative means to evaluate the mediastinum and has reduced the number of more invasive procedures needed.[76]

NSCLC TREATMENT

Treatment of NSCLC is stage specific. Within a given stage, several relevant factors direct therapeutic decision-making, including histology and molecular profiling of the tumor. Patient characteristics, such as goals of care, performance status (PS), comorbid conditions, and relevant social factors must also be taken into account.

STAGE I AND II NSCLC

Surgery

Approximately one-third of all patients with lung cancer present with stage I or II disease. The treatment of choice for fit patients is anatomic surgical resection, which can result in cure for many patients. The preferred surgical procedure is lobectomy, although for patients in whom disease crosses a major fissure or involves the proximal mainstem bronchus, pneumonectomy may be required. Lobectomy traditionally has been the procedure of choice, even for patients with small, peripheral lesions, because wedge resections are associated with increased local recurrence and decreased survival.[82] Lobectomy should include resection of bronchial, hilar, and selected mediastinal nodes, on the basis of published guidelines (at least nodes 4R and 7 for right-sided tumors; at least nodes 5/6 and 7 for left-sided tumors). More recently, sublobar resection in the form of an anatomic segmentectomy has been explored and has shown comparable oncologic outcomes to lobectomy, though randomized data are not yet available.[83] Patients with peripheral chest-wall invasion (T3N0; stage IIB) should have an en bloc resection of the involved ribs and underlying lung. Five-year survival rates as high as 50% have been reported.[84] Research is ongoing regarding the management of the small, lesions with ground-glass appearance discovered on low-dose, noncontrast-enhanced, thin-slice, helical CT. For example, because pure AIS does not feature lymphatic or hematogenous spread, it has been proposed that wedge resection without lymph node dissection may be adequate for localized tumors.

Preoperative Evaluation

The suitability of a patient for a definitive resection depends on two factors: the stage of the lesion and the ability of the patient to withstand surgery. A detailed discussion of the preoperative

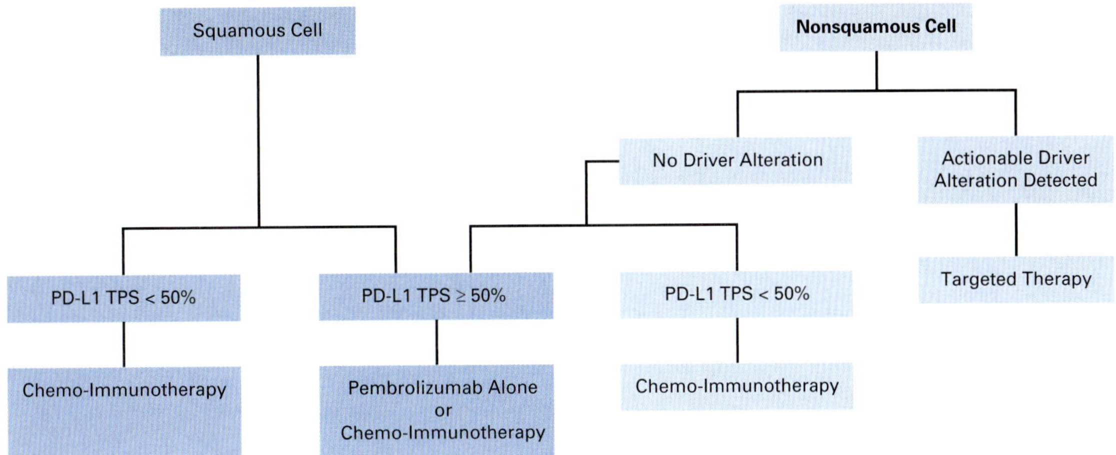

Fig. 11-5 Treatment paradigms for advanced non-small cell lung cancer by cancer subtype and PD-L1 tumor proportion score (TPS).

evaluation and comorbid conditions are beyond the scope of this chapter; however, assessment of pulmonary reserve is important. It should be emphasized that a certified general thoracic surgeon, working as part of a multidisciplinary thoracic oncology team, is best qualified to determine whether a patient is a surgical candidate. Preoperative evaluation for a thoracotomy starts with spirometry.[85] The forced vital capacity is most commonly used to assess suitability for surgery; a predicted postoperative forced vital capacity of < 1 L or a preoperative value of < 2 L for a pneumonectomy or < 1.5 L for a lobectomy usually suggests the patient is at risk for perioperative complications. Diffusion capacity should be measured if there is concern that the forced vital capacity may not be adequate or that the patient has signs or symptoms of interstitial lung disease. A low diffusion capacity (< 50% of predicted) suggests an increased risk of postoperative morbidity or mortality.

Pulmonary status should be optimized as much as possible before surgery. Treatment of bronchitis with antibiotics, bronchodilators, and/or oral corticosteroids is helpful. The patient should quit smoking, if applicable, and preoperative training with incentive spirometry and weight reduction should be considered when appropriate.

Radiotherapy

For patients with medical contraindications to surgery but with adequate pulmonary function, conventional fractionated radiotherapy (eg, 6,000 cGy, or rads, in 30 fractions of 200 cGy each) results in cure for approximately 20% of patients, with outcomes varying by stage. Advances in imaging and radiation delivery have resulted in the use of stereotactic radiation for lung tumors. With this technology, radiation delivery to surrounding normal lung parenchyma is substantially less than that seen with conventional radiotherapy. Therefore, it is possible to administer much higher, ablative doses of radiation over a few fractions. Stereotactic radiation entails radiation to the primary tumor but typically not to the draining lymph nodes. Because of a higher risk of adverse effects, such as bronchial stenosis, hemoptysis, and fistula formation, stereotactic radiation is usually not performed when the tumor lies within 2 cm of the proximal bronchial tree.[86] This technique is also usually restricted to tumors < 5 cm.

To date, outcomes with this technique appear promising. In an analysis of 676 patients treated with stereotactic body radiation for stage I and II NSCLC, the 2-year rate of local recurrence was 4.9% and the 5-year rate was only 10.5%.[87] In a prospective trial, stereotactic radiation was superior to standard radiotherapy for inoperable stage I lung cancer, with a decreased risk of treatment failure (hazard ratio [HR], 0.32).[88] The 5-year rate of distant failure was 19.9%. Radiation is often reserved for patients felt to be medically inoperable, but a single-arm phase II study of patients with operable T1-T2, N0, M0 NSCLC demonstrated a 4-year local control rate of 96%.[89] Randomized studies comparing surgery and radiation are underway. In contrast to surgically resected early-stage tumors (see Adjuvant Chemotherapy section), the role of chemotherapy after radiation therapy for medically inoperable early-stage NSCLC is unclear. Other locally ablative treatments, including radiofrequency ablation and microwave ablation, are used in specific clinical situations and are under investigation.[90]

Secondary Lung Cancer

The risk of second lung cancers developing is high (approximately 2% to 3% annually) for patients with resected stage I NSCLC. Aside from smoking cessation, no dietary changes or supplements have been proven to decrease the risk of a second lung cancer developing.[21-23,91]

PANCOAST TUMORS

Pancoast, or superior sulcus, tumors in the upper lobe adjoining the brachial plexus are frequently associated with Horner syndrome (ptosis, miosis, and anhidrosis) or shoulder and arm pain; the latter is caused by rib destruction, involvement of the seventh cervical vertebra or T1 nerve roots, or both. The SWOG Intergroup phase II trial involving patients with T3-4, N0-1, M0 superior sulcus NSCLC established the current standard of care, which consists of cisplatin plus etoposide and concomitant radiation therapy (45 Gy) followed by attempted surgical resection and then two cycles of consolidation chemotherapy after surgery.[92] Among patients with available surgical specimens, 54 (65%) showed either a complete pathologic response or minimal microscopic disease on pathologic evaluation. The 2-year survival rate was 55% for all eligible patients and 70% for patients who had a complete resection.

ADJUVANT CHEMOTHERAPY

The rationale for adjuvant chemotherapy for patients with early-stage lung cancer is based on the observation that distant metastases are the most common site of failure after potentially curative surgery. Several randomized trials have evaluated the role of adjuvant chemotherapy after surgical resection of early-stage NSCLC (Table 11-7).[93-100] In a pooled analysis of five of these trials, there was a 5.4% absolute survival benefit at 5 years (HR, 0.89).[101] Importantly, the benefit of adjuvant chemotherapy varied considerably by disease stage. For stage IA NSCLC, adjuvant chemotherapy was associated with a trend toward worse survival (HR for death, 1.40). Patients with resected stage IB NSCLC were randomly assigned to receive postoperative chemotherapy or undergo standard observation in the CALGB 9633 trial. Although the study results, overall, were negative, the subset of patients with tumors ≥ 4 cm demonstrated a significant survival difference in favor of adjuvant chemotherapy (HR, 0.69).[97] The role of adjuvant chemotherapy for resected stage II and III NSCLC is well established (Table 11-7). Cisplatin was partnered with vinca alkaloids or etoposide in these adjuvant studies, but it is common practice to use modern partners such as paclitaxel, docetaxel, gemcitabine (in squamous histology) or pemetrexed (in nonsquamous histology). Although treatment with these agents is included in current guidelines, data demonstrating a survival benefit with them are lacking. In the randomized, phase II TREAT trial, patients with resected stages IB-pT3N1 NSCLC were randomly assigned to receive cisplatin with either vinorelbine or pemetrexed. This study did not meet its primary end point of improving overall survival (OS), though dose delivery was superior with pemetrexed compared with vinorelbine (90% *v* 64%).[101]

Molecularly Target Agents

There is growing interest in incorporating molecularly targeted agents into the treatment of early-stage NSCLC. At this time, however, such an approach cannot be recommended outside a clinical trial. In the NCIC JBR.19 trial, which was terminated early, administration of the EGFR inhibitor gefitinib after resection of stages I to III NSCLC did not improve survival.[102] Surprisingly, a subset analysis of the small number of patients with tumors harboring activating *EGFR* mutations—a population expected to derive particular benefit from such an approach—suggested the possibility of a detrimental effect from gefitinib. In the RADIANT trial, patients with stage IB to IIIA NSCLC were randomly selected to receive erlotinib or placebo for 2 years.[103] In patients whose tumors harbored an EGFR mutation, a trend toward increased disease-free survival was observed with erlotinib but the change was not statistically significant. Multiple late-stage randomized trials are ongoing to examine the role for targeted therapy and immunotherapy in the postoperative setting.

Neoadjuvant Chemotherapy

A neoadjuvant approach, with delivery of systemic therapy before surgical resection has two potential advantages: (1) there is improved tolerability when chemotherapy is administered before surgery; and (2) a neoadjuvant approach allows for immediate treatment of micrometastatic disease, provides insight into chemosensitivity, and may facilitate resection.

Two small randomized studies published in 1994 raised considerable interest in the role of neoadjuvant chemotherapy.[104,105] In these trials, each of which involved only 60 patients, surgery alone was compared with surgery plus preoperative chemotherapy for stage IIIA disease and the addition of neoadjuvant chemotherapy improved survival. In a larger randomized French trial, preoperative chemotherapy with mitomycin, ifosfamide, and cisplatin plus surgery was compared with surgery alone for patients with resectable stages I (except T1N0), II, and IIIA (including N2) NSCLC. No benefit with neoadjuvant chemotherapy was found.[106] A subset analysis suggested a survival advantage for neoadjuvant chemotherapy for N0 and N1 disease but not for N2 disease. A European intergroup study randomly assigned patients to surgery alone or to receive three cycles of platinum-based chemotherapy followed by surgery. There was a numeric improvement in survival but it did not meet statistical significance.[107]

Collectively, randomized trials have shown that patients tolerate preoperative chemotherapy better, dose delivery is better, and that a higher percentage of patients complete preoperative compared with postoperative therapy. One study has demonstrated a survival advantage for preoperative therapy.[108] In addition, a meta-analysis of the HR for neoadjuvant chemotherapy in 15 randomized, controlled trials showed a significant benefit of preoperative chemotherapy on survival (HR, 0.87) with an absolute survival improvement of five percentage points at 5 years (from 40% to 45%) that is comparable to the LACE meta-analysis of adjuvant chemotherapy clinical trials.[109]

KEY POINTS

- Preoperative evaluation should include determinations of lung function.
- Treatment of stages I and II NSCLC involves surgical resection (if the patient is a candidate) or radiation therapy (specifically stereotactic radiotherapy, if the patient is not a surgical candidate).
- Anatomic resection such as lobectomy is preferred, though there may be a role for sublobar resection in patients with limited pulmonary reserve.
- Optimal management of Pancoast tumors consists of concurrent chemoradiation followed by surgical resection.
- Adjuvant chemotherapy consisting of a cisplatin-based combination is indicated for patients with stages II and IIIA disease after surgical resection; though controversial, it should be discussed with patients with larger tumors > 4 cm with negative lymph nodes. Cisplatin is the preferred platinum compound in this curative setting.

Table 11-7 **Adjuvant Therapies After Surgical Resection of Early-Stage Non-Small-Cell Lung Cancer**

Study	Stages*	Intervention	Patients (No.)	5-Year OS (%)	Median OS (months)	Hazard Ratio for Death	*P*
ALPI[95]	I-IIIA	Cisplatin, mitomycin, vindesine	606		55.2	0.96	.589
		Surgery alone	603		48		
IALT[96]	IB-IIIB	Cisplatin + (etoposide, vindesine, or vinorelbine)	932	44.5		0.86	<.03
		Surgery alone	935	40.4			
CALGB 9633[97]	IB	Carboplatin + paclitaxel	173	60	95	0.83	.125
		Surgery alone	171	58	78		
NCI-C JBR.10[255]	IB-II	Cisplatin + vinorelbine	242	67	Not reported	0.78	.04
		Surgery alone	240	56	Not reported		
ANITA[99]	IB-IIIA	Cisplatin + vinorelbine	407		65.7	0.80	.017
		Surgery alone	433		43.7		
TREAT[101]	IB-IIIA	Cisplatin + pemetrexed	67	75 (3-year OS)	Not reached	0.594	.424
		Cisplatin + vinorelbine	65	77 (3-year OS)	59		

Abbreviations: ALPI, Adjuvant Lung Project Italy; ANITA, Adjuvant Navelbine International Trialist Association; CALGB, Cancer and Leukemia Group B; IALT, International Adjuvant Lung Cancer Trial; NCI-C, National Cancer Institute of Canada; OS, overall survival.

*These studies used American Joint Commission on Cancer staging prior to 8th edition.

LOCALLY ADVANCED STAGE III NSCLC

Treatment of locally advanced, stage III NSCLC is one of the most controversial issues in the management of lung cancer. In large part, this is due to the heterogeneity of the disease and the patient population. Treatment of locally advanced NSCLC should be managed by an experienced, multidisciplinary team and could include systemic chemotherapy, immunotherapy, radiation therapy, and surgery, in various combinations and sequences. Interpretation of the results of clinical trials involving patients with locally advanced disease has been clouded by several issues, including changing diagnostic techniques, different staging systems, and the heterogeneity of stage III lung cancer: the same stage can be applied to a patient with bulky, symptomatic, unresectable NSCLC and a patient with incidental lymph node involvement.

Microscopic Stage IIIA NSCLC

Occasionally, despite appropriate preoperative staging, patients thought to have stage I or II disease are found to have N2 nodal involvement at the time of surgery. As outlined in the previous section on Adjuvant Chemotherapy, there is a survival benefit with adjuvant cisplatin-based chemotherapy for patients with completely resected stage III NSCLC. In addition, postoperative radiation therapy (PORT; 50 to 54 Gy) may be considered, usually after completion of adjuvant chemotherapy. In a PORT meta-analysis, this approach reduced locoregional recurrence but did not prolong survival.[110] However, in a more contemporary review of the National Cancer Database, patients who received PORT after complete surgical resection and adjuvant chemotherapy for N2 disease had prolonged survival compared with those not receiving PORT.[111]

Resectable Stage III NSCLC

The optimal treatment of resectable, nonbulky, stage IIIA NSCLC generally consists of systemic treatment (chemotherapy) combined with a local approach (radiation therapy and/or surgery). Possible combinations include surgery followed by adjuvant chemotherapy with or without thoracic radiation (for incidentally noted stage III); neoadjuvant chemotherapy (or chemoradiation) followed by surgery (with or without postoperative thoracic radiation), or concurrent or sequential chemotherapy with definitive radiation. In general, the accepted standard remains concurrent definitive chemoradiation, though there are differences in practice for resectable stage III disease and more data are needed.

The potential benefit of adding surgery to combined chemoradiation for stage IIIA disease was evaluated in a randomized, phase III Intergroup trial (INT 0139).[112] In this study 396 patients with stage T1-3N2M0 NSCLC were randomly assigned to concurrent chemoradiation (45 Gy) plus two cycles of cisplatin plus etoposide, followed by either surgical resection or continuation of radiation to 61 Gy total plus an additional two cycles of cisplatin/etoposide. Although progression-free survival (PFS) was significantly longer in the surgery arm (12.8 *v* 10.5 months), there was no significant difference in OS (23.6 *v* 22.2 months). There were more treatment-related deaths in the surgery arm (8% *v* 2%), with the majority of deaths among patients who required pneumonectomy. In patients who underwent lobectomy, and not pneumonectomy, there was a survival benefit to trimodality therapy, but this was a post hoc, exploratory subset of patients.

Unresectable Stage III NSCLC

The standard treatment of locally advanced, stage III NSCLC is concurrent chemoradiation and this would be the preferred treatment for all eligible patients with unresectable disease, such as bulky stage IIIA or stage IIIB/IIIC NSCLC. Randomized studies have demonstrated an improvement in median and long-term survival with chemotherapy followed by radiation therapy compared with radiation therapy alone.[113,114]

The results from two randomized studies, one conducted in Japan and the other by the Radiation Therapy Oncology Group (RTOG), showed a survival advantage with concurrent chemoradiation compared with a sequential approach, albeit at the expense of increased toxicity. In the Japanese trial, two cycles of mitomycin C plus vindesine plus cisplatin (MVP) were given concurrently or sequentially with 56 Gy of radiation.[115] Patients in either arm who experienced a response received another two cycles of MVP after radiation therapy was completed. The response rate and median survival were significantly improved with concurrent chemoradiotherapy (84% *v* 66%, *P* = .0002; 17 *v* 13 months, *P* = .04). The confirmatory randomized RTOG 9410 trial also showed improved survival with concurrent cisplatin, vinblastine, and radiation therapy compared with sequential chemoradiation (median survival, 17 *v* 13 months; *P* = .08).[116] Notably, the concurrent approach appeared to provide particular benefit to patients older than 70 years.

The two most commonly used chemotherapy regimens used with definitive radiation for NSCLC are (1) cisplatin plus etoposide (at full dose) and (2) carboplatin plus paclitaxel (at low, weekly doses).

Cisplatin plus etoposide was studied in a multicenter phase II study of patients with stage IIIB NSCLC.[117] In this study, the 5-year survival rate was 15% and treatment was notable for myelosuppression and a relatively high rate of radiation esophagitis (20% grade 3 to 4). Initially, chemoradiation was complemented with consolidation chemotherapy, but the current role of consolidation is unclear. SWOG 9504 demonstrated promising results with consolidation docetaxel following full-dose cisplatin plus etoposide and concurrent radiation therapy, but these results were not confirmed in a randomized trial.[118-120] Indeed, consolidation docetaxel after concurrent chemoradiation led to more febrile neutropenia, pneumonitis, and hospitalizations, and cannot be recommended.

A randomized phase III trial compared cisplatin plus etoposide with weekly carboplatin plus paclitaxel.[121] In this study, 200 patients with stage III NSCLC received 60 to 66 Gy thoracic radiation and were randomly assigned to receive either concurrent, full-dose cisplatin plus etoposide or weekly carboplatin plus paclitaxel. Neither arm received consolidation chemotherapy, which is a potential limitation to interpreting the carboplatin plus paclitaxel arm, where consolidation is often favored. There was no significant difference in OS between the two arms. The 3-year survival rate was notably higher with cisplatin plus etoposide, though the toxicity rates were also higher, including the incidence of grade 2 or higher radiation pneumonitis (33.3% *v* 18.9%) and grade 3 or higher esophagitis (20% *v* 6.3%).

Modern platinum doublets have also been explored. In the phase III PROCLAIM trial, 598 patients with stage IIIA/IIIB nonsquamous NSCLC were randomly assigned to receive thoracic radiation (60 to 66 Gy) with either concurrent cisplatin plus etoposide for two cycles followed by two cycles of consolidation platinum-based doublet chemotherapy or concurrent cisplatin plus pemetrexed for three cycles followed by four cycles of pemetrexed consolidation. This superiority study did not meet its primary end point. Cisplatin plus pemetrexed did not improve survival over cisplatin plus etoposide (HR, 0.98; median, 26.8 *v* 25.0 months), though the cisplatin plus pemetrexed arm had a lower incidence of any drug-related grade 3 to 4 adverse events (64.0% *v* 76.8%), including neutropenia (24.4% *v* 44.5%).[122]

The optimal chemotherapy to deliver with radiation remains unclear. Escalating radiation, however, appears to be an inferior approach. Results of a phase III trial[121] showed standard 60-Gy thoracic radiotherapy is superior to a 74-Gy radiation dose with chemotherapy in terms of OS and locoregional control for treatment of stage III NSCLC.[122] These results were not explained simply by an increase in toxicity.

Immunotherapy in Stage III NSCLC

Although definitive chemoradiation is a potentially curative treatment approach, long-term survival is unfortunately only achieved in a subset of patients. Efforts to improve survival had been largely unsuccessful until the recent incorporation of immunotherapy in this setting. Based in part on preclinical evidence demonstrating synergy between radiation and use of checkpoint inhibitors, the randomized phase III PACIFIC study explored the role of the PD-L1 inhibitor durvalumab as a consolidation therapy after concurrent chemoradiation.[123] In this trial, 713 patients with unresectable stage III NSCLC who had completed definitive thoracic radiation therapy (54 to 66 Gy) with at least two cycles of concurrent platinum-based chemotherapy and had not progressed were randomly assigned 2:1 to receive durvalumab 10 mg/kg or placebo every 2 weeks for up to 12 months. After a median follow-up of 25.2 months, the use of durvalumab significantly improved PFS from 5.6 months to 17.2 months (HR, 0.51) and also led to an improvement in OS (HR, 0.68). The incidence of new lesions was lower with durvalumab, including the development of new brain metastases (6.3% with durvalumab v 11.8% with placebo). The incidence of grade 3 or 4 adverse events was slightly higher with durvalumab (30.5% v 26.1%), with similar rates of pneumonitis (4.8% v 2.6%). Given acceptable tolerability and a clear improvement in survival, incorporation of durvalumab in appropriate patients has emerged as standard of care in this setting.

Treatment of patients with stage III NSCLC does not lend itself well to algorithms and requires input from an experienced, multidisciplinary team. Optimal management typically includes multimodality therapy with chemotherapy for all eligible patients with incorporation of some combination of radiation therapy, surgery, and immunotherapy. More work is needed to clarify which patients benefit from specific treatment approaches, and the role of targeted therapy is still under investigation.

KEY POINTS

- If microscopic N2 (or N1) disease is detected at surgery, postoperative chemotherapy should be administered. For N2 disease detected at surgery, PORT can be considered.
- The current standard treatment of locally advanced, stage III NSCLC remains concurrent platinum-based chemoradiation therapy.
- Consolidation with the PD-L1 inhibitor durvalumab after concurrent chemoradiation for unresectable stage III NSCLC improves PFS and OS and should be considered for all patients without a contraindication.

STAGE IV NSCLC

The majority of patients with NSCLC present with stage IV disease, for which the goal of treatment is largely palliative, not curative. Systemic therapy can prolong survival and improve quality of life, though it is important to review the goals and limitations of treatment with each patient. Historically, a similar treatment approach was used for all patients with advanced NSCLC; however, current treatment recommendations are guided by the presence or absence of an activating genomic alteration. When present, targeted therapy may be a preferred option, though the level of evidence for each specific target will vary. For some targets, FDA-approved agents have shown promising activity and, in some cases, offer superior outcomes to chemotherapy. For others targets, the evidence supporting targeted therapy may still be evolving but identification of these alterations may influence later lines of therapy or facilitate involvement in a clinical trial. When no actionable alterations are identified, after appropriate testing, early incorporation of immunotherapy improves outcomes. For all patients, optimizing palliation and supportive measures remains an important consideration.

Oligometastatic NSCLC

Although the presence of distant metastases is consistent with stage IV lung cancer, the extent of disease may play a role in management. This stems from the recognition that stage IV lung cancer still represents a spectrum of disease and some advanced cancers can still have a more indolent course.[124] The current AJCC staging system allows for identification of patients with a single extrathoracic metastasis in a single organ (M1b). For patients with NSCLC who have a limited number of metastases, or oligometastatic NSCLC, there may be a benefit to definitive therapy at all sites of disease. In a randomized phase II study, 49 patients with oligometastatic NSCLC, defined here as three or fewer sites of metastases, were randomly assigned to receive definitive local consolidative therapy after receiving first-line systemic therapy. Median PFS favored the local consolidative arm (11.9 v 3.9 months; HR, 0.35). The optimal definition of oligometastatic disease and the importance of specific sites of disease involvement will need additional refinement. Although more study is needed, local consolidation is an appropriate consideration for a subset of patients with limited sites of disease and a good PS.

TARGETED THERAPY IN NSCLC

Epidermal Growth Factor Receptor

Epidermal growth factor receptor (EGFR) belongs to the HER/erbB family of growth factor receptors, which includes EGFR (HER1 or erbB1), HER2/neu (erbB2), HER3 (erbB3), and HER4 (erbB4). These cell-surface proteins consist of an extracellular ligand-binding domain, a transmembrane structure, and an intracellular tyrosine kinase domain. The binding of ligand to receptor activates receptor dimerization and tyrosine kinase autophosphorylation, initiating a cascade of intracellular events and leading to increased cell proliferation, angiogenesis, metastasis, and a decrease in apoptosis. Inappropriate pathologic activation of this receptor-signal transduction pathway can be caused by specific EGFR-activating mutations (Fig 11-2).[33,34]

In NSCLC, activating mutations in the *EGFR* tyrosine kinase domain, seen in approximately 28% of lung adenocarcinomas, are centered around exons 18 to 21.[125] At diagnosis, these mutations are typically mutually exclusive of other driver alterations (though not always) and are associated with certain clinicopathologic features (ie, female sex, East Asian race, never or light smoking history, and adenocarcinoma histology), though *EGFR* mutations can regularly be detected in patients without these characteristics. Mutations in exons 19 and 21 ("classic" activating *EGFR* mutations) account for approximately 90% of *EGFR* mutations. Exon 19 mutations are most commonly in-frame deletions of amino acids 747 to 750. Exon 21 mutations are characteristically L858R substitutions. Other sensitizing mutations exist as well and when a sensitizing *EGFR* mutation is identified in advanced NSCLC, TKIs targeting EGFR are the preferred initial therapy. Activating insertions in exon 20 account for a smaller subset of *EGFR* mutations seen in NSCLC but still have transforming potential. Unfortunately, tumors harboring *EGFR* exon 20 insertions are generally resistant to the currently approved EGFR TKIs, likely because of the homology between the exon 20 mutant EGFR and wild-type EGFR.[35] Several agents are in development for this specific patient subset.

NSCLC harboring a sensitizing *EGFR* mutation is sensitive to treatment with an EGFR TKI. There are currently five different

Table 11-8 Select First-Line Randomized Trials of EGFR Tyrosine Kinase Inhibitor Therapy

Study	Intervention	EGFR+ Patients	ORR (%)	Median PFS (months)	HR for Progression	*P*
IPASS[126,256]	Gefitinib	132	71.2	9.5	0.48	< .001
	Carboplatin + paclitaxel	129	47.3	6.3		
WJTOG 3405[129]	Gefitinib	86	62.1	9.2	0.489	< .001
	Cisplatin + docetaxel	86	32.2	6.3		
NEJSG G002[130]	Gefitinib	114	73.7	10.8	0.30	< .001
	Carboplatin + paclitaxel	114	30.7	5.4		
OPTIMAL[131]	Erlotinib	83	83	13.1	0.16	< .001
	Carboplatin + gemcitabine	82	36	4.6		
EURTAC[132]	Erlotinib	86	58	9.7	0.37	< .001
	(Cisplatin or carboplatin) + (gemcitabine or docetaxel)	87	15	5.2		
LUX-Lung 3[133]	Afatinib	230	56	11.1	0.58	.001
	Cisplatin + pemetrexed	115	23	6.9		
LUX-Lung 6[257]	Afatinib	242	66.9	11	0.28	< .001
	Cisplatin + gemcitabine	122	23.0	5.6		
LUX-Lung 7[258]	Afatinib	160	70	11.0	0.73	.017
	Gefitinib	159	56	10.9		
ARCHER[136]	Dacomitinib	227	75	14.7	0.59	< .001
	Gefitinib	225	72	9.2		
FLAURA[127]	Osimertinib	279	80	18.9	0.46	<.001
	Erlotinib or gefitinib	277	76	10.2		

Abbreviations: EGRF, epidermal growth factor receptor; HR, hazard ratio; ORR, objective response rate; PFS, progression-free survival

EGFR TKIs approved for the initial treatment of EGFR-mutant NSCLC. Erlotinib and gefitinib are first-generation EGFR TKIs; these are reversible EGFR inhibitors that bind to mutant and wild-type EGFR. Afatinib and dacomitinib are second-generation EGFR TKIs; these bind irreversibly to mutant and wild-type EGFR as well as to HER2.[117,118] Osimertinib is the only available third-generation EGFR TKI, and it is an irreversible, mutant-selective inhibitor. In *EGFR*-mutant NSCLC, EGFR TKI therapy has been consistently superior to platinum-doublet chemotherapy, with markedly higher response rates and significantly improved PFS (Table 11-8). EGFR TKI therapy can be associated with rash, diarrhea, and paronychia, related to EGFR expression in nontumor tissue, but consistently has lower rates of grade 3 or higher toxicity than chemotherapy. There have also been studies comparing EGFR TKIs, with second-generation TKIs providing superior results to first-generation TKIs (though with more toxicity, including diarrhea and rash). The third-generation TKI osimertinib was also compared with first-generation TKI therapy in the randomized FLAURA trial.[127] Osimertinib had a superior PFS of 18.9 months compared with 10.2 months in the control arm (HR, 0.46). Duration of response was greater with osimertinib (17.2 *v* 8.5 months) and the incidence of grade 3 or higher adverse events was lower with osimertinib (34% *v* 45%). With longer follow up, a survival advantage was seen with osimertinib (HR, 0.80), where median survival was 38.6 months compared to 31.8 months with erlotinib or gefitinib.[128]

Osimertinib is now approved as initial therapy for *EGFR*-mutant NSCLC.

Less common *EGFR* mutations were included in three trials of afatinib: LUX-Lung 2, LUX-Lung 3, and LUX-Lung 6.[136] Although not all known *EGFR* mutations predicted response (including de novo T790M and exon 20 insertions), several did confer sensitivity, including S768I, L861Q, and G719X. Afatinib is FDA approved for NSCLC harboring nonresistant *EGFR* mutations, including these less common variants.

Despite an initial dramatic response to EGFR inhibitors among patients with *EGFR*-mutant NSCLC, resistance generally develops within 2 years.[137] Following initial use of first or second generation EGFR TKIs, approximately half of these cases are associated with a secondary *EGFR* exon 20 T790M mutation, which results in steric hindrance to EGFR-TKI binding (analogous to the T315I mutation in chronic myeloid leukemia) and altered ATP handling.[138,139] A subset of *EGFR*-mutated tumors can develop acquired resistance with a histologic transformation to SCLC and may respond to chemotherapy regimens active in that disease.[141] This appears to be much more likely in tumors that harbor inactivated *RB1* and *TP53*.[142]

Osimertinib still binds to mutant EGFR in the presence of the T790M mutation. In patients with *EGFR*-mutant NSCLC with the T790M mutation after progression on prior EGFR-TKI therapy, osimertinib demonstrated significant activity with a response rate of 61% and a median PFS of 9.6 months.[143] The confirmatory phase III trial randomly assigned patients with T790M-positive NSCLC whose disease progressed after treatment with an EGFR TKI to receive osimertinib or carboplatin plus pemetrexed.[144] Osimertinib was associated with a longer PFS (8.5 *v* 4.2 months; HR, 0.42) and a higher response rate (71% *v* 31%). The rate of grade 3 or higher adverse events was lower with osimertinib (23%) than chemotherapy (47%). Osimertinib has been approved and is now standard of care when T790M is identified as the mechanism of acquired resistance to early-generation EGFR TKIs.

Mechanisms of acquired resistance to osimertinib are still under investigation.[140, 145] At this time, chemotherapy would be a standard option at the time of progression after osimertinib (or resistance to a first- or second-generation TKI that is not mediated by T790M). Although the role of continuing osimertinib with subsequent lines of therapy is not clear, the IMPRESS study explored the role of continuing gefitinib during cytotoxic chemotherapy.[146] In this trial, 265 patients with *EGFR* mutation–positive NSCLC that had progressed after initial benefit from gefitinib were treated with cisplatin plus pemetrexed. Patients were randomly assigned 1:1 to daily gefitinib or placebo during chemotherapy. Unfortunately, continuation gefitinib was associated with an inferior survival compared with placebo (13.4 *v* 19.5 months; HR, 1.44).

Anaplastic Lymphoma Kinase–Positive NSCLC

Rearrangements in the anaplastic lymphoma kinase (*ALK*) gene can lead to a fusion oncogene with transforming potential and are detected in approximately 2% to 7% of NSCLCs. Although there are multiple described fusion partners involved in this rearrangement, the most common sequence involves a chromosome 2p inversion that results in fusion of the protein encoded by the echinoderm microtubule-associated protein-like 4 (*EML4*) gene with the intracellular signaling portion of the ALK receptor tyrosine kinase. Analogous to *EGFR* mutations, *EML4-ALK* fusions result in constitutive tyrosine kinase activity, dependence of the cancer cell on activated downstream mitogenic pathways, and sensitivity to ALK inhibition.[36] *ALK* fusions are more commonly described in patients with adenocarcinoma histology, younger age, and a history of light or never smoking.[37] *ALK* rearranged NSCLC can be identified using IHC, fluorescence in situ hybridization, or next-generation sequencing.[38,39] Specific fusion variants may impact disease course and are the focus of ongoing study.[40]

The first TKI approved for NSCLC harboring an *ALK* gene rearrangement was crizotinib, after it demonstrated a response rate of 57% in a phase I study that included 82 patients, most of whom were previously treated.[147] The subsequent randomized phase III PROFILE 1007 trial compared second-line crizotinib to docetaxel in patients with ALK-positive NSCLC that had progressed after chemotherapy.[148] Crizotinib had a superior PFS (7.7 *v* 3.0 months; HR 0.49) and response rate (65% *v* 20%) as well as a greater improvement in global quality of life. When compared with first-line chemotherapy in the PROFILE 1014 trial, crizotinib was again associated with improved outcomes.[149] The median PFS with crizotinib was 10.9 months compared with 7.0 months with platinum plus pemetrexed (HR, 0.45) and the response rate was 74% compared with 45%.

Following disease progression after crizotinib therapy, multiple agents have demonstrated efficacy, including ceritinib, alectinib, and brigatinib.[150–152] All three of these agents have also been studied in the first-line setting. In the ASCEND-4 study, treatment-naïve patients who were ALK positive were randomly assigned to treatment with ceritinib or platinum plus pemetrexed (with maintenance pemetrexed).[153] Ceritinib had a superior PFS of 16.6 months compared with 8.1 months with chemotherapy (HR, 0.55). In the ALEX trial, 303 ALK-positive patients were randomly assigned to first-line alectinib or first-line crizotinib.[154] Investigator-assessed PFS was notably longer with alectinib (HR, 0.43), with a median PFS of 34.8 months, compared with 10.9 months with crizotinib therapy.[155] Brigatinib has also been studied in the first-line setting. In the ALTA-1L study, 275 ALK-positive patients were randomly assigned to treatment with first-line brigatinib or crizotinib.[156] Brigatinib had a superior PFS (HR, 0.49) with a much higher intracranial response rate (78% *v* 29%).

Acquired resistance is still a significant clinical challenge with all ALK TKIs. Unlike resistance to first- and second-generation EGFR TKIs, there is not a dominant mechanism for resistance to ALK TKIs. Solvent-front point mutations in *ALK* have been described in a subset of cases, though other mechanisms have been identified.[157] Lorlatinib has in vitro activity against a broad spectrum of ALK TKI resistance mutations and is now approved for the treatment of ALK-rearranged NSCLC in patients whose disease has progressed on treatment with crizotinib and another ALK inhibitor or has progressed on treatment with first-line alectinib or ceritinib. In a phase I-II trial, lorlatinib demonstrated activity in *ALK*-rearranged NSCLC, including tumors with known resistance mutations that had progressed on alectinib.[158] In patients who had received two or more *ALK* TKIs, the response rate was 42% (n = 11 of 26 patients).

ROS-1–Positive NSCLC

ROS-1 gene rearrangements are oncogenic drivers present in about 1% of NSCLC tumors.[42] *ROS-1* is an orphan tyrosine kinase of the insulin receptor family located on chromosome 6 and with notable sequence homology to *ALK*. Gene rearrangements of *ROS-1* lead to constitutive activation of this tyrosine kinase. Like many oncogene-addicted lung cancers, *ROS-1*–rearranged tumors commonly arise in younger nonsmokers with lung adenocarcinoma histology. Targeted therapy has also proven effective in ROS-1–positive NSCLC. Crizotinib was approved by the FDA for the treatment of advanced NSCLC with an *ROS-1* fusion after a single-arm study showed a high response rate (72%) with a median PFS of 19.2 months.[159] The other ROS-1 TKI approved for ROS-1–positive NSCLC is entrectinib. In an analysis of 53 patients across three separate phase I/II trials, the overall response rate was 77.4%, with a median PFS of 19.0 months.[160] It is worth noting that although there is significant sequence homology between ALK and ROS-1, and crizotinib is approved in both settings, not all ALK inhibitors are effective ROS-1 inhibitors. For example, alectinib is a potent ALK TKI but has no notable activity at ROS-1.

BRAF-Positive NSCLC

BRAF

BRAF mutations are present in 2% to 4% of lung adenocarcinomas. Unlike *EGFR* mutations and *ALK* rearrangements, *BRAF*-mutant lung adenocarcinoma is frequently seen in patients with or without a smoking history.[40] Unlike melanoma, in which the majority of *BRAF* mutations are V600E, only about half of the *BRAF* mutations in NSCLC are the clinically relevant V600E. Presence of the *BRAF* V600E mutation in metastatic melanoma predicts response to dabrafenib, a BRAF inhibitor, and trametinib, a MEK inhibitor. The mutation has a similar predictive role in NSCLC. In a phase II trial of dabrafenib plus trametinib, among 57 patients with previously treated *BRAF* V600E–positive NSCLC, the response rate was 63.2% and the median PFS was 9.7 months.[161] Outcomes appeared better with combined *BRAF* V600E and MEK inhibition than seen in a separate trial exploring dabrafenib alone, which resulted in a lower, but still substantial, 32% overall response rate and 56% 12-week disease-control rate. In a subsequent cohort of treatment-naïve, *BRAF* V600E–positive patients, the combination of dabrafenib plus trametinib had similar outcomes with a response rate of 64% (including two patients with a complete response) and a PFS of 10.9 months.[162]

Other Driver Alterations (*RET*, *MET*, *HER2*, *NTRK*)

NSCLC has an increasing number of relevant but less common molecular subtypes.[43] As more driver alterations are uncovered, molecular testing practices and therapeutic interventions will need to evolve further. A partial list of potentially actionable genomic alterations relevant to the treatment of NSCLC would include fusions in *NTRK1-3* and *RET* and mutations in *MET* and *HER2*. In these settings, the optimal sequence of therapy is not yet known but targeted therapy warrants consideration.

NTRK fusions have been described in < 1% of lung cancers, but when present, they predict response to NTRK inhibitors. Larotrectinib is a selective NTRK inhibitor approved in a tumor agnostic manner for use in advanced cancers harboring an *NTRK* fusion. In a report of 55 patients with *NTRK* fusion–positive cancer (n = 4 with lung cancer), the response rate was 75% with no drug-related grade 3 or 4 adverse events.[51] Entrectinib is another potent NTRK inhibitor with efficacy across tumor types and approval with a tumor-agnostic indication. In an analysis of 54 NTRK-positive patients (n = 10 with NSCLC), the response rate was 57.4%, with a median PFS of 11.2 months.[163] Entrectinib is also highly CNS penetrant, with an intracranial response rate of 54.5%.

RET gene fusions have been identified in 1% to 2% of NSCLCs, and are more frequently seen in younger patients with no smoking history.[44] Fusions in *RET* are rare but potentially actionable alterations in NSCLC. Cabozantinib is a multikinase TKI approved for the treatment of renal cell carcinoma and medullary thyroid cancer. In a phase II study in *RET* fusion–positive NSCLC, cabozantinib had a response rate of 28%.[164] Other, more selective RET inhibitors are currently in development.

MET exon 14 skipping mutations represent approximately 2.5% of NSCLCs and occur more frequently in the rare sarcomatoid histology of NSCLC (approximately 20% to 30% frequency). These juxtamembrane splice-site mutations lead to decreased MET degradation and appear to be potent oncogenic drivers.[45] *MET* exon 14 skipping mutations have been associated with response to crizotinib, yet another target for this versatile TKI. In a study of 17 patients with *MET* exon 14 skip mutations, 58.8% of patients had a response and 29.4% had a confirmed response.[165]

HER2 mutations have been described in approximately 1% to 2% of NSCLCs. *HER2* can be amplified in lung cancer as it is in breast cancer, but the *HER2* mutations found in NSCLC are distinct from *HER2* amplification and most commonly are insertions in exon 20.[46] The antibody-drug conjugate ado-trastuzumab emtansine has shown promising efficacy in *HER2*-mutant NSCLC.[166] In an 18-patient cohort, the response rate was 44% and responses were seen in patients with *HER2* exon 20 insertions and point mutations.

Although larotrectinib and entrectinib are approved with a tumor agnostic indication, it is worth noting that many of these driver alterations best described in NSCLC have also been observed in other cancer types. For example, *ALK* fusions can be seen in anaplastic large-cell lymphomas,[47] and inflammatory myofibroblastic tumor[48] and *ROS-1* fusions have been noted in thyroid carcinoma[49] and pancreatic cancer.[50] These findings support an approach that, in some cases, a tumor's molecular characteristics, and not anatomic site or histology, may ultimately guide treatment selection in oncology. This is still an area of active study, however, and not always the case (ie, *BRAF* mutations in colorectal cancer do not predict sensitivity to BRAF inhibitors).[52]

KEY POINTS

- For *EGFR*-mutant NSCLC, approved first-line options include osimertinib, dacomitinib, afatinib, erlotinib, and gefitinib.
- Acquired resistance to first- and second-generation EGFR TKIs is often mediated by the T790M resistance mutation in exon 20 of *EGFR*, and osimertinib is indicated in this setting.
- For *ALK*-rearranged NSCLC, approved first-line options include alectinib, ceritinib, and crizotinib.
- Crizotinib and entrectinib are approved for *ROS-1*–positive NSCLC.
- The combination of dabrafenib and trametinib is approved for the treatment of NSCLC harboring a *BRAF* V600E mutation.
- Larotrectinib and entrectinib are approved in tumors with an *NTRK1-3* fusion.
- Targeted therapy has shown great promise in tumors with activating genomic alterations in *MET*, *RET*, and *HER2* and warrant consideration, though participation in a clinical trial is preferred when possible.

First-Line Immunotherapy

The introduction of checkpoint inhibitors, specifically antibodies targeting PD-1 and PD-1 ligand (PD-L1), has dramatically changed the treatment paradigm for NSCLC (Fig 11-5). Although initial studies were in previously treated patients, immunotherapy has now become part of first-line treatment of NSCLC. In the KEYNOTE-024 trial, 305 patients with PD-L1 expression on at least 50% of tumor cells (ie, a tumor proportion score [TPS] of 50%) and wild-type *EGFR* and *ALK* were randomly assigned to receive either pembrolizumab alone or platinum-based chemotherapy.[167] Crossover from the chemotherapy group to the pembrolizumab group was allowed at disease progression. The primary end point of PFS was superior in the pembrolizumab arm compared with chemotherapy arm, with a median PFS of 10.3 versus 6.0 months (HR, 0.50). Survival was also significantly improved in the pembrolizumab arm (HR, 0.60). The response rate was higher with pembrolizumab (44.8% *v* 27.8%), and treatment-related adverse events of any grade were less frequent (73.4% *v* 90.0% of patients), as were serious treatment-related adverse events (26.6% *v* 53.3%). Pembrolizumab is FDA approved as first-line treatment of stage IV NSCLC with a PD-L1 TPS of at least 50%.

KEYNOTE-042 compared first-line pembrolizumab monotherapy with chemotherapy in patients with PD-L1 positive NSCLC using a PD-L1 TPS cutoff of 1%.[168] The study met its primary end point of improved OS in the pembrolizumab arm, with a median OS of 16.7 months versus 12.1 months (HR, 0.81). The benefit was driven, however, by patients with a PD-L1 TPS of ≥ 50%. In the exploratory subset of patients with a PD-L1 TPS of 1% to 49%, there was not a clear difference between pembrolizumab and chemotherapy. On the basis of this study, pembrolizumab was approved for advanced NSCLC with a PD-L1 TPS of ≥ 1%, but its role in tumors with a TPS of 1% to 49% is less clear.

In the Checkmate 026 trial, 541 patients whose tumors were PD-L1 positive (defined as expression in 1% of cells using the Dako 28-8 PD-L1 IHC clone) were randomly assigned to nivolumab or platinum-based chemotherapy.[169] The primary end point was PFS in patients with ≥ 5% PD-L1 expression. Among these patients, nivolumab did not improve median PFS compared with investigators' choice of chemotherapy and there was no difference in survival (median, 14.4 months for nivolumab *v* 13.2 months for chemotherapy; HR, 1.02).

Chemotherapy-Immunotherapy Combinations

Although pembrolizumab has established a new standard of care in tumors with ≥ 50% PD-L1 expression, combinations of checkpoint inhibitors with cytotoxic therapy have also shown great promise in patients across the spectrum of PD-L1 expression (Fig 11-5). Concurrent administration of chemotherapy and immunotherapy has several potential advantages.[170] Chemotherapy can lead to the depletion of immunosuppressive cells and promote neoantigen presentation to facilitate an immune-mediated antitumor response. Recent data also show pemetrexed administration can induce an immune activation gene-expression signature.[171] Early trials of combined chemotherapy with PD-L1 inhibitors demonstrated the potential for long-term survival with no significance increase in the expected toxicity profile.[172]

The first approved chemotherapy-immunotherapy combination for NSCLC was carboplatin, pemetrexed, and pembrolizumab in nonsquamous NSCLC. Initial approval was based on results of the KEYNOTE-021 trial: 123 patients with treatment-naïve, nonsquamous NSCLC were randomly assigned to the triplet of carboplatin, pemetrexed, and pembrolizumab or the doublet of carboplatin plus pemetrexed.[173] The primary end point of response rate was superior with the addition of pembrolizumab (55% *v* 26%). In the confirmatory phase III KEYNOTE-189 study, 616 patients with treatment-naïve, nonsquamous NSCLC were randomly assigned 2:1 to platinum (carboplatin or cisplatin), pemetrexed, and pembrolizumab (with pembrolizumab and pemetrexed maintenance) or platinum, pemetrexed, and placebo (with placebo and pemetrexed maintenance).[174] The response rate was higher with pembrolizumab in the overall study population (48% *v* 19%) and in all PD-L1 subsets: 61% versus 23% with PD-L1 TPS ≥ 50%, 48% versus 21% with PD-L1 TPS 1% to 49%, and 32% versus 14% in PD-L1–negative tumors. Survival also favored chemo-immunotherapy with an HR of 0.49, also seen across PD-L1 subsets. It is worth noting that both KEYNOTE-021 and KEYNOTE-189 excluded patients with activating alterations in *EGFR* or *ALK*.

Another approved chemo-immunotherapy combination is the four-drug regimen of carboplatin, paclitaxel, bevacizumab, and atezolizumab. In the IMpower 150 study, this regimen was compared with carboplatin, paclitaxel, and bevacizumab.[175] Unlike KEYNOTE-189, IMpower 150 included patients with *EGFR* or *ALK* alterations, though only after progressing on the appropriate TKI therapy. The addition of atezolizumab to the backbone of carboplatin, paclitaxel, and bevacizumab led to an improvement in PFS (8.3 *v* 6.8 months; HR, 0.62) as well as a significant increase in survival (19.2 *v* 14.7 months; HR, 0.78). This combination has also been approved for treatment-naïve, nonsquamous NSCLC, independent of PD-L1 expression. Its FDA approval does not include the exploratory subset of EGFR- or ALK-positive NSCLC, though approvals outside of the United States do include this subset.

Chemo-immunotherapy has also improved outcomes in squamous NSCLC. In KEYNOTE-407, 559 patients with untreated, stage IV squamous NSCLC were treated with carboplatin plus either paclitaxel or nab-paclitaxel (investigator's choice) and were randomly assigned to receive either pembrolizumab or placebo, with pembrolizumab or placebo maintenance for up to 31 cycles.[176] The response rate was higher with pembrolizumab in the overall study population (58% *v* 38%) and in PD-L1–high (60% *v* 33%), PD-L1–low (50% *v* 41%) and PD-L1–negative (63% *v* 40%) subsets. Survival also favored the addition of pembrolizumab (HR, 0.64). This regimen has been approved as initial therapy for squamous NSCLC independent of PD-L1 expression.

Immunotherapy as Second-Line Therapy

Although immunotherapy in NSCLC currently is incorporated in standard first-line therapy, its initial approval was in the second-line setting after multiple randomized trials showed PD-1 and PD-L1 inhibitors were superior to second-line docetaxel. For patients who do not receive immunotherapy initially, it should be considered in the second-line setting, though the preferred strategy is early incorporation, given the suboptimal cross-over rates seen in KEYNOTE-024.[167] Three PD-1/PD-L1 antibodies are currently approved for second-line treatment of advanced NSCLC (Table 11-9): nivolumab (a PD-1), pembrolizumab (a PD-1), and atezolizumab (a PD-L1). All these agents were compared with second-line docetaxel and were associated with an improved OS. Pembrolizumab is approved for PD-L1–positive (TPS ≥ 1%) NSCLC, whereas nivolumab and atezolizumab are approved independent of PD-L1 expression. The PD-L1 inhibitor avelumab was also compared with docetaxel but did not improve survival.[177]

No direct comparisons exist among these agents. No clear role is recognized for use of these agents as monotherapy in patients whose disease has progressed after treatment with a PD-1 or PD-L1 inhibitor in the front-line setting, either alone or with chemotherapy. The role of immunotherapy in patients with actionable genomic alterations is unclear. Some patients with *EGFR* mutations were among the long-term survivors in the phase I study of nivolumab, showing that durable benefit from immunotherapy is possible in this subset of patients.[180] However, the likelihood of response is low. In a retrospective analysis of patients with EGFR mutations or *ALK* rearrangements, the response to PD-L1 inhibition was reported as only 3.6%, compared with 23.3% in an *EGFR* and *ALK* wild-type population.[183] Patients with *EGFR* and *ALK* alterations were excluded from the first-line randomized trials of pembrolizumab and the combination of pembrolizumab, carboplatin, and pemetrexed.[167,174] EGFR- and ALK-positive patients (who had previously received TKI therapy) were included in the IMpower 150 first-line study of carboplatin, paclitaxel, bevacizumab, and atezolizumab and subset analysis results were encouraging, but the analysis was exploratory and the sample size was small.[175] Immunotherapy, however, should not supplant TKI therapy. A phase II study explored the role of first-line pembrolizumab in patients with *EGFR*-mutant, PD-L1–positive NSCLC and reported no responses.[184]

KEY POINTS

- For tumors without an activating alteration in *EGFR* or *ALK* and with high PD-L1 expression (≥ 50%), pembrolizumab monotherapy is an approved and appropriate option after demonstrating an improvement in survival over platinum-doublet chemotherapy.
- The addition of pembrolizumab to platinum plus pemetrexed improved PFS and survival in patients with nonsquamous NSCLC (*EGFR* and *ALK* wild type) across all PD-L1 subsets.
- A carboplatin, paclitaxel, bevacizumab, and atezolizumab combination improved survival over carboplatin, paclitaxel, and bevacizumab in nonsquamous NSCLC and is also approved as initial therapy independent of PD-L1 expression.
- Pembrolizumab also improved outcomes, including survival in squamous NSCLC, when added to platinum combination therapy with paclitaxel or nab-paclitaxel.
- For patients who do not receive immunotherapy as part of first-line therapy (which is preferred for patients without a driver alteration), pembrolizumab (for PD-L1, TPS ≥ 1%), nivolumab (independent of PD-L1), and atezolizumab (independent of PD-L1) improved survival compared with docetaxel and are approved as monotherapy.

First-Line Platinum-Doublet Chemotherapy

Most patients with advanced NSCLC should receive either targeted therapy or immunotherapy (alone or with chemotherapy) as their initial therapy. For patients who are not candidates for immunotherapy, platinum-doublet chemotherapy remains a relevant option. Until recently, there was not felt to be a clinically significant advantage of any specific platinum-based doublet regimen over another. The landmark ECOG 1594 study randomly assigned 1,207 patients with treatment-naïve NSCLC to cisplatin plus paclitaxel, cisplatin plus gemcitabine, cisplatin plus docetaxel, or carboplatin plus paclitaxel.[185] The response rate and survival were similar across all arms. Data now support different treatment approaches for specific histologic subtypes of NSCLC, based on efficacy (pemetrexed and gemcitabine) and safety (bevacizumab). A phase III trial of > 1,700 patients with chemotherapy-naïve disease compared pemetrexed plus cisplatin and gemcitabine plus cisplatin.[186] Although OS was similar in the two arms, in a prespecified subset analysis, survival was statistically superior for cisplatin plus pemetrexed compared with cisplatin plus gemcitabine for patients with adenocarcinoma (12.6 *v* 10.9 months) and large-cell carcinoma histology (10.4 *v* 6.7 months). Conversely, patients with squamous cell histology experienced a significant improvement in survival with cisplatin plus gemcitabine compared with cisplatin plus pemetrexed (10.8 *v* 9.4 months).

Meta-analyses have suggested that cisplatin may have a modest benefit in terms of survival as compared with carboplatin for patients with advanced disease, albeit with a different toxicity profile.[187] In one direct comparison, patients in a phase III trial of the Spanish Lung Cancer Group were randomly assigned to paclitaxel with either cisplatin or carboplatin. Efficacy end points showed superiority of the cisplatin-based regimen with approximately a 1-month improvement in survival.[188] In metastatic, incurable disease, where the goal is palliation, carboplatin is an appropriate agent, because administration of cisplatin with higher rates of renal insufficiency, neuropathy, and hearing loss may significantly affect quality of life.

Maintenance Chemotherapy

Results from early randomized studies did not show a survival difference with prolonged (more than six) cycles of chemotherapy compared with fewer (four to six) cycles.[189-193] More recent trials have challenged that paradigm. Two maintenance strategies have been investigated: so-called switch maintenance and continuation maintenance. The goal of continuation maintenance is to delay progressive disease by continuing an effective agent. The aim of switch maintenance is to initiate a new second-line agent early to delay onset of progressive disease.

Three trials have been reported that suggest a benefit with prolonged therapy. In one study, patients who had stable or responsive disease after their initial four cycles of gemcitabine plus carboplatin were randomly assigned to receive maintenance docetaxel immediately after induction chemotherapy or at progression.[192] Median PFS for immediate docetaxel was significantly greater than for delayed docetaxel (5.7 *v* 2.7 months; $P = .001$). Median survival for immediate docetaxel also was greater than for delayed docetaxel, although the difference was not significant (12.3 *v* 9.7 months). Interestingly, the median survival for patients assigned to treatment with immediate docetaxel and those assigned to delayed docetaxel treatment who received the specified therapy at the time of progression was identical. These findings raise the question of whether switch-maintenance therapy may be similar to early use of second-line therapy at the first sign of progressive disease. An important finding from this study is that only 62.8% of patients in the delayed docetaxel arm received their assigned treatment. The most common reason for not receiving docetaxel at the time of progression was disease progression itself.

Switch-maintenance pemetrexed was studied in a large randomized trial.[193] A total of 633 patients with stable or responsive disease were randomly assigned 2:1 to observation or pemetrexed after induction chemotherapy with platinum-based, non-pemetrexed chemotherapy. Switch maintenance with pemetrexed improved survival (13.4 *v* 10.6 months; HR, 0.79) and PFS. The improvement in survival was observed primarily among patients with nonsquamous histology (15.5 *v* 10.3 months).

A phase III clinical trial (PARAMOUNT) explored continuation-maintenance pemetrexed. Patients with advanced nonsquamous NSCLC were randomly assigned to four cycles of cisplatin and pemetrexed followed by observation, compared with continuation-maintenance pemetrexed every 3 weeks until progression or intolerable toxic effects occurred.[194] Continuation-maintenance with pemetrexed improved PFS and OS, with a median OS of 16.9 months compared with 14.0 months after induction.

Table 11-9 Checkpoint Inhibitors as Second-Line Therapy (*v* Docetaxel) in Non-Small-Cell Lung Cancer, ITT

Study	Type of NSCLC	Response Rate (%)	Median PFS	Median OS	1-Year OS (%)
Nivolumab Checkmate 017[178]	Squamous	20 (*v* 9)	3.5 (*v* 2.8)	9.2 (*v* 6.0)	42 (*v* 24)
Nivolumab Checkmate 057[179]	Nonsquamous	19 (*v* 12)	2.3 (*v* 4.2)	12.2 (*v* 9.4)	51 (*v* 39)
Pembrolizumab KEYNOTE 010[181]	PD-L1+	18 (*v* 9)	3.9 (*v* 4.0)	10.4 (*v* 8.5)	43 (*v* 35)
Atezolizumab OAK[182]	NSCLC	14 (*v* 13)	2.8 (*v* 4.0)	13.8 (*v* 9.6)	55 (*v* 41)
Avelumab JAVELIN[177]	NSCLC	15 (*v* 11)	2.8 (*v* 4.2)	10.5 (*v* 9.9)	

Abbreviations: NSCLC, non-small-cell lung cancer; OS, overall survival; PFS, progression-free survival.

Bevacizumab

Bevacizumab is a monoclonal antibody that targets vascular endothelial growth factor and inhibits the process of angiogenesis. Bevacizumab has been approved for the management of nonsquamous NSCLC on the basis of results from the Eastern Cooperative Oncology Group (ECOG) 4599 phase III trial of 878 patients randomly assigned to chemotherapy (paclitaxel and carboplatin) or to chemotherapy plus 15 mg/kg bevacizumab every 3 weeks.[195] Median survival for patients who received chemotherapy plus bevacizumab was 12.3 months, compared with 10.3 months for patients who received chemotherapy alone. Bevacizumab also improved both PFS (6.2 *v* 4.5 months) and response rate (35% *v* 15%). However, because of grade 3 to 4 bleeding episodes observed in a phase II study,[196] use of bevacizumab is restricted to patients with nonsquamous histology (because of higher levels of severe hemoptysis observed in squamous NSCLC).

A second randomized study of bevacizumab involving > 1,000 patients has been conducted (the Avastin in Lung [AVAIL] trial).[197] Unlike the ECOG study, this study involved gemcitabine and cisplatin and patients were randomly assigned to chemotherapy plus placebo, chemotherapy with 7.5 mg/kg bevacizumab every 3 weeks, or chemotherapy with 15 mg/kg bevacizumab every 3 weeks. The study met its primary end point of PFS; however, the absolute benefit was modest (median PFS, 6.7 and 6.5 months *v* 6.1 months), with no improvement in survival. It is unclear whether the lack of survival benefit is a result of the differences in chemotherapy doublets between the ECOG study and the AVAIL trial, differences in bevacizumab dose, or differences in study design, of which there were many.

Cetuximab and Necitumumab

In contrast to EGFR-TKIs, the effect of anti-EGFR monoclonal antibodies in NSCLC is less well defined and is not associated with the presence of activating *EGFR* mutations. Two phase III clinical trials incorporating anti-EGFR monoclonal antibodies have been performed. Patients with NSCLC in the BMS099 trial were randomly assigned to treatment with platinum plus taxane chemotherapy with or without cetuximab.[198] No difference in survival was noted. Patients in the First-line in Lung cancer with ErbituX (FLEX) trial were randomly assigned receive cisplatin plus vinorelbine with or without cetuximab.[199] The cetuximab-containing arm demonstrated a statistically significant improvement in OS (HR, 0.87), with an increase in median survival from 10.1 to 11.3 months. Whether differences in the chemotherapy regimen, geographic setting, or inclusion criteria (FLEX mandated EGFR-positive tumors, defined as at least one cell staining positive by IHC) underlie the different results of the BMS099 and FLEX trials is not known. As for first-line treatment in stage IV squamous cell NSCLC, another EGFR monoclonal antibody, necitumumab, modestly improved OS when added to cisplatin and gemcitabine. In the SQUIRE trial, 1,093 patients received cisplatin plus gemcitabine and were randomly assigned to receive necitumumab.[200] The addition of necitumumab modestly improved survival (median survival, 11.5 , 9.9 months; HR 0.84).

Chemotherapy in Older Patients

Treatment of patients age 65 years or older tends to be complicated by comorbid conditions and by patients taking multiple medications. However, studies show that fit older patients are likely to benefit as much from chemotherapy as their younger counterparts. Evidence from a phase III study in which patients older than 70 years who had advanced disease were randomly assigned to best supportive care or to weekly vinorelbine indicated that patients who received vinorelbine had better scores on quality-of-life scales than did the control group, as well as fewer lung cancer–related symptoms. However, patients in the chemotherapy group experienced more severe toxicity-related symptoms.[201] There was a significant survival advantage for patients who received vinorelbine (median survival, 28 *v* 21 weeks). More recently, it has been shown that, despite an increase in toxic effects, platinum-based doublet chemotherapy yields superior outcomes to single-agent chemotherapy in fit elderly individuals. In a phase III trial conducted by the Intergroupe Francophone de Cancerologie Thoracique, 451 previously untreated patients ages 70 to 89 (median, 77) years with ECOG PS of 0 to 2 were randomly assigned to carboplatin plus paclitaxel or monotherapy with vinorelbine or gemcitabine.[202] In each arm of the study, 27% of patients had an ECOG PS of 2. Median survival was 10.3 months in the carboplatin plus paclitaxel arm, compared with 6.2 months in the monotherapy arm. Subset analyses of other randomized trials showed the response rate, toxicity, and survival for fit older patients receiving platinum-based treatment of NSCLC appear to be similar to the same variables for younger patients. For patients ≥ 70 years old, however, comorbidity is greater and the frequencies of leukopenia and neuropsychiatric toxicity are higher. Hence, advanced age alone should not preclude appropriate treatment.

Second- and Third-Line Therapy Beyond Immunotherapy

For patients whose disease progresses on platinum-doublet therapy and immunotherapy (either concurrent or in some sequence), a standard treatment option would be docetaxel. In two randomized trials, second-line docetaxel was evaluated for patients who did not respond to first-line platinum-doublet chemotherapy. Docetaxel significantly prolonged survival compared with best supportive care.[203] Moreover, docetaxel also improved quality of life and reduced weight loss and the need for pain medications. Previous exposure to paclitaxel did not affect response to docetaxel, suggesting non–cross-resistance between the two agents. In a second study, docetaxel was compared with either vinorelbine or ifosfamide.[204] Although OS was not significantly different among the three groups, the 1-year survival associated with docetaxel was notably better than that associated with the control treatment (32% *v* 19%).

Ramucirumab is a monoclonal antibody that targets VEGFR2. This antiangiogenesis agent, in combination with docetaxel, has been approved for the treatment of metastatic NSCLC with progression of disease on or after platinum-based treatment. Unlike bevacizumab, which is contraindicated in squamous histology NSCLC, ramucirumab is approved and has shown benefit in both squamous and non-squamous subtypes.

Approval was based on results from the randomized, phase III REVEL trial, in which 1,253 patients with stage IV NSCLC after progression on platinum-based chemotherapy were randomly assigned to docetaxel therapy with or without ramucirumab.[205] Survival (10.5 *v* 9.5 months), PFS (4.5 *v* 3.0 months), and response rates (23% *v* 14%) were all improved with the addition of ramucirumab.

A phase III study compared pemetrexed with docetaxel.[206] Although no difference in survival was observed (1-year survival was 29.7% in both arms), patients randomly assigned to receive docetaxel were more likely to have febrile neutropenia (12.7% *v* 1.9%), infections (3.3% *v* 0%), and hospitalizations for neutropenic fevers (13.4% *v* 1.5%) than patients who received pemetrexed, resulting in the FDA approval of pemetrexed as second-line therapy for NSCLC.

The irreversible EGFR-TKI afatinib received FDA approval for the treatment of advanced squamous NSCLC as second-line treatment after platinum-doublet chemotherapy. Approval was based on findings of a large randomized, phase III study (LUX-LUNG 8).[207] In this trial, 795 patients with advanced squamous cell lung cancer were randomly assigned to afatinib or erlotinib. PFS was the primary end point and was significantly longer with afatinib than with erlotinib (median, 2.4 *v* 1.9 months). Survival was also modestly greater in the afatinib group than in the erlotinib group (7.9 *v* 6.8 months).

KEY POINTS

- Pemetrexed is an appropriate platinum partner in nonsquamous histology; gemcitabine is appropriate for treatment of tumors with squamous histology.
- Bevacizumab prolongs survival when administered with carboplatin plus paclitaxel to eligible patients with advanced nonsquamous NSCLC, as demonstrated in a large, randomized trial.
- Fit elderly patients tolerate chemotherapy and derive the same survival benefit as their younger counterparts.
- The addition of the VEGFR2 antibody ramucirumab to second-line docetaxel improves survival.

SCLC MANAGEMENT

EPIDEMIOLOGY

SCLC accounts for approximately 13% of new lung cancer diagnoses in the United States. The incidence has decreased over the past few decades, with a peak in the early 1990s when it represented as many as 25% of lung cancer diagnoses.[26] There has also been a shift in demographics. In the 1970s, only 28% of patients with SCLC were female, whereas in the early 2000s, 50% of patients were female. These changes in incidence and demographics are most likely related to tobacco use, as are geographic variations in the incidence of SCLC, which has a strong dose-response relationship with smoking. As noted earlier in this chapter, SCLC is also characterized by a high incidence of paraneoplastic syndromes.

ESTABLISHING A DIAGNOSIS

Staging

Staging of SCLC uses the same AJCC TNM staging system used in NSCLC (Tables 11-1 and 11-5). The staging system has been validated in SCLC and carries prognostic value.[208] However, because of the aggressive nature of this disease and the limited role of surgery, a working staging system—a two-stage system used by the Veterans' Affairs Lung Study Group—is often used in clinical practice.[209] In this staging schema, (1) patients with limited-stage SCLC (or limited-disease SCLC) are patients with tumor limited to one hemithorax with regional nodes that can be included in a single, tolerable radiotherapy port; and (2) patients with extensive-stage SCLC (or extensive-disease SCLC) are those with tumor that does not meet the criteria for limited stage, including those with distant metastases or malignant pericardial or pleural effusions.

It is worth noting that defining a tolerable radiotherapy port is done in conjunction with a radiation oncologist and may vary based on an individual patient's pulmonary function. The Veterans' Affairs staging system is a functional system that primarily identifies patients who are candidates for definitive radiotherapy.

Common sites of metastases include the brain, liver, bone marrow, and bone. For this reason, a full staging work-up consists of the following: CBC count; liver-function tests; CT scan with contrast of chest and upper abdomen; CT or MRI of the brain; and a PET scan (or, if not available, a bone scan).

SCLC is associated with a high incidence of brain metastases and contrast enhanced MRI is a preferred imaging modality to CT because CT is unlikely to detect asymptomatic brain metastases.[210] The extent of staging will vary based on the clinical circumstance. If a patient appears to be a candidate for aggressive, potentially definitive therapy, a full staging work-up is appropriate, though bone marrow aspiration is not recommended unless an otherwise unexplained hematologic abnormality is present (eg, nucleated RBCs seen on peripheral-blood smear, neutropenia, or thrombocytopenia). If the patient is known to have extensive-stage SCLC, not all studies may be required, though some studies may influence management (eg, radiation for brain metastases, bone-targeted agents for bone metastases).

SCLC TREATMENT

SCLC is a chemosensitive and radiosensitive tumor with remarkably high response rates to multiple regimens. Unfortunately, it is characterized by rapid relapse and, after recurrence, it is a much more refractory disease. For those with limited-stage SCLC, definitive therapy offers a chance at cure for a small subset of patients. For those with extensive-stage disease, treatment is palliative, and < 5% of patients with extensive-stage disease survive > 2 years. For those patients with a poor PS, there may still be a palliative role for systemic therapy, given the high response rates with chemotherapy, though it is important to discuss the limitations of therapy with patients.

TREATMENT OF LIMITED-STAGE SCLC

Unlike NSCLC, there is little role for surgical resection in SCLC, which is often disseminated or locally advanced at the time of diagnosis. For a stage I SCLC, there are limited retrospective data demonstrating good outcomes with surgical resection.[208,211] Stage I SCLC, though, is exceedingly rare and before pursuing surgery, extensive staging, including invasive mediastinal staging, is appropriate. If a proper staging work-up does show stage I SCLC, surgery is reasonable, in part to confirm the diagnosis, because other neuroendocrine tumors, such as atypical carcinoid, may have an appearance similar to SCLC in a small, limited biopsy specimen. After surgery, adjuvant chemotherapy is recommended, though not on the basis of high-level evidence. Commonly, despite proper staging, histopathologic analysis upstages the disease by identifying involved lymph nodes, in which case chemoradiation (as discussed in the next paragraph) is an appropriate consideration.

For most patients with limited-stage SCLC, the recommended treatment will be concurrent, definitive chemoradiation. Radiation therapy to the thorax in addition to chemotherapy is associated with a small but significant improvement in long-term survival for patients with limited-stage disease, providing an additional 5% improvement in 3-year survival compared with chemotherapy alone.[212] Chemotherapy given concurrently with thoracic radiation is more effective than sequential chemoradiation. The concurrent approach showed a trend toward an improvement in survival, with a median of 27.2 months compared with 19.7 months in the sequential arm (P = .097); however, it was associated with substantially more esophagitis and hematologic toxicity. To decrease the morbidity associated with such treatment, as well as to improve overall outcome, investigative efforts have focused on optimizing the radiation fields, fractionation, and schedule. In one randomized study, twice-daily hyperfractionated radiation was compared with a once-daily schedule; both were administered concurrently with four cycles of cisplatin and etoposide. Survival was significantly higher with the twice-daily regimen (median survival, 23 *v* 19 months; 5-year survival, 26% *v* 16%), albeit at the expense of more grade 3 esophagitis.[213]

Cisplatin plus etoposide is the current standard regimen used in combination with radiation for limited-stage SCLC. A randomized trial compared cisplatin plus etoposide with the triplet of cyclophosphamide, epirubicin, and vincristine (CEV) given concurrently with radiation in 214 patients with limited-stage SCLC. Survival favored cisplatin plus etoposide (14.5 *v* 9.7 months) with an increase in 5-year survival from 3% with CEV to 10% with cisplatin plus etoposide. With concurrent chemoradiation, response rates are high; 97% of patients achieve a response and 40% achieve a complete response. Long-term survival, however, is uncommon and the 5-year survival rate is < 25%. This discordance between initial sensitivity and frequent relapse has been the subject of intense research. Despite the high risk of recurrence, prolonged or maintenance therapy has not improved outcomes and radiographic observation is the current standard after definitive chemoradiation.

FIRST-LINE TREATMENT OF EXTENSIVE-STAGE SCLC

Most patients with SCLC will present with extensive-stage disease, and most patients with limited-stage SCLC will experience disease relapse. For extensive-stage SCLC, the cornerstone of treatment is platinum-based chemotherapy. In a randomized trial of cisplatin plus etoposide compared with cyclophosphamide, adriamycin, and vincristine (CAV), there was no significant difference in survival but cisplatin and etoposide was favored for practical reasons and offered a response rate of 61% and a complete response rate of 10%.[214] Responses to chemotherapy are frequent and can be rapid, with the median time to best response at only 4.6 weeks. Unfortunately, responses are transient; the median time to progression was only 4 months, with an OS of 8.6 months. Despite the predictable relapse, randomized studies have not shown a survival benefit for prolonged administration of chemotherapy or for consolidation chemotherapy; the optimal duration of treatment is four to six cycles.

There have been surprisingly few changes to the treatment of this highly lethal disease over the past several decades. The only notable FDA approval in the first-line setting was carboplatin, which was not based on an improvement in survival. The COCIS meta-analysis of individual patient data compared patients with SCLC who received cisplatin versus carboplatin. There was no difference in response rate, PFS, or survival, based on choice of platinum, though the toxicity profile of these two drugs include important differences. Although cisplatin remains the standard of care in limited-stage SCLC, carboplatin and cisplatin are both appropriate options in the treatment of patients with extensive-stage SCLC. Many trials have failed to improve on the outcomes seen with platinum plus etoposide. Although initial results of studies featuring irinotecan plus cisplatin showed an improvement in survival in a Japanese population (compared with etoposide plus cisplatin), these results were not confirmed in US studies.[215,216]

The first study to demonstrate an improvement in OS in the first-line treatment of extensive-stage SCLC in several decades was IMpower 133, a randomized phase III trial of carboplatin plus etoposide with the PD-L1 inhibitor atezolizumab.[217] In this global study, 403 patients with extensive-stage SCLC received four cycles of carboplatin plus etoposide and were randomly assigned 1:1 to receive either concurrent atezolizumab or placebo followed by atezolizumab or placebo maintenance. The addition of atezolizumab led to a significant improvement in OS (12.3 *v* 10.3 months; HR, 0.70) as well as an improvement in PFS (HR, 0.77). More immune-related adverse events occurred with atezolizumab, but the rate of serious adverse events was similar between the two arms (37.4% with atezolizumab *v* 34.7% with placebo). Importantly, the median number of cycles of chemotherapy was four in both arms, suggesting that concurrent atezolizumab improved survival without limiting the ability to deliver chemotherapy. Other trials are exploring similar strategies incorporating immunotherapy in this setting.

PROPHYLACTIC CRANIAL IRRADIATION

Brain metastases are the first site of relapse for approximately one-third of patients who have relapsing SCLCs. Another third of such patients will have both brain and systemic metastases as the first sites of relapse, and the remaining one-third will have systemic-only disease. Because of the morbidity and cognitive decline associated with brain metastases, the role of prophylactic cranial irradiation (PCI) has been studied in numerous randomized trials. A meta-analysis of patients with SCLC in complete remission (primarily those with limited-stage disease) concluded that PCI was associated with a 5.4% increase in survival at 3 years.[218]

A study from the European Organization for Research and Treatment of Cancer also showed a survival benefit for patients with extensive-stage disease who had any response to induction chemotherapy.[219] Patients with extensive-stage SCLC who had a response to chemotherapy were randomly assigned to undergo PCI or no additional therapy. Irradiation was associated with an increase in median survival from 5.4 to 6.7 months and an improvement in the 1-year survival rate (27.1% *v* 13.3%) in addition to a lower risk of brain metastases (risk of metastases at 1 year, 14.6% *v* 40.4%). One limitation of the study was the lack of baseline brain imaging and MRI surveillance. A recent trial mirrored this study design but required brain imaging at baseline and during surveillance. In that randomized trial of 224 patients with extensive-stage SCLC, there was no difference in survival between patients who received PCI and those who were radiographically observed, with a median survival of 11.6 months with PCI and 13.7 months with observation.[220] With no survival advantage to PCI and a risk of neurocognitive toxicity, the role of PCI in managing extensive-stage SCLC is now under debate.

CONSOLIDATIVE THORACIC RADIATION

SCLC is a radiosensitive tumor and given the high local recurrence rates after initial chemotherapy for extensive-stage SCLC, the role of thoracic radiation after chemotherapy has been explored. A randomized clinical trial of 498 patients with extensive-stage SCLC with a response to platinum-based induction chemotherapy showed that thoracic radiotherapy, when added to PCI, significantly increased PFS.[221] The primary end point of the study was an improvement in survival at 1 year. The study did not meet its primary end point; survival at 1 year was not significantly prolonged (33% *v* 28%; *P* = .066) and the median survival was the same in both arms (8 months). However, in a secondary analysis, there was a significant improvement in 2-year survival (13% *v* 3%; *P* = .04). Some of the features of the overall patient population were atypical for extensive-stage SCLC, such as 46% rate of isolated intrathoracic progression in the control group. Thus, thoracic radiotherapy could be considered for patients with extensive-stage SCLC that responds to platinum-based chemotherapy; though, in view of the atypical features of the trial population, more studies are required before this approach can be considered the standard of care.

SECOND-LINE THERAPY

The chance of response to second-line agents correlates with the timing of relapse after induction chemotherapy. Patients who experience relapse > 3 months after completing first-line chemotherapy are considered to have sensitive disease and are more likely to have a response. Patients who experience disease progression during or within 2 to 3 months after receiving a first-line regimen are considered to have resistant disease.[222]

For those with sensitive disease, revisiting platinum plus etoposide is an option. The only drug approved for second-line therapy for SCLC in the United States is topotecan, which is associated with a response rate of approximately 25% and survival of approximately 6 months.[223] Multiple studies have not improved on these modest outcomes. A phase III trial compared the novel anthracycline amrubicin with topotecan as second-line treatment of SCLC. Although amrubicin was associated with a higher response rate than topotecan (31.1% *v* 16.9%) and an improvement in PFS (4.1 *v* 3.5 months; HR, 0.802; *P* = .018), there was no difference in survival, with a median survival of 7.5 months with amrubicin and 7.8 months with topotecan (HR, 0.880; *P* = .170). Amrubicin is not approved in the United States but is available in Japan. Temozolomide also has modest activity in second- or third-line treatment of extensive-stage SCLC, including among patients with platinum-refractory disease and brain metastases.[224,225] As in glioma, tumor methylguanine methyltransferase methylation status may predict benefit.

Immune checkpoint inhibitors have been studied in relapsed extensive-stage SCLC, and have shown some evidence of efficacy. The Checkmate-032 study explored the activity of nivolumab with or without the CTLA-4 inhibitor ipilimumab in relapsed SCLC.[226] In an analysis of the subset of patients who received nivolumab monotherapy as third-line therapy, the response rate was 11.9%.[227] On the basis of these data, nivolumab received accelerated approval as third-line monotherapy by the FDA. Pembrolizumab was also approved in this setting, on the basis of a combined analysis of two single-arm studies that demonstrated a response rate of 19% when pembrolizumab was given as third-line monotherapy.[228] Median

KEY POINTS

- SCLC is characterized by high response rates and high relapse rates.
- The AJCC TNM staging system is appropriate, but the functional staging system proposed by the Veterans' Authority Lung Study Group is often used clinically. Limited-stage SCLC can be encompassed in a tolerable radiotherapy port; extensive-stage disease cannot.
- For limited-stage SCLC, the standard approach is cisplatin plus etoposide with definitive radiation therapy.
- For extensive-stage SCLC, the standard approach is cisplatin or carboplatin with etoposide.
- The addition of the PD-L1 inhibitor atezolizumab to carboplatin plus etoposide with atezolizumab maintenance therapy improves PFS and OS.
- PCI reduces the incidence of symptomatic brain metastases and prolongs disease-free survival and OS for patients with limited-stage disease, though its role in extensive-stage SCLC is unclear.
- For relapsed SCLC, the approved second-line therapy is topotecan. Nivolumab and pembrolizumab are approved as third-line therapies.

PFS was only 2.0 months, but responses were durable, with 61% of responses lasting ≥ 18 months. Studies seeking to confirm this activity and to explore additional strategies implementing use of immunotherapy are underway.

PALLIATION FOR PATIENTS WITH LUNG CANCER

For patients with a good PS, systemic therapy can play an important palliative role by reducing symptoms and improving quality of life (Table 11.10). This is particularly the case in highly responsive tumors, such as SCLC or NSCLC with an actionable driver alteration. Other ways to offer palliation for patients with lung cancer merit consideration.

PALLIATIVE CARE

Palliative care specialists can provide valuable insight and guidance on symptom management and psychosocial support but are often involved late in the disease course. In a landmark trial, 151 patients with newly diagnosed, metastatic NSCLC were randomly assigned to early integration with a palliative care team or standard oncologic care alone.[229] Early referral to palliative care led to improvements in quality of life and fewer patients with depressive symptoms. Though there were fewer patients who received aggressive end-of-life care in the palliative care arm (33% *v* 54%), survival was longer in patients with an early referral to palliative care (11.6 *v* 8.9 months).

BONE-TARGETED AGENTS

Bone metastases are common in NSCLC and SCLC and are an important potential cause of patient morbidity. Supportive medications have been effective at preventing this morbidity. Bisphosphonates (eg, zoledronate) have resulted in the reduction of skeletal-related complications such as pain, hypercalcemia, pathologic fractures, and spinal cord and nerve compression, as well as improvements in the quality of life for patients with metastatic bone disease who are likely to have a prolonged clinical course.[230] However, a small risk of osteonecrosis of the jaw is seen. Denosumab, a monoclonal antibody to the receptor activator of nuclear κ B ligand, was noninferior to zoledronate in delaying or preventing skeletal-related complications for patients with advanced cancer, including patients with lung cancer, in a randomized, double-blind study of denosumab compared with zoledronic acid in the treatment of bone metastases for patients with advanced cancer (excluding breast and prostate cancer) or multiple myeloma.[231] The incidence of osteonecrosis is similar to that with bisphosphonates.

RADIATION THERAPY

Palliative radiation therapy often is helpful for controlling pain related to bone metastases or for improving neurologic function for patients with brain metastases. Radiation therapy to the thorax may also help control hemoptysis, SVC syndrome, airway obstruction, laryngeal-nerve compression, and other local complications. Different modalities of radiation, such as stereotactic body radiation therapy, may have relative advantages over conventional radiation therapy, but dose and modality will vary by the specific clinical situation.

MANAGEMENT OF PLEURAL EFFUSIONS

Palliative thoracentesis should be performed for patients who are symptomatic from pleural effusions, and management with intermittent thoracentesis can frequently be effective if the effusion does not reaccumulate quickly. When reaccumulation is rapid, pleurodesis may be considered. The two most common methods of a pleurodesis are through a chest tube or via thoracoscopy. Common sclerosing agents include doxycycline, talc, and bleomycin; talc is the most effective. Unfortunately, the procedure is effective in only approximately 50% of cases and is associated with discomfort and a prolonged hospital stay. For these reasons, long-term drainage through a semipermanent catheter is being used more frequently.[232] Effective systemic therapy may reduce the effusion.

KEY POINTS

- Early integration with palliative medicine specialists improves quality of life for patients with metastatic lung cancer, and also extends survival.
- Every attempt should be made to palliate the symptoms of patients with lung cancer. In addition to systemic anticancer therapies, approaches include management of bone metastases, incorporation of palliative radiation when appropriate, and addressing dyspnea caused by pleural effusions.

THYMIC MALIGNANCIES

The thymus contains two major cell populations: epithelial cells and lymphocytes. A number of different tumors can arise in the anterior mediastinum, including thymoma, Hodgkin and non-Hodgkin lymphomas, carcinoid tumors, and germ cell neoplasms. Thymomas are malignant neoplasms originating within the epithelial cells of the thymus, which often contain admixtures of lymphocytes.[233] Thymic carcinomas also are tumors of the thymic epithelium, but they are associated with a paucity of lymphocytes and are more aggressive and have a worse prognosis.

Thymomas are the most common (approximately 20% to 30%) of all anterior mediastinal tumors in adults. Most thymomas are well encapsulated, but they are considered malignant because of their invasive potential. Cytokeratin is a useful diagnostic marker to distinguish thymomas from nonepithelial cell malignancies. Although they usually present in the fourth and fifth decades of life, cases have been reported from infancy into the ninth decade. At presentation, one-third of patients have local symptoms such as cough, SVC syndrome, and dysphagia. Distant metastases are uncommon, with the most common metastatic site being the pleura. Several paraneoplastic syndromes have been associated with thymoma. Myasthenia gravis—an autoimmune disorder caused by circulating acetylcholine-receptor antibodies resulting in acetylcholine-receptor deficiency at the motor end plate—occurs in approximately one-third of patients with thymoma, although it is rarely seen with thymic carcinoma. Myasthenia gravis is characterized by diplopia, dysphagia, weakness of the ocular muscles, and easy limb fatigability (with proximal weakness more pronounced than distal weakness). Interestingly, thymomas associated with myasthenia gravis tend to be less aggressive, and histologically, they tend to have a larger ratio of lymphocytes to epithelial cells. Surgical removal of all thymic tissue, not just tumor tissue, usually results in an attenuation of the severity of myasthenia gravis, although not all patients achieve resolution of all symptoms. Patients should have their serum antiacetylcholine receptor antibody levels measured before surgery to determine whether they have myasthenia gravis, to allow proper management and avoid respiratory failure during surgery.

Other paraneoplastic syndromes include pure red cell aplasia, vasculitides, hypogammaglobulinemia, and other autoimmune disorders. Thymectomy may result in normalization of the bone marrow for ≤ 40% of patients with pure red cell aplasia, although the procedure rarely results in a return to normal immunoglobulin levels for patients with immunodeficiency. The Masaoka staging for thymoma is based on encapsulation of the tumor and invasion into surrounding organs and distant sites outside the chest (Table 11-11).[234] Important prognostic factors include World Health Organization histologic grade, complete resection status, and size.[233,235] Negative prognostic factors include tumor size > 10 cm; tracheal or vascular compromise; age < 30 years; presence of hematologic paraneoplastic syndromes; incomplete surgical resection; and thymic carcinoma histology.

The treatment of choice for thymoma is resection. Long-term survival for patients with encapsulated, noninvasive (stage I) tumors is excellent, approaching 90% to 95% at 10 years. The role played by postoperative radiation after a complete (R0) resection is controversial, but sometimes the procedure is used for completely resected stage II to stage IV thymoma. Adjuvant radiation therapy is often recommended for patients with invasive disease.[236]

The optimal management of incompletely resected or unresectable thymoma is controversial. Achieving an R0 resection is an important prognostic indicator. Thymoma is generally a chemosensitive tumor; thus, debulking with chemotherapy for locally advanced thymoma to attempt to increase the potential for an R0 resection is sometimes performed. Given the small number of affected patients, no randomized trials have been performed to identify the best chemotherapy regimen for inoperable or recurrent thymoma. Commonly used regimens include combined cisplatin, doxorubicin, and

Table 11-10 Palliative Approaches for Complications of Lung Cancer

Complication	Palliative Approach
Superior vena cava syndrome	Systemic alone (mild symptoms)
	Concurrent chemoradiation therapy (if potentially curable disease)
	Radiation therapy to the thorax (patients with non-small-cell lung cancer)
	Placement of stent
Pleural effusion	Intermittent thoracentesis
	Pleurodesis
	Long-term catheter drainage
	Systemic chemotherapy
Bronchial obstruction	High-dose endobronchial radiation therapy
	Placement of stent
	Neodymium-yttrium-aluminum-garnet endobronchial laser therapy
	Electrocautery
	Photodynamic therapy
Cachexia	Megestrol acetate (160 to 800 mg/d)
Bone metastases	Bisphosphonates (namely, zoledronate)
	RANK-ligand inhibitor (denosumab)
Brain metastases	Corticosteroids
	Resection or stereotactic radiation with or without whole-brain radiation
	Whole-brain radiation therapy (for multiple metastases)

Abbreviation: RANK, receptor activator of nuclear κ B

cyclophosphamide;[237] combined etoposide, ifosfamide, and cisplatin;[238] and combined cisplatin and etoposide.[239]

Thymic carcinomas are aggressive and characterized by a high degree of histologic anaplasia and architectural atypia. Several different subtypes have been described, although more than half are undifferentiated. These tumors often metastasize to regional lymph nodes and distant sites; thus, they have a worse prognosis than thymomas, with 5-year survival rates of 20% to 30%. Responses to carboplatin and paclitaxel have been described.[240] Phase II studies of pembrolizumab have shown promising activity, with response rates > 20% but immune-related toxicity was also noted and at higher incidence than some other cancers, such as NSCLC.[241]

KEY POINTS

- Thymomas are often encapsulated, well differentiated, and associated with paraneoplastic syndromes such as myasthenia gravis.
- The optimal treatment of thymoma is thymectomy and complete surgical resection, in which case the survival is excellent.
- The most important prognostic factors after resection are Masaoka stage, histology, complete resection status, and size.
- Thymic carcinomas are more aggressive than thymomas.
- Platinum-based chemotherapy remains standard therapy for unresectable or recurrent thymoma or thymic carcinoma.

MESOTHELIOMA

Mesothelioma arises from mesothelial cells—the cells that form the serosal lining of the pleura, pericardium, and peritoneal cavities.[242,243] Although benign mesotheliomas have been described, most are malignant and have an aggressive clinical course. Malignant mesotheliomas are rare, with approximately 2,500 new cases diagnosed annually in the United States. Although approximately 80% are associated with exposure to asbestos, only approximately 5% of asbestos workers are diagnosed with mesothelioma. In contrast to lung cancer and asbestosis, smoking does not increase the risk of mesothelioma. The various types of asbestos are divided into two major groups: serpentine, represented by chrysotile, the most common form of asbestos in the Western world; and rodlike amphiboles, which include crocidolite, the most oncogenic type of asbestos.

Carcinogenic effects of asbestos appear to result from its physical properties rather than from its chemical structure, with long, rodlike fibers of narrow diameter being more likely to induce tumors in laboratory animals. It has been postulated that chrysotile asbestos fibers are less carcinogenic because the fibers can be partially digested and removed from the lungs, whereas amphibole asbestos is more resistant to solubilization by cellular enzymes and therefore accumulates in the lungs. The fibers cause mutagenic changes by several different mechanisms, including direct physical effects on chromosomes; the production of hydroxyl radicals and superoxide anions leading to DNA strand breaks and deletions; stimulation of EGFR autophosphorylation, activation, and signal transduction; and increased production of inflammatory cytokines. The expression of the simian virus 40 large-tumor antigen in mesothelioma cells and not in nearby normal cells, as well as the capacity of antisense T-antigen treatment to arrest mesothelioma cell growth in vitro, suggest that simian virus 40 may also contribute to the development of mesothelioma, particularly for patients exposed to asbestos.[244] Mesothelioma also has been associated with exposure to thorium dioxide, a radiologic contrast agent, and its radiation effects. Three histologic variants of mesothelioma have been described: (1) epithelial, which is the most common form and is associated with the best prognosis; (2) sarcomatoid; and (3) mixed.

To distinguish mesotheliomas from metastatic adenocarcinomas, the periodic acid–Schiff stain is frequently used before and after diastase digestion. Neutral mucopolysaccharides that are strongly positive on periodic acid–Schiff staining are found in intracellular secretory vacuoles and in intra-acinar vacuoles in most adenocarcinomas, but are rarely found in most mesotheliomas. In addition, immunohistochemical staining for CD15, Ber-EP-4, TTF1, and carcinoembryonic antigen are usually absent in mesotheliomas but are positive in most adenocarcinomas, whereas mesothelioma is characterized by staining for calretinin, Wilms tumor antigen (WT1), vimentin, CK5/6, mesothelin, or HBME-1 (an antimesothelial cell antibody).[243]

Mesothelioma most commonly develops in the fifth to seventh decade, and affects men and women in a 5:1 ratio. The onset of disease occurs 20 to 50 years after exposure. Family members also are at higher risk of mesothelioma, presumably because of exposure to asbestos fibers brought home on the clothing and bodies of individuals who work with asbestos. The typical presentation consists of dyspnea or chest-wall pain secondary to a pleural effusion. Most mesotheliomas (60%) occur on the right side, and bilateral involvement of the chest wall is present at the time of diagnosis in < 5% of cases. Repeated cytologic examination of pleural fluid may be negative, necessitating either a thoracoscopy or thoracotomy, despite the risk of seeding the biopsy site or surgical scar with tumor.

Mesothelioma tends to be locally invasive. For approximately 20% of patients, a chest-wall mass develops over tracts resulting from thoracentesis, chest tubes, or thoracotomy. Direct involvement of the ribs, diaphragm, pericardium, and vertebrae is common. Although various staging classifications have been described, the TNM staging system adopted by the AJCC is most commonly used and its prognostic value was confirmed by the International Association for the Study of Lung Cancer and the International Mesothelioma Interest Group.[245]

Table 11-11 Modified Masaoka Clinical Staging of Thymoma[234]

Masaoka Stage	Diagnostic Criteria
I	Macroscopically and microscopically completely encapsulated
II	(A) Microscopic transcapsular invasion
	(B) Macroscopic invasion into surrounding fatty tissue or grossly adherent to but not through mediastinal pleura or pericardium
III	Macroscopic invasion into neighboring organs (ie, pericardium, great vessels, lung)
	(A) Without invasion of great vessels
	(B) With invasion of great vessels
IV	(A) Pleural or pericardial dissemination
	(B) Lymphatic or hematogenous metastasis

Evaluation of surgical resectability often includes echocardiography to delineate cardiac involvement and MRI to delineate diaphragmatic involvement, in addition to chest CT and PET scans. The choice of surgical resection for mesothelioma is controversial and has not been shown conclusively to improve survival. Surgical approaches include extrapleural pneumonectomy (EPP) and pleurectomy with decortication (P/D). EPP includes en bloc resection of the parietal pleura, lung pericardium, and diaphragm. P/D involves only careful resection of the visceral and parietal pleura.[246] A retrospective comparison of patients with malignant pleural mesothelioma compared EPP and P/D. Operative mortality was higher with EPP (7% *v* 4%) and survival favored P/D, though many confounders were inherent in this analysis. The prospective Mesothelioma and Radical Surgery (MARS) trial randomly assigned patients who completed induction chemotherapy to EPP and radiation or to no EPP.[247] The study was not found to be feasible but the limited data did not provide any suggestion of benefit to EPP. Overall, postoperative radiation may offer improved local control, though its impact on survival is not clear.[248]

The role of preoperative (neoadjuvant) chemotherapy is also being explored. Results of a multicenter phase II trial of neoadjuvant pemetrexed and cisplatin followed by EPP and hemithoracic radiation showed a median survival in the overall population of 16.8 months (n = 77 patients) and of 29 months for patients completing all therapy (n = 40 patients; 2-year survival, 61%).[249]

The prognosis is poor for patients who have unresectable disease at presentation; median survival is approximately 12 months. Effusions may be controlled by thoracoscopy with talc pleurodesis. Pleurectomy with decortication, although rarely curative, also can be used to control effusions. Smaller doses of radiation (21 Gy in three fractions) may prevent seeding of the surgical wound by mesothelioma cells. Single-agent chemotherapy yields response rates of 5% to 20%, with active agents including doxorubicin, cisplatin, pemetrexed, and gemcitabine.[250] Combination chemotherapy has increased response rates as initial systemic treatment. A phase III study in which cisplatin was compared with cisplatin plus pemetrexed demonstrated a 9-month median survival for patients treated with cisplatin alone and a 12-month survival for patients treated with the combination ($P = .02$).[251] The response rate with cisplatin plus pemetrexed was 41.3% compared with cisplatin alone, which had a response rate of 16.7%. In a randomized, phase III trial, bevacizumab added to cisplatin and pemetrexed improved survival (18.8 *v* 16.1 months).[252] More grade 3 or higher hypertension (23% *v* 0%) and thrombotic events (6% *v* 1%) were noted with bevacizumab. Cisplatin and pemetrexed with bevacizumab should be considered a new standard of care in patients with unresectable malignant pleural mesothelioma who are bevacizumab eligible, though bevacizumab is not yet FDA approved in this setting. No standard salvage therapy exists for recurrent mesothelioma, though pembrolizumab has shown some encouraging activity, with a response rate of 20% and median duration of response of 12 months in a single-arm study.[253]

KEY POINTS

- Approximately 80% of pleural mesotheliomas are associated with exposure to asbestos, including indirect exposure.
- The epithelial histologic form of mesothelioma is associated with a better prognosis than the sarcomatoid or mixed histology forms.
- Surgical options include extrapleural pneumonectomy and pleurectomy with decortication, though the impact of surgery on survival is not clear and extrapleural pneumonectomy has been associated with significant morbidity.
- First-line chemotherapy for patients with mesothelioma consists of cisplatin and pemetrexed with the addition of bevacizumab for unresectable mesothelioma in patients eligible to receive bevacizumab.

Acknowledgment

The following authors are acknowledged and thanked for their contribution to prior versions of this chapter: Joan H. Schiller, MD, FASCO; David E. Gerber, MD; Jonathan W. Riess, MD; and David R. Gandara, MD, FASCO.

GLOBAL ONCOLOGY PERSPECTIVE: LUNG CANCER

Herbert Loong, MD (Prince of Wales Hospital, Hong Kong, China); and Tony Mok, MD (The Chinese University of Hong Kong, Hong Kong, China)

Lung cancer is the most common cancer diagnosed and the greatest cause of cancer-related death worldwide.[259] Variations in trends of population growth, aging and smoking behavior, as well as distinctive ethnic makeup of the population of different regions and accessibility to health care also have implications on lung cancer prevalence and survival.

Wu et al[135] reported on their analysis of data including lung cancer incidence and mortality extracted from GLOBOCAN. In 2012, there were 1.82 million and 1.59 million new lung cancer cases and deaths worldwide, respectively.[135] The Human Development Index (HDI) is a composite measure encompassing population health, knowledge and living standards of a country.[260] Incidence was highest in countries with a high HDI and lowest in countries with a low HDI. In most countries with a high HDI, as lung cancer incidence in men decreased gradually (ranging from −0.3% in Spain to −2.5% in the United States each year), incidence in women continued to increase (ranging from 1.4% each year in Australia to 6.1% in recent years in Spain).[135]

The distribution of histologic types or subtypes of lung cancer varies widely between countries.[135] Overall, the incidence of adenocarcinoma was higher than that for squamous cell carcinoma in men (ratio of adenocarcinoma to squamous cell carcinoma, > 1). However, in some countries, including Belarus, India, the Netherlands, and the Russian Federation, squamous cell carcinoma has a higher incidence.[261] The pattern of higher incidence of adenocarcinoma compared with squamous cell carcinoma was more evident among women, with a more than five-fold difference reported for women in China, Japan, and Saudi Arabia.[261] Globally, the incidence of adenocarcinoma has stabilized in men but continues to increase in women.[261] Increasing incidence of adenocarcinoma in smokers has been linked to design changes in cigarettes that have promoted deeper inhalation since the late 1950s.[262] Studies from Southeast Asia, where prevalence of smoking among women remains low, have suggested that the increase in adenocarcinoma in women can be attributed to second-hand smoke and cooking fumes.[264,265] Moreover, in the United States, blacks, primarily men, with adenocarcinoma and squamous cell carcinoma have lower survival rates than do white people and other racial/ethnic groups.[265]

Identification of somatic mutations at a molecular level has become an important cornerstone of pathologic work-up for patients with lung cancer.[266] This approach can open opportunities for use of targeted therapies. The frequencies of genetic alterations (ie, mutations, amplifications, or translocations) vary considerably across published studies and by histologic subtype. In East Asia, where the burden of *EGFR* mutations is much higher in adenocarcinoma than in the United States and Europe, the frequencies of other mutations are also different (Fig 11-6). Kohno et al[267] and Li et al[32] have reported that *ERBB2, RET, BRAF,* and *ROS1* mutation frequencies in adenocarcinoma are essentially the same in East Asian and white populations, whereas there are significantly more *KRAS* mutations in the white population (20% to 30% *v* 8% to 10% respectively). Moreover, in a pooled analysis of a spectrum of somatic mutations in lung cancer in the United States, the frequencies of *EGFR* and *KRAS* mutations have been reported as being comparable between blacks and whites.[268]

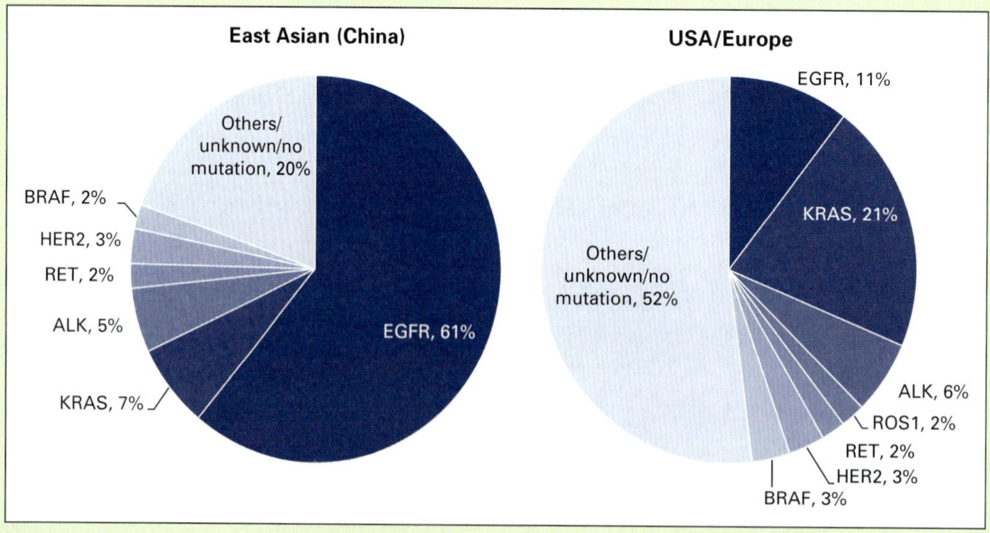

Fig. 11-6 Comparison of mutations and their frequencies between East Asian and western populations in the United States (USA) and Europe.

Reduction of burden of lung cancer can be achieved through different approaches. The key driver of lung cancer incidence is smoking. Thus, tobacco control programs are of paramount importance in combating the burden of lung cancer globally. This becomes even more critical in socioeconomically less developed countries, which have limited access to screening and treatment measures. Various countries and regions across the world, including California in the United States,[269] and Hong Kong,[272] have benefited from decreasing smoking prevalence due to coordinated tobacco control programs. These regions are likely to experience continued reductions in lung cancer incidence, particularly among men, over the coming years. Because there is a lag period between smoking prevalence and resultant disease, it is likely that countries without strong anti-tobacco programs, such as China, will face an increasing burden of lung cancer in the coming decades.[271]

Early detection through screening in a large proportion of high-risk populations with low-dose CT reduces mortality rates. In countries that can afford to implement screening, it is expected that the incidence of lung cancer, including a higher proportion of early-stage cancer, may increase because of early detection, but overall mortality rates should decrease over time. This widespread implementation of screening likely will be restricted to countries with the financial means to pay for these tests. Overall, regardless of the geographic location or socioeconomic status of a particular country or region, a comprehensive yet affordable lung cancer control policy including coordinated strategies to reduce exposures to recognized risk factors as well as implementation of screening for at-risk populations is necessary to curb the growing incidence of this deadly disease.

In the void of an efficient early detection strategy, Most patients present with advanced (stage III or IV) disease. This is not dissimilar between the Asian and Western populations. The only exception would be in rural areas where basic diagnostic and treatment facilities are lacking and, therefore, an even higher incidence of advanced disease is expected. However, the increasing trend of screening by low-dose CT scan in Asian and Western countries will likely increase the incidence of asymptomatic patients with stage I disease.

Treatment of lung cancer is now based on molecular genomic and PD-L1 status. There is no major difference between Asian and Western countries in the practice of using molecular biomarker as official standard for selection of therapy. However, the extent and methods of testing could be different. In most Asian countries, both *EGFR* mutation and *ALK* translocation are routinely tested, whereas *ROS-1* and *BRAF* V600E mutation are tested only in selective centers. In contrast, many centers in the United States would test for all four biomarkers, and, not infrequently, multigene genome profiling by next-generation sequencing is used as the standard testing method.

For patients harboring *EGFR* mutation, the standard first-line therapy is EGFR TKI. The first generation EGFR TKIs, gefitinib and erlotinib, are associated with PFS of 10 to 14 months.[272] The second-generation EGFR TKIs, afatinib and dacomitinib, are more potent in EGFR inhibition, thus the two randomized phase III studies comparing first- and second-generation EGFR TKIs reported improvement in PFS with the latter.[135,258] However, the EGFR TKI–related toxicities are more severe. Osimertinib is a third-generation EGFR TKI with the benefit of CNS penetration and T790M inhibition, and this would allow longer disease control. In a study comparing osimertinib with a first-generation TKI in first-line therapy, median PFS of 18.9 month versus 10.2 months, respectively, was reported.[127] Efficacy in CNS control was also superior. Therefore, osimertinib has become the preferable first-line treatment in United States. However, its cost is approximately four times higher than that of the first-generation EGFR TKI. For this reason, in Asian countries where reimbursement is not available, only a fraction of patients would choose osimertinib as first-line therapy. The paradigm may change over time, but the chance for low- to middle-income Asian countries to fully reimburse osimertinib remains relatively remote.

Similar to *EGFR* mutation, first-line treatment of *ALK* translocation–positive lung cancer is TKIs. Crizotinib was the first approved treatment, with a median PFS of 10.9 months.[149] With the advent of second-generation ALK inhibitors including ceritinib, alectinib, and brigatinib, most patients would receive one of these second-generation drugs as first-line therapy. The ALEX study that compared alectinib with crizotinib as first-line therapy has confirmed the significant superiority in PFS, reaching 34.8 months.[154] There is no difference in treatment outcome between Asian and non-Asian populations. The interesting point is that the standard dosage in Japan is 300 mg twice daily compared with the standard dosage of 600 mg twice daily in other countries. The Japanese ALEX phase III study had demonstrated similar efficacy. The reason for the difference in dosage is not based on pharmacogenomics difference but rather on local regulation of maximum dose of solvent allowed in the drug.

For patients without a driver oncogene, treatment options would include an anti-PDL1 inhibitor, chemotherapy, or combination of both. Selection is based on status of PD-L1 expression, which is generally classified as < 1%, 1% to 49%, and ≥ 50%. For the PD-L1 > 50% population, the standard therapy is single-agent pembrolizumab.[167] Although this is the standard in countries that offer reimbursement, only a limited number of patients from low- and middle-income countries can afford the high cost. Combination of chemotherapy and anti–PD-L1 therapy is the standard treatment of patients with PD-L1 expression between 1% and 49% in Western countries, but again, this remains a treatment option in Asia due to the high cost. To date, there is no significant difference between Asian and non-Asian populations in reference to efficacy and safety.

12

HEAD AND NECK CANCERS

Francis P. Worden, MD; Michelle L. Mierzwa, MD, and Keith A. Casper, MD

Recent Updates

- Cetuximab and radiation demonstrated inferior survival and local control compared with cisplatin and radiation in p16-positive locally advanced oropharyngeal cancer. (Gillison M, *Lancet* 2019; Mehanna H, *Lancet* 2019)
- Pembrolizumab improved survival compared with investigator's choice of standard therapies in patients with platinum-refractory, previously treated recurrent or metastatic head and neck squamous cell carcinoma. (Cohen E, *Lancet* 2019)
- Larotrectinib is approved for the treatment of solid tumors that have NTRK-activating fusions without a known resistance mutation in patients whose disease is either metastatic or where surgical resection is likely to result in severe morbidity. (Drilon A, *N Engl J Med* 2018)
- The combination of dabrafenib and trametinib is approved for the treatment of patients with locally advanced or metastatic anaplastic thyroid cancer with BRAF V600E mutation and with no satisfactory locoregional treatment options. (Subbiah V, *J Clin Oncol* 2018)

OVERVIEW

The term "head and neck cancer" refers to a heterogeneous group of malignant tumors arising from the epithelial lining of the upper aerodigestive tract. The specific primary sites are subdivided by anatomic boundaries: lip and oral cavity, pharynx (comprising the nasopharynx, oropharynx, and hypopharynx), larynx, and nasal cavity and paranasal sinuses (Table 12-1; Fig 12-1). Squamous cell cancer is the most common histologic type, accounting for 85% to 95% of head and neck cancers.

Etiologic factors include tobacco and alcohol use and viruses, such as the human papillomavirus (HPV) and the Epstein-Barr virus (EBV) (Table 12-2). Head and neck cancers are generally categorized as early-stage disease (localized to the primary site without neck nodal involvement), locoregionally advanced disease (large bulky tumors [T3-T4] with or without nodal involvement or smaller primary tumors with nodal involvement), or metastatic disease. Involvement of the neck nodes is prognostically significant, reducing the cure rate for patients with a given tumor stage by approximately 50%. Exceptions in staging occur with HPV-positive tumors, where favorable prognostic disease can include the involvement of neck nodes < 6 cm. Early-stage disease at times may be treated with single modality therapy (ie, surgery or radiation), whereas locally advanced disease is generally treated with multimodality therapy, which commonly includes radiation and chemotherapy.

Within the aerodigestive tract, second primary malignancies (SPMs) occur most frequently in the lung, followed by the esophagus. The risk and distribution of SPMs vary significantly according to the subsite of the index cancer and are highest for hypopharyngeal cancers. When

Table 12-1 **Head and Neck Cancer: Primary Sites**	
Anatomic Area	**Primary Cancer Site**
Oral cavity and lip	Floor of mouth
	Oral tongue
	Buccal mucosa
	Alveolar ridges
	Hard palate
	Retromolar trigone
Pharynx	Nasopharynx (includes superior surface of soft palate)
	Oropharynx (includes inferior surface of soft palate, uvula, base of tongue, tonsil, posterior pharyngeal wall)
	Hypopharynx (pyriform sinus, postcricoid, posterior wall)
Larynx	Supraglottic larynx (false cords, arytenoids, epiglottis)
	Glottic larynx (includes commissures)
	Subglottic larynx
Nasal cavity and paranasal sinuses	Nasal cavity
	Maxillary sinuses
	Ethmoid sinuses
	Frontal sinuses
	Sphenoid sinuses

solitary distant lesions are identified on imaging, patients with early-stage cancers (ie, with no involved neck nodes) are more likely to have a SPM rather than metastases, and treatment should be with curative intent. Systemic therapy by itself is palliative and is the mainstay for metastatic head and neck squamous cell carcinomas (HNSCCs).

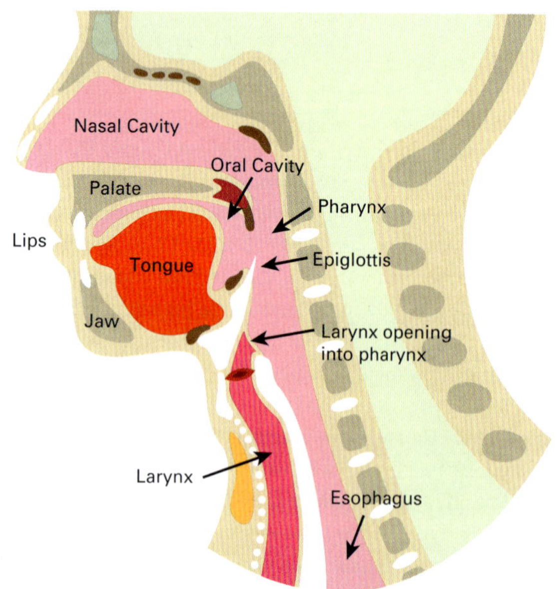

Fig. 12-1 Head and neck cancer regions.

Reused with permission from the website of the National Cancer Institute (https://www.cancer.gov).

The other two anatomic sites included in the head and neck region are the thyroid and salivary glands. Surgical resection remains the standard of care for localized thyroid cancers and salivary gland tumors. Depending on the pathologic findings, radioactive iodine has a role in localized thyroid cancers and for external-beam radiation in salivary gland tumors. For patients with well-differentiated thyroid cancer, radioactive iodine is the first treatment of choice for metastatic disease if radiolabeled thyroid imaging is positive. Two tyrosine kinase inhibitors (TKIs) are approved for treatment of radioactive iodine–refractory disease. Similarly, two TKIs are approved for the management of medullary thyroid cancer. No standard systemic therapies are recognized for patients with unresectable or metastatic salivary gland cancers with the exception of mammary analog secretory carcinoma (MASC), which is treated with a pan-TRK inhibitor.

EPIDEMIOLOGY

In 2019, head and neck cancer accounts for about 4% of all cancers in the United States. It is estimated that 65,410 people (48,000 men and 17,410 women) will develop carcinomas of the head and neck. The median age at diagnosis is approximately 60 years, and it is also estimated that 14,620 people will die of their disease (10,980 men and 3,640 women). Worldwide, head and neck cancer accounts for > 550,000 cancer cases and 380,000 deaths from cancer annually.

Head and neck cancers affect men and women in a ratio of 2.5:1, although the ratio varies according to the primary site (eg, 4:1 for cancer of the oropharynx, 7:1 for cancer of the larynx). Oropharyngeal cancer incidence has increased significantly since

Table 12-2 **Characteristics of Virus- and Nonvirus-Associated Head and Neck Cancers**

Characteristic	HPV-POSITIVE	Nonviral	EBV-POSITIVE
Anatomic site	Oropharynx	All sites	Nasopharynx, type: (WHO types I, II, and III: 80%)
Anatomic subsite	Lingual and palatine tonsils, base of tongue	Tonsils, base of tongue, larynx, hypopharynx, lateral tongue, retromolar trigone, buccal mucosa, nasopharynx (WHO type I: 20%)	Pharyngeal walls, fossa of Rosenmüller
Presenting Symptoms	Sore throat, chronic dysphagia, persistent odynophagia, and otalgia	Oropharynx: Sore throat, chronic dysphagia, persistent odynophagia, and otalgia Oral cavity: mouth sores, a nonhealing ulcer, or pain Nasopharynx: ear fullness, otalgia, or otitis media; a diagnosis in an adult patient that mandates careful assessment of the nasopharynx	Eustachian tubes invaded by nasopharyngeal disease: ear fullness, otalgia, or otitis media–a diagnosis in an adult patient that mandates careful assessment of the nasopharynx
		Hypopharyngeal or supraglottic laryngeal cancers: sore throat, hoarseness, difficulty swallowing, or neck mass; diagnosed with more advanced disease due to delay in symptoms Glottic larynx: hoarseness; diagnosed in earlier stages due to early onset of symptoms	More advanced tumors: double vision due to invasion of cavernous sinuses and the branches of the third, fourth, and particularly sixth cranial nerves
Percentage virus associated	60%-70%	WHO I: 16-20%	WHO I: 4% WHO II and III: 96%
Associated histopathology	Basaloid, nonkeratinizing	Keratinizing, (for nasopharyngeal WHO type I)	WHO type II (nonkeratinizing) and III (undifferentiated cancer)
Viral transmission	Sexual	Tobacco and alcohol	Oral
Viral genome	Episomal/integrated	–	Episomal/integrated
Viral oncogenes	*E6* and *E7*	–	*LMP-1* and *EBNA1*
Tumor markers	p16 positive	p16 negative, EBER negative	EBER positive
Cofactors	Possibly marijuana	Poor oral hygiene and poor nutrition	Diet and genetics
Clinical presentation	Rapidly growing neck mass, sore throat	Neck mass, hoarseness, tongue ulcer, sore throat	Nasal and sinus congestion, neck mass
Prognosis controlled for stage	Improved	Poorer when compared with HPV-positive tumors or EBV-positive	Improved

Abbreviations: EBER, Epstein-Barr encoding region; EBV, Epstein-Bar virus; HPV, human papillomavirus.

the 1980s, more so in developing countries and often in younger individuals. This increase is due to the association of HPV infections with this cancer, particularly among men. The prognosis for HPV-related head and neck cancers is much improved over those head and neck tumors that are unrelated to HPV infections. Overall, the age-adjusted incidence and mortality rates for head and neck cancer are highest among black men, and the stage-specific survival rates are lowest for this group.

RISK FACTORS

TOBACCO AND ALCOHOL

Epidemiologic data document a multiplicative risk relationship between tobacco and alcohol. Age younger than 18 years at onset and a duration of smoking of > 35 years are significant risk factors. Approximately 75% of head and neck cancers can be attributed to tobacco and alcohol use. Smokeless tobacco and other orally chewed carcinogens (eg, betel quid, a combination of betel leaf, lime, and areca nut, commonly used in India and parts of Asia) are associated with the development of cancers of the oral cavity. Black, air-cured tobacco (used in cigars and pipe tobacco) is more irritating to the respiratory mucosa than blonde or flue-cured tobacco (used in cigarettes) and is associated with a higher risk for head and neck cancer. Marijuana use may also carry a higher risk for developing head and neck cancers.

DIET AND GENETIC SYNDROMES

Diets low in vitamins A and B and poor oral and dental hygiene are believed to elevate the risk for head and neck cancer. Plummer-Vinson syndrome, which is most commonly seen in postmenopausal women older than 50 years, is associated with iron-deficiency anemia, hypopharyngeal webs, dysphagia, and a higher risk for squamous cell cancers in the postcricoid region of the hypopharynx, oral cavity, and esophagus. Genetic factors and nutritional deficiencies may play important roles in the development of this premalignant condition. Two inherited syndromes, Fanconi anemia and dyskeratosis congenital, are also linked with development of head and neck cancers.

OCCUPATIONAL EXPOSURES

Tumors of the sinonasal tract primarily originate from the maxillary sinus, and such cancers are associated with various occupational exposures (eg, nickel, radium, mustard gas, and chromium, byproducts of leather tanning and woodworking).

VIRUSES

Human Papillomavirus

In the United States between 1984 and 1989, only 16% of oropharyngeal cancers were related to HPV; however, between 2000 and 2019, this percentage increased to 70% of oropharyngeal cancers, revealing a four-fold increase within two decades. This trend was striking, given the decrease in tobacco use in the United States. The incidence of oropharyngeal cancers among men younger than 60 years, with no or minimal use of alcohol or tobacco, continues to increase.

The transforming potential results from viral proteins E6 and E7, which inactivate the tumor-suppressor proteins p53 and retinoblastoma protein (pRb) and result in loss of cell-cycle regulation, cellular proliferation, and chromosome instability (Fig 12-2). Tumoral expression of p16 protein reflects biologically relevant HPV infection, is not genotype specific, and is an excellent surrogate for HPV status for oropharynx primaries. Expression of p16 is upregulated when HPV E7 oncoprotein degrades pRb, whereas p16 expression in HPV-negative tumors is silenced by epigenetic promoter methylation or genetic mutation.

Immunohistochemical analysis of tumoral p16 protein expression performs numerically better than detection of HPV DNA, which will detect HPV but does not necessarily reflect E7 activity. Thus, the 8th edition of the AJCC Cancer Staging Manual (hereafter, AJCC) has adopted p16 overexpression by immunohistochemistry, defined as ≥ 75% tumor expression with at least a moderate staining-intensity marker, as a surrogate for HPV positivity in oropharyngeal cancers. Because the same survival benefit does not extend to HPV-positive or p16-positive tumors from non-oropharyngeal head and neck sites, p16 staining is not recommended for any other squamous cell head and neck cancers.

Patients with HPV-related oropharynx carcinomas have strikingly better survival rates than those with HPV-negative tumors.

Epstein-Barr Virus

Nasopharyngeal cancer is strongly associated with EBV. Cancer of the nasopharynx is especially common among individuals from endemic areas in southern China and northern Africa, where WHO

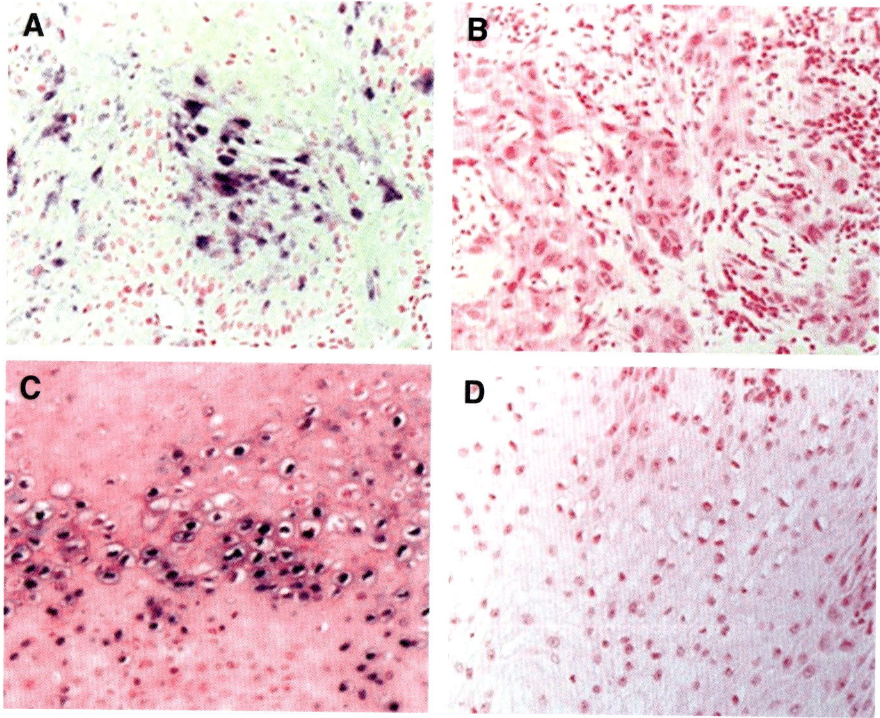

Fig. 12-2 Pathogenesis of human papillomavirus (HPV).

Permission to reuse given by the Creative Common license for Senba, M., & Mori, N. (2012). Mechanisms of virus immune evasion lead to development from chronic inflammation to cancer formation associated with human papillomavirus infection. Oncology Reviews, *6(2), e17.*

type II (nonkeratinizing) and III (undifferentiated cancer) nasopharyngeal cancers are more common. Epstein-Barr encoding region (EBER) in situ hybridization is the method of choice for the detection of EBV. WHO type I (keratinizing) nasopharyngeal cancer is more common in Western countries and appears to more likely be related to tobacco exposure or possibly HPV. Emerging data also suggest a posttreatment plasma EBV DNA level is an excellent prognostic marker; however, this has not been standardized and is not yet considered standard of care.

KEY POINTS

- Tobacco and alcohol use are the major risk factors for squamous cell cancer of the head and neck, and the use of both results in a multiplicative increase in risk.
- There is evidence for a causal association between high-risk oncogenic HPV and cancers of the oropharynx (eg, tonsil, base of tongue); a causal association also exists between EBV and nasopharyngeal carcinomas.
- p16 and EBER are prognostic biomarkers for HPV- and EBV-related tumors, respectively. The survival prognosis is substantially better for p16-positive and EBER-positive cancers than for HPV-negative and EBER-negative cancers.
- The incidence of second primary cancers for patients with a history of squamous cell cancer of the head and neck is 3%–7% annually; common sites include the head and neck, lung, and esophagus.

HEAD AND NECK CARCINOGENESIS

MOLECULAR PROGRESSION MODEL

A molecular progression model of multistep carcinogenesis has been elucidated for the transformation of normal mucosa to invasive squamous cell cancer (Fig 12-3) and summarized here. The earliest genetic alteration noted during transition from normal mucosa to hyperplastic mucosa is the loss of genetic material containing tumor-suppressor genes (ie, loss of heterozygosity or allelic imbalance) from chromosome region 9p21 and inactivation (promoter hypermethylation) of the pl6 tumor-suppressor gene.

The next step during the transition from hyperplastic mucosa to dysplasia is the loss of genetic material containing tumor-suppressor genes (ie, loss of heterozygosity or allelic imbalance) 3p and 17p with inactivation (promoter hypermethylation) of the p53 gene.

Transition from dysplasia to carcinoma in situ is associated with loss of chromosome regions 11q, 13q, and 14q. During transition to invasive squamous cell carcinoma, there is loss of chromosome regions 6p, 8p, and 4q.

More than half of patients with tobacco- and alcohol-associated HNSCC have disease with the TP53 gene mutation and downregulation of p16 protein. In contrast, HPV-associated HNSCC characteristically demonstrates wild-type TP53 and RB1 genes and upregulation of p16 protein levels.

ORAL PREMALIGNANCY (INTRAEPITHELIAL NEOPLASIA)

Leukoplakia

Leukoplakia are the most common precancerous lesions in the oral mucosa; the majority (approximately 80%) of leukoplakia are benign. The clinical presentation of these lesions includes white plaques distributed on the patient's lip, buccal mucosa, floor of the mouth, hard palate, tongue, and soft palate (Fig 12-4).

Erythroplakia

Erythroplakia are associated with a 90% incidence of severe dysplasia, carcinoma in situ, or invasive disease. The clinical presentation of these lesions includes a red, velvety patch that is separated from the surrounding normal tissue by a distinct interface, and occasionally has a pebbled or granular appearance. This patch occurs on the tongue, lower lip, floor of the mouth, buccal mucosa, and oral commissure (Fig 12-5).

KEY POINTS

- The earliest genetic alteration during transition from normal mucosa to hyperplastic mucosa is the loss of genetic material containing tumor-suppressor genes known as a loss of heterozygosity or allelic imbalance.
- A causal association between high-risk oncogenic HPV and cancers of the oropharynx (eg, tonsil, base of tongue) is well documented; a causal association also exists between EBV and nasopharyngeal carcinomas.
- p16 and EBER are prognostic biomarkers for HPV- and EBV-related tumors, respectively. Overall survival rates are substantially higher for p16-positive and EBER-positive cancers than for HPV-negative and EBER-negative cancers.
- The incidence of second primary cancers for patients with a history of squamous cell cancer of the head and neck is 3% to 7% annually; common sites include the head and neck, lung, and esophagus.

CLINICAL PRESENTATION, DIAGNOSIS, AND STAGING

In general, cancers of the oral cavity, pharynx, and larynx are characterized by disease confined to the primary site with or without spread to regional nodes at the time of diagnosis and late metastatic spread. Less than 10% of patients have distant disease at presentation. Thus, initial disease staging and management focus on the extent of locoregional involvement and the effect of the choice of treatment on speech and swallowing function, as well as on the risk for recurrence.

PRESENTING SIGNS AND SYMPTOMS

Clinical signs and symptoms vary with the anatomic site affected (Table 12-2). The discovery of a painless lump in the neck

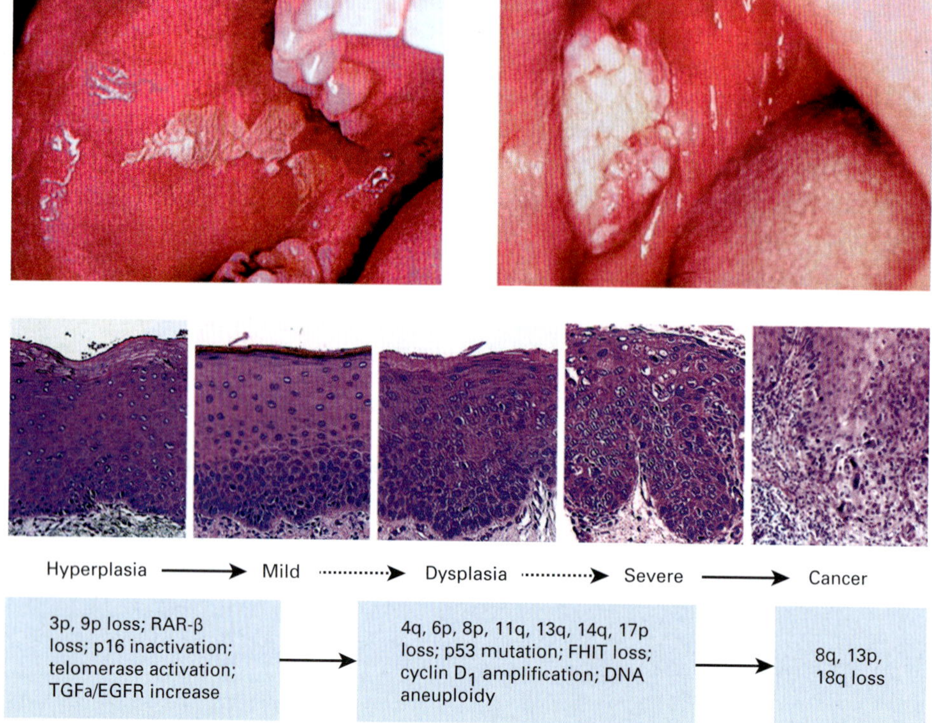

Fig. 12-3 Molecular progression model of multistep carcinogenesis.

Leukoplakia-carcinoma progression models in the oral cavity. Top panels, the clinical progression of a patient's white oral leukoplakia lesion (left) to an oral cancer (right) that developed 3 years after complete leukoplakia resection. Middle panels, histological progression from hyperplasia to invasive cancer. Bottom panels, a molecular progression model, in which the accumulation of genetic alterations is more important than the order. The apparent loss of heterozygosity at 11q may represent allelic imbalance via cyclin D1 amplification at 11q13. Some molecular alterations, such as an autocrine growth loop involving transforming growth factor-α (TGF-α) and epidermal growth factor receptor (EGFR) overexpression, can occur in carcinogen-exposed histologically normal epithelium. Molecular alterations will differ depending on carcinogenic exposure [eg, to cigarette smoke, betel nuts, or human papillomavirus (especially for oropharyngeal cancer)], and on genetic susceptibility (eg, affected by certain glutathione S-transferase genotypes and by helicase defects involved with DNA-repair genes).

Abbreviation: FHIT, fragile histidine triad.

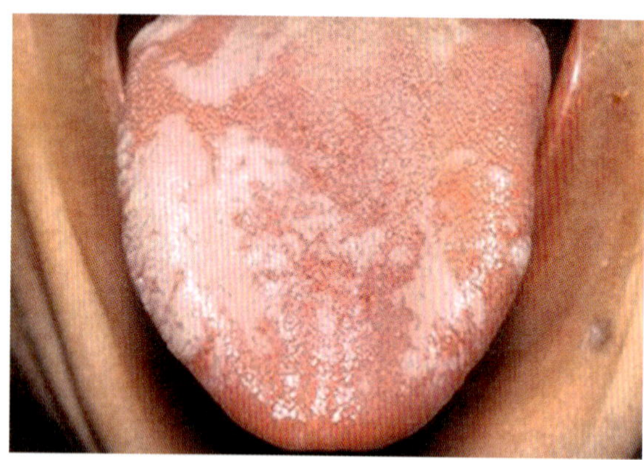

Fig. 12-4 Leukoplakia.

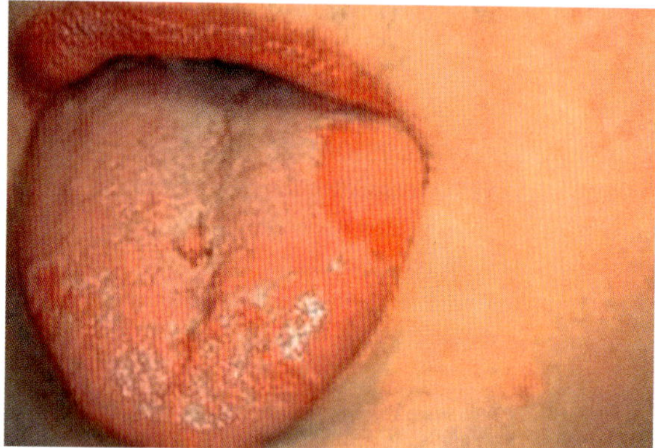

Fig. 12-5 Erythroplakia.

is a common presenting symptom for a patient with head and neck cancer. The location of cervical adenopathy, denoted by dividing the neck into levels, may direct the physician to the primary site (Fig 12-6). Higher-level nodes (eg, level V) may indicate a nasopharyngeal primary, whereas level II or III nodal involvement more likely dictates a primary from the oral cavity, larynx, or oropharynx. Lymph nodal drainage associated with head and neck is shown in Table 12-3.

DIAGNOSTIC EVALUATION

Because lymph nodes track along the internal jugular vein, examination of the neck for enlarged lymph nodes is facilitated by rotating the head to the side during examination to promote relaxation of the sternocleidomastoid muscle on that side.

Endoscopy

A comprehensive examination of the head and neck with the assistance of mirrors or fiberoptic scopes is central to the evaluation.

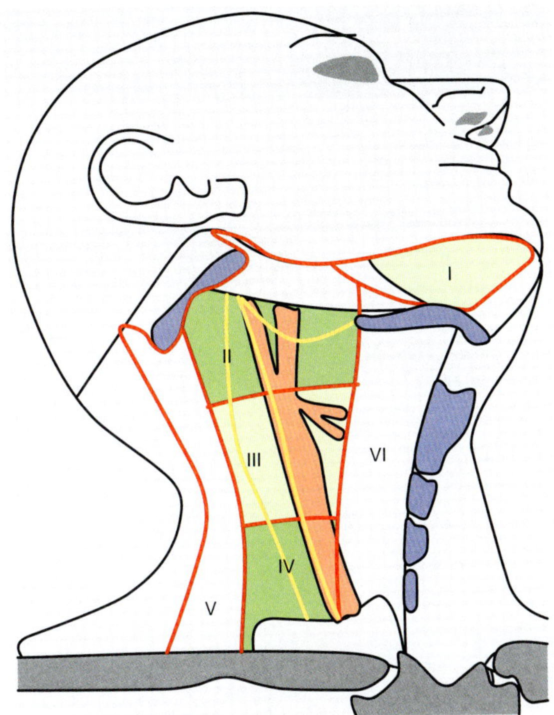

Fig. 12-6 Cervical lymph node levels.

From Moergel M, Jahn-Eimermacher A, Krummenauer F, et al. Effectiveness of adjuvant radiotherapy in patients with oropharyngeal and floor of mouth squamous cell carcinoma and concomitant histological verification of singular ipsilateral cervical lymph node metastasis (pN1-state)—a prospective multicenter randomized controlled clinical trial using a comprehensive cohort design. Trials. 2009;10:118. PMID 20028566. © *Moergel et al; licensee BioMed Central Ltd. 2009.*

Examination under anesthesia often is important for patients with tumors of the larynx or pharynx. Triple endoscopy (ie, laryngoscopy or pharyngoscopy plus bronchoscopy and esophagoscopy) to rule out synchronous tumors is primarily indicated for patients with evidence of diffuse mucosal abnormalities in the setting of a malignant neck node without a clear primary site (ie, lower neck nodes), which increases the likelihood of lung or esophageal primary tumors.

Imaging

High-quality computed tomography (CT) scan performed with contrast medium is sufficient in most HNSCC cases. Magnetic resonance imaging (MRI) is primarily reserved for skull-based tumors and those arising from the sinuses and nasopharynx.

A chest radiograph is taken to rule out a second primary lung cancer or to document chronic obstructive pulmonary disease or possible metastases. A high-resolution CT scan is more sensitive than a chest radiograph for identifying a new primary site or metastases, and it could have a specific indication for patients presenting with bulky N2 or N3 neck disease.

Formal imaging of the liver and bones should be carried out only if clinically indicated on the basis of symptoms or a biochemical abnormality, such as hypercalcemia, elevations in serum alkaline phosphatase, or elevations in liver function tests. Body CT scans and bone scans or 18-fluorodeoxyglucose (FDG)-positron emission tomography (PET)/CT imaging are appropriate parts of the workup for patients with nasopharyngeal cancer with lymph node involvement, because the incidence of distant metastases approaches 60%, and bone is the most common site of metastasis. FDG-PET is also appropriate when the primary site is unknown to evaluate an equivocal finding on cross-sectional imaging. In approximately 30% of cases, the primary site of disease can be located with PET imaging. PET scans should be ordered with cross-sectional imaging of the primary site and neck with contrast, which may be useful for identifying spread to regional nodes in the N0 neck; identification would alter radiation portals or the choice of neck dissection to be performed. FDG-PET is also used to establish a baseline for evaluating response following definitive treatment with chemoradiation (eg, oropharyngeal and nasopharyngeal primaries).

Tissue Diagnosis

Needle aspiration of a lymph node is preferred to excisional biopsy, especially for an apparently malignant node with an occult primary lesion. If an excisional biopsy is necessary, it should be performed in the setting of an appropriate neck dissection. Excisional biopsies alone raise the risk for tumor seeding. A surgeon capable of performing a neck dissection should be involved if squamous cell cancer is suspected.

Table 12-3 Lymph Nodal Drainage in Head and Neck Cancers

Primary Cancer	Lymph Node
Oral cavity	Submental and submandibular areas (level I), upper and midneck (levels II and III) after (level I)
Oropharyngeal	Upper and midneck (levels II and III)
Laryngeal (except glottis)	Upper and midneck (levels II and III)
Nasopharyngeal	Upper neck and posterior triangle (levels II and V)
Primary lesion below the clavicle or in the thyroid	Disease confined to the lower part of the neck or supraclavicular area (levels IV and V)
Glottic larynx	Spread to neck uncommon
Paranasal sinuses	Spread to neck uncommon

Table 12-4 *American Joint Committee on Cancer Staging, 8th Edition*[68]: Non–HPV-Associated (p16-Negative) Tumors of the Lip and Oral Cavity, Oropharynx, Hypopharynx, and Larynx

Primary Tumor	TX	Primary tumor cannot be assessed
	Tis	Carcinoma in situ
Lip	T1	Tumor ≤ 2 cm in greatest dimension
	T2	Tumor > 2 cm but ≤ 4 cm in greatest dimension
	T3	Tumor > 4 cm in greatest dimension
	T4	Lip: Tumor invades through cortical bone, inferior alveolar nerve, floor of mouth, or skin of face (ie, chin or nose)
Oral cavity	T1	Size < 2 cm and depth of invasion < 0.5 cm
	T2	Size < 2 cm and depth of invasion > 0.5 cm, but < 1 cm; size > 2 cm but < 4 cm and depth of invasion < 1 cm
	T3	Size > 4 cm or DOI > 1 cm
	T4a	Moderately very local advanced disease, eg, invasion of cortical bone, deep (extrinsic) muscle of tongue (genioglossus, hyoglossus, palatoglossus, and styloglossus), maxillary sinus, skin of face
	T4b	Very advanced local disease; tumor invades masticator space, pterygoid plates, or skull base and/or encases the internal carotid artery
Oropharynx (p16-negative)	T1	Tumor ≤ 2 cm in greatest dimension
	T2	Tumor > 2 cm but ≤ 4 cm in greatest dimension
	T3	Tumor > 4 cm in greatest dimension or extension to the lingual surface of epiglottis
	T4a	Tumor invades the larynx, deep/extrinsic muscle of tongue, medial pterygoid, hard palate, or mandible
	T4b	Tumor invades lateral pterygoid muscle, pterygoid plates, lateral nasopharynx, or skull base, or encases carotid artery
Hypopharynx	T1	Tumor limited to one subsite of hypopharynx and ≤ 2 cm in greatest dimension
	T2	Tumor invades more than one subsite of hypopharynx or an adjacent site, or measures > 2 cm but ≤ 4 cm in greatest diameter without fixation of hemilarynx
	T3	Tumor > 4 cm in greatest dimension or fixation of hemilarynx
	T4a	Tumor invades thyroid/cricoid cartilage, hyoid bone, thyroid gland, esophagus, or central compartment soft tissue
	T4b	Tumor invades prevertebral fascia, encases carotid artery, or involves mediastinal structures
Larynx-supraglottis	T1	Tumor limited to one subsite of supraglottis with normal vocal cord mobility
	T2	Tumor invades mucosa of more than one adjacent subsite of supraglottis or glottis or region outside the supraglottis (eg, mucosa of base of tongue, vallecula, medial wall of pyriform sinus) without fixation of the larynx
	T3	Tumor limited to larynx with vocal cord fixation and/or invades any of the following: postcricoid area, pre-epiglottic tissues, paraglottic space, and/or minor thyroid cartilage erosion (eg, inner cortex)
	T4a	Tumor invades through the thyroid cartilage and/or invades tissues beyond the larynx (eg, trachea, soft tissues of neck including deep extrinsic muscle of the tongue, strap muscles, thyroid, or esophagus)
	T4b	Tumor invades prevertebral space, encases carotid artery, or invades mediastinal structures

Table 12-4 **continued**		
Glottis	T1	Tumor limited to the vocal cord(s) with normal mobility
	T2	Tumor extends to supraglottis and/or subglottis, and/or with impaired vocal cord mobility
	T3	Tumor limited to the larynx with vocal-cord fixation and/or invades paraglottic space, and or minor thyroid cartilage erosion
	T4a	Tumor invades through the thyroid cartilage and/or invades tissues beyond the larynx (eg, trachea, soft tissues of neck including deep extrinsic muscle of the tongue, strap muscles, thyroid, or esophagus)
	T4b	Tumor invades prevertebral space, encases carotid artery, or invades mediastinal structures
	T4b	Tumor invades prevertebral space, encases carotid artery, or invades mediastinal structures
Clinical classification for non-HPV-associated (p16-negative) lip and oral cavity, oropharynx, hypopharynx, and larynx	NX	Regional lymph nodes cannot be assessed
Regional lymph nodes (cN)	N0	No regional lymph node metastasis
	N1	Metastasis in a single ipsilateral lymph node, ≤ 3 cm in greatest dimension, no ENE
	N2a	Metastasis in a single ipsilateral lymph node, > 3 cm but ≤ 6 cm in greatest dimension, no ENE
	N2b	Metastasis in multiple ipsilateral lymph nodes, none ≤ 6 cm in greatest dimension, no ENE
	N2c	Metastasis in bilateral or contralateral lymph nodes, ≤ 6 cm in greatest dimension, none > 6 cm in greatest dimension, no ENE
	N3a	Metastasis in a lymph node, > 6 cm in greatest dimension, no ENE
	N3b Pathologic classification for non–HPV-associated (p16-) lip and oral cavity, oropharynx, hypopharynx, and larynx	Metastasis in a lymph node, > 6 cm in greatest dimension, with ENE
Regional lymph nodes (pN)	N1 Single ipsilateral lymph node, < 3 cm, no ENE	
	N2a	Single ipsilateral or contralateral lymph node, < 3 cm, with ENE; single lymph node 3-6 cm, no ENE
	N2b	Multiple ipsilateral lymph nodes, < 6 cm, no ENE
	N2c	Bilateral or contralateral lymph nodes, < 6 cm, no ENE
	N3a	Any lymph node > 6 cm, no ENE
	N3b	Any single lymph node > 3 cm with ENE; any multiple/bilateral/contralateral lymph node with ENE
	Mx	Distant metastasis cannot be assessed
Distant metastasis (M)	M0	No distant metastasis
	MI	Distant metastasis
	Stage 0	Tis

Table 12-4 continued

Clinical and pathologic stage grouping for non–HPV-associated	Stage I	T1	N0	M0
	Stage II	T2	N0	M0
	Stage III	T3	N0	M0
	Stage IVA	T1	N0	M0
		T2	N1	M0
		T3	N1	M0
		T4a	N0	M0
	Stage IVB	T4a	N1	M0
		T1	N2a,b,c	M0
		T2	N2a,b,c	M0
		T3	N2a,b,c	M0
		T4a	N2a,b,c	M0
		T4b	Any N	M0
		Any T	N3a,b	M0
	Stage IVC	Any T	Any N	M1

Republished with permission of Springer, from AJCC Cancer Staging Manual, 8th Edition (2017); permission conveyed through Copyright Clearance Center, Inc.[69]
Abbreviations: ENE, extranodal extension; DOI, depth of invasion; HPV, human papillomavirus.

STAGE CLASSIFICATION

Staging for nonviral-associated HNSCC is outlined in Table 12-4 and staging for HPV-positive oropharyngeal cancer is described in Table 12-5. A summary of the changes comparing the 7th and 8th editions of the AJCC for oral cavity and oropharynx is presented in Table 12-6.

GENERAL RULES FOR CLINICAL STAGING

The stage groupings for all primary sites are based on the tumor, node, and metastasis (TNM) classification of the AJCC 8th edition and of the Union for International Union Against Cancer (UICC). The TNM system is based on clinical examination, radiographic information, and pathologic findings.

For p16- tumors, T0 has been eliminated. In addition to previously included size and sites of local invasion, oral cavity T stage has been updated to incorporate depth of invasion (not tumor thickness). Extrinsic muscle infiltration has been eliminated from T4. Primary tumors of the oral cavity and oropharynx that are ≥ 4 cm are classified as T3; those with massive local invasion of adjacent structures are classified as T4. Vocal cord paralysis in the setting of a primary tumor of the larynx or hypopharynx indicates a stage of no less than T3.

For nasopharyngeal cancers, T2 disease includes adjacent muscle involvement including medial and lateral pterygoid and prevertebral muscle involvement, and T4 disease now involves soft tissue involvement. N3a and N3b are now considered N3 (Tables 12-7 and 12-8). The Ho staging system is commonly used in Asia to stage nasopharyngeal cancers, and definitions for component stages vary between the Ho and AJCC staging system. This must be taken into consideration for interpreting published data on such trials. For all primary sites (Table 12-4) except the nasopharynx and p16-positive oropharyngeal cancers (Table 12-5), the TNM stage grouping is the same.

Cancers of unknown primary origin in patients who are HPV or EBV positive (ie, p16 positive or EBER positive) are regarded as oropharyngeal cancers or nasopharyngeal cancers, respectively, and are staged as T0, N appropriate disease; Tx has been eliminated (Table 12-9). For HPV-unrelated or p16-negative disease, the general nodal staging system now incorporates extranodal extension (ENE) into the N staging (N3b) to reflect the poorer prognosis associated with tumors clinically (skin invasion, dense tethering to adjacent structures, nerve invasion with dysfunction; eg, cranial nerve, brachial plexus) or pathologically determined to have extension outside of the lymph nodes, into surrounding connective tissue with or without stromal reaction. Pathologically, it is classified as microscopic (< 2 mm) or macroscopic (> 2 mm), and increases N by one step. Radiographic evidence of ENE supports the clinical evidence of ENE, but alone is insufficient.

For p16-negative disease, the term "early-stage disease" refers to stages I and II disease and to low-volume stage III disease (ie, T1 or T2 and N0 or N1); the terms "locally" or "locally regionally advanced disease" refer to stages III and IV disease, specifically a large primary tumor (T3 or T4) or the presence of multiple or bulky neck nodes (N2 or N3).

UNRESECTABLE T4 LESIONS

Primary criteria for unresectability include base-of-skull involvement fixation to the prevertebral fascia carotid encasement involvement of the pterygoid musculature. Additional criteria include, 1) inability to perform an adequate reconstruction for a functional result, 2) a low likelihood of achieving the negative, and 3) margin requirement for total glossectomy.

For p16- disease, assignment to the stage IVB category has implications for prognosis (ie, less favorable) and treatment (ie, primary surgical management not planned). For these primary sites, stage IVB disease now includes patients with T4b, any N category, and no metastasis (M0), or any T category and N3 (any neck node > 6 cm in greatest diameter). Stage IVC includes any T and N category as well as M1 disease.

HPV-RELATED OROPHARYNGEAL CANCERS

The AJCC staging system was updated to account for p16 status in staging of oropharyngeal tumors, given the marked difference in prognosis between patients with p16-positive and p16-negative tumors. The new staging system for p16-positive oropharyngeal tumors now combines T4a and T4b into a single T4 category. N1 disease indicates one or more ipsilateral lymph nodes, none > 6 cm; N2 disease indicates contralateral or bilateral nodal disease; and N3 nodes are those > 6 cm.

The new system has three stages for nonmetastatic disease: (1) early stage, or stage I (T0-T2, N0-N1); (2) locally advanced disease, or stage II (T0-T2, N2 or T3,N0-N2) or stage III (T4 or N3); and (3) metastatic disease, or stages or stage IV (M1).

Unknown primary cancers that are HPV- or EBV-positive are treated as oropharyngeal or nasopharyngeal cancers, respectively.

KEY POINTS

- Many presenting signs and symptoms are associated with a particular primary site (eg, hoarseness may refer to the larynx or hypopharynx, and a unilateral otitis media may refer to the nasopharynx).
- The location of pathologic lymph nodes in the neck may suggest the primary site.
- The initial staging evaluation for head and neck cancer includes comprehensive examination of the head and neck, imaging of the primary site and neck, chest imaging, and routine laboratory screenings.
- Early-stage disease is primarily defined as disease limited to a small primary tumor (T1 or T2) with low risk nodal involvement. Locally or locoregionally advanced disease is generally defined as the presence of a large primary tumor (T3 or T4) or the presence of large, multiple, or contralateral regional node involvement (N2 or N3).
- Criteria for unresectable disease include base of skull involvement, fixation to the prevertebral fascia, carotid encasement, and involvement of the pterygoid musculature.

PRINCIPLES OF DISEASE MANAGEMENT

TNM stage groupings are helpful for defining prognosis and treatment options. Figure 12-7 outlines treatments for newly diagnosed stages I, II, or low bulk III disease. Because of their curative potential, surgery and RT are the central treatment modalities for head and neck cancers. Although chemotherapy may enhance the effects of RT, chemotherapy by itself is not curative.

Management of the primary site and management of the neck are separate but related concerns that influence decisions about which modality is used or the integration of combined-modality therapy. Management of head and neck cancer is best served by multidisciplinary treatment planning that involves not only a surgeon, medical oncologist, and radiation oncologist but also dentists, prosthodontists, nutritionists, pharmacists, advanced practice providers, nurses, audiologists, speech and swallowing therapists, physical and occupational therapists, social workers, and psychiatrists.

NEWLY DIAGNOSED HPV-NEGATIVE STAGES I, II, AND LOW-BULK III (p16-NEGATIVE T1 OR T2, N0 OR N1, AND M0) OR HPV-POSITIVE STAGE I DISEASE

Single-modality treatment with surgery or radiation is typically used for previously untreated p16-negative stage I, stage II, or low-bulk stage III disease—essentially, a small primary tumor with or without a single ipsilateral node measuring ≤ 3 cm in diameter, and for p16-positive stage I disease of the oropharynx (Fig 12-7). Cure rates for this group are quite favorable, ranging from 52% to 100%, depending on the primary site. Tumors that are upstaged or have positive margins may require additional surgery or adjuvant chemoradiation.

The chosen modality depends on local expertise, anticipated functional outcome, and patient preference. RT is associated with excellent control rates and voice-function outcome, but it requires a 7-week course, is associated with late-term toxicities and fibrosis, and may be more expensive.

NEWLY DIAGNOSED, HIGHER-VOLUME HPV-NEGATIVE STAGES III AND IVA/IVB DISEASE OR HPV-POSITIVE STAGE II, III

If a higher-volume, p16-negative, stage III or a stage IV tumor (Fig 12-7) is resectable, the standard approach is surgery followed by adjuvant RT with or without concomitant chemotherapy based on pathologic risk features (see Surgical Management of Head and Neck Cancer), or combined chemotherapy and radiotherapy, if organ preservation is preferred. For p16-negative disease, if the tumor is unresectable, the approach is RT and concomitant chemotherapy. However, when surgery is not possible, cure rates with chemoradiotherapy are less favorable, ranging from 10% to 65%, depending on the primary site and disease extent. Data from

Table 12-5 AJCC Cancer Staging Manual, 8th Edition[68]: HPV-Associated (p16-Positive) Oropharyngeal Cancer

Oropharynx (p16-positive)	T0	No primary identified
	T1	Tumor $\leq$ 2 cm in greatest dimension
	T2	Tumor $>$ 2 cm but $\leq$ 4 cm in greatest dimension
	T3	Tumor $>$ 4 cm in greatest dimension or extension to the lingual surface of epiglottis
	T4	Tumor invades the larynx, deep/extrinsic muscle of tongue, medial pterygoid, hard palate, or mandible, or beyond
Clinical classification for HPV-associated (p16-positive) oropharyngeal cancer		
Regional lymph nodes (cN)	NX	Regional lymph nodes cannot be assessed
	N0	No regional lymph node metastasis
	N1	$\geq$ 1 ipsilateral lymph nodes, none $>$ 6 cm
	N2	Contralateral or bilateral lymph nodes, none $>$ 6 cm
	N3	Lymph node(s) $>$ 6 cm
Pathologic classification for HPV-associated (p16-positive) oropharyngeal cancer		
Regional lymph nodes (pN)	NX	Regional lymph nodes cannot be assessed
	pN0	No regional lymph node metastasis
	pN1	Metastases in $\leq$ 4 lymph nodes
	pN2	Metastases in $>$ 4 lymph nodes

Anatomic stage groups for clinical TNM grouping of HPV-associated (p16-positive) oropharyngeal cancer	Stage I	T0	N1	M0
		T1	N0	
		T1	N1	M0
		T2	N0	M0
		T2	N1	M0
	Stage II	T0	N2	M0
		T1	N2	M0
		T2	N2	M0
		T3	N0	M0
		T3	N1	M0
		T3	N2	M0
		T0	N3	M0
		T1	N3	M0
		T2	N3	M0
		T3	N3	M0
	Stage III	T4	N0	M0
		T4	N1	M0
		T4	N2	M0
		T4	N3	M0
	Stage IV	Any T	Any N	M1

Abbreviation: HPV, human papillomavirus.

Table 12-6 Comparison of the AJCC Cancer Staging Manual 7th Ed.[69] and 8th Ed.[68] Staging Systems for Oral Cavity and Oropharyngeal Cancers

Change	7th Ed. (2010)	8th Ed. (2017) Oral Cavity	8th Ed. (2017) HPV-Negative Oropharynx	8th Ed. (2017) HPV-Positive Oropharynx
T-stage	T0: no primary	T0 deleted	T0 deleted	T0 if proven p16-positive disease without evidence of primary tumor. All locally advanced combined to T4
	T1: size < 2 cm	T1: size < 2 cm and DOI < 5 mm		
	T2: size 2-4 cm	T2: size < 2 cm and DOI 5-10 mm or size 2-4 cm and DOI < 10 mm		
	T3: size > 4 cm	T3: size > 4 cm or > 10 mm DOI		
	T4: T4a: moderately advanced (extrinsic tongue muscle involvement constituted T4a) T4b: very advanced	T4a: extrinsic tongue muscle infiltration now deleted		
		Clinical *N*-stage		
	N0: no LN involved	N1-N2 is same as previous and ENE(-)		Previous N1, N2a, N2b combined to N1 (< 6 cm with or without ENE) N2c now called N2
	N1: single ipsi LN < 3 cm	N3 now with subcategories: N3a is previous N3 (> 6 cm) and ENE(-) N3b is any ENE(+), either clinical or radiographic		
	N2:	Pathologic *N*-stage		
	N2a: single ipsi LN, 3-6 cm	Microscopically evident ENE(+) LNs results in upstaging		
	N2b: multiple ipsi LNs, all < 6 cm			N1: < 4 LNs involved
	N2c: any bi or ctr LNs, all < 6 cm			N2: > 4 LNs involved
	N3: any LN > 6 cm			N3 deleted
Stage grouping	Clinical or pathologic TNM used for same grouping system	Same as previous		Separate clinical and pathologic TNM groupings

Abbreviations: bi, bilateral; ctr, contralateral; DOI, depth of invasion; ENE(+), extranodal extension present; ENE(-) extranodal extension absent; ipsi; LN, lymph node.

randomized trials support integrated chemotherapy and RT as standard treatment options for patients with advanced, resectable cancers of the larynx and hypopharynx (with the intent of avoiding total laryngectomy) and for patients with p16-negative or p16-positive cancers of the oropharynx when a nonsurgical approach is chosen.

The most standard chemoradiation regimens for organ preservation, unresectable tumors, and adjuvant therapy are summarized in Table 12-10. When primary chemoradiation therapy is used, surgery is reserved for persistent disease or for recurrence of resectable disease. For locally advanced, resectable cancers of the oral cavity, primary surgical management with appropriate reconstruction and/or postoperative RT is the mainstay of treatment, because anticipated functional outcomes are favorable even for more advanced tumors.

KEY POINTS

- Single-modality treatment with surgery or RT is typically used with curative intent for previously untreated p16-negative stage I, stage II, or low-bulk stage III (T1-2, N0, N1:single node ≤ 3 cm) disease or p16-positive stage I (T1-2, N0-1).

- Combined-modality treatment after surgery and RT: or chemoradiotherapy is used with curative intent for previously untreated, higher-volume, p16-negative stage III (T3, N0-1) and stage IVA/B disease, or p16-positive stages I (multiple nodes or single node > 3 cm), II, and III disease, though chemoradiotherapy is generally preferred over surgery + RT for p16-positive disease.
- Metastatic disease below the clavicle and locoregional recurrent disease without a surgical or radiation option are generally incurable and treated with palliative intent.

SURGICAL MANAGEMENT OF HEAD AND NECK CANCER

SURGERY OF THE PRIMARY TUMOR

Surgery is used as an upfront, definitive modality as well as a salvage option in many types of head and neck cancer. Complete extirpation of the primary tumor with negative margins defines an adequate surgical resection. Nodal surgery (typically a neck dissection) is also required for most head and neck cancers but is dependent on numerous patient factors and tumor characteristics.

Recent surgical advances have been made, particularly with the use of the surgical transoral robot (TORS). This approach can provide improved visualization and may minimize the morbidity and functional sequela of surgery. Despite these advances, resection of the primary tumor may necessitate removal of key structures, such as the larynx, tongue, eye, or mandible. These considerations are frequently dictated by the site of primary disease, size of the tumor, and the structures involved with disease. The potential adverse effects on cosmesis and function underscores the importance of optimal reconstruction and associated postoperative rehabilitation as part of the treatment strategy. The anticipated adverse effects are also important to consider when discussing surgery with the patient as a possible definitive treatment approach. For example, advanced p16-positive oropharynx cancers have equivalent survival outcomes whether addressed with definitive surgery or with definitive chemoradiation; therefore, functional deficits are important to consider when discussing surgery with a patient, even when a TORS approach is being considered.

Table 12-7 **WHO Classification Criteria of Nasopharyngeal Carcinoma**

WHO Classification	Former Terminology
Type I: Keratinizing squamous cell carcinoma	Squamous cell carcinoma
Type II: Nonkeratinizing carcinoma	Transitional cell carcinoma
Without lymphoid stroma	Intermediate cell carcinoma
With lymphoid stroma	Lymphoepithelial carcinoma (Regaud)
Type III: Undifferentiated carcinoma	Anaplastic carcinoma
Without lymphoid stroma	Clear-cell carcinoma
With lymphoid stroma	Lymphoepithelial carcinoma (Schminke)

Neck dissection plays an integral role in the surgical management of head and neck cancers. The extent of neck dissection depends on a variety of factors, including the location of the primary tumor, extent of clinically positive lymph nodes, and extracapsular extension of nodal disease into surrounding structures (eg, the sternocleidomastoid muscle, internal jugular vein). Neck dissections are typically classified as either radical, modified radical, or selective, as follows: A radical or comprehensive neck dissection includes the en bloc removal of all five lymph node levels along with the resection of the sternocleidomastoid muscle, the internal jugular vein, and the spinal accessory nerve (Fig 12-6). If any or all of these structures are preserved the procedure is considered a modified radical neck dissection. A selective neck dissection removes only specific nodal levels. For example, a larynx cancer is typically addressed with a bilateral level 2-4 selective neck dissection.

SURGERY OF THE NECK

Neck dissection is frequently indicated in patients with no clinically apparent neck disease. In a randomized controlled trial, D'Cruz et al[1] evaluated whether early-stage oral cavity cancers (cT1-2N0) should be treated with elective neck dissection or therapeutic neck dissection at the time of nodal relapse. At 3 years, elective nodal dissection resulted in a better overall survival (OS; 80% *v* 67.5%) and disease-free survival (69.5% *v* 45.9%) compared with the therapeutic neck dissection group.

Sentinel lymph node biopsy can also be used to identify patients with early-stage N0 oral cavity cancer. Reconstruction is frequently required for surgery involving advanced-stage disease. Improvements in reconstructive techniques have enabled large extirpations with good functional results. A variety of free flaps, frequently composed of skin, muscle, and/or bone (and, occasionally, multiple flaps in the same patient), can successfully address many defects that arise from surgery. In addition, customized obturators and prosthetics can be used alone or in combination with free-flap reconstruction to optimize function.

KEY POINTS

- Function-conserving procedures are applicable for select patients in whom negative margins can be achieved with preservation of structures important for function.
- Conservative or debulking surgery is not part of routine clinical practice for head and neck cancer.
- Comprehensive neck dissections involve removal of all five lymph node levels and are usually performed with therapeutic intent. Selective neck dissections involve removal of fewer than all five levels and are generally done electively to improve staging precision.

Table 12-8 **Classification Criteria and Staging According to the 7th and 8th Editions of the UICC/AJCC Staging System for Nasopharyngeal Carcinoma**[70]

7th Edition	8th Edition
T category	
T1: Nasopharynx, oropharynx, or nasal cavity without parapharyngeal extension	T1: Nasopharynx, oropharynx, or nasal cavity without parapharyngeal extension
T2: Parapharyngeal extension	T2: Parapharyngeal extension, adjacent soft-tissue involvement (medial pterygoid, lateral pterygoid, prevertebral muscles)
T3: Bony structures of skull base and/or paranasal sinuses	T3: Bony structures (skull base, cervical vertebra) and/or paranasal sinuses
T4: Intracranial, cranial nerves, hypopharynx, orbit, infratemporal fossa/masticator space	T4: Intracranial extension, cranial nerve, hypopharynx, orbit, extensive soft-tissue involvement (beyond the lateral surface of the lateral pterygoid muscle, parotid gland)
N category	
N0: No regional lymph node metastasis	N0: No regional lymph node metastasis
N1: Unilateral cervical, unilateral or bilateral retropharyngeal lymph nodes above the supraclavicular fossa; ≤ 6 cm	N1: Retropharyngeal (regardless of laterality). cervical: unilateral, ≤ 6 cm, and above caudal border of cricoid cartilage
N2: Bilateral metastasis in lymph nodes, ≤ 6 cm in greatest dimension, above the supraclavicular fossa	N2: Cervical: bilateral, ≤ 6 cm, and above caudal border of cricoid cartilage
N3a: > 6 cm in dimension	N3: > 6 cm and/or below caudal border of cricoid cartilage (regardless of laterality)
N3b: Supraclavicular fossa	
Stage/group	
I: T1 N0 M0	I: T1 N0 M0
II: T2 N0-1 M0, T1 N1 M0	II: T2 N0-1 M0, T1 N1 M0
III: T1-3 N2 M0, T3 N0-1 M0	III: T3 N0-2 M0, T1-2 N2 M0
IVA: T4 N0-2 M0	IVa: T4 or N3 M0
IVB: any T N3 M0	IVb: any T, any N M1
IVC: any T, any N M1	

[Adapted from Tang et al[70]]

PRINCIPLES OF RT

The curability of head and neck cancer with RT is inversely related to tumor bulk, with HPV-positive cancers showing increased radiosensitivity compared with HPV-negative tumors. The rate of disease control with RT alone decreases with increasing T stage, which explains why RT can be used as a single modality to treat early-stage disease but is generally applied as an adjunct to surgery or combined with chemotherapy for more advanced tumors.

RADIATION DOSE AND FRACTIONATION

Definitive Radiation

Standard, once-daily fractionation consists of 2 Gy/d with a total dose of ≥ 70 Gy to the primary site and gross adenopathy and 50 to 60 Gy to uninvolved nodal stations at risk (other biologically equivalent fractionation schemes may be used). Altered fractionation schedules consist of more RT doses with lower dose per fraction, with the goals of improving locoregional control and widening the therapeutic index. Altered fractionation RT alone is associated with improvements in OS when compared with conventional, single-fraction RT alone.

Hyperfractionation refers to twice-daily treatment, and accelerated fractionation (AF) typically refers to six fractions per week separated by > 6 hours to allow for normal tissue repair. RTOG 0129 was designed to test the efficacy and toxicity of cisplatin plus accelerated fractionation (AF) with a concomitant boost versus standard fractionation (SF). Patients with locally advances HNSCC were randomly assigned to 70 Gy in 35 fractions over 7 weeks (SF) or 72 Gy in 42 fractions over 6 weeks (AF). Cisplatin doses were 100 mg/m^2 once every 3 weeks for two (AF) or three (SF) cycles. The clinical trial established no benefit from combined concurrent chemoradiation with SF or AF in OS (hazard ratio [HR], 0.96, *P* = .37; 5-year, 57% *v* 60%; 8-year estimate, 48% *v* 48%), progression-free survival (PFS; HR, 1.02, *P* = .52; 5-year, 49% *v* 50%; 8-year estimate, 42% *v* 41%), locoregional failure rate (HR, 1.08, *P* = 0.78; 5-year, 31% *v* 34%; 8-year estimate, 37% *v* 39%).[2]

Table 12-9 **AJCC *Cancer Staging Manual, 8th ed.*: Cancers of Unknown Primary: Viral and Nonviral**[71]

Stage	HPV-Positive/p16-Postive CUP	EBV-Positive CUP	Nonviral-Related CUP
I	T0 N1 M0	NA	NA
II	T0 N2 M0	T0 N1 M0	NA
III	T0 N3 M0	T0 N2 M0	T0 N1 M0
IV	Clinical: T0 N1-3 M1	IVA T0 N3 M0	IVA T0 N2 M0
	Pathologic: T0 N1-2 M1	IVB T0 N1-3 M1	IVB T0 N3 M0
			IVC T0 N1-3 M1

NOTE. The unknown primary of the neck is considered respectively as nasopharynx or oropharynx if EBV positive or HPV/p16 positive; therefore, stages I-IV is recognized for HPV-positive/p16 CUP, whereas EBV-positive CUP comprises stages II-IV. The prognosis is dismal for nonviral-related CUP; therefore, stages I and II are not included.
Abbreviations: CUP, cancer of unknown primary; EBV, Epstein-Barr virus; HPV, human papillomavirus; NA, not applicable.
[Taken from Denaro et al[71]]

Adjuvant RT

Adjuvant RT doses are typically 60 Gy, delivered in standard, once-daily fractionation, after surgery and neck dissection and should begin no later than 6 weeks from the postoperative date. Areas of positive margin or nodal extracapsular extension are boosted to 66 Gy. Uninvolved, nondissected nodal regions considered at risk are typically treated with 50 to 56 Gy. Locoregional control and OS advantage have been demonstrated with adjuvant RT started within 6 weeks of surgery.

Technical Aspects of RT

Intensity-modulated radiotherapy is regularly used in the treatment of head and neck cancer. This therapy delivers therapeutic radiation doses specifically around the tumor and the at-risk lymph nodes, with improved conformality, defined as the ratio of the dose to tumor relative to the dose to normal tissues. Advantages include increased normal-tissue sparing and preservation of anatomic structures (eg, the pharyngeal constrictor muscles necessary for swallowing and the salivary glands). Patients treated with intensity-modulated radiotherapy have less incidence of xerostomia than do patients treated with conventional RT, but they experience higher rates of fatigue during treatment.

Another more recent advancement is the use of proton-beam therapy. In proton-beam therapy, Bragg peak refers to the physical properties of a proton beam that allow rapid decrease in RT dose beyond the tumor, leading to lower normal-tissue doses. Phase II data demonstrated efficacy, safety, and favorable toxicity profiles in base of skull malignancies, periorbital tumors, nasopharynx cancer, and reirradiation, and studies in other head and neck malignancies are ongoing. However, there are not yet phase III data in head and neck cancer to suggest improved tumor control or decreased toxicity associated with the use of proton-beam therapy.

RADIATION-RELATED TOXICITY

Acute and late-term RT toxicities are noted in Table 12-11. Adequate saliva is an important component of oral hygiene; thus, careful dental assessment is recommended before the start of RT, followed by ongoing dental prophylaxis and fluoride treatments.

RT at the doses outlined previously is associated with predictable acute mucosal and skin toxicities, including mucositis, desquamation, pain, odynophagia, dysgeusia, and thick phlegm or mucus. More-aggressive dosing and fractionation schedules and the addition of concomitant chemotherapy generally increase the severity of these acute toxicities. Any acute and late toxicities greater than grade 3 of 70% to 85% and 40% to 50%, respectively, are associated with a 20% feeding-tube dependence at 1 year in HPV-negative patients and 5% for HPV-positive patients.[2,3] Xerostomia can be a late sequelae of RT. Pain management, nutritional support, swallowing evaluation and therapy, and aggressive oral care are required during therapy.

KEY POINTS

- Compared with standard schedules, altered-fractionation RT improves locoregional control of advanced tumors, albeit with increased acute local toxicity.
- Head and neck RT commonly cause acute toxicities, including mucositis, edema, and xerostomia. Other potential toxicities include hypothyroidism, Lhermitte syndrome, long-term induration and fibrosis, and osteoradionecrosis of the mandible.
- IMRT delivers radiation around the tumor and high-risk lymph nodes conformally; it is associated with less dry mouth after treatment than that seen with conventionally planned RT.

PRINCIPLES OF CHEMOTHERAPY

Cisplatin is the most widely used cytotoxic drug to treat HNSCC. Other drugs with activity include fluorouracil (FU), taxanes (ie, paclitaxel and docetaxel), methotrexate, and cetuximab. The reported response proportions with chemotherapy vary with the setting (untreated or pretreated) and with the drugs used (single agent or combination).

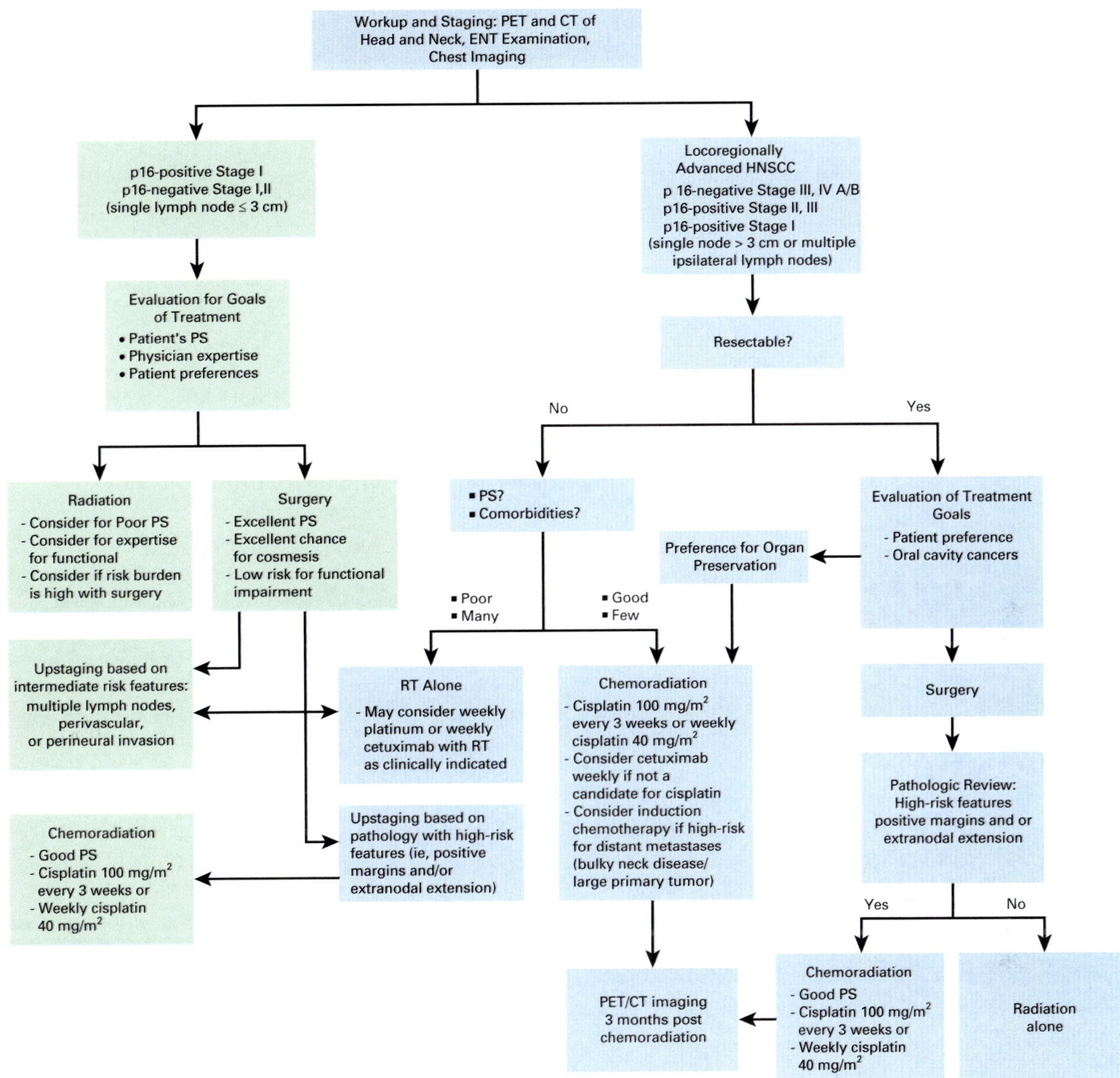

Fig. 12-7 **Treatment algorithm for localized and locally advanced head and neck squamous cell carcinoma (HNSCC).**
Abbreviations: CT, computed tomography; ENT, ear, nose, and throat; PET, positron emission tomography; PS, performance status; RT, radiation therapy.

Platinum-based regimens are most commonly used as first-line therapy with chemoradiation, with induction regimens, and with disease that is metastatic or incurable. The anticipated major response rate in patients with previously untreated disease is 60% to 90%, with clinical complete responses in 20% to 50% of patients. By contrast, the activity of platinum-based drug combination therapy in patients with recurrent disease is 30% to 40%, and complete responses are rare. Rates of complete and partial responses from single-agent therapy are approximately half the rate of those observed with combination chemotherapy.

When the goal for therapy is to control or cure locoregional disease, the chemotherapy literature can be divided into the following four groups: (1) induction or neoadjuvant chemotherapy administered prior to definitive local therapy (surgery, RT, or chemoradiotherapy); (2) chemoradiation in the setting of locally advanced, unresectable disease; (3) local curative therapy (surgery) followed by adjuvant chemoradiation; and (4) organ-preservation techniques, as an alternative to total surgical resections, to preserve speech and swallowing function for patients with resectable cancers of the oropharynx, larynx, and hypopharynx.

INDUCTION CHEMOTHERAPY

Historically, induction chemotherapy has not provided improvements in locoregional control or survival when compared with standard-of-care treatments for HNSCC. Cisplatin and fluorouracil (FU) in one subset analysis, however, demonstrated potential survival benefit. The next phase of induction studies compared the addition of taxanes to cisplatin and FU versus

Table 12-10 **Concurrent Chemoradiotherapy Standard of Care**

Site of Disease	Regimen
Larynx	RT/cisplatin[23]
Oropharynx	RT/cisplatin or RT/carboplatin/FU[25,26,5] Consider RT/cetuximab if not candidates for platinum therapy[17,19]
Nasopharynx	RT/cisplatin followed by cisplatin/FU[3]
Unresectable disease	RT/cisplatin[4]
Postoperative adjuvant	RT/cisplatin[1,2]

Abbreviations: FU, fluorouracil; RT, radiation therapy.

cisplatin and FU followed by definitive RT or chemoradiation. Results from three phase III, randomized controlled trials comparing three or four cycles of induction docetaxel and cisplatin and FU with standard cisplatin (100 mg/m^2) plus FU (1,000 mg/m^2/d by continuous infusion for 5 days) are summarized in Table 12-12.[4-6] These three trials, along with a meta-analysis of five randomized trials representing 1,772 patients comparing cisplatin and FU induction therapy with a paclitaxel or docetaxel and cisplatin and FU (TPF) regimen established TPF as the standard of care for HNSCC when induction chemotherapy is followed by RT alone or chemoradiation with weekly carboplatin.[7]

SEQUENTIAL THERAPY

To test whether induction chemotherapy improved survival, three randomized, phase III trials comparing TPF followed by chemoradiation versus chemoradiation alone were conducted and demonstrated no survival benefit (Table 12-13).[8-10] Induction chemotherapy with TPF followed by chemoradiation or RT is a treatment option for patients with locally advanced HNSCC. With the exception of treatment of nasopharyngeal and laryngeal primaries, induction chemotherapy is considered a category 3 recommendation guideline, per the National Comprehensive Cancer Network (NCCN).[11] Induction chemotherapy may be considered for patients for whom there is need to rapidly reduce bulky neck disease in an effort to improve morbidity and to possibly delay the onset of distant metastasis. It should not be used in the context of improving OS.

CONCOMITANT CHEMOTHERAPY AND RT

The major role for chemotherapy in patients with nonmetastatic disease is as a radiation sensitizer. Therefore, the main focus has been on drugs that show activity against the disease and radiation-enhancement properties (eg, cisplatin, carboplatin, cetuximab, and FU). Combined modality therapy with chemotherapy and RT is considered standard treatment of patients with locally advanced, unresectable HNSCC who are able to tolerate the anticipated added treatment-related toxicity and, in some cases, may preserve organ function.

Chemoradiation is considered standard of care in organ preservation of the larynx and oropharynx and for advanced locoregional nasopharyngeal cancers. In addition, cisplatin (100 mg/m^2) administered every 21 days with RT is standard of care for patients with locally advanced HNSCC who are not candidates for surgery upfront.[12] Toxicities, including hearing loss, protracted nausea and vomiting, renal dysfunction, and peripheral neuropathy, may preclude patients from receiving all three doses. A minimum of 200 mg/m^2 is required for efficacy. In efforts to reduce toxicity, cisplatin can be administered weekly (40 mg/m^2) with RT. Although randomized, prospective data are lacking to fully substantiate the use of weekly platinum or to determine if weekly regimens are less toxic than

Table 12-11 **Acute and Late Grade 3+ Toxicities of Modern Definitive Chemoradiation With Cisplatin Reported per RTOG 1016 and HN 002 (Acute Toxicities Only)**

Acute Toxicity	> Grade 3 (%)	Late Toxicity	> Grade 3 (%)
Dry mouth	49	Dry mouth	32
Dysphagia	18-37	dysphagia	4
Mucositis	21-41	Weight loss	4
Dehydration	4-37	Hearing impairment	6
Dermatitis	3-8	Pain	2
Pain	7-15	Osteoradionecrosis	2
Weight loss	4-8		
Hearing impairment	3-4		

NOTE. Acute and late toxicities of RT alone are typically less severe than chemoradiation.

Table 12-12 **Induction Chemotherapy Clinical Trials Followed by Definitive Radiation in Patients With Head and Neck Squamous Cell Carcinoma**

Study	No. of Patients	Population	Study Arm	Primary Outcome	Secondary Outcome
GORTEC9 2000-01	213	Larynx and hypopharynx (requiring laryngectomy) for organ preservation	IC with TPF *v* IC with PF followed by definitive radiation	3-year laryngeal preservation: 70.3% *v* 57.5% (*P* = .03)	Overall response rate: 80% *v* 59.2% (*P* = .002)
TAX 32310	358	Unresectable oropharynx, hypopharynx, oral cavity, and larynx	IC with TPF *v* IC with PF, both followed by definitive radiation	Median PFS, 11 months *v* 8.2 months. Median OS, 18.8 months	CRR: 33% *v* 19.9% (*P* = .004)
TAX 32411	501	Oropharynx, larynx, hypopharynx, and oral cavity for organ preservation (T3-4, N2-3 disease only)	IC with TPF *v* IC with PF both followed by weekly carboplatin (AUC 1.5) with radiation	5-year OS: 52% *v* 42% (*P* = .014)	Median PFS: 38.1 months *v* 13.2 months (HR 0.75; 95% CI, 0.60 to 0.94)

Abbreviations: AUC, area under the curve; CRR, complete response rate; HR, hazard ratio; IC, induction chemotherapy; OS, overall survival; PF, cisplatin, fluorouracil; PFS, progression-free survival; TPF, docetaxel, cisplatin, fluorouracil.

bolus-dose regimens, most experts agree that weekly cisplatin may be administered without compromising survival.

When possible, large, bulky (T4 or N3) tumors should be treated with combined high-dose cisplatin and RT. A published meta-analysis demonstrated that chemoradiation regimens were associated with an 8% absolute benefit in survival at 5 years compared with RT alone (HR, 0.81; 95% CI, 0.76 to 0.88; *P* < .0001).[13] An updated analysis of 87 trials involving > 16,000 patients showed the same absolute benefit for survival with concomitant treatment (HR, 0.81; *P* < .0001), and multitherapy chemotherapy (eg, cisplatin and FU) does not offer an advantage over single-agent cisplatin when combined with RT.[14] Once-daily fractionation RT for 7 weeks with high-dose cisplatin (100 mg/m^2 on days 1, 22, and 43) is equivalent to accelerated boost RT (42 fractions for 6 weeks) in combination with two cycles of cisplatin (100 mg/m^2 on days 1 and 22), per the RTOG 0129 trial.[2]

Epidermal growth factor receptor (EGFR) is highly expressed on HNSCC, and expression is inversely associated with prognosis. In a multicenter trial, the EGFR inhibitor cetuximab, when administered weekly with RT, demonstrated significant improvements in locoregional failure-free survival and OS when compared with RT alone in patients with advanced head and neck cancers.[15] The updated median OS for patients treated with cetuximab and RT was 49.0 (95% CI, 32.8 to 69.5) months compared with 29.3 (95% CI, 20.6 to 41.4) months in the RT-alone group (HR, 0.73; 95% CI, 0.56 to 0.95; *P* = .018). Five-year OS was 45.6% in the cetuximab and RT group and 36.4% in the RT-alone group. Survival was improved in patients who experienced at least a grade 2 acneiform rash compared with patients with grade 0 or 1 rash (HR, 0.49; 95% CI, 0.34 to 0.72; *P* = .002).[16]

Unlike cisplatin, when administered with RT, cetuximab has no effect on distant metastases. The only indication for cetuximab with RT instead of platinum-based chemotherapy is in the treatment of patients with good performance status, for whom the use of cisplatin is precluded (ie, severe hearing loss, creatinine clearance < 30 mL/min, or severe peripheral neuropathy), or due to patient preference because of concern for cisplatin-related toxicities.

Cetuximab should never be delivered in combination with chemotherapy and RT. RTOG trial 0522 directly compared cisplatin and RT with or without cetuximab.[3] After a median of 3.8 years, there was no statistically significant improvement in the 3-year PFS (61.2% *v* 58.9%; *P* = .76) and OS (72.9% *v* 75.8%; *P* = .32) or distant metastasis (13.0% *v* 9.7%; *P* = .08) with the addition of cetuximab to cisplatin and RT.

ADJUVANT CHEMORADIATION

Adjuvant chemoradiation applies mainly to patients with advanced, resectable oral cavity cancers, because surgery remains the standard of care and good reconstructive options exist for these tumor types. Adjuvant treatment is also administered after surgical resection of laryngeal and oropharyngeal primaries when upfront chemoradiation is not considered.

Two phase III randomized, controlled trials have clarified the role of chemoradiation in the postoperative adjuvant setting. The RTOG[17] and the EROTC[18] trials addressed the question of whether the addition of cisplatin to standard postoperative RT (based on pathologic criteria) would improve the outcome for patients compared with postoperative RT alone. In both studies, toxicity was greater with concomitant chemoradiation therapy (Table 12-14). Although the treatment was similar in these two studies, the high-risk pathologic features were not uniform, and the study populations differed. RTOG trial high-risk criteria were having more than two positive lymph nodes, extracapsular extension of nodal disease, or positive margins; and EORTC trial high-risk criteria were having positive margins, extracapsular extension of nodal disease, vascular embolism, or perineural disease; for oral cavity or oropharynx primary sites, high risk was defined as positive nodes at level IV or V.

Survival differences were statistically significant in the EORTC trial but not in the RTOG trial, in part due to the differences in entry criteria. A pooled analysis of both studies indicated the subsets of patients in both trials who experienced a significant benefit from cisplatin with RT had either microscopically involved margins or extracapsular extension of disease in neck nodes.[19] The presence of either or both of these risk factors is considered an absolute indication for adjuvant chemoradiation.

A reanalysis of the RTOG trial, with a median follow-up of 9.4 years, demonstrated a significant advantage for chemoradiation with locoregional control of disease and disease-free survival in patients with either positive margins or extracapsular nodal extension, but with only a trend for OS benefit.[20] Cisplatin (100 mg/m^2) administered on days 1, 22, and 43 during RT is the standard-of-care chemoradiation regimen for adjuvant therapy. Per the NCCN Guidelines for Head and Neck Cancer, weekly cisplatin (40 mg/m^2) with RT may be considered.

KEY POINTS

- No strong, definitive data are available to demonstrate that induction chemotherapy followed by chemoradiation therapy leads to better survival compared with chemoradiation alone.
- For patients with unresectable HNSCC, chemoradiation with high-dose cisplatin significantly improves survival compared with RT alone and is the standard of care.
- In locally advanced laryngeal cancer (T2 to low-volume T4), locoregional control and larynx preservation were significantly improved with concomitant cisplatin and RT, compared with induction chemotherapy followed by RT or RT alone.
- Cetuximab added to RT improves survival compared with RT alone in locally advanced head and neck cancer, but there are insufficient data to support replacing chemoradiation with cisplatin therapy as the standard of care.
- Chemoradiation with high-dose cisplatin is the standard of care for postoperative adjuvant treatment of patients with positive resection margins or ENE of disease.

COMBINED-MODALITY TREATMENT: ORGAN PRESERVATION

For patients with locally advanced squamous cell cancer of the larynx, hypopharynx, or oropharynx, chemoradiation therapy yields better disease control compared with RT alone, though acute toxicities are greater. Successful applications of chemotherapy and RT strategies (ie, management of mucositis, weight loss, hematologic toxicities, and swallowing dysfunction necessitating the need for a feeding tube) for organ preservation requires a team approach that includes the head and neck surgeon, radiation oncologist, and medical oncologist, as well as a nutritionist, swallowing therapist, oncology nurses, advanced care practitioners, pharmacists, and social workers. Close monitoring with comprehensive head and neck examinations and timely integration of salvage surgery, when necessary, are part of the treatment plan and necessary to avoid compromising survival.

PET imaging 3 months after treatment is useful in the assessment of patients with node-positive disease who were treated with chemoradiation therapy. Rather than all patients proceeding to adjuvant neck dissection, given the high negative predictive value of FDG-PET, observation can be considered for patients with non–FDG-avid neck lymph nodes measuring < 1 cm. Evaluation of functional and quality-of-life outcomes is also required to assess the overall benefit of organ-preservation therapies.

LARYNX AND HYPOPHARYNX

The US Department of Veterans Affairs Laryngeal Cancer Study Group (VALCSG) was the first, randomized organ preservation study to demonstrate no significant difference in survival between chemotherapy and RT versus surgery.[21] Patients with locally advanced, resectable T2 to T4 laryngeal cancers were randomly assigned to induction chemotherapy with three cycles of cisplatin and FU followed by RT, or total laryngectomy followed by RT. Total laryngectomy was avoided for approximately two-thirds of survivors who received chemoradiation. Long-term follow-up of > 10 years continued to demonstrate no significant difference in survival between the groups. On multivariate analysis, T4 and N2 disease were both significant predictors of treatment failure, with 56% of T4 cases eventually requiring laryngectomy. The pattern of failure differed between the two treatment groups, with a significant reduction in distant failures in those receiving induction chemotherapy but higher rates of local failure. In the surgery control arm, higher rates of distant metastases were noted, but fewer local failures.

The EORTC performed a similar study involving patients with advanced, resectable (T2 to T4) cancer of the hypopharynx.[22] No difference in survival between the two groups was noted, and the 5-year estimate of successful larynx preservation (ie, local control and no tracheostomy or feeding tube) was 35%.

In follow-up to the VALCSG study, the Intergroup RTOG 91-11 trial addressed two unresolved issues: the optimal sequencing of chemotherapy and RT (induction chemotherapy followed by RT or concomitant chemotherapy and RT) and the precise contribution of chemotherapy added to RT.[23] A total of 547 patients with T2 to low-volume T4, locally advanced squamous cell cancer of the larynx were randomly assigned to one of three treatment arms: RT alone (70 Gy); concomitant cisplatin (100 mg/m^2), RT (70 Gy) on days 1, 22, and 43, or three cycles of induction cisplatin and FU followed by RT. The primary end point was larynx preservation, which was significantly higher for the concomitant-treatment arm (88%) compared with the induction arm (75%; $P = .005$) and the RT-alone arm (70%; $P < .001$). Locoregional control also was significantly better with concomitant treatment compared with the other two treatments (78% *v* 61% and 56%, respectively). OS rates did not differ among the three groups; grade 3-4 toxicities were highest in the concurrent chemoradiation arm

Table 12-13 **Sequential Therapy Clinical Trials in Patients With Head and Neck Squamous Cell Carcinoma**						
Study	**No. of Patients**	**Population**	**Study Arm**	**Primary Outcome**	**Secondary Outcome**	**Grade 3-4 Toxicity (%)**
PARADIGM13	145 (Study terminated early due to poor accrual)	Unresectable or T3/4 or N2/3 (except for T1,N2), or candidates for organ preservation	IC with TPF x 3 cycles: response evaluation. NR: weekly docetaxel with RT. PR: weekly carboplatin with RT *v* high-dose cisplatin every 3 weeks with RT	3-year OS: 73% *v* 78% (HR, 1.09; *P* = .77)	Febrile neutropenia in the IC followed by chemoradiation (16 patients) compared with the chemoradiation arm	Mucositis IC: 47 CRT: 16 Febrile neutropenia IC: 23 CRT: 1 PEG tube placement: IC: 79 CRT: 85
DeCIDE14	280 (planned: 400)	N2/N3 disease	Docetaxel/FU/ hydroxyurea plus radiation *v* TPF three cycles followed by docetaxel/FU/ hydroxyurea plus radiation	3-year OS 75% *v* 73% (*P* = NS)	3-year distant failure: 10% *v* 19% (*P* = .025)	Mucositis IC: 9 CRT: 47 Neutropenia IC: 11 CRT: 2 PEG tube placement: IC: 79
Hitt et al 15[10]	439	Unresectable; primary sites: oropharynx, oral cavity, larynx, hypopharynx; greater than measurable lesion	IC with TPF or PF three cycles followed by high-dose cisplatin every 3 weeks with radiation *v* high-dose cisplatin every 3 weeks with radiation	Median PFS: 14.6 months/ 14.4 months *v* 13.8 months (*P* = .56) TTF 7.9 months/7.9 months *v* 8.2 months (*P* = .90)	No statistically significant differences for overall survival	Stomatitis: IC: 44 CRT: 37 Febrile neutropenia IC: 10 CRT: 1

Abbreviations: CR, complete responder; CRR, complete response rate; CRT, concomitant chemoradiation; FU, fluorouracil; HR, hazard ratio; IC, induction chemotherapy; NR, nonresponder; NS, not significant; OS, overall survival; PEG, percutaneous endoscopic gastrostomy; PF, cisplatin, fluorouracil; PFS, progression-free survival; PR, partial responder; TPF, docetaxel, cisplatin, fluorouracil; TTF, time to treatment failure.

(77%), followed by the induction arm (66%), and were lowest in the RT alone arm (51%). Mature follow-up data at 5 and 10.8 years are reported in Table 12-15. Concomitant cisplatin and RT remain the standard treatment options for organ preservation; however, laryngectomy-free survival did not differ between the induction arm and the concurrent arm, suggesting that either treatment paradigm is acceptable.[24]

Based on these data, the standard-of-care regimen for larynx preservation is cisplatin (100 mg/m^2) administered on days 1, 22, and 43 during RT, with surgery reserved for patients with persistent or recurrent disease after treatment. Patients with large T4a tumors with poor pretreatment laryngeal function are often treated with total laryngectomy, because no randomized data exist.

OROPHARYNX ORGAN PRESERVATION

Chemoradiation has become standard practice for most resectable, advanced oropharynx cancers, because disease-control outcomes compare favorably with those obtained historically with primary surgical management. Site-specific, randomized prospective data are lacking, however.

A retrospective multivariate analysis of patients treated in the RTOG 0129 trial revealed significantly improved 3-year survival among patients who were HPV positive compared with patients who were HPV negative (84% *v* 57%).[2] Per the ASCO Radiation Oncology Evidence-Based Clinical Practice Guidelines,[25] intermittent bolus-dose cisplatin (100 mg/m^2) delivered with definitive radiation (70 Gy) is considered standard

Table 12-14 **Summary of Clinical Studies of Adjuvant Therapy After Surgery for Locally Advanced Head and Neck Squamous Cell Carcinoma**

Study	No. of Patients	Study Population	Study Arms (Adjuvant Treatment After Surgery)	Primary Outcomes	Secondary Outcomes	Toxicities
EORTC 229312[18]	334	T3-4 with negative margins (except T3,N0 of larynx) or T1-2, N2-3; T1-2, N0-1 with high-risk features (ENE, positive margin, PNI, LVI) or OC/OP with LN+ at levels IV or V	Postoperative radiation alone *v* cisplatin (100 mg/m^2) three cycles with radiation	5-year PFS: 36% *v* 47% (HR, 0.75; *P* = .04)	5-year OS 40% *v* 53% (HR, 0.70; *P* = .02) 5-year local or regional relapses 31% *v* 18% (*P* = .007)	Incidence of grade 3 or higher: 21% radiation alone arm, 41% chemoradiotherapy arm. Severe mucosal events similar in both arms
RTOG 95011[20]	459	Locally advanced high-risk (> 2 LNs positive, positive ENE, and/or positive margins)	Postoperative radiation alone *v* cisplatin (100 mg/m^2) three cycles, with radiation	10-year DFS 19% *v* 20% (*p* = NS)	10-year OS 27% *v* 29% (*P* = NS) in patients with ENE and/or positive margin LRC 33% *v* 21% (*P* = .02) DFS 12% *v* 18% (*P* = .05) OS 20% *v* 27% (*P* = .07)	Incidence of grade 3 or higher: 34% radiation alone arm, 77% chemoradiotherapy arm

Abbreviations: DFS, disease-free survival; ENE, extranodal extension; HR, hazard ratio; LN, lymph nodes; LRC, locoregional control; LVI, lymphovascular invasion; NS, not significant; OC, oral cavity; OP, oropharynx; OS, overall survival; PFS, progression-free survival; PNI, perineural invasion.

of care for locally advanced oropharyngeal cancers. Although it was the intention to deliver three cycles of cisplatin with radiation in the control arm, a retrospective analysis of RTOG 0129 established that at least 200 mg/m^2 of cisplatin (total dose) was required to attain maximum survival benefit.[2] For patients who are not fit to receive high-dose cisplatin, concurrent weekly cisplatin with definitive RT may be delivered, though prospective randomized data demonstrating the efficacy of RT with weekly cisplatin compared with intermittent cisplatin are lacking.

Two studies have reaffirmed that high-dose cisplatin and RT is standard of care for patients with HPV-positive oropharyngeal carcinomas. The RTOG 1016 trial[26] randomly assigned patients with p16-positive oropharynx cancers of all stages to RT with concurrent cetuximab or two cycles of high-dose cisplatin. The study was designed as a noninferiority trial with the hypothesis that cetuximab would reduce toxicity while maintaining survival rates. The 5-year OS, PFS, and locoregional failure rates all favored patients who were treated in the cisplatin and RT arm, and the number of overall acute and late grade 3-4 toxicities were similar between the two groups. Similar to RTOG 1016, the DE-ESCALATE HPV trial[27] randomly assigned the same population (but included only those with smoking histories of ≤ 10 pack-years) to high-dose cisplatin plus RT versus cetuximab and RT. The primary outcome was overall severe (grade 3-5) acute and late adverse events. However, both short-term and long-term graded toxicities did not differ. The 2-year OS favored the cisplatin and RT arm (97.5% *v* 89.4%; HR, 5.0; 95% CI, 1.7 to 14.7; *P* = .001].

Concomitant bolus doses of carboplatin (70 mg/m^2 daily for 4 days) and FU (600 mg/m^2 as a daily 24-hour infusion for 4 days) on days 1, 22, and 43 with radiation (70 Gy; 35 fractions) may be administered as an alternative to high-dose cisplatin.[28] This randomized trial treated only patients with oropharyngeal carcinomas and compared chemoradiation to RT alone. Carboplatin and FU with RT provided a statistically significant advantage over RT. The incidence of severe, late (grade 3-4) toxicities was higher (14%) in the combined arm as compared with the RT alone arm (9%), with cervical fibrosis being more severe in those receiving chemotherapy. Cetuximab should only be considered when patients are not eligible to receive either cisplatin or carboplatin-based regimens, because cetuximab and RT have not been compared with alternative chemoradiation regimens.

Chemoradiation is considered an evidence-based standard treatment option and is particularly applicable for the management of T3 to T4 or N2 to N3 disease located at the base of the tongue or tonsils.

Given the low volume and favorable prognosis of early-stage disease, radical surgery (total glossectomy) or chemoradiation should be avoided, in general, in patients with T1-2, N0-1 HPV-negative disease or in patients with T1-2, N0-1 HPV-positive disease, when N1 is a single node < 3 cm. Preservation of speech and swallowing function can be attained with RT or surgery. Per the NCCN guidelines, RT, TORS, or open resection at T1 or T2 oropharyngeal primaries without neck nodal involvement is appropriate. For N0 disease, strong consideration for neck dissection should be given because oropharyngeal tumors often harbor disease in the neck. For patients with HPV-positive N1 disease (a single node < 3 cm) or HPV-negative disease, a neck dissection should be performed along with surgery to the primary. Bilateral neck dissections are required for tumors arising from the midline.

Multiple trials are ongoing to evaluate the role of TORS in oropharynx cancer, but no randomized data exist to evaluate surgery compared with definitive chemoradiation.

Given the favorable prognosis of HPV-related oropharyngeal cancer, recent efforts have focused on attempts to de-intensify the definitive standard modalities of RT and chemotherapy. RT de-escalation to 60 Gy with concurrent weekly cisplatin also shows promising high rates of locoregional control, as do studies selecting patients for lower radiation dosages with concomitant systemic therapy if they demonstrate complete responses to induction chemotherapy. These data are considered exploratory. At this time, any de-intensification approach, although potentially attractive for reducing long-term toxicities, should be considered investigational.

KEY POINTS

- Induction chemotherapy with cisplatin, 5-FU, and docetaxel (TPF) is considered the standard induction regimen when induction chemotherapy is recommended. When induction chemotherapy is administered, TPF improves local control of disease over PF.
- No definitive data demonstrate that induction chemotherapy followed by chemoradiation therapy leads to better survival compared with chemoradiation alone.
- For patients with unresectable HNSCC, chemoradiation with high-dose cisplatin significantly improves survival compared with RT alone and is the standard of care.
- In locally advanced laryngeal cancer (T2 to low-volume T4a), local-regional control and larynx preservation is best achieved with concomitant cisplatin and RT, though induction chemotherapy followed by RT is a reasonable alternative as long-term data show no difference in laryngectomy-free survival for either treatment paradigm.
- Cetuximab added to RT improves survival compared with RT alone in locally advanced head and neck cancer, and should not replace chemoradiation with cisplatin therapy as the standard of care.
- Chemoradiation with high-dose cisplatin is the standard of care for postoperative adjuvant treatment of patients with positive resection margins or extracapsular extension of nodal disease.

NASOPHARYNGEAL CANCER

OVERVIEW

WHO type I (keratinizing squamous cell cancer) is more common in Western countries and has a locoregional behavior more similar to that of other smoking-related head and neck cancers. WHO types II (nonkeratinizing, differentiated) and III (undifferentiated cancer), both of which can occur with lymphoid stroma (previously called lymphoepithelioma), predominate in endemic areas (such as southern China and northern Africa) and have a higher propensity for distant metastases. More than 90% of cases of WHO types II and III disease are associated with EBV. If tumors are EBV positive, the presence of HPV is rarely if ever seen. However, many EBV negative nasopharyngeal cancers are often HPV positive.

RT is the historic mainstay of treatment of disease above the clavicle. The same drugs used in the management of squamous cell cancers arising from other sites in the head and neck, such as cisplatin, FU, and the taxanes, also are active against nasopharyngeal cancer.

The clinical behavior of nasopharyngeal cancer varies somewhat according to its histologic subtype and biomarkers. WHO types II and III respond more favorably to definitive chemoradiation compared with patients with WHO type I disease. EBV-positive, HPV-negative disease is more likely to recur distantly, whereas HPV-positive, EBV-negative disease is more likely to recur locally.

THERAPY

Chemoradiation

Numerous randomized studies and multiple meta-analyses have established that cisplatin-based chemoradiation therapy is the cornerstone of therapy for newly diagnosed, advanced, locoregional nasopharyngeal cancer. Although this treatment is widely used, disagreement remains regarding the role of adjuvant chemotherapy in this setting. Table 12-16 summarizes the studies[29-32] with the longest follow-up time demonstrating the marked improvements with chemoradiation over RT alone. The Intergroup[29] study was criticized because the relative contributions of the concurrent cisplatin and the adjuvant therapies could not be determined, and the trial results may be less applicable to endemic areas where WHO type I histologic subtypes are infrequent. Subsequent follow-up studies in endemic areas confirmed the significant survival advantage afforded by cisplatin chemotherapy concurrent with RT, as compared with RT alone.

Adjuvant Chemotherapy

The benefit of adjuvant chemotherapy, theoretically used to suppress distant metastases common in nasopharyngeal cancer, is not universally accepted. A trial by Chen et al[33] compared weekly chemoradiation with or without adjuvant chemotherapy in 251 patients with nonmetastatic stage III or IV nasopharyngeal carcinoma. The primary end point was failure-free survival. After a median follow-up of 37.8 months, the estimated 2-year failure-free survival rate was 86% in the chemoradiation plus adjuvant chemotherapy arm and 84% in the chemoradiation-only group (P = .13). Critics, however, believe the study was not designed as a noninferiority study against the standard of care (ie, high-dose cisplatin and RT).

A meta-analysis of 20 trials has suggested the benefit of adjuvant chemotherapy after concurrent chemoradiation, which has led NRG Oncology to conduct an ongoing international study (NRG 001), which will hopefully answer this important question. This trial uses plasma EBV DNA to prognosticate which patients are at risk for recurrence after definitive chemoradiation. Patients who

Table 12-15 **RTOG 91-11 Results: 5- and 10-Year Outcomes**

Treatment Arm	Time (years)	LFS (%)	LP (%)	DM (%)	DFS (%)	OS (%)
Cis/FU followed by RT	5	44	71	14.7	37.7	58.1
	10	29 (*P* = .02 as compared with CRT)	68	16.6	20.4	38.8
CRT	5	47	83.6	13.6	38	55.1
	10	24 (*P* = .68 as compared with induction; *P* = .03 as compared with RT alone)	81.7 (*P* = .005 as compared with induction; *P* < .001 as compared with RT alone)	16.1	21.6 (*P* = .04 as compared with RT alone)	27.5 (*P* = .08 as compared with induction; *P* = .53 as compared with RT alone)
RT alone	5	34	66	22	28	53.8
	10	17	64	24	14.8	31.5 (*P* = .29 as compared with induction)

Abbreviations: cis, cisplatin; CRT, concomitant chemoradiation; DFS, disease-free survival; DM, distant metastases; FU, fluorouracil; LFS, laryngectomy-free survival; LP, larynx preservation; OS, overall survival; RT, radiotherapy; RTOG, Radiation Therapy Oncology Group.

clear EBV DNA during definitive treatment are randomly assigned to observation or standard adjuvant treatment. In a second arm, patients with posttreatment EBV DNA in the blood are randomly assigned to two different adjuvant chemotherapy regimens.

Sequential Chemotherapy

Sequential therapy defined as induction chemotherapy followed by RT or chemoradiation is not well defined. Sun et al[34] conducted a phase III study with patients with stage III-IVB disease and demonstrated improvement in failure-free survival with docetaxel 60 mg/m^2, cisplatin 60 mg/m^2, and FU 600 mg/m^2 by continuous infusion on days 1 through 5 for three cycles (TPF) followed by concurrent cisplatin 100 mg/m^2 and RT, as compared with concurrent cisplatin and RT alone (80% *v* 72%; HR, 0.68; 95% CI, 0.48 to 0.97) as well as 3-year OS (92% *v* 86%; HR, 0.59; 95% CI, 0.36 to 0.95). The TPF dosing was lower than standard TPF dosing (see the section on Induction Chemotherapy), and some believe this regimen in not optimal treatment of patients with EBV-negative disease. Overall, induction chemotherapy is easier to deliver than chemotherapy delivered after chemoradiation. Induction therapy, however, comes with greater financial burden and more hematologic toxicity. It should be considered for large, bulky disease (ie, T4 tumors, N3 nodal involvement, or nodes extending into the supraclavicular regions). Confirmation from ongoing studies is needed to accept sequential chemotherapy as standard practice.

Currently in the United States, the standard of care for treatment of patients with AJCC 8th edition stages II (T2 N0–1 M0, T1 N1 M0), III (T3 N0–2 M0, T1–2 N2 M0), and IVa (T4 or N3 M0) nasopharyngeal cancer is RT (70 Gy) with concurrent high-dose cisplatin on days 1, 22, and 43, followed by three courses of adjuvant cisplatin and infusional FU.[29] Treatment with weekly cisplatin (30 to 40 mg/m^2) concurrent with RT may also be considered as an alternative to high-dose cisplatin with RT. RT alone is indicated for stage I disease.

The general management of recurrent or metastatic nasopharyngeal carcinoma is with a platinum-based doublet. In one randomized, phase III study, patients treated with gemcitabine and cisplatin experienced an improved median PFS of 7.0 (range, 4.4 to 10.9) months compared with 5.6 (range, 3.0 to 7.0) months in patients receiving FU and cisplatin (HR, 0.55; 95% CI, 0.44 to 0.68; $P < .0001$).[35] Gemcitabine and cisplatin are designated by the NCCN as recommended front-line therapy for recurrent or metastatic disease (category 1).

KEY POINTS

- WHO type I nasopharyngeal cancer (keratinizing) is more commonly found in the United States, whereas WHO types II (nonkeratinizing, differentiated cancer) and III (undifferentiated cancer) overwhelmingly predominate in endemic areas, such as southern China and northern Africa, and are associated with EBV.
- The standard of care (according to stage) is RT alone for stage I and chemoradiation therapy with cisplatin followed by three cycles of adjuvant cisplatin and FU for stage II to IVa nasopharyngeal cancer. However, results with regard to the benefits of adjuvant or induction chemotherapy are inconclusive.
- Cisplatin and gemcitabine is an active combination therapy for the treatment of recurrent or metastatic nasopharyngeal cancer; it is more efficacious than treatment with cisplatin and FU.

Table 12-16 Summary of Clinical Studies in Patients With Locally Advanced Nasopharyngeal Cancer

Study (Location)	No. of Patients	AJCC Stage (Year)	Study Arm	Median Follow-Up (months)	Primary Outcome	Secondary Outcome	Grade 3-4 Toxicity (%)
Al-Sarraf, et al.[29] (USA)	147	III-IV (1992)	Cisplatin (100 mg/m^2) every 3 weeks with radiation plus adjuvant chemotherapy cisplatin (80 mg/m^2) plus FU (1,000 mg/m^2) for 3 cycles *v* radiation alone	60	OS: 67% *v* 37% (*P* = .001)	PFS	RT alone
						58% *v* 29% ($P \leq .001$)	Stomatitis: 28
							Leukopenia: 1
							Nausea/vomiting: 10
							CRT:
							Stomatitis: 37
							Leukopenia: 36
							Nausea/vomiting: 31
Chan, et al.[30,31] (Hong Kong)	350	Ho's N2/N3 or node > 4 cm	Weekly cisplatin (40 mg/m^2) with radiation *v* radiation alone (no adjuvant chemotherapy)	66	OS: 90% *v* 80% (*P* = .049)	PFS	RT alone
						60% *v* 52% (*P* = .16)	Stomatitis: 36
							Leukopenia: 0
							Nausea/vomiting: 0
							CRT:
							Stomatitis: 49
							Leukopenia: 13
							Nausea/vomiting: 12
Lin, et al.[32] (Taiwan)	284	III-IV (1992)	Cisplatin (20 mg/m^2/d) for 4 days plus FU (400 mg/m^2/d) for 4 days for 2 cycles with radiation *v* radiation alone (no adjuvant chemotherapy)	65	OS: 72% *v* 54% (*P* = .002)	PFS	RT alone
						72% *v* 53%	Stomatitis: 35
						(*P* = .001)	Leukopenia: 0
						DMFS	Nausea/vomiting: 0
						79% *v* 70%	CRT:
						(*P* = .058)	Stomatitis: 45
							Leukopenia: 4.3
							Nausea/vomiting: 4

Abbreviations: AJCC, American Joint Committee on Cancer; CRT, concomitant chemoradiation; DFS, disease-free survival; DMFS, distant metastases-free survival; FU, fluorouracil; OS, overall survival; PFS, progression-free survival; RT, radiation therapy.

CANCER OF UNKNOWN PRIMARY SITE

Although a malignant neck lymph node without a clear primary tumor is a common occurrence in the head and neck, for most patients, the primary site will be found after comprehensive examination of the head and neck, assessment under anesthesia, and diagnostic imaging. The location of the lymph node in the neck directs the examiner toward the likely potential primary sites. FDG-PET imaging should be part of the standard evaluation for squamous cell carcinoma of unknown primary site; it can help identify the primary site in approximately 30% of cases.

Fine-needle aspiration (FNA) of the lymph node is the first choice for initial biopsy. If negative, repeating FNA with consideration of a core needle biopsy, if feasible, is appropriate. Viral testing of the nodal specimen (HPV and EBV) should be performed. If positive, the tumor staging classification on staging becomes T0. These patients should undergo work up, with their tumor treated as oropharyngeal or nasopharyngeal primaries, respectively. If viral staining is negative, the tumor staging classification becomes Tx. If the histologic diagnosis remains inconclusive, subsequent excisional biopsy should be performed in such a way that the incision can be incorporated into an appropriate neck dissection. Open biopsy done inappropriately may contaminate the surgical field and create a larger problem.

If pathologic findings from the neck indicate a diagnosis of squamous cell cancer and a primary lesion above the clavicle is suggested (in particular, if the lymph node is high in the neck), a comprehensive head and neck examination under anesthesia is the next step. Directed biopsies should be performed for suspicious mucosal areas as well as locations known to be a source of occult tumors, such as the hypopharynx, base of the tongue, and nasopharynx. In addition, bilateral simple tonsillectomies are recommended on the basis of increasing incidence of tonsillar cancers associated with HPV.

The skin, upper part of the esophagus, and lung are other potential sources of squamous cell cancer spread to the neck. If the findings on biopsy specimen of a cervical lymph node indicate an adenocarcinoma, the primary lesion sites, such as the thyroid gland, salivary gland, or sites below the clavicle, should be considered.

Lymphoma is another important diagnostic possibility and may require a core needle biopsy for diagnostic purposes. Similarly, distinguishing lymphoma from anaplastic and undifferentiated or poorly differentiated cancers can be difficult on the basis of cytologic analysis alone and may require additional immunohistochemical studies or more tissue.

The choice of treatment of patients with squamous cell cancer in a neck node of unknown primary site is controversial and evolving. Historically, either surgery or RT was used to treat patients with low-bulk disease in a single lymph node, whereas both modalities were necessary for patients with more advanced disease. The extent of radiation to the potential primary sites requires clinical judgment regarding the likely source of the tumor, because a larger portal will increase the morbidity associated with treatment. Findings from clinical series indicate that with longitudinal follow-up, the primary site ultimately will be found for approximately 30% of patients. Long-term survival is better for patients in whom the primary lesion remains occult than for those in whom it does not.

The mainstay of treatment is still neck dissection followed by RT with concomitant cisplatin when extracapsular extension of nodal disease is present. However, the vast majority of these cases are now p16-positive tumors arising from the oropharynx, so definitive chemoradiation can also be considered another standard treatment option.

KEY POINTS

- The search for the primary site should include FDG-PET/CT imaging and an examination under anesthesia with directed biopsies of the base of tongue, nasopharynx, and hypopharynx and bilateral, simple tonsillectomies.
- After FNA biopsy of the lymph node, HPV and EBV testing should be performed. If positive, tumors should be treated as oropharyngeal or nasopharyngeal primaries, respectively.
- Standard treatment consists of neck dissection followed by RT to include the likely primary sites, and concurrent cisplatin is added if extracapsular extension of nodal disease is present.
- In selected patients, chemoradiation therapy is another primary treatment option.

INCURABLE RECURRENT OR DISTANT METASTATIC DISEASE

SYSTEMIC THERAPY

Recurrent or persistent disease that is not subject to additional surgery or RT after definitive therapies have been delivered or disease that involves distant organs is considered incurable. Cisplatin, carboplatin, docetaxel, paclitaxel, FU, and methotrexate are the most commonly used cytotoxic agents to treat recurrent or metastatic HNSCC in the front-line and second-line settings; cetuximab is an active targeted agent that also commonly is used as a second-line regimen.

Historically, randomized trials comparing combination chemotherapy and single-agent therapy show a near doubling of the response rate with platinum-based combinations, but unless a clinical complete response is achieved, the duration of response is brief (2 to 4 months) and does not have a significant effect on OS. Toxicity is generally greater when combination chemotherapy is used. Combination chemotherapy should be limited to patients with a good performance status (eg, Eastern Cooperative Oncology Group performance status of 0 to 1), who are better able to tolerate the added toxicity.

Immunotherapy may be better for patients with more limited performance statuses, because single-agent therapy (pembrolizumab or nivolumab) is relatively well tolerated in most patients (Fig 12-8). Keynote 040 and Checkmate 141 only enrolled patients primarily with performance status of 0-1 who had failed platinum-based therapies. The number of grade 3-4 adverse events, however, was much higher with the standard-of-care chemotherapy arms (36% chemotherapy *v* 13% pembrolizumab) and (35% chemotherapy *v* 13% nivolumab). In general, factors associated with poor response to systemic therapy are well known and include poor performance status, the presence of comorbidities, bulky locoregional disease or high tumor volume, and prior treatment of recurrent disease. PD-1 inhibitors are associated with immune-related toxicities. The most common adverse events in both Keynote 040 and Checkmate 141 were fatigue, rash, and skin-related toxicities. In addition, the Checkmate study reported stability in several quality-of-life measures in those receiving nivolumab and declines in measures in those receiving chemotherapy. As newer data emerge, treatment with single-agent immunotherapy in the upfront setting is likely to become an accepted standard.

Taxane doublets do not provide improvements in survival compared with other chemotherapeutic regimens. Results from an Eastern Cooperative Oncology Group study showed that survival rates with paclitaxel (175 mg/m^2) and cisplatin (75 mg/m^2) treatment did not differ significantly (9 *v* 8 months) from standard cisplatin (100 mg/m^2) and FU (1,000 mg/m^2 by continuous infusion over 4 days); the 1-year survival rate was 30% compared with 41%, respectively, although the paclitaxel regimen was generally better tolerated.[36] The grade 3-5 toxicities overall were higher in the cisplatin and FU arm, most likely because of the higher dosage of cisplatin in this arm. More patients in the FU arm experienced mucositis or cutaneous hand-foot syndrome. FU is metabolized by dihydropyridine

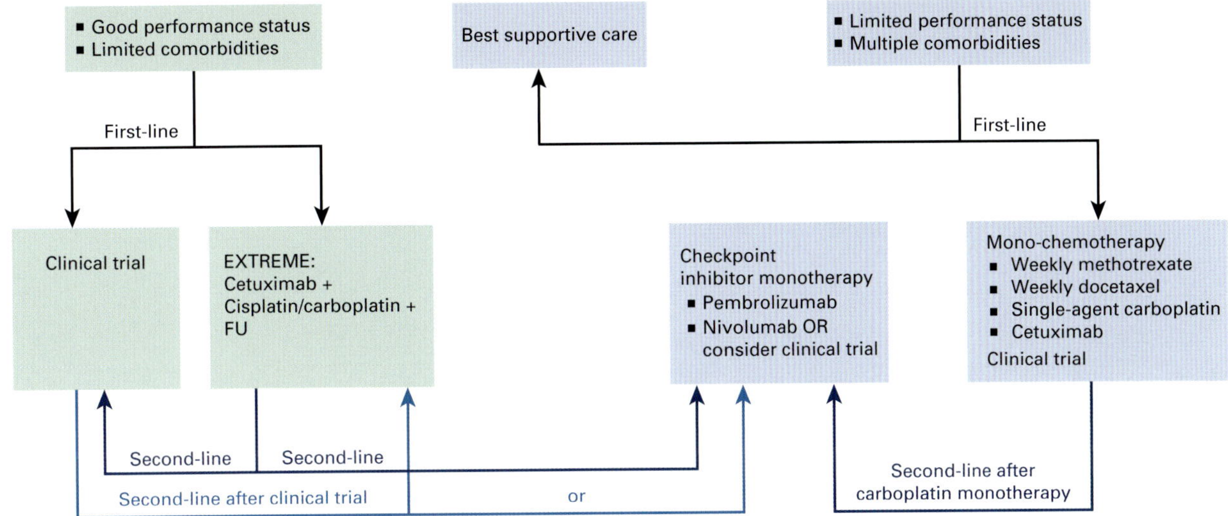

Fig. 12-8 Treatment algorithm for metastatic head and neck squamous cell carcinoma (HNSCC).

Abbreviation: FU, fluorouracil.

dehydrogenase and those with homozygous loss of gene that encodes for this protein are at much higher risk for a severe cutaneous adverse event developing. Exposure to 5-FU also increases the risk of cardiac ischemic events developing and must be used with caution in patients with histories of unstable angina.

Cetuximab is the only molecularly targeted drug to be approved for use in the United States for platinum-refractory, metastatic or recurrent head and neck cancer in combination with chemotherapy or as monotherapy. In a randomized trial in which the combination of cisplatin and placebo was compared with cisplatin and cetuximab in 123 patients, no significant difference was found in median PFS (2.7 *v* 4.2 months; *P* = .27), although the rate of major response (complete plus partial) was significantly higher for patients who received cisplatin and cetuximab (10% *v* 26%; *P* = .03).[37]

In the phase III EXTREME trial, 440 patients with recurrent or metastatic HNSCC were randomly assigned to either the intervention arm (cisplatin or carboplatin with FU and cetuximab) or standard arm (cisplatin or carboplatin with FU) as first-line treatment.[5] Cetuximab and the platinum and FU combination significantly prolonged the median OS from 7.4 months to 10.1 months (HR for death, 0.80; 95% CI, 0.64 to 0.99; *P* = .04), significantly prolonged the median PFS from 3.3 months to 5.6 months (HR for progression, 0.54; *P* < .001), and increased the response rate from 20% to 36% (*P* < .001). This is the first trial to show any improvement in OS when compared with the standard regimen of cisplatin and FU and has been designated by the NCCN as front-line therapy (category 1) for metastatic or refractory HNSCC (non-nasopharyngeal).

Cetuximab, as a single agent, demonstrated a 13% response rate and a disease-control rate of 46% in patients with metastatic or recurrent head and neck cancers who experienced progression while receiving platinum therapy. Grades 1 to 4 acneiform rash and dry skin were the most bothersome adverse effects of this agent, occurring in > 50% all of patients. Hypomagnesemia is not uncommon and must be monitored, especially in those with histories of cardiac arrhythmias. Because cetuximab is not a fully humanized antibody, care must be taken to monitor for acute and delayed anaphylactic reactions that could lead to cardiopulmonary arrest.

CHECKPOINT INHIBITORS

Pembrolizumab and nivolumab, monoclonal antibodies directed at programmed cell death 1 protein, were approved by the FDA for the treatment of platinum-refractory recurrent or metastatic HNSCC on the basis of the results of three large clinical trials. Nivolumab is approved for intravenous administration of 240 mg every 2 weeks or 480 mg every 4 weeks, and Pembrolizumab 200 mg every 3 weeks.

Pembrolizumab

KEYNOTE-040 was a randomized, phase III study in which patients were randomly assigned 1:1 to pembrolizumab 200 mg every 3 weeks intravenously or the physician's choice of standard intravenously administered doses of docetaxel, methotrexate, or cetuximab. Patients treated with pembrolizumab had an improved median OS of 8.4 months (95% CI, 6.4 to 9.4) versus 6.9 months (95% CI, 5.9 to 8.0) in patients treated with standard treatment (HR. 0.80; 95% CI, 0.65 to 0.98; *P* = .0161). The response rate in the pembrolizumab arm was 14.6% (95% CI, 10.4 to 19.6) compared with 10.1% (95% CI, 6.6 to 14.5) in those treated with standard-of-care chemotherapy (*P* = .0610).[38]

Nivolumab

CheckMate 141 was a randomized, phase III study in which patients were randomly assigned 2:1 to nivolumab 3 mg/kg every 2 weeks or the physician's choice of weekly docetaxel, methotrexate, or cetuximab. Patients receiving nivolumab demonstrated an improved median OS of 7.5 months (95% CI, 5.5 to 9.1) versus 5.1 months (95% CI, 4.0 to 6.0) in patients treated with standard

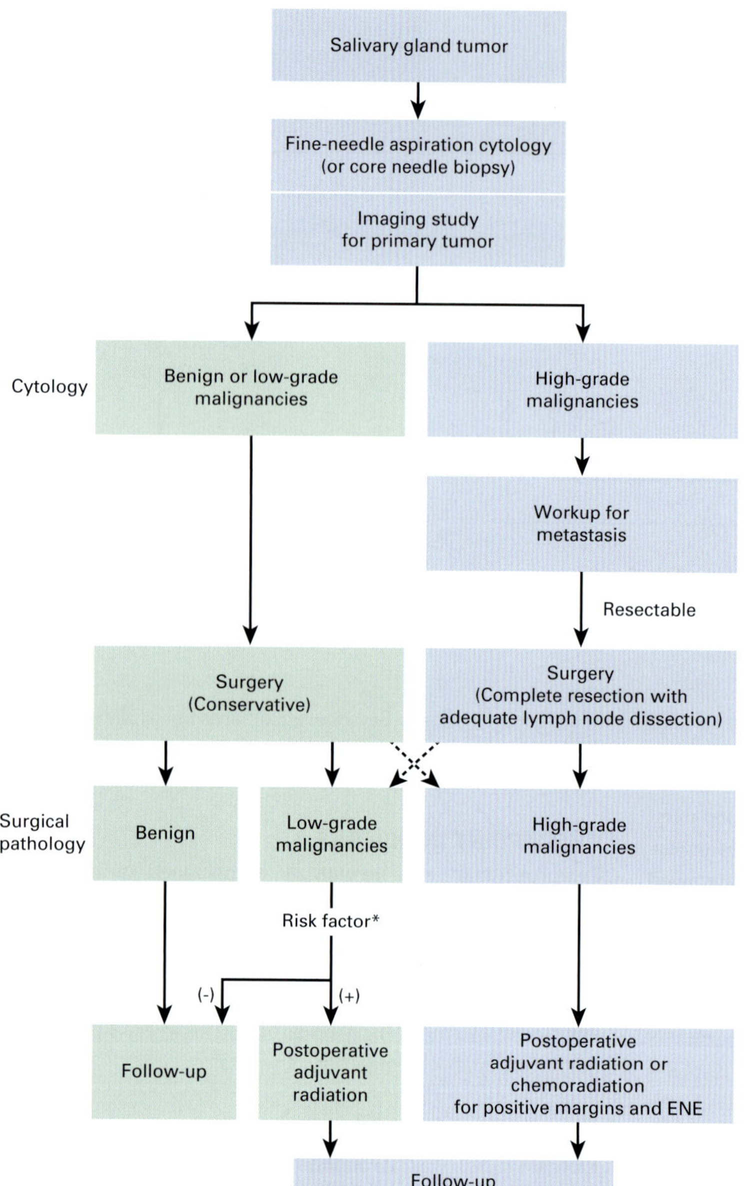

Fig. 12-9 Treatment algorithm of local and locally advanced salivary gland tumors.

Abbreviation: ENE, extranodal extension.

*Multiple lymph nodes, perineural spread.

Permission to reuse given by the Creative Common license for Jang JY, Choi N, Ko Y, et al. Treatment outcomes in metastatic and localized high-grade salivary gland cancer: high chance of cure with surgery and post-operative radiation in T1-2 N0 high-grade salivary gland cancer. BMC Cancer. *2018; 18:672, 1-12.*

treatment ($P = .01$). The response rate to nivolumab was 13.3%. At 1 year, 36.0% of patients in the nivolumab arm were alive compared with 16.6% of patients treated with standard therapy.[39] Though patients with HPV-positive (p16-positive) disease and those whose tumors expressed programmed death ligand 1 (PDL-1) of > 1% appeared to have somewhat improvement in survival with nivolumab than with chemotherapy in an exploratory analysis, those whose tumors did not express PDL-1 or were p16 negative also attained benefit. Hence, PDL-1 expression is not required for administration of checkpoint inhibitors in the second-line, recurrent or metastatic cancer setting.

REIRRADIATION FOR SECOND PRIMARY OR RECURRENT HEAD AND NECK TUMORS

Reirradiation is increasingly feasible with the greater availability of conformal technology. Building on the improved disease control seen with concurrent chemoradiation for primary treatment, this approach also has been investigated in the recurrent-disease setting. Patterns of failure analysis have suggested that essentially all locoregional failures after reirradiation occur in the reirradiated gross tumor volume; therefore, the current approach to reirradiation is typically to treat gross disease plus margin only. Patient selection for reirradiation remains an important area of investigation because some of these individuals are at risk for higher complications, including spinal cord myelopathy, osteoradionecrosis of the mandible or bone, and carotid artery rupture that can occur in up to 3% of patients.

Patients with a > 2-year interval between RT courses and those who have undergone resection are most likely to benefit from reirradiation. Stereotactic body RT is frequently used in the reirradiation setting and commonly dosed at five fractions of 8 Gy each.

KEY POINTS

- In the recurrent or metastatic cancer setting, combination chemotherapy leads to increased response rates compared with weekly single-agent therapy, but it has not demonstrated an improvement in survival and comes at the expense of increased toxicity.
- Cetuximab and cisplatin and FU combination demonstrated a survival benefit compared with cisplatin and FU combination and is considered the standard first-line chemotherapy regimen in the recurrent or metastatic setting.
- Nivolumab and Pembrolizumab are indicated as second-line therapy in patients who have failed platinum-based chemotherapy in the recurrent/metastatic setting.
- Reirradiation in the form of stereotactic body RT or fractionated RT with or without concurrent chemotherapy may provide long-term survival for a select subset of patients.

SALIVARY GLAND TUMORS

Cancers of the major salivary glands (parotid, submandibular, sublingual) and the minor salivary glands are uncommon, accounting for < 10% of epithelial head and neck tumors. Tobacco and alcohol use are not risk factors for tumors of the salivary glands, but there may be an association with prior exposure to radiation. The WHO classification lists 24 histologic subtypes of malignant epithelial salivary tumors. Their small numbers, as well as their histologic and prognostic heterogeneity, make them difficult to study.

Pleomorphic adenomas (PAs) are the most common salivary gland tumor. They have a variable appearance architecturally. PAs are diagnosed by FNA, and surgery is the treatment of choice because these tumors can transform into carcinomas (carcinoma ex-pleomorphic).

The most common types of salivary gland cancers are adenoid cystic carcinoma and adenocarcinoma, which originate from the intercalated ducts, and mucoepidermoid carcinoma, which originates from the secretory ducts. A histologic reading of high-grade mucoepidermoid or adenocarcinoma correlates with aggressive behavior and greater likelihood of eventual metastasis, whereas low-grade cancers of these histologies are more likely to be cured with initial local therapies.

Figure 12-9 depicts the workup and treatment of salivary gland tumors. Surgery is the mainstay of treatment of all primary and recurrent resectable disease with adjuvant RT, as indicated by the presence of adverse pathologic features. On the basis of their experience with HNSCC, medical oncologists tend to recommend the addition of cisplatin or other chemotherapy as a radiosensitizer

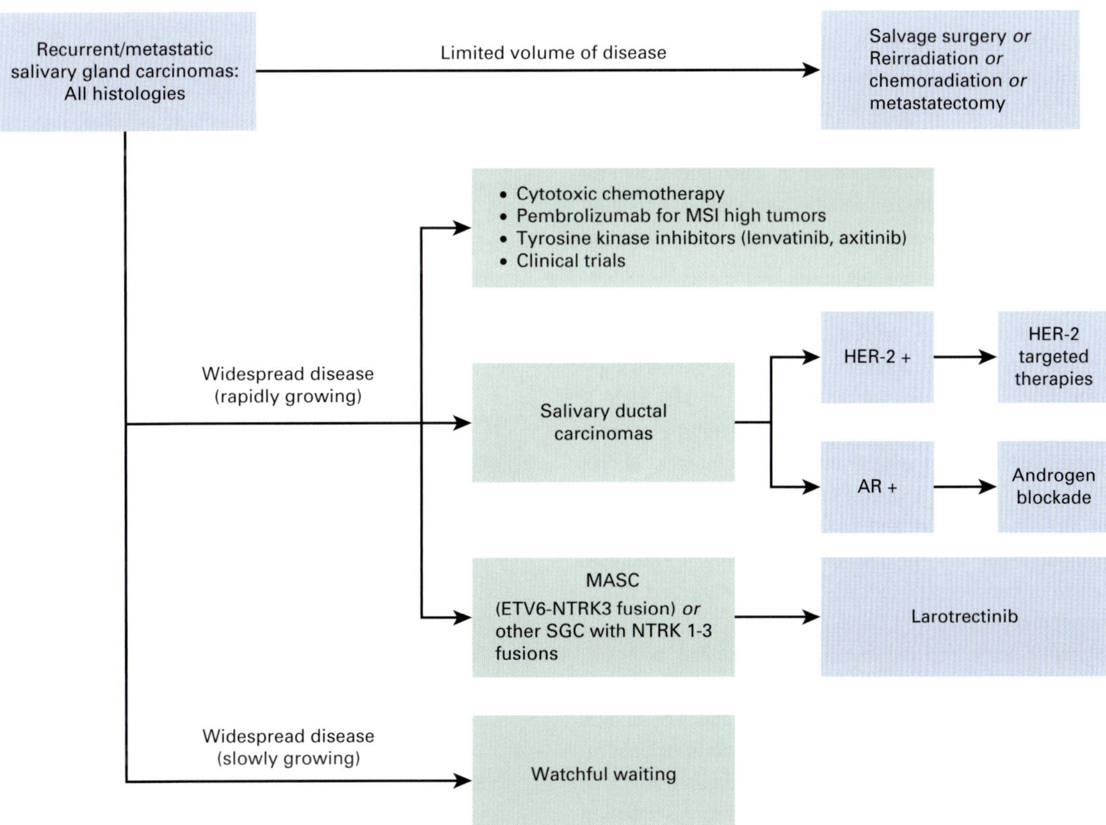

Fig. 12-10 Management of recurrent/metastatic salivary gland tumors.

Abbreviations: +, positive; –, negative; AR, androgen receptor; CTX, chemotherapy; MASC, mammary analogue secretory carcinoma; SGC, salivary gland carcinoma.

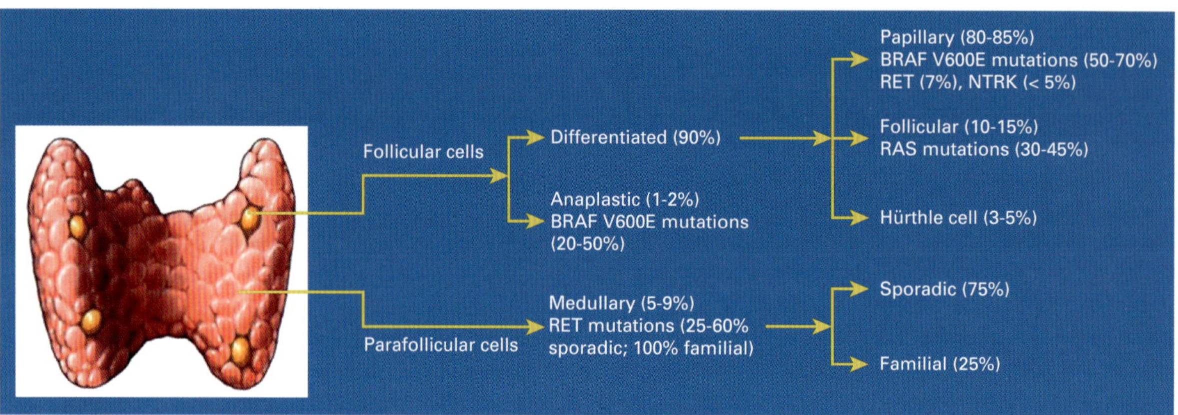

Fig. 12-11 Classification of thyroid cancers.

to improve locoregional control when poor-risk features are present (eg, positive margins, extracapsular nodal spread), but no definitive, randomized data support this addition. An ongoing cooperative group trial is attempting to answer this question. Figure 12-10 depicts treatment of incurable salivary gland cancers. Definitive radiation-based therapy is used for unresectable tumors. Neutron-beam therapy has shown promise in this setting, especially for adenoid cystic cancer, but toxicity is a concern and the RTOG-MRC randomized trial that suggested therapeutic benefit with neutron compared with photon therapy had significant methodologic limitations.

Adenoid cystic cancer, most commonly found in the minor salivary glands, is prone to neurotropic spread. It has the highest propensity of all histologic subtypes for distant metastases, yet it can grow indolently. Therefore, palliative chemotherapy should be attempted only for a symptomatic patient or when substantial tumor growth can be appreciated on serial imaging within 6 months. In this setting, combinations of cyclophosphamide, doxorubicin, and cisplatin or these chemotherapies as single agents can be considered. Antiangiogenic agents, such as lenvatinib and axitinib, have also been studied and higher response and disease-control rates were documented than those reported with cytotoxic chemotherapy. Pembrolizumab can also be considered if tumors are MSI high.

Salivary duct carcinoma is an aggressive subtype of adenocarcinoma with a rapid appearance of metastases. Microscopically, it looks similar to ductal breast cancer, is commonly androgen-receptor positive, and may also overexpress HER2 and androgen receptors on immunohistochemical analysis. Responses to antiandrogen blockade or HER2-targeted therapies have been reported.

A subtype of acinic cell carcinoma, now classified as MASC, harbors an ETV6-NTRK3 fusion protein. Larotrectinib, an inhibitor of tropomyosin kinase receptors TrkA, Trk B, and Trk C, was recently approved by the FDA for patients with neurotrophic receptor tyrosine kinase (NTRK) gene fustions.[40] Results from three multicenter, open-label, single-arm clinical trials demonstrated an overall response rate of 75%, with a 22% complete response rate, and ≥ 6-month duration of response of 73% in patients with NTRK fusions. Salivary gland tumors were the most commonly treated tumors. Hence, it is now reasonable to test all salivary gland tumors for NTRK fusions, especially if the histology is less clear.

THYROID CANCERS

Until recently, thyroid cancer was the most rapidly increasing cancer diagnosis among the US population. This increase was believed to be associated with highly sensitive diagnostic tests that could detect very small cancers. The increase has now dropped from 7% annually during the 2000s to 1.5% annually from 2011 to 2015. In 2019, an estimated 52,070 adults (14,260 men and 37,810 women) will be diagnosed with thyroid cancer. It is the most common cancer in women ages 20 to 34 years. Women are three times more likely to have thyroid cancer than men, but women and men die at similar rates, suggesting that male patients have a worse prognosis than female patients. The overall 5-year survival rate for thyroid cancer is 98%, depending on the type and stage of disease. Thyroid cancers are classified on the basis of the two main parenchymal cells of origin: the follicular cells involved in thyroid hormone production and the parafollicular cells that produce calcitonin (Fig 12-11).

KEY POINTS

- Surgery is the mainstay of treatment of salivary gland tumors, followed by RT for those tumors with high-risk features; pleomorphic adenomas should be surgically resected because of their potential for malignant transformation.
- Metastatic adenoid cystic cancer and selected other salivary gland cancers are often characterized by an indolent natural history and are followed with serial imaging.
- Systemic treatment should be delayed until substantial tumor growth can be appreciated on serial imaging studies

within 6 months or if disease is located such that symptom development is imminent (eg, bronchial obstruction).

- Salivary ductal tumors are histologically similar to breast cancer and can overexpress androgen receptors and HER2. Such tumors may be treated with antiandrogen blockade or HER2-targeted therapies.
- MASCs are characterized by the presence of ETV6-NTRK3 fusion proteins; larotrectinib is the treatment of choice for MASC tumors that are metastatic or for tumors for which surgery is likely to result in severe morbidity.

DIFFERENTIATED THYROID CANCERS

Etiology

The only well-documented etiologic factor for differentiated thyroid cancer (DTC) is radiation exposure, with an inverse relationship between age at exposure and risk for development of a thyroid malignancy. The thyroid gland of children younger than 10 years is highly vulnerable to developing thyroid cancer if it is exposed to ionizing radiation. The risk for the development of thyroid cancer is much higher for individuals who have been exposed to radioactive iodine isotopes from nuclear reactor accidents and atomic bomb testing, as well as for children and young adults who have received external RT for other cancers (eg, Hodgkin lymphoma, neuroblastoma, or Wilms tumor). More than 90% of well-differentiated thyroid cancers, however, are unrelated to radiation exposure. Approximately 5% of DTCs are associated with hereditary syndromes such as Gardner syndrome (familial adenomatous poylposis), Cowden syndrome, Pendred syndrome, Werner syndrome, and Carney complex.

Clinical Presentation and Workup

The sporadic DTCs are usually asymptomatic for a long time and present as a solitary nodule. The familial papillary thyroid cancers appear to be clinically more aggressive than the sporadic ones. The familial DTCs are usually multifocal and bilateral and have a tendency to recur both locoregionally and in distant sites.

Papillary thyroid cancer and its variants tend to recur locally in the regional lymph nodes, whereas follicular and Hürthle cell cancers tend to recur distantly, especially in bone and lung. Several factors have been widely accepted as being associated with a poor prognosis: being older than 45 years, male sex, poorly differentiated histology, tumor size > 1.5 cm, and extrathyroidal extension at diagnosis. Involvement of the regional lymph nodes is associated with greater risk for nodal recurrence but does not confer a worse prognosis for survival. The 10-year survival rate for DTC is excellent (90%). The median age at diagnosis is 45 years, and the median age at death is 75 years.

Most thyroid cancers are detected as incidental thyroid nodules found on physical examination or by the patient presenting to the physician with a neck mass. The diagnostic evaluation should include high-resolution ultrasonography to aid performing FNA biopsy and to assess the number and characteristics of the nodules, including whether the nodules are solid or cystic. FNA has high sensitivity and specificity and is the test of choice when evaluating solitary thyroid nodules.

Routine thyroid scanning with ^{123}I or technetium-99 is not recommended. This test provides information on whether a nodule is functional; however, the majority of benign and malignant nodules are "cold" or nonfunctioning, meaning that the test is nonspecific and not cost-effective. However, all patients with a thyroid nodule and suspected familial medullary thyroid cancer should have calcitonin level testing.

Treatment

Surgery. The mainstay of treatment is thyroid surgery for DTC. The extent of initial surgical therapy is controversial. Some experts recommend removal of the entire thyroid gland, with the caveats that removal of only the affected lobe and the isthmus is necessary for patients with better risk (eg, young patients with small tumors) and that total thyroidectomy is associated with a greater risk for complications, such as recurrent laryngeal nerve injury leading to vocal cord paralysis and hypocalcemia secondary to hypoparathyroidism. After surgery, administration of radioactive iodine, followed by levothyroxine suppression of TSH, are the standards of care. Treatments with external-beam RT for localized disease and antiangiogenic agents for the widespread, metastatic disease are reserved for palliative setting.

Radioactive Iodine. A single dose of radioactive iodine is usually recommended to ablate any normal thyroid remnant and destroy any microscopic deposits of the remaining thyroid cancer after a total thyroidectomy. Use of iodinated contrast medium, an iodine-rich diet, and inadequate elevation of the level of TSH (thyrotropin) can all undermine the effectiveness of radioactive iodine treatment, and human recombinant thyrotropin has replaced the need for a patient to be put into a hypothyroid state.

Dosing strategies for radioactive iodine—ablative, compared with higher therapeutic doses—are determined by the patient's prognostic risk, and they range from 50 to 75 mCi for ablation of remnants after total thyroidectomy for low-risk patients, 100 to 150 mCi for the treatment of locoregional lymph nodes, and 150 to 250 mCi for the treatment of lung and bone metastases. Ablation of remnants enables improved surveillance because normal thyroid cells are also removed, which could cause false-positive results on whole-body iodine scans or false-positive elevations of serum thyroglobulin. In the absence of all normal thyroid tissue, the serum thyroglobulin is a highly sensitive and specific tumor marker. After total thyroidectomy and ablation of remnants, the serum TSH level generally should be suppressed to below normal levels with levothyroxine, because this hormone is a potential growth factor for microscopic cancer deposits.

Six to 12 months after initial therapy, measurement of the serum thyroglobulin should be performed while the patient is receiving suppressive doses of levothyroxine. If the serum thyroglobulin is undetectable and the findings of ultrasound imaging of the neck are negative, an annual analysis of thyroglobulin levels and physical examination are sufficient for most low-risk patients. With no detectable level of serum thyroglobulin during treatment with suppressive doses of levothyroxine at 1 year after surgery and ablation, the thyroglobulin level should be determined after two doses of recombinant human TSH. If the level increases to > 2 ng/mL, a search for remaining disease is warranted. Diagnostic whole-body imaging with iodine scanning should be performed. If this is negative, recombinant human TSH stimulated FDG-PET scanning has been shown to be helpful for localizing disease in > 60% of such cases.

If metastases develop, radioactive iodine is the treatment of choice. Complete response to treatment has been observed for 45% of patients with distant metastases, although a higher complete response rate has been noted for younger patients and those with small pulmonary metastases.

Treatment of Radioactive Iodine–Refractory DTC

Once DTC no longer takes up iodine on scanning or patients have received a maximum of 600 mCi of radioactive iodine, such tumors are deemed radioactive iodine refractory. Some thyroid tumors grow slowly, so a period of careful observation is reasonable before committing to treatment. Interest in targeted therapies has been stimulated by the discovery of activating point mutations of the BRAF gene that occur early, are associated with more advanced disease at diagnosis, and independently predict recurrence. Point mutations of the BRAF gene are found in 45% of thyroid papillary carcinomas. BRAF serine-threonine kinase can lead to activation of the mitogen-activated protein kinase signaling pathway. Two multitargeted tyrosine kinase inhibitors have been approved by the FDA for the treatment of radioactive iodine–refractory DTC: sorafenib and lenvatinib, independent of mutational status. If the disease does not respond to treatment with sorafenib or lenvatinib, alternative tyrosine kinase inhibitors, as noted in the NCCN compendium, may be considered. In addition, genetic profiling can also be considered for patients with papillary thyroid cancers. Such patients can harbor BRAF mutations that can be amenable to treatment with dabrafenib or vemurafenib when antiangiogenic agents are no longer an option. Cytotoxic chemotherapy has no role in the treatment of this disease.[41]

Sorafenib. Sorafenib targets proto-oncogene BRAF, rearranged during transfection receptor (RET), vascular endothelial growth factor receptor (VEGFR) 1 to 3, and proto-oncogene c-KIT. Sorafenib was approved by the FDA on the basis of the positive results of the phase III, placebo-controlled DECISION trial.[42] A total of 417 patients who had locally advanced or metastatic thyroid cancer that was refractory to radioactive iodine and had progression within the past 14 months were randomly assigned to receive 400 mg of oral sorafenib twice daily or matching placebo. Patients receiving placebo were allowed to receive sorafenib open label if they had disease progression.

Sorafenib extended the median PFS from 5.8 months (placebo arm) to 10.8 months (sorafenib arm; $P < .0001$). Median OS was not statistically significant, due to the crossover effect. The disease control rate (complete response plus partial response plus stable disease > 6 months) was 54% in the sorafenib arm, compared with 38% in the placebo arm ($P < .0001$). No complete responses and 12% partial responses were reported. The most common grade 3 or 4 toxicities included hand-foot syndrome (76%), hypertension (41%), fatigue (50%), and diarrhea (69%).

Lenvatinib. Lenvatinib inhibits VEGFR 1 to 3, fibroblast growth factor receptor 1 to 4, platelet-derived growth factor α, RET, and KIT. It was approved by the FDA on the basis of the positive results of the SELECT trial, a phase III, placebo-controlled trial.[43] In a 2:1 design, 261 patients were randomly assigned to lenvatinib 24 mg daily and 131 patients were randomly assigned to placebo. Patients receiving placebo were allowed to receive lenvatinib upon disease progression. The median PFS was 18.3 months, compared with 3.6 months, favoring lenvatinib with an HR for progression or death of 0.21 (95% CI, 0.14 to 0.31; $P < .001$). The response rate to lenvatinib was 64.8%, with four complete responses and 165 partial responses. Treatment-related adverse events (grade 3 or higher) occurred in 75.9% of patients taking lenvatinib versus 9.9% in those taking placebo. The most common toxicities included hypertension (68%), diarrhea (59%), fatigue (59%), anorexia (50%), and weight loss (46%).

ANAPLASTIC THYROID CANCER

Anaplastic or "giant cell" variant thyroid cancer is associated with an extremely poor prognosis, with the best available therapy producing a median survival of < 1 year. Well-differentiated thyroid cancer precedes anaplastic thyroid cancer (ATC) or coexists with approximately 50% of ATC. Patients with ATC are older, generally in their 60s or 70s, and the distribution between the sexes is balanced. From 20% to 50% of ATCs harbor activating BRAF V600 mutations.

Distinguishing the tumor from a large-cell lymphoma of the thyroid is of fundamental importance. Clinically, ATC is characterized by a rapidly growing mass in the thyroid that invades the trachea or larynx and causes symptoms of dysphagia, hoarseness, or hemoptysis. Between 20% and 50% of patients have distant metastases at the time of presentation (most often pulmonary), and the remainder usually manifest metastases within 1 or 2 months of diagnosis. Most deaths are a result of aggressive locoregional spread and upper airway respiratory failure.

The treatment of choice is surgical resection if feasible, although these tumors are typically unresectable at presentation, and the patient often requires an urgent tracheostomy. Initial external-beam RT, both for definitive treatment and as an adjuvant (often with doxorubicin sensitization), is commonly used and considered the standard of care. Chemotherapy alone has limited efficacy, and radioactive iodine generally plays no role in the treatment of these tumors.

The combination of dabrafenib, a BRAF inhibitor, and trametinib, a MEK inhibitor, has been FDA approved for the treatment of BRAF V600E-mutated ATCs. In an open-label, phase II study, this combination produced a 69% response rate and estimated 12-month PFS and OS rates of 79% and 80%, respectively.[44] The most significant adverse events included fatigue (38%), pyrexia (37%), and nausea (35%).

MEDULLARY THYROID CANCER

Medullary thyroid cancer (MTC) is a neoplasm of the calcitonin-producing cells that reside in the thyroid. It constitutes approximately 5% to 9% of all thyroid cancers and is associated with a mutation in the RET proto-oncogene. Both sporadic and familial types occur. The 10-year survival rate for patients with MTC ranges from 75% to 85%. Approximately half of patients with MTC present with disease localized to the thyroid gland, whereby total thyroidectomy often results in complete cure. Ten-year survival rates for these patients is 95.6%. CT and PET imaging are useful to detect nodal and distant metastases in this disease, but radioactive iodine scans are not useful.

The sporadic form is more common (75% of cases) and tends to occur in an older age group (40 to 45 years). The clinical presentation of the sporadic type of MTC is usually a painless thyroid mass; however, high calcitonin levels may result in a watery, secretory diarrhea as the primary symptom. The diagnosis is made on the basis of a constellation of a thyroid mass, a high calcitonin level, and a FNA specimen that stains positive for calcitonin.

Three distinct familial syndromes account for the remaining 25% of cases. They tend to occur in a younger age group (15 to 25 years). The RET mutation is transmitted in the germline, and familial MTC may be part of multiple endocrine neoplasia type 2A (MTC, pheochromocytoma, and parathyroid hyperplasia) or type 2B (MTC, pheochromocytoma, and intestinal and mucosal ganglioneuromatosis with characteristic marfanoid habitus); it also may be a familial form of MTC not associated with multiple endocrine neoplasia. For the familial syndromes, a dominant inheritance pattern is recognized, and family members of patients with newly diagnosed cases of the disease should be screened for RET mutations, because germline mutations are substantially higher than might be expected on the basis of family history alone. Screening for pheochromocytoma (catecholamine excess) is important to exclude a familial syndrome, and all patients with germline mutations must be referred for a genetic counseling evaluation. Prophylactic total thyroidectomy will prevent MTC in young, at-risk family members (based on RET gene testing), even in the absence of clinically detectable thyroid abnormalities.

The treatment of choice for MTC is total thyroidectomy with bilateral central compartment node dissection and unilateral neck dissection (at the least). RT has disappointing efficacy for macroscopic disease, and postoperative RT is not routinely used.

After resection of all disease in the neck, patients should be monitored with two tumor markers: calcitonin and carcinoembryonic antigen levels. Patients whose calcitonin levels double within 6 months have a worse prognosis.

Local recurrences are usually treated surgically. Metastatic disease (commonly to the mediastinum, lung, bone, and liver) often follows an indolent course, and in this case, observation is reasonable. MRI is required to monitor liver disease because metastases may be small and not readily visualized with CT scans. Palliative surgery, including tumor debulking, or RT may be used as indicated for symptom control or to manage tumor encroachment on critical structures.

Vandetanib and cabozantinib are FDA-approved agents for the treatment of patients with locally advanced MTC unamenable to surgery or for those with metastatic disease. No data exist comparing these agents head to head; thus, the choice of which agent to use first may depend on expected adverse effects, and the indications for starting therapy will need to be individualized and balanced with toxicity profiles and quality-of-life outcomes.

Vandetanib is an oral inhibitor that targets VEGFR, RET, and EGFR. Vandetanib was FDA approved on the basis of the positive results of a phase III, placebo-controlled trial for patients with symptomatic or progressive unresectable, locally advanced or metastatic MTC.[45] In the trial, 331 patients with advanced MTC were randomly assigned 1:1 to receive vandetanib 300 mg daily versus placebo. The primary end point was PFS. There was a statistically significant improvement in PFS with vandetanib as compared with placebo (HR, 0.46; 95% CI, 0.31 to 0.69; $p < .001$). The objective response rate, disease-control rate, and biochemical response were also favorable with vandetanib. Common adverse events of any grade included diarrhea (56%), rash (45%), nausea (33%), hypertension (32%), and headache (26%). QT prolongation (14%), torsades de pointes, and sudden death are serious adverse effects that have resulted in a black box warning for this drug.

Cabozantinib is an oral TKI that targets MET, VEGFR 2, and RET. Cabozantinib was approved for patients with progressive MTC, based on the positive results of a randomized, double-blind, phase III placebo-controlled trial.[46] In the trial, 330 patients were enrolled and randomly assigned 2:1 to cabozantinib (140 mg/d) or placebo. The primary end point was PFS. There was a statistically significant improvement in PFS of 11.2 months with cabozantinib compared with 4 months with placebo. Response rates were 28% for cabozantinib and 0% for placebo ($p < .001$). Common adverse effects of cabozantinib included diarrhea (63%), palmar-plantar erythrodysesthesia (50%), decreased weight (48%) and appetite (46%), nausea (43%), and fatigue (41%), prompting dose reductions in 79% of patients. Patients assigned to cabozantinib therapy achieved a statistically significant improvement in PFS of 11.2 months, compared with 4.0 months for the placebo arm ($P < .001$). This drug has black box warnings for serious adverse effects of GI perforations (3%) and fistula formation (1%).

KEY POINTS

- For DTCs, poor prognostic features include age > 45 years, male sex, poorly differentiated histology, tumor size > 1.5 cm, and extrathyroidal extension at diagnosis. In contrast, involvement of the regional lymph nodes does not confer a worse prognosis for survival.
- Radioactive iodine is the treatment of choice for metastatic disease for DTC. Radioactive iodine generally has no role in the treatment of anaplastic or medullary thyroid cancers.
- Sorafenib and lenvatinib are approved by the FDA for the treatment of locally recurrent or metastatic, progressive DTC that no longer responds to radioactive iodine treatment.
- Screening for germline RET gene mutation in patients with MTC should be considered because total thyroidectomy, based on the results of genetic testing, often results in complete cures for young, at-risk family members.
- The combination of dabrafenib and trametinib has been approved by the FDA for the treatment of BRAF V600E-mutated ATCs.
- Vandetanib and cabozantinib have been approved by the FDA for the treatment of symptomatic or progressive, locally advanced or metastatic MTCs.

MANAGEMENT OF DISEASE IN THE ELDERLY

Elderly patients present with age-specific problems such as multiorgan dysfunction, depression, alteration of mental status, reduced nutritional status, and limited social support, all of which can interfere with the diagnosis and treatment of cancer. A multidisciplinary team with both oncologic and nononcologic providers is needed to optimize a treatment strategy in elderly patients. Biological age is more important than chronologic age and takes into account comorbid illnesses and performance status. In a large, single-institution study, the percentage of patients with head and neck cancer with moderate to severe comorbidity was 21%, and there was a significant relationship between severity of comorbidity and OS. A comprehensive geriatric assessment can be used to evaluate functional status, mental status, medications, nutritional status, social support, and comorbid illnesses to provide physicians with a better sense of a patient's life expectancy and tolerance to different treatment modalities when making therapeutic decisions.

Surgery remains an appropriate option for the management of head and neck cancer in elderly patients once a full risk assessment is completed and medical optimization is initiated. Postsurgical mortality is associated with older age, severity of comorbid illnesses, and length of the operation.

RT is a potentially curative option for patients diagnosed with early-stage disease or those with nonmetastatic disease who are deemed ineligible for surgical resection. RT can be safely administered in an elderly population, and most patients are able to complete their planned treatment. No data demonstrate poorer tolerance or the need to reduce radiation dose because of age.

Patients age ≥ 70 years derived little or no incremental survival benefit from adding chemotherapy to RT; however, the use of chemoradiation in patients older than 65 years has steadily increased during the past two decades. This trend has further increased with the use of cetuximab with RT. However, the OS benefit in an older patient population is not clear,[15] meaning that platinum should be still be administered if patients are potential candidates. In some patients, the benefit of chemoradiation may be offset by acute, often severe, treatment-related toxicities, particularly among older patients and those with comorbid medical conditions or poor performance status. Older patients can be more susceptible to the toxic effects of chemotherapy because of potential delayed clearance from renal or hepatic impairment, decreased bone marrow reserve, malnutrition, and cognitive impairment.

SURVIVORSHIP

Studies involving survivors of head and neck cancer have mainly focused on social supports, tobacco and alcohol use, the risk for second primary cancers, functional status, and depression and how these factors influence quality of life. Chronic pain, xerostomia, impairments of speech and swallowing, alterations of taste and smell, and poor cosmesis are some of the long-term sequelae associated with treatment of head and neck cancer. These variable, long-term toxicities can have a profound psychosocial effect on cancer survivors and their families. Sadly, suicide rates in patients with head and neck cancer, including survivors, are three times more frequent than that of the general population. Advances in reconstructive techniques and organ-preservation strategies are having a positive effect on quality of life relative to the functional and cosmetic consequences of radical local therapies of the past. Nevertheless, quality-of-life and survivorship issues must continue to be a focus of future research.

KEY POINTS

- Older patients can safely be treated with radiation-based therapy for head and neck cancer but require additional attention for management of comorbid illnesses.
- Measures of biological rather than chronologic age are relevant when determining appropriate treatment of patients with locally advanced head and neck cancer.
- Survivors of head and neck cancer can experience issues with swallowing, breathing, pain, and neck mobility that require ongoing management.

Acknowledgment

The following authors are acknowledged and graciously thanked for their contribution to prior versions of this chapter: Arlene A. Forastierre, MD, FASCO; Shanthi Marur, MD; Bhoomi Mehrotra, MD; Shrujal Baxi, MD, MPH; and David G. Pfister, MD, FASCO.

Global Perspective: Head and Neck Cancers

Jan B. Vermorken, MD, PhD (University of Antwerp, Antwerp, Belgium) Petr Szturz, MD, PhD (University Hospital Brno, Brno, Czech Republic)

Originating from the upper part of the aerodigestive tract, head and neck cancer histologically corresponds to squamous cell carcinoma in most cases.[47] According to worldwide incidence estimates for 2018, cancers of the lip, oral cavity, oropharynx, larynx, and hypopharynx account for approximately 700,000 new cases and 350,000 cancer deaths.[48] These figures propel head and neck cancer to the forefront of global health care needs. It has an important socioeconomic impact that goes beyond a mere medical diagnosis. Herein, we focus on differences between the developed, high-income countries (HICs) and the developing, low- to middle-income countries (LMICs) in terms of tumor biology, epidemiology, risk factors, prevention, clinical presentation, and treatment approach. The United States and another 80 countries with gross national income per capita > $12,000 belong to the former group, whereas nine of 10 most populated regions belong to the latter one (137 developing countries in total).[49,50]

BIOLOGY

In the biology of HNSCC, one of the major achievements was the identification of HPV-positive oropharyngeal cancer as a separate entity with a markedly better prognosis than its nonviral-related counterpart. In the locally advanced setting, survival is particularly encouraging in nonsmokers and in those with only a light tobacco smoking history (≤ 10 pack-years); for early, recurrent, and metastatic diseases, fewer data are available.[51-54] Moreover, HPV-positive oropharyngeal cancer has a typical clinical presentation distinct from the majority of HNSCC cases, driven by tobacco exposure (smokeless tobacco use and active or passive smoking) and alcohol consumption. HPV-positive oropharyngeal cancer manifests with smaller primaries (mainly in the tonsils and the base of tongue) and larger lymphadenopathies; it usually affects younger male patients with a higher socioeconomic status and risky sexual behavior.[55] Consequently, a much higher burden of this disease has been observed in the developed countries, above all in North America and Europe, with > 40% of attributable oropharynx cancer cases (> 50% in North America), compared with < 20% in the developing world.[56]

EPIDEMIOLOGY

In the United States, the incidence of oropharyngeal cancer has been increasing substantially in men over the past four decades and more recently in women. Simultaneously, the incidence of oral cavity cancer leveled off to such an extent that the age-adjusted incidence curves of these two HNSCC subtypes crossed near the turn of the century.[57,58] Although reports of oral cavity cancer recently have been increasingly once again, the contrasting temporal trends of oropharyngeal and oral cancers reflect the still-uncontrolled HPV epidemic on the one hand and effective tobacco prevention strategies on the other. In addition, the latter causal relationship probably also holds true for the decreasing incidence of laryngeal cancer from the 1990s onward.[58-60] A similar epidemiologic landscape has been ascertained in some other economically developed regions, except for some Asian countries where the oropharyngeal cancer rates declined.[60] Despite possible difficulties with data collection, cancer rates are different in the resource-limited world.

We compared the epidemiology of HNSCC in the United States as the third most populated country and a HIC with that of HNSCC in the nine most populated, LMICs. Source data pertain to the estimated number of new cases in 2018 available online at from GLOBOCAN (https://gco.iarc.fr) and, in part, were published in full text.[48] Altogether, HNSCC was diagnosed in < 3% of the US patients with cancer with the following subsite distribution: lip and oral cavity, 44%; larynx, 28%; oropharynx, 22%; and hypopharynx, 5%. A rather similar distribution can be found in three upper-middle-income economies, namely, Brazil, Russia, and Mexico, and in one lower-income economy (Indonesia). China and Nigeria have an equivalently low overall incidence of HNSCC but have a higher proportion of larynx cancer than the aforementioned regions. In contrasting, India, Pakistan, and Bangladesh have a high incidence of HNSCC (15% to 20% of all new cancer cases), which is, in fact, the most common cancer type in these countries except for Pakistan, where it is the second most common tumor. The subtype distribution is linked to smokeless tobacco consumption and strongly favors the oral cavity (up to 70% of HNSCC cases in Pakistan), with only approximately 10% of oropharyngeal cancers. Chewing and other forms of unburned tobacco consumption is popular in these regions, with about 20% to 30% of regular users.[61]

One of the hallmarks of modern oncology care in the developed countries is molecularly targeted agents. However, it seems that a substantial portion of these drugs have gained attention not because of their efficacy but because of their excessive price tags, as evidenced by alarming cost-effectiveness analyses. In this respect, the reimbursement of some expensive medicines has sometimes been criticized for a lack of clinically meaningful positive influence on OS and/or quality of life.[62] Illustrative is annual spending on all cancer medicines reaching 133 billion US dollars globally in 2017, with the United States accounting for 46%. This is in line with the number of newly approved anticancer medicines irrespective of cancer type. In 2017, patients in the United States had access to

46 of 55 drugs launched between 2012 and 2016, as opposed to merely five new agents accessible in India. Of course, this does not say anything about the real benefit conveyed by these products and the situation varies from country to country. Some developing regions (eg, Mexico, n = 22 drugs) may even be more advanced than the developed ones (eg, Poland, n = 18 drugs).[63] However, it should be remembered that the people's needs in the developing world are different, not rarely depending on basic human rights to clean drinking water and sanitation. This is seen especially in low-income economies, where the total expenditure on health per person per year may decrease to as low as $10.[64]

HNSCC TREATMENT

Whereas in the HICs, future directions of oncology aim at the cutting-edge of clinical and laboratory research, improvement in the quality of cancer care in the developing world can be accomplished without excessive costs by pursuing investments in traditional anticancer modalities, including classic cytotoxic chemotherapeutics, RT, and surgery, and into their quality assurance. From this perspective, clinical practice recommendations should reflect the available resources and infrastructure according to geographic areas. Guidelines incorporating modern immunotherapeutic approaches and, in some cases, even drugs showing marginal benefits in the context of incurable diseases have been adopted in developed countries but have limited value in less-privileged socioeconomic areas. Addressing this issue, the recently launched ASCO resource-stratified guidelines provide applicable solutions to confront the cancer burden in LMICs, including primary and secondary prevention, workup, and treatment.[65] Spatial epidemiologic heterogeneity, such as the increasing proportion of HPV-positive oropharyngeal cancers in the United States or high prevalence of oral cancer in India, steers research interests but does not necessarily mean different treatment approaches. Despite high hopes for de-escalating strategies in prognostically favorable HPV-positive oropharyngeal cancers, results of recent phase III trials were discouraging, largely failing to show that HPV is a predictive factor for a presumed less-intensive therapy.[26,27]

HNSCC PREVENTION

Finally, we discuss preventive measures according to epidemiologic background. Although some results of smoking prevention programs can already be seen, alcohol and tobacco remain the major etiological factors for HNSCC worldwide, increasing the risk for secondary tumors as well. Prevention of HPV-related oropharyngeal cancer requires a specific approach. The vaccination of girls at ages 11 to 12 years represents a recommended and validated protection against cervical, vaginal, and vulvar cancers. A similarly protective effect can be expected in the case of oropharyngeal cancer, thus extending the indication to preteen boys, albeit supported by less evidence.[66]

On the other hand, prevention programs in the developing regions primarily need to address the lack of awareness and education about the harmful health effects of tobacco, namely the smokeless forms known as *paan* and *gutkha*, which are still believed by many locals to have beneficial effect on oral cleaning, digestion, germ killing, and tension relief.[61] Unlike the successful implementation of cervical cancer screening, secondary prevention of HPV-positive oropharyngeal cancer has not been established so far. In the case of oral cancer, a periodic oral examination during a dental check-up, a self-examination, and dedicated screening programs in high-risk populations rank among the possibilities of effective prevention strategies.[67]

Head and neck cancers remain a global health issue. Strategies enhancing prevention and treatment outcomes should be based on joint efforts at the level of educational programs, research activities, and rational resource allocations. Western countries have been recognized as the leading innovators in oncology. However, to prevent new cancer cases and optimize the maturing health care system, the developing world can also learn from the challenges Western societies have been facing, including the HPV epidemic and debatable drug regulations.

13

GASTROINTESTINAL CANCERS

Blase Polite, MD, FASCO and Daniel Catenacci, MD

Recent Updates

GI CANCERS

- The first tumor-agnostic drug approval by the US Food and Drug Administration (FDA) was granted May 23, 2017, for pembrolizumab for adult and pediatric patients with unresectable or metastatic, microsatellite instability–high (MSI-H) or mismatch repair–deficient (dMMR) solid tumors, including GI tumors, that have progressed after prior treatment and who have no satisfactory alternative treatment options or with MSI-H or dMMR colorectal cancer that has progressed after treatment with a fluoropyrimidine, oxaliplatin, and irinotecan. (Le D, *Science* 2017)

ESOPHAGEAL SQUAMOUS CELL CARCINOMA

- The phase III, randomized, KEYNOTE-181, second-line study evaluated the anti-PD1 antibody pembrolizumab versus paclitaxel for treatment of esophageal cancer. Significant improvement in survival was noted only in esophageal squamous cell cancers with tumors having a PD-L1 combined positivity score (CPS) ≥ 10, which led to FDA approval for this subgroup of patients on July 30, 2019. (Kojima T, *ASCO Gastrointestinal Cancer Symposium* 2019) Nivolumab versus chemotherapy in patients with advanced oesophageal squamous cell carcinoma refractory or intolerant to previous chemotherapy (ATTRACTION-3): a multicentre, randomised, open-label, phase 3 trial. (Kato K, *Lancet Oncol* 2019)

GASTROESOPHAGEAL ADENOCARCINOMA

- The phase III, randomized FLOT4 study of the three-drug combination of fluorouracil (FU) and leucovorin plus oxaliplatin and docetaxel improved patient overall survival when compared with combined epirubicin, cisplatin, and FU in the perioperative treatment (four cycles before surgery and four cycles after surgery) of locally advanced gastric and esophagogastric adenocarcinomas. (Al-Batran SE, *Lancet* 2019)
- Despite demonstrated survival improvement of the anti-VEGFR2 antibody ramucirumab, either alone (REGARD study; Fuchs CS, *Lancet* 2013) or in combination with paclitaxel (RAINBOW study; Wilke H, *Lancet Oncol* 2014) in the second-line setting without selection by any biomarker, ramucirumab did not improve survival in the first-line setting when combined with cisplatin and 5-FU plus capecitabine. (RAINFALL study; Fuchs CS, *Lancet Oncol* 2019)
- The third-line or higher TAGS randomized, placebo-controlled, phase III study evaluating the oral cytotoxic agent trifluridine/tipiracil versus best supportive care alone, without selection by any biomarker, confirmed an improvement in overall survival to 5.7 months from 3.6 months (hazard ratio, 0.69; P = .00058), leading to FDA approval on February 25, 2019. (Shitara K, *Lancet Oncol* 2018)

- The third-line, KEYNOTE-059, phase II, single-arm study evaluated the anti-PD1 antibody pembrolizumab without patient selection by any biomarker, which led to conditional FDA approval on September 22, 2017, only for treatment of patients having tumors with a PD-L1 immunohistochemistry combined positivity score (CPS) ≥ 1. (Fuchs CS, *JAMA Oncol* 2018) However, the JAVELIN Gastric-300 randomized, open-label, phase III study evaluating the anti-PD-L1 antibody avelumab versus physician's choice chemotherapy in the second- or third-line setting, without patient selection by any biomarkers, was negative, including the PD-L1+ subset analysis. (Bang YJ, *Ann Oncol* 2018)
- The second-line, KEYNOTE-061, randomized, placebo-controlled, phase III study evaluating pembrolizumab versus paclitaxel, without selection by any biomarker, was negative and was also negative when restricted to patients having PD-L1 CPS ≥ 1 tumors. (Shitara K, *Lancet* 2018) In an unplanned subset analysis, patients with CPS ≥ 10 tumors appeared to derive benefit from pembrolizumab treatment; however in the KEYNOTE-181 study, which included patients with esophageal adenocarcinoma, there was no observed survival benefit in the CPS ≥ 10 subgroup or any other adenocarcinoma subgroup analysis. (Kojima T, *ASCO Gastrointestinal Cancer Symposium* 2019)
- The first-line, KEYNOTE-062, randomized, placebo-controlled, three-armed, phase III study for patients with PD-L1 CPS ≥ 1 tumors did not show benefit in the comparison between chemotherapy plus pembrolizumab versus chemotherapy plus placebo, including in the preplanned, coprimary end point subgroup of PD-L1 CPS ≥ 10 tumors. In the pembrolizumab open-label monotherapy arm, results for patients with tumors of CPS > 1 were reported to be noninferior to chemotherapy; however, there were clearly patients who experienced worse survival and others improved survival compared with the chemotherapy plus placebo arm; the survival benefits were more pronounced in the PD-L1 CPS ≥ 10 subgroup. (Tabernero J, *ASCO 2019*) Much or most of the benefit derived in both arms containing pembrolizumab was attributable to the MSI-H subgroups. (Shitara K, *ESMO* 2019)

HEPATOCELLULAR CARCINOMA

- The RESORCE study confirmed the benefit of regorafenib in second-line treatment compared with placebo for advanced hepatocellular carcinoma (HCC), which led to FDA approval on April 27, 2017. (Bruix J, *Lancet* 2017)
- The REFLECT study confirmed noninferiority of lenvatinib in first-line treatment compared with sorafenib for advanced HCC, which led to FDA approval on August 16, 2018. (Kudo M, *Lancet* 2018)
- The CELESTIAL study confirmed the benefit of cabozantinib in second- and third-line treatment compared with placebo for advanced HCC, which led to FDA approval on January 14, 2019. (Abou-Alfa GK, *N Engl J Med* 2018)
- The REACH-2 study confirmed the benefit of ramucirumab in the second-line treatment of patients with α-fetoprotein concentration > 400 ng/mL compared with placebo for advanced HCC, which led to FDA approval in this indication on May 10, 2019. (Zhu AX, *Lancet Oncol* 2019)
- The CHECKMATE-040 study demonstrated efficacy of the anti-PD1 antibody nivolumab in a second-line, single-arm study for advanced HCC, which led to accelerated conditional approval by the FDA on September 22, 2017. (El-Khoueiry A, *Lancet* 2017) However, the follow-up, randomized, phase III, first-line CHECKMATE-459 study of nivolumab versus sorafenib did not show significantly improved survival. (Yau T, *ESMO* 2019)
- The KEYNOTE 224 study demonstrated efficacy of pembrolizumab in a second-line, single-arm study for advanced HCC, leading to accelerated conditional approval by the FDA on November 9, 2018. (Zhu AX, *Lancet Oncol* 2018) However, the follow-up, randomized, phase III, second-line KEYNOTE-240 study of pembrolizumab versus placebo did not show significantly improved survival. (Finn RS, *ASCO* 2019)
- The IMbrave150 study confirmed benefit of atezolizumab plus bevacizumab in first-line treatment compared to sorafenib for advanced HCC. (Galle PR, *ASCO Gastrointestinal Cancer Symposium* 2020)

BILIARY TRACT CARCINOMA

- The randomized, phase III BILCAP study of adjuvant capecitabine versus observation in resected biliary tract cancer demonstrated an improved survival and can be considered a standard of care. (Primrose JN, *Lancet Oncol* 2019)
- The second- or third-line, randomized, phase III ClalDHy study of the IDH1 inhibitor ivosidnib versus placebo for *IDH1*-mutant cholangiocarcinoma met its primary end point of progression-free survival (PFS), and improved quality of life also was reported. (Abou-Alfa GK, *ESMO* 2019)
- Other molecular subsets of intrahepatic cholangiocarcinoma have demonstrated promise in phase II, nonrandomized studies, including from the ROAR basket study using the combination of the anti-BRAF and anti-MEK agents vemurafenib and trametinib, respectively, for *BRAF* mutant tumors (Wainberg ZA, *ASCO Gastrointestinal Cancer Symposium* 2019) and the FIGHT-202 study of the anti-FGFR2 agent pemibatinib for *FGFR2* fusion. (Vogel A, *ESMO* 2019)

PANCREATIC CANCER

- Given that up to 20% of patients with exocrine pancreatic neoplasms have germline alterations, universal testing for germline mutations is now recommended. (Lowery MA, *J Natl Cancer Inst* 2018)
- The PRODIGEE-24 Trial has established FOLFIRINOX (leucovorin, 5-fluorouracil, irinotecan, oxaliplatin) as the standard of care for the adjuvant treatment of patients with good performance status after resection of pancreatic cancer. (Conroy T, *N Engl J Med* 2018)
- On the basis of the POLO trial, patients with *BRCA1/2* germline mutations who do not progress on ≥ 16 weeks of treatment with an oxaliplatin-containing regimen should be considered for olaparib maintenance therapy. (Golan T, *N Engl J Med* 2019)

COLORECTAL CANCER

- On the basis of the IDEA Collaborative, emerging clinical consensus suggests 3 months of adjuvant therapy is a reasonable alternative for patients with T1-3, N1 disease. If 3 months of therapy is chosen, many expert panels favor capecitabine and oxaliplatin over 5-fluorouracil, leucovorin, oxaliplatin (FOLFOX). Patients with either T4 or N2 disease should still receive 6 months of adjuvant chemotherapy. (Grothey A, *N Engl J Med* 2018)

- Patients with MSI-H/dMMR tumors refractory to standard therapy should be considered for immunotherapy with either single-agent PD-1 inhibitors or combination of PD-1 and CTLA-4 inhibitors. (Overman MJ, *Lancet Oncol* 2017; Overman MJ, *J Clin Oncol* 2018)
- On the basis of results from the BEACON trial, patients with BRAF V600E mutant tumors that progress while receiving frontline chemotherapy should be considered for treatment with the triplet therapy of encorafenib, binimetinib, and cetuximab or with a doublet regimen of encorafenib and cetuximab. (Kopetz S, *N Engl J Med* 2019)
- Results of the phase III ADORE trial established a 6-year disease-free survival advantage of FOLFOX versus bolus 5-FU as adjuvant therapy for patients with postoperative stage II or III rectal cancer who had received neoadjuvant chemoradiation. (Hong YS, *J Clin Oncol* 2019)

GASTROENTEROPANCREATIC NEUROENDOCRINE TUMORS

- Capecitabine and temozolomide versus temozolomide alone has shown impressive PFS and response rates for patients with metastatic pancreatic neuroendocrine tumors. (Kunz PL, *ASCO Annual Meeting, Abstract 4004*, 2018)

OVERVIEW

In 2019, approximately 328,030 new cancers of the digestive system will be diagnosed in the United States, which makes it the most common physiologic system afflicted by cancer and more common than breast cancer (n = 271,270), lung and respiratory tract cancers (n = 246,440), and genitourinary cancers (n = 295,290). Approximately 165,460 patients will die annually of GI malignancies, including 51,020 patients with colon cancer, 45,750 patients with pancreatic cancer, 31,780 patients with liver and intrahepatic bile duct cancers, and 27,220 patients with gastroesophageal cancers (GECs).[1]

The spectrum of diseases encountered in this field varies from rather indolent malignancies, such as low-grade neuroendocrine tumors with overall survival (OS) measured in years, to very aggressive and rapidly fatal cancers, such as pancreatic and hepatocellular carcinomas, for which, in advanced stages, survival is measured in months. Several cancers of the digestive tract are linked to hereditary syndromes that require genetic counseling of patients and family members. Medical oncologists are feeling significant pressure to keep current with the advances in the development of medical therapies, which now routinely include targeted agents beyond conventional chemotherapy in most GI malignancies, as well as the identification of specific biomarkers that allow tailoring medical therapy to subsets of patients. The complexity associated with the diagnosis and treatment of GI cancers is further increased because most of these malignancies require multidisciplinary management involving close interaction among gastroenterologists, interventional radiologists, surgeons, advanced practice providers, radiation oncologists, and medical oncologists. One of the medical oncologist's key roles, therefore, is to coordinate the multidisciplinary team and counsel the patient on various potential and sometimes competing treatment options for his or her disease.

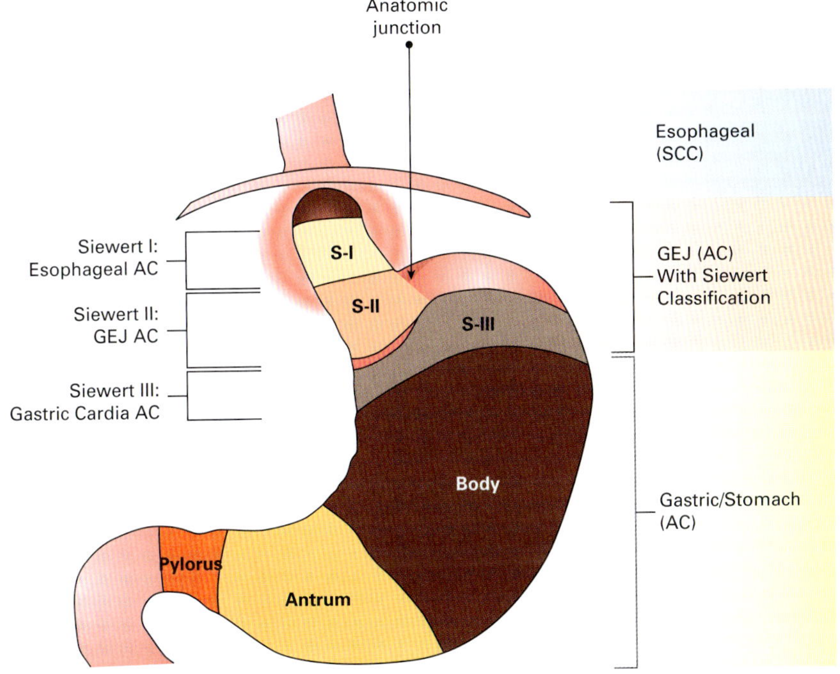

Fig. 13-1 Anatomical distribution of gastroesophageal cancers.

Abbreviations: AC, adenocarcinoma; GEJ, gastroesophageal junction; SCC, squamous cell carcinoma.

GASTROESOPHAGEAL CANCER

GECs exhibit great variation in histology, geographic distribution, and incidence over time. Esophageal adenocarcinoma (AC) and gastroesophageal junctional (GEJ) ACs, so-called type I and II Siewert tumors,[2] respectively, had often been grouped along with esophageal squamous cell cancer (SCC) as esophageal cancer, whereas proximal gastric cardia AC was grouped with distal gastric AC (Fig 13-1). However, recent data suggest molecular features clearly differentiate esophageal SCC from esophageal AC and that SCCs resemble SCCs of other organs more than they do esophageal AC, whereas esophageal AC predominantly resembles the chromosomal instability (CIN) found in the gastric cardia AC and distal gastric AC.[3-5] As such, recent classification generally comprises three main gastroesophageal subtypes, reflecting current understanding of anatomy, histology, etiology, and molecular biology[6-8]:

- esophageal SCC;
- GEJ AC, which includes ACs in the distal esophagus AC (type I Siewert), at the GEJ AC (type II Siewert), and in the gastric cardia AC (type III Siewert); and
- distal gastric AC.

Numerous histologic subtypes have been described, particularly pertinent to gastric AC but also for GEJ AC, including histologic differentiation (ie, well, moderate, poor), Lauren classification (ie, intestinal, diffuse, mixed type), presence of signet-ring cells or not, and a whole host of other subtypes in the WHO criteria.[9] Despite the noted differences between GEJ AC and gastric AC, these two subtypes are often grouped together as gastroesophageal adenocarcinoma (GEA) in both the locally advanced and metastatic settings, when considering therapy. However, with improved understanding of the molecular biology and interpatient heterogeneity within GEA, treatment strategies are emerging to direct personalized therapeutics to patients, including established anti-HER2 and anti-PD1 therapies, as well as other potential targets under continued evaluation.

KEY POINTS

- Beyond known histopathological and epidemiologic distinctions, molecular features differentiate esophageal SCC from esophageal AC, with SCCs resembling SCCs of other organs more than they do esophageal AC, whereas esophageal AC predominantly resembles the CIN type found in gastric AC.
- There are three main GEC subtypes reflecting current understanding of anatomy, histology, etiology, and molecular biology. These are esophageal SCC, GEJ AC, and distal gastric AC. In the United States, the incidences of esophageal SCC and distal GA is decreasing, and the incidence of GEJ AC is increasing rapidly, likely as an effect of lifestyle changes.
- The Cancer Genome Atlas (TCGA) project proposed a molecular classification dividing GEJ AC and GA (together, GEA) into four subtypes: tumors positive for Epstein-Barr virus, microsatellite instability–high (MSI-H) unstable tumors, genomically stable tumors, and tumors with CIN.

EPIDEMIOLOGY, ETIOLOGY, AND PREVENTION

In the United States, GECs, together, represent the fourth most common GI cancer (after colorectal, pancreatic, and hepatobiliary cancers), with the third highest mortality rate.[10] Worldwide, they are the third most common cancer and second leading cause of cancer mortality.[11] Historically, the most common types of GECs were esophageal SCC of the upper to middle esophagus and distal gastric AC.[12] However, during the past three to four decades, particularly in western countries, including the United States, the incidences of esophageal SCC and distal gastric AC have decreased. In contrast, the incidence of GEJ AC has reciprocally increased rapidly during this same period in the Western world, paralleling the rise of gastroesophageal reflux disease (GERD) in the general population, with notable association with patients with a high body mass index.[13,14]

KEY POINT

- The incidence of GEC correlates with socioeconomic status and is clearly dependent on environmental factors. The worldwide incidences of gastric cancer and esophageal SCC are in decline; however, there is an increase in more proximal gastric and gastroesophageal cancers.

Esophageal Squamous Cell Carcinoma

In the United States, SCC of the esophagus is infrequent, constituting approximately 1% of all cancers and approximately 6% of GI malignancies. Esophageal SCC is more likely to occur in patients who are black. These tumors are associated with achalasia, caustic injury, tylosis, Plummer-Vinson syndrome, cigarette smoking, and excessive alcohol consumption. Infection with human papillomavirus (HPV) has been correlated with an increased incidence of SCC of the upper cervical esophagus.[15] Patients with esophageal SCC are at risk for synchronous or metachronous head and neck or lung SCC, which are molecularly more similar to esophageal SCC than to GEJ AC. With increased awareness and decreased exposure to risk factors, including smoking and alcohol use, the incidence of esophageal SCC has decreased significantly in recent decades in the United States. However, worldwide, there remains high incidence, particularly in portions of Iran, Russia, and northern China.[12]

Esophagogastric Junction Adenocarcinoma

GEJ ACs typically arise in metaplastic epithelium—a condition known as Barrett esophagus (BE).[14] Murine carcinogenesis models suggest migration of precursor cells from the gastric cardia proximally into the distal esophagus.[16,17] This premalignant condition is characterized by the replacement of stratified squamous epithelium by columnar epithelium that develops as a consequence of chronic GERD. The incidence of BE is 10% to 20% among symptomatic patients who undergo endoscopy and 30% to 50% for patients with peptic strictures. Risk factors associated with BE include GERD, white or Hispanic race, male sex, advanced age, smoking, diabetes mellitus, Western diet, and obesity.[14,18] However, there is heterogeneity in carcinogenesis and not all tumors arise within a BE background. Approximately 60% of GEJ AC cases have evidence of precursor BE. In a nationwide population study from Denmark, the relative risk of AC among patients with BE was 11.3 (95% CI, 8.8 to 14.4) compared with the risk in the general population.[19] The annual risk of GEJ AC was 0.12% (95% CI, 0.09 to 0.15). Detection of low-grade dysplasia on the index endoscopy was associated with an incidence of AC of 5.1 cases per 1,000 person-years. Risk estimates for patients with high-grade dysplasia (HGD) were slightly higher. In contrast, the incidence among patients without dysplasia was 1.0 case per 1,000 person-years.

There is an inverse association between *Helicobacter pylori* infection and GEJ AC, potentially as a result of the reduced acidity associated with atrophic gastritis.[20] Whether rigorous medical management of GERD with long-term use of proton-pump inhibitors (PPIs) can affect the natural history of the disease or the development of malignancy has long been debated.

A recent, large prevention study, ASPECT, evaluated this question in patients with BE ≥ 1 cm and no HGD or esophageal AC.[21] A total of 2,563 patients were randomly assigned to high-dosage (40 mg twice daily) or low-dosage (20 mg once daily) esomeprazole PPI acid suppression, alone or combined with aspirin 300 mg/d. The primary composite end point was time to all-cause mortality, esophageal AC, or high-grade dysplasia. The combination of aspirin with high-dose PPI had the strongest effect, compared with low-dose PPI with no aspirin.[21]

Another recent, large, population-based retrospective analysis of Nordic countries evaluating 942,906 patients with GERD reported that medical and surgical treatments of GERD were associated with a similar reduced esophageal AC risk, with the risk decreasing to the same level as that in the background population over time, supporting the hypothesis that effective treatment of GERD might prevent esophageal AC.[22] Other than antireflux medication[21] and antireflux surgery,[22] the typical treatment of patients with BE is surveillance using upper endoscopy and collecting a biopsy specimen to examine tissue for evidence of dysplasia.[18] HGD is an indication for more aggressive management, including surgical resection.[23,24]

Gastric AC

In the United States, gastric AC is seen twice as often in men as in women and more frequently in black men than in white men, and its incidence increases with age, starting at 50 years.[25] The incidence of gastric AC has varied considerably during the past century. In the United States, the incidence of gastric AC has decreased approximately 75% during the past few decades.[14] Although gastric AC rates have declined worldwide, it is still prevalent in regions of the world where the storage of fresh foods and the quality of water are poor and in some industrialized nations as well (eg, Japan).[6] Gastric AC is a major health issue in Japan and Korea, and both countries have nationwide screening programs. In Japan and Korea, gastric AC is associated with a better prognosis than in western cultures. When controlling for baseline tumor characteristics, patient demographics, and surgical factors, there is a difference in survival that remains unexplained.[26] Studies of migrant populations have supported evidence for the effect of environmental influences on the development of gastric AC.[27,28] Factors associated with an increased risk of gastric AC include nutritional factors such as high salt and nitrate intake, a diet low in vitamins A and C, the consumption of large amounts of smoked or cured foods, lack of refrigerated foods, and poor-quality drinking water.[29] Occupational exposure to rubber and coal also increases the risk. Cigarette smoking, *H. pylori* infection,[30,31] Epstein-Barr virus,[32] radiation exposure, and prior gastric surgery for benign ulcer disease also have been implicated as risk factors. Together, these data support the concept that gastric AC is strongly influenced by nutritional, socioeconomic, and medical factors rather than dominated by genetic predisposition. Awareness and decreased exposure to these factors have contributed to the decline in incidence and mortality rate of gastric AC in the United States.

Genetic risk factors include type A blood, pernicious anemia, a family history of gastric AC, hereditary nonpolyposis colon cancer (HNPCC), Li-Fraumeni syndrome, and hereditary diffuse gastric cancer (HDGC) caused by mutations in the E-cadherin gene, *CDH1*. HDGC is a genetic predisposition syndrome characterized by a family history of gastric AC characterized by poorly cohesive, diffuse-type histology, often with early onset of disease (generally younger than age 40 years). The cumulative risk of the development of diffuse gastric AC by the age of 80 years for *CDH1* mutation carriers is 70% for men and 56% for women. Women are also at higher risk for the development of lobular breast cancer, with a cumulative risk of 42% by age 80 years.[33] Individuals with a germline mutation in *CDH1* should undergo a risk-reducing prophylactic gastrectomy to prevent future development of HDGC.[34] The optimal timing of prophylactic gastrectomy is unknown and is usually highly individualized. The current consensus is that the procedure should be discussed and offered to carriers of pathogenic germline *CDH1* mutation in early adulthood, generally between ages 20 and 30 years.

Results from several studies have demonstrated an increased likelihood of *H. pylori* infection in patients with gastric AC, particularly cancer of the distal stomach.[30,31] Although cancer does not develop in most people with *H. pylori* infections, the increased risk for patients who are infected has raised the issue of whether treatment of *H. pylori* might decrease the risk of gastric AC. Although the role of *H. pylori* in gastric carcinogenesis is well defined, no definitive evidence shows that mass eradication could reduce the incidence of gastric cancer.[35] A large Chinese study showed no benefit in the prevention of gastric AC with the eradication of *H. pylori*.[36] By contrast, a meta-analysis suggested that eradication, indeed, could reduce the risk of gastric AC.[37] At present, treatment of patients with this infection should be reserved for those with demonstrated ulcers, gastritis, or other symptoms.[38]

KEY POINTS

- Individuals who carry a germline *CDH1* mutation are at significant lifetime risk for the development of gastric cancer and should undergo risk-reducing prophylactic gastrectomy as early as in their 20s.
- At present, treatment of patients with *H. pylori* infection should be reserved for those with demonstrated ulcers, gastritis, or other symptoms.

CLINICAL PRESENTATION, DIAGNOSIS, AND STAGING OF GEC

The most common clinical presentation of esophageal SCC and GEJ AC is dysphagia. Cachexia and substantial weight loss are complications of this presenting symptom, which cause many patients to be debilitated at the time of the diagnosis. Another common presentation is occult or frank bleeding (usually manifested by melena, iron-deficiency anemia, and fatigue).[6] Other symptoms include treatment-refractory heartburn. Patients with more proximal tumors can have tracheobronchial invasion and may present with laryngeal nerve paralysis, cough, and/or postobstructive pneumonia.[39]

Because of vague symptoms that go unaddressed for some time, it is unfortunately common for patients with GEA to present with synchronous metastatic disease when symptoms become more severe, persistent, and compounded by metastatic spread. Common sites of disseminated disease are liver, lung, distant lymph nodes, bone, and peritoneum. Carcinomatoses are common and seen in approximately 30% of patients with GA and 10% to 15% with GEJ AC (particularly diffuse and mixed-type histology, and tumors with signet-ring features), and result in the formation of ascites and abdominal pain culminating in severe anorexia, dysfunctional bowel, and, ultimately, frank partial or complete bowel obstructions.[6]

An upper endoscopic examination should be performed to obtain a diagnostic biopsy. Diffuse-type gastric AC may be elusive on routine upper endoscopy because there is no obvious mass. Therefore, repeated endoscopy with endoscopic ultrasound and other specialized endoscopic techniques may be required to arrive at a confirmed diagnosis if there is still high clinical suspicion of gastric AC. Computed tomography (CT) imaging of the chest, abdomen, and pelvis should be performed with tomographic slices through the liver to evaluate the extent of disease in the upper abdomen, with focus on potential liver metastases and celiac lymphadenopathy. A thorough clinical examination with careful attention paid to the lymph nodes in the supraclavicular regions is essential.

For patients without obvious metastatic disease by CT scan, additional staging should include endoscopic ultrasound (EUS), which is a standard component when evaluating patients with GEC eligible for locoregional therapy to determine depth of invasion of the primary tumor.[40,41] In addition, EUS enables the biopsy of suspicious lymph nodes to confirm the presence of lymph node metastases. Positron emission tomography (PET), preferably as a PET/CT scan, is part of the routine pretreatment diagnostic workup for patients with GEC. PET allows for the determination of lymph node status and the detection of occult sites of distant metastatic spread; therefore, it may spare the patient the morbidity of an aggressive locoregional treatment approach.[42-44] Given the similar risk factors for lung and esophageal SCC, consideration of two separate primaries is important for patients with a primary esophageal SCC and with a solitary lung lesion at staging. It should be noted that diffuse-type gastric AC tumors can be negative on PET staging scans. Patients with GEA, particularly distal gastric AC and patients with proximal gastric cardia AC, having ≥ stage T3 disease and/or lymph node–positive (N+) disease on EUS have high risk of occult peritoneal dissemination despite otherwise negative CT and PET scans. Diagnostic laparoscopy can identify up to 20% to 30% of occult peritoneal metastases in these cases; therefore, this is considered a standard staging procedure in this common scenario to accurately stage disease in patients before initiating therapy.[44,45]

Staging has evolved through various editions of the American Joint Committee on Cancer (AJCC) manual but maintains three distinct staging systems for each of esophageal SCC, GEJ AC, and gastric AC, on the basis of the extent of involvement of the esophagus and stomach. Within GEJ AC, subdivision into three Siewert types (type I, esophageal AC; type II, GEJ; and type III, gastric cardia), largely for surgical anatomic planning, was named after the German surgeon who defined these.[2] The Siewert types are now often used as criteria for enrollment in clinical trials. However, practically speaking, these distinctions are difficult to accurately characterize by upper endoscopy, because tumors often span these artificial boundaries. Recently, the eighth edition of the AJCC staging manual incorporated consideration of clinical staging at diagnosis prior to any therapy or surgery (c-stage), pathologic stage after neoadjuvant therapy (yp-stage), or pathologic stage in those without neoadjuvant therapy (*p*-stage), and the prognostic estimates by stage for each scenario.[7,8,46-50]

KEY POINTS

- Common presenting symptoms for GEC include dysphagia, anorexia, early satiety, nausea, dyspepsia, pain, bleeding, and hematemesis.
- CT and PET imaging, along with upper endoscopy and EUS procedures, are critical to determine the location and stage of the tumor.

TREATMENT

Local Disease

Historically, primary surgical resection alone was standard, except for proximal esophageal SCC, for which definitive chemoradiotherapy (CRT) replaced surgery if surgery was technically not feasible. However, the results of surgical resection alone with muscle-invasive or node-positive disease were discouraging, spawning a series of clinical trials to determine the efficacy of chemotherapy with or without radiation and before or after surgery.

GECs limited to the mucosa (high-grade dysphagia or tumors invading the lamina propria or muscularis mucosae) may be managed with endoscopic mucosal resection because there is a relatively low risk of occult regional lymph node metastasis (Fig 13-2).[51-53] For lesions that have penetrated the submucosa without lymph node involvement on staging studies (tumor invading the submucosa [T1b]), surgical resection with lymphadenectomy is recommended because of the approximately 15% to 40% risk of occult lymph node involvement.

For any lesions ≥ T3 (tumor invading the muscularis propria [T3]) and/or N+ disease amenable to surgical resection, multimodal management with chemotherapy with or without radiation therapy (RT), before and/or after surgery, has become the standard, given high-risk of micrometastastic dissemination.[39,54,55] It is controversial whether patients with T2N0 GECs (ie, tumor invading the muscularis propria [T2]) should have perioperative therapy versus surgery alone, because some studies have included these patients for eligibility and other studies have not, and some reports suggested lack of benefit in the setting of adequate surgery.[56-59] Currently, a discussion of potential risks and benefits of perioperative therapy plus surgery versus surgery alone with the patient and family is prudent, and a personalized approach for patients with T2N0 disease is recommended, including enrollment in a clinical trial if available.

Surgery. The preferred curative treatment approach for patients with locally advanced GEC is surgical resection.[60] For distal esophageal SCC and GEJ AC, the two most commonly used surgical techniques are transhiatal esophagectomy and a transthoracic approach (eg, an Ivor-Lewis resection). Transhiatal esophagectomy is generally reserved for patients with tumors of the lower esophagus. A transthoracic approach uses a combination of thoracotomy and laparotomy, particularly used in midesophageal tumors. The results associated with the two approaches are similar.[61-63] Reports suggest a higher retrieval rate of lymph nodes with an Ivor-Lewis approach.[64,65] The surgical approach is determined by the experienced surgeon on the basis of the tumor location and patient details, including transthoracic esophagectomy with two-field lymphadenectomy, transhiatal esophagectomy with lower mediastinal and upper abdominal lymphadenectomy, and proximal, subtotal or total gastrectomy. Minimally invasive approaches via laparoscopy and robotic surgeries are becoming more common for GEC, without evidence for detriment in efficacy.[66-70]

The number of lymph nodes removed is important.[71-73] A D2 lymphadenectomy is defined as the contiguous resection of the second tier of lymph nodes along the branches of the celiac trunk (eg, common hepatic artery, left gastric artery, and splenic artery). After 15-year follow-up of a randomized Dutch trial that included 1,078 patients with distal gastric AC, D2 lymphadenectomy was associated with lower locoregional recurrence (12% *v* 22%) and gastric cancer–related death rates (37% *v* 48%) than D1 (fewer lymph nodes removed) surgery.[74] Although D2 dissection was associated with higher operative morbidity, these data suggest D2 lymphadenectomy should be considered the surgical standard of care. Larger meta-analyses have confirmed this, particularly among patients who have undergone D2 resection who did not undergo resection of the spleen or distal pancreas and nodal stations around these ("modified D2"), as well as for patients with higher risk T3/T4 or node-positive cancers.[75,76]

Operative mortality rates for GEC should be < 5% when the operation is performed by an experienced surgeon at a high-volume center.[77] Historically, survival has been poor for patients with GEC treated with surgery alone, with 5-year survival rates ranging from 5% to 34%,[39] leading to several studies evaluating the benefit of perioperative therapies.

Neoadjuvant, Adjuvant, or Perioperative Treatment. The relatively advanced nature of disease at the time of diagnosis (stages II and III, at least muscle invasive or node-positive disease) and poor outcomes of surgery alone led to investigations to improve outcomes using various neoadjuvant, adjuvant, or perioperative (a course of both neoadjuvant and adjuvant therapies) approaches for the treatment GEC. Combined-modality treatment involves surgery with either chemotherapy or RT, or both (trimodality). A universal treatment of choice for patients with locally advanced GEC has been elusive due to lack of consensus. Particularly controversial is the classification of GEJ tumors as either esophageal or gastric cancer, versus its own entity, as well as which modality(ies) to add to surgery and whether these should be done before and/or after surgery. Furthermore, the different incidences of each of the subtypes of GEC (ie, esophageal SCC, GEJ AC, and gastric AC) geographically

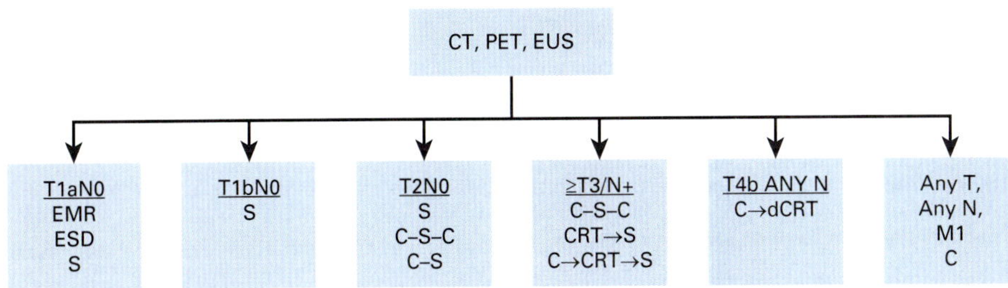

Fig. 13-2 Treatment algorithm based on clinical stage.

Abbreviations: C, chemotherapy; CRT, chemoradiotherapy; CT, computed tomography; dCRT, definitive chemoradiotherapy (no surgery); EMR, endoscopic mucosal resection; ESD, endoscopic submucosal dissection; EUS, endoscopic ultrasound; PET, positron emission tomography; S, surgery.

led to different makeup of these tumor types within various studies, making cross-trial comparisons challenging and potentially misleading. For instance, GEA studies from Asia are almost exclusively of distal gastric AC, without any patients with proximal GEJ AC enrolled, whereas in western countries, GEJ AC accounts for at least half of patients enrolled in GEA studies. Similarly, different makeup of esophageal SCC and AC within different esophageal studies also makes comparison across studies challenging because these subtypes have a different biology, natural history, and sensitivities to the perioperative therapies. As such, various combinations of variables (eg, the tumor site inclusion, the modalities included, nuanced details of type of chemotherapy or RT, doses and the timing of treatment as related to surgery) were studied in large GEC trials across centers and countries in parallel, each compared with surgery alone. This ultimately has led to a fragmented treatment approach, with each approach deemed to be more effective than surgery alone, but it remains unclear which, if any, is superior.[55] However, accumulating evidence from molecular analyses[3,4] and from comparative clinical trials has led to some consensus regarding the practical management of each of the GEC subtypes,[55] summarized in Table 13-1 and discussed in the following paragraphs. Ongoing, prospective comparative studies will continue to define the optimal therapeutic approach to be combined with surgery.

Esophageal SCC

Local recurrence rates of muscle-invasive or node-positive esophageal SCC are high with surgery alone, similar to other SCC tumor sites.[39,60] Without neoadjuvant therapy before surgery, particularly RT, local recurrence can be as high as 40% to 45%.[78] Chemotherapy sensitization of RT led to evaluation of neoadjuvant trimodality CRT studies.[79,80] The chemotherapy agents historically administered with RT were 5-FU, a platinum drug (cisplatin or carboplatin), and/or mitomycin C,[81] and later combination with taxanes.[82] With these combinations, the pathologic complete response (pCR) rate, which is associated with better outcome,[83] but potentially misleading as a surrogate end point,[84] was approximately 30% to 40% for esophageal SCC. Data from the CROSS phase III trial, which enrolled patients with esophageal SCC (25%) and AC (75%), confirmed the superiority of a neoadjuvant CRT approach compared with surgery alone for patients with localized esophageal SCC.[85] In a cross-trial comparison, the toxicity of the carboplatin and paclitaxel regimen was mild and appeared less severe than the toxicity that occurred with the 5-FU and platinum combination used in CALGB 9781,[86] making carboplatin and paclitaxel a preferred regimen. These results confirm the use of trimodality therapy as standard of care for patients with locally advanced esophageal SCC.[87]

Adjuvant therapy after esophagectomy is difficult to tolerate, and no convincing data justify the routine use of adjuvant chemotherapy after surgery. RT has no role as the sole postoperative modality. Current guidelines recommend surveillance alone for patients with esophageal SCC (and also those with GEJ AC) after completion of neoadjuvant CRT then surgery, including even those who have residual disease after neoadjuvant CRT (ypT+ or ypN+), despite the recognition that these patients have a poor prognosis, particularly so for patients with node-positive disease, for whom long-term survival rate is < 20%.[88] However, there is some controversy about the suggestion of possible benefit of adjuvant chemotherapy in these pathologic nonresponders.[89] A recent meta-analysis lends some support to adjuvant chemotherapy after previous neoadjuvant CRT then surgery.[89] Clinical trials should be encouraged for these high-risk patients.

Given the favorable pCR rate (approximately 50%) with CRT in esophageal SCC, definitive CRT is considered a standard option for patients with localized and locally advanced esophageal SCC who are not considered appropriate surgical candidates. Decisions regarding surgical appropriateness involve several factors, including, but not limited to, proximal

Table 13-1 Preferred Standard Curative-Intent Options of Perioperative Therapy for Locally Advanced Gastroesophageal Cancers Amenable for Surgery

Disease Subtype	Trial Name	Strategy	Median OS, (months)	3-year DFS (%)	5-year OS (%)
SCC	CROSS[85,87]	CRT[a]→ S	81.6	62	58
	FFCD 9102[78,92]	dCRT[b]	19	34 (2-year)	NR
GEJ AC	CROSS[85,87]	CRT →S	43.2	48	43
	FLOT4[c] [95]	C→S→C	50	57	45
GA	FLOT4[95]	C→S→C	50	57	45
	CLASSIC[d] [108]	S→ C	Not reached	75	78

Abbreviations: AC, adenocarcinoma; C, chemotherapy; CRT, chemoradiotherapy; dCRT, definitive chemoradiotherapy; DFS, disease-free survival; GA, gastric adenocarcinoma; GEJ, esophagogastric junction adenocarcinoma; NR, not reported; S, surgery; SCC, esophageal squamous cell carcinoma.

[a]Chemoradiotherapy: weekly carboplatin and paclitaxel for 5 weeks, with daily radiation therapy 41.4 Gy.

[b]Radiation therapy 46 Gy.

[c]FLOT chemotherapy: four cycles of biweekly 5-fluorouracil, leucovorin, oxaliplatin, and docetaxel before and after surgery.

[d]Only Korean patients enrolled. All other listed studies were conducted in Western countries.

tumors, age, comorbidities, performance status, and need for laryngectomy. Patients with T4b disease (invading other adjacent structures, such as aorta, vertebral body, trachea), trachealesophageal fistula, or cervical esophageal SCC are not candidates for curative-intent surgery. In addition to patients not suitable for surgery, definitive CRT (without surgery) may also be considered a viable option for routine esophageal SCC treatment in those responding to CRT.[90,91] Supporting this notion, surgically treated patients in the FFCD 9102 phase III trial had significantly lower rates of locoregional recurrence (34% *v* 43%) and were significantly less likely to require palliative intervention for dysphagia (24% *v* 46%) compared with definitive CRT without surgery. There were no differences in OS or in longitudinal quality of life among survivors with 2 years of follow-up.[92] Patients who have a clinical response after CRT may choose, therefore, not to proceed to resection immediately, opting to wait for local recurrence and progression in the hope of avoiding an esophagectomy altogether. However, it is recommended to have a discussion regarding these potential risks and benefits. As noted, a salvage esophagectomy if or when recurrence is observed is associated with similar survival compared with proceeding directly to esophagectomy as planned, but with higher surgical morbidity, including anastomotic leak of 25% (for salvage esophagectomy) versus 3% if performed shortly after completion of combined modality therapy.[91,93]

KEY POINTS

- Combined-modality CRT is the standard neoadjuvant approach to the treatment of locally advanced esophageal SCC. Definitive CRT (without surgery) can be a valid treatment option for patients with esophageal SCC if a clinical CR is achieved, given similar OS with trimodality therapy, but is associated with lower locoregional control and more need for palliative procedures.
- After trimodality therapy (CRT followed by surgery), adjuvant therapy is not recommended outside of a clinical trial, and surveillance alone is the standard of care.

Esophagogastric Junction Adenocarcinoma

As noted, management of GEJ AC has been an area of contention, largely due to the borderline location between the esophagus and stomach.[2] As such, tumors from the GEJ have been included in clinical trials for esophageal cancer (including SCC) as well as for gastric cancer proper, and, in some cases, studied as a unique entity, leading to heterogeneous trials with varying eligibility and, ultimately, heterogeneous treatment practices.

One standard approach remains to consider GEJ, particularly type I and II Siewert tumors, as esophageal cancer and treat it with neoadjuvant CRT as detailed in the preceding section on esophageal SCC. Rationale to support this approach includes a lower rate of complete (R0) resection with surgery alone compared with distal gastric cancer and, therefore, the need for locally focused RT to enhance R0 resection rates. Initial evidence to support the utility of neoadjuvant CRT for GEJ AC was based on many smaller studies, analyzed as meta-analyses.[80] Eventually, the CROSS study with doublet chemotherapy (carboplatin and paclitaxel) was the first stand-alone phase III study to support this approach, with 75% of patients enrolled having GEJ AC (type I or II Siewert tumors) and the other 25% having esophageal SCC. For patient with GEJ AC, the pCR rate was 23% (21% intention to treat), and median OS was 43.2 months with CRT followed by surgery, versus 27.1 months with surgery alone. For these reasons, the neoadjuvant CRT approach is listed as an option for treatment in guidelines and as a preferred approach in the National Comprehensive Cancer Network (NCCN) guidelines. The optimum chemotherapy to use is unresolved, because a recent study, CALGB 80803, suggested leucovorin, fluorouracil, and oxaliplatin (FOLFOX) chemotherapy had better clinical outcomes.[94] FOLFOX and the doublet chemotherapy of carboplatinum and paclitaxel are accepted options.

In contrast, another school of thought considers GEJ AC predominantly as a systemic problem with more potential for distant disease dissemination and, therefore, takes into account disease-site differences within GEC. These differences include the etiology and molecular classification and also the recognized differences in sensitivity to different therapies (eg, SCC is more sensitive to RT), clinical outcomes, and patterns of disease recurrence across esophageal SCC and GEJ AC. Specifically, there is more distant disease recurrence with AC compared with SCC, suggesting that a focus locally with both RT and surgery is not addressing the main problem. Meanwhile, optimizing systemic chemotherapy (eg, with potent triplet chemotherapy) to address systemic micrometastatic disease is less feasible with concurrent CRT. Moreover, when dissecting the CROSS study further, although there was a trend for better OS than surgery alone in the AC subgroup, CRT with doublet chemotherapy was not statistically significant in multivariate analysis,[87] supporting the concern for predominantly systemic disease recurrence.[55] As such, there has been focus on optimizing triplet chemotherapeutic regimens with the "sandwich" approach of perioperative chemotherapy before and after surgery, as discussed later in the section on distal gastric AC, in attempt to eliminate micrometastatic systemic disease present at the time of diagnosis. Indeed, the most recent advance for GEA was the FLOT4 study that evaluated perioperative 5-FU, leucovorin (LV), oxaliplatin, and docetaxel (FLOT) for four cycles before and four cycles after surgery.[95] The study demonstrated improved median OS of 50 months compared with 35 months with the previous standard of epirubicin, cisplatin, and 5-FU (ECF) from the MAGIC study.[95,96] More than 50% of patients enrolled had proximal esophageal and GEJ AC; the remaining patients had distal gastric AC. For this reason, FLOT is considered a standard option for all locally advanced GEA, including the proximal AC tumors,[95] and a preferred option in Europe.

In terms of which of the two options (neoadjuvant CRT or perioperative chemotherapy) is superior, there is not consensus.[97]

A prospective study (the ESOPEC study [ClinicalTrials.gov identifier: NCT02509286]) is evaluating perioperative FLOT compared with neoadjuvant CRT with carboplatin and paclitaxel (the CROSS regimen) solely in patients with proximal GEJ AC, which may help consolidate treatment practice.[98] However, the study will not be completed until approximately 2024. Until then, both options remain reasonable standards of care for GEJ AC, with evidence to support either. Finally, another triplet regimen, FOLFIRINOX (5-fluoropyrimidine, leucovorin, irinoecan, and oxaliplatin) has been investigated in the perioperative setting for locally advanced GEA in a phase II study, given the non-overlapping toxicities of irinotecan and oxaliplatin versus oxaliplatin and docetaxel. This study demonstrated similar efficacy of negative margins and pathologic response grade with improved tolerabiliaty. This FOLFIRINOX regimen could be important particularly in patients having pre-exisiting neuropathy or in patients wishing to limit alopecia, compared to FLOT.[99]

KEY POINT

- Neoadjuvant CRT then surgery (trimodality therapy) versus perioperative triplet chemotherapy are both standard options to treat locally advanced GEJ AC tumors to decrease risk of recurrence. The optimal approach between these two strategies is unresolved and head-to-head studies are ongoing that are evaluating this question.

Gastric AC

Patients with locally advanced gastric AC have high recurrence risk with surgery alone. Different perioperative approaches to the management of locally advanced gastric AC (and GEJ AC, as discussed in the preceding section) are used, with the specific approach varying again due to fragmented clinical trial and treatment strategies over the years. Based on contemporary studies, emerging standard options include perioperative (neoadjuvant and adjuvant) triplet chemotherapy with FLOT (United States,[95] United Kingdom, and much of Europe), or adjuvant chemotherapy alone after D2 resection (Asia).[108] For patients who have had resection without adequate, modified D2 lymphadenectomy (at minimum) for whatever reason, with or without completion of neoadjuvant chemotherapy, inclusion of adjuvant CRT is reasonable (Table 13-1).

Perioperative chemotherapy administered before and after surgery for resectable gastric and GEJ ACs also has shown a significant OS benefit compared with surgery alone, initially in the MAGIC trial with the ECF regimen,[96] with cisplatin and 5-FU,[100] and, most recently, with FLOT replacing the previous ECF regimen on the basis of results from the FLOT4 study.[95] The FLOT regimen was compared with perioperative epirubicin, cisplatin, and capecitabine.[95] This phase III study, accruing patients with ≥ T2 and/or N+ disease from 2010 to 2015, enrolled 716 patients and demonstrated a significant improvement in median OS (35 months with ECF or epirubicin, cisplatin, and capecitabine *v* 50 months with FLOT; hazard ratio [HR], 0.77; P = .012). The study demonstrated approximately equal toxicity in both arms, suggesting FLOT is a more effective three-drug chemotherapy regimen in the perioperative setting. The study included all patients with GEA, including 56% with GEJ AC (24% type I, 34% type II or III) and 44% with distal gastric AC, and updated analyses showed benefit across all subgroups including type I Siewert tumors (HR, 0.6).[95] Therefore, triplet FLOT represents a standard of care for all GEAs.

It should be noted that in these perioperative studies, only approximately 50% of patients received all the intended adjuvant chemotherapy.[95,96,100] A remaining unresolved issue is how to approach patients postoperatively who, on the basis of poor pathologic response, clearly did not derive benefit from neoadjuvant FLOT therapy. Moreover, the question of whether pCR, associated with better survival,[101,102] requires additional adjuvant therapy. The strategy within the perioperative FLOT4 study was to proceed with four more adjuvant cycles, as tolerated. Additional investigation is necessary to better direct an optimal approach for the scenarios of excellent response and poor response to the neoadjuvant component—whether it is to continue more FLOT, to change to other therapy, or to surveil only, despite poor prognosis. Indeed, the utility of any adjuvant chemotherapy after completion of neoadjuvant therapy and surgery has been questioned, and this requires additional investigation. For now, the standard approach is to complete the adjuvant therapy, if possible, in all scenarios (or consider a clinical trial to address these issues). Completing the adjuvant therapy component is potentially supported in the CRITICS study, discussed later in this section.[103] In contrast to perioperative triplet chemotherapy, sequencing different agents in doublets adjuvantly (5-FU and irinotecan then docetaxel and cisplatin, compared with 5-FU alone) was not effective in the ITACA-S phase III study.[104] Finally, adding ECF triplet chemotherapy to CRT adjuvantly was not effective,[105] supporting the notion that the neoadjuvant therapy component is important for survival benefit, potentially because of the relatively low rate of completion of adjuvant therapy (approximately 50% of patients complete therapy in most studies).

However, although neoadjuvant therapy is preferred before surgery in the United States, large studies from Asia demonstrated benefit of adjuvant chemotherapy after D2 resection without neoadjuvant treatment.[106-109] The Korean CLASSIC study, which included 1,035 patients with D2-resected stage II or III distal gastric AC, identified adjuvant therapy with capecitabine plus oxaliplatin (CapeOx) as superior to surgery alone, with significant improvement in OS.[108] The superior outcomes of patients in eastern countries are clearly highlighted here with the CLASSIC study, as compared with outcomes in western countries, but it is challenging to compare perioperative FLOT as studied in the West to adjuvant CapeOx as studied in the East.[95,108] In addition to these individual trials supporting adjuvant chemotherapy, a meta-analysis of 17 trials with 3,838 patients confirmed that adjuvant chemotherapy without radiation after gastric AC resection was associated with a significant survival benefit.[110] Although doublet platinum and capecitabine is an option, per the CLASSIC study, FLOT therapy should be considered, given the known superior survival advantage demonstrated with triplet therapy, albeit in a perioperative, not solely adjuvant, study (Table 13-1). Regardless, for patients who had surgery at diagnosis without neoadjuvant treatment and/or who cannot tolerate adjuvant triplet FLOT therapy, results of the CLASSIC study provide evidence that doublet chemotherapy adjuvantly for 4 to 6 months can improve survival compared with surgery alone, and this should be considered in these scenarios.

Although postoperative CRT, supported by meta-analyses,[111] had been considered a standard approach, mostly in the United States, contemporary randomized studies have demonstrated no improvement over chemotherapy alone in randomized comparative studies of patients who had adequate D2 (or modified D2) lymphadenectomy. The historic INT-0116 randomized, phase III trial, examined adjuvant CRT (RT plus concurrent 5-FU) compared with surgery alone.[112] The study has been criticized for the low rate of D2 (or even D1) lymph node dissections. In fact, < 50% of patients underwent a D1 or D2 resection. In addition, only the rate of local recurrence, not the rate of distant metastasis, was reduced in the adjuvant CRT group, suggesting the adjuvant RT therapy could have mainly compensated for what is certainly now considered inferior surgery.

Three contemporary studies have since confirmed no benefit of adjuvant CRT after adequate D2 resection. The Korean Adjuvant Chemoradiotherapy in Stomach Tumors (ARTIST) trial evaluated the CRT in patients with GA who underwent gastrectomy with D2 lymph node dissection.[113] Patients were randomly assigned to either six cycles of chemotherapy with capecitabine and cisplatin (XP), or two cycles of XP followed by CRT (with capecitabine), followed by two more cycles of XP. Neither disease-free survival (DFS) nor OS was different between the two arms, but subsets of patients with node-positive disease and intestinal-type GA did have a significantly improved DFS with the addition of RT therapy in unplanned subset analyses. The ARTIST2 trial, which assessed CRT in the subset of lymph node–positive disease, also was negative compared with chemotherapy alone adjuvantly for recurrent disease. In ARTIST2, the 3-year DFS rate was 78% with adjuvant chemotherapy versus 73% with adjuvant CRT. Finally, the large, randomized Dutch trial, Chemoradiotherapy After Induction Chemotherapy in Cancer of the Stomach (CRITICS) Study, determined that adjuvant CRT therapy is no better than perioperative chemotherapy (MAGIC regimen)[103] and results suggested postoperative CRT does not improve patient survival compared with this chemotherapy regimen. The postoperative MAGIC regimen has since been replaced by the even better FLOT regimen. Upfront surgery should not be a preferred option; rather, perioperative therapy, including chemotherapy before and after surgery, is preferred. However, in the setting of surgery first with inadequate lymph node harvest, for any reason, adjuvant CRT remains an option for these patients in attempt to decrease recurrence in any potentially involved, residual regional lymph nodes.

Some have argued that because it is difficult to deliver the intended treatment to all patients postoperatively, a total neoadjuvant approach for GEA could realize the RT benefit. In addition to the aforementioned ESOPEC study specifically for EJG AC, The TOPGEAR study, initiated in 2009, is evaluating whether neoadjuvant CRT therapy added to perioperative chemotherapy (via the MAGIC approach, and later amended to include FLOT) will be superior to the chemotherapy alone (the majority of patients were accrued before FLOT4 results were reported and the study was amended to allow use of FLOT for both arms) for patients with GEA.[114] Other prospective studies, like CRITICS-II, are ongoing and assessing neoadjuvant triplet chemotherapy for four cycles versus triplet chemotherapy for four cycles, then CRT versus CRT only, each followed by surgery.[115]

A recent meta-analysis demonstrated that MSI-H tumors have a good prognosis compared with microsatellite stable (MSS) tumors.[116] Importantly, this meta-analysis, including several perioperative phase III studies, also demonstrated that MSI-H tumors appear to have a negative outcome with chemotherapy as compared with surgery alone, similar to stage II, MSI-H colorectal cancer (CRC). Thus, there is a current push to test for MSI-H tumors in this setting, to prospectively evaluate the question of surgery alone versus chemotherapy versus immunotherapy.

KEY POINTS

- Randomized trials have demonstrated a survival benefit from preoperative and postoperative (perioperative FLOT regimen) chemotherapy for patients with GEA compared with ECF or adjuvant chemotherapy (CapeOx) without radiation for tumors with at least muscle invasion (≥ T2) and/or node-positive disease (≥ N1) in patients having had D2 lymphadenectomy, compared with surgery alone.
- Three prospective, randomized studies have demonstrated that adjuvant radiotherapy does not add to the benefit of standard perioperative or adjuvant chemotherapy and should not be used.

Immunotherapy. The wave of excitement from immune checkpoint inhibitors across tumors has included GEC. At this time, however, evaluations have been solely in the metastatic setting; these are summarized in the next section. After approval of pembrolizumab in the United States for GEA in MSI-H tumors in second-line or higher setting, and for GEA programmed death ligand 1 (PD-L1)-positive tumors in the third-line or higher setting, a number of studies with numerous, different anti-programmed death 1 (PD1)/PD-L1 agents have been launched for GEC in the perioperative setting. As noted, MSI-H tumors appear to derive negative benefit from perioperative chemotherapy alone,[116] and studies evaluating checkpoint blockade are ongoing. The results of these phase II and phase III studies will not be available for several years, because many have just been initiated. There is hope that these could improve outcomes for at least a subset of patients with locally advanced disease.

KEY POINT

- Immunotherapy checkpoint inhibitors are not currently standard to use in the perioperative setting, but ongoing studies are evaluating this approach, particularly in MSI-H tumors.

TREATMENT OF METASTATIC DISEASE

Unfortunately, many patients present with synchronous metastatic disease at initial diagnosis, and there is a high risk of recurrence even after curative-intent therapy; > 50% of patients have had their cancer recur within 2.5 to 3 years. There is no role for routine resection of the primary tumor without resection of the metastatic disease, even when there is limited single-site metastases.[117] However, when there is limited metastatic involvement, recent data for GEA suggest that resection of all disease after aggressive neoadjuvant treatment may warrant additional investigation, but this is not routinely recommended.[118] As such, the intent of treatment of metastatic GEC is to control the disease, prolong life, and provide palliation, while limiting toxicities from the therapy. Notably, many phase III studies evaluating novel therapies for GEA have not included type I Siewert esophageal AC, despite the similar biology of these tumors with the type II and III disease, as discussed previously.

Palliative systemic therapy is associated with an improved quality of life as well as improved median OS to approximately 10 to 12 months (14 to 16 months in HER2-positive patients) over best supportive care, with median OS historically of approximately 3 months.[119,120] To date, chemotherapy, targeted therapy, and immunotherapy have each contributed to improved median OS over three and even four lines of therapy (Fig 13-3). Ancillary support, including palliative RT of symptomatic localized metastases like bone lesions, as well as RT and/or endoluminal stenting for refractory or symptomatic primary tumors, also contributes to improved or maintained quality of life and OS.

KEY POINT

- There are three main GEC subtypes reflecting current understanding of anatomy, histology, etiology, and molecular biology: esophageal SCC; GEJ AC including EA, junctional, and gastric cardia tumors; and distal GA.

Chemotherapy

Many agents have demonstrated some activity in GEC, including fluoropyrimidines (intravenous FU and oral capecitabine), platinum agents, taxanes, irinotecan, trifluridine/tipiracil, and—now used to a lesser extent—anthracyclines,[121,122] mitomycin C, methotrexate, vinorelbine, and gemcitabine.[120,123] Treatment commonly is administered as a combination of two

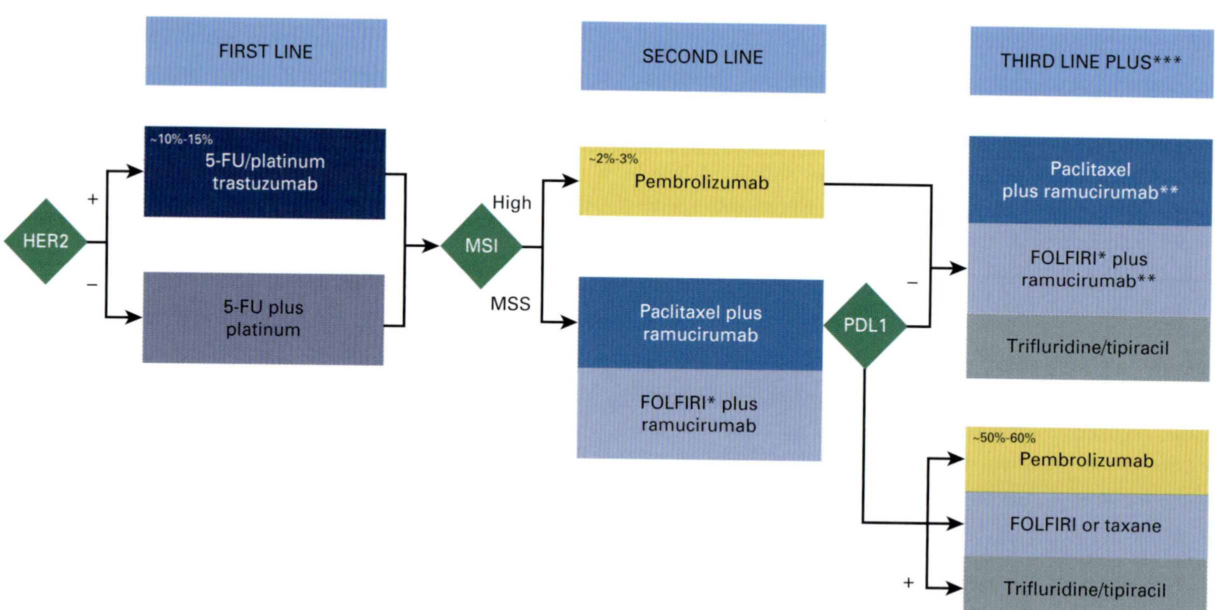

Fig. 13-3 Palliative therapeutic strategy for gastroesophageal adenocarcinoma in the advanced metastatic setting. HER2 status determined by immunohistochemistry (IHC) and reflex fluorescence in situ hybridization if equivocal (IHC2+); MSI status determined by either IHC, PCR, or next-generation sequencing.

Abbreviations: FOLFIRI, 5-fluorouracil, oxaliplatin, irinotecan, and leucovorin; FU, fluorouracil; MSI, microsatellite instability; MSS, microsatellite stable.

*FOLFIRI may be substituted for paclitaxel in the second line (or third line for MSI-High patients) if residual oxaliplatin neuropathy precludes taxane use.

**Ramucirumab in the third line only if not used in second lne.

***No studies have been conducted to date to determine optimal sequencing of recently approved third line therapies, see text for discussion and approach.

(preferred) or three drugs or, less frequently, as single-agent therapy, depending on the patients performance status. The utility of chemotherapy treatment regimens is similar across gastroesophageal subtypes, but most studies in western countries have predominantly focused on GEA.

In most clinical trials assessing single-agent therapy, the response rate has ranged from 10% to 20%, and there is likely some benefit compared with best supportive care. Doublet-chemotherapy regimens have yielded response rates as high as 40% to 50% and are associated with increased OS when compared with single-agent therapies.[120] Standard contemporary doublet regimens have emerged for the first-line setting, including FOLFOX and FOLFIRI, because they achieve similar outcomes but with less toxicity and more convenient dosing schedules.[124-127]

Triplet regimens, on the other hand, are generally discouraged at this time because they do not lead to significantly better OS but do come with higher rates of toxicity.[128] A large, randomized, phase III study, REAL-2, evaluated various iterations of triplet fluoropyrimidines and platinums with epirubicin. This study demonstrated that results with oral capecitabine were similar to those with continuous-infusion FU, and results with oxaliplatin were similar to those with cisplatin.[129] Although 5-FU plus capecitabine and cisplatin plus oxaliplatin are considered, therefore, interchangeable, the combination of epirubicin, oxaliplatin, and capecitabine (EOX) was found to be less toxic and at least as active as the ECF combination, with all EOX efficacy parameters actually trending toward superiority, and both oxaliplatin arms less toxic than the cisplatin arms. This and other studies comparing oxaliplatin versus cisplatin have largely supplanted the use of cisplatin in western countries because of better tolerability and similar or better efficacy. The use of epirubicin has also fallen out of favor,[126,130] because it is not believed to add significant efficacy.[121,122] As for other triplet regimens, taxane, platinum, and fluoropyrimidines have been used in various doses and schedules, including FLOT; docetaxel, cisplatin, and fluorouracil; and docetaxel, oxaliplatin, and 5-FU,[118,131] as well as modified versions that are more tolerable.[132] Another triplet regimen that has been evaluated with promising results is a fluoropyrimidine, leucovorin, oxaliplatin, and irinotecan (FOLFOXIRI or FOLFIRINOX).[133-135] However, other than in select circumstances, the general consensus is that the preferred approach is tandem doublet regimens throughout the course of care, rather than upfront triplet regimens, because the former are more tolerable and have similar results. In sum, a combination regimen with a platinum agent (oxaliplatin preferred) plus a fluoropyrimidine as a backbone can be considered first-line standard of care in the palliative treatment of advanced GEC. Irinotecan has clearly demonstrated activity and could be used in the setting of quick recurrence (usually defined as < 6 months from surgery or completing adjuvant therapy) after platinum and taxane perioperative therapy (eg, FLOT; carboplatin and paclitaxel plus RT) or if there are contraindications to platinum and taxane, such as severe baseline neuropathy (Fig 13-3).

The utility of second-line chemotherapy in the palliative management of GEC had long been questioned. Eventually, studies evaluating chemotherapy versus best supportive care clearly demonstrated improvement in OS with either irinotecan or taxane after failure of first-line, combined fluoropyrimidine and platinum therapy.[136-140] Head-to-head comparison between two commonly used second-line therapies, paclitaxel and irinotecan, demonstrated similar efficacy and each is a reasonable option.[138,139] Although there is a drop off in the number of eligible patients proceeding to second-line therapy, approximately 60% of patients have preserved performance status and do derive benefit from continued treatment. As discussed in a later section, anti-VEGFR2 therapy with ramucirumab has also demonstrated benefit in the second-line setting, either alone or in combination with chemotherapy.

Similarly, the utility of chemotherapy in the third-line and higher treatment setting was similarly debatable for the approximately 20% to 30% of patients still otherwise eligible for palliative therapy with preserved performance status, but there is now support for continued therapy for these patients. This includes irinotecan-based regimens after failure of prior platinum and taxane regimens,[138,139,141-143] or taxane for those whose disease previously progressed while being treated with platinum- and irinotecan-based regimens. As such, physician's choice standard chemotherapy is a common control therapy, composed of taxane or irinotecan in third-line studies evaluating novel treatments, as discussed later in the chapter. Importantly, a large, phase III, placebo-controlled, randomized study, TAGS, evaluated oral trifluridine and tipiracil versus best supportive care and recently reported a modest survival advantage (median OS, 3.6 to 5.7 months) in a third-line (27% of patients) or higher (63% of patients) setting, and oral trifluridine plus tipiracil are an option for therapy in these settings and gained FDA approval on February 25, 2019.[144]

KEY POINTS

- A combination regimen with a platinum agent (oxaliplatin preferred) plus a fluoropyrimidine as a backbone can be considered first-line standard of care in the palliative treatment of advanced GEC.
- Approximately 60% of patients have preserved performance status and derive benefit from continued treatment with palliative therapy in the second-line setting.
- Third-line chemotherapy has demonstrated benefit compared with best supportive care or placebo, including with trifluridine plus tipiracil (TAS-102) and should be considered for patients with preserved performance status after two or more lines of therapy.

Targeted Therapy

To date, there are no standard targeted approaches for esophageal SCC, although immunotherapy for esophageal SCC was approved by the FDA on July 30, 2019, for second-line CPS ≥ 10 tumors.[145-149] Molecular characterization of GEA has identified mutations and copy number variations in a number of readily targetable genes, including *HER2*, *EGFR*, *FGFR2*, *MET*, and *PI3K/mTOR*, along with other oncogenes, biomarkers, and immune-oncologic checkpoints that may serve as actionable therapeutic targets.[3,4,150,151] To date, targeted therapy for HER2-positive GEA tumors in the first-line setting, MSI-H tumors in the second-line setting, VEGFR2 for all patients in the second-line setting, and PD-L1+ tumors in the third-line or higher setting are standards in the palliative treatment journey for GEA (Fig 13-3).

HER2. Approximately 10% to 15% of GAs and about 15% to 25% of GEAs overexpress or amplify HER2.[152] The first targeted therapy to demonstrate benefit in GEA was trastuzumab, the humanized monoclonal antibody against HER2, added to standard cisplatin and fluoropyrimidine chemotherapy in *HER2* gene-amplified and overexpressing tumors. In the pivotal phase III Trastuzumab in Gastric Cancer [TOGA]) trial,[153] 584 patients were randomly assigned to receive a fluoropyrimidine plus cisplatin 80 mg/m^2 on day 1 with or without trastuzumab. The addition of trastuzumab to cisplatin and a fluoropyrimidine increased median OS from 11.1 months to 13.8 months ($P = .0046$). In addition, secondary end points such as PFS and overall response rate (ORR) were also improved in the trastuzumab arm. There were no significant differences in toxicity between the two treatment arms. An asymptomatic decrease in ejection fraction occurred in 4.6% and 1.1% in the trastuzumab and chemotherapy-alone arms, respectively. As a result of findings of the TOGA trial, trastuzumab added to standard chemotherapy is the standard of care in patients with metastatic, HER2-overexpressing GEA. It is common practice in the United States to use the FOLFOX chemotherapy backbone with trastuzumab, again with routine exclusion of the 5-FU bolus, given the better tolerability compared with cisplatin and more convenient 5-FU dosing schedule.[154] The HELOISE study evaluated higher-dose trastuzumab (an 8 mg/kg load followed by 10 mg/kg every 3 weeks) in higher-risk HER2-positive patients with GEA, but it was not more effective than standard dosing.[155]

In contrast to the positive results for trastuzumab in the first-line setting of HER2-positive GEA, two phase III trials evaluating other anti-HER2 therapeutic agents in the first-line setting were negative.

- The first was the LOGIC trial, which evaluated lapatinib, an oral HER2 and EGFR kinase inhibitor, versus placebo added to cisplatin and fluoropyrimidine chemotherapy for first-line therapy and was negative for the primary end point of OS.[156] However, lapatinib increased objective response from 39% to 53% and modestly increased median PFS from 5.4 to 6 months. The absolute level of gene amplification positively correlated with outcome,[157] as previously described,[158,159] signifying heterogeneity of benefit within the current HER2-positive classification. Recently, the degree of amplification has been shown to correlate closely with absolute protein expression level and to be closely associated with clinical benefit.[160,161] The variations in absolute amplification or expression of patient tumors across various first-line trials, as well as lack of antibody-dependent, cell-mediated cytotoxicity with lapatinib as compared with trastuzumab,[162-164] serve as two potential explanations when contrasting outcomes of ToGA and LOGIC.
- Another first-line study, JACOB,[165] compared pertuzumab, an inhibitor of HER2 dimerization with HER3, in combination with chemotherapy plus trastuzumab, versus chemotherapy plus tratuzumab and placebo, and was negative for improved OS. It is notable, however, that for both arms of this contemporary study of HER2-positive patients, 2-year survival was 30% to 35%, and 3-year survival was 20% to 25% with plateauing of the curve, emphasizing the momentous advance that tratuzumab has had for a significant subset of patients with HER2-positive disease.

There have been no large-scale, second-line or higher studies for only patients with HER2-positive disease failing first-line trastuzumab-based therapy that are confirmed to retain *HER2* amplification. However, in the second-line setting for patients whose HER2-positive disease (as determined by original testing before first-line therapy) failed first-line trastuzumab-based therapy, two phase III studies were conducted and were negative for improved survival.

- The first was the TyTAN study, evaluating lapatinib plus paclitaxel versus paclitaxel alone.[166] Despite the negative outcome in the intention-to-treat population, the subgroup of patients with high HER2 expression (3+ on IHC testing) exhibited a survival benefit with the addition of lapatinib to paclitaxel versus placebo, again supporting the observations that higher-level expression or amplification is more sensitive to anti-HER2 therapy.
- The second large, second-line study, GATSBY, evaluated trastuzumab emtansine, the antibody-drug conjugate combining trastuzumab with the cytotoxic emtansine, a microtubule inhibitor. This study also did not show an improved survival compared with taxane (choice of paclitaxel or docetaxel) therapy.[167]

Together, the results of these studies demonstrate no evidence to support continuing HER2 blockade beyond progression in GEA, based on HER2 status derived at diagnosis of advanced disease before first-line therapy. However, conversion of previously HER2-positive to HER2-negative disease is becoming a recognized possibility in approximately 15% to 70% of cases, depending on the report.[168-171] In one recent phase II study, T-ACT, 69% of patients who underwent biopsy just before starting second-line therapy no longer had *HER2* amplification, despite being HER2-positive before first-line therapy.[171] The assumption that "once HER2 positive always HER2 positive" in GEA is clearly erroneous and likely led to a number of patients enrolled to TyTAN and GATSBY who no longer had HER2-positive cancer. There remains, then, the question of the utility of continued anti-HER2 therapy for the subset of patients with persistently positive HER2 tumors after failure of first-line anti-HER2 therapy, and this is an area of continued interest and future studies.

Though HER2 overexpression as a consequence of gene amplification predicts benefit from trastuzumab in the first-line setting, the definition of positivity and trial inclusion criteria within HER2-selecting trials have evolved over time. Current clinical diagnostic testing requires evaluation by a combination of IHC (membranous reactivity in > 10% of cancer cells in a surgical specimen or a cluster of at least five cells in a biopsy specimen), and fluorescence in situ hybridization (FISH; with an HER2-to-CEP17 ratio ≥ 2).[172] IHC 0/1+ should be considered negative irrespective of FISH positivity, and IHC3+ is considered positive, whereas IHC2+ requires reflex to FISH assessment. Higher throughput assays, including next-generation sequencing, have emerged with potential to refine diagnostic accuracy as well as having multiplexing capability to assess for other relevant aberrations.[151,173] Assessment of amplification by cell-free DNA is also emerging as a potential noninvasive strategy, as well as potentially for serial assessment of HER2 status over time in a noninvasive manner.[174] Intrapatient molecular heterogeneity at baseline diagnosis is becoming a well-recognized phenomenon, with obvious implications for targeted therapy, including anti-HER2 therapy.[175,176] Consideration of biopsy of a metastatic lesion may assist with optimal targeted-therapy decisions.[175] Similarly, molecular evolution over time with anti-HER2 therapy in the first-line setting, referred to as 'HER2-conversion', may be best identified by repeated testing via tissue or blood biopsy at the time of progression, and this is under investigation.[168]

KEY POINTS

- The addition of trastuzumab to chemotherapy is standard of care in HER2-positive (IHC 3+ or IHC2+/FISH+) metastatic GEA.
- Unfortunately, other HER2 inhibitors, including lapatinib, pertuzumab, and trastuzumab emtansine, have failed in the first- and second-line settings.

VEGFR2. Ramucirumab, a VEGFR2 antibody, demonstrated benefit as monotherapy or in combination with paclitaxel in the second-line setting.[177,178] In the REGARD trial, 472 patients whose disease had not responded to failed first-line fluoropyrimidine and platinum therapy were randomly assigned in a 2:1 ratio to receive single-agent ramucirumab or placebo.[177] Median OS was 5.2 months for the ramucirumab group and 3.8 months for the placebo group. Aside from a higher rate of hypertension, no relevant differences were seen in recorded adverse effects between ramucirumab and placebo. The RAINBOW trial (n = 665 patients) compared second-line therapy with paclitaxel plus placebo with paclitaxel plus ramucirumab for those in whom disease progressed after exposure to a platinum- and fluoropyrimidine-based regimen.[178] OS was 9.6 months in the ramucirumab arm compared with 7.4 months with paclitaxel alone. Patients in the ramucirumab arm had a significantly higher response rate (28% *v* 16%; $P = .001$) and improved PFS (4.4 months *v* 2.9 months; $P < .0001$) than patients in the paclitaxel plus placebo arm. Despite the activity of ramucirumab seen in these second-line–setting therapies in which this was an approved standard option, studies in the first-line setting, including the phase III RAINFALL study and others, did not show benefit to adding ramucirumab to first-line chemotherapy.[179-181] Similarly, the phase III AVAGAST study, in which bevacizumab plus standard chemotherapy was evaluated versus chemotherapy alone, was negative for OS.[182,183]

With the introduction of either standard triplet FLOT chemotherapy or neoadjuvant platinum- and /taxane-based CRT in the perioperative setting for GEA, those patients with quick disease recurrence or progression (defined as < 6 months from the time of completion of surgery or adjuvant therapy) may not be suited for the RAINBOW regimen of paclitaxel plus ramucirumab. This is also the case for those patients who may receive triplet taxane-based first-line therapy as discussed previously or those with limiting oxaliplatin-related neuropathy. In these cases, evidence supports the use of second-line FOLFIRI plus ramucirumab with safety from colon cancer,[184] and retrospective analyses in patients with GEA.[185]

KEY POINT

- The VEGFR antibody ramucirumab has shown efficacy in second-line phase III trials in advanced GEA and is now a standard-care option either alone or with paclitaxel therapy. However, several studies evaluating antiangiogenesis inhibitors in the first-line setting did not show an OS benefit.

Other Targets. Claudins are structural components of tight junctions that seal intercellular space and are overexpressed in GEA. *CLDN18* amplification is found in 3% of patients with GA in the TCGA and 3% of patients also harbor oncogenic gene fusions between *CLDN18* and *ARHGAP26*, an RhoA inhibitor. These fusions impair cell to extracellular membrane adhesion and, in doing so, promote migration. Claudiximab (IMAB362) is a chimeric IgG1 monoclonal antibody against CLDN18.2 that is intended to enhance T-cell infiltration and antibody-dependent, cell-mediated cytotoxicity. The phase II FAST study evaluated claudiximab in combination with EOX first-line therapy in patients with claudin expression > 2+ in ≥ 40% of cells and demonstrated benefits in PFS and OS, most pronounced in those with high expression in > 70% of cells of CLDN18.2.[186] Additional evaluation is planned in a phase III study called SPOTLIGHT (ClinicalTrials.gov identifier: NCT03504397).

EGFR monoclonal antibodies added to chemotherapy in unselected patients did not improve patient survival, including in the two first-line GEA studies, EXPAND with cetuximab and REAL-3 with panitumumab, and the second-line or higher GEC study COG with gefitinib.[187-189] The consistently negative data from these trials confirm there is no role for EGFR inhibitors in GEC, at least in unselected patients.[190,191]

Similarly, MET tyrosine kinase (hepatocyte growth factor receptor,) pathway inhibitors were assessed by selecting MET-expressing tumors in two large, first-line GEA studies. Each study used different diagnostic antibodies and scoring systems, but both evaluated HGF ligand–blocking antibodies.[192,193] The RILOMET-1 study, in which rilotumumab anti-HGF antibody plus first-line ECF therapy was evaluated versus ECF plus placebo, was negative despite a previous positive, randomized phase II study.[194] The METGastric study evaluated the single-arm, anti-MET antibody onartuzumab, which is another ligand-blocking antibody, and was also negative, confirming lack of efficacy of this strategy for GEA.[193] Tumors with *MET* gene amplification remain a small subset that may derive benefit from MET-directed therapies, but these require additional investigation.[195]

Similarly, many other strategies have failed, including mammalian target of rapamycin (mTOR) inhibition,[196,197] PARP inhibition,[198] matrix metalloproteinase inhibition,[193] STAT3 inhibition,[194] and others. Combinations of inadequate selection of the appropriate patients along with unsuccessful therapeutic efficacy are themes of these failed targeted therapy strategies, no doubt compounded by intrapatient molecular heterogeneity.[175]

Immunotherapy

Immunotherapy with the anti–PD-1 monoclonal antibody pembrolizumab has become standard for GEA in two settings to date: in the second-line setting or higher for MSI-H tumors,[199] and in the third-line setting and higher for PD-L1–positive tumors.[200] An unprecedented approval of pembrolizumab was made for any solid tumor harboring MSI-H, including GEA. Although this genomic event is relatively rare in advanced GEA, amounting to only 2% to 3% of stage IV cases, the response rate is 45% to 60% for monotherapy pembrolizumab, with long-lasting control and, therefore, a preferred standard option in the second-line setting for this subset of tumors.

The KEYNOTE-059 trial evaluated pembrolizumab in the third-line setting or higher in patients in a single-arm study with both PD-L1–negative and -positive tumors, on the basis of the prior success of the pilot KEYNOTE-012 trial.[200,201] Of note, the definition of PD-L1 positivity in this study used the pharmDx IHC assay (PD-L1 IHC 22C3) and determined PD-L1 positivity on the basis of the CPS assessment of tumor cells and tumor-infiltrating lymphocytes. The KEYNOTE-059 study considered patients' tumors to be PD-L1 positive if CPS was ≥ 1, which amounts to approximately 50% to 60% of patients. The CPS may aid prediction of response to therapy, given that the CPS incorporates assessment of the tumor microenvironment in addition to actual tumor cells.[200] In the KEYNOTE-059 study, patients with MSS and PD-L1–positive tumors achieved a response rate of 13.3%, leading to FDA approval on September 22, 2017, for pembrolizumab therapy for these patients. In a strictly Asian phase III study, ATTRACTION-02, 493 patients with advanced GEA whose disease had progressed while receiving two or more lines of therapy were treated with nivolumab, an anti–PD-1 monoclonal antibody, or placebo, and demonstrated significant efficacy over control in all patients without specific biomarker selection, with a median OS of 5.3 months versus 4.14 months with placebo. This study enrolled only Asian patients, and nivolumab has not been approved in western countries to date.[202] A third study, JAVELIN-300, of patients in the third-line therapy setting evaluated avelumab, an anti–PD-L1 antibody, compared with physician's choice of either irinotecan or taxane therapy.[203] This study, unfortunately, demonstrated worse survival compared with control chemotherapy, including in PD-L1–positive tumors.

In the second-line setting, unfortunately, the KEYNOTE-061 study evaluating pembrolizumab versus paclitaxel was negative in the original intention-to-treat population (all patients), as well as in the amended primary end point of PD-L1 positivity (CPS >1).[204] Interestingly, an unplanned subgroup analysis of CPS ≥ 10, amounting to approximately 15% of patients, demonstrated survival benefit, and this has also recently been reported for esophageal SCC in the KEYNOTE 181 study, as noted previously, but did not appear to show benefit in the esophageal AC subset even if CPS >10.[145,148]

In the first-line setting, the three-arm KEYNOTE-062 study of cisplatin and a fluoropyrimidine with pembroluzmab or placebo or pembrolizumab open-label monotherapy in patients with PD-L1 CPS ≥ 1 failed to demonstrate superiority of those treatments over chemotherapy alone.[205] In the comparison of chemotherapy with or without pembrolizumab, there was no difference in survival in either the intention-to-treat PD-L1 (CPS ≥ 1) or the amended, preplanned CPS ≥ 10 groups. Survival was not improved in the pembrolizumab monotherapy arm compared with chemotherapy alone in either tumors with PD-L1 CPS ≥ 1 or the CPS ≥ 10 groups. There appeared to be worse survival with pembrolizumab in a subset of patients, and a better survival in a different subset of patients. Studies suggest that anti–PD-1/PD-L1 checkpoint agents do have modest activity in GEA, but the effect is more pronounced in a small subset of patients appropriately selected by biomarkers.[206] These subsets including MSI-H tumors. In addition, the greater the PD-L1 expression, the greater the probability of benefit.

KEY POINTS

- The first tumor-agnostic FDA drug approval was granted on May 23, 2017, for pembrolizumab for treatment of patients with unresectable or metastatic, MSI-H or mismatch repair deficient (dMMR) solid tumors, including GEA.
- Pembrolizumab has demonstrated efficacy in the third-line or higher setting of GEA having PD-L1 CPS ≥ 1 and received conditional FDA approval on September 22, 2017. The ATTRACTION-02 study demonstrated improved survival of nivolumab compared with placebo in the third-line setting in Asian patients only, and, therefore, has not been approved by the FDA. The third-line JAVELIN-300 study, comparing avelumab versus irinotecan or taxane, demonstrated worse survival with avelumab. With recent approvals of several options simultaneously, the optimal sequencing of third-line therapies including chemotherapy (irinotecan or taxane), trifluridine/tipiracil, or pembrolizumab (for PD-L1 CPS > 1 only) remains unknown.
- The phase III, randomized, KEYNOTE-181 second-line study evaluated the anti-PD1 antibody pembrolizumab versus paclitaxel for esophageal cancer, and significant improvement in survival was noted only in esophageal SCCs with tumors having PD-L1 CPS ≥ 10, which led to FDA approval for this subgroup of patients on July 30, 2019. The randomized, phase III, second-line

ATTRACTION-3 study of anti-PD1 antibody nivolumab versus taxane also demonstrated improved survival in advanced esophageal SCC.

- The KEYNOTE-062 study in the first-line setting failed to show a benefit of pembrolizumab added to chemotherapy versus chemotherapy alone, in either the intention-to-treat PD-L1 CPS ≥ 1 or the amended, preplanned CPS ≥ 10 groups. Pembrolizumab monotherapy appears to have benefit in a subset of patients, whereas a different subset appears to have worse outcome, compared with standard chemotherapy. Additional work in delineating which patients (eg, those with MSI-H tumors) will benefit from earlier implementation of anti–PD-1 therapies is ongoing, as are other studies like Checkmate 649, in which FOLFOX with or without nivolumab is being evaluated.

PALLIATIVE CARE FOR PATIENTS WITH ADVANCED GEC

It is important to monitor and maintain patients' nutritional status in light of weight loss and continued difficulty with alimentation before and during perioperative treatment and surgery, as well as in the advanced metastatic setting. To palliate tumor-related esophageal or gastric outlet obstruction in the advanced setting, several palliative options exist including radiation, esophageal stents, laser therapy, endoscopic dilation, and/or gastric or jejunal tube feeding. However, > 80% of patients derive benefit from systemic palliative chemotherapy. Therefore, chemotherapy could be administered first, then radiation or stenting in the event of refractory symptoms, either if chemorefractory at the outset, or if symptoms developed at some point after an initial response to chemotherapy (which could be several months or even years later). For refractory bleeding from the primary tumor, endoscopic cautery, interventional radiology embolization, and RT are all options to address this not uncommon issue. Because thromboembolic events are common in advanced disease, balancing anticoagulation and intact primary tumors often is challenging and clinical discretion as to the more pressing issue is recommended. Oral anticoagulants lead to higher risk of bleeding compared with subcutaneous low-molecular-weight heparin, if the primary tumor is in place, and this should be considered when treating thromboembolic events. Carcinomatosis and ascites are common with GEC, particularly gastric AC, and partial or complete bowel obstructions are frequently experienced by patients with these conditions. Venting gastrostomy tube, peritoneal drain placement, and somatostatin analogs can be palliative in this subset of patients, particularly if symptoms are refractory to a trial of palliative first-line chemotherapy.[207] Having patients see palliative care doctors to manage the diverse set of these cancer-related symptoms and pain is encouraged, as is seeing a nutritionist to assist with dietary issues. Oxaliplatin-induced neuropathy is common, and duloxetine has demonstrated palliative benefit. OPTIMOX strategy (ie, intermittently adding and stopping oxaliplatin over time to limit cumulative neuropathy), as described in colon cancer, is often routinely used in patients with GEA. Recent approvals of immune checkpoint blockade require consideration of all potential toxicities and treatments related to them.

CANCERS OF THE LIVER AND BILIARY TREE

HEPATOCELLULAR CARCINOMA

Epidemiology and Etiology

Primary hepatobiliary cancers, which include hepatocellular carcinomas (HCCs), cholangiocarcinomas, and gallbladder cancers, represent the highest global incidence of solid-organ tumors and are responsible for approximately 1 million deaths annually, although they are uncommon in western cultures (particularly HCCs).[11] The risk factors for HCC are well known (Table 13-2) and include cirrhosis of any etiology. Hepatitis B virus infections account for approximately 60% of all liver cancer incidence in developing countries and for approximately 23% of liver cancer in developed countries; the corresponding percentages for hepatitis C virus infections are 33% in developing countries and 20% in developed countries. Hepatitis B infection can be decreased by vaccination. Hepatitis C now has effective therapy to eradicate the viral infection, which may lead to fewer cases of HCC in the coming years. In the United States and several other western countries with low-risk populations, alcohol-related cirrhosis and, possibly, nonalcoholic fatty liver disease, associated with obesity, are thought to account for most liver cancers. The total mortality from HCC in the United States has been increasing due alcohol-related cirrhosis and, possibly, nonalcoholic fatty liver disease, despite the encouraging reduction in mortality associated with hepatitis C virus–related HCC.

Table 13-2 **Risk Factors for Hepatocellular Carcinoma**

Risk Factor
Hepatitis B and C infection
Excessive alcohol consumption
Autoimmune hepatitis
Nonalcoholic fatty liver disease
Primary biliary cirrhosis
Androgenic steroids
Aflatoxins
Tobacco use
Nitrosylated compounds
Thorotrast
Hemochromatosis
α-1 antitrypsin deficiency
Wilson disease
Porphyria
Glycogen-storage disease

Clinical Presentation and Diagnosis

There is a protean array of presentations of HCC, from asymptomatic disease found at screening to decompensated cirrhosis or paraneoplastic syndromes. Guidelines disseminated from several consensus conferences and professional organizations have recommended HCC surveillance in patients with cirrhosis who are at high risk for development of HCC.[208] Ultrasound and serum α-fetoprotein (AFP) are the most commonly used modalities for HCC surveillance. Data suggest that an elevated subfraction of AFP, the lens culinaris agglutinin-reactive fraction of AFP-L3%, is a more reliable indicator of the presence of a HCC in combination with CT scan or magnetic resonance imaging (MRI) in patients with hepatitis C–related cirrhosis than is the total AFP.[209] Making the diagnosis with imaging alone versus with a confirmatory biopsy has long been deliberated, and debate remains whether to routinely incorporate biopsy into standard diagnostic practices.[210-212]

HCC is graded as well differentiated, moderately well differentiated, and poorly differentiated. The most important pathologic issue is the distinction between the fibrolamellar variant and the more traditional HCC. Fibrolamellar cancer is generally seen in younger patients, is much more likely to be resectable, and is less commonly associated with infection or cirrhosis.[213] In contrast, traditional HCC is found more often in men older than 65 years.

KEY POINT

- HCC is an important cancer and global incidence can be reduced by vaccination against hepatitis B virus; treatment of hepatitis C is curative, which may lead to reduced incidence of HCC in the coming years.

Treatment

Localized HCC. The Barcelona-Clinic Liver Cancer staging classification and treatment schedule has served as a paradigm on how to stage and treat HCC.[214] The treatment of choice for patients with localized HCC is surgical resection or transplantation. However, resection is not possible in most cases, and transplantation is limited by organ availability. Less than 25% of the tumors are resectable, often because of underlying liver disease and inadequate hepatic reserve.[215] The predominant reasons for nonresectability are the multifocal nature of the disease in the liver and detection late in the disease course, the latter of which occurs because of the long, asymptomatic latency until diagnosis. Attempts at administration of systemic cytotoxic chemotherapy have been unsuccessful in demonstrating improvement in survival in patients with localized disease. Nonetheless, locally ablative chemoembolization (transcatheter arterial chemoembolization [TACE]) has proven to be useful and has been associated with improved outcome in randomized trials. Locally ablative treatments are generally reserved for unresectable, localized disease. These approaches include TACE, transarterial radioembolization, alcohol injection, radiofrequency ablation, and external beam radiotherapy or stereotactic radiotherapy. In a recent meta-analysis of three randomized studies, transarterial radioembolization and TACE resulted in similar outcomes in unresectable HCC.[216] Percutaneous ablation achieves complete remission (CR) in > 80% of tumors < 3 cm in diameter, but in only 50% of tumors of 3 to 5 cm.[217] Although these response rates are high, it is unclear whether these techniques result in a survival benefit. A pooled analysis of eight comparative studies suggested that radiofrequency ablation was superior to other locally percutaneous ablative techniques.

For the subset of patients who can undergo surgical resection or ablation with curative intent, there is currently no benefit to adjuvant systemic therapy. On the basis of the benefits of sorafenib, an oral inhibitor of VEGFR and *Raf* in the advanced setting, the STORM trial tested whether patients would benefit from sorafenib after resection or ablation; there were no differences in recurrence-free survival or OS.[218]

Liver transplantation represents the ultimate local therapy for nonmetastatic or liver-only unresectable HCC. For patients with substantial cirrhosis, liver transplantation provides an excellent option for early-stage tumors because the procedure is therapeutic for both the cancer and for the underlying pathology. Once patients have passed the high-risk peritransplantation phase, the prognosis is similar to that for patients who have had resection of more localized disease.[219] Patients with known extrahepatic disease and gross vascular invasion are not candidates for liver transplantation.

KEY POINTS

- The Barcelona-Clinic Liver Cancer staging classification and treatment schedule has served as a paradigm on how to stage and treat HCC.
- Locally ablative treatments are generally reserved for unresectable, localized disease. These approaches include TACE, transarterial radioembolization, alcohol injection, radiofrequency ablation, and EBRT or stereotactic radiotherapy.

Advanced HCC. There is no role for systemic cytotoxic chemotherapy for advanced unresectable disease; it has not demonstrated improved survival compared with best supportive care. First-line therapy for advanced, unresectable HCC with sorafenib was approved by FDA in 2007 on the basis of results from the SHARP trial (Table 13-3).[220] Similar findings were observed in the parallel Asian study.[220,221] Diarrhea, weight loss, hand-foot skin reaction, and hypophosphatemia were more common than in control subjects receiving placebo in these studies. Because both studies included only patients with Child-Pugh class A disease (Table 13-4), questions regarding the activity and tolerability of sorafenib in patients with more severe liver dysfunction have been raised. In clinical practice, generally patients with Child-Pugh class A and perhaps class B7 scores should be routinely considered for sorafenib therapy. However, a prospective, noninterventional study, Global Investigation of Therapeutic Decisions in Hepatocellular

Table 13-3 Current Clinical Trials Paradigm for Hepatocellular Carcinoma

Treatment Line	Outcome	Notes	Study
First			
Sorafenib *v* placebo	Superiority study	First approved first-line therapy, December 1, 2007	SHARP study[220]
Lenvatinib *v* Sorafenib	Noninferiority study	Approved August 16, 2018	REFLECT study[220]
Atezolizumab plus bevacizumab *v* Sorafenib	Superiority Study	FDA approval submitted 2/2020	IMbrave 150 study[228b]
Second			
Regorafenib *v* Placebo	Superiority study	First approved second-line therapy, April 27, 2017	RESOURCE study[229]
Ramucirumab *v* Placebo	Superiority study	AFP ≥ 400 ng/mL eligible; approval pending	REACH-2 study[231]
Nivolumab		Conditional approval September 22, 2017	Checkmate040 study[236]
Pembrolizumab		Conditional approval December 17, 2018	Keynote 224 study[240]
Second and Third			
Cabozantinib *v* placebo	Superiority study	Approved January 14, 2019	CELESTIAL study[233]

Abbreviation: AFP, α-fetoprotein.

Carcinoma, created a large, global database of > 3,000 patients with unresectable HCC treated with sorafenib. The database has enabled evaluation of a broad assessment including patients with Child-Pugh class B disease with more advanced liver dysfunction.[222] Per the report, safety and dosing during treatment were generally consistent across patients irrespective of liver function, although, as expected, liver function was a strong prognostic factor.

It is unclear at this point whether the observed efficacy of sorafenib is more related to its VEGFR–, *Raf*–, or other inhibitory capacity. In the last decade, contemporary trials focusing on targeted therapies, including antiangiogenesis, signal transduction inhibitors, and immune checkpoint inhibitors, either as single agents or in combinations, have led to significant progress compared with treatment with sorafenib. Interestingly, several other multitargeted tyrosine kinase inhibitors with antiangiogenic activity have been inferior to sorafenib in head-to-head studies, including sunitinib,[223] brivanib in the BRISK-FL study,[224] and linifanib.[225] Combinations of sorafenib with erlotinib (an anti-EGFR tyrosine kinase) in the SEARCH study or with everolimus were also negative.[226,227] Recently, in the REFLECT study, lenvantinib appeared to be noninferior, but with less toxicity and higher response rate, lenvantinib has become a preferred choice for the treatment of first-line HCC.[228]

In the second-line and subsequent settings, a flurry of recent positive studies has dramatically changed the treatment landscape of HCC (Table 13-3). Regorafenib was examined against best supportive care in second-line treatment of patients who had advanced HCC that progressed or were intolerant to sorafenib in the RESOURCE study.[229] Patients who received regorafenib for 21 days and then had 7 days of no treatment experienced a median OS of 10.6 months, versus 7.8 months with placebo (HR, 0.63; 95% CI, 0.5 to 0.79; $P < .0001$), which led to FDA approval on April 27, 2017.[229] The most common, clinically relevant grade 3 or 4 treatment-emergent events were hypertension (n = 57 patients [15%] in the regorafenib group *v* nine patients [5%] in the placebo group), hand-foot skin reaction (n = 47 patients [13%] *v* one [1%]), fatigue (n = 34

Table 13-4 Child-Pugh Scoring System

Measure	1 Point	2 Points	3 Points
Total bilirubin, pmol/L (mg/dL)	< 34 (< 2)	34-50 (2-3)	> 50 (> 3)
Serum albumin, g/dL	> 3.5	2.8-3.5	< 2.8
PT INR	< 1.7	1.71-2.30	> 2.30
Ascites	None	Mild	Moderate to severe
Hepatic encephalopathy	None	Grades I to II (or suppressed with medication)	Grades III to IV (or refractory)

NOTE. Chronic liver disease is classified into Child-Pugh class A to C, by adding the points: A = 5 to 6, B = 7 to 9, C = 10 to 15. The score uses five clinical measures of liver disease. Each measure is scored 1 to 3, with 3 indicating the most severe derangement.
Abbreviation: PT INR, prothrombin time international normalized ratio.

patients [9%] *v* nine patients [5%]), and diarrhea (n = 12 patients [3%] *v* no patients). The REACH phase III study evaluated the efficacy of the anti-VEGFR2 monoclonal antibody ramucirumab (8 mg/kg) administered intravenously every 2 weeks in patients with HCC whose disease progressed on prior sorafenib therapy. In the intention-to-treat population, the median OS was improved with ramucirumab compared with placebo, but the difference was not statistically significant (9.2 *v* 7.6 months; *P* = .1391).[230] However, a prespecified subset analysis demonstrated a significant median OS benefit of 7.8 months for patients with an AFP level ≥ 400 ng/mL who were treated with ramucirumab compared with 4.2 months for patients treated with placebo (HR, 0.67; 95% CI, 0.51 to 0.90; *P* = .0059). Indeed, in the follow-up REACH-2 phase III study, 292 patients with an AFP level ≥ 400 ng/mL were randomly assigned 2:1 to ramucirumab (n = 197) or placebo (n = 95).[231] Ramucirumab treatment significantly improved median OS to 8.5 months versus 7.3 months compared with placebo (HR, 0.71; 95% CI, 0.531 to 0.949; *P* = .0199), which led to approval in this indication on May 10, 2019. Grade 3 or worse treatment-emergent adverse events that occurred in at least 5% of patients in either group were hypertension (n = 25 [13%] in the ramucirumab group *v* five [5%] in the placebo group), hyponatremia (n = 11 [6%] *v* 0), and increased aspartate aminotransferase level (n = 6 [3%] *v* 5 [5%]). Serious adverse events of any grade and cause occurred in 68 patients (35%) in the ramucirumab group and 28 patients (29%) in the placebo group. A pooled analysis of patients with AFP level ≥ 400 ng/mL (n = 542) from the REACH and REACH-2 studies demonstrated improved median survival to 8.1 months from 5.0 months with placebo (HR, 0.694; 95% CI, 0.571 to 0.842; *P* = .0002).[232] The CELESTIAL phase III study evaluated 707 patients who were randomly assigned in a 2:1 ratio to receive oral cabozantinib (60 mg once daily) or matching placebo, which led to FDA approval on January 14, 2019.[233] Eligible patients had received previous treatment with sorafenib, had disease progression after at least one systemic treatment for HCC, and may have received up to two previous systemic regimens for advanced HCC. At the second planned interim analysis, the median OS was 10.2 months with cabozantinib versus 8.0 months with placebo (HR, 0.76; 95% CI, 0.63 to 0.92; *P* = .005). Most patients had only one prior systemic therapy (72%) compared with two prior systemic therapies (27%), with more pronounced OS benefit in the second line (HR, 0.74; 95% CI, 0.59 to 0.92) compared with third line (HR, 0.9; 95% CI, 0.63 to 1.29). Grade 3 or 4 adverse events occurred in 68% of patients in the cabozantinib group and 36% in the placebo group. The most common high-grade adverse events were palmar–plantar erythrodysesthesia (17% with cabozantinib *v* 0% with placebo), hypertension (16% *v* 2%), increased aspartate aminotransferase level (12% *v* 7%), fatigue (10% *v* 4%), and diarrhea (10% *v* 2%). Unfortunately, there have been a number of negative phase III studies evaluating targeted therapies in the second-line setting compared with placebo of other kinase inhibitors, including brivanib in the BRISK-PS study,[234] as well as tivantinib in patients with Met-expressing tumors by IHC.[235]

Finally, two immune checkpoint inhibitors have been conditionally approved in the second-line setting of HCC on the basis of results of single-arm phase II studies. Approval of nivolumab, an anti–PD-1 inhibitor, was based on a 154-patient subgroup of CHECKMATE-040, a multicenter, open-label, phase I and phase II dose-escalation trial conducted in patients with HCC and Child-Pugh class A cirrhosis whose disease progressed while receiving sorafenib treatment or who were intolerant to sorafenib.[236] Approval of pembrolizumab, also a PD-1 inhibitor, was also based on results of KEYNOTE 224, a single-arm, multicenter trial enrolling 104 patients with HCC. Toxicity for both nivolumab and pembrolizumab were similar to those reported previously in other approved tumor types. Unfortunately, in a follow-up randomized phase III study, KEYNOTE 240, pembrolizumab did not improve survival significantly compared with placebo.[237] In that study, 413 patients were randomly assigned 2:1 (n = 278 patients received pembrolizumab and n = 135 received placebo). The HR for OS was 0.78 and progression-free survival (PFS) was 0.78 in favor of pembrolizumab; however, these differences did not meet significance per the prespecified statistical plan.

In the first-line setting, phase Ib study cohort, patients with unresectable or metastatic HCC received first-line treatment with atezolizumab (a PD-L1 inhibitor) at 1,200 mg plus bevacizumab 15 mg/kg intravenously every 3 weeks until loss of clinical benefit or unacceptable toxicity. For the primary end point of response rate, 34% of patient achieved response, with responses observed in all clinically relevant subgroups, including patients with AFP level ≥ 400 ng/mL, extrahepatic spread, and/or macrovascular invasion. Of 23 confirmed responses, 19 were ongoing (≥ 6 months in 11 patients). The 6-month PFS rate was 71% and median duration of response (range, 1.6+ to 22.0+ months) and median OS were not yet been reached. Unfortunately, CheckMate 469, a randomized study of the anti-PD1 antibody nivolumab compared with sorefenib in the first-line setting in 1,009 patients with unresectable HCC, did not meet its primary end point of OS.[238]

Immunotherapy has great promise in HCC, with improved response rates and impressive duration of response in those having response. However, to date, monotherapy checkpoint blockade has not demonstrated definitive benefit in all patients in larger, phase III, randomized studies compared with sorafenib in first-line or placebo in second-line settings. Biomarkers to identify those who may derive the most benefit are ongoing. A number of phase III first- and later-line studies of various combinations are ongoing or completed.[228b]

With the recent simultaneous approvals of several therapies in the same second-line indication, as well as levantinib in the first-line setting, the optimal sequencing of these therapies is not well established (Table 13-3). Moreover, several ongoing phase III studies are evaluating these agents in the first-line setting, including immune checkpoint inhibitors either alone or in combination with anti–PD-1 plus anti-CTLA4, or in combination with antiangiogenic monoclonal antibodies or tyrosine kinase inhibitors like bevacizumab, sorafenib, or lenvantinib.

The findings are eagerly awaited and likely will change the treatment paradigm further.

KEY POINTS

- The SHARP study established the first standard systemic therapy of oral sorafenib for HCC.[220]
- The RESORCE study confirmed the benefit of regorafenib in second-line treatment compared with placebo for advanced HCC, which led to FDA approval on April 27, 2017.[230]
- The REFLECT study confirmed noninferiority of lenvatinib in first-line treatment compared with sorafenib for advanced HCC, which led to FDA approval on August 16, 2018.[228]
- The CELESTIAL study confirmed the benefit of cabozantinib in second- and third-line treatment compared with placebo for advanced HCC, which led to FDA approval on January 14, 2019.[233]
- The REACH-2 study confirmed the benefit of ramucirumab in the second-line treatment of patients with AFP level > 400ng/mL compared with placebo for advanced HCC, which led to approval in this indication on May 10, 2019. [239]
- The CHECKMATE-040 study demonstrated efficacy of the anti-PD1 antibody nivolumab in a second-line, single-arm study for advanced HCC, which led to accelerated conditional approval on September 22, 2017. [236] However, the follow-up, randomized, phase III, first-line CHECKMATE-459 study of nivolumab versus sorafenib did not show significantly improved survival.[238]
- The KEYNOTE 224 study demonstrated efficacy of the anti-PD1 antibody pembrolizumab in a second-line, single-arm study for advanced HCC leading to accelerated conditional approval on November 9, 2018. [240]However, the follow-up, randomized, phase III, second-line KEYNOTE-240 study of pembrolizumab versus placebo did not show significantly improved survival.[237]
- Immunotherapy with checkpoint blockade has great promise in HCC, with improved response rates and impressive duration of response in those having response with anti-PD1 monotherapy. However, to date, treatment with monotherapy checkpoint blockade has not demonstrated definitive survival benefit in all patients in larger, phase III, randomized studies compared with sorafenib in the first-line setting or placebo in the second-line setting. Biomarkers to identify those who may derive the most benefit are ongoing.
- The treatment paradigm of advanced HCC is in flux with the addition of all of these agents relatively simultaneously without direction on the best sequencing approach. Several first-line phase III studies with immune checkpoint inhibitors and various combinations of tyrosine kinase inhibitors are ongoing and will possibly change the paradigm in the coming years.
- The IMbrave150 study confirmed benefit of atezolizumab plus bevacizumab in first-line treatment compared to sorafenib for advanced HCC.[228b]

BILIARY CANCERS

Epidemiology and Etiology

Biliary tract cancers include a diverse group of cancers, including intrahepatic cholangiocarcinoma (IHCC), hilar cholangiocarcinoma, extrahepatic cholangiocarcinoma (EHCC), and gallbladder cancer (Fig 13-4). Historically, these were considered a uniform entity, but they now are recognized to be quite distinct in terms of etiology, molecular biology, and, most recently, treatment.[241-245] In western countries, cholangiocarcinoma is associated with metabolic syndrome, inflammatory bowel disease, primary sclerosing cholangitis, and hepatolithiasis, whereas the liver fluke and hepatitis B virus are important risk factors in Asian countries.[246,247] Cholangiocarcinoma is most common in women older than 50 years, and long-term survival is highly dependent on the effectiveness of surgical therapy. A number of risk factors for gallbladder cancer have been described and include:[248]

- obesity,
- female sex,
- family history,
- middle age,
- gallstones causing chronic inflammation,
- porcelain gallbladder (ie, hardened gallbladder due to calcium deposits),
- ethnicity (highest in Mexican, Lain Americans, and Native Americans),
- choledochal cysts (ie, bile-filled sacs along the common bile duct),
- gallbladder polyps,
- abnormalities of the bile ducts causing backflow, and
- primary sclerosing cholangitis.[248]

Recent molecular studies have demonstrated distinct molecular profiles between the anatomic sites and geographic or etiologic subsets.[249-252] Cancers of the extrahepatic bile duct and gallbladder are relatively rare, with only 11,740 cases diagnosed annually in the United States, resulting in approximately 3,830 deaths annually.[253] The low mortality rate for biliary cancers overall can be explained by the fact that approximately 50% of gallbladder cancers are incidental findings on cholecystectomy, which, because they commonly are diagnosed at an early stage, can have a good prognosis (3-year OS, 70% to 100%).

Unfortunately, US statistics do not give specific numbers for IHCCs but classify them under "hepatobiliary tumors"; the actual incidence of biliary cancers as a whole is definitely higher, perhaps approaching the incidence of esophageal cancers, with approximately 15,000 cases per year.[254] ACs of unknown primary site involving the liver are more commonly recognized as primary IHCCs, which has also led to an increase in incidence of the disease.[255]

CLINICAL PRESENTATION, DIAGNOSIS, AND TREATMENT

Cholangiocarcinomas typically present with jaundice, pain, anorexia, abnormal laboratory test results, or with a mass evident on CT scan or ultrasound or that is visualized endoscopically. Gallbladder cancer often presents as vague postprandial right upper quadrant pain and is diagnosed as gallstones, with incidental finding of gallbladder cancer at the time of resection and/or in the pathology specimen. The location of the primary tumor often dictates which of these symptoms predominantly occur, such as painless jaundice with EHCC that is quite similar that seen with pancreatic cancer.

The primary treatment is surgical resection, if localized and technically feasible. Because of the location of these tumors, they are frequently difficult to resect; therefore, specialized surgical intervention should always be sought. The cure rate for patients with early-stage disease ranges from 60% to 70%; however, for patients with more advanced disease, the 5-year survival rate is only 10% to 25%.[245,256,257] It is important to note that when a gallbladder cancer is found after laparoscopic cholecystectomy, reresection of the adjacent liver segment and lymphadenectomy are indicated for all disease stages except stage I.[258,259]

The role of neoadjuvant or adjuvant therapy with chemotherapy or CRT is not well established; there have been few randomized studies. With respect to chemotherapy alone, in the phase III PRODIGE 12-ACCORD 18 trial, gemcitabine plus oxaliplatin was evaluated and compared with observation in 196 patients randomly assigned 1:1 after curative-intent resection of biliary tract cancers; there was no significant difference in relapse-free survival.[260] However, in the recent BILCAP study,[261] patients with completely resected cholangiocarcinoma or gallbladder carcinoma were randomly assigned 1:1 to capecitabine 1,250 mg/m^2/d (capecitabine given twice daily) or observation. The median OS was 51 (95% CI, 35 to 59) months for capecitabine and 36 (95% CI, 30 to 45) months for observation (HR, 0.80; 95% CI, 0.63 to 1.04; *P* = .097), and although negative in the intent-to-treat analysis, after excluding patients not enrolled and treated per protocol, the difference became significant at 25.9 (95% CI, 19.8 to 46.3) months in the capecitabine group and 17.4 (95% CI, 12.0 to 23.7) months in the observation group.

Although the role of RT—either alone or in combination with chemotherapy—has been evaluated in several studies, which found no substantial benefit,[262,263] the intergroup study S0809 evaluated adjuvant chemotherapy for four cycles of gemcitabine and capecitabine every 21 days followed by concurrent capecitabine and RT in a single-arm study. For all patients, the 2-year survival rate was 65% (95% CI, 53% to 74%); it was 67% and 60% in patients who underwent R0 and R1 surgery, respectively. Median OS was 35 months (R0, 34 months; R1, 35 months). Local, distant, and combined relapse occurred in 14, 24, and nine patients, respectively. Adjuvant therapy is also supported by results of a meta-analysis, which demonstrated that the greatest benefit for adjuvant therapy was in patients with biliary cancers who had lymph node–positive disease (odds ratio, 0.49; *P* = .004) and in those who had a positive microscopic resection margin (odds ratio, 0.36; *P* = .002).[264] A number of web-based nomograms predicting the benefit of adjuvant chemotherapy and CRT have been developed for biliary tract cancers and also for specific subsets (IHCC, hilar cholangiocarcinoma, EHCC, and gallbladder), which can serve as guidelines in the absence of definitive phase III data in this setting.[265-268] However, to our knowledge, there are no randomized studies in the adjuvant setting that have evaluated CRT in resected biliary tract cancers. Despite this, there is consensus that for patients who have undergone resection but with positive microscopic margins, radiation should be included the adjuvant treatment planning.

KEY POINTS

- Resection, when feasible, is the mainstay of treatment hepatobiliary tumors.
- The randomized phase III BILCAP study of adjuvant capecitabine versus observation in resected biliary tract cancer demonstrated improved survival and can be considered a standard of care.
- Therapy in the adjuvant setting, therefore, requires discussion of the paucity of level I evidence for concurrent radiation.
- Neoadjuvant approaches are being studied and may be particularly important for "borderline resectable" disease. Ultimately, localized disease should be discussed in a multidisciplinary tumor board setting to identify the optimal approach for a given patient.

The efficacy of systemic chemotherapy alone in advanced biliary tract cancers is poor, with response rates ranging from 10% to 40% for single-agent and combination chemotherapy regimens.[256] Although the curative-intent surgical approaches for IHCC, EHCC, and gallbladder cancers differ, systemic chemotherapy does not currently distinguish among these anatomically diverse cancers. Most of the regimens used are gemcitabine or fluoropyrimidine based and follow treatment strategies established in pancreatic cancer. A pooled analysis of clinical trials in biliary cancers documented higher response rates and longer time to tumor progression for gemcitabine-based combination regimens with fluoropyrimidines and with platinum agents than for gemcitabine alone.[256] The phase III trial, the ABC-02 (Advanced Biliary Cancer) trial, randomly assigned 410 patients with advanced biliary tract cancers to receive first-line gemcitabine 1,000 mg/m^2 on days 1, 8, and 15 every 4 weeks for six cycles or gemcitabine 1,000 mg/m^2 plus cisplatin 25 mg/m^2 on days 1 and 8 every 3 weeks for eight cycles.[269] The addition of low-dose cisplatin did not result in significant differences in grade 3 or 4 toxicities. The PFS was

8.4 months in the gemcitabine and cisplatin arm and 6.5 months in the gemcitabine- only arm (HR, 0.72; 95% CI, 0.57 to 0.90; P = .003). This translated into an OS benefit, with median OS of 11.7 months in the gemcitabine and cisplatin arm compared with 8.3 months in the gemcitabine-only arm (HR, 0.70; 95% CI, 0.54 to 0.89; P = .002). Adverse events were similar in the two groups, with the exception of more neutropenia in the cisplatin plus gemcitabine group; the number of neutropenia-associated infections was similar in the two groups. This trial established combined gemcitabine and cisplatin as a new standard of care in the treatment of advanced biliary cancers. Gemcitabine plus oxaliplatin has been studied, and oxaliplatin may be substituted in patients who are not candidates for cisplatin therapy.[270]

Recently, molecular profiling has revealed targeted therapeutic options for cholangiocarcinoma, particularly IHCC with MSI-H, *FGFR2* fusions (15% of patients), *BRAF* mutation (5% of patients), and *IDH1* mutation (15% of patients).[252,271] The second- or third-line, randomized, phase III ClaIDHy study of the IDH1 inhibitor ivosidnib versus placebo for *IDH1*-mutant cholangiocarcinoma met its primary end point of PFS, and also reported improved quality of life.[272] Other molecular subsets of IHCC have demonstrated promise in phase II nonrandomized studies, including from the ROAR basket study using the combination of the anti-BRAF and anti-MEK agents vemurafenib and trametinib, respectively, for *BRAF*-mutant tumors[273] and the FIGHT-202 study of the anti-FGFR2 agent pemibatinib for *FGFR2* fusion.[274-279]

KEY POINTS

- The combination of gemcitabine and platinum combination therapy, based on the ABC-02 study, is a standard-of-care treatment option for patients with advanced biliary tree cancers.
- The second- or third-line randomized phase III ClaIDHy study of the IDH1 inhibitor ivosidnib versus placebo for *IDH1*-mutant cholangiocarcinoma met its primary end point of PFS and also reported improved quality of life.
- The first tumor-agnostic FDA drug approval was granted May 23, 2017, for pembrolizumab for patients with unresectable or metastatic, MSI-H or dMMR solid tumors, including biliary tract cancers.
- Other molecular subsets of IHCC have demonstrated promise in phase II nonrandomized studies, including from the ROAR basket study using the combination of anti-BRAF and anti-MEK agents vemurafenib and trametinib, respectively, for *BRAF*-mutant tumors and the FIGHT-202 study of anti-FGFR2 agent pemibatinib for FGFR2 fusion.

PANCREATIC CANCER

EPIDEMIOLOGY AND ETIOLOGY

Exocrine pancreatic cancer is a substantial health problem in the United States, with an annual incidence of 56,770 cases and death occurring in 45,750 patients annually, with only 9% surviving 5 years. Rates are better for those with localized disease, for whom the 5-year survival rate is > 35%, but they are still dismal for those with metastatic disease, with a 5-year survival of only 3%.[280] The nonhereditary risk factors for pancreatic cancers include older age, diabetes, chronic pancreatitis, intraductal pancreatic mucinous neoplasms, cigarette smoking, obesity, physical inactivity, and a diet high in saturated fats.[281] More recent data suggest pathogenic germline alterations may be present in up to 20% of unselected exocrine pancreatic cancers and has led to the recommendation for universal testing of patients with pancreatic cancer for germline mutations regardless of family history.[282] Common germline mutations and associated genomic syndromes are listed in Table 13-5. There is no agreed upon approach for screening patients for pancreatic cancer with an identified germline mutation, but screening typically involves alternating magnetic resonance cholangiopancreatography and endoscopic ultrasound procedures. Several ongoing trials are attempting to define the best screening algorithms.

There is no standard surveillance or screening for pancreatic cancer. Pancreatic intraepithelial neoplasias, which are microscopic lesions of the pancreas, and intraductal papillary mucinous neoplasms and mucinous cystic neoplasms, which are both macroscopic lesions often found incidentally during imaging for other reasons, are thought to be precursors of invasive pancreatic cancer, especially those involving the main pancreatic duct.[283,284] The American Gastroenterological Association has issued management guidelines for these lesions.[285] More than 90% of pancreatic cancers harbor activating genetic mutations of the oncogene *KRAS*, which is integrated in signaling pathways of various receptor kinases, such as EGFR and the insulin-like growth factor receptor I. In addition, > 50% of pancreatic cancers harbor mutations in at least one of three tumor suppressor genes: *p16/CDKN2A*, *TP53*, and *SMAD4* (previously known as *DPC4*). *BRCA* mutations are less common and found in approximately 5% of pancreatic cancers, but they recently have been found to have therapeutic implications, as will be discussed in more detail in this section under Frontline Therapy.[283,284]

Table 13-5 Germline Mutations Associated With Pancreatic Cancer

Mutated Gene	Syndrome
BRCA1, BRCA2	Hereditary breast and ovarian syndrome
ATM	Ataxia-telangiectasia
PALB2	Hereditary breast cancer
PRSS1	Hereditary pancreatitis
STK11	Peutz-Jaghers
CDKN2A	Familial atypical multiple mole and melanoma syndrome
MLH1, MLH2, MSH6	Lynch syndrome

CLINICAL PRESENTATION AND DIAGNOSIS

Symptoms associated with pancreatic cancer at the time of presentation commonly include abdominal pain with or without back pain, cachexia, and/or jaundice. Initial symptoms are often vague and can vary based on location, with pancreatic head lesions more likely to cause jaundice, and tail lesions, which often can be asymptomatic and, thus, delay diagnosis. When evaluating patients with adult-onset diabetes without other risk factors or worsening diabetes without an obvious cause, physicians should consider pancreatic cancer as a possible diagnosis.[286]

The most common diagnostic tests used for pancreatic cancer are triple-phase CT scan so arterial and venous structures are clearly evaluable, MRI, EUS, and endoscopic retrograde cholangiopancreatography. Tissue is best obtained by EUS-guided biopsy and, for those patients presenting with biliary obstruction and not planned for immediate surgery, placement of a biliary stent. Although pancreatic cancer is staged using the standard TNM methodology, in practice, it is often classified as resectable, borderline resectable, locally advanced unresectable, or metastatic (Fig 13-5).

KEY POINTS

- Exocrine pancreatic cancer is a common disease with incidence nearly equaling the mortality rate and 5-year survival rate of < 10%.
- Several lifestyle risk factors have been associated with the risk of pancreatic cancer.
- Current guidelines recommend that all patients diagnosed with pancreatic cancer should be evaluated for germline mutations found in as many as 20% of patients.
- Best surveillance screening for affected relatives continues to be the subject of ongoing trials, and family members should be referred to centers with expertise in this area.
- Presenting symptoms are vague but often include abdominal or back pain, jaundice, and cachexia.
- Staging should include CT scan of chest abdomen and pelvis with appropriate arterial phasing to assess the abdominal vasculature.
- Pathologic diagnosis is best obtained by EUS biopsy, and patients with biliary obstruction not planned for immediate surgery should get biliary stenting.
- Although formal TNM staging exists, in practice, tumors are best classified as resectable, borderline resectable, locally advanced unresectable, and metastatic.

TREATMENT

General Principles

The most important component in the management of a patient newly diagnosed with nonmetastatic pancreatic

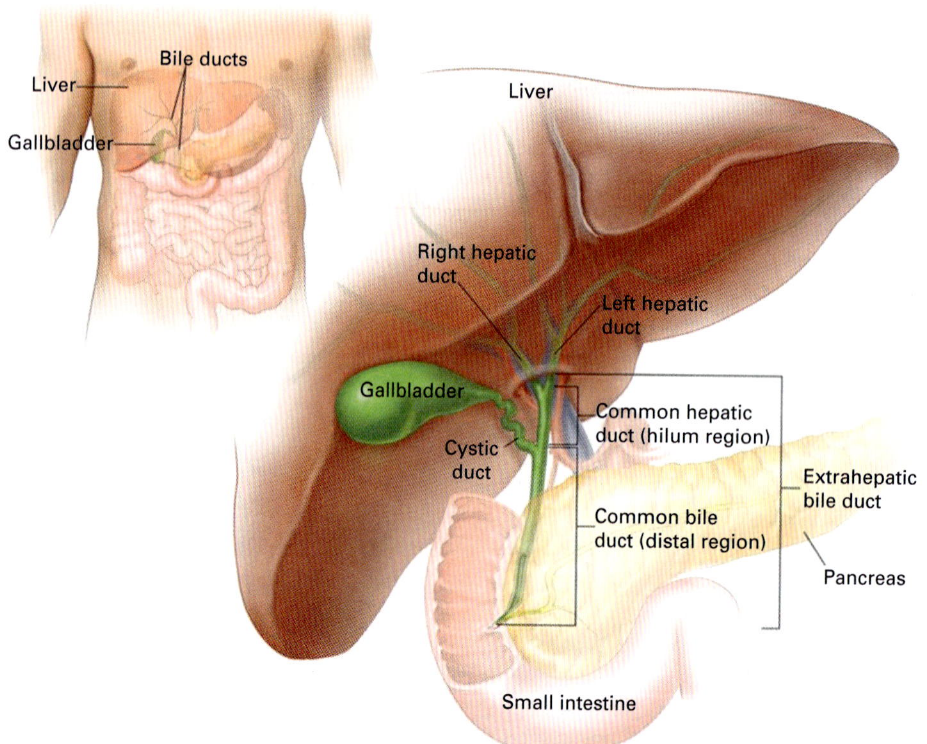

Fig. 13-4 Hepatobiliary anatomy.

Abbreviations: CT, computed tomography; EUS, endoscopic ultrasound; SMA, superior mesenteric artery; SMV, superior mesenteric vein.

cancer is the involvement of a multidisciplinary team at a center with high-volume experience with this cancer. The continuum, defined in Figure 13-5, is complex and often requires the opinion of several surgeons and expert radiologists and endoscopists. Although surgery has been the mainstay of treatment of pancreatic cancer and remains the only curative approach, cure rates remain dismal. This has led to the incorporation of more highly active chemotherapy regimens such as FOLFIRINOX into the adjuvant setting and, increasingly, in the neoadjuvant setting. The duration and sequence of these therapies and their role in converting previously unresectable cancers into resectable ones are the subject of multiple studies, and the field is rapidly evolving.

Resectable Pancreatic Cancer: Adjuvant Therapy

The appropriate adjuvant treatment of resectable pancreatic cancer has come into clearer focus over the last several years, although some controversy remains regarding the role for RT. A German phase III trial (CONKO-1), including 364 patients, demonstrated the superiority of adjuvant chemotherapy with gemcitabine compared with surgery alone for patients with resected pancreatic cancer, regardless of whether a tumor-free resection margin could be obtained.[287,288] An update of this study demonstrated a significant improvement in 5-year OS of 20.7% (95% CI, 14.7 to 26.6) compared with 10.4% (95% CI, 5.9 to 15.0) for gemcitabine compared with surgery alone.[289] Building on CONKO-1, the ESPAC-4 study compared adjuvant gemcitabine with gemcitabine plus capecitabine in a large phase III study of 732 patients.[290] This study did demonstrate a modest improvement in survival with the combination adjuvant therapy; the median survival was 28.0 months, versus 25.5 months with gemcitabine alone (HR, 0.82; 95% CI, 0.68 to 0.98, $P = .032$) and a 5-year OS of 29% (95% CI, 22.0 to –35.2) versus 16% (95% CI, 10.2 to –23.7). The recently completed phase III Adjuvant Therapy for Patients with Resected Pancreatic Cancer study comparing gemcitabine with gemcitabine plus nab-paclitaxel in the adjuvant setting did not show a survival advantage.[291]

One of the most important and practice-changing trials was the phase III PRODIGE-24 trial, which compared 6 months of adjuvant FOLFIRINOX with gemcitabine therapy and showed an improvement in median survival from 35 months to 54 months (HR, 0.66; 95% CI, 0.49 to –0.89) with a 3-year OS of 63.4% versus 48.6%.[292] This is the longest median survival ever seen in a phase III trial of adjuvant therapy for pancreatic cancer. This is now clearly the standard of care for patients with resected pancreatic cancer fit for this regimen.

The role of CRT in the adjuvant treatment setting for pancreatic cancer remains controversial and has been made more difficult by the excellent results seen in the PRODIGE-24 trial. The ESPAC-1 study was a complex trial (2 × 2 design) that compared adjuvant chemotherapy and adjuvant CRT each with no such therapy. The trial showed no benefit (and perhaps harm) with CRT but a benefit for chemotherapy.[293] The RTOG 0848 trial of gemcitabine versus gemcitabine and erlotinib followed by either additional chemotherapy or CRT is ongoing. ASCO guidelines offer a moderate recommendation that adjuvant CRT be considered for patients who have completed 4 to 6 months of adjuvant systemic therapy and have microscopically positive margins (R1) and/or node positive disease after resection.[294]

KEY POINTS

- Six months of modified FOLFIRINOX treatment is the new standard of care for resected pancreatic cancer.
- For those patients not felt to be candidates for modified FOLFIRINOX, 6 months of treatment with gemcitabine and capecitabine can be considered.
- There is no defined role for adjuvant RT in resected pancreatic cancer, but RT can be considered in those patients with postresection R1 disease and/or node-positive disease after 4 to 6 months of adjuvant systemic therapy.
- Although surveillance tumor markers and imaging are often used in clinical practice, there is no evidence that they improve patient survival, and they should not be considered the standard of care. The focus at surveillance visits should be on symptoms and nutrition.
- There are numerous active studies testing neoadjuvant chemotherapy and CRT for resectable and borderline resectable pancreatic cancer, but until these studies are complete, these treatments should not be considered the standard of care and should preferably be administered in the context of a clinical trial.

Neoadjuvant Therapy: Resectable and Borderline Resectable Pancreatic Cancer

At this time, neither neoadjuvant chemotherapy nor CRT is considered the standard of care for resectable or borderline resectable pancreatic cancer, but these are areas with active trial research. Many centers have adopted these approaches in hope of improving R0 resection rates, improving selection of those patients who will likely benefit from surgery, and possibly treating micrometastatic disease earlier in the treatment process. For those interested, there are several pertinent trials, such as the phase II and phase III PREOPANC studies and the ongoing SWOG 1505 study.[295-297] If neoadjuvant strategy is used outside of a clinical trial, it should include frequent assessments of the patient's tolerance of therapy and close consultation with a pancreatic surgeon.

Locally Advanced, Unresectable Pancreatic Cancers

For patients with locally advanced, unresectable disease, current ASCO guidelines recommend 6 months of initial systemic chemotherapy with a combination regimen, in those who can tolerate it, with consideration of CRT in those who do not progress after induction therapy.[298] As in the case of those with resectable disease, the role of CRT in this setting remains controversial. The international LAP07 phase III trial randomly assigned patients with locally advanced, unresectable pancreatic cancer to treatment with gemcitabine with or without erlotinib. Patients with at least stable disease after 4 months were randomly assigned a second time to either continue with the same chemotherapy as in the first phase or to proceed to CRT with capecitabine as a radiation sensitizer. This study closed at the first planned interim analysis because of lack of efficacy. No OS or PFS benefit was observed with the switch from chemotherapy to consolidating CRT. A subsequent analysis to evaluate the effect of RT on locoregional tumor control found that patients in the radiation arm had significantly less local tumor progression (34% *v* 65%; $P < .0001$) and a longer time before reintroduction of chemotherapy (159 *v* 96 days; $P = .05$).[299]

In general, at the end of either definitive chemotherapy or chemotherapy and CRT, patients should again be evaluated by a multidisciplinary team with high-volume expertise in pancreatic cancer to determine whether the patient may be a candidate for surgical resection.

KEY POINTS

- Although the exact definition of locally advanced, unresectable disease remains a moving target, > 180° encasement of the superior mesenteric artery or direct involvement of the inferior vena cava or celiac trunk are often considered contraindications to successful surgical resection.
- Determination of unresectability must be done in conjunction with a multidisciplinary team at a high-volume pancreatic cancer center.
- Treatment should include initial multiagent chemotherapy with consideration of CRT in those who do not progress. The exact duration of therapy is not well defined.
- After definitive therapy, the patient should be revaluated by the multidisciplinary team to determine if the cancer is now potentially resectable.

Treatment of Metastatic Pancreatic Cancer: Frontline Therapy

All patients with metastatic pancreatic cancer should be considered for early referral to a palliative care specialist, if available. Because these patients often have symptoms from their cancer that are due to direct involvement of the celiac plexus, biliary obstruction, and gastric outlet obstruction, involvement of specialists in interventional pain management and interventional endoscopy is also often required.

Until recently, single-agent gemcitabine was considered the standard of care for patients with metastatic pancreatic cancer.[300] Subsequently, many clinical trials have tried improve upon gemcitabine monotherapy. In several negative phase III trials, agents added to gemcitabine consisted of several conventional chemotherapy drugs, such as FU, cisplatin, oxaliplatin, irinotecan, or pemetrexed. Novel biologic agents also were used, such as matrix metalloproteinase inhibitors, farnesyl-transferase inhibitors, or the VEGF inhibitor bevacizumab and the EGFR antibody cetuximab.[301]

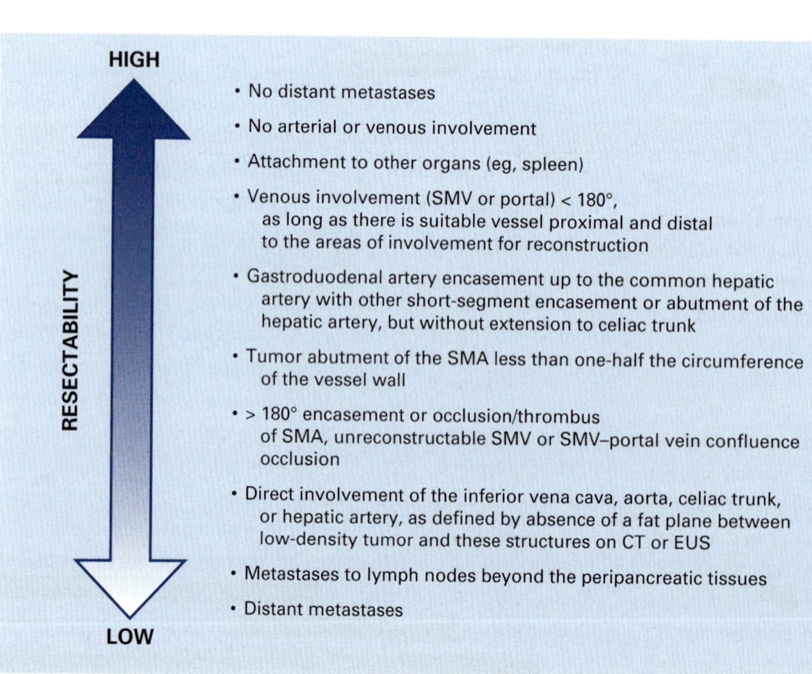

Fig. 13-5 Determining resectability for pancreatic cancer.

Abbreviations: CT, computed tomography; EUS, endoscopic ultrasound; SMA, superior mesenteric artery; SMV, superior mesenteric vein.

Adapted and reproduced with permission from: Ryan DP, Mamon H. Treatment for potentially resectable exocrine pancreatic cancer. In: UpToDate, Post TW (Ed), UpToDate, Waltham, MA. (March 11, 2020.) Copyright © 2019 UpToDate, Inc. For more information visit www.uptodate.com.

A new standard of care in the treatment of metastatic pancreatic cancer was defined in 2011 by the results of a French study of 342 patients comparing gemcitabine with FOLFIRINOX.[302] The median OS was an unprecedented 11.1 months in the FOLFIRINOX group as compared with 6.8 months in the gemcitabine group (HR, 0.57; 95% CI, 0.45 to 0.73; $P < .001$), median PFS was 6.4 months in the FOLFIRINOX group and 3.3 months in the gemcitabine group (HR, 0.47; 95% CI, 0.37 to 0.59; $P < .001$), and the objective response rate was 31.6% for FOLFIRINOX compared with 9.4% for the gemcitabine group ($P < .001$). More adverse events were noted in the FOLFIRINOX group, but despite this, overall quality-of-life scores were superior in the FOLFIRINOX arm. These results established FOLFIRINOX as the new standard of care for patients with advanced pancreatic cancer, good performance status, absence of biliary obstruction, and no infectious complications. It should be noted that the trial excluded patients with an Eastern Cooperative Oncology Group (ECOG) performance status (PS) ≥ 2 and in patients older than 75 years. More recent trials with FOLFIRINOX in pancreatic cancer have modified the original regimen by eliminating the 5-FU bolus and reducing the irinotecan dose from 180 mg/m^2 to 150 mg/m^2 without appearing to compromise its effectiveness. This modified FOLFIRINOX regimen was used in the practice changing PRODIGE-24 adjuvant study.[292]

An alternative first-line therapy for advanced pancreatic cancer was established in 2013 when the addition of nab-paclitaxel to gemcitabine was found to be superior to gemcitabine alone in a phase III trial.[303] In this study, median OS was 8.5 months in the nab-paclitaxel and gemcitabine group compared with 6.7 months in the gemcitabine- alone group (HR, 0.72; 95% CI, 0.62 to 0.83; $P < .001$); the response rate, according to independent review, was 23% compared with 7% ($P < .001$). Rates of neutropenia, febrile neutropenia (3% *v* 1%), neuropathy, and fatigue were significantly higher in the nab-paclitaxel arm.

Finally, in the recently published POLO study,[304] 154 patients with metastatic pancreatic cancer, a germline *BRCA1* or *BRCA2* mutation, and who had received and not progressed on ≥ 16 weeks of a platinum-containing regimen, were randomly assigned to receive maintenance therapy with the PARP inhibitor olaparib, or placebo. The median PFS was significantly longer in the olaparib group than in the placebo group (7.4 *v* 3.8 months; HR, 0.53; 95% CI, 0.35 to 0.82; $P = .004$).[304] Survival data are not yet mature.

Both modified FOLFIRINOX and the gemcitabine and nab-paclitaxel combination are appropriate treatment options for patients with metastatic pancreatic cancer. We would caution against the tendency for cross-trial comparisons, given potential differences in the underlying populations. Decisions regarding first-line treatment, therefore, depend on patient factors and clinician preference. It could be reasonable to establish a three-tiered approach toward metastatic pancreatic cancer: otherwise healthy, medically fit patients with good ECOG performance status (< 2) and those with a germline *BRCA1/2* mutation could preferentially be treated with FOLFIRINOX as first-line therapy and potentially nab-paclitaxel and gemcitabine as second-line therapy. Patients with poor performance status, advanced age, and significant comorbidities could still be considered candidates for single-agent gemcitabine therapy. In between these extremes lies a group of patients who could be considered for nab-paclitaxel and gemcitabine as first-line therapy. Figure 13-6 lays out a potential treatment alogorithm.

Treatment of Metastatic Pancreatic Cancer: Second-Line Therapy and Beyond

There is no agreed-upon standard-of-care regimen for patients who progress on first-line treatment of metastatic pancreatic cancer and completed trials did not include patients treated with the more recent FOLFIRINOX and gemcitabine and nab-paclitaxel frontline regimens. In general, treatment choice is often based on first-line regimen, performance status, and organ function. These patients should always be considered for enrollment in a clinical trial. In the CONKO-003 trial, 168 patients who had progressed on first-line gemcitabine were randomly assigned to 5-FU or 5-FU with oxaliplatin. The oxaliplatin regimen is not FOLFOX but rather a regimen consisting of weekly infusional 5-FU and oxaliplatin given on days 8 and 22, followed by a 3-week break. Median OS was 5.9 months in the arm with the 3-week break from therapy compared with 3.3 months in the 5-FU arm (HR 0.66; 95% CI, 0.48 to 0.91; $P = .1$).[305] The NAPOLI-1 trial evaluated nanoliposomal irinotecan in patients with metastatic pancreatic cancer refractory to gemcitabine.[306] Patients in the combination nanoliposomal irinotecan plus 5-FU and LV arm had a significantly improved OS compared with patients in the 5-FU and LV arm—6.1 months compared with 4.2 months (HR, 0.67; 95% CI, 0.49 to 0.92; $P = .012$).

An important update in the ASCO 2018 guideline statement is the recommendation for the PD-1 immune checkpoint inhibitor pembrolizumab as second-line therapy for patients with dMMR/MSI-H cancer.[307]

KEY POINTS

- All patients with metastatic pancreatic cancer should be referred to a palliative care specialist, if available.
- Either modified FOLFIRINOX or gemcitabine and nab-paclitaxel are considered appropriate frontline regimens. Choice should be based on patient performance status, underlying organ dysfunction, and presence or absence of germline *BRCA1/2* mutation (such patients should preferentially receive FOLFIRINOX).
- Patients with *BRCA1/2* germline mutations who do not progress on ≥ 16 weeks of an oxaliplatin-containing regimen should be considered for olaparib maintenance therapy.

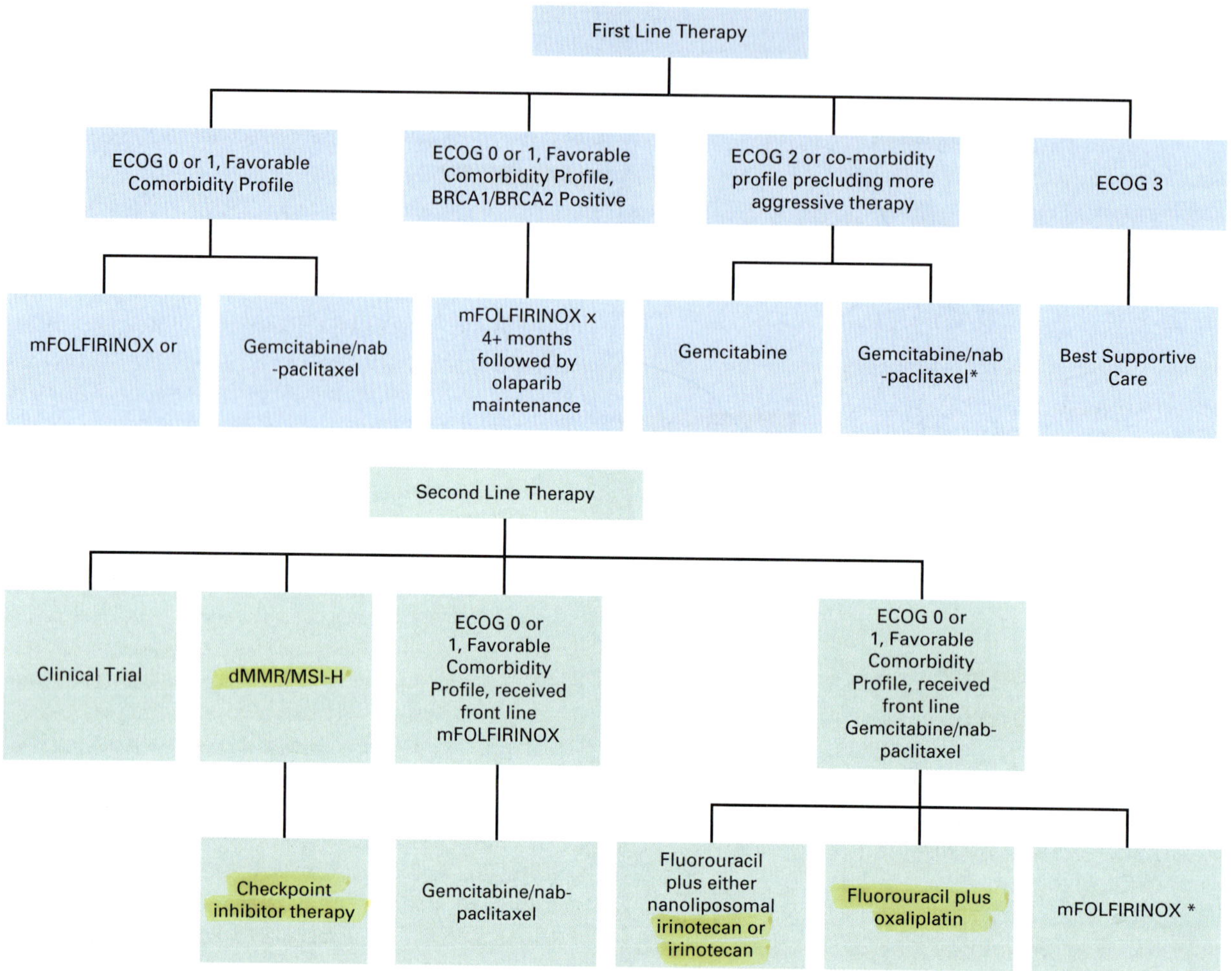

Fig. 13-6 Treatment algorithm for metastatic pancreatic cancer.

Abbreviations: dMMR, mismatch-repair deficient; ECOG, Eastern Cooperative Oncology Group; mFOLFIRINOX, modified regimen of leucovorin, fluorouracil, irinotecan, and oxaliplatin; MSI-H, microsatellite instability-high.

*Only for those patients deemed medically fit.

- There is no agreed-upon standard-of-care second-line regimen. Second-line treatment should be based on frontline treatment and the patient's overall functional status. All these patients should be considered for a clinical trial, if available.

COLORECTAL CANCER

EPIDEMIOLOGY AND ETIOLOGY

CRC affects approximately 145,600 patients in the United States every year. Among all cancers, it is the second leading cause of death in the United States (n = > 51,000) and affects men and women equally (second only to lung cancer, which results in 155,870 deaths annually).[308] The 5-year relative survival rates for localized cancer is nearly 90%; for distant disease, it is almost 15%. The incidence of CRC is higher in developed countries than in developing countries. In the past decade, there has been a decrease in the incidence and mortality rate of CRC in the United States, likely secondary to improved adherence to screening recommendations.[1] Findings from epidemiologic studies indicate that during the past two decades, the anatomic distribution of CRC may have shifted from the distal to the proximal colon, but that there has also been a particularly sharp increase in rectal cancer incidence among those younger than 50 years.[309] These results indicate strong environmental associations for CRC. However, data from prospective, interventional studies indicate the association among dietary fiber, calcium, fat intake, and CRC is not clear.[310,311] Additional environmental factors include the intake of alcohol and tobacco, hormone replacement in women (protective), total calorie consumption, and physical activity as it relates to obesity.[312-315]

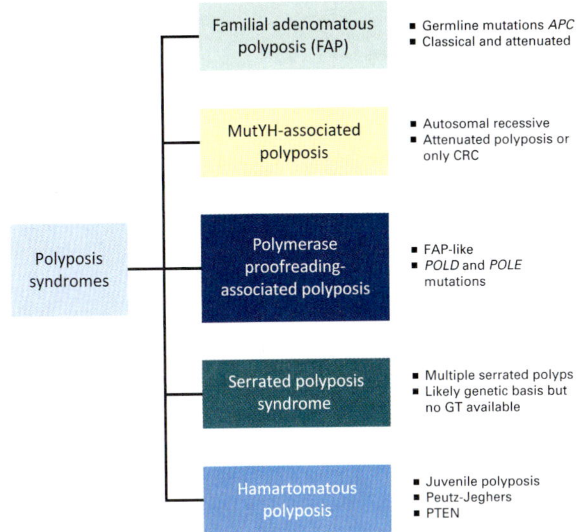

Fig. 13-7 Polyposis syndromes.

Abbreviations: CRC, colorectal cancer; GT, genetic testing.

FAMILIAL SYNDROMES

The two most common inherited forms of CRC are those associated with HNPCC and the familial adenomatous polyposis (FAP) syndrome. These two recognized genetic syndromes are distinct in molecular biology and in clinical characteristics. Several other inherited polyposis syndromes are shown in Figure 13-7.

FAP Syndrome

The first syndrome to be recognized was FAP, which is caused by an inherited mutation in the adenomatous polyposis coli (*APC*) gene, a key regulator of the Wnt-signaling pathway. Mutations of the *APC* gene lead to the formation of a dysfunctional protein, which cannot bind to β-catenin; thus, β-catenin can then activate the transcription of various oncogenes. Patients with mutated *APC* have hundreds to thousands of colonic polyps, predisposing them to malignant tumors at a young age. Although FAP represents a small percentage (approximately 0.5% to 1%) of the overall number of cases of CRC, somatic *APC* (or β-catenin) mutations activating the Wnt-signaling pathway have been found in the majority (80% to 85%) of sporadic CRCs. Additional gene expression studies along the adenoma-carcinoma sequence have provided an important genetic model in which specific genetic mutations, leading to invasive CRCs, have been clearly elucidated (Fig 13-8).[316]

Hereditary Nonpolyposis Colon Cancer

HNPCC is an inherited autosomal-dominant disease with high penetrance; it is the most common hereditary colorectal syndrome, accounting for approximately 5% of CRCs. CRC generally develops at an early age in these patients (median age, 45 years) and commonly in the proximal colon. Other associated malignancies with the genetic syndrome include ovarian, pancreatic, breast, biliary, endometrial, gastric, genitourinary, and small bowel primary cancers. Although the Amsterdam and Bethesda Criteria (Table 13-6) traditionally have been used to identify patients who should be considered for genetic testing, there is a push for universal germline testing in all patients diagnosed with CRC.

HNPCC is caused by mutations in a group of genes that code for DNA MMR enzymes, including MSH-2, MLH-1, PMS-2, MSH-6, and EPCAM (deletion causes loss of expression of MSH2).[317] The defect in MMR allows spontaneous genetic mutations to accumulate in the colonic mucosa, which predispose for the development of dysplasia and, eventually, for invasive cancers. Tumor testing can be done in one of two ways and this often creates confusion in terminology. MSI designation is derived from a polymerase chain reaction–based tumor test in which a panel of microsatellite markers (so-called Bethesda markers) are used to test for MSI, and tissue is classified as MSI-H if two or more of five core markers show instability. A second, and now more common test, is to perform IHC analysis of the four MMR proteins listed at the beginning of this paragraph. If any one of them is not expressed on IHC, then the tumor is classified as having a dMMR. Although dMMR and MSI-H are often used interchangeably, this is technically not accurate.

Although a patient with dMMR or an MSI-H tumor could have HNPCC, only 20% actually do when additional germline testing is done. This means that in the majority of patients, these abnormalities are somatic alternations confined to the tumor itself. Approximately 10% to 15% of sporadic colon cancers have aberrations in the MMR enzymes and the prevalence is approximately 15% in stage II, 8% in stage III, and 4% to 5% in stage IV CRCs.[318] These sporadic cases are generally caused by epigenetic silencing of *MLH1*.[319] These patients will also often lack expression of *PMS2* and usually have a mutation in *BRAF*. Figure 13-9 shows a flow diagram to distinguish between

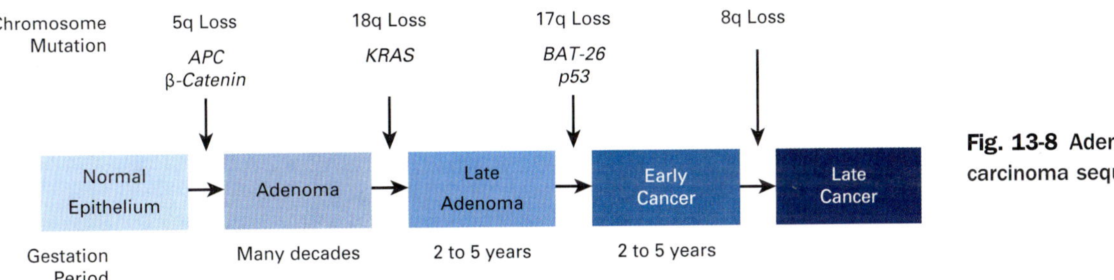

Fig. 13-8 Adenoma to carcinoma sequence.

Table 13-6 Clinical Criteria to Determine Likelihood of HNPCC

Criteria
Amsterdam II Criteria (all criteria must be met)
At least three relatives with an HNPCC-associated cancer (colorectal, cancer of the endometrium, small bowel, ureter, or renal pelvis)
One relative should be a first-degree relative of the other two
Malignancies should include at least two successive generations
At least one family member should be diagnosed before age 50 years
Familial adenomatous polyposis is excluded
Tumors should be verified by pathologic examination
Revised Bethesda Criteria to identify patients with CRC who should undergo pathologic examination for HNPCC (any criterion is sufficient)
CRC in a patient younger than 50 years
Synchronous or metachronous CRC, or associated with another HNPCC-associated tumor (ie, endometrial, stomach, small intestine, ovarian, pancreatic, biliary tract, ureter or renal pelvis, brain, sebaceous gland adenoma, or keratoacanthoma)
Pathologic features of an MSI-high cancer (eg, tumor-infiltrating lymphocytes, Crohn's-like lymphocytic reaction, mucinous/ signet-ring differentiation, medullary growth pattern) in a patient younger than 60 years
Development of CRC in an individual who has a first-degree relative with CRC and/or HNPCC-related extracolonic cancer and/or colorectal adenoma, with one of the cancers diagnosed before the patient reaches age 50 years or an adenoma diagnosed before age 40 years
CRC in two or more first- or second-degree relatives with HNPCC-related tumors, regardless of age

Abbreviations: CRC, colorectal cancer; HNPCC, hereditary nonpolyposis colorectal cancer; MSI-H, microsatellite instability-high.

patients with sporadic and familial dMMR CRCs, which is useful if universal germline testing is not being performed.

Regardless of whether universal germline screening is done for patients with CRC, routine testing for dMMR by IHC or for MSI by polymerase should be done on the tumors of all patients with CRC, because this has implications for the treatment of early-stage cancers and is the basis for FDA approval of checkpoint inhibitors for patients with more advanced disease, as will be discussed in more detail in this chapter.

Other Polyposis and CRC Syndromes

There are other polyposis and CRC syndromes (Fig 13-7). Inflammatory bowel disease (IBD), particularly ulcerative colitis, is associated with an increased risk for colon cancer, estimated to be 5% to 10% by 20 years after the time of diagnosis of IBD. IBD also is associated with a high incidence of synchronous cancers, affecting 10% to 20% of cases. Crohn disease also may have a role in increasing risk for CRC, particularly cancer in the ileocolic region. However, in the absence of colonic involvement

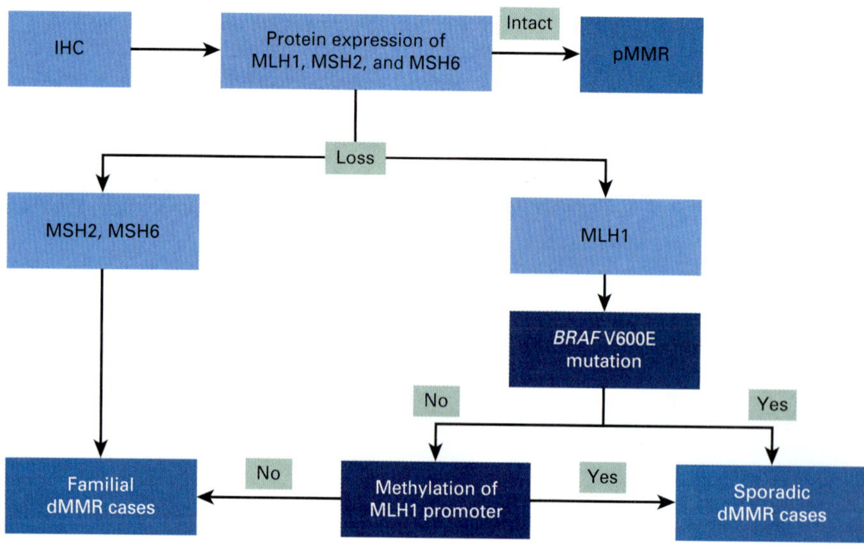

Fig. 13-9 Mismatch repair testing algorithm.

Abbreviations: dMMR, mismatch-repair deficient; IHC, immunohistochemistry; pMMR, mismatch-repair proficient.

Table 13-7 **Four Consensus Molecular Subtypes**[320]

Subtype	CMS1-MSI Immune	CMS2-Canonical	CMS3-Metabolic	CMS4-Mesenchymal
Incidence	14%	37%	13%	23%
Genomic aberrations	MSI, CIMP high, hypermutation	SCNA high	Mixed MSI status, SCNA low, CIMP low	SCNA high
Mutations	*BRAF* mutations		*KRAS* mutations	
Gene expression pathways/cellular processes	Immune infiltration and activation	WNT and MYC activation	Metabolic deregulation	Stromal infiltration, TGF-β activation, angiogenesis
Clinical outcomes	Worse survival after relapse			Worse relapse-free and overall survival

Abbreviations: CIMP, CpG island methylator phenotype; CMS, consensus molecular subtype; MSI, microsatellite instability; SCNA, somatic copy number alteration; TGF, transforming growth factor.

by Crohn disease, there is no increased risk of colon cancer. The risk for the development of a subsequent cancer is 3% for patients with a history of adenomatous polyps.

CRC GENETIC ABERRATIONS

In 2015, a consensus statement was released evaluating data from 18 colorectal data sets including the TCGA and other public and proprietary sources. Four consensus molecular subtypes (CMS) were arrived at (Table 13-7): CMS1 (MSI immune, 14%) with hypermutated microsatellite unstable and strong immune activation; CMS2 (canonical, 37%) with marked WNT and MYC activation; CMS3 (metabolic, 13%) metabolic dysregulation; and CMS4 (mesenchymal, 23%) with transforming growth factor β activation and angiogenesis.[320] With the exception of CMS1, which has clear prognostic and predictive implications for cancer treatment, as will discussed later in this section, the other three CMSs have not yet been incorporated into clinical decision-making but form the basis for continued attempts to personalize therapy for CRC.

SCREENING

Table 13-8 shows the screening recommendations recommended by the US Preventive Service Task Force (see also Chapter 1: Epidemiology and Prevention). These differ somewhat from those made by the American Cancer Society and US Multi-Specialty Task Force. The most recent change is that the American Cancer Society has proposed starting screening at age 45 years instead of 50 years (a qualified recommendation) and the US Multi-Specialty Task Force has suggested starting earlier screening at age 45 years for black patients. Fecal immunochemical test (FIT)-DNA screening has also begun to appear in the recommendations for patients every 3 years.[321] The sensitivity for detecting CRC is 92.3% with DNA testing and 73.8% with FIT (P = .002). The sensitivity for detecting advanced precancerous lesions is 42.4% with DNA testing and 23.8% with FIT (P < .001).

Screening should be more regular for patients at high risk, including those with inherited syndromes, IBD, previous adenomatous polyps or CRC, and strong family histories. Individuals with HNPCC should have screening by total colonoscopy every 1 to 3 years beginning between ages 20 and 25 years, because of the lack of a visible premalignant lesion in this population and the higher risk for right-sided colon cancers.[322] Individuals with FAP should start screening colonoscopies as early as age 10 years. If a colon cancer or severe dysplasia is found in patients with IBD, the general recommendation is for a near-total or a subtotal colectomy because of the high incidence of synchronous and metachronous cancers in this population.[323] Surgery can be less extensive for patients with sporadic cancers. For patients with HNPCC, a more extensive surgery can be recommended, particularly for women beyond childbearing age, for whom hysterectomy and oophorectomy should be considered. Finally, patients with a strong family history (one first-degree relative diagnosed before the age of 60 years or two first degree relatives diagnosed at any age) of colon cancer or advanced adenomatous polyps (> 1 cm, or high-grade dysplasia, or with villous elements) should start screening with colonoscopy no later than age 40 years or 10 years younger than the youngest first-degree relative and should undergo screening every 5 years.

KEY POINTS

- Screening for CRC is underused. Screening endoscopy and fecal occult blood test/FIT testing reduce CRC–associated death over the long term.
- All individuals should have their tumors evaluated for MMR proteins or for MSI status. Those with dMMR/MSI-H tumors suggestive of a germline origin should be referred for genetic screening.
- If universal screening for germline mutations is not performed in all colon cancer patients, clinicians should follow the revised Bethesda Criteria to determine who should be recommended for genetic screening.

STAGING

Colorectal Cancer

Cancer staging using the eighth edition of the AJCC manual (2017) is shown in Table 13-9. Important areas to note that are included in the seventh and eighth editions but differ from the sixth edition are the T4B category (invasion or adherence to other organs or structures) and the N1c category (tumor deposits in subserosa, mesentery, or nonperitonealized pericolic and perirectal tissues without regional lymph nodes). In effect, T4B places a patient in the very high-risk IIC or IIIC category, depending on nodal status, and N1C (recorded as present or absent and not counted) is considered the risk equivalent to N1 lymph nodes (one to three regional lymph nodes). The eighth edition also includes nodal micrometastases (tumor clusters > 0.2 mm in diameter) as being lymph node positive and has added the M1C category (peritoneal metastases), creating a stage IVC category.

TREATMENT OF CRC

Early-Stage Colon Cancer (Stages 0 and I)

Nearly all patients with stage 0 disease (carcinoma in situ or intramucosal cancer) are cured by endoscopic resection alone; note, however, that the lymph nodes are not adequately assessed by this technique. The primary treatment of virtually all invasive, nonmetastatic CRCs is surgery, which alone is curative for > 85% of patients who have stage I or low-risk stage II disease.

Stage II Colon Cancer

For patients with stage II disease, the role of adjuvant chemotherapy remains controversial because of the heterogeneity of this disease stage. Current ASCO recommendations dating back to 2004 suggest that not all patients with stage II tumors should receive adjuvant chemotherapy but that a discussion should be had with patients about their individual benefit-to-risk ratio when using adjuvant chemotherapy in stage II colon cancer.[324] The identification of prognostic factors might help distinguish patients at high risk for relapse and identify patients with high-risk stage II disease who may more likely benefit from adjuvant treatment. In addition to T4 status, all major groups (ASCO, NCCN, European Society of Medical Oncology [ESMO]) consider inadequate nodal sampling (< 12 or 13 nodes), lymphovascular invasion, perineural invasion, and clinical obstruction or perforation to be high-risk stage II disease that may warrant chemotherapy. Poorly differentiated tumors must be evaluated in the context of their MSI/dMMR status.

Apart from aforementioned clinical risk factors, molecular determinants of prognosis, such as MSS have been evaluated. Remarkably consistent results from retrospective analyses of large adjuvant trials and pooled data sets have confirmed that patients with stage IIA colon cancer and dMMR/MSI-H tumors

Table 13-8 **Screening Guidelines for Colon and Rectal Cancer**[563]
Beginning at age 50, both men and women at average risk for the development of colorectal cancer should use one of the screening tests below. The tests designed to find both early cancer and polyps are preferred if these tests are available and the person is willing to have one of these more invasive tests.
Tests that find polyps and cancer
Flexible sigmoidoscopy every 5 years[a]
Colonoscopy every 10 years
Double-contrast barium enema every 5 years[a]
CT colonography (virtual colonoscopy) every 5 years[a]
Tests that mainly find cancer
Fecal occult blood test every year[a,b]
Fecal immunochemical test every year[a,b]
Stool DNA test every 3 years[a]
People should talk to their doctor about starting colorectal cancer screening earlier and/or being screened more often if they have any of the following colorectal cancer risk factors:
A personal history of colorectal cancer or adenomatous polyps
A personal history of chronic inflammatory bowel disease (Crohn disease or ulcerative colitis)
A strong family history of colorectal cancer or polyps (> 1 cm, or high-grade dysplasia, or with villous elements) in a first-degree relative (parent, sibling, or child) younger than age 60 years or in two or more first-degree relatives of any age:
Start screening with colonoscopy no later than at age 40 years or at 10 years younger than the youngest first-degree relative, and then undergo screening every 5 years
A known family history of hereditary colorectal cancer syndromes such as familial adenomatous polyposis or hereditary nonpolyposis colon cancer

Abbreviation: CT, computed tomography

[a]Colonoscopy should be done if test results are positive.

[b]For fecal occult blood test or fecal immunochemical test used as a screening test, the take-home, multiple-sample method should be used. A fecal occult blood test or fecal immunochemical test done during a digital rectal examination in the doctor's office is not adequate for screening.

have excellent prognosis (> 95% long-term DFS) and do not benefit from treatment with 5-FU adjuvant chemotherapy.[325-328] For patients with dMMR/MSI-H stage IIB with *BRAF* mutations and certainly those with stage IIC and stage III disease, adjuvant therapy with a fluoropyrimidine and oxaliplatin should be given. Duration of such treatment is discussed in more detail in the following paragraphs. Efforts to develop a molecular profile of predictive variables that could potentially guide adjuvant treatment decisions in stage II colon cancer have not proved very useful clinically.[325,329,330] These tests include gene expression signatures such as the Oncotype DX Colon[325] and ColoPrint,[329] as well as molecular detection assays of micrometastasis in morphologically unaffected lymph nodes.[330] At this time, none of these assays is routinely recommended for use in clinical practice as a decision tool for adjuvant therapy in stage II colon cancer, because they remain prognostic tests but are not able to predict which patients derive benefit from chemotherapy.

KEY POINTS

- Stage II colon cancer is a heterogeneous disease and there is no one-size-fits-all answer for who should get chemotherapy.
- The role of adjuvant therapy in stage II colon cancer should involve risk stratification and shared decision-making.
- Patients with stage IIA colon cancer and dMMR/MSI-H have an excellent prognosis and do not require adjuvant therapy.
- Patients with stage IIB *BRAF*-mutant and IIC dMMR/MSI-H colon cancer should be considered for adjuvant fluoropyrimidine- and oxaliplatin-based therapy.
- Patients with stage IIA disease without any risk factors should be counseled about the low absolute benefit, if any, of chemotherapy.
- Patients with stage IIA disease and high-risk factors and those with stage IIB (T4a) disease should be counseled regarding their higher risk of tumor recurrence and the potential benefit of fluoropyrimidine chemotherapy.
- Patients with stage IIC disease are at very high risk for tumor recurrence and should be urged to consider adjuvant fluoropyrimidine- and oxaliplatin-based therapy.

Stage III Colon Cancer

Adjuvant Chemotherapy. The initial trial presented in the early 1990s that established adjuvant chemotherapy as standard of care in stage III colon cancer used a combination of FU and levamisole administered for 12 months.[331] A 10% to 20% absolute improvement in 5-year survival was documented for patients receiving postoperative, adjuvant FU-based chemotherapy. Evidence from subsequent trials demonstrated that FU combined with LV provides a superior outcome, with 6 months of therapy being adequate to achieve this survival benefit.[332]

Table 13-9 **Staging, Incidence per Stage, and Treatment Recommendations for Invasive Colon Cancer**

Characteristic	Stage I	Stage II	Stage III	Stage IV
Staging	T1, N0, M0	A: T3, N0, M0	A: T1-2, N1/N1c, M0; T1, N2a, M0	A: Any T, Any N, M1a
	T2, N0, M0	B: T4a, N0, M0	B: T3-4a, N1/N1c, M0; T2/3, N2a, M0; T1-2, N2b, M0	B: Any T, Any N, M1b
		C: T4b, N0, M0	C: T4a, N2a, M0; T3-4a, N2b, M0; T4b, N1-2, M0	C: Any T, Any N, M1c
Definition	Invades submucosa (T1) or muscular propria (T2)	Invades subserosa, nonperitonealized pericolic/perirectal tissues (T3), or penetrates the surface of the visceral peritoneum (T4a), or directly invades or is adherent to other organs or structures (T4b)	Involves 1-3 (N1-N1a: 1, N1b: 2 to 3) or more (N2-N2a: 4-6, N2b: > 6) lymph nodes; N1c for tumor deposits in subserosa, mesentery, or pericolic/ perirectal tissue without lymph node metastasis	M1a: distant metastasis confined to one organ or site; M1b: distant metastasis in more than one organ or site; M1c: metastasis to peritoneal surface is identified alone or with other site or organ metastases
Incidence, %	15	25	35	25
Usual treatment	Surgery	Surgery with or without chemotherapy	Surgery with chemotherapy	Chemotherapy with or without surgery

Table 13-10 Comparison of Oxaliplatin Adjuvant Trials

Outcome	MOSAIC	NSABP C-07	XELOXA
5-year DFS, %	73.3 *v* 67.2 (5.9)	69.4 *v* 64.2 (5.2)	66.1 *v* 59.8 (6.3)
HR (95% CI)	0.8 (0.68 to 0.93)	0.82 (0.7 to 0.97)	0.8 (0.69 to 0.93)
5-8 Year OS, %	79 *v* 76 (3)	80 *v* 78 (2)	73 *v* 67 (6)
HR (95% CI)	0.84 (0.71 to 1.00)	0.88 (0.75 to 1.02)	0.83 (0.7 to 0.99)
Grade ≥ 3e neurotoxicity, %	12.5 during therapy	8 during therapy	11
	1.3 at 1 year	0.5 at 1 year	
Total oxaliplatin	1,020 mg/m^2	765 mg/m^2	1,040 mg/m^2

Abbreviations: DFS, disease-free survival; HR, hazard ratio; OS, overall survival.

For more than a decade, the standard in adjuvant therapy remained unchanged because of the lack of novel agents with relevant activity in CRC. This changed when oxaliplatin, irinotecan, and the oral FU prodrug capecitabine were used for the treatment of advanced CRC, with combination regimens of FU plus either irinotecan or oxaliplatin demonstrating high antitumor efficacy.

Worldwide, six phase III trials were conducted to evaluate the value of these three novel chemotherapeutic agents in the adjuvant setting. The results of the pivotal Multicenter International Study of Oxaliplatin/5-FU/Leucovorin in the Adjuvant Treatment of Colon Cancer trial (MOSAIC) clearly demonstrated that oxaliplatin plus infusional FU and LV (FOLFOX) is superior to FU with LV in terms of 3-year DFS and, ultimately, for OS with longer follow-up.[333] Results of the National Surgical Adjuvant Breast and Bowel Project C-07 trial and XELOXA trial confirmed the role of oxaliplatin plus intravenous or oral FU-based regimens in the adjuvant therapy of colon cancer.[334,335] A comparison of these trial results is shown in Table 13-10.

Although irinotecan- and oxaliplatin-based regimens are thought to be equally effective as palliative therapy for advanced CRC, for unknown reasons, none of the three phase III trials using combination regimens of irinotecan, FU, and LV demonstrated significantly superior efficacy regarding 3-year DFS when compared with FU and LV alone.[336-338] Similarly, despite their activity in the metastatic setting, several trials examining the addition of bevacizumab in an unselected population and cetuximab in a *KRAS* wild-type (WT) population did not show benefit of adding these agents to the standard 6-month FU- and oxaliplatin-based regimens.[339-342]

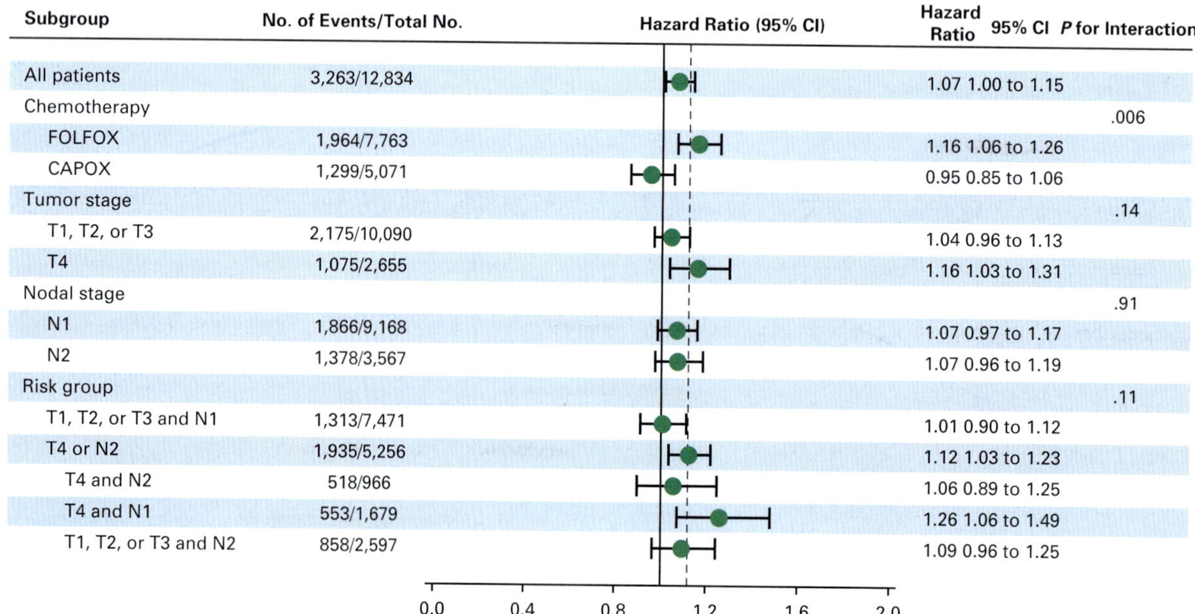

Fig. 13-10 Forest plots for DFS of 3 months versus 6 months of therapy in the IDEA Collaborative.

Abbreviations: CAPOX, capecitabine and oxaliplatin; DFS, disease-free survival; FOLFOX, leucovorin, fluorouracil, and oxaliplatin.

From The New England Journal of Medicine, Grothey A, Sobrero AF, Shields AF, et al., Duration of Adjuvant Chemotherapy for Stage III Colon Cancer, 378(13):1177-1188, Copyright © (2018) Massachusetts Medical Society. Reprinted with permission from Massachusetts Medical Society.

To mitigate the long-term neurotoxic adverse effects of oxaliplatin-based adjuvant therapy (10% to 15% of patients can develop grade 3 neuropathy, resulting in, for example, an inability to button shirts or walk without difficulty), the International Duration Evaluation of Adjuvant chemotherapy (IDEA) collaboration was established to prospectively combine and analyze data from six randomized trials conducted around the world to answer the question of whether a 3-month course of oxaliplatin-based adjuvant therapy is noninferior to the current standard 6-month treatment of patients with stage III colon cancer.[343] The final combined, published analysis included 12,834 patients from 12 countries. The primary end point of noninferiority was not met (HR, 1.07; 95% CI, 1.00 to 1.15); however, the absolute difference in 3-year DFS was only 0.9% (75.5% *v* 74.6%). Importantly, grade 2 or higher neurotoxicity during therapy and in the month after treatment was significantly lower in the 3-months group than in the 6-months group. Preplanned subgroup analyses included specific tumor penetration, nodal status groups, and chemotherapy regimen (FOLFOX or capecitabine and oxaliplatin [CAPOX]). The forest plots are shown in Figure 13-10.

Current ASCO clinical guidelines recommend that patients with T4 or N2 disease should receive 6 months of therapy and that for all other patients, either 6 months of adjuvant chemotherapy or a shorter duration of 3 months may be offered on the basis of a potential reduction in adverse events and no significant difference in DFS with the 3-month regimen.[344] On the basis of the subgroup analyses, many expert panels, including NCCN, would favor CAPOX over FOLFOX if 3 months of therapy is chosen. The ASCO guideline panel also favored CAPOX over FOLFOX but chose not to make it a formal recommendation. Data presented at the ASCO 2019 Annual Meeting revealed the same findings of 3 versus 6 months for stage II cancers when an oxaliplatin regimen is chosen.[345]

KEY POINTS

- By strict scientific criteria, 6 months of adjuvant CAPOX or FOLFOX remains the standard of care for stage III colon cancer.
- Emerging clinical consensus suggests 3 months of adjuvant therapy is a reasonable alternative for patients with T1-3, N1 disease and stage II patients, given the small absolute differences in DFS and the significant decrease in clinically significant neurologic and other toxicities.
- If 3 months of therapy is chosen, many expert panels favor CAPOX over FOLFOX.
- Six months of therapy with either regimen remains the preferred treatment for those with T4 or N2 disease.
- Irinotecan, anti-VEGF agents such as bevacizumab, and anti-EGFR antibodies such as cetuximab, regardless of *RAS* status, should not be used in the adjuvant setting.
- Table 13-11 lists a testing schedule and lifestyle changes recommended for patients with CRC.

ADVANCED CRC (STAGE IV)

Stage IV CRC is generally not considered curable with the exception of a small subset of patients with isolated sites of metastases (see the section on Oligometastatic CRC later in the chapter). For decades, standard first-line therapy consisted of 5-FU and LV, with response rates of approximately 20% and a median survival of approximately 1 year. In the late 1990s and early 2000s, the addition of oxaliplatin and irinotecan to the backbone of FU and LV resulted in an improvement in median OS to nearly 24 months when patients received active first-line and second-line therapy. The introduction of biologic agents,

Table 13-11 Surveillance Survivorship for Colorectal Cancer

Recommendation
Testing Schedule
Carcinoembryonic antigen measurement and history and physical examination every 3 months for 2 years, then every 6 months to 5 years
CT scans yearly to years 3-5, depending on risk
Colonoscopy 1 year after initial diagnosis, then in 3 years if findings are normal, and then every 5 years for life
In families without an identified familiar risk syndrome, all first-degree relatives should undergo screening colonoscopy starting 10 years younger than when the patient was diagnosed but no later than age 40 years and should undergo screening colonoscopy every 5 years
Lifestyle Changes
Increased exercise after diagnosis and avoidance of a Western-style diet; diets with a low glycemic load are associated with a reduced risk of cancer recurrence and improved OS[312-314,346]
Patients with classes II and III obesity (BMI > 35 kg/m^2) have a modestly increased risk of recurrence[315]
Lower serum vitamin D levels have been associated with an increased risk of recurrence, but prospective studies are lacking to show that increasing vitamin D to normal levels can improve outcomes in the adjuvant setting[347]

Abbreviations: BMI, body mass index; OS, overall survival.

such as bevacizumab, cetuximab, and panitumumab, have further enhanced the efficacy of systemic medical therapy. The emphasis of current advances in medical therapy is on the development of predictive biomarker signatures, which can help guide treatment decisions for specific patient subpopulations.

The availability of various active agents for the treatment of metastatic CRC (mCRC) has resulted in an abundance of therapeutic options that now demand a goal-oriented, strategic approach to therapy to maximize patient benefit. Figure 13-11 lays out a possible sequencing strategy. When treating a patient with mCRC, the first determination is whether stage IV disease is potentially curable by a surgical resection of metastases either at the time of diagnosis or after downsizing initially unresectable metastases by neoadjuvant chemotherapy. This will guide the choice and timing of chemotherapy because, in this scenario, the most appropriate treatment is conceivably the one that generates the highest response rates and carries the greatest potential to downsize metastases. If the patient's disease does not appear curable, the main goals of systemic chemotherapy are to extend the duration of the patient's life and to maintain quality of life for as long as possible. In this scenario, treatment regimens that offer the longest PFS and OS, as well as a favorable toxicity profile, are preferred.

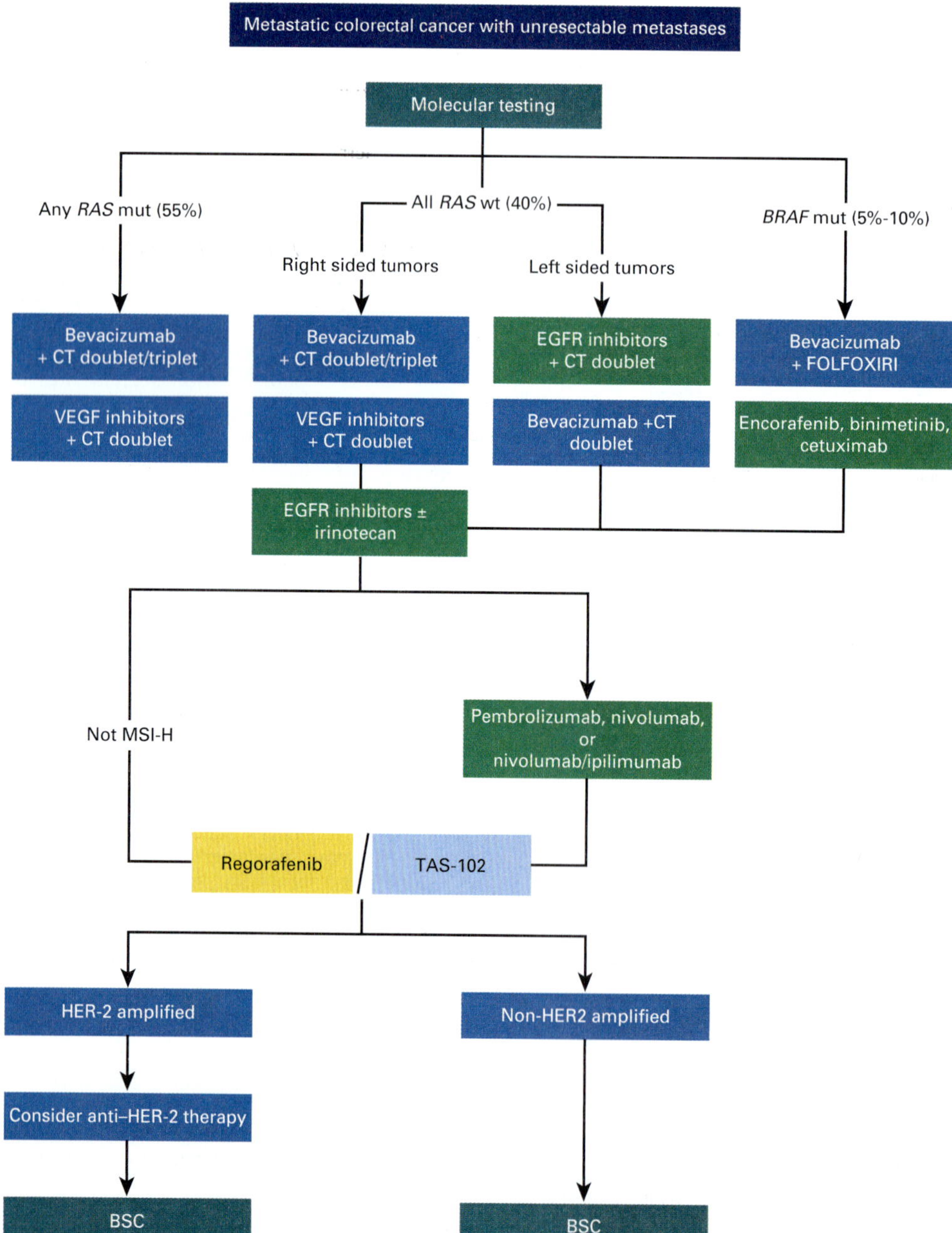

Fig. 13-11 Treatment algorithm for metastatic colorectal cancer.

Abbreviations: BSC, best supportive care; CT, computed tomography; FOLFOXIRI, leucovorin, fluorouracil, oxaliplatin, and irinotecan; MSI-H, microsatellite instability-high; mut, mutation; wt, wild type.

Irinotecan and Oxaliplatin

In the late 1990s and early 2000s, several trials established the benefit of oxaliplatin- and irinotecan-containing regimens in the frontline metastatic setting (ie, FOLFOX, FOLFIRI, IFL, CAPOX).[346-354] The main lessons learned over time was that an infusional or oral fluoropyrimidine-based regimen was superior to bolus 5-FU–based regimens, especially when combined with irinotecan, and that oxaliplatin was ineffective as a single agent and needed to be combined with other chemotherapy agents such as a fluoropyrimidine or irinotecan.

Comparing Irinotecan- and Oxaliplatin-Based Regimens

In the 2000s, several trials established the superiority of FOLFOX and FOLFIRI over bolus 5-FU regimens in the metastatic setting and smaller trials suggested an equivalency between FOLFOX and FOLFIRI.[355-357] The choice between FOLFOX and FOLFIRI in the clinic should be based mainly on the expected adverse effect profile. Because the benefit of subsequent-line therapy in CRC has been well established, patients should receive all active cytotoxic drugs in the course of their therapy to optimize outcome.[358]

Bevacizumab

Bevacizumab, a recombinant, humanized monoclonal antibody to vascular endothelial growth factor (VEGF)-A, has demonstrated clinical efficacy for the treatment of mCRC. In a large phase III, placebo-controlled trial with 813 patients, irinotecan, bolus FU, and LV (IFL protocol) was compared with IFL plus bevacizumab (5 mg/kg every 2 weeks) as first-line therapy for advanced CRC.[359] The addition of the anti-VEGF antibody led to a significantly increased response rate (45% *v* 35%; *P* = .0036), PFS (10.6 *v* 6.2 months; HR, 0.54; *P* < .00001), and median OS (20.3 *v* 15.6 months; HR, 0.66; *P* = .00004). This trial was the first phase III validation of an antiangiogenic agent as an effective treatment option in a human malignancy. Subsequently, bevacizumab also has been shown to enhance the efficacy of oxaliplatin-based regimens in first- and second-line treatments, as well as in combination with FU and LV alone or with irinotecan.[360-362] It is important to note that bevacizumab does not appear to have significant single-agent activity in mCRC.[360]

The main adverse effects observed with bevacizumab consist of hypertension (a class-effect of all agents targeting VEGF signaling), bleeding, GI perforations (in 1.5% to 2% of patients), and poor wound healing, as well as arterial thrombotic events in approximately 4% to 5% of patients.[363] In addition to arterial thrombotic events, a meta-analysis identified a 33% higher incidence of venous thrombotic events in patients receiving bevacizumab compared with the nonbevacizumab control arm in randomized trials,[364] although another, more recent analysis refuted this claim.[365] Bevacizumab should be used with extreme caution, if at all, in patients with a strong history of an arterial thrombotic event. Bevacizumab should also be used with caution in patients with recent surgeries or who are being planned for surgery (at least 4 weeks between bevacizumab and surgery is recommended, if possible) and those with obstructing primary tumors. A history of a venous thromboembolic event is not considered an absolute contraindication to bevacizumab therapy. On the basis of its well-documented efficacy and relative moderate toxicity, bevacizumab has emerged as a standard component of first-line chemotherapy for advanced CRC. Discussion on its use in right- versus left-sided tumors is in the section titled Tumor Sidedness.

Anti-EGFR Antibodies: Cetuximab and Panitumumab

Data from various clinical trials and translational studies now have opened the door to individualized treatment approaches in CRC by identifying patients who are most likely to benefit from monoclonal antibodies against EGFR, namely, cetuximab and panitumumab. It is increasingly clear that patients with advanced CRC must have a tumor that is WT for *KRAS* exons 2, 3, and 4 and *NRAS* exons 2, 3, and 4 (referred to as "extended RAS") for EGFR monoclonal antibodies to be effective (Fig 13-12).[366-371] Mutations in *RAS* (approximately 55% of tumors) result in constitutively active signaling downstream from the EGFR, thereby negating the effect of blocking the receptor. The CRYSTAL trial was a large phase III trial of 1,198 patients with untreated metastatic colon cancer and in which compared FOLFIRI and cetuximab were compared with FOLFIRI alone. Among patients with pan-RAS WT tumors, response rate (57% *v* 40%), median PFS (9.9 *v* 8.4 months), and OS (23.5 *v* 20 months) were all improved with the addition of cetuximab.[370] The PRIME trial of FOLFOX with or without panitumumab yielded similar results. NCCN guidelines now call for expanded *RAS*-mutation testing before EGFR monoclonal antibodies are used for patients with CRC and all patients with metastatic colon cancer should have extended *RAS* and *RAF* testing performed at the time of diagnosis if they are being considered for active therapy.[371] Use of either agent with either chemotherapy backbone (FOLFOX or FOLFIRI) is an acceptable standard of care for the frontline treatment of extended *RAS* WT tumors. Additional negative predictive biomarkers (discussed under Tumor Sidedness) may include *BRAF*-mutant and HER-2–amplified tumors as well as right-sided tumors.

The main toxic effects of anti-EGFR monoclonal antibodies are an acneiform skin rash, hypomagnesemia, diarrhea, and hypersensitivity reactions, the latter of which is particularly relevant for the chimeric antibody cetuximab. Prophylactic treatment of the skin rash with oral doxycycline and topical corticosteroids was investigated in the randomized phase II STEPP trial,[372] and skin toxicities were reduced from 62% in the reactive group to 29% in the preemptive group. Preemptive therapy should be considered for all patients receiving anti-EGFR therapies.

Head-to-Head Comparison Between EGFR Monoclonal Antibodies and Bevacizumab

Initial reports suggested an overadditive activity when bevacizumab was combined with cetuximab in salvage therapy.[373]

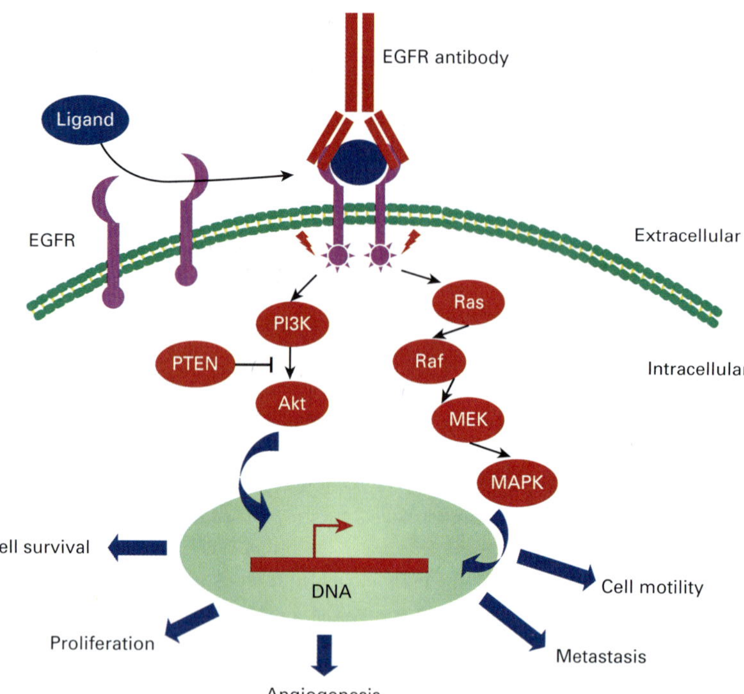

Fig. 13-12 EGFR pathway.

Results of subsequent larger, randomized, first-line trials, however, suggested an antagonistic effect of the combination of EGFR monoclonal antibodies with bevacizumab in the context of concurrent chemotherapy.[374,375] Thus, combinations of bevacizumab and EGFR monoclonal antibodies should not be used in clinical practice outside of a clinical trial at this time.

The choice of anti-EGFR therapy versus bevacizumab in the frontline metastatic setting for patients with extended *RAS* WT tumors has been addressed by two phase III trials. The FIRE-3 trial randomly selected 592 patients with conventionally assessed *KRAS* exon 2 WT CRC to receive FOLFIRI plus cetuximab or FOLFIRI plus bevacizumab. The primary end point of the investigator-assessed response rate was not reached. In addition, no difference in PFS was noted (10.0 *v* 10.3 months); in fact, the PFS curves were almost completely superimposable. Surprisingly, however, a statistically significant difference was found in OS, with a difference in median OS of 3.7 months in favor of FOLFIRI and cetuximab.[376] An updated analysis, which accounted for additional mutations in *KRAS* and *NRAS*, demonstrated an even larger difference in median OS (33.1 *v* 25.0 months; HR, 0.70; *P* = .0059)—again without a statistically significant difference in response rate and PFS.[376]

Data from the larger US Intergroup study, CALGB/Southwest Oncology Group (SWOG) 80405, were released in 2014. This study compared chemotherapy (FOLFOX or FOLFIRI) with cetuximab or bevacizumab as first-line therapy for 1,137 patients with *KRAS* exon 2 WT mCRC.[378] In contrast to the FIRE-3 trial, no difference in OS was noted between the two treatment arms, not even when any *RAS*-mutated cancers were excluded. Both treatment arms showed long median OS: 31.2 months for chemotherapy plus bevacizumab and 32.0 months for chemotherapy plus cetuximab (HR, 0.9; *P* = .40). Note that the outcome parameters of FIRE-3 and CALGB/SWOG 80405 were more alike than different, with the exception of the poor performance of the bevacizumab arm in FIRE-3 (Table 13-12).

Tumor Sidedness

Colon tumors present with substantial heterogeneity in molecular features, which is strongly associated with tumor location. Left-sided tumors often present with WT *BRAF* (*BRAF*-WT), *KRAS* point mutations (codons 12, 13, and 61), and extensive copy number alterations, as well as other structural genomic aberrations, including CIN and loss of heterozygosity. Right-sided tumors are enriched for *BRAF* V600E point mutations, are WT for *KRAS*, and have a diploid copy number, MSI, DNA hypermutation, and extensive DNA hypermethylation associated with CpG island methylator phenotype (Fig 13-13).

On the basis of these molecular differences, left- and right-sided colon tumors are now becoming increasingly recognized as two unique cancer types that may benefit from different therapeutic strategies. A post hoc analysis of the CALGB 80405 data found sidedness to be prognostic; median survival of right- versus left-sided tumors was 31.4 versus 24.2 months, respectively (*P* = .01).[379] The trial also suggested that sidedness was predictive of response to cetuximab versus bevacizumab (P_{int} = .05) with cetuximab having an OS advantage for left-sided tumors (*P* = .01) and a suggestion of improved survival of bevacizumab for right-sided tumors (*P* = .08). An analysis of the CRYSTAL and FIRE-3 studies similarly showed a survival advantage for cetuximab over chemotherapy alone or chemotherapy plus

Table 13-12 **Comparison of Outcome Parameters of FIRE-3 and CALGB/SWOG 80405**

Outcome	FIRE 3 CT + Bev v CT + Cetux	CALGB/SWOG 80405 CT + Bev v CT + Cetux
Primary end point	Response rate	Overall survival
CT backbone	All FOLFIRI	FOLFOX 74%/FOLFIRI 26%
ITT (*KRAS* WT exon 2), no.	295 *v* 297	559 *v* 578
RR, %	58 *v* 62 (*P* = .183)	57.2 *v* 65.6 (*P* = .02)
PFS, months	10.3 *v* 10.0; HR, 1.06 (*P* = .547)	10.8 *v* 10.4; HR, 1.04 (*P* = .55)
Median OS, months	25.0 *v* 28.7; HR, 0.77 (*P* = .017)	29.0 *v* 29.9; HR, 0.92 (*P* = .34)
RAS WT, no.	201 *v* 199	256 *v* 270
RR, %	58.7 *v* 65.3; OR, 1.33 (*P* = .18)	53.8 *v* 68.6 (*P* < .01)

Abbreviations: Bev, bevacizumab; Cetux, cetuximab; CT, chemotherapy; FOLFIRI, leucovorin, fluorouracil, and irinotecan; FOLFOX, leucovorin, fluorouracil, and oxaliplatin; HR, hazard ratio; ITT, intention to treat; OR, odds ratio; OS, overall survival; PFS, progression-free survival; RR, recurrence rate; WT, wild type.

bevacizumab for left-sided tumors.[380] NCCN and ESMO guidelines currently recommend anti-EGFR therapy rather than bevacizumab for left-sided, extended *RAS* WT tumors and they should not be used as first-line therapy for patients with right-sided, extended *RAS* WT tumors.

5-FU, Oxaliplatin, and Irinotecan Regimens

FOLFOXIRI regimens have high activity but also increased toxicity. The largest of these trials was the TRIBE trial, in which FOLFOXIRI and bevacizumab were compared with FOLFIRI and bevacizumab alone.[381] The triplet combination improved median OS (29.8 *v* 25.8 months; HR, 0.8; 95% CI, 0.65 to 0.98; *P* =.03), and 5-year survival was doubled to 25% versus 12.5%. There was also a suggestion that patients with *BRAF*-mutant tumors of poor prognosis had improved median OS (19 *v* 10.7 months; HR, 0.54; 95% CI, 0.24 to 1.20) that did not reach statistical significance, likely secondary to the small number of patients with this mutation (n = 28). A subsequent phase II trial, OLIVIA, of FOLFOXIRI with bevacizumab versus FOLFOX with bevacizumab also showed higher response rates and longer PFS and improved rates of liver resection.[382] Another phase III trial, STEAM, confirmed the benefit of the triplet regimen for PFS and liver resection rates, and the recently presented TRIBE2 study of FOLFOXIRI with bevacizumab versus FOLFOX with bevacizumab suggested an OS advantage with early results.[383,384] At this point, given the increased toxicity in a noncurative

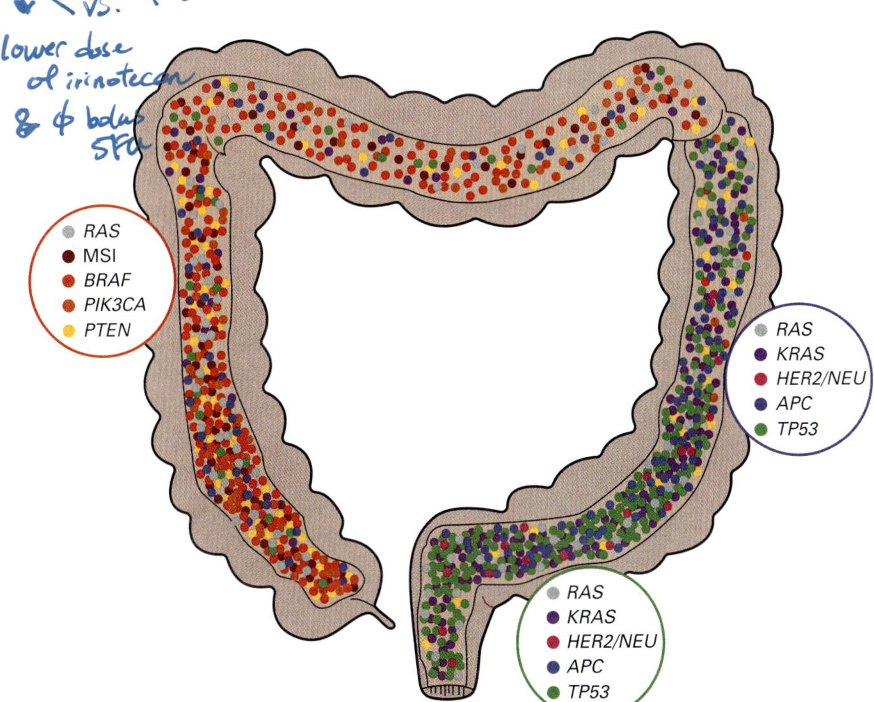

Fig. 13-13 Molecular alterations by tumor sidedness in colorectal cancer.
Abbreviation: MSI, microsatellite instability.

treatment setting for most patients, the triplet regimen should be reserved for patients needing rapid clinical response, either because of symptoms or for conversion to liver resectability, and should be considered for those with *BRAF* mutations.

Stop-and-Go Strategies

Because the treatment-limiting toxicity of oxaliplatin-based first-line therapy is cumulative neurotoxicity, proactive strategies have to be used to maximize treatment duration for patients who start palliative therapy with FOLFOX. Therefore, induction-maintenance approaches with a limited number of oxaliplatin-containing treatment cycles up front and maintenance therapy with a fluoropyrimidine and bevacizumab combination can be considered a standard of care. This concept is supported by several prospective trials and most prominently by the Dutch CAIRO3 study.[385] In this trial, 558 patients who had achieved at least stable disease after an 18-week (six-cycle) induction therapy of capecitabine and oxaliplatin plus bevacizumab were randomly assigned to a complete chemotherapy-free interval or maintenance therapy with low-dose continuous capecitabine (625 mg/m^2 twice daily) plus bevacizumab (7.5 mg/kg every 3 weeks). All prospectively defined outcome parameters in this strategy trial were in favor of the maintenance therapy arm, even with a strong trend toward improvement in OS. Toxicity associated with maintenance was mild and manageable. Thus, an induction-maintenance approach with a limited duration of oxaliplatin-based therapy and prolonged fluoropyrimidine and bevacizumab therapy may be considered an option to minimize toxicity in patients with advanced CRC. Importantly, this and other trials established that oxaliplatin could be reintroduced at the time of progression and still yield acceptable response rates.

Benefit in the Elderly

Although most patients with mCRC will tolerate and receive bevacizumab in the context of an irinotecan- or oxaliplatin-based combination regimen, it is unclear whether specific subgroups—in particular, elderly patients—could benefit from a bevacizumab-and-fluoropyrimidine combination alone. This question was addressed in the AVEX phase III trial.[386] In this study, 280 patients age ≥ 70 years (median age, 76 years) who were not deemed to be candidates for oxaliplatin- or irinotecan-based first-line chemotherapy regimens were randomly selected to receive capecitabine alone or to receive bevacizumab every 3 weeks. PFS, the primary end point, was significantly longer with bevacizumab and capecitabine than with capecitabine alone (median, 9.1 *v* 5.1 months; HR, 0.53; 95% CI, 0.41 to 0.69; $P < .0001$). Although the study was underpowered to demonstrate a statistically significant improvement in OS, the median survival in the bevacizumab arm of 20.7 months (compared with 16.8 months for capecitabine alone) is remarkable given the age of the patient population and the limited postprogression therapies patients received. The combination of a fluoropyrimidine plus bevacizumab can be considered as an acceptable standard of care for elderly patients who are not eligible for irinotecan or oxaliplatin but have no contraindication to receiving bevacizumab.

KEY POINTS

- All patients with metastatic colon cancer being considered for multiagent chemotherapy should have their tumors undergo extended *RAS*- and *BRAF*-mutation testing. In addition, all tumors should be tested for dMMR/MSI-H status and should be considered for HER-2–amplification testing.
- Either FOLFOX or FOLFIRI is an appropriate first-line chemotherapy backbone for patients with mCRC. Eventual exposure to all appropriate agents is what is most important.
- In patients with left-sided extended *RAS* WT tumors, anti-EGFR therapy should be preferentially used, and anti-EGFR therapy should be avoided in patients with right-sided tumors, for which bevacizumab is preferred.
- FOLFOXIRI and bevacizumab should be considered in patients with large, symptomatic tumor burden, those with *BRAF* V600E–mutant tumors, and those being considered for conversion of unresectable hepatic metastases.
- Induction-maintenance approaches with a limited number of oxaliplatin-containing treatment cycles upfront and maintenance therapy with a fluoropyrimidine plus bevacizumab combination can be considered a standard of care. Those whose disease progresses on maintenance therapy can still have oxaliplatin reintroduced.
- For patients who are not candidates for either oxaliplatin- or irinotecan-containing regiments, the combination of a fluoropyrimidine plus bevacizumab can be considered as an acceptable standard of care.

Anti-VEGF Therapy Beyond First-Line Progression

It has been suggested that prolonged inhibition of the VEGF-mediated proangiogenic system is required to maximize treatment benefit for patients who are receiving anti-VEGF therapy, particularly because the mechanism and onset of secondary resistance could differ between chemotherapy and bevacizumab.[387] Additional evidence supporting the concept of prolonged VEGF inhibition as an optimized treatment approach in CRC comes from the ML18147 phase III trial, which tested the efficacy of bevacizumab beyond progression (BBP) added to chemotherapy in mCRC.[388] A total of 820 patients who had received first-line palliative therapy with a bevacizumab-based combination were randomly assigned at progression to either continue bevacizumab with another standard chemotherapy backbone or stop bevacizumab. The primary end point of the study, improvement in OS, was reached with an HR of 0.81 (95% CI, 0.69 to 0.94) and a median improvement of 1.4 months (11.2 *v*

9.8 months; $P = .0062$). This effect was confirmed in all evaluated subgroups and supported by the results of PFS, which demonstrated superiority for the BBP arm (HR, 0.68; median 5.7 *v* 4.1 months; $P < .0001$). No increase in response rate was seen in the BBP group, and the response rates seen in both arms in second-line therapy were low, approximately 4% to 5%. No new or unexpected safety issues emerged for bevacizumab. Confirmatory results were seen with two alternative anti-VEGF therapies: Ziv-aflibercept (formerly known as VEGF-Trap), a VEGF receptor decoy fusion protein, and ramucirumab, a human monoclonal antibody directed against VEGFR-2.[184,389] It should be noted that there is no role for bevacizumab to be used as a single agent either as a maintenance or as a subsequent-line therapy.

Oral Agents in Salvage Therapy of CRC

Regorafenib, a small-molecule inhibitor of multiple cell-signaling kinases (eg, VEGFR1-3, KIT, RET, FGFR1-2, PDGFR-β, and BRAF), has documented efficacy in salvage therapy in advanced CRC. Regorafenib was investigated in a placebo-controlled, randomized, phase III trial in a salvage therapy setting. Efficacy results of the trial demonstrated a benefit in OS for patients receiving regorafenib compared with placebo (6.4 *v* 5.0 months).[390] The activity of regorafenib was also reflected in an improvement of PFS (1.9 *v* 1.7 months). The most common severe toxicities observed with regorafenib were hand-foot syndrome, fatigue, diarrhea, and hypertension. Regorafenib is FDA approved as a salvage therapy option in patients with advanced CRC who have previously been treated with a fluoropyrimidine, oxaliplatin, irinotecan, a VEGF inhibitor, and, if pan-*RAS* WT, an EGFR monoclonal antibody. Dose modifications to reduce the toxicity of this regimen were addressed in the randomized, phase II ReDOS trial.[391]

Trifluridine/tipiracil is a novel oral anticancer agent consisting of trifluorothymidine (FTD) as the antitumor component, which is incorporated and retained in the DNA of cancer cells, and tipiracil hydrochloride, which prevents the degradation of FTD. An international phase III study of 800 patients was launched in the same setting with a 2:1 randomization favoring trifluridine/tipiracil.[392] The primary end point of the trial was met, with an improvement of OS (median OS, 7.1 *v* 5.3 months). The most common grade 3/4 adverse event was neutropenia in about 40% of patients, with 4% having febrile neutropenia. Trifluridine/tipiracil received FDA approval in September 2015 for the treatment of patients with mCRC who have previously been treated with fluoropyrimidine-, oxaliplatin-, and irinotecan-based chemotherapy, an anti-VEGF biologic product, and an anti-EGFR monoclonal antibody, if pan-*RAS* WT. This puts trifluridine/tipiracil in the same clinical setting as regorafenib. It remains to be seen how these two agents will be sequenced in clinical practice. The two agents have distinctly different adverse-effect profiles (trifluridine/tipiracil: neutropenia; regorafenib: hand-foot skin reaction, fatigue) but similar efficacy data.

An evidence-based treatment algorithm in the palliative management of CRC including biologic agents based on molecular testing for *RAS* and *BRAF* is outlined in Figure 13-11. It highlights that in the salvage setting, regorafenib and trifluridine/tipiracil can both be considered and could be sequenced in patients whose disease is considered appropriate for continued antitumor therapy.

PD-1/PD-L1 Immune Checkpoint Inhibitors in CRC

Immune checkpoint inhibitors targeting the PD-1 pathway by binding to PD-1 or its ligand(s) (PD-L1/L2) have shown proof of efficacy in various malignancies since 2014, and several antibodies targeting this system have already received FDA approval in noncolorectal malignancies such as melanoma and non–small-cell lung cancer.[393] PD-1/PD-L1 inhibitors allow the patient's immune system to recognize cancer cells by blocking immunosuppressive mechanisms generated by tumor cells, in particular, when these tumor cells carry a high DNA mutation burden with consecutive expression of many neoantigens. MSI-H/dMMR CRCs carry 10 to 100 times as many somatic mutations as do MSS/MMR-proficient (pMMR) tumors.[394] In addition, MSI-H/dMMR colon cancers are commonly characterized by dense lymphocytic infiltrates, indicating a potential activation of the host's immune system.[395] On the basis of these observations, a pivotal pilot study was initiated that investigated the role of pembrolizumab, an antibody against a PD-1, in heavily pretreated patients with advanced CRC, with cohorts identified by their MSI status (MSI-H/dMMR *v* MSS/pMMR).[196] In addition, a cohort of patients with MSI-H/dMMR noncolorectal cancer was included in the study. Single-agent pembrolizumab showed a remarkable activity only among patients with MSI-H/dMMR cancers independent of their histologic origin. In MSI-H/dMMR CRCs, patients experienced a > 60% response rate and a > 90% disease control rate, with some experiencing durable response for more than a year.[396] These findings have led to the initiation of several studies with PD-1/PD-L1 antibodies, which target the approximately 4% to 5% mCRCs characterized as MSI-H/dMMR. Furthermore, for the first time, the FDA granted organ site–agnostic approval of pembrolizumab for any dMMR solid tumor. For CRC, pembrolizumab is approved for MSI-H/dMMR tumors after prior treatment with a fluoropyrimidine, oxaliplatin, and irinotecan.

Similarly, the FDA approved both nivolumab and nivolumab plus ipilimumab for treatment of patients with metastatic colon cancer with MSI-H/dMMR tumors. This was based on the results of the CHECKMATE-142 study, which showed an ORR of 34% (CR, 9%) and disease control rate of 62% in the single-agent nivolumab arm.[397] Among the 119 patients treated with the combination of ipilimumab and nivolumab, the ORR was 55% and disease control rate was 80%.[398] The two arms were not randomized, so caution is needed in comparing the results. At this point, there is no specific guidance on which PD-1 inhibitor should be used or whether it should be used in combination with ipilimumab or as single agent. Although the completed trials to date have used these therapies in patients refractory to most standard agents, ongoing trials are evaluating these agents in the frontline metastatic setting with or without chemotherapy. It must be emphasized that these agents should not be used in patients with pMMR tumors outside of a clinical trial.

BRAF-Mutant Tumors

BRAF encodes a protein, GTPase, downstream of RAS. *BRAF* V600E mutations can be found in approximately 5% to 10% of patients with advanced CRC.[399] They are mutually exclusive with *RAS* mutations and have been consistently found to be associated with a poor prognosis.[370,400,401] Even in the era of modern combination therapy, the median survival of patients with *BRAF*-mutated, stage IV CRC is only 12 to 14 months.[370] Whether activating *BRAF* mutations can be considered negative predictive markers for the activity of EGFR antibodies has long been unclear because of their strong negative prognostic effect and their low prevalence. A meta-analysis of nine phase III trials and one phase II trial, which all randomly assigned patients to treatment with or without EGFR inhibitors, showed no benefit for the use of EGFR antibodies with regard to PFS, OS, or response rate.[402] Thus, the use of EGFR inhibitors for patients with tumors containing activating *BRAF* mutations should not be considered a first choice, if at all.

In a randomized phase II study including 106 patients, those with *BRAF*-mutant CRC whose disease had progressed on at least one line of therapy were randomly assigned to treatment with irinotecan and cetuximab with or without the *BRAF* V600E inhibitor vemurafenib. Patients assigned to the three-drug regimen had significantly improved PFS (median, 4.4 months) compared with irinotecan and cetuximab alone (2 months; HR, 0.42; 95% CI, 0.26 to 0.66; $P < .001$).[403] Results of the phase III BEACON trial of second- or third-line cetuximab and the *BRAF* inhibitor encorafenib with or without the *MEK* inhibitor binimetinib compared with irinotecan (with or without 5-FU) and cetuximab have been recently published.[404] Improvement was demonstrated in response rate (26% *v* 2%; $P < .001$) and OS (9.0 *v* 5.4 months; HR, 0.52; 95% CI, 0.39 to 0.7; $P < .0001$) of the triplet regimen compared with irinotecan and cetuximab alone. The doublet regimen of cetuximab and encorafenib also performed well. Current NCCN guidelines recommend this triplet regimen in second-line treatment of patients with *BRAF* V600E–mutated mCRC. As reported from the TRIBE trial, an aggressive regimen of FOLFOXIRI plus bevacizumab should be considered as frontline treatment of patients with *BRAF*-mutant tumors.

HER2

HER2 is overexpressed in approximately 5% of metastatic colon cancers. The HERACLES trial treated patients with mCRC patients with *KRAS* WT/*HER2*–positive disease (IHC 3+ or IHC 2+ with FISH ratio > 2.0) with trastuzumab and lapatinib. Despite 74% of these patients receiving more than four lines of therapy, the ORR was 30% and the disease control rate was 60%.[405] Similar findings were seen in the MyPathways trial, in which patients with *HER2*-positive disease were treated with trastuzumab and pertuzumab therapy.[406] Among the 37 patients with colon cancer, most of whom had received more than four prior therapies, 38% had tumor response and the disease control rate was 49% with a median duration of response of > 11 months. An evolving story is whether patients with *RAS*-mutant /*HER2*-overexpressed tumors respond to anti-HER2 therapy (they do not appear to) and similarly, whether patients with extended *RAS* WT/*HER2*-overexpressed tumors respond to anti-EGFR antibodies (they also do not appear to). More data are needed before these findings can be incorporated into routine clinical practice.

KEY POINTS

- Continuing anti-VEGF therapy beyond first-line progression on bevacizumab is supported by the trial literature.
- Patients with *BRAF* V600E–mutant tumors should be considered for treatment with the triplet regimen of encorafenib, binimetinib, and cetuximab or the doublet regimen of encorafenib and cetuximab.
- Patients with MSI-H/dMMR tumors should be considered for immunologic therapy with either single-agent PD-1 inhibitors or a combination of PD-1 and CTLA-4 inhibitors.
- Patients with *HER2*-amplified cancers should be evaluated for trials with agents directed against HER2.
- Either regorafenib or trifluridine/tipiracil should be considered for patients with disease refractory to all other approved agents. The decision of which agent to use first should be based on the adverse-effect profile.

Oligometastatic CRC

All patients with potentially resectable metastatic disease should be evaluated by a multidisciplinary team at a center with high-volume expertise in treating oligometastatic disease. If there is any question about potential resectability, referral is appropriate. When pooling data for all patients who have a hepatic resection, the average 5-year survival rate is approximately 30%, with a less favorable prognosis for patients with multiple lesions, a short interval between the diagnosis of the primary tumor and recurrence, and the presence of stage III disease at the time of initial diagnosis.[407-409]

Preoperative chemotherapy can be used to downsize initially unresectable metastases to make them amenable for a surgical approach. The OS of patients who undergo successful neoadjuvant therapy with subsequent R0 resection of liver metastases approaches the survival of patients with initially resectable metastases.[407,410] Thus, the initial therapeutic approach for a patient with limited metastatic disease should always include consideration of a potentially curative option.

The benefit for chemotherapy in the setting of clearly resectable hepatic disease either in adjuvant or the neoadjuvant therapy is low, with no clear survival advantage. In a European phase III trial of resectable, liver-limited mCRC, 364 patients were randomly assigned to either proceed directly to surgery or to receive FOLFOX chemotherapy for 3 months followed by resection and then followed by 3 additional months of FOLFOX.[411] Patients meeting the eligibility criteria of the trial who received perioperative chemotherapy had a significant improvement in 3-year PFS compared with patients in the surgery-alone arm (36.2% *v* 28.1%; HR, 0.77; *P* = .041). After a median follow-up of 8.5 years, no difference in OS was seen in this study.[412] It is important to note that the 5-year survival in this group of patients with resectable metastatic disease is approximately 50%.

The role of biologic agents (ie, EGFR and VEGF inhibitors) in the context of pre- or perioperative therapy for potentially resectable liver metastases is unclear. Initial data suggest some benefit for the addition of cetuximab to chemotherapy (FOLFOX or FOLFIRI) in this setting,[413] but more recent results from a randomized trial conducted in the United Kingdom suggested an unexplained detrimental effect when cetuximab was added to chemotherapy in the perioperative setting.[414] No randomized trial to our knowledge has tested the role of bevacizumab in the context of liver resection. If bevacizumab is used in the preoperative setting, it needs to be discontinued approximately 6 weeks before planned surgery to reduce the risk of wound-healing complications.[415] It is important to note there are substantial data to support disease resection outside of the liver, with the lung being the next most common site for secondary resection.

Liver-Directed Therapies. Hepatic arterial infusion has been evaluated in multiple prospective trials. Although excellent response rates and control of hepatic metastases have been achieved, a meta-analysis of 10 randomized trials enrolling > 1,000 patients found no differences in OS.[416] Similarly, radioembolization using yttrium plus systemic chemotherapy was evaluated in three parallel, multinational trials in patients with liver-limited disease and despite improved response rates and liver-specific PFS, no improvement in OS, PFS, or hepatic resection rates was seen.[417] Combinations of surgical resection and radiofrequency ablation are used at some specialty centers, as is the use of external beam radiotherapy. This again emphasizes the importance of having patients evaluated at centers with high-volume expertise in treating these patients.

Peritoneal-Only Metastases. An older, randomized Dutch trial that compared cytoreductive surgery and hyperthermic intraperitoneal chemotherapy (HIPEC) to systemic 5-FU chemotherapy for patients with CRC with peritoneal-only disease reported improved survival for the cytoreductive surgery and HIPEC group.[418] The relevance of the trial was questioned because of the use of the older, less aggressive systemic chemotherapy (ie, 5-FU alone) and because the relative value of HIPEC added to the cytoreductive surgery could not be determined. At ASCO 2018, results from the PRODIGE-7-ACCORD-15 trial was presented on patients with peritoneal-only colorectal metastases randomly assigned to cytoreductive surgery plus 6 months of systemic chemotherapy or to the same with the addition of HIPEC using oxaliplatin.[419] The trial showed no difference in OS between the two groups, with a median OS of > 41 months in both groups and a 5-year survival of 40%. In subgroup analysis, there was a trend of HIPEC benefit in those with intermediate-volume peritoneal disease. At this time, HIPEC cannot be recommended for patients with CRC peritoneal-only metastases. Cytoreductive surgery is an option, but patients should be seen at centers with specialization in assessing patients for this type of procedure.

KEY POINTS

- All patients with isolated metastatic disease should be considered for surgical resection and discussion should take place in a multidisciplinary setting conducted at a center with high-volume expertise in treating these cancers.
- Patients with initially unresectable disease can be considered for conversion therapy with multiagent neoadjuvant chemotherapy.
- The benefit of neoadjuvant, perioperative, or adjuvant chemotherapy in patients with clearly resectable metastatic disease, although often used, has not been substantiated by randomized clinical trials to improve OS.
- Liver-directed therapies with either intrahepatic chemotherapy or radioembolization have not shown a survival advantage in multi-institution trials and should not be considered standard of care outside of careful patient selection in experienced centers.
- Patients with peritoneal-only CRC should be evaluated at specialized centers for cytoreductive surgery, but HIPEC should not be routinely used.

TREATMENT OF NONMETASTATIC RECTAL CANCER

Cancers arising in the rectum are associated with a higher overall risk of recurrence than those associated with similar stages of colon cancer. The reason for local recurrence in rectal cancer is believed to be the anatomic location of the rectum and the challenge this presents to the surgeon to achieve clear, circumferential resection margins. In general, stage II and III rectal cancer, unlike colon cancer, is treated with trimodality therapy of chemotherapy, RT, and surgery.

Staging

Staging of rectal cancer consists of either transrectal endoscopic ultrasound or rectal MRI to determine clinical T and N staging. Both are considered appropriate, but more recent data suggest more information can be gleaned from the rectal MRI, including more precise T staging and better evaluation of the likely circumferential resection margin.[420] Both approaches are contingent on the technical competence of the endoscopist or the reading radiologist and on the availability of modern MRI equipment. Imaging of the chest and upper abdomen should also be performed to rule out metastatic disease. There is no role for routine PET scan in the staging of rectal cancer.

Treatment

There is increasing evidence to suggest that local excision should be restricted to patients with stage T1 rectal cancer without high-risk factors.[421] For all other stages, total mesorectal excision has emerged as the preferred surgical technique. This technique honors natural tissue planes and decreases the chance for local seeding and subsequent recurrence.[422] In combination with preoperative or postoperative chemoradiation, 5-year local recurrence rates of < 5% to 10% can be achieved.[423-426]

The recognition of the significant morbidity and the potential mortality associated with local relapse led to the use of preoperative and postoperative RT as additional regional treatment options designed to reduce local recurrence. Two different approaches have been used in this regard: short-term, high-dose radiation commonly delivered as 5 Gy daily for 5 days (5 × 5) immediately before surgery; or prolonged combined-modality therapy with radiosensitizing chemotherapy administered concurrently with radiation to a total dose of 50.4 Gy (45 + 5.4 Gy local boost) over 5 to 6 weeks, followed by a 3- to 4-week treatment break before curative surgery.[424,426,427]

It is important to note that only the longer CRT approach repeatedly has been demonstrated to downstage tumors and cause tumor shrinkage, which might allow sphincter-preserving surgery. Both treatment approaches, however, have been associated with a decrease in locoregional failure. Prevention of local recurrence has not uniformly been associated with improved OS. However, the results of one Swedish trial, in which 1,168 patients were randomly assigned to either 5 days of high-dose RT (to 25 Gy) in the week before surgery or to surgery alone, demonstrated a reduction in local recurrences (11% *v* 27%; *P* < .001) and a survival advantage at 5 years (58% *v* 48%; *P* = .004) for preoperative RT.[426] A subsequent Dutch trial, using the same radiation technique in combination with quality-controlled total mesorectal excision surgery, confirmed a low rate of local recurrence (at 2 years, 2.4% *v* 8.4%; *P* < .001) but did not demonstrate a survival benefit.[424] It is of note, however, that the local recurrence rate of tumors > 10 cm from the anal verge was not significantly affected. Although the shorter, high-dose preoperative radiation strategy is most commonly used in Scandinavia and other European countries, US oncologists have historically preferred combined-modality therapy as preoperative or postoperative chemoradiation. Findings from two studies of postoperative adjuvant CRT demonstrated that FU-based chemotherapy plus RT was more effective than RT or surgery alone in preventing both local and distant recurrence.[428,429] Results from another trial showed that prolonged infusion of FU was superior to bolus administration during RT, providing a 3-year DFS advantage.[430] This finding confirms that protracted delivery of chemosensitizing agents concomitantly with radiation is the best option for combined-modality therapy. In clinical practice, capecitabine administered twice daily parallel to RT (common dosage, 825 mg/m^2 twice daily on days of RT) has become a widely used substitute for the continuous infusion of FU. Two phase III studies confirmed the noninferiority of capecitabine as a radiosensitizer compared with protracted infusion of 5-FU as neoadjuvant therapy in rectal cancer.[431,432] Either infusional 5-FU or capecitabine are acceptable choices to give with RT, and the choice depends on patient preferences for convenience and the clinical team's determination of whether the patient is likely to adhere to an oral regimen.

The long-standing question about whether preoperative or postoperative CRT results in improved outcomes was definitively answered by the results of a large German randomized trial that compared standard continuously infused FU plus radiation either before or after quality-controlled total mesorectal excision surgery.[426] Patients undergoing preoperative combined-modality therapy had a lower rate of local recurrence (6% *v* 13% at 5 years), a lower rate of acute and chronic toxicities, and a significantly higher rate of sphincter preservation compared with postoperative chemoradiation (*P* = .006), but there was no survival advantage to the preoperative approach. This trial established preoperative neoadjuvant chemoradiation with FU as a radiosensitizer as a new standard of care for stages II and III rectal cancers. It is important to note that for those patients who undergo upfront surgery (because of presumed stage I disease) and are found to have stage II or stage III disease, postoperative CRT should be given.

Subsequent studies have tried to further improve the local control rate by incorporating additional radiosensitizing agents, such as oxaliplatin, and biologic agents into the preoperative treatment phase.[433-436] Data call into question the potential role of oxaliplatin as a radiosensitizer when added to fluoropyrimidines in the neoadjuvant CRT of rectal cancer.[437-439] Consistent results from Italian, French, and US phase III trials showed addition of oxaliplatin to fluoropyrimidine (5-FU or capecitabine) as a component of neoadjuvant CRT did not increase the rate of pCR with the use of oxaliplatin, but it significantly increased toxic effects, mainly diarrhea. Only a German trial, which used a slightly different schedule of oxaliplatin administration, showed superiority of the oxaliplatin arm in terms of pathologic response.[435] However, the overwhelming body of evidence at this time suggests oxaliplatin should not be used as part of neoadjuvant CRT for rectal cancer outside of a clinical trial.

Two smaller phase III trials compared neoadjuvant CRT, following the German rectal protocol, with short-course RT (5 × 5 Gy) as neoadjuvant treatment of localized rectal cancer. The two trials demonstrated that both treatment approaches are valid options in the preoperative setting of rectal cancer, with similar rates of local recurrence and OS.[440,441]

Role of Adjuvant Chemotherapy

The role of adjuvant chemotherapy, particularly after neoadjuvant RT, has been disputed by results of individual trials and by a meta-analysis of four studies.[442] The meta-analysis included subgroups of patients from trials, two of which were completed a decade ago. The trials used 5-FU–based adjuvant chemotherapies administered according to outdated regimens no longer considered standards of care, such as the Mayo Clinic regimen and its variations. Neoadjuvant therapy was heterogeneous and included CRT and radiation alone. The authors found no difference in distant relapse and OS associated with the use of adjuvant therapy. A consistent problem in many of these studies and in clinical practice is that it is difficult for patients to complete chemotherapy after surgery; completion rates of ≤ 50% often are seen. Results of the recently published ADORE trial conducted in Korea in patients who had received neoadjuvant CRT and had a postoperative stage II or III cancer were randomly assigned to adjuvant bolus 5-FU or FOLFOX. Six-year DFS was 68.2% in the FOLFOX arm versus 56.8% in the bolus 5-FU arm (HR, 0.63; 95% CI, 0.43 to 0.93; *P* = .018).[443] Although some experts advocate that those with a pCR at the time of surgery do not need additional adjuvant chemotherapy, this is not the standard of care and NCCN guidelines currently recommend all such patients receive adjuvant chemotherapy.

Total Neoadjuvant Therapy Approaches

A current approach of interest is the so-called total neoadjuvant treatment (TNT) approach, where all chemotherapy and CRT are completed before surgery. The theoretical advantage to this approach is that micrometastatic disease is treated earlier, tumor downstaging is enhanced, and compliance with the full chemotherapy regimen may be increased, leading to greater dose intensity of treatment. In one trial, 108 patients were randomly assigned to CAPOX plus RT followed by surgery followed by four cycles of CAPOX or to a TNT approach of four cycles of CAPOX followed by CAPOX plus RT followed by surgery. pCR did not differ between the groups, but grade 3 toxicity was much lower in the TNT approach (19% *v* 54%) and compliance with all four cycles of chemotherapy was higher (94% *v* 57%).[444] In a multicenter trial, 259 patients were sequentially assigned to neoadjuvant FU-sensitized RT followed by zero, two, four, or six cycles of FOLFOX therapy before total mesorectal excision. Patients who received six cycles of FOLFOX therapy before surgery (ie, TNT) experienced 38% pCR, significantly greater than the 18% pCR experienced by the group who received standard CRT alone (*P* = .0036).[445] Chemotherapy was also completed by 98% of the patients in the six-cycle group. The recently published phase II CAO/ARO/AIO-12 trial compared sequencing of neoadjuvant FOLFOX chemotherapy before (induction) or after (consolidation) CRT. The study found increased pCR rates in the consolidation chemotherapy arm (25% *v* 17% in the induction group).[446] The ongoing OPRA trial is examining the question of sequence of chemotherapy in the TNT approach (ie, before or after CRT but before surgery) in a randomized fashion. The European RAPIDO trial is comparing short-course RT followed by CAPOX chemotherapy with the standard CRT surgery chemotherapy approach. Current NCCN guidelines include TNT as an option for treatment of rectal cancer; however, pending current trial results, we do not know the optimum regimen, the best way to sequence, and the impact on long-term outcomes of DFS and OS.

Removing a Modality of Therapy

Retrospective and prospective data have prompted the question of whether all patients with locally advanced rectal cancer need surgery and whether all need RT. In terms of nonoperative management, data from Brazil have suggested high rates of rectal preservation and excellent DFS and OS among patients with a complete clinical response to neoadjuvant therapy compared with a population of patients with pCR who underwent surgery.[447] These findings were confirmed in a meta-analysis of 23 studies[448] including 867 patients and in a large, international, multicenter registry, which suggested local regrowth rates in the nonoperative management group of 15% to 25%, most of which could be successfully salvaged.[449] This approach is being prospectively studied in the aforementioned OPRA trial of TNT. It should be cautioned that although nonoperative management is intriguing, it is not considered the standard of care and should only be considered in the context of a clinical trial or as suggested by NCCN guidelines in centers with experienced multidisciplinary teams and only after careful discussion with the patient.

Another approach being tested is whether RT can be eliminated in a subset of patients with locally advanced rectal cancer. The phase III FOWARC trial conducted in China compared FOLFOX alone with FOLFOX and RT or 5-FU and RT followed by surgery and demonstrated similar rates of local recurrence, 3-year DFS, and OS.[450] This strategy is also being studied in the Intergroup PROSPECT (N1048) trial. To date, this approach remains experimental and should not be used outside the context of a clinical trial.

Role of Biologics

Several studies have sought to enhance the efficacy of preoperative RT by adding biologic agents to a fluoropyrimidine backbone. Results with bevacizumab suggest improved response rates in some studies but at the cost of perineal wound- and anastomotic-healing complications.[451,452] Results with cetuximab and panitumumab have been disappointing with respect to pCR rates and toxicity.[453,454]

KEY POINTS

- Rectal cancer should be staged with either endorectal ultrasound or rectal MRI, on the basis of local availability and technical competence of the endoscopist or reading radiologist. However, MRI is becoming the preferred staging approach.
- Imaging of chest and upper abdomen should also be performed to rule out metastatic disease. There is no role for routine PET scan in the staging of rectal cancer.
- Neoadjuvant CRT using either infusional 5-FU or capecitabine followed by total mesorectal excision is the standard treatment approach for stage II and III rectal cancer but short-course RT is an acceptable neoadjuvant alternative.
- Patients with stage II or III rectal cancer should receive systemic therapy with FOLFOX or CAPOX given either before (TNT) or after surgery.
- Elimination of either surgery or RT for rectal cancer remains investigational and should not be considered the standard of care.

- Oxaliplatin, bevacizumab, cetuximab, or panitumumab should not be added to the CRT backbone for patients with rectal cancer.

SQUAMOUS CELL ANAL CARCINOMAS

EPIDEMIOLOGY AND ETIOLOGY

Cancers of the anus are relatively uncommon in the United States. The male-to-female ratio is approximately 2:3.5. The most clear causal relationship for anal cancer is infection with HPV (mainly HPV-16); > 90% of anal cancers are associated with HPV infection.[455] One large study found a strong positive correlation between the amount of sexual activity and the risk of anal cancer.[456] The association between AIDS and anal cancer has been known for some time, but the exact etiologic relationship has not been elucidated. The incidence of anal cancer in patients infected with HIV is increased > 40 times compared with the general population and, unlike other HIV-associated cancers, has not decreased since the introduction of highly active antiretroviral therapy.[457] Additional risk factors for anal cancers are smoking and chronic inflammation or fistulas in the context of IBD.

The efficacy of a quadrivalent HPV vaccine (HPV-6, 11, 16, and 18) against anal intraepithelial neoplasia was prospectively investigated in a double-blind, randomized study of 602 healthy homosexual men, ages 16 to 26 years.[458] The rate of grade 2 or 3 anal intraepithelial neoplasia related to infection with HPV-6, 11, 16, or 18 was reduced by 54.2% (95% CI, 18.0 to 75.3) in the intention-to-treat population and by 74.9% (95% CI, 8.8 to 95.4) in the per-protocol efficacy population. These intriguing findings, which could lead to a decrease in the incidence of anal cancers through HPV vaccination, prompted the Advisory Committee on Immunization Practices to recommend, in October 2011, the routine use of the HPV vaccine in boys age 11 to 12 years.[459]

Most anal cancers are squamous cell cancers or cloacogenic cancers, with a few adenocarcinomas that should be treated as rectal cancers. Involvement of the inguinal lymph nodes is found in as many as 63% of cases. The most important prognostic factors are the T stage (T1, < 2 cm; T2, 2 to 5 cm; T3, > 5 cm; T4, invasion into adjacent organs) and the lymph node status. In a pooled analysis of four randomized trials with a total of 644 patients, tumor diameter > 5 cm and lymph node involvement were associated with poorer 5-year DFS ($P < .0001$) and 5-year OS ($P = .0001$). In stratified analyses, lymph node involvement had more adverse influence on DFS and OS than did tumor diameter. Patients with > 5 cm tumor and lymph node metastases had the worst DFS (only 30% at 3 years compared with 74% for the best group, which had < 5 cm primary and N0 status), and OS (only 48% at 4 years compared with 81% for the best group (< 5 cm primary and N0 status). Men had worse DFS ($P = .02$) and OS ($P = .016$).[460]

STAGING

In general, staging involves physical examination and biopsy to determine size of the primary and the presence of inguinal lymphadenopathy. Imaging of the chest and upper abdomen should be performed to rule out metastatic disease, especially in those with T3/T4 or lymph node–positive disease, as well as CT or MRI imaging of the pelvis in all patients to assess regional lymph nodes. PET/CT scan should be strongly considered for anal cancer, because a meta-analysis suggested PET imaging changed nodal staging in nearly 30% of the patients.[461] Because the presence of inguinal or pelvic lymph nodes will change the radiation strategy, information provided by the PET is important in treatment planning. NCCN guidelines suggest using PET scan in staging anal cancers. Women with anal cancer should also be evaluated for cervical cancer.

TREATMENT OF NONMESTASTIC DISEASE

In the distant past, treatment of patients with anal cancers was surgical abdominal perineal resection. This treatment option was curative for only approximately 50% of patients and was associated with a high morbidity rate. Today, the standard approach to treatment of anal squamous cell cancers is combined-modality chemotherapy and radiation. Local excision is reserved for patients with small lymph node–negative tumors (T1N0) that are well differentiated. Even here, long-term efficacy data are lacking. Patients with adenocarcinoma of the anus should be treated as patients with rectal cancer and not as patients with anal cancer.

In initial CRT trials, combinations of FU and mitomycin C with radiation yielded a high rate of response, including pCR.[457,462] Eventually, it was recognized that surgical resection was not necessary, and it is used today only as salvage therapy for patients with local recurrences after RT. The expectation is that the CR rate with combined-modality therapy will be between 70% and 80%, with an overall 5-year survival rate of > 65%. However, a substantial number of patients will still experience either local recurrence or metastatic disease. Strategies to improve upon the existing 5-FU and mitomycin standard have not been successful. An induction 5-FU and cisplatin strategy was tested in a phase III RTOG trial involving 682 patients and that compared the mitomycin C and FU and radiation standard to an intensified treatment approach consisting of induction chemotherapy with cisplatin and FU followed by cisplatin and FU during RT.[463] Both the 5-year locoregional recurrence rate (25% *v* 33%) and the distant metastasis rates (15% *v* 19%) trended in favor of the mitomycin-based treatment. The cumulative rate of colostomy was significantly better for mitomycin-based than for cisplatin-based therapy (10% *v* 19%; $P = .02$). An updated analysis with long-term follow-up identified the standard mitomycin-based arm as significantly superior in OS.[464] Results of a more recent phase III comparison between FU combined with either mitomycin or cisplatin in combination with RT did not find a significant difference in outcome,[465] so the inferior results of the RTOG trial for the cisplatin arm could be related to the delay in radiation because of its initial induction chemotherapy component. This trial, the ACT II, also did not show the benefit of adjuvant 5-FU and cisplatin chemotherapy, thus neither induction nor consolidation chemotherapy has a role in locally advanced anal cancer.

Table 13-13 Anal Cancer Follow Up

Follow-Up
Every 3 to 6 months for 5 years with first examination 12 weeks after completing chemotherapy and radiation therapy
Digital rectal examination
Anoscopy
Inguinal node palpation
Computed tomography scan of chest, abdomen, and pelvis yearly to year 3 for those with T3/T4 disease or those with node-positive disease and in those with positive disease on the 12-week examination

In clinical practice, the well-established combined-modality approach using FU and mitomycin C plus radiation remains the standard of care. Mitomycin carries an FDA boxed warning for severe bone marrow suppression that is often delayed (nadir occurs often at 4 weeks) and can be prolonged. Patients' blood cell counts should be carefully monitored during and after the completion of therapy. Cisplatin plus FU can be used for patients with contraindications to mitomycin, usually those related to baseline bone marrow deficiency. Intensity-modulated RT for anal cancer is being evaluated in an effort to reduce short- and long-term toxicity from RT.[346] Intensity-modulated RT should only be used by radiation oncologists experienced in delivering this therapy for anal cancer to avoid undertreatment of the cancer.

The treatment of anal cancer for patients with HIV is somewhat more complex. Standard, aggressive, combined-modality therapies should be used for patients with a CD4 count > $200 \times 10^9/mm^3$ who have no signs or symptoms of other HIV-related diseases. For patients with more severe HIV-related problems, reduced doses of radiation, chemotherapy, or both should be considered to maintain local disease control.[466]

FOLLOW-UP AFTER TREATMENT

Evaluation of anal cancer too early after the completion of CRT can result in premature declaration of treatment failure and unnecessary abdominoperineal resections. The most recent data from the aforementioned ACT II trial suggest tumor regression can be seen up to 26 weeks after therapy completion;[467] therefore, persistent disease prior to 26 weeks should not be deemed a treatment failure. Table 13-13 lists recommended steps for follow-up of anal cancer after treatment.

TREATMENT OF RECURRENT AND METASTATIC DISEASE

For those patients with locally recurrent or persistent disease at 26-week post-therapy evaluation, surgical resection is the preferred treatment modality, with evidence of 5-year survival rates of nearly 50%.[468] The appropriate treatment of patients with metastatic disease is not known and approaches generally follow those for squamous cell carcinoma from other sites. While we await the final peer-reviewed publication, the recent presentation of the phase II InterAACT trial results provides strong evidence for the use of carboplatin and paclitaxel as the first-line treatment of patients with metastatic anal cancer.[469] In this trial, 91 patients were randomly assigned to 5-FU and cisplatin or carboplatin and paclitaxel. The trial used a "pick the winner" design and response rate was the primary end point. Response rates were similar at nearly 60%, as was PFS, but OS was significantly improved at 20 months compared with 12.3 months for carboplatin and paclitaxel compared with 5-FU and cisplatin (HR, 2.0; $P = .014$). The incidence of serious adverse events was also lower in the carboplatin plus paclitaxel arm. Recently published and ongoing studies also have suggested a role for immunotherapy in this cancer. In a trial of 39 patients treated with nivolumab, ORR was 24%, including two complete responders, and 46% had stable disease for a disease control rate of 70%. Median survival was 11.5 months.[470] Combinations of nivolumab and ipilimumab are being tested in this disease as well.

KEY POINTS

- HPV vaccination reduces the incidence of anal intraepithelial neoplasia, but the benefit in reducing the rate of anal cancer has yet to be determined.
- Mitomycin C plus FU with radiation remains the standard approach for localized anal squamous cell cancers, but 5-FU and cisplatin can be considered for those with underlying bone marrow toxicity.
- Responses to chemotherapy and RT can be seen up to 26 weeks after treatment, so early declaration of failure should be avoided.
- Salvage surgery is the treatment of choice for those with locally recurrent or persistent disease at the 26-week evaluation.
- There is no role for induction or adjuvant chemotherapy in locally advanced disease.
- There is no standard regimen for patients with metastatic disease, but early trial results favoring carboplatin and paclitaxel are encouraging.
- Initial data from treatment with immunotherapy agents are promising and confirmatory trials are ongoing.

APPENDICEAL MUCINOUS CANCER AND GOBLET CELL CARCINOIDS OF THE APPENDIX

Appendiceal mucinous cancers and goblet cell carcinoids (GCCs) have their own terminology (Table 13-14) and staging system (Table 13-15).[471,472] The key histologic feature for appendiceal cancer is to determine if it is low grade or high grade and, if high grade, whether signet-ring cells are present. GCCs are classified by the Tang criteria, which puts them into three categories:

- typical GCC (group A),
- signet-ring cell type (group B), and
- AC (eg, GCC poorly differentiated carcinoma; group C)

Table 13-14 **Appendiceal Mucinous Cancers and Goblet Cell Carcinoids**

Diagnostic Terminology	Histologic Criteria
Serrated polyp with or without dysplasia	Serrated crypt profiles confined to the mucosa with intact muscularis mucosae. When present, dysplasia can be classified as low grade or high grade
LAMN	Mucinous neoplasm with low-grade cytology and any of the following:
	Loss of the lamina propria and muscularis mucosae
	Fibrosis of the submucosa
	"Pushing" diverticulum-like growth into the wall
	Dissection of acellular mucin in the wall
	Mucin and/or neoplastic cells outside of the appendix
HAMN	Mucinous neoplasm with high-grade cytology present (at least focally) and lacking infiltrative invasion
Mucinous adenocarcinoma	Mucinous neoplasm with infiltrative invasion. Patterns of infiltrative invasion include:
	(1) Infiltrative glands, incomplete glands, or single infiltrative tumor cells associated with extracellular mucin and desmoplastic stroma
	(2) "Small cellular mucin pool" pattern characterized by small dissecting pools of mucin containing floating nests, glands, or single neoplastic cells
	Grade assessment is based on AJCC criteria
Mucinous adenocarcinoma with signet ring cells	Mucinous neoplasm with a signet-ring cell component accounting for ≤ 50% of the tumor cells
	Mucinous neoplasm with a signet-ring cell component accounting for > 50% of the tumor cells

Abbreviations: AJCC, American Joint Committee on Cancer; HAMN, high-grade appendiceal mucinous neoplasm; LAMN, low-grade appendiceal mucinous neoplasm; PSOGI, Peritoneal Surface Oncology Group International.

Treatment usually consists of surgical debulking with consideration of HIPEC, although the use of HIPEC is not universally accepted. Systemic therapy, following colon cancer criteria and not neuroendocrine criteria, is usually recommended for high-grade and poorly differentiated tumors, although rigorous clinical trials are lacking to guide therapy. Patients with appendiceal or GCC should have tumor pathology reviewed by expert pathologists and should be seen by a multidisciplinary team specializing in these cancers.

GASTROENTEROPANCREATIC NEUROENDOCRINE TUMORS

EPIDEMIOLOGY, CLASSIFICATION, AND STAGING

The gastroenteropancreatic (GEP) neuroendocrine tumor (NET) incidence rate is 3.56 per 100,000 individuals in the United States and has increased significantly over the last > 40 years, as has median OS. Five-year survival rates for metastatic grade 1 and 2 GEP-NET range from 28% for rectal to 69% for small-intestine NETs.[280] Although there are many different historical classification systems for GEP-NETs, in practice and in the recent clinical trial literature, they tend to be divided between pancreatic and nonpancreatic NETs. They are then additionally classified into low-, intermediate-, and high-grade tumors on the basis of either mitotic rate per 10 high-power field or KI-67 labeling (Table 13-16). A recent change in the 2017 WHO classification system for pancreatic NETs created a category of well-differentiated grade 3 tumors, which are tumors that have a high-grade proliferation index but a more well-differentiated appearance on histology. They are treated more in line with the well-differentiated than the poorly differentiated small-cell and large-cell subtypes. Staging is slightly different for each location but follows general TNM AJCC principles.

CLINICAL GENETICS

Although most pancreatic NETs are sporadic, they have been clearly associated with multiple endocrine neoplasia type 1, Von Hippel-Lindau disease, neurofibromatosis 1, and tuberous sclerosis.

CLINICAL PRESENTATION AND WORKUP

The majority of NETs are nonfunctional; therefore, patients often exhibit few symptoms and are often found incidentally at the time of imaging for unrelated reasons. Workup for metastatic GEP typically involves gallium GA-68 dotatate PET imaging, which has largely replaced somatostatin receptor–based imaging because of its better sensitivity and specificity. CT imaging with arterial phase liver or MRI with gadoxetate disodium are the preferred anatomic imaging. If the primary is not identified with these modalities, then upper and lower endoscopy, pancreatic EUS, and/or CT or MRI enterography can be used to better identify pancreatic, duodenal, gastric, or small-bowel origin. Laboratory workup often includes measuring serum chromogranin-A and 24-hour urine 5-hydroxyindoleacetic acid levels. In pancreatic NETs, additional functional markers such as glucagon, gastrin, vasoactive intestinal peptide, or insulin

Table 13-15 Morphologic Criteria

Group	Morphologic Criteria
A: Typical GCC	Well-defined goblet cells arranged in clusters or cohesive linear pattern
	Minimal cytologic atypia
	Minimal to no desmoplasia
	Minimal architectural distortion of the appendiceal wall
	Degenerative change with extracellular mucin is acceptable
B: Adenocarcinoma (eg, GCC, signet-ring cell type)	Goblet cells or signet-ring cells arranged in irregular large clusters, but lack of confluent sheets of cells
	Discohesive single-file or single-cell infiltrating pattern
	Significant cytologic atypia
	Desmoplasia and associated destruction of the appendiceal wall
C: Adenocarcinoma (eg, GCC, poorly differentiated carcinoma type)	At least focal evidence of goblet cell morphology
	A component (> 1 low-power field or 1 mm^2) not otherwise distinguishable from a poorly differentiated
	Adenocarcinoma, which may appear as either gland forming, confluent sheets of signet ring cells, or undifferentiated carcinoma

NOTE. The classification is based on morphologic features at the primary site (appendix) only.
Abbreviation: GCC, goblet cell carcinoid.

levels can be determined depending on the clinical presentation. Pathologic findings should be reviewed by pathologists with expertise in evaluating these tumors and should include either KI-67 labeling (preferred) and/or mitotic rate per 10 high-power field.

TREATMENT

LOCOREGIONAL THERAPIES

Surgery is the main treatment of patients with nonmetastatic tumors. There is no role for adjuvant therapy in these patients. In patients with advanced disease, cytoreductive surgery (debulking) for palliative purposes (decreasing the amount of hormone-producing tissue) should be considered for these tumors. Such surgery includes hepatic resection or resection of other intra-abdominal and thoracic metastases. Surgical palliation of bowel obstruction from tumor masses or mesenteric fibrosis associated with carcinoid tumors may substantially improve quality of life. Hepatic surgery for liver metastasis may allow patients to remain disease free for prolonged periods and may reduce hormone production even if the resection is not complete.

Liver-directed therapy, such as TACE, high-frequency radioablation, or surgical resection, commonly is used for these tumor types.[473] These techniques are particularly useful for reducing symptoms caused by local growth of the tumor or by hormone production and should be regarded as nonsurgical debulking. These procedures also are associated with a greater likelihood of prolonged tumor regression.

SOMATOSTATIN ANALOGS

Somatostatin analogs have been used for some time to control the secretion of 5-hydroxyindoleacetic acid and other

Table 13-16 Nomenclature and Classification of Neuroendocrine Tumors[564]

Differentiation and Grade	Mitotic Count (per 10 HPF[a])	Ki-67 Index (%)[b]
Well differentiated		
Low grade (grade 1)	< 2	< 3
Intermediate grade (grade 2)	2-20	3-20
PanNET G3[b]	> 20	> 20
Poorly differentiated		
High grade (grade 3)	> 20	> 20
Small-cell and large-cell type		

Abbreviation: HPF, high-power field (×40 magnification).
[a]×40 magnification.
[b]Only applies to pancreatic neuroendocrine tumors.

peptides.[474,475] Although octreotide has long been used and is indicated for the palliation of symptoms related to excess hormone secretion, more recently, the analogs have been assessed for their antitumor activity, despite their poor tumoricidal effect, resulting in few regressions. In the PROMID study, a prospective, placebo-controlled, randomized trial of 85 patients with midgut NETs, the use of long-acting octreotide (30 mg intramuscular injection monthly) was associated with significant delay in tumor progression and a trend toward improvement in OS.[476] An alternative long-acting somatostatin analog, lanreotide, was evaluated in advanced NETs in the CLARINET trial.[477] In contrast to the aforementioned PROMID study, which included mainly patients with low-grade, midgut NETs, CLARINET enrolled patients with NETs from the pancreatic, midgut, or hindgut or of an unknown origin that were well or moderately differentiated and had a Ki-67 index < 10%. A total of 204 patients were randomly assigned to lanreotide or placebo. PFS was not reached in the lanreotide arm compared with a PFS of 18 months in the placebo arm (HR, 0.47; 95% CI, 0.30 to 0.73; $P < .001$). The 2-year PFS rates were 65.1% and 33.0% for the lanreotide and placebo arms, respectively. OS was not different between the arms, likely because crossover was allowed in the study and because of potential differences in subsequent treatments. Lanreotide was approved by the FDA in December 2014. The excellent PFS of 18 months in the placebo group should be noted from the CLARINET study, as should the findings that lanreotide was associated with increased rates of diarrhea, abdominal pain, and cholelithiasis. This argues that in asymptomatic patients with a low burden of metastatic disease, watchful waiting is a perfectly appropriate option.

Somatostatin analogs are the first-line therapy for all patients with advanced, well-differentiated NETs in need of systemic therapy. The indication to start therapy in asymptomatic patients is not well defined but should be strongly considered in those with progressive disease on interval imaging or those with a large baseline burden of disease.

TREATMENT OF CARCINOID SYNDROME

In addition to the use of surgical and nonsurgical debulking and somatostatin analogs for carcinoid syndrome, patients with carcinoid syndrome symptoms refractory to standard therapy may benefit from telotristat etiprate, which targets an enzyme involved in excess serotonin production, tryptophan hydroxylase. In a phase III trial, patients with carcinoid syndrome uncontrolled by somatostatin analog treatment experienced a 35% reduction in the number of bowel movements with telotristat etiprate compared with placebo (17%; $P < .001$).[478] Patients in the telotristat etiprate arm also had a lower frequency of flushing episodes and less intense abdominal pain compared with placebo, although these differences were not statistically significant.

SYSTEMIC TREATMENTS FOR SOMATOSTATIN REFRACTORY DISEASE

^{177}Lu-DOTA0-Tyr3-octreotate is a peptide receptor radionuclide therapy that has been available in Europe since 2000. This therapy was tested in the randomized, phase III trial, NETTER-1, in which patients with progressive, somatostatin receptor-positive midgut NETs were randomly assigned to receive four doses of ^{177}Lu-DOTA0-Tyr3-octreotate over 8 weeks along with 30 mg of octreotide every 28 days compared with octreotide alone 60 mg every 28 days.[479] With a median follow-up of 30 months, the median PFS was not reached in the ^{177}Lu-DOTA0-Tyr3-octreotate plus octreotide arms and was 8.4 months in the octreotide arm (HR, 0.21; 95% CI, 0.13 to 0.34; $P < .0001$). An early analysis also suggests a possible survival analysis for lutetium ^{177}Lu dotatate. Serious adverse events include irreversible myelotoxicity and 2% to 3% rate of myelodysplastic syndrome and a 0.5% rate of acute leukemia. Acute events include nausea related to the amino acid infusion required for renal protection, which has improved with new amino acid formulations.

ADDITIONAL SYSTEMIC TREATMENTS FOR PANCREATIC NETS

Pancreatic NETs are more sensitive to cytotoxic chemotherapy compared with other GEP-NETs. In an important phase II trial presented at the ASCO 2018 Annual Meeting by the ECOG-ACRIN group (study E2211), 144 patients with metastatic or unresectable pancreatic cancer were randomly assigned between temozolomide alone or temozolomide with capecitabine. Median PFS was 22.7 months in the combination arm versus 14.4 months in the temozolomide arm (HR, 0.58; 95% CI, 0.36 to 0.93) with a response rate of 33% in the combination arm.[480]

Novel biologics—including VEGF inhibitors such as sunitinib and signal transduction inhibitors such as mTOR inhibitors—have shown efficacy in pancreatic NETs.[481] Data from a placebo-controlled, phase III trial with sunitinib (37.5 mg/d) versus best supportive care for 169 patients with advanced pancreatic NET cancer, all of which had progressed in the past 12 months,[481] demonstrated that PFS increased from 5.5 months with placebo to 11.4 months in the sunitinib group (HR, 0.42; 95% CI, 0.26 to 0.66; $P < .001$). Median OS favored sunitinib but was not statistically significant (38.6 *v* 29.1 months).[482] In a parallel, placebo-controlled, phase III trial of 410 patients with advanced low- to intermediate-grade pancreatic NETs, the mTOR inhibitor everolimus (10 mg/d) likewise improved median PFS from 4.6 months to 11.0 months (HR, 0.35; 95% CI, 0.27 to 0.45; $P < .001$).[483] OS data showed a nonsignificant improvement in median OS of 44.0 months in the everolimus arm and 37.7 months in the placebo arm (HR, 0.94; 95% CI, 0.73 to 1.20; $P = .300$).[484] On the basis of these positive trial results, sunitinib and everolimus gained FDA approval in 2011 for the treatment of pancreatic NETs.

Multiple systemic therapy options now exist for patients with metastatic pancreatic NETs. The correct sequencing of these agents remains unknown at this time and will need to involve shared decision-making regarding the differing toxicities of each of the agents.

NONPANCREATIC GI NETS

Everolimus added to octreotide initially demonstrated only modest activity for patients with NETs with only a borderline statistically significant improvement in PFS.[485] The RADIANT-4 study was a randomized, phase III trial of everolimus versus placebo for patients with advanced, progressive, well-differentiated, nonfunctional lung and GI NETs.[486] Patients in the everolimus arm had a median PFS of 11.0 months compared with 3.9 months with placebo ($P < .001$). There were very few partial responses (2% and 1% for everolimus and placebo, respectively). OS favored everolimus, but was not significant (HR, 0.73; 95% CI, 0.48 to 1.11). On the basis of these results, the FDA approved everolimus for these tumors in February 2016.

Unlike pancreatic NETs, nonpancreatic GEP tumors are not responsive to cytotoxic chemotherapy. For those patients refractory to somatostatin analogs, the clinician has the choice between everolimus or lutetium ^{177}Lu. Many are choosing lutetium ^{177}Lu because of its long PFS, but this is not based on clear level I evidence. As above, shared decision-making regarding the different toxicity and costs of these agents is needed.

POORLY DIFFERENTIATED GEP TUMORS

For patients who have poorly differentiated GEP tumors, the selection of chemotherapy is similar to that for small-cell lung cancer, with the most consistent regression observed using combination etoposide and platinum agents. Ongoing trials are comparing capecitabine and temozolomide with platinum etoposide for these tumors, and the success of immunotherapy in small-cell cancers has led to an interest for these poorly differentiated tumors as well.

KEY POINTS

- GEP tumors are a heterogeneous group of tumors that have a variable course of illness depending on stage, site of origin, and histologic grade based on mitotic rate and Ki-67 index labeling.
- Surgery is the primary treatment of tumors amenable to resection, and there is a role for cytoreductive surgery as well for patients with metastatic and unresectable disease. There is no role for adjuvant therapy in patient undergoing complete surgical resection.
- The oral tryptophan hydroxylase inhibitor, telotristat ethyl is a new option for patients with somatostatin-refractory carcinoid syndrome–related diarrhea.
- For asymptomatic patients with metastatic low-grade tumors and low tumor burden, a watch-and-wait strategy is appropriate.
- Somatostatin analogs octreotide and lanreotide are standard first-line treatment options for most well or moderately differentiated neuroendocrine cancers that exhibit uptake on functional imaging.
- Peptide receptor radionuclide therapy with lutetium ^{177}Lu dotatate is an emerging therapy for patients with GEP who have progressed on octreotide analogs.
- Capecitabine and temozolomide is a systemic chemotherapy option for patients with pancreatic NETs. Nonpancreatic NETs do not appear to be responsive to cytotoxic chemotherapy.
- Everolimus and sunitinib are targeted therapy options in pancreatic NETs and everolimus is approved for nonpancreatic GI NETs. The optimal sequencing of these agents has not been established.

Acknowledgment

The following authors are acknowledged and graciously thanked for their contribution to prior versions of this chapter: Axel Grothey, MD; Joleen M. Hubbard, MD; and Manish A. Shah, MD, FASCO.

GLOBAL ONCOLOGY PERSPECTIVE: GI CANCERS, ASIA PERSPECTIVE

Kohei Shitara, MD; and Hiroya Taniguchi, MD (Department of Gastroenterology and Gastrointestinal Oncology, National Cancer Center Hospital East, Japan)

EPIDEMIOLOGY AND RISK FACTORS FOR GASTRIC AND ESOPHAGEAL CANCER

Gastric cancer is the fifth common cancer and the third leading cause of cancer-related death worldwide. The incidence of gastric cancer is high in eastern Asian countries such as Japan, China, and Korea, as well as eastern Europe and Latin America (Fig 13-14).[487] There has been a gradual decrease in the incidence and mortality rate of gastric cancer in the last several decades. Most gastric cancers are ACs.[488]

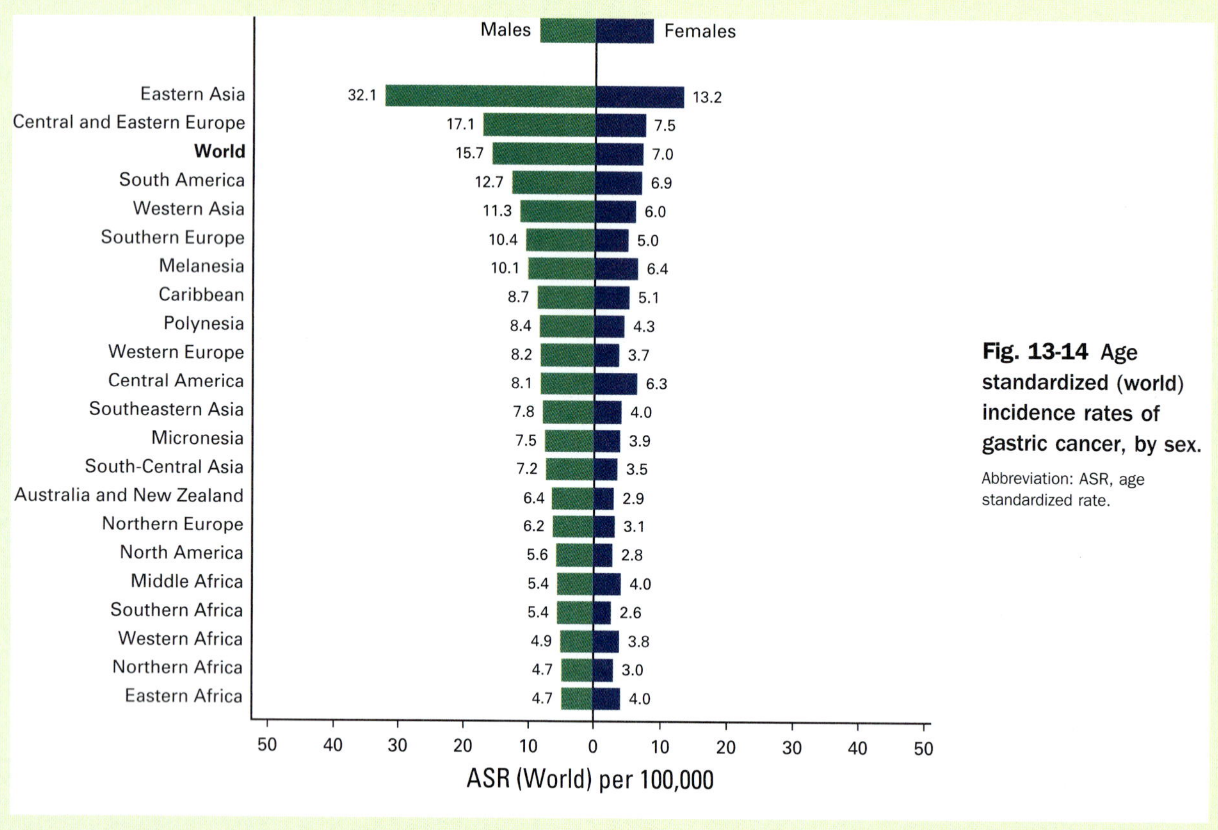

Fig. 13-14 Age standardized (world) incidence rates of gastric cancer, by sex.

Abbreviation: ASR, age standardized rate.

The major risk factors for gastric cancer include environmental factors, host factors, and genetic factors.[489,490] Among the environmental factors, diet including smoked and salty foods and pickled vegetables, which are more frequently consumed in Asia than in the United States, appear to be the most important. Among host factors, *H. pylori* infection, which commonly occurs in early childhood and persists thereafter, is of importance because it leads to chronic atrophic gastritis by inflammation and gastric cancer.[491,492] *H. pylori* infection is more common in eastern Asia than North America or western Europe (Fig 13-15).[493]

The incidence for conventional gastric cancer arising in the stomach body has been declining recently in North America, Europe, and Asian countries,[487] presumably due to decline in *H. pylori* infections by improved sanitation and use of antibiotics. Furthermore, the availability of fresh foods and a reduction in smoking may also have contributed to the declines.[494,495] In contrast, gastroesophageal junction cancers have been increasing in the United States and European countries, which is thought to be due to increasing obesity.[496,497]

Hereditary factors are associated with a small fraction of gastric cancer with no large difference between Asia and the United States or Europe.[498] E-cadherin (*CDH1*) germline mutation is known to cause early onset of diffuse histology of gastric cancer.[494] Also, Lynch syndrome with a mutation within MMR genes also is associated with increased frequency of gastric cancer. Other rare gene mutations related to hereditary gastric cancer include *TP53* mutation in Li-Fraumeni syndrome, *STK11* mutation in Peutz-Jeghers syndrome, *APC* mutation in familial adenomatous polyposis, and *BRCA2* mutation.[498]

Esophageal cancer is the seventh most common cancer and the sixth most common cause of death from cancer worldwide.[487] The age-standardized rate of esophageal cancer is higher in eastern Asia than in western Europe or North America (Fig 13-16).[487] There are two main histologic types of esophageal cancer: SCC and AC. SCC accounts for 90% of esophageal cancer worldwide, especially in eastern Asian countries.[499] In contrast, ACs are most common in the regions with

Prevalence of
Helicobacter pylori
Unknown
< 40%
40%-49%
50%-69%
>70%

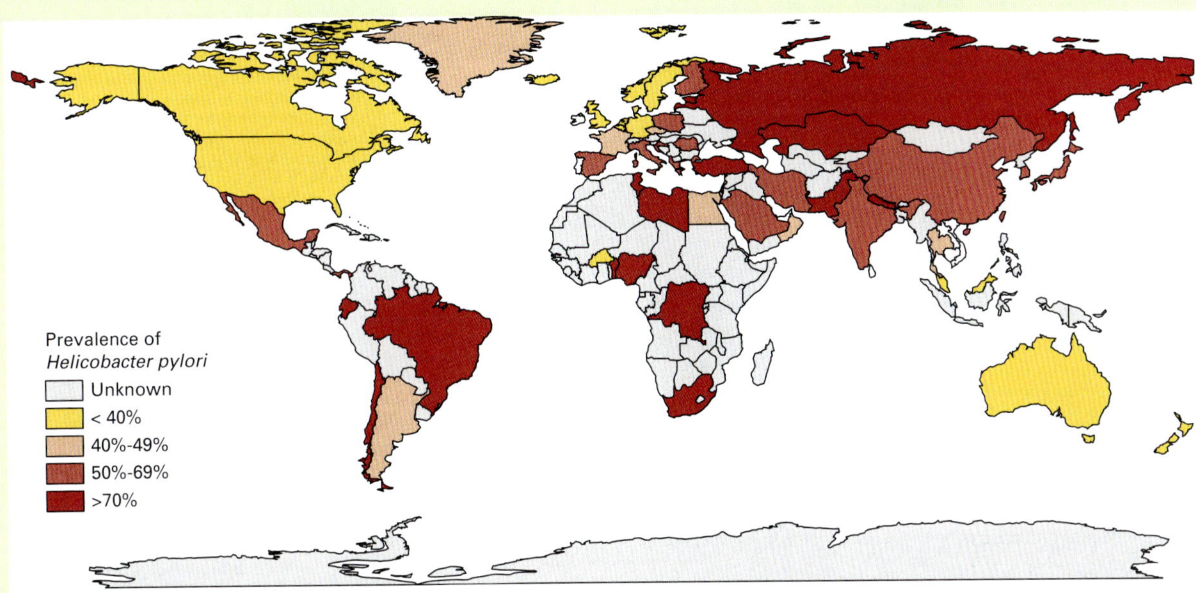

Fig. 13-15 Prevalence of Helicobacter pylori.

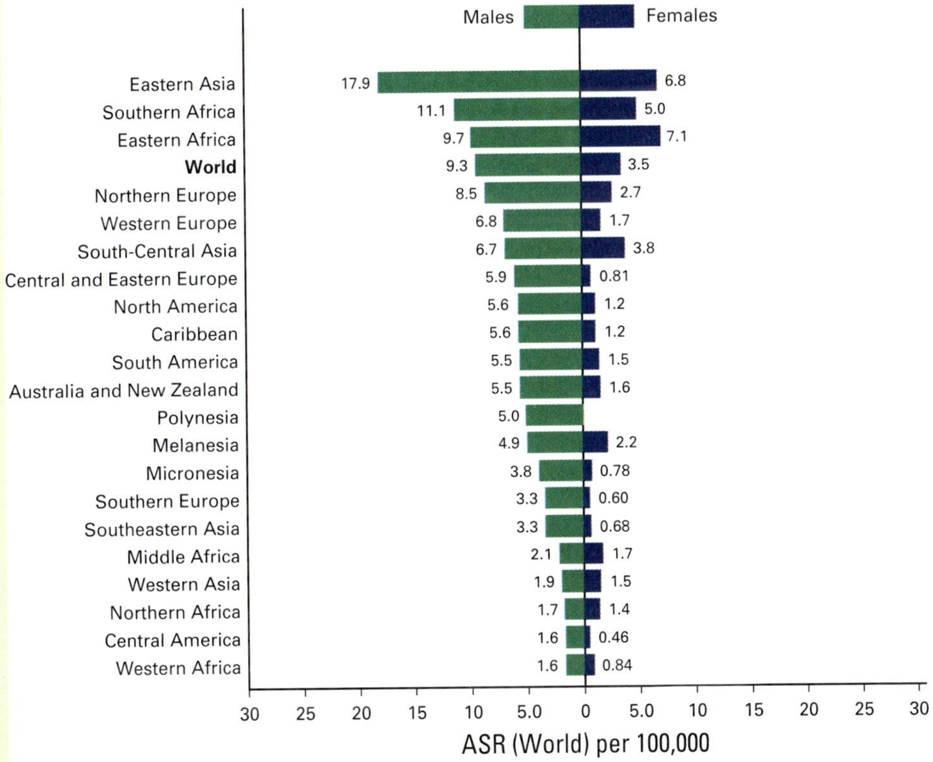

Males
Females
Eastern Asia 17.9 6.8
Southern Africa 11.1 5.0
Eastern Africa 9.7 7.1
World 9.3 3.5
Northern Europe 8.5 2.7
Western Europe 6.8 1.7
South-Central Asia 6.7 3.8
Central and Eastern Europe 5.9 0.81
North America 5.6 1.2
Caribbean 5.6 1.2
South America 5.5 1.5
Australia and New Zealand 5.5 1.6
Polynesia 5.0
Melanesia 4.9 2.2
Micronesia 3.8 0.78
Southern Europe 3.3 0.60
Southeastern Asia 3.3 0.68
Middle Africa 2.1 1.7
Western Asia 1.9 1.5
Northern Africa 1.7 1.4
Central America 1.6 0.46
Western Africa 1.6 0.84
30 25 20 15 10 5.0 0 5.0 10 15 20 25 30
ASR (World) per 100,000

Fig. 13-16 Age standardized (world) incidence rates of esophageal cancer, by sex.

Abbreviation: ASR, age standardized rate.

lower overall esophageal cancer incidence rates, such as the United States and European countries.[500,501] Although the exact reason for the regional differences in incidence and major histologic subtype remains unclear, different risk factors might contribute to it. The incidence of SCC has been decreasing in Europe and North America due to a reduction in alcohol use and smoking. Meanwhile, increasing obesity in western countries is associated with increasing incidence of gastroesophageal reflux and Barrett's esophagus, as well as esophageal or GEJ AC.[500,501]

MOLECULAR CHARACTERISTICS OF GASTRIC AND ESOPHAGEAL CANCER

There is no large difference in molecular characteristics of these cancers by ethnicity. TTCGA project proposed four subtypes of gastric cancer:

- Epstein–Barr virus–positive gastric cancer,
- MSI-H gastric cancer,
- genomically stable (GS) gastric cancer, and
- gastric cancer with CIN.[3]

The CIN group is associated with relatively high frequencies of gene amplifications of receptor tyrosine kinases[502,503] Meanwhile, the Asian Cancer Research Group classified gastric cancer into four molecular subtypes:

- MSI-H,
- MSS with epithelial-to-mesenchymal transition features,
- MSS/TP53 mutant (MSS/TP53), and
- MSS/TP53 WT (MSS/TP53)

These groupings have a stronger prognostic impact than TCGA classification.[504] Molecular profiles of gastric cancer have been also investigated in metastatic gastric cancer in Japan.[502,503,505,506] These profiles or incidences are not largely different from prior reports mainly conducted outside Japan. One study showed that non-Asian gastric cancer was associated with higher expression of multiple signaling pathways related to T-cell functions than was Asian gastric cancer, although detailed clinical factors such as HPV infections have not yet been analyzed.[507]

The TCGA project also investigated the molecular profile of esophageal cancer.[4] Gene expression profiles in SCC are similar to those of squamous-type lung cancer or head and neck tumor. Meanwhile, molecular profiles of esophageal AC resemble those of CIN subtype in gastric cancer AC. Commonly detected gene alterations of Japanese esophageal cancers with SCC histology in the GI-SCREEN project were not largely different from previously mentioned molecular profiles in the TCGA project.[508]

MANAGEMENT OF LOCALIZED GASTRIC AND ESOPHAGEAL CANCER

Greater than 60% of Japanese gastric cancers are diagnosed as stage I disease.[509] In Japan and Korea, where the incidence of gastric cancer is high, screening by endoscopy, which achieves early detection of gastric cancer, is included in routine practice. Meanwhile, there is no routine screening practice for esophageal cancers, thus patients present with more advanced disease, even in Japan. In contrast to gastric cancer, only 15% of Japanese patients with esophageal cancers are diagnosed with stage I disease at the initial presentation.[509]

Various guidelines for management of patients with gastric cancer or esophageal cancers have been published and updated periodically (eg, NCCN guidelines, the ESMO Clinical Practice guidelines, and Japanese guidelines or Japanese Society of Medical Oncology-ESMO guidelines).[510-516]

In Japan, gastrectomy with D2 lymph node dissection is the standard surgical procedure,[514] which has also been recommended in western countries where possible.[511,513] The ACTS gastric cancer trial demonstrated that adjuvant chemotherapy with S-1 as one of the oral fluoropyrimidines significantly improved prognosis and decreased disease recurrence after D2 gastrectomy compared with surgery alone in Japanese patients with stage II and III gastric cancer.[106] Furthermore, adjuvant S-1 plus docetaxel showed better relapse-free survival compared with S-1 after D2 gastrectomy in patients with stage III gastric cancer in the START-2 trial (66% *v* 50%) at the interim analysis, which may establish S-1 plus docetaxel as the Japanese standard adjuvant treatment for patients with sufficient general status after D2 gastrectomy.[517] Meanwhile, another randomized trial, mainly conducted in Korea, also showed improvement in relapse-free survival with adjuvant capecitabine plus oxaliplatin after D2 gastrectomy, compared with surgery alone.[518]

However, a major issue in postoperative treatment is the difficulty in delivering intensive treatment, thus more and more trials have investigated a neoadjuvant or perioperative approach, even in Asian countries.[95,519] In western countries, preoperative treatments have been more extensively investigated. Standard treatment of gastric cancer, esophageal cancers, or GEJ cancer in western countries includes neoadjuvant or perioperative chemotherapy or neoadjuvant CRT, followed by surgical resection.[511,513] The recent randomized, phase III FLOT4 trial confirmed survival benefit of a twice-weekly FLOT regimen compared with a thrice-weekly regimen of epirubicin, cisplatin, and capecitabine as perioperative chemotherapy for resectable esophagogastric junction or gastric cancer AC.[95] Thus, perioperative FLOT is recommended for patients with sufficient performance status.[509,511]

The utility of perioperative CRT has also been investigated in several trials. The CROSS trial demonstrated improved OS with neoadjuvant CRT plus surgery versus surgery alone in patients with SCC and AC of the esophagus or GEJ.[85] Although efficacy of CRT was observed in both histologic types, the magnitude of improvement of survival was more apparent in the SCC subgroup. In Japan, neoadjuvant chemotherapy followed by definitive surgery is the standard treatment of esophageal cancers, based on results of the JCOG9007 trial.[520]

KEY POINTS

- Patients with gastric cancer in Asian countries are frequently diagnosed at an earlier stage of disease than patients in non-Asian countries.
- Surgery followed by adjuvant chemotherapy is the standard treatment of gastric cancer in Asian countries, whereas perioperative chemotherapy is more commonly used in western countries.
- Neoadjuvant chemotherapy is the standard treatment of esophageal cancers with squamous histology in Japan, whereas neoadjuvant CRT is standard in western countries.

SYSTEMIC TREATMENT OF UNRESECTABLE GASTRIC AND ESOPHAGEAL CANCER

Standard treatment of unresectable gastric cancer or esophageal cancers is still systemic chemotherapy including molecular targeting agents or immune checkpoint inhibitors, where available.[509-515] Patients in Asian countries usually had better outcomes in randomized trials, which is suspected to be due to better performance status, lower tumor burdens, and higher proportions of patients with subsequent treatments.[521,522] 5-FU or oral fluoropyrimidines with platinum agents are common first-line chemotherapy regimens for gastric cancer.[509-515] Among oral fluoropyrimidines, S-1 has been mainly developed in Japan.[523,524] S-1 has been also approved in European countries to treat advanced gastric cancer. Because of toxicities observed with S-1, clinical studies in Europe and the United States recommended the dosage of S-1 for subsequent trials as 25 mg/m^2 twice daily,[525,526] which was lower than standard S-1 dose in Asian countries (40 mg/m^2). The difference in toxicity is suspected to be caused by different polymorphisms of the CYP2A6 gene among Asians and non-Asians. The polymorphisms affect the conversion of the S-1 prodrug tegafur to FU as the active drug. CYP2A6 polymorphisms are associated with pharmacokinetics or outcomes after S-1–containing treatment, even among Asian patients.[144,178]

In contrast, the standard dose of capecitabine, which is commonly used as one of the agents in the standard chemotherapy (ie, capecitabine plus cisplatin or oxaliplatin), in several global trials is similar between Asian and non-Asian countries. Paclitaxel and the anti-VEGFR2 monoclonal antibody ramucirumab showed a survival benefit compared with paclitaxel monotherapy as a second-line treatment of advanced gastric cancer in the global RAINBOW trial.[178] Thus, this combination is recommended in Asian and western countries, where available.[509-515] Results of a subgroup analysis of Japanese patients also suggest clinical benefit of the paclitaxel and ramucirumab combination.[521] Recently, the global TAGS trial demonstrated a survival benefit of trifluridine/tipiracil as a new oral agent for chemotherapy-refractory gastric cancer. The trial showed no large ethnic difference according to regions.[200] Now FTD/TPI is approved by the FDA and in Japan.

A difference in immunologic profiles of Asian gastric cancer and non-Asian gastric cancer has been suggested.[505] However, trial comparisons between Asian trials with PD-1 blockade by nivolumab and the global trial with pembrolizumab mainly conducted in western countries showed a similar response rate or PFS.[204,527] Also, the randomized studies of PD-1 blockade for gastric cancer and esophageal cancers showed no remarkable differences of efficacy according to regions; this will be further analyzed in ongoing randomized studies. Thus, detailed immunologic profiles such as PD-L1 expression or mutation burdens may be more important rather than ethnicity itself to predict outcomes after PD-1 blockade, which should be further evaluated in larger patient cohorts.

EPIDEMIOLOGY AND RISK FACTORS FOR CRC

The incidence and mortality of CRC is rising rapidly in Asia. Worldwide, CRC is the third most commonly diagnosed and the second most common cause of cancer-related death.[487] In Asia, it is the second most common cancer, and epidemiologic trends in CRC vary among different Asian countries.[528] Eastern Asia has the highest incidence rates within the Asian region. Economically advanced countries, such as Hong Kong, Singapore, and South Korea, have seen a decrease in CRC mortality rates, which could be attributed to a widespread adoption of screening programs[529]; in Japan, the CRC mortality rate has been stable.[509] However, the incidence of CRC in these countries has increased, possibly due to changes in lifestyle risk factors.

The etiology of colon cancer is different from that of rectal cancer. High intake of dietary fat and animal foods and low levels of physical activity are well-established risk factors for colon cancer in western societies. On the other hand, cigarette smoking and polluted surface-water sources are reported to be risk factors for distal colon and rectal cancer, which is of importance as risk factors among populations from lower- and middle-income countries, particularly those in Asia.[530,531] The age effects on incidence generally increase in western and Asian populations, and there is an increased risk of CRC as their younger cohorts reach older ages.[532] These findings are consistent with the life-course argument that macroenvironmental changes associated with socioeconomic development have specific effects that extend over the life course.

The most common test used as a screening tool in organized screening programs was the fecal occult blood test. In countries with screening programs that arose opportunistically, colonoscopy was most commonly used for screening.[533]

MOLECULAR CHARACTERISTICS OF CRC

There are no large differences in molecular characteristics by ethnicity itself. The genomic landscape of CRC is not different between the West and Asia. Comprehensive genomic sequencing showed that the overall mutation spectrum of Japanese patients is similar to that of populations in western countries.[534] It was interesting to note that there is no difference in the prevalence of *KRAS* mutations, whereas incidence of a tumor *BRAF* V600E mutation in eastern Asian patients appears to be a little lower than among white patients (approximately 5% *v* 10%, respectively).[535,536] The frequency of DNA dMMR in stage II/III CRC is also > 10% in the United States[537]; it is approximately 5% in Japan.[538]

MANAGEMENT OF RESECTABLE CRC

Colon adenomas or some T1 colon ACs can be treated by endoscopic resection. Endoscopic treatment methods have evolved over the years from snare polypectomy to endoscopic mucosal resection, and now to endoscopic submucosal dissection (ESD). ESD is a well-established method in Asian countries and is increasingly practiced, but there is still lack of experience in the United States.[539,540] Lesions with a maximum diameter of ≥ 2 cm are one of the suggested indications for ESD in guidelines. Additional surgical resection is recommended for positive vertical margin; tumor invading the submucosa (depth of submucosal invasion ≥ 1,000 μm); positive lymphovascular invasion, including high-grade component such as signet-ring cell carcinoma or mucinous carcinoma; and high budding grade at the site of deepest invasion by pathologic assessment.

Radical surgery involves colon resection and regional lymph node dissection is the standard of care for resectable CRC. If patients have pathologically diagnosed stage III or high-risk stage II disease, adjuvant chemotherapy with oxaliplatin-based combination chemotherapy for 6 months is recommended in western countries, which is also widely accepted in Asian countries.[541,542] IDEA collaboration including the Japanese ACHIEVE trial demonstrated similar recurrence-free survival in 3 months and 6 months of CapeOx, especially in low-risk (T1-3 and N1) stage III colon cancer.[342,543] Therefore, CapeOx for 3 months is listed as one of the options in Japanese guidelines. Fluoropyrimidine monotherapy is also one of the options in Japan because a better prognosis is reported there than in western countries, partially because the standard procedure for colectomy in Japan involves complete tumor resection and an extended D3 lymph node dissection that includes pericolic, intermediate, and mostly central lymph nodes.[544] By contrast, many surgeons in other high-income countries feel the increased complexity of the procedure and the longer duration of surgery provide an increased risk generally, particularly in overweight or obese patients, which are more common in Europe and North America.

The treatment algorithm for locally advanced rectal cancer is different between Asia and western countries. In Japan, lateral lymph node dissection is routinely performed and radiation is not routinely used.[545] In China, most surgeons did not use neoadjuvant treatment in the past; however, during the past 10 years, more physicians have accepted neoadjuvant treatment, but the use of radiation is still adopted only for small populations, based on the results of a study that compared chemotherapy alone with CRT and that found no difference in recurrence-free survival.[546] In South Korea and other Asian countries, neoadjuvant CRT is a mainstay for the treatment of locally advanced rectal cancer.[547]

KEY POINTS

- Endoscopic submucosal dissection is established in Asian countries for en bloc resection for lesions at risk for submucosally invasive CRC.
- Surgery followed by adjuvant chemotherapy is the standard treatment in United States as well as in Asian countries for advanced colon cancer.
- Neoadjuvant CRT followed by surgery is increasing as the standard treatment in Asian countries as it currently is in western countries.

SYSTEMIC TREATMENT OF UNRESECTABLE CRC

Various guidelines for the management of patients with mCRC have been published and updated periodically, including the following:

- NCCN guidelines,[548,549]
- ESMO clinical practice guidelines,[550]
- Pan-Asian adapted ESMO guidelines,[551] and
- local guidelines in each country.

Patients in Asian countries usually had similar survival outcomes as patients in western countries in randomized trials. Standard treatment of mCRC is still systemic chemotherapy including a fluoropyrimidine, oxaliplatin, irinotecan, and molecular targeting agents, where available. The choice of backbone chemotherapy depends on factors such as patient preference, toxicity, and drug availability. FOLFOX, CapeOx, and FOLFIRI are common first- or second-line chemotherapy regimens in western countries as well as Asian countries. S-1 is also used in combination with oxaliplatin or irinotecan in Japan.[552,553] *RAS* mutation testing and, in some countries, *BRAF* V600E testing are recommended for mCRC, and one of the bevacizumab or anti-EGFR antibodies, cetuximab or panitumumab, is used in combination with cytotoxic agents. Especially for left-sided tumors, anti-EGFR therapy with FOLFOX or FOLFIRI is recommended in Asian guidelines on the basis of retrospective analyses in western countries as well as Asian trials.[554,555]

In second-line treatment, patients who receive an oxaliplatin-based fluoropyrimidine regimen in the first-line setting receive irinotecan-based regimen as a second-line treatment and vice versa with a molecular antibody. The modified XELIRI (mXELIRI) regimen (irinotecan plus capecitabine) can be used for second-line chemotherapy.[390] The Chinese Society of Clinical Oncology guidelines basically do not recommend continuation of bevacizumab in second-line therapy, whereas Japanese guidelines recommend continuation of anti-VEGF therapy (including ramucirumab and aflibercept) as one of the treatment options. Pembrolizumab is approved for MSI-H/dMMR CRC in some Asian countries.

As later-line treatment, regorafenib and trifluridine/tipiracil are the standard of care, on the basis of the reproducible results from separate phase III trials in western countries (including Japan)[392,556] and Asia.[557,558] In China, an oral VEGFR inhibitor, fruquintinib, demonstrated survival benefit compared with placebo and is one of the treatment options for chemotherapy-refractory CRC.[559]

Irinotecan-induced toxicity is associated with the activity of the enzyme UGT1A1, especially with genetic polymorphisms UGT1A1*28 and UGT1A1*6. In Asian patients, the frequency of the UGT1A1*28 variant is much lower than that in white patients, whereas the UGT1A1*6 variant is more common in Asian populations than in patient populations in western countries.[560] Approximately 10% of Japanese patients are either homozygous or simultaneously heterozygous for UGT1A1*6 or UGT1A1*28, which is associated with the severity of irinotecan-induced toxicities.[561] With regard to the other markers of chemotherapy sensitivity and toxicity, a Japanese study showed that patients with dihydropyrimidine dehydrogenase deficiency experienced serious toxicity, including death, after 5-FU treatment; the incidence of dihydropyrimidine dehydrogenase deficiency in healthy Japanese volunteers is extremely low (0.1% to 0.7%).[562] For other examples of the ethnic difference in toxicity profile, the incidence of hand-foot skin reaction and liver dysfunction with regorafenib treatment is higher in Japanese and Asian populations than in western populations, but incidence of diarrhea was slightly lower in phase III trials.

KEY POINTS

- There is no striking difference for the efficacy of chemotherapeutic agents between east Asian and western patients with mCRC.
- There are some ethnic differences in the toxicity profiles of some agents; for example, irinotecan and regorafenib.

14

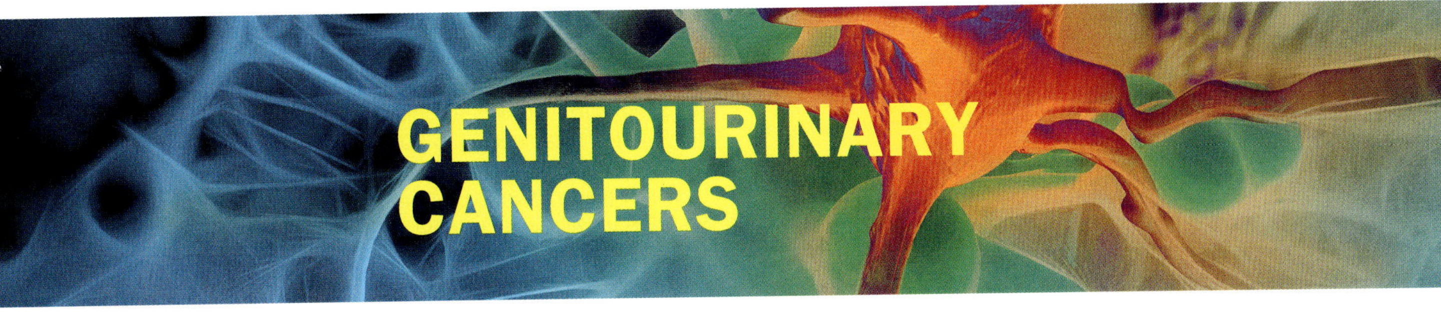

David J. Einstein, MD, and Marc B. Garnick, MD

Recent Updates

PROSTATE CANCER

- Two prospective, randomized clinical trials showed an improvement in overall survival (OS) with the addition of the androgen receptor antagonists apalutamide (TITAN Trial) or enzalutamide (ENZAMET Trial) to androgen deprivation therapy (ADT) in patients with metastatic castration-sensitive prostate cancer, compared with ADT alone. (Chi KN, *N Engl J Med* 2019; Davis ID, *N Engl J Med* 2019) A third randomized trial (ARCHES) also showed improved radiographic, progression-free survival (PFS) with the addition of enzalutamide to ADT relative to ADT alone. (Armstrong AJ, *J Clin Oncol* 2019) Apalutamide and enzalutamide received US Food and Drug Administration (FDA) approvals for treatment in these settings.
- Three prospective, randomized clinical trials—ARAMIS, PROSPER and SPARTAN—showed an improvement in metastasis-free survival with the addition of darolutamide, enzalutamide, and apalutamide, respectively, to ADT in patients with nonmetastatic castration-resistant prostate cancer (nmCRPC), leading to FDA approvals for all three drugs for nmCRPC. (Hussain M, *J Clin Oncol* 2018; Smith MR, *N Engl J Med* 2018; Fizazi K, *N Engl J Med* 2019)
- Men with metastatic castration-resistant prostate cancer who are beginning treatment with the androgen signaling inhibitors abiraterone or enzalutamide are much less likely to have prostate-specific antigen (PSA) or radiographic responses if androgen receptor-variant 7 (AR-V7) is detected in circulating tumor cells by either of two commercially available assays, compared with those who do not have detectable AR-V7. (Armstrong AJ, *J Clin Oncol* 2019)
- In men suspected to have prostate cancer, on the basis of elevated PSA level, the PRECISION trial showed that magnetic resonance imaging (MRI) followed by MRI-targeted biopsy led to more frequent diagnosis of clinically significant prostate cancer and less frequent diagnosis of clinically insignificant prostate cancer, compared with standard transrectal ultrasonography-guided biopsy. (Kasivisvanathan V, *N Engl J Med* 2018)

BLADDER CANCER

- Erdafitinib, a tyrosine kinase inhibitor targeting fibroblast growth receptors (FGFR)-1 through FGFR-4, demonstrated a 40% response rate in a phase II study of patients with previously treated, advanced and FGFR-altered urothelial carcinoma, earning accelerated FDA approval on the basis of the presence of FGFR alterations in a companion diagnostic test. (Loriot Y, *N Engl J Med* 2019)
- Enfortumab vedotin, an antibody-drug conjugate targeting Nectin-4, demonstrated a 44% response rate in a phase II study of patients with previously treated advanced urothelial carcinoma. (Rosenberg JE, *J Clin Oncol* 2019 [supplement]) It received an FDA accelerated approval.

- Pembrolizumab demonstrated a 40% complete response rate in patients with non-muscle-invasive bladder cancer (carcinoma in situ with or without papillary tumors) unresponsive to Bacillus Calmette-Guerin (BCG) in a single-arm phase II study (Balar AV, *J Clin Oncol* 2019 [supplement]), with half of these responses persisting at one year, earning FDA approval.
- The phase III POUT trial demonstrated that adjuvant gemcitabine plus platinum improved 2-year disease-free survival compared with surveillance followed by chemotherapy at the time of recurrence in patients with high-risk, resected, upper-tract urothelial carcinoma. (Birtle AJ, *J Clin Oncol* 2018)
- Alterations in DNA-damage response and repair genes are independently associated with response to programmed death-1 (PD-1)/programmed death-ligand 1 (PD-L1) inhibitors in metastatic urothelial carcinoma. (Teo MY, *J Clin Oncol* 2018)
- Prior to cystectomy, neoadjuvant PD-1/PD-L1–inhibitor monotherapy with pembrolizumab or atezolizumab resulted in 42% and 29% rates of pathologic complete response, respectively. (Necchi A, *J Clin Oncol* 2018; Powles T, *J Clin Oncol* 2018)

RENAL CANCER

- In contrast with data from the cytokine era, the CARMENA trial demonstrated that sunitinib alone was noninferior to cytoreductive nephrectomy followed by sunitinib for metastatic clear-cell renal cell carcinoma with intermediate or poor risk, according to the Memorial Sloan Kettering Cancer Center prognostic model. (Mejean A, *N Engl J Med* 2018)
- The combination of PD-1/PD-L1 inhibitors with vascular endothelial growth factor inhibitors has been explored in several trials. The KEYNOTE-426 trial demonstrated improved OS with pembrolizumab plus axitinib relative to sunitinib regardless of PD-L1 status, leading to FDA approval for this combination as first-line therapy for advanced renal cell carcinoma (RCC). (Rini BI, *N Engl J Med* 2019) The IMmotion 151 trial demonstrated that atezolizumab plus bevacizumab improved PFS compared with sunitinib in first-line treatment of metastatic RCC with PD-L1 ≥ 1% expression on tumor-infiltrating immune cells. (Motzer RJ, *J Clin Oncol* 2019) The JAVELIN Renal 101 trial showed that avelumab plus axitinib improved PFS relative to sunitinib regardless of PD-L1 status. (Motzer RJ, *Ann Oncol* 2018)

OVERVIEW

Genitourinary malignancies—including cancers of the prostate, bladder, ureters, kidneys, testes, and penis—are a heterogeneous group of tumors with major public health implications. Prostate cancer is the second most common cancer among men worldwide and the fourth most common cancer overall. Bladder cancer incidence is increasing in developing nations, reflecting increased rates of tobacco smoking decades prior. In this chapter, we discuss the medical oncologist's approach to genitourinary malignancies. We discuss risk stratification and, in some cases of low-risk cancers, active surveillance instead of intervention. In more advanced settings, we discuss established treatment protocols as well as emerging biomarkers and therapies. The spectrum of treatments for genitourinary malignancies is wide and includes not only chemotherapy but hormonal therapies, molecularly targeted therapies, and immunotherapies, in addition to local therapies such as surgery and radiation.

PROSTATE CANCER

EPIDEMIOLOGY

Approximately one American man in nine will be diagnosed with prostate cancer during his lifetime, and it is the most common cancer in American men other than skin cancer.[1] It has been estimated that approximately 15% to 17% of men older than 50 years are harboring occult prostate cancer, and this percentage increases with each decade of advancing age.[2] Autopsy series show that nearly 70% of men older than 80 years have occult prostate cancer. Only about one in 41 will die of prostate cancer, but this still makes it the second leading cause of cancer death in American men. In the United States in 2019, there will be an estimated 174,650 new cases of prostate cancer and 31,620 associated deaths.[1] The 6:1 ratio of incidence to mortality demonstrates that although the disease is lethal for some men, the majority of men with prostate cancer die of other causes. These data highlight the variable biology and clinical course of prostate cancer. Many prostate cancers do not require immediate intervention, because the risk of death from noncancer-related causes exceeds that of the cancer; other prostate cancers require multimodality approaches, both to eradicate the tumor locally and to eliminate micrometastases.

Although the frequency of histologic cancers at autopsy is similar throughout the world, the clinical incidence is significantly higher in Western countries, suggesting a role for environmental factors. High consumption of dietary fats, in particular the fatty acid α-linoleic acid, is believed to increase risk by two- to three-fold. Several potential protective dietary factors for prostate cancer incidence have been proposed, including tomatoes (which contain lycopenes), cruciferous vegetables, carotenoids, fish, long-chain marine omega-3 fatty acids, soy, and polyphenols. The association with dietary animal fat intake is most robust.

Although poorer outcomes have been observed in black men with prostate cancer compared with white men, it is unclear to what extent this is related to intrinsic differences in disease biology versus inadequate access to health care. A recent study of the SEER Prostate Active Surveillance/Watchful Waiting database found that black men were twice as likely to die of Gleason score 6 prostate cancer compared with nonblack men but no more likely to die of Gleason score ≥ 7 prostate cancer.[3] In addition, when the numbers of black men are adequately represented in clinical research studies, no differences in clinical outcomes compared with other racial groups are seen.[4]

Of note, although some have reported an association between vasectomy and development of prostate cancer, the largest review to date has not demonstrated any association.[5] Testosterone supplementation appears associated with an increased incidence of low- to intermediate-risk prostate cancer, likely due to increased screening, but not high-risk prostate cancer (and, in fact, significantly lower risk).[6]

KEY POINTS

- Prostate cancer is a common diagnosis, and although metastatic disease develops in a small percentage of affected patients, this translates into a large absolute number of deaths due to prostate cancer.
- Whether black men tend to have biologically more aggressive prostate cancer than nonblack men is controversial. Disparities in access to care likely explain at least some of the difference in outcomes.
- There is no clear causal link between vasectomy and prostate cancer, nor does testosterone supplementation appear to increase the risk of aggressive prostate cancer.

HEREDITY

Current estimates suggest that 5% to 10% of all cases of prostate cancer are hereditary.

- A rare but recurrent mutation (G84E) in *HOXB13* (rs138213197), a homeobox transcription factor, is strongly associated with early-onset, familial prostate cancer, suggesting that rare genetic variants exist that contribute to familial clustering of prostate cancer.
- Germline alterations in DNA repair genes are more common and are especially enriched in metastatic disease.

A more recent study of 692 men with metastatic prostate cancer unselected for family history of cancer analyzed germline DNA for mutations in 20 DNA repair genes associated with autosomal dominant cancer predisposition syndromes.[7] Eighty-four germline DNA repair gene mutations presumed to be deleterious were identified in 82 men (11.8%). Mutations were found in 16 genes, including *BRCA2*, *ATM*, *CHEK2*, *BRCA1*, *RAD51D*, and *PALB2*. Mutation frequencies did not differ according to family history of prostate cancer or age at diagnosis. The overall frequency of DNA damage-repair germline mutations in men with metastatic prostate cancer exceeded the prevalence in men with localized prostate cancer (4.6%). The authors suggest these findings, along with the activity of poly-ADP ribose polymerase (PARP) inhibitors (currently olaparib and rucaparib have US Food and Drug Administration [FDA] breakthrough designations but not full approval) and platinum-based chemotherapy in men with metastatic prostate cancer and DNA repair gene mutations, provide an argument for considering the routine evaluation of men with metastatic prostate cancer for the presence of germline mutations in DNA repair genes. Results presented at a recent international symposium on genetics of prostate cancer are summarized in Table 14-1.

Guidelines for screening patients with prostate cancer for germline alterations are rapidly evolving.[8] Strong family history of cancer consistent with a *BRCA1/2*-related syndrome or Lynch syndrome should certainly prompt genetic counseling. National Comprehensive Cancer Network (NCCN) prostate cancer guidelines[9] recommend consideration of germline testing for:

- any patient with metastatic, regional, or high-risk localized prostate cancer, regardless of family history.
- patients with low- to intermediate-risk prostate cancer with intraductal histology (new in NCCN 2019 guidelines) or a "strong family history" of prostate cancer, meaning:
  - a brother or father or multiple family members diagnosed with prostate cancer at age < 60 years
  - known family history of high-risk germline alterations
  - two or more relatives with breast, ovarian, or pancreatic cancer (suggesting *BRCA2* alteration)
  - two or more relatives with colorectal, endometrial, gastric, ovarian, pancreatic, small-bowel, urothelial, kidney, or bile duct cancer (suggesting Lynch syndrome)
  - Ashkenazi Jewish ancestry, which could also prompt genetic testing

KEY POINTS

- Prostate cancer is one of the most hereditable cancers. Clinicians should take a full history of malignancies in the family and be familiar with the link between prostate cancer and germline alterations in *BRCA2* and mismatch repair genes, which are enriched among men with metastatic prostate cancer.
- Guidelines for referral to genetic counseling are frequently changing, but at minimum, clinicians should

Table 14-1 Risk Estimates for Prostate Cancer by Genes Associated With Hereditary Cancer Syndromes

Gene	Risk of PCa	Risk of Aggressive PCa	Risk of Early-Onset PCa	Specific Outcomes
BRCA1	1.07-3.81		1.82	5.16
BRCA2	3.18-8.6	3.18-4.38	7.33	HR for death, 2.4-5.48
Mismatch repair genes	1.99-3.67		2.48	
HOXB13	2.8-8.47		2.7-10.11	

Abbreviations: HR, hazard ratio; PCa, prostate cancer.

consider genetic counseling for all patients with metastatic castration-resistant prostate cancer (mCRPC), those with strong family histories as outlined in the preceding paragraphs, or those with alterations in DNA damage repair or mismatch repair genes identified from tumor sequencing.

ANATOMY

The peripheral zone is palpable by digital rectal examination (DRE) and is the site of origin of 70% of prostate cancers (Fig 14-1). The transition zone surrounds the urethra and cannot be assessed by DRE. Up to 20% of all prostate cancers develop in the transition zone; however, benign prostatic hypertrophy is more common than prostate cancer in the transition zone. The anterior portion of the prostate gland is especially important because this area is generally not biopsied as part of a routine prostate needle biopsy. It should be evaluated either by magnetic resonance imaging (MRI) or targeted, directed biopsy in settings where the prostate-specific antigen (PSA) level continues to rise in the setting of continued negative biopsy specimens, and often harbors, in these circumstances, high-grade cancers.

When counseling men considering treatment options with either a surgical approach or radiation, the anatomic location of the positive biopsy specimens is instructive. In the standard 12-core biopsy, generally two biopsy cores are obtained from the base of the gland, midportion, and apical region (Fig 14-2). The possibility of seminal vesicle involvement with a preponderance of positive biopsy specimens in the base of the gland is a concern, especially because the base is in the anatomic region of the seminal vesicle. Therefore, a clinician should consider obtaining an MRI to look for seminal vesical involvement if the bulk of positive biopsy specimens are from the base. And, if seminal vesical involvement is suspected, then primary radiation plus androgen deprivation therapy (ADT) is typically used in lieu of prostatectomy.

Likewise, apical disease poses the problem of having a higher rate of positive surgical margins, harboring an anterior tumor (not necessarily biopsied during a standard biopsy procedure), and incontinence due to the necessity of creating an anastomosis between the bladder neck and the penile urethra, in near the external urinary sphincter. Therefore, patients with a bulk of positive biopsy specimens from the apex may not be optimal candidates for prostatectomy. In addition, the possibility of an anterior tumor in this instance may prompt an MRI to investigate for undersampled disease via standard transrectal ultrasound (TRUS) biopsy. These considerations may aid decision-making regarding the initial treatment approach.

KEY POINTS

- Prostate cancer is typically diagnosed via TRUS biopsy using a standard 12-core template to sample the posterior peripheral zone.
- Anatomic location can help predict pattern of spread and treatment-related risks. Disease near the base of the gland may extend into the seminal vesicles. Disease in the apex may increase risk of positive surgical margins and urinary incontinence.

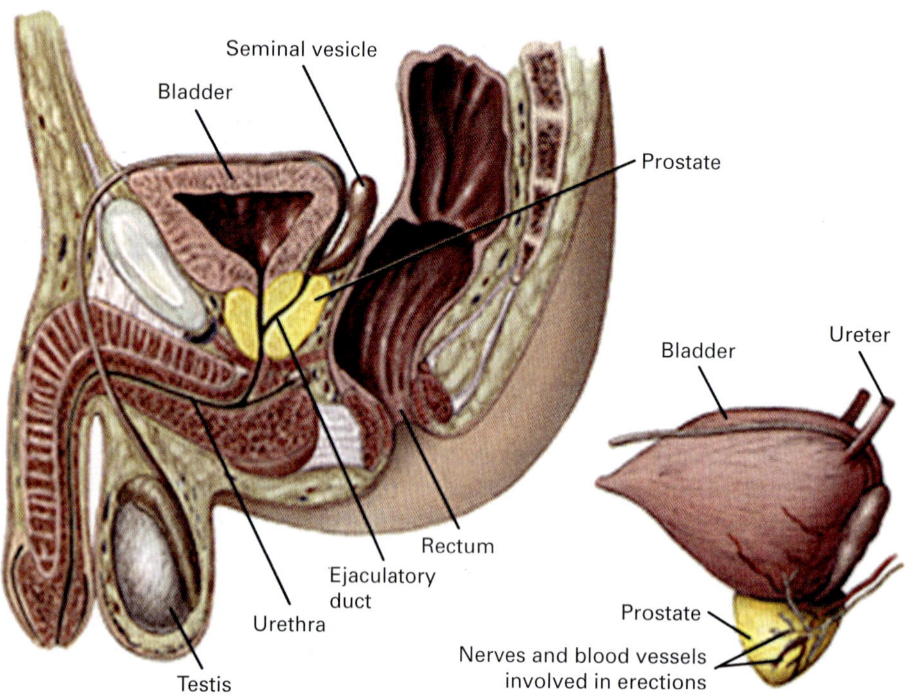

Fig. 14-1 Cross sectional view of prostate gland and surrounding anatomic organs.

Permission to reuse given by Dr. Marc B. Garnick from Garnick, MB., and Fair., WR. Combating Prostate Cancer. Scientific American. 1998 Dec; 279(6):74-83.

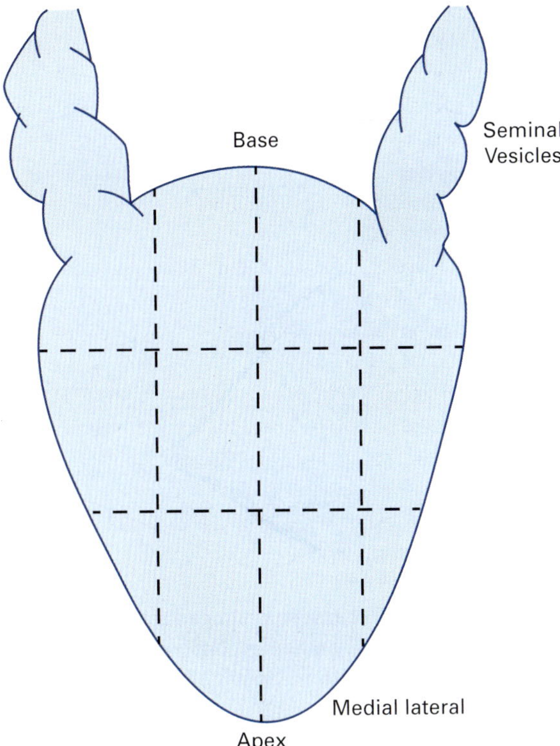

Fig. 14-2 Standard template for 12-core TRUS (transrectal ultrasound-guided) biopsy of the prostate.

PATHOLOGY AND MOLECULAR PATHOGENESIS

Androgens are the primary regulators of prostate cancer cell growth and proliferation. Prostate cancer rarely develops in castrated men or in those who have hypopituitarism before age 40 years. The androgen receptor (AR), located on chromosome Xq11-13, is a member of a superfamily of ligand-dependent transcription factors that have a similar structure with different functional domains. The development of prostate cancer involves a multistep process in which androgen-receptor signaling plays a key role. Specific genetic changes have been identified in tumors representing different clinical states. Gene expression profiling has identified numerous molecular abnormalities that may differ between primary, metastatic, and castration-resistant prostate cancers (CRPCs). As such, the targets relevant for the treatment of early-stage disease may not be the same as those for late-stage tumors.

The typical immunohistochemistry (IHC) profile of prostate cancer is as follows:

- negative for cytokeratins 7 and 20,
- positive for AR and PSA, and
- positive for the NKX 3.1 homeobox protein.

NKX 3.1 positivity is retained even in some advanced treatment-resistant prostate cancers that have lost AR and/or PSA expression. In cases of a mass involving both prostate and bladder, this profile can help differentiate prostate cancer from urothelial cancer, which is typically positive for cytokeratins 20 and (usually) 7, as well as GATA3, and negative for PSA and NKX 3.1 (and typically, but not always, negative for AR).

The Gleason grading system is used to describe the morphology of adenocarcinomas of the prostate. Using the original system, the morphology was described using a score of 1 to 5 for the primary and secondary growth patterns within the tumor. Prostate cancers often contain a variety of different Gleason patterns within the same tumor.

Pattern 1 tumors were the most differentiated, with discrete glandular formation, whereas pattern 5 lesions were the most undifferentiated, with virtually complete loss of the glandular architecture. In 2005, a consensus conference modified Gleason grading to include the use of IHC. This resulted in a narrow definition of Gleason 3 pattern (discreet glandular units) and widened the scope of Gleason 4 pattern. The Gleason score is determined by adding the Gleason grade of the two most predominant histologies. A tertiary (third most prevalent) Gleason pattern 5 is associated with adverse pathologic features and biochemical recurrence (BCR) in some series, and so this may now be reported separately and also replaces the secondary pattern in reporting biopsy results (ie, a finding of Gleason 3+4+5 in a biopsy specimen would be reported as Gleason 3+5) so as not to miss this important finding. A higher Gleason score is associated with more aggressive disease and a greater probability of extracapsular extension, nodal involvement, and the subsequent development of metastases. Figure 14-3 shows a new prostate cancer five-group grading system.

Prostatic intraepithelial neoplasia is an epithelial cellular proliferation within benign-appearing glands and acini. Approximately 50% of men with prostatic intraepithelial neoplasia, as demonstrated in prostate biopsy specimen(s), will be diagnosed with prostate cancer in 5 years, depending on the frequency of biopsy procedures. More than 99% of prostate cancers are adenocarcinomas; < 1% are pure ductal and mucinous variants. Other histologic subtypes include small-cell carcinoma and rare mesenchymal tumors (ie, rhabdomyosarcomas in younger patients and leiomyosarcomas in older patients). Urothelial carcinomas of the prostate are confined to the periurethral ducts and are more common among patients who have been successfully treated for nonmuscle-invasive bladder cancer. Lymphomas and leukemias may rarely occur in the prostate gland.

During the course of treatment of advanced prostate cancer, multiple genomic and transcriptomic alterations can occur as mechanisms of treatment resistance. Despite resistance to castration and androgen-signaling inhibitors, most prostate cancers remain dependent on AR signaling, but a subset may become "androgen indifferent" and are generally characterized by alterations in *RB1* and *p53* (Fig 14-4). Some, but not all, of these tumors may exhibit neuroendocrine differentiation, with positive synaptophysin and/or chromogranin A staining. The extreme of neuroendocrine differentiation is "small-cell" morphology, histologically similar to small-cell carcinoma of the lung or other extrapulmonary sites. Neuroendocrine prostate cancer is associated with amplification of the genes, aurora kinase A *(AURKA)* and N-myc *(MYCN)*,

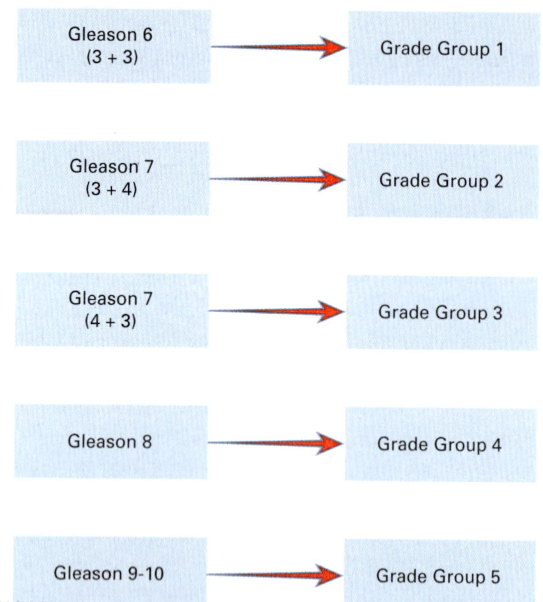

Fig. 14-3 Gleason scoring and WHO prognostic groups.

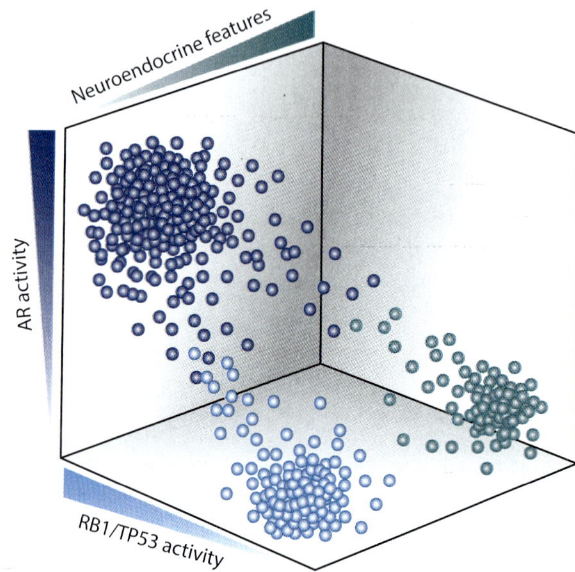

Fig. 14-4 Relationship between androgen receptor signaling, tumor suppressor genes, and neuroendocrine features in metastatic castration-resistant prostate cancer.

This depicts a conceptual representation of the spectrum of profiles that include AR signaling, loss of tumor suppressor genes, and development of neuroendocrine features during prostate cancer progression. Individual dots represent hypothetical patients, but different subclones may also be present within one individual.[154]

Abbreviation: AR, androgen receptor.

Permission to reuse given by Dr. David J. Einstein.

offering the opportunity for targeted therapy.[10] Clinically, the emergence of neuroendocrine differentiation of prostate cancer, including the transformation to small-cell cancer, should be considered in men who develop castration-resistant disease after ADT for high-grade Gleason cancers, especially when visceral involvement including liver metastases are diagnosed and when radiographic progression occurs in the absence of an increase in serum PSA level. Ongoing research is aimed at better defining and treating androgen-indifferent and neuroendocrine prostate cancer.

KEY POINTS

- Prostate cancer can be characterized by its typical IHC profile: cytokeratin 7/20-negative, PSA-positive, AR-positive, and NKX3.1-positive.
- As treatment resistance occurs, different phenotypes may emerge. Most CRPC is still driven by AR signaling, even after developing resistance to subsequent AR-directed therapies.
- Some advanced CRPC may become "androgen indifferent," often harboring alterations in *Rb1* and *p53*. These may be admixed with AR-driven tumors. A subset of these cases may have neuroendocrine features, with the most extreme exhibiting small-cell morphology.
- Small-cell prostate cancer is a rare subset and classically occurs with rapid visceral spread in the absence of increase in serum PSA level after a period of hormonal therapy for high-grade initial disease (de novo small-cell prostate cancer is extremely rare). It is characterized primarily by morphology, but it can also be positive on synaptophysin and/or chromogranin A staining.

PREVENTION

A number of chemoprevention strategies have been studied in prostate cancer. The Prostate Cancer Prevention Trial (PCPT) was a randomized, double-blind, multicenter study designed to investigate the use of finasteride, a 5-α reductase inhibitor, to prevent prostate cancer in men age ≥ 55 years.[2] More than 18,000 men were enrolled, of whom half received 5 mg of finasteride daily for 7 years and half received placebo. The unique aspect of this study was an end-of-protocol prostate needle biopsy for men in the placebo group, which included many men with PSA values that never went above 4 ng/mL and who had a normal DRE during the conduct of the study—a population of men who, in normal clinical practice, would never undergo a biopsy procedure. The results provided compelling evidence that no cut point of PSA values is identified above or below which indicates the presence or absence of prostate cancer but underscores that there is a continuum of risk according to PSA values.

The results initially demonstrated relative risk of 0.7 in prostate cancer risk among men treated with finasteride compared with placebo (10.5% *v* 14.9%), but a higher frequency of high-grade lesions for this same group, although the clinical significance of the high-grade disease was uncertain. An updated analysis of the PCPT trial was consistent with that of the earlier studies, with no statistical differences in the death rate from high-grade prostate cancer in the finasteride group.[11]

A complementary study called REDUCE (albeit with differing entry criteria) using the 5-α reductase inhibitor dutasteride showed similar results to the PCPT of prostate cancer reduction of low-risk cancers, but an increase in high-grade cancers.[12] Results of these studies are summarized in Figure 14-5.

In 2011, an FDA advisory committee analysis of both trials confirmed a relative reduction of approximately 25% in the overall incidence of prostate cancer. The analysis noted, however, that this was limited to tumors with a modified Gleason score ≤ 6 and that many of the detected cancers were diagnosed by prostate biopsy in response to an elevated PSA level or to an abnormal DRE. The reassessment of the PCPT and REDUCE trials confirmed a significantly increased incidence of high-grade prostate cancers, and the committee estimated that use of a 5-α reductase inhibitor for prevention of prostate cancer would result in one additional high-grade cancer to avert three to four potentially clinically relevant lower-grade cancers. The advisory committee concluded that finasteride and dutasteride do not have a favorable risk-benefit profile for chemoprevention of prostate cancer in healthy men (Fig 14-5). In a recent population-based cohort study, the all-cause and prostate cancer–specific mortality rates were increased in patients treated with 5-α reductase inhibitors, possibly related to a delay in diagnosis due to the decrease in PSA level that occurs with treatment.[13]

According to findings of the Physicians'' Health Study II randomized controlled trial evaluating supplementation with vitamins E and C in 14,641 male physicians in the United States, initially age ≥ 50 years, supplementation did not reduce the risk of prostate cancer.[14] The Selenium and Vitamin E Cancer Prevention (SELECT) trial evaluated 35,553 men in a double-blind, 2 × 2 factorial study of selenium (200 μg daily) and vitamin E alone (400 IU daily) and in combination for men age ≥ 50 years (black men) or age ≥ 55 years (all other men) with a serum PSA level ≤ 4 ng/mL and a normal DRE. The end point was clinical incidence of prostate cancer. With a median follow-up of 5.46 years, there were no significant differences in the development of prostate cancer in any cohort ($P > .15$). At a median follow-up of 7 years, there was a 17% increased risk of prostate cancer in the vitamin E group (Fig 14-6) but not in the selenium plus vitamin E group, suggesting that vitamin E supplementation at 400 IU daily significantly increases the risk of prostate cancer development.[15]

Early Detection and Screening

Prostate Cancer Screening. A screening procedure, by definition, is intended to be performed on asymptomatic patients with no signs or symptoms of the organ being evaluated. Moreover, the patients so screened may be diagnosed with the disease being screened for and may be treated for that disease. The outcomes of the population of patients who have been included in the screening intervention are then compared with the population of patients who were not screened. In evaluating the outcomes of prostate cancer detection, this has been the most important element in determining whether screening does or does not improve outcomes in a similar population of patients who were never screened. This type of study answers the questions: Is an earlier diagnosis of the disease beneficial? And if so, should such a screening study inform clinical practice? The following paragraph outlines the sobering fact that despite PSA screening studies involving hundreds of thousands of men, so far, none has demonstrated a conclusive improvement in overall survival (OS) as a result of screening.

In 2012, the US Preventive Services Task Force (USPSTF) recommended against the routine screening for all men, regardless of age, ethnicity, or family history of prostate cancer. This recommendation was softened in 2018; however, it was not based on increased effectiveness of screening but rather a diminution of treatments offered to men who had a screen-detected cancer by offering them participation in active surveillance protocols, thereby limiting harm from treatments.

The historical role of PSA testing as a screening method for the detection of prostate cancer is instructive to review. In 2010, there were no widely accepted standards for PSA-based

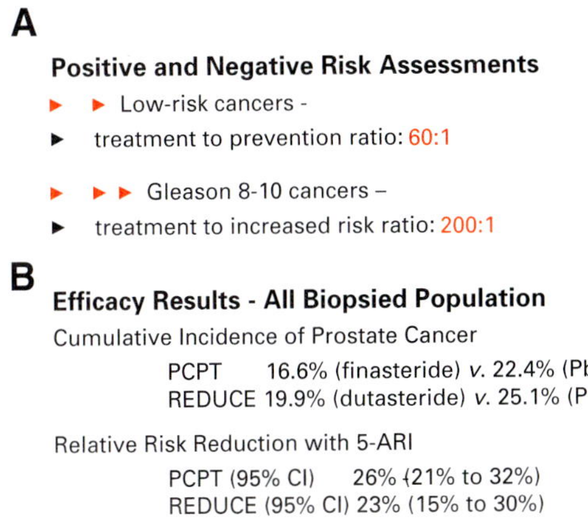

A
Positive and Negative Risk Assessments
▸ Low-risk cancers -
treatment to prevention ratio: 60:1
▸▸ Gleason 8-10 cancers –
treatment to increased risk ratio: 200:1
B
Efficacy Results - All Biopsied Population
Cumulative Incidence of Prostate Cancer
PCPT 16.6% (finasteride) v. 22.4% (Pbo)
REDUCE 19.9% (dutasteride) v. 25.1% (Pbo)
Relative Risk Reduction with 5-ARI
PCPT (95% CI) 26% (21% to 32%)
REDUCE (95% CI) 23% (15% to 30%)

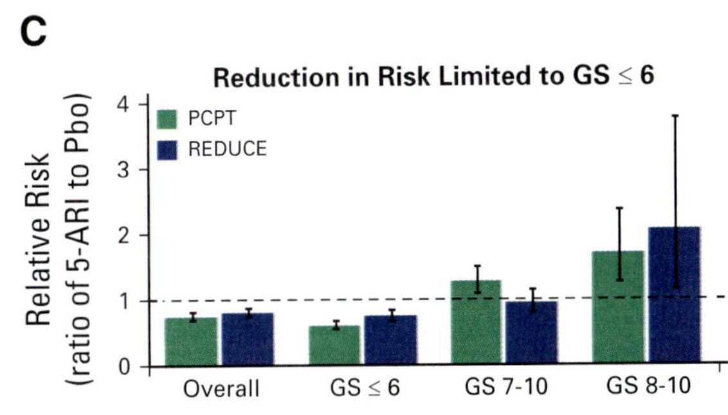

Fig. 14-5 The effects of 5-alpha reductase inhibitors for prostate cancer prevention.

(A) Data obtained from the PCPT trial and prepared by FDA analysis. For every 60 men treated with finasteride, one low grad prostate cancer would be avoided; for every 200 men treated, on high grade prostate cancer would occur. (B) Provides data on the cumulative incidence of cancer in both the PCPT and REDUCE trials; and the relative reduction of cancer incidence in both studies. (C) Vertical lines represent 95% CIs.

Abbreviations: ARI, α reductase inhibitor; FDA, US Food and Drug Administration; GS, Gleason score; Pbo, placebo; PCPT, Prostate Cancer Prevention Trial.

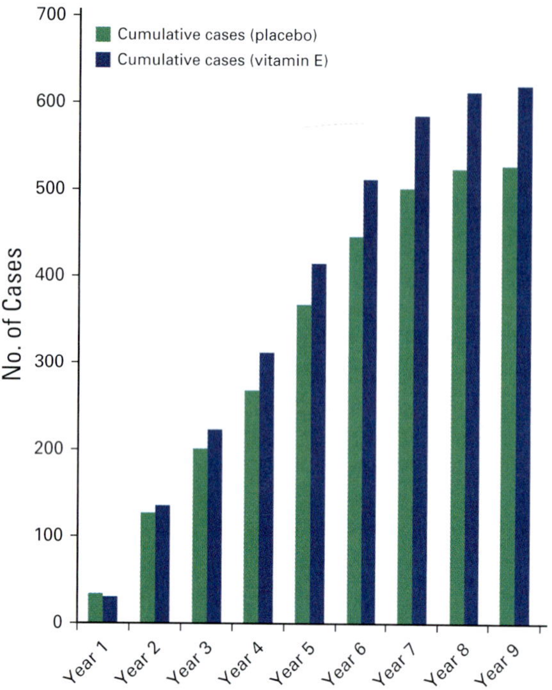

Fig. 14-6 Histogram of prostate cancers in SELECT study.

Vitamin E led to an increase in the number of prostate cancers in the SELECT study.

screening recommendations for the detection of prostate cancer. There were multiple, competing and conflicting recommendations at that time related to PSA screening, frequency of testing if testing was selected, the role of PSA testing, and the performance of a DRE. The guidelines published by the USPSTF in 2008 did not recommend for or against prostate cancer screening using PSA testing, because there was insufficient evidence to allow an assessment of the benefits and harms of screening. The scientific bases for the eventual recommendation by the USPSTF in 2012 to recommend against the routine use of PSA testing for prostate cancer screening for all men (regardless of age, race, or family history) were published in 2009. The bases of the recommendation were the lack of data and negative data from large randomized studies that failed to show a survival advantage for men who are screened versus those who receive standard care, without planned screening. These publications suggested that PSA testing might produce more harm than good and provided a basis for the 2012 recommendation that a physician not discuss prostate screening using PSA testing with patients. However, the 2018 recommendations (presented later in this section) have softened this position and have recommended shared decision-making.

For male patients age ≥ 55 years, recommendations published in 2012 led to a standard of care that did not require prostate cancer screening using PSA testing or discussing with this class of patients the option of being screened for prostate cancer using PSA testing. Three level I, large, international randomized evaluations that evaluated such outcomes in nearly 700,000 men did not show any improvements in survival, and most did not demonstrate any meaningful improvements in cancer-specific survival (Table 14-2).

Increased use of active surveillance programs was one reason that the 2018 recommendations of the USPSTF were altered to a C recommendation for PSA testing for men ages 55 to 69 years (a grade D recommendation was continued for men age ≥ 70 years). This recommendation indicates a discussion and shared decision-making should occur between the clinician and patient regarding PSA testing so that each man has the opportunity to understand the potential benefits and harms of screening and to incorporate his values and preferences into his decision. There was also an acknowledgment that more investigations are necessary to understand the role of PSA screening practices in populations at higher risk of prostate cancer, including black men and men with a family history of prostate cancer in a first-degree relative.

The USPSTF, in issuing their final 2018 guidelines summarized the risks and benefits of PSA testing for the early diagnosis of prostate cancer as follows:[16]

- Benefits
  - In men aged 55 to 69 years, may prevent approximately 1.3 deaths from prostate cancer over approximately 13 years per 1,000 men screened.
  - Screening may prevent approximately three cases of metastatic prostate cancer per 1,000 men screened.
- Harms
  - Harms include erectile dysfunction, urinary incontinence, and bowel symptoms.
  - Approximately one in five men who undergo radical prostatectomy develop long-term urinary incontinence.
  - Two in three men will experience long-term erectile dysfunction.
  - Harms of screening in men > 70 are at least moderate and greater than in younger men.

Prostate-Specific Antigen. PSA is a single-chain glycoprotein that functions as a kallikrein-like serine protease, causing liquefaction of seminal coagulum. It is prostate specific, but not prostate cancer specific, and an elevated PSA concentration may occur as a result of prostatitis, nonmalignant enlargement of the gland, biopsy of the prostate, ejaculation, and prostate cancer. A DRE does not alter PSA levels appreciably. The half-life of PSA is estimated to be 2 to 3 days, and levels should remain undetectable if the prostate has been removed.

- A PSA level > 4 ng/mL has predictive value for the diagnosis of prostate cancer, however, lower PSA values may also be associated with prostate cancer, as well as high-grade cancers, as demonstrated in the Prostate Cancer Prevention Trial.[2]
- For men with a PSA value between 4 ng/mL and 10 ng/mL, a PSA velocity of at least 0.75 ng/mL/y is suspicious for cancer.
- PSA measurements should be made on at least three to four consecutive occasions, usually separated by 6 months over at least 12 to 18 months, because of variability.

Table 14-2 **Randomized Trials of Prostate Cancer Screening**		
Study	**No. of Men Randomly Assigned to PSA Testing (± DRE)**	**Results**
European Randomized Screening Study for Prostate Cancer[91]	Approximately 182,000 ages 50-74 years; n = 162,243 ages 55-69 years	No OS benefit
	PSA every 4 years *v* no screening	Absolute cancer death risk reduction of 0.71/ 1,000 men screened; with additional follow-up, 1.2/1,000 men screened; no OS benefit
Prostate Lung Colorectal Ovarian Study[92]	76,693	No OS benefit; no cancer-specific survival benefit
	PSA every year for 6 years plus DRE *v* usual care	2 deaths/10,000 men screened group *v* 1.7 deaths/10,000 in control group; similar data with additional follow-up
Clustered randomized study of single PSA testing[93]	Approximately 408,825	One-time PSA testing did not alter prostate cancer mortality rate between screened and unscreened men (0.3/1,000 screened *v* 0.31/1,000 in unscreened)

Abbreviations: DRE, digital rectal examination; OS, overall survival; PSA, prostate-specific antigen

- Because 5-α reductase inhibitors including finasteride and dutasteride are associated with a lowering of the PSA level when used for treatment of benign prostatic hyperplasia, failure to have a substantial decrease in PSA level (approximately 50%) or an increase in PSA level while receiving these agents can be associated with prostate cancer.

An abnormal DRE necessitates a referral to a urologist for additional diagnostic evaluation. The sensitivity, specificity, and positive-predictive value have been determined for DRE and PSA (using a cutoff of 4 ng/mL). The positive-predictive value of an abnormal DRE is 21%, whereas 25% of men with an elevated PSA level and abnormal DRE have cancer. Conditions that mimic prostate cancer on DRE include acute and granulomatous prostatitis and a prostatic calculus. When establishing a diagnosis, a TRUS is used to ensure biopsy specimens encompass all portions of the gland. A TRUS has no role in screening. The diagnosis of prostate cancer is established by examination of a specimen obtained with a TRUS-guided needle biopsy using a biopsy gun. An extended-pattern 12-core biopsy is recommended (Fig 14-2), and additional biopsies may be performed if clinically indicated. Ongoing studies are evaluating multiparametric MRI (mpMRI) of the prostate using the structured Prostate Imaging Reporting and Data System to detect and localize prostate cancer.

A recent study compared patients who were suspected of having prostate cancer, on the basis of an elevated PSA value but who had not yet undergone biopsy.[17] Men were randomly assigned to undergo an MRI. Abnormalities identified by MRI underwent targeted biopsy, and if there were no MRI abnormalities, biopsy was not performed, versus a standard TRUS-guided biopsy with 10 to 12 cores sampled. Findings from data on the 500 men participating in the study included:

- More high-grade cancers with MRI guidance
  - 38% of participants had clinically significant cancer when biopsy was prompted by MRI versus 26% undergoing standard TRUS biopsy
- 13% fewer low-grade cancers in the MRI group
- 28% avoided biopsy (no MRI abnormalities; hence, no biopsy)

These data are prompting the increased use of MRI as the first diagnostic step in the evaluation of PSA-suspected prostate cancer, but longer follow-up is needed to determine the safety of eliminating standard template biopsies based on MRI and to determine the cost-effectiveness of this strategy.

Improving Specificity and Sensitivity of PSA Testing

A variety of additional modifications to PSA testing have been developed to help improve its sensitivity and specificity, especially when PSA values are between 4 and 10 ng/mL. These tests are often used to help assess whether a prostate needle biopsy should be performed (Table 14-3).

KEY POINTS

- There are no universally accepted protocols for prostate cancer prevention or screening.
- 5-α Reductase inhibitors decrease the incidence of prostate cancer but thus far have not shown a convincing reduction in prostate cancer–specific mortality rate. There is some ongoing concern about 5-α reductase inhibitors increasing risk of high-grade prostate cancer.
- PSA-based prostate cancer screening has shown, at most, a small reduction in prostate cancer–specific mortality rate and no convincing effect on overall

mortality. Screening could be more effective if targeted to higher-risk men and to the age groups most likely to benefit—younger men, rather than older men—but further studies evaluating this are underway.

- For men undergoing evaluation for elevated PSA concentration, a prebiopsy MRI may help triage who requires biopsy, limiting biopsies to those with a greater likelihood of clinically significant cancer. However, this is not yet standard of care, and longer-term follow-up will be needed to see whether omitting standard 12-core biopsies in a patient with no high-grade lesions on MRI (appropriately performed and interpreted) risks under-diagnosis of clinically significant cancer.
- When clinicians have adopted MRI-targeted biopsies thus far, it has typically been in one of two scenarios: (1) to supplement the standard 12-core biopsy approach, or (2) if PSA level increases significantly in the absence of aggressive disease in standard core biopsy specimens, or negative standard biopsy specimens, possibly indicating a possible anterior gland tumor.

TUMOR STAGING

The TNM system describes the extent of the primary tumor (T), status of the regional nodes (N), and presence or absence of distant metastases (M) (Table 14-4).[18]

Clinical T stage is assigned by DRE. Radiographic evidence of extracapsular extension is not formally part of the staging guidelines but clinicians may opt to intensify therapy for patients with radiographically more advanced tumors. In particular, there has been increased use of mpMRI in staging, which incorporates T2-weighted, diffusion-weighted, and dynamic contrast-enhanced MRI imaging for the detection, staging, and management of prostate cancer. The Prostate Imaging Reporting and Data System assessment uses a 5-point scale based on the mpMRI findings to determine the likelihood of a clinically significant cancer in the prostate gland.

Pathologic T stage is assigned on the basis of examination of a radical prostatectomy specimen for patients who undergo surgery. Margin positivity, which is influenced by surgical technique and anatomic extent of disease, should be specified in the pathology report. Nodal involvement can also be assessed.

Tumors detected in a biopsy specimen on the basis of an elevated PSA level and no palpable disease detected by DRE are designated T1c. T2 disease is confined to the prostate (pathologic substaging to T2a, T2b, or T2c is no longer performed). In T3 disease, tumor extends through the prostate capsule (T3a) or invades the seminal vesicles (T3b), whereas tumors are considered T4 if they invade adjacent structures or organs.

RISK STRATIFICATION

Localized prostate cancer is clinically heterogeneous. Many groups have developed prognostic models based on the combination of the initial T stage, Gleason score, and baseline PSA level. These algorithms are used to predict disease extent (ie, organ confined *v* nonorgan confined), node status (negative or positive), and the probability of success using a PSA-based definition of failure specific to the local therapy under consideration. Specific nomograms have been developed for radical prostatectomy, external-beam radiation therapy (EBRT), and brachytherapy (ie, radioactive seed implantation). The eighth edition of the AJCC Cancer Staging Manual (AJCC) includes prognostic groupings that incorporate anatomic stage and PSA (Table 14-5).[19]

Using T stage, Gleason score, and PSA value, discrete risk categories have been defined and form the basis for treatment

Table 14-3 Improving PSA Testing

Test	What Is Measured	Usefulness
Free/bound PSA	Amount of PSA bound to serum proteins; lower values of free PSA more indicative of prostate cancer	Somewhat useful and may prompt biopsies if free PSA is ≤ 10%
Select MDx	Prostate cancer-specific mRNA in urine	If elevated, may prompt a biopsy for slightly elevated PSA values
PSA density	PSA value divided by volume of gland	Values of > 0.15 more likely associated with prostate cancer
Prostate Health Index	PSA, free PSA, [-2] proPSA	
4K	Three forms of PSA plus human kallikrein 2 (hK2)	May help distinguish presence of low-risk disease and potentially lessen need for biopsy
PSA velocity	Rate of change of PSA over time; many differing definitions but should include at least four values over 18 months, each 6 months apart	Changes of > 2 units in 1 year prior to a diagnosis of prostate cancer may indicate high-grade cancer

Abbreviations: PSA, prostate-specific antigen.

Table 14-4 **Staging of Prostate Cancer**[93]

Stage	Definition
Primary tumor (T)	
Clinical T (cT)	
TX	Primary tumor cannot be assessed
T0	No evidence of primary tumor
T1	Clinically inapparent tumor that is not palpable
T1a	Tumor incidental histologic finding in ≤ 5% of tissue resected
T1b	Tumor incidental histologic finding in > 5% of tissue resected
T1c	Tumor identified by needle biopsy found in one or both sides, but not palpable
T2	Tumor is palpable and confined within prostate
T2a	Tumor involves ≤ 50% of one side
T2b	Tumor involves > 50% of one side but not both sides
T2c	Tumor involves both lobes
T3	Extraprostatic tumor that is not fixed or does not invade adjacent structures
T3a	Extracapsular extension (unilateral or bilateral)
T3b	Tumor invades seminal vesicle(s)
T4	Tumor is fixed or invades adjacent structures other than seminal vesicles (eg, external sphincter, rectum, bladder, levator muscles, and/or pelvic wall)
Pathologic (pT)[a,b]	
pT2	Organ-confined
pT3	Extraprostatic extension
pT3a	Extraprostatic extension (unilateral or bilateral) or microscopic invasion of bladder neck
pT3b	Seminal vesicle invasion
pT4	Tumor is fixed or invades adjacent structures other than seminal vesicles, such as external sphincter, rectum, bladder, levator muscles, and/or pelvic wall
Regional lymph nodes (N)	
Clinical	
NX	Regional lymph nodes were not assessed
N0	No positive regional nodes
N1	Metastasis in regional node(s)
Distant metastasis (M)[c]	
M0	No distant metastasis
M1	Distant metastasis
M1a	Nonregional lymph node(s)
M1b	Bone(s)
M1c	Other site(s) with or without bone disease; most advanced

[a]There is no pathologic T1 classification.
[b]Positive surgical margin should be indicated by an R1 descriptor (residual microscopic disease).
[c]When more than one site of metastasis is present, the most advanced category (M1c) is used.

decision-making (Fig 14-7).[20] ASCO guidelines differ slightly from NCCN criteria but are broadly similar. Historically, patients were categorized as low, intermediate, and high risk. However, both the low- and intermediate-risk groups have been subdivided in more recent updates (as well as the high-risk group in NCCN criteria) using additional factors such as PSA density and number of involved cores.

Genomic biomarkers have been developed in an effort to refine clinical risk stratification. In particular, some clinicians may use these tests to help the patient decide between active surveillance and definitive therapy (Fig 14-8). However, no genomic risk score has yet been demonstrated to have predictive value for treatment decision-making in a prospective study.

Role of Imaging in Staging

Prostate cancers spread by local extension through the capsule and seminal vesicles, the lymphatic system to regional nodes, or hematogenously to bone and visceral sites. Staging imaging typically consists of a CT scan or MRI of the abdomen and pelvis, plus bone scan. More-sensitive imaging techniques have been developed but are not yet in routine use in this setting.

Guidelines issued by the American Urological Association (AUA), American Society for Radiation Oncology, Society of Urologic Oncology, and ASCO recommend no routine staging imaging in patients with low-risk disease.[20] For patients with intermediate-risk disease, the guidelines suggest staging imaging if patients have two of three risk factors present: palpable nodule on DRE (cT2), Gleason score 7, and PSA concentration > 10 ng/mL. Other guidelines use thresholds based on nomograms for prediction of lymph node involvement. A follow-up CT scan and/or MRI may be helpful for evaluating suspicious areas of the skeleton on bone scan, as well as for identifying healing fractures, arthritis, Paget disease, bone infections, and other inflammatory bone conditions that may mimic blastic metastases. All patients with high-risk disease should have staging imaging.

MANAGEMENT OF PROSTATE CANCER BY RISK

Localized prostate cancers are those confined to the prostate gland without nodal involvement or metastases. Treatment selection considers whether the disease can be eradicated by a treatment directed solely at the prostate, whether a combined local and systemic approach is necessary for cure, or whether therapy is not needed or can be deferred because of a low risk of progression. In general, therapy is aimed at complete local control to decrease the potential for recurrence while preserving optimal bowel, bladder, and sexual function.

Tumors confined to the prostate are generally managed by radical prostatectomy, radiation therapy (RT), or, in some cases, active surveillance. An assessment of the patient's life expectancy, overall health status, and tumor characteristics should be undertaken before a treatment decision is made. Life expectancy can be estimated with nomograms, including one from the Social Security database. Patients with life expectancy of < 5 years do not benefit from treatment of low-risk prostate cancer and therefore should undergo watchful waiting and additional workup only if the patient becomes symptomatic.

Low Risk

For patients with very low-risk localized prostate cancer, active surveillance is the preferred management option. For patients with low-risk localized prostate cancer, active surveillance, interstitial prostate brachytherapy, EBRT, and radical prostatectomy are appropriate monotherapy treatment options. Prostate brachytherapy should not be offered to men with significant lower urinary tract symptoms or who have had repeated episodes of prostatitis or urinary infections, because brachytherapy may be more likely to exacerbate these symptoms. The AUA symptoms score index for assessment of urinary symptoms (developed to assess urinary symptoms of benign prostatic hyperplasia) or the

Table 14-5 **Anatomic Stage and Prognostic Groups**[a94]

Group	T	N	M	PSA Level (ng/mL)	Grade Group	Gleason Score
I	cT1a-c	N0	M0	< 10	1	≤ 6
	cT2a	N0	M0	< 10	1	≤ 6
	pT2	N0	M0	< 10	1	≤ 6
IIA	cT1a-c	N0	M0	10 < 20	1	≤ 6
	cT2a	N0	M0	10 < 20	1	≤ 6
	cT2b-c	N0	M0	< 20	1	≤ 6
IIB	T1-2	N0	M0	< 20	2	7
IIC	T1-2	N0	M0	< 20	3	7
	T1-2	N0	M0	< 20	4	8
IIIA	T1-2	N0	M0	320	1-4	≤ 8
IIIB	T3-4	N0	M0	Any PSA	1-4	≤ 8
IIIC	Any T	N0	M0	Any PSA	5	9 or 10
IV	Any T	N1	M0	Any PSA	Any	Any Gleason
	Any T	N0	M1	Any PSA	Any	Any Gleason

Abbreviation: PSA, prostate-specific antigen.

[a]Changes from AJCC Cancer Staging Manual: T4N0M0 is now stage III; WHO grade should be used to record tumor grade.

Republished with permission of Springer, from AJCC Cancer Staging Manual, 8th Edition (2017); permission conveyed through Copyright Clearance Center, Inc.

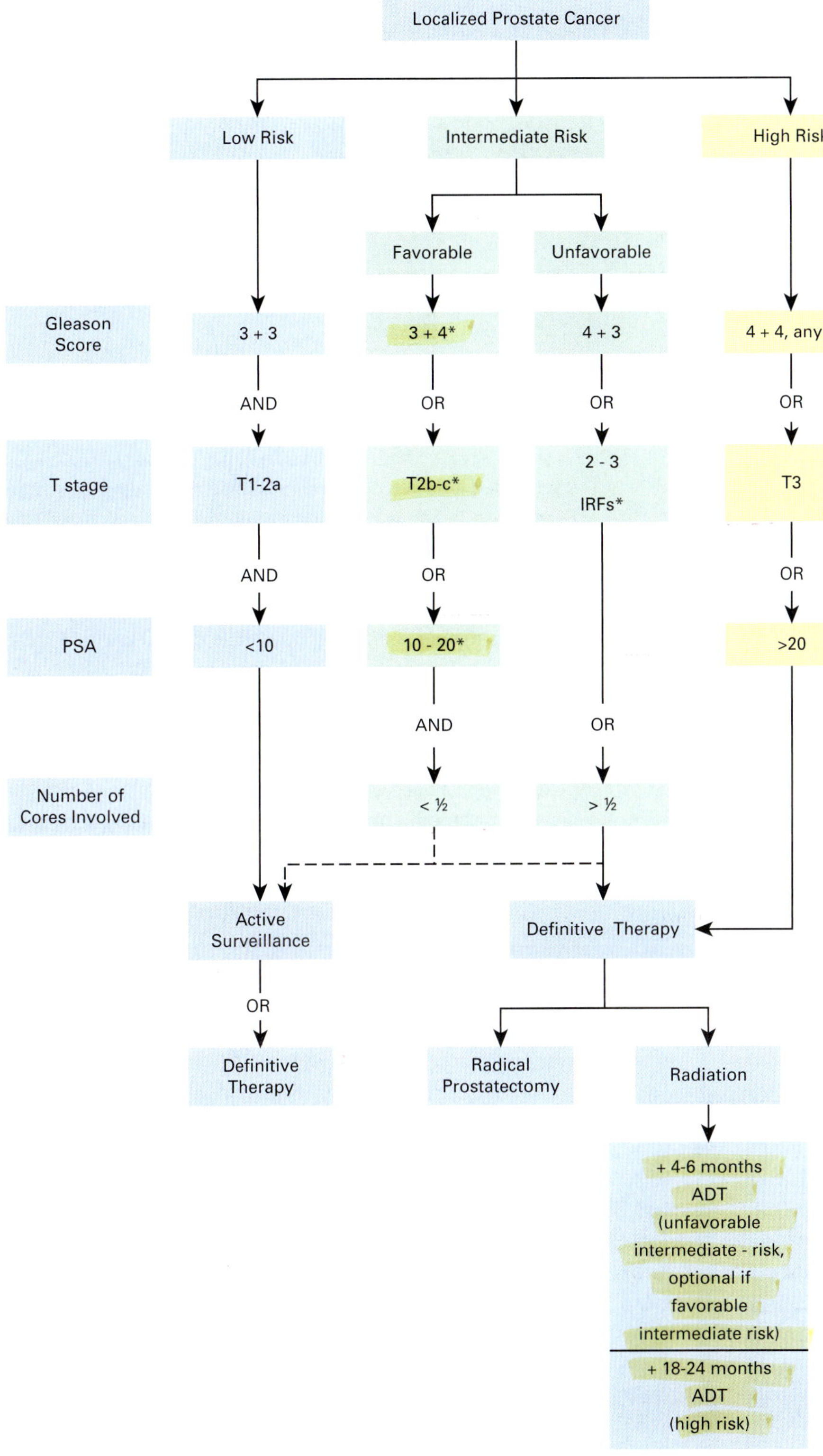

Fig. 14-7 Approach to treatment options in newly diagnosed localized prostate cancer according to risk stratification.

Various forms of radiation are discussed in the text. Short course of ADT (4-6 months) is recommended for intermediate-risk category (especially if unfavorable) and long course (18-24 months) for high-risk category.

Abbreviations: ADT, androgen deprivation therapy; EBRT, external-beam radiation therapy; IRF, intermediate risk factor; PSA, prostate-specific antigen.

*IRFs.

Permission to reuse given by Harvard Medical School Annual Report on Prostate Diseases.

EPIC-26 instrument can be used to quantify the current symptom burden a patient is experiencing. This information can then be incorporated into initial therapy decisions for men opting for localized treatment with external-beam radiation or prostatectomy, and these instruments can be used to track changes in symptoms after treatment.

Intermediate and High Risk

For patients with intermediate-risk or high-risk localized prostate cancer, definitive therapy with either prostatectomy or RT is recommended as long as the patient's life expectancy is ≥ 5 years (intermediate risk) or ≥ 10 years (high risk), or if the patient is symptomatic. Patients with favorable intermediate-risk prostate

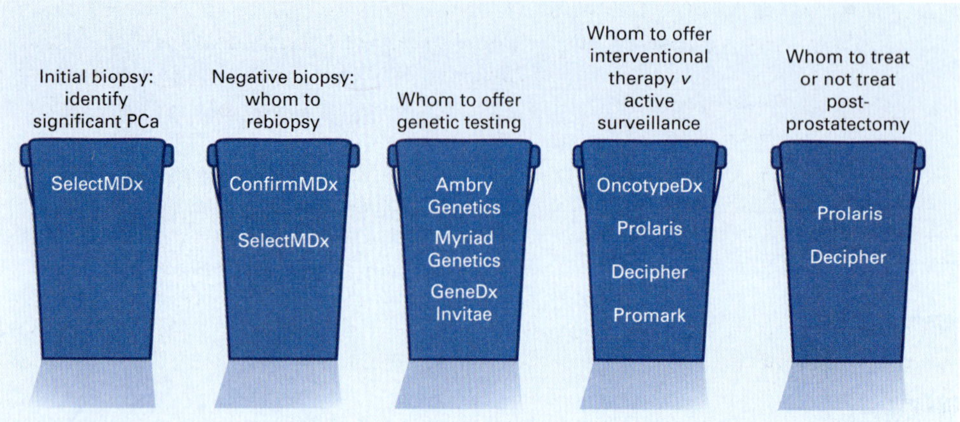

Fig. 14-8 Available genomic and gene expression tests for prostate cancer and their intended uses.

Abbreviation: PCa, prostate cancer.

cancer may be considered for active surveillance, but this is primarily for patients with comorbidities or who strongly prefer to defer definitive therapy (Fig 14-7). The rate of subsequent upgrading may be increased for favorable intermediate-risk patients compared with low-risk patients on active surveillance, but it is not clear whether OS or cancer-specific survival is affected.

The treatment decision is guided primarily by adverse effect profiles. With few randomized trials, comparisons among treatments have been limited by selection bias and differences in outcomes reporting, both with respect to cancer control and quality of life (QOL). Nomograms and other prognostic models have been developed to assist decision-making, whereas QOL assessments have become more standardized.

- Overall, prostatectomy is primarily associated with urinary incontinence and erectile dysfunction, with the incontinence typically improving in the months after surgery and erectile function dependent on baseline function as well as surgical approach (nerve-sparing *v* non–nerve-sparing surgery).
- Radiation is more associated with irritative urinary and bowel symptoms in the months after treatment.[21]

Reported complication rates for each modality vary widely in the literature. The differences are related to the different definitions used, whether the patient or physician is reporting, and the time from the treatment to the assessment of symptoms. Health-related quality-of-life (HRQOL) studies are more accurately defining the patient's satisfaction with the different treatments for localized prostate cancer. For example, in one study, adjuvant hormone therapy was associated with worse QOL outcomes among patients receiving brachytherapy or external radiotherapy; prostatectomy was associated with worse urinary incontinence, but urinary irritation and obstruction improved, particularly in patients with a large prostate.[22] Thus, prostatectomy may be the preferred modality in patients with significant baseline urinary obstructive symptoms; radiation may worsen obstructive symptoms in the short term.

Erectile dysfunction can occur as a result of radiation and especially surgery. However, all patients in the Protect study were noted to have decreases in erectile function over time, even those in the active monitoring group, highlighting that many men in this age range will be expected to have decreases in erectile function for reasons other than prostate cancer treatment.[21] These analyses have led to the development of HRQOL nomograms that may help guide treatment choice in an individual patient with localized prostate cancer.

Node-Positive (Regional) Prostate Cancer

Some aggressive local tumors may have already metastasized to pelvic lymph nodes at the time of diagnosis. These may be diagnosed clinically, by suspicious appearance on CT scan and/or MRI, or pathologically, by examination of biopsy specimen or at time of prostatectomy with lymph node dissection. Suspicious nodes located above the aortic bifurcation are considered outside of the pelvis and therefore are staged as M1 disease (stage IVB) rather than N1 (stage IVA).

Some nodes may be borderline. In this case, the clinician may choose to obtain a biopsy specimen for clarification. Alternatively, treatment with a neoadjuvant ADT may be started before planned definitive radiation. Then, if a repeated CT scan or MRI after approximately 3 months of ADT shows that any suspicious nodes have decreased in response to ADT, this strongly implies presence of prostate cancer and may be treated as such.

- Most commonly, these patients are treated with definitive RT to the prostate and pelvic lymph nodes plus long-course ADT (extrapolating ADT data from the high-risk localized setting), because population-based data have shown improved long-term survival compared with ADT alone.
- Node-positive patients and patients undergoing RT were included in the STAMPEDE trial comparing ADT with ADT plus abiraterone for castration-sensitive disease (see the section Metastatic Prostate Cancer later in the chapter).[23] In subgroup analyses, nodal status did not seem to affect OS or failure-free survival benefit, but planned RT seemed to have a significant interaction with the addition of abiraterone on improvement in failure-free survival. Currently, NCCN guidelines prefer ADT alone for patients with localized and regional disease undergoing RT,

although some clinicians may discuss risks and benefits of adding abiraterone especially in the higher-risk, node-positive patients. Longer follow-up will be needed.

- Alternatively, prostatectomy and extended lymphadenectomy may be performed, but with a likely plan for adjuvant RT and ADT after surgery (trimodality therapy) for selected patients. The increased toxicity of trimodality therapy may only be justified if a patient has significant obstructive urinary symptoms that could actually be palliated by surgery.

The treatment of patients with positive lymph nodes found at the time of prostatectomy with lymph node dissection (ie, "surprise" positive lymph nodes) is discussed later in the chapter.

KEY POINTS

- Patients with localized prostate cancer can be risk-stratified on the basis of three clinical factors: T stage, Gleason score, and PSA level. Genomic testing of the cancer specimen may provide additional information about risk and progression, but this is not yet prospectively validated for decision-making.
- Prostatectomy, RT, and ADT all have unique adverse effect profiles. Prostatectomy can lead to urinary incontinence and erectile dysfunction, but it can help improve significant obstructive symptoms. Radiation tends to lead to irritative urine and bowel symptoms. ADT can cause vasomotor symptoms, fatigue, loss of libido, weight gain, muscle loss, and bone thinning, most of which reverse after discontinuation of ADT and recovery of testosterone.

TREATMENT MODALITIES

Watchful Waiting and Active Surveillance

Watchful waiting is a policy of no therapeutic intervention after a diagnosis has been established until symptomatic disease progression is evidenced by changes in symptoms, local tumor growth, or the development of symptomatic metastases. In contrast with active surveillance, watchful waiting involves no monitoring of PSA levels or scheduled serial biopsies. Watchful waiting is most appropriate for men with limited life expectancy, based on age and/or comorbid conditions. The approach evolved from studies of predominantly older men with well-differentiated tumors in whom tumor progression occurred over a protracted time, and in which, during the follow-up interval, a substantial proportion of men died of nonprostate cancer–related illnesses.

Active surveillance (with delayed intention to treat) is a recommended option for men with low-risk prostate cancer to receive no immediate treatment interventions in an effort to reduce overtreatment and the resulting adverse effects of therapy. Active surveillance protocols include scheduled PSA testing, DREs, and periodic, repeated prostate needle biopsies (or more recent use of repeat mpMRIs after the initial prostate biopsies). Most protocols require a repeated biopsy at 1 year to account for the sampling error of a 12-core biopsy. Treatment is offered if or when changes in Gleason score, volume of tumor, or serum PSA suggest increasing disease activity (Table 14-6).

Radical Prostatectomy

The goal of radical prostatectomy is to completely excise the cancer while maintaining urinary control and preserving potency. After the prostate has been removed, PSA levels should decline to undetectable; any detectable or increasing PSA level after prostatectomy is an indication of recurrent or residual cancer. Cancer control is assessed by PSA relapse-free survival, time to objective progression (local or systemic), cancer-specific survival, and OS.

Robotic prostatectomy has become common, with the majority of procedures using robot-assisted laparoscopic prostatectomy rather than the historically more common open radical prostatectomy. Despite initial enthusiasm and widespread acceptance of this technique by community and academic urologic centers, little data exist to suggest improvements in oncologic or functional outcomes when compared with the more traditional approaches. In fact, the skill of the operating surgeon in his or her specific modality (open *v* robot assisted) should be a major determinant in which approach is selected.

Management of Erectile Dysfunction. As discussed earlier, most men will experience erectile dysfunction after radical prostatectomy, even in settings where one neurovascular bundle is spared during surgery. Less frequent loss of erectile function may occur when both neurovascular bundles are spared. Methods for treating this include use of PDE-5 inhibitors (eg, sildenafil and tadalafil) often administered in the immediate postoperative period to help minimize penile shortening. Some experts advocate daily doses, with increases in dosing prior to anticipated sexual activity, although data supporting this practice are limited. Use of vacuum pumps is often effective but must be judiciously used, especially in the immediate postoperative period because disruption of the bladder neck–penile anastomosis can occur. Direct injections of alprostadil or insertion of drug pellets containing alprostadil into the penis or penile urethra may result in more effective achievements of erections. When regaining erection function is not achieved by these methods, patients may be considered for implantation of a penile prosthesis, of which several varieties are available, each with advantages and disadvantages. Patients will find it helpful to understand these potential options before surgery and set appropriate expectations, because this adverse effect is likely to occur and often be irreversible without interventions.

Management of Urinary Incontinence. Development of urinary incontinence after radical prostatectomy is an adverse effect that more commonly can result in patient-reported poorer QOL and regret. Performing Kegel exercises of pelvic floor muscles can speed recovery if routinely practiced. After prostatectomy, many men use a male diaper to maintain their current lifestyle without being limited by incontinence. Surgical approaches to reduce incontinence should be considered when the severity of the bother is high due to the leakage itself or

Table 14-6 **Randomized Trials of Early Versus Delayed Selective Intervention in Prostate Cancer**

Study	No. of Participants	Outcomes and Comments
Scandinavian Prostate Cancer Group Study Number 4 (SPCG-4)[95]	695 Random assignment to either radical prostatectomy or watchful waiting	Prostatectomy associated with a relative risk of death of 0.55 and absolute risk reduction of 11.7 percentage points. Clinically detected prostate cancer included, so results are not generalizable to screen-detected prostate cancer
Prostatectomy Versus Observation for Early Prostate Cancer (PIVOT)[4]	731 Random assignment to either treatment with surgery or observation was made after prostate cancer diagnosis,	No difference in either overall survival or cancer-specific survival
Prostate Testing for Cancer and Treatment (ProtecT)[96]	1,643 After PSA-based screening diagnosis, patients were randomly assigned to surgery, radiation therapy, or active monitoring and intervention only in the event of PSA or disease progression	No difference in either overall survival or cancer-specific survival. Slightly increased risk of metastasis in the active monitoring group. Of note, no serial biopsies were performed in the active monitoring group (differing from active surveillance), and not all patients had low-risk prostate cancer

Abbreviation: PSA, prostate-specific antigen.

urinary odor, which can be particularly bothersome to patients. Procedures include bulbourethal sling surgery and the implantation of an artificial urinary sphincter if the amount of urinary leakage is interfering with normal daily activities and is not controllable with diapers or pads or is accompanied by urinary odor. Like erectile dysfunction, urinary incontinence must be recognized as a potential complication before surgery to ensure that patient expectations are aligned with possible outcomes.

Radiation Therapy

Radiation can be administered using external-beam techniques, an implant of radioactive seeds, or a combination of the two. Contemporary EBRT incorporates three-dimensional conformal treatment planning with intensity modulation to maximize the administered dose to the tumor while minimizing the exposure of surrounding normal structures. These techniques allow for the safe administration of higher doses, which, in turn, have resulted in improved outcomes. Whether to include clinically negative pelvic nodes in the radiation field remains an unanswered question. In long-term follow-up, one randomized trial demonstrated improved progression-free survival (PFS) with whole-pelvis RT with neoadjuvant ADT versus whole-pelvis RT with adjuvant ADT or prostate-only RT with neoadjuvant ADT,[24] but most clinicians and trials currently use both neoadjuvant and adjuvant ADT. Most EBRT protocols involve approximately 5 to 8 weeks of treatment, five times per week. Stereotactic radiosurgery (eg, Cyberknife) offers a more condensed schedule of only five treatments (hypofractionation) and otherwise appears comparable to standard EBRT. Protons are heavier than the photons emitted by standard external-beam radiation and therefore discharge their energy over a shorter distance, thereby limiting damage to surrounding normal tissue (ie, a narrow Bragg peak). In theory, this would optimize delivery of radiation to the tumor and prevent toxicity to nearby organs, but the technique so far has not improved clinical outcomes despite being significantly more costly (Table 14-7).

Treatment to pelvic lymph nodes in addition to the prostate can be considered for patients with substantial risk of lymph node involvement, although including nodes in the radiation field was not associated with superior outcomes in two randomized trials. For patients with radiographically evident lymph node involvement, the radiation field should include the pelvic lymph nodes and may still offer a chance of long-term disease control or, at minimum, decreased chance of symptomatic local relapse.

The use of interstitial radiation or implantation of radioactive seeds, also known as brachytherapy, is typically used either as monotherapy for gland-confined, low- to intermediate-risk disease or as a boost together with EBRT for gland-confined high-risk disease. An acute toxicity associated with implantation is irritative urinary symptoms, including urinary frequency. Long-term complications including stricture and irritative symptoms can be bothersome, especially in men who had symptoms of lower urinary tract symptoms prior to receiving treatment. Four prospective randomized trials have demonstrated that RT doses < 70 Gy are inadequate for the curative treatment of clinically localized prostate cancer and doses of 78 to 79 Gy provide improved cancer control. Studies that have evaluated addition of ADT to RT (with or without a brachytherapy boost) suggest some improvements in local control and biochemical freedom from relapse.

Compared with surgery, RT is associated with a higher frequency of bowel complications, mainly loose stools and diarrhea, as well as irritative urinary symptoms, but lower rates of

Table 14-7 **Radiation Therapy Modalities Relative to Prostate Diseases**

<table>
<tr><th>Treatment</th><th>Ideal Candidates</th><th>Treatment Time and Recovery</th><th>Adverse Effects</th><th>Advantages</th><th>Disadvantages</th></tr>
<tr><td rowspan="2">Standard EBRT, 3D-CRT, and IMRT</td><td rowspan="5">Older patients or those with multiple medical conditions; patients whose cancer has spread outside the prostate capsule; men who have had a TURP</td><td rowspan="2">35 to 45 treatments (five times a week for 7-9 weeks); each treatment takes approximately 15 minutes</td><td rowspan="5">Bowel problems (eg, diarrhea, blood in stool, rectal leakage, rectal pain), frequent urination, blood in the urine, urinary incontinence (increases over time), impotence (develops slowly), fatigue</td><td>3D-CRT and IMRT are very well-understood therapies with well-documented outcomes</td><td>Length of treatment makes it inconvenient, especially for men living far from a treatment facility or those who travel frequently</td></tr>
<tr><td>IMRT may, in theory, enable more accurate targeting of the tumor than 3D-CRT, so there is less damage to surrounding healthy tissue. The intensity of each of the beams can be adjusted</td><td>In rare cases, the radiation may miss part of the tumor if the beam is too narrowly focused</td></tr>
<tr><td rowspan="3">Proton beam therapy</td><td rowspan="3">35 to 45 treatments (five times a week for 7-9 weeks); each treatment takes approximately 15 minutes</td><td rowspan="3">May be able to deliver more radiation to the prostate and less to surrounding tissues, causing less damage to nearby structures; protons release their energy after traveling a certain distance, limiting damage to the tissue they pass through</td><td>Available at a limited number of sites in the United States</td></tr>
<tr><td>May not be covered by insurance</td></tr>
<tr><td>More research is needed to determine whether it reduces adverse effects</td></tr>
<tr><td rowspan="2">Stereotactic body radiation therapy (eg, CyberKnife, Gamma Knife)</td><td rowspan="4">Older patients or those with multiple medical conditions; patients whose cancer has spread outside the prostate capsule; men who have had a TURP</td><td rowspan="2">Usually five outpatient treatments, each lasting 60-90 minutes. May require fewer treatments if combined with another form of radiation</td><td rowspan="4">Bowel problems (eg, diarrhea, blood in stool, rectal leakage, rectal pain), frequent urination, blood in the urine, urinary incontinence (increases over time), impotence (develops slowly), fatigue</td><td rowspan="2">Corrects for small movements and changes in the prostate during the course of treatment</td><td>Limited availability</td></tr>
<tr><td>Short-term data suggest equal efficacy to other forms of radiation therapy</td></tr>
<tr><td rowspan="2">TomoTherapy (a slightly different type of stereotactic radiation therapy)</td><td rowspan="2">Number of treatments varies depending on tumor characteristics. Each treatment lasts approximately 25 minutes</td><td>Integrates CT scanning at each visit to correct for changes in the prostate</td><td rowspan="2">Device has not been commercially available for long. It is not available in all areas</td></tr>
<tr><td>Beams rotate 360° around the patient for greater accuracy</td></tr>
</table>

Table 14-7 continued

Treatment	Ideal Candidates	Treatment Time and Recovery	Adverse Effects	Advantages	Disadvantages
Permanent seed implants (ie, brachytherapy)	Men with early-stage cancer and prostate volume < 60 mL	Half-day to full-day outpatient procedure with anesthesia	Impotence and urinary and bowel problems	Radiation is concentrated in the prostate, potentially sparing the urethra, bladder, rectum, and nerves	Small risk that unlinked seeds will migrate or be passed in the urine. Rarely, seeds enter the bloodstream and travel to the lungs or other parts of the body
					May cause urinary toxicity, which may last a long time
High-dose brachytherapy	Immediate- and high-risk patients	Usually three treatments over a few days; treatments last approximately 15 minutes	Pain and rectal irritation usually resolve in approximately a month	Can be used with external-beam radiation in high-risk patients	Limited availability
					Needles remain in place until after the final treatment
					Requires a hospital stay

Abbreviations: 3D-CRT, three-dimensional conformal radiation therapy; EBRT, external-beam radiation therapy; IMRT, intensity-modulated radiation therapy; TURP, transurethral resection of the prostate.

urinary incontinence and sexual dysfunction. Because urinary symptoms may worsen with radiation, patients with significant baseline urinary obstructive symptoms may be better candidates for prostatectomy; if they do undergo RT, then symptoms can be improved with a combination of several months of neoadjuvant ADT, standard therapies like α-blockers, and transurethral resection of the prostate in refractory cases.

Management of Proctitis. The development of rectal proctitis commonly occurs throughout the lifetime of patients who have had curative doses of radiation for prostate cancer. It is often accompanied by sporadic rectal bleeding, which can occur months to years after completion of RT and is often self-limited in duration. Endoscopic findings include telangiectasias in the distal rectum that are often cauterized at the time of endoscopic examination. Administration of rectal suppositories containing steroids or mesalamine can also lessen the effects of proctitis. Judicious evaluations of the distal rectal mucosa should be performed routinely, especially because a small but finite increase in the incidence of rectal cancers after RT is observed.

Management of Radiation Cystitis. Cystitis can manifest as hematuria and/or dysuria. It can be diagnosed symptomatically and treated with nonsteroidal anti-inflammatories in mild cases or, in more severe cases, a cystoscopy may be indicated. Intractable cases may respond to the use of hyperbaric oxygenation. Suspicion for urothelial cancer should be raised in the setting of persistent hematuria and urinary irritative symptoms, and cystoscopy and urine cytology should be strongly considered if these symptoms develop after the first few months after RT.

Focal Therapy

Cryosurgery is a minimally invasive procedure aimed at local control with low complication rates and favorable functional outcomes. This approach often is considered for patients whose disease is not suitable for radical surgery or who have local recurrences after RT. Sufficient long-term follow-up is lacking to estimate efficacy in terms of prostate cancer–specific mortality. High-intensity focused ultrasound, a hyperthermia therapy, is another minimally invasive treatment, but it is not currently recommended for definitive prostate cancer treatment, because the available data do not demonstrate any significant improvement compared with surgery and because there is significant incidence of residual tumor in treated areas 2 years after initial treatment.

Neoadjuvant and Adjuvant ADT

Although neoadjuvant ADT before surgery leads to a reduction in the rate of positive surgical margins, it has not had an effect on overall outcome in older trials and is not recommended for routine clinical use. Clinical trials involving neoadjuvant ADT are ongoing. The benefit of immediate adjuvant ADT after surgery in men with localized disease at high risk for relapse is not proven.

In contrast to surgery, the role of neoadjuvant and concurrent ADT for patients receiving radiation is well established. Several randomized trials (Table 14-8) have demonstrated an OS benefit with the addition of ADT to RT in patients with high-risk disease.

Although the addition of ADT to RT for high-risk disease has thus been established as a standard of care, the optimal duration of ADT is less well defined. As shown in Table 14-8, three trials have evaluated short versus prolonged courses of ADT.

Table 14-8 Randomized Trials of Radiation and ADT in High-Risk Localized Prostate Cancer

Trial	No. of Participants	Study Population	Design	Outcome	Notes
RTOG 86-10[97]	471	T2-T4 (at least 5 × 5 cm), N0-1	EBRT *v* EBRT plus ADT (4 months)	Improved disease-specific mortality at 10 years with ADT (23% *v* 36%)	OS benefit not statistically significant
EORTC 22863[98]	415	T1-T2 with WHO grade 3 histology, or T3-T4. All N0	EBRT *v* EBRT plus ADT (3 years)	Improved 10-year OS with ADT (58% *v* 40%)	
RTOG 85-31[99]	977	T3, N0-1	EBRT *v* EBRT plus ADT (indefinite)	Improved 10-year OS (49% *v* 39%)	No benefit to ADT seen in Gleason score 2-6 disease. No OS benefit seen in N1 disease
RTOG 9202[99,100]	1,554	T2c-T4	EBRT plus ADT (4 *v* 24 months)	Improved OS (29.8% *v* 27.1%) and 15-year DFS (15.7% *v* 10%) with prolonged ADT	Low RT dose by modern standards
EORTC 22961[101]	970	T1-T2, N1-2, or T2c-4, N0-2	EBRT plus ADT (6 *v* 36 months)	Improved 5-year mortality rate with prolonged ADT (15.2% *v* 19%)	
Nabid et al[102]	630	NCCN high-risk (T3-T4, Gleason score > 7, and/or PSA > 20 ng/mL), N0	EBRT plus ADT (18 *v* 36 months)	No statistically significant difference in OS between 18 *v* 36 months of ADT (86% *v* 91%)	Not powered as a noninferiority study, upper bound of OS hazard ratio CI was 1.56. Improved quality-of-life scores with 18 months of ADT

Abbreviations: ADT, androgen-deprivation therapy; DFS, disease-free survival; EBRT, external-beam radiation therapy; NCCN, National Comprehensive Cancer Network; OS, overall survival; RT, radiation therapy.

Two have shown superiority of prolonged ADT, whereas one showed comparable outcomes with medium-course versus prolonged ADT (although not powered as a noninferiority study). Thus, the typical course of ADT in practice is 18 to 24 months (although studies have evaluated durations as long as 36 months) and can be customized depending on patient tolerability and comorbidities.

The addition of ADT to RT has not been shown to improve OS for patients with intermediate-risk disease, but two trials have demonstrated an improvement in biochemical disease-free survival (DFS) with 4 to 6 months of ADT.[25,26] Thus, ADT is typically also offered to intermediate-risk patients but for a shorter time (4 to 6 months). Ongoing trials are testing the value of ADT in addition to more modern RT protocols, and the newest NCCN guidelines suggest ADT may be optional for patients with favorable intermediate-risk disease.

ADT is typically started 2 months before RT, although earlier or later timing of RT relative to ADT does not appear to affect long-term outcomes. It is uncertain whether the addition of bicalutamide to castration improves outcomes, but on the basis of analyses in more advanced disease (see the section titled Metastatic Prostate Cancer Therapy), some clinicians will add bicalutamide for the first 4 to 6 months of ADT or until after RT is completed, especially in high-risk disease.

KEY POINTS

- Patients with low-risk disease may be offered active surveillance, which uses serial PSA measurements, DREs, and biopsy specimens to detect any presence of higher-risk disease, at which point definitive therapy can be offered. Sequential MRI may also be helpful. This strategy results in less treatment-associated morbidity and similar long-term cancer survival compared with immediate therapy.
- Patients with intermediate- and high-risk disease typically should receive definitive therapy, assuming a life expectancy of at least 5 (high-risk) to 10 (intermediate-risk) years (or if symptomatic). Definitive therapies include radical prostatectomy and RT. Long-term cancer survival is similar with either strategy, but adverse effect profiles differ.

- For patients with intermediate- or high-risk disease undergoing RT, the addition of ADT improves biochemical DFS (intermediate risk) and OS (high risk). Duration is typically 4 to 6 months for intermediate-risk disease and 18 to 24 months for high-risk disease. ADT may be optional for favorable intermediate-risk disease.
- Patients with clinical or pathologic (biopsy specimen) evidence of pelvic lymph node involvement are typically treated with definitive RT plus long-course ADT, although no randomized data exist, and prostatectomy followed by adjuvant RT and ADT may also be an option.
- Patients with preexisting urinary symptoms should avoid brachytherapy and may experience symptomatic benefit from radical prostatectomy.
- There is little to no advantages for robotic prostatectomy versus other surgical approaches and for proton therapy versus conventional RT for clinically localized prostate cancer.

THERAPY FOR RECURRENT OR ADVANCED DISEASE

Pathologic Node-Positive Disease

A finding of positive lymph nodes at the time of prostatectomy indicates aggressive disease at high risk for recurrence. However, not all patients will experience disease recurrence. Clinicians may choose to use adjuvant ADT with or without adjuvant RT (see the section titled Local Failure). Adjuvant ADT is justified by a trial demonstrating improved OS and prostate cancer–specific survival in patients with positive lymph nodes at the time of prostatectomy.[27] Only retrospective data are available for the use of adjuvant RT in such patients, but this is often considered as well, given benefits seen in other high-risk situations. In addition, modeling has indicated that immediate (adjuvant) RT may be better than delayed (salvage) RT if the risk is sufficiently high to justify some overtreatment of patients in whom disease would never have recurred.[28]

Biochemical Recurrence

The disease state of increasing PSA level or biochemical relapse refers to men who have no detectable metastases on a scan and in whom the PSA level increases after radical prostatectomy, RT, or both (Fig 14-9). It does not refer to an increase in PSA level for patients in whom disease is managed by watchful waiting. BCR is generally defined by the absence of metastases on conventional imaging, plus:

- after radical prostatectomy (regardless of adjuvant or salvage RT): any detectable PSA confirmed by a second detectable PSA level, because no normal prostate tissue should be left; and
- after primary RT: a PSA level that has increased by 2 ng/dL above the nadir PSA value after RT ("Phoenix criteria").
    - Of note, PSA level may transiently increase after RT, because of recovery of testosterone after ADT and/or the so-called PSA bounce that may be induced by prostate inflammation in the months after RT (18 to 24 months).

Issues in management include whether the increasing PSA value represents a local recurrence that could be eliminated with additional treatment to the prostate bed, or metastatic disease, or both.

In most cases, an increasing PSA level represents micrometastatic disease that is not detectable on conventional imaging studies. The time to development of metastases is highly variable. PSA doubling time, time to biochemical progression, and Gleason score can be used to prognosticate regarding time

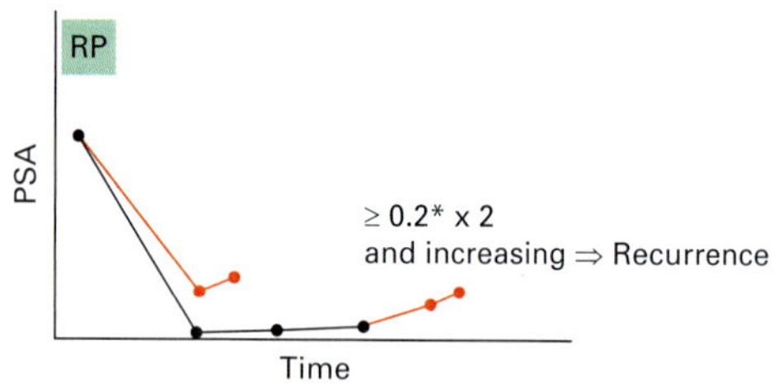

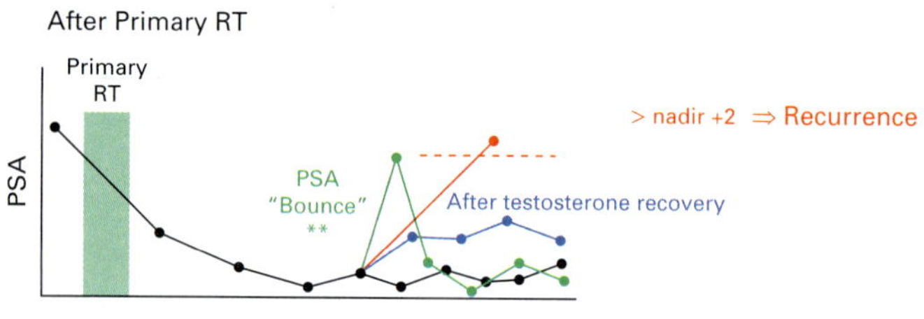

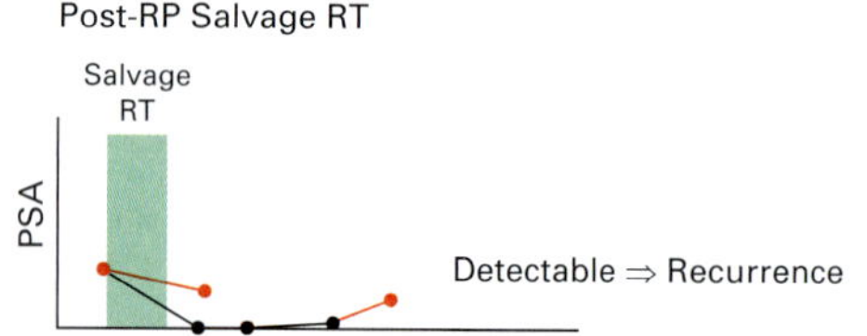

Fig. 14-9 PSA outcomes after primary therapies for localized prostate cancer-defining biochemical recurrence (BCR).

Abbreviations: PSA, prostate-specific antigen; RP, radical prostatectomy; RT, radiation therapy.

*Ultrasensitive PSA assays define biochemical recurrence as any measurable PSA value after radical prostatectomy.

**PSA "bounce" observed only in absence of ADT

to development of metastases. PSA doubling times of < 9 to 10 months are generally associated with development of metastases within months, whereas PSA doubling times of 1.5 to 2 years are generally associated with many years of metastasis-free survival. Thus, treatment is often targeted to those with fastest PSA doubling times, although it is not clear that these prognostic markers can be used to predict benefit from treatment versus surveillance (Fig 14-10).

Local Failure

Adjuvant and Salvage RT. Adjuvant RT to the prostatic bed is considered for patients with certain high-risk features at the time of radical prostatectomy (Fig 14-9). Salvage RT is similar but refers to RT at the time of PSA recurrence (BCR) after prostatectomy, thus limiting RT to only those patients with definitive evidence of recurrence. Three prospective, randomized trials suggested that immediate postoperative RT in men with advanced pathologic features (stage pT3a or pT3b) and/or positive surgical margins improves biochemical PFS, and, in one study, OS. In practice, some physicians might choose to use adjuvant RT for very high-risk pathology (eg, seminal vesicle involvement and positive margins) and use early salvage RT in more ambiguous cases (1- to 2-mm positive margin) to avoid the risk of overtreatment. Early salvage RT at low PSA levels appears to be superior to later RT at higher PSA levels. Salvage RT may increase prostate cancer–specific survival, but one study suggested the benefit was limited to men with a PSA doubling time of < 6 months.

The role of hormonal therapy with RT in the salvage or adjuvant settings has also been studied. In combination with salvage RT, high-dose bicalutamide (150 mg daily) for 24 months offered an OS benefit relative to placebo.[29] However, high-dose bicalutamide is associated with cardiac toxicities and gynecomastia. Many clinicians give 6 months of luteinizing hormone-releasing hormone (LHRH) analog–based ADT on the basis of the benefits seen in the primary treatment setting and as well as a randomized trial for patients undergoing salvage RT that demonstrated a PFS benefit with 6 months of ADT relative to RT alone.[30]

Salvage Prostatectomy. Patients treated initially with RT may be considered for salvage prostatectomy if they were surgical candidates at the time of diagnosis, have a life expectancy > 10 years, and have no metastatic disease. Biopsy-specimen confirmation of persistent disease in the gland and no evidence of spread are essential before surgery is considered. Despite refinements in case selection, incontinence rates remain high and virtually all patients are

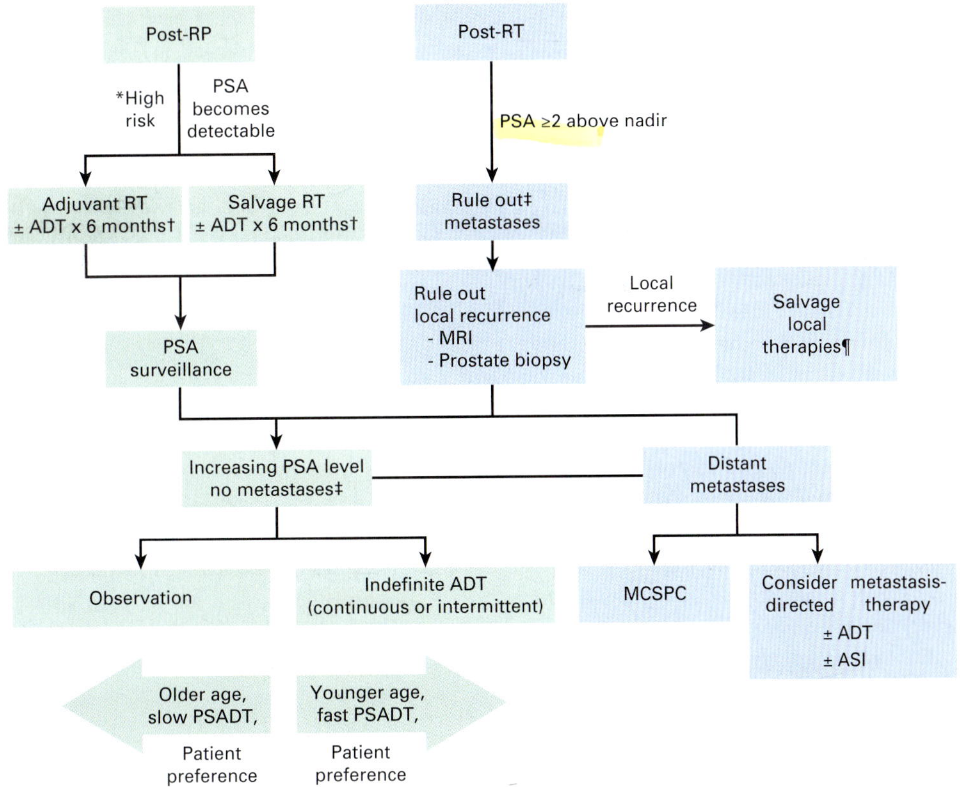

Fig. 14-10 Management options after primary therapy.

Management options for biochemical recurrence (BCR) after primary therapy

Abbreviations: ADT, androgen-deprivation therapy; ASI, androgen signaling inhibitor; mCSPC; metastatic castration-sensitive prostate cancer; MRI, magnetic resonance imaging; PSA, prostate-specific antigen; RP, radical prostatectomy; RT, radiation therapy.

*High risk defined as pT3b, or R1 (positive margin).†Use and duration of ADT is variable. 6 months is common, but patients with low PSAs may not benefit.‡Consider using ultrasensitive diagnostic imaging if available (eg, PET using 18-fluciclovine, 11-choline, or 68-gallium PSMA as tracer); if not available, conventional imaging modalities. ¶Salvage therapies may include brachytherapy, cryotherapy, radiofrequency ablation, HIFU (high intensity focused ultrasound), or salvage prostatectomy.

impotent after the procedure. Salvage treatments, including cryotherapy and brachytherapy for postradiation recurrent prostate cancer, may be considered for select patients. MRI is most useful for detecting recurrence in the prostate after RT, and a confirmatory diagnosis is then made via prostate biopsy specimen. Of note, biopsies should not be done for several months after RT because the effect of radiation is prolonged and residual cancers cells may persist at these earlier time points.

Systemic Therapy for Biochemically Recurrent Prostate Cancer

As discussed in more detail in the section titled ADT for Metastatic Castration-Sensitive Prostate Cancer, the standard systemic treatment of prostate cancer is ADT. Although PSA level almost always declines in response, the clinical benefit of ADT in this setting has not been conclusively established. One trial attempted to answer this question by randomly assigning patients with BCR (as well as those ineligible for curative treatment due to age, comorbidities, or locally advanced disease) to early ADT at the time of BCR, versus delayed ADT at the time of metastatic disease.[31] Although OS was improved with early ADT in the entire cohort, there was no OS benefit in the BCR-only group. In addition, the trial was underenrolled, with too few events to allow definitive conclusions. NCCN guidelines currently recommend observation as the preferred management of nonmetastatic castration-naïve disease (ie, BCR), but with ADT as another option. Thus, the decision of when to start ADT for BCR is a difficult one and must factor in patient preferences in the absence of clear evidence-based guidelines.

If the decision is made to begin ADT in a patient with increasing PSA value but no evidence of metastases, data suggest that intermittent androgen suppression (for 8 months in each cycle, restarting ADT when PSA is > 10 ng/mL) may be a reasonable alternative to continuous androgen suppression, but only in the setting of nonmetastatic disease. The goal is to minimize adverse effects of chronic ADT, including hot flashes, loss of libido, bone loss, and muscle atrophy, but it is not clear to what extent this strategy, in fact, does improve patients' QOL overall.

Nonmetastatic Castration-Resistant Prostate Cancer

Some patients will go on to develop nonmetastatic castration-resistant prostate cancer (nmCRPC), meaning increasing PSA level despite castration-level testosterone values but without overt radiographic evidence of metastases by conventional bone scan and CT imaging. Several randomized trials have demonstrated that the addition of second-generation AR antagonists in this setting delayed the onset of radiographic metastatic disease (metastasis-free survival) compared with ongoing ADT alone (Table 14-9).

On the basis of these outcomes, the FDA approved enzalutamide (also FDA approved for mCSPC and mCRPC) as well as apalutamide (also approved for mCSPC) and darolutamide for patients with nmCRPC (Fig 14-11). Interestingly, the novel end point of metastasis-free survival had recently been established to be a strong surrogate of OS in localized prostate cancer.[32] OS data are immature for these studies. However, as previously discussed, it is not yet clear that starting men on early ADT and then proceeding to one of these agents before development of metastatic disease will prolong survival relative to starting ADT (and subsequent therapies) only at the time of metastatic disease. The potential benefit needs to be weighed against toxicity. Apalutamide was associated with increased risk of rash, hypothyroidism, and fracture; enzalutamide was associated with increased risk of hypertension, myocardial infarction, fatigue, falls, and fractures; darolutamide was associated with increased risk of fatigue. However, patient-reported outcomes were mostly similar in these trials between the active treatment and placebo arms. In addition, these drugs carry significant financial cost (to patients, insurers, and society). Finally, the proper interpretation of both of these studies is complicated by the inclusion of node-positive patients in the SPARTAN study.

The Role of Local Therapy Outside the Prostate for BCR

Patients with BCR at some point may develop oligometastatic recurrence, in which case local therapies such as targeted RT, cryoablation, or radiofrequency ablation may be used in an effort to delay the need for systemic therapy (Fig 14-10). This strategy was demonstrated to delay the need for ADT in a randomized trial,[33] although more objective measures and survival data will be needed. In conjunction with this approach, more sensitive imaging modalities have been developed to detect oligometastatic disease earlier in the disease course. Positron emission tomography (PET) imaging with fluciclovine was approved by the FDA for this purpose and can be used in the setting of negative CT scan or MRI and bone scan. Of note, for patients who underwent primary RT, fluciclovine is often taken up in the residual prostate, limiting its ability to discern local recurrence; MRI is best for evaluating for local recurrence.

KEY POINTS

- Detectable PSA after radical prostatectomy or increase in PSA concentration by 2 ng/dL or more above PSA nadir after RT is an indicator of recurrent prostate cancer. In the absence of evidence of metastatic disease on standard bone scan and CT imaging, this is termed BCR or biochemical relapse.
- Salvage RT may be used for patients who experience BCR after radical prostatectomy, typically combined with 6 months of ADT. Conversely, salvage prostatectomy is less commonly performed after primary RT.
- The optimal timing of systemic therapy for BCR is unclear. ADT will lower PSA level in this setting but its impact on OS relative to ADT at the time of metastatic disease is still unknown.
- Patients with BCR who are treated with ADT and whose PSA levels increase without evidence of metastases on standard bone scan and CT imaging have disease that

Table 14-9 Randomized Trials for nmCRPC

Trial	No. of Participants	Study Population	Design	Outcome	Notes
ARAMIS[103]	1,509	nmCRPC, PSADT ≤10 months and PSA ≥ 2 ng/mL	Continued ADT plus darolutamide *v* placebo	Improved metastasis-free survival with darolutamide (40.4 *v* 18.4 months)	OS data not yet mature
PROSPER[104]	1,401	nmCRPC, PSADT ≤10 months and PSA ≥ 2 ng/mL	Continued ADT plus enzalutamide *v* placebo	Improved metastasis-free survival with enzalutamide (36.6 *v* 14.7 months)	OS data not yet mature
SPARTAN[105]	1,207	nmCRPC, PSADT ≤10 months	Continued ADT plus apalutamide *v* placebo	Improved metastasis-free survival with apalutamide (40.5 *v* 16.2 months)	OS data not yet mature

Abbreviations: ADT, androgen-deprivation therapy; nmCRPC, nonmetastatic castration-resistant prostate cancer; PSA, prostate-specific antigen; PSADT, prostate-specific antigen doubling time.

has progressed to nmCRPC. The addition of the second-generation AR antagonists apalutamide, darolutamide, or enzalutamide prolongs metastasis-free survival in this setting.

THERAPY FOR METASTATIC PROSTATE CANCER

Castration- or hormone-sensitive metastatic prostate cancer is defined by metastases on an imaging study (either at the time of diagnosis or after local therapy) in patients who have non-castration levels of testosterone. At this point, the risk of death from prostate cancer exceeds that of noncancer-related mortality.

ADT for Metastatic Castration-Sensitive Prostate Cancer

The growth of prostate cancer is highly reliant on the activity of androgens on the AR, and downstream signaling and targeting the AR with ADT is the standard systemic treatment approach for relapsed prostate cancer. More than 90% of male hormones originate in the testes, with the remaining hormones synthesized in the adrenal gland. ADT options can be divided into castrating therapies, meaning those that lower serum testosterone levels (such as gonadotropin-releasing hormone agonists or antagonists, and estrogens, as well as surgical castration), and noncastrating therapies, primarily antiandrogens that do not lower testosterone but block androgen action at the level of the AR. Medical or surgical castration is associated with gynecomastia, impotence, loss of

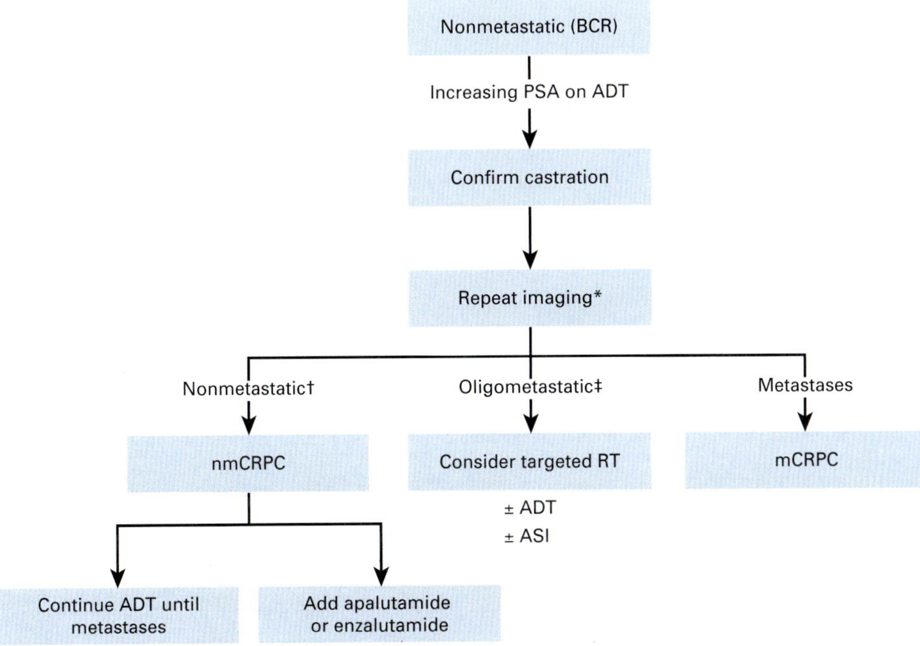

Fig. 14-11 Treatment options for nmCRPC.

Abbreviations: ADT; androgen-deprivation therapy; BCR, biochemical recurrence; mCRPC, metastatic castration-resistant prostate cancer; nmCRPC, nonmetastatic castration-resistant prostate cancer; PSA, prostate-specific antigen; RT, radiation therapy.

*Consider using ultrasensitive diagnostic imaging if available (eg, PET with 18-fluciclovine, 11-choline, or PSMA tracer); if not available, conventional imaging modalities, but low yield if PSA <5 ng/mL. †In nmCRCP studies, patients were included who had pelvic lymph nodes up to 2 cm in diameter. ‡Oligometastatic disease is variably defined as 1-5 metastases.

libido, weakness, fatigue, hot flashes, loss of muscle mass, anemia, depression, and loss of bone over time. Resistance and aerobic exercise can improve muscle mass, strength, and physical function. There have been conflicting data regarding the risk of cardiovascular mortality and dementia in patients with prostate cancer who are receiving ADT.

Prolonged castration can result in osteoporosis or exacerbate underlying osteopenia. Dual-energy x-ray absorptiometry scans can be used at baseline and over time to screen for the development of osteopenia and osteoporosis, although there are no high-quality data to guide who should be screened and how frequently. NCCN guidelines recommend using the National Osteoporosis Foundation guidelines for screening and treatment in the general population but also mention a recommendation from the International Society for Clinical Densiometry to obtain dual-energy x-ray absorptiometry scans at baseline and after 1 year of ADT.[34] Again, there are no high-level data to guide treatment recommendations in this population, but the Fracture Risk Assessment Tool (FRAX) score can be used with ADT considered "secondary osteoporosis" in this algorithm.

- In practice, some clinicians might obtain a baseline bone mineral density scan at the start of long-term ADT (typically in conjunction with primary RT for high-risk localized or regional disease), especially for patients ≥ 70 years or older or with additional risk factors for osteoporosis and repeat this after 1 year of ADT. Any patient who had a FRAX score justifying treatment would then be treated unless testosterone recovery was imminent. FRAX score is calculated with several clinical factors and estimates the 10-year probability of fracture.[35]

Response to ADT can be measured by a decline in PSA values, decrease in the size of nodal or visceral metastases, and improvement in cancer-related symptoms. Overall, 60% to 70% of patients with abnormal PSA levels will have normalization of the value to < 4 ng/mL after castration, 30% to 50% of measurable tumor masses will regress by ≥ 50%, and approximately 60% of patients will have palliation of symptoms. Serial bone scans will show improvement in only 30% to 40% of patients, and a scintigraphic flare on serial bone scans can occur after ADT between 3 and 6 months after initiation of therapy; this should not be confused with progression of skeletal metastases. The PSA value measured at 7 months after initiating therapy is prognostic, with dramatically shorter median survival for patients with a PSA concentration > 4 ng/mL and dramatically longer median survival for those with a PSA concentration < 0.2 ng/mL at this point.

Treatment with an LHRH agonist initially increases serum testosterone level for up to a few weeks after treatment initiation, although the clinical relevance of this is debatable. Because of this, antiandrogens are sometimes used concurrently to block potential effects of the testosterone surge, starting approximately 2 weeks prior to LHRH agonist, especially if a patient has high-risk metastatic lesions (eg, imminent spinal cord compression or urinary obstruction). Alternatively, a gonadotropin-releasing hormone antagonist or surgical castration could be used to avoid testosterone flare. The combination of an antiandrogen and an LHRH analog also has the additional potential to block the effects of adrenal androgens, which can contribute from 5% to 45% of the residual androgens present in tumors after surgical castration alone. In a meta-analysis, nonsteroidal antiandrogens conferred a small but significant improvement in 5-year survival over castration therapy alone. However, because of the additional toxicity of this combination, combination treatment is generally not continued after the flare period. If bicalutamide is given as long-term therapy, it may paradoxically begin to act as an AR agonist. Therefore, for patients whose PSA level increases while the patient is receiving bicalutamide, bicalutamide should be withdrawn and may result, in approximately 20% of patients, in a decrease in PSA level over 1 to 2 months ("antiandrogen withdrawal").

Typical adverse effects of bicalutamide include gynecomastia, for which prophylaxis or treatment with tamoxifen (10 mg daily) or RT can be considered, and elevations in transaminase levels, for which periodic monitoring of liver function tests is mandatory. High doses of bicalutamide (150 mg) generally should be avoided given evidence of cardiotoxicity (Table 14-10), and the typical dosing is 50 mg daily, whether used with an LHRH analog or as monotherapy. Monotherapy is not a standard-of-care choice for systemic treatment of metastatic prostate cancer, but it can be used in patients who decline or do not tolerate castration therapy, or for patients who are significantly debilitated and have other life-limiting comorbidities.

Chemotherapy for Metastatic Castration-Sensitive Prostate Cancer. Based on the results of three randomized trials (Table 14-11), the addition of docetaxel to ADT is now a standard-of-care option for patients with metastatic castration-sensitive prostate cancer (mCSPC). However, the benefit may be limited to patients with high-volume metastatic disease, which was defined in the CHAARTED trial as presence of four or more bone metastases with at least one outside the axial skeleton (ie, skull, ribs, or extremities), or presence of visceral metastases. Similar benefits were not seen in the CHAARTED trial in patients with low-volume metastatic disease, even with longer follow-up, or in the prior GETUG study. STAMPEDE investigators recently presented an abstract of their analysis of the effect of docetaxel by volume of metastases; they found no difference between low- and high-volume disease, using the CHAARTED definition. How can these differing results be reconciled? One major difference between the two trials is the relative percentages of patients with recurrent versus de novo metastatic disease. Recurrent metastatic disease may carry a better prognosis, and a substantial proportion of patients with low-volume metastases in the CHAARTED trial had recurrent disease, whereas few patients in the STAMPEDE trial did. Thus, the apparent benefit of docetaxel in low-volume disease may be limited to those with de novo low-volume disease, not recurrent low-volume disease (Fig 14-12 and Fig 14-13).

Febrile neutropenia can occur with docetaxel, although routine primary prophylaxis with granulocyte colony-stimulating factor (G-CSF) was left to investigator discretion in clinical trials. In practice, patients with additional risk factors (ie, prior chemotherapy, persistent neutropenia, bone marrow involvement by tumor, liver or renal dysfunction, and older age) could be considered for primary prophylaxis. Docetaxel can also cause edema that is refractory to diuresis; this is prevented with steroid prophylaxis. In the CHAARTED trial, QOL decreased during docetaxel treatment but was similar or better in patients treated with ADT alone at later points.

Abiraterone for mCSPC. After the publication of trials demonstrating the efficacy of adding docetaxel to ADT for first-line treatment of mCSPC, two other studies demonstrated a similar improvement in OS with the addition of abiraterone and prednisone to ADT for mCSPC versus ADT alone. The limited data currently available to directly compare these two strategies–adding either chemotherapy or abiraterone to first line ADT for mCSPC–are derived from the multiarm STAMPEDE trial and thus far indicate no difference in any comparative outcomes.[36] In contrast with the CHAARTED study, no study of abiraterone plus prednisone made a distinction between high-volume versus low-volume metastatic disease, but the LATITUDE study included only high risk patients as defined by having two of three of the following: visceral disease, at least three bone metastases, and Gleason score ≥ 8 (Table 14-12). At this point, intensifying first-line therapy for mCSPC with the addition of either docetaxel or an androgen-signaling inhibitor to ADT can be considered the standard of care (Fig 14-12 and Fig 14-13). The effect of sequential docetaxel followed by abiraterone and prednisone in the CSPC setting is under investigation. Although the adverse effect profile and possible financial costs patients may encounter differ between these two strategies, most patients with metastatic disease will eventually receive both agents at some point in the disease course, and sequencing should be determined by patient and physician preference until more definitive data provide superiority of simultaneous versus sequential therapies.

Table 14-10 Increased Risk of Cardiac Arrest and Heart Failure With Bicalutamide 150 mg/d[153]

AEs During Treatment	Bicalutamide 150 mg/d, No. (%) (n = 4,022)	Placebo, No. (%) (n = 4,031)
Cardiac arrest	19 (0.5)	7 (0.2)
Heart failure	61 (1.5)	36 (0.9)
Cardiac arrest		
During treatment	12 (0.30)	5 (0.12)
After treatment	11 (0.27)	7 (0.17)
Total	23 (0.57)	12 (0.30)
Heart failure		
During treatment	15 (0.37)	1 (0.02)
After treatment	6 (0.15)	4 (0.10)
Total	21 (0.52)	5 (0.12)

NOTE. Review of combined data from trials 23, 24, and 25 (N = 8,113).
Abbreviation: AE, adverse event.

AR Antagonists for mCSPC. Three recent trials have tested the addition of either apalutamide or enzalutamide to standard ADT for mCSPC (Table 14-13). Apalutamide and enzalutamide have both received FDA approval for use in mCSPC treatment. In addition, these trials were the first to evaluate intensification of AR-directed therapy together with docetaxel, although none was specifically designed to answer the question of whether docetaxel plus AR antagonists are more effective than either alone, in combination with ADT.

Prostate-Directed Therapy for Metastatic Prostate Cancer

Conventionally, the presence of metastatic disease excluded the consideration for radical prostatectomy or definitive prostate RT. However, interest in prostate-directed therapy is growing even in the setting of metastatic disease. Some reports have described long-term remissions using prostate-directed therapy plus targeted RT and ADT for oligometastatic prostate cancer. The definition of oligometastatic disease is likely to evolve as increasingly sensitive imaging techniques are used in this setting, and this disease state is defined by a different number of metastatic sites in different studies (see the section titled Biochemical Recurrence). The HORRAD and STAMPEDE trials have assessed the efficacy of prostate RT in more diffuse metastatic disease treated with ADT alone.[37,38] Neither trial demonstrated an increase in OS in the populations overall, but there was an increase in OS in patients with low-volume disease (per the CHAARTED criteria) in STAMPEDE in a preplanned subgroup analysis. Thus, there may be a role for definitive prostate RT in the setting of low-volume mCSPC. Ongoing studies are evaluating whether patients with mCSPC should undergo treatment of the primary tumor with surgery or RT, and whether treatment with docetaxel, abiraterone, or other systemic therapies, or metastasis-directed RT will improve survival.

Metastatic Castration-Resistant Prostate Cancer

The treatment of patients with disease that progresses during ADT requires documentation that the patient is medically castrate (defined as serum testosterone level < 50 ng/dL). Despite castration resistance, castration is continued during all subsequent therapies because this decreases the availability of AR ligand and possible direct antagonism of tumor LHRH receptors. Despite the development of mCRPC, AR signaling continues to play a major role in many prostate cancers. Mechanisms leading to persistent AR activation despite castrate testosterone levels include AR overexpression, ligand-independent activation, de novo synthesis of intratumoral androgens, and alterations in the AR, including splice variants and circulating subcastrate levels of androgens.

The development of new classes of agents including novel nonsteroidal antiandrogens, cytochrome P450 (CYP) 17 inhibitors,

Table 14-11 Randomized Trials of ADT Plus Docetaxel for mCSPC

Trial	No. of Participants	Study Population	Design	Outcome	Notes
CHAARTED[106]	790	mCSPC (recurrent or de novo)	ADT *v* ADT plus docetaxel, 6 cycles	Improved OS with docetaxel (58 *v* 47 months; 51 *v* 34 months in high-volume disease)	No OS benefit seen in low-volume group.[107] Mostly de novo mCSPC
GETUG-AFU 15[108]	385	mCSPC	ADT *v* ADT plus docetaxel (≤ 9 cycles)	No statistically significant OS improvement with docetaxel (62 *v* 49 months)	Fewer patients enrolled with high-volume disease than in CHAARTED. High-volume subset demonstrated nonsignificant improvement in OS with docetaxel (underpowered comparison)
STAMPEDE[45]	2,962	High-risk localized or high-risk BCR or mCSPC (recurrent or de novo)	ADT *v* ADT plus docetaxel, 6 cycles	Improved OS with docetaxel (81 *v* 71 months)	Benefit was seen across subsets including M0 patients, although few events in this group. No benefit seen with addition of zoledronic acid

Abbreviations: ADT, androgen-deprivation therapy; BCR, biochemical recurrence; mCSPC, metastatic castration-sensitive prostate cancer; OS, overall survival.

and AR-targeted compounds has led to improvements in survival for patients with mCRPC. Abiraterone acetate and enzalutamide are associated with prolonged survival and improved QOL. Additional AR pathway-targeted agents are under investigation in patients with mCRPC. Before the availability of these novel agents, ketoconazole and other agents were used, with a minority of patients exhibiting long-term response.

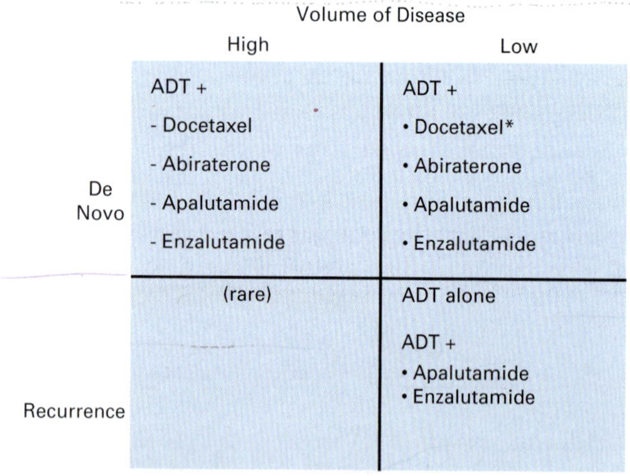

	Volume of Disease: High	Volume of Disease: Low
De Novo	ADT + - Docetaxel - Abiraterone - Apalutamide - Enzalutamide	ADT + • Docetaxel* • Abiraterone • Apalutamide • Enzalutamide
Recurrence	(rare)	ADT alone ADT + • Apalutamide • Enzalutamide

Fig. 14-12 Population of patients with mCSPC studied in trials of treatment intensification.

Abiraterone is always administered with prednisone.

Abbreviations: ADT, androgen-deprivation therapy; mCSPC, metastatic castration-sensitive prostate cancer.

*Per STAMPEDE post hoc analysis. No benefit seen in low-volume disease in the CHAARTED trial, but a substantial percentage of patients with recurrent disease was included in that trial.

For patients who have previously received primary localized therapy and now present with overt symptomatic metastatic disease (after PSA and radiologic progression) at the time of initiating ADT, characterization of the anatomic location and symptoms is important. The presence of new-onset back pain should raise concern for possible spinal cord or cauda equina disease, and, if clinically indicated, an MRI of the spine should be performed. In approximately 10% to 15% of patients, disease will relapse with aggressive local or distant metastases. In circumstances where the PSA level appears to be disproportionately low for the tumor burden present or the presence of visceral metastases, a repeated biopsy of a metastatic site may indicate a neuroendocrine or small-cell phenotype. It is believed that neuroendocrine clones may emerge under pressure of intensive androgen blockade, although ongoing research is characterizing this spectrum of prostate cancer.

Abiraterone and Enzalutamide for mCRPC. Androgen-signaling inhibitors like abiraterone and enzalutamide are AR-targeting therapies that remain effective even after the onset of castration resistance (Fig 14-14). Abiraterone acetate is an oral CYP17 (17α hydroxylase and 17,20 lyase) inhibitor that inhibits androgen and glucocorticoid biosynthesis (Fig 14-15). Feedback loops during

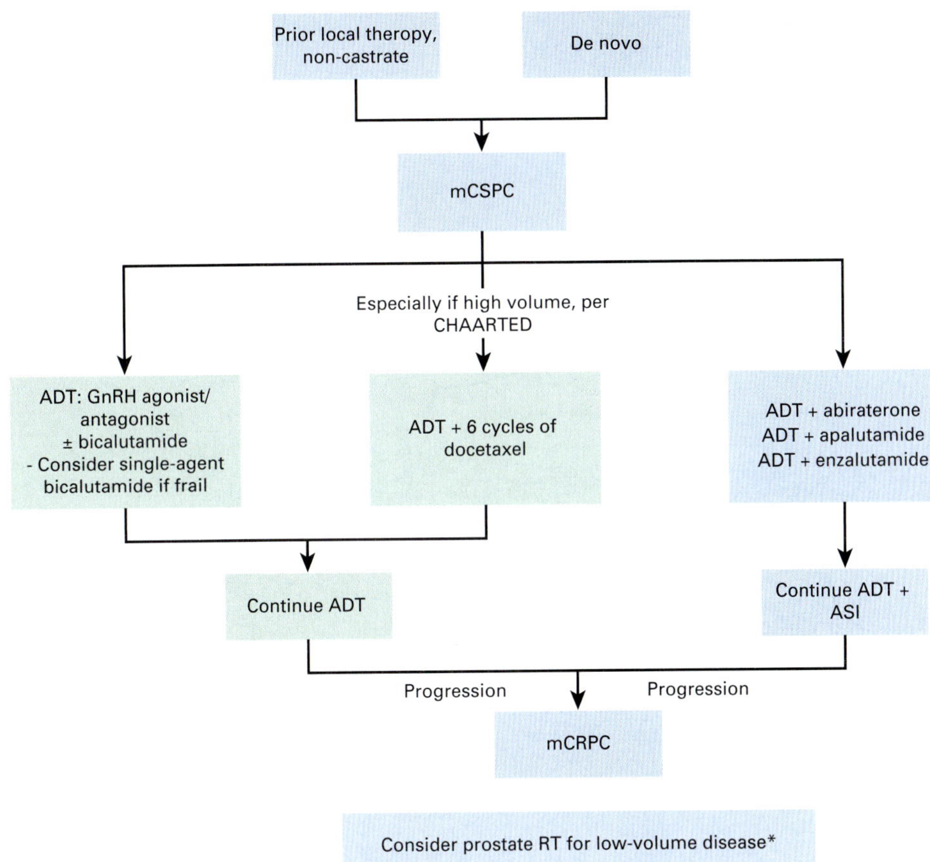

Fig. 14-13 Systemic treatment options for mCSPC.

Abiraterone is always administered with prednisone.

Abbreviations: ADT, androgen-deprivation therapy; ASI, androgen signaling inhibitor; GnRH, gonadotropin-releasing hormone; mCRPC, metastatic castration-resistant prostate cancer; mCSPC; metastatic castration-sensitive prostate cancer; RT, radiation therapy.

*Supported by a pre-specified subgroup analysis from STAMPEDE, but comparison arm was ADT alone. Efficacy in setting of intensified therapy (ADT + docetaxel or + ASI) is unknown.

treatment result in adrenocorticotropic hormone–mediated excess mineralocorticoid activity including hypertension, fluid retention, and hypokalemia, and low-dose prednisone is administered concurrently to prevent this. Potassium level and blood pressure should be monitored during treatment. Hypertension may be treated with standard antihypertensive mineralocorticoid receptor antagonists like eplerenone if standard agents are ineffective.

The FDA label includes directions to give concurrent prednisone 5 mg twice daily in the setting of castration-resistant disease but only 5 mg daily in the setting of castration-sensitive disease. However, given the potential adverse effects of higher-dose steroids, another off-label option is to start treatment for all patients at 5 mg daily and then increase to twice daily if adrenocorticotropic hormone–mediated adverse effects develop. Abiraterone is taken on an empty stomach because fatty food may increase absorption; however, toxic levels were never reached in studies, so patients should not fear overabsorption due to taking this drug with food. Giving a lower-than-recommended dose of abiraterone together with food is being investigated as a strategy to decrease the cost of abiraterone therapy.

Table 14-12 Randomized Trials of ADT Plus Abiraterone and Prednisone for mCSPC

Trial	No. of Participants	Study Population	Design	Outcome	Notes
LATITUDE[109]	1,199	De novo high-risk mCSPC	ADT plus placebo *v* ADT plus abiraterone and prednisone	Improved OS with addition of abiraterone and prednisone (not reached *v* 34.7 months)	High-risk based on 2 of 3 of: Gleason 8+, 3+ bone lesions, visceral metastases
STAMPEDE[40]	1,917	High-risk localized or high-risk BCR or mCSPC (recurrent or de novo)	ADT plus placebo *v* ADT plus abiraterone and prednisone (plus RT for localized or N+ disease)	Improved 3-year OS with addition of abiraterone and prednisone (83% *v* 76%)	Benefit was seen across subsets including M0 tumors, although there were few events in this group

Abbreviations: ADT, androgen-deprivation therapy; BCR, biochemical recurrence; mCSPC, metastatic castration-sensitive prostate cancer; OS, overall survival; RT, radiation therapy.

Table 14-13 Randomized Trials of ADT Plus Androgen Receptor Antagonists for mCSPC

Trial	No. of Participants	Study Population	Design	Outcome	Notes
ARCHES[110]	1,150	mCSPC (recurrent or de novo)	ADT *v* ADT plus enzalutamide. Docetaxel allowed at investigator discretion in either trial arm	Improved radiographic PFS with addition of enzalutamide (not reached *v* 19 months)	rPFS benefit seen regardless of docetaxel use and/or disease volume. OS data immature
ENZAMET[111]	1,125	mCSPC (recurrent or de novo)	ADT *v* ADT plus enzalutamide. Docetaxel allowed at investigator discretion in either trial arm	Improved OS with addition of enzalutamide (median OS not yet estimable; 80% *v* 72% OS at 3 years)	Possibly limited benefit of enzalutamide in docetaxel-treated patients. Possible increased docetaxel toxicity with addition of enzalutamide
TITAN[112]	1,052	mCSPC (recurrent or de novo)	ADT *v* ADT plus apalutamide. Docetaxel allowed at investigator discretion in either trial arm	Improved OS and radiographic PFS with apalutamide (82% *v* 74% OS; 68% *v* 48% rPFS)	rPFS benefit seen regardless of docetaxel use and/or disease volume. Possibly limited OS benefit of apalutamide in docetaxel-treated patients

Abbreviations: ADT, androgen-deprivation therapy; mCSPC, metastatic castration-sensitive prostate cancer; OS, overall survival; PFS, progression-free survival; rPFS, radiography progression-free survival; RT, radiation therapy.

Abiraterone acetate was FDA approved in 2011 for men with mCRPC after docetaxel treatment, on the basis of OS benefit relative to placebo. It was subsequently FDA approved in 2012 for treatment before docetaxel treatment, on the basis of improved OS relative to placebo (Table 14-14). Enzalutamide is a highly potent, oral AR antagonist that also prevents translocation of the AR to the nucleus and inhibits AR binding to DNA. It was FDA approved in 2012 for the treatment of mCRPC after docetaxel treatment and in 2014 for use in patients with mCRPC before docetaxel treatment (Table 14-14). Toxicities include fatigue and hypertension, and because enzalutamide is a strong CYP3A4 inducer, there can be significant interactions with medications metabolized via this pathway, for example, direct oral anticoagulants and fentanyl. There is an increased risk of falls and possibly seizures associated with enzalutamide (although the latter has been questioned in postmarketing studies), and it is generally avoided in patients with history of falls or seizures.

Although abiraterone and enzalutamide have changed the landscape for the management of CRPC, approximately 15% to 25% of patients have primary resistance and a high degree of cross-resistance, with response rates of 15% to 30% when patients are switched to the alternative agent and more brief responses even in those who do respond. The specific sequencing of abiraterone and enzalutamide does not appear to affect survival.[39] Detection in circulating tumor cells of the AR-splice variant AR-V7, which lacks the ligand-binding domain, in men with CRPC is associated with resistance to enzalutamide and abiraterone, although notably, depending on the assay used, resistance is not 100%.[40] In contrast, the presence of AR-V7 in circulating tumor cells from men with mCRPC does not appear to be associated with resistance to taxane chemotherapy. AR-V7 is only one of many potential mechanisms of resistance. Thus, clinicians may choose to check AR-V7 status via one of two commercially available assays when deciding between AR-directed therapy and taxane therapy; alternatively, they may simply try a second-line androgen-signaling inhibitor and evaluate PSA response before proceeding to taxane therapies.

Chemotherapy for mCRPC. In 2004, two randomized trials were reported that compared docetaxel-based therapy with mitoxantrone and prednisone in patients with mCRPC. A significant improvement in OS was demonstrated for patients who received docetaxel, with a median survival of > 18 months. Docetaxel was also superior to mitoxantrone with respect to pain response rate, PSA response rate, and QOL indices. On the basis of these study results, the FDA approved the use of docetaxel (75 mg/m^2 every 21 days) together with prednisone as frontline therapy for men with mCRPC (Fig 14-14).

Cabazitaxel is a microtubule-stabilizing taxane that was FDA approved as second-line chemotherapy after docetaxel therapy, on the basis of the results of a phase III trial in patients who had received treatment with docetaxel and demonstrated improved OS with cabazitaxel (25 mg/m^2) versus mitoxantrone. Grade 3 to 4 neutropenic fever was the major serious toxicity in patients

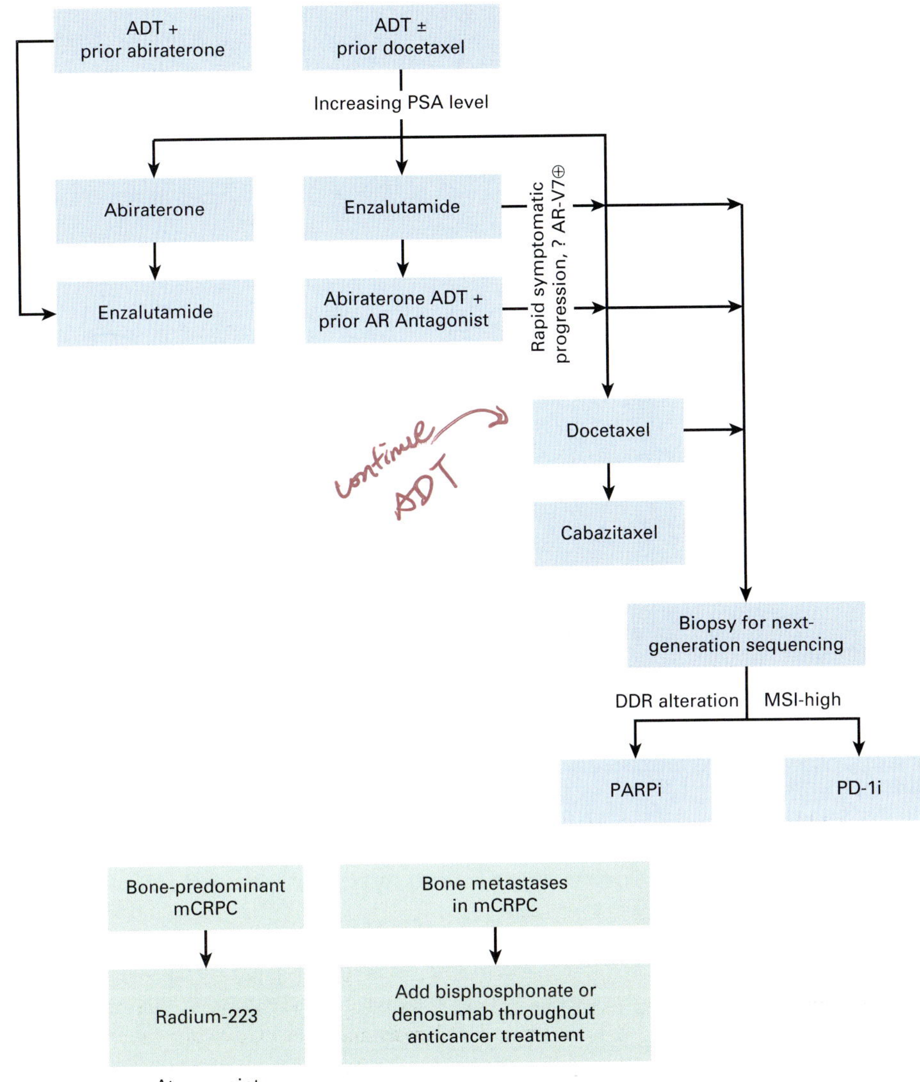

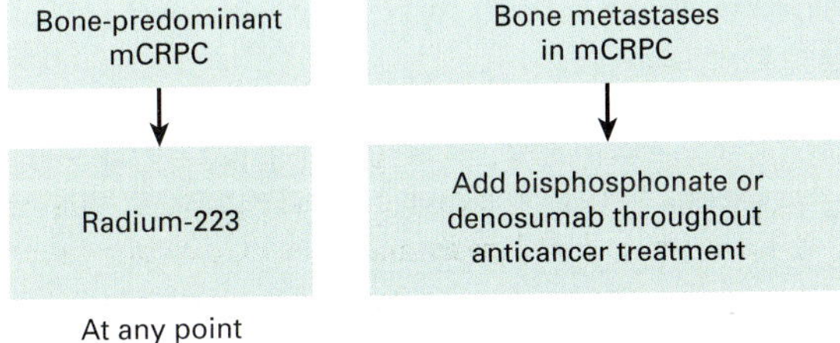

Fig. 14-14 **Treatment options for mCRPC.**

Abiraterone is always administered with prednisone.

Abbreviations: ADT, androgen-deprivation therapy; AR, androgen receptor; DDR, DNA damage repair; mCRPC, metastatic castration-resistant prostate cancer; MSI, microsatellite instability; PSA, prostate-specific antigen.

*Consider AR-V7 testing prior to initiating second line androgen signaling inhibitors, and consider using docetaxel in lieu of second-line ASI for patients in whom AR-V7 is detected.

who received cabazitaxel, and primary prophylaxis with G-CSF should be given routinely for patients using standard dosing. A subsequent study demonstrated that cabazitaxel 20 mg/m^2 is noninferior in terms of survival and is less toxic.[41] Mitoxantrone and other regimens that have demonstrated activity in mCRPC may be beneficial as possible additional therapies for patients with a good performance status if they have used all other available treatment options and cannot enroll in a clinical trial.

In patients with small-cell histologies, platinum-containing chemotherapy combination regimens like cisplatin or carboplatin plus etoposide or carboplatin plus docetaxel, are recommended. ADT should be continued during treatment of small-cell carcinoma because of intratumoral and intertumoral heterogeneity.

Immunotherapy. A variety of studies using various immune-based therapies suggested a benefit in survival for men with mCRPC. Sipuleucel-T is an autologous cellular vaccine composed of prostatic acid phosphatase and granulocyte-macrophage colony-stimulating factor. After cells are harvested and tagged with the therapy, it is administered intravenously every 2 weeks for a total of three infusions and is designed to elicit an immune response to prostatic acid phosphatase. In patients with minimally symptomatic mCRPC, OS was improved. No significant effect on PSA values or PFS was observed in the phase III trial, leading to controversy in the field regarding whether it is truly effective. On the basis of this 4.1-month improvement in OS, sipuleucel-T was approved by the FDA in 2010.

Other immune-based therapies have been assessed in mCRPC and were not effective. Checkpoint inhibitors such as inhibitors of CTLA-4 and PD-1/PD-L1 have had limited efficacy in advanced CRPC after failure of standard therapies. However, a small percentage of patients with metastatic prostate cancer have microsatellite-high/mismatch repair–deficient status. The FDA approved the PD-1 inhibitor pembrolizumab for such patients regardless of primary tumor type in 2017, and some patients have had dramatic responses to pembrolizumab when no other treatment options were available.[42] Responses to PD-1/PD-L1 inhibition have also been seen in a small number of patients with prostate cancer without microsatellite-high/mismatch repair–deficient status, sometimes in combination with other agents, and this is an active area of research.

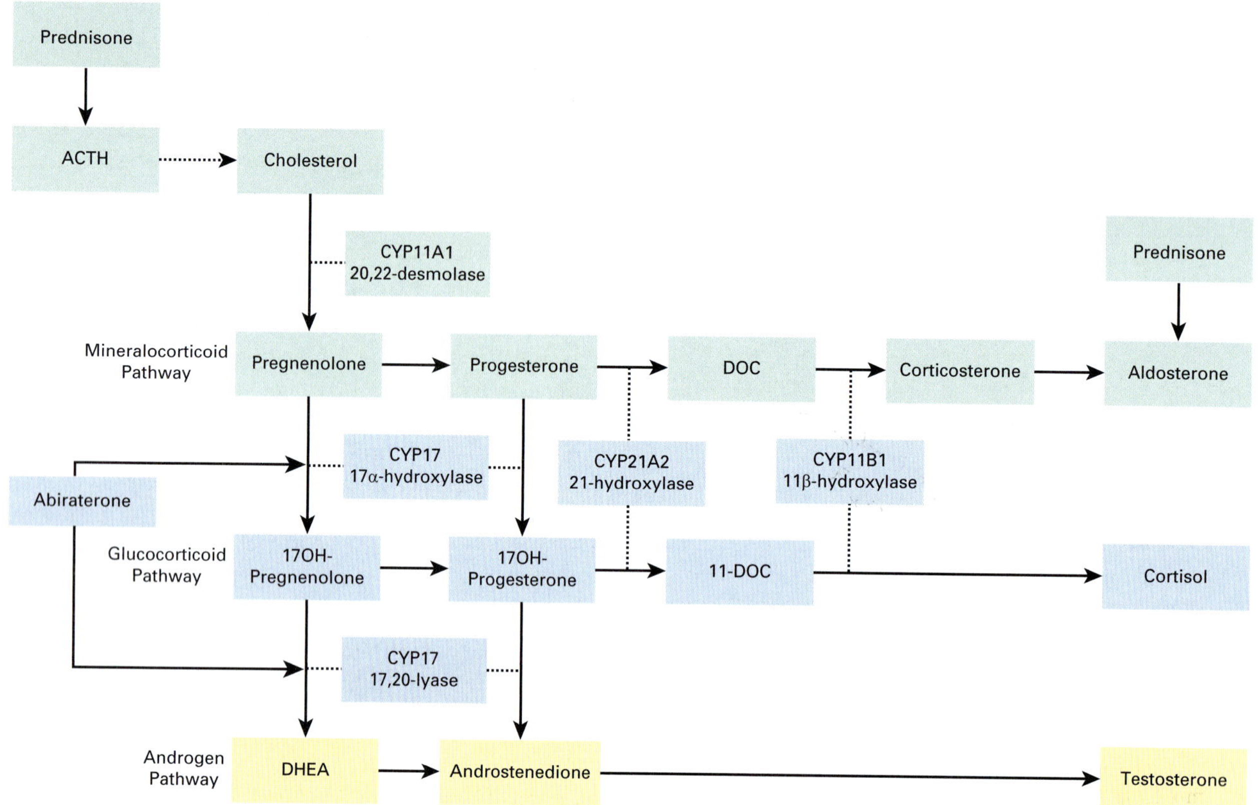

Fig. 14-15 Biochemical pathways resulting from abiraterone administration and prednisone.
Administration of prednisone prevents a compensatory ACTH surge and thus decreases downstream symptoms of excess mineralocorticoid production (hypertension, hypokalemia and edema)
Abbreviations: ACTH, adrenocorticotropic hormone; DHEA, dehydroepiandrosterone; DOC, 11-deoxycorticosterone.

Table 14-14 Phase III Randomized Trials of Abiraterone and Enzalutamide in mCRPC

Trial	No. of Participants	Study Population	Design	Outcome
COU-AA-301[113]	1,195	mCRPC postdocetaxel	Abiraterone plus prednisone *v* placebo	Improved OS with abiraterone plus prednisone (15.8 *v* 11.2 months)
AFFIRM[114]	1,199	mCRPC postdocetaxel	Enzalutamide *v* placebo	Improved OS with enzalutamide (18.4 *v* 13.6 months)
COU-AA-302[115]	1,088	mCRPC predocetaxel	Abiraterone plus prednisone *v* placebo	Improved OS with abiraterone plus prednisone (34.7 *v* 30.3 months)
PREVAIL[116]	1,717	mCRPC predocetaxel	Enzalutamide *v* placebo	Improved OS with enzalutamide (35.3 *v* 31.3 months)

Abbreviations: mCRPC, metastatic castration-resistant prostate cancer; OS, overall survival.

Novel Targeted Therapies. A phase II study of olaparib, a PARP inhibitor, in 50 patients with mCRPC after treatment with docetaxel and one or more AR directed therapies demonstrated a response (a composite of radiographic or PSA response or conversion of circulating tumor cells from 5 cells/7.5 mL blood to < 5 cells/7.5 mL blood) in 33% of evaluable patients, with 12 patients receiving the treatment for > 6 months.[43] Responses were enriched among patients with biallelic somatic or germline *BRCA2* loss or *ATM* aberrations. Additional studies are ongoing to further define the role for PARP inhibitors in patients with mCRPC and DNA repair gene alterations. The addition of platinum chemotherapy to docetaxel may also be effective in patients with alterations in DNA repair genes because their tumors are less able to repair the platinum-induced double-stranded breaks. Ongoing research will hopefully clarify biomarkers of response to either PARP inhibition or platinum therapy (Fig 14-14).

Bone-Targeted Therapy. Involvement of bone occurs at some point in the disease course of a vast majority of patients with metastatic prostate cancer. In some patients, metastatic disease is confined to or predominantly involves bone (Fig 14-14). Bone metastases may be asymptomatic or painful, and they can eventually lead to pathologic fracture, spinal cord compression, need for RT, or need for surgery to bone, all of which are collectively termed "skeletal-related events" (SREs).

The α-emitter radium-223 is a bone-seeking radionuclide that has been approved by the FDA for treatment of patients with mCRPC and symptomatic bone metastases with no known visceral metastatic disease, on the basis of results of the ALSYMPACA trial (Table 14-15). Patients included in the study had received treatment with docetaxel, were unfit for docetaxel, or refused docetaxel, and toxicity included myelosuppression and GI symptoms. This study led to the FDA approval in 2013 of radium-223 dichloride. Notably, the ERA223 trial randomly assigned men with mCRPC with no prior treatment of mCRPC to treatment with abiraterone with or without radium.[44] The study was unblinded early due to an increased fracture risk and poorer OS in the combination arm. An updated analysis demonstrated that the treatment arms had similar survival, but there was an increased risk of fragility fractures in the combination arm and a low rate of treatment in the study overall with bone-targeting agents to prevent SREs. The FDA subsequently recommended avoiding concurrent treatment with radium-223 and abiraterone plus prednisone. Other combination therapies involving radium-223 are still being assessed in prospective clinical trials.

Bisphosphonates or denosumab, a fully humanized anti-RANKL monoclonal antibody, may be approved by the FDA in two situations:

- Men receiving long-course ADT in combination with RT for localized prostate cancer who are found to have baseline or treatment-induced osteopenia or osteoporosis. In this case, the goal is to increase bone mineral density and prevent osteoporosis-related fractures.
- Men with mCRPC and bone metastases. In this case, the goal is to prevent SREs. Use of bisphosphonates in mCSPC did not improve SREs or OS in the STAMPEDE trial.[45]

Renal insufficiency, osteonecrosis of the jaw, and hypocalcemia are potential adverse effects of bisphosphonates. Patients with significant dental disease or who require dental procedures should not be treated with bisphosphonates until after dental clearance. Monthly or every 3-month dosing of zoledronic acid is indicated for bone metastases, whereas yearly infusions can be used for treatment of osteoporosis.

In a phase III trial, denosumab, a RANKL inhibitor, was superior to zoledronic acid for prevention of SREs (Table 14-15). Hypocalcemia was more common in patients treated with denosumab, and osteonecrosis of the jaw occurred infrequently in both arms. Denosumab can be used in patients with renal impairment. Of note, the approved dose and schedule of denosumab for prevention of SREs in patients with mCRPC (120 mg every month) differ from those approved for fragility fracture prevention (60 mg every 6 months). Extrapolating from data showing equivalence of zoledronic acid every 3 months versus monthly in preventing SREs in patients with bone metastases from any cancers,[46] some clinicians may use denosumab every 3 months off-label instead of monthly for mCRPC with bone metastases. Bisphosphonates may be stopped or given less frequently after 2 years of therapy, due to an increased risk of atypical femoral fractures and osteonecrosis of the jaw. Denosumab may be continued indefinitely given an increase in bone turnover markers after stopping therapy, especially in the metastatic setting, although the clinical significance of this is unclear.

Both denosumab and zoledronic acid are given with calcium to mitigate the risk of hypocalcemia, and typically this is also given in combination with vitamin D (especially in patients being treated for osteoporosis).

Palliation

An important aspect of patient care is the palliation of pain. Durable relief in selected sites can be achieved with EBRT delivered in a focal or hemibody technique. Systemic therapies can also provide palliation, especially nonsteroidal anti-inflammatory medications. The combination of mitoxantrone and prednisone is FDA approved for the palliation of pain. Bone-seeking radiopharmaceutical agents such as radium-223 reduce the pain of skeletal metastases, as discussed previously.

KEY POINTS

- Treatment of metastatic prostate cancer is palliative, not curative, but with sequential treatments, patients may experience years of disease control.
- Compared with ADT alone, the addition of docetaxel, abiraterone plus prednisone, or the AR antagonists apalutamide or enzalutamide to treatment for patients with mCSPC significantly prolongs OS. Docetaxel seems to have the most benefit for patients with high-volume disease (four or more bone metastases with one or more outside the spine and pelvis, or visceral—not nodal—metastases).
- In the setting of mCRPC, abiraterone, enzalutamide, sipuleucel-T, docetaxel, radium-223, and cabazitaxel all prolong OS. Unfortunately, cross-resistance to AR-directed therapies occurs after exposure to abiraterone or enzalutamide for a prolonged period, and the efficacy of enzalutamide after abiraterone or abiraterone after enzalutamide is limited.

Table 14-15 **Randomized Phase III Trials of Bone-Directed Therapy for mPCa**

Trial	No. of Participants	Study Population	Design	Outcome	Notes
ALSYMPCA[117]	921 (809 in interim analysis)	mPCa postdocetaxel or ineligible or declined docetaxel	Radium-223 *v* placebo	Improved OS with radium-223 (14.0 *v* 11.2 months)	Also improved bone pain
Fizazi et al.[118]	1,904	mCRPC, no prior bisphosphonate	Monthly denosumab plus placebo *v* monthly zoledronic acid plus placebo	Improved time to first skeletal-related event (20.7 *v* 17.1 months)	

Abbreviations: mCRPC, metastatic castration-resistant prostate cancer; mPCa, metastatic prostate cancer; OS, overall survival.

SURVIVORSHIP AND ELDERLY CONSIDERATIONS

With early detection and treatment, many men will be cured of prostate cancer by RT or surgery. A variety of adverse effects may develop in these patients that are related to therapy, including urinary incontinence, erectile dysfunction, and posttreatment psychosocial issues. Prostate cancer is predominantly a disease of older men with coexisting medical issues, and ADT is associated with numerous adverse effects that may be particularly pronounced in older men, including decreased libido, impotence, decreased lean body mass and muscle strength, increased fat mass, decreased QOL, and osteoporosis. It also has been recognized that metabolic complications such as insulin resistance, hyperglycemia, and metabolic syndrome can occur in patients receiving long-term ADT (≥ 12 months), potentially contributing to an increased risk of cardiovascular events. Men receiving long-term ADT may be monitored for the development of diabetes, and those in whom an adverse lipid profile develops should be treated according to the established guidelines for hyperlipidemia. It has been suggested that men (especially those with preexisting cardiovascular diseases) who receive as little as 6 months of ADT with RT may have an increased risk of cardiovascular-related mortality, but this observation was not confirmed in other retrospective analyses or in a meta-analysis. Other studies suggest that men with previous cardiovascular disease may be at increased risk of cardiovascular morbidity while receiving ADT. One report suggested that cardiovascular disease risk may be highest in the first 6 months of ADT in men who experienced two or more cardiovascular events before therapy. Data are conflicting regarding the association of ADT and dementia, including Alzheimer disease in men with prostate cancer, and there is evidence to suggest an association between ADT and the development of depression.[47] None of these studies has established a causal link and no randomized trials have demonstrated significantly increased risk of cardiovascular mortality, dementia, or depression, although they were not powered for these outcomes. In practice, the potential risks of ADT are likely justified for patients with intermediate- to high-risk localized or metastatic disease in which clear survival advantages have been established, and clinicians should be judicious about use of ADT in lower-risk prostate cancer and low-risk BCR prostate cancer.

BLADDER CANCER

EPIDEMIOLOGY

An estimated 80,470 new cases of bladder cancer (n = 61,700 in men and n = 18,770 in women)and 17,670 bladder cancer–related deaths (n = 12,870 in men and n = 4,800 in women) occurred in the United States in 2019.[48] The incidence of bladder cancer is three to four times higher in men than in women and the median age at diagnosis is 73 years. The approximate 5:1 ratio of incidence to mortality reflects the frequency of noninvasive tumors compared with muscle-invasive tumors and metastatic disease. Although white Americans have a two-fold higher incidence of bladder cancer, black Americans have a higher mortality rate, with a higher incidence of high-grade and muscle-invasive tumors. The difference in mortality does not appear to be related to the intensity and quality of care received.

Risk factors for bladder cancer include:

- tobacco use,
- occupational exposures,
- urinary tract diseases, and
- pharmaceutical drug use.

Cigarette smoking is strongly associated with an increased risk of bladder cancer among men and women. In the United States, the risk of bladder cancer in former smokers and current smokers compared with the risk in never-smokers has increased over time. Although smoking cessation is associated with a reduced risk of bladder cancer, the risk as compared with that in never-smokers remains elevated for those who have quit even after ≥ 10 years of smoking. This risk increases in proportion to the amount and duration of cigarette exposure with heavy smokers (> 20 cigarettes smoked per day and/or > 40 years of smoking), resulting in up to a five-fold higher relative risk compared with nonsmokers.

Occupational exposure to aromatic amines (particularly 2-naphthylamine, benzidine, and polycyclic aromatic hydrocarbons) is associated with an increased incidence of bladder cancer (eg, workers in dyestuff manufacturing and rubber and aluminum industries).

Infection with the trematode *Schistosoma haematobium* leads to chronic irritation of the urothelium and to an increased risk of both squamous and urothelial carcinomas. Other chronic urinary tract infections, including stones and cystitis, also may lead to chronic inflammation and to an increased risk of bladder cancer.

Heavy use of phenacetin-containing analgesics is associated with tumors of the renal pelvis and ureter, and cyclophosphamide also has been associated with an increased risk of urothelial carcinoma.

These myriad risk factors lead to field changes within the urothelium that predispose individuals to the development of recurrent tumors, as well as to the involvement of new locations in the urothelial tract (polychronotropism). Hereditary nonpolyposis colon cancer syndrome, also known as Lynch syndrome, is associated with an increased risk for the development of bladder and other urothelial cancers, most notably upper tract tumors.

The three general categories of disease—nonmuscle invasive, muscle invasive, and metastatic—differ in tumor biology, clinical phenotype, management, and prognosis, as follows:

- For nonmuscle-invasive tumors, the goal is to prevent recurrence and progression to muscle-invasive disease necessitating cystectomy or to an incurable state characterized by metastatic disease.
- For muscle-invasive disease, the goal is to maximize the chance for cure using a multimodality approach incorporating chemotherapy with surgery or RT.
- The management of metastatic disease requires the use of established prognostic and predictive factors to determine the therapeutic objectives and potential for treatment-related toxicity.

The main goals are prolongation of survival and palliation of symptoms because the cancer is incurable. Bladder preservation may be considered in select patients using a trimodality approach: a maximal transurethral resection of bladder tumor(s) followed by concurrent chemotherapy and RT. The anatomic location of the bladder neoplasm will dictate the appropriateness of this approach.

KEY POINTS

- Urothelial carcinoma is predominantly a disease of older men and is associated with smoking as well as industrial exposures, chronic catheters, and chronic bladder infections, including schistosomiasis in endemic areas. Upper tract (ureteral and renal pelvis) urothelial carcinoma may be associated with Lynch syndrome.
- The entire urothelial tract is at risk from these carcinogenic exposures, so patients with urothelial carcinoma in one area are at risk for separate primaries in other areas and at other times.

PATHOLOGY

Urothelial carcinoma may occur throughout the urinary tract (ie, in any structure lined by the urothelium), with > 90% of tumors originating in the bladder. Upper urinary tract tumors, including the renal pelvis and ureter, account for 5% to 7% of urothelial carcinomas, with renal pelvis tumors constituting the majority.

Lesions of mixed histology generally are variants of urothelial carcinoma. Such variants include micropapillary, sarcomatoid, rhabdoid, and plasmacytoid differentiation of urothelial cancer. Tumors with plasmacytoid differentiation may often have lepidic growth (ie, proliferation along tissue planes without invasion), appearing as vague infiltrative processes on imaging rather than discrete metastatic deposits.

In the United States, 92% of lower urinary tract tumors are urothelial carcinomas, 5% are squamous cell cancers, 2% are adenocarcinomas, and 1% are small-cell carcinomas. Adenocarcinomas may be of urachal origin, occurring at the junction of the urachal ligament and bladder dome. In Northern Africa and other parts of the world where there is a high prevalence of infection with *S. haematobium,* up to 75% of tumors are pure squamous cell carcinomas, although urothelial carcinoma is becoming more prevalent in those regions, too.

KEY POINTS

- Most bladder and ureter cancers are of urothelial (transitional cell) histology. There are several variants of urothelial carcinoma, most of which are treated similarly as pure urothelial carcinoma.
- Rare bladder cancers can have pure adenocarcinoma, squamous cell, or small-cell histology. These are generally not treated as urothelial carcinoma.

BIOLOGY

Molecular profiling has demonstrated that urothelial tumors evolve through divergent pathways corresponding to the clinical phenotypes of nonlethal, recurrent nonmuscle-invasive lesions and lethal, muscle-invasive, and metastatic disease. Although approximately 70% of these low-grade lesions will recur, only 10% to 15% will progress to invasive lesions. Progression of low-grade lesions to invasive disease is characterized by structural and functional alterations in the tumor suppressors *p53* and *Rb*, in addition to chromosome aberrations. Alterations in *p53* and *Rb* also are frequently seen in high-grade muscle-invasive tumors. Despite radical cystectomy and the use of perioperative chemotherapy, up to 50% of muscle-invasive tumors will progress to local and distant metastases. This ability to invade and metastasize is not only a function of alterations in the tumor cells but also involves the interactions of the tumor cells with the local microenvironment.

However, the role of *p53* status as a prognostic or predictive biomarker remains limited. A phase III study of adjuvant chemotherapy after cystectomy guided by *p53* status failed to confirm both the prognostic value of *p53* and the benefit of chemotherapy in *p53*-positive tumors, but it was limited by methodologic issues.[49] Thus, loss of tumor suppressor genes is not currently used for clinical decision-making.

Data suggest mutations in DNA damage repair genes in urothelial cancers may predict response to platinum-based chemotherapy as well as to immune checkpoint inhibitors (Table 14-16).[50] DNA damage repair alterations are also under investigation as predictive biomarkers for benefit from poly-ADP ribose inhibitors. Tumor mutational burden also appears to enrich for responses to immune checkpoint inhibitors.[51,52] Bladder cancer has one of the highest mutational burdens among cancers, similar to other cancers caused by exogenous mutagens. In addition to DNA sequencing, whole-genome mRNA expression profiling has resulted in the identification of intrinsic subtypes of muscle-invasive bladder cancer, including luminal and basal subtypes.

DIAGNOSIS AND STAGING

The most common presenting symptom is hematuria. Irritative voiding symptoms including dysuria in a patient with risk factors such as tobacco use may be related to carcinoma in situ (CIS) or a bladder tumor. Less frequently, patients present with symptoms related to distant metastases. Urine cytology can be helpful in evaluating patients with irritative symptoms (especially heavy smokers). The diagnosis is established by cystoscopy and biopsy. As of 2011, the USPSTF concluded there was insufficient evidence to make a recommendation on screening for bladder cancer.

The T staging for bladder cancer is as follows:

- Papillary urothelial neoplasms of low malignant potential.
- Ta tumors are noninvasive papillary lesions that tend to recur but not invade.
- Tis, or CIS, is the precursor of a more aggressive and potentially lethal invasive variant.
- T1 tumors invade the subepithelial connective tissue, including lamina propria or muscularis mucosa.
- T2 tumors invade the muscle.
- pT2a tumors invade superficial muscle.
- pT2b tumors invade deep muscle.
- T3 tumors invade perivesical tissue.
- pT3a are evident microscopically.
- pT3b are evident macroscopically (extravesical mass).
- T4 tumors invade the prostate, seminal vesicles, uterus, vagina, pelvic, and/or abdominal wall.

The major problem with staging is that the correlation of depth of invasion determined by cystoscopy and transurethral resection of bladder tumor (TURBT) with the results of cystectomy is only 50% to 60%. A TURBT specimen is mainly useful for determining presence or absence of muscle-invasive (T2) disease but cannot give information about more advanced invasion, because the urologist must avoid bladder perforation during the procedure. Muscularis propria must be present in the TURBT specimen; if it is not, then a repeated TURBT is generally recommended, balancing risks of understaging with the risks of bladder perforation with aggressive TURBT. Noninvasive imaging with CT or MRI can identify extravesical or nodal disease and is more reliable if done prior to the transurethral resection with a distended bladder; immediately after TURBT, local adenopathy may be inflammatory. Fluorodeoxyglucose (FDG)-PET/CT imaging may have a role in the staging of muscle-invasive disease and in the detection of metastatic bladder cancer,[53] but the urinary excretion of FDG limits its usefulness in local staging. The histologic grading system of low grade and high grade is more relevant for nonmuscle-invasive tumors, because virtually all muscle-invasive neoplasms are high grade.

Urothelial Cancers in Bladder Diverticula

Urothelial cancers arising in bladder diverticula, though uncommon, pose diagnostic and therapeutic challenges. Because of the limited presence of a musularis propria layer, bladder perforation is a potential complication if a transurethral resection is contemplated. The traditional pathologic stage T2 is often eliminated and the cancer is staged as either Ta, Tis, T1, or T3+, indicating extradiverticular extension. A conservative approach for disease without extradiverticular extension has been recommended and includes diverticulectomy or, in lesions that are anatomically amenable, partial cystectomy. Partial or radical cystectomy is often recommended for extradiverticular extension.

KEY POINTS

- Bladder cancer may present as painless hematuria or irritative urinary symptoms, and it is typically diagnosed via TURBT.
- Based on TURBT pathology, bladder cancer is broadly divided into nonmuscle-invasive tumors and muscle-invasive tumors. Muscularis propria must be present in the TURBT specimen to enable this assessment; otherwise, repeated TURBT is considered.

THERAPY FOR NONMUSCLE-INVASIVE BLADDER CANCER

The following section is specifically provided to the medical oncologist to enhance the understanding of the management issues that patients face with the diagnosis of nonmuscle-invasive bladder cancer, because most medical oncologists do not actively treat these patients until muscle-invasive disease is detected.

Up to 80% of patients with newly diagnosed bladder cancer present with nonmuscle-invasive disease (which includes papillary urothelial neoplasm of low malignant potential, CIS, and low- and high-grade urothelial cancers), with 70% confined to the mucosa (Ta or Tis) and 30% involving the submucosa (T1). Patients initially will be diagnosed by either having a positive urinary cytology or after an evaluation for hematuria or dysuria. The initial cystoscopic evaluation is via flexible cystoscopy performed during an office visit to allow the urologist to systematically evaluate the entire urothelial surface and identify abnormal and erythematous areas. This is then followed by a formal TURBT as well as random bladder biopsies in areas that do not look abnormal to the urologist on visual inspection. This is performed under general or spinal anesthesia and enables bladder resection including muscle specimens to be obtained; random biopsies of both normal and erythematous appearing areas, prostatic urethral evaluation, as well as assessment for determination of need for upper tract evaluations.

Table 14-16 Potential Biomarkers in Urothelial Carcinoma

Biomarker	Description	Prognostic or Predictive Role
p53 or *Rb* alteration	Tumor suppressor gene loss or alteration assessed by immunohistochemistry	May indicate poor prognosis, but unclear predictive role
Genomic subtyping, gene expression classification	Gene expression clustering analysis	Neoadjuvant chemotherapy may be most helpful for basal tumors. Luminal tumors have favorable prognosis, claudin-low tumors have poor prognosis; neither seemed to benefit from neoadjuvant chemotherapy. May also have a role in predicting response to immune checkpoint inhibitors
DNA damage repair	Genomic alterations in nucleotide excision repair, homologous recombination, or mismatch repair	DNA damage repair alterations may predict response to cisplatin. Possible role of alterations in *ERCC2*, *ATM*, *RB1*, and *FANCC*. May also have a role in predicting response to immune checkpoint inhibitors
Immune checkpoint expression	Expression of PD-1/PD-L1 by immunohistochemistry on tumor cells and/or tumor-infiltrating T cells	High PD-L1 expression on immune cells may predict response to PD-1/PD-L1 inhibition, but results are inconsistent
Tumor mutational burden	Overall number of somatic mutations by next-generation sequencing	High tumor mutational burden may correlate with response to PD-1/PD-L1 inhibition

Patients will receive constant bladder irrigation after this procedure and will be discharged home with a catheter for approximately 1 week. The determination of the presence or absence of muscle-invasive disease is made by pathologists and requires presence of muscle in the biopsy specimen to enable accurate assessment. For nonmuscle-invasive disease, an assessment of risk is performed on the basis of clinical and pathologic features.[54] AUA guidelines suggest a treatment algorithm according to this risk assessment (Fig 14-16).

A single dose of intravesical chemotherapy (mitomycin C or epirubicin) within 24 hours of TURBT may decrease tumor recurrence, and this is recommended for patients with suspected or known low- or intermediate-risk bladder cancer (unless there was extensive resection or suspected perforation). The greatest effect appears to be in patients with single, small, low-grade tumors and may decrease recurrences even when additional adjuvant intravesical therapy is given.

Low-risk disease includes small (< 3 cm), solitary, low-grade Ta lesions without CIS. Treatment typically involves a single dose of intravesical therapy just after the resection.

High-risk lesions include CIS, high-grade lesions, T1 lesions, or large (> 3 cm) or multiple lesions. Intermediate risk is any lesion not meeting low- or high-risk criteria. Very high-risk disease may require early consideration of cystectomy rather than intravesical therapy, including large or multiple T1 high-grade lesions, co-occurring T1 high-grade with carcinoma in situ or involving prostatic urethra, or micropapillary histology.

The diagnosis of intermediate- or high-risk disease at the time of TURBT is then followed (usually within 4 weeks) with the so-called induction course of intravesical bacillus Calmette-Guérin (BCG). This consists of six weekly instillations of BCG (alone or with addition of intravesical interferon [IFN]). A repeated TURBT, again obtaining specimens involving muscularis propria, is then performed approximately 4 weeks after, during which where biopsy specimens are collected again of the previously identified lesions, along with a repeated urinary cytology.

Patients in whom a complete remission is achieved (ie, negative cytologic results and no evidence of residual cancer in the biopsy specimens of previous disease) may begin a 3-year program of maintenance BCG therapy. The first such treatment is started approximately 3 months after the second TURBT and then every 6 months thereafter. In contrast to the induction program, maintenance treatments are done weekly for 3 weeks. Approximately 1 month after each maintenance program, repeated cytology and office cystoscopies are performed for continued surveillance. The maintenance program continues for 3 years if possible. Unfortunately, both the local and systemic adverse effects of intravesical BCG (with or without IFN) are so significant that nearly 75% of patients are unable to tolerate and complete the entire program.

Regarding the management of noninvasive bladder cancer with intravesical BCG, it is not uncommon for relapse to occur at the ureteral orifices, ureter, or urethra—areas that are less accessible to intravesical treatment. As such, monitoring must include periodic evaluations of the remaining urothelium with cytology and imaging to ensure relapses or new primary tumors are identified and treated when diagnosed

Potential adverse effects of intravesical BCG include the following:

- cystitis, including urinary frequency, dysuria, hematuria, and/or fever; and
- systemic complications, including arthralgia, osteomyelitis, sepsis, and multiorgan dysfunction due to granulomatous involvement.

Patients who do not achieve a complete response (CR) after induction BCG and second TURBT may be considered BCG refractory. If muscle-invasive disease is detected, definitive bladder therapy is considered. In those with persistent but nonmuscle-invasive disease, a second induction course of BCG can be considered. Use of second-line intravesical therapies such as gemcitabine, docetaxel, valrubicin, or other investigational agents may be considered. Checkpoint inhibitors are under investigation in this setting, and intravenous pembrolizumab demonstrated a 38.8% CR rate in the phase II KEYNOTE-057 trial, earning FDA approval in patients with BCG-unresponsive NMIBC.[55] Intravesical checkpoint inhibitors are under investigation.

KEY POINTS

- Nonmuscle-invasive bladder cancer is stratified according to risk of recurrence.

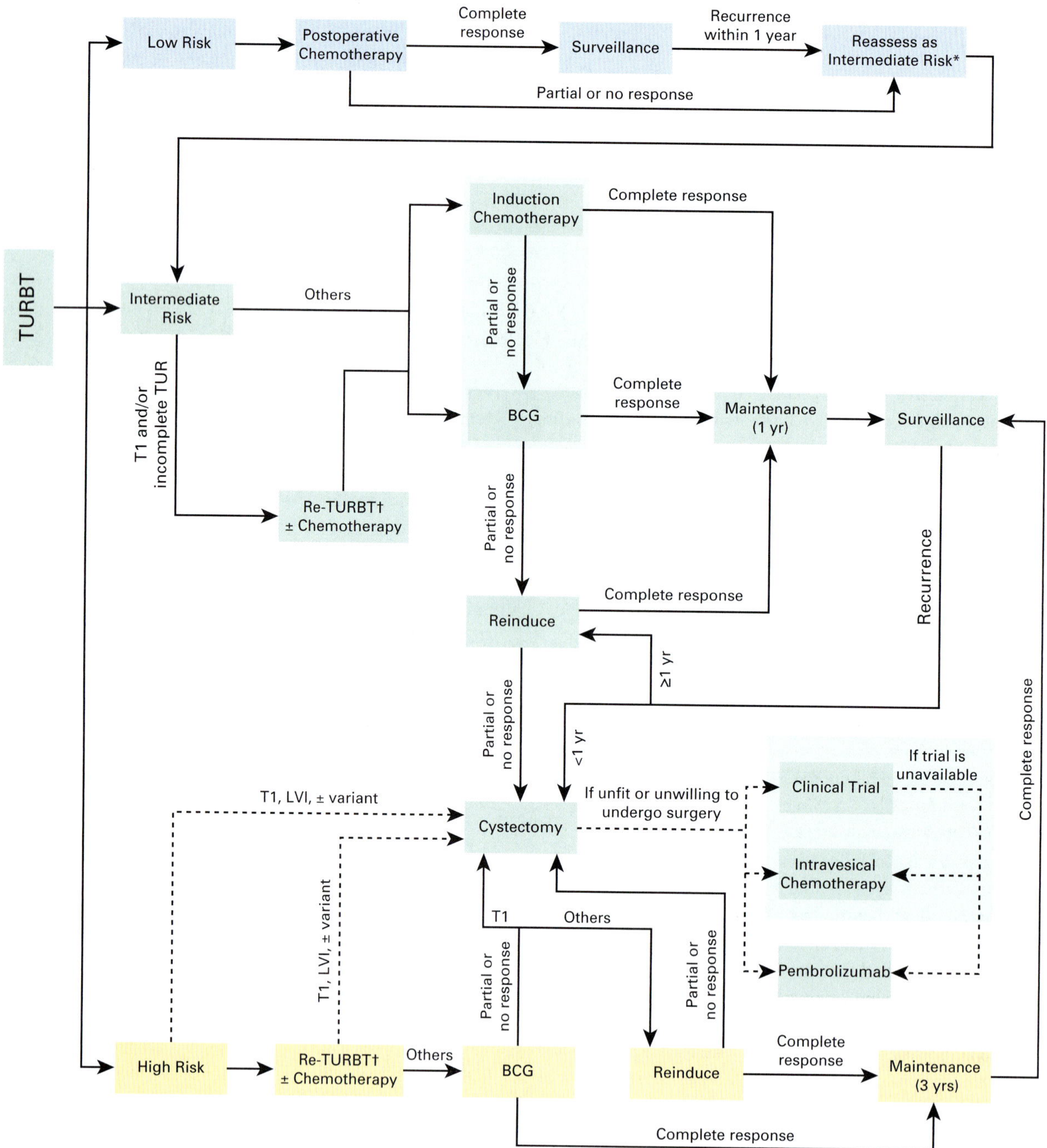

Fig. 14-16 Non-muscle invasive bladder cancer: AUA/SUO treatment algorithm.

Abbreviations: AUA, American Urological Association; BCG, bacillus Calmette-Guérin; LVI, lymphovascular invasion; SUO, Society of Urologic Oncology; TUR, transurethral resection; TURBT, transurethral resection of bladder tumor.

*Consider fulguration in low-volume disease recurrence; otherwise reassess as intermediate risk. †Timely re-TURBT (within 6 weeks) should be performed if there are concerns regarding an incomplete resection and/or if bladder-sparing treatment (eg, intravesical therapy or surveillance) is being planned.

- For low-risk tumors, surveillance (cystoscopy and urine cytology) is most appropriate.
- For intermediate- and high-risk tumors, intravesical BCG decreases risk of recurrence, and surveillance is also crucial. Definitive bladder therapy (cystectomy or RT) is considered in situations of particularly high-risk nonmuscle-invasive tumors or for BCG-refractory tumors.

Urothelial Carcinoma in Prostate Urethra and Prostate Gland

The diagnosis of carcinoma or CIS of the prostatic urethra poses diagnostic and therapeutic challenges. Increased morbidity follows resection of the prostatic urethra, yet it is important for appropriate staging. In addition, it is more challenging to treat the prostatic urethra with intravesical therapies because these are administered via Foley catheter, essentially bypassing exposure of the drug to the prostatic urethra. Patients may undergo a transurethral resection of the prostate with the expectation that more accurate staging may result and the prostate will be exposed to optimal concentrations of BCG. If prostatic stromal invasion is found, surgical management would include cystoprostatectomy. The pathologic finding of urothelial cancer in the prostate or prostatic urethra requires a discussion about additional therapy with primary urethrectomy, as well.

TREATMENT OF MUSCLE-INVASIVE BLADDER CANCER

Although most patients present with nonmuscle-invasive disease, approximately 20% to 40% of patients either present with more advanced disease or experience disease progression after therapy for nonmuscle-invasive disease (Fig 14-17). Staging for patients with muscle-invasive disease includes a CT scan of the abdomen and pelvis, chest imaging, and, if, clinically indicated, a bone scan. FDG-PET can be used to rule out distant metastases, but because FDG is excreted through the urinary tract, FDG-PET is less helpful for evaluating local extension and local nodal involvement.[53]

Cystectomy

The standard treatment of a muscle-invasive tumor is a radical cystectomy with bilateral pelvic lymphadenectomy that includes removal of the bladder, prostate, seminal vesicles, and proximal urethra for men, and removal of the bladder, urethra, and uterus (including bilateral salpingo-oophorectomy), as well as possible excision of a portion of the anterior vaginal wall, for women. The pelvic lymph node dissection is a necessary part of the radical cystectomy surgery, with a more extended lymph node dissection associated with an improvement in outcome. The three main types of urinary diversions include an ileal conduit that drains to an appliance on the anterior abdominal wall, a continent cutaneous reservoir constructed from detubularized bowel segments, and an orthotopic neobladder (Fig 14-18). More men are candidates for continent urethral reservoirs than women because of anatomic considerations. It is not clear that continent reconstruction after radical cystectomy is associated with an improvement in QOL as compared with conduit diversion. In fact, most patients report a favorable QOL regardless of the type of diversion used. Of note, urinary diversion may result in hypokalemic hyperchloremic metabolic acidosis, and use of ileum for a conduit may result in malabsorption of vitamin B_{12}, requiring parenteral supplementation.

Prognosis varies inversely with higher T stage, lymphatic or vascular invasion in the primary tumor, and lymph node involvement. Approximately two-thirds of patients remain recurrence free after cystectomy with long-term follow-up, but prognosis worsens with nonorgan-confined disease and/or nodal involvement. Multivariate nomograms have been developed to predict outcome after radical cystectomy. A partial cystectomy can provide adequate local control of invasive bladder cancer in select patients. Less invasive surgical techniques, including laparoscopic and robotic radical cystectomy, have been evaluated and robot-assisted techniques may be similar to standard open surgery in terms of operative, pathologic, oncologic, complication, and most functional outcomes. The use of bladder-sparing protocols as alternatives to surgery in the management of muscle-invasive bladder cancer is reviewed in the Bladder Preservation section.

Perioperative Chemotherapy

The use of perioperative chemotherapy in the management of invasive and locally advanced bladder cancer has been studied in the neoadjuvant and adjuvant settings. The potential advantages for neoadjuvant chemotherapy include evaluation of response to therapy in vivo with assessment of the pathologic response in the cystectomy specimen, tumor downstaging to allow for a less-complicated surgery, and the delivery of full-dose chemotherapy without the potential problems associated with postoperative recovery. The major advantages for the use of adjuvant chemotherapy include treatment based on pathologic criteria with the ability to select those patients at higher risk who are most likely to benefit from chemotherapy and to avoid the unnecessary treatment of patients with lower-risk disease (Fig 14-17).

Platinum Eligibility. Cisplatin is the backbone of perioperative and palliative chemotherapy regimens. However, medical comorbidities, especially renal dysfunction, may pose a challenge to treating with cisplatin-based therapy. Cisplatin ineligibility has been defined by expert consensus[56] as patients with any of the following:

- WHO or Eastern Cooperative Oncology Group performance status ≥ 2;
- estimated creatinine clearance < 60 mL/min;
- Common Terminology Criteria for Adverse Events, version 4, grade ≥ 2 audiometric hearing loss or peripheral neuropathy; or
- New York Heart Association class III heart failure

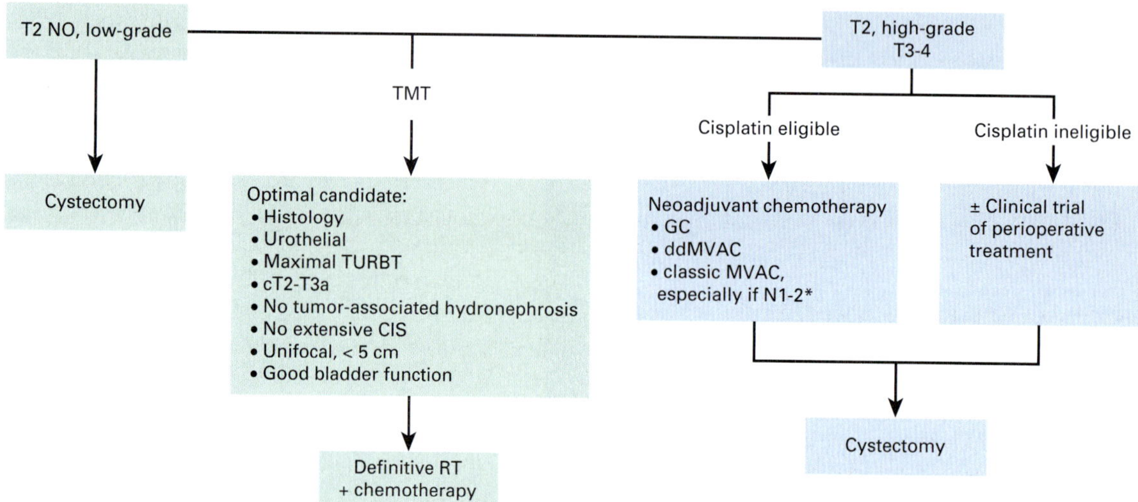

Fig. 14-17 Treatment options for muscle invasive bladder cancer.

Abbreviations: CIS, carcinoma in situ; ddMVAC, dose-dense methotrexate, vinblastine, doxorubicin, and cisplatin; GC, gemcitabine and cisplatin; RT, radiation therapy; TMT, trimodality therapy; TURBT, transurethral resection of bladder tumor.

*If N+ disease is established or suspected prior to scheduled radical cystectomy and patient has not received nevo-adjuvant therapy, radical cystectomy and pelvic lymphadenectomy is still a treatment option. There is no level 1 evidence for adjuvant chemotherapy in the post-cystectomy node-positive setting, but many clinicians would consider its use.

However, these criteria are not based on prospective data. Renal impairment poses a particular problem, because 30% to 50% of patients undergoing radical cystectomy have an estimated creatinine clearance below the threshold of 60 mL/min,[57] meaning that the standard of care would not be offered to almost half of all patients. In addition, different equations for estimating creatinine clearance or glomerular filtration rate may result in different estimates, and the commonly used Cockroft-Gault equation, in particular, may result in lower estimates of renal function than alternative equations, with unclear implications for clinical decision-making. Second, cisplatin-based therapy may be feasible in patients with borderline renal function, as shown in observational studies, and some clinicians will use split-dose regimens, albeit without strong evidence that this is safer than standard dosing. Finally, the risk of cisplatin nephrotoxicity may be related to factors other than calculated creatinine clearance and is not likely to be a dichotomous outcome, so risk-prediction models may be helpful.

Neoadjuvant Chemotherapy. Neoadjuvant chemotherapy is the standard of care for patients with muscle-invasive bladder cancer who are eligible for both cystectomy and cisplatin-based therapy (Table 14-17). A US phase III Intergroup trial randomly assigned patients with T2-4aN0M0 bladder cancer to neoadjuvant methotrexate, vinblastine, doxorubicin, and cisplatin (MVAC) plus cystectomy (n = 153 patients) or to cystectomy alone (n = 154 patients).[58] Median survival of patients assigned to surgery alone was 46 months compared with 77 months among patients assigned to MVAC plus cystectomy. The survival benefit of neoadjuvant MVAC was associated with tumor downstaging to pT0 (38% in those patients who received MVAC compared with 15% of those who received cystectomy), with an 85% 5-year survival for patients who experienced a pathologic CR to neoadjuvant chemotherapy. A meta-analysis of neoadjuvant chemotherapy showed a significant OS benefit for platinum-based combination chemotherapy, with a 14% reduction in the risk of death and 5% absolute survival benefit at

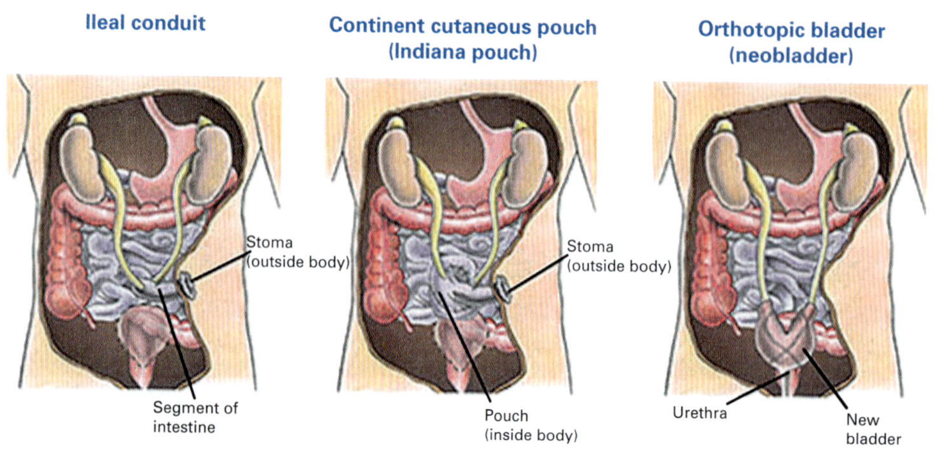

Fig. 14-18 Three types of urinary diversions commonly performed at time of radical cystectomy for bladder cancer.

Ileal conduit (left), continent cutaneous pouch (center), and orthotopic bladder (right).

5 years (OS increasing from 45% to 50%). This effect did not vary between subgroups of patients or type of local treatment.

Two single-arm, phase II studies using dose-dense MVAC with pegfilgrastim support demonstrated promising pathologic response rates in patients with cT2-cT4a, N0-1, M0 muscle-invasive bladder cancer,[59,60] with much less myelotoxicity than seen in the classic MVAC regimen. In addition, this decreases the time needed to deliver neoadjuvant chemotherapy before surgery.

Although it has not been studied in randomized trials in the neoadjuvant setting, the combination of gemcitabine and cisplatin (GC) is frequently used instead of MVAC, as an extrapolation of evidence in the metastatic setting that GC offers equivalent response rates and less toxicity compared with classic MVAC.[61] Nonrandomized data have compared neoadjuvant dose-dense MVAC versus GC and vary as to whether pathologic CR rates differ between the two regimens. Thus, the shorter treatment time of dose-dense MVAC compared with GC is weighed against the added potential toxicity (especially anthracycline cardiotoxicity) in deciding which regimen to use in a cisplatin-eligible patient.

Neoadjuvant Treatment Remains Effective for Patients With Node-Positive Disease. Current guidelines limit the use of perioperative chemotherapy to patients eligible for cisplatin. Substitution of carboplatin for cisplatin in the neoadjuvant setting is associated with inferior outcomes and is not recommended, nor is nonplatinum-based therapy. Thus, renal insufficiency or coexisting medical problems may limit the both the efficacy and ability to administer perioperative chemotherapy.

Interestingly, a recent, single-arm, phase II study tested single-agent pembrolizumab as neoadjuvant therapy prior to cystectomy in both cisplatin-eligible and -ineligible patients. Twenty-one of 50 participants experienced pathologic CR, which was especially enriched among patients with PD-L1 positivity or high tumor mutational burden.[51] Similarly, atezolizumab demonstrated a 29% rate of pathologic CR.[62] (It is important to remember that a small minority of patients may have pathologic CR simply from a complete resection by TURBT.) Neither is yet approved for this indication, but many trials are currently testing this strategy, especially in combination with chemotherapy or other immune-based study drugs.

Adjuvant Chemotherapy. Although many physicians favor the use of adjuvant chemotherapy for patients with nodal involvement and extravesical tumor extension, definitive trials are lacking. Unfortunately, most of the adjuvant studies that have been performed have major limitations, including suboptimal statistical methodology due to underpowered trials and early termination, as well as the use of older chemotherapy programs that did not include cisplatin. In addition, cystectomy is a major operation entailing substantial postoperative recovery for many patients, limiting or delaying the ability to deliver adjuvant chemotherapy.

The largest adjuvant phase III study published to date, EORTC 30994, randomly assigned patients with pT3-pT4 or N+ M0 bladder cancer after radical cystectomy to immediate (four cycles of GC, dose-dense MVAC, or classic MVAC) compared with six cycles of chemotherapy at relapse.[63] The trial was closed after recruitment of only 284 of 660 planned patients. Although no significant improvement in OS with immediate treatment compared with deferred treatment was observed, median PFS was prolonged from 0.99 years to 3.11 years with the addition of adjuvant chemotherapy. Several meta-analyses have concluded there is an OS benefit with adjuvant chemotherapy, but the validity of the meta-analysis is clearly limited by the flawed trials from which the analyses are derived. In sum, adjuvant chemotherapy may be offered to high-risk patients who have not received neoadjuvant chemotherapy, with the caveat that strong evidence is lacking.

As in the neoadjuvant setting, patients who are not eligible for cisplatin are generally not treated with any adjuvant chemotherapy. Randomized trials are underway to test the effectiveness of checkpoint inhibitors in this setting.

Bladder Preservation

Although neoadjuvant chemotherapy in combination with cystectomy improves OS, the role of chemotherapy alone in bladder preservation is problematic because of the inability to definitively determine which bladders are truly without residual tumor. In addition, pathologic CR rates after neoadjuvant chemotherapy at the time of cystectomy are only 20% to 40%. At a minimum, chemotherapy alone cannot replace definitive treatment of the bladder by surgery or RT.

Table 14-17 Standard Neoadjuvant Chemotherapy Regimens

Classic MVAC (28-day cycle)	Dose-dense MVAC (14-day cycle)	Gemcitabine and Cisplatin
Methotrexate on days 1, 15, and 22	Methotrexate on day 1	21-day regimen:
Vinblastine on days 2, 15, and 22	Vinblastine on day 2	Cisplatin on day 1 or 2
Doxorubicin on day 2	Doxorubicin on day 2	Gemcitabine on days 1 and 8
Cisplatin on day 2	Cisplatin on day 2	28-day regimen:
	G-CSF on days 4-10 or pegylated G-CSF after chemotherapy	Cisplatin on day 1 or 2
		Gemcitabine on days 1, 8 and 15

Abbreviation: G-CSF, granulocyte colony-stimulating factor; MVAC, methotrexate, vinblastine, doxorubicin, and cisplatin.

Although radical cystectomy with neoadjuvant chemotherapy remains the standard of care for muscle-invasive bladder cancer, many patients are either ineligible for cystectomy, based on medical comorbidities, or prefer a bladder-sparing approach. For appropriately selected patients, a trimodality treatment consisting of transurethral resection (as complete as safely possible) followed by definitive RT plus radiosensitizing chemotherapy for select patients has resulted in long-term DFS and OS rates approaching those seen in radical cystectomy series (Fig 14-17). Trimodality treatment is now included as a category 1 recommendation in NCCN guidelines, alongside cystectomy.[64] Appropriate patients are those who had:

- a unifocal urothelial carcinoma < 5 cm,
- undergone a visibly complete TURBT,
- no extensive CIS,
- no T4 disease or tumor-associated hydronephrosis, and
- good bladder function and capacity.

One trial attempted to randomly assign patients to cystectomy versus trimodality treatment but closed due to poor accrual, so no formal comparison can be made between cystectomy and trimodality treatment. An analysis of long-term outcomes of selective bladder preservation in 348 patients at the Massachusetts General Hospital demonstrated 5-year disease-specific survival and OS rates of 64% and 52%, respectively, with preservation of the bladder in > 70% of patients.[65]

The optimal radiosensitizing regimen is unknown. The majority of trimodality protocols have used cisplatin-based chemotherapy (typically weekly cisplatin monotherapy); however, other agents such as paclitaxel and gemcitabine have been used as well. In the largest randomized study to compare chemoradiotherapy using fluorouracil and mitomycin with RT alone in muscle-invasive bladder cancer, the chemoradiotherapy arm was associated with an improvement in 2-year locoregional DFS from 54% to 67%.[66] It is unknown which radiosensitizing chemotherapy is optimal and whether "induction therapy" with standard systemic doses of chemotherapy (ie, GC) prior to chemoradiation is beneficial. Many bladder-sparing protocols include an early evaluation of response to treatment with cystoscopy after RT; patients who show less than a CR go on to receive salvage cystectomy. Approximately one-third of patients started on a bladder-sparing protocol will ultimately require cystectomy for a less-than-complete response or for recurrent muscle-invasive tumors.

QOL is another important consideration. RT can induce disturbances in the function of the bladder, anal sphincter, and large bowel. The morbidity of RT has decreased with the availability of better imaging, allowing for a boost to the primary tumor and a reduction in fraction size. An evaluation of late pelvic toxicity after bladder-sparing therapy in patients with invasive bladder cancer who received treatment in four prospective Radiation Therapy Oncology Group (RTOG) protocols showed low rates of substantial late pelvic toxicity (7% of patients with late grade 3 or greater pelvic toxicity: 5.7% genitourinary and 1.9% GI) at a median follow -p of 5.4 years. The main disadvantage for bladder preservation is the requirement for lifelong surveillance as a result of the risk of recurrence or development of a new bladder cancer. However, many of these new or recurrent tumors are noninvasive and can be treated endoscopically with or without intravesical therapies (Fig 14-16).

KEY POINTS

- The most established standard-of-care for muscle-invasive bladder cancer is neoadjuvant cisplatin-based therapy followed by radical cystectomy and lymph node dissection. The optimal neoadjuvant chemotherapy regimen is not known, but the most commonly used are GC and dose-dense MVAC.
- For cisplatin-ineligible patients undergoing cystectomy, no perioperative chemotherapy is currently recommended.
- Maximal transurethral resection of the bladder tumor followed by definitive RT plus radiosensitizing chemotherapy, also known as "bladder-sparing" or trimodality therapy, may offer similar long-term disease control for appropriately selected patients. Historically, this has been considered only for patients ineligible for or declining cystectomy, but on the basis of nonrandomized data, is now considered a reasonable alternative to cystectomy in all eligible patients.

THERAPY FOR METASTATIC BLADDER CANCER

Patients may develop either de novo metastatic bladder cancer or metastatic recurrence after prior therapy for localized disease (Fig 14-19). GC is the most commonly used first-line therapy for metastatic bladder cancer. GC appears to have similar response rates as MVAC (approximately 50%), and similar median OS of about 14 to 15 months, but GC is less toxic.[61] For patients eligible for combination chemotherapy but not platinum agents (ie, those with rapidly fluctuating renal function), gemcitabine plus taxanes may offer similar response rates and OS.

Platinum-Ineligible Patients

As noted, many patients are not eligible for cisplatin. Multiple phase II trials have suggested an improvement in outcome with cisplatin- compared with carboplatin-based chemotherapy, but in contrast to neoadjuvant therapy, it is acceptable in the metastatic setting to substitute carboplatin for patients with renal impairment that precludes cisplatin treatment. Combination platinum-based therapy offers superior response rates to PD-1/PD-L1 inhibitors and remains the standard first-line therapy for platinum-eligible patients.

Chemotherapy-Ineligible Patients

Many patients are ineligible for combination chemotherapy because of poor performance status. For such patients, atezolizumab and pembrolizumab are now FDA-approved options for first-line treatment of locally advanced or metastatic bladder cancer in cisplatin-ineligible patients. The IMvigor

210 study was a phase II trial that evaluated the anti-PD-L1 antibody atezolizumab as first-line treatment in cisplatin-ineligible patients with locally advanced and metastatic urothelial carcinoma (cohort 1).[52] The objective response rate was 23% and median OS was 15.9 months. Response rates were improved in patients with a high tumor mutational burden. In a similar patient population including elderly patients and those with a poor performance status, the KEYNOTE-052 trial evaluated the anti-PD-1 antibody pembrolizumab and demonstrated promising activity, with an overall response rate of 24%.[67] Immune-related adverse events were reported with both agents but are generally manageable with appropriate attention and early intervention, as appropriate.

Of note, two randomized phase III trials (KEYNOTE-361 and IMvigor130) that involved PD-1/PD-L1 monotherapy arms reported decreased OS for patients with tumors with low PD-L1 expression, relative to chemotherapy-containing arms. Therefore, both trials stopped enrollment of patients with PD-L1–low tumors to the PD-1/PD-L1 inhibitor monotherapy arms, and the FDA issued a warning against frontline use of PD-1/PD-L1 monotherapy in patients with PD-L1–low tumors. However, the clinical implications of this were limited because response rates to first-line, platinum-based chemotherapy regimens are superior to that of PD-1/PD-L1 inhibitors. Thus, for platinum-eligible patients, the first-line standard of care remains platinum-based chemotherapy, and for platinum-ineligible patients, PD-1/PD-L1 inhibitors may be used regardless of PD-L1 status, due to limited alternatives.

Second-Line Therapies

Before the advent of PD-1/PD-L1 inhibitors, there was no accepted standard of care for second-line chemotherapy in advanced bladder cancer. Evaluations of single agents, such as ifosfamide, docetaxel, gemcitabine, paclitaxel, and pemetrexed, have demonstrated response rates between 9% and 27%, with a PFS in the range of 2 to 3 months and no documented improvement in OS. Although multidrug regimens have been associated with higher response rates, this does not appear to translate into an improvement in survival.

However, PD-1/PD-L1 inhibitors now represent the standard of care for second-line treatment of advanced urothelial carcinoma. Atezolizumab, avelumab, durvalumab, pembrolizumab, and nivolumab have all been FDA approved for second-line treatment. Atezolizumab and pembrolizumab have been tested in randomized phase III trials against standard second-line chemotherapies (Table 14-18), and pembrolizumab demonstrated an OS benefit of approximately 3 months.[68]

Many ongoing trials are seeking to expand the role of checkpoint inhibitors in urothelial carcinoma. PD-1/PD-L1 inhibitors are being tested for BCG-refractory, nonmuscle-invasive bladder cancer in the neoadjuvant and adjuvant settings for muscle-invasive bladder cancer undergoing cystectomy, and as maintenance after first-line platinum-based chemotherapy for metastatic disease. Other trials are testing combinations of PD-1/PD-L1 inhibition together with standard chemotherapy in the neoadjuvant and metastatic settings: combinations of PD-1/PD-L1 inhibitors with other immune checkpoint inhibitors (eg CTLA-4) and vaccines, and combinations with several other targeted therapies as well as RT.

Several targeted therapies have demonstrated responses in advanced and previously treated urothelial carcinoma:

- Erdafitinib is a tyrosine kinase inhibitor of fibroblast growth factor receptor (FGFR)-1 through FGFR-4, alterations of which are frequently seen in advanced urothelial carcinoma. In a phase II, single-arm trial in patients with advanced urothelial carcinoma and prior chemotherapy (with or without prior PD-1/PD-L1 treatment) and FGFR alterations, the confirmed response rate was 40%—3% with CR.[69] On the basis of these results, the FDA granted accelerated approval for patients with platinum-resistant advanced urothelial carcinoma and FGFR alterations detected by the companion diagnostic kit. Treatment-related adverse events were seen frequently, most commonly hyperphosphatemia, hyponatremia, stomatitis, and asthenia. Ophthalmologic monitoring is recommended due to risk of detachment of the retinal pigment epithelium. No randomized survival data are yet available.
- Enfortumab vedotin is an antibody-drug conjugate targeting Nectin-4, which is highly overexpressed in urothelial carcinomas. In a phase II, single-arm trial in patients with advanced urothelial carcinoma and previous platinum and anti–PD-1/PD-L1 treatment, the confirmed overall response rate was 44%, with 12% CRs.[70] The FDA granted accelerated approval in 2019 for use in patients with locally advanced or metastatic urothelial cancer and prior platinum-containing chemotherapy and PD-1/PD-L1 inhibitor. No randomized survival data are yet available.

PARP inhibitors are also under investigation. In highly selected patients with metastatic urothelial carcinoma, resection of metastatic disease can result in long-term disease control.

KEY POINTS

- For patients with metastatic bladder cancer, first-line therapy consists of platinum-based chemotherapy for eligible patients, typically GC. In contrast with perioperative chemotherapy, carboplatin may be substituted for cisplatin-ineligible patients.
- For chemotherapy-ineligible patients, first-line PD-1/PD-L1 inhibitors may be considered.
- PD-1/PD-L1 inhibitors are now standard as second-line therapy after failure of platinum-based chemotherapy.
- Other later-line therapies include single-agent chemotherapies and the newly approved targeted therapy erdafitinib for patients with FGFR alterations.

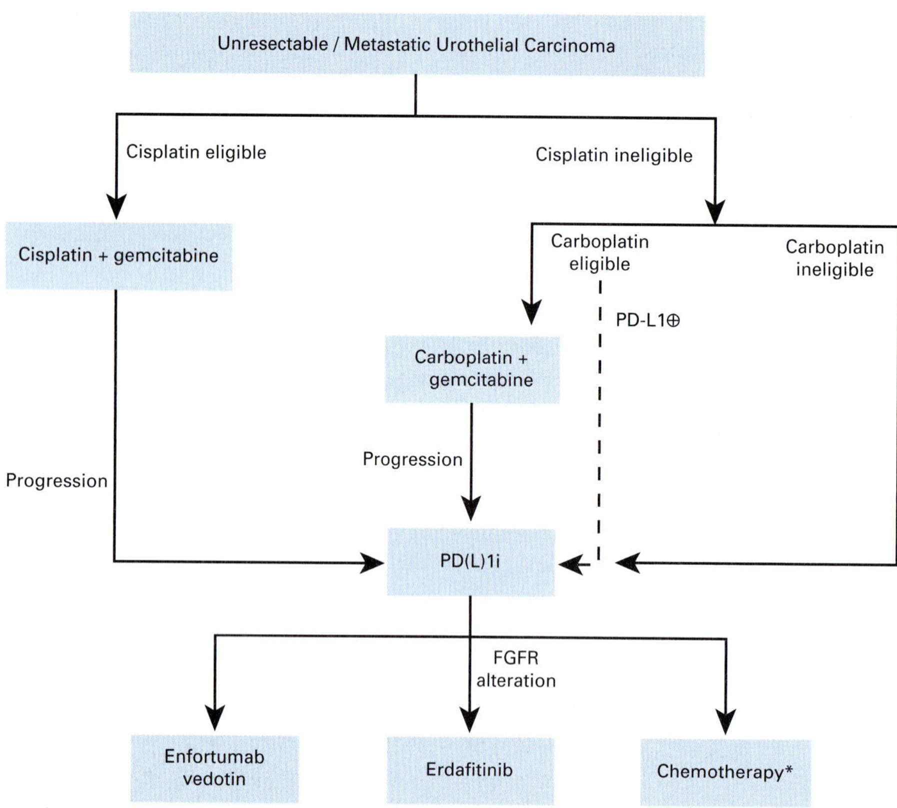

Fig. 14-19 Flow chart of advanced urothelial cancer. Treatment opitions for advanced (unresectable or metastatic) urothelial carcinoma.

*Later-line chemotherapy includes taxances or pemetrexed (or vinflunine in Europe).

OTHER UROTHELIAL TRACT CANCERS

Upper-Tract Urothelial Carcinoma

Cancers of the renal pelvis, ureter, and proximal urethra also are of urothelial origin and should be treated on the basis of primary histology. Upper urinary tract tumors may have a worse outcome as compared with urothelial carcinomas that arise in the bladder. They can also arise in the setting of Lynch syndrome. Comprehensive genomic profiling of upper tract tumors has revealed novel mutations, differing mutational frequencies, and expression subtypes with unique molecular profiles as compared with bladder cancer. Upper-tract urothelial carcinomas may first be detected by imaging or retrograde pyelogram. Selective ureter cytology and/or brushings of lesions may be performed during the pyelogram. Unfortunately,

Table 14-18 Phase III Trials for Second-Line Treatment of UC

Trial	No. of Participants	Study Population	Design	Outcome	Notes
KEYNOTE-045[68]	542	Locally advanced or metastatic UC after platinum therapy	Pembrolizumab *v* physician's choice chemotherapy	Improved OS with pembrolizumab (10.3 *v* 7.4 months)	OS higher in patients with > 10% tumor PD-L1 expression. Fewer severe treatment-related AEs with pembrolizumab *v* chemotherapy
IMvigor211[119]	931	Locally advanced or metastatic UC after platinum therapy	Atezolizumab *v* physician's choice chemotherapy	OS did not differ significantly (11.1 *v* 10.6 months)	Fewer severe treatment-related AEs with atezolizumab *v* chemotherapy

Abbreviations: AE, adverse event; OS, overall survival; UC, urothelial carcinoma.

unlike bladder cancer, great difficulty exists in the clinical staging of upper tract urothelial carcinomas, and management decisions generally rely on tumor grade. Ultimately, the definitive diagnosis is made after nephroureterectomy. Lymph node dissection is not done routinely for clinically node-negative patients, but it may be performed in the presence of radiographically suspicious lymphadenopathy. Node-positive disease is considered stage IV, but resection is still performed if possible, because long-term remission is still possible.

No definitive data were available on the role of perioperative chemotherapy until a recent abstract from the randomized POUT study.[71] Patients who had undergone nephroureterectomy for high-risk upper tract urothelial carcinoma (pT2-4 and/or node-positive) were randomly assigned to adjuvant GC versus GC at the time of recurrence. DFS was significantly prolonged with adjuvant chemotherapy compared with no adjuvant chemotherapy; OS data are not yet mature. Neoadjuvant chemotherapy may also be reasonable, extrapolating from bladder cancer, but there are no randomized data in this setting. In addition, upper-tract disease may be diagnosed simply on the basis of suspicious imaging and/or cytology, so pathologic information on risk may not be available until resection is performed.

Because approximately 20% to 50% of patients with resected upper-tract urothelial carcinoma will eventually develop bladder cancer, surveillance cystoscopy is necessary. The two theories for the multifocal nature of urothelial carcinoma include the field cancerization effect and monoclonality (ie, tumor cells spreading from their origin to multiple sites). Thus, simultaneous or metachronous primary tumors of the urothelium at multiple sites may occur, and monitoring is required, including follow-up cystoscopies and imaging of the upper tracts.

Nonurothelial Bladder Cancer

Less than 5% of bladder cancers in the United States have nonurothelial histology, including squamous cell carcinoma, adenocarcinoma, and small-cell carcinoma. Squamous cell carcinoma of the bladder is typically related to chronic urinary tract infections, RT, prior cyclophosphamide therapy, and, possibly, chronic indwelling catheters. In endemic areas, schistosomiasis can cause urothelial carcinoma as well as squamous and adenocarcinoma bladder cancers. Adenocarcinomas may originate from remnant urachal tissue, especially if they are located in the bladder dome.

The primary treatment modality for all localized nonurothelial bladder cancers is cystectomy, and the role of chemotherapy and/or RT as neoadjuvant or adjuvant therapy is not well defined. The chemotherapy used for urothelial carcinoma has been considered to be less effective in nonurothelial histology tumors. Neoadjuvant RT may have a role for squamous cell carcinomas, which have a greater tendency for local recurrence than metastatic spread. For patients with pure small-cell or adenocarcinoma, chemotherapy regimens that have demonstrated activity in other sites with similar histology generally are used (eg, etoposide and cisplatin for small-cell carcinoma of the lung may be used for the treatment of small-cell carcinoma of the bladder), either as perioperative therapy for localized disease or as palliative systemic therapy for metastatic disease, but results are often discouraging and these patients generally have a poor prognosis.

KEY POINTS

- Upper-tract (ureteral and renal pelvis) urothelial carcinoma may be diagnosed initially by imaging, urine cytology, and/or biopsy via retrograde ureteroscopy, but often a nephroureterectomy is required for pathologic diagnosis as well as treatment.
- Perioperative chemotherapy may be considered for high-risk tumors on the basis of extrapolation from bladder cancer or from one randomized trial of adjuvant platinum-based chemotherapy.
- Pure nonurothelial bladder cancers are typically treated with cystectomy; the role of perioperative chemotherapy and/or RT is not well defined.

SURVIVORSHIP AND ELDERLY CONSIDERATIONS

Bladder cancer is predominantly a disease of older individuals with coexisting medical issues, which strongly affect management decisions. Although most patients are diagnosed with nonmuscle-invasive disease, lifelong surveillance including urine cytology, cystoscopy, and periodic imaging is required. For those with muscle-invasive disease, the requirement for a radical cystectomy for most patients necessitates a urinary diversion procedure, and in patients receiving neoadjuvant cisplatin-based chemotherapy, the potential for short- and long-term chemotherapy-related adverse effects, including peripheral neuropathy, hearing loss, and renal dysfunction, as well as others, exists. Although life expectancy is limited in patients with metastatic disease, chemotherapy-related adverse effects can have a substantial effect on QOL. Many older patients are not candidates for perioperative chemotherapy secondary to the normal physiologic decline in renal function with aging, baseline hearing loss, and other comorbidities such as cardiac disease. Additional advancements in immuno-oncology, such as with checkpoint inhibitors, may enable treatment of older patients who otherwise would be unable to receive standard chemotherapy. For example, 21% of the patients treated with atezolizumab in the first-line setting in the IMvigor 210 study were ≥ 80 years old. Although radical cystectomy is a major surgical procedure, evidence supports the ability to safely perform a radical cystectomy in older individuals, including octogenarians.

KEY POINTS

- Bladder cancer is predominantly a disease of older patients and frequently occurs in patients with other smoking-related comorbidities. Thus, many "standard" therapies like cisplatin and cystectomy are actually unavailable to a significant portion of patients.

- Bladder-sparing or trimodality therapy is now considered as an equal alternative to cystectomy and is be increasingly offered to appropriately selected patients who wish to preserve their bladders and avoid urinary diversion; previously it was reserved primarily for patients ineligible for cystectomy, because of comorbidities.
- Cisplatin should be offered to any eligible patient regardless of age, but this requires careful assessment of baseline neuropathy, hearing, and kidney function, and serial assessment during and after treatment. New systemic treatment modalities (ie, immune checkpoint inhibitors, antibody-drug conjugates, and targeted therapies) will offer more treatment options to cisplatin-ineligible patients.

RENAL CANCER

EPIDEMIOLOGY

Renal cell carcinomas (RCCs) account for 90% of all malignant neoplasms of the kidney, with an estimated 73,820 newly diagnosed cases of kidney tumors (n = 44,120 men; n = 29,700 women) and 14,770 deaths (n = 9,820 men; n = 4,950 women) in 2019.[72] Renal cancers were historically called the "internist's tumor," on the basis of its protean clinical presentations, including fatigue, weight loss, and anemia. Today, < 10% of cases present with the classic triad of hematuria, abdominal pain, and a palpable mass. Between 1993 and 2004, the proportion of patients diagnosed with stage I RCC increased from 43.0% to 57.1%, whereas the proportion of patients diagnosed with stage IV disease decreased from 27.4% to 18.7%, indicating an increase in incidental diagnoses as a result of the increased use of imaging for other diagnostic purposes. Risk factors for RCC include smoking, obesity, hypertension, and acquired cystic kidney disease, which is associated with end-stage renal disease. Tobacco use (longer duration and exposure) is associated with an increased risk of advanced RCC. Environmental toxins such as cadmium and asbestos have also been associated with increased risk of RCC. Approximately 2% of cases are associated with inherited syndromes.

KEY POINTS

- RCC is the most common type of kidney tumor. The classic triad of hematuria, abdominal pain, and a palpable mass is rarely seen in modern practice. Incidental diagnoses are increasing.
- Risk factors include smoking, obesity, hypertension, environmental exposures, hereditary kidney cancer syndromes, and acquired cystic kidney disease leading to end-stage renal disease.

PATHOLOGY AND MOLECULAR PATHOGENESIS

The Heidelberg classification of renal tumors introduced in 1997 correlated histopathologic features with genetic abnormalities. The classification of adult epithelial kidney tumors has expanded to include less common histologies that are associated with distinct clinical outcomes. The most common types of renal cancer in adults are clear cell (75% of cases) and papillary (10% of cases) RCCs. More rare types include chromophobe (≤ 5% of cases), collecting-duct and renal medullary (each in ≤ 1% of cases), and translocation (< 1% of cases) carcinomas. Oncocytomas consist of neoplastic cells and can grow similarly to RCC, but they have benign behavior and are not considered truly malignant. However, presence of oncocytoma should prompt thorough evaluation for coexisting RCC, and patients should have ongoing surveillance despite a relatively low risk of subsequent RCC development. Sarcomatoid differentiation, which is associated with a worse prognosis, can occur in any major histologic subtype.

RCCs can have a variable natural history that reflects the biology of the histologic tumor type. The clinical course of clear-cell carcinomas, which make up the majority of renal tumors, is typically aggressive, although some patients can have an indolent course with stable metastases for years or metastases occurring decades after complete resection of a primary tumor. Molecular studies are attempting to identify markers that may predict prognosis. Papillary tumors are divided into type I and type II lesions according to architectural, cytologic, and genetic features. Type II papillary RCC is associated with more aggressive clinicopathologic features and a worse outcome. Chromophobe carcinomas also are typically indolent and uncommonly result in metastases and cancer-related death, although tumor necrosis and sarcomatoid differentiation predict a more aggressive phenotype versus chromophobes lacking these characteristics. Collecting-duct carcinomas have a very aggressive clinical course, with more than half of patients presenting with metastases and a median survival of only a few months for patients with metastatic disease.

Von Hippel-Lindau (VHL) disease is an autosomal-dominant familial cancer syndrome that predisposes individuals to renal clear-cell cancers, retinal angiomas, hemangioblastomas of the spinal cord and cerebellum, and pheochromocytomas, as well as to other rare neoplasms (Table 14-19). Frequent loss of at least one allele on chromosome 3p in renal tumors from patients with VHL disease led to the identification of the *VHL* tumor-suppressor gene. This gene encodes a protein that promotes the ubiquitination and destruction of hypoxia-inducible factor-α (HIF-α; Fig 14-20). Several proteins encoded by HIF-α are involved in angiogenesis, such as VEGF and platelet-derived growth factor B chain (PDGF-B). When the VHL protein is lost in renal cancers, VEGF, PDGF-B, and other proteins are overexpressed, promoting angiogenesis and tumor cell growth. Defects in the *VHL* gene, including mutation or gene silencing through methylation, also occur in the majority of tumors from patients with sporadic clear-cell carcinomas. Tumor angiogenesis is also stimulated by other growth factors that activate AKT and mammalian target of rapamycin (mTOR) signaling, which also increases HIF-α expression. Therapies that target VHL-regulated and AKT-signaling pathways have demonstrated substantial antitumor activity.

Several other genetic syndromes may be associated with RCC (Table 14-20). Genetic counseling is recommended for patients with renal cancer who are age 45 years or younger, and may be considered in patients with multifocal or bilateral renal masses, and/or if personal or family history is potentially consistent with an inherited renal cancer syndrome (Table 14-20).[73]

KEY POINTS

- The most common type of RCC is clear cell. Papillary RCC is the most common nonclear-cell type.
- Clear-cell RCC is driven by increased angiogenesis, which is frequently associated with loss of VHL tumor suppressor activity. This results in increased VEGF activity, among other pathways, providing the rationale for inhibition of VEGF as a key treatment modality in RCC.

SCREENING

Certain populations may be eligible for kidney cancer screening. Patients with end-stage renal disease who have been on dialysis for ≥ 3 years may be screened for acquired cystic disease, which can be a premalignant condition. Screening is indicated for some inherited renal carcinoma syndromes. Patients with known hereditary kidney cancer syndromes may be screened, but the screening protocol depends on the syndrome and the nature of the anticipated kidney tumors.

STAGING

CT scan with contrast medium is a reliable method for detecting and staging renal cancers. MRI is useful when renal function is poor, as well as to evaluate for local invasion or to assess the renal vein and inferior vena cava for thrombus. MRI can also help distinguish a benign tumor known as angiomyolipoma, which contains fat. Although negative FDG-PET imaging does not reliably exclude renal cancer, it may be useful in evaluating for local recurrence and distant metastases. Staging is performed using the American Joint Committee on Cancer (AJCC) staging classification (Table 14-21).

MANAGEMENT OF LOCALIZED RENAL CANCER

Surgical excision by open or laparoscopic nephrectomy is the primary treatment for patients with localized disease, either by radical nephrectomy or nephron-sparing partial nephrectomy for small tumors (Fig 14-21). The role for lymphadenectomy remains controversial and does not clearly improve OS. Tumor extension into the renal vein or inferior vena cava, indicating stage III disease, does not preclude resection, and cardiopulmonary bypass may be required; approximately 50% of such patients have prolonged survival with a successful resection. There is no benefit to postoperative RT for patients with locally advanced disease. Signs and symptoms of hepatic dysfunction may occur in patients with localized renal cancer (ie, without evidence of metastatic disease). This is a paraneoplastic phenomenon referred to as Stauffer syndrome. Although rare, patients with this syndrome should undergo resection, which leads to reversal of the hepatopathy.

Small renal masses are defined as incidentally image-detected, contrast-enhancing renal tumors ≤ 4 cm in diameter that are generally consistent with stage T1a RCC. A biopsy should be considered with suspicion of hematologic, metastatic, inflammatory, or infectious etiology,[73] but it is not required with a solid mass consistent with RCC in a patient for whom active surveillance is planned. Active surveillance is used for patients with significant comorbidities and limited life expectancy, especially for those with lesions < 2 cm. No validated protocols for active surveillance exist, but serial imaging is generally performed every 3 to 6 months for the first 2 years to establish growth rate, then every 6 to 12 months afterward. Triggers for intervention are unclear, but may include size > 3 cm, median growth rate > 5 mm/y, or increased stage.[73]

A partial nephrectomy may be performed for patients in whom an intervention is indicated and with a tumor amenable to this approach. Partial nephrectomy is associated with less risk of renal dysfunction than radical nephrectomy in patients with baseline normal renal function. Percutaneous thermal ablation or radiofrequency ablation may be considered as an alternative to partial nephrectomy in patients with cT1a masses < 3 cm, although these techniques may have an increased likelihood of tumor persistence or local recurrence compared with surgery.[74]

In contrast, radical nephrectomy should be considered for complex masses that would make partial nephrectomy technically challenging in a patient with no baseline renal dysfunction or proteinuria, and a normal contralateral kidney.

KEY POINTS

- After radiographic evaluation of a localized kidney mass, the decision to biopsy versus to perform partial or radical nephrectomy depends on the level of suspicion, the size of the lesion, and the age and comorbidities of the patient.
- Small renal masses are incidentally detected, contrast-enhancing tumors < 4 cm. Options for management include active surveillance, partial nephrectomy, and percutaneous ablation.
- Complex masses may require radical nephrectomy, with some increased subsequent risk of renal impairment.

METASTATIC RCC

Patients with metastatic RCC may have a varied, unpredictable, and in some cases, protracted clinical course. One prospective, phase II study of patients with treatment-naive, asymptomatic, metastatic RCC with a primary end point of time to initiation of

Table 14-19 Genomic Alterations in Inherited and Sporadic Renal Tumors

Genomic Alteration	Type of Renal Tumor	Syndrome
VHL	ccRCC	Von Hippel-Lindau (autosomal dominant): • Hemangioblastomas of CNS • Retinal angiomas • Pheochromocytomas • Pancreatic serous cystadenomas and neuroendocrine tumors
Chromosome 3 translocations or BRCA1-associated protein 1 (*BAP1* gene)	ccRCC	Familial ccRCC
MET (germline and somatic)	Hereditary or sporadic type I papillary RCC	Hereditary papillary renal carcinoma (autosomal dominant): • Bilateral multifocal papillary renal tumors.
Fumarate hydratase (germline)	Type II papillary RCC	Hereditary leiomyomatosis and RCC • Autosomal dominant • Uterine fibroids
Succinate dehydrogenase (germline)	ccRCC or chromophobe RCC	Hereditary paraganglioma and pheochromocytoma (autosomal dominant): • Paragangliomas • Pheochromocytomas • Bilateral and/or multifocal kidney tumors
Xp11.2 (*TFE* gene)	ccRCC or papillary RCC	Early-onset RCC
Folliculin (*FLCN* gene)	Chromophobe RCC or mixed chromophobe-oncocytoma renal tumors	Birt-Hogg-Dubé syndrome: hair-follicle hamartomas of the face and neck • Renal and pulmonary cysts • Slow-growing bilateral kidney tumors
Hamartin (*TSC1*) or Tuberin (*TSC2*)	Angiomyolipomas, rare ccRCC	Tuberous sclerosis complex: • Bilateral multifocal kidney tumors
SMARCB1 (germline)	Medullary carcinoma	

Abbreviations: ccRCC, clear-cell renal cell carcinoma; RCC, renal cell carcinoma.

systemic therapy made at the discretion of the treating physician and patient reported a median time of surveillance of 14.9 months. Having more adverse risk factors and more metastatic sites was associated with a shorter surveillance time. Thus, a subset of patients with metastatic RCC can safely be on a surveillance program prior to systemic therapy. One nomogram used to predict survival based on patients treated in the cytokine era includes the following as poor prognostic variables: no prior nephrectomy, low Karnofsky performance status (< 80%), low hemoglobin level, high "corrected" serum calcium level, and high serum lactate dehydrogenase (LDH) level. The median survival was 24 months (good risk), 12 months (intermediate risk), and 5 months (poor risk) for patients with 0, 1 to 2, or 3 or more risk factors, respectively. Newer prognostic models for patients with metastatic RCC treated with contemporary targeted therapies have generally included these prognostic factors in addition to others, such as platelet count, alkaline phosphatase, and number and sites of metastases. Although the International Metastatic Renal-Cell Carcinoma Database Consortium model (risk factors: anemia, thrombocytosis, neutrophilia, hypercalcemia, Karnofsky performance status < 80%, and < 1 year from diagnosis to treatment) has been externally validated in patients treated with first-line, VEGF-targeted treatment, prospective validation has not yet been performed. This risk-stratification scheme was used to define eligibility for a pivotal study of first-line nivolumab plus ipilimumab, described later in the section titled Immune Checkpoint Inhibitors.

The spectrum of FDA-approved therapies is displayed in Figure 14-22, along with targets of tyrosine kinase inhibitor (TKI) therapies.

Role of Surgery in Metastatic Disease

Cytoreductive nephrectomy should be considered as an initial treatment for patients with metastatic disease or to relieve

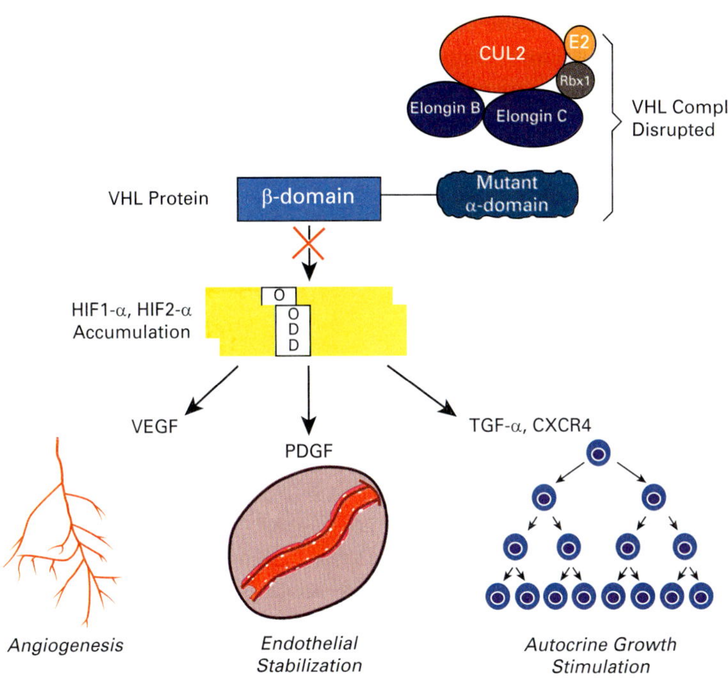

Fig. 14-20 VHL pathways for oncogenes activation.

Pathways of oncogene activation in any loss of VHL function with emphasis on HIF activation.

Abbreviations: CUL2, Cullin 2 (protein encoded by CUL2 gene); CXCR4, chemokine receptor type 4 (also known as fusin or CD 184); E2, a ubiquitin-conjugating enzyme; HIF, hypoxia inducible factor; PDGF, platelet derived growth factor; Rbx1,evolutionary conserved protein that interacts with cullin; TGFα, transforming growth factor alpha; VHL, Von Hippel-Lindau.

symptoms or control bleeding. Two prospective, randomized studies demonstrated improved survival for patients subsequently treated with IFN-α-2b. The role for cytoreductive nephrectomy is less well defined in the contemporary era. This question was addressed in the CARMENA trial, which randomly assigned patients with confirmed de novo, metastatic clear-cell RCC and intermediate or poor risk by the Memorial Sloan Kettering Cancer Center prognostic model to standard care (nephrectomy followed by sunitinib) versus sunitinib without nephrectomy.[19] OS in the sunitinib-only group was noninferior to that of the standard-care group at the planned interim analysis. This trial was limited by unequal allocation of large tumors to the surgery arm, failure of some patients in both arms to undergo assigned interventions, and selection bias with a particularly poor-risk population enrolled in the study. There was also concern that patients with symptomatic primary tumors might have been preferentially selected to undergo nephrectomy rather than enrolled in the study, thus limiting generalizability to this population. Therefore, patient selection is key and nephrectomy may still be appropriate for some patients, especially those without poor-risk disease or in patients experiencing symptoms (eg, hematuria, pain) from the renal mass. An alternative strategy is to treat with systemic therapy and perform an early evaluation of response to therapy, reserving cytoreductive nephrectomy for patients without evidence of primary refractory disease.

Table 14-20 Factors More Common in Hereditary RCC Useful for Referral for Genetic Evaluation

Factor
Early age at RCC diagnosis (≤ 45 years)
Bilateral renal cancer
Multifocal renal cancer
Strong family history of RCC (two or more relatives in same blood line)
RCC with personal or family history of one or more tumor type[a]
Unusual skin conditions (eg, leiomyomas, fibrofolliculomas, angiofibromas)
Family history of kidney cancer syndrome

Abbreviation: RCC, renal cell carcinoma.
[a]Pheochromocytoma, brain/spinal hemangioblastoma, pancreatic neuroendocrine tumor, retinal tumor, papillary cystadenoma, endolymphatic sac tumor, GI stromal tumor, uterine fibroid (age ≤ 35 years), uveal and cutaneous melanomas, and solid cancer occurring in childhood.

The use of neoadjuvant antiangiogenic agents in patients with locally advanced RCC has demonstrated tumor downsizing as well as the use of partial nephrectomy in a subset of patients who would otherwise have required a radical nephrectomy. Use of embolization is often recommended preoperatively for large primary tumors and for the resection of metastatic lesions because of the highly vascular nature of RCC. Surgical excision of oligometastatic disease at presentation or after prolonged disease-free intervals may be appropriate in select patients.

Systemic Therapies

Available systemic therapies for RCC include the following (Figs 14-22 and 14-23):

- agents targeting VEGF receptor (VEGFR), including monoclonal antibodies and TKIs,
- agents targeting mTOR, and
- immune-based therapies, including cytokines and checkpoint inhibitors.

Table 14-21 American Joint Committee on Cancer Staging of Bladder Cancer

T	N	M	Stage
Ta	N0	M0	0a
Tis	N0	M0	0is
T1	N0	M0	I
T2a	N0	M0	II
T2b	N0	M0	II
T3a, T3b, T4a	N0	M0	IIIA
T1-T4a	N1	M0	IIIA
T1-T4a	N2, N3	M0	IIIB
T4b	N0	M0	IVA
Any T	Any N	M1a	IVA
Any T	Any N	M1b	IVB

Adjuvant Therapy

Three major trials have tested the use of anti-VEGF TKIs for resected RCC (Table 14-22). Only one demonstrated a DFS benefit with treatment compared with placebo, and this resulted in FDA approval for sunitinib as adjuvant therapy. However, sunitinib also increases toxicity, and no data demonstrating OS benefit are yet available.

Immunotherapy

Cytokines. Until 2006, immunotherapy had represented the primary treatment of patients with advanced renal cancer. The most extensively studied agents were IFN-α and aldesleukin (human recombinant interleukin-2 [IL-2]). IFN-α demonstrated low but reproducible response rates of 10% to 20% with occasional durable responses. Response rates > 30% have been reported for patients with small-volume disease primarily limited to the lung. A dose response to IFN-α is suggested, because few responses are associated with a dose < 3 million U/d, with maximal benefit seen in the dose range of 5 million to 20 million U/d.

Therapy with IL-2 results in major responses in 10% to 15% of patients with clear-cell histology, with durable responses in 4% to 5% of cases. Prolonged and durable responses occur more commonly in patients with a good performance status and young age. Toxicity associated with high-dose, bolus IL-2 is related to increased vascular permeability and often necessitates treating patients in an intensive-care setting. IL-2 has been associated with a 4% incidence of treatment-related death. IL-2 remains the only therapy associated with durable CRs and may be most appropriate for young, good-risk patients. There is no proven role for administration of cytokine therapy in the adjuvant setting.

Immune Checkpoint Inhibitors. Anti–CTLA-4 and anti–PD-1/PD-L1 therapies have recently become standard treatments for advanced kidney cancer. The PD-1 inhibitor nivolumab prolonged

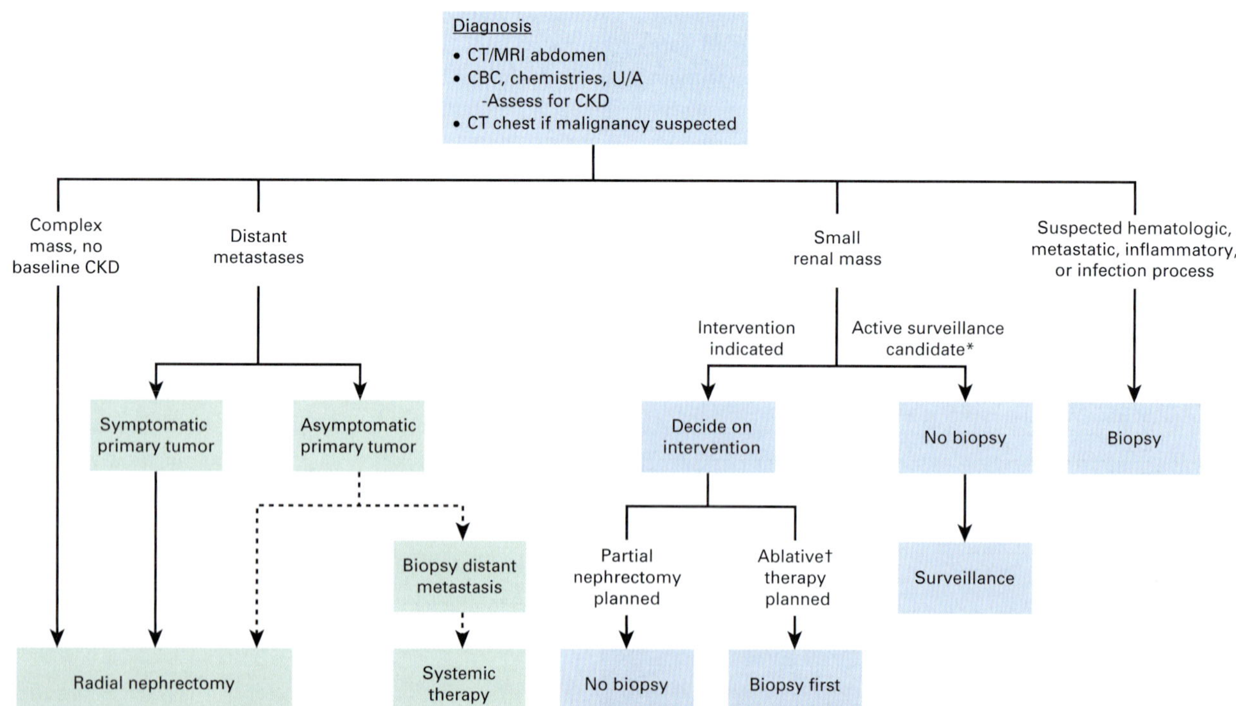

Fig. 14-21 Diagnostic and treatment approaches to the patient with a kidney mass.

Abbreviations: CKD, chronic kidney disease; CT, computed tomography; MRI, magnetic resonance imaging; U/A, urinalysis.

*Criteria for observation of small renal masses (see text). †Ablative approaches include catheter embolization, radio frequency ablation, radiation.

OS in comparison with everolimus in patients with metastatic RCC after prior angiogenic therapy (25.0 months *v* 19.6 months),[75] and it received FDA approval for this indication. Subsequently, the combination of nivolumab with the CTLA-4 inhibitor ipilimumab demonstrated improved OS in comparison with sunitinib in treatment-naïve patients with intermediate- or poor-risk advanced RCC (per International Metastatic Renal-Cell Carcinoma Database Consortium criteria described previously),[76] thus changing the standard of care for first-line treatment and earning FDA approval. The safety profiles of nivolumab and ipilimumab were manageable, with fewer grades 3 to 5 adverse events seen with the combination (46%) as compared with sunitinib (63%). However, systemic corticosteroids were required in 60% of patients treated with nivolumab and ipilimumab. Of note, this was only the second RCC treatment regimen demonstrated to improve OS, the other being temsirolimus. Trials are ongoing evaluating perioperative PD-1 blockade for patients with high-risk localized disease in an effort to prevent or delay metastatic recurrence.

Immunotherapy Combination Strategies. Several recent trials have also tested the combination of VEGF-targeted agents with PD-1/PD-L1 inhibitors, because VEGF-targeted agents are active in kidney cancer (discussed in more detail in the section titled VEGF Targeted Treatments) and may also have immunomodulatory effects. IMmotion151 is a phase III trial that randomly assigned treatment-naïve patients to atezolizumab plus bevacizumab versus sunitinib.[77,78] PFS was prolonged with atezolizumab plus bevacizumab compared with sunitinib, regardless of PD-L1 status. Subsequently, the phase III JAVELIN Renal 101 trial demonstrated improved PFS with the combination of axitinib and avelumab relative to sunitinib, regardless of PD-L1 status,[70] and the phase III KEYNOTE-426 trial demonstrated improved OS in addition to PFS with the combination of pembrolizumab and axitinib versus sunitinib. This regimen, only the third to have a demonstrated OS benefit for RCC, is now FDA approved. Thus, the standard frontline treatment of locally advanced or metastatic RCC now includes the combination anti-VEGFR and anti–PD-1/PD-L1 therapy, and biomarkers will be needed to see which patients benefit from the addition of either VEGF or CTLA-4 blockade to PD-1/PD-L1 blockade. Because combined CTLA-4 and PD-1/PD-L1 blockade is associated with significant immune-related adverse events, other ongoing trials are testing a strategy of first-line PD-1/PD-L1 inhibitor monotherapy followed by the addition of CTLA-4 blockade only for patients who have a suboptimal response to PD-1/PD-L1 monotherapy.

VEGF-Targeted Treatments

Bevacizumab. Increased expression of VEGF in clear-cell renal carcinomas led to investigations of bevacizumab, a humanized VEGF-neutralizing antibody in metastatic RCC before and after cytokine therapy (Table 14-23). The addition of bevacizumab to IFN for first-line therapy significantly improved overall response rate and PFS in two phase III randomized trials. Hypertension and asymptomatic proteinuria are the most common adverse events.

Tyrosine Kinase Inhibitors. Several TKIs have been developed to target the kinase domain of the VEGF receptor, downstream of the action of bevacizumab. The multikinase TKIs sorafenib, sunitinib, and pazopanib have been approved by the

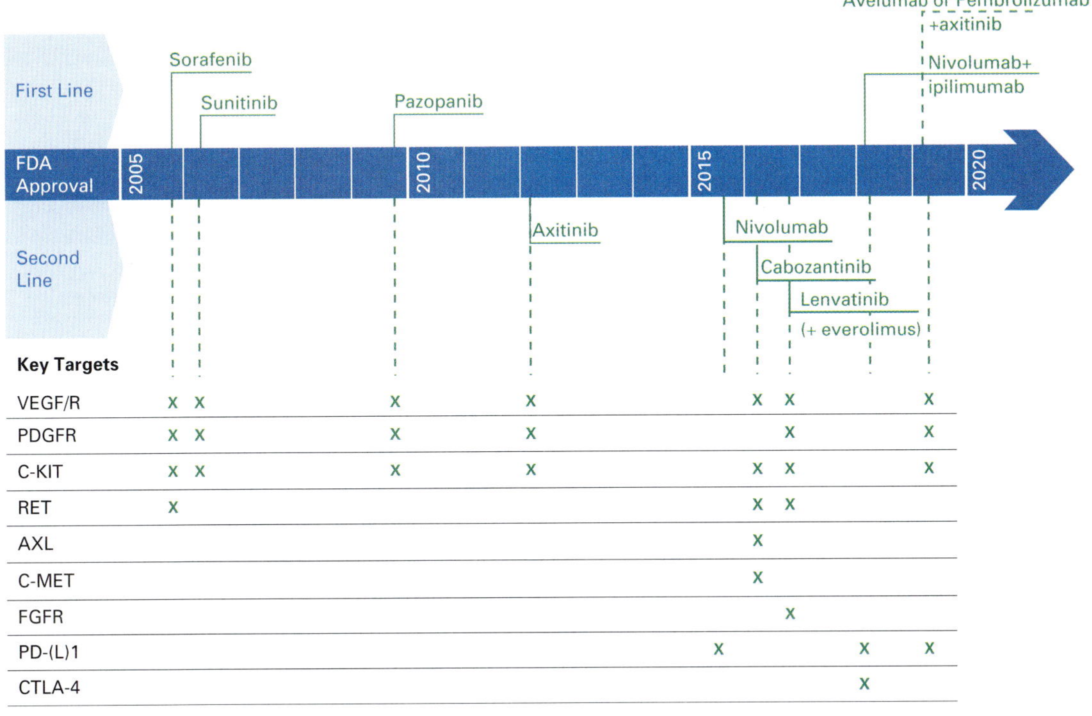

Fig. 14-22 Chronology, approvals and targets of FDA approved therapies for advanced kidney cancer.
Abbreviation: FDA, Food and Drug Administration.

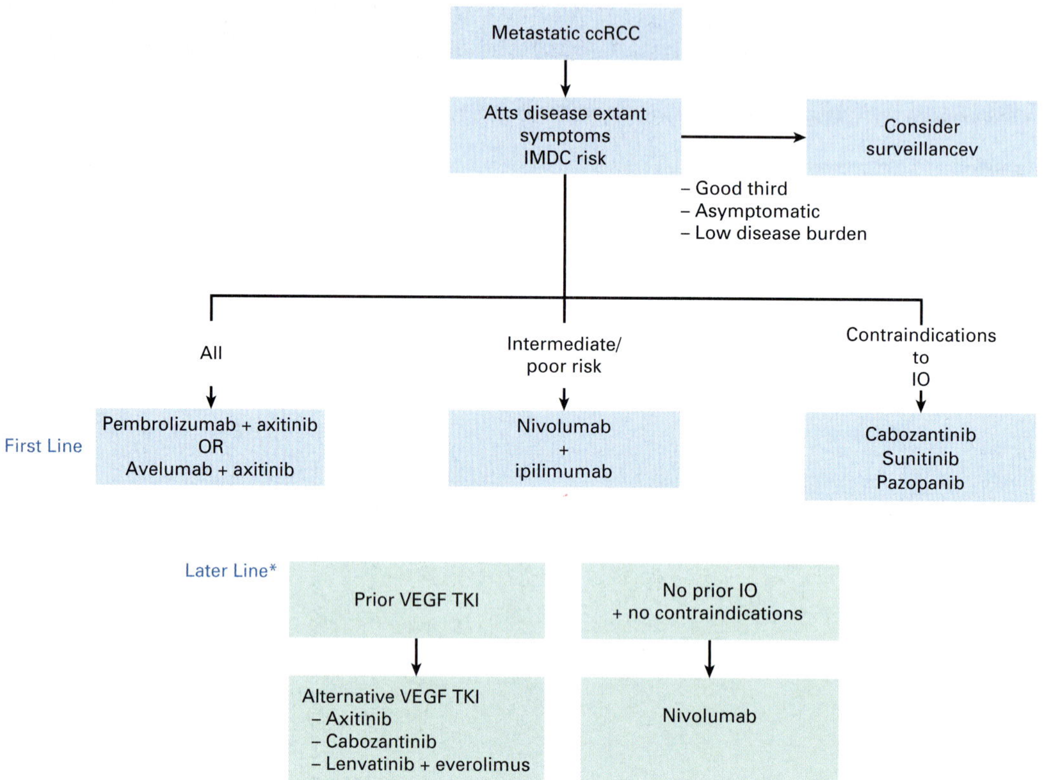

Fig. 14-23 Treatment options for metastatic clear-cell renal cell carcinoma.

Abbreviations: Atts, assess disease; ccRCC, clear-cell renal cell carcinoma; Courrier surveillance, consider; IMDC, International Metastatic Renal-Cell Carcinoma Database Consortium; IO, immunotherapy; Phon, prior; TKI, tyrosine kinase inhibitor.

FDA for first-line therapy in RCC. Sunitinib monotherapy has been a standard comparator arm in several recent first-line trials but may increasingly be an outdated standard of care.

The major toxicities of sunitinib are fatigue, oral lesions, hand-foot syndrome (also known as palmar-plantar erythrodysesthesia), hypertension, and diarrhea. Alternative dosing schedules including 2 weeks on and 1 week off may be associated with improved tolerability and similar efficacy as standard dosing. A randomized, phase III noninferiority trial compared the efficacy and safety of pazopanib and sunitinib as first-line therapy. The PFS for patients treated with pazopanib was noninferior to those treated with sunitinib, and the OS was similar. The safety profile favored

Table 14-22 Randomized Phase III Trials of Adjuvant TKIs for RCC

Trial	No. of Participants	Study Population	Design	Outcome	Notes
ASSURE[120]	1,943	Resected RCC, pT1b or greater and grade 3-4	Sunitinib *v* sorafenib *v* placebo for 1 year	No improvement in DFS or OS	Increased toxicity in TKI arms
PROTECT[121]	1,538	Resected RCC: pT2 grade 3-4; pT3-T4 any grade; or pN1	Pazopanib *v* placebo for 1 year	No improvement in DFS	Initial pazopanib dose reduced for toxicity, although improved DFS in group treated at initial dose
S-TRAC[122]	615	Resected RCC: stage 3 (pT3 or pN1) or greater	Sunitinib *v* placebo for 1 year	Improved DFS with sunitinib (6.8 *v* 5.6 years)	Higher-risk population than in ASSURE. Increased toxicity with sunitinib

Abbreviations: DFS, disease-free survival; OS, overall survival; RCC, renal cell carcinoma; TKI, tyrosine kinase inhibitor.

pazopanib, with less fatigue (55% v 63%), hand-foot syndrome (29% v 50%), and thrombocytopenia (41% v 78%). A higher incidence of increased alanine aminotransferase level was seen with pazopanib (60% v 43%). HRQOL measures favored pazopanib, with less fatigue and soreness of the mouth, hands, and feet. However, this trial did not allow dose reductions and alternative dosing schedules frequently used to ensure tolerability of sunitinib, as discussed previously. Other toxicities from this class of drugs include rash; myelosuppression, including thrombocytopenia; hypothyroidism; and congestive heart failure. Pazopanib therapy may also be associated with serious hepatotoxicity. Sunitinib-associated hypertension, defined as a maximum or mean systolic blood pressure > 140 mm Hg, was associated with an improvement in clinical outcome, suggesting that the development of hypertension during therapy may be a biomarker of response to sunitinib.

Previous studies had shown that patients whose disease progressed while taking a VEGF-targeted therapy could experience a response to another VEGF-targeted therapy. The AXIS trial compared the VEGF selective receptor TKI axitinib to sorafenib in patients whose disease had progressed during first-line therapy.[79] The overall median PFS was 6.7 months for patients who received axitinib compared with 4.7 months for patients treated with sorafenib. Therefore, axinitinib was FDA approved in 2012 for treatment of advanced RCC after failure of one prior systemic therapy.

Targeted therapies have also been directed against several identified mechanisms of resistance to VEGF-directed therapy. Cabozantinib is a TKI that targets MET and AXL in addition to VEGFR. The METEOR trial demonstrated that cabozantinib was superior to everolimus in OS and PFS in previously treated patients with metastatic RCC.[80] Subsequently, the CABOSUN trial showed that cabozantinib improved PFS relative to sunitinib in treatment-naïve patients, although the difference in OS was not statistically significant.[81] On the basis of these trials, cabozantinib is now FDA approved as first-line therapy for metastatic RCC or after failure of prior antiangiogenic therapy. Cabozantinib may have particular efficacy in patients with bone metastases. Finally, lenvatinib is a TKI that inhibits FGF receptor in addition to VEGF. Lenvatinib combined with everolimus improved PFS versus everolimus alone in patients previously treated with antiangiogenic therapy.[82] This combination was FDA approved in 2016 for treatment of advanced RCC after one prior antiangiogenic therapy.

mTOR Inhibitors. The mTOR protein is frequently activated in RCC, which can result in increased production of HIF-1α and HIF-2α. Consequently, agents that inhibit mTOR have been studied in patients with metastatic RCC. The mTOR inhibitor temsirolimus improved OS compared with IFN (10.9 months v 7.3 months) in treatment-naïve patients with poor-risk metastatic RCC. This led to FDA approval of single-agent temsirolimus in 2007. However, ipilimumab plus nivolumab is a new treatment option also applicable to poor-risk patients.

Everolimus is an orally administered mTOR inhibitor. Compared with placebo, everolimus improved PFS in previously treated patients with metastatic RCC (4.0 months v 1.9 months). This study was the first phase III, randomized trial to demonstrate efficacy of second-line therapy for patients whose disease progressed while taking a VEGF inhibitor, and it led to FDA approval in 2009 for treatment of advanced RCC after failure of either sunitinib or sorafenib. Adverse reactions from mTOR inhibitors include rash, asthenia, mucositis, nausea, edema, myelosuppression, hyperlipidemia, hypercholesterolemia, hyperglycemia, and drug-induced pneumonitis.

Chemotherapy

In general, RCC is highly resistant to single-agent and combination chemotherapy, except for patients with sarcomatoid or collecting-duct carcinomas. Gemcitabine plus platinum may have activity in metastatic collecting-duct carcinoma, analogous to treatment of upper-tract urothelial carcinoma. VEGF-targeted agents have also shown activity in clear-cell RCC with varying degrees of sarcomatoid differentiation.

KEY POINTS

- Although adjuvant sunitinib may improve DFS in high-risk, resected localized RCC and is FDA approved for this indication, no OS benefit has yet been demonstrated and toxicity is increased.
- First-line systemic therapy for metastatic clear-cell RCC includes combination immune checkpoint blockade or combination PD-1/PD-L1 inhibition plus VEGF inhibition. TKIs directed against the VEGFR are also a standard first-line therapy but are increasingly being replaced in this setting by combination therapies.
- The role of cytoreductive nephrectomy in the setting of metastatic disease remains undefined in the modern era. For patients without symptomatic primary tumors who are being treated with first-line sunitinib, cytoreductive nephrectomy may not offer a survival benefit.
- Second-line therapy for metastatic disease includes similar agents as in first-line therapy, with the choice of therapies dependent on prior treatment. PD-1 inhibition may be used after antiangiogenic therapy, and alternate antiangiogenesis inhibitors may still be active after prior antiangiogenic therapy.

NON–CLEAR-CELL RENAL CELL CARCINOMA

Most treatment strategies in RCC have been tested primarily or exclusively in clear-cell RCC, and high-level evidence for treatment of rare non–clear-cell RCC histologies is lacking. For localized disease, the standard treatment remains nephrectomy. For advanced disease, targeted therapies may be offered; immunotherapy and chemotherapy are generally ineffective. Selected data regarding targeted therapies for non–clear-cell RCC are listed in Table 14-24. Better therapies are needed for patients with non–clear-cell RCC, and clinical trials are preferred when available.

Table 14-23 **Key Phase III Trials of Antiangiogenic Therapy in Metastatic RCC**

Trial	No. of Participants	Study Population	Design	Outcome	Notes
Motzer et al.[123]	750	Treatment-naïve metastatic RCC	Sunitinib *v* interferon-α	Improved PFS with sunitinib (11 *v* 5 months)	Improved OS with sunitinib in long-term follow-up (26.4 *v* 21.8 months)
Sternberg et al.[124]	435	Treatment-naïve and cytokine-treated metastatic RCC	Pazopanib *v* placebo	Improved PFS with pazopanib (9.2 *v* 4.2 months)	PFS benefit seen regardless of prior treatment.
AXIS[79]	723	Previously treated metastatic RCC	Axitinib *v* sorafenib	Improved PFS with axitinib (6.7 *v* 4.7 months)	OS did not differ in long-term follow-up (20.1 *v* 19.2 months)
METEOR[80]	658	VEGFR-treated metastatic RCC	Cabozantinib *v* everolimus	Improved PFS with cabozantinib (7.4 *v* 3.8 months)	More toxicity with cabozantinib. Improved OS with cabozantinib in long-term follow-up
CABOSUN[81]	157	Treatment-naïve intermediate/high-risk metastatic RCC	Cabozantinib *v* sunitinib	Improved PFS with cabozantinib (8.6 *v* 5.3 months)	No significant OS difference in long-term follow-up
Motzer et al.[82]	153	VEGFR-treated metastatic RCC	Lenvatinib plus everolimus *v* lenvatinib *v* everolimus	Improved PFS with lenvatinib plus everolimus (14.6 months) or lenvatinib (7.4 months) *v* everolimus (5.5 months)	Marginally improved OS with lenvatinib plus everolimus *v* everolimus, but underpowered. Increased toxicity with combination therapy

Abbreviations: OS, overall survival; PFS, progression-free survival; RCC, renal cell carcinoma.

Activation of the c-MET signaling pathway in papillary RCCs has led to trials with agents that target the c-MET tyrosine kinase receptor or its ligand, hepatocyte growth factor, in patients with metastatic papillary RCC. MET-driven disease can be defined by chromosome 7 copy gain, focal *MET* or *HGF* gene amplification, or MET kinase domain mutations. As shown in Table 14-24, several MET inhibitors have been investigated in this disease.

Special Considerations in the Patient With Metastatic RCC

Approximately one-third of patients with advanced RCC have bone metastases and these are predominantly osteolytic. Treatment with bone-targeting agents, such as zoledronic acid (which requires dose adjustment for renal impairment) or denosumab, has been shown to decrease the risk of SREs in patients with bone metastases. As discussed in the Prostate Cancer section, dosing schedules may vary. Brain metastases are a frequent complication in patients with metastatic clear-cell renal cancer. Surgical resection or stereotactic radiosurgery are feasible alternatives to whole-brain radiation and may result in long-term survival. Patients with treated brain metastases may safely receive systemic therapy. Limited studies also suggest that patients with severe renal impairment or end-stage renal disease who are on hemodialysis may safely be treated with selected targeted therapies.

SURVIVORSHIP AND ELDERLY CONSIDERATIONS

Radical nephrectomy is a significant risk factor for chronic kidney disease. With the normal physiologic decline in renal function attributed to aging, older patients have a greater decline in kidney function compared with younger patients. Nephron-sparing approaches should be considered in appropriately selected patients in an effort to preserve renal function; however, despite similar tumor sizes, fewer older patients are treated with a partial nephrectomy. Although checkpoint inhibitors and agents targeting the VEGF and mTOR pathways have substantially improved the outcome for patients with advanced kidney cancer, these drugs are associated with a new spectrum of adverse effects, including immune-related adverse events, hypertension, hand-foot syndrome, thyroid dysfunction, hyperglycemia, hyperlipidemia, dysphonia, and pneumonitis, as well as others, as compared with conventional cytotoxic therapy. Monitoring for and management of these new toxicities is critical to ensure patients tolerate treatment and derive the greatest benefit from these effective therapies. With the substantial improvement in survival associated with targeted therapies in RCC, special attention to long-term adverse effects, including cardiac disease, thyroid dysfunction, renal insufficiency, and infection risk, and others, is needed. Older patients with preexisting medical issues such as hypertension or heart disease must be monitored closely for worsening hypertension and left ventricular-function decline during treatment. For example, patients with a history of hypertension and coronary artery disease are at increased risk for cardiotoxicity related to sunitinib. An analysis of age and efficacy and toxicity from phase III trials of sorafenib, sunitinib, temsirolimus, and bevacizumab, and from an expanded-access experience with sunitinib and sorafenib, suggests that outcomes and major toxicities are similar for patients ages ≥ 65 years and younger patients. Prospective studies of immune-based and targeted agents in the elderly with advanced RCC with particular attention to adverse effects are most certainly needed.

KEY POINTS

- Non–clear-cell RCCs have been underrepresented in clinical trials and the optimal treatment strategy is not well defined. Targeted agents include standard anti-VEGF TKIs as well as an emerging role for *MET* inhibition in papillary RCC.
- Bone metastases may be treated with systemic therapy plus bone-protective agents such as bisphosphonates or denosumab. Brain metastases and oligometastases can be treated with local therapies (eg, surgery, RT, or ablation) followed by systemic therapy, sometimes with long-term disease control.
- Elderly patients with comorbidities may benefit from active surveillance of appropriate RCCs or nephron-sparing approaches (eg, partial nephrectomy or stereotactic body RT) when treatment is required. For those being treated for advanced RCC, attention must be paid to the unique toxicities of checkpoint inhibitors and/or targeted therapies in the setting of concomitant hypertension, diabetes, chronic kidney disease, and thyroid disease, among others.

GERM CELL TUMORS

Germ cell tumors are the most common malignancies among men between ages 15 and 35 years, although there is a second peak in patients > 60 years old (primarily seminomas). It is estimated that 9,560 cases and 410 deaths related to germ cell tumors occurred in the United States in 2019.[83] Germ cell tumors most frequently originate in the gonads (testis or ovary) and less commonly in the retroperitoneum and mediastinum or CNS (primary extragonadal germ cell tumors); For a discussion of germ cell tumors in women, see Chapter 15: Gynecologic Cancers.) Retroperitoneal tumors in the absence of a primary testicular cancer may represent pure extragonadal germ cell tumors. Occasionally, an orchiectomy in these circumstances may show no distinct cancer but rather remnants of a scar ("scar carcinoma" or "burnt-out primary," which has been attributed to rapidly proliferating testicular cancer, which metastasized, leaving only a scar at its site of origin. Primary mediastinal germ cell tumors are not associated with testicular involvement. Primary extragonadal germ cell neoplasms also arise rarely in the sacrum, pineal gland, paranasal sinuses, and liver, and may be associated with several concomitant hematologic abnormalities including refractory thrombocytopenia or acute megakaryocytic (M7) leukemia. Regardless of the stage or extent of disease, the therapeutic objective is cure, which requires an integrated multidisciplinary approach (Table 14-25).

Table 14-24 Targeted Agents for Non-Clear-Cell RCC

Agent	Primary Target	Histology	Outcome
Sunitinib	VEGFR	Papillary, chromophobe, translocation	Improved PFS with sunitinib *v* everolimus (8.3 *v* 5.6 months), but poor-risk patients may have better PFS with everolimus
Temsirolimus	mTOR	Papillary, chromophobe	Improved OS with temsirolimus *v* IFN (11.6 *v* 4.3 months)
Everolimus	mTOR	Papillary, chromophobe, translocation	See above comments on sunitinib. No clear difference between sequencing sunitinib followed by everolimus *v* everolimus followed by sunitinib
Crizotinib	MET	Type I papillary RCC	In 4 of 23 patients with *MET* alteration, 2 had PR
Foretinib	MET, VEGF	Papillary RCC	In 10 patients with germline *MET* alteration, 5 had PR. Overall, RR was 13.5%; median PFS was 9 months
Savolitinib	MET	Papillary RCC	In 44 patients with *MET*-driven papillary RCC, 8 had PR. Phase III trial of savolitinib *v* sunitinib in MET-driven papillary RCC is planned

Abbreviations: IFN, interferon; PFS, progression-free survival; PR, partial response; RCC, renal cell carcinoma; RR, response rate.

EPIDEMIOLOGY

Risk factors include both abdominal and inguinal cryptorchidism, spermatic or testicular dysgenesis, and a family history that confers a four- to 10-fold increase in risk. Orchiopexy or surgical correction of abdominal cryptorchidism results in an improved ability to monitor the testis; and treatment of an undescended testis before puberty or during infancy decreases the risk of testicular cancer as compared with correction after puberty. Factors associated with increased risk for testicular cancer mortality include age older than 40 years, nonwhite race, and lower socioeconomic status. Testicular seminoma occurs more frequently in men with HIV, and the treatment is the same as for the HIV-negative population. Klinefelter syndrome is a risk factor for the development of mediastinal germ cell tumors. CIS (intratubular germ cell neoplasia) is a common finding when testicular germ cell tumors are diagnosed. Men in whom in situ disease is identified during a testicular biopsy as part of an infertility evaluation have a 50% risk of an invasive tumor within 5 years. Asynchronous testicular primary germ cell tumor occurs in 2% of patients, with seminoma as the most common histology and a 3% lifetime risk of developing a contralateral testis cancer. Regular self-examination of the remaining testis is recommended. Surveillance with scrotal ultrasonography should be considered to evaluate testicular complaints in men with a previous diagnosis of testicular cancer.

BIOLOGY

Germ cell tumors are derived from the malignant transformation of premeiotic germ cells. To create a pluripotential tumor, these transformed germ cells must be able to differentiate in a manner similar to the totipotential zygote without the reciprocal genetic information that results from fertilization. An isochromosome of the short arm of chromosome 12, i(12p), is present in 80% of all histologic subtypes, including CIS and primary extragonadal tumors. The remaining 20% of cases have excess 12p genetic copy number, tandem duplication, or transposition, which indicates that one or more genes on 12p are involved in malignant transformation. Most germ cell tumors are hyperdiploid, often triploid or tetraploid, implying that endoreduplication is important in the early steps of malignant transformation.

KEY POINTS

- The most well-known risk factor for testicular cancer is history of undescended testis (cryptorchidism). Early surgical correction can help mitigate this risk.
- Genes on chromosome arm 12p appear to be involved with germ cell tumor pathogenesis, and isochromosome 12p is a common finding that may help differentiate germ cell tumors from other tumor types in ambiguous situations.

DIAGNOSIS

A painless testicular mass is highly suggestive of a testicular tumor; however, the majority of patients present with diffuse testicular swelling, induration, hardness, pain, or some combination of these findings. For patients who present with scrotal or testicular pain, the initial therapy prescribed is often antibiotics for presumed infectious epididymitis or orchitis. Scrotal ultrasonography should be performed when any concern is present about the possibility of a testicular tumor. If the ultrasound is abnormal and a testicular tumor is suspected, levels of biologic tumor markers (human chorionic gonadotropin [hCG], α-fetoprotein [AFP], and LDH) should be determined, followed by a radical inguinal orchiectomy with removal of the testis and ligation of the spermatic cord at the level of the internal ring is performed. Because the testes originate in the genital ridge and migrate through the abdomen and

Table 14-25 Germ Cell Tumor WHO Classification[125]

Germ Cell Tumors Derived From Germ Cell Neoplasia In Situ
Noninvasive germ cell neoplasia
Germ cell neoplasia in situ
Specific forms of intratubular germ cell neoplasia
Tumors of a single histologic type (pure forms)
Seminoma
Seminoma with syncytiotrophoblast cells
Nonseminomatous germ cell tumors
Embryonal carcinoma
Yolk sac tumor, postpubertal type
Trophoblastic tumors
Choriocarcinoma
Nonchoriocarcinomatous trophoblastic tumors
Placental site trophoblastic tumor
Epithelioid trophoblastic tumor
Cystic trophoblastic tumor
Teratoma, postpubertal type
Teratoma with somatic-type malignancy
Nonseminomatous germ cell tumors of more than one histologic type
Mixed germ cell tumors
Germ cell tumors of unknown type
Regressed germ cell tumors
Germ cell tumors unrelated to germ cell neoplasia in situ
Spermatocytic tumor
Teratoma, prepubertal type
Dermoid cyst
Epidermoid cyst
Well-differentiated neuroendocrine tumor (monodermal teratoma)
Mixed teratoma and yolk sac tumor, prepubertal type
Yolk sac tumor, prepubertal type

Adapted with permission from Elsevier.

inguinal canal into the scrotum, the vascular and lymphatic drainage of the testes is to the renal or great vessels and the retroperitoneal nodes, respectively. A testicular biopsy or transscrotal orchiectomy is contraindicated because the normal vascular and lymphatic drainage is disturbed. Levels of αAFP, β-hCG, and LDH also should be determined before orchiectomy. Less common presentations include unilateral or bilateral gynecomastia (as a result of elevated levels of β-hCG), hyperthyroidism due to homology between β-hCG and thyroid-stimulating hormone, persistent back pain related to retroperitoneal nodal disease, superior vena cava syndrome from primary mediastinal tumors, supraclavicular adenopathy, and hemoptysis from extensive pulmonary metastases.

KEY POINTS

- Suspicious testicular symptoms should be evaluated by ultrasound. If the results are suggestive, then diagnosis is made via orchiectomy, never via specimens collected during percutaneous biopsy. Tumor-marker levels are determined beforehand and, if elevated, measurement must be repeated after surgery.
- For patients who present with life-threatening symptoms (eg, bleeding brain metastases or pulmonary metastases causing respiratory failure), highly elevated AFP or β-hCG level, and a typical pattern of spread, systemic therapy should be started immediately. Resection of a suspicious testicular lesion can be delayed until after starting or completing chemotherapy but should still be performed to establish a pathologic diagnosis and remove a potential sanctuary site.

PATHOLOGY

Germ cell tumors are classified histologically into seminomas and nonseminomas. Seminomas, which account for approximately half of testicular germ cell tumors, retain totipotentiality and are exquisitely sensitive to RT and chemotherapy. Nonseminomas are composed of the following cell types: embryonal carcinoma, teratoma, choriocarcinoma, and yolk sac tumors, and are very responsive to chemotherapy but not RT.

Table 14-26 shows the WHO Classification for Germ Cell Tumors. Embryonal carcinoma is the most undifferentiated, with totipotential capacity to differentiate into extraembryonic malignant cell types, such as yolk sac tumors and choriocarcinoma, and somatic cell types, such as teratoma. Teratoma is composed of somatic cells from two or more germ cell layers (ie, ectoderm, mesoderm, or endoderm) and thus can differentiate into tissue types such as cartilage, muscle, mucinous glandular epithelium, and others. The presence of any component of nonseminoma with seminoma is treated as a nonseminomatous germ cell tumor. In addition, an abnormal serum AFP level is not typically seen in seminoma and should prompt a search for a nonseminomatous component (either not identified in the orchiectomy specimen or present in metastatic foci). Borderline AFP elevations can be caused by liver disease, but an occult nonseminomatous component should be ruled out. Most nonseminomas show mixed histologies, including embryonal carcinoma, yolk sac tumors, teratoma, and choriocarcinoma. When reporting histology, all subtypes present must be noted, starting with the most prevalent and ending with the least common component.

Seminomas are positive for placental alkaline phosphatase (PLAP), CD117 (c-kit), OCT-4, and SALL-4 (Fig 14-24). They are negative for cytokeratins and CD30. Embryonal carcinoma, however, almost universally expresses cytokeratins, epithelial membrane antigen, CD30, OCT-4, and SALL-4; approximately 50% express PLAP. Yolk sac tumors are positive for cytokeratins, AFP, and SALL-4, but negative for CD117 and CD30. Immunohistochemical analysis and testing for i(12p) may be useful in the evaluation of patients with midline tumors of uncertain histogenesis. Serum markers consistent with germ cell tumors may also be helpful, although elevation of β-hCG level is more specific than elevated levels of AFP or LDH.

KEY POINTS

- Germ cell tumors are divided into seminomas and nonseminomas. Seminomas must be composed entirely of seminoma; any component of other histology results in a diagnosis of nonseminoma, and an elevated AFP level should prompt a thorough search for nonseminomatous component.
- Seminomas are highly sensitive to chemotherapy and RT. This has implications for therapy and evaluation of residual masses after therapy.
- Nonseminomas can be mixes of multiple histologies, including malignant germ cell tumors (embryonal carcinoma, yolk sac tumor, choriocarcinoma) and teratoma. Malignant nonseminomatous germ cell tumors are generally chemotherapy sensitive. Teratoma is neither chemotherapy nor RT sensitive. By itself, teratoma does not usually metastasize, but it can dedifferentiate over time into malignant histologies including (but not limited to) teratocarcinoma.

PATTERNS OF SPREAD

The primary lymphatic drainage for testicular germ cell tumors is to the retroperitoneal lymph nodes (primary landing zones). The right testicular artery originates from the aorta, and the right testicular vein drains into the inferior vena cava. The left testicular artery originates near the left renal artery, and the left testicular vein terminates in the left renal vein. Right-sided tumors spread to the interaortocaval lymph nodes immediately below the renal blood vessels, and left-sided tumors spread to the para-aortic lymph nodes immediately below the left renal artery and vein. Cross-metastases are more commonly seen

Table 14-26 **Staging of Testicular Germ Cell Tumors**[93]	
Stage	**Definition**
Primary Tumor (T)	
Clinical T (cT)	Note: Except for Tis confirmed by biopsy and T4, the extent of the primary tumor is classified by radical orchiectomy
cTX	Primary tumor cannot be assessed
cT0	No evidence of primary tumor
cTis	Germ cell neoplasia in situ
cT4	Tumor invades scrotum with or without vascular or lymphatic invasion
Pathologic T (pT)	
pTX	Primary tumor cannot be assessed
pT0	No evidence of primary tumor
pTis	Germ cell neoplasia in situ
pT1	Tumor limited to testis (including rete testis invasion) without lymphovascular invasion (subclassification only applies to pure seminoma)
pT1a	Tumor < 3 cm
pT1b	Tumor ≥ 3 cm
pT2	Tumor limited to testis (including rete tesis invasion) with lymphovascular invasion;
	OR Tumor invading hilar soft tissue or epididymis or penetrating visceral mesothelial layer covering the external surface of tunica albuginea with or without lymphovascular invasion
pT3	Tumor invades the spermatic cord with or without lymphovascular invasion
pT4	Tumor invades the scrotum with or without lymphovascular invasion
Regional lymph nodes (N) clinical	
cNX	Regional lymph nodes cannot be assessed
cN0	No regional lymph node metastasis
cN1	Metastasis with a lymph node mass ≤ 2 cm in greatest dimension;
	OR Multiple lymph nodes, none > 2 cm in greatest dimension
cN2	Metastasis with a lymph node mass > 2 cm but not > 5 cm in greatest dimension;
	OR Multiple lymph nodes, any one mass > 2 cm but not > 5 cm in greatest dimension
cN3	Metastasis with a lymph node mass > 5 cm in greatest dimension
Pathologic (pN)	
pNX	Regional lymph nodes cannot be assessed
pN0	No regional lymph node metastasis
pN1	Metastasis with a lymph node mass ≤ 2 cm in greatest dimension and fewer than five nodes positive, none > 2 cm in greatest dimension
pN2	Metastasis with a lymph node mass > 2 cm but not > 5 cm in greatest dimension;
	OR more than five nodes positive, none > 5 cm in greatest dimension; or evidence of extranodal extension of tumor
pN3	Metastasis with a lymph node mass > 5 cm in greatest dimension
Distant metastases (M)	
M0	No distant metastasis
M1	Distant metastasis
M1a	Nonretroperitoneal nodal or pulmonary metastasis
M1b	Nonpulmonary visceral metastases

Table 14-26 continued

Stage	Definition
Serum tumor markers (S)	
SX	Marker studies not available or not performed
S0	Marker study levels within normal limits
S1	LDH level is < 1.5 times ULN and hCG level (mIU/mL) is < 5,000 and AFP (ng/mL) is < 1,000
S2	LDH level is 1.5 to 10 times ULN or hCG is 5,000 to 50,000 or AFP is 1,000 to 10,000
S3	LDH level is > 10 times ULN or hCG is > 50,000 or AFP is > 10,000
Anatomic stage/prognostic groupings	
Stage 0	pTis N0 M0 S0
Stage I	pT1-4 N0 M0 SX
Stage IA	pT1 N0 M0 S0
Stage IB	pT2 N0 M0 S0
Stage IB	pT3 N0 M0 S0
	pT4 N0 M0 S0
Stage IS	Any pT/TX N0 M0 S1-3
Stage II	Any pT/TX N1-3 M0 SX
Stage IIA	Any pT/TX N1 M0 S0
	Any pT/TX N1 M0 S1
Stage IIB	Any pT/TX N2 M0 S0
	Any pT/TX N2 M0 S1
Stage IIC	Any pT/TX N3 M0 S0
	Any pT/TX N3 M0 S1
Stage III	Any N M1 SX
Stage IIIA	Any N M1a S0
	Any N M1a S1
Stage IIIB	Any pT/TX N1-3 M0 S2
	Any pT/TX Any N M1a S2
Stage IIIC	Any pT/TX N1-3 M0 S3
	Any N M1a S3
	Any N M1b Any S

Abbreviations: AFP, α-fetoprotein; hCG, human chorionic gonadotropin; LDH, lactate dehydrogenase; ULN, upper level of normal.

Republished with permission of Springer, from AJCC Cancer Staging Manual, 8th Edition (2017); permission conveyed through Copyright Clearance Center, Inc.

from right to left but may occur in either direction if there has been a prior inguinal surgery like hernia repair. Invasion of the epididymis or spermatic cord may be associated with iliac nodal involvement, and inguinal metastases may be seen with scrotal invasion or if there has been disturbance of the normal lymphatic drainage related to prior surgery such as a vasectomy or orchiopexy. A full understanding of lymphatic drainage has informed the development of retroperitoneal templates for right- and left-sided tumors that are often used when a retroperitoneal lymphadenectomy is performed and helps minimize fertility consequences of the operation. Additional metastatic sites include retrocrural, mediastinal, and supraclavicular lymph nodes; the lungs; and, less commonly, the liver, CNS, and bone.

KEY POINTS

- The testicles descend from the retroperitoneum embryologically; therefore, the lymphatic drainage is to the retroperitoneal lymph nodes rather than inguinal or pelvic lymph nodes. This has implications for surveillance and treatment.
- If prior inguinal or transcrotal surgeries have been performed, then the lymphatic drainage may be

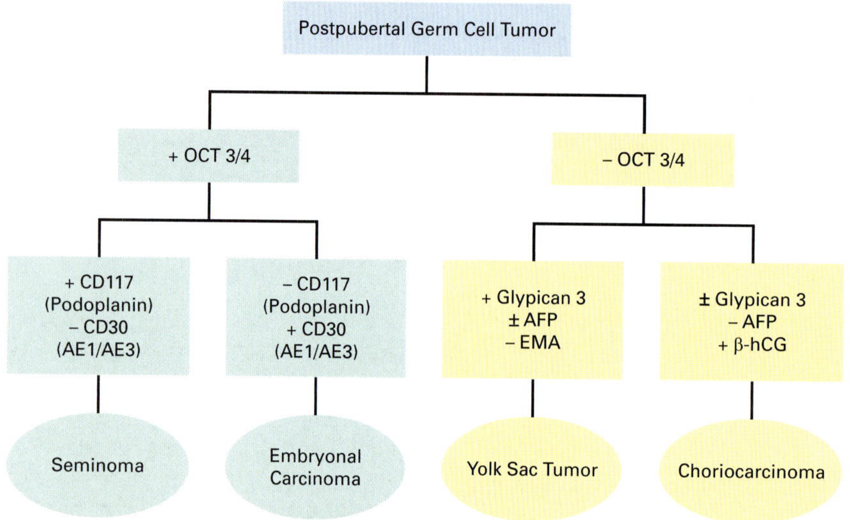

Fig. 14-24 Pathological and immunohistochemical classifications of testicular germ cell tumors.

Abbreviations: AFP, α-fetoprotein; EMA, epithelial membrane antigen; hCG, human chorionic gonadotropin.

disrupted; therefore, the pattern of metastasis can be less predictable.

- From the retroperitoneal lymph nodes, testicular cancer may spread to mediastinal and other lymph nodes. Pulmonary metastases are much more common than other visceral metastases and do not carry as poor a prognosis as other visceral involvement.

STAGING

Pretreatment Evaluation

The extent of disease evaluation for patients with newly diagnosed germ cell tumors includes a chest radiograph, CT scan of the abdomen and pelvis, and measurement of tumor-marker levels. Indications for a CT scan of the chest include an abnormal chest radiograph, known mediastinal disease, and risk for pulmonary metastases. A bone scan and MRI of the brain are indicated only if related symptoms are present or for patients with very high serum β-hCG levels. Measurement of tumor markers, including AFP, hCG, and LDH, is used to establish the diagnosis and may assist in determining histologic subtype. Sperm banking should be performed before treatment is pursued, when practical, but also with an appreciation that many men with testicular cancer will have low sperm counts associated with their disease.

Stage Groupings

A tumor-node-metastasis (TNM) staging classification system was developed by the AJCC and incorporates serum tumor markers, including AFP, β-hCG, and LDH (Table 14-27). Adverse factors include mediastinal primary site; degree of elevation of AFP, β-hCG, and LDH; and presence of nonpulmonary visceral metastases. On the basis of these findings, advanced germ cell tumors are risk stratified as follows: good risk, accounting for 60% of germ cell tumors and resulting in a 5-year survival rate of 91%; intermediate risk, accounting for 26% of germ cell tumors and a 5-year survival rate of 79%; and poor risk, accounting for 14% of germ cell tumors and a 5-year survival rate of 48%. All seminomas are either good or intermediate risk (Table 14-28). Regardless of the initial risk stratification, patients with advanced germ cell tumors who survive and remain without disease > 2 years after their diagnosis have an excellent chance of remaining disease free in subsequent years, although late relapses of seminoma can occur.

Tumor Markers

Tumor-marker levels are measured before, during, and after treatment. An initial increase in tumor-marker levels may occur with chemotherapy, particularly in the setting of bulky advanced disease. The serum half-lives of AFP and β-hCG are 5 to 7 days and 24 to 48 hours, respectively, and a slow decline in marker level after orchiectomy or during chemotherapy implies residual active disease. In the absence of radiographic metastases, markers should be checked approximately 4 weeks (four AFP half-lives) after orchiectomy to assess for residual disease (stage IS) that would require systemic treatment. Elevated or increasing AFP and/or β-hCG levels that occur without radiologic or clinical findings imply micrometastatic disease and should be managed with consideration of additional systemic therapy. Other conditions associated with elevated AFP levels include hepatocellular carcinoma, liver damage, and other GI malignancies. β-hCG elevations may occur as a result of treatment-related hypogonadism or cross-reactivity with pituitary hormones, including luteinizing hormone as well as some GI tumors, including gastric cancer. This cross-reactivity is generally less of an issue with current assays specific for the β subunit of hCG. Hyperthyroidism may be associated with elevated levels of β-hCG related to homology between β-hCG and thyroid-stimulating hormone. A spurious elevation in hCG also has been associated with marijuana use. With these exceptions, increased levels of AFP are pathognomonic of a nonseminoma and not seen in seminoma, whereas elevated levels of β-hCG may be seen in both seminoma and nonseminoma. AFP elevation in the setting of a diagnosis of seminoma should prompt re-evaluation of the pathology and often treatment of presumed nonseminoma; low levels of AFP elevation that do not change may indicate an alternative etiology such as liver damage. LDH levels can increase in patients with advanced seminoma or nonseminoma and are used for staging and assessment of outcome. However, LDH is very nonspecific and as a result, NCCN guidelines do not recommend using LDH as a surveillance marker (Table 14-27).

KEY POINTS

- Prior to orchiectomy, tumor-marker levels should be measured and patients should undergo cross-sectional imaging of the abdomen and pelvis as well as chest radiograph. MRI of the head is only indicated for patients with suspicious symptoms or in the setting of widespread metastases and/or highly elevated β-hCG value.
- Advanced (metastatic) germ cell tumors are risk stratified according to primary site, pattern of spread, and degree of serum tumor marker elevation.

SEMINOMA

Stage I

Approximately 70% of patients with seminoma have stage I disease. After radical inguinal orchiectomy, standard treatment options include surveillance, adjuvant infradiaphragmatic RT to include the para-aortic nodes, and single-agent carboplatin, recognizing that approximately 85% of these patients will not have required treatment and that the long-term survival is nearly 100% regardless of the initial option chosen. Observational studies of patients with clinical stage I seminoma indicate a 15% to 20% likelihood of disease relapse, mostly in the retroperitoneum; however, the median time to relapse is 14 months, which is longer than for clinical stage I nonseminomatous tumors, and late relapses at > 5 years may occur. A contralateral tumor in the remaining testis should be considered when relapses occur.

On the basis of the excellent outcome for patients with stage I seminoma and the potential for long-term radiation-related toxicity, including secondary malignancies, surveillance represents a preferred strategy for the management of patients with clinical stage I disease (Fig 14-25; Table 14-29).[2-5] Adjuvant RT or single-agent chemotherapy reduces recurrence risk but increases late toxicity, and patients whose disease is managed with active surveillance can almost always be cured with deferred treatment at the time of relapse. RT can be used but is to be avoided in the setting of inflammatory bowel disease or a horseshoe kidney. RT using a para-aortic field as compared with a dogleg field is associated with reduced toxicity and a low rate of recurrence. Including a pelvic field should be considered for men with a prior history of scrotal surgery (eg, vasectomy), because out-of-field recurrences can occur if the possibility of aberrant lymphatic drainage is not addressed. A randomized trial comparing RT with single-dose carboplatin in the adjuvant treatment of stage I seminoma showed a noninferior relapse-free rate for single-dose carboplatin (area under the curve, 7), with a reduced risk of a second primary germ cell tumor in the carboplatin arm. Two cycles of carboplatin may further reduce the risk of recurrence. Although chemotherapy represents a potential strategy for the management of clinical stage I disease, concerns have been raised on the basis of the relatively short follow-up period (median, 6.5 years) to evaluate for late relapse and late toxicity. In a retrospective report on patients who experienced a relapse after adjuvant carboplatin, 15% of the relapses occurred > 3 years after adjuvant treatment.

In seminoma, stage IS disease is rare, and low levels of LDH or β-hCG may be attributable to other causes. In this circumstance, patients should have ongoing surveillance to monitor for the development of radiographically apparent metastases, and alternative explanations for tumor marker elevation should be sought.

Stage IIA/B

Patients with stage IIA and nonbulky IIB disease (2 to 3 cm) are treated with 30 to 36 Gy of radiation to the para-aortic and ipsilateral iliac lymph nodes. Chemotherapy is preferred for patients with clinical stage IIB seminoma with bulkier disease (> 3 cm). Chemotherapy will cure > 90% of the patients who

Table 14-27 **Risk Stratification According to the International Germ Cell Consensus Classification**[126]

Germ Cell Tumor	Risk Stratification
Seminoma	Good risk
	Any primary and any markers and no nonpulmonary visceral metastases
	Intermediate risk
	Any primary and any markers and nonpulmonary visceral metastases
Nonseminoma	Good risk
	Testis or retroperitoneal primary and good-risk markers and no nonpulmonary visceral metastases
	Intermediate risk
	Testis/retroperitoneal primary and intermediate- risk markers and no nonpulmonary visceral metastases
	Poor risk
	Mediastinal primary site or testis or retroperitoneal primary with either nonpulmonary visceral metastases or poor-risk markers

Table 14-28 Serum Markers in Germ Cell Tumors

Histology	Serum Marker		
	AFP[a]	β-hCG[b]	LDH[c]
Seminoma	Never	+/– (Typically < 100)	+/–
Nonseminoma			
Choriocarcinoma	+/–	+++	+/–
Embryonal carcinoma	+/–	++	+/–
Teratoma	–	–	–
Yolk sac tumor	+++	+/–	+/–

Abbreviations: AFP, α-fetoprotein; hCG, human chorionic gonadotropin; LDH, lactate dehydrogenase.
[a]Half life: 5-7 days.
[b]Half life: 1-2 days.
[c]Half life: varies by isoform.

experience disease relapse after RT; approximately 99% of patients with early-stage seminoma are cured.

Advanced Seminoma

Patients with retroperitoneal masses > 5 cm (stage IIC), supradiaphragmatic lymphadenopathy, visceral disease, bulky retroperitoneal tumors, tumor-related back pain, and mediastinal extragonadal presentations are treated with primary chemotherapy. Approximately 90% of patients with advanced seminoma will be classified as having a good prognosis and receive treatment with good-risk chemotherapy, with an 86% 5-year survival, whereas only 10% of patients have intermediate-risk disease, due to extragonadal primary or nonpulmonary visceral metastases. Pure seminomas are never classified as poor risk (see the section titled Management of Advanced Germ Cell Tumors by Risk Classification) (Fig 14-25; Table 14-29).

Postchemotherapy Residual Masses

Surgery after chemotherapy is technically more difficult for patients with seminoma, because of a dense desmoplastic reaction after chemotherapy in seminoma that does not occur for patients with nonseminomas. Postchemotherapy residual masses usually represent fibrosis rather than persistent seminoma and may continue to shrink in the absence of any additional interventions over months to years. Options have included surgery for postchemotherapy masses > 3 cm or close observation with CT imaging and intervention if there is evidence of disease progression (Fig 14-26). FDG-PET is a predictor for viable tumors in postchemotherapy seminoma. The specificity, sensitivity, and negative predictive value of FDG-PET are improved if performed 6 weeks after the end of the last chemotherapy cycle compared with before 6 weeks. In summary, FDG-PET is recommended in patients with a residual mass > 3 cm and normal tumor-marker levels. A positive FDG-PET scan indicates viable seminoma, for which surgery or RT is indicated.

KEY POINTS

- Stage I seminomas are generally managed with active surveillance. Alternatives include adjuvant chemotherapy (one to two cycles of carboplatin) or RT, which decrease risk of recurrence but result in some degree of overtreatment and have long-term toxicities. OS is excellent regardless of immediate versus delayed intervention. Thus, adjuvant treatment is typically offered only to patients who are eager to reduce their chance of recurrence (and the need for more intensive therapy) or who may have difficulties adhering to a surveillance schedule, with the understanding that OS will not likely be improved.
- Stage IIA and nonbulky IIB seminomas can be treated with radiation to the retroperitoneal lymph nodes.
- Stage IIB and advanced seminomas (stages IIC and III) are treated according to the risk stratification scheme for advanced germ cell tumors, with most falling into the good-risk category and a minority being intermediate risk due to nonpulmonary visceral metastases. Seminomas are never considered poor risk.

NONSEMINOMATOUS GERM CELL TUMORS

Stage I Disease

Approximately 30% to 40% of patients with nonseminomatous germ cell tumors present with stage I disease. Management options include surveillance, retroperitoneal lymph node dissection (RPLND), or primary chemotherapy.

Surveillance is a preferred option for adherent patients with stage IA (pT1 tumors; ie, those with no vascular or lymphatic invasion or with invasion into the tunica vaginalis, spermatic cord, or scrotum) who have a low risk for recurrence (Fig 14-25; Table 14-30). Absence of a predominant embryonal carcinoma component in the primary tumor is also favorable. Approximately 20% of patients will experience a recurrence of the disease (most commonly in the retroperitoneum) and will need chemotherapy. Most recurrences of nonseminomatous germ cell tumors will occur within 2 years of orchiectomy, and these patients must have meticulous follow-up that includes a history, physical examination, and measurement of serum tumor markers every 2 months, as well as a chest radiograph at months 4 and 12 and an abdominal and pelvic CT scan every 4 to 6 months during the first year (Table 14-30). Although the intervals for follow-up increase during subsequent years, it is important to remember that late recurrences can occur. Compliance with this surveillance schedule, and with salvage therapy as indicated, produces cure rates of 98% to 99% and spares the 75% to 80% of patients without micrometastatic disease from additional therapy. The potential long-term risk of secondary cancers associated with exposure to low-dose ionizing radiation with medical imaging procedures has generated

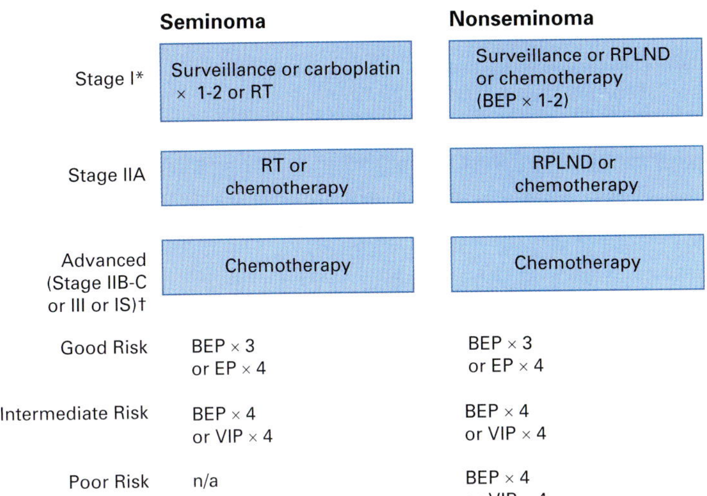

Seminoma
Nonseminoma
Stage I*
Surveillance or carboplatin × 1-2 or RT
Surveillance or RPLND or chemotherapy (BEP × 1-2)
Stage IIA
RT or chemotherapy
RPLND or chemotherapy
Advanced (Stage IIB-C or III or IS)†
Chemotherapy
Chemotherapy
Good Risk
BEP × 3 or EP × 4
BEP × 3 or EP × 4
Intermediate Risk
BEP × 4 or VIP × 4
BEP × 4 or VIP × 4
Poor Risk
n/a
BEP × 4 or VIP × 4

Fig. 14-25 Approach to management of germ cell tumors of the testis.

Approach to management of germ cell tumors based upon risk classification and stage.

Abbreviations: BEP, bleomycin, etoposide, and cisplatin; EP, etoposide and cisplatin; n/a, not applicable; RPLND, retroperitoneal lymph node dissection; RT, radiation therapy; VIP, etoposide, ifosfamide, and cisplatin.

*See text for high-risk criteria in stage I disease. †See text for advanced germ cell tumor risk stratification criteria

particular concern for young patients with germ cell tumors. Although one report suggested that the risk of secondary cancers was not associated with the amount of diagnostic radiation, the observation period was relatively short at only 11 years. To minimize radiation exposure from these repeated radiographic evaluations, MRI evaluations of the abdomen and pelvis can be substituted using specialized imaging protocols.

Patients with stage I disease for whom the risk of disease recurrence is high (> 50%) based on pathologic features—including embryonal carcinoma predominance (> 50%), and/or the presence of lymphatic, vascular, scrotal, or spermatic-cord invasion (stage IB)—may be considered for an ejaculatory nerve-sparing RPLND by a surgeon experienced in the procedure. RPLND is also considered for patients with a substantial teratoma component in the testis, because teratoma is a not responsive to chemotherapy. In a nerve-sparing RPLND, the sympathetic chains, postganglionic sympathetic nerve fibers, and hypogastric plexus are identified and spared, as feasible, to increase the likelihood of preserved antegrade ejaculation (non–nerve-sparing techniques may result in retrograde ejaculation and therefore impaired fertility). Surveillance in a compliant patient with stage IB is an accepted option and is preferred by some experts in the field. Low recurrence rates have been demonstrated in studies evaluating the use of short-course primary chemotherapy with one or two cycles of combination bleomycin, etoposide, and cisplatin (BEP) in patients with clinical stage I nonseminomatous germ cell tumors; however, some experts have concerns regarding the many men exposed to unnecessary chemotherapy, resulting in a potential for long-term adverse effects. The decision to recommend adjuvant chemotherapy after a RPLND is made on the basis of pathologic findings, as described for patients with pathologic stage II disease. Patients without evidence of clinical disease and persistently elevated levels of tumor markers, including β-hCG, AFP, or both after orchiectomy (stage IS), should receive standard chemotherapy for advanced disease rather than surgery.

Stage II Disease

The standard treatment of a patient with stage IIA disease (retroperitoneal nodes < 2 cm in diameter) is a modified, bilateral RPLND. In this procedure, the dissection becomes unilateral at the level of the inferior mesenteric artery. Experience with the technique is essential because, depending on the location of the tumor, an ejaculatory nerve-sparing procedure can be performed.

Approximately 20% to 25% of patients who have undergone a primary RPLND will have pathologic N1 (metastases with node diameter of ≤ 2 cm or five or fewer involved nodes)—in other words, an occult nodal metastasis that was not detected on preoperative imaging. In these patients, the risk of relapse is approximately 20%, thus surveillance is preferred in an adherent patient. With modern CT imaging, it would be rare to have occult N2 or N3 disease discovered at the time of primary RPLND (radiographic N2 or N3 disease would be treated with chemotherapy). The likelihood of micrometastatic disease outside the templated dissection is ≥ 50% for patients with pathologic N2 (an involved node diameter of > 2 cm, more than five involved nodes, or any extranodal extension). Assuming that serum tumor-marker levels return to normal after surgery, these patients should receive two cycles of adjuvant chemotherapy, which results in a 98% to 99% likelihood of cure. In patients with pathologic N3 (node diameter > 5 cm), three to four cycles of chemotherapy are administered. In circumstances wherein disease recurs or if the serum tumor-marker levels do not normalize, indicating residual active disease, then three to four cycles of chemotherapy and subsequent surgical excision of residual macroscopically documented disease, if present, are indicated (assuming that after chemotherapy, tumor-marker levels normalize), as is required for any patient with disseminated disease. Most patients with clinical stage IIB disease (nodes > 2 cm but not > 5 cm in diameter) are generally advised to receive primary chemotherapy rather than undergo RPLND.

Table 14-29 National Comprehensive Cancer Network Guidelines: Seminomas

Clinical Stage	Year (at month intervals)				
	1	2	3	4	5
Stage I seminoma: surveillance after orchiectomy					
H&P	Every 3-6 months	Every 6 months	Every 6-12 months	Annually	Annually
Abdominal Pelvic CT scan	At 3, 6, and 12 months	Every 6 months	Every 6-12 months	Every 12-24 months	
Chest radiograph	As clinically indicated, consider chest CT scan with contrast in symptomatic patients				
Stage I seminoma: surveillance after adjuvant treatment (chemotherapy or radiation)					
H&P	Every 6-12 months	Every 6-12 months	Annually	Annually	Annually
Abdominal Pelvic CT scan	Annually	Annually	Annually		
Chest radiograph	As clinically indicated, consider chest CT scan with contrast in symptomatic patients				
Stage IIA and non-bulky IIB seminoma: surveillance after radiotherapy or chemotherapy					
H&P	Every 3 months	Every 6 months	Every 6 months	Every 6 months	Every 6 months
Abdominal Pelvic CT scan	At 3 months, then at 6-12 months	Annually	Annually	As clinically indicated	
Chest radiograph	Every 6 months	Every 6 months			
Bulky clinical stage IIB, IIC, and stage III seminoma: surveillance after chemotherapy					
H&P and markers	Every 2 months	Every 3 months	Every 6 months	Every 6 months	Annually
Abdominal Pelvic CT scan	Every 4 months	Every 6 months	Annually	Annually	As clinically indicated
Chest radiograph	Every 2 months	Every 3 months	Annually	Annually	Annually

Abbreviation: CT, computed tomography; H&P, history and physical examination.
Adapted from NCCN® Guidelines.

Advanced Nonseminoma

Clinical stage IIC disease (nodes > 5 cm in diameter) and stage III disease should also be treated with chemotherapy (see section titled Management of Advanced Germ Cell Tumors by Risk Classification). Approximately 70% to 80% of patients with metastatic disease will be cured with cisplatin-based chemotherapy combined with surgery to resect residual disease as an integral part of management. The therapeutic objective is cure, with distinct approaches for disease deemed good risk (ie, high probability of cure is approximately 90%) and poor risk (ie, lower probability of cure is as low as 50%). For patients with good-risk disease, the goal is to minimize toxicity without compromising cure, whereas management of poor-risk disease focuses less on minimizing toxicity and more on increasing the probability of cure.

Postchemotherapy Surgery

Surgery after chemotherapy is an integral part of the treatment of patients with nonseminomatous germ cell tumors and should be considered for individuals with residual radiographic abnormalities but with normal serum tumor markers after treatment (Fig 14-26; Table 14-30). RPLND is the standard surgery for patients with evidence of disease in the retroperitoneum. All residual masses at all sites should be excised, because the histology at one site does not adequately predict the histology at other sites. Approximately 45% of residual masses will consist of necrotic debris or fibrosis, 40% will consist of mature teratoma, and 15% will harbor viable germ cell tumor.

In the case of residual viable germ cell tumor, some would treat with two additional cycles of chemotherapy. However, patients who have had a complete resection (no positive margins), < 10% viable tumor cells, and good-risk initial disease have a good prognosis and may not need adjuvant chemotherapy.

Although histologically benign, teratoma arises from malignant germ cells and may grow and undergo malignant degeneration over time; surgical removal is mandatory. In addition, a minority of resected teratomas will have malignant transformation to cell types including teratocarcinoma, rhabdomyosarcoma, adenocarcinoma, and others. Surgical resection is the mainstay of treatment; however, chemotherapy for metastases of a particular cell type may result in major responses and long-term survival in select patients.

Surgery is still important in patients with minimal residual disease after completion of first-line chemotherapy. In patients with minimal residual tumor masses (largest diameter of the residual mass on transaxial plane, ≤ 20 mm) after chemotherapy, approximately 66% will have complete fibrosis or

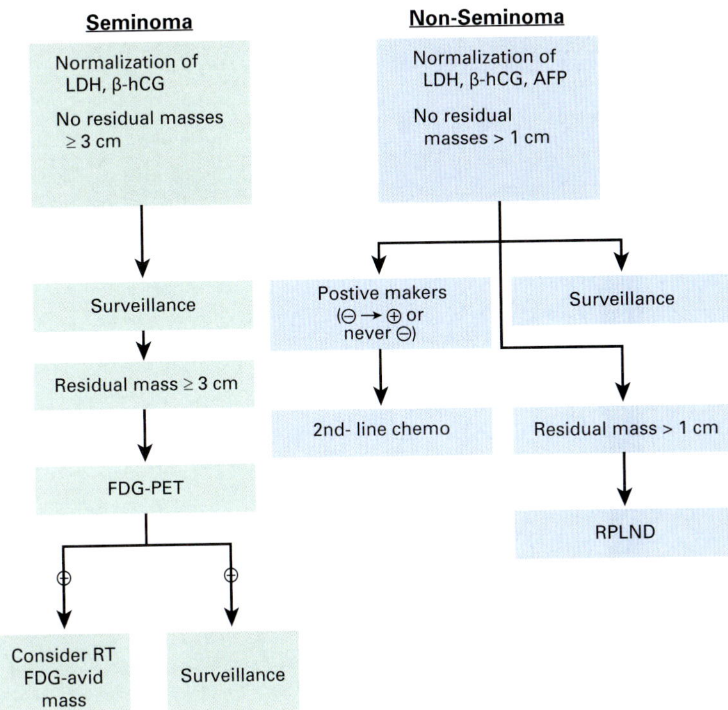

Fig. 14-26 Recommended follow-up postchemotherapy in advanced testicular cancer.

Abbreviations: AFP, α-fetoprotein; FDG, fluorodeoxyglucose; hCG, human chorionic gonadotropin; LDH, lactate dehydrogenase; PET, positron emission tomography; RPLND, retroperitoneal lymph node dissection; RT, radiation therapy.

necrosis, but 25% will have teratoma, and approximately 5% may have viable malignant germ cell tumor. Thus, approximately 33% of patients had vital tumor tissue with teratoma at risk for growth and/or malignant transformation and viable germ cell tumor at risk for progression. Many experts advocate for no surgery if retroperitoneal lymph nodes have normalized (residual mass < 1 cm) on CT scan, with a reported 15-year recurrence-free and cancer-specific survival of 90% and 97%, respectively, for a nonsurgical approach. With nonseminomatous germ cell tumors, FDG-PET scans are unable to distinguish fibrosis from teratoma, thereby limiting the utility of PET imaging in determining the histology of residual masses after chemotherapy.

Typically, RPLND is only performed in the setting of normal serum levels of tumor markers (with the caveat that borderline elevations in AFP or hCG may not be due to cancer, and LDH is very nonspecific). For patients who have elevated serum marker levels that do not normalize after second-line chemotherapy, RPLND may be considered selectively, because approximately 20% to 40% of patients will have teratoma present that could be surgically cured. However, this should not be used in patients with elevated hCG level and increasing tumor-marker levels, because these patients have a poor prognosis.

KEY POINTS

- Stage I nonseminomas are generally treated with active surveillance. Alternatives include RPLND or chemotherapy. Higher-risk features for recurrence include a substantial component of embryonal carcinoma and lymphovascular invasion.
- Stage IIA nonseminoma may be treated with RPLND, in which case the need for adjuvant chemotherapy is determined by the pathologic findings.
- Stage IIB and advanced (stages IIC and III) nonseminomas are treated with chemotherapy according to the risk-stratification scheme for germ cell tumors. Stage IS (ie, increasing levels of serum tumor markers in the absence of radiographic metastatic disease) is treated as stage II disease. Residual disease > 1 cm after chemotherapy should be resected, because of risk of residual viable tumor cells and/or teratoma.

MANAGEMENT OF ADVANCED GERM CELL TUMORS BY RISK CLASSIFICATION

The treatment of germ cell tumors is based on the International Germ Cell Consensus Classification, developed in 1996 (Table 14-31).

Good Risk

Approximately 60% of patients with nonseminomatous germ cell tumors present with good-risk disease. Patients with good risk include those with stage II or III disease with testis or primary extragonadal retroperitoneal primary tumors, no nonpulmonary visceral metastases, and good-risk tumor markers. The majority of patients with advanced seminoma have good-risk disease. According to results of clinical trials, > 90% of these patients will be cured with the use of combination chemotherapy, including cisplatin and etoposide with or without bleomycin (Fig 14-25).[26-31]

Table 14-30 **National Comprehensive Cancer Network Guidelines: Nonseminomas**					
	Year (at month intervals)				
Clinical Stage	**1**	**2**	**3**	**4**	**5**
Stage I without risk factors, NSGCT: active surveillance					
H&P and markers	Every 2 months	Every 3 months	Every 4-6 months	Every 6 months	Annually
Abdominal	Every 4-6 months	Every 6 months	Annually	As clinically indicated	
Pelvic CT scan					
Chest radiograph	At month 4 and 12	Annually	Annually	Annually	Annually
Stage I with risk factors, NSGCT: active surveillance					
H&P and markers	Every 2 months	Every 3 months	Every 4-6 months	Every 6 months	Annually
Abdominal	Every 4 months	Every 4-6 months	Every 6 months	Annually	As clinically indicated
Pelvic CT scan					
Chest radiograph	Every 4 months	Every 4-6 months	Every 6 months	Annually	As clinically indicated
Stage IA/B NSGCT: treated with 1 cycle of adjuvant BEP chemotherapy or primary RPLND					
H&P and markers	Every 3 months	Every 3 months	Every 6 months	Every 6 months	Annually
Abdominal	Annually	Annually			
Pelvic CT scan					
Chest radiograph	Every 6-12 months	Annually			
Stage II-III NSGCT: surveillance after complete response to chemotherapy ± postchemotherapy RPLND					
H&P and marker	Every 2 months	Every 3 months	Every 6 months	Every 6 months	Every 6 months
Abdominal	Every 6 months	Every 6-12 months	Annually	As clinically indicated	
Pelvic CT scan					
Chest radiograph	Every 6 months	Every 6 months	Annually	Annually	
Pathologic stage IIA/B NSGCT: after primary RPLND and treated with adjuvant chemotherapy					
H&P and markers	Every 6 months	Every 6 months	Annually	Annually	Annually
Abdominal	4 months after RPLND	As clinically indicated			
Pelvic CT scan					
Chest radiograph	Every 6 months	Annually	Annually	Annually	Annually
Pathologic stage IIA/B NSGCT: after primary RPLND and NOT treated with adjuvant chemotherapy					
H&P and markers	Every 2 months	Every 3 months	Every 4 months	Every 6 months	Annually
Abdominal	At 3-4 months	Annually	As clinically indicated		
Pelvic CT scan					
Chest radiograph	Every 2-4 months	Every 3-6 months	Annually	Annually	Annually

Abbreviations: BEP, bleomycin, etoposide, and cisplatin; CT, computed tomography; H&P, history and physical examination; NSGCT; nonseminomatous germ cell tumor; RPLND, retroperitoneal lymph node dissection.

Summaries of the trials are as follows:

- Four cycles of etoposide plus cisplatin or three cycles of BEP achieve a durable CR in approximately 90% of patients with good-risk disease.
- The elimination of bleomycin can compromise cure if only three cycles of therapy with etoposide and cisplatin are given or adequate doses of etoposide are not administered.

Three cycles of BEP are considered the standard therapy for good-risk germ cell tumors, but four cycles of etoposide and cisplatin—without bleomycin—is considered an acceptable alternative, especially for patients with risk factors for lung toxicity, based on two randomized trials suggesting similar OS but higher CR rates with BEP.

- Although carboplatin has less toxicity, it cannot be substituted for cisplatin, because it is less effective.

Bleomycin is associated with Raynaud phenomenon and pulmonary toxicity, although clinically significant pulmonary toxicity is rare.[36] Risk factors for bleomycin-induced lung toxicity include older age, a history of smoking, and impaired renal function.

Although bleomycin is not very myelosuppressive, the combination of etoposide and cisplatin does have significant myelosuppressive effects, and the risk of febrile neutropenia with etoposide and cisplatin may exceed 20%. Although NCCN guidelines would suggest primary prophylaxis with granulocyte growth factors for regimens with > 20% of febrile neutropenia, there have been some concerns about growth factors increasing the risk of lung toxicity of bleomycin.

Variability exists in practice about treatment modification for myelosuppression: some advocate for no delays in treatment regardless of myelosuppression, whereas others would consider a delay for absolute neutrophil count < 1,000 cells/uL. There is also variability in practice about use of granulocyte growth factors: some prefer to use them only if febrile neutropenia or dose delays due to neutropenia occur during therapy, whereas others would use them as primary prophylaxis, because the effect of growth factors on bleomycin-induced lung injury is not well established.

Etoposide carries some risk of secondary leukemia, and cisplatin carries well-known risks of renal toxicity, neuropathy, and ototoxicity, as well as some increase in thrombotic risk and long-term increase in cardiovascular events due to vascular irritation.

Intermediate Risk

The intermediate-risk group includes patients with nonseminomatous tumors with intermediate-risk tumor markers, as well as patients with seminoma who have nonpulmonary visceral metastases. These patients compose 20% to 30% of those with germ cell tumors and have a 5-year survival rate of approximately 80%. A regimen that includes four cycles of BEP is the standard treatment (Fig 14-25). An alternative regimen of four cycles of etoposide, ifosfamide, and cisplatin (VIP) is also acceptable and may be preferred in case of a contraindication to bleomycin, but it is more toxic and requires inpatient care.

Poor Risk

Patients with poor-risk disease include those with nonseminomatous germ cell tumors with nonpulmonary visceral metastases, poor-risk tumor markers, or primary mediastinal site. These patients compose 10% to 20% of those with nonseminomas and have a 5-year survival of approximately 50%. For patients with poor-risk disease, the standard of care remains four cycles of conventional-dose BEP. In patients with primary mediastinal nonseminomatous germ cell tumors, a report from Indiana University demonstrated a high rate of postoperative pulmonary failure and mortality after BEP, with a suggestion to substitute ifosfamide for bleomycin (ie, the VIP regimen) in the treatment of these patients who will undergo a major thoracic surgery,[45] but many experts still use BEP and may omit the last two doses before surgery. In this case, the anesthesiologist should be made aware of the prior history of bleomycin treatment and should use low fraction of inspired oxygen (FIO_2) during the surgery due to the unfortunate and often fatal complication of acute respiratory distress syndrome in patients previously treated with bleomycin who have diminished pulmonary function (decrease in diffusing capacity of the lungs for carbon monoxide [DLCO]) who were exposed to high FIO_2 and excessive hydration in the operative period.

Surveillance schedules after initial treatment are outlined in Table 14-30 and Table 14-31.

KEY POINTS

- Good-risk advanced germ cell tumors are treated with three cycles of BEP or four cycles of etoposide and cisplatin.
- Intermediate- and poor-risk advanced germ cell tumors are treated with four cycles of BEP or four cycles of VIP. Omission of bleomycin is not acceptable unless the patient is receiving VIP.

SECOND-LINE THERAPY FOR GERM CELL TUMORS

In 20% to 30% of patients with advanced germ cell tumors, the disease will not achieve a durable response to first-line chemotherapy regimens, including cisplatin and etoposide with or without bleomycin. These patients remain curable, although, unfortunately, the chance of cure is lower. Most relapses occur within 2 years of first-line chemotherapy. Late relapses (after 2 years) may also occur. In seminoma, this distinction does not influence treatment, but in nonseminomas, late relapses may be treated with a combination of chemotherapy and surgery with more favorable results than chemotherapy alone.

Paclitaxel, ifosfamide, and cisplatin (TIP) was evaluated as second-line therapy for patients with favorable prognostic features for response, including testis primary tumor site and a prior CR to a first-line chemotherapy program (Table 14-32).[84] Four cycles of TIP as second-line therapy resulted in a 70% CR rate to treatment, with a 63% durable CR rate and a 2-year PFS rate of 65%. The high level of activity with TIP as salvage therapy is related, in part, to the criteria used to select patients who are more likely to benefit from conventional-dose second-line therapy. Ifosfamide-based therapy has been associated with significant hematologic, renal, and neurologic toxicities, and the use of granulocyte growth factors is standard.

Table 14-31 **Chemotherapy Regimens for First-Line Treatment of Germ Cell Tumors**

BEP	VIP
Bleomycin	Etoposide (VP-16)
Etoposide	Ifosfamide plus mesna
Cisplatin	Cisplatin

EP is simply BEP minus the bleomycin.

The use of high-dose chemotherapy with peripheral stem cell rescue may be considered as second-line therapy for patients who do not have an initial CR to induction chemotherapy and as third-line therapy in those who experience a relapse after second-line therapy. The use of high-dose carboplatin and etoposide followed by peripheral-blood stem cell transplantation or autologous bone marrow transplantation rescue with a repeated course of therapy given after hematopoietic reconstitution was evaluated as second-line therapy in 65 patients with testicular cancer. Resection of residual disease was performed in selected patients after high-dose chemotherapy. At a median follow-up of 39 months, 37 of the 65 patients (57%) were continuously disease free, and three additional patients were disease free with surgery. The use of sequential, dose-intensive paclitaxel, ifosfamide, carboplatin, and etoposide with stem cell rescue was evaluated in 107 patients with germ cell tumors whose disease was resistant to cisplatin and who had unfavorable prognostic features for response to conventional-dose salvage therapy, including primary extragonadal site, incomplete response to first-line therapy, or relapse or incomplete response to ifosfamide- and cisplatin-based conventional-dose salvage therapy.[85] A total of 54 patients (50%) achieved a CR, and eight (8%) achieved a partial response with negative tumor markers. With a median follow-up of 61 months, the 5-year DFS was 47%; OS was 52% with no relapses occurring after 2 years.

Patients with primary mediastinal (extragonadal) germ cell tumors treated with high-dose chemotherapy and stem cell rescue demonstrate worse outcomes, and these patients should be enrolled in clinical trials at specialized centers. Treatment-related morbidity after high-dose therapy can be substantial, and all patients should be referred to major treatment centers specializing in this approach.

It is unclear whether standard-dose chemotherapy or high-dose chemotherapy should be used for patients whose disease recurs after prior chemotherapy. Two prospective, phase III trials that evaluated the role of high-dose chemotherapy versus standard-dose salvage therapy demonstrated mixed results. An important, ongoing phase III trial of initial salvage chemotherapy for patients with germ cell tumors (TIGER) randomly assigns patients with relapsed disease to TIP for four cycles (standard-dose chemotherapy) versus the paclitaxel, ifosfamide, carboplatin, and etoposide (high-dose chemotherapy) regimen (Fig 14-27).

KEY POINTS

- Germ cell tumors refractory to first-line chemotherapy are still curable, but the prognosis is worse.
- Options for second-line chemotherapy include standard-dose regimens such as TIP and high-dose chemotherapy with autologous stem cell rescue. Which strategy is superior is unknown, but high-dose chemotherapy is generally reserved for patients with poor prognosis features or as third-line therapy.
- Residual masses after second-line chemotherapy in nonseminomas should still undergo resection, as in the first-line setting.
- Pulmonary toxicity must be managed in patients treated with bleomycin, by continued monitoring of symptoms and DLCO. Bleomycin is discontinued if there are suggestive symptoms. Small asymptomatic drops in DLCO are common, but discontinuation is generally recommended for drops of ≥ 25%. For bleomycin-treated patients who subsequently require surgery, low intraoperative FiO_2 and minimal hydration should be used.

ASSOCIATED MALIGNANT DISEASE

Malignant transformation of a teratoma to somatic malignancies, including rhabdomyosarcoma, adenocarcinoma, primitive neuroectodermal tumor, and leukemia, as well as others, has been well described. The presence of i(12p) or excess 12p copy number in these tumors establishes the clonal germ cell tumor origin. The finding of i(12p) or excess 12p genetic material by either molecular or cytogenetic studies correlates with response to cisplatin therapy. Mediastinal nonseminomatous germ cell tumors also are associated with the presence of myeloproliferative disorders, including acute nonlymphocytic leukemia and acute megakaryocytic leukemia. A minority of patients with poorly differentiated carcinomas of unknown primary origin have a CR to cisplatin-based chemotherapy. The presence of additional clinical features, including male sex, predominant midline tumor, relatively young age, and elevated levels of serum tumor markers, has suggested that the minority of patients with poorly differentiated carcinomas of unknown primary origin may have germ cell tumors. Clinical features as well as molecular and cytogenetic studies are important in the management of carcinomas of unknown primary or midline tumors of uncertain histogenesis.

SEX CORD STROMAL TESTICULAR TUMORS

Nongerm cell testicular tumors are rare and comprise sex cord stromal tumors, including Leydig cell tumors, Sertoli cell tumors, granulosa cell tumors, and other extremely rare histologies. Leydig cell tumors are the most common among sex cord and stromal tumors. Unlike the more common germ cell varieties, Leydig cell tumors arise from interstitial cells of Leydig, one of the cell types that make up the interstitium along with cells of the seminiferous tubules. Two peaks of incidence are observed, in young childhood (ages 3 to 9 years) and mid to later adult life (ages 30 to 60 years). The clinical presentation is a painless testicular mass and can be accompanied by gynecomastia and other endocrine abnormalities. Ultrasonography shows a hypoechoic mass with areas of hypervascularity. Mutations in the luteinizing hormone receptor may be associated with Leydig cell hyperplasia. Levels of the common germ cell markers (serum and IHC), AFP, LDH, and hCG are normal. Specific diagnosis is established by IHC

Table 14-32 **Selected Treatment Regimens for Relapsed Germ Cell Tumors after First-Line Bleomycin, Etoposide, and Cisplatin Combination or Etoposide, and Cisplatin**

Chemotherapy	Regimen	Agents	Results
Standard dose	TIP[84]	Paclitaxel (Taxol)	Limited to patients with favorable prognostic factors
		Ifosfamide plus mesna	ORR, 63%; 2-year PFS, 65%
		Cisplatin	
	VelP	Vinblastine	Disease-free rate, 36% (including patients undergoing subsequent resection of masses); median survival, 12.7 months
		Ifosfamide plus mesna	
		Cisplatin	
High-dose with autologous stem cell rescue	TI-CE[85]	Two cycles of conventional-dose paclitaxel (Taxol) and ifosfamide plus mesna, followed by G-CSF followed by stem cell collection (leukapheresis)	Limited to patients with unfavorable prognostic factors
		3 cycles of high-dose carboplatin and etoposide followed by stem cell rescue each cycle	5-year DFS, 47%; OS, 52%

Abbreviations: DFS, disease-free survival; G-CSF, granulocyte colony-stimulating factor; ORR, overall response rate; PFS, progression-free survival; TI-CE, paclitaxel, ifosfamide, carboplatin, and etoposide; TIP, paclitaxel, ifosfamide, and cisplatin; VeIP, vinblastine, ifosfamide, and cisplatin.

staining with inhibin and melan-A. Staining for calretinin and vimentin is sometimes positive. Treatment is surgical removal, and long-term survival is generally very good. In the rare circumstance of metastatic disease, chemotherapy and RT are of limited usefulness.

SURVIVORSHIP

Cardiovascular Disease and Myocardial Infarctions

Long-term testicular cancer survivors appear to have a moderately increased risk of myocardial infarction associated with cisplatin-containing chemotherapy and/or infradiaphragmatic radiation. Short-term risk of venous thrombotic disease may also increase as a result of increased plasma von Willebrand factor levels and endothelial damage. In addition to chemotherapy-induced endothelial damage, cardiovascular toxicity also is likely related to metabolic syndrome and gonadal dysfunction.

Secondary Malignancies

Patients with testicular cancer treated with RT or chemotherapy have an increased risk of secondary malignancies for at least 35 years after treatment. Increased risks have been seen for cancers of the stomach, gallbladder, bile ducts, pancreas, bladder, kidney, and thyroid, as well as for soft-tissue sarcoma, nonmelanoma skin cancer, and myeloid leukemia.

Decreased Sperm Count and Other Late Effects

Patients with newly diagnosed testicular cancer are at risk for decreased sperm counts or impaired sperm motility, even before any treatment. With treatment, infertility can result from retrograde ejaculation after RPLND or as a result of RT or chemotherapy. Some, but not all, patients will have long-standing chemotherapy-induced oligospermia or azoospermia. Patients who are scheduled to have a RPLND, RT, or chemotherapy are advised to bank sperm. Other late effects of treatment include ototoxicity, chronic neurotoxicity, renal impairment, pulmonary toxicity, and anxiety disorder. In light of a young age at diagnosis and high cure rates, patients with testicular cancer require specialized follow-up care with close attention to monitoring for late effects of cancer and cancer therapy.

KEY POINTS

- Teratoma may undergo malignant transformation into teratocarcinoma, adenocarcinoma, or other histologies, generally as a late complication of unresected teratomatous components of nonseminomas. In a situation of diagnostic uncertainty, presence of isochromosome 12p points to a likely germ cell tumor origin.
- Nongerm cell testicular cancers are rare and include sex cord tumors, the most common being Leydig cell tumors. These can cause endocrinopathies and are typically cured via orchiectomy.
- Most patients with testicular cancer have long-term survival and are treated relatively early in life, so early and late complications of treatment are important to monitor and intervene, especially those related to the cardiovascular system. Cisplatin-based chemotherapy and/or RT may increase cardiovascular risks, risk of secondary malignancies, and infertility, among others. Patients treated with chemotherapy and/or RT should

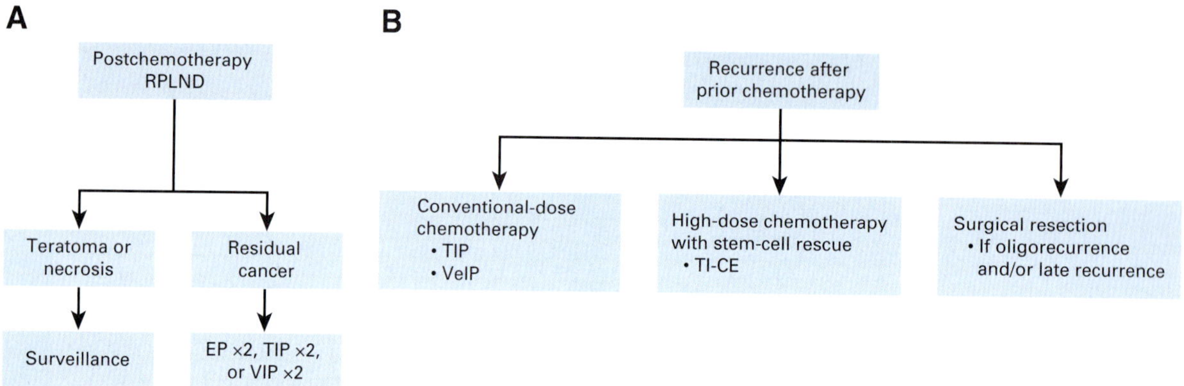

Fig. 14-27 Management following pathology from retroperitoneal lymph node dissection (RPLND).

Abbreviations: EP, etoposide and cisplatin; TI-CE, paclitaxel, ifosfamide, carboplatin, and etoposide; TIP, paclitaxel, ifosfamide, and cisplatin; VeIP, vinblastine, ifosfamide, and cisplatin; VIP, etoposide, ifosfamide, and cisplatin.

monitor and treat other cardiovascular risk factors including hypertension and adhere to age-appropriate cancer screening. These risks further justify avoidance of adjuvant therapies for most patients with stage I disease.

PENILE CANCER

EPIDEMIOLOGY, RISK FACTORS, AND HISTOLOGY

Penile cancer is rare in industrialized nations, with fewer than one case per 100,000 men per year and, in the United States, approximately 2,320 new cases and 380 deaths in 2018.[86] It is more prevalent in developing nations, and it is also more common among the elderly.

Positive associations have been described between penile cancer and human papillomavirus (HPV) infection, as have negative associations between penile cancer and circumcision that could be mediated by decreased rate of HPV infection in circumcised men. Phimosis, HIV infection, and tobacco exposure have also been described as risk factors, among others.

The vast majority of penile cancer is of squamous cell histology, although a few subtypes are identified, including verrucous carcinoma, papillary carcinoma, warty carcinoma, basaloid carcinoma, and sarcomatoid carcinoma. Warty and basaloid carcinoma may be more associated with HPV infection, especially HPV 16.

STAGING

A deep biopsy is necessary to obtain a specimen for adequate diagnosis and staging. Staging is according to AJCC criteria (Table 14-33). Invasiveness (increased T stage) or high-risk features (ie, lymphovascular invasion, perineural invasion, high grade) are classified as stage II, whereas clinical node involvement is classified as at least stage III.

Although many cases present with inguinal adenopathy, only approximately half will be due to nodal metastasis. Infection and/or inflammation, often with an odiferous component, can commonly cause adenopathy in conjunction with penile cancer. Clinical staging is performed based on the physical examination, although imaging can be helpful in the absence of overt adenopathy on examination, and PET imaging can be used in node-positive patients to evaluate for distant spread. Pathologic staging should be performed for men with high-risk features in the primary tumor. The standard method is with inguinal lymph node dissection, but this carries significant potential of morbidity, including lymphedema. Alternatives include fine-needle aspiration of any palpable lymphadenopathy or dynamic sentinel node biopsy (with lymphoscintigraphy or fluorescent dye labeling) at experienced centers.

For men with a negative clinical examination, the NCCN recommends lymph node staging based on pathologic features in the primary tumor, as follows:[87]

- low-risk (pTis, Ta, or T1a, grade 1): surveillance;
- intermediate-risk (pT1a, grade 2): sentinel node biopsy or inguinal lymph node dissection, with close surveillance also reasonable; and
- high-risk (pT1b or greater): sentinel node biopsy or inguinal lymph node dissection.

For men with palpable lymphadenopathy, strategies include:

- empirical antibiotics followed by re-evaluation, and
- fine-needle aspiration. If negative, an excisional biopsy or inguinal node dissection can be used in patients with sufficiently high risk.

Because distant metastasis occurs rarely and typically late in the disease course, if at all, imaging for detection of distant metastases may only be needed in patients with bulky regional nodal metastases or concerning symptoms.

KEY POINTS

- Penile cancer is a rare disease associated with age, lack of circumcision, HPV and/or HIV infection, and tobacco use.

- Penile cancer is typically of squamous histology.
- The primary pattern of spread is local invasion followed by inguinal lymph node metastasis. However, inguinal nodes may frequently be enlarged due to concomitant inflammation and infection. Evaluation of the inguinal nodes depends on the invasiveness of the primary tumor and whether the nodes are palpable.

TREATMENT BY STAGE

Stage 0: Tis or Ta, N0, M0

Also known as erythoplasia of Queyrat on the glans or Bowen disease on the shaft, penile CIS is a precursor lesion to invasive disease. There are no high-level data to guide decision-making, but treatment options include Mohs surgery, laser surgery, cryosurgery, and topical 5-fluorouracil cream or imiquimod cream.

Stages 1 and 2: T1a, N0, M0 or T1b-T3, N0, M0

Treatment options include circumcision for tumors limited to foreskin or, for more infiltrating tumors, surgical resection or RT.

Stage 3: T1-3, N1-2, M0

As noted, inguinal adenopathy may be due to infection or inflammation rather than cancer involvement. In the event of confirmed inguinal lymph node metastasis without distant metastases, bilateral ilioinguinal dissection is appropriate. If two or more nodes are involved, additional pelvic lymph node dissection may be considered.

Stage 4: T4 or N3 or M1

Distant metastasis is rare and occurs late in the disease course. There is no standard treatment of advanced penile cancer. Surgery and/or RT may be used for local palliation. Neoadjuvant chemotherapy has been used for patients with advanced tumors and/or adenopathy. A regimen of neoadjuvant TIP was tested in a phase II study of node-positive penile cancer patients and demonstrated a 50% response rate.[88]

Adjuvant Therapy

There are no high-level studies to guide treatment in the setting of high-risk, resected penile cancer. Adjuvant chemotherapy may be considered for patients who did not receive neoadjuvant chemotherapy and have high-risk features including pelvic lymph node involvement, extranodal extension, bilateral inguinal node involvement, or four or more nodes involved. TIP or other cisplatin-based therapy may be used. For patients who have received neoadjuvant TIP and have residual disease with extranodal extension or bilateral lymph node involvement, adjuvant RT to the inguinal/pelvic area may be considered.

Recurrent Disease

Local recurrence may be treated with penectomy if not already performed, or in some circumstances with a second penis-preserving treatment. Inguinal recurrence may be treated with neoadjuvant chemotherapy followed by node dissection or chemoradiation, but the prognosis is poor. For distant metastatic disease, cisplatin-based treatment may be used; the described neoadjuvant TIP regimen is considered the standard first-line therapy for patients with adequate performance status and renal function, despite lack of high-level data in the metastatic setting. Immune checkpoint inhibitors are being studied for this disease, but no data are available yet. High-dose methotrexate with leucovorin rescue has also been reported to provide benefit in an anecdotal case.

KEY POINTS

- Penile cancer is managed according to degree of tumor invasion and lymph node involvement. The primary treatment modality is surgery.
- Intermediate- or high-risk penile cancers should undergo assessment of lymph node involvement.
- Perioperative chemotherapy (such as the TIP regimen) and/or RT may be used for advanced tumors, but high-level evidence is lacking.

MALIGNANT ADRENAL TUMORS

Malignant adrenal tumors are extremely rare cancers, with only limited information to guide specific treatment recommendations. Malignant adrenal cortical carcinoma is derived from the adrenal cortex, with approximately 60% of cases associated with hormone secretion leading to symptoms and signs of hypercortisolism, virilization, and mineralocorticoid excess. Localized disease is managed with surgery. The overall prognosis is poor, particularly in patients with larger tumors (> 5 cm) and/or evidence of local invasion. The adrenocorticolytic agent mitotane is commonly used for patients with metastatic disease; however,

Table 14-33 **Penile Cancer: American Joint Committee on Cancer Staging**[94]

T	N	M	Stage
Tis	N0	M0	0is
Ta	N0	M0	0a
T1a	N0	M0	I
T1b	N0	M0	IIA
T2	N0	M0	IIA
T3	N0	M0	IIB
T1-3	N1	M0	IIIA
T1-3	N2	M0	IIIB
T4	Any N	M0	IV
Any T	N3	M0	IV
Any T	Any N	M1	IV

Republished with permission of Springer, from AJCC Cancer Staging Manual, 8th Edition (2017); permission conveyed through Copyright Clearance Center, Inc.

response rates are low with no clear survival benefit. Although several studies suggest higher response rates with chemotherapy plus mitotane, it is not at all clear that this translates into an improvement in outcome. There may be a benefit for mitotane in the adjuvant setting, and it is commonly used in patients at high risk of recurrence after surgery. In the advanced setting, the FIRM-ACT study compared mitotane plus a combination of etoposide, doxorubicin, and cisplatin every 4 weeks or streptozocin every 3 weeks and demonstrated significant improvements in response and PFS with toposide, doxorubicin, and cisplatin plus mitotane, but no difference in OS.[89] A phase 1b study of the PD-L1 inhibitor avelumab in previously treated adrenal cortical carcinoma demonstrated limited overall response rate but approximately a 50% disease control rate.[90]

Malignant pheochromocytomas arise from chromaffin tissue of the adrenal medulla and are extremely rare, accounting for approximately 10% of all pheochromocytomas. Functional pheochromocytomas secrete catecholamines and lead to an array of clinical symptoms, including the classic triad of headache, diaphoresis, and tachycardia (and episodic hypertension). The typical initial diagnostic test is either 24-hour urine collection for fractionated metanephrines and catecholamines or plasma-fractionated metanephrines (collected through an intravenous catheter placed 20 to 30 minutes prior and with the patient supine), being sure to stop all antiadrenergic medications beforehand. If abnormal, localization is performed with dedicated adrenal imaging. No curative therapy exists for malignant pheochromocytoma, and the mainstay of management includes surgical resection of the tumor, with preoperative α- and β-adrenergic blockade. Close collaboration with endocrinologists is essential. Data are limited, and no definitive recommendations regarding systemic therapy can be made; however, the association of pheochromocytomas with VHL has led to the use of VEGFR-targeted agents in this disease.

KEY POINTS

- Malignant adrenal tumors are extremely rare.
- After resection of localized adrenal cortical carcinoma, patients at high risk of recurrence may be considered for adjuvant mitotane.
- Adding mitotane to chemotherapy in the advanced setting increases response rates but not survival.
- Malignant pheochromocytoma is treated surgically, similarly to nonmalignant pheochromocytoma.

Acknowledgment

We wish to acknowledge and thank previous authors of this chapter, Matthew I. Milowsky, MD; and David M. Nanus, MD.

Global Oncology Perspective: Genitourinary Cancers

Cora N. Sternberg, MD; Dario Trapani, MD, and Alex Eniu, MD (Weill Cornell Medicine, New York, NY; Istituto Europeo di Oncologia, Milan, Italy; and Cancer Institute "Ion Chiricuta," Cluj-Napoca, Romania)

The United Nations has established sustainable development goals (SDGs).[128] Health- related SDGs comprise a comprehensive set of objectives for the well- being of humankind. For cancer, a noncommunicable disease, member states have committed to purse sustainable development to reduce associated cases of mortality by one-third by 2030, providing efforts to ensure universal health coverage. The term universal health coverage implies that everyone can have access to health care when they need it and where they live. However, disparities in life expectancy, effective control of the national disease burden, and chances to receive quality treatments still exist today.[129] Disparities in cancer outcomes are related to inequalities in access to care, resulting in wide gaps in cancer outcomes. Patients and their families can be thrust into extreme poverty due to cancer-related health expenditures. Catastrophic health expenditures affect primarily the poor and vulnerable populations in low- and middle-income countries (LMICs).[130]

According to WHO, disparities in access to cancer care are described across the entire cancer continuum: late-stage presentation and inaccessible diagnosis and treatment are common in LMICs. In 2017, only 26% of low-income countries reported having pathology services generally available in the public sector. More than 90% of high-income countries (HICs) have reported treatment services are available compared with < 30% of low-income countries. In low-income countries, the availability of pathology and surgery services for cancer and the availability of subsidized antineoplastic chemotherapy has been estimated to be as low as 30%. In theory, universal access to health care is everyone's ideal. Availability of a public health system, with equal access for everyone, however, is highly dependent on the country in which one resides.

Stronger and resilient health systems are capable of providing timely access to quality and safe treatments, built on evidence-based, robust governance systems.[131] Disparities in access to cancer care are described across the cancer continuum, from the control of risk factors and prevention to therapy and optimal palliative care.

Worldwide, genitourinary (GU) tumors accounted for 13% of all newly diagnosed tumors and 8% of cancer-related deaths in 2018.[127] Prostate cancer was the second most frequently diagnosed tumor and the most prevalent cancer in men. Overall, > 2 million people received a diagnosis of a GU cancer in 2018 and > 750,000 died of a GU cancer. Clear differences in outcome occurred in high-income countries (HICs) and LMICs (Table 14-34). For all GU tumors, a different life expectancy was reported across the different income areas. For instance, all mortality-to-incidence ratios were higher in LMICs as compared with HICs, suggesting a worse outcome in these populations.

Table 14-34 Global Landscape of Genitourinary Malignancies, 2018[127]

Tumor Type	Incidence (no.)	No. of Deaths	MIR[a]	MIR in HICs	MIR in LMICs
Prostate	1,276,106	358,989	0.28	0.19	0.42
Bladder	549,393	199,922	0.36	0.29	0.46
Kidney	403,262	175,098	0.43	0.34	0.55
Testicular	71,105	9,507	0.13	0.05	0.22
Penile	34,475	15,138	0.44	0.26	0.50

Abbreviations: HIC, high-income country; LMIC, low- to middle income country; MIR, mortality-to-incidence ratio.
[a]MIR is used as a parameter to estimate the health system performance for cancer care.

Few effective screening strategies exist for most GU tumors; thus, disparities in outcomes are primarily related to differences in education, awareness of risk factors, and social behavioral control (eg, cigarette smoking).[132] Cancer presentation at more advanced disease stage, lack of quality diagnostics, timely referral to specialists and appropriate treatments, as well as treatment abandonment due to the unaffordability of care, all contribute to the disparities in outcomes.

PROSTATE CANCER

Prostate cancer is a special case because overdiagnoses and overtreatments are commonly described in HICs as a result of uncontrolled PSA testing in the general population at average risk.[133] In addition, more aggressive biology of the disease in black African men is reported, partially justifying the differences in outcomes.[134] In central Africa, for example, prostate cancer is the most frequently diagnosed cancer in men and the primary cause of cancer mortality, with a mortality-to-incidence ratio of

0.61—among the highest in the world (Fig 14-26).[127,135] The reasons for this high burden and aggressiveness are not fully understood and warrant additional investigation of prostate cancer in LMICs to address similarities and differences in treatment approaches, including active surveillance policies, as well as the use of frontline chemotherapy and endocrine therapy alone or in combination. Until recently, men of African ancestry were thought to have more aggressive prostate cancer. In the United States, the incidence of prostate cancer is twice that of white men, and the mortality rate is approximately 2.5 times higher. Black men have been studied less frequently in genomic studies and have had less access to health care than white men.[136] Recent studies, however, reveal black men may respond better than white men to abiraterone, a hormonal drug frequently used in treatment of this disease.[137] However, despite the significant contribution in disease control of the new antihormone agents, cost may represent a major issue to access for enzalutamide and abiraterone, proved to be not cost-effective in LMICs and largely unaffordable.[138] According to one report, in 2019, enzalutamide and abiraterone could cost $10,000 per month in the United States, resulting in an annual cost of approximately $120,000 per patient. In fact, a lower-dose schedule of abiraterone has been proposed on the basis of pharmacokinetic and pharmacodynamic effects and included in NCCN guidelines as a more affordable option of treatment. The use of low- dose abiraterone, from 1,000 mg daily to 250 mg daily, would reduce the burden of costs by 75%, resulting in large benefits for patients and health systems. Interestingly, cost can be optimized with the preference for the generic abiraterone that appeared in the market at a cost discounted by 72%. Eventually, when hormone blockade is required, in any setting of prostate cancer care, nonpharmacologic hormone manipulations can still be realized in some patients, including bilateral orchiectomy for androgen ablation (Table 14-35 and Fig 14-28).

Table 14-35 **Age-Standardized 5-Year Net Survival for Prostate Cancer From CONCORD- 3**

5-Year Survival Range (%)	Countries
100	Puerto Rico, Martinique, United States
90-99	Brazil, Costa Rica, Canada, Israel, Japan, Korea, Australia, New Zealand, Europe[a]
80-89	Argentina, Ecuador, Uruguay; Malaysia, Singapore, Taiwan, Kuwait, Turkey, Europe[b]
< 80	Slovakia, China, Mauritius, Bulgaria, Thailand, India

NOTE. Data are from 5,864,878 men (age range: 15-99 years) diagnosed during 2010 to 201414 from 290 registries in 62 countries.
[a]European countries in this range: Iceland, Ireland, Finland, Latvia, Lithuania, Norway, Sweden, Italy, Portugal, Spain; Austria, Belgium, France, and Germany.
[b]European countries in this range: Denmark, Estonia, United Kingdom, Croatia, Malta, Slovenia, Czech Republic, Netherlands, Switzerland, Poland, Romania, and Russia.

BLADDER CANCER

Bladder cancer epidemiology presents some specific features in LMICs when associated with communicable disease (eg, *Schistosoma* infection).[139] In Egypt, bladder cancer is the second most diagnosed tumor in men, second only to liver cancer.[127] Both tumors are associated with transmissible causes of cancer, namely urinary schistosomiasis and virus-associated chronic hepatitis, respectively.[140] In this case, the most prevalent histology of bladder cancer is the squamous cell subtype, with different management and a worse prognosis than transitional cell carcinoma. A correlation between national income and bladder cancer survival has been reported,[141] more probably related to the need for a multimodal and multidisciplinary network of health providers to optimize the delivery of quality care, along with robust capacity to provide supportive care. Accordingly, this tumor can be significantly affected by the quality of the health care system, particularly in providing proper comprehensive, multidisciplinary integrated care. Notably, the cost for the management of bladder cancer is the highest per patient, from diagnosis to death, due to the high recurrence and progress rates in bladder cancer.[142] The lifetime cost in patients with nonmuscle-invasive disease is estimated as nearly US$100,000 to $200,000, and the total economic burden is estimated at 4.9 billion euros across the European Union. In the curative setting, the availability of financial and human resources is critical for the delivery of quality services, representing a trigger of disparities. Recently, an international shortage of BCG for the management of nonmuscle-invasive bladder cancer necessitated rationalizing and improvement of efficiency and cost-effectiveness of treatments.[143] Solutions have been provided, such as using one-third the dose and reducing the number of induction and maintenance courses of BCG therapy.

TESTICULAR CANCER

Testicular cancer is the most frequently diagnosed tumor in young men aged 20 to 35 years.[127] Testicular cancer is a highly curable disease, even when diagnosed in more advanced stages.[144] Treatment of testicular cancer is based on inexpensive essential medicines (chemotherapy) and supportive care.[145] However, disparities in the outcome between HICs and LMICs are still wide. This is clearly unacceptable for the young population affected in the most critical phase of family planning and professional productivity.[146]. In HICs in 2018, approximately 5% of patients diagnosed with testicular cancer, mainly germ cell tumors, died of their cancer.[127] This is in line with the benefit of multimodal treatments, resulting in high rates of cured patients. Introduction of cisplatin-based combination therapies in the late 1970s brought a significant decrease in mortality rates, with survival rates reaching 95%.[147]. However, in LMICs, almost one in four men with a diagnosis of testicular cancer did not survive in 2018. In low-income countries, mainly African countries, the mortality rate for this tumor approached 35% of diagnosed patients—more than one in three.[127] Critically, approximately 80% of deaths occurred in Africa, Asia, Central and South America, and the Caribbean. The majority of young men diagnosed with testicular cancer live in settings where the prognosis is poorer because access to proper health care is suboptimal.

PENILE CANCER

Penile cancer is a rare tumor in Western populations. The majority of the diagnoses occur in LMICs, where mortality is 2.5 times higher than in HICs.[127] Complexity is added in HIV-related penile cancer, because HIV infection is a modifying factor for high-risk HPV infections, enhancing and accelerating cancerogenesis.[140] In the context of HIV control and public health interventions for

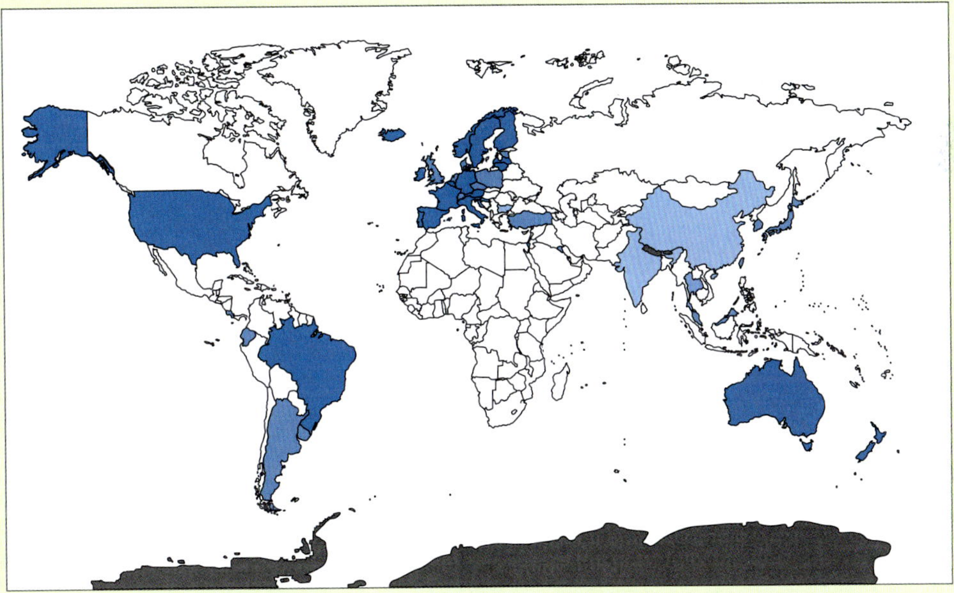

Fig. 14-28 Global map of survival for prostate cancer.
Data are from CONCORD-3. Light blue, 5-year overall survival < 80%; dark blue: 5-year overall survival > 90%.

cervical cancer, control of penile cancer can be expected to be optimized, with more widespread implementation of HPV vaccinations, as well as circumcision of male newborns.[148]

KIDNEY CANCER

Data on the epidemiology of kidney cancer are generally fragmentary, with difficulties in differentiating non–clear-cell histology from other tumor types. Registration according to the localization, histologic subtype, and stage at presentation from registries is often misleading.[149] In the absence of an effective strategy for early diagnosis, kidney cancer can present with vague symptoms, often as advanced disease. Surgery remains the cornerstone of treatment because no effective (neoadjuvant treatments significantly increase survival and there is no role for RT in early stages. For patients with metastatic disease, access to the majority of TKIs and virtually all the immune checkpoint inhibitors can present numerous barriers, including the unaffordability or nonreimbursement in many countries dominated by public health systems that struggle in setting priorities for the increasing cancer burden.[150] Currently, no medicine for the treatment of advanced disease is mentioned in the WHO list of essential medicines. This warrants additional investigation to improve the outcome of patients with advanced kidney cancer with tailored approaches to substantially improve access to affordable, quality, valuable medicines.

DISPARITY IN CARE

No easy response exists to address the disparities in the outcome of GU cancers worldwide. The gap between HICs and LMICs is vast and unacceptable, exposing vulnerable populations to a high risk of further impoverishment and to catastrophic health expenditure for them, their families, and subsequent generations.[151] The call of the United Nations, endorsed by WHO, to advocate for and support the realization of universal health coverage touches on every patient and every oncologist and must be framed on solid evidence that also enables research in and inclusiveness of LMICs, reorienting and reshaping the research agenda.[128] Many questions are still unanswered, but undoubtedly, more people die, suffer more, and struggle more in LMICs because of cancer, creating an unacceptable situation of global disparities.

What can be done? Is this disparity actionable? ASCO, ESMO, and their partner societies are collaborating to tackle cancer disparities through a value- based, priority-setting exercise with an emphasis on cancer medicines.[152] Also, efforts to provide adapted guidelines to the available resources have been emphasized, with the realization of resource-adapted guidelines as well as consensus guidelines that adhere to national and regional unique regulatory environments and actual potential of accessing treatments. A comprehensive, value- based, and context- appropriate approach must be pursued. Patients with GU cancer, as with all the patients, cannot be neglected because they are living in an LMIC or because of poverty. The time for action is now and we must all contribute to eliminate disparities in cancer care.

15

GYNECOLOGIC CANCERS

Don S. Dizon, MD, FACP, FASCO

Recent Updates

- The US Food and Drug Administration (FDA) approved bevacizumab in the first-line treatment of stage III or IV ovarian cancer, in combination with carboplatin and paclitaxel followed by its use as maintenance treatment, based on the results of the Gynecologic Oncology Group 218 trial. (Burger RA, *J Clin Oncol* 2018)
- The PD-1 targeting agent pembrolizumab was approved by the FDA for the treatment of recurrent or metastatic cervical cancer following disease progression on or after chemotherapy in patients whose tumors are positive for PD-L1. (Chung HC, *J Clin Oncol* 2019)
- The 2018 International Federation of Gynecology and Obstetrics staging system for cervical cancer now incorporates nodal involvement as stage IIIC disease, on the basis of either radiologic or pathologic information. (Bhatla N, *Int J Gyncaecol Obstet* 2018)
- The role of poly-ADP ribose phosphorylase inhibitors in the treatment of ovarian cancer continues to expand from treatments in recurrent disease to expanding options as maintenance treatment for women with newly diagnosed stage 3 or 4 disease following a response to platinum-based chemotherapy. (Moore, *N Eng J Med* 2018; Ray-Coquard, *Ann Oncol* 2019; Gonzalez-Martin, *N Eng J Med* 2019; Coleman, *N Eng J Med* 2019)
- The FDA expanded approval of the human papillomavirus vaccine for use in men and women ≤ 45 years old. The expansion of coverage was based on a study that showed vaccination was highly effective for women ≤ 45 years old.
- For women with newly diagnosed cervical cancer that is amenable to surgical excision, minimally invasive surgery (MIS) should be avoided. A randomized trial and separate database analysis both showed that compared with open laparoscopy, MIS is associated with significantly worse overall survival.

OVERVIEW

Each year, > 110,000 women are diagnosed with a gynecologic cancer, and > 32,000 die of their disease.[1] Although endometrial cancer is the most common gynecologic cancer, ovarian cancer remains the most fatal of the gynecologic malignancies. In this chapter, the epidemiology and clinical characteristics of the major gynecologic cancers are reviewed and established approaches to prevention and treatment are described. Areas of ongoing controversy in the management of these diseases also are reviewed.

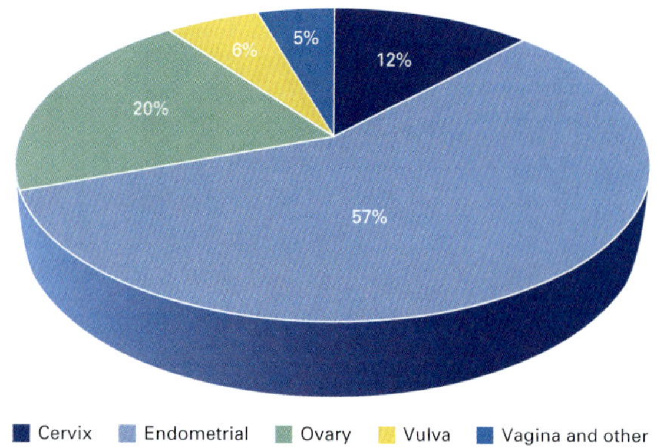

Fig. 15-1 Incidence of gynecologic cancers.
Adapted from Siegel et al.[1]

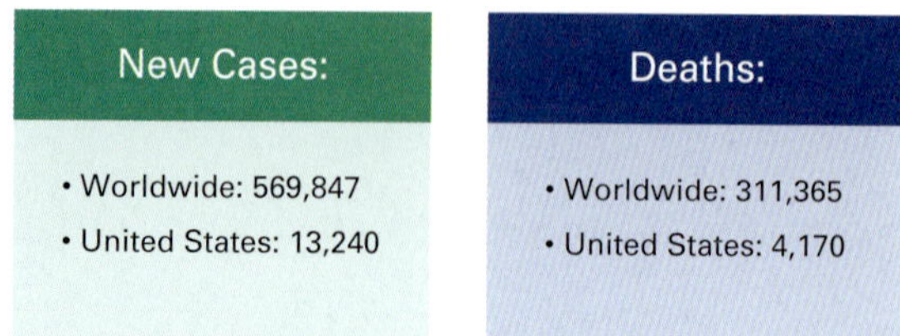

Fig. 15-3 Cervical cancer statistics for 2018.[2,73]

CERVICAL CANCER

EPIDEMIOLOGY AND PREVENTION

Within the United States, cervical cancer is the third most common gynecologic malignancy. The disease is more common worldwide, particularly in resource-poor regions where screening and prevention programs have not been fully established (Figs 15-1–15-3) and where cervical cancer is the leading cause of cancer death in women. The relatively slow growth rate of most cancers of the cervix, and the causal association with high-risk human papillomavirus (HPV) infection (Fig 15-4), means that HPV vaccination, HPV testing, and Papanicolaou smear screening (Fig 15-5) all offer opportunities for cancer prevention or early detection of preinvasive changes in the cells of the surface of the cervix, and thus can prevent the development of invasive cancer (Fig 15-6).

Risk factors for the development of cervical cancer include smoking (which increases the risk for persistent cervical dysplastic changes) and immunocompromised status (eg, HIV infection). Use of an intrauterine device has been associated with a lower risk for cervix cancer, independent of HPV status.

The vast majority of cervical cancers are either squamous cell carcinomas or adenocarcinomas, although there are rarer subtypes, including clear-cell and neuroendocrine cancers. These rare histologic types confer a worse prognosis and treatment often will require a specialized multidisciplinary approach.

It is widely recommended that women and men who are eligible for HPV vaccination receive it (Table 15-1). The recombinant 9-valent HPV vaccine received expanded approval to include men and women from age 9 through 45 years (it initially was approved for people ≤ 26 years old) on the basis of data from a randomized trial showing efficacy against HPV vaccination in women aged ≥ 26 years.[3] The vaccine is not effective in women with active HPV infection or cervical dysplasia.

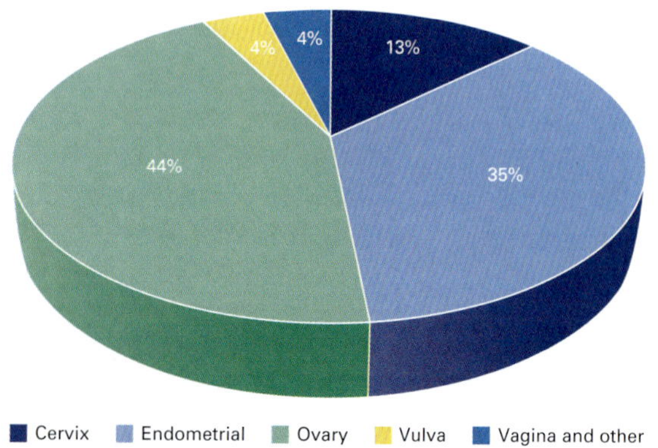

Fig. 15-2 Mortality from Gynecologic Cancers.
Adapted from Siegel et al.[1]

PATHOGENESIS

HPV infection is the leading cause of cervical cancer in women, accounting for > 90% of all cases in the United States annually. Approximately 70% of all cervical cancers are due to infection with high-risk HPV 16 or 18. Cervical cancer development requires four major steps (Fig 15-7). Notably, progression does not happen swiftly, taking up to 5 years to go from persistent infection to preinvasive disease. It also does not affect the majority of women with an HPV infection; cervical cancer will develop in < 10% of women infected.[4]

CLINICAL PRESENTATION AND STAGING

Most women are asymptomatic at early stages of cervical cancer. Symptoms of vaginal bleeding (ie, intermenstrual or postcoital), pelvic pain, and vaginal discharge, typically suggest the presence of more advanced disease.

Cervical cancer is staged by the International Federation of Gynecologic Oncology (FIGO) system, which was updated in October 2018. This version incorporates nodal involvement as

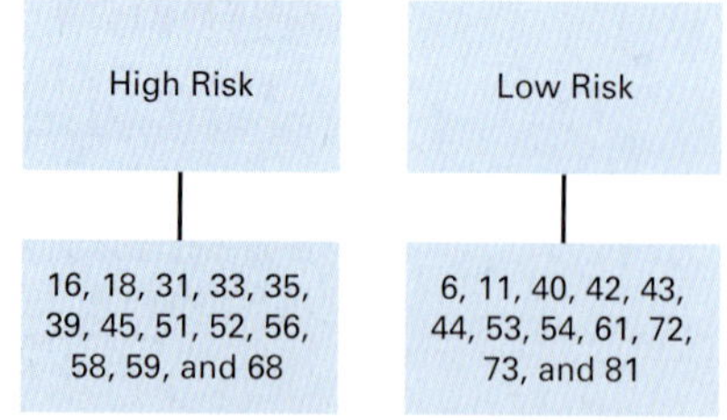

Fig. 15-4 Human papillomavirus serotypes and their risk for progression to cervical cancer.

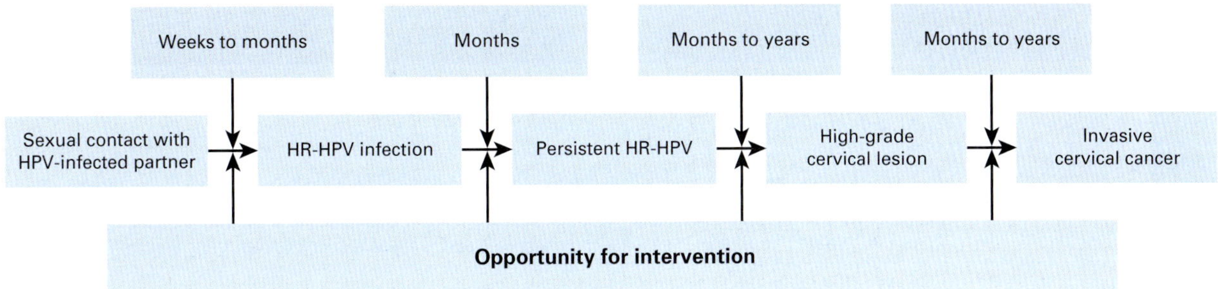

Fig. 15-5 Human papillomavirus infection and progression to cervical cancer.

Abbreviations: HPV, human papillomavirus; HR, high risk.

stage IIIC disease, with clarification if disease was detected radiologically or pathologically (Table 15-2).[5] In clinical practice in the United States, advanced imaging such as MR and PET are often used for staging (including to assess nodes) which yields important information for treatment planning.

CURRENT TREATMENT PRACTICE

Early Invasive Cervical Cancer

Early invasive cervical cancer is defined as stage IA or IB1 disease. For patients with stage IA or IB1 disease, long-term survival is excellent, with 5-year relative survival rates > 90%. The primary treatment is surgical (Fig 15-8). Results of two important clinical trials indicated women undergoing surgery for early-stage cervical cancer should undergo an open laparotomy rather than a minimally invasive approach.[6,7] In the Laparoscopic Approach to Cervical Cancer trial, > 600 women with stage IA1, IA2, or IB1 cervical cancer were randomly assigned to minimally invasive (MIS) or an open abdominal radical hysterectomy. Compared with open surgery, MIS was associated with a lower rate of disease-free (hazard ratio [HR], 3.74; 95% CI, 1.63 to 8.58) and overall (HR, 6.0; 95% CI, 1.77 to 20.3) survival.[6] For women with the lowest-risk disease (ie, lesion < 2 cm with no evidence of lymph node involvement) and who desire fertility preservation, options such as conization or removal of the cervix alone (ie, trachelectomy) are reasonable options to radical hysterectomy. Adjuvant treatment may be recommended as well, on the basis of final pathologic findings (Table 15-3; Fig 15-9).

Locally Advanced Cervical Cancer

Women with stage IB2 to IVA disease are characterized as having locally advanced cervical cancer. For these patients, the long-term survival rates range from approximately 70%, with greater odds of relapse if pelvic or para-aortic nodes are involved.[8] A multidisciplinary approach to treatment planning is critical to determine the approach associated with the best chance of cure for these patients. However, one should avoid surgery followed by chemoradiation for these patients, because multimodality treatment carries a high risk of short- and long-term toxicities (eg, bowel and bladder dysfunction). The primary approach to management is given in Figure 15-10.

Metastatic and Recurrent Cervical Cancer

The prognosis is poor for patients with de novo metastatic (stage 4B) cervical cancer and for those who have recurrence after primary treatment. For carefully selected patients who have an isolated pelvic recurrence within a previously irradiated field, an en bloc resection of the recurrence, which requires bowel and/or bladder resection (ie, pelvic exenteration), can be considered for potentially curative intent, though careful patient selection is key. For those who are not surgical candidates, standard first-line treatment of these

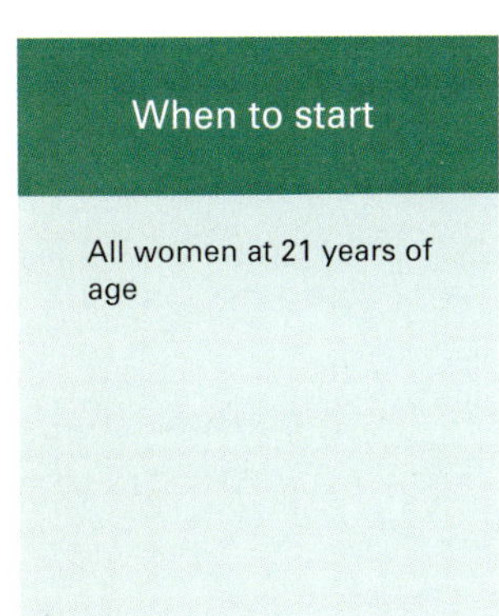

When to start
All women at 21 years of age
Frequency of screening
21 to 29 years: Every 3 years with cervical cytology at ages 30 to 65 years:
-Every 3 years with cervical cytology **OR**
-Every 5 years with high-risk HPV testing alone **OR**
-Every 5 years with cotesting (cervical cytology plus HR-HPV testing)
Screening not needed for:
Women < 21 years old or > 65 years old
Women who had hysterectomy and do not have a history of high-risk cervical changes

Fig. 15-6 Screening guidelines for cervical cancer.[74]

Abbreviations: HPV, human papillomavirus; HR, high risk.

Table 15-1 **HPV Vaccination**	
Vaccine	**Nonavalent (V503)**
HPV types included	6, 11, 16, 18, 31, 33, 45, 52, 58
Indications	
Schedule	Age 9-14 years: 2 doses (the second 6-12 months after the first) or 3-dose series (see below)
	Age 15-45 years: 3 doses (the second and third at 2 and 6 months, respectively, after the first)
Trade name	Gardasil 9 (Merck & Co, Kenilworth, NJ)
Status	Available

Abbreviation: HPV, human papillomavirus.

patients is systemic therapy with cisplatin, paclitaxel, and bevacizumab, based on the results of GOG 240, which showed that compared with chemotherapy alone, the addition of bevacizumab to chemotherapy increased overall survival (OS) by nearly 4 months.[9] Given the palliative nature of treatment, however, it is reasonable to substitute carboplatin for cisplatin because of its more tolerable toxicity profile, particularly in patients who were previously treated with cisplatin plus radiation therapy (RT).[10] In 2018, the FDA approved the immune checkpoint inhibitor pembrolizumab for treatment of women with advanced or cervical cancer after progression during or after chemotherapy for patients with PD-L1–positive disease or are otherwise found to have microsatellite instability high (MSI-H)/deficient mismatch repair (dMMR) tumors. The approval for treatment of PD-L1–positive cervical cancer was based on results of the KEYNOTE-158 phase II trial, in which > 90 women were enrolled and provided pembrolizumab for up to 2 years of treatment.[11] The overall response rate (ORR) was 12% and among women with PD-L1–positive tumors, it was 14.6%. Progression-free survival (PFS) at 6 months was 25% and median OS was 9.4 months. The assessment of PD-L1 is determined by the Combined Positive Score, which represents the number of PD-L1 staging tumor cells, lymphocytes, or macrophages relative to all viable tumor cells. A Combined Positive Score of one or more is considered positive. In the Keynote 158 trial, the PD-L1 IHC 22C3 pharmDx quantitative assay was used.

Approach to Women With Rare Cervical Cancers

Clear-cell and neuroendocrine tumors (including large- and small-cell carcinomas) account for 4% and up to 2% of all

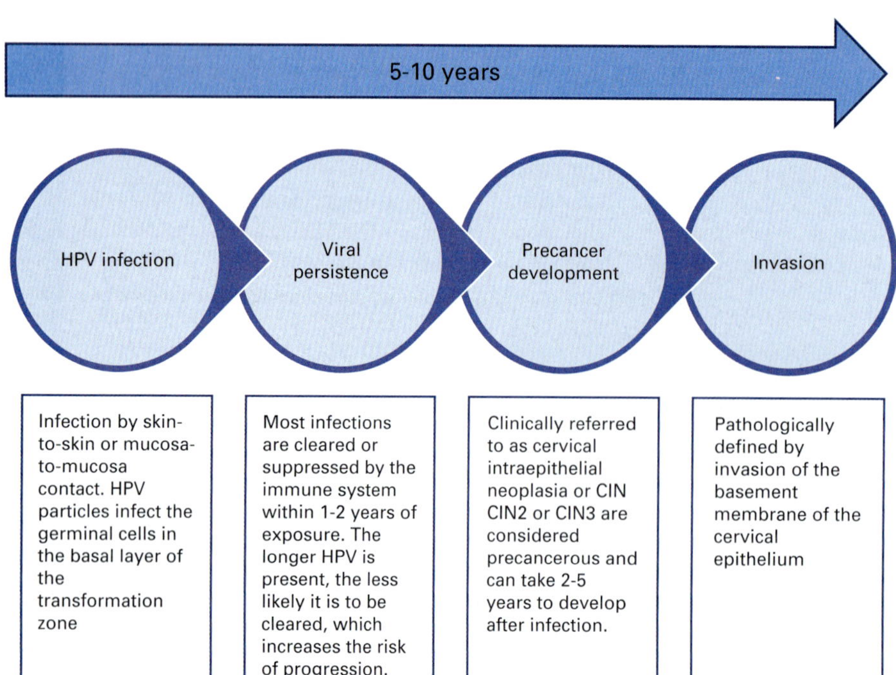

Fig. 15-7 Stepward progression from HPV infection to cervical carcinoma.

Abbreviations: CIN, carcinoma in situ; HPV, human papillomavirus; HR, high risk.

Table 15-2 **Cervical Staging**

AJCC Category	FIGO 2009	FIGO 2018	Criteria
Tumor			
Tx			Tumor cannot be assessed.
T0			No evidence of primary tumor
T1	I		Cervical cancer confined to the uterus
T1a	IA		Cancer detected by microscopy. Pathology shows maximum stromal invasion of 5 mm and horizontal spread ≤ 7 mm.
T1a1	IA1		Stromal invasion ≤ 3 mm
T1a2	IA2		Stromal invasion > 3 mm but ≤ 5 mm
T1b	IB		Cervical lesion is clinically visible or is microscopically larger than a T1a2 lesion.
T1b1	IB1		FIGO 2009: Lesion is ≤ 4 cm. FIGO 2018: Lesion ≥ 5 mm depth of stromal invasion, < 2 cm in greatest dimension
T1b2	IB2		FIGO 2009: Lesion is > 4 cm. FIGO 2018: Lesion is ≥ 2 cm and < 4 cm in greatest dimension.
		IB3	Lesion is ≥ 4 cm.
T2	II		Lesion invades beyond the uterus but does not involve PSW or lower third of vagina.
T2a	IIA		Tumor without parametrial invasion
T2a1	IIA1		Lesion is ≤ 4 cm.
T2a2	IIA2		Lesion > 4 cm
T2b	IIB		Tumor involves the parametria.
T3	III		Tumor involves the PSW and/or extends to the lower third of the vagina and/or causes hydronephrosis or nonfunctioning kidney.
T3a	IIIA		Tumor involves the lower third of the vagina but does not involve the PSW
T3b	IIIB		Tumor extends to the PSW and/or causes hydronephrosis or nonfunctioning kidney.
T4	IVA		FIGO 2009: Tumor involves the bladder mucosa, rectum, and/or extends beyond the true pelvis. FIGO 2018: Spread to adjacent organs
Nodes			
Nx	—		Nodes cannot be assessed.
N0	—		No regional node metastases
N0(i+)	—		Isolated tumor cells in regional lymph nodes ≤ 0.2 mm
N1	—	IIIC	Regional node metastases FIGO 2018: Positive pelvic and/or para-aortic node involvement, notation used for method of detection as radiologic (r) or pathologic (p)
		IIIC1	Pelvic lymph node metastases only
		IIIC2	Para-aortic lymph node metastases (± pelvic node involvement)
Metastases			
M0			No distant metastases
M1	IVB		Distant metastases (includes peritoneal spread or nodal involvement in the supraclavicular, mediastinal, or other distant nodal basins; visceral involvement)

Abbreviations: —, not used in FIGO 2009 system; AJCC, American Joint Committee on Cancer; FIGO, International Federation of Gynecology and Obstetrics; PSW, pelvic side wall.

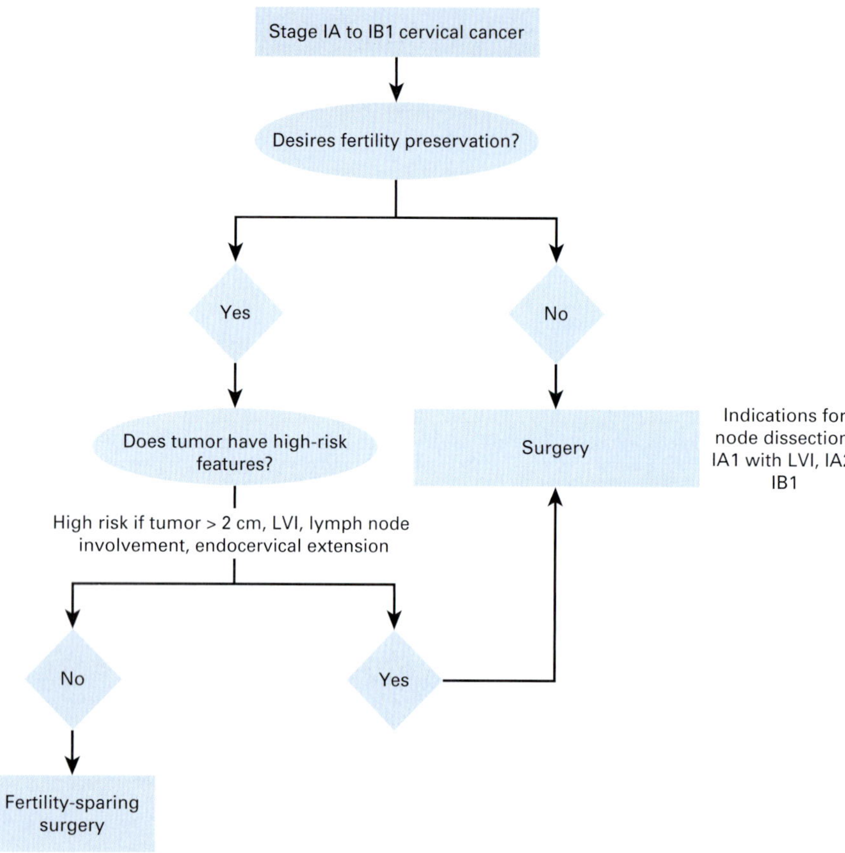

Fig. 15-8 Approach to early-stage cervical cancer.

Women with stage IA to IB1 cervical cancer are typically treated with surgery. Some patients may be candidates for fertility-sparing surgery, as indicated in the figure.

Abbreviation: LVI, lymphovascular invasion.

cervical cancers in the United States, respectively.[12] As such, there are no prospective trials to inform treatment, and clinical practice is extrapolated from the treatment of small-cell lung cancer, with platinum-based therapy typically administered. These patients are typically younger than patients with squamous cell carcinomas, are more likely have metastatic disease, and have poorer survival outcomes for all stages of disease.

SURVIVORSHIP

In general, the prognosis for women treated for cervical cancer is good, particularly for women diagnosed with localized disease: 5-year survival estimates are 66% and 91%, respectively.[2] Among women with regional node involvement, however, > 40% will die within 5 years.[2] Regardless of their risk of recurrence, women completing curative-intent treatment should be uniformly followed for recurrent disease with serial pelvic examinations every 3 to 6 months for 5 years and then annually.[13] As in other solid tumors, imaging should only be performed if clinically indicated. The general tenets of survivorship care espoused in the Institute of Medicine report[14] holds true for all woman treated for gynecologic cancers, including cervical cancer. Specific issues to the treatment of cervical cancer depend on the primary treatment modality.

Women treated with chemoradiation often develop premature genitourinary symptoms of menopause. For these

Table 15-3 Indications for Adjuvant Pelvic Radiotherapy in Early-Stage Cervical Cancer

Tumor Size, cm	Lymphovascular Space Invasion	Depth of Cervical Stromal Invasion
Any	Present	Deep one-third
≥ 2	Present	Middle one-third
≥ 5	Present	Superficial one-third
≥ 4	Absent	Middle or deep one-third

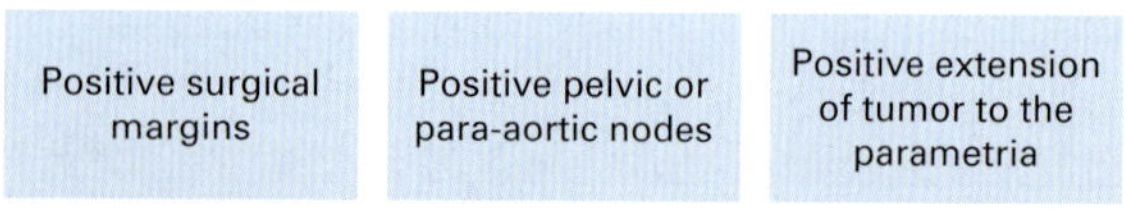

Positive surgical margins

Positive pelvic or para-aortic nodes

Positive extension of tumor to the parametria

Fig. 15-9 Indications for adjuvant chemoradiation for women with early-stage cervical cancer.

When administered, a dose of cisplatin 40 mg/m^2/wk is given during radiation therapy.

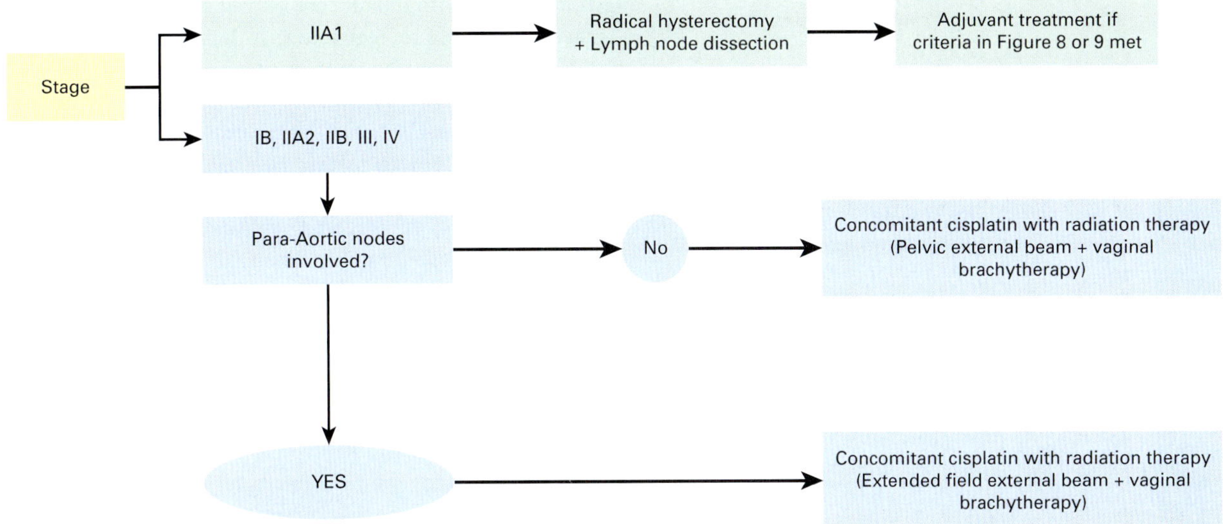

Fig. 15-10 Approach to locally advanced cervical cancer. Women with stage IIA1 disease are candidates for primary surgery. For these patients, the role of radiation with or without chemotherapy is based on final pathologic findings. For women with more advanced disease, imaging (typically positron-emission tomography/computed tomography scan) is required to evaluate for nodal involvement. Women with imaging evidence of pelvic node involvement should be offered a lymph node dissection to better define the field for radiation therapy. The presence of para-aortic node involvement (either suspected or pathologically confirmed) warrants the use of extended-field external-beam radiation therapy.

women, hormone replacement therapy should be offered, because there are no data to suggest it is associated with worse outcomes.[15] The choice of agent must take in to account whether the uterus is present; if it is, combined hormone therapy should be prescribed.

For women undergoing RT, a mainstay of treatment is vaginal dilators. Although there are no high-quality data to support its effectiveness, it is supported as a useful tool to prevent and treat vaginal tightening, adhesions, and shortening.[16]

Patients undergoing a pelvic and/or para-aortic lymph node dissection are also at risk for lower extremity lymphedema even years after surgery. Education and prompt referral for decongestive therapy are the hallmarks of management.[17]

SPECIAL POPULATIONS

Women With Renal Insufficiency

The treatment of women with renal insufficiency, whether acute or chronic, represents a major medical dilemma. All patients require a workup to rule out correctable causes of renal dysfunction, including ureteral obstruction due to cervical cancer. It is critical that any obstruction be addressed before treatment to allow for cisplatin therapy. For those women with chronic renal in sufficiency, consultation with a nephrologist is critical to determine the most appropriate therapy. If cisplatin cannot be administered, the use of an alternative agent such as carboplatin, gemcitabine, or fluorouracil can all be considered.

Older Women With Cervical Cancer

For women older than 65 years who present with cervical cancer, curative intent treatment should be offered, although they are at risk for more severe toxicities. In one study that included 75 women 65 years or older at the time of diagnosis, > 60% of those treated with chemoradiation (n = 30) completed treatment.[18] However, a higher percentage of those receiving cisplatin (n = 7 of 18) discontinued treatment because of toxicities, compared with those treated with carboplatin (n = 3 of 12).

KEY POINTS

- Cervical cancer is a sexually transmitted disease associated with a chronic infection of oncogenic types of HPV. HPV strains 16 and 18 account for 70% of cervical cancers.
- HPV vaccination represents an opportunity to reduce the worldwide occurrence of cervical cancer. The 9-valent vaccine available in the United States can be administered to men and women from ages 9 to 45 years.
- Although vaccination against HPV is now available, cervical cancer screening with Papanicolaou smear still remains an important part of health maintenance in women.
- The approach to invasive cervical cancer depends on whether a patient presents with early-stage or locally advanced disease. The FIGO staging of cervical cancer is defined by the tumor characteristics and nodal involvement.
- For women with early-stage cervical cancer, the treatment is primarily surgical. The indications for

adjuvant treatment using radiation with or without concomitant chemotherapy will depend on final pathologic findings, including tumor grade, presence of lymphovascular invasion, depth of stromal invasion, as well as whether there are positive surgical margins, and parametrial or nodal involvement.

- For most women with locally advanced cervical cancer, cisplatin plus RT are administered as curative treatment.
- For women with de novo metastatic (stage 4B) or recurrent cervical cancer, first-line treatment consists of cisplatin (or platinum-based chemotherapy), paclitaxel, and bevacizumab. Patients whose disease progresses after first-line therapy are candidates for pembrolizumab, provided their tumor is positive for PD-L1 expression or they are found to have MSI-H tumors.

ENDOMETRIAL CANCER

EPIDEMIOLOGY AND PREVENTION

Endometrial cancer is the fourth most common cancer in US women. Most (75%) women diagnosed with endometrial cancer are postmenopausal and approximately 70% of patients will present with early-stage, uterine-confined disease. Although the risk for endometrial cancer is 40% lower for black women than for white women in the United States, the mortality rate for black women is approximately 50% higher. Black women present with more advanced-stage disease and have a higher incidence of tumors of aggressive histology. The cause of this mortality discrepancy between black women and white women is likely complex, involving environmental, socioeconomic, and biological factors.

High body mass index (and thus, endogenous excess estrogen) was more likely to be associated with type I tumors than with type II tumors, but obesity also increases the risk of nonendometrioid histologies. Although women taking tamoxifen face a three- to seven-fold greater risk of endometrial cancer (compared with women who do not take the drug), its benefits for the treatment and prevention of breast cancer outweigh this risk. Symptoms include dysfunctional uterine bleeding and, as a result, routine pelvic (or transvaginal) ultrasound surveillance in otherwise asymptomatic women who received tamoxifen is not indicated.

Histologic subtypes of endometrial cancer include endometrioid adenocarcinoma, papillary serous carcinomas, adenosquamous carcinomas, and clear-cell carcinomas. Uterine carcinosarcomas are often included in the epithelial category; staging and treatment of these tumors are similar to the approach for more typical endometrial cancers. Because the predictive value of mismatch repair protein loss for the use of immune checkpoint inhibitors, immunohistochemistry testing for MMR is recommended, particularly for endometrioid histologies. Patients whose tumors show loss of MMR protein expression should be referred for genetic screening for hereditary non–polyposis colon cancer (HNPCC) syndrome. Prevention strategies have focused on the importance of healthy lifestyles, given the data indicating obesity is an independent risk factor for endometrial carcinoma.[19]

PATHOGENESIS

Historically, endometrial cancers have been classified as either type I or type II cancers (Table 15-4). The major risk factors for type I endometrial carcinoma are those typically associated with increased estrogen exposure. An integrated genomic analysis of endometrial cancer was conducted as part of The Cancer Genome Atlas and, based on mutation frequencies, tumors could be stratified into four groups:

Table 15-4 Clinico-pathologic classification of endometrial adenocarcinoma

Characteristic	Type I	Type II
Histology	Endometrioid	Serous
		Clear cell
		Carcinosarcoma
Estrogen dependent	Yes	No
Precursor	Endometrial intraepithelial carcinoma	Unknown
Prognosis	Good	Poor
Molecular alterations	PTEN loss (≤ 60%)	p53 mutation (90%)
	PIK3CA mutation (30%-40%)	HER2 overexpression (26%-80%)
	K-ras mutation (10%-20%)	PTEN loss (25%)
	FGFR2 mutation (12%-16%)	PIK3CA mutation (50%)
	Mismatch repair protein loss (20%-45%)	
	Peta-catenin accumulation (≤ 50%)	

(1) POLE ultramutated,
(2) MSI (hypermutated),
(3) copy-number low (endometrioid), and
(4) copy-number high (serous-like).[20]

These subgroups are associated with PFS, with POLE-type tumors having the best prognosis and those with low copy number (serous-like) having the worst prognosis.

CLINICAL PRESENTATION AND STAGING

The most common symptom associated with endometrial cancer is postmenopausal bleeding and blood-tinged discharge from the vagina. Therefore, all postmenopausal women with abnormal uterine bleeding require evaluation by endometrial sampling. Type II endometrial cancers may or may not present with bleeding, and for these patients, the presence of nonspecific symptoms (eg, abdominal pain, bloating, sexual dysfunction, changes in bowel or bladder habits) often herald more advanced disease.

Endometrial cancer is surgically staged, and all patients should be evaluated by a gynecologic oncologist. The standard surgical staging procedure for endometrial cancer includes hysterectomy, bilateral salpingo-oophorectomy, pelvic washings, and examination of the entire abdominal cavity. Whether nodal evaluation (including pelvic and para-aortic lymph node dissection) is necessary for all patients is controversial, but many recommend nodal staging for patients with risk factors such as deep invasion, lymphovascular space invasion, and grade 3 tumors (which include the higher-risk histologies: papillary serous and clear cell). In many centers, sentinel lymph node biopsy is now performed. The staging systems (American Joint Committee

Table 15-5 Endometrial Staging

AJCC Category	FIGO Stage	Criteria
Tumor		
Tx		Tumor cannot be assessed.
T0		No evidence of primary tumor
T1	I	Tumor confined to the uterine corpus.
T1a	IA	Tumor invades < 50% of the myometrium.
T1b	IB	Tumor invades ≥ 50% of the myometrium.
T2	II	Tumor invades the cervical stroma but does not extend beyond the uterus.
T3	III	Tumor involves the serosa, adnexa, vagina, or peritoneum.
T3a	IIIA	Tumor involves the serosa and/or adnexa (direct extension or metastasis).
T3b	IIIB	Tumor involves the vagina or parametria.
T4	IVA	Tumor involves the bladder or bowel mucosa.
Nodes		
Nx	–	Nodes cannot be assessed.
N0	–	No regional node metastases
N0(i+)	–	Isolated tumor cells in regional lymph nodes ≤ 0.2 mm
N1	IIIC1	Pelvic node metastases
N1mi	IIIC1	Pelvic node metastasis > 0.2 mm but ≤ 2.0 mm in diameter
N1a	IIIC1	Pelvic node metastasis > 2.0 mm
N2	IIIC2	Regional node metastasis to para-aortic nodes, with or without pelvic node metastases
N2mi	IIIC2	Para-aortic node metastasis > 0.2 mm but ≤ 2.0 mm in diameter
N2a	IIIC2	Para-aortic node metastasis > 2.0 mm in diameter
Metastases		
M0		No distant metastases
M1	IVB	Distant metastases (includes involvement of inguinal nodes, peritoneal cavity, bone, visceral organs)

Abbreviations: AJCC, American Joint Committee on Cancer; FIGO, International Federation of Gynecology and Obstetrics.

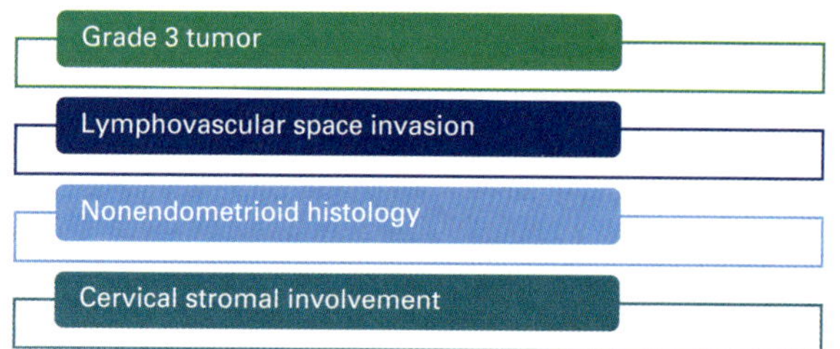

Fig. 15-11 Pathologic factors denoting high-risk endometrial cancer.[75]

on Cancer and FIGO) are listed in Table 15-5, with FIGO being the more commonly used staging system.

CURRENT TREATMENT PRACTICE

Adjuvant Treatment

For patients who undergo surgery with curative intent, there is no single approach to adjuvant therapy and the approach considers the presence or absence of high-risk pathologic factors (Fig 15-11). Patients with low-risk disease do not require additional treatment. However, the approach to patients with stage I, high-intermediate (Fig 15-12) and high-risk disease continues to evolve, and an individualized approach is often recommended. An algorithm to treatment decisions based on National Comprehensive Cancer Network guidelines is provided in Figure 15-13.

Three trials sought to clarify the appropriate adjuvant therapy for endometrial cancer, but the results have failed to do so. GOG 249 was a prospective, phase III study of patients with GOG-defined high-intermediate-risk, stage II (any histology), and stage I-II serous or clear-cell cancer. Patients were randomly assigned to whole pelvic radiation with or without vaginal brachytherapy versus adjuvant paclitaxel/carboplatin chemotherapy plus intravaginal brachytherapy.[21] With a median follow-up of 24 months, relapse-free survival (RFS) was the same in both treatment arms (82% pelvic radiation, 84% vaginal brachytherapy plus chemotherapy). GOG 258 enrolled women with stage III and IVA endometrial cancer and randomly assigned them to six cycles of paclitaxel/carboplatin chemotherapy or to an investigational regimen consisting of chemoradiation (cisplatin plus tumor-volume–directed RT) followed by paclitaxel/carboplatin for four cycles.[22] There were no differences in RFS between the two arms. Although local relapse rates were lower in the investigational arm, distant relapse rates were higher. PORTEC 3 enrolled women with stage I, grade 3 or clear-cell or serous histology plus myometrial invasion or stage II or III cancers and randomly assigned them to a standard treatment of pelvic radiation (plus vaginal brachytherapy if there was cervix involvement) or to cisplatin and radiation followed by paclitaxel/carboplatin for four cycles.[23] There were no differences in RFS or OS between the two arms. However, on subset analysis, there was a significant difference in RFS favoring the investigational arm.

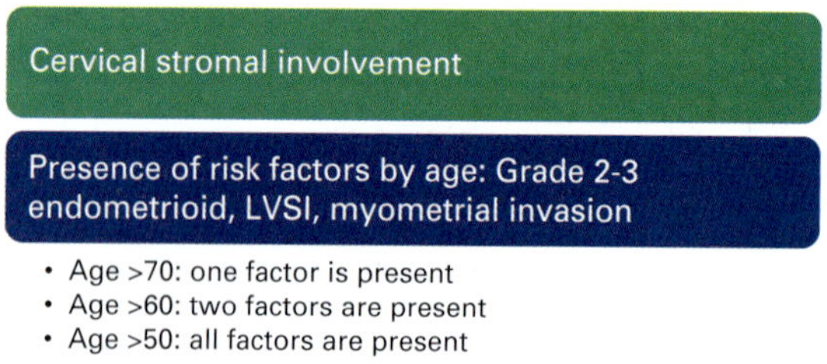

Cervical stromal involvement

Presence of risk factors by age: Grade 2-3 endometrioid, LVSI, myometrial invasion

- Age >70: one factor is present
- Age >60: two factors are present
- Age >50: all factors are present

Fig. 15-12 **High- to intermediate-risk factors in early-stage endometrial cancer.**

These factors help identify patients who may benefit from adjuvant radiation therapy.

On the basis of the results of PORTEC 3 and GOG 258, the role of chemoradiation in endometrial cancer is not clear. Future clinical trials will hopefully clarify the roles of chemotherapy and/or RT in these patients.

Advanced (Inoperable), Recurrent, or Metastatic Disease

Endometrial cancer is a hormonally sensitive malignant disease, regardless of tumor grade, and responses of up to 38% have been reported. Clinical features that are predictors of response to endocrine therapy include grade 1 or 2 histology, a long disease-free interval from diagnosis, and the presence of estrogen or progesterone receptors on the tumor cells. Strategies include the use of megestrol acetate, tamoxifen, aromatase inhibitors, or an alternating regimen of tamoxifen followed by megestrol acetate. Another strategy combines the mTOR inhibitor everolimus with letrozole. This was evaluated in a phase II trial conducted by NRG Oncology.[24] Among 38 patients, the ORR was 32%, with no patients stopping treatment because of toxicity.

For chemotherapy-naïve patients, carboplatin and paclitaxel are often prescribed. For patients requiring second-line therapy, there is no standard treatment. For patients with MMR protein loss or MSI-H, pembrolizumab was approved by FDA in May 2017. In 2019, the FDA approved the combination of lenvatinib plus pembrolizumab as an additional option on the basis of the results of a single-arm phase II study.[25] At 13-month follow-up, the ORR was 30%. Grade 3 toxicities included hypertension (34%) and diarrhea (8%).

SURVIVORSHIP

Women treated for endometrial cancer should be followed with a pelvic examination as part of their routine surveillance using a risk-based strategy (Table 15-6).[13] For women who experience premature menopause related to treatment, estrogen therapy is indicated because data do not show replacement is associated with negative cancer-related outcomes. Treatment also carries an increased risk of vaginal and sexual health complaints, as well as lower extremity lymphedema. Guidance discussed previously in this chapter for women treated for cervical cancer remains relevant for this population as well.

KEY POINTS

- Endometrial carcinomas are the most common gynecologic cancer. The major risk factors for endometrial carcinoma are those typically associated with increased estrogen exposure.
- For women who undergo surgical treatment, adjuvant therapeutic options include RT and/or chemotherapy. Postoperative risk factors are used to help determine who should be offered adjuvant treatment.
- Patients with high- or intermediate-risk disease are candidates for RT. Their risk is predominantly for a local relapse; hence, RT is administered to reduce the risk of this happening.
- Patients at high risk of recurrence should be offered chemotherapy and/or RT; an individualized approach is recommended.
- Patients with an endometrioid adenocarcinoma should be tested for MMR protein deficiency. This information may be important to identify patients who experience disease relapse as appropriate for treatment with pembrolizumab. It also is important to identify patients with Lynch syndrome.

UTERINE SARCOMAS

EPIDEMIOLOGY AND PREVENTION

Uterine sarcomas make up < 10% of all uterine cancers. The most common of these are leiomyosarcoma (LMS) and low-grade endometrial stromal sarcoma. Other variants include undifferentiated sarcoma and adenosarcomas. Unfortunately, there are no preventive strategies against these mesenchymal tumors. Of note, carcinosarcomas are not considered true sarcomas but a dedifferentiated carcinoma. As such, they are staged and treated as an endometrial adenocarcinoma.

PATHOGENESIS

Little is known about the pathogenesis of uterine sarcomas.

CLINICAL PRESENTATION AND STAGING

Uterine sarcomas typically present with nonspecific symptoms, including abnormal uterine bleeding, a pelvic mass, or abdominal pain or pressure. However, these are not pathognomic of sarcoma and are also common complaints among women ultimately diagnosed with leiomyomas. Uterine sarcomas are staged differently from endometrial adenocarcinoma, with separate staging for adenosarcoma and all other sarcomas (Table 15-7).

CURRENT TREATMENT PRACTICE

Leiomyosarcoma

LMS is a high-risk cancer of the uterine smooth muscle with a propensity for early hematogenous dissemination. Patients with uterus-limited disease have a 50% to 70% risk for recurrence. Despite this high risk of recurrence, there are no data to suggest adjuvant treatment affords a survival advantage. As a result, the standard of care is surgical. Tumor size is a prognostic indicator and a cutoff of 5 cm is used; nodal involvement is rarely encountered if disease is confined to the uterus. Adjuvant RT can be considered but has no impact on survival outcomes.

For patients with advanced, recurrent, or metastatic LMS, an anthracycline-based regimen is indicated. If contraindications to anthracyclines are present, gemcitabine plus docetaxel is a typical alternative; otherwise, the regimen is often used as a second-line therapy. Other active agents include doxorubicin, gemcitabine, ifosfamide, trabectedin, pazopanib, and dacarbazine.

Endometrial Stromal Sarcoma

Low-grade endometrial stromal sarcomas nearly always express estrogen and progesterone receptors. Although the risk for recurrence is approximately 30% for women with disease limited to the uterus at time of diagnosis, 10-year survival rates exceed 90% because of the indolent pace of progression. The treatment of choice is surgical and recurrence rates appear to be lower among women who have bilateral oophorectomy at the time of diagnosis. For patients who require medical therapy, endocrine therapy is typically administered.

Adenosarcoma

Adenosarcomas are tumors of mixed histology in which the sarcomatous portion looks similar to low-grade endometrial stromal sarcoma, and the "adeno" portion appears benign. Prognosis and management are similar to that for low-grade endometrial stromal sarcoma, unless there is evidence of sarcomatous overgrowth. Adenosarcomas with sarcomatous overgrowth are high-risk cancers, the prognosis and treatment of which are driven by the high-grade portion of the tumor. Surgery is the primary treatment of choice, with systemic or RT reserved for recurrent or metastatic disease.

High-Grade or Undifferentiated Uterine Sarcoma

High-grade endometrial stromal sarcomas are hormone-receptor negative and behave aggressively. Molecular diagnostics can distinguish these tumors from undifferentiated uterine sarcomas (Table 15-8); thus far, however, such classification does not dictate different treatment choices. Because of their rarity, there are no prospective studies addressing active agents for these tumors. Retrospective data and sarcoma treatment guidelines support treatment with doxorubicin-based or gemcitabine/docetaxel treatment. Enrollment in clinical trials for soft-tissue sarcomas is encouraged.

SURVIVORSHIP

The approach to women treated for uterine sarcoma is similar to the approach of women treated for endometrial cancer, with one exception: women with endometrial stromal sarcoma should not be prescribed hormone therapy, because these tumors express estrogen and progesterone receptors. Otherwise, the follow-up of patients may include routine chest radiograph and periodic imaging, as done for other soft-tissue sarcomas.

KEY POINTS

- Sarcomas are a heterogenous group of diseases accounting for 4% of all uterine cancers.
- Surgery is the mainstay of treatment for uterine sarcoma. There is no evidence that adjuvant treatment improves survival outcomes and adjuvant treatment is typically not indicated.

EPITHELIAL OVARIAN CANCER, FALLOPIAN TUBE CANCER, AND PRIMARY PERITONEAL CANCER

Epithelial cancers arising from the ovary, fallopian tube, or peritoneum (collectively referred to as ovarian cancer for the rest of this section) are the leading cause of gynecologic cancer death in the United States. Epithelial adenocarcinomas can be histologically subclassified as serous, endometrioid, mucinous, clear-cell, and low-grade serous carcinomas. A rare variant, small-cell carcinoma hypercalcemia-type, is a highly malignant type that typically affects women in their second decade. In 2014, mutations in *SMARCA4*, which plays a role in chromatin modification, was identified as a critical driver of these tumors.[26] Subsequent work also found loss of *SMARCA2*, as well.[27]

EPIDEMIOLOGY AND PREVENTION

In the normal-risk population, ovarian cancer will develop in approximately one woman in 70 in the United States. The mean age at diagnosis is 63 years. Increasing age is the strongest risk factor for the development of ovarian cancer. Family history is the next strongest risk factor after age. A woman with one first-degree relative with ovarian cancer has a relative risk of 3.6 for the development of ovarian cancer, meaning her lifetime risk for ovarian cancer is approximately 5%. Carriers of deleterious mutations in *BRCA1* or *BRCA2* have a lifetime risk of ovarian cancer estimated at 16% to 60%. Women with genetic mutations that are part of the HNPCC syndrome also are at increased risk for ovarian cancer, although the lifetime risk likely varies depending on the specific MMR enzyme mutation. Other germline mutations associated with increased risk for ovarian cancer include *BRIP1, RAD51C,* and *RAD51D.* Emerging data are elucidating whether there is a clinically relevant increased risk of ovarian cancer associated with other germline mutations. Other risk factors are shown in Figure 15-14.

At this time, there are no data to support the routine use of ovarian cancer screening of any type. However, women with a known genetic mutation associated with an increased risk of ovarian cancer are candidates for prophylactic bilateral salpingo-oophorectomy for risk reduction. Several studies indicate that performing a bilateral risk-reduction salpingo-oophrectomy may substantially reduce the risk for ovarian cancer for women who are carriers of deleterious *BRCA1* or *BRCA2* mutations (an approximately 80% lower risk for ovarian, fallopian tube, and peritoneal cancers, with average follow-up of 5.6 years from the surgery, and 77% reduction in all-cause mortality). For women without a mutation in *BRCA 1/2,* removal of the fallopian tubes during a pelvic procedure for benign indications—usually

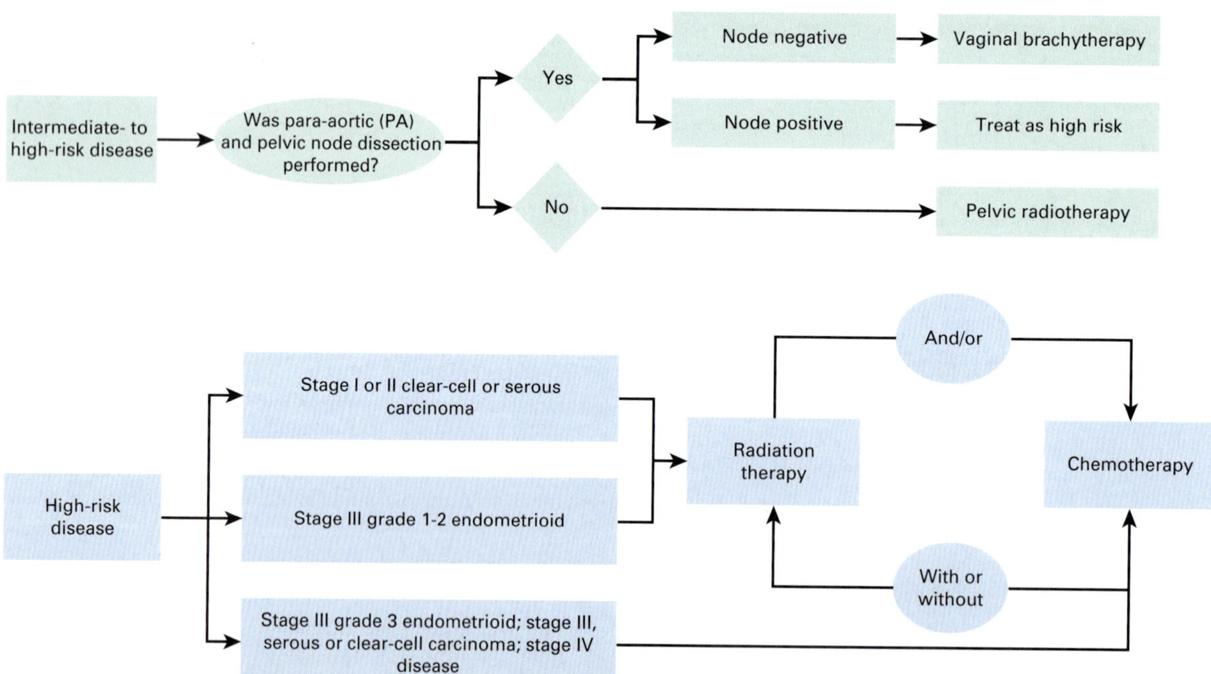

Fig. 15-13 Approach to endometrial cancer. Adjuvant treatment is offered to women on the basis of the presence of intermediate-to high- or high-risk features.

The primary modality of treatment is radiation therapy, which reduces the risk of a local recurrence. For women at high risk, adjuvant chemotherapy is often used. However, there is no consensus on the optimal approach to treatment, and an individualized treatment approach is recommended.

Table 15-6 Surveillance Guidelines for Women Treated for Endometrial Cancer					
		Pelvic Examination Frequency by Year			
Risk	Clinical Features	0-1	2-3	4-5	>5
High	Serous carcinoma (all stages) Clear-cell carcinoma (all stages) Stage III Stage IV	Every 3 months	Every 3 months	Every 6 months	Annually
Intermediate	Endometrioid carcinoma, grade 1-2, stage IB to II Endometrioid carcinoma, grade 3, stage IA	Every 3 months	Every 6 months	Every 6 months	Annually
Low	Endometrioid carcinoma, grade 1-2, stage IA	Every 6 months	Every 6-12 months	Annually	Annually

hysterectomy or tubal sterilization—referred to as an opportunistic salpingectomy, is being performed. However, removal of the tubes does not completely negate the risk of ovarian cancer.[28]

PATHOGENESIS

Contemporary data implicate the fallopian tube as the origin of high-grade serous ovarian cancer because high-grade intraepithelial carcinomas have been identified in the fimbria of women with a *BRCA 1/2* mutation who underwent bilateral salpingo-oophorectomy. Older case-control studies reported that endometriosis is associated with a three-fold increased risk of clear-cell carcinoma of the ovaries and a two-fold increase in the risk of low-grade or endometrioid carcinomas.

CLINICAL PRESENTATION AND STAGING

Patients with early-stage ovarian cancer often have nonspecific symptoms, including irregular menses (if premenopausal), urinary frequency, persistent bloating, and constipation. Most patients with advanced disease will present with symptoms reflecting advanced disease, including abdominal pain, bloating, dyspnea, emesis, early satiety, anorexia, and constipation. It is not uncommon for the initial presentation to include bloating related to large-volume ascites.

The definitive diagnosis of ovarian, fallopian tube, or primary peritoneal cancer is made by surgical exploration with stage assigned on the basis of the FIGO system (Table 15-9). Prognosis is linked to the amount of residual tumor after surgical cytoreduction (debulking surgery). Optimal cytoreduction has been defined as no residual tumor measuring > 1 cm at the end of the surgical procedure, although a more contemporary definition is no gross residual disease (R0 cytoreduction). Women who have > 1-cm disease at the end of surgery are deemed to have a suboptimal cytoreduction, conferring a worse prognosis.

ASCO and Society of Gynecologic Oncology practice guidelines recommend that all women with suspected epithelial ovarian cancer undergo evaluation by a gynecologic oncologist.[29] Women whose disease burden and medical status make it likely that an optimal cytoreduction will be possible with acceptable morbidity should be offered primary debulking surgery. Others should be offered neoadjuvant chemotherapy after histologic confirmation of the diagnosis of invasive epithelial ovarian, fallopian tube, or peritoneal cancer.

CURRENT TREATMENT PRACTICE

The approach to treating women with ovarian cancer is guided by whether patients are surgical candidates at presentation and, ultimately, by disease stage (Fig 15-15).

Early-Stage Ovarian Cancer

Patients with stage I ovarian cancer are classified as having early-stage ovarian cancer. Historically, women with stage II disease were included in this category, but contemporary data show it is associated with a less favorable prognosis. As a result, they are often considered in the group with advanced ovarian cancer and treated as such.

Not all women with early-stage ovarian cancer require adjuvant treatment. Patients with stage IA or IB grade 1 or 2 cancers have 5-year disease-free survival rates > 90% with surgery alone and can be spared the toxicity of adjuvant treatment. For patients with stage IA or IB grade 3 tumors, all women with stage IC disease, and those with clear-cell carcinoma, adjuvant chemotherapy is recommended. An analysis of data from > 900 patients with high-risk, early-stage

Table 15-7 Uterine Sarcoma Staging

Leiomyosarcoma and Endometrial Stromal Sarcomas		
AJCC Category	**FIGO Stage**	**Criteria**
Tumor		
Tx		Tumor cannot be assessed.
T0		No evidence of primary tumor
T1	I	Tumor limited to the uterus.
T1a	IA	Tumor size ≤ 5 cm
T1b	IB	Tumor size < 5 cm
T2	II	Tumor extends beyond uterus, within the pelvis.
T2a	IIA	Tumor without parametrial invasion
T2a	IIA	Tumor involves the adnexa.
T2b	IIB	Tumor involves other tissue in the pelvis.
T3	III	Tumor has infiltrated abdominal tissue.
T3a	IIIA	Tumor involves one site.
T3b	IIIB	Tumor has multisite extension.
T4	IVA	Tumor invades bladder or rectum.
Adenosarcoma		
Tumor		
Tx		Tumor cannot be assessed.
T0		No evidence of primary tumor
T1	I	Tumor limited to the uterus.
T1a	IA	Tumor limited to endometrium or endocervix.
T1b	IB	Tumor invades ≤ 50% of myometrium.
T1c	IC	Tumor invades > 50% of myometrium.
T2	II	Tumor extends beyond the uterus, within the pelvis.
T2a	IIA	Tumor involves the adnexa.
T2b	IIB	Tumor involves other tissue in the pelvis.
T3	III	Tumor has infiltrated abdominal tissue.
T3a	IIIA	Tumor involves one site.
T3b	IIIB	Tumor has multisite extension.
T4	IVA	Tumor invades bladder or rectum.
Nodes (all sarcoma)		
Nx	–	Nodes cannot be assessed.
N0	–	No regional node metastases
N0(i+)	–	Isolated tumor cells in regional lymph nodes ≤ 0.2 mm
N1	IIIC	Metastases to pelvic and/or para-aortic nodes
Metastases		
M0		No distant metastases
M1	IVB	Distant metastases (excludes adnexa, pelvic or abdominal tissues)

Abbreviations: –, criteria is not used in FIGO staging; AJCC, American Joint Committee on Cancer; FIGO, International Federation of Gynecology and Obstetrics.

Table 15-8 **Molecular Characteristics That May Help Distinguish Endometrial Sarcoma and Undifferentiated Uterine Sarcoma**

Tumor Type	Molecular Findings
Low-grade ESS	ER, PR positive
	Strongly positive for CD10
	t(7;17) Results in fusion of Zinc proteins (JAZF1/JJAZ1)
High-grade ESS	ER, PR positive
	CD10 negative
	Cyclin D1 positive
	BCOP (VCL6 coexpressor) positive
	t(10;17) Results in a 14-3-3 fusion to FAM22
	ZC3H7B-BCOR gene fusion
Undifferentiated uterine sarcoma	Variable
	Cycle D1 positive
	CD10 positive

Abbreviations: ER, estrogen receptor; ESS, endometrial stromal sarcoma; PR, progesterone receptor.

disease showed that adjuvant platinum-based chemotherapy led to an 11% improvement in 5-year PFS and an 8% improvement in 5-year OS compared with a strategy of observation.[30] Although patients are often recommended to undergo six cycles of therapy, the optimal duration of therapy is not clear. However, one randomized trial of women with stage I-II ovarian cancer showed those who received three cycles of therapy had a trend toward a higher risk of recurrence compared with women who received six cycles, though there was no difference seen in OS.[31]

Advanced Ovarian Cancer

For women with stage II or higher ovarian cancer who undergo primary surgical cytoreduction, a series of randomized, phase III trials have established combination platinum (cisplatin or carboplatin) and taxane (paclitaxel or docetaxel) chemotherapy as the standard of care for first-line treatment. Results generally have shown a significant improvement in overall survival with combination platinum/taxane regimens. The angiogenesis inhibitor bevacizumab, in combination with platinum and taxane chemotherapy and then used as single-agent maintenance treatment, has been approved by the FDA.

For patients who undergo an optimal cytoreduction (ie, residual disease ≤ 1 cm), intraperitoneal (IP) chemotherapy remains a reasonable option, although the toxicity of treatment, including abdominal pain, excessive nausea, and worsening neuropathy, have limited its adoption. In addition, if bevacizumab is administered in the upfront setting, there may be no advantage with IP therapy. This was shown in GOG 252, which compared one IP arm with two arms of IV treatment, with all patients receiving bevacizumab, and showed no survival advantage to IP therapy.[32]

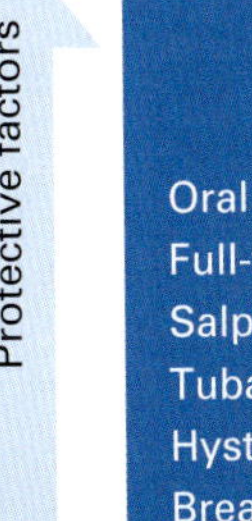

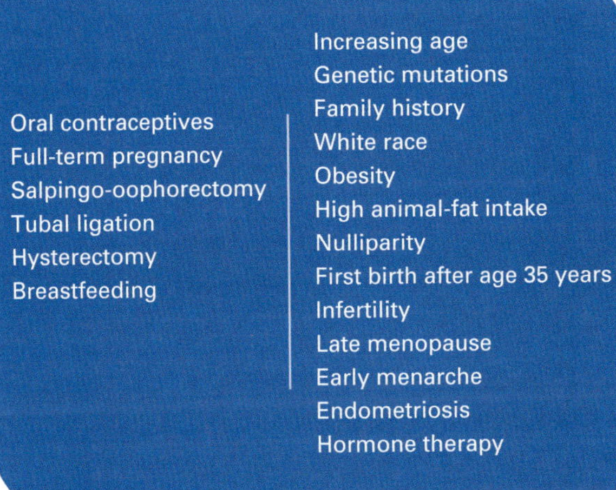

Fig. 15-14 Protective and associated risk factors for ovarian cancer.

Table 15-9 **Ovarian Cancer Staging**		
AJCC Category	**FIGO Stage**	**Characteristics**
Tumor		
Tx		Tumor cannot be assessed.
T0		No evidence of primary tumor
T1	I	Tumor limited to ovaries.
T1a	IA	Tumor limited to one ovary with capsule intact.
T1b	IB	Tumor involves both ovaries, but capsules are intact.
T1c	IC	Tumor involves one or both ovaries, with any of the following:
T1c1	IC1	Surgical spill
T1c2	IC2	Capsule ruptured before surgery or tumor on ovarian or fallopian tube surface
T1c3	IC3	Malignant cells in ascites or peritoneal washing
T2	II	Tumor involves one or both ovaries or fallopian tubes with pelvic extension below pelvic brim or primary peritoneal cancer.
T2a	IIA	Tumor extension and/or implants on the uterus and/or fallopian tube(s) and/or ovaries
T2b	IIB	Tumor extension to and/or implants on other pelvic tissues
T3	III	Tumor involves one or both ovaries or fallopian tubes, or primary peritoneal cancer, with microscopically confirmed peritoneal metastasis outside the pelvis and/or metastasis to the retroperitoneal (pelvic and/or para-aortic) lymph nodes.
T3a	IIIA2	Microscopic peritoneal involvement extending above the pelvis with or without positive retroperitoneal lymph nodes
T3b	IIIB	Visible metastases ≤ 2 cm
T3c	IIIC	Visible metastases > 2 cm (includes extension of tumor to capsule of liver and spleen without parenchymal involvement of either organ)
Node		
Nx	–	Nodes cannot be assessed.
N0	–	No regional node metastases
N0(i+)	–	Isolated tumor cells in regional lymph nodes ≤ 0.2 mm
N1	IIIA1	Metastases involves the retroperitoneal nodes.
N1a	IIIA1i	Nodal metastases ≤ 10 mm in greatest dimension
N1b	IIIA1ii	Nodal metastases > 10 mm in greatest dimension
Metastases		
M0		No distant metastases
M1	IV	Distant metastases
M1a	IVA	Pleural effusion (diagnosed by positive cytology)
M1b	IVB	Distant metastases (visceral, bone, nodes outside of abdominal cavity, transmural intestinal involvement)

Abbreviations: –, criteria not used in FIGO staging; AJCC, American Joint Committee on Cancer; FIGO, International Federation of Gynecology and Obstetrics.

The typical schedule of administration of carboplatin and paclitaxel (CP) is to use it every 3 weeks. Alternative approaches use a dose-dense schedule with either carboplatin and paclitaxel administered weekly (wCP), or with carboplatin administered every 21 days with weekly paclitaxel (CwP). These regimens were compared in the ICON8 phase III trial and, although presented only in abstract form, there was no difference in PFS among the three arms reported.[33] Compared with CP, CwP and wCP both had a higher frequency of grade 3 or 4 toxicities (63% and 53% *v* 42%, respectively).

The use of neoadjuvant chemotherapy in advanced ovarian cancer is favored for patients in whom a complete cytoreduction seems unlikely or when other circumstances are present that make patients poor surgical candidates at the time of diagnosis. ASCO and the Society of Gynecologic Oncology published

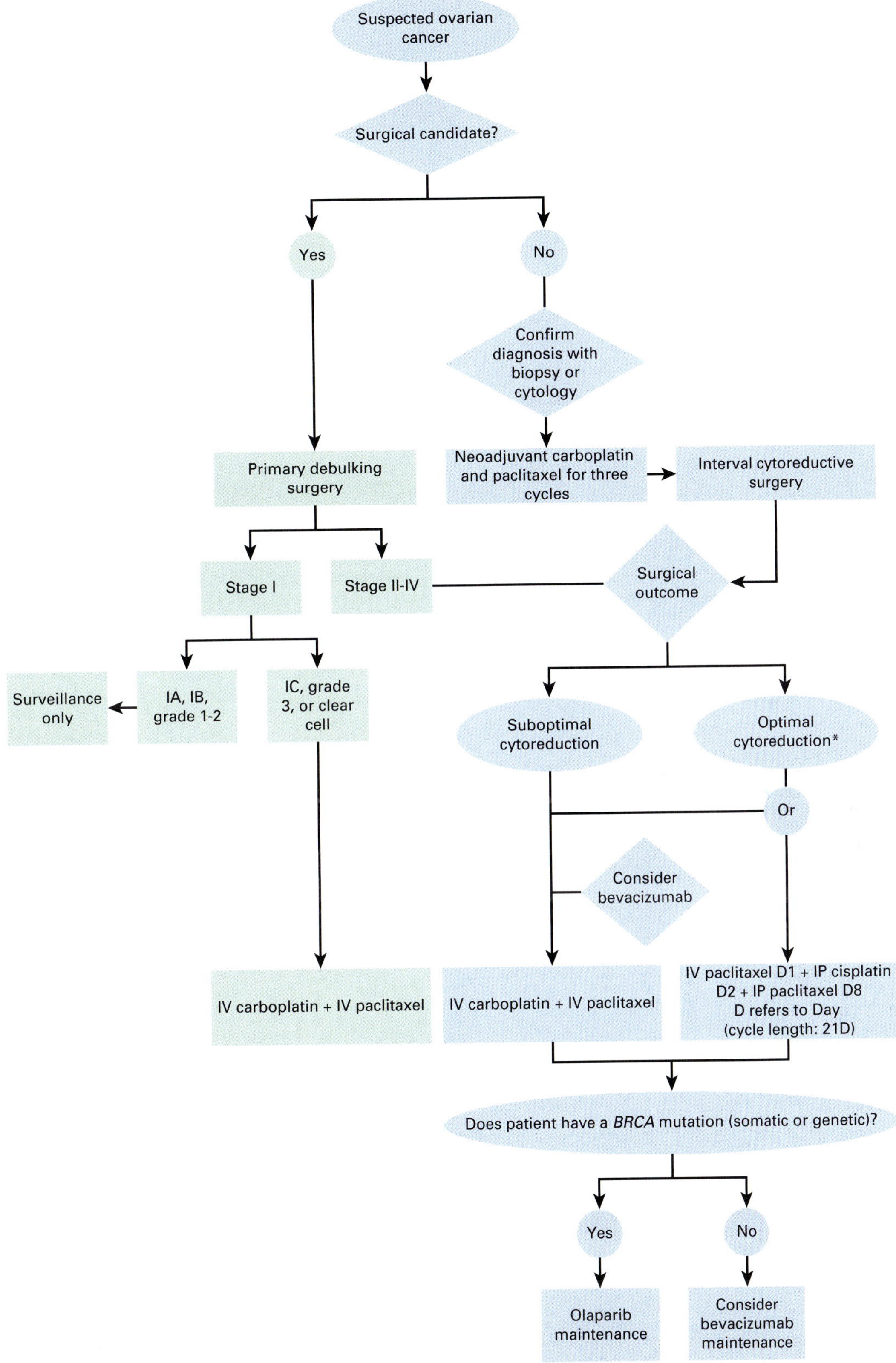

Fig. 15-15 Approach to ovarian cancer.

Abbreviations: IP, intraperitoneal; IV, intravenous.

*For women undergoing neoadjuvant chemotherapy and who achieve an optimal cytoreduction at interval surgery, heated intraperitoneal chemotherapy delivered at the time of surgery and then followed by IV carboplatin and paclitaxel was associated with a survival advantage compared with IV chemotherapy alone.

Table 15-10 Seminal phase 3 trials of Maintenance PARP Inhibitors in the First-Line Treatment of Advanced Ovarian Cancer

	Trial			
	PAOLA1	**PRIMA**	**SOLO1**	**VELIA**[a]
Characteristic				
Volunteers	All comers	All comers	BRCA-mutation associated	All comers
Intervention	Olaparib + bevacizumab	Niraparib	Olaparib	Veliparib
Comparator	Bevacizumab	Placebo	Placebo	Placebo
Hazard ratio for progression-free survival (*v* Comparator)				
All comers	0.59	0.62	–	0.68
BRCA 1/2 positive	0.31	0.40	0.31	0.44
HRD (any)	0.33	0.43	–	–
HRD positive (no BRCA)	0.43	0.50	–	0.57
HRD negative/unknown	0.92	–	–	0.81
HRD proficient	–	0.68	–	–
HRD unknown	0	0.85		–

Abbreviations: –, results not reported; HRD, Homologous Recombination Deficiency.

[a]VELIA enrolled volunteers in three arms: chemotherapy plus veliparib followed by maintenance placebo (combination only); chemotherapy plus veliparib followed by maintenance veliparib (veliparib throughout); or chemotherapy without maintenance (control).

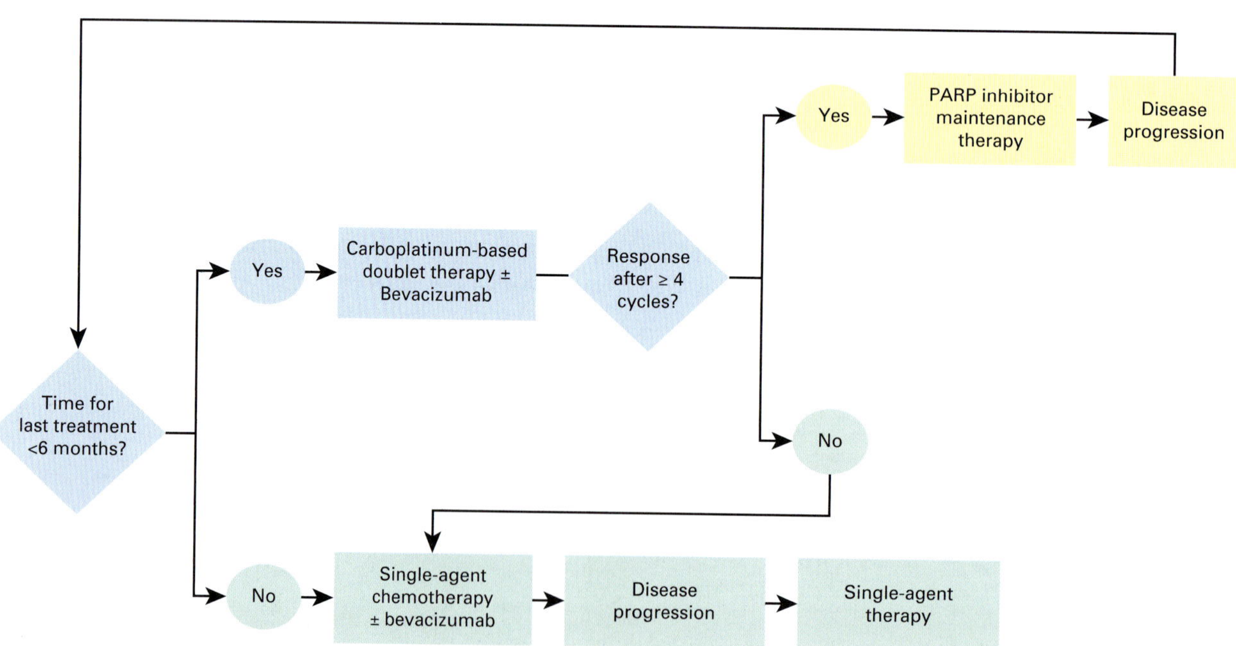

Fig. 15-16 Approach to recurrent ovarian cancer.

The treatment of ovarian cancer can be stratified by the time to recurrence from last platinum-based therapy or the platinum-free interval. For women with platinum-sensitive disease, retreatment with a platinum (usually carboplatin) containing doublet is favored. Data support the concomitant use of bevacizumab with chemotherapy. Once a response is achieved, bevacizumab can be continued as maintenance therapy. However, contemporary clinical trials have established a role for PARP inhibitors as maintenance therapy after a response to platinum-based treatment, particularly if bevacizumab is not used. For women with platinum-resistant disease, single-agent chemotherapy is preferred, with or without the addition of bevacizumab.

Abbreviation: PARP, poly-ADP ribose phosphorylase.

Table 15-11 PARP Inhibitors for Treatment of Recurrent Ovarian Cancer

Agent	Trial	Efficacy: PFS *v* Control
Recurrent platinum-sensitive disease, maintenance therapy after response to chemotherapy		
Niraparib	NOVA (n = 546)	BRCA 1/2 positive; HR, 0.27
		HRD positive; HR, 0.38
		BRCA wild-type, HRD negative; HR, 0.45
Rucaparib	ARIEL-3 (n = 564)	BRCA 1/2 positive; HR, 0.23
		HRD positive; HR, 0.32
		LOH high; HR, 0.44
		BRCA wild-type, low LOH; HR, 0.58
Olaparib	SOLO-2 (n = 295)	BRCA 1/2 positive; HR, 0.30
Recurrent disease as a treatment line		FDA approval
Olaparib		BRCA 1/2 positive; after ≥ 3 prior lines
Rucaparib		BRCA 1/2 positive or evidence of LOH in tumor, after ≥ 2 prior lines

Abbreviations: FDA, Food and Drug Administration; HR, hazard ratio; HRD, homologous recombination deficiency; LOH, loss of heterozygosity; PFS, progression-free survival.

clinical practice guidelines on the role of neoadjuvant chemotherapy supporting its use in appropriate candidates.[29]

For those who undergo surgery following neoadjuvant therapy (ie, an interval cytoreduction), the optimal treatment in the adjuvant setting is not yet clear. For women who have an optimal cytoreduction, limited data suggest that IP treatment may play a role; one randomized trial reported an OS advantage with heated intra-peritoneal chemotherapy.[34] Otherwise, the current approach for treatment of these patients disease is to continue platinum-taxane therapy (with or without bevacizumab), typically to complete a total of six cycles.

All women who complete adjuvant therapy should be offered maintenance therapy, although the optimal choice of treatment is not clear. Although bevacizumab is approved in this setting, randomized trials do not show treatment affects OS, although it improves PFS.

Poly-ADP ribose phosphorylase (PARP) inhibitors have emerged as another option for maintenance treatment of advanced ovarian cancer (Table 15-10). The impact of maintenance olaparib after completion of a platinum-based regimen was demonstrated in the SOLO1 trial that included 391 volunteers with advanced (stage III or IV) high-grade endometrioid or serous carcinomas and a known genetic or somatic *BRCA 1/2* mutation, who were randomly assigned in a 2:1 ratio to olaparib (300 mg twice daily) or placebo to be taken for a maximum of 2 years.[35] Compared with placebo, the risk of disease progression or death at 3 years was significantly reduced with maintenance olaparib (27% *v* 60%, respectively; HR, 0.30; $P < .001$). These data led to the FDA approval of olaparib in this setting.

Table 15-12 Olaparib and Rucaparib are FDA Approved as a Single-Agent Treatment

Drug	Dose	Eligibility
Olaparib	300 mg twice daily	Known germline BRCA-mutation carrier
		≥ 3 prior treatment lines
Rucaparib	600 mg twice daily	Known germline or somatic BRCA mutation or positive HRD status
		≥ 2 prior lines

Abbreviation: HRD, homologous recombination deficiency.

Results of three subsequent trials consistently showed benefits of PARP inhibition for all patients after a response to adjuvant platinum:

- In the PAOLA1 trial, 806 volunteers were randomly assigned to maintenance olaparib plus bevacizumab versus bevacizumab.[36] Compared with bevacizumab, combination with olaparib significantly improved PFS (median, 22.1 *v* 16.6 months, respectively; HR, 0.59; 95% CI, 0.49 to 0.72), with benefits seen in subgroups with a known *BRCA1/2* mutation and those with Homologous Recombination Deficiency (HRD).
- In the PRIMA trial, 733 volunteers were randomly assigned to maintenance niraparib therapy or to placebo.[37] Compared with placebo, niraparib resulted in significant improvement in PFS in those with HRD (median, 21.9 *v* 10.4 months; HR, 0.43; 95% CI, 0.31 to 0.59), without HRD (8.1 *v* 5.4 months; HR, 0.68, 95% CI, 0.49 to 0.94), and in the entire population (median, 13.8 *v* 8.2 months; HR, 0.62; 95% CI, 0.50 to 0.76). The benefits extended to those with HRD due to a *BRCA 1/2* mutation and those without it.
- In the VELIA trial, 1,140 volunteers were randomly assigned to one of three treatment arms: chemotherapy plus placebo followed by placebo maintenance (control), chemotherapy plus veliparib followed by placebo maintenance (combination only), or chemotherapy plus veliparib followed by veliparib maintenance (veliparib throughout).[38] Compared with the control group, PFS was significantly prolonged in

Table 15-13 **FDA-Approved PARP Inhibitors**

Agent; Reference[a]	Patients	Comparator	PFS (months)	HR; *P*
Niraparib; Mirza et al[40]	n = 553	Placebo	gBRCA: 21 *v* 5.5	0.27; < .0001
	High-grade serous tumors		No gBRCA: 9.3 *v* 3.9	0.45; < .0001
	Response after ≥ 4 cycles		HRD+:12.9 *v* 3.8	0.38; < .0001
			HRD−:6.9 *v* 3.8	0.58; .02
Rucaparib; Coleman et al[41]	n = 375	Placebo	gBRCA: 16.6 *v* 5.4	0.23; < .0001
	High-grade serous tumors		HRD+:13.6 *v* 5.4	0.32; < .0001
	Response to platinum		ITT: 10.8 *v* 5.4	0.36; < .0001
Olaparib; Ledermann et al[76]	n = 265	Placebo	Overall: 8.4 *v* 4.8	0.35; < .0001
	≥ 2 prior platinum-based regimens		mBRCA: 11.2 *v* 4.3	0.18; < .001
	Complete or partial response to most recent platinum			

Abbreviations: gBRCA, germline BRCA status; HR, hazard ratio; HRD, homologous recombination deficiency; ITT, intention to treat; mBRCA, BRCA mutation; PFS, progression-free survival; PARP, poly-ADP ribose phosphorylase.

[a]Randomized trial results of the Food and Drug Administration–approved PARP inhibitors as maintenance treatment for women with recurrent ovarian cancer after a response to platinum-based treatment. Of note, the use of PARP inhibitors in this context does not require the presence of a genetic or somatic mutation in *BRCA1* or *BRCA2*.

those receiving veliparib throughout, with benefits seen in the *BRCA 1/2* cohort (median, 34.7 *v* 22 months, respectively; HR, 0.44; 95% CI, 0.28 to 0.68), in the HRD cohort (31.9 *v* 20.5 months; HR, 0.57; 95% CI, 0.43 to 0.76), and in the intention-to-treat group (23.5 *v* 17.3 months; HR, 0.68; 95% CI, 0.56 to 0.83). There was no significant difference in PFS in the combination-only group compared with control treatment, suggesting that the benefit of veliparib is as a maintenance treatment, which would be consistent with the results of other PARP inhibitors.

Although impressive, none of the PARP-inhibitor trials have reported OS. This remains an area of intense investigation.

Table 15-14 **Serum Tumor Markers in Ovarian Germ Cell Tumors**

Marker	Tumor Type
Human chorionic gonadotropin	Embryonal cell carcinoma
	Choriocarcinoma
	Mixed germ cell tumors
	Dysgerminoma
α Feto-protein	Yolk sac tumors
	Embryonal cell carcinoma
	Polyembryoma carcinoma
	Mixed germ cell tumors
	Immature teratomas
Lactate dehydrogenase	Dysgerminoma

Recurrent Ovarian Cancer

The approach to recurrent ovarian cancer is often based on whether the recurrent disease is platinum resistant (defined as progressing within < 6 months of completing first-line platinum-based therapy) or platinum sensitive (defined as recurrence ≥ 6 months after the completion of first-line platinum-based therapy) (Fig 15-16). All patients with recurrent ovarian cancer are appropriate candidates for clinical trial participation because no current strategy is known to result in long-term disease control or cure.

For women with a platinum-sensitive disease recurrence, the typical recommendation is to offer retreatment with a carboplatin in combination with paclitaxel, liposomal doxorubicin, or gemcitabine, with or without bevacizumab, which can then be continued as maintenance therapy. An additional option after a response to platinum-based treatment is to stop all intravenous therapy in favor of a PARP inhibitor (Table 15-11). Notably, the use of a PARP inhibitor in this context is not restricted only to those harboring a genomic or somatic mutation in *BRCA1* or *BRCA2*, which was used to select volunteers in the SOLO-2 trial[39]; rather, trials that evaluated niraparib[40] and rucaparib[41] showed that compared with placebo, treatment benefitted all patients. The primary adverse effects are similar with all the commercially available agents and include GI toxicities (eg, diarrhea, nausea, anorexia) and myelosuppression (eg, neutropenia, anemia, thrombocytopenia).

For women with a platinum-resistant disease recurrence, use of sequential single-agent chemotherapy is often advised. However, data from a randomized trial showed that, compared with single-agent therapy (ie, weekly paclitaxel, liposomal doxorubicin, or weekly topotecan), the combination of bevacizumab plus chemotherapy improved PFS,[42] which led to the approval of bevacizumab in this setting.

For women who have previously received chemotherapy and have a known genetic or somatic mutation in *BRCA* or other evidence of homologous recombination deficiency, both olaparib and rucaparib are FDA approved as a single-agent treatment (Table 15-12).

Women With a Germline or Somatic Mutation in BRCA

All women should be referred for genetic counseling at diagnosis because the information can affect treatment in the first and/or subsequent line of treatment. For those who present with advanced ovarian cancer, for those whose disease recurs and responds to platinum, all three FDA-approved PARP inhibitors showed consistent and statistically significant benefits in PFS (Table 15-13). A subsequent trial specifically evaluated the magnitude of benefits of maintenance PARP inhibition among women with mBRCA-positive recurrent ovarian cancer.[39] Compared with placebo, olaparib (dosed in tablet formulation) significantly improved PFS (5.5 *v* 19.1 months, respectively; HR, 0.30; $P < .0001$) and the time to first subsequent treatment or death (7.1 *v* 27.9 months respectively; HR, 0.28; $P < .0001$).

SURVIVORSHIP

Despite standard treatment, women are at a high risk of cancer relapse. Surveillance consists of physical and pelvic examination every 3 months for the first 3 years, then every 4 to 6 months to year 5, and then annually. Whether a CA125 value is determined as part of follow-up should be individualized, not mandatory. One randomized trial showed no survival or quality-of-life advantage to routine monitoring of CA125 for detection of relapse, because early treatment based on increasing CA125 levels did not improve survival.[43] Women treated for ovarian cancer may experience physical and emotional adverse effects, even months after treatment has ended. These include fear of recurrence, depression, paclitaxel-induced neuropathy, and fatigue. Prompt evaluation and referral are necessary to help women adjust to survivorship.

SPECIAL POPULATIONS

For older women with ovarian cancer, combination therapy of a platinum and a taxane should be used if treatment is indicated. This was shown in the Elderly Women with Ovarian Cancer–1 trial presented at the 2019 ASCO Annual Meeting. In this trial, 120 study volunteers with stage III or IV ovarian cancer considered vulnerable on the basis of a validated scoring system were randomly assigned to single-agent carboplatin (arm 1), weekly carboplatin plus weekly paclitaxel (arm 2) or to a control arm using carboplatin plus paclitaxel on an every-3-week schedule (arm 3).[44] More than 90% of them either had a suboptimal cytoreductive surgery prior to enrollment or did not undergo surgery. Compared with arm 3, OS was significantly worse in arms 2 and 3 (median, 17.3 and 7.4 months *v* not being reached, respectively).

KEY POINTS

- Ovarian cancer is the most fatal of all gynecologic malignancies. Gynecologic oncologists play a key role in their management, particularly as it relates to surgical cytoreduction.
- Risk factors for ovarian cancer include increasing age, nulliparity, family history, early menarche, and late menopause. Use of oral contraceptives, tubal ligation, breastfeeding, and higher parity are protective.
- For women who are not candidates for surgery because of tumor burden or morbidity, neoadjuvant chemotherapy is a reasonable option.
- Women who undergo an optimal cytoreduction should receive six cycles of platinum-taxane adjuvant therapy. Exceptions to this include women with stage IA or IB, grade 1 or 2 cancers.
- Women whose disease relapses can be stratified as having platinum-sensitive or platinum-resistant disease. This can help devise treatment strategies with retreatment using a platinum-based regimen favored for women with platinum-sensitive disease and the use of a nonplatinum single agent for those with platinum-resistant disease.
- When their disease is diagnosed, all women should undergo genetic testing for hereditary risk. Those who harbor a mutation in *BRCA1* or *BRCA2* are candidates for maintenance olaparib after completion of adjuvant (or first-line) chemotherapy.
- The PARP inhibitors are indicated as maintenance therapy after a response to retreatment with platinum-based therapy (regardless of whether a *BRCA* mutation is present). Both olaparib and rucaparib can be used to treat relapsed ovarian cancer in women with a genetic *BRCA* mutation. Rucaparib also is approved for use in women with tumor-associated defects in homologous recombination deficiency (mutation in *BRCA* or high loss of heterozygosity).

OTHER TUMORS OF THE OVARY

Low Malignant Potential Tumors

Low malignant potential (LMP) tumors of the ovary (also referred to as borderline ovarian tumors) are noninvasive ovarian cancers. The primary approach is surgical because most women have early-stage disease at diagnosis. Because their outcomes are excellent (ie, 5-year overall survival rates > 95%), adjuvant therapy is not indicated. Medical therapy is often reserved for patients whose tumor is not resectable at diagnosis (either initially or at relapse); for such patients, chemotherapy or endocrine therapy is used. Whether patients treated for an LMP tumor should be offered estrogen therapy is controversial. However, most oncologists consider this to be an endocrine-sensitive cancer and as such, estrogen therapy is not typically administered.

Sex-Cord Stromal Cell Tumors

The sex-cord stromal tumors are subclassified as granulosa cell tumors and the androgen-producing tumors, such as Sertoli-Leydig cell tumors. Adult-type granulosa cell tumors are generally stage I at diagnosis and are classically diagnosed in women between the ages 40 to 70 years. Most granulosa cell tumors have a somatic mutation in *FOXL2*, which may be useful in diagnosis. Serum inhibin levels, particularly inhibin B, may be elevated in granulosa cell tumors and should be measured as part of the disease evaluation. The treatment of granulosa cell tumors is surgical resection; adjuvant therapy is not generally recommended. For those whose disease relapses, surgical resection is strongly favored. For those who are not surgical candidates, a platinum-based combination is often administered for treatment. Bevacizumab appears to have activity in this disease as well, as demonstrated in a phase II trial; an objective response was seen in six of 36 patients and median PFS was 9 months.[45] Sertoli-Leydig tumors commonly present before age 40 years. More than 90% are stage I at diagnosis, and as with granulosa cell tumors, surgery is the preferred treatment. Platinum-based chemotherapy may be considered for patients with poorly differentiated tumors and for patients with advanced or recurrent disease.

Germ Cell Tumors

Germ cell tumors of the ovary account for 2% to 3% of ovarian cancers and usually affect adolescent girls and young women; 50% are dysgerminomas; other histologic types include yolk sac tumors (endodermal sinus tumors), teratomas (immature, mature, and monodermal types), embryonal cell tumors, polyembryoma nongestational choriocarcinomas, and mixed germ cell tumors. These cancers typically can be followed with serum tumor markers (Table 15-14). Dysgerminomas are more likely to be confined to one ovary at diagnosis and carry a favorable prognosis. Adjuvant chemotherapy is typically not administered to patients with stage I dysgerminomas who have had complete staging surgery and those with stage I, grade 1 immature teratomas, because they can generally be cured with surgery. For all others, adjuvant treatment is indicated, which includes three to four cycles of bleomycin, etoposide, and cisplatin. For germ cell tumors that relapse after initial chemotherapy, high-dose chemotherapy with stem cell rescue may cure some women.

KEY POINTS

- Sex-cord stromal tumors are rare gynecologic malignancies that typically affect younger women.
- The primary treatment of sex-cord stromal tumors is surgical excision. Medical therapy is often reserved for patients with tumors that are not resectable at diagnosis (either initially or at relapse).
- For women with germ cell tumors, systemic treatment with platinum-based chemotherapy is often recommended after surgery. Exceptions to this rule include stage I dysgerminomas following complete staging surgery and stage I, grade 1 immature teratomas, because they rarely relapse.

GESTATIONAL TROPHOBLASTIC DISEASE

Gestational trophoblastic disease (GTD) comprises diseases of the human placenta that occur in women of childbearing age. There is a spectrum of malignant potential, from lesions with very low malignant potential (ie, complete and partial hydatidiform moles) to invasive tumors with metastatic potential (ie, invasive moles and placental-site trophoblastic tumors) to tumors with exceedingly high risk for systemic metastases (ie, gestational choriocarcinoma). Despite the risk for metastatic disease, nearly all women with GTD can be cured with the appropriate use of chemotherapy, careful monitoring for treatment response, and surveillance for relapse using sensitive β-human chorionic gonadotropin (hCG) assays. Given the rarity of this disease and the highly curative nature with appropriate treatment, all patients should be referred to a specialized center.

Malignant GTD is also referred to as gestational trophoblastic neoplasia (GTN). All patients with GTN require FIGO staging and WHO risk assessment (Tables 15-15 and 15-16).[46] Treatment of GTN is then based on risk classification (Fig 15-17). For those patients requiring chemotherapy, response is assessed by longitudinal assessment of the quantitative level of the serum hCG. Treatment is continued for several cycles after a negative hCG level is achieved. The finding of a plateau or increase in hCG while receiving treatment indicates relapse and, if seen, all patients require restaging and additional treatment.

SURVIVORSHIP

After normalization of hCG level, patients should have their level rechecked at monthly intervals for 12 months; physical examination should be performed every 6 to 12 months. Most women who required chemotherapy will resume menses during surveillance. It is strongly recommended that women use contraception to avoid pregnancy during the first year after treatment. Beyond that, patients can be counseled that pregnancy after GTN is typically uncomplicated, although there is a 1% to 2% risk of GTD developing again. The risk of relapse after treatment of GTD depends on risk. Survivorship issues after treatment of GTD should follow the principles in place for the curative treatment of other solid tumors, because their prognosis is typically excellent.

Table 15-15 **FIGO Staging of Gestational Trophoblastic Neoplasia**

FIGO Stage	Description
I	Tumor confined to the uterus
II	Extends to the adnexa or vagina, but limited to the genital structures
III	Lung metastases (with or without genital tract involvement)
IV	All other metastatic sites

Table 15-16 WHO Scoring of Gestational Trophoblastic Neoplasia

Parameter	Characteristic			
Risk factor scoring	0	1	2	4
Age	≤ 40	> 40	–	–
Antecedent pregnancy	Mole	Abortion	Term	
Interval from index pregnancy, months	< 4	4-6	7-12	> 12
Pretreatment hCG, mIU/mL	$< 10^3$	$> 10^3$-10^4	$> 10^4$-10^5	$> 10^5$
Largest tumor size, cm	–	3-4	≥ 5	
Site of metastases including uterus	Lung	Spleen, kidney	GI tract	Brain, liver
No. of metastases identified	–	1-4	5-8	> 8
Prior chemotherapy	–	–	Single drug	≥ 2 drugs

KEY POINTS

- GTNs are the malignant tumors within the category of GTD. If suspected or diagnosed, all patients require FIGO staging and WHO scoring.
- The medical treatment of GTN is based on the WHO score. Patients with low-risk disease (WHO score 0 to 4) have a good prognosis and can be treated with single-agent chemotherapy. Both methotrexate and actinomycin D are used in this situation.
- For patients with disease of poor prognosis, combination chemotherapy is preferred. The most commonly used regimen is a sequential treatment using etoposide, methotrexate, and actinomycin D during week 1, followed by cyclophosphamide and vincristine during week 2 of a 14-day cycle.
- GTN is highly curable regardless of stage at presentation. However, given the rarity of this disease, referral to a specialty center is advised.

VULVAR CANCER

The majority of vulvar cancers are squamous cell carcinoma. There are approximately 6,000 cases annually in the United States, and these occur mostly in postmenopausal, older women (median age, 68 years). Risk factors include smoking, vulvar dystrophy, HPV infection, history of cervical cancer, and prior immunodeficiency syndromes. The primary approach to vulvar cancer is surgical. Patients with lymph node involvement are at greater risk for recurrence and death (5-year survival rate, 25% to 41%) and are often treated with adjuvant external-beam RT with or without concomitant sensitizing cisplatin. For patients with locally advanced disease that cannot be completely resected, primary chemoradiation using weekly cisplatin is used; patients who have an excellent clinical response to chemoradiation may be considered subsequently for resection of residual disease. For those who experience a local recurrence, surgical re-excision should be considered. If unresectable, RT is administered, provided patients were not previously treated with RT. For all other patients (including those with metastatic disease), palliative chemotherapy can be used, although there are no prospective data evaluating the efficacy of systemic chemotherapy for metastatic vulvar cancer. Agents such as cisplatin, carboplatin, paclitaxel, vinorelbine, and erlotinib are reasonable options for patients who are fit for chemotherapy. Pembrolizumab also can be used in this setting for PD-L1–positive disease or MSI-H/dMMR.

SURVIVORSHIP

After treatment of vulvar cancer, all patients should be followed with serial physical examinations, including pelvic examination. The schedule is similar to that for cervical cancer.

KEY POINTS

- Most vulvar cancers are squamous cell carcinomas. The primary treatment is surgical.
- For patients with locally advanced disease that cannot be completely resected, primary chemoradiation with weekly cisplatin is used.

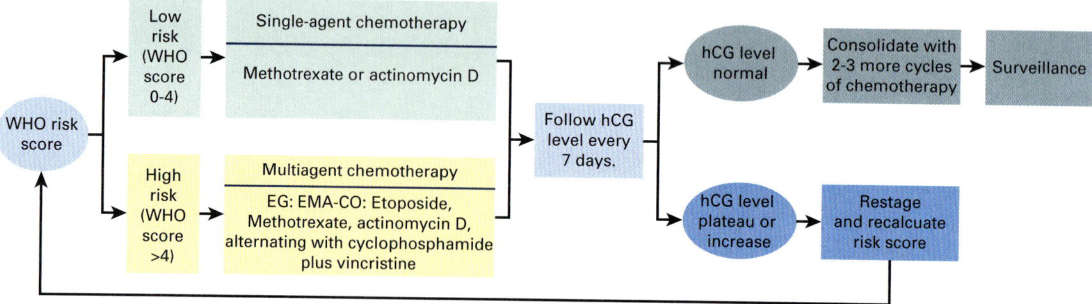

FIG 15-17 Approach to gestational trophoblastic neoplasia (GTN).

Regardless of stage or risk score, it is important to know that patients are curable. Given the rarity of these neoplasms, prompt referral to a specialist in GTN is recommended. Note: Patients with brain metastases are at a high risk of complications during treatment, including hemorrhage. If brain involvement is noted, neurosurgical and/or radiation therapy referral should be obtained before beginning medical treatment.

Abbreviations: CO, cyclophosphamide and vincristine; EMA, etoposide, methotrexate, and actinomycin D; hCG, human chorionic gonadotropin.

VAGINAL CANCER

Primary vaginal cancers arising from the vagina and cervix are rare and represent 1% to 2% of vaginal malignancies. Most vaginal carcinomas are squamous cell carcinomas and affect women in the sixth and seventh decade of life. Because of the increase in the incidence of HPV infections, there has been an increase in women diagnosed with vaginal cancer before the age of 40 years. Other risk factors include smoking, early age at first intercourse, multiple lifetime sexual partners, prior sexually transmitted diseases, and a history of prior cervical cancer. Other vaginal cancer histologic types are extremely rare and include clear-cell carcinoma, melanoma, sarcoma, and adenocarcinoma. It is important to consider metastatic or recurrent disease from other sites (ie, cervix, vulva, ovary, breast, endometrium, or uterus) in the evaluation of a new vaginal lesion, because metastatic disease is more common than primary vaginal carcinoma. There are no prospective studies on which to base treatment recommendations for vaginal carcinomas. As with vulvar cancers, primary treatment is surgical; if not feasible, treatment using radiotherapy with or without concomitant cisplatin is used. Although there are no prospective comparison data showing chemoradiation to be superior to radiation alone, many physicians extrapolate the data from randomized trials in cervical cancer, and interpret data from retrospective studies in vaginal cancer, to support the recommendation of chemoradiation. Patients with unresectable, metastatic disease may be offered palliative cytotoxic chemotherapy, but there are no prospective data to establish which agents are active.

SURVIVORSHIP

As with vulvar cancer, after treatment of vaginal cancer, all patients should be followed with serial physical examinations, including a pelvic examination, following a schedule similar to that for cervical cancer.

KEY POINTS

- Vaginal cancers are typically squamous cell carcinomas and should be considered for definitive surgical resection.
- For patients with a history of a primary cancer, it is critical to rule out a vaginal tumor is actually a metastatic lesion.
- For patients who are not amenable to surgical treatment, RT affords palliation.

Acknowledgment

The following authors are acknowledged and graciously thanked for their contribution to prior versions of this chapter: Martee Leigh Hensley, MD, FASCO; and Maurie Markman, MD FASCO.

GLOBAL ONCOLOGY PERSPECTIVE: Gynecologic Cancers in Latin America

Angélica Nogueira-Rodrigues, MD, PhD (Federal University of Minas Gerais, Belo Horizonte, Minas Gerais, Brazil)

Gynecologic cancer is the second most common cancer in Latin American women, after breast cancer. It is estimated there will be approximately 115,070 new cases diagnosed in the region yearly.[47] This gynecologic cancer burden is huge, primarily because of the high incidence of cervical cancer: a total of 56,187 new cervical cancer cases are diagnosed every year, corresponding to approximately half of all gynecologic cancers diagnosed in the region. These data confirm that cervical cancer continues to be a public health challenge in Latin America.

In addition, with an estimated 30,000 new cases per year, the incidence of endometrial cancer is increasing in Latin America, probably due to more westernized lifestyles and higher rates of overweight and obesity, as well as longer life expectancy.[48] According to Globocan, the current incidence of other cancers in Latin America arising in the gynecologic tract is approximately 23,000, 4,000, and 2,000 for ovarian cancer, vulvar cancer, and vaginal cancers, respectively.[46]

CERVICAL CANCER PREVENTION: HPV VACCINE UPTAKE

The HPV vaccine is considered one of the most important advances for Latin American women's health. However, its implementation has faced more hurdles than initially expected in Latin America. After the introduction of the vaccine in Brazil in 2014, the Pan American Health Organization stated that HPV immunization is now available to > 80% of adolescent girls in the Americas. However, this does not mean that 80% of girls in the region are being vaccinated[49]; instead, it indicates that 80% of adolescent girls live in one of the countries that offer the HPV vaccine through public immunization programs.

To date, Argentina, Brazil, Chile, Colombia, Dominican Republic, Ecuador, Guatemala, Honduras, Mexico, Panama, Paraguay, Peru, Puerto Rico, and Uruguay have included HPV vaccination in their national recommendations. In 2015, Venezuela included HPV vaccination in its national public immunization policy, but the vaccine remains unavailable as of March 2019. An alarming situation in Latin America is the reduction in uptake of the first vaccine dose in the years after the introduction of HPV vaccination into national immunization calendars. According to the Brazilian Ministry of Health, vaccination coverage with at least one dose decreased from 92% of the target population (girls aged 11 to 13 years) in 2014 (year of implementation) to 69.5% (girls aged 9 to 11 years) in 2015, a dramatic reduction of 23% in 1 year. A similar trend was observed in Guadalajara, Mexico, which saw a 22% reduction in the first-dose uptake from 2009 to 2013. Colombia has faced the deepest decrease in adherence.

In 2013, Colombia had reached a first-dose coverage rate of 97.5%, the second-best rate worldwide, after Australia. However, according to the National Vaccine Program Office, after the "Carmen de Bolivar episode," in which families in one Colombian town claimed the vaccine made girls sick, the coverage decreased to a mere 20.4% by the end of 2014. Furthermore, similar to trends observed in the United States and other high-income countries, the rates of second and third doses are far below first-dose rates in Latin America, as well.

No other vaccine has seen similar decline in uptake in the first few years of implementation as the HPV vaccine has in Latin America, indicating that, despite Latin America's history of successful immunization campaigns and strong national programs, the HPV vaccine has distinct characteristics that must be considered when devising optimal implementation strategies.[50-52]

CERVICAL CANCER EPIDEMIOLOGY

Most cervical cancer cases are squamous cell carcinoma, but the relative and absolute incidence of adenocarcinoma has increased in recent years, and adenocarcinoma now accounts for approximately 20% of invasive cervical cancer in screened populations worldwide. However, the increase in adenocarcinoma incidence has been slower in the developing world, with a suboptimally screened population. In a cohort of 60,883 Brazilian patients with cervical cancer, the trend in adenocarcinoma relative increase was confirmed: 9.1% in 2000 to 13.3% in 2009—an increase of 46.2% in 10 years. However, 89.4% of cases are still squamous cell carcinoma and 10.6% (n = 6,458) are adenocarcinoma.[53]

CERVICAL CANCER: DIAGNOSIS AND TREATMENT DELAYS

Scarce data exist about gynecologic cancers in some Latin American countries. The epidemiologic and clinical scenario of the Brazilian population probably has common denominators with Latin America, and even with other low- and middle-income countries (LMICs), and may be of interest for cancer control planning in the region. According to an analysis of a large Brazilian cohort (193,000 women affected with gynecologic cancers between 2000 and 2015 in the country, from data from the Brazilian National Cancer Institute), 79.76% of patients with cervical cancer had stage II-IV disease at diagnosis, and time from diagnosis to first treatment exceeded 30 days in 78.4% of patients with cervical cancer. Similar delays in the start of treatment were observed in vulvar and vaginal cancers. A high percentage of early deaths (13.2%) was seen in this cohort.[54]

OVARIAN CANCER

In Latin America and the Caribbean, ovarian cancer is the eighth most common malignant tumor in women, with an estimated incidence of 23,300 cases per year.[47] The Brazilian National Cancer Institute (INCA) appraises that in 2019 there will be 6,150 new cases of ovarian cancer in Brazil, with 5.95 cases per 100,000 women, making this cancer the seventh most common among women in the country. About 70% of the cases are diagnosed at an advanced stage (FIGO stage III and IV), similar to high-income countries.[54]

Among women with ovarian cancer, mutation prevalence varies according to ethnicity, genetic testing criteria used, age at cancer diagnosis, and family history of the disease. In Brazil, mutation prevalence in the general Brazilian population has not been established, but several studies have performed comprehensive *BRCA* mutation testing and described mutation prevalence among breast and ovarian cancer affected patients, totaling 2,090 individuals tested in studies.[58-65] Using established mutation testing criteria,[66,67] many of these reports show an overall mutation prevalence of 19% to 22%. Among all mutations identified, approximately 5% are large gene rearrangements. An interesting observation that stands out from the preliminary data on the mutational landscape in Brazil is that certain variants are likely more common or even exclusive from certain Brazilian regions, which could be explained by distinctive patterns of immigration that occurred in different regions of Brazil.[60,68-72] It is important to highlight that the general population prevalence of *BRCA1* and *BRCA2* is unknown and the vast majority of unaffected *BRCA* carriers in Brazil have yet to be tested and identified. Despite the importance of early diagnosis and timely intervention to improving health outcomes, there are several barriers limiting access to genetic cancer-risk assessment and genetic testing for individuals with a high risk of hereditary ovarian cancer in Brazil and other Latin American countries.

ACCESS TO TREATMENT OF GYNECOLOGIC CANCERS

Focusing on interdisciplinary treatment, RT resources in Latin America need to be expanded. Access to radiation facilities is far from optimal. RT facilities are available in only 70% of Latin American countries, and only three countries in Africa and Latin America regions meet the International Atomic Energy Agency's (IAEA) recommendation of 250,000 population per megavoltage machine (MVM). In Latin America, LMICs have a distribution of 1.64 million inhabitants per MVM, as opposed to 0.64 and 0.49 million inhabitants per MVM in upper-middle– and high-income countries, respectively.[55] Brazil for example, has a shortage of radiation machines as well as human resources. In a study by De Araujo et al,[77] based on more strict criteria using the IAEA recommendation, the deficit of radiation machines and radiation oncologists in 2015 was 225 units and 387 professionals.

Regarding surgery, one concern is that there is no formal subspecialization in gynecologic oncology in many countries in Latin America. Some patients are treated by general gynecologists, who sometimes are not trained in oncological principles or on the decision-making process.[56]

Access to systemic treatment varies greatly in the region. Olaparib is the only PARP inhibitor approved in Brazil as of September 2019. Olaparib is currently approved in the country according to SOLO1 and SOLO2 trials criteria; however, despite being approved, it is not included yet in the list of obligatory drugs that must be provided by the supplementary health system, and it is not available in the public health system. Immunotherapy is currently unavailable in Brazil for patients with gynecologic cancers, as of September 2019. Access to clinical trial registration and implementation in Latin America is limited compared with access in high-income countries.[57]

Because of the epidemiologic relevance of gynecologic cancers, it is imperative to implement gynecologic cancer prevention policies, improve RT resources, and augment equitable patient access to specialized and well-equipped cancer centers with trained professionals.

16

MELANOMA AND OTHER SKIN CANCERS

Stergios J. Moschos, MD, and Georgia Sofia Karachaliou MD, MSc

Recent Updates

- Adjuvant therapy of up to 1 year of single-agent nivolumab or pembrolizumab were each approved by the US Food and Drug Administration (FDA) for patients with completely resected, stage III-IV melanoma on the basis of significant relapse-free survival (RFS) improvement compared with adjuvant high-dose ipilimumab or placebo, respectively (CheckMate 238 and KEYNOTE-054 trials). (Weber J, *N Engl J Med 2017*; Eggermont AMM, *N Engl J Med* 2018)
- Adjuvant therapy of up to 1 year of concurrent dabrafenib and trametinib was FDA-approved for patients with completely resected stage III, *BRAFV600*-mutant melanoma on the basis of significant RFS and overall survival (OS) improvement compared with placebo (COMBI-AD trial). (Long GV, *N Engl J Med* 2017)
- Treatment with concurrent encorafenib and binimetinib was approved by the FDA for patients with unresectable stage III-IV *BRAFV600*-mutant melanoma on the basis of significant RFS improvement compared with vemurafenib alone. In the same trial, single-agent encorafenib was associated with significantly longer OS compared with single-agent vemurafenib (COLUMBUS). (Dummer R, *Lancet Oncol* 2018)
- Patients with untreated (ie, active), asymptomatic, parenchymal brain metastases had durable responses from concurrent ipilimumab and nivolumab (CheckMate 204, Tawbi HA, *N Engl J Med* 2018); concurrent dabrafenib and trametinib also resulted in intracranial responses in patients with *BRAFV600*-mutant parenchymal brain metastases, although the responses, especially intracranially, were less durable (COMBI-MB). (Davies MA, *Lancet Oncol* 2017)

OVERVIEW

This chapter primarily focuses on cutaneous melanoma (CM), with sections dedicated to nonmelanoma skin cancers, including basal cell carcinoma (BCC), squamous cell carcinoma (SCC), and Merkel cell carcinoma (MCC), as well as mucosal melanoma and ocular melanoma.

CUTANEOUS MELANOMA

EPIDEMIOLOGY

CM accounts for 232,100 (1.7%) of all new cancer cases. However, the melanoma-specific mortality rate is only 0.7% of all cancer-related deaths,[1] because of screening, early detection, and adequate surgical management of early-stage disease. In the United States, CM is the fifth most common cancer among men and sixth among women.[2] At the time of new melanoma diagnosis, 84% of CMs are localized (stages I and II), 8% are regional (stage III), and only 4% are distant-metastatic (stage IV). Thus, most early-stage CMs are highly treatable and do not cause death. Figure 16-1 shows annually projected incidence, mortality, and mortality-to-incidence ratios from the Annual Surveillance and Health Services Research, American Cancer Society data between 2002 and 2019 for CM.

RISK FACTORS

Almost half of the newly diagnosed patients with CM in the United States are between 55 and 74 years old (44.9%). However, melanoma incidence is increasing across all age groups. Geography and ethnicity play a role in risk for CM development. Australians and New Zealanders have the highest incidence of CM development, followed by US Americans and Northern Europeans (> 9.0 per 100,000 persons).[1] Within the United States, non-Hispanic whites have a 25-fold higher risk of CM development than blacks and approximately a six-fold higher risk than Hispanic whites.

The most important risk factors for CM include:

- Ultraviolet (UV) light exposure, the most well-characterized risk factor for CM. Higher number of tanning bed sessions and sunburns increase the risk for development of CM.[3]
- Various forms of immunosuppression increase the risk of CM; for example, malignancy-associated immunosuppression (eg, non-Hodgkin lymphoma, chronic lymphocytic leukemia), virally-induced immunosuppression (eg, HIV infection), and iatrogenic immunosuppression among recipients of a solid-organ transplant.
- Skin phenotype, a polygenic trait with various polymorphisms among pigment-associated genes (eg, *MC1R*, *TYR*, *TYRP1*, *ASIP*) that regulate the amount and type of melanin present in the skin, has also been associated with CM development. For example, people with light skin (Fitzpatrick skin types I and II), red hair, and light eye color have increased risk for CM.[4]
- Precursor melanoma lesions known to harbor cancer-associated mutations, such as atypical or common nevi (odds ratio [OR], 17.40 and 1.02, respectively), personal history of melanoma (OR, 12.78), personal history of nonmelanoma skin cancers (relative risk [RR], 4.28)[4], and family history of CM are also associated with increased risk for CM.[5]
- Certain genes bearing germline mutations or gene variants are associated with a higher risk for development of familial melanoma, as discussed in the Familial Melanoma section of this chapter.

KEY POINTS

- CM accounts for 1.7% of all new cancer diagnoses worldwide annually; 0.7% of all cancer-related deaths annually are due to CM.
- Projected melanoma-specific mortality rates have begun to decline since 2016, whereas incidence continues to rise steadily.
- Both CM incidence and mortality rates are higher in men than in women.
- UV light exposure is the most well-characterized risk factor for CM.

BIOLOGY

Melanocytes are derived from the neural crest cells and they resemble dendritic cells and neurons. Their dendritic shape, along with the vesicles (ie, melanosome) and molecules they secrete, imply that melanocytes have a prominent function within their microenvironment.[6] Melanin is the principle multiprotein pigment structure within melanosomes and has complex physicochemical properties that protect against UV radiation–induced DNA damage. The primary purpose of the melanocyte is to respond to UV radiation–induced damage that occurs within keratinocytes, by activating production of melanin. However, the intermediate enzymatic steps leading up to melanin production are pro-oxidative, and therefore lead to higher levels of oxidative stress and reactive oxygen species (ROS) within melanocytes. In fact, melanin paradoxically inhibits enzymes involved in various types of DNA repair.[7]

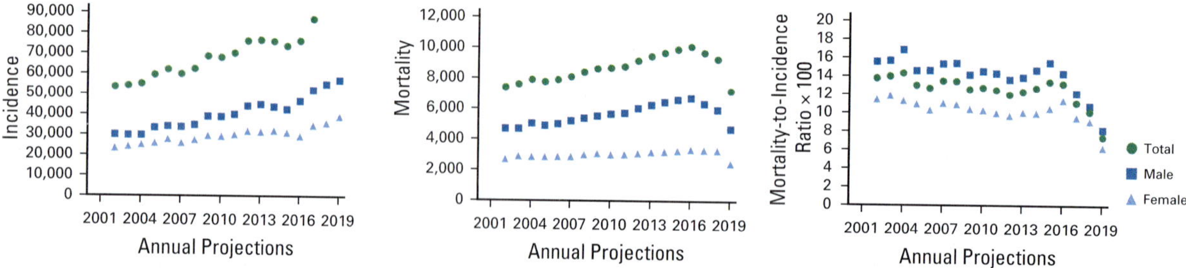

Fig. 16-1 Annually projected incidence, mortality, and mortality-to-incidence ratios from the Annual Surveillance and Health Services Research, American Cancer Society, data between 2002 and 2018.

Siegel R, *CA Cancer J Clin* 2019 and similar annual reports published by the American Cancer Society regarding Annual Cancer Statistics since 2002.

Conditions such as high UV radiation exposure, or p16 deficiency that generate more ROS within melanocytes can lead to melanocyte transformation. The process of uncontrolled melanin production by melanoma cells can explain the genotoxic, immunosuppressive, mutagenic, and tumor-promoting effects of melanin. High oxidative stress and defects in DNA repair may lead to genomic instability and can account for the high somatic mutation burden seen in CM compared with other cancers (Fig 16-2).[8]

Progression from benign nevi to dysplastic nevi, to melanoma in situ, to invasive melanoma is associated with increases in the number of somatic mutations and copy number alterations in melanomas arising from nevi. *BRAV600E* is the most frequent, somatically mutated gene codon identified in benign nevi. More genetic events (eg, *NRASQ61*, mutations in the promoter for the telomerase transcriptase gene [*TERT*], mutations or gene copy number deletions of the *CDKN2A* locus) occur even before invasive melanoma is detected (ie, melanoma in situ). Invasive melanomas are associated with a higher frequency of activating mutations in oncogenes (*BRAFV600E, NRASQ61, CDK4K22, RB1Y498, PPP6CR264, PIK3CA*), genetic aberrations in tumor suppressor genes (CDKN2A locus, *PTEN, TP53*), and genes encoding for chromatin remodeling complexes (ARIDs, *SMARCA4, PBRM1, EZH2*), and increased expression of genes encoding for proteins involved in the MAPK signaling pathway.[9]

Sporadic Melanoma

The Cancer Genome Atlas (TCGA) Project in CM (N = 333) confirmed the mutational landscape of CM that had been previously reported (ie, 52% *BRAFV600* codon, 31% *CDKN2A* gene loss, 28% *RAS* oncogenic mutations, 15% *TP53*, 14% *NF1* mutations, and 13% *CDKN2A* gene locus mutations).[8] Genetic or epigenetic aberrations in melanoma cells have consequences regarding the host immune response. Decreased protein expression of tumor-suppressor genes (eg, *PTEN, CDKN2A, APC/CTNNB1*) or mutations in distinct oncogenes (eg, *NRASQ61*) are associated with decreased incidence of tumor-infiltrating lymphocytes (TILs), poor response to systemic therapies, and worse prognosis.[10] Coexistence of these genetic aberrations, or lack thereof, along with other more frequently mutated genes (eg, *BRAFV600*)[11] may enable identification of patient subgroups who may benefit from single, as opposed to combination, strategies in the future.

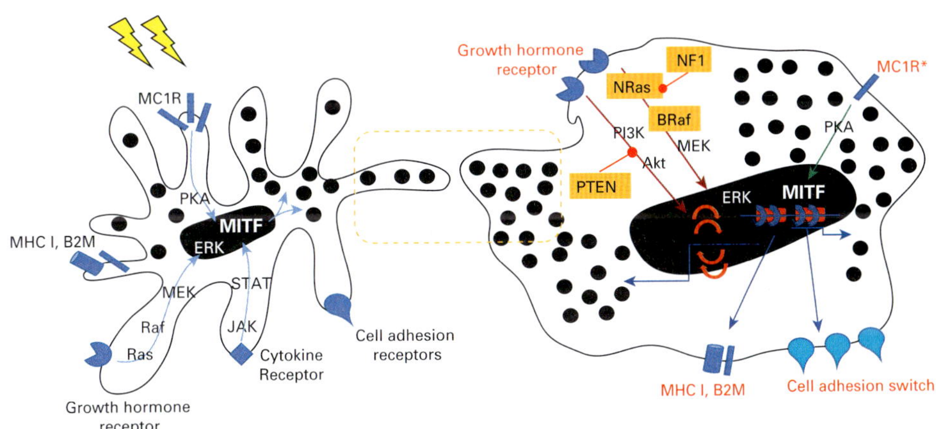

Fig. 16-2 Melanocyte-to-melanoma transition and implications for therapy.

The most well-studied role of melanocytes is the production of melanin that is packaged within melanosomes (black-filled circles) and secreted to nearby keratinocytes in response to UV radiation (yellow lightning bulbs). The process is highly regulated in part via the melanocortin 1 receptor (MC1R) that activates the master melanocyte transcriptional regulator, MITF. Melanocytes also respond to growth factors (eg, HGF, PDGF, SCF) via growth-factor receptors (eg, EGFR, PDGFR, KIT, VEGF) by means of a highly regulated process in response to UV exposure or skin wound. Growth factor-mediated stimuli signal via the Ras-Raf-Mek-Erk pathway and, to a lesser extent, others (eg, PI3K-Akt-mTOR). Melanoma cells share several common antigens with melanocytes (yellow dotted square), given that, on most occasions, they also produce melanin (eg, MAGE family, Melan A-MART1, GAGE family).[8] Antigens from these shared proteins can be immunogenic and stimulate a strong immune response. The implications of these shared antigens for melanoma therapy are many-fold. First, they can be a sign of original diagnosis, recurrence, and immunotherapy-related response (ie, vitiligo induced by ipilimumab or high-dose interferon). Second, common antigens shared between melanocytes and melanoma cells explain antitumor responses to immunotherapies in patients with melanomas having low somatic mutation burden. Third, melanoma vaccines historically have been one of the first treatments to target these antigens.[157] Fourth, clinical research efforts to augment host immune response to these antigens by disrupting central thymic tolerance are necessary and ongoing (eg, RANKL inhibition).[158] Fifth, if such antigens are not expressed (eg, amelanotic melanoma), there are ongoing efforts to enhance immunogenicity by targeting epigenetic modifiers (eg, histone deacetylase [HDAC] inhibitors).[159] Aggressive melanomas: (1) have increased proliferative capacity [eg, *CDKN2A* locus (epi)genetic aberrations]; (2) escape senescence (eg, *TERT* gene promoter mutations); (3) upregulate autonomous cell growth independent of membrane receptor signaling (eg, *PTEN* loss, *NRASQ61* mutation, *BRAFV600* mutations, *NF1* highly functional mutations); (4) exhibit deficiencies in DNA repair and alter melanin production (mutations or polymorphisms in the *MC1R* gene [MC1R*]); and (5) accumulate epigenetic changes with altered patterns of gene expression that affect immunogenicity (expression of major histocompatibility complex [MHC] class I, β2-microglobulin [B2M]) and interaction with cell partners from keratinocytes to melanoma cells themselves (eg, loss of E-cadherin and P-cadherin, upregulation of N-cadherin, MelCam, and αVβ integrins).

In addition, the TCGA in CM showed that the MEK1/2 proteins are activated in both *BRAF* and *RAS* hot-spot mutation subtypes, whereas ERK1/2 protein activation was the highest in the *RAS* hot-spot mutation subtype.[8] The high level of activation of MEK1/2 accounts for the clinical benefit of concurrent BRAF and MEK inhibition in *BRAFV600*-mutant melanoma. In addition, gene expression profiling identified a prominent subgroup termed "immune-high" (51%), which had the best overall prognosis among the other two subgroups (microphthalmia-associated transcription factor [*MITF*]-low [18%], and keratin-high [31%]). The approximate 50% incidence of CM bearing TILs (ie, inflamed) at least partially accounts for the high incidence of antitumor responses to immunotherapies (see Systemic Therapies for Advanced Melanoma later in this chapter).

Familial Melanoma

Although the majority of CMs are sporadic, approximately 10% of patients with CM have familial melanoma. Table 16-1 lists several genes associated with an increased risk of familial melanoma. The *CDKN2A* gene locus is the most well-studied and strongest genetic factor for familial CM. Carriers of *CDKN2A* germline mutations have 60-fold higher risk of CM development, in part due to the high penetrance of the gene (60% to 90%).[12] Carriers of germline mutations in the *BRCA1*-associated protein 1 (*BAP1*) gene are also at high risk for development of CM (OR, 17.3).[13] Carriers of the *MITF* Mi-E318K variant, the master regulator of melanocyte development, have a higher risk for development of either multiple primary melanomas and/or renal cell carcinoma.

Carriers of the melanocortin-1 receptor (*MC1R*) gene variant have a moderate risk for CM; variants corresponding to red hair color have a higher risk than the non–red hair variants (OR, 2.4 *v* 1.2). Furthermore, the number of *MC1R* variants increases the RR for CM among *CDKN2A* mutation carriers.[14] Patients with a family history of at least two relatives with CM and/or pancreatic cancer, breast cancer, or early age of onset of multiple primary melanomas should be offered genetic counseling.

KEY POINTS

- Familial CMs represent only a small minority of melanomas; most CMs are sporadic.
- Germline mutations in the *CDKN2A* gene locus are associated with increased risk (odds ratio) for the development of CM.
- *BRAFV600* is the most frequent mutation in sporadic melanomas, followed by *NRASQ61*, *CDKN2A*, *TERT*, and *NF1*.

SCREENING AND PREVENTION

The broad availability of smartphones with high-resolution cameras is changing the early evaluation of atypical pigmented skin lesions, with technology now supplementing, but not replacing, routine skin screening.[15] The question of whether skin examination for CM detection increases melanoma-specific OS has been investigated. The SCREEN project was a massive, population-based skin cancer screening program conducted only in the German state of Schleswig-Holstein and not in the 3 nearby German states or Denmark. More than 1,700 physicians and > 360,000 participants, older than 20 years participated for the duration of the intervention (2003-2004). In the years before the start of the project, feasibility of physician training, screening test performance, and documentation of screen examinations was evaluated. The mortality rate before (1998 to 2000) and after (2007 to 2008) the intervention was calculated for Schleswig-Holstein, three neighboring German states (Hamburg, Mecklenburg-Vorpommern, and Lower Saxony), and the neighboring country of Denmark. Schleswig-Holstein, the only state where the intervention was applied, was the only state with an almost 50% decline in melanoma-specific mortality in the period after intervention.[16] Atypical nevi, personal history of melanoma, and multiple (≥ 40) nevi were associated with increased risk of melanoma detection. A screening strategy that focused on only three risk factors—age ≥ 35 years, family history, and congenital nevi—reduced the number of persons needed to screen to detect one melanoma from the originally screened 360,000 participants to 178.[17] Other studies have supported similar results.[18]

Apart from early detection, sunscreens, antioxidants, anti-inflammatory drugs, vitamins, and supplements have been considered for chemoprevention in CM.[19] Only regular sunscreen use has the highest level of clinical evidence for melanoma prevention. A prospective study in Queensland of 1,621 participants who were randomly assigned to daily use of sunscreen (sun protection factor, 16) versus any other sun protective factor at the discretion of the investigators showed that sunscreen use significantly reduced the development of invasive melanomas (hazard ratio [HR], 0.27; 95% CI, 0.08 to 0.97]).[20]

KEY POINTS

- Population-based skin cancer screening programs have identified risk factors that can render melanoma screening cost-efficient to select high-risk patients.
- The use of sunscreens has the highest level of clinical evidence for melanoma prevention.

CLINICAL PRESENTATION

Staging System

Stage at diagnosis, as defined in the American Joint Committee on Cancer (AJCC) 2018 staging system, is the most significant predictor of OS.[21] The SEER Program 5-year OS rates for localized (stages I to II), regional (stage III), and distant metastatic melanoma (stage IV) that was diagnosed between 2009 and 2015 were 99%, 65%, and 25%, respectively. The current AJCC Staging System version:

Table 16-1 **Genes Associated With a High Risk of Cutaneous Melanoma Development**

Gene	Function	OR	Reference
CDKN2A	Encodes for the p16^INK4A^ and p14^ARF^ cell-cycle inhibitors	64.8	Helgadottir et al[12]
BAP-1	Ubiquitin C terminal hydrolase; deubiquitinates various proteins, including histone H2A	17.3	Carbone et al[13]
MITF (*Mi-E318K* variant)	Transcription factor and master regulator of melanocyte development	4.8	Bertolotto et al[141]
PARK 2	Encodes RPR E3 ubiquitin ligase	3.9	Hu et al[142]
MC1R	G-protein-coupled receptor, signals melanocortin production		Williams et al[143]
Red hair color		2.4	
Other		1.3	
SLC45A2	Transporter protein that mediates melanin synthesis	2.0	Ibarrola-Villava et al[144]
IRF4	Lymphocyte-specific transcription factor that regulates interferons		Gibbs et al[145]
With solar elastosis		1.5	
With neval remnants		0.6	
TERT (promoter)	Ribonucleoprotein polymerase that maintains polymerase ends	1.2	Read et al[146]

Abbreviation: OR, odds ratio.

- retains the major histopathologic parameters of the primary melanoma (Breslow depth of invasion for thin [T1], intermediate [T2, T3], and thick [T4] melanoma; ulceration) and regional lymph node status (N) staging (number of metastasis-containing regional lymph nodes; presence of satellite, microsatellite, or in transit lesions);
- simplifies reporting of the Breslow depth of invasion value to the nearest 0.1 mm;
- reclassifies thin melanomas (T1a and T1b) by Breslow depth of invasion of either < 0.8 versus ≥ 0.8 mm and the presence or absence of ulceration (T1a melanomas have both < 0.8 mm Breslow depth of invasion and are nonulcerated);
- simplifies terminology of locoregional (satellite, and in transit disease) or regional lymph node involvement (clinically occult *v* clinically detected);
- introduces the fourth substage for stage III, identified by "D"; and
- refines distant metastatic disease (M) by introducing a D substage (central nervous system [CNS] metastases) and takes into consideration biochemical changes (eg, elevated serum lactate dehydrogenase) across each M1 substage.

The highlights of the 2018 CM staging system are listed in Table 16-2 along with diagnostic and treatment inventions.

Other Prognostic Factors

Younger women, Caucasian subjects, and immunocompetent patients have an overall better prognosis compared with older men, black patients, and immunosuppressed individuals, respectively. Several histopathologic features not included in the 2018 AJCC staging system remain important prognostic factors, such as the mitotic rate of the primary CM[22] and density of TILs, either if TIL density is measured in the primary CM,[23,24] regional lymph nodes,[8] or distant metastatic sites.[25]

An increasing number of molecular assays have been used to evaluate the prognosis of patients with stage I to II CM. However, they still lack validation in prospective studies. The DecisionDx-Melanoma (Castle Biosciences, Friendswood, TX) is based on a retrospective analysis of RNA extracted from archival, formalin-fixed, paraffin-embedded primary melanoma tissue and tested for a 31-gene expression profiling signature. This test categorizes patient risk as Class 1 (A or B) and 2 (A or B). In a retrospective analysis of 259 patients with CM who had negative sentinel lymph node (SLN) mapping, patients whose disease was classified as Class 2 by the DecisionDx-Melanoma test had worse RFS and OS than any other class. In patients with stage I and IIA CM, the 31-gene expression test predicted RFS independent of Breslow thickness.[26] However, Breslow thickness and SLN status remain stronger prognostic indicators. Therefore, the clinical utility of the DecisionDx-Melanoma test is not yet clear, and routine application in stage I to II melanoma is not recommended at this time.

Patient Evaluation

Clinical. The initial evaluation of a patient with a recent diagnosis of CM involves obtaining a thorough history and physical examination. The evaluation includes a family history of CM (invasive CM or pancreatic cancer in three or more affected members on one side of the family) or other cancers (ie, uveal melanoma, renal cell carcinoma, mesothelioma). Also, a prior personal history of (1) multiple CMs (three or more), including one primary melanoma at age < 45 years; (2) regressing pigmented skin lesions, raising the possibility for melanoma of unknown primary; and (3) or non-melanoma skin cancers. Patients diagnosed with CM between 15 and 30 years of age have a higher incidence of *BRAFV600E* somatic mutations. Constitutional symptoms can be a sign of advanced

Table 16-2 **Highlights of Eighth Edition of the American Joint Committee on Cancer Staging System for Cutaneous Melanoma**

Stage	Clinical Descriptor	T	N	M	Surgery	Scans
0	No invasive melanoma					
I						
IA	Breslow < 0.8 mm and nonulcerated	1A	0	0	SLN mapping under debate	Not recommended
	Breslow 0.8-1.0 mm, or Breslow < 0.8 mm and ulcerated	1B			SLN mapping	
IB	Breslow < 2 mm and nonulcerated	2A				
II	Breslow > 1 mm					
IIA	Breslow < 2 mm and ulcerated, or Breslow > 2 mm and nonulcerated	2B, 3A	0	0	SLN mapping	Not recommended
IIB	Breslow > 2 mm and ulcerated, or Breslow > 4 mm and nonulcerated	3B, 4A				Consider
IIC	Breslow > 4 mm and ulcerated	4B				
III	LN positive					
IIIA	Breslow < 1 mm, or Breslow < 2 mm and nonulcerated and ≤ 3 LN, nonpalpable	1, 2A	1A, 2A	0	CLND	Recommended
IIIB	Breslow < 2 mm and nonulcerated, and satellite, in transit, or one palpable LN (≤ 3 LNs total)	0, 1, 2A	1B, 1C, 2B		CNLD	
IIIB	Breslow > 1 mm and ulcerated or Breslow > 2 mm and nonulcerated and one LN (microscopic or palpable)	0, 2B, 3A	1A-2B		CNLD	
IIIC	Breslow 2 mm and nonulcerated and ≥ 1 LN (one palpable or ≥ 4 nonpalpable)	0, 1A-3A	2C, N3		CNLD	
IIIC	Breslow > 2 mm and ulcerated, or Breslow > 4 mm and nonulcerated and any nodal disease	3B-4A	≥ 1		CLND	
IIIC	Breslow > 4 mm and ulcerated and at least one nonpalpable LN	4B	1A-2C		CLND	
IIID	Breslow > 4 mm and ulcerated and ≥ 4 LNs (or ≥ 2 palpable LNs)	4B	3		CLND	
IV[a]	Distant metastatic disease					
IVA	Skin, soft tissue, lymph node	Any	Any	1	Consider if oligometastatic	Yes
IVB	Lung					
IVC	Non-CNS visceral sites					
IVD	CNS					

NOTE. Summary of recommendations for SLN biopsy and CLND.
Abbreviations: CLND, completion lymph node dissection; LN, regional lymph node; SLN, sentinel lymph node.
[a]Each M1 substage is split into 0 or 1 on the basis of absence or presence of elevated serum lactate dehydrogenase.
Republished with permission of Springer, from AJCC Cancer Staging Manual, 8th Edition (2017); permission conveyed through Copyright Clearance Center, Inc.

melanoma, and new-onset headaches can be a sign of CNS metastases. The physical examination can be remarkable for the presence of chronically sun-damaged skin (eg, actinic keratosis, solar elastosis, lentigines) or other nonmelanoma skin cancers suggesting that CM may have high somatic mutation burden. Alternatively, multiple atypical pigmented lesions suggest that CM may have risen from nevi. Infrequently, vitiligo, a lymphocyte-mediated destruction of normal melanocytes, cutaneous, and subcutaneous nodules may indicate satellite, in transit disease, epidermotropic/cutaneous, or subcutaneous metastases. Blood tests have little prognostic significance for patients with stage I to III melanoma. However, high WBC count, neutrophilia, monocytosis, low absolute lymphocyte count, and elevated serum lactate dehydrogenase have been associated with worse prognosis in patients with stage IV melanoma.[21]

Surgical Staging. A patient with a recently diagnosed primary CM should undergo wide excision concurrent with SLN mapping and biopsy, when indicated. Wide excision with 1- to 2-cm margins decreases the incidence of a local recurrence.[27] SLN mapping is the recommended method to complete the regional surgical staging by assessing the incidence of regional lymph node metastases for patients at risk for regional nodal involvement (≥ T1b). SLN biopsy should be offered to all patients with at least T2 lesions. SLN biopsy could also be considered for patients with thinner lesions—in particular, young patients whose disease may also bear aggressive histopathologic features (eg, high mitotic rate, ulceration, T1b lesions).[28] In experienced hands, the use of standardized probes (eg, technetium-99 sulfur colloid and intraoperative vital blue dye around the primary tumor) results in an overall SLN identification rate of 95% and with low morbidity. SLN status is an independent prognostic factor for OS. At a median follow-up of 20 months, 15% of patients with positive SLN(s) who did not undergo completion lymph node dissection (CLND) had a nodal recurrence. The Multicenter Selective Lymphadenectomy Trial-I (MSLT-I) is a prospective phase III study in which 2,001 patients with at least T2 CM but no clinically detectable nodal disease were enrolled. Patients were randomly assigned to undergo immediate CLND if SLN mapping was positive, versus no SLN mapping, at the time of study entry. MSLT-I showed no difference in 10-year OS rate.[29] These data suggest SLN mapping has only prognostic information and control of the regional, non-clinically detectable disease may not have an impact on OS.

Radiographic Staging. Radiographic staging in CM has considerably lower sensitivity and specificity compared with SLN mapping, because it cannot detect microscopic (ie, ≤ 3 mm) lymph node involvement. The use of whole-body fluorodeoxyglucose positron emission tomography (FDG-PET) and computed tomography (CT) coregistered with nonintravenous contrast CT scan is superior compared with FDG-PET alone regarding sensitivity and specificity to screen for distant metastases in patients with stage III disease.[30] The use of PET/CT or diagnostic CT scan with intravenous contrast for initial staging of low-risk patients (stages I-II) at the time of diagnosis is controversial, although it has increased in popularity over time. Interestingly, approximately 23% of patients with low-risk melanoma had positive PET/CT scans at original diagnosis in a single study.[31]

Surveillance After Original Diagnosis and Therapy. Any surveillance strategy should consider patterns of recurrence after resection of the primary lesion and/or nodal staging or resection. Approximately half of recurrences are within the regional lymph node bed, 20% are locoregional, and 30% involve distant metastases. Most recurrences are within the first 2 years of CM diagnosis and with a decreasing risk between the second and fourth year. All patients should be followed with a medical history and physical examination, including skin and lymph node examinations every 3 to 6 months for the first 3 to 5 years and then annually for their lifetime. Patients should have skin screening for additional primary melanomas and other nonmelanoma skin cancers at least annually for their lifetime. Table 16-2 lists recommendations for radiographic imaging according to the stage at diagnosis.

KEY POINTS

- Clinical evaluation of the patient with newly diagnosed CM should include a full medical history, including a family and personal history of melanoma and other cancers.
- Physical examination should include skin and lymph node examinations.
- Surgical management includes wide excision concurrent with SLN biopsy when indicated. SLN status is an independent prognostic factor for OS.
- Radiographic imaging with whole-body PET/CT scans can be considered for patients with stage III disease to screen for locoregional and distant metastases.
- Patients should be clinically followed every 3 to 6 months for the first 3 to 5 years and then annually for their lifetime.

TREATMENT

Tis to T4 (Stages 0 to II)

Several large, randomized control studies have established optimal wide-excision margins for Tis to T4 melanoma.[32] Surgical margins are clinically defined from the edges of the primary tumor, or primary melanoma scar, and are not based

Table 16-3 **Recommended Wide and Deep Excision Margins for Tis to T4 Melanoma**

Breslow Depth of Invasion (mm)	Wide Surgical Margin (cm)	Deep Surgical Margin
In situ	0.5-1	Excised to the depth within the adipose layer
≤ 1.0	1	
> 1.0 and ≤ 2.0	1-2	Excised to the depth immediately above muscle fascia
> 2.0	2	

on the histopathologic margins reported by the pathologist. Fewer standardized criteria are available regarding the optimal depth of wide excision. Table 16-3 provides the recommended wide- and deep-excision margins relative to the depth of invasion in primary CM.

At this time, the only available US FDA-approved systemic adjuvant treatment for completely resected stage IIB/IIC disease is high-dose interferon α2b (IFNα2b; 20 MU/m^2 administered intravenously, Monday through Friday, for 4 weeks, followed by 10 MU/m^2 administered subcutaneously on Mondays, Wednesdays, and Fridays for up to 48 weeks); the approval was based on the results from three randomized, phase III, Eastern Cooperative Oncology Group (ECOG)-led adjuvant trials (E1684, E1690, and E1694).[33-35] It is important to emphasize that in the 1980s and 1990s, the "high-risk" definition involved patients with either regional lymph node–negative, deep primary (Breslow depth of invasion > 4 mm), or regional lymph node-positive disease (any T). Therefore, the results from these trials did not solely include patients with stage IIB/IIB melanoma. The clinical benefit from high-dose interferon (HDI) in stage IIB/IIC melanoma is unknown in the current era of more effective immunotherapies for stage IV disease. At this time, two ongoing studies are testing the efficacy of pembrolizumab and nivolumab in patients with CM (ClinicalTrial.gov identifiers NCT03553836/KEYNOTE-716 and NCT03405155, respectively).

KEY POINTS

- Melanoma with deep Breslow thickness (ie, ≥4 mm), ulceration, even without positive regional lymph nodes (stage IIC), has a high risk of recurrence.
- The only available systemic adjuvant treatment for stage IIB/IIC melanoma is high-dose IFNα2b, based on the results from three randomized, phase III, ECOG-led adjuvant trials that enrolled patients with completely resected stage IIB to III melanoma.
- Ongoing adjuvant clinical trials are investigating the efficacy of PD-1 inhibitors in patients with stage II melanoma who are at high risk for relapse.

Stage III Disease

Role of Surgery.

Clinically occult (normal) regional lymph nodes. MSLT-II, a randomized phase III study (N = 1,939 patients), aimed to address the question of whether immediate CLND after positive SLN mapping in patients without clinical evidence of regional lymphadenopathy increased the rate of regional disease control and/or prolonged OS. This was an important question because CLND could identify additional positive lymph nodes (21%) following positive SLN mapping at the cost of permanent morbidities (eg, lymphedema).[36] Melanoma-specific OS was not prolonged in the CLND group; however, regional disease control was improved in the CLND group.[37] Lack of OS benefit was also seen in the German DeCOG-SLT, a multicenter, randomized phase III trial that included 483 patients.[38] Lack of OS benefit after control of regional disease implies that patient's outcome is not solely influenced by eradication of the regional clones. Perhaps regional nodal disease may not be the "launching pad" for development of distant metastatic disease, as was previously thought.[39]

On the basis of the results of the MSLT-2 and DeCOG-SLT studies, CLND is no longer considered the standard recommended treatment for all patients with positive SLN biopsy specimens (ie, nonclinically detected). CLND can be discussed and offered to select patients with positive SLNs. ASCO guidelines recommend a balanced discussion about the risks and benefits of foregoing CLND in favor of watchful observation with serial nodal ultrasound.[28] Many centers have primarily adopted the observation approach, given the lack of OS benefit with CLND. It is also important to note that staging will be influenced by the decision to avoid CLND in these patients.

Clinically Detected Regional Lymph Nodes.

Therapeutic lymph node dissection and the role of adjuvant radiation therapy. Therapeutic lymph node dissection (level I to III dissection in the axilla, superficial groin dissection in the groin, and level II to V radical lymph node dissection in the neck) is the standard treatment for patients with clinically detected stage III melanoma and no radiographic evidence of distant metastases, because it offers the best opportunity for locoregional control. Patients with sizeable nodal tumor burden or extracapsular extension still have a high risk for regional and distant relapse following CLND, and with considerable morbidity (eg, pain, lymphedema, impaired function).

Adjuvant radiation can be considered in select patients with high-risk features for locoregional relapse (eg, multiple regional nodes involved, matted nodes, extracapsular extension within the affected nodes), given the significantly lower incidence of lymph node in-field relapse in the radiation therapy–treated patients as opposed to observation that was seen in the randomized, multicenter, phase III ANZMTG 01.02/TROG 02.01 trial (HR, 0.52; 95% CI, 0.31 to 0.88]).[40]

Isolated Limb Infusion and Perfusion. Therapeutic isolated limb perfusion and isolated limb infusion are surgical techniques that achieve temporal regional vascular isolation to enable regional delivery of chemotherapies at doses many-fold higher than those administered systemically, which would otherwise cause irreversible bone marrow toxicity. Patients with advanced locoregional CM involving an extremity are eligible. The most frequently used cytotoxic agent is melphalan (10 mg/L in lower-limb tissue perfused and 13 mg/L in upper-limb tissue perfused) and the usual perfused time is 60 to 90 minutes. Local complications include myotoxicity, neuropathy, erythema, edema, blistering, and desquamation, and depend on the temperature of the infused drug. Systemic complications depend on the level of systemic drug leakage and include nausea, vomiting, and bone marrow toxicity. Experienced academic institutions have high overall response rates (81% for heated isolated limb perfusion; 43% for isolated limb infusion) and low mortality rates. The procedure requires a hospital stay.[41] OS benefit has not been demonstrated in clinical trials, but isolated limb-directed therapy is an useful option in select patients.

KEY POINTS

- CLND did not improve OS after a positive SLN biopsy specimen in two randomized clinical trials and is not considered as standard of care across all patients with clinically occult stage III melanoma. CLND decreases incidence of regional lymph node recurrence and can be considered in select patients.
- For patients with stage III melanoma and clinically detected regional lymph nodes, therapeutic lymph node dissection of the regional nodal basin should be discussed and offered, in addition to resection of the clinically involved node.

Role of Systemic Therapy.

Adjuvant therapy. Table 16-4 summarizes important data from pivotal randomized phase III clinical trials that led to the FDA approval of systemic therapies for patients with completely resected high-risk for relapse melanoma. Seminal randomized phase III studies have drastically changed the standard of care treatments for patients with stage III melanoma. Nearly all FDA-approved adjuvant therapies are administered for up to 1 year, an interval that was set by convention in the first successful adjuvant trial in CM, E1684.[34] Experimental drugs in all clinical trials were tested in patients with stage III melanoma and were compared against placebo, with the exception of CheckMate 238, which also included patients with completely resected stage IV melanoma and compared adjuvant nivolumab, a monoclonal antibody targeting PD-1, against adjuvant ipilimumab, a monoclonal antibody targeting CTLA-4.[43]

Adjuvant pembrolizumab (200 mg administered intravenously every 3 weeks for 18 doses), a monoclonal antibody targeting PD-1, and adjuvant nivolumab (3 mg/kg administered intravenously every 2 weeks) are the two FDA-approved, frontline adjuvant treatments for patients with completely resected stage III/IV melanoma; approval was granted on the basis of significant RFS benefit compared with placebo (HR, 0.57; 95% CI, 0.43 to 0.74) or adjuvant high-dose ipilimumab (HDIp; 10 mg/kg administered intravenously every 3 weeks for up to four doses and then every 12 weeks; HR, 0.65; 95% CI, 0.51 to 0.83), as reported from the KEYNOTE-054 and CheckMate 238 studies, respectively. At a median follow-up of 1.3 years (KEYNOTE-054) or minimal follow-up of 2 years (CheckMate 238), no OS benefit in favor of the experimental arm has been reported.[44,45] It is unclear whether, with longer follow-up for CheckMate 238 and EORTC 1325, OS will be significantly improved favoring the investigation arm. If there is no OS benefit in favor of the PD-1 inhibitor arms, such a finding may imply that the control arm that did not receive PD-1 inhibitors could be effectively treated at the time disease recurs, despite the delay in delivering a more effective treatment (ie, PD-1 inhibitor). In contrast, administration of adjuvant dabrafenib (150 mg administered orally twice daily), a BRAF inhibitor, and trametinib (2 mg administered orally once daily), a MEK inhibitor, in patients with completely resected nonmicroscopic (stage IIIA > 1 mm) stage III *BRAFV600*-mutant melanoma has shown both significant RFS and OS compared with observation (COMBI-AD trial, median follow-up 2.8 years; RFS HR, 0.47 [95% CI, 0.39 to 0.58] and OS HR, 0.57 [95% CI, 0.42 to 0.79]).[46]

Randomized, phase III adjuvant clinical trials in the pre–PD-1 inhibitor era have established that HDIp (EORTC 18071), HDI (E1684, E1690), and pegylated high-dose IFNα2b (6 μg/kg administered subcutaneously every week for 8 weeks followed by 3 μg/kg administered subcutaneously for up to 5 years; EORTC 18991) as superior compared with observation or placebo in terms of RFS in patients at high risk for CM relapse.[33,34,42,47] However, only the EORTC 18071 and the E1684 adjuvant studies have shown significant OS benefit (HR, 0.72 [95% CI, 0.58 to 0.88], and HR, 0.84 [95% CI, 0.58 to 1.22], respectively). E1609 is the only three-arm, randomized, phase III adjuvant study that compared OS between each of the two different adjuvant ipilimumab regimens (HDIp and low-dose ipilimumab [LDIp], 10 mg/kg administered intravenously every 3 weeks for four doses and then every 12 weeks) and HDI which at the time of study design was the standard of care adjuvant treatment for stage III melanoma. Only LDIp resulted in significant OS compared with HDI (HR, 0.78; 95% CI, 0.61 to 0.99]). Surprisingly, the rate of discontinuation due to adverse events was significantly lower in the HDI arm.[48] At this time, HDIp remains the only FDA-approved treatment for stage III melanoma. Given the higher clinical benefit and significantly lower toxicity of pembrolizumab and nivolumab in the adjuvant setting, it is unclear what the role of adjuvant LDIp is in stage III melanoma. High toxicity rate, the lack of OS benefit seen with pegylated high-dose IFNα2b, and the inferior OS benefit of HDI compared with LDIp may additionally reduce the use of adjuvant interferons in patients at high risk for relapse stage III melanoma.

At this time, there are no level I data supporting an optimal choice between PD-1 inhibitors and a combination of dabrafenib and trametinib for adjuvant treatment in patients at high risk for relapse of *BRAFV600*-mutant, stage III melanoma. Patients with this melanoma subtype require a balanced discussion regarding the risks and potential benefit of each systemic treatment. A retrospective multicenter analysis of 149 patients who received adjuvant PD-1 inhibitor–based treatments for completely resected stage III/IV melanoma that subsequently recurred was performed. The majority of these recurrences occurred while the patient was receiving treatment (71%) and were distant metastases (57%). If locoregional relapse occurred, the most frequent strategy was surgery alone (60%); if distant relapse occurred, the most frequent treatment was ipilimumab-based therapy (42%) followed by BRAF/MEK-targeted therapy (39%). Antitumor responses to BRAF/MEK inhibitors were significantly

Table 16-4 **Summary of Clinical Data From Key Randomized Clinical Trials in Patients With Completely Resected Melanoma at High Risk for Relapse**

Study	Stage	Drug(s) Tested	No. Eligible Pts	Mdn F/U (years)	Study Arm (A, B, or C) Comparison		Toxicities in Treatment Arm (% grade ≥ 3)	Discontinuation Rate Due to Drug-Related AEs (%)
					RFS, HR (95% CI)	OS, HR (95% CI)		
E1684[34]	T4+ or N+	HDI *v* obs	280	6.9	0.76[a] (0.53 to 1.08)	0.84[a] (0.58 to 1.22)	Constitutional (48), myelosuppression (24), hepatotoxicity (15), neurologic (28)	41
EORTC 18991[147]	III	PEG-IFNα2b[b] *v* obs	1,256	7.6	0.87[a] (0.76 to 1.00)	0.96 (0.82 to 1.11)	Fatigue (16), hepatotoxicity (11), depression (7)	31
EORTC 18071[42]	III > 1mm	HDIp *v* placebo	951	5.3	0.76[a] (0.64 to 0.89)	0.72[a] (0.58 to 0.88)	Any immune-related Aes (43), diarrhea (10), colitis (8), hypophysitis (5), ↑LFTs (4)	40
E1609[48]	IIIB-M1b	HDIp[c] (A) *v* HDI[d] (B) and LDIp (C) *v* HDI (B)	1,670	4.8	A *v* B 0.84 C *v* B 0.85	A *v* B 0.88 C *v* B 0.78[a]	Any grade ≥ 3 Arm A, 67 Arm B, 68 Arm C, 54	Arm A, 54 Arm B, 20 Arm C, 35
KEYNOTE-054[44]	III	Pembro[e] *v* placebo	1,019	1.3	0.57[a] (0.43 to 0.74)	Not reported	Any immune-related (7), colitis (2), T1DM (1), hepatitis (1)	14
CheckMate 238[45]	III-M1c	Nivo[f] *v* HDIp	906	2 (minimum)	0.65[a] (0.51 to 0.83)	Not reported	Diarrhea (1.5), rash (1), ↑ALT (1)	5
COMBI-AD[46]	All III except IIIA (< 1 mm)	D+T[g] *v* obs	870	2.8	0.47[a] (0.39 to 0.58)	0.57[a] (0.42 to 0.79)	Hypertension (6), pyrexia (5), fatigue (4), ↑ALT (4), ↑AST (4)	24-25

Abbreviations: AE, adverse event; ALT, alanine aminotransferase; AST, aspartate aminotransferase; D+T, dabrafenib plus trametinib; HDI, high-dose interferon; HDIp, high-dose ipilimumab; HR, hazard ratio; LDIp, low-dose ipilimumab; LFT, liver function test; Mdn F/U, median follow-up; nivo, nivolumab; Obs, observation; OS, overall survival; PEG-IFNα2b, pegylated interferon-α2b; pembro, pembrolizumab; Pts, Patients; RFS, relapse-free survival; T1DM, type 1 diabetes mellitus.

[a]Statistically significant ($p<0.05$).

[b]Dosing: 6 μg/kg administered subcutaneously each week for 8 weeks followed by 3 μg/kg administered subcutaneously for ≤ 5 years.

[c]Dosing: 10 mg/kg administered intravenously every 3 weeks for four doses and then every 12 weeks.

[d]Dosing: 20 MU/m^2 administered intravenously, Monday through Friday, for 4 weeks, followed by 10 MU/m^2 administered subcutaneously on Monday, Wednesday, and Friday for ≤ 48 weeks.

[e]Dosing: 200 mg administered intravenously every 3 weeks for 18 doses.

[f]Dosing: 3 mg/kg administered intravenously every 2 weeks.

[g]Dosing: dabrafenib, 150 mg administered orally twice daily; trametinib, 2 mg administered orally once daily.

higher than the responses seen to ipilimumab-based treatments, especially if adjuvant PD-1 inhibitors had been discontinued and disease relapse occurred (90% *v* 40%).[49]

KEY POINT

- Up to 1 year concurrent dabrafenib and trametinib (in *BRAFV600*-mutant disease), nivolumab, or pembrolizumab are adjuvant treatment options for patients with completely resected stage III melanoma, based on improved RFS and reasonable tolerability. Of these treatment options, only concurrent dabrafenib and trametinib has also demonstrated improved OS benefit compared with placebo. Longer follow-up is required to assess whether pembrolizumab or nivolumab also improve OS.

Neoadjuvant therapy. In contrast to most other solid cancers, preoperative (neoadjuvant) administration of systemic drugs for bulky stage III melanoma has only recently begun to be considered. Previously, there were few effective systemic therapies for melanoma to potentially transform a patient's melanoma from unresectable to resectable. Analysis of pooled data was recently reported from six neoadjuvant clinical trials in clinical stage III melanoma for patients with nodal metastases who underwent definitive surgery as part of the International Neoadjuvant Melanoma Consortium. Of the 184 patients whose data were analyzed, 133 received immunotherapy and 51 targeted therapy. Despite differences between neoadjuvant immunotherapy and BRAF/MEK inhibitor therapy trials in terms of substage (IIIB *v* IIIC), anatomic location of involvement (axilla *v* groin), treatment duration of the neoadjuvant strategy, the median time to surgery, and the median follow-up after surgery, the incidence of complete pathologic response was high (38% to 47%). The 12-month RFS rate was higher in patients with stage IIIB disease than in those with stage IIIC disease (84% *v* 67%) and in patients who received immunotherapies versus those who received targeted therapies (83% *v* 65%). Across all patients, 1- and 2-year RFS rates were higher in patients who achieved complete pathologic response (95% *v* 62% and 89% *v* 48%, respectively).[50] Two of these neoadjuvant clinical trials had a two-arm randomized design in which the comparator arm included patients who received the same regimen in the adjuvant setting.[51,52] Despite the small number of patients enrolled and the short follow-up, neoadjuvant administration of systemic treatments significantly prolonged RFS compared with adjuvant setting. Although the underlying mechanism remains elusive, future, larger, prospective randomized studies testing the neoadjuvant versus adjuvant treatment approach (eg, the S1801 Intergroup Study, a randomized phase II study of adjuvant *v* neoadjuvant pembrolizumab for clinically detectable stage III-IV high-risk melanoma) may challenge the clinical benefit of the half-century-old concept of the "surgery first, chemotherapy afterward" approach.

KEY POINTS

- Results of small phase II clinical studies of systemic treatments in which patients with stage III melanoma were randomly assigned to receive systemic treatment in the neoadjuvant as opposed to adjuvant setting suggest early RFS benefit favoring the neoadjuvant approach. The presumed mechanism and confirmation of this signal in larger clinical studies are currently under investigation.
- Neoadjuvant administration of the recently FDA-approved targeted therapies and immunotherapies is associated with high incidence of complete pathologic responses. Complete pathologic response is associated with longer RFS benefit irrespective of systemic treatment type.

Stage IV Melanoma

Overview of Biology. Few studies with matched (ie, same-patient) primary and metastatic melanoma tumors are available to investigate what makes advanced melanomas biologically distinct from their primary lesion. This is an essential question because it influences treatment decisions for patients with unresectable stage III-IV melanoma. Beyond the well-described, frequently mutated *BRAF*, *NRAS*, *PTEN*, *CDKN2A*, and *TP53A* genes, infrequent mutations in a few other genes (eg, *RAC1*, *SPEN*) may have prognostic significance in metastatic melanoma.[53] Whereas important mutated oncogenes that are present early in melanoma development (eg, *BRAFV600E*, *NRASQ61*) are retained at a high frequency between primary and metastatic tumors in the same patient, other somatically mutated tumor-suppressor genes (eg, *CDKN2Ap16*) are more frequent in distant metastases. The finding that the *BRAFV600E* mutation is also present in metastases is the molecular basis for targeting a protein present in earlier stages of melanoma development, such as BRAFV600.[9] Considerable intratumoral genetic heterogeneity of large metastatic melanoma lesions provides a molecular explanation regarding the lower responses seen to any systemic therapies in advanced, high tumor burden melanoma.[54]

Two reports that analyzed at least two metastatic melanoma tumors from the same patient, using gene expression profiling and targeted panel sequencing, showed that both intertumoral (ie, molecular differences between different metastatic lesions) heterogeneity and homogeneity are seen in advanced melanoma.[25,55] Molecular homogeneity between extracranial and intracranial metastases may account for concordance in extracranial and intracranial responses seen with combination ipilimumab and nivolumab administration in patients with active brain metastases (CheckMate 204).[56] Intratumoral heterogeneity (ie, molecular differences between different parts of the same tumor) is an adverse prognostic factor as well as a predictor of poor response to available systemic therapies. Epigenetic heterogeneity, which is not solely driven by genetic aberrations but also influenced by the physicochemical factors, such as pH, hypoxia, and cues derived from the metastatic organ–specific niche, is poorly understood at this time. Knowledge about the biology of metastatic melanoma has tremendous implications in the treatment approach to advanced melanoma, as discussed in the following paragraphs.

Surgery. In appropriately selected patients (eg, those with oligometastatic melanoma), curative-intent metastasectomy was a standard treatment option before 2010. Analysis of the SEER database for patients diagnosed with advanced melanoma between 1986 and 2006 (N = 4,229) showed that approximately one-third of patients underwent metastasectomy. These patients were usually younger and had more recently diagnosed advanced melanoma. Patients who underwent metastasectomy had longer OS compared with patients who did not undergo metastasectomy, irrespective of M1 substage (M1a *v* all others). Selection bias to perform metastasectomy was an obvious flaw of the study. It also implied, however, that patients with oligometastatic melanoma might have an inherently better prognosis than patients with multiple distant metastases.[57] A single-institution study conducted at the Royal Marsden Hospital NHS Foundation Trust showed that since 2011, there were fewer excisions for in transit melanoma and more abdominal metastasectomies.[58] Surgery continues to have an important treatment role in selective patients with advanced melanoma, both for palliative intent and for disease control.

Radiation Therapy. Hypofractionated radiation therapy (≥ 2.5 Gy/fraction) is a standard treatment option in the palliative care of patients with advanced melanoma who have symptomatic lesions (eg, pain, mass effect, hemorrhage, bone destruction) that are not amenable or responsive to systemic treatments or surgery. Advances in imaging techniques, patient mobilization, and instrumentation have enabled radiation oncologists to provide even higher doses per fraction, sparing adjacent normal tissues from toxicity via a variety of radiation delivery methods (eg, external beam radiation therapy, stereotactic radiosurgery, intensity-modulated radiation therapy). Stereotactic radiosurgery should be considered in patients with limited parenchymal brain metastases,[59] reserving the use of whole-brain irradiation for patients with more extensive CNS disease for palliation. Concurrent administration of MAPK inhibitors with radiation therapy can significantly worsen radiation therapy–related toxicities. Therefore, concomitant use of MAPK inhibitors and radiation therapy should be avoided.[60] Radiation can induce immunogenic cell death through the release of tumor-associated antigens. The synergy of radiation with immunotherapy is being investigated in clinical trials, including the ABC-X Study, RADVAX, and BOOSTER MELANOMA trials.

KEY POINTS

- Surgical resection can be considered in select patients with metastatic melanoma for disease control (ie, oligometastatic disease) or with palliative intent.
- Radiation therapy is a standard palliative treatment option in advanced melanoma; stereotactic radiotherapy can be considered for disease control in select patients with oligometastatic disease or limited CNS disease.
- Concurrent administration of MAPK inhibitors with radiation therapy worsens radiation therapy–related toxicities.
- Concurrent administration of radiation therapy with immune checkpoint inhibitors is currently under clinical investigation.

Systemic Therapy. Effective systemic treatments for advanced melanoma have prolonged OS and reduced melanoma-specific mortality over the last 2 to 3 years (Fig 16-1). In 2010, there were only two systemic treatment options for advanced melanoma: dacarbazine and high-dose bolus interleukin-2 (IL-2). Since 2011, three treatment combinations targeting the MAPK pathway (vemurafenib and cobimetinib; dabrafenib and trametinib; encorafenib and binimetinib), three immune checkpoint inhibitors (ipilimumab, nivolumab, and pembrolizumab), and one oncolytic virotherapy administered intratumorally (talimogene laherparepvec [TVEC]) have been FDA-approved. The increasing number of options has generated questions about their comparative safety and efficacy, optimal combinations, and optimal sequences, and about rationally combining them with a growing number of investigational drugs currently in clinical development. The following sections elaborate on the essential data from pivotal clinical trials that led to the FDA approval of these drugs and provide recommendations regarding optimal use, sequence, mechanisms of resistance, and the potential for rechallenge.

Immunotherapy. Use of systemic therapies to augment host immune response to melanoma has been ongoing since at least the 1960s.[61] In retrospect, high-throughput and histopathologic analyses of cutaneous melanoma tumor samples as part of the TCGA and other projects have explained the immunogenicity of this tumor in terms of the high somatic mutation burden, the aberrant expression of various melanoma-associated and other cancer-testis antigens, as well as the increased frequency of TILs.[8] Various cytokines, growth factors, and melanoma vaccines constituted the early immunotherapies that were tested in metastatic melanoma with overall low success before the advent of immune checkpoint inhibitors.[61] Table 16-5 lists key clinical studies in advanced melanoma that led to the FDA approval of various immunotherapies over the last 30 years.

High-Dose IL-2. High-dose bolus IL-2 (HDIL2) was the first treatment to be FDA-approved in advanced melanoma. IL-2, previously known as T-cell growth factor, plays an essential role in T-cell survival, proliferation, and activation. HDIL2 was approved in 1988 on the basis of the durability of antitumor responses (6% and 10% incidence of complete response and partial response, respectively) from several nonrandomized, single-arm, phase II studies.[62] The median OS of 11.4 months was the new bar set for any new systemic treatments in advanced melanoma. Given HDIL2's severe adverse effects (AEs), development of strict guidelines for administration of HDIL2 have been developed.[63]

Ipilimumab. Historically, MDX-020-010 was the first randomized phase III trial (N = 676) in advanced melanoma that tested the clinical benefit of LDIp (3 mg/kg administered intravenously every 3 weeks for up to four infusions) alone and in combination with an HLA-A*0201-restricted gp100 vaccine.[64] Both ipilimumab-treated arms had longer RFS and OS compared with the gp100 vaccine-treated arm. Although the median OS seen in the ipilimumab-treated arms from this trial was comparable with that seen with HDIL2, the convenient outpatient administration of the LDIp regimen every 3 weeks and its less severe acute toxicities compared with those of HDIL2 broadened the use of LDIp to a far larger group of medical oncologists, because it did not require them to be IL-2 specialists or refer their patients to HDIL2-specialized centers for treatment. Interestingly, a randomized trial of HDIp (10 mg/kg administered intravenously every 3 weeks for up to 4 infusions) versus LDIp in patients with advanced melanoma resulted in prolonged OS in favor of the high dose (median OS, 15.7 *v* 11.5 months; HR, 0.84; 95% CI, 0.70 to 0.99), but at the expense of higher incidence of treatment-related toxicities (37% *v* 18%).[65] Despite the higher clinical benefit of HDIp in stage IV melanoma and given the fact that this trial was conducted before the advent of PD-1 inhibitors, LDIp remains the FDA-approved standard of care. Ipilimumab monotherapy is not recommended as standard first-line therapy, due to the superiority of anti-PD-1 agents, as detailed in the next section.

PD-1 Inhibitors. Pembrolizumab is the first PD-1 inhibitor to be approved by the FDA for ipilimumab-refractory (and MAPK inhibitor–refractory, if *BRAFV600*-mutant) advanced melanoma, based on the results of the KEYNOTE-002 study.[66] In the KEYNOTE-002 study, the two different doses of pembrolizumab (2 mg/kg and 10 mg/kg) were administered intravenously every 3 weeks and were tested against investigator's choice chemotherapy (1:1:1 randomization; N = 540). Both pembrolizumab arms significantly prolonged 6-month PFS compared with the investigator's choice chemotherapy. Given the nonsignificant difference in the PFS between high-dose and low-dose pembrolizumab, FDA approved the 2 mg/kg dose

Table 16-5 Summary of Clinical Data From Key Randomized Clinical Trials of Immunotherapy Drugs in Patients With Unresectable Stage III or Distant Metastatic Melanoma

Study	Drug(s) (study arms)	No. Pts[a]	Mdn F/U (months)	ORR, % (study arms)	Study Arm (A, B, or C) Comparisons		Comments
					RFS, HR	OS, HR	
Meta-analysis 1985-1993[62]	HDIL2[b]	270	62	16	Not reported	Not reached	CR, 6%; if CR MDR, not reached PR, 10%; if PR MDR, 5.9 months Median OS, 11.4 months
MDX-020-010[64]	LDIp+V (A) *v* LDIp+PBO (B) *v* PBO+V (C)	676	17.2-27.8	5.7 (A) *v* 11 (B) *v* 1.5 (C)	A *v* C, 0.81 B *v* C, 0.64	A *v* C, 0.68[k] B *v* C, 0.66[k]	HLA-A*0201 patients only 3 (Arm A): 1 (Arm B): 1 (Arm C) Median OS (LDIp alone), 10.1 months
KEYNOTE-002[66]	HDPembro[c] (A) *v* LDPembro[d] (B) *v* chemotherapy (C)	540[e]	28	26 (A) *v* 21 (B) *v* 4 (C)	A *v* C, 0.47[k] B *v* C, 0.58[k]	A *v* C, 0.74[k] B *v* C, 0.86 A *v* B 0.87	No difference in PFS between HDPembro *v* LDPembro No difference in OS between LDPembro and chemotherapy Median OS (LDPembro), 13.4 months
CheckMate 037[68]	Nivo[f] (A) *v* chemotherapy (B)	370[e]	~24	27 (A) *v* 10 (B)	A *v* B, 1.0	A *v* B, 0.95	Median OS (nivo), 15.7 months
KEYNOTE-006[67]	Pembro[g] q2w (A) *v* pembro q3w (B) *v* LDIp (C)	811	22.9	37 (A) *v* 36 (B) *v* 13 (C)	A *v* C, 0.61[k] B *v* C, 0.61[k] A *v* B, 0.95	A *v* B, 0.68[k] A *v* C, 0.68[k] A *v* B, not reported	1 (Arm A): 1 (Arm B): 1 (Arm C) Median OS (both pembro arms), 32.7 months[148]
CheckMate 064[149]	Nivo→LDIp[h] (A) LDIp→nivo (B)	140	14.7-19.8	56 (A) *v* 32 (B)	Not reached	0.48	Median OS (nivo→LDIp), not reached
CheckMate 067[70]	Nivo-ipi[i] (A) *v* nivo+PBO (B) *v* LDIp+PBO (C)	945	18.6-46.9	58 (A) *v* 44 (B) *v* 21 (C)	A *v* C, 0.44[k] B *v* C, 0.53[k] A *v* B, 0.79	A *v* C, 0.54[k] B *v* C, 0.65[k] A *v* B, 0.84	Patients (%) who received ipi after progression in A *v* B (6% *v* 28%)[70] Median OS (ipi-nivo), not reached (minimum f/u, 48 months) Longer OS of arm A *v* arm B in patients with *BRAFV600*-mutation
CheckMate 204[56]	Nivo-ipi	94	14	Intracranial 56 Extracranial 50	N/A	N/A	Only the asymptomatic cohort for CNS symptoms was reported 1-yr PFS: 56.6%; OS rate, 81.5%
OPTiM[j73]	TVEC intratumoral injections v GM-CSF sc injections *v* GM-CSF	436	49	19.3 *v* 1.4	0.42	0.79[k]	2 (TVEC): 1 (GM-CSF) randomization Median OS (TVEC), 23.3 months

Abbreviations: CR, complete response; GM-CSF, granulocyte-macrophage colony-stimulating factor; HDIL2, high-dose bolus interleukin-2; HDPembro, high-dose pembrolizumab; HR, hazard ratio; ipi, ipilimumab; LDIp, low-dose ipilimumab; LDPembro, low-dose pembrolizumab; Mdn F/U, median follow-up; MDR, median duration of response; N/A, not applicable; nivo, nivolumab; ORR, overall response rate; OS, overall survival; PBO, placebo; pembro, pembrolizumab; PFS, progression-free survival; PR, partial response; q2w, every 2 weeks; q3w, every 3 weeks; RFS, relapse-free survival; TVEC, talimogene laherparepvec; V, vaccine.

[a]Only eligible and/or randomly assigned patients.

[b]Dosing: 600,000 IU/kg/dose administered intravenously over 15 minutes every 8 hours for a maximum of 14 doses per cycle per admission; each cycle is separated by a minimum of 9 days.

[c]Dosing: 10 mg/kg administered intravenously q3w.

[d]Dosing: 2 mg/kg administered intravenously q3w.

[e]Ipilimumab-refractory and BRAF-inhibitor refractory (if *BRAFV600*-mutant).

[f]Dosing: 3 mg/kg administered intravenously q2w.

[g]Dose: 10 mg/kg administered intravenously.

[h]Dosing: 3 mg/kg administered intravenously q3w for up to four doses.

[i]Dosing: nivolumab 1 mg/kg administered intravenously q3w plus ipilimumab 3 mg/kg administered intravenously q3w followed by nivolumab 3 mg/kg q2w.

[j]Unlike other studies, OPTiM enrolled patients with IIIB-M1c melanoma, used durable response rate as the primary end point, and time-to-treatment failure as opposed to PFS.

[k]Statistically significant ($p \leq 0.05$).

administered every 3 weeks. Pembrolizumab was subsequently approved by the FDA as a front-line treatment for patients with advanced melanoma, on the basis of results from the randomized KEYNOTE-006 trial (N = 834) that compared pembrolizumab (10 mg/kg administered intravenously either every 2 or every 3 weeks) versus ipilimumab (3 mg/kg administered intravenously every 3 weeks).[67] Based on dosing data from KEYNOTE-002 and KEYNOTE-006, the FDA-approved dose of pembrolizumab is 2 mg/kg administered intravenously every 3 weeks.

Nivolumab was FDA-approved on the basis of data from CheckMate 037, a randomized (2:1) study that compared the efficacy of single-agent nivolumab (3 mg/kg administered intravenously every 2 weeks) with investigator's choice chemotherapy in a similar patient population to the one enrolled in the KEYNOTE-002 study. Despite fewer patients and shorter median follow-up compared to the KEYNOTE-002, the study met its primary end point of significantly higher and durable (ie, minimum follow-up of 24 weeks) antitumor responses favoring nivolumab.[68] Nivolumab was similarly approved in the front-line setting on the basis of the CheckMate 066 trial, a randomized phase III study of patients without any *BRAFV600* codon mutations. As part of this trial, nivolumab significantly prolonged PFS and OS compared with dacarbazine.[69]

CTLA-4– and PD-1–Inhibitor Sequencing. The optimal sequence of PD-1 versus CTLA-4 inhibitor monotherapies was investigated in CheckMate 064, a multicenter phase II study in patients with advanced melanoma who had been naïve to immune checkpoint inhibitors. In this study, 140 patients were randomly assigned to initiate ipilimumab treatment (3 mg/kg administered intravenously every 3 weeks for up to four infusions) followed by nivolumab (3 mg/kg administered intravenously every 2 weeks for a total of six infusions), on weeks 13 to 25, or to nivolumab followed by ipilimumab therapy. At a median follow-up of 14.7-19.8 months, the median OS was not reached for the patients receiving nivolumab followed by ipilimumab, whereas the corresponding median OS was 16.9 months for the group treated with the reverse sequence (HR, 0.48; 95% CI, 0.29 to 0.80). The OS superiority in the nivolumab followed by ipilimumab group versus the group that was treated with the reverse sequence is in line with the lack of OS seen for both low-dose pembrolizumab and nivolumab compared with investigator's choice chemotherapy in an updated analysis for the corresponding KEYNOTE-002 and CheckMate 037 trials.[66,70] However, these results are confounded by the allowable crossover in both trials.

CTLA-4– and PD-1–Inhibitor Combinations. CheckMate 067 tested the efficacy and toxicity profile of the combination of ipilimumab plus nivolumab versus each drug alone in patients with immune checkpoint inhibitor–naïve advanced melanoma.[71] The ipilimumab and nivolumab combination was associated with unprecedented antitumor responses compared with nivolumab alone or LDIp alone (57.6%. *v* 43.7% *v* 19%, respectively), without significant difference in PFS and OS between the combination arm and the nivolumab-alone arm (PFS HR, 0.79 [95% CI, 0.65 to 0.97]; OS HR, 0.84 [95% CI, 0.67 to 1.05]). Post hoc analysis of the systemic treatments after exit from the trial showed that patients in the nivolumab-alone arm received salvage ipilimumab-containing regimens more frequently than patients who were randomly assigned to the combination arm (28% *v* 6%).[71] This implies that ipilimumab may potentially "salvage" the majority of patients who received nivolumab alone, such that the OS may not be significantly different. Finally, an unplanned subgroup analysis of patients with *BRAFV600*-mutant melanomas who received the combination of nivolumab and ipilimumab versus nivolumab alone showed that the combination treatment prolonged OS (HR, 0.62; 95% CI, 0.44 to 0.88).[71]

Talimogene Laherparepvec. TVEC is a type 1 herpes simplex virus that has been genetically modified to attenuate viral pathogenicity (via deletion of the neurovirulence factor ICP34.5) in favor of greater immunogenicity via insertion and expression of the gene encoding for the human granulocyte-macrophage colony-stimulating factor (GM-CSF). In line with an immune-mediated mechanism of action,[72] analysis of TVEC-injected and noninjected distant lesions from patients with melanoma showed that TVEC was able to break local immune tolerance in the microenvironment of injected lesions by suppressing T regulatory cells, myeloid-derived suppressor cells, and activating melanoma antigen-specific effector T cells. The effect of TVEC in distant non-injected melanoma lesions was also present but much weaker.[72]

A randomized (2:1) phase III study tested the clinical benefit of intralesional TVEC injections versus systemic GM-CSF injections in patients with ≥ 1 cm lesions amenable for direct or ultrasound-guided injection(s). In this heterogeneous patient group (IIIB-M1c), incidence of antitumor responses lasting at least 6 months was significantly higher in patients in the TVEC-treated arm compared with those in the systemic GM-CSF-treated arm (19.3% v 1.4%). At a median follow-up of 49 months, both median time-to-treatment-failure and OS were significantly longer in the TVEC-treated arm as opposed to the GM-CSF–treated arm. From these results, the FDA approved TVEC for patients with stage IIIB to IV melanoma.[73]

KEY POINTS

- PD-1 blockade with pembrolizumab or nivolumab are first-line immunotherapy treatment options for patients with advanced melanoma, with improved OS in prospective, randomized phase III clinical trials.
- Concurrent ipilimumab and nivolumab is a highly effective first-line immunotherapy combination with improved PFS and OS compared with LDIp alone; dual checkpoint blockade is an effective first-line immunotherapy treatment option in select patients and should be considered for patients with small, asymptomatic CNS metastasis.

Targeted Therapies. Table 16-6 lists pivotal clinical trials that led to the FDA approval of the three BRAF/MEK inhibitor combinations in advanced *BRAFV600*-mutant melanoma.

Table 16-6 Summary of Clinical Data From Key Randomized Clinical Studies in Patients With BRAFV600-Mutant Melanoma

Study	Drugs	No. Pts[a]	Mdn F/U (months)	ORR (%)	PFS, HR (95% CI)	OS, HR (95% CI)	Comments
BRIM-3[150]	V[b] *v* DTIC[c]	675	9.2-13.4	48 *v* 5	0.26[h] (0.20 to 0.33)	0.81[h] (0.7 to 1.0)	1:1 Randomization; allowed crossover; stopped early Median PFS (V *v* DTIC), 5.3 *v* 1.6 months Median OS with and without censoring at crossover (V), 10.3 and 13.6 months, respectively
BREAK-3[74]	D[d] *v* DTIC	250	11.8-17.0	50 *v* 6	0.30[h] (0.18 to 0.51)	0.61 (0.25 to 1.48)	3:1 Randomization; allowed crossover; stopped early; 5-year OS rate (D *v* DTIC), 24% *v* 22%, respectively
COMBI-d[78]	D+T[e] *v* D+PBO	423	Not reported (≥ 36 months F/U for living patients)	68 *v* 55	0.71[h] (0.57 to 0.88)	0.75[h] (0.58 to 0.96)	1:1 Randomization 3-year PFS and OS rate (D+T), 22% and 44%, respectively Median OS, not reported
COMBI-v[79]	D+T v V	704	10-11	64 *v* 51	0.56[h] (0.46 to 0.69)	Not reported	1-year OS rate (D+T), 72% Median PFS (D+T), 11.4 months
coBRIM[151]	V+C[f] *v* V+PBO	495	18.6	70 *v* 50	0.58[h] (0.46 to 0.72)	0.70[h] (0.55 to 0.90)	1:1 Randomization Median PFS (V+C), 12.6 months Median OS (V+C), 22.5 months 4-year OS rate (V+C), 34.7%
COLUMBUS[82]	E450+B[g] (A) *v* E300 (B) *v* V (C)	577	36.8	63 *v* 51 *v* 40	A *v* C 0.51[h] B *v* C 0.68[h] A *v* B 0.77[h]	A *v* C 0.61[h] B *v* C 0.76[h] A *v* B 0.81	1:1:1 Randomization Median OS (E450+B), 33.6 months 2-year OS rate (E450+B), 57.6%

Abbreviations: B, binimetinib; BRIM, BRAF inhibitors in melanoma; C, cobimetinib; coBRIM, cobimetinib combined with BRAF inhibitors in melanoma; COMBI, dabrafenib in combination trametinib; D, dabrafenib; DTIC, dacarbazine; E450 and E300, encorafenib administered at 450 mg or 300 mg orally, once daily, respectively; F/U, follow-up; HR, hazard ratio; Mdn, median; ORR, overall response rate; OS, overall survival; PBO, placebo; PFS, progression-free survival; T, trametinib; V, vemurafenib.

[a]Only eligible, randomly assigned patients.

[b]Dosing: 960 mg orally twice daily.

[c]Dosing: 1,000 mg/m^2 administered intravenously every 3 weeks.

[d]Dosing: 150 mg orally twice daily.

[e]Dosing: 2 mg orally once daily.

[f]Dosing: 60 mg orally every day for 21 days on, 7 days off.

[g]Dosing: 45 mg orally twice daily.

[h]Statistically significant ($p \le 0.05$).

Vemurafenib followed by dabrafenib were the first two BRAF inhibitors that were FDA-approved for patients with *BRAFV600*-mutant advanced melanoma on the basis of results from the BRIM-3 and BREAK-3 randomized phase III studies, which tested each BRAF inhibitor against dacarbazine.[74,75]

Single-agent MEK inhibitors were clinically developed because direct inhibition of a downstream effector of an oncogenic protein, such as BRAFV600, adds clinical benefit to BRAF inhibitors, especially in distinct *BRAFV600*-mutant patient subgroups.[76] In line with this, early clinical studies using single-agent MEK inhibitors showed that although MEK inhibition alone has activity in *BRAFV600*-mutant melanoma, all clinical end points (ie, antitumor responses, PFS, and OS) were inferior to that of single-agent BRAF inhibitors.[77] Part of the explanation about the inferior results is the inherent weakness of a drug that targets a downstream effector of an oncogenic protein, MEK, which is usually nonmutated in melanoma.[8] This, along with the essential physiologic role of MEK signaling in normal cells, makes dose escalation of even high-affinity MEK inhibitors challenging, due to frequent toxicities. COMBI-d, COMBI-v, and coBRIM are three randomized phase III clinical studies that have tested the dabrafenib and trametinib combination (150 mg administered orally twice daily plus 2 mg administered orally once daily, respectively) and the vemurafenib and cobimetinib combination (960 mg administered orally twice daily plus 60 mg administered orally daily, respectively, on a 21-days on, 7-days off schedule) versus a single-agent BRAF inhibitor (COMBI-d or COMBI-v, and coBRIM) in patients with advanced *BRAFV600*-mutant melanoma. All three studies have shown a higher activity of the combination strategy over single-agent BRAF inhibition across all clinical end points (ie, RR, PFS, and OS).[78-80] A landmark 4-year analysis over longer follow-up for COMBI-d and coBRIM showed that approximately 35% of patients who received BRAF/MEK inhibitor combination treatment are still alive at 4 years after treatment initiation, and approximately 15% remain free of progression.

Encorafenib plus binimetinib is the most recent FDA-approved BRAF/MEK inhibitor combination for *BRAFV600*-mutant melanoma. Encorafenib is a novel ATP-competitive inhibitor that binds its target at least 15 times longer than dabrafenib and vemurafenib (the dissociation half-life from the target for encorafenib, dabrafenib, and vemurafenib is 30 hours, 120 minutes, and 30 minutes in a biochemical assay, respectively).[81] Binimetinib is a selective allosteric ATP-noncompetitive inhibitor of MEK1/2 with a shorter half-life than that of the other two FDA-approved MEK inhibitors. Paradoxically, concurrent administration of encorafenib plus binimetinib allowed for higher dosing of encorafenib (450 mg administered orally once daily [E450]) compared with the maximum tolerated dose identified in the phase I study of encorafenib (ie, 300 mg administered orally once daily [E300]).[81]

A randomized phase III study, COLUMBUS part 1, tested concurrent E450 plus binimetinib (45 mg administered orally twice daily) against E300 and against vemurafenib alone (960 mg administered orally twice daily) in patients with *BRAFV600*-mutant, BRAF inhibitor–naïve advanced melanoma.[82] E450 plus binimetinib showed a superior antitumor response, PFS, and OS compared with vemurafenib alone. At a 36.8 month follow-up, the median OS for E450 plus binimetinib combination was 33.6 months. When compared with E300, the E450 plus binimetinib combination resulted in higher antitumor responses and significantly longer PFS but no significant difference in OS. A secondary analysis showed E300 was superior to vemurafenib alone across all important clinical end points (ie, RR, PFS, and OS).[82] The superiority of OS favoring E300 over vemurafenib alone and the lack of OS difference between the E450 plus binimetinib arm versus the E300 arm can be explained by the superior pharmacodynamic profile of encorafenib compared with vemurafenib and the more important impact of BRAF as opposed to MEK inhibition as part of the concurrent BRAF/MEK blockade for patients with *BRAFV600*-mutant melanoma.[81]

There are no FDA-approved targeted treatments for patients with non–*BRAFV600*-mutant melanoma, who comprise 50% to 60% of the CM population.[8] A high proportion of melanomas in this group have hotspot mutations in the *NRASQ61* codon. Constitutive activation of RAS, a signaling molecule upstream from RAF proteins, involves more than one signaling pathway, in contrast with BRAFV600, which predominantly dysregulates a single pathway (ie, MAPK).[8] It is important to emphasize that several of these pathways are also crucial for normal cell physiology and that direct NRASQ61 inhibitors currently are not available. Several approaches have indirectly targeted constitutively activated NRAS by blocking distinct downstream signaling pathways, such as the MAPK pathway. NEMO was a randomized (2:1) phase III study that tested the efficacy of binimetinib (45 mg administered orally twice daily) compared with dacarbazine (1,000 mg/m^2 administered intravenously every 3 weeks) in patients with advanced *NRASQ61*-mutant melanoma. Although the study met its primary end point showing that binimetinib significantly prolongs PFS compared with dacarbazine, the difference (2.8 *v* 1.5 months.) was not clinically meaningful; furthermore, no OS difference was observed.[83] The results emphasize the challenges when the target cannot be directly pharmacologically inhibited; therefore, the alternative approach of blocking only one of the several downstream effectors of RAS signaling does not lead to a meaningful clinical benefit.

KEY POINTS

- Four randomized, phase III clinical studies in patients with *BRAFV600*-mutant metastatic melanoma have shown significant PFS and OS benefit favoring concurrent BRAF/MEK inhibition compared with single-agent BRAF inhibitor.
- Differences in potency among the three different BRAF inhibitors matter. Single-agent encorafenib is the first BRAF inhibitor to show OS benefit compared with single-agent vemurafenib.

Chemotherapy. Before 2010, cytotoxic chemotherapy, along with HDIL2, had been a mainstay in the treatment of advanced melanoma. After the initial FDA approval of dacarbazine in 1975, subsequent trials using combination chemotherapy regimens or biochemotherapy did not show any OS benefit, despite higher toxicity rates.[84] EORTC 18032 tested the efficacy and toxicity of escalated-dose temozolomide (150 mg/m^2 once daily for 7 days, followed by 7 days off) against standard-dose dacarbazine (1,000 mg/m^2 administered intravenously every 3 weeks) in patients with advanced melanoma. No significant differences in PFS or OS were seen between the two arms. However, antitumor responses were significantly higher with temozolomide compared with dacarbazine (14.5% *v* 10%).[85] Although the FDA never approved temozolomide for treatment of advanced melanoma, the convenience of administering a pill over an infusion, the ability of temozolomide to better penetrate the blood-brain barrier, and the significantly higher antitumor responses with temozolomide favor its use in patients whose quality of life may depend on antitumor response. To date, chemotherapies are being used as salvage therapies in patients whose disease has progressed from immunotherapies or targeted therapies (if *BRAFV600*-mutant), although early data suggest the clinical benefit is small.[86]

Systemic Treatments in the Management of Melanoma Brain Metastases. Results of several phase II trials in patients with untreated parenchymal brain metastases show that treatments do not cause any severe neurologic AEs that require corticosteroids for management, especially if brain metastases are asymptomatic. Overall, intracranial antitumor responses are similar to same-patient extracranial antitumor responses and are overall higher in patients that receive either combination targeted therapies or immunotherapies.[56, 87-90] The similar response between extracranial and intracranial disease is supported by translational studies showing that same-patient intracranial and extracranial lesions are biologically similar.[25,55] Intracranial responses are more durable in patients with asymptomatic parenchymal brain metastases who were treated with concurrent ipilimumab and nivolumab as opposed to concurrent dabrafenib and trametinib, because disease in patients with *BRAFV600*-mutant melanoma who receive concurrent dabrafenib and trametinib tends to relapse earlier in the brain as opposed to extracranial sites.[56,87] Nevertheless, the clinical benefit for patients with leptomeningeal disease or symptomatic brain metastases was disappointingly low irrespective of whether single-agent PD-1 inhibitors, combination PD-1 and CTLA-4 inhibitors, or concurrent BRAF/MEK blockade were administered.[88] Overall, data from these studies have provided alternative options to traditional local treatments. Asymptomatic patients with excellent performance status and parenchymal brain metastases of < 3 cm maximum diameter may be spared local treatments in the front-line setting; such patients can be treated alternatively with either a combination of ipilimumab and nivolumab or a combination of dabrafenib and trametinib (if *BRAFV600*-mutant). However, the optimal sequence or combination of local and systemic therapies remains poorly defined, and multidisciplinary care is essential for these patients.

KEY POINTS

- Patients with untreated, asymptomatic parenchymal brain metastases can be safely and effectively treated with concurrent ipilimumab and nivolumab.
- Intracranial responses are durable in patients with asymptomatic parenchymal brain metastases treated with concurrent ipilimumab and nivolumab; combination of dabrafenib and trametinib results in less durable intracranial responses.
- Multidisciplinary care is more frequently required for patients with symptomatic brain metastases, given that the clinical benefit from systemic treatments is less.

Toxicities From Systemic Treatments in Advanced Melanoma. Pooled analysis from all phase III trials that tested single-agent nivolumab versus ipilimumab (3 mg/kg) plus nivolumab (1 mg/kg) showed that the overall incidence of treatment-related, serious AEs was much higher with combination versus single-agent treatment (55.4% *v* 9.9%). Table 16-7 lists the incidence of organ-specific treatment-related AEs of any grade that occur with the combination treatment versus with single-agent nivolumab. The timing and number of treatment-related AEs are associated with the overall response rates: higher response

Table 16-7 **Incidence and Timing of Organ-Specific Adverse Events From Combination Therapy With Ipilimumab-Nivolumab Versus Nivolumab Alone**

Affected System	Median Onset for Combination Therapy (weeks; %)	Median Onset for Single-Agent Nivolumab (weeks; %)
Skin	2; 64	5; 33
Gastrointestinal	5; 47	7.3; 14
Hepatic	6.1; 29	7.7; 4
Endocrine	7.4; 30	10.4; 8
Pulmonary	10.6; 8	8.9; 2
Renal	10.2; 4	15.1; 2

rates were associated with longer time to AE development (> 12 weeks *v* ≤ 12 weeks from treatment initiation) and more AEs (one or more AEs *v* none).[91] Lower dose of ipilimumab (1 mg/kg), as compared with the FDA-approved 3 mg/kg ipilimumab dose, concurrently administered with PD-1 inhibitors significantly reduced serious AEs in patients with advanced melanoma in two studies, KEYNOTE-029 and CheckMate 511. In both studies, clinical benefit was not significantly different between high (3 mg/kg) and low (1 mg/kg) ipilimumab-containing regimens.[92,93] Therefore, reduced doses of ipilimumab can be considered for vulnerable patient subgroups who would otherwise be candidates for concurrent PD-1 and CTLA-4 inhibitor blockade (eg, older subjects).

Immune checkpoint inhibitor toxicities are generally reversible with corticosteroids and other immunomodulatory agents. Autoimmune endocrinopathies can be managed with hormone replacement therapy. Grade 3 toxicities warrant suspension of immune checkpoint inhibitors; for grade 4 toxicities (endocrine-related will be excepted), permanent discontinuation is generally recommended. Steroid-refractory gastrointestinal AEs may require vedolizumab treatment, whereas steroid-refractory hepatic AEs may require mycophenolate mofetil. Furthermore, a small proportion of toxicities may be fatal, particularly pneumonitis and myocarditis.[94] A pooled analysis of phase II and phase III trials showed that discontinuation of concurrent ipilimumab and nivolumab due to treatment-related toxicity does not significantly diminish treatment efficacy.[95] Retreatment with PD-1 inhibitors after toxicity resulting from concurrent PD-1 and CTLA-4 blockade, or CTLA-4 monotherapy, was associated with a variable response rate (35% in patients who had a flare of autoimmune disease *v* 31% in patients without flare). However, these AEs were well managed. and antitumor responses were high.[96] Patients with preexisting autoimmune disorders who were treated with PD-1 inhibitors frequently experienced a flare of their underlying autoimmune disorder; however, the type of flare was usually a mild exacerbation of their preexisting symptoms that could be managed with corticosteroids, as opposed to an extension of their underlying autoimmune disorder. Although response rates were comparable to those patients without preexisting autoimmune diseases (ie, 33%), patients receiving immunosuppressant therapy had a lower frequency of responses compared to those not receiving immunosuppressants (15% *v* 44%).[96] ASCO, the European Society for Medical Oncology, the Society for Immunotherapy of Cancer, and the National Comprehensive Cancer Network have published clinical practice guidelines for the management of immune-mediated AEs in patients treated with immune checkpoint inhibitors.[97] These guidelines provide recommendations for specific organ-based toxicities. Similar guidelines exist for the management of toxicities from high-dose bolus IL2.[63]

In contrast with the lack of significant differences in toxicity between nivolumab and pembrolizumab, there are class-specific differences in treatment-related toxicities of any grade between combinations of BRAF inhibitors and MEK inhibitors (Table 16-8). Other uncommon AEs associated with MEK inhibitors that warrant careful and timely assessment are decreased left ventricular ejection fraction, central serous retinopathy, interstitial lung disease, and pneumonitis.[77] Within each drug class, there are differences in the incidence of certain AEs. For example, vemurafenib tends to cause diarrhea, transaminitis, photosensitivity, secondary nonmelanoma skin cancers, and hypertension more frequently than do other BRAF inhibitors. Encorafenib tends to cause vomiting, alopecia, palmar-plantar erythrodysesthesia, and myalgias more frequently than do dabrafenib and vemurafenib, whereas encorafenib tends to cause photosensitivity, fatigue, and pyrexia

Table 16-8 **Differences in Treatment-Related Adverse Effects of Any Grade Between Combinations of BRAF Inhibitors and MEK Inhibitors**

Adverse Effect	BRAF Inhibitors (%)	MEK Inhibitor (%)
Diarrhea	12-34	40-43
Alopecia	26-37	17 (trametinib only)
Palmar-plantar erythrodysesthesia	14-47	NR
Hyperkeratosis	29-39	NR
Skin papilloma	9-18	NR
Secondary nonmelanoma skin cancer	9-18	NR
Photosensitivity	4-30	NR
Fatigue	26-35	22-26
Headache	19-26	NR
Arthralgia	27-45	NR
Myalgia	22-27	NR
Acneiform dermatitis	3-4	19-36
Peripheral edema	5	26-36

Abbreviation: NR, not reported.

less frequently. Trametinib tends to cause rash, dry skin, and alopecia more frequently than does binimetinib, but also less frequently cause acneiform dermatitis, peripheral edema, nausea, vomiting, and serum creatinine kinase elevation. The treating physician needs to have a balanced discussion with the patient regarding the specific AEs of each drug, given that certain options may be more favorable for some patients than for others. Concurrent treatment with BRAF and MEK inhibitors has distinct toxicity profiles from either monotherapy. Irrespective of the choice of the doublet, common AEs of any grade include nausea (30% to 41%), diarrhea (24% to 36%), rash (23% to 39%), fatigue (29% to 32%), and arthralgias (24% to 32%). AEs from certain BRAF/MEK doublets remain a concern: combination vemurafenib and cobimetinib tends to cause diarrhea (56%), transaminitis (23%), rash (39%), and photosensitivity (28%) more frequently; combination dabrafenib and trametinib tends to cause pyrexia (51%), chills (30%), and back pain (9%) more frequently; the encorafenib and binimetinib doublet tends to cause vomiting (30%) and retinal detachment (13) more frequently, and cause pyrexia (18%) hypertension (11%), and fatigue (29%) less frequently. Irrespective of the treatment combination, certain AEs warrant particular attention, such as pyrexia, decreased left ventricular ejection fraction, hypertension, and QTc prolongation. Pyrexia (≥ 38°C) can occur in > 50% of patients early during the course of combined treatment with dabrafenib and trametinib (median time to onset, 19 days), can last for more than a week (median duration, 9 days), and can recur. Early treatment can involve nonsteroidal anti-inflammatory drugs and hydration; however, high-grade and prolonged pyrexias may require the use of systemic corticosteroids. Excellent reviews regarding the optimal management of other AEs in patients who receive MAPK inhibitors are available.[98] Knowledge about class-specific, drug-specific, and regimen-specific AEs is key to the selection of the most appropriate doublet therapy, dose modification or reduction, or even switching to another doublet if toxicity, but not disease progression, is the issue.

KEY POINTS

- Toxicities from immune checkpoint inhibitors are generally reversible with dose suspension, and use of corticosteroids and/or other immunomodulatory agents. The exception is endocrine toxicities that may require permanent hormone replacement. For serious AEs, suspension or discontinuation of immune checkpoint inhibitors is recommended.
- Discontinuation of immunotherapy because of severe AEs does not affect overall clinical benefit.
- Addition of a MEK inhibitor to a BRAF inhibitor decreases the frequency of specific BRAF inhibitor–associated AEs (ie, dermatologic: alopecia, palmar-plantar erythrodysesthesia, hyperkeratosis, skin papillomas, secondary nonmelanoma skin cancers; and arthralgias), does not change others (eg, QTc prolongation), but increases incidence or severity of other AEs (eg, nausea, vomiting, diarrhea, transaminitis, serum creatinine kinase increase, and reduction in left ventricular ejection fraction). Physicians need to be aware of drug- and class-specific AEs for optimal early selection of the BRAF/MEK combination, as well as appropriate dose reductions, delays, or even treatment discontinuations, if necessary.

Sequencing of Therapy, Initial Treatment Selection, and Stopping Therapy. Immune checkpoint inhibitors and MAPK pathway inhibitors (if *BRAFV600*-mutant) are at the forefront of systemic treatments for advanced melanoma, whereas chemotherapy or HDIL2 use is primarily limited in patients who have disease progression while receiving these treatments. To date, there is no level I clinical evidence about the optimal sequence of systemic therapies in advanced *BRAFV600*-mutant melanoma. EA6134 is an ongoing, prospective, randomized phase III trial comparing initial treatment with dabrafenib plus trametinib followed by ipilimumab plus nivolumab at progression versus the reverse therapy sequence in patients with *BRAFV600*-mutant melanoma.

Another question is whether front-line concurrent PD-1/CTLA-4 blockade should be a universal strategy for any patient with advanced melanoma or if single-agent immune checkpoint blockade is sufficient. The KEYNOTE-006, CheckMate 064, and CheckMate 067 trials have clearly shown that if a single-agent immune checkpoint inhibitor is appropriate, front-line PD-1 inhibition is superior to front-line ipilimumab. The answer regarding the optimal upfront combination schedule is complicated and considers patient preferences and perception about the severity of life-threatening, treatment-related toxicities, total tumor burden, requirement for a prompt response if tumor volume and location of metastatic tumors (eg, brain) cause life-threatening symptoms, and overall performance status.

Once secondary resistance to MAPK inhibitors develops, rechallenge after several months following the end of initial MAPK inhibitor treatment can be beneficial. A multicenter retrospective analysis of patients (N = 116) who had previously received MAPK inhibitors and whose disease subsequently progressed showed that rechallenge with MAPK inhibitors is associated with high antitumor response rates (42%). Of interest, responses upon rechallenge were usually higher in patients who had longer intervals between the first treatment and rechallenge.[99]

PD-1 inhibitors may have long-lasting, durable responses after stopping treatment. An analysis of patients who received at least one dose of pembrolizumab as part of the phase I pembrolizumab study (KEYNOTE-001; N = 655) and stopped treatment following a complete response after 2 years (n = 67) showed that responses are durable after stopping.[100] Less is known about outcomes after rechallenge of patients with metastatic disease progression whose disease had previously responded to PD-1 inhibitors but treatment was stopped due to patient preference.

KEY POINTS

- There is no current, level I clinical evidence regarding the optimal sequence of systemic treatments in patients with advanced *BRAFV600*-mutant melanoma. Either immunotherapy or BRAF/MEK targeted therapy are reasonable first-line treatment options.
- Treatment with single-agent PD-1 inhibitor or concurrent PD-1 and CTLA-4 inhibition are first-line immunotherapy options; the decision to treat with single or dual checkpoint blockade can be individualized on the basis of tumor burden, CNS disease status, performance status, tumor-associated symptoms, and patient preference.
- Immunotherapy can result in durable complete responses after stopping therapy. Treatment discontinuation of immunotherapy should be discussed with patients who have a complete confirmed response.

SURVIVORSHIP

The number of melanoma survivors living in the United States has increased over the last few years (Fig 16-1). As of 2016, CM is the third and fifth most common tumor among male and female survivors, respectively. Patients with previously diagnosed CM have a 1% to 8% lifetime risk of developing another invasive melanoma. Melanoma survivors also tend to be diagnosed with nonmelanoma skin cancers more frequently. Patients with lymphedema had significantly lower scores on the majority of the health-related, quality-of-life measures. Younger patients reported financial issues, ranging from poor performance at work requiring career change to financial difficulties associated with the cost of lymphedema therapy, whereas young men and women reported worse social functioning and poorer body image scores.[101] Female long-term melanoma survivors had a higher frequency of fatigue, nausea, insomnia, appetite loss, and constipation.

MELANOMA IN OLDER ADULTS

Among patients diagnosed with CM, 30.7% are > 60 years old.[102] Older men have significantly higher CM incidence and mortality rate than older women. CM among patients > 60 years old is biologically and clinically different from the CM among younger patients. Melanoma in older adults usually has a greater Breslow thickness of invasion, a lower incidence of positive SLNs, and is less frequently of the superficial spreading melanoma histologic subtype. The incidence of positive SLNs is lower in older patients. Melanomas in older adults have a higher incidence of somatic mutations of the UV radiation–signature type, implying chronically sun-damaged skin. In this patient population, *BRAFV600K* and *NRASQ61* mutations are more frequently seen. Despite the under-representation of older patients with melanoma in the pivotal studies that led to the FDA approval of various systemic treatments, older patients respond at least as well as younger patients. Nevertheless, the incidence of severe AEs from targeted therapies and perhaps immune checkpoint inhibitors tends to be higher in older patients than in younger individuals.[103]

Treatment of older patients with advanced melanoma should consider geriatric assessment tools to determine the level of fitness and, therefore, eligibility for the potentially higher-risk, higher-benefit combined modality treatment. In cases of oligometastatic melanoma, upfront surgery (ie, metastasectomy), if possible, is a reasonable approach as an attempt to delay initiation of systemic treatments, which are usually administered for the patient's remaining life and are usually associated with AEs. In patients with *BRAFV600*-mutant melanoma, the risks and benefits from a concurrent BRAF/MEK blockade versus single-agent PD-1 inhibitor or concurrent PD-1/CTLA-4 inhibitor have not been well studied. If the geriatric assessment indicates that the patient is fit, the patient may well consider the combination of ipilimumab plus nivolumab; otherwise, a single-agent PD-1 inhibitor should be the first strategy.

NONCUTANEOUS MELANOMA

EPIDEMIOLOGY AND RISK FACTORS

Although most prevalent in the skin, melanocytes can be found in other organs of the body and can give rise to noncutaneous melanomas. Non-CMs comprise 5% of all melanomas. Approximately 3% to 5% are ocular, and the remaining 1% to 2% are mucosal. The majority of mucosal melanomas are located in the head and neck (55%; conjunctival, sinonasal, and oral), and less frequently in the anorectal (24%) and vulvovaginal area (18%).

HISTOPATHOLOGY, BIOLOGY, AND PROGNOSIS

Mucosal Melanoma

Oncogenic *BRAF* and *NRAS* mutations are less frequent in mucosal melanomas (6.4%, and 13.8%, respectively) than in CM, although the incidence of *KIT* mutations is higher; these tumors have a much lower somatic mutation burden than CM.[104] Two large mucosal melanoma cohorts from Germany (N = 444)[105] and China (N = 706; Peking University)[106] have provided significant insights about the prognostic significance of various histopathologic factors. These cohorts showed that depth of the primary lesion, the number of positive regional lymph nodes, and sites of distant metastases are important prognostic factors for OS.

Uveal Melanoma

The human adult choroid tissue does not have the classic lymphatic system drainage seen in other tissues. The transformation of choroidal melanocytes to melanoma leads to two possible uveal melanoma subtypes with respect to their propensity to metastasize distantly. These two types are classified as low risk (class 1) or high risk (class 2) for metastatic disease by gene expression profiling.[107] DecisionDx-UM (Castle Biosciences) is a commercially available, 15-gene expression profiling diagnostic assay used for risk stratification in uveal melanoma.

Activating mutations in any of the two G-protein-pathway–associated *GNAQ* and *GNA11* genes are present in the majority of uveal melanomas and are thought to be early events in tumorigenesis. Genetic aberrations of BAP1, a enzyme that removes single ubiquitin moieties from various substrates including histones, are associated with the more aggressive class 2 type.[108] Gene expression analysis of 80 uveal melanomas as part of TCGA project has also shown low (ie, < 15%) incidence of tumors bearing T-cells expressing immune-exhaustion markers.[109] These molecular characteristics have provided the basis for several clinical trials, as discussed later in the Treatment section.

Once uveal melanoma becomes metastatic, the prognosis is poor, with median OS ranging between 11.3 and 13.4 months. Multivariate analysis has shown that ECOG performance status ≥ 1, high serum lactate dehydrogenase level, and short time from primary tumor diagnosis to the metastasis are poor prognostic factors for survival.

TREATMENT

Mucosal Melanoma

Resection of the primary lesion with negative surgical margins is an important prognostic factor and can be curative in select cases. The utility of SLN mapping is controversial. Lymph node dissection is considered if there is clinical or radiologic evidence of nodal involvement. Metastatic mucosal melanoma has a worse prognosis than CM, irrespective of the anatomic site of origin. Table 16-9 lists various studies of systemic treatments for patients with mucosal melanoma. Overall, the clinical benefit is inferior to that in CM. This may be explained by the lower incidence of PD-L1 positivity seen in these trials,[110] and, perhaps, the lower incidence of TILs. Authors of retrospective studies have suggested that single-agent anti–PD-1 and combination PD-1/CTLA-4 blockade may result in antitumor response rates of 23% and 37%, respectively.[110]

KIT-targeted therapies have been investigated in melanomas bearing *KIT* genetic aberration, including the mucosal subtype. In a 25-patient phase II study imatinib (400 mg administered orally once daily) was associated with a 21% incidence of confirmed antitumor responses. All responses occurred in patients with mutations as opposed to gene amplifications. Unfortunately, most responses were short (median time to progression, 3.7 months), and median OS was 12.5 months.[111]

Uveal Melanoma

Eye enucleation has been the standard-of-care treatment for patients with uveal melanoma. The Collaborative Ocular

Table 16-9 Summary of Clinical Data From Key Phase II Studies in Mucosal Melanoma

Study	Drug(s)	No. Pts	Median F/U (months)	ORR (%)	PFS, Median (range), Months	OS, Median (range), Months	Comments
Lian et al.[152]	Obs *v* HDI *v* chtx	189	26.8	N/A (adjuvant)	5.4 *v* 9.4 *v* 20.8	21.2 *v* 40.4 *v* 48.7	
Postow et al.[153]	Ipi (various doses)	30	9.9	6.7 (irRC)	Not reported	6.4 (1.8-26.7)	Mutations in *BRAFV600E* (5%), *KIT* (16%), *NRAS* (30%)
Del Vecchio et al.[154]	Ipi (3 mg/kg)	69	21.8	12 (irRC)	4.3 (3.4-5.2)	6.4 (4.1-8.7)	
Hamid, et al.[155]	Pembro (various doses and schedules)	84	Not reached	22 (Ipi-naive)	2.8 (2.8-3.0)	14.0 (6.1-24.3)	PD-L1-positive (70%)
				15 (Ipi-treated)	2.8 (2.6-5.1)	10.2 (6.1-17.1)	*BRAFV600E*-mutant (8%)
Shoushtari et al.[156]	Nivo (0.3-10 mg/kg q2-3wks) Pembro (2-10 mg/kg q2-3wks)	35	10.6	23	3.9	12.4	Mutations in *BRAFV600E* (0), *KIT* (6), and *NRAS* (11)
D'Angelo et al.[110]	Nivo	86	6.2-8.6	23.3	3.0 (2.2-5.4)	Not reported	PD-L1-positive (20%), *BRAFV600E* (6%)
	Ipi-Nivo	35		37.1	5.9 (2.2-NR)		
	Ipi	36		8.3	2.7 (2.6-2.8)		

Abbreviations: Chtx, chemotherapy; F/U, follow-up; HDI, high-dose Interferon-alpha2b; Ipi, ipilimumab; irRC, immune-related (ir) response criteria (RC); N/A, not applicable; Nivo, nivolumab; NR, not reached; Obs, observation; ORR, overall response rate; Pembro, pembrolizumab; PFS, progression-free survival.

Melanoma Study is the largest trial of patients (N = 1,317) with ocular melanoma to address whether local radiation is noninferior to eye enucleation. Patients with no evidence of metastatic disease were randomly assigned to eye-preserving ^{125}I plaque radiotherapy versus enucleation; there was no difference in melanoma-specific OS.

Molecular assays have enabled better identification of patients at high risk for distant metastatic uveal melanoma. Adjuvant clinical trials in this high-risk group are underway; at this time, results from only nonrandomized, single-arm studies are available.

Metastatic uveal melanoma has a poor prognosis. A retrospective analysis of 521 patients who were diagnosed with metastatic uveal melanoma in a single institution and were followed up to 2011 showed poor OS, irrespective of whether the patient received treatment or not (median OS was 6.3 months *v* 1.7 months, respectively).[112] In a selected patient population, adoptive cell therapies have shown a proof-of-principle efficacy, suggesting that immunotherapies can have a role in this aggressive disease.[113] A multicenter study in patients with metastatic uveal melanoma (N = 50) showed that concurrent CTLA-4/PD-1 blockade was associated with some clinical benefit (antitumor response rate, 12.5%; median PFS, 3.7 months; median OS, 12.7 months). Significantly less benefit was seen after treatment with single-agent PD-1/PD-L1 inhibitors (antitumor response rate, 3.6% to 4.7%).[114,115] Despite advances in knowledge about the biology of uveal melanoma, little clinical benefit has been demonstrated so far with targeted therapies including MEK inhibitors.[116,117]

KEY POINTS

- Non-CMs account for 5% of all melanomas and consist of ocular and mucosal melanomas.
- *KIT* mutations are more frequent in mucosal melanomas compared with CM; the incidence of oncogenic *BRAF* and *NRAS* mutations is low.
- A commercially available gene expression profiling test (DecisionDx-UM) classifies uveal melanomas into two types (low-risk class 1 and high-risk class 2) on the basis of their propensity to metastasize.
- *GNAQ* and *GNA11* mutations are present in the majority of uveal melanomas and are thought to be early events in tumorigenesis; genetic aberrations of *BAP1* are associated with the more aggressive class 2 type.
- Combination of ipilimumab and nivolumab is associated with higher response rates compared with single-agent PD-1 inhibitors; however, the clinical benefit from immunotherapy is much lower in uveal melanoma.

NONMELANOMA SKIN CANCERS

Table 16-10 lists the important characteristics of nonmelanoma skin cancers. Nonmelanoma skin cancer can arise from any skin cell subtype. Basal cell carcinomas (BCC) and squamous cell carcinomas (SCC) comprise nearly 99% of nonmelanoma skin cancer and are by far the most frequently diagnosed skin cancers. Less common (1%) skin cancer types include Merkel cell carcinoma (MCC), Kaposi sarcoma, cutaneous lymphoma, skin adnexal tumors, and various types of sarcomas (eg, carcinosarcoma, fibrosarcoma). Approximately 5.4 million BCC and SCC are diagnosed each year in the United States, affecting 3.3 million Americans; an increase in diagnoses and treatments represent an increasing public health challenge.

BCC, SCC, and MCC share common risk factors, such as high UV radiation exposure, skin phototype (low Fitzpatrick skin type), male sex, advanced age, and immunosuppression. For SCC and MCC, human papillomavirus and Merkel cell polyomaviruses also play an etiopathogenic role, respectively. Several histopathologic analyses across the three nonmelanoma skin cancers have detected a high incidence of PD-1–positive lymphocytes that infiltrate PD-L1–expressing tumors; these studies established the translational rationale for the successful use of PD-1/PD-L1 pathway inhibitors in each of these three cancers.[118-120] Due to the high frequency of these cancers and the increasing costs of diagnostics and treatment, considerable research on chemoprevention is ongoing. Apart from large public health care campaigns to encourage use of broad-spectrum (UVA/UVB) sunscreens and adoption of sun-clever practices, large randomized clinical trials have identified a handful of chemopreventive agents that reduce incidence of skin cancer development compared with standard-of-care practices.[121,122]

Newly diagnosed SCC and BCC can be stratified on the basis of relapse risk and metastatic potential according to the NCCN guidelines. Large size (> 20 mm for trunk and extremities, and 10 mm for face), poorly defined borders, prior recurrence, immunosuppression, and poor histology are associated with high risk for relapse and distant metastases. In the case of SCC and MCC that have higher propensity for metastases, SLN mapping should be considered for complete staging.

Nonmelanoma skin cancers are overall curable diseases, and surgical resection of the lesion is the primary treatment modality. Surgical removal offers the best outcome compared with any other local treatment modalities (eg, cryotherapy, photodynamic therapy, radiotherapy, 5-fluorouracil, imiquimod) in terms of lesion response and probability for relapse. For lesions located on the face, Mohs micrographic surgery can provide the best cosmetic outcome. There are no standards for optimal wide-excision margins, although NCCN recommends excision of low-risk SCC and BCC with 4- to 6-mm and 4-mm clinical margins, respectively. Radiation therapy is recommended for patients who are not surgical candidates or who are at high risk for relapse, or in cases in which surgery did not achieve negative margins. Radiation therapy can also be considered in patients with SCC and MCC who have positive lymph nodes and cannot

Table 16-10 Important Characteristics of the Three Most Frequent Nonmelanoma Skin Cancers

Characteristic	Squamous Cell Carcinoma	Basal Cell Carcinoma	Merkel Cell Carcinoma
New diagnosis	> 1 million/year	~ 4.3 million/year	~ 2,000/year
Cell origin	Stem cells in the hair follicle bulge and basal layer of interfollicular epidermis	Undifferentiated CD200+ basal cells of the hair follicle outer root sheath	Merkel cells in the basal epidermal layer of skin
Precursor lesion	Solar keratosis, Bowen disease, keratoacanthoma	Not known	Not known
Risk factors	UV radiation exposure, skin phototype, ionizing radiation, chronic wounds/scars, immunosuppression, HPV infection, smoking, genetic defects in DNA repair	UV radiation exposure, tanning bed, skin phototype, male sex, age > 50 years, immunosuppression, basal cell nevus syndrome	UV radiation exposure, skin phototype, age > 70 years, male sex, immunosuppression, MCPyV
Biology	High somatic mutations burden (*TP53, NOTCH-1/2/4, CDKN2A, EGFR*), high degree of PD-1+ tumor-infiltrating lymphocytes	Mutations in *PTCH1*, smoothened homolog, high degree of PD-1+ tumor-infiltrating lymphocytes	Low somatic mutation burden if MCPyV positive, high somatic mutation burden if MCPyV negative, high degree of PD-1+ tumor-infiltrating lymphocytes
Prevention	Broad-spectrum sunscreens Nicotinamide	Broad-spectrum sunscreens Nicotinamide Calcipotriol + 5-fluorouracil	Broad-spectrum sunscreens
Propensity to metastasize, %	1.4	0.0029-0.55	40
Median OS, if distant metastatic	2.2 years	10 months	9.5 months

Abbreviations: HPV, human papillomavirus; MCPyV, Merkel cell polyomavirus; OS, overall survival; UV, ultraviolet.

be considered for systemic chemotherapy or radical lymph node surgery.

Considerable advances in the systemic management of patients with nonmelanoma skin cancers have been achieved since 2012; these advances have challenged the use of cytotoxic chemotherapies for these cancers that was common practice before 2012. Driven by the unique biology of BCC in which constitutive activation of the hedgehog pathway is seen secondary to mutations in hedgehog pathway–associated genes (eg, *PTCH1*, *SMO*), there are currently two FDA-approved hedgehog inhibitors for patients with locally advanced or metastatic BCC. The approval was based on large phase II nonplacebo-controlled clinical trials (BOLT and STEVIE).[123,124] Both targeted therapies, sonidegib (200 mg) and vismodegib (150 mg), are orally available and are administered once daily. Antitumor responses were > 50% in both drugs, and they are higher in patients with locally advanced disease. Class-specific AEs for hedgehog inhibitors are muscle spasms (49% to 64%), alopecia (43% to 62%), dysgeusia (38% to 54%), weight loss (27% to 33%), asthenia (8% to 28%), appetite loss (19% to 25%), diarrhea (17% to 24%), nausea (16% to 33%), and fatigue (16% to 29%). Given the cumulative constitutional symptoms, treatment with hedgehog inhibitors is frequently discontinued or interrupted. Nevertheless, the median OS for the metastatic BCC cohort for vismodegib was 33.4 months, whereas it was not reached for sonidegib.

Two PD-L1 inhibitors were recently approved by the FDA for treatment of locally unresectable and distant metastatic SCC and MCC on the basis of > 40% antitumor responses enduring longer than 6 months seen in large clinical trials (EMPOWER-CSCC-1, JAVELIN, respectively).[125,126] These treatments have significantly limited use of cytotoxic chemotherapies in the front-line setting for these two nonmelanoma skin cancers. More specifically, cemiplimab (3 mg/kg administered intravenously every 3 weeks) was associated with 44% and 49% overall response rate for locally advanced and metastatic SCC, respectively. At a medical follow-up of 9 months (locally advanced disease) and 17 months (metastatic disease), median OS has not been reached. Avelumab (10 mg/kg administered intravenously every 2 weeks) administered in the front-line setting was associated with a 62% confirmed overall response rate.[126] In the chemotherapy-refractory setting, avelumab was associated with a 32% confirmed overall response rate.[127] Similar to avelumab antitumor responses to pembrolizumab are also durable in metastatic MCC.[128]

KEY POINTS

- Nonmelanoma skin cancers are by far the most frequently diagnosed cancers. This has implications for increasing health care costs, in particular for BCC and SCC.
- Surgery is the cornerstone therapy for management of most nonmelanoma skin cancers.
- Unlike MCC, SCC and BCC have a low metastatic potential.
- The two hedgehog inhibitors, sonidegib and vismodegib, have been approved for treatment of locally advanced or metastatic BCC.
- Two PD-L1 inhibitors, cemiplimab and avelumab, have been approved for patients with locally advanced or distant metastatic SCC and MCC, respectively.

Acknowledgment

The following authors are acknowledged and graciously thanked for their contribution to prior versions of this chapter: Lynn M. Schuchter, MD, FASCO; and Tara C. Mitchell, MD.

Global Oncology Perspective: Melanoma and Other Skin Cancers

Jean Rene V. Clemenceau, MD (Hospital Angeles del Pedregal, Mexico City, Mexico)

Melanoma causes most skin cancer–related deaths worldwide.[129] Melanoma is not the most common of the skin cancers, but it is one of the most dangerous.

INCIDENCE AND SURVIVAL TRENDS

Variations in incidence trends depend on population and ethnicity, and in different regions, accessibility to health care has implications for melanoma prevalence and survival. Bray et al[129] reported on the analysis of data including melanoma incidence and mortality extracted from GLOBOCAN. In 2018, there were 287,723 new cases (1.6% of all cancers) and 60,712 deaths (0.6% of all cancer deaths). The highest melanoma incidence is in Australia (39 cases per 100,000 inhabitants per year) and New Zealand (34 cases per 100,000 inhabitants), followed by the United States with 17 cases per 100,000 inhabitants.[130] In Latin America, a prevalence of 1.7 cases per 100,000 inhabitants is estimated by the International Agency for Research on Cancer (IARC), with an extensive variability of zero cases per 100,000 in countries such as Belize to 7.6 cases per 100,000 in Uruguay.[131,132] In Mexico, the prevalence of malignant melanoma is unknown; estimations are two cases per 100,000 inhabitants, according to IARC.[130] The Malignant Neoplasm Histopathological Record in Mexico for 1995 reported an incidence of 11,107 cases, 1.5% of the reported cancers.[133]

The anatomic site and distribution of melanoma of the skin vary between countries. Using a retrospective database, Lino-Silva et al[134] analyzed a total of 1,219 patients with cutaneous melanoma whose data were collected from a cancer referral institute, and the results were compared with those from developed countries. Median age was 57 years, and 713 (58.5%) were women. The most common melanoma subtype was acral lentiginous melanoma (ALM; n = 538 patients [44.1%]). The median Breslow thickness was 5.2 mm. Among the 837 patients with complete data, the 5-year, melanoma-specific survival (DSS) was 52.3%. Factors associated with worse DSS on univariate analysis were Breslow thickness, recurrence, ulceration, positive margin, ALM, and male sex. Multivariate analysis identified Breslow thickness, positive margin, recurrence, and male sex as independent risk factors for DSS.

Patients had worse prognosis in Mexico compared with data from the SEER database. Male sex and ALM are independent risk factors for worse survival.

An analysis to determine the frequency of *BRAFV600E* mutations in a population of patients with malignant melanoma from northeastern Mexico[135] showed a mean frequency of 54.6%, similar to that reported in the white populations. Two studies exploring *BRAFV600E* mutations found a frequency ranging from 6.4%[136] to 73%[135] explained by the heterogeneity of the populations analyzed (from the center and northeast of Mexico, respectively) and the size of the sample analyzed (< 50 patients).[137] In this sample of patients, nodular melanoma accounted for the highest number of cases with *BRAFV600E* mutations. In this study, the patients studied from central part of Mexico had the highest prevalence of *BRAFV600E* mutation (41.8%). This might be related to the sample supply and the general ethnic mix in the country.

PREVENTION OF MELANOMA OF THE SKIN

Reduction of incidence and mortality rate of skin melanomas can be achieved via at least three different approaches: genetic testing, limiting the amount of sun exposure, and self-examination of the skin. No public screening programs are in place for melanoma in most low- and middle-low–income countries.

GENETIC TESTING

Puig et al[138] analyzed *CDKN2A* locus and *MC1R* mutations in 186 Latin American patients from Argentina, Brazil, Chile, Mexico, Uruguay, and in 904 Spanish patients with familial and sporadic multiple primary melanoma. They compared the data to establish a scientific basis for melanoma genetic counseling in Latin America. Overall, 24% and 14% of melanoma-prone families in Latin America and Spain, respectively, had mutations in the *CDKN2A* locus. Latin American families had *CDKN2A* locus mutations more frequently ($P = .014$) than did Spanish families. Of patients with sporadic multiple primary melanoma, 10% of those from Latin America and 8.5% of those from Spain had mutations in the *CDKN2A* locus ($P = .623$). The most recurrent *CDKN2A* locus mutations were c.-34G>T and p.G101W. Latin American patients had fairer hair ($P = .016$) and skin ($P < .001$) and a higher prevalence of *MC1R* variants ($P = .003$) compared with Spanish patients.

DECREASING THE AMOUNT OF SUN EXPOSURE

The most well-described key driver of skin melanomas is sun exposure. Thus, sun-exposure control programs are of importance in combating the melanoma burden globally. This becomes even more critical in less socioeconomically developed countries that have limited access to screening and treatment measures.

EARLY DIAGNOSIS AND TREATMENT

Patients with thin, low-risk primary skin melanomas have an excellent long-term prognosis and higher quality of life than those whose disease is diagnosed at later stages. From an economic standpoint, treatment of early-stage melanoma consumes a small fraction of the health care resources needed to treat advanced disease. Consequently, early diagnosis of melanoma is in the best interest of patients, payers, and health care systems.[139] In Mexico, patients are often diagnosed with advanced (stage III/IV) disease.

Biopsy specimens are globally used to confirm the presence of melanoma. A biopsy may involve the removal of a mole, lump, or taking a sample with a needle (fine-needle biopsy or core biopsy). The sample is sent to a pathology laboratory. Test results are discussed by a skin cancer multidisciplinary team that includes dermatologists, surgeons, pathologists, radiologists, oncologists, and nurses.

SCANS

The contribution of nuclear medicine to treatment of patients with melanoma is increasing. In intermediate-thickness N0 melanomas, lymphoscintigraphy provides a roadmap for SLN biopsy. With the introduction of single-photon emission computed tomography images with integrated CT (SPECT/CT), three-dimensional anatomic environments for accurate surgical planning are now possible. SLN identification in intricate anatomic areas (eg, pelvic cavity, head and neck) has been improved using hybrid radioactive and fluorescent tracers, and preoperative lymphoscintigraphy and SPECT/CT together with modern intraoperative portable imaging technologies for surgical navigation (eg, free-hand SPECT, portable gamma cameras). Furthermore, PET/CT today provides three-dimensional roadmaps to resect FDG–avid melanoma lesions. Simultaneously, in advanced-stage melanoma and recurrences, FDG PET/CT is useful in clinical staging and treatment decision-making, as well as in the evaluation of therapy response.[140] Ultrasound, CT, and magnetic resonance imaging also are used to monitor any spread of the cancer.

Targeted Therapies

Targeted therapies for melanoma are not widely accessible in Mexico. If melanoma is shown to have a *BRAFV600* mutation, targeted therapy with a BRAF inhibitor will be suitable. AEs of these drugs include rash, joint pain, fever, liver strain, and ECG changes.

BRAF inhibitors in Mexico are used alone or in combination with a MEK inhibitor with the intention of producing longer responses than BRAF inhibitors alone. MEK inhibitors may cause high blood pressure, changes in eyesight, and weakness of the heart muscle. Generally, targeted treatment should be continued as long as it is working.

Palliative and supportive care is available in some major cancer centers in Mexico. Many places are lacking the basic diagnostic and treatment facilities for palliative and supportive care, although patients often present with advanced (stage III/IV) melanoma.

17

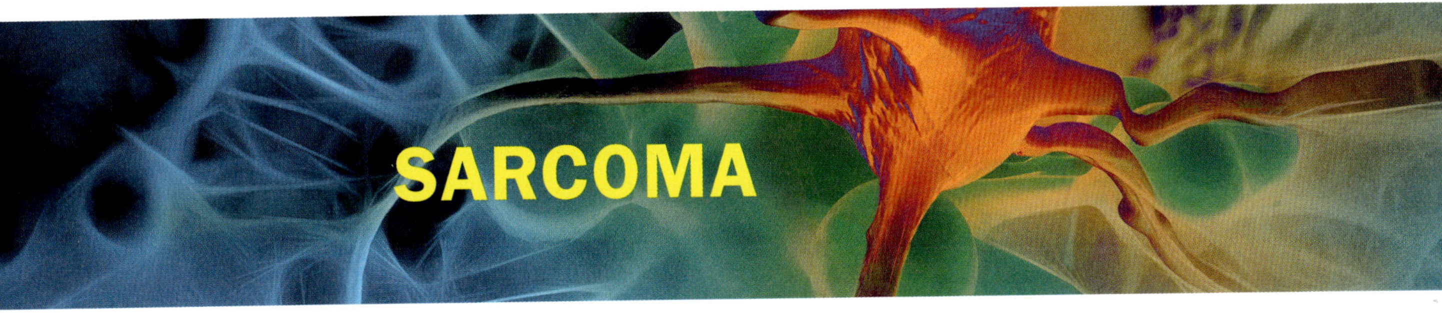

SARCOMA

Lee P. Hartner, MD

Recent Updates

SARCOMA WITH MICROSATELLITE INSTABILITY

- Pembrolizumab, a monoclonal antibody directed against PD-1, was approved by the US Food and Drug Administration (FDA) for treatment of unresectable or metastatic, microsatellite instability-high (MSI-H) or mismatch repair deficient adult and pediatric cancers that have progressed through prior treatments and for which no satisfactory alternative is available. This approval is histology agnostic and includes bone and soft-tissue sarcoma with the MSI-H phenotype. (Marcus L, *Clin Cancer Res* 2019)

DESMOID TUMOR

- Sorafenib, a multitargeted tyrosine kinase inhibitor active against VEGFR2, PDGFRB, and RAF, was shown in a randomized phase III clinical trial to improve progression-free survival (PFS) compared with placebo. Notably, and not uncharacteristically for desmoid tumor, placebo was not without beneficial effect. (Gounder MM, *N Engl J Med* 2018)
- Pazopanib, a multitargeted, oral tyrosine kinase inhibitor targeted against VEGFR, was compared with methotrexate and vinblastine in a randomized phase II clinical trial and found to significantly improve the 6-month nonprogression rate (from 50% to 86%) in a group of patients with documented progressive disease at study entry. (Toulmonde M, *Lancet Oncol* 2018)

OSTEOSARCOMA

- Regorafenib, known to be effective in the treatment of sunitinib-refractory GI stromal tumor, was shown in a randomized phase II clinical trial to improve median PFS and also PFS at 24 weeks. (Davis LE, *J Clin Oncol* 2019)

SOFT-TISSUE SARCOMA

- Olaratumab, a monoclonal antibody directed against PDGFRA, did not improve overall survival when given in combination with doxorubicin, as compared with doxorubicin alone. PFS was inferior to single-agent doxorubicin. The provisional FDA approval for this agent was withdrawn. (Tap W, 2019 ASCO Annual Meeting)
- Larotrectinib, a small-molecule inhibitor of tropomyosin receptor kinases (TRK) was approved by the FDA for treatment of cancers positive for fusions involving one of three TRK kinases. Soft-tissue sarcoma is among several cancer types known to rarely harbor TRK fusions. (Drilon A, *N Engl J Med* 2018)

OVERVIEW

Sarcoma is the term used for cancers of bone and soft tissue. Most sarcomas arise from mesoderm-derived cells. These cancers are uncommon, constituting < 1% of cancers occurring in adults and approximately 15% of cancers in children. Sarcomas are heterogeneous, with > 50 subtypes recognized in the WHO classification of tumors of soft tissue and bone.[1] In adults, soft-tissue sarcomas (STSs) are about four times more common than sarcomas of bone (13,040 compared with 3,450 cases, respectively, in 2018).[2] Approximately 40% of patients diagnosed with sarcoma will die of the disease, with the majority dying of metastatic disease.[2]

Appropriate multidisciplinary treatment is essential for patients presenting with sarcoma. In most cases, complete surgical removal of the primary tumor is required for cure. Surgery is also used in the management of oligometastatic disease, particularly in the lung. Radiation therapy (RT) is also important in many sarcoma subtypes to reduce the risk of local tumor recurrence after surgery for localized disease or for palliation of tumor-related symptoms. Chemotherapy in the adjuvant setting plays a more limited role but is critically important in selected subtypes, such as osteosarcoma, Ewing sarcoma and pediatric rhabdomyosarcoma. It does not have as much benefit in other types of sarcoma but is used selectively on the basis of patient- and disease-specific considerations.

Recently, there have been important advances in the treatment of sarcoma. With appropriate multidisciplinary management, the rates of long-term survival of localized osteosarcoma and Ewing sarcoma have improved from < 20% to > 70%. Similar gains in cure rates have occurred in patients with pediatric rhabdomyosarcoma but have been less impressive in other STS subtypes. Great improvement in long-term survival rates of patients with metastatic GI stromal tumor (GIST) has occurred after the introduction of tyrosine kinase inhibitor therapy, with 20% to 30% of patients surviving 9 to 10 years after initiation of treatment.[3]

EPIDEMIOLOGY AND ETIOLOGY

The most common subtypes of sarcoma include GIST, leiomyosarcoma, liposarcoma, and undifferentiated pleomorphic sarcoma (UPS). Osteosarcomas and chondrosarcomas are the two most common sarcomas arising from bone in adults. Ewing sarcoma can arise in either bone or soft tissue. Figure 17-1 indicates the relative frequency of some of the more common sarcoma subtypes.

Most sarcomas occur in the absence of a genetic cancer predisposition syndrome or exposure to specific environmental factors. The incidence of sarcoma generally increases with age, though there are exceptions for some subtypes. Ewing sarcoma, rhabdomyosarcoma (embryonal and alveolar subtypes), and osteosarcoma occur more frequently in children and young adults. Adults younger than 35 years are at increased risk for synovial sarcoma and desmoplastic small round cell tumor.

Many genetic syndromes are associated with sarcoma. Examples are:

- Li-Fraumeni syndrome (*TP53* mutation);
- retinoblastoma (*RB1* gene deletion);
- neurofibromatosis type 1 (*NF1* mutation);
- Gardner syndrome (*APC* mutation);
- McCune-Albright syndrome (*GNAS1* mutation);
- Bloom, Rothmund-Thomson, and Werner syndromes (associated with loss of helicase function);
- Costello syndrome (*HRAS* mutation); and
- Nijmegen breakage syndrome (*NBN* mutation).[1]

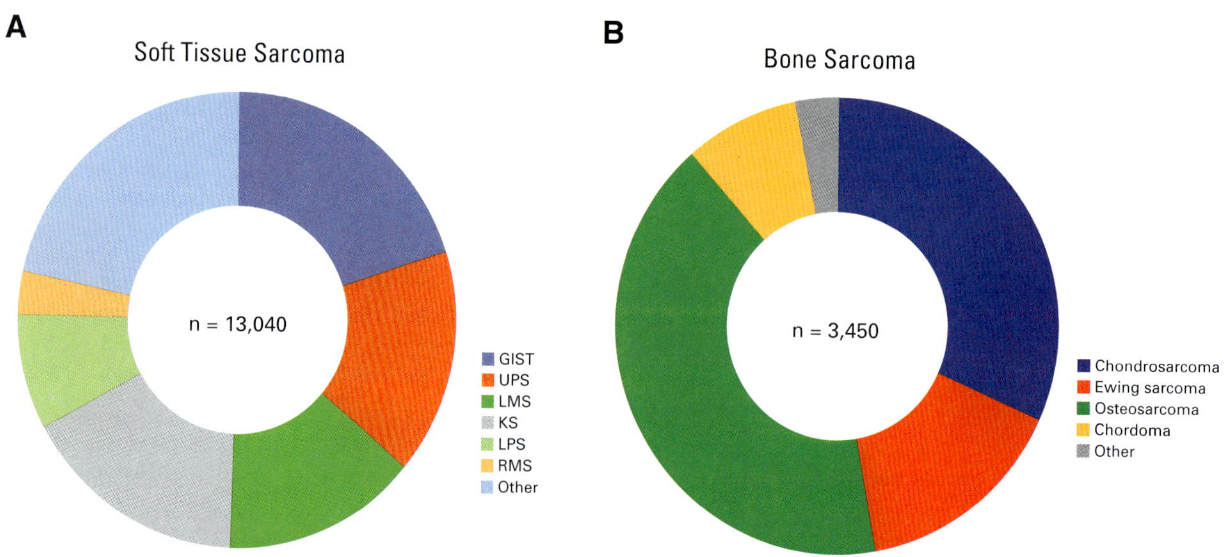

Fig. 17-1 Soft-tissue and bone sarcomas: relative frequency.

The number of estimated cases and breakdown of subtypes for soft-tissue and bone sarcomas is indicated. The area of each circle is proportional to the frequency of such tumors. GIST, GI stromal tumor; KS, Kaposi sarcoma; LPS, lipsarcoma; RMS, rhabdomyosarcoma; UPS, undifferentiated pleomorphic sarcoma.

In an international genomic study of > 1,000 patients with sarcoma, recognized pathogenic germline variants were detected in approximately 10% of patients, and a significant minority had multiple genomic variants, suggesting an interacting contribution of rare mutations to sarcoma risk.[4] People with Li-Fraumeni syndrome are at significant risk for the development of osteosarcoma or STS. In one large study of patients with sarcoma, germline *TP53* mutations were present in approximately 3% of cases.[5]

Referral for genetic counseling and testing should be considered in:

- individuals younger than 46 years with STS or osteosarcoma, and
- individuals with a family history of STS, osteosarcoma, breast cancer, CNS tumor, or adrenocortical carcinoma in a first-or second-degree relative occurring before age 56 years.[6]

Referral for genetic counseling and testing should also be considered in patients with multiple cancers of the listed types, regardless of age at diagnosis. The most common secondary cancers in patients with retinoblastoma syndrome are leiomyosarcoma and osteosarcoma. Individuals with neurofibromatosis type 1 have a 5% to 10% risk for the development of an STS (malignant peripheral nerve sheath tumor or GIST) in their lifetime. Desmoid tumors (aggressive fibromatosis) are associated with Gardner syndrome.

Some epidemiologic evidence associates occupational exposure to vinyl chloride or exposure to the imaging agent Thorotrast with the development of hepatic angiosarcoma, but few other environmental exposures are linked to sarcoma.[7] Studies have suggested that exposure to dioxins or phenoxyacetic acid herbicides, such as Agent Orange, increases the risk for sarcoma, but others have not; meta-analyses of such data have been inconclusive.[8-11]

There is also a small but measurable long-term risk for STS or bone sarcoma to develop after exposure to therapeutic radiation.[12] The median latency in one series was 8.6 years (range, 6 months to 44 years).[13] Angiosarcoma tends to have a shorter latency than other radiation-associated sarcomas—a particular concern for breast cancer survivors treated with breast radiation. Analysis of sarcoma incidence in survivors of atomic bomb blasts suggested moderate levels of ionizing radiation, lower than typically administered for therapy, also increased the risk for bone sarcoma and STS.[14,15] The prognosis of radiation-induced sarcoma does not appear to be worse than that of sporadic STS of the same stage and subtype. Local control can be challenging because of the long-term effects of radiation on tissue planes and wound healing, and the inability to deliver additional cytotoxic doses of radiation.

Other risk factors for the development of STS include lymphedema (angiosarcoma) and human herpesvirus 8 infection (HHV-8; Kaposi sarcoma [KS]). KS is causally associated with HHV-8 and occurs in the setting of immune dysregulation, most notably HIV infection, but also in elderly Mediterranean men and in immunosuppressed transplant recipients in the absence of HIV.

GENETIC CHARACTERISTICS

Sarcomas exhibit a wide range of genetic abnormalities, including complex chromosomal aberrations, chromosomal translocations involving transcription factors, overexpression of ligands to receptor kinases, gene mutations resulting in activated cellular kinases, gene amplification, and regulatory protein inactivation, among others (Table 17-1).[16]

Approximately 30% to 40% of sarcomas have defined, recurring, specific genetic alterations that contribute to pathogenesis. These alterations are important for diagnostic purposes,

Table 17-1 Representative Genetic Alterations in Sarcomas[1,15]

Class of Alteration	Sarcoma Subtype	Genetic Change	Frequency (%)
Activating mutation	GI stromal tumor	*KIT* or *PDGFRA* mutation	> 90
Ligand expression	Dermatofibrosarcoma protuberans	PDGF	~100
	Giant cell tumor of the bone	RANK ligand	~100
Inactivation/deletion	Myxofibrosarcoma Malignant peripheral nerve sheath tumor	*NF1* mutation *NF1* deletion	~10-20, > 90
Gene amplification	Well-differentiated and dedifferentiated liposarcoma	*CDK4, MDM2*	> 90
Translocation	Synovial sarcoma	t(X;18) *SYT-SSXI* or *SYT-SSX2*	> 90
	Ewing sarcoma	t(11;22) *EWSR1-FLI1*	> 85
		t(21;22) *EWSR1-ERG*	5-10
	Alveolar rhabdomyosarcoma	t(2;13) *PAX3-FOXO1*	~70
		t(1;13) *PAX7-FOXO1*	~15

especially in cases where histologic findings do not point to a definite diagnosis. Modern analysis of chromosome translocations using fluorescence in situ hybridization or polymerase chain reaction can be performed on paraffin-embedded, fixed tissue.

Tumor genome sequencing identifies potentially actionable mutations in < 20% of patients with STS, and the impact on survival is yet to be defined.[17] Two important, low-frequency actionable genetic alterations seen in sarcoma are NTRK fusions and high microsatellite instability (MSI-H).

KEY POINTS

- Sarcomas account for approximately 1% of cancer in adults; the incidence of sarcomas of soft tissue are three to four times more common than of bone.
- Individuals with certain genetic cancer susceptibility syndromes have an increased risk for sarcoma.
- Therapeutic radiation confers a small but definite risk for the development of sarcoma.
- HHV-8 infection is associated with KS.
- Approximately 30% to 40% of sarcomas have defined, recurring, specific genetic alterations such as chromosomal translocation, gene amplification, or mutation that contributes to pathogenesis.

CLINICAL PRESENTATION AND DIAGNOSIS

STSs generally present as growing masses that are sometimes associated with pain, whereas bone sarcomas are often associated with pain in the region of bone involvement. STSs are generally differentiated from benign tumors, such as lipomas, by either their texture (generally firmer) or their location (typically deep to subcutaneous fat). Lipomas remain at least 100 times as common as their neoplastic counterpart. Magnetic resonance imaging (MRI) is useful in the evaluation of suspected sarcoma and can help differentiate clearly benign from potentially malignant masses. Core needle biopsy is the preferred method of biopsy when sarcoma is suspected. Fine-needle aspiration is not adequate, because it does not allow for accurate assessment of subtype and grade; its role is limited to confirming recurrence. When diagnostic material cannot be obtained by core needle biopsy, incisional biopsy is performed, with the understanding that the subsequent oncologic resection will need to encompass the prior biopsy site and scar.

Dermal vascular neoplasms such as angiosarcoma and KS often appear as indistinct red, purple, blue, or brown discoloration in the skin (Fig 17-2). Often, a mass-like lesion is not present. Angiosarcoma occurring in the dermis in the elderly and KS occurring in the setting of HIV/AIDS frequently involve the head and neck and are often multicentric. KS occurring in the absence of HIV infection (often referred to as "classic KS") frequently involves the legs and feet. Advanced KS (usually in the setting of AIDS) may involve lymph nodes (resulting in severe edema), the oropharynx, the GI tract, or the respiratory tract.

KEY POINTS

- STSs often present as painless, enlarging masses.
- Bone sarcomas are usually associated with pain.
- Core needle or incisional biopsy is required to obtain sufficient tumor material for definitive diagnosis and sarcoma subtype classification.
- KS can present with dermal-only disease or with visceral disease.

PATHOLOGIC FEATURES, STAGING, AND PROGNOSTIC FACTORS

Because of the diversity of sarcoma subtypes and their differential diagnoses, such as sarcomatoid carcinoma (which is treated as a carcinoma, not a sarcoma), uterine carcinosarcoma, melanoma, or lymphoma, the pathologist is a critical contributor to patient care. Important considerations for sarcoma staging include an evaluation of sarcoma grade and histologic subtype. It is important to recognize that pathologists may use different grading systems, with two grades (low and high), three grades (low, intermediate, and high), or four grades (grades 1 to 4, with higher numbers indicating more aggressive disease).

Evaluation of the local extent of sarcoma is generally accomplished by MRI or computed tomography (CT) of the site of the primary tumor. For patients with high-grade sarcoma, a chest CT scan is usually performed to evaluate for the presence of lung metastasis and to serve as a baseline for future comparison. CT scan of the abdomen and pelvis is performed for sarcomas originating in the abdomen, pelvis, or retroperitoneum. It is also needed for specific subtypes that can spread via lymphatics in addition to the bloodstream. This includes epithelioid sarcoma, dedifferentiated liposarcoma, and myxoid round-cell liposarcoma. Myxoid liposarcoma may also spread to the spine or bone, for which additional imaging (eg, spine MRI or technetium bone scan) is needed to fully stage the disease. For high-grade bone sarcomas, radionuclide bone scan or positron-emission tomography is recommended to evaluate the presence of metastases to bone. In the absence of symptoms, the yield from routine imaging of the brain in patients with tumors originating outside the head-and-neck region or the left side of the heart is low. Positron-emission tomography has relatively low accuracy in staging STSs, because of false-negative and false-positive findings.

The American Joint Committee on Cancer (AJCC) staging system for STS includes the tumor grade, size, and location, as well as the presence of nodal disease or overt metastatic disease (Table 17-2).[18] The preferred histopathologic grading system, as used in the 8th edition of the AJCC Cancer Staging Manual, is a three-tier (low, intermediate, and high) classification.[19]

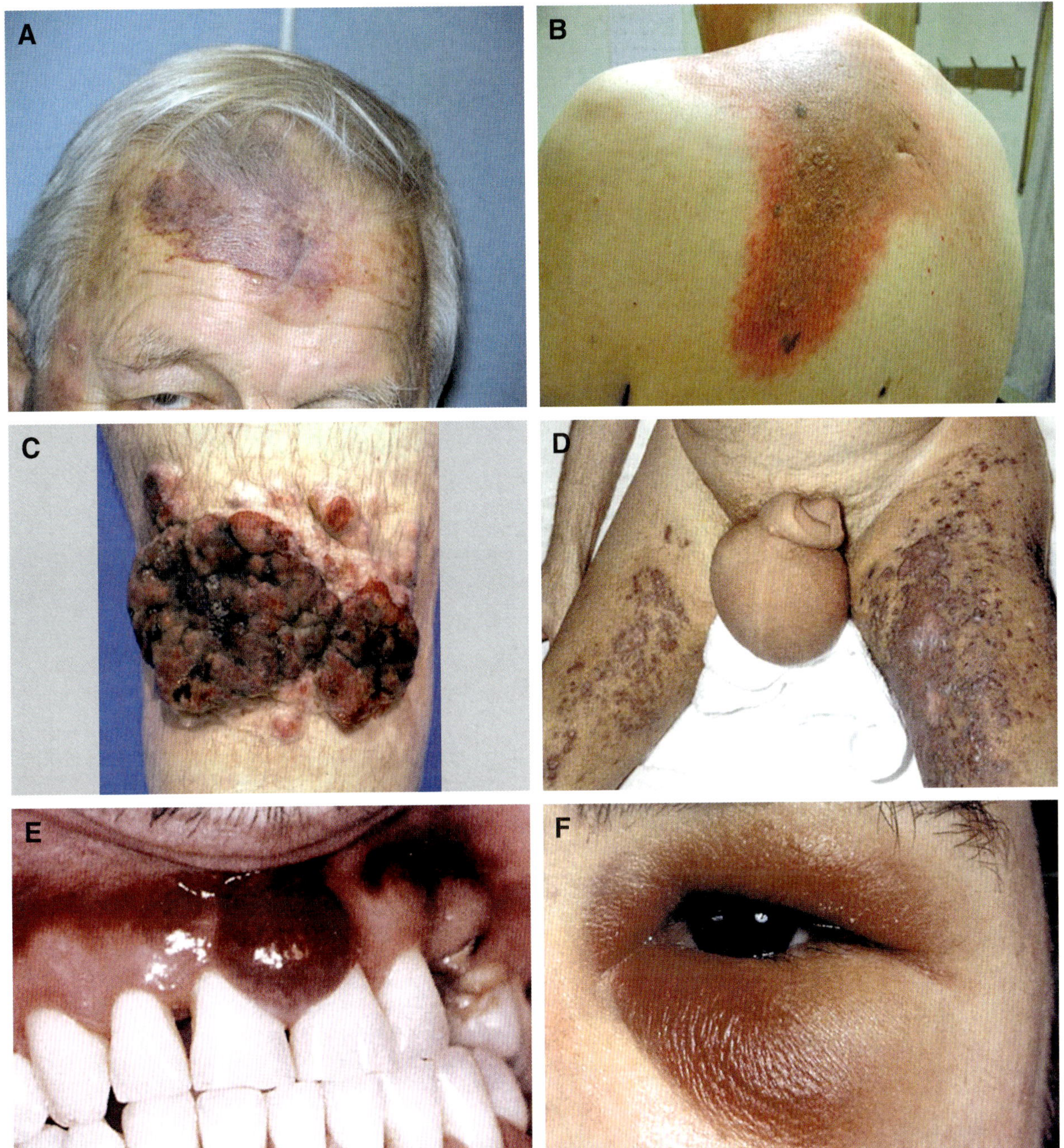

Fig. 17-2 Selected manifestations of angiosarcoma and Kaposi sarcoma.

(A) Angiosarcoma involving the scalp. (B) Angiosarcoma arising in prior radiation field. (C) Angiosarcoma associated with chronic lymphedema. (D) Kaposi sarcoma involving thighs, causing lymphedema and scrotal edema. (E) Kaposi sarcoma of gingiva. (F) Kaposi sarcoma of head, causing periorbital erythema and edema.

Nodal metastatic disease is an unfavorable prognostic feature, but it is associated with better overall survival (OS) than bloodborne metastatic disease. Nodal metastatic disease is observed in < 10% of patients with STS; however, certain subtypes of sarcoma, including angiosarcoma, clear-cell sarcoma, epithelioid sarcoma, extraskeletal Ewing sarcoma, pediatric rhabdomyosarcoma, and synovial sarcoma, have a relatively higher propensity to spread through lymphatics. Sentinel-node biopsy evaluations have been studied in the management of localized clear-cell, epithelioid, and synovial sarcomas, but the yield of positive nodes is low.[20]

Histology, grade, size, and completeness of resection are the most important factors in determining the risk for relapse. Of primary importance in determining OS is tumor grade; OS also

Table 17-2 American Joint Committee on Cancer Staging System for Soft-Tissue Sarcoma Arising in Trunk, Extremity, or Retroperitoneum[16]

Stage	Three-Grade System (grade)	T	N	M
IA	1	T1	N0	M0
IB	1	T2, T3, T4	N0	M0
II	2 and 3	T1	N0	M0
IIIA	2 and 3	T2	N0	M0
IIIB	2 and 3	T3, T4	N0	M0
	Any grade	Any	N1	M0
IV	Any grade	Any	Any	M1

Abbreviations: M0, no distant metastasis; M1, distant metastasis; N0, no lymph node metastasis; N1, lymph node metastasis; T1, tumor ≤ 5 cm in greatest dimension; T2, tumor > 5 cm and ≤ 10 cm in greatest dimension; T3, tumor > 10 cm and ≤ 15 cm in greatest dimension; T4, tumor > 15 cm in greatest dimension.

Republished with permission of Springer, from AJCC Cancer Staging Manual, 8th Edition (2017); permission conveyed through Copyright Clearance Center, Inc.[18]

depends on the initial size and location of the tumor. As the size of the primary tumor increases, the risk for relapse increases, even within a given stage (Table 17-3), and the 8th edition of AJCC Cancer Staging Manual[18] now includes five categories of size for STS.[21,22] It is important to recognize that sarcomas of different primary sites (and typically different histologic subtypes) are associated with different patterns of distant and local failure (Table 17-4). A nomogram using tumor histology, grade, size, depth, and patient age is available to help estimate the risk for death resulting from STS after definitive local therapy.[23] A separate validated nomogram to help estimate risk of recurrence and death after resection of retroperitoneal STS is available.[24]

The AJCC staging system for bone cancers is presented in Table 17-5. Primary malignant lymphoma of bone and multiple myeloma are not included in the bone cancer staging system. Metastases of osteosarcomas to lymph nodes are extremely unusual and constitute stage IV disease. Patients with osteosarcoma with metastases only to the lungs have lower-stage disease, because surgical resection of lung metastases can be curative.

KEY POINTS

- Tumor grade is a key factor in sarcoma staging, treatment, and patient prognosis. Patients with low-grade sarcoma have low risk for metastases and excellent prognosis. Patients with high-grade (grade 3) sarcoma are at high risk for metastases.
- The risk of sarcoma metastasis increases with increasing size of the sarcoma.
- Staging STS or bone sarcoma should include imaging of the lung because the lung is the most common location for metastases. Staging disease in patients diagnosed with intermediate- or high-grade bone sarcoma includes evaluation of bone for presence of metastases.

Table 17-3 5-Year Disease-Free Survival Rates According to Size of High-Grade Soft-Tissue Sarcoma

Tumor Size (cm)[a]	5-Year DFS Rate (%)
2.6-4.9	77
5.0-9.9	62
10.0-14.9	51
15.0-20.0	42
> 20.0	17

Abbreviation: DFS, disease-free survival.

[a]Tumors ≤ 5 cm were generally treated with surgery; tumors > 5 cm were typically treated with surgery and radiation.

TREATMENT OF NON-GIST STS

GENERAL PRINCIPLES

Surgery

The primary curative treatment of most STS is surgery. A planned oncologic resection to remove the tumor intact with a rim of normal tissue at the surgical margin (R0 resection) results in a lower risk for local relapse and better long-term patient survival than removal in which sarcoma touches the surgical margin (R1 resection).[25]

Radiation

Radiation to the site of the primary tumor is a standard of care for all intermediate- or high-grade STS of the extremities or body wall that are > 5 cm. RT significantly improve rates of local control and to reduce the need for amputation in patients with extremity STS. Radiation is usually administered after resection of low-grade STS that are > 5 cm and involve the extremities or body wall if the tumor is resected with a close (< 1 cm) or positive surgical margin and reoperation would result in significant morbidity.

Table 17-4 **Site of Recurrence According to Primary Site of Soft-Tissue Sarcoma**

Primary Site	Local	Lung	Other	Multiple Sites
Extremity	10	70	15	5
Trunk	41	29	12	18
Retroperitoneum	30	17	6	47

NOTE. Data are reported as percentages.

Table 17-5 **American Joint Committee on Cancer Staging System for Bone**[16]

Stage	Grade (four tiers)	T	N	M
IA	1 to 2 (low)	T1	N0	M0
IB	1 to 2 (low)	T2, T3	N0	M0
IIA	3 to 4 (high)	T1	N0	M0
IIB	3 to 4 (high)	T2	N0	M0
III	3 to 4 (high)	T3	N0	M0
IVA	Any	Any	N0	M1a
IVB	Any	Any	N1	Any
	Any	Any	Any	M1b

Abbreviations: M0, no distant metastasis; M1a, lung metastasis; M1b, other distant metastasis; N0, no lymph node metastasis; N1, lymph node metastasis; T1, tumor ≤ 8 cm in greatest dimension; T2, tumor > 8 cm in greatest dimension; T3, discontinuous tumor in primary bone site.

Republished with permission of Springer, from AJCC Cancer Staging Manual, 8th Edition (2017); permission conveyed through Copyright Clearance Center, Inc.[18]

Patients with STS < 5 cm occurring in an extremity or body wall do not uniformly require adjuvant radiation after an R0 resection.[26] One exception to the general guidelines for adjuvant RT is when there is well-differentiated liposarcoma or atypical lipomatous tumor that arises in a location amenable to additional surgery in a case of local recurrence. Adjuvant RT is not used in this situation (even for close or positive margins) because this subtype of sarcoma has an indolent clinical course and negligible risk for metastasizing. RT using external-beam radiation[27] or brachytherapy[28] has been shown in randomized studies to significantly reduce the risk of local recurrence for STSs of the extremities.

For intermediate and high-grade STS, radiation can be given either before or after surgery. A Canadian randomized study of preoperative RT compared with postoperative RT demonstrated similar rates of local disease control. The risk for wound complications (delayed healing, infection, or need for reoperation) was increased (most significantly in the leg) with preoperative radiation, but the treatment field was smaller and the radiation dose was lower than with postoperative radiation.[29] The risk for late complications, including fibrosis and lymphedema, appears greater with the larger field treated and higher dose used in postoperative RT.[30] One nonrandomized phase II study of preoperative image-guided RT for extremity STS suggested that late-effect radiation toxicity (eg, fibrosis, edema, joint stiffness) may be significantly reduced by narrowing gross target volume exposed to high-dose radiation using three-dimensional conformal or intensity-modulated techniques without a significant increase in local recurrence risk.[31] The timing of radiation should be decided in conjunction with the orthopedic or surgical oncologist.

In contrast to the benefit of radiation for STS of the extremities or body wall, no clear role exists for RT for retroperitoneal or visceral STS resected with clear or microscopically positive margins; the doses that can be administered postoperatively for abdominal STS generally are not tumoricidal, because of the dose limits for radiation for normal organs. Preoperative RT may be considered for high-grade or large abdominal or retroperitoneal STS because the tumor serves as its own tissue expander, pushing normal abdominal components, such as the bowel, out of the radiation field. This anatomic feature increases the likelihood that a tumoricidal dose of radiation can be delivered to the abdomen. However, neoadjuvant radiation does not clearly improve survival in this patient population.[32] Intraoperative RT mostly has been used for local control when STS extends to the surgical margin adjacent to critical structures or after resection of local recurrence in a previously irradiated field; it is not widely available. New techniques such as image-guided RT or proton or carbon ion radiation are useful for treatment of STS in anatomic areas with little tolerance for radiation scatter, such as the spine, sacrum, and base of the skull. Postoperative RT may be used in highly selected cases in which the area at risk is small and regrowth of sarcoma in that location would cause significant morbidity.

KEY POINTS

- Surgical resection remains the standard of care for most STSs.
- Adjuvant or neoadjuvant external-beam RT is used for larger STSs (> 5 cm in greatest dimension) arising in extremities or the body wall.
- Adjuvant RT may be used for smaller STSs in areas in which local recurrence would be difficult to manage using surgery.
- Adjuvant RT is usually avoided in the initial treatment of well-differentiated liposarcoma or atypical lipomatous tumors of the extremity or body wall, because of the low risk for metastatic disease in this histologic type of sarcoma and the possibility for repeated resection if there is local recurrence.
- Adjuvant RT is not generally recommended after resection of retroperitoneal or visceral STS.

ADJUVANT CHEMOTHERAPY

The role of chemotherapy in the preoperative or postoperative setting for adult STS remains controversial. Adjuvant chemotherapy is generally not used to manage STS < 5 cm or confined to a superficial location, because of the low risk for metastases. Notable exceptions to this rule are extraskeletal Ewing sarcoma and pediatric rhabdomyosarcoma, which are discussed later in this chapter.

Many older trials of adjuvant chemotherapy enrolled patients with AJCC stage IIB or III disease, because of the high risk for metastases. However, most studies have included relatively few patients with a variety of STS histologies. Furthermore, many different chemotherapy agents and combinations have been tested in these trials. Not surprisingly, such studies yielded conflicting results. Multiple meta-analyses have been performed in an effort to resolve these data. The most recently published meta-analysis showed a statistically significant survival benefit associated with use of the combination of anthracycline and ifosfamide, with an odds ratio of 0.56 and absolute average OS risk reduction of 10%.[33] Adjuvant treatment with doxorubicin without ifosfamide was associated with an absolute reduction in STS recurrence risk of 9% but was not associated with a significant improvement in OS.

In contrast, more modern trials have been randomized prospective trials. However, these trials have also come to conflicting conclusions. For example, an Italian randomized, multisite study of epirubicin and ifosfamide given for five cycles as compared with no adjuvant chemotherapy after resection of high-grade STS > 5 cm (median diameter, 10 cm) of the extremities or the pelvic girdle observed an OS benefit for patients who received adjuvant chemotherapy.[34] With longer follow-up, the 5-year OS remained superior for the study arm that used adjuvant chemotherapy (66% *v* 46%; *P* = .04).[35]

An OS benefit from adjuvant chemotherapy was not confirmed in a larger randomized study performed in Europe.[36] The study included STS occurring at any site, but the majority arose from the extremity or proximal limb girdle. The study was designed to enroll only patients with grade 2 or 3 tumors; however, 6% of the patients had grade 1 STS. Less than 75% of the patients randomly assigned to adjuvant chemotherapy completed five cycles of treatment, and the dose of ifosfamide used (5 g/m^2 per cycle) was lower than the dose used in the aforementioned Italian trial. However, a retrospective analysis of the data set from this larger European Organization for Research and Treatment of Cancer (EORTC) trial and a previous EORTC randomized adjuvant chemotherapy trial reported a significant improvement in relapse-free survival for patients age ≥ 30 years receiving chemotherapy but not for younger patients.[37]

Taken together, these studies indicate adjuvant anthracycline and ifosfamide chemotherapy is likely associated with a small but meaningful benefit. However, this must be balanced against the significant toxicity associated with these regimens. They are associated with high rates of grade 3/4 hematologic toxicity as well as significant risk of nonhematologic toxicity. Therefore, adjuvant chemotherapy is not considered a routine standard of care for all patients, but rather something that can be considered on a case-by-case basis for medically fit patients with high-grade extremity and body wall STS.

Adjuvant therapy is not indicated for some patients. Adjuvant chemotherapy for patients with STSs that arise from visceral or abdominal sites has not shown a survival benefit, and surgery alone remains a good standard of care. In addition, a number of STS subtypes (eg, alveolar soft part sarcoma, epithelioid sarcoma, clear cell sarcoma, extraskeletal myxoid chondrosarcoma, hemangiopericytoma) are known to have poor sensitivity to doxorubicin and ifosfamide chemotherapy, for which the risks of adjuvant chemotherapy outweigh the potential benefit.

In contrast to adjuvant therapy for adult-type STS, adjuvant or neoadjuvant chemotherapy and RT have greatly improved OS for patients with pediatric rhabdomyosarcoma (eg, embryonal sarcoma, alveolar rhabdomyosarcoma) and extraskeletal Ewing sarcoma regardless of the age of the patient at the time of diagnosis. Although these sarcomas typically are seen in the pediatric population and are found less frequently in adults, treatment of adults follows the same schedules of therapy as those for pediatric patients when feasible. Neoadjuvant or adjuvant chemotherapy should be administered to all patients with embryonal or alveolar rhabdomyosarcoma or extraskeletal Ewing sarcoma who have a good clinical performance status, adequate organ function, and sufficient bone marrow reserve to tolerate such therapy. The treatment of extraskeletal Ewing sarcoma is similar to that of Ewing sarcoma occurring in bone (see the section on Ewing sarcoma).

On the basis of phase III data, combination vincristine, dactinomycin, and cyclophosphamide form the backbone of adjuvant chemotherapy for most patients with primary, pediatric-type rhabdomyosarcomas[38]; although for adult patients, doxorubicin is often substituted for dactinomycin until a cumulative dose of approximately 450 mg/m^2 is reached. In contrast to embryonal and alveolar rhabdomyosarcoma, for which chemotherapy is recommended, pleomorphic rhabdomyosarcoma is an "adult-type," high-grade STS; thus, the role of adjuvant chemotherapy is less clearly defined. Spindle cell or sclerosing rhabdomyosarcoma is an uncommon variant that affects children and adults; it has a high rate of metastasis and relative resistance to chemotherapy in adults. Standard chemotherapy for this disease has not been established.

KEY POINTS

- Adjuvant chemotherapy with an anthracycline (doxorubicin or epirubicin) and ifosfamide reduces the risk of sarcoma recurrence and may improve OS in patients with chemotherapy-sensitive STS subtypes who have a high risk for the development of metastases.
- Patients with localized extraskeletal Ewing sarcoma should receive neoadjuvant or adjuvant chemotherapy as given to patients with skeletal Ewing sarcoma if not medically contraindicated.
- Embryonal and alveolar rhabdomyosarcoma are aggressive cancers with a propensity for nodal and distant metastases. They are best managed using surgery, adjuvant RT and/or multiagent chemotherapy at centers with experience in treating these "pediatric" STSs.

METASTATIC NON-GIST STS

Anthracyclines

As single drugs or in combination, anthracyclines such as doxorubicin and the alkylating agent ifosfamide yield the best response rates for metastatic non-GIST STS (rates of 10% to 25% for each drug in various studies).[39] Doxorubicin and ifosfamide are not synergistic, although the combination may be used when patients are symptomatic and rapid reduction in tumor burden is desired for palliation.

Doxorubicin and Ifosfamide

A randomized EORTC trial of doxorubicin 75 mg/m^2 combined with ifosfamide 10 g/m^2 per cycle demonstrated an improved objective response rate (26% with the combination and 14% with doxorubicin alone) and PFS (7.4 months *v* 4.6 months) but similar OS as single-agent doxorubicin.[40] Because of toxicity, 18% of patients receiving the combination discontinued treatment before completing six cycles, compared with 3% of patients receiving doxorubicin alone. The rate of death from toxic effects was low (< 2%) and similar in the two treatment arms. On basis of the results, the authors recommended sequential single-agent therapy in the palliative setting when the patient has minimal symptoms from STS, and to consider combination therapy if sarcoma regression would relieve acute symptoms or improve the likelihood of tumor control from surgery or radiation.

Doxorubicin and Olaratumab

An open-label, randomized phase II trial of doxorubicin 75 mg/m^2 administered on day 1 in combination with olaratumab (a human recombinant monoclonal antibody directed against platelet-derived growth factor receptor α [PDGFRA]) administered on days 1 and 8 of each cycle, as compared with doxorubicin alone, demonstrated significant improvement in median PFS and OS in adults with locally advanced or metastatic STS not previously treated with an anthracycline.[41] Up to eight cycles of doxorubicin-containing therapy were given. After that, patients in the olaratumab arm continued maintenance therapy with olaratumab alone. The combination did not improve PFS but it increased OS by about 12 months (26.5 months *v* 14.7 months). Eighteen percent of the patients in the combination arm had an objective tumor response, compared with 12% in the doxorubicin-alone arm. On the basis of the results of this study, the US Food and Drug Administration (FDA) provisionally approved olaratumab in combination with doxorubicin as treatment of adults with STS not curable by surgery or radiation and for whom treatment with an anthracycline is appropriate. However, the results of a follow-up, phase III, randomized, double-blind clinical trial were reported at the 2019 ASCO annual meeting.[42] In that study, the combination of olaratumab and doxorubicin did not improve OS compared with doxorubicin alone. PFS was actually inferior in the combination arm. On the basis of that result, the FDA withdrew the prior approval for olaratumab.

Pegylated liposomal doxorubicin has also been studied and is active in the treatment of metastatic STS. Studies have shown varying degrees of efficacy associated with this agent. It is generally better tolerated than conventional doxorubicin and is easier to administer to older patients.[43]

Gemcitabine and Docetaxel

At least four studies have demonstrated activity of the combination of gemcitabine and docetaxel in leiomyosarcoma.[44-46] This combination is also active against undifferentiated pleomorphic sarcoma. PFS and OS rates were improved for patients who received gemcitabine and docetaxel compared with gemcitabine alone, even at a higher gemcitabine dose.[46] However, the docetaxel dose used in this study (100 mg/m^2 per cycle) is too high for routine use, and many physicians recommend a docetaxel dose of 75 mg/m^2 per cycle.[46] A phase III trial confirmed activity of docetaxel administered at 75 mg/m^2 with gemcitabine for uterine leiomyosarcoma; an objective tumor response rate of 32% and median PFS of 6 months was demonstrated.[47] No benefit in response rate, PFS, or OS was seen in this trial from the addition of bevacizumab to gemcitabine and docetaxel. Gemcitabine and docetaxel have also been compared with doxorubicin in the first-line treatment of unresectable or metastatic STS in a randomized phase III trial.

This study found no difference in the proportion of patients alive and free of disease progression at 24 weeks.[48]

Duration of Front-Line Therapy

No consensus is available as to the duration of front-line therapy for metastatic disease. Some physicians treat until progression or toxicity, whereas others administer a defined number of cycles or to maximum clinical or tumor response and then closely follow patients off therapy for symptoms or signs of tumor progression. In the aforementioned uterine leiomyosarcoma trial, approximately 25% of patients with objective tumor response or stable disease stopped therapy as a personal preference after receiving a median of nine cycles of chemotherapy. The median time to progression after stopping treatment in this group was 6 months; this ranged up to 19.5 months, illustrating that some patients may have prolonged tumor control after chemotherapy.

Second-Line and Later Chemotherapy

Trabectedin is a cytotoxic agent that was approved by the FDA for use in patients with unresectable or metastatic leiomyosarcoma or liposarcoma after prior treatment with an anthracycline-containing regimen. An early, randomized, open-label, phase II study of trabectedin in patients with advanced or metastatic leiomyosarcoma or liposarcoma demonstrated a longer median PFS and time to progression in patients treated with a 24-hour infusion once every 3 weeks than with a 3-hour infusion once weekly for 3 of 4 weeks per cycle.[49] Treatment with trabectedin led to a 45% reduction ($P < .001$) in risk for sarcoma progression or death compared with dacarbazine in a randomized, open-label, international phase III study of trabectedin administered over 24 hours compared with dacarbazine treatment of patients with advanced or metastatic leiomyosarcoma or liposarcoma.[50] Objective response rates were < 10% and not significantly different between the two arms. The median PFS was 4.2 months with trabectedin, compared with 1.5 months with dacarbazine. There was no significant difference in OS. Principal adverse events of trabectedin are neutropenia, anemia, thrombocytopenia, increased transaminase levels, increased creatine kinase level, fatigue, and nausea. Treatment with trabectedin led to a 1.2% incidence of rhabdomyolysis and a 2.1% incidence of treatment-related death; this did not occur in the dacarbazine-treated arm. Trabectedin is a vascular irritant and may result in tissue necrosis after extravasation; therefore, it should be infused through a central venous catheter. Elderly patients (older than 70 years) do not have increased adverse-event rates from trabectedin compared with younger individuals.[51]

Eribulin is an antimitotic agent that inhibits microtubule function and, in a phase III randomized, open-label trial, has demonstrated improvement in OS compared with dacarbazine in patients with previously treated, locally advanced or metastatic leiomyosarcoma or liposarcoma.[52] A planned subgroup analysis stratified by sarcoma subtype identified a statistically significant improvement in PFS and OS in patients with liposarcoma treated with eribulin as compared with dacarbazine. There was a 1.2-month difference in median PFS and a 7-month difference in OS in favor of eribulin. No difference in PFS or OS was seen in patients with leiomyosarcoma. On the basis of these results, the FDA approved eribulin as treatment of patients with unresectable or metastatic liposarcoma who have previously received an anthracycline. Patients treated in the phase III study had previously received at least an anthracycline and one other chemotherapy. Eribulin 1.4 mg/m^2 was administered over 2 to 5 minutes on days 1 and 8 of a 21-day cycle. The most frequent adverse events were neutropenia, fatigue, nausea, alopecia, and constipation. Eribulin did not demonstrate significant antitumor activity in synovial sarcoma or in a cohort with undifferentiated, unspecified, and fibrohistiocytic sarcomas in a four-cohort, single-arm, phase II trial.[53]

Tyrosine Kinase Inhibitors

Pazopanib, an oral multikinase inhibitor that targets VEGF receptors, PDGFRA and PDGFRB, among others, was approved as treatment of patients with locally advanced or metastatic STS after treatment with standard chemotherapy. This was based on results of a phase III, randomized, placebo-controlled trial that demonstrated significant improvement in median PFS in patients receiving pazopanib as compared with placebo (20 *v* 7 weeks).[54] Objective sarcoma responses were infrequent—6% in the group receiving pazopanib. Median OS was not significantly different between patients taking pazopanib compared with those taking placebo (12.5 *v* 10.7 months). Patients with liposarcoma or GIST were not included in the trial. Notable severe toxicities were experienced by more patients taking pazopanib than those taking placebo and included fatigue, anorexia, nausea, mucositis, hypertension, diarrhea, rash or desquamation, hypopigmentation, and decline in cardiac ejection fraction. The recommended starting dose is 800 mg daily. Adverse effects are frequent and careful monitoring is essential to avoid dose reduction.[55]

Larotrectinib is a highly selective inhibitor of the three tropomyosin receptor kinases (TRK1, TRK2, and TRK3). The genes (*NTRK1*, *NTRK2*, and *NTRK3*) encoding these kinases can be constitutively activated by chromosomal translocations, which can be seen in a variety of different cancers. Larotrectinib was FDA approved for treatment of solid tumors with a known NTRK fusion without a resistance mutation. This approval was made on the basis of a 55-patient study that found this agent was associated with a 75% response rate in these cancers. Notably, this study included 18 patients with STS.[56]

Immunotherapy

PD-1 and PD-L1 inhibitors have been studied in the treatment of advanced STS but do not yet have a standard role in the treatment of any sarcoma subtype. Studies have shown evidence of potential efficacy, but with the exception of MSI-H STS, immunotherapy is not a standard treatment of advanced STS. For example, pembrolizumab was found in a small phase II trial to have activity against UPS and liposarcoma. This trial enrolled a total of 40 patients with advanced STS. The response rate was

40% in the UPS cohort and 20% in the liposarcoma cohort.[57] There was no evidence of activity in synovial sarcoma, leiomyosarcoma, or in bone sarcoma. On the basis of these results, trials are ongoing not only with pembrolizumab but also with other PD-L1 and PD-1 inhibitors in the treatment of advanced STS.

Histology-Specific Treatment

Because sarcomas are a biologically heterogeneous group of diseases, it is not surprising that specific sarcoma subtypes are preferentially sensitive to certain agents (Table 17-6). Ifosfamide is particularly active for synovial sarcoma and myxoid liposarcoma and appears to be less active for leiomyosarcomas. Dacarbazine has modest activity against leiomyosarcoma, and paclitaxel as well as pegylated liposomal doxorubicin[43] are active against angiosarcomas. Studies have demonstrated activity of sunitinib and cediranib against alveolar soft-part sarcoma.[58-60] The combinations of temozolomide and bevacizumab, as well as sunitinib, have activity in solitary fibrous tumor.[61,62]

Desmoid Tumor

Desmoid tumor is a benign but locally aggressive soft-tissue tumor that can occur in the setting of familial adenomatous polyposis, or sporadically. It follows an unpredictable course, with spontaneous regression seen in 33% of patients in one recently reported phase III trial not uncommonly occurring.[63] Treatment is indicated for patients with symptomatic disease and/or rapidly progressive disease. Until recently, the evidence supporting activity of such agents was limited to small case series. More recently, however, two randomized controlled trials have confirmed benefit associated with both sorafenib and pazopanib in the treatment of this disease. Sorafenib, a multi-targeted tyrosine kinase targeting both RAF kinases and cell-surface kinase receptors (including VEGF receptors, among others), improved PFS compared with placebo in patients with progressive disease.[63] The study enrolled 87 patients; the median PFS was 9.4 months for placebo and it has not yet been reached for patients treated with sorafenib. Common adverse effects associated with sorafenib included rash, hypertension, fatigue, and pain. Of the patients treated with sorafenib, 18% had to stop treatment for toxicity reasons. In another clinical trial, pazopanib was compared with methotrexate and vinblastine chemotherapy in a randomized trial and improved the 6-month nonprogression rate from 50% to 86%.[64] Other effective agents include liposomal doxorubicin, imatinb, tamoxifen, sulindac, and the combination of methotrexate and vinblastine.

Connective-Tissue Tumors

Improved understanding of the biology of certain connective-tissue tumors has led to the clinical introduction of serine-threonine and tyrosine kinase inhibitors in the management of disease. Angiomyolipomas are benign tumors that often occur in patients with tuberous sclerosis and that, on occasion, can lead to serious morbidity or death. Loss of tuberous sclerosis complex results in constitutive activation of the mammalian target of rapamycin complex 1 (mTORC1), which is thought to be responsible for tumor growth. Everolimus is an inhibitor of mTORC1, and treatment of patients with angiomyolipomas resulted in an objective tumor response rate of 42% in patients using everolimus 10 mg daily compared with 0% in those using placebo in a double-blind, randomized trial.[65] Everolimus is approved for the treatment of angiomyolipoma associated with tuberous sclerosis and not requiring immediate surgery. Inhibitors of mTORC1 (eg, sirolimus and everolimus) also have activity in other perivascular epithelioid cell tumors, including lymphangioleiomyomatosis.[66]

Other examples of rare connective-tissue tumors significantly affected by inhibitors of kinases include dermatofibrosarcoma protuberans, with overexpression of PDGF, and tenosynovial giant-cell tumor/pigmented villonodular synovitis (TGCT/PVNS), with overexpression of colony-stimulating factor 1. Both of these tumors may be effectively controlled using imatinib.[67,68] In addition, pexidartinib, a selective inhibitor of

Table 17-6 **Agents With Activity Against Specific STS Subtypes**

Tumor Type	Agent
Undifferentiated pleomorphic sarcoma	Pembrolizumab
Leiomyosarcoma	Trabectedin, gemcitabine/docetaxel
Myxoid liposarcoma	Trabectedin, ifosfamide
Dedifferentiated liposarcoma	Palbociclib, eribulin
Synovial sarcoma	Ifosfamide
Angiosarcoma	Paclitaxel, bevacizumab, PLD, sunitinib
Alveolar soft parts sarcoma	Cedirinib, sunitinib
Solitary fibrous tumor	Bevacizumab/temozolomide, sunitinib
Desmoid tumor	Sorafenib, pazopanib, imatinib
Angiomyolipoma, PEComa	Everolimus, temsirolimus, sirolimus
Dermatofibrosarcoma protruberans	Imatinib

Abbreviations: PEComa, perivascular epithelioid cell tumor; PLD, pegylated liposomal doxorubicin.

CSF-1, has been approved by the FDA for treatment of TGCT/PVNS not amenable to surgical resection. This agent had a 25-week response rate of 39% compared with 0% for placebo.[69] It is a reasonable option but has been associated with risk of significant hepatotoxicity and currently can only be prescribed via a Risk Evaluation and Mitigation Strategy program. Cyclin-dependent kinase 4 (CDK4) is frequently amplified along with MDM2 in well-differentiated and dedifferentiated liposarcoma. Treatment of patients with well-differentiated or dedifferentiated liposarcoma using the selective CDK4 inhibitor palbociclib resulted in one objective tumor response and a median PFS of 18 weeks in two separate, single-arm, open-label, phase II trials.[70,71] The most common adverse events were neutropenia, anemia, and thrombocytopenia. Improved molecular and cytogenetic methods, including next-generation sequencing of sarcomas, are leading to additional associations of recurrent molecular changes within specific sarcoma subtypes. These changes will need to be validated as important drivers of oncogenesis, and new drugs targeting these changes will need to be evaluated in prospective, controlled trials before a "targeted" therapy is adopted as standard treatment.

KEY POINTS

- Doxorubicin and ifosfamide are the most effective single drugs for metastatic non-GIST adult STSs. The benefit of these two drugs appears additive, not synergistic. The combination has not been shown to improve OS in patients with metastatic disease but is a reasonable option for selected patients. Sequential single-agent treatment of metastatic disease is a reasonable approach for many patients with metastatic disease.
- Gemcitabine and docetaxel is active in advanced or metastatic STS, with efficacy similar to doxorubicin.
- Trabectedin is active in patients with leiomyosarcoma or liposarcoma who have received prior treatment with an anthracycline. Eribulin is active in patients with liposarcoma who have received prior treatment with an anthracycline.
- Pazopanib is approved for treatment of advanced or metastatic non-GIST STS (excluding liposarcoma) after treatment with chemotherapy, on the basis of improvement in PFS as compared with placebo.
- Both sorafenib and pazopanib are effective in the treatment of desmoid tumors requiring treatment, based on disease progression or tumor-related symptoms.

KAPOSI SARCOMA

Treatment of KS is aimed at disease control and alleviation of tumor-related symptoms and complications. No treatment is clearly curative. Specific treatment recommendations vary on the basis of disease extent and presence or absence of concurrent HIV infection. Asymptomatic lesions may be observed without direct therapy. In patients with HIV infection and KS, introduction of antiretroviral therapy (ART) resulting in a decline in viral load and an increase in CD4 cell count frequently leads to regression in Kaposi lesions with durable clinical response rates > 60%.[72] This is standard for all patients with HIV/AIDS and is the only treatment needed in some cases. Occasionally, and sometimes dramatically, patients with KS who subsequently receive ART experience a sudden flare or burst in KS lesion growth. [73] This phenomenon, known as immune reconstitution inflammatory syndrome (IRIS), resulting from immune response against pathogens, may occur within weeks to a few months after initiation of ART. In a cohort study of 150 patients with HIV-associated KS who began ART as the sole treatment of KS, 10 (6.6%) had progressive IRIS-associated KS. In such instances, ART usually can be successfully continued, although chemotherapy also may be required for a time to control KS growth.[74]

The decision to provide specific antitumor local or systemic treatment of KS should be based on several factors, including:

- assessment of disease abundance,
- site of the disease,
- rate of disease progression,
- patient-specific psychologic factors, and
- presence of organ dysfunction.[75]

Local Treatment

Local treatment may be possible for patients who have limited, nonbulky, and accessible lesions. Alitretinoin gel (0.1%) is the only topical, patient-administered therapy approved by the FDA for the treatment of KS.[76]

Other local treatments for KS include intralesional chemotherapy, RT, laser therapy, and cryotherapy, all of which can be effective at controlling local tumor growth. RT has a role in the treatment of KS, particularly when the disease is bulky and symptomatic and when rapid tumor shrinkage is required.[77] In a series of 36 patients with KS of the feet, a fractionation schedule of three fractions per week at 3.5 Gy per fraction (up to a total dose of 21.0 Gy) yielded an overall response rate of 91% (complete response, 80%).[78] Although discomfort from RT was frequent, it usually resolved without intervention within 2 weeks of completion of therapy.

Systemic Chemotherapy

Patients with KS-associated edema, extensive mucocutaneous disease, or symptomatic pulmonary or GI disease need a rapid response, which is achieved best with systemic chemotherapy. Many cytotoxic chemotherapy agents have moderate activity in KS, including bleomycin, vinca alkaloids, etoposide, taxanes, and anthracyclines.[75] Most of the reports of drug activity in classic or HIV-associated KS are from small retrospective series, case reports, or relatively small phase II trials. Few larger randomized studies of chemotherapy for KS have been conducted. Because many anticancer agents are also metabolized by CYP450, the potential for drug reactions with ART is high.

Liposomal formulations of doxorubicin and daunorubicin are the standard front-line treatments for patients with extensive or advanced disease or for those who require rapid tumor shrinkage. For HIV-related KS, each of the two available liposomal anthracyclines proved superior to conventional chemotherapy (bleomycin and vincristine, with or without nonliposomal doxorubicin) in terms of response rates and toxicity profiles based on the results of randomized prospective clinical trials.[79-81] Liposomal doxorubicin also has significant activity in classic KS and is usually given at a dose of 20 mg/m^2 every 3 weeks.[82]

Patients with KS whose tumors initially respond well to this treatment may require additional therapy. Among 98 patients who received pegylated liposomal doxorubicin, after a median follow-up of 50 months, 13% had experienced a relapse, most within the first year of stopping chemotherapy.[83] Low-dose weekly paclitaxel is an established second-line therapy for KS treatment and has shown efficacy even for patients with HIV-associated KS and anthracycline-resistant disease. For patients in whom one previous systemic chemotherapy regimen had failed, the response rates in two trials were 59% and 71%, respectively, and the median duration of response in these studies was 8.9 months and 10.4 months, respectively.[84,85] Drug-related adverse events occurring in the majority of patients were grade 4 neutropenia and alopecia. Oral etoposide, vinorelbine, gemcitabine, bevacizumab, and imatinib have also been evaluated individually in patients with anthracycline-treated KS and demonstrated objective responses, but no randomized comparison of these agents has been reported.

KEY POINTS

- KS may be followed without the use of antineoplastic therapy when the disease burden is limited and asymptomatic.
- ART is standard front-line treatment of all patients with HIV-associated KS
- Immune reconstitution after introduction of ART in patients with HIV-associated KS may result in tumor flare in 5% to 10% of cases.
- Liposomal anthracycline is a standard first-line chemotherapy for patients requiring treatment of KS because of tumor growth, tumor symptoms, or involvement of visceral organs.
- Paclitaxel is active in anthracycline-resistant KS.

GI STROMAL TUMORS

BIOLOGY AND PRESENTATION

GISTs are sarcomas characterized by the presence of the CD117 (KIT) and/or DOG-1 (discovered on GIST) immunohistochemical markers, and most express stem cell marker CD34. Most GISTs have activating mutations in the *KIT* or *PDGFRA* gene.[86] Approximately 10% to 15% of GISTs use alternative mechanisms for pathogenesis, including loss of function of the succinate dehydrogenase complex, inactivating mutation in neurofibromin-1 and activating mutation in *BRAF*.[87] Rarely, NTRK fusions can also be seen in these tumors.[88] These latter three types of GISTs were previously referred to as wild-type GIST.

GISTs are currently the most common form of sarcoma (incidence, 5 to 10 cases per million persons in the United States). These tumors arise from the interstitial cells of Cajal, the pacemaker cells of the GI tract. Approximately 65% of GISTs occur in the stomach, 25% in the small bowel, and the remainder arise in other sites along the GI tract or in the abdomen. GISTs occurring in the setting of neurofibromatosis predominantly appear in the small intestine, including the duodenum, as multifocal tumors and frequently exhibit a low mitotic rate.[89]

In some cases, GISTs are found unexpectedly during an endoscopy study in the absence of symptoms. Often, symptoms are nonspecific, such as bloating and early satiety. They also can present with bleeding causing significant anemia, and less commonly can cause frank bowel obstruction. CT is the imaging study of choice, and biopsy is performed in patients with metastatic disease or when the diagnosis is not clear based on imaging findings.

The primary treatment of localized GISTs is surgery, but many will recur in the peritoneum, liver, or both. Nodal, bone, and pulmonary metastasis from GIST have been described but are rare. GISTs are included in the 8th edition of the AJCC Cancer Staging Manual.[18] Tumors are staged on the basis of size, location (gastric *v* small bowel), mitotic rate, involvement of lymph nodes and presence of metastasis. The involvement of lymph nodes or presence of metastasis is classified as stage IV disease. GISTs are graded by mitotic rate. A low mitotic rate is five or fewer mitoses per 5 mm^2 (50 microscopic fields using ×40 magnification); a high mitotic rate is more than five mitoses per 5 mm^2.

The approximate risk for GIST recurrence based on the above variables is shown in Table 17-7. The occurrence of tumor rupture before or during surgery is associated with a high risk for GIST recurrence.

LOCALIZED DISEASE

Adjuvant Therapy

The role of imatinib in the adjuvant setting has been the subject of several studies. A large, randomized, prospective, placebo-controlled trial of imatinib after surgery for patients with GIST > 3 cm was stopped early because of a beneficial effect of imatinib on delaying disease recurrence; this led to the approval of imatinib in the adjuvant setting in the United States and Europe (the latter only for patients at substantial risk for relapse).[90] Only 3% of patients who received imatinib experienced disease progression at 1 year (the end of the mandated treatment), compared with 17% of patients who were assigned to the placebo arm. However, there was no demonstrable OS benefit, likely owing to the high response rate in patients receiving

Table 17-7 Risk for GIST Recurrence After Resection

Stage	Tumor Size (cm)	Mitotic Rate	Location	Observed Rate of Recurrence (%)
I	≤ 5	Low	Small bowel	0-4
IA	≤ 5	Low	Stomach	0-2
IB	> 5-10	Low	Stomach	3-4
II	> 5-10	Low	Small bowel	24
	< 2	High	Stomach	Insufficient data
	> 2-5	High	Stomach	16
	> 10	Low	Stomach	12
IIIA	> 5-10	High	Stomach	55
	> 10	Low	Small bowel	52
	≤ 2	High	Small bowel	50
IIIB	> 10	High	Stomach	86
	> 2-5	High	Small bowel	73
	> 5-10	High	Small bowel	85
	> 10	High	Small bowel	90

Adapted from the AJCC Cancer Staging Manual, 8th edition, published by Springer Science and Business Media.[18].

imatinib after recurrence was detected and the short follow-up of the study (a median of 15 months).

The SSG XVIII trial, a large, randomized, open-label trial of imatinib taken for 1 year compared with 3 years after complete resection of high-risk GIST (> 50% risk of tumor recurrence) detected an approximate 20% improvement in relapse-free survival at 5 years for the cohort receiving 3 years of adjuvant imatinib (65% *v* 48%).[91] Importantly, OS was significantly better at 5 years in the group receiving adjuvant therapy for 3 years compared with 1 year (92% *v* 82%). High risk was defined by tumor size > 10 cm, mitotic count more than 10 per 50 high-power field, tumor size > 5 cm with mitotic count more than five per 50 high-power field or tumor rupture.

Imatinib therapy can be associated with intolerable adverse effects, and one-quarter of the patients assigned to take imatinib for 3 years discontinued treatment early for reasons other than disease recurrence. Periorbital edema, muscle cramps, leukopenia, and elevation in serum creatinine level were more common in patients assigned to 3 years of imatinib. On the basis of information currently available, it is reasonable to discuss adjuvant imatinib therapy for at least 3 years with patients who are at high risk for tumor relapse. Finally, adjuvant imatinib is not recommended for "wild-type" GIST or those with the *PDGFR D824V* mutation, because these are not sensitive to imatinib.

Neoadjuvant Therapy

The primary treatment of localized GIST is surgery. Imatinib can be considered a neoadjuvant therapy for patients who have high predicted morbidity associated with primary surgery. In that setting, optimal response to imatinib can take approximately 6 months, based on data in advanced disease. No evidence is available that neoadjuvant imatinib improves outcomes compared with adjuvant imatinib. If neoadjuvant therapy is given, mutation testing to confirm the presence of a responsive *KIT/PGDRF* mutation is recommended beforehand to ensure the tumor is likely to respond.

ADVANCED DISEASE

Imatinib, Sunitinib, and Regorafenib

Cytotoxic chemotherapy (including intraperitoneal chemotherapy) is ineffective in the treatment of GIST. However, imatinib has remarkable activity against most *KIT* or *PDGFRA*-mutation–positive GIST. In early-phase studies of imatinib therapy for metastatic GIST, response rates were approximately 60%, at least 10 times the rates associated with previously available therapy.[92] In randomized phase II and phase III studies, a once-daily dose of 400 mg was as effective as 600 mg or 800 mg of imatinib daily.[93,94] As a result, 400 mg daily of oral imatinib is the standard treatment of metastatic GIST. The *KIT* phenotype of a GIST predicts the responsiveness of the tumor to imatinib. Patients with mutations in exon 11 of *KIT* have a greater chance of response to imatinib than patients with exon 9 *KIT* mutations or wild-type *KIT*.[86] Tumors that harbor the *PDGFR* mutation *D842V* are particularly insensitive to imatinib, although other mutations in *PDGFR* are imatinib-sensitive. The mutation in *KIT* (or in *PDGFRA*), and not mere expression of the protein, appears to correlate with sensitivity to imatinib and other tyrosine kinase inhibitors in GIST.

Patients with GIST harboring an activating mutation in exon 9 of *KIT* may benefit from a higher starting dose of imatinib (400 mg twice daily), based on the demonstration of a small, but statistically significant, improvement in median PFS compared with patients receiving 400 mg of imatinib daily.[95] A meta-analysis of two large, randomized trials comparing imatinib 400 mg daily with 400 mg twice daily in the treatment of advanced or metastatic GIST confirmed a small PFS advantage and detected a higher objective response rate associated with the higher dose in patients with the exon 9 *KIT* mutations.[96] However, with a median follow-up of > 40 months, documented GIST progression or death in patients with exon 9 mutations occurred in 40 of 42 and 42 of 49 patients randomly assigned to 400 mg and 800 mg daily, respectively. There was no improvement in OS. There was no difference in outcome between the standard- and high-dose groups among patients with the more common exon 11 *KIT* mutations. Dose-limiting adverse effects of imatinib include nausea and vomiting, diarrhea, rash, mucositis, and/or diuretic-resistant peripheral edema. At imatinib doses > 800 mg daily, dose-limiting toxicities are frequently encountered.

After disease progression while receiving imatinib 400-mg daily dosing, a conventional approach is to increase the dose to a total daily dose of 800 mg (or 600 mg if the higher dose is not tolerated). Approximately one-third of patients may have some degree of tumor control after escalation of imatinib dose.[93,94]

For patients with imatinib-refractory disease or in patients intolerant of imatinib, sunitinib is the standard second-line therapy, because this agent was superior to placebo in a randomized phase III study in this setting.[97] The median duration of PFS in the arm receiving sunitinib was 24 weeks, compared with 6 weeks in patients treated with placebo; however, objective tumor responses were infrequent (< 10% of patients). OS was superior in the sunitinib arm compared with the placebo-treated arm. Patients less likely to benefit from sunitinib had primary mutations in exon 11 of *KIT* and/or development of secondary mutations, rendering GIST resistant to both imatinib and sunitinib. The most frequently reported adverse effects of sunitinib were fatigue, diarrhea, skin discoloration, and nausea, each occurring in > 20% of patients. Hypertension and hypothyroidism are also known toxicities of sunitinib; they should be treated immediately when identified. Rare cases of fatal liver or cardiac events have been reported, and patients should be monitored closely while receiving therapy.

Regorafenib, at a dose of 160 mg daily for 3 of every 4 weeks, is approved for treatment of GIST after the development of resistance to imatinib and sunitinib, based on results of a randomized, blinded, placebo-controlled trial.[98] Median PFS was 5 months for patients receiving regorafenib compared with 1 month for patients receiving placebo. The most common, severe, adverse regorafenib-related events were hypertension and hand-foot skin reaction, which occurred in 24% and 20% of patients, respectively. Dose escalation of regorafenib has been associated with lower incidence of adverse effects in patients with colorectal cancer, but there are no data regarding efficacy of this approach in patients with advanced GIST.

Surgery

Surgery can play a role in the treatment of metastatic disease. In some patients with multifocal metastatic disease, progression is identified in a limited number of sites, with other sites remaining under control. Patients with this pattern of disease progression can be treated successfully with resection of progressing sites coupled with continued imatinib therapy. It is essential to continue imatinib in such patients because of the risk of rapid progression without systemic treatment.

Patients with multiple sites of disease progression, indicative of generalized resistance to imatinib, are not appropriate candidates for surgical resection, because they almost universally will experience additional progression within a few months after surgery.[99] Resumption of imatinib after progression after second- or third-line therapy may be considered in patients with GIST previously controlled (responsive or stable for > 6 months) by imatinib if a clinical trial is not available. In one small, randomized, placebo-controlled trial, median PFS was delayed 1 month in patients receiving imatinib rather than placebo; however, allowing for crossover from placebo to imatinib after progression, there was no difference between the arms in OS.[100]

KEY POINTS

- Most GISTs have activating mutations in the *KIT* or *PDGFRA* gene.
- Surgery is the best curative treatment of primary GIST.
- For patients with localized GIST at high risk (> 50%) of recurrence, imatinib 400 mg daily for at least 3 years after surgery delays time to recurrence and improves OS.
- Imatinib at a dose of 400 mg daily is the standard of care in first-line therapy for metastatic GIST with sensitive mutations. For progressive disease, treatment with an increased dose of imatinib may be tried.
- Patients with exon 9 *KIT*-mutant GISTs may benefit from a higher initial starting dose of imatinib (ie, 400 mg twice daily) when tolerated; GIST tumors with *PDGFRA D842V* mutations are resistant to imatinib.
- Sunitinib is approved for second-line therapy for patients with imatinib-refractory GIST or who cannot tolerate imatinib.
- Regorafenib is approved for third-line therapy of GIST after failure of imatinib and sunitinib.
- Surgical resection may be appropriate, in conjunction with tyrosine-kinase inhibitor therapy, for patients with progressive metastatic disease limited to one or a few sites.

BONE SARCOMAS

OSTEOSARCOMA

Osteosarcomas are the most common tumors of bone, with two peaks of incidence: one between ages 10 and 20 years and a smaller peak between ages 60 and 80 years. Disease in the latter age group is sometimes associated with Paget disease of bone. Osteosarcomas generally arise in the metaphysis of the bone (between the bone end [epiphysis] and the shaft [diaphysis]). They are characterized by lytic and blastic features in admixed bone. If the tumors extend to soft tissue, they can cause both a periosteal reaction (Codman triangle; Fig 17-3) and ossification in a pattern perpendicular to the surface of the bone.

Adjuvant and/or neoadjuvant chemotherapy is the standard of care for most patients with osteosarcomas. It has resulted in significant improvement in 5-year survival rates from about 20% with surgery alone to as high as 80% in patients with responsive disease. Neoadjuvant chemotherapy is often preferred because it allows for assessment of histologic response, which is a major prognostic factor in localized high-grade osteosarcoma. Nearly all patients with localized osteosarcoma benefit from chemotherapy. The exception is superficial low-grade osteosarcomas, for which adjuvant chemotherapy is not indicated. For conventional osteosarcomas, six cycles of cisplatin and doxorubicin were found to be as effective as a more complex seven-drug regimen in one randomized, multicenter study.[101]

Data regarding the use of methotrexate remain somewhat controversial in adult patients. However, the combination of doxorubicin, cisplatin and high-dose methotrexate is a standard therapy in patients younger than 40 years who have normal cardiac and renal function. In older adults, high-dose methotrexate is associated with delayed clearance, increased risk of nephrotoxicity, and acute lung injury. Given these risks and the unclear benefit associated with this agent, methotrexate is not a standard component of treatment of adults aged ≥ 40 years.

Muramyl tripeptide, a nonspecific immune stimulator, improved OS when used in the adjuvant setting in one large cooperative group study; however, the compound is unavailable for use in the United States, though it was approved for adjuvant use in patients younger than 30 years in Europe.[102,103]

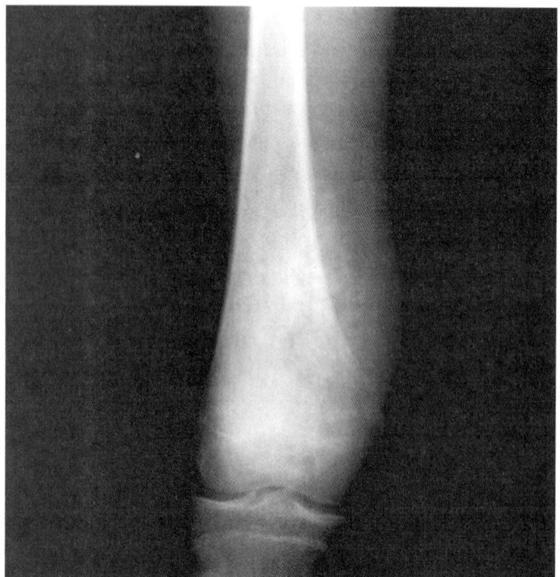

Fig. 17-3 Codman's triangle in distal femoral osteosarcoma. Codman's triangle seen along the distal femur laterally in this radiograph, in the area of the associated soft-tissue mass.

The response of osteosarcomas to neoadjuvant chemotherapy is best assessed by pathologic examination at the time of operation, which provides prognostic information. This examination assesses for the percentage of viable tumor in the total volume of the resection specimen. Presently, there is no evidence that changing therapy improves OS in patients with osteosarcoma who have a poor response to preoperative chemotherapy. EURAMOS-1, a large, international, randomized, phase III trial, evaluated the addition of interferon in patients with < 10% viable tumor (good histologic response) and the addition of ifosfamide and etoposide in patients with ≥ 10% viable tumor (poor histologic response) after two cycles of methotrexate plus doxorubicin plus cisplatin [MAP]). Pegylated interferon α-2b did not improve event-free survival (EFS).[104] There was no reduction in osteosarcoma relapse or survival benefit from the addition of ifosfamide and etoposide to MAP in patients with a poor histologic response to preoperative MAP.[105] The 3-year EFS rate was 55% in the control group and 53% in the group receiving ifosfamide and etoposide.

Because patients with poorly responding osteosarcoma treated with full-course chemotherapy have higher survival rates than patients who do not receive additional chemotherapy, all patients should be offered six cycles of chemotherapy for treatment of primary osteosarcoma, regardless of histologic response. The addition of zoledronate to combination chemotherapy did not improve the EFS or OS rates in patients with localized or metastatic osteosarcoma in a randomized, open-label, phase III trial.[106] EFS at 3 years was 63% in the control group and 57% in the group receiving zoledronate.

RT is not commonly used as an adjuvant or neoadjuvant treatment of localized high-grade osteosarcoma. It can be used for patients who have undergone positive-margin surgery but has no role for those who have undergone negative-margin surgery.

Osteosarcomas typically metastasize to the lung. Resection of pulmonary metastases (stage IVA disease) can be curative in a significant minority of patients—one of the few examples of this in solid tumor oncology.[107] Patients with fewer than three pulmonary metastases who are > 2 years from diagnosis to the development of lung metastases have the best survival rates after metastasectomy.

Ifosfamide plus etoposide with or without methotrexate has activity in relapsed osteosarcoma.[108,109] Gemcitabine (with or without docetaxel) also has some activity in this setting.[110] More recently, tyrosine kinase inhibitors have demonstrated activity in the treatment of advanced osteosarcoma. Regorafenib was compared with placebo in a randomized, phase II clinical trial in patients with known progressive disease, many of whom had previously been treated with chemotherapy for metastatic disease. PFS at 24 weeks was 35% for regorafenib-treated patients, compared with 0% in the placebo-treated patients.[111] The most common toxicities encountered were hypertension, hand/foot syndrome, asthenia, and diarrhea.

> **KEY POINTS**
>
> - Chemotherapy is used in the neoadjuvant and adjuvant settings to treat osteosarcoma. Doxorubicin and cisplatin are commonly used as standard therapy, and high-dose methotrexate can be included in treatment of children and young adults (< 40 years) with normal renal function. The addition of ifosfamide and etoposide to first-line chemotherapy does not improve survival.
> - Pathologic response to neoadjuvant chemotherapy is an important prognostic variable in patients with localized osteosarcoma but does not change recommendations for additional therapy.
> - Resection of lung metastases (metastasectomy) should be considered for patients with osteosarcoma. The patients who are most likely to benefit are those who have a relatively prolonged disease-free interval and three or fewer lung metastases.
> - More recent data support treatment with the tyrosine kinase inhibitor regorafenib for patients with metastatic osteosarcoma.

CHONDROSARCOMA

Chondrosarcomas are the second most common primary tumor of bone and usually affect patients older than 60 years. On radiographs, chondrosarcomas generally appear as a radiolucent area with obvious bony destruction and a moderate number of discrete calcified areas. They most often involve the medullary cavity and have scalloped edges consistent with a multinodular growth pattern. Metastases from conventional chondrosarcoma often involve the lung, follow an indolent growth rate, and may be managed by surgery if limited in number.

There is no role for chemotherapy in the management of most chondrosarcomas, which are typically low- to intermediate-grade tumors that resemble cartilage both macroscopically and microscopically and are highly chemotherapy resistant. Although chondrosarcomas have activating mutations in different receptor tyrosine kinases as well as mutations in *IDH1* and *IDH2*, treatment based on these alterations remains under study. Dedifferentiated chondrosarcoma occasionally responds to chemotherapy used for osteosarcoma. Patients with mesenchymal chondrosarcoma, another high-grade variant that resembles Ewing sarcoma on routine staining, may benefit from chemotherapy used for treatment of Ewing sarcoma. Extraskeletal mesenchymal chondrosarcoma is not a cartilaginous tumor but rather a soft-tissue malignancy that often occurs in deep soft tissues; it has a relatively indolent growth rate, has a high risk of dissemination, and is relatively chemotherapy resistant.[1]

EWING SARCOMA

Ewing sarcoma typically occurs in the bones of children and less commonly in adults. Extracranial (peripheral) primitive neuroectodermal tumor arises in soft tissues and is more common than skeletal Ewing sarcoma in adults. Askin tumor is a Ewing-like neoplasm that typically arises in the soft tissues of the chest or pleura of young adults. These tumors are part of a spectrum of diseases referred to as the Ewing sarcoma family of tumors (ESFT), which are characterized by varying degrees of differentiation and are always considered high grade.

On microscopy, Ewing sarcoma appears as monotonous sheets of small, round, blue cells that express high levels of a cell-surface glycoprotein (CD99) and the nuclear factor FLI-1, which can be detected using immunohistochemistry (Fig 17-4). However, expression of CD99 and FLI-1 is not specific for Ewing sarcoma, and molecular studies may be performed to detect the characteristic chromosome translocations present in the disease. Most Ewing sarcomas have reciprocal translocation involving *EWSR1* and *FLI-1*, with a small minority involving *EWSR1* and *ERG* or other less commonly seen partners. Skeletal Ewing sarcoma usually affects the shaft of the bone in an infiltrative pattern called "onion-skinning," which is easily visible on CT scans (Fig 17-5).

Treatment

Multimodality therapy with surgery, chemotherapy, and radiation is the standard of care for ESFT and results cure rates of > 50% in patients with localized disease. Approximately 20% to 30% of patients with metastases may be long-term survivors after multimodal therapy.[112,113] Local treatment of the primary site of disease is usually performed after an initial 12 weeks of chemotherapy. Complete resection of the tumor is preferred, which reduces the risk for local recurrence and secondary radiation-associated malignancy. Radiation is administered as an adjuvant for the treatment of microscopic residual tumor or as definitive local therapy if surgery cannot be performed with acceptable morbidity. Radiation-induced sarcomas develop in

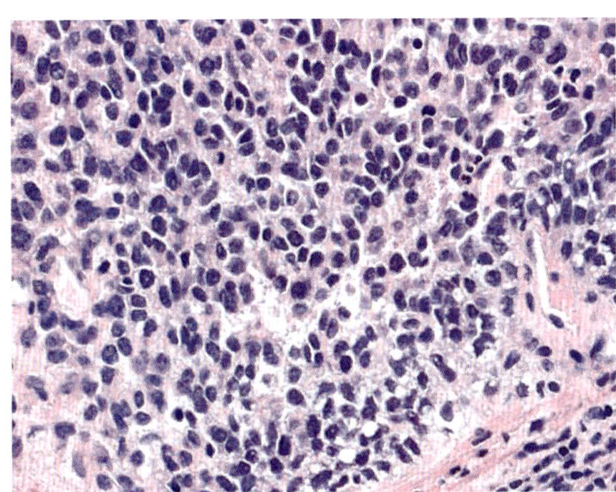

Fig. 17-4 Ewing sarcoma on histologic micrograph.

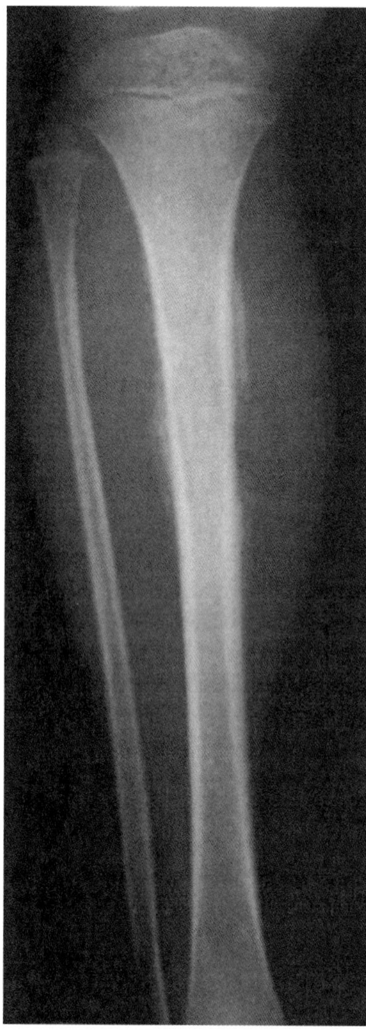

Fig. 17-5 Radiograph showing "onion skinning."

approximately 1% to 2% of long-term survivors of Ewing sarcoma who were treated with radiation for local tumor control.[112,113]

The addition of ifosfamide and etoposide to the combination of vincristine, doxorubicin, and cyclophosphamide (VDC) is the standard chemotherapy for this malignancy, and this regimen yielded improvement in relapse-free survival and OS compared with combination vincristine, doxorubicin, dactinomycin, and cyclophosphamide in patients with nonmetastatic Ewing sarcoma.[112] A randomized trial of cyclophosphamide, vincristine and doxorubicin given in cycles alternating with ifosfamide and etoposide administered every 2 weeks, as compared with every 3 weeks, for a total of 14 cycles in patients younger than 50 years with localized Ewing sarcoma demonstrated improvement in recurrence-free survival. There was an absolute difference of 8% at 5 years for the arm receiving dose-dense treatment, which resulted in fewer distant relapses.[114] The toxicity profile and frequency did not differ between arms. Secondary malignancies, including acute leukemia, osteosarcoma, and lymphoma, occurred in approximately 3% of patients.

Late recurrence of Ewing sarcoma > 5 years after initial diagnosis occurs in approximately 10% to 15% of children and adolescents, with approximately 25% of the late recurrences developing > 10 years after diagnosis.[115] Patients treated for cure of Ewing sarcoma should be evaluated every 2 to 4 months for 3 years, then every 6 months for 2 years, then annually for symptoms and signs of sarcoma recurrence and long-term complications of therapy.

Metastatic Disease

For metastatic Ewing sarcomas, a study showed the simpler combination of VDC was as effective as the five-drug combination used for primary disease, probably because patients progressing on the three-drug regimen could cross over to ifosfamide and etoposide at the time of progression.[112] In patients receiving VDC, dactinomycin is usually substituted for doxorubicin after a cumulative dose of 375 to 450 mg/m^2 has been administered. Assuming patients have received the standard multidrug regimen for Ewing sarcoma, options for therapy are limited, and these patients are good candidates for clinical trials. Relapsed or refractory ESFT may respond to treatment with cyclophosphamide plus topotecan or irinotecan plus temozolomide.[116,117]

GIANT-CELL TUMOR OF BONE

Giant-cell tumor of bone (GCT) is considered a benign disease, though it often causes severe morbidity from destruction of bone. In a small number of cases, metastatic disease is diagnosed (primarily to the lungs). The tumor is composed of malignant stromal cells that secrete receptor activator of nuclear factor κ B (RANK) ligand and recruit multinucleated osteoclast-like cells that result in bone lysis.

Patients usually present with lytic bone destruction, pain, and restricted mobility of the joint adjacent to the lesion. Current primary management involves complete curettage of the lesion, often followed by intralesional adjuvant therapy with heat, freezing, or chemicals (eg, phenol). About 10% to 20% of tumors will recur locally, often necessitating joint resection and replacement; metastasis occurs in approximately 1% of cases. Denosumab, an inhibitory monoclonal antibody to RANK ligand, administered monthly, resulted in lack of tumor progression in the large majority of patients in a phase II trial.[118] Significant adverse events that occurred during denosumab treatment included osteonecrosis of the jaw in 1% of patients, hypocalcemia in 5%, and hypophosphatemia in 3%. On the basis of the high rate of tumor control and relatively low rate of adverse effects from denosumab treatment of GCT, the FDA approved denosumab 120 mg administered subcutaneously monthly (after initial treatment with 120 mg on days 1, 8, and 15 in the first month to rapidly achieve higher serum levels of denosumab) for treatment of patients with unresectable GCT or in situations in which complete resection would result in severe morbidity in adults and skeletally mature adolescents.

KEY POINTS

- Chondrosarcomas are the second most common bone sarcoma in adults. They are generally low to intermediate grade and are chemotherapy resistant.
- Neoadjuvant and adjuvant chemotherapy using five drugs (VDC plus ifosfamide and etoposide) is standard treatment of localized Ewing sarcoma of bone or soft tissue. RT may be used in the case of positive tumor margin during surgery or as definitive local therapy for unresectable, localized disease.
- Metastatic Ewing sarcoma may be treated with vincristine, doxorubicin, dactinomycin, and cyclophosphamide.
- Metastatic bone sarcomas may be cured by appropriate multidisciplinary management.
- GCT causes osteoclast activation resulting in lysis of bone and carries a small risk of metastasis. Denosumab blocks differentiation and activation of osteoclasts in GCT and halts additional bone destruction in most cases.

SURVIVORSHIP

Survivors of childhood cancer are at risk for the development of secondary cancers, including sarcomas. The Childhood Cancer Survivor Study identified a nine-fold higher risk for a secondary sarcoma among survivors of childhood cancer compared with the general population.[119] Moreover, the significant improvement in long-term survival rates of children and adults with sarcoma, especially Ewing sarcoma, osteosarcoma, and rhabdomyosarcoma, from multimodality treatment comes at a heavy cost for a minority of patients. Serious late effects of treatment include secondary malignancy, infertility, cardiomyopathy, nephropathy, neuropathy, hearing impairment, and limb dysfunction. The cumulative incidence of secondary malignancy in children treated for sarcoma is about 1% to 3% at 10 to 20 years, with the highest risk in patients who received chemotherapy and radiation. Children treated for sarcoma have a three- to six-fold higher risk for secondary cancer than do those in an age-matched general population.[120,121]

Adults with sarcoma treated with chemotherapy and/or RT are also at risk for long-term complications, including secondary malignancies and radiation-induced fibrosis and lymphedema. Symptomatic cardiomyopathy develops in approximately 1% to 2% of patients treated for sarcoma with doxorubicin and ifosfamide, and renal tubular and/or glomerular dysfunction develops in 5% to 10%, with the risk related to the cumulative dose received. Infertility is most often related to exposure to alkylating agents and affects postpubescent men more often than women. The Children's Oncology Group has guidelines for the long-term follow-up of survivors of childhood, adolescent, and young adult cancer.

Acknowledgment

The following authors are acknowledged and graciously thanked for their contributions to prior versions of this chapter: Robert G. Maki, MD, PhD, FACP, FASCO; and Scott Schuetze, MD, PhD.

GLOBAL PERSPECTIVE IN SARCOMA

Hans Gelderblom, MD, PhD (Leiden University Medical Center, Leiden, Netherlands)

Introduction

Sarcomas represent a challenging and diverse group of tumors: consisting of 80 different subtypes and divided into soft tissue (approximately 85% of cases) and bone (approximately 15%) sarcomas.[1] The tumors have their mesenchymal cell of origin in common and account for 1% of adult cancers and 10% to 20% of cancers in the pediatric population. With the lack of adequate cancer registries in most lower-income countries and many middle-income countries, it is hard to objectively study the difference in epidemiology, biology, and treatment of sarcoma between countries. However, general principles may apply and are discussed in the following paragraphs on STS, GISTs, and bone sarcoma.

SOFT TISSUE SARCOMA

The most frequently observed STS subtypes across the 50 different subtypes in the western world, including the United States, are liposarcoma, leiomyosarcoma, and undifferentiated pleiomorphic sarcoma, followed by synovial sarcoma, fibrosarcoma, angiosarcoma, malignant peripheral nerve-sheath tumors, and other even more rare subtypes. Specific pathologic subtyping is often based on molecular diagnostics, additional immunohistochemical staining, and vast experience with state-of-the-art diagnostics by a dedicated pathologist in sarcoma. This is often not available in research settings without access to advanced technology. KS is most often HIV related and, therefore, more common in endemic areas such as Africa. Although most risk factors for sarcoma are unknown and presumably not related to smoking status, diet, other environmental factors, and race, it is not expected that there are large regional differences in biology worldwide: at least cancer registries in the western world are comparable for STS. Because some sarcomas tend to develop in younger persons, it can be expected that developing countries with a younger age distribution may show a relative larger contribution of, for example, synovial sarcomas and desmoplastic round cell tumors that are known to occur in younger patients. Also, because of the limited access to health care, stage at presentation is higher in lower-income countries. Stage is related to outcome of sarcoma; thus, cure rates in lower- and middle-income countries (LMICs) are lower than the 50% 5-year OS observed in high-risk sarcoma in the western world.[122,123] High-risk STS is commonly defined as high grade, deep seated, and > 5 cm. The primary treatment of high-risk STS is surgery in combination with pre- or postoperative RT. Adjuvant or neoadjuvant chemotherapy is proposed in selected cases. This recommendation is universal in western countries and probably difficult to achieve in developing countries, therefore impairing outcome. Many large western countries produce their own guidelines and they all are in line with the European Society for Medical Oncology (ESMO) guidelines that are updated every 3 years.[124] The National Comprehensive Cancer Network (NCCN) guidelines are comparable, in general, with the ESMO guidelines as well, acknowledging minor differences such as choice of chemotherapy in the palliative setting.

Treatment patterns in Europe and the United States were recently published, both for the general population[125,126] as well as for the elderly population.[127,128] Although no formal comparison was made, one of the conclusions (also based on discussions with sarcoma experts) is that treatment patterns and outcomes are similar with maybe a US preference for combination of doxorubicin and ifosfamide in the younger population and gemcitabine and docetaxel in the elderly population, whereas monotherapy doxorubicin in North European countries and metronomic chemotherapy in elderly may be more frequent in Europe. The novel drugs for metastatic STS (ie, pazopanib, trabectedin, and eribulin) are available in most high-income countries but have only a modest effect of a few months on median OS.

GIST

The annual incidence of clinically relevant GIST is comparable between the European Union and the United States: one per 100,000 persons, accounting for one-quarter of all STSs. Here, also, clinical guidelines do not differ essentially between ESMO and NCCN. Adequate surgery, as needed after neoadjuvant treatment, is the standard. The currently available drugs imatinib, sunitinib, and regorafenib have revolutionized the outcome for these patients. Imatinib is given in the first line and has the longest duration of activity and is recommended in the adjuvant setting for 3 years for high-risk GIST. Soon, the patent of imatinib for GIST will expire; moreover, imatinib has been on the WHO Essential Medicines List since 2015. Both factors hopefully will stimulate use in LMICs. Adequate diagnosis and molecular testing in all cases are mandatory and both need to be improved, especially in these countries, where outcome is presumably worse.

BONE SARCOMA

Osteosarcoma, chondrosarcoma, and Ewing sarcoma are the main malignant bone tumors; incidence is approximately 0.3 per 100,000 persons annually. For Ewing sarcoma and osteosarcoma, the incidence is much higher in adolescence. Secondary osteosarcoma at older age, due to RT, will be higher in countries offering this treatment routinely (eg, for locally advanced rectal and breast cancers). Chondrosarcoma generally can be cured with surgery alone, whereas cure rates for localized osteosarcoma and Ewing sarcoma have increased from 15% to 60% since the 1980s, with multimodal chemotherapy. These patients are generally treated following pediatric protocols that are more or less the same in the western world, but also in many parts of Asia and South America. There is no second-line palliative treatment with proven survival benefit.

In conclusion, biology, incidence, outcome, and treatment of sarcoma are comparable between the United States and most of Europe, including higher-income countries in the rest of the world. Sarcoma treatment is difficult and needs an experienced team of clinicians, including pathologists and radiologists. It has been shown repeatedly that outcome for this disease is better in specialized centers. In Europe, a network of centers of excellence with national and European endorsement has been set up (www.EURACAN.ern-net.eu). The aim of this network is to help middle-income European countries (eg, by video consultancy and education to improve outcome). Similar efforts are needed in the rest of the world for LMICs.

18

CENTRAL NERVOUS SYSTEM TUMORS

Matthias Holdhoff, MD, PhD

Recent Updates

Gliomas

- Phase III randomized controlled data of elderly patients (in this trial defined as 65 years of age or older) showed a benefit in overall survival from the addition of temozolomide to short-course hypofractionated radiation over radiation alone. However, the study did not compare short-course hypofractionated radiation plus temozolomide with standard 6-week radiation plus temozolomide and results should be interpreted with caution. (Perry JR, *N Engl J Med* 2017)

Brain Metastases

- A growing body of evidence supports efficacy of small molecule inhibitors and checkpoint inhibitors in the treatment of CNS metastases for which these therapies are known to be effective systemically. (nccn.org)

OVERVIEW

Primary CNS tumors consist of a diverse range of pathologic entities. Metastatic tumors represent the majority of CNS tumors. Among primary brain cancers, tumors of neuroepithelial tissue comprise most of the malignant primary CNS tumors such as astrocytic tumors (including glioblastoma), oligodendroglial tumors, and embryonal tumors (eg, medulloblastoma). The updated 2016 WHO classification broadly categorizes CNS tumors into several groups, for the first time with the incorporation of molecular features in addition to histology.[1] The new WHO classification is especially helpful to differentiate, on the basis of molecular markers, astrocytomas from oligodendrogliomas, which are now understood as different disease entities, each with a distinct biology, prognosis, and treatment approach. The treatment of cancers within the CNS presents specific challenges, including drug delivery, because of the blood-brain barrier (BBB), relatively low incidence, and often exclusion from early-phase clinical trials. Surgery and radiation have remained the mainstay in many CNS tumors; however, the role for chemotherapy has evolved in several of these cancers. The current understanding and evidence-based treatment of the most common cancers of the CNS as they are encountered in clinical oncology practice are outlined in this chapter.

EPIDEMIOLOGY

Primary malignant CNS tumors are the most common solid tumor in children and are the leading cause of death resulting from cancer in children. CNS tumors are the third leading cause of cancer-related death for adolescents and young adults (ages 15 to 39 years). The median age-adjusted incidence for primary brain tumors is 5.7 cases per 100,000 population per year in children, 11.2

and 44.5 per 100,000 population for ages 15 to 39 years and 40 years or older, respectively. Of all primary brain tumors, approximately one-third are meningiomas, one-third are gliomas, and the remainder are a variety of other benign and malignant tumors (Fig 18-1). Malignant brain tumors occur more frequently in men, whereas meningiomas are more common in women. Of all primary gliomas, 56.6% are glioblastomas. In children, embryonal tumors such as medulloblastoma are the most common CNS tumors.[2]

It has been difficult to identify environmental factors associated with primary brain tumors. Ionizing radiation is the only environmental risk factor reliably considered to increase the risk of brain tumors.[3] The risk of primary CNS lymphoma, but not other types of primary brain tumors, is increased for patients with immunodeficiency conditions such as HIV infection.[4]

Genetic predisposition to primary CNS tumors is relatively uncommon, although they may be associated with several familial cancer syndromes (Table 18-1).[5] For example, astrocytomas are associated with Li-Fraumeni syndrome, neurofibromatosis type 1, tuberous sclerosis, and Lynch syndrome. Medulloblastoma is associated with Li-Fraumeni syndrome, basal cell nevus syndrome, and familial adenomatous polyposis.

KEY POINTS

- Exposure to ionizing radiation is a well-established risk factor for primary CNS tumors.
- Most patients with primary CNS tumors have no identifiable risk factor. The exceptions are those patients who have a primary CNS tumor associated with one of the familial cancer syndromes, including neurofibromatosis, Li-Fraumeni syndrome, Lynch syndrome, and familial adenomatous polyposis.
- Immunodeficiency is a risk factor for primary CNS lymphoma.

PRESENTATION

The presenting symptoms of a brain tumor are related to mass effect, parenchymal infiltration, hydrocephalus, and/or tissue destruction.

- Headaches are the most common presenting symptom in patients with brain tumors. The classic symptom for these is new onset of headaches, especially if they are more severe in the morning and are associated with nausea, vomiting, or focal neurologic deficits.
- Seizures occur more frequently with low-grade gliomas. However, seizures may be associated with any CNS tumor.
- Focal neurologic deficits are related to the location of the tumor.
- Altered mental status can be a presenting symptom.
- Personality changes and/or psychiatric problems can be the presenting symptom, often preceding the tumor diagnosis by months or years, particularly with low-grade gliomas and primary CNS lymphoma (PCNSL).
- Posterior fossa masses and, less commonly, supratentorial masses may obstruct the third or fourth ventricle, resulting in hydrocephalus, causing headache, nausea, vomiting, somnolence, lethargy, or coma.

DIAGNOSIS AND STAGING

DIAGNOSTIC IMAGING

Magnetic resonance imaging (MRI) is more sensitive than computed tomography (CT) for confirming the presence of a brain tumor. In T1-weighted MRI scans, a brain tumor appears as a mass lesion that may enhance with contrast; there may also be signal abnormality on T2-weighted scans, especially prominent on fluid attenuation and inversion recovery images. Contrast enhancement is indicative of BBB disruption, and it usually increases with higher grades of malignant disease. Ring enhancement is characteristic of glioblastoma and is a consequence of central tumor necrosis. However, some low-grade tumors, for example, pilocytic astrocytoma, may also demonstrate contrast enhancement. Conversely, some high-grade tumors may not enhance with contrast. Contrast enhancement does not reflect the true extent of disease, because the BBB may remain intact at the rim of the infiltrating tumor. Although MRI is generally much more helpful in evaluating brain tumors, CT imaging can be helpful in certain situations, such as in assessing hemorrhage or tumor involvement of the bone.

DIAGNOSTIC PATHOLOGY

For nearly all patients, the definitive diagnosis of a CNS tumor requires a surgical biopsy or resection with histologic and molecular examination of the tissue. However, some patients, those with brainstem gliomas, for example, may not be candidates for biopsy because of the operative risk, and imaging can be diagnostic in some cases.

Since 1993, the WHO classification system has used a four-tiered histologic grading system based on the degree of malignancy of the respective grade. Primary brain tumors typically remain localized to the brain, and a staging system, as is common in systemic cancers, does not exist.

- Grade I tumors include well-circumscribed tumors with low proliferative potential.
- Grade II tumors are more infiltrative and cellular. Although relatively slow growing, they tend to progress to higher grades of malignancy.
- Grade III tumors demonstrate histologic evidence of malignancy, such as cytologic atypia and increased mitotic activity.
- Grade IV tumors are more cytologically malignant, mitotically active, and prone to necrosis. Endothelial and vascular proliferation may also be seen.

The most recent edition of the WHO Classification of CNS tumors (2016) integrates molecular markers in the classification

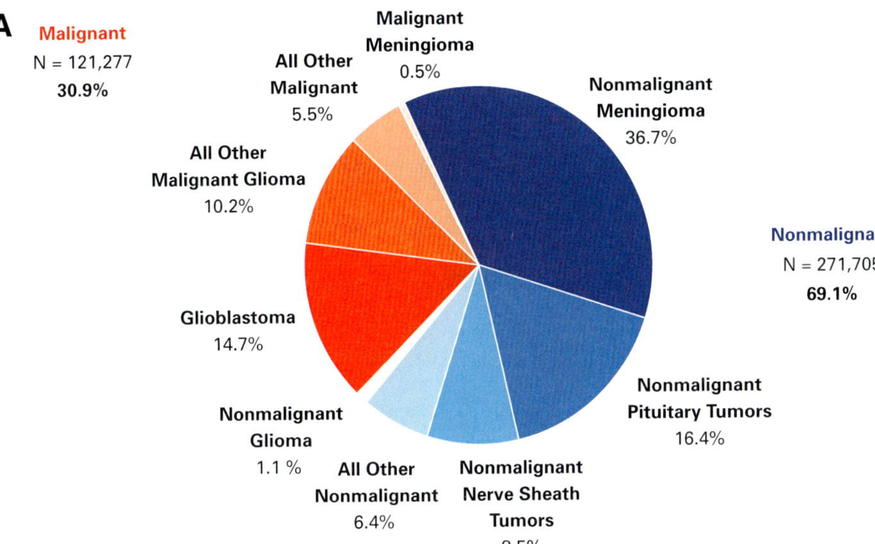

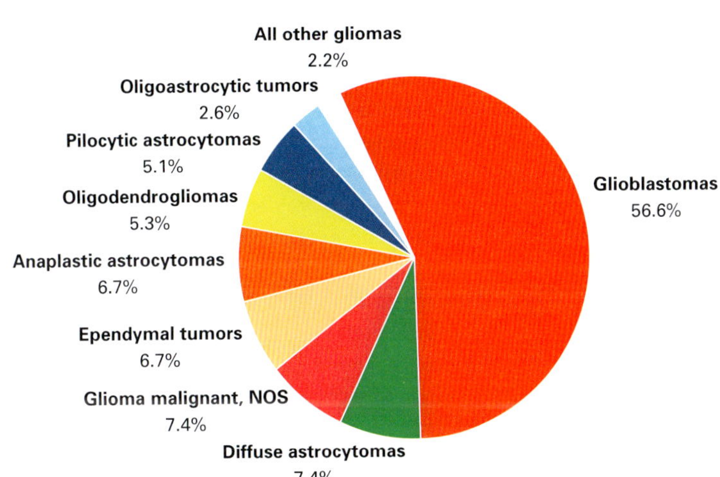

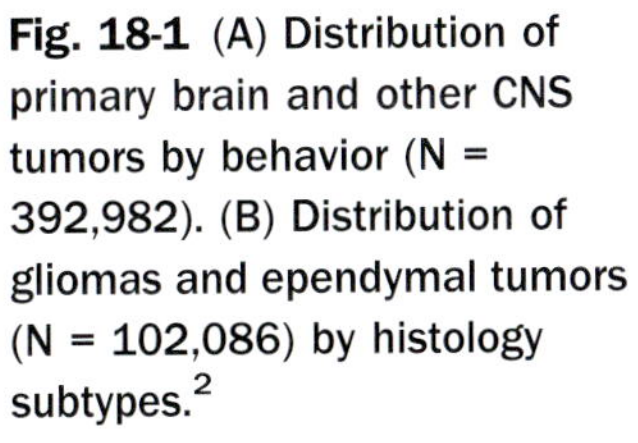

Fig. 18-1 (A) Distribution of primary brain and other CNS tumors by behavior (N = 392,982). (B) Distribution of gliomas and ependymal tumors (N = 102,086) by histology subtypes.[2]

NOS, not otherwise specified.

Reprinted with permission from Oxford University Press.

for the first time.[1] Examples include the classification of gliomas on the basis of the presence of *IDH* mutation and/or 1p/19q codeletion, as well as the creation of a new entity, diffuse midline gliomas that are H3K27M mutant, which is more commonly seen in children. Clinically relevant markers are discussed for each tumor type in the respective sections in this chapter.

PATHOGENESIS

CLINICALLY RELEVANT MARKERS IN GLIOMAS

Research in the last decade has rapidly increased understanding of the pathobiology of diffuse gliomas. Several molecular abnormalities have been discovered that seem to play key roles in glioma development. Precise molecular characterization of diffuse gliomas is still subject to discussion and extensive research, but diffuse gliomas are currently considered to fall within three broad categories (Fig 18-2):

1. **Gliomas with *IDH* mutation and 1p/19q codeletion.** These gliomas consist predominantly of oligodendroglial tumors. This category of tumors, compared with the other two groups, is associated with an improved overall prognosis and better response to radiation and chemotherapy. The 5-year survival rate of patients with these tumors typically ranges from 50% to 80%, although with aggressive treatment consisting of radiation and procarbazine, lomustine, and vincristine (PCV) chemotherapy, median survivals of 12 to 18 years have been observed. (N.B. The percentages and outcome figures presented in the category descriptions are approximations to illustrate the significant differences in biological behavior and outcome among the three molecularly defined groups of gliomas. Data are based on the Central Brain Tumor Registry of the United States [CBTRUS] database. Of note, specific outcome data for these molecular subgroups are not available yet in the current version of the CBTRUS statistical report.[2])
2. **Gliomas with *IDH* mutation and *ATRX* mutation without 1p/19q codeletion.** These gliomas predominantly consist of grade II and grade III astrocytomas, along with

Table 18-1 **Genetic Syndromes Associated With Primary CNS Tumors**

Genetic Syndrome	Gene Alteration(s)	Associated Primary CNS Tumors
Basal cell nevus (Gorlin) syndrome	*PTCH1*	Medulloblastoma
Cowden syndrome	*PTEN*	Gangliocytoma
Li-Fraumeni syndrome	*TP53*	High-grade glioma, medulloblastoma
Neurofibromatosis 1	*NF1*	Malignant peripheral nerve sheath tumor, low-grade astrocytoma (usually pilocytic astrocytoma)
Neurofibromatosis 2	*NF2*	Vestibular schwannoma (frequently bilateral), meningioma
Tuberous sclerosis	*TSC1, TSC2*	Subependymal giant cell astrocytoma
Familial adenomatous polyposis	*APC*	Medulloblastoma
Lynch syndrome (hereditary nonpolyposis colorectal cancer)	*MSH2, MLH1, MSH6, PMS2*	Glioblastoma
Von Hippel–Lindau syndrome	*VHL*	Hemangioblastoma

so-called secondary glioblastomas (ie, glioblastoma that has arisen from a lower-grade glioma). The 5-year survival rate of patients with these tumors typically ranges from 25% to 50%.

3. **Gliomas arising from mutations other than in the *IDH* or *ATRX* genes and without 1p/19q codeletion.** These gliomas consist predominantly of primary glioblastoma (ie, de novo glioblastoma). Compared with the other two categories, these gliomas overall have a less favorable prognosis and are less responsive to chemotherapy. The 5-year survival rate of patients with these tumors is overall approximately 5%.

IDH MUTATION

Mutations in the *IDH* gene are probably early genetic abnormalities in glioma development. *IDH1* mutations result in the excess accumulation of 2-hydroxyglutarate, an oncometabolite, which contributes to the formation and progression of gliomas.[6,7] *IDH* mutations were first described in glioblastomas, but they have since been found in most WHO grade II and III gliomas (Fig 18-3) and are a clear indicator of favorable prognosis in high-grade glioma.[8]

In addition, *IDH* mutations have been demonstrated to independently predict survival benefit from the addition of combination chemotherapy (ie, PCV) to radiation therapy (RT) for patients with anaplastic oligodendroglioma and anaplastic oligoastrocytoma.[9] Multivariate analysis of this study, which only included anaplastic (WHO grade III) tumors, demonstrated that the survival advantage from the addition of PCV to RT in *IDH*-mutated tumors is observed in both 1p/19q codeleted and non-codeleted subsets; however, the chemotherapy benefit seems much more significant in the patients with codeletion.

1P/19Q CODELETION

Most oligodendrogliomas and anaplastic oligodendrogliomas (along with some histologic oligoastrocytomas and anaplastic oligoastrocytomas) show a combined loss of the short arm of chromosome 1 (1p) and the long arm of chromosome 19 (19q). This codeletion of 1p/19q is secondary to an unbalanced pericentromeric translocation event and seems to be instrumental in the development of oligodendrogliomas.[10] Several candidate genes have been identified, including *CIC* and *FUBP1*, which may represent the genetic alteration underlying the 1p/19q codeletion.[11]

Many studies have demonstrated that 1p/19q codeletion is associated with a favorable prognosis in patients with oligodendrogliomas.[10] More recently, 1p/19q codeletion has been determined not only to indicate a better prognosis in patients

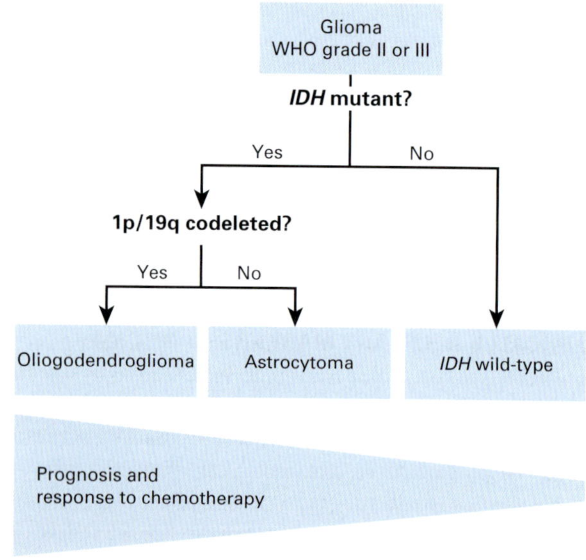

Fig. 18-2 Significance of *IDH* mutation and 1p/19q codeletion status in WHO grade II and III gliomas.
Simplified after WHO classification of CNS tumors.[1]

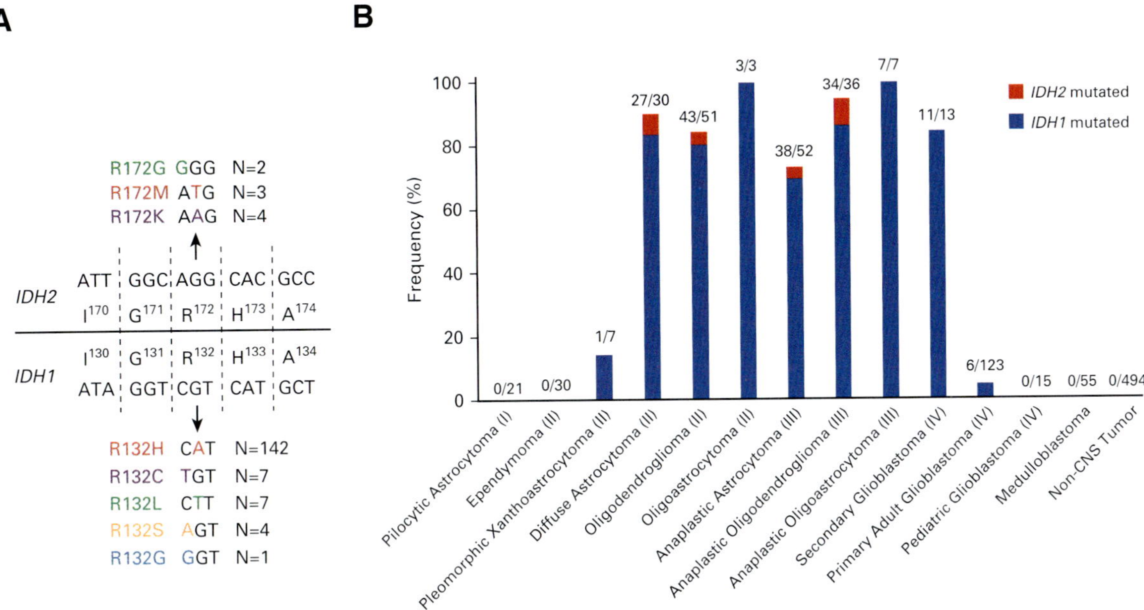

Fig. 18-3 ***IDH1*** **and** ***IDH2*** **mutations in human gliomas.**

(A) Mutations at codon R132 in *IDH1* and R172 in *IDH2* that were identified in human gliomas, along with the number of patients who carried each mutation. Codons 130 to 134 of *IDH1* and 170 to 174 of *IDH2* are shown. (B) The number and frequency of *IDH1* and *IDH2* mutations in gliomas and other types of tumors. The roman numerals in parentheses are the tumor grades, according to histopathological and clinical criteria established by WHO.[8]

with anaplastic oligodendrogliomas but also predict improved survival with addition of combination chemotherapy (ie, PCV) to radiation compared with RT alone.[12,13]

ATRX MUTATION

Somatic mutations in the *ATRX* gene are commonly seen in grade II and grade III astrocytomas and are mutually exclusive with 1p/19q codeletions. Astrocytic tumors with *IDH* mutation are typically *ATRX* mutant. Although no current therapeutic options are available to target the *ATRX* gene, astrocytomas with mutant *ATRX* are typically *IDH* mutant and may have a more favorable prognosis compared with astrocytomas without *ATRX* loss.[14]

O6-METHYLGUANINE–DNA METHYLTRANSFERASE PROMOTER METHYLATION

O^6-methylguanine–DNA methyltransferase (*MGMT*) is an enzyme that plays a crucial role in DNA repair. Alkylating agents such as temozolomide lead to methylation of nucleotide bases in genomic DNA. Although some of these lesions are fixed by base excision repair, O6-methylguanine is a cytotoxic lesion that requires *MGMT* for its repair.

Hypermethylation of the *MGMT* promoter–associated CpG island has been described in approximately 30% to 40% of glioblastomas. *MGMT* promoter methylation prevents transcription of the *MGMT* gene and subsequent expression of the DNA repair enzyme. Consequently, patients with *MGMT* promoter–methylated tumors are expected to receive more benefit from temozolomide than patients whose tumors lack it. The favorable prognosis of patients with *MGMT* promoter–methylated glioblastoma is well described, along with its association with a greater likelihood of benefit from temozolomide.[15]

KEY POINTS

- *IDH* mutations are common in grade II and III gliomas, and they are typically found in glioblastomas that arise out of lower-grade gliomas. *IDH* mutations are associated with younger age and comparatively favorable prognosis.
- 1p/19q codeletion and *IDH* mutation independently predict response to chemotherapy and prognosis in oligodendrogliomas. Tumors that are *IDH* mutated without 1p/19q codeletion may have a mutation in *ATRX*, which is commonly seen in grade II and grade III astrocytomas.
- Patients with glioblastoma whose tumor is *MGMT* promoter methylated have a better prognosis than patients whose tumors lack *MGMT* methylation. Furthermore, *MGMT* promoter methylation predicts a greater benefit from temozolomide.

ASTROCYTOMAS

GLIOBLASTOMA (WHO GRADE IV)

Glioblastomas (WHO grade IV) are the most common primary brain cancers in adults. Histopathological hallmarks include increased cellularity, nuclear pleomorphism, frequent mitoses, as well as necrosis and neovascularization. The median age at diagnosis is approximately 65 years.[2] Most glioblastomas develop de novo and are typically *IDH* wild-type. These patients are typically of older age (median age, 59 years) and have a median survival of approximately only 15 months with standard treatment. About 12% of glioblastomas harbor an *IDH* mutation, which is associated with younger age (median age, 32 years) and a comparatively better prognosis.[8] *IDH* mutations are common in patients with so-called secondary glioblastomas, which are first diagnosed at lower histologic grades before eventually meeting the criteria of glioblastoma (WHO grade IV). *MGMT* promoter methylation is also associated with a prolonged survival of patients with glioblastoma compared with those without methylation (18.2 months *v* 12.2 months; $P < .001$).[15]

Surgery

The initial step of treatment is best possible safe neurosurgical resection. In general, overall outcome is better in patients who can undergo a gross total resection (removal of all contrast-enhancing tissue[16]); but due to tumor location and comorbidities, many tumors are only amenable to a partial resection or biopsy. Unfortunately, even in the absence of residual contrast enhancement, the extremely infiltrative nature of this tumor makes true complete surgical resection impossible and virtually all patients have residual cancer that requires additional therapy.

Radiation

RT has remained the backbone of the treatment of newly diagnosed glioblastoma. Early phase III data showed that postoperative involved-field RT improved survival over supportive care alone (median survival, 35 weeks *v* 14.5 weeks).[17] Currently, involved-field radiation (only to areas of tumor involvement, not the whole brain) consisting of 60 Gy delivered in 30 fractions is considered standard. However, a shorter course of hypofractionated radiation over 3 weeks (40 Gy in 15 fractions) has been evaluated in a phase III clinical trial of elderly patients with glioblastoma, because of the poorer prognosis of these patients. This trial demonstrated that the shorter course of radiation produced outcomes similar to those for standard radiation (60 Gy in 30 fractions) in elderly patients.[18]

Multiple attempts to improve the therapeutic efficacy of radiation by using altered fraction schemes so far have not produced substantially better results.

Chemotherapy

Temozolomide. In a phase III clinical trial, patients with newly diagnosed glioblastoma were randomly assigned after surgery to receive radiotherapy alone (daily fractions of 2 Gy given 5 d/wk for 6 weeks, for a total of 60 Gy) or radiotherapy plus concurrent daily oral temozolomide (75 mg/m^2 daily, 7 d/wk from the first to the last day of radiotherapy) followed by six cycles of adjuvant temozolomide (150 to 200 mg/m^2 daily for 5 days of each 28-day cycle). Median survival and 2-year survival rates for patients receiving temozolomide were increased by 2.5 months (from 12.1 months to 14.6 months) and 16.1% (from 10.4% to 26.5%), respectively (Fig 18-4).[19] These results have established chemoradiation with temozolomide followed by adjuvant temozolomide as the standard of care for newly diagnosed glioblastoma after surgery.

Within the same phase III trial, a companion, correlative laboratory study demonstrated that *MGMT* promoter methylation, detected in 35% of cases, was associated with superior survival, regardless of treatment received, and greater efficacy of temozolomide (Fig 18-5).[15] In both the initial and 5-year analyses of this trial, survival differences between patients receiving radiation plus temozolomide and those receiving radiation alone were greatest in patients with *MGMT* promoter–methylated glioblastoma (median survival, 23.4 months *v* 15.3 months; $P = .004$). However, there was still a significant, although much more modest, survival benefit from the addition of temozolomide to radiation versus radiation alone in patients whose tumors did not have *MGMT* promoter methylation detected (median survival, 12.6 months *v* 11.8 months; $P = .035$).[20]

Alternative adjuvant temozolomide regimens have been assessed, but they have not demonstrated superiority over the standard combined regimen. As an example, a phase III randomized clinical trial compared standard adjuvant temozolomide (150 to 200 mg/m^2 of body surface area for 5 days during each 28-day cycle) to a dose-dense regimen of temozolomide (75 to 100 mg/m^2 on days 1 to 21 every 4 weeks).[21] There was no difference in median survival, regardless of *MGMT* methylation status. However, the dose-dense regimen was associated with more toxicity.

A recently published, German, randomized study (CeTeG/NOA-04 trial) compared treatment with combined lomustine and temozolomide during and after radiation with standard therapy (chemoradiation with temozolomide followed by adjuvant temozolomide) in patients with newly diagnosed *MGMT* promoter–methylated glioblastoma.[22] In this trial, > 650 patients were screened to enroll 141 patients aged 18 to 70 years. Eligible patients were randomly assigned to receive lomustine 100 mg/m^2 on day 1, followed by temozolomide 100 to 200 mg/m^2 on days 2 through 6 every 42 days, or standard therapy. A modified intent-to-treat analysis that included all 129 patients showed similar overall survival (OS) of 37.9 versus 31.4 months in the combination versus the standard therapy arm (hazard ratio [HR], 0.90; 95% CI, 0.58 to 1.41). In prespecified analysis of the data, using matching by treatment center and recursive partitioning analysis class, 32 of the randomly assigned patients were excluded, leaving 109 patients for analysis. Among these patients, survival was superior in the combination therapy arm compared with the standard therapy arm (48.1 *v* 31.4 months; HR, 0.60, 95% CI, 0.35 to 1.03); however progression-free survival (PFS) was similar (HR, 0.91; 95% CI, 0.57 to 1.44). Grade 3 and 4 hemolytic toxicity was greater in the combination versus the standard therapy arm, as was nausea (30% *v* 19%). These data need to be interpreted with great caution because the study was small for a prospective randomized trial and it excluded many randomly assigned patients in the prespecified analysis.

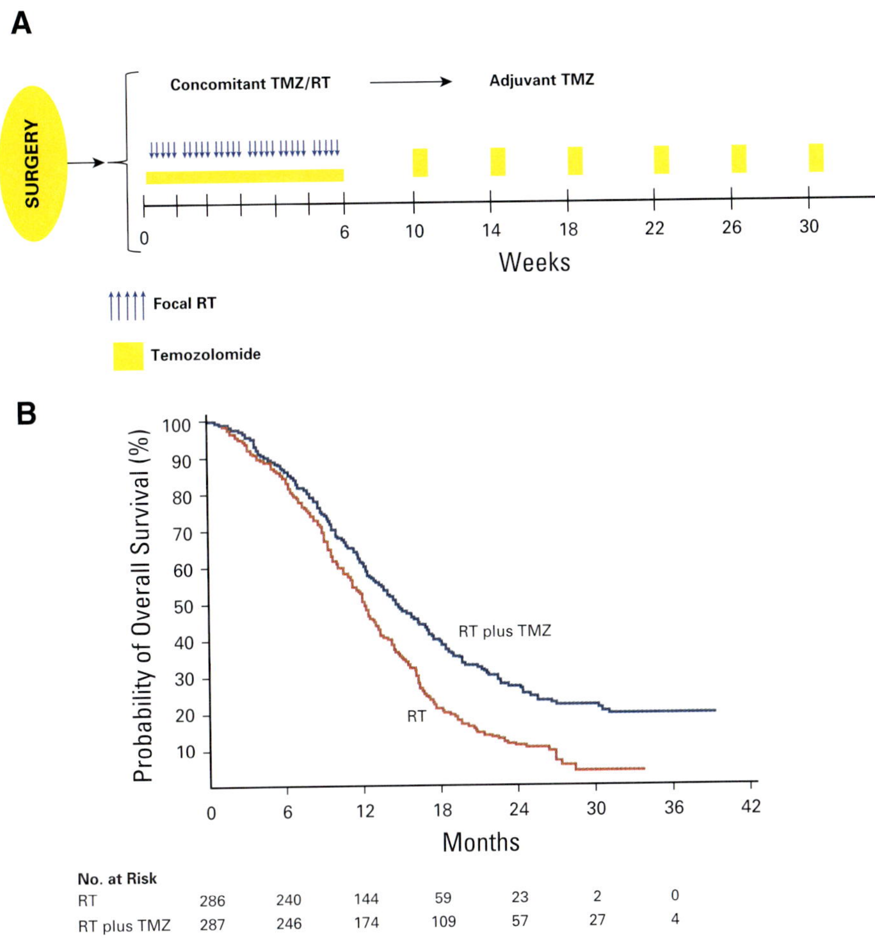

Fig. 18-4 Radiation therapy (RT) and temozolomide (TMZ) for newly diagnosed glioblastomas.

(A) Treatment schema. (B) Overall survival.[21]

From The New England Journal of Medicine, *Radiotherapy plus Concomitant and Adjuvant Temozolomide for Glioblastoma, Vol 352(10), Stupp R, Mason WP, van den Bent M, et al., Pg. 987-996. Copyright © (2009) Massachusetts Medical Society. Reprinted with permission from Massachusetts Medical Society.*

Temozolomide in Older Adults. There has been significant discussion about optimal treatment of older adults with glioblastoma. The landmark EORTC/NCIC trial that defined the role of temozolomide in the adjuvant treatment of glioblastomas excluded patients older than age 70 years; however, patients between ages 60 and 70 years did have an improvement in 2-year survival with combined therapy when compared with radiation alone (21.8% *v* 5.7%).[19,20] An international phase III trial evaluating hypofractionated RT alone versus hypofractionated RT plus temozolomide in elderly patients with glioblastoma demonstrated that the addition of temozolomide to RT significantly improved OS (median, 9.3 months *v* 7.6 months *P* < .0001) and PFS (median, 5.3 months *v* 3.9 months; *P* < .0001) compared with RT alone.[23] As would be expected, patients with *MGMT*-methylated tumors had the most benefit from the addition of temozolomide to RT (median OS almost doubled). However, it is of note that in this trial, patients with unmethylated *MGMT* promoter also had a smaller but significant benefit from the addition of temozolomide to radiation. Because hypofractionated and not standard 6-week radiation was used in the trial, it remains unclear how standard chemoradiation would compare with the results with hypofractionated RT and temozolomide in this patient population.

Some older patients with poor performance status and multiple comorbidities may not be candidates for concurrent RT and chemotherapy. Two phase III clinical trials have explored single-modality therapy (radiation alone *v* temozolomide alone) for newly diagnosed glioblastoma.[24,25] One trial demonstrated that temozolomide alone as initial therapy is at least noninferior to standard doses of radiation alone in elderly patients (8.6 months *v* 9.6 months; noninferiority *P* = .033). Furthermore, patients with *MGMT*-methylated tumors had prolonged event-free survival with temozolomide compared with RT (8.4 months *v* 4.6 months; *P* < .05), whereas the opposite was true for patients with *MGMT*-unmethylated tumors (3.3 months *v* 4.6 months; *P* < .05).[25] The second trial also noted similar OS between elderly patients who received temozolomide and those who received hypofractionated RT. The trial demonstrated an improvement in survival with temozolomide compared with standard doses of radiation (60 Gy; median survival, 8.3 months *v* 6.0 months; *P* = .01) but no difference in survival when compared with a hypofractionated course of radiation (34 Gy; median survival, 8.3 months *v* 7.4 months; *P* = .12).

Pseudoprogression

It is essential to consider so-called pseudoprogression before initiating alternative therapy. Pseudoprogression is best described in glioblastomas, when concern for tumor progression arises after chemoradiation. Pseudoprogression can mimic true tumor growth,

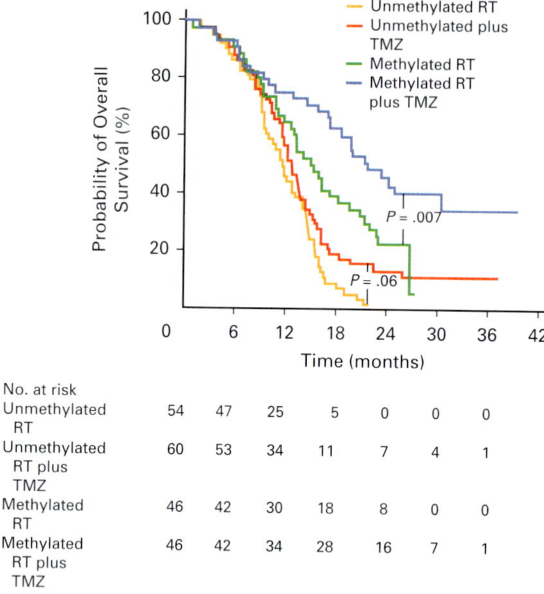

Fig. 18-5 Survival in patients with glioblastoma related to *MGMT*-promoter methylation status by *MGMT*-promoter methylation status and treatment (RT alone or RT plus TMZ).[17]

Abbreviations: MGMT, O6-methylguanine–DNA methyltransferase; RT, radiation therapy; TMZ, temozolomide.

From The New England Journal of Medicine, *MGMT gene silencing and benefit from temozolomide in glioblastoma. Vol 352(10), Hegi ME, Diserens AC Gorilia T, et al. Pg. 997-1003. Copyright 2005. Massachusetts Medical Society. Reprinted with permission from Massachusetts Medical Society.*

especially in patients whose tumors exhibit *MGMT* promoter methylation.[26] In a study of 103 patients with newly diagnosed glioblastoma, pseudoprogression was noted in 91% of patients with *MGMT* promoter methylation versus only 41% in patients with unmethylated tumors. On MRI, both progression and pseudoprogression are characterized by increased contrast enhancement, T2-weighted signal abnormality, and mass effect, with or without clinical deterioration (Fig 18-6). No currently available imaging method can reliably distinguish the difference. Postradiation changes that are within the radiation treatment field can often be observed initially (typically for the first 3 months after radiation) to assess whether the changes represent pseudoprogression rather than actual tumor growth. However, repeated tissue biopsy may be needed to more definitively determine if the patient has active or progressive tumor or treatment effect or necrosis. Although tissue diagnosis is the current gold standard, even it can be challenging, because tissues often comprise a mixture of treatment effect or necrosis and tumor, which can lead to significant interobserver variability in diagnosis.[27]

Tumor-Treating Fields

Tumor-treating fields (TTFs) is a device that delivers alternating electromagnetic fields to electrodes placed on the shaved scalp. It is approved by the US Food and Drug Administration (FDA) for use in the treatment of patients with newly diagnosed (after concurrent chemoradiation) and recurrent glioblastoma. A randomized phase III trial of temozolomide with or without TTFs alongside adjuvant temozolomide enrolled 695 patients who had completed concurrent chemoradiation. The final data demonstrated a significant increase in median OS of the patients treated concurrently with temozolomide and TTFs, compared with patients treated with temozolomide alone (21 months *v* 16 months; $P < .00062$).[28] However, this trial was not blinded and a sham intervention was not considered feasible. Quality of life and gross cognitive function were comparable in the two arms. On the basis of these data, the FDA has approved TTFs for use in newly diagnosed glioblastoma after concurrent chemoradiation.

Bevacizumab

The addition of bevacizumab to standard chemoradiation with temozolomide for treatment of newly diagnosed glioblastomas has been assessed in two large, phase III trials.[29,30] Both illustrated an improvement in PFS but no improvement in OS. One of the studies showed improvements in several measures of quality of life,[29] whereas the other revealed worsened neurocognitive function and decreased quality of life after the use of bevacizumab.[30] Both studies indicated a higher rate of adverse events, including thromboembolic events and hypertension, with the use of upfront bevacizumab compared with placebo.

Recurrence

No uniform standard of care exists for the treatment of recurrent glioblastoma. Treatment options are tailored to the individual clinical setting. Participation in clinical trials should be considered. Unfortunately, all standard therapies have limited benefit, and a focus on symptom control with end-of-life care may be appropriate.

It is of note that radiographic pseudoprogression may mimic tumor progression in patients with glioblastoma treated with radiation with or without temozolomide and should be considered before switching therapy, especially in patients with *MGMT* promoter–methylated tumors (see the previous section on Pseudoprogression).

For patients with resectable disease who have good neurologic function and performance status, a second resection may be reasonable (with or without placement of carmustine wafers).[31] In 2009, the FDA approved bevacizumab as treatment of recurrent glioblastoma after failure of RT and temozolomide.[32] Nitrosoureas (lomustine or carmustine) may also be used to treat recurrent glioblastoma.[33] A phase III clinical trial demonstrated that the addition of bevacizumab to lomustine did not improve survival when compared with lomustine alone, conveying that although bevacizumab may improve PFS, it does not increase OS.[34]

The use of irinotecan with bevacizumab has been investigated, but no evidence shows it improves survival; however, it does increase toxicity.[32] No data show bevacizumab improves survival in glioblastoma, but its use can be of benefit to some patients with significant, symptomatic edema and mass effect who have difficulties tolerating high doses or a long course of steroids. Complicating considerations for bevacizumab include that patients need a long washout period (ideally ≥ 6 weeks) after being considered for repeated surgery and that the drug increases the risk for hemorrhage, bowel perforation, venous thromboembolism, hypertension, and nephrotic syndrome.

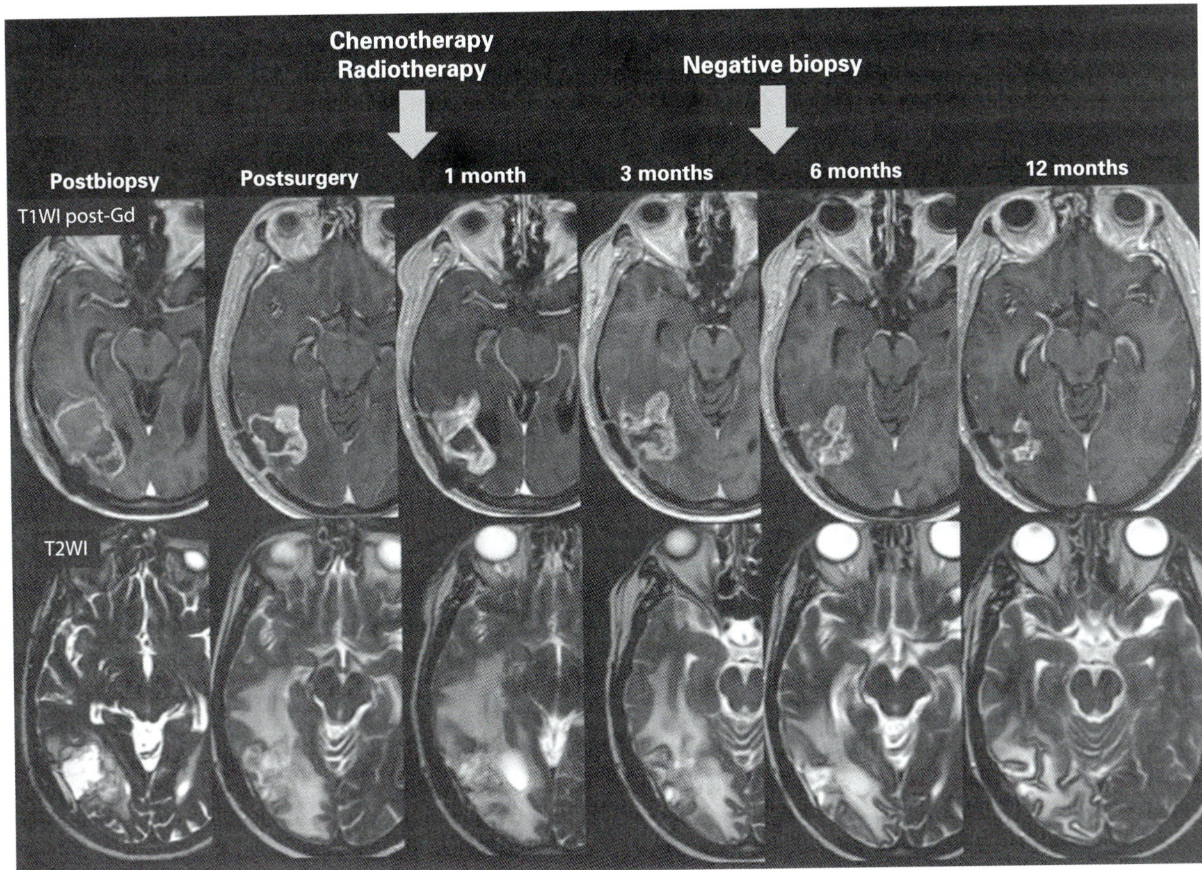

Fig. 18-6 Magnetic resonance images (MRIs) showing pseudoprogression in a 59-year-old man with glioblastoma.

MRI obtained 1 month after concurrent radiation and temozolomide demonstrated an expansion of the right temporal lesion. Reductions in both the enhancing portion and the surrounding abnormal hyperintense area in the T2-weighted imaging were seen in the follow-up MRI examination.

Abbreviations: T2WI, T2-weighted image; T1WI post-Gd, T-weighted image postgadolinium.

Reprinted with permission from American Journal of Neuroradiology. Copyright 2011.

TTFs are also approved by the FDA for the treatment of recurrent glioblastoma. Results from a phase III, randomized trial of TTFs compared them with physician's choice of chemotherapy for patients with recurrent glioblastoma demonstrated no difference in OS. Although it did not provide a survival advantage, TTFs was considered comparable to chemotherapy or bevacizumab and was associated with fewer serious adverse events and better quality of life.[35] However, the benefit of TTFs is debated because no evidence from phase III clinical trials is available to demonstrate that chemotherapy itself extends survival in this patient population. The trial was not blinded and there was no sham intervention.

ANAPLASTIC ASTROCYTOMA (WHO GRADE III)

Anaplastic astrocytomas (WHO grade III) are differentiated from lower-grade astrocytomas by the presence of increased mitotic activity. Anaplastic astrocytomas have a high propensity to transform into glioblastomas. The median age at diagnosis is approximately 55 years. The prognosis of patients with anaplastic astrocytoma varies greatly with *IDH*-mutation status. Patients with *IDH*-mutated tumors have a median survival of 65 to 112 months, whereas patients with *IDH* wild-type tumors have a median survival of only 20 months. In fact, astrocytomas that are *IDH* wild-type typically show clinical behavior similar to that of glioblastomas and are considered to be "astrocytomas with molecular features of glioblastomas," on the basis of work published by the cIMPACT-NOW working group.[36]

KEY POINTS

- The current standard of treatment of glioblastoma in patients younger than 70 years is maximum safe resection followed by radiation with concurrent and adjuvant temozolomide.
- Phase III data also support the use of concurrent chemoradiation in older adults, on the basis of results of a trial with hypofractionated RT plus temozolomide versus treatment with hypofractionated RT alone.
- Pseudoprogression may mimic tumor progression in patients with glioblastoma treated with RT with or without temozolomide and should be considered before

- switching therapy, especially in patients with *MGMT*-methylated tumors.
- Tumor-treating fields are FDA approved for newly diagnosed and recurrent glioblastoma.
- There is no evidence that bevacizumab improves survival in glioblastoma.

Surgery

As in glioblastoma, the initial step of treatment is best possible, safe neurosurgical resection of all contrast-enhancing tissue for the goal of gross total resection.

Radiation

Similar to patients with glioblastoma, postoperative RT has been demonstrated to prolong survival in patients with anaplastic astrocytoma and is a standard component of treatment.[37] Most practitioners currently treat with 55.8 to 60 Gy in 1.8- to 2.0-Gy fractions.

Chemotherapy

The role of adjuvant chemotherapy in anaplastic astrocytoma remains controversial; results from earlier trials must now be revisited in light of new data regarding tumor genetics. Most importantly, *IDH*-mutant anaplastic astrocytomas carry a much better prognosis as well as likely better response to treatment (including RT and chemotherapy). A phase III international trial (EORTC 26053 [CATNON trial]) is ongoing, in which patients with anaplastic glioma without 1p/19q codeletion are randomly assigned to either RT alone or RT with temozolomide during and/or after RT. Interim results indicate improved OS with post-RT temozolomide (reduction for OS HR, 0.645; $P = .0014$), further supporting adjuvant chemotherapy.[38] It is expected that final results from this study will provide more data regarding an optimal treatment regimen (concomitant temozolomide and/or adjuvant temozolomide). In addition, the benefit from the addition of temozolomide was primarily and possibly only seen in *IDH* mutant and/or *MGMT* promoter–methylated tumors. The final data from the CATNON trial are expected to more clearly define which patients may benefit and which regimen should be used for the treatment of these tumors.

Although studies do support improved survival with PCV in *IDH*-mutant, noncodeleted tumors, the survival advantage appears much more pronounced in codeleted tumors (ie, oligodendrogliomas).[9] Because of its lower toxicity and probable efficacy (based on data in glioblastoma and interim data of the CATNON study), temozolomide (both concurrent with and after radiation as adjuvant chemotherapy) is often similarly used in *IDH*-mutant, noncodeleted anaplastic astrocytomas.

Recurrence

Similar to glioblastoma, no uniform therapy is available for patients with anaplastic astrocytomas, and treatment options are tailored to the individual clinical setting. Repeated surgery may be considered in select cases, either for diagnostic purposes (eg, possible progression to glioblastoma, differentiation of active tumor *v* treatment effect) and/or for debulking. Temozolomide or nitrosourea-based regimens may be options. Also repeated RT with or without concomitant temozolomide is considered in certain situations.

KEY POINTS

- Anaplastic astrocytomas have a high propensity to progress into glioblastomas.
- Although standard therapy has not yet fully been established, anaplastic astrocytomas (both *IDH* wild-type and *IDH* mutant) are currently often treated like glioblastoma, with maximal safe resection followed by RT with concurrent and adjuvant temozolomide.
- Final data from the ongoing CATNON are expected to inform treatment decisions in anaplastic astrocytomas, including selection of patients who may benefit from the addition of temozolomide to radiation and regarding the optimal treatment regimen.

DIFFUSE ASTROCYTOMA (WHO GRADE II)

Most WHO grade II astrocytomas are diffuse astrocytomas. These tumors are diffusely infiltrative and cellular, and they tend to eventually progress to higher-grade astrocytomas. Controversy exists as to what constitutes a high-risk, low-grade glioma. Older studies described prognostic factors in diffuse astrocytoma including older age (≥ 40 years), tumor diameter ≥ 6 cm, Karnofsky performance status < 70, tumors that cross the midline, presence of enhancement on imaging, and neurologic deficits prior to surgery.[39,40] Integration of prognostic markers into the 2016 WHO classification has simplified and improved risk stratification of low-grade gliomas. Mutations of *IDH1* or *IDH2* are favorable prognostic markers. Absence of codeletion of 1p/19q differentiates these tumors from "true" oligodendrogliomas, which harbor the codeletion.[41,42] Tumors with *IDH* mutation but no codeletion have an intermediate prognosis, whereas tumors lacking both *IDH* mutation and 1p/19q codeletion have the worst survival and are prognostically closer to glioblastoma (regardless of WHO histologic grade).

Surgery

Symptomatic diffuse astrocytomas typically are resected to debulk the tumor, if feasible. The surgical management of small, asymptomatic diffuse astrocytomas is more controversial. Either upfront surgical resection or a watch-and-wait approach may be considered.

Radiation

A phase III clinical trial has evaluated the role of immediate RT versus delayed RT in patients with low-grade glioma (this was the so-called "nonbeliever trial").[43] Patients were randomly assigned to receive either 54 Gy of radiation immediately after surgery or no immediate radiation. In the latter arm, RT was administered at the time of progression. This study demonstrated that RT beginning immediately after diagnosis extends the time to recurrence compared with delayed RT at time of tumor progression (median PFS, 5.3 years *v* 3.4 years; $P < .0001$). However, there was no change in median OS (7.4 years *v* 7.2 years; $P = .87$).

In the absence of a clear OS benefit, rationale exists for delaying RT in an attempt to prevent radiation-induced neurologic damage. Prospective data had initially demonstrated that tumor growth, the use of antiepileptic drugs, and radiation fraction sizes > 2 Gy were associated with neurocognitive decline. By contrast, RTOG 9802, a phase III trial of RT alone versus RT followed by chemotherapy with PCV, demonstrated minimal long-term neurotoxicity. In fact, a majority of patients showed improvement in neurocognitive testing over time.[44] Thus, for patients with minimal symptoms or well-controlled seizures, it is acceptable to either treat at the time of initial diagnosis or defer RT until evidence of symptomatic tumor growth is observed.

Chemotherapy

The role of adjuvant chemotherapy for patients with low-grade astrocytoma remains under investigation. Results from a phase III trial in which RT alone was compared with RT followed by chemotherapy with PCV suggested that chemotherapy is associated with superior median OS (13.3 *v* 7.8 years; $P = .003$).[44] Information on 1p/19q codeletion status was not available for this study. Comparison of outcomes based on histology illustrated that greater benefit from chemotherapy with PCV was seen in patients with oligodendrogliomas or oligoastrocytomas when compared with patients with histologic astrocytomas, in whom there was no statistically significant benefit noted; however, these data represent a historical subgroup analysis of the overall data of this trial (Fig 18-7).

The toxicity associated with PCV and the lack of evidence of a clear benefit from the addition of PCV to RT has limited its general acceptability in the adjuvant treatment of low-grade astrocytomas. Many practitioners prefer the use of temozolomide in the treatment of diffuse astrocytomas, as temozolomide is the only drug that improved survival in glioblastomas (ie, grade IV astrocytomas). However, data supporting initial therapy with temozolomide in low-grade gliomas are limited.

KEY POINTS

- Diffuse astrocytomas can be indolent tumors; however, they tend to progress to high-grade astrocytomas eventually.
- Prognosis and survival of patients with diffuse astrocytoma is highly dependent on *IDH*-mutation status (having *IDH* mutation is favorable).
- Maximal safe resection is recommended if the diffuse astrocytoma is large and/or symptomatic.
- No clear overall survival advantage is seen with immediate postoperative RT compared with delayed RT at time of progression. Similarly, higher doses of RT do not improve survival.
- In asymptomatic patients, delaying treatment such as surgical resection and RT (after biopsy confirmation of the diagnosis) may be considered.

GRADE I ASTROCYTOMAS

Grade I astrocytomas are relatively uncommon in adults and include pilocytic astrocytoma and subependymal giant cell astrocytoma. These well-circumscribed tumors are typically seen in children and young adults and are often associated with excellent outcomes.[45]

Pilocytic astrocytomas are most frequently present in the cerebellum (40%), followed by supratentorial regions (35%). Tandem duplication at chromosome 7q34 occurs in 66% of pilocytic astrocytomas, resulting in a *BRAF-KIAA1549* gene that is unique to these tumors.[46] Radiographically, pilocytic astrocytomas are frequently cystic, with an associated contrast-enhancing mural nodule. Pilocytic astrocytomas are potentially curable with complete surgical resection.

Subependymal giant cell astrocytomas (SEGA) are periventricular tumors that occur in approximately one in 10 patients with tuberous sclerosis and are the most frequent cause of decreased life expectancy in this disease. Acutely symptomatic SEGA (ie, those associated with increasing ventricular enlargement) should be surgically resected. Asymptomatic SEGA may either be surgically resected or treated with a mammalian target of rapamycin–complex inhibitor such as everolimus, which is approved by the FDA for this indication.[47]

Even if surgical resection is incomplete, grade I astrocytomas typically remain indolent. RT may be considered in such circumstances but is typically deferred until significant tumor progression. Cytotoxic chemotherapy is of uncertain value.

KEY POINTS

- Grade I astrocytomas are more common in children and young adults. Surgical resection is often curative.
- Everolimus is FDA approved for treatment of SEGA.

OLIGODENDROGLIAL TUMORS

Tumors containing oligodendroglial elements are relatively uncommon, accounting for only 7.9% of gliomas (oligodendrogliomas, 5.3%; oligoastrocytic tumors, 2.6%; Fig 18-1). Nevertheless, they are important to note because of their unique natural history, comparatively favorable prognosis, and sensitivity to chemotherapy. Key molecular features of oligodendroglial tumors include *IDH* mutation and 1p/19q codeletion. Some tumors, based on histopathology, have oligodendroglial as well as astrocytic features and were historically referred to as oligoastrocytomas or "mixed" tumors. Analysis of large genomic data sets showed that most oligoastrocytomas can be

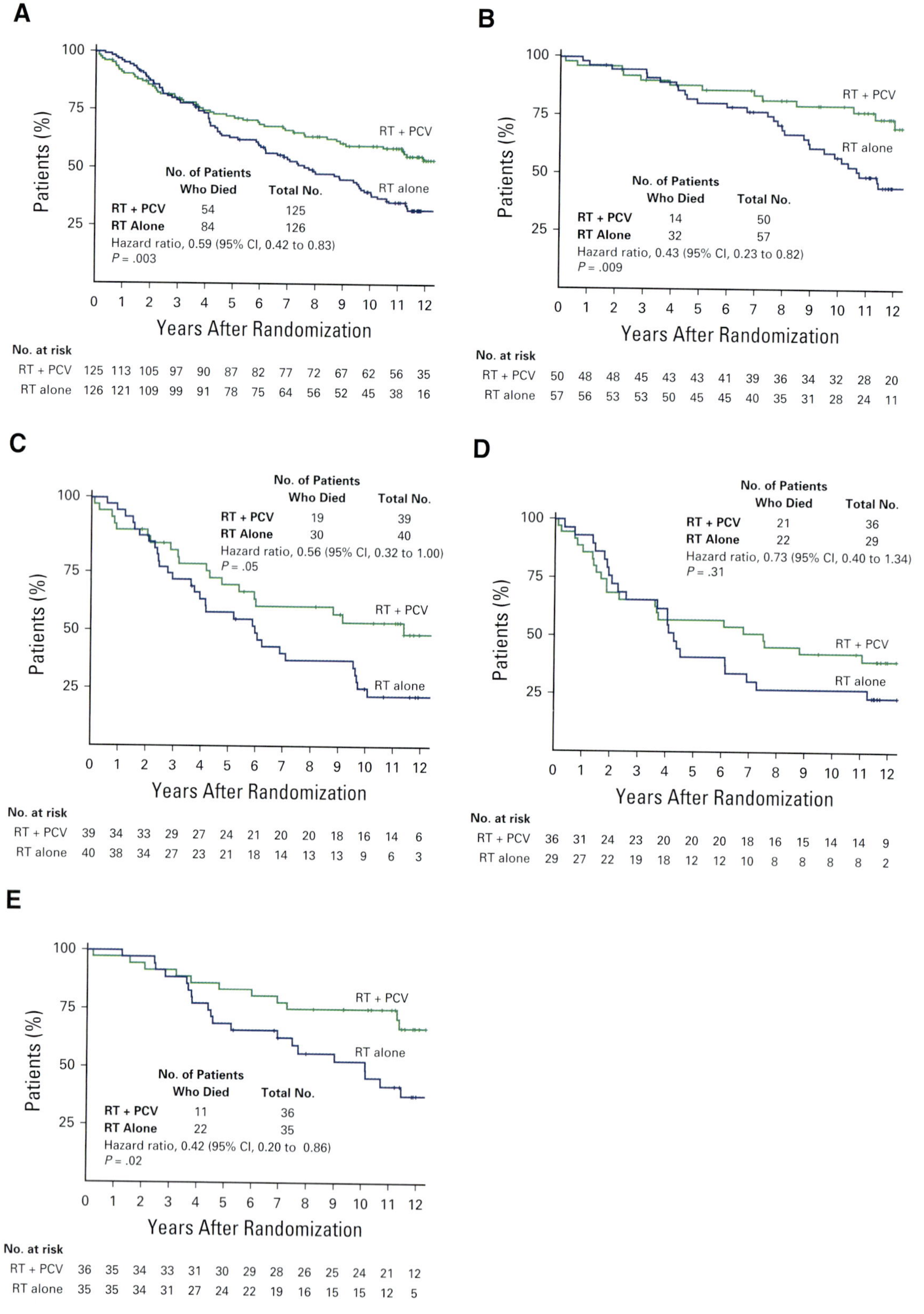

Fig. 18-7 Differential benefit from the addition of PCV chemotherapy to radiation related to histopathology in low-grade gliomas.[44] (A) Overall survival. (B) Overall survival, grade II oligodendroglioma. (C) Overall survival, grade II oligoastrocytoma. (D) Overall survival, grade II astrocytoma. (E) Overall survival among patients with *IDH1* R132H mutation.

Abbreviations: PCV, procarbazine, lomustine, and vincristine; RT, radiation therapy.

From The New England Journal of Medicine, *Radiation plus Procarbazine, CCNU, and Vincristine in Low-Grade Glioma. Vol 374(10), Buckner JC, Shaw EG, Pugh SL, et al. Pg. 1344-1355.*

categorized more accurately, on the basis of molecular features, into oligodendrogliomas (if 1p/19q codeleted) or astrocytomas (not codeleted; *ATRX* mutant), and the category of mixed gliomas has virtually disappeared since publication of the new 2016 WHO classification of CNS tumors.[1]

ANAPLASTIC OLIGODENDROGLIOMAS, WHO GRADE III

Anaplastic oligodendrogliomas are grade III gliomas that typically demonstrate high cellularity, nuclear pleomorphism, and frequent mitoses. Abundant endothelial proliferation and tumor necrosis may also be seen, but these tumors are not graded differently; a grade IV does not exist for oligodendrogliomas in the WHO classification of 2016. The median age at diagnosis is approximately 50 years. Mass effect or seizures are typically seen at presentation. MRI reveals a variably contrast-enhancing mass in most patients.

Treatment of anaplastic oligodendroglioma includes optimal surgical debulking followed by RT with or without chemotherapy. Support for the use of chemotherapy and RT after resection of anaplastic oligodendroglioma comes from two phase III trials (Fig 18-8), one conducted in North America (RTOG 9402) and the other in Europe (EORTC 26951). In the North American trial, patients with anaplastic oligodendroglioma and anaplastic oligoastrocytoma were randomly assigned to receive PCV for four cycles prior to RT or to RT alone.[12] Patients with *IDH*-mutant, codeleted tumors benefited from the addition of PCV to RT (median survival, 14.7 years *v* 6.8 years). PCV improved survival in patients with *IDH*-mutant, noncodeleted tumors, but the survival advantage was less substantial (5.5 years *v* 3.3 years).[9] For patients without *IDH* mutation, chemotherapy did not significantly prolong survival.

In the European trial, patients received PCV after RT. Results were similar to the North American results. Some long-term results demonstrated longer median survival in patients with 1p/19q codeleted tumors who received both RT and PCV compared with those who received RT alone. In contrast, patients with noncodeleted tumors did not have statistically significant improvement in OS with the addition of PCV.[13] Taken together, these two randomized trials support the standard use of RT and chemotherapy with PCV for patients with anaplastic oligodendroglioma with *IDH* mutation and 1p/19q codeletion.

It is currently unclear how the standard regimen for high-grade astrocytomas—RT and concomitant temozolomide followed by adjuvant temozolomide—compares with the data on RT and PCV in these cancers. Temozolomide is overall better tolerated and, prior to publication of the two aforementioned studies, patients were commonly treated with RT and temozolomide. An ongoing prospective trial (the CODEL study) is comparing RT followed by PCV with chemoradiation with temozolomide followed by adjuvant temozolomide in patients with oligodendrogliomas (both high and low grade). This study will eventually answer the question of how the two regimens compare.

OLIGODENDROGLIOMAS, WHO GRADE II

Oligodendrogliomas are grade II gliomas typically characterized histologically as well as by presence of an *IDH* mutation and codeletion of 1p/19q. The disease course of oligodendrogliomas is more indolent than that of grade II astrocytomas. Considerations regarding timing of therapy are similar to those in low-grade astrocytomas (see the section Diffuse Astrocytoma, WHO Grade II). The phase III clinical trial RTOG 9802 defined patients as at high risk for early progression if they were age ≥ 40 years

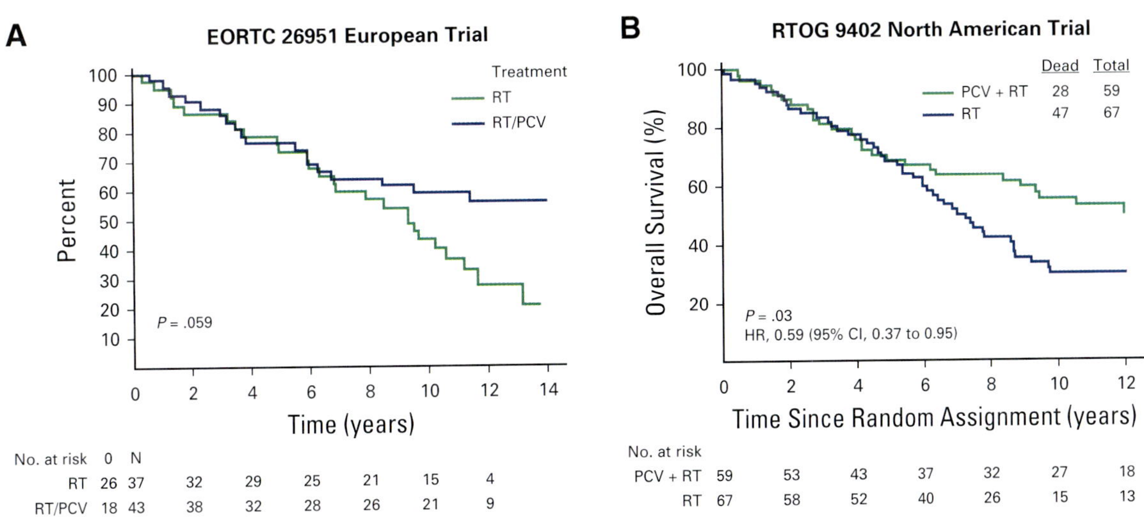

Fig. 18-8 Survival benefit from the addition of PCV chemotherapy in patients with 1p/19q codeleted oligodendrogliomas or oligoastrocytomas.

These two independently conducted clinical trials showed virtually the same result of a significant survival benefit when PCV chemotherapy was added to RT, compared with RT alone.[12,13]

Abbreviations: HR, hazard ratio; PCV, procarbazine, lomustine, and vincristine; RT, radiation therapy.

Permission to reuse van den Bent MJ, Brandes AA, Taphoorn MJB, et al. Adjuvant Procarbazine, Lomustine, and Vincristine Chemotherapy in Newly Diagnosed Anaplastic Oligodendroglioma: Long-Term Follow-Up of EORTC Brain Tumor Group Study 26951. J Clin Oncol. *2013 31:3, 344-350; Cairncross JG, Wang M, Jenkins RB, et al. Benefit From Procarbazine, Lomustine, and Vincristine in Oligodendroglial Tumors Is Associated With Mutation of IDH.* J Clin Oncol. *2014 Mar 10; 32(8): 783-790.*

and/or if they were younger than 40 years and had undergone subtotal resection or biopsy instead of a gross total resection. Patients meeting these eligibility criteria were then randomly assigned to receive either RT alone or RT followed by chemotherapy with PCV. The study showed that the addition of chemotherapy with PCV significantly improved survival (Fig 18-7).[44]

KEY POINTS

- Oligodendroglial tumors are characterized by both *IDH* mutation and 1p/19q codeletion and have a more indolent course than astrocytomas.
- In patients with anaplastic oligodendroglioma with *IDH* mutation and 1p/19q codeletion, chemotherapy with PCV after RT significantly improves OS.

EPENDYMAL TUMORS

Ependymal tumors are rare CNS tumors that usually arise from the ependymal lining of the ventricular system of the brain or the central canal in the spinal cord. In children, this tumor is more commonly found in the posterior fossa; in adults, the tumor is somewhat more common in the spinal cord. Supratentorial lesions outside the ventricular system are infrequent. Ependymomas are currently separated into five categories by the WHO classification: Subependymomas and myxopapillary ependymomas are rare grade I; ependymomas are grade II; ependymomas, RELA fusion-positive are grade II or III, and are seen mostly in children; and anaplastic ependymomas are grade III. Initial treatment is maximal safe, complete resection, if possible. Incompletely resected, anaplastic, or disseminated tumors are usually treated with RT. Currently, no published, randomized controlled trials for patients with ependymomas are available that could guide management. Studies have shown that ependymomas may respond to platinum-based chemotherapy regimens, but the exact clinical benefit of chemotherapy remains to be defined, and response rates are, overall, considerably low.[48,49] Clinical research is underway to identify options for systemic therapy for this group of tumors.

MEDULLOBLASTOMA

Medulloblastoma is the most common malignant brain tumor in children, but young adults and also older adults are also at risk, although at lower frequency. Medulloblastomas develop in the posterior fossa. They may be located in either the cerebellar hemispheres or the vermis and may involve the fourth ventricle. Obstructive hydrocephalus is relatively common because of this proximity of the tumor to the fourth ventricle. Symptoms at presentation may include the following:

- loss of balance,
- incoordination,
- diplopia,
- dysarthria, and
- signs of hydrocephalus such as headache, nausea, vomiting, and gait instability.

Molecular pathology studies have demonstrated discrete subtypes of medulloblastoma with variable prognoses. The following genetically defined subtypes have been incorporated into the new WHO 2016 classification:

- WNT-activated,
- sonic hedgehog (SHH)-activated,
- group 3, and group 4 medulloblastomas (Fig 18-9).[50]

The WNT-activated group has the best prognosis, with long-term survival in > 90% of patients. Patients in the SHH group and group 4 have an intermediate prognosis, and group 3 patients, with overexpression of *MYC*, have the worst prognosis. Although the molecular characterization has not yet resulted in specific therapies, the aberrant pathways identified may eventually lead to targeted treatments for the respective entities.

Maximal surgical resection is important because residual tumor after surgery confers a worse prognosis. Worse prognosis is also seen with positive cerebrospinal fluid (CSF) cytology or presence of leptomeningeal metastases on MRI. Surgery alone is not curative; however, surgical resection followed by RT to the craniospinal axis with a boost to the site of the primary tumor (usually the posterior fossa) may be curative.

Postradiation chemotherapy is a mainstay of treatment in children with medulloblastoma, particularly because this limits the total dose of radiation required in treating the still-developing CNS. On the basis of this experience, adults with medulloblastoma are usually offered chemotherapy, if post-radiation blood cell counts permit. However, no prospective data show an added benefit from chemotherapy in adults who have received full-dose craniospinal radiation. Chemotherapy regimens for adult patients are often modeled after the experience in pediatric patients. Weekly vincristine treatment during RT, frequently used in children, is often omitted in adults because of poor tolerability of the drug and concerns about lack of efficacy. Adjuvant chemotherapy regimens include cisplatin, cyclophosphamide, and vincristine,[51] or cisplatin, lomustine, and vincristine,[51] but there is no unifying standard of care and the role for chemotherapy after craniospinal RT remains controversial.

Vismodegib, a small-molecule inhibitor of the SHH pathway, has demonstrated activity in patients with recurrent SHH-type medulloblastoma,[52] and high-dose chemotherapy with autologous stem cell transplantation may result in longer survival in some selected patients.[53,54]

With appropriate initial therapy, 5-year event-free survival is achieved in > 80% of patients with average-risk medulloblastoma, and 36% in patients with disseminated disease at diagnosis.[51]

KEY POINTS

- Ependymomas are rare. Treatment consists of optimal surgical resection. In patients with incompletely resected or disseminated tumors, RT is a standard

Molecular Subgroups of Medulloblastoma

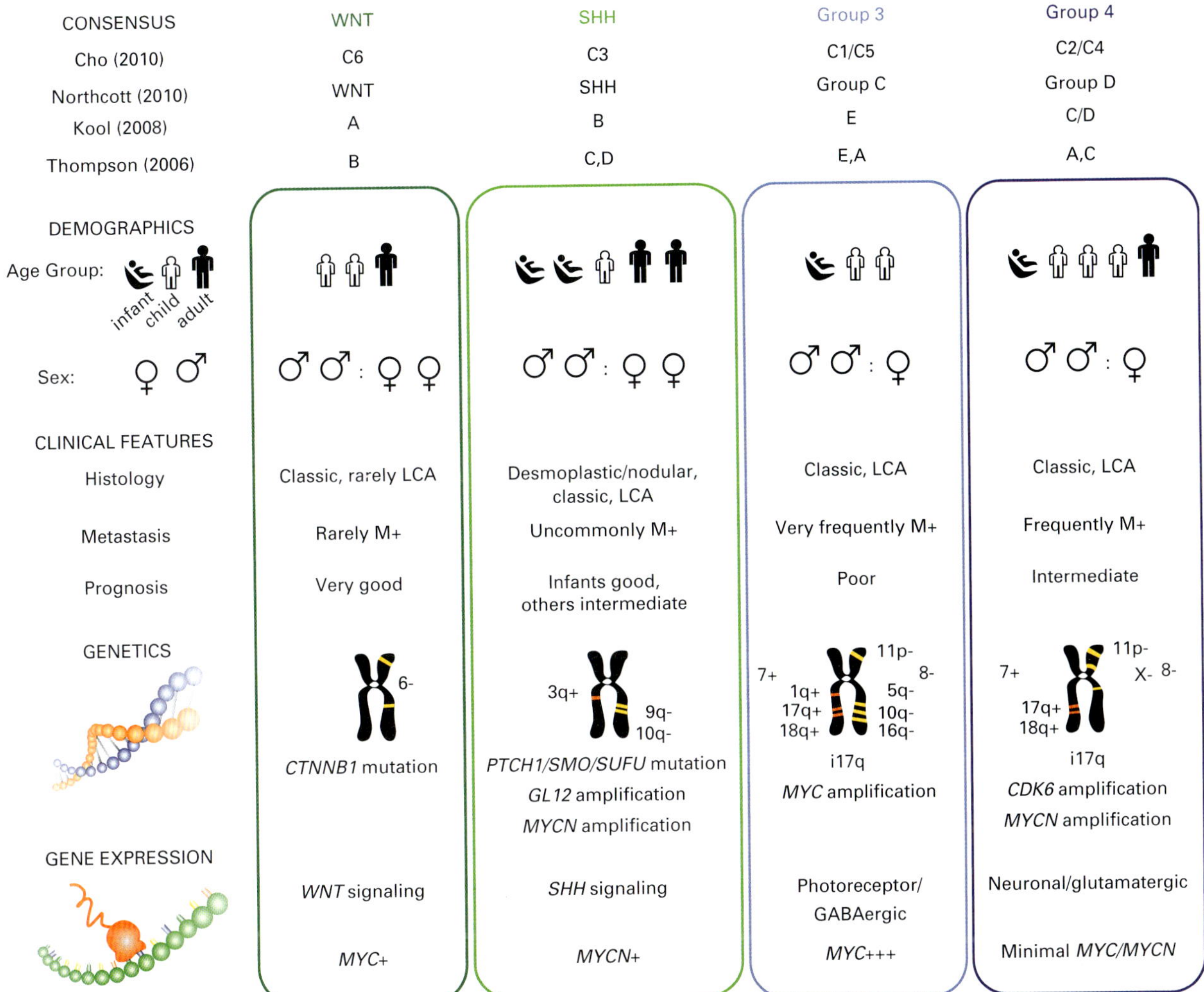

CONSENSUS
WNT
SHH
Group 3
Group 4
Cho (2010)
C6
C3
C1/C5
C2/C4
Northcott (2010)
WNT
SHH
Group C
Group D
Kool (2008)
A
B
E
C/D
Thompson (2006)
B
C,D
E,A
A,C
DEMOGRAPHICS
Age Group:
infant
child
adult
Sex:
CLINICAL FEATURES
Histology
Classic, rarely LCA
Desmoplastic/nodular, classic, LCA
Classic, LCA
Classic, LCA
Metastasis
Rarely M+
Uncommonly M+
Very frequently M+
Frequently M+
Prognosis
Very good
Infants good, others intermediate
Poor
Intermediate
GENETICS
6-
CTNNB1 mutation
3q+
9q-
10q-
PTCH1/SMO/SUFU mutation
GL12 amplification
MYCN amplification
7+
1q+
17q+
18q+
11p-
8-
5q-
10q-
16q-
i17q
MYC amplification
7+
17q+
18q+
11p-
X-
8-
i17q
CDK6 amplification
MYCN amplification
GENE EXPRESSION
WNT signaling
MYC+
SHH signaling
MYCN+
Photoreceptor/ GABAergic
MYC+++
Neuronal/glutamatergic
Minimal MYC/MYCN

Fig. 18-9 Comparison of the various subgroups of medulloblastoma, including their affiliations with previously published papers on medulloblastoma molecular subgrouping.[50]

Abbreviations: LCA, large cell/anaplastic; M+, metastatic; SHH, sonic hedgehog.

Permission to reuse given by the Creative Common license for Taylor, M.D., Northcott, P.A., Korshunov, A. et al. Molecular subgroups of medulloblastoma: the current consensus. Acta Neuropathol *123, 465–472 (2012).*

option. The role of chemotherapy has remained unclear and there currently is no unifying standard of care.

- Medulloblastomas typically occur in the cerebellum of children, but it can also present in adults.
- Treatment of medulloblastoma includes maximal safe resection followed by irradiation of the craniospinal axis (with a boost to the posterior fossa). Platinum-based chemotherapy regimens are considered, especially in higher-risk patients, if postradiation blood cell counts permit.

MENINGIOMA

Meningiomas are usually benign and originate in the dura covering the brain and spinal cord. Patients with meningiomas may present with typical features of mass lesions in the brain, including seizures or focal neurologic deficits. Asymptomatic meningiomas may also be incidentally detected on CT or MRI scans that are obtained for other reasons. The tumors have a characteristic appearance on MRI, usually consisting of uniform contrast enhancement along the dura and distinct separation from brain parenchyma.

Many incidentally discovered meningiomas do not require treatment. For patients with an asymptomatic benign meningioma (WHO grade I), observation may be appropriate. Epidemiologic evidence suggests that as many as two-thirds of these patients will not have symptoms over time.[55]

In cases of substantial mass effect with or without symptoms, the treatment of choice is usually complete resection. Surgery is often feasible if the meningioma is located over the cortical convexity, olfactory groove, anterior sagittal sinus, or posterior fossa. However, the possibility of resection may be limited for tumors in other sites, including sphenoid, parasagittal, orbital, tentorial, or clival locations. Under those circumstances, external-beam RT or focal stereotactic radiotherapy may be useful for tumor control.

Meningiomas may occasionally have atypical histologic features or be malignant. Patients with atypical (WHO grade II) or malignant meningiomas (WHO grade III) are commonly treated with surgical resection followed by RT, either external-beam RT or stereotactic radiosurgery. Those who experience relapse despite optimal surgery and RT often have progressive debilitation before death. Although several pharmaceutical approaches have been assessed, they have had minimal, if any, efficacy.[56]

KEY POINTS

- For many patients with meningioma, observation is appropriate. For patients who are symptomatic, surgical removal of the tumor is the most common treatment.
- Atypical and malignant meningiomas are rare but have a more aggressive course with recurrences that may require repeated resection and RT.
- Currently, no systemic regimens have more than minimal, if any, efficacy for the treatment of meningiomas.

PRIMARY CNS LYMPHOMA

PCNSL is a variant of non-Hodgkin lymphoma that involves the CNS without evidence of systemic disease. More than 95% of primary CNS lymphomas are diffuse large B-cell lymphomas. Primary CNS lymphomas constitute approximately 2% to 3% of all brain tumors. The tumor is more common in men, and the median age at diagnosis in immunocompetent patients is approximately 67 years.[57] Most patients diagnosed with primary CNS lymphoma are immunocompetent; however, patients with a compromised immune system (eg, those who have undergone solid organ transplantation, have congenital immunodeficiency, or have HIV infection) are at increased risk for this disease. Epstein-Barr virus (EBV) is frequently associated with primary CNS lymphoma in immunocompromised individuals, and EBV DNA may be found within the tumor.

Patients present with a variety of symptoms characteristic of either focal or multifocal mass lesions. MRI usually shows homogenous, contrast-enhancing tumors within the periventricular deep white matter. Multifocality is common because these tumors grow diffusely. Heterogeneous contrast enhancement is sometimes seen, especially in patients with a compromised immune system or after exposure to immunosuppressant agents such as corticosteroids. It is important to consider CNS lymphoma in the differential diagnosis of brain tumors, because their treatment differs significantly from that of other primary brain cancers. Administration of corticosteroids may result in complete disappearance of the contrast-enhancing lesion, making diagnosis difficult. Consequently, when CNS lymphoma is considered in the differential diagnosis, corticosteroids should be avoided unless mass effect is causing serious and immediate complications. Obtaining specimens of suspected lesions by biopsy is critically important because many malignant and nonmalignant CNS conditions can mimic a CNS lymphoma. As with systemic lymphoma, the role of surgery is restricted primarily to obtaining appropriate tissue for diagnosis.

Staging evaluation includes slit-lamp examination of the eyes (to assess for ocular lymphoma, present at diagnosis in approximately 25% of patients); MRI of the spine; positron emission tomography/CT imaging or CT scan of the chest, abdomen, and pelvis to rule out systemic lymphoma; lumbar puncture, if safe; and HIV testing. PCNSLs typically do not involve the bone marrow and the role for a bone marrow biopsy as part of the standard workup is controversial.

High-dose methotrexate-based regimens with typical methotrexate doses of between 3.5 and 8 mg/m^2 have remained the backbone of treatment of CNS lymphoma. Several combination regimens are used in clinical practice, including high-dose methotrexate with rituximab or with rituximab plus temozolomide, or with vincristine, procarbacine, and rituximab, or high-dose methotrexate and cytarabine.[58-62] The different regimens have not been formally compared in prospective trials and efficacy cannot be conclusively compared. Overall response rates of the different regimens have been reported to be between 35% and 95%. Whether some patients may be cured of PCNSL is controversial.[63] Approximately 30% of patients achieve a durable complete response, raising the question if some of these patients may be cured. However, late relapses, even after ≥ 10 years, can occur.

Controversy still remains regarding the role of consolidation therapy after induction with high-dose methotrexate-based therapy. Encouraging data are reported with the use of autologous stem cell transplantation.[60,64] A currently ongoing trial comparing autologous transplant with high-dose chemotherapy as consolidation therapy in newly diagnosed PCNSL is expected to shed more light on a potential role of autologous transplant in the setting of newly diagnosed PCNSL setting (ClinicalTrial.gov identifier: NCT01511562; CALGB-51101). A possible role of low-dose radiation for consolidation in patients with newly diagnosed PCNSL has also been studied.[65]

A number of additional drugs show promising activity in PCNSL, including ibrutinib[66], lenalidomide[67], temozolomide, pemetrexed, and, possibly, PD-1 inhibitors. Additional research is needed to determine the best clinical use of these new agents.

Strategies for the treatment of recurrent disease include reinduction with high-dose methotrexate-based regimens; in select cases, high-dose chemotherapy with autologous stem cell transplantation; chemotherapy including temozolomide; ibrutinib; lenalidomide; combinations with rituximab; rituximab; and whole-brain RT (WBRT). WBRT historically played a central role in the initial treatment of PCNSL, but responses are typically short lived and there is significant risk of later neurotoxicity.[68] Several studies have demonstrated that RT may be eliminated from first-line therapy.[58,69] However, hyperfractionation of RT with lower doses is being evaluated in hope of balancing efficacy with decreased neurotoxicity.

The aforementioned doses of methotrexate (3.5 to 8.0 g/m^2) are potentially lethal if not followed by active measures to reduce associated toxicity. Multiple doses of leucovorin must be administered starting approximately 24 hours after treatment to minimize toxicity to normal cells ("leucovorin rescue"), and hyperhydration with urinary alkalinization with intravenous sodium bicarbonate is used to enhance methotrexate excretion. Methotrexate levels must be monitored to confirm effective elimination. Prolonged exposure may be secondary to accumulation of methotrexate in third-space fluid collections (eg, pleural effusions). Such fluid collections should be drained prior to treatment with methotrexate, if possible. In patients who are unable to clear methotrexate sufficiently quickly, administration of glucarpidase can be considered, which cleaves the methotrexate and neutralizes its toxic effect.

KEY POINTS

- Primary CNS lymphomas are usually diffuse large B-cell lymphomas.
- EBV is frequently associated with primary CNS lymphoma in immunocompromised individuals.
- When CNS lymphoma is considered in the differential diagnosis, corticosteroids should be held prior to biopsy, if clinically feasible, because they can lead to a nondiagnostic biopsy results, which, in turn, can delay treatment.
- High-dose methotrexate-based chemotherapy has remained the backbone of therapy for newly diagnosed primary CNS lymphoma.
- Autologous stem cell transplantation can be considered for consolidation in patients with good functional status who respond to a methotrexate-based chemotherapy regimens.

METASTATIC DISEASE TO THE NERVOUS SYSTEM

BRAIN METASTASES

Brain metastases from systemic cancers are 10 times more common than from primary brain tumors. The incidence of brain metastases has been reported as 9% to 17% in various studies; autopsy series suggest that the true incidence of brain metastases in adults may be > 20%. Brain metastases are most commonly associated with cancers of the lung, breast, melanoma, or an unknown primary cancer. These lesions result from hematogenous spread and are most common at the junction of the gray and white matter, where the caliber of blood vessels narrows, thereby trapping tumor emboli. A total of 80% of brain metastases occur in the cerebral hemispheres, 15% occur in the cerebellum, and 5% in the brainstem.[70] It has been reported that > 80% have more than one and approximately 50% three or more brain metastases seen on MRI.[71]

The management of brain metastases requires an individualized approach because these patients have highly heterogeneous primary disease processes. Considerations for therapy depend on multiple variables, such as the number and location of the brain metastases, histology of the primary cancer, tumor molecular characteristics, degree of extracranial disease, and performance status.

Radiation

Two randomized, prospective studies have shown that surgery plus WBRT is superior to WBRT alone in patients with one surgically accessible brain metastasis. In one trial, patients who received surgery plus RT survived 6 months longer than patients who received radiation alone (median, 40 weeks *v* 15 weeks; $P < .01$).[72] Many patients with one or two brain metastases, however, are not surgical candidates, because of complicating factors such as an inaccessible tumor location.

Stereotactic radiosurgery (SRS) is increasingly being used in addition to or in place of surgery for patients with a limited number of metastases. Local control rates with SRS are high, ranging from 80% to 90%.[73] In a phase III clinical trial, patients with one to three brain metastases were treated with WBRT either with or without a SRS boost. Patients who received SRS in addition to WBRT therapy were more likely to maintain a stable or higher performance score at 6 months (43% *v* 27%; $P = .03$). Patients with a single brain metastasis also seemed to have a survival advantage (6.5 months *v* 4.9 months; $P = .04$).[74] After surgery, radiation to the resection cavity with SRS has been shown to decrease local recurrence compared with surgery alone. One phase III trial randomly assigned 132 patients who had undergone a complete resection of one to three brain metastases (maximum diameter of resection cavity, < 4 cm) to either SRS of the resection cavity or observation.[75] Freedom from local recurrence at 1 year was 43% in the observation group and 72% in the SRS group (HR, 0.46; $P = .015$), indicating that SRS significantly lowers local recurrence. SRS may be preferred as an independent treatment in patients who have surgically inaccessible lesions who cannot undergo craniotomy because of the operative risk or who have more than one lesion in different parts of the brain. Limitations include the inability to obtain tissue diagnosis or reduce mass effect; also, lesions must generally be < 3 to 4 cm to be safely treated. Furthermore, SRS may increase cerebral edema, resulting in mass effect that requires either corticosteroid treatment or resection of necrotic tissue.

In patients who have undergone a surgical resection or SRS, the role of WBRT is controversial. In a phase III clinical trial, patients with one to three brain metastases were treated with either surgery or SRS and then randomly assigned to either WBRT (30 Gy in 10 fractions) or observation. WBRT reduced the incidence of intracranial progression (48% *v* 78%; $P < .001$) and neurologic death (28% *v* 44%; $P < .002$); however, OS was similar in the two groups (10.9 months *v* 10.7 months; $P = .89$).[76] Similar results have been found in other studies.[77-79] Many studies have raised concerns regarding cognitive impairment with the addition of WBRT. Another phase III trial compared the survival and cognitive outcomes of patients receiving WBRT or SRS after metastasis resection. Patients with one resected brain metastasis were randomly assigned to either postoperative SRS or WBRT. Median OS was similar between the two groups (12.2 months for SRS and 11.6 months for WBRT), and cognitive deterioration occurred sooner and more frequently with WBRT.[80] With these results, ways to limit the cognitive toxicity of WBRT are being investigated. Data from a placebo-controlled phase III clinical trial suggest that memantine concurrent with WBRT may delay cognitive decline.[81]

Definitive therapy with either surgical resection or SRS may not be an option in several situations. Patients with tumors that almost always disseminate widely, such as small-cell lung cancer, are not candidates for either surgical resection or SRS. These patients and others with multiple brain metastases should receive WBRT as standard therapy.

Systemic Therapy

Classic chemotherapy plays a limited role in the treatment of brain metastases, in part due to poor drug delivery via the BBB/blood-tumor barrier. However, chemotherapy may be curative in specific tumors, such as lymphoma and germ-cell tumors; chemotherapy may be incorporated into the treatment plan for both brain and systemic metastatic disease in these patients, often in combination with RT.

A growing body of evidence shows efficacy of small molecules and/or checkpoint inhibitors in cancers in which the respective agents are known to be effective. Examples include BRAF/MEK inhibitor combinations (eg, vemurafenib and cobimetinib; dabrafenib and trametinib) or checkpoint inhibitors (eg, ipilimumab and nivolumab; pembrolizumab) in melanoma.[82-87] In ALK rearrangement-positive, non–small-cell lung cancer, alectinib and brigatinib have shown efficacy[88]; in EGFR-sensitizing mutant tumors, erlotinib, gefitinib, and afatinib have shown efficacy; and in EGFR T790 mutant tumors, treatment with osimertinib,[89] as well as immunotherapy with pembrolizumab have shown efficacy.[86] Chemotherapy plus small-molecule inhibitor combinations (eg, capecitabine with or without lapatinib) are used in select patients with breast cancer.[90]

KEY POINTS

- Brain metastases are by far the most common cancers in the CNS.
- Surgical resection and SRS benefit patients with a single brain metastasis who have a good Karnofsky performance score and controlled or absent systemic tumor.
- SRS is increasingly being used in addition to or in place of surgery for patients with a limited number of metastases.
- Small molecules and immunotherapies are increasingly used in cancers for which the respective medications are effective.

LEPTOMENINGEAL METASTASES

Leptomeningeal metastases occur in approximately 5% of patients with cancer and are more frequently recognized as patients with cancer live longer and as diagnostic studies improve.[91] Leptomeningeal disease is most common with breast cancer, lung cancer, and melanoma. The tumor reaches the leptomeninges by hematogenous spread or by direct extension from preexisting tumor deposits within the dura or brain parenchyma. Tumor cells are disseminated throughout the neuraxis by the flow of the CSF. Patients present with signs and symptoms referable to one or more of the following:

- Local injury to nerves traveling through the spinal fluid (cranial nerve palsies, weakness, paresthesias, or pain).
- Direct invasion into the brain or spinal tissues or interruption of blood supply to those tissues (focal findings or seizures).
- Obstruction of normal CSF flow pathways, increased intracranial pressure, and hydrocephalus (headache, nausea, vomiting, and dizziness).
- Interference with cognitive function (encephalopathy).

The diagnosis is made by MRI or CSF analysis. Initial analysis of CSF demonstrates malignant cells in 50% of affected patients; however, in nearly 10% of patients with leptomeningeal involvement, the cytologic examination remains persistently negative.[92] Increasing the number of lumbar punctures (up to six) and the volume of CSF removed (10 mL per lumbar puncture) increases the yield of positive cytology. CSF analysis usually demonstrates mild protein elevation, pleocytosis, and possible low glucose concentrations. Radiographic studies may demonstrate diffuse and/or nodular contrast enhancement of the leptomeninges or hydrocephalus without a mass lesion.

In patients with leptomeningeal disease from solid tumors, median survival is typically short, often 4 to 6 weeks without therapy. Death results from progressive neurologic dysfunction. Palliative care may be the most appropriate for patients with poor performance status, significant neurologic dysfunction, and/or uncontrolled systemic disease. Corticosteroids and analgesics may offer limited temporary improvement. RT may be considered for the treatment of symptomatic sites. Ventriculoperitoneal shunting can be considered for palliative relief of refractory symptomatic hydrocephalus.

For patients who have minimal systemic disease, no significant neurologic deficits, and an acceptable performance status, a more aggressive approach may be considered. Unfortunately, no specific treatment has definitively demonstrated an improvement in OS. Imaging to assess for normal CSF flow should be considered because blockage of flow by tumor deposits in the subarachnoid space reduces drug delivery and increases the risk of toxicity of intrathecal therapy. In the presence of CSF flow abnormalities, RT may be attempted to attain normal CSF flow. RT may also be used to treat areas of bulky disease and other symptomatic sites.

If CSF flow is normal, intrathecal chemotherapy may provide some disease control in patients with nonbulky leptomeningeal involvement of their cancer. Drugs can be administered intrathecally through an Ommaya reservoir or by repeated lumbar punctures.

It is of note that leptomeningeal involvement from hematologic malignancies may have a much better response to systemic (eg, high-dose methotrexate in secondary CNS lymphoma) and intrathecal chemotherapy.

KEY POINTS

- Leptomeningeal metastases are manifested by progressive symptoms and signs of injury to brain parenchyma, cranial nerves, and/or spinal nerves.
- Treatment of leptomeningeal metastases from solid tumors is often limited to symptom control. Radiation to symptomatic areas and, in select cases, with symptomatic hydrocephalus, shunt placement may alleviate symptoms.

COMPLICATIONS AND IMPORTANT SUPPORTIVE CARE AGENTS IN CNS TUMORS

CEREBRAL EDEMA

Corticosteroids, antiepileptic drugs, and anticoagulant drugs are important ancillary agents for the treatment of patients with brain tumors. Corticosteroids are indispensable for controlling cerebral edema. Unfortunately, the long-term use of these agents can result in substantial toxic effects, including myopathy, hyperglycemia, peripheral edema, and Cushing syndrome. Dexamethasone is often the drug of choice because of its minimal mineralocorticoid activity and long half-life. Corticosteroids are generally recommended for temporary relief of symptoms and should be started at the minimum dose necessary and tapered as quickly as deemed possible, especially in asymptomatic patients. Bevacizumab may also be considered in select cases to control severe edema, including edema secondary to radiation necrosis.[93]

SEIZURES

Antiepileptic drugs are administered for the treatment of seizures. Clinical trials have demonstrated that some antiepileptic agents, including phenytoin, phenobarbital, and carbamazepine, induce common hepatic enzyme systems, such as cytochrome P450 enzymes. Induction of these enzymes results in decreased exposure to chemotherapy agents and other drugs metabolized by the same enzyme systems, including warfarin and small-molecule inhibitors. In contrast, valproate inhibits cytochrome P450 and may reduce chemotherapy metabolism, with a consequent increase in toxicity. Newer antiepileptic drugs, such as levetiracetam, zonisamide, lacosamide, lamotrigine, topiramate, and pregabalin, do not typically interact with current treatment regimens. These agents are preferred when feasible, because they may avoid the enzyme interactions previously noted.

Clinical trials have not yet demonstrated a discernible benefit for the use of routine prophylactic antiepileptic therapy for patients with no history of seizure.[94] Similarly, no clear evidence supports the efficacy or lack of efficacy of antiepileptic therapy in the postcraniotomy setting.[95] Prospective, randomized trials have demonstrated a lack of efficacy of perioperative seizure prophylaxis;[96] however, the heterogeneity of included patients and the use of older antiepileptic agents in these trials have led to limited acceptance of these results. If antiepileptics are initiated perioperatively, current practice recommendations are to taper and discontinue use after the first postoperative week.[97] Patients who have had a seizure should continue to receive antiepileptic therapy after surgery.

VENOUS THROMBEMBOLISM

Clinically apparent venous thromboembolism (VTE) or pulmonary emboli that require anticoagulation may occur in 20% to 30% of patients with primary brain tumors. The reason for this high risk is likely multifactorial and includes hypercoagulability of malignancy as well as immobility of many patients with brain tumor. Presumably, the surgical injury of brain parenchyma also results in the release of procoagulant proteins that lead to a higher risk of thrombosis. Spontaneous bleeding during anticoagulation occurs in only 2% of patients with malignant glioma and does not appear to be higher than the rate seen in nonanticoagulated patients.[98] Low-molecular-weight heparin is generally considered more effective than warfarin in patients with active malignancy.[99] Patients with CNS tumors should receive anticoagulation for established VTE as recommended for other patients with cancer. Anticoagulation should be avoided in the setting of active intracranial bleeding (or, especially, hemorrhagic brain tumors), thrombocytopenia, or coagulopathy. Clinical trials evaluating newer oral anticoagulants, including factor Xa inhibitors (eg, apixaban, edoxaban, and rivaroxaban) and direct thrombin inhibitors (eg, dabigatran) have not yet conclusively assessed the safety of these drugs in patients with brain tumors. Additional clinical evaluation is necessary before these drugs can be recommended for routine use in this population.

Acknowledgment

The following authors are acknowledged and graciously thanked for their contribution to prior versions of this chapter: Rajiv S. Magge, MD; and Howard A. Fine, MD.

GLOBAL ONCOLOGY PERSPECTIVE: CNS TUMORS

Lawrence Cher, MBBS BSc(Med) (Heidelberg, Melbourne, Victoria, Australia)

Neuro-oncology practice around the world varies widely, which can be due to variations in epidemiology; imaging and diagnostic techniques; surgical technologies and training; as well as access to radiation and chemotherapy. In addition, neuro-oncologic practices may vary between regions, unrelated to access to resources.

EPIDEMIOLOGY

Recent reviews of epidemiologic studies in brain tumors have shown differences within populations. For example, studies showed differing international rates of gliomas, which were higher in Western industrialized nations than in developing nations, and more common among white people than those of African or Asian descent; this holds true in the United States as well.[100] In the study by de Robles et al,[101] limitations of the available studies suggested there is a need for better and more accurate incidence and prevalence studies from multiple world regions in a standardized manner to accurately address the global nature of the challenges in neuro-oncology. Another study, based on tumor registries, also reported variations when comparing Europe and Asia but likewise showed increasing incidence in South America over time.[102]

Germ-cell tumors are more common in Japan and account for 2.7% of total CNS tumors[103]; the equivalent CBTRUS provides a figure of 0.6% in the United States for an equivalent period.[104] Similar findings were noted in a pediatric Korean study using the Korea Central Cancer Registry.

Some of these differences may be due to underascertainment. In certain developing countries, access to CT and MRI technology may vary dramatically depending on socioeconomic factors and urban versus rural settings. Also, there likely are genomic differences that affect the incidence of different tumor types.

PATHOLOGY

WHO has established classification systems for multiple tumor types with the aim of providing a system of classifying and grading tumors in a manner that is accepted and can be implemented worldwide. In the most recent classification in 2016,[7] the inclusion of molecular findings was introduced, given the strength of the data showing the importance of this information for prognosis and treatment. However, the ability to perform testing is limited in developing countries.

TREATMENT OPTIONS

There are significant variations of access to therapies around the world. Specialized neurosurgery with access to neuronavigation is widely available in Western countries, as well as many Asian countries, but is not universal. Radiation techniques using linear accelerators are also readily available, although specialized facilities such as those with proton RT are much more limited. Access to temozolomide is now more readily available given the availability of generics.

The implementation of therapies can vary widely and is significantly limited in less developed settings. Evidence is limited; however, presentations at the combined ASNO/Asian Society of Neuro-Oncology/Cooperative Trials Group for Neuro-Oncology meeting in 2016[105] described significant limitations of availability of resources in Thailand, the Philippines, Malaysia, and Indonesia.

The work of de Roxas et al[106] on the diagnosis and management of CNS tumors at Philippines General Hospital is illustrative. Of patients with CNS tumor who were admitted to hospital, 56% had surgery alone. The largest group had meningioma (45%); 80% of patients had nonmalignant tumors and 30% of patients did not undergo biopsy. Of the 22.5% planned to have combination therapy with chemoradiotherapy, only 13.1% actually received the planned treatment. This is likely in part due to the inability to pay for such therapies. Many patients may not have been seen by either the neurology or neurosurgery teams. In addition, there is also evidence that Asian patients are more sensitive to the myelosuppressive effects of nitrosourea-based therapies and require a lower dose with increased cycle length.[107]

The difficulties noted in Africa were addressed by Ngulde et al.[108] Epidemiology data are limited, and the risk associated with HIV infections or environmental exposure is not well documented. In addition, many patients do not consult doctors trained in Western medicine. Traditional medical practitioners are more numerous and more readily available. Traditional beliefs about cancer also affect patients accessing modern hospitals. Neurosurgeons are particularly uncommon, and so tissue-based diagnostics are also limited, as are access to modern RT and chemotherapy.

Newer therapies such as TTFs are only available in certain countries—predominantly the United States, Israel, Japan, and countries in Europe. It is not available, for example, in Australia, even for those willing to pay for it, because TTF requires significant support infrastructure and the health economics of this treatment remain controversial. The National Comprehensive Cancer Network guidelines[109] include a recommendation for the use of TTF in combination with chemoradiotherapy in those with supratentorial glioblastoma, but TTF is not recommended in the published European Association of Neuro-Oncology guidelines.[110] A cost-benefit analysis suggested that the incremental cost-effectiveness ratio expressed as cost per life-years gained was $613,198.03, based on costs in the French health care system.[111]

19

LEUKEMIAS AND OTHER MYELOID NEOPLASMS

Mark R Litzow, MD, and Aditi Shastri, MD

Recent Updates

Acute Myeloid Leukemia Updates

- Venetoclax, a Bcl-2 inhibitor, is approved for the treatment of newly diagnosed acute myeloid leukemia (AML) in combination with hypomethylating agents (ie, azacitidine, decitabine) or low-dose cytarabine for patients ≥ 75 years old or who are unfit for standard induction therapy. (DiNardo CD, *Blood* 2019)
- Glasdegib, a hedgehog pathway inhibitor, is approved for the treatment of newly diagnosed AML in combination with low-dose cytarabine for patients ≥ 75 years old or who are unfit for standard induction therapy on the basis of an improved overall survival (OS) benefit. (Savona MR, *Clin Cancer Res* 2018; Cortes JE, *Am J Hematol* 2018)
- *IDH1* mutations occur in 6% to 10% of patients with relapsed/refractory (R/R) AML. The inhibitor of mutant IDH1, ivosidenib, is approved for the treatment of R/R AML with an *IDH1* mutation as detected by a US Food and Drug Administration (FDA)-approved companion diagnostic test on the basis of the demonstration of complete response with or without partial hematologic recovery and conversion from transfusion dependence to independence. (DiNardo CD, *N Engl J Med* 2018)
- *IDH2* mutations occur in 10% to 15% of patients with R/R AML. The IDH2 inhibitor enasidenib blocks the enzymatic activity of mutant IDH2 and lowers the levels of the oncometabolite 2-hydroxyglutarate. Enasidenib is approved for the treatment of R/R AML with an *IDH2* mutation as detected by an FDA-approved test. (Amatangelo MD, *Blood* 2017; Stein EM, *Blood* 2017)
- Gilteritinib, a highly selective FLT3/AXL inhibitor, is approved for the treatment of R/R AML with an *FLT3* mutation as detected by an FDA-approved test based on a high overall response rate of up to 52% (Perl AE, *Lancet Oncol* 2017). The FDA approval was based on the overall response rate (complete response plus complete response with partial recovery of blood cells) of 21% with gilteritinib in the phase III study of gilteritinib versus salvage chemotherapy. (unpublished data)

Myelodysplastic Syndromes Updates

- Luspatercept is a TGF-β inhibitor. A phase III, randomized, double-blinded study comparing luspatercept with placebo in patients with low- to intermediate-risk myelodysplastic syndrome, anemia, and ring sideroblasts and *SF3B1* mutations (90%) showed a reduced transfusion burden in patients treated with luspatercept (37.9% *v* 13.2%; $P < .0001$). This agent is currently awaiting FDA approval. (Fenaux P, *Blood* 2019; Fenaux P, *N Engl J Med* 2020)

Myeloproliferative Neoplasms Updates

- Fedratinib, a JAK2 selective inhibitor, has been approved by the FDA for the treatment of intermediate-2 or high–risk myelofibrosis. Oral fedratinib given daily at a dose of 400 mg achieved a splenic response (≥ 35% reduction in splenic volume) in 46 of evaluable patients (55%; 95% CI, 44 to 66). Wernicke's encephalopathy is a rare and fatal complication of the treatment. (Harrison

CN, *Lancet Haematol* 2017; https://www.fda.gov/drugs/resources-information-approved-drugs/fda-approves-fedratinib-myelofibrosis)

Acute Lymphoblastic Leukemia

- In adults with B-cell acute lymphoblastic leukemia (B-ALL) who are positive for minimal residual disease (MRD) after chemotherapy, treatment with blinatumomab converted 78% of patients to MRD negativity and patients who were MRD responders had improved relapse-free survival and OS compared with MRD nonresponders. (Gökbuget N, *Blood* 2018)
- A phase II, single-arm global study of the chimeric antigen receptor T-cell therapy tisagenlecleucel was conducted with 75 children and young adults with CD19+ R/R B-ALL and demonstrated an 81% MRD negative remission rate with event-free survival and OS rates of 73% and 90%, respectively, at 6 months and 50% and 76%, respectively, at 12 months. (Maude SL, *N Engl J Med* 2018)
- A recently published US intergroup trial confirmed that use of a pediatric regimen for adolescents and young adults with acute lymphoblastic leukemia up to age 40 years was feasible and effective, resulting in improved survival rates compared with historical controls. (Stock W, *Blood* 2019)

Chronic Lymphocytic Leukemia

- There are three randomized, phase III trials testing ibrutinib with or without an anti-CD20 monoclonal antibody in comparison with conventional chemoimmunotherapy in treatment-naïve (TN) chronic lymphocytic leukemia (CLL):
  - The ECOG-ACRIN study compared ibrutinib plus rituximab (IR) with fludarabine, cyclophosphamide, and rituximab (FCR) in younger patients with TN CLL (age < 70 years). (Shanafelt T, *N Engl J Med* 2019)
  - The Alliance study was a three-arm trial comparing bendamustine plus rituximab (BR) with IR or ibrutinib alone in older patients with TN CLL (age ≥ 65 years). (Woyach JA, *N Engl J Med* 2018)
  - The ILLUMINATE trial compared IR with chlorambucil plus obinutuzumab in older patients with TN CLL. (Moreno C, *Lancet Oncol* 2018)

  All three studies demonstrated superior progression-free survival (PFS) in the ibrutinib-based arms compared with conventional chemoimmunotherapy. In the Alliance study, there was no PFS difference between two ibrutinib arms with or without rituximab. These results establish ibrutinib as effective first-line therapy for CLL regardless of age. Ibrutinib has been approved as monotherapy for CLL and can be given as any line of therapy.
- Duvelisib, a dual inhibitor of PI3K-δ and γ isoforms, is approved for the treatment of R/R CLL after at least two prior lines of therapy, on the basis of the demonstration of improved PFS compared with ofatumumumab in a randomized phase III trial. (Flinn IW, *Blood* 2018)

OVERVIEW

The term "leukemia" describes a number of related cancers characterized by increased growth and/or impaired maturation of the blood-forming organs. Leukemias are classically defined by their rapidity of growth (acute *v* chronic) and by the origin of the healthy cell the leukemia most resembles (myeloid *v* lymphoid). Thus, the four major forms of leukemia are acute myeloid leukemia (AML), acute lymphoblastic leukemia (ALL), chronic myeloid leukemia (CML), and chronic lymphocytic leukemia (CLL). Other leukemias include some of the mature B-cell, T-cell, or natural killer (NK)-cell neoplasms such as B-cell prolymphocytic leukemia, hairy cell leukemia, and the chronic T-cell leukemias. Approximately 61,780 new cases of leukemia were expected in the United States in 2019, with 22,840 leukemia-related deaths (Table 19-1; Fig 19-1).[1,2]

In addition to these four major forms of leukemia, we also discuss in this chapter the myelodysplastic syndromes (MDSs) and the myeloproliferative neoplasms (MPNs), which, together with AML, encompass disorders WHO classifies as myeloid neoplasms.[3] MDS is a heterogeneous group of clonal stem cell disorders characterized by peripheral-blood cytopenias and an inherent tendency for leukemic transformation, with an estimated 30,000 to 40,000 new cases occurring annually in the United States. MPNs are clonal stem cell diseases with proliferation of one or more hematopoietic cell lineages. Besides CML, the classic MPNs include polycythemia vera (PV), essential thrombocythemia (ET), and primary myelofibrosis (PMF).[3,4] Chronic neutrophilic leukemia, chronic eosinophilic leukemia, and unclassifiable MPNs are other diseases currently recognized by WHO as MPNs. Mastocytosis is now considered a separate entity in the WHO 2016 classification.[3] Several other entities, such as chronic myelomonocytic leukemia, atypical CML, and juvenile myelomonocytic leukemia show myelodysplastic and myeloproliferative features and are classified as MDS/MPN neoplasms, as are MDSs/MPNs with ring sideroblasts and thrombocytosis and unclassifiable MDS/MPN. All B- and T-cell subtypes and CLL, including classic CLL of B-cell origin and the rarer subtypes of lymphocytic leukemia, including hairy cell leukemia, prolymphocytic leukemia, and chronic T-cell/NK cell leukemias, also are discussed (Table 19-2).[3]

ETIOLOGY

The cause of leukemia is usually unknown. However, in addition to a familial/genetic predisposition in some individuals, exposure to certain infectious pathogens, radiation, chemicals, and chemotherapeutic agents has been associated with an increased incidence of leukemia (Table 19-3).

GENETIC PREDISPOSITION

Genetic predisposition for the development of leukemia is well established. Single germline mutations in several genes (eg, *GATA2, RUNX1, CEBPA, SRP72)* have been identified as causes of familial nonsyndromic MDS/AML predisposition syndromes.[5]

Type of Leukemia	No. of New Cases	No. of Deaths
Acute lymphocytic leukemia	5,930	1,500
Chronic lymphocytic leukemia	20,720	3,930
Acute myeloid leukemia	21,450	10,920
Chronic myeloid leukemia	8,990	1,140
Other leukemia	4,690	5,350

Table 19-1 **2018 US Leukemia Estimates**[98]

Syndromes characterized by defective DNA repair, such as Fanconi anemia, ataxia telangiectasia, and Bloom syndrome, also have an increased incidence of acute leukemia.[6] Similarly, bone marrow–failure syndromes associated with ribosomal abnormalities, including Diamond-Blackfan anemia and Schwachman-Diamond syndrome, also have an increased incidence of acute leukemia. Dyskeratosis congenita is due to mutations of the telomerase complex and associated with reticular rash, mucosal leukoplakia, and dyskeratosis of the nails. Acute leukemia also may develop in patients with dyskeratosis congenita. The same is true for germline mutations in *TP53* and abnormalities in chromosome number, such as those associated with Klinefelter and Down syndromes. A high rate of concordant leukemia has long been noted in identical twins, particularly infants. Although concordant leukemia often was thought to reflect a shared, inherited, or genetic susceptibility, molecular analyses have provided evidence that leukemias from twin pairs have a common clonal origin, with initiation of leukemia in one twin fetus and the spread of clonal progeny to the cotwin via vascular anastomoses and the need for additional postnatal exposures and/or genetic events to produce clinical disease.[7]

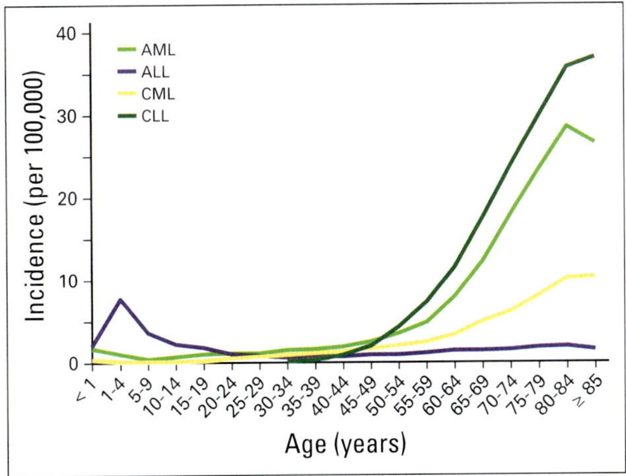

Fig. 19-1 Incidence of acute and chronic leukemias in the United States.

Surveillance and Results, 2000 SEER Cancer Registry estimates of age-specific incidence rates of acute myeloid leukemia (AML), acute lymphoblastic leukemia (ALL), chronic myeloid leukemia (CML), and chronic lymphocytic leukemia (CLL) in the United States, SEER 18 areas, 2009–2013. Rates are given per 100,000 and are age-adjusted to the 2000 US standard population.[2]

ONCOGENIC VIRUSES

Human T-cell lymphotropic virus type 1 is a causative agent of adult T-cell leukemia and lymphoma. This enveloped, single-stranded RNA virus is found in geographic clusters in southwestern Japan, the Caribbean, intertropical Africa, the Middle East, South America, and Papua New Guinea. It spreads horizontally by sexual contact or through blood products or vertically from mother to fetus. Although it is endemic in these geographic areas, adult T-cell leukemia will develop in only 3% to 5% of patients infected with the virus and has a very long latency period, estimated at 30 years or more.[8] Epstein-Barr virus is associated with the endemic African form of Burkitt lymphoma and leukemia.[9] The immunodeficiency-related type of Burkitt lymphoma is seen most often in patients with HIV infection and is more common when the CD4 T-cell count is $> 200/\mu L$—that is, early in the progression of HIV infection. The association of HIV with the endemic form of Burkitt lymphoma is less clear.[9]

RADIATION

Ionizing radiation is leukemogenic.[10] The incidences of AML, CML, and ALL were increased in individuals who received radiation therapy for ankylosing spondylitis and in survivors of the atomic bomb blasts at Hiroshima and Nagasaki. The highest rates of leukemia were associated with higher doses of radiation, particularly if the radiation was absorbed over a shorter time. Younger individuals seem more susceptible to the leukemogenic effects of radiation. The incidence of leukemia peaks between 5 and 10 years after radiation exposure, regardless of patient age. The incidence of chromosomal aberrations has been reported to be higher than expected for individuals living in areas with high natural background radiation (often because of radon), but a higher incidence of acute leukemia has not been consistently observed.

Concern has been raised about the possible leukemogenic effects of extremely low-frequency, nonionizing electromagnetic fields emitted by high-energy wires and step-down transformers. Several studies have been conducted with mixed results, and if any leukemogenic effect of such radiation exists, the magnitude of the effect is likely small.[11]

Table 19-2 **2016 World Health Organization Classification of Acute Leukemia**[3]

Type of Leukemia	Classification
Acute myeloid leukemia and related neoplasms	AML with recurrent genetic abnormalities
	AML with t(8;21)(q22;q22.1); *RUNX1-RUNX1T1*
	AML with inv(16)(p13.1q22) or t(16;16)(p13.1;q22); *CBFB-MYH11*
	APL with *PML-RARA*
	AML with t(9;11)(p21.3;q23.3); *MLLT3-KMT2A*
	AML with t(6;9)(p23;q34.1); *DEK-NUP214*
	AML with inv(3)(q21.3q26.2) or t(3;3)(q21.3;q26.2); *GATA2, MECOM*
	AML (megakaryoblastic) with t(1;22)(p13.3;q13.3); *RBM15-MKL1*
	Provisional entity: AML with BCR-ABL1
	AML with mutated *NPM1*
	AML with biallelic mutations of *CEBPA*
	Provisional entity: AML with mutated RUNX1
	AML with myelodysplasia-related changes
	Therapy-related myeloid neoplasms
	AML, NOS
	AML with minimal differentiation
	AML without maturation
	AML with maturation
	Acute myelomonocytic leukemia
	Acute monoblastic/monocytic leukemia
	Pure erythroid leukemia
	Acute megakaryoblastic leukemia
	Acute basophilic leukemia
	Acute panmyelosis with myelofibrosis
	Myeloid sarcoma
	Myeloid proliferations related to Down syndrome
	Transient abnormal myelopoiesis
	Myeloid leukemia associated with Down syndrome
Blastic plasmacytoid dendritic cell neoplasm	
Acute leukemias of ambiguous lineage	Acute undifferentiated leukemia
	MPAL with t(9;22)(q34.1;q11.2); *BCR-ABL1*
	MPAL with t(v;11q23.3); *KMT2A* rearranged
	MPAL, B/myeloid, NOS
	MPAL, T/myeloid, NOS

Table 19-2 continued

Type of Leukemia	Classification
B-lymphoblastic leukemia/lymphoma	B-lymphoblastic leukemia/lymphoma, NOS
	B-lymphoblastic leukemia/lymphoma with recurrent genetic abnormalities
	B-lymphoblastic leukemia/lymphoma with t(9;22)(q34.1;q11.2); *BCR-ABL1*
	B-lymphoblastic leukemia/lymphoma with t(v;11q23.3); *KMT2A* rearranged
	B-lymphoblastic leukemia/lymphoma with t(12;21)(p13.2;q22.1) *ETV6-RUNX1*
	B-lymphoblastic leukemia/lymphoma with hyperdiploidy
	B-lymphoblastic leukemia/lymphoma with hypodiploidy
	B-lymphoblastic leukemia/lymphoma with t(5;14)(q31.1;q32.3); *IL3-IGH*
	B-lymphoblastic leukemia/lymphoma with t(1;19)(q23;p13.3); *TCF3-PBX1*
	Provisional entity: B-lymphoblastic leukemia/lymphoma, BCR-ABL1-like
	Provisional entity: B-lymphoblastic leukemia/lymphoma with iAML21
T-lymphoblastic leukemia/lymphoma	*Provisional entity: early T-cell precursor lymphoblastic leukemia*
Provisional entity: natural killer cell lymphoblastic leukemia/lymphoma	

Abbreviations: AML, acute myeloid leukemia; APL, acute promyelocyte leukemia; MPAL, mixed phenotype acute leukemia; NOS, not otherwise specified.

CHEMICALS

Extensive occupational exposure to benzene and benzene-containing compounds may lead to marrow damage that eventually can manifest as aplastic anemia, MDS, or AML.[12] Benzene is widely used in industry, particularly as starting material for chemicals used to make plastics, resins, synthetic fibers, dyes, detergents, drugs, and pesticides, and is a component of crude oil, gasoline, and cigarette smoke. Other associations between occupational exposure to chemicals and subsequent leukemia are not as persuasive. Most studies have found a small but consistent increase in AML development among cigarette smokers.[13,14]

DRUG- AND THERAPY-RELATED LEUKEMIAS

Therapy with antineoplastic agents is a major identifiable cause of acute leukemia, with alkylating agents being most commonly associated with therapy-related leukemia.[15] Among the various alkylating agents, melphalan and the nitrosoureas seem to be particularly associated with increased risk; however, all alkylating agents are likely leukemogenic, with an increased incidence of leukemia observed after prolonged exposure and dose-intense regimens.

The leukemias associated with alkylating agents often present initially as MDS before progressing to AML; they have no other distinct morphologic features and, on cytogenetic examination, frequently exhibit whole or partial loss of chromosomes 5 or 7 or, less often, trisomy 8. These leukemias typically develop 4 to 6 years after chemotherapy. Patients treated with topoisomerase II inhibitors also are at risk for therapy-related leukemia. In contrast to leukemias associated with alkylating agents, disease caused by topoisomerase II inhibitors tends to have a shorter latency period (1 to 2 years), lacks a myelodysplastic phase, carries a monocytic morphology, and frequently involves 11q23.3 abnormalities; less commonly, translocations of 21q22 are involved.[16] Acute promyelocytic leukemia has been associated with prior exposure to leukemogenic agents as well. Patients with lymphoma who undergo autologous hematopoietic stem cell transplantation (HSCT) are at increased risk for leukemia, with a cumulative incidence as high as 10%.

Overall, approximately 50% of patients with therapy-related neoplasms have adverse cytogenetics, and approximately one-third have *TP53* mutations, which partly explains why these neoplasms tend to have lower therapeutic response rates than do de novo disease.[17,18]

KEY POINTS

- Leukemias, MDS, and MPNs encompass a diverse group of clonal diseases of the hematopoietic system.
- Familial/genetic predisposition and exposure to certain infectious pathogens, radiation, chemicals, and chemotherapeutic agents have been associated with an increased incidence of these hematopoietic neoplasms.

Table 19-3 **Etiologic Considerations in Genetic Predisposition of Leukemia and Related Disorders**
Possible Etiologies
Germline mutations (eg, in *GATA2*, *RUNX1*, *CEBPA*, and *SRP72*)
Fanconi anemia
Ataxia telangiectasia
Bloom syndrome
Diamond-Blackfan anemia
Schwachman-Diamond syndrome
Dyskeratosis congenita
Li-Fraumeni syndrome
Klinefelter syndrome
Down syndrome
Oncogenic viruses
Human T-cell lymphotropic virus type 1
Epstein-Barr virus
Ionizing radiation
Environmental chemicals
Benzene
Cigarette smoke
Chemotherapy/radiotherapy
Alkylating agents
Topoisomerase II inhibitors
Radiation therapy

ACUTE MYELOID LEUKEMIA

AML arises from malignant transformation of an immature hematopoietic precursor followed by clonal proliferation and accumulation of the transformed cells,[19] which typically display myeloid-specific markers. AML can be classified according to cytogenetic and molecular abnormalities, which have important prognostic relevance (Table 19-4). The goal of AML therapy is to develop a treatment plan tailored to the molecular characteristics of the disease while also taking into consideration individual patient comorbidities and preferences.

PATHOBIOLOGY OF AML

AML is a clonally derived hematologic malignancy that originates from an aberrant hematopoietic stem cell (HSC) that has an increased capacity for self-renewal and profoundly altered patterns of differentiation. A pioneering study by Fialkow et al[20] established the clonal nature of AML in humans. Since then, understanding of the biology of the disease has greatly expanded.

The current understanding is that disturbed gene expression in HSCs causes a differentiation block and increased self-renewing capacity, which give rise to a leukemic stem cell (LSC).[21,22] The clonal evolution of AML starts from the LSCs where founder or so-called driver mutations arise that initiate the leukemogenesis process but lack the entire arsenal of mutations required for leukemogenesis. Genes such as *DNMT3A*, *TET2*, and *ASXL1* involved in the regulation of DNA modification and of the chromatin state are present in the preleukemic stem and progenitor cells.[23-26] Progression to AML is accompanied by a stepwise accumulation of additional mutations, including those assumed to be part of the pathogenesis of the disease (the drivers) and random mutations (so-called passengers) that confer a strong proliferative advantage to the LSCs and the blasts derived therein. The acquisition of individual mutations and subsequent clonal evolution are highly dynamic processes. This is indicated by studies of relapsed AML, in which typically either the founding clone gained additional mutations and evolved into the relapsed clone, or a subclone present at diagnosis survived chemotherapy, acquired additional mutations, and expanded at relapse.[24,27-29] Although debulking chemotherapy helps reduce the percentage of blasts, newer targeted therapies are often directed toward the mutations that ensure the LSCs survival and proliferative advantage.

Advancement of genomic profiling has expanded our understanding of AML and transformed treatment approaches. A large-scale genomic analysis of > 1,500 AML patients revealed 11 molecularly defined subgroups with distinct biologic mechanisms and survival.[30] These findings, along with development of targeted therapy, reclassify disease subgroups by AML-related genetic changes, inform treatment decisions (ie, *FLT3*, *IDH1/2*), and provide clues for the ordinal nature of mutations (ie, *DNMT3A*, followed by *NPM1* and another AML disease allele). In the past, patients were routinely profiled for the

Table 19-4 **Cytogenetic Risk and Treatment Outcomes in Younger Adults with Newly Diagnosed Acute Myeloid Leukemia**[51,52]

Cytogenetic Risk	CR Rate (%)		5-Year Relapse Risk (%)		5-Year Survival (%)	
	SWOG	MRC/NCRI	SWOG	MRC/NCRI	SWOG	MRC/NCRI
Favorable	84	91	–	35	55	65
Intermediate	76	86	–	51	38	41
Unfavorable	55	63	–	76	11	14

Abbreviations: –, data not available; CR, complete remission; MRC, Medical Research Council; NCRI, National Cancer Research Institute; SWOG, Southwest Oncology Group.

presence of mutations in *FLT3*, *CEBPA*, *NPM1*, and *TP53* genes.[31] With several targeted-therapy agents approved for the treatment of AML in the period 2016 through 2018, a more expansive role for molecular profiling for assessment and treatment of active disease as well as minimal residual disease (MRD) is anticipated.

PROGNOSIS

AML is highly heterogeneous, and responses to AML therapy vary substantially among individual patients. Many factors have been independently associated with failure to achieve remission with intensive chemotherapy and/or with shortened survival; these include older age, poor performance status, prior cytotoxic chemotherapy or radiation therapy, disease evolution from an antecedent hematologic disorder (eg, "secondary" AML), and increased WBC count.

In contrast, extramedullary disease, although common, is not an independent prognostic factor.[32] AML can be classified into good, intermediate, and poor prognosis groups on the basis of cytogenetics and molecular profiling of the disease (Table 19-5).

The following paragraphs provide an idea of some of the important cytogenetic and molecular features of each category mentioned in Table 19-5.

Good and Intermediate Prognosis AML

Of patients younger than 60 years who have leukemia, core binding factor (CBF) leukemias make up 10% to 15% of cases and have a favorable prognosis along with acute promyelocytic leukemia. The CBF leukemias consist of t(8,21) causing a fusion gene *RUNX1-RUNX1T1*, and inv (16) or t(16,16), due to the fusion of *CBFB* to *MYH11* t(8,21), is frequently accompanied by loss of the sex chromosome (particularly Y) or deletion of chromosome 9 (del 9q). Inv(16) is accompanied by trisomies, such as 22, 8, and 21.

Of patients with AML patients aged 16 to 60 years, 35% to 40% have a normal karyotype at presentation. These patients may have accompanying mutations in *FLT3*, *NPM1*, *CEBPA*, *IDH1*, *IDH2*, *ASXL1*, and *TP53* in validated assays and a host of other mutations on comprehensive profiling. Prognostic and therapeutic significance of these mutations are presented in Table 19-5. *NPM1* mutations occur concurrently with *FLT3*-

Table 19-5 **2017 European LeukemiaNet Cytogenetic/Molecular Risk Stratification of Acute Myeloid Leukemia**[34]

Risk Level	Subset
Favorable	t(8;21)(q22;q22.1); *RUNX1-RUNX1T1*
	inv(16)(p13.1q22) or t(16;16)(p13.1;q22); *CBFB-MYH11*
	Mutated *NPM1* without *FLT3*-ITD or with *FLT3*-ITD^{low+}
	Biallelic mutated *CEBPA*
Intermediate	Mutated *NPM1* and *FLT3*-ITD^{high§}
	Wild-type *NPM1* and *FLT3-ITD* (normal karyotype)
	Wild type *NPM1* without *FLT3*-ITD or with *FLT3*-ITD^{low} (without adverse-risk genetic lesions) t(9;11)(p21.3;q23.3); *MLLT3-KMT2A*$^{\#}$
	Cytogenetic abnormalities not classified as favorable or adverse
Adverse	t(6;9)(p23;q34.1); *DEK-NUP214*
	t(v;11)(v;q23.3); *KTM2A* rearranged
	t(9;22)(q34.1;q11.2); *BCR-ABL1*
	inv(3)(q21.3q26.2) or t(3;3)(q21.3;q26.2);
	GATA2, *MECOM (EVI1)*
	−5 or del(5q); −7; −17/abnl(17p)
	Complex karyotype*, monosomal karyotype
	Wild-type *NPM1* and *FLT3*-ITD^{high}
	Mutated *RUNX1*^
	Mutated *ASXL1*^
	Mutated *TP53*

+Low: low allelic ratio (< 0.5).
§High: high allelic ratio (≥ 0.5).
#Takes precedence over rare, concurrent adverse-risk gene mutations.
*Three or more unrelated chromosomal abnormalities in the absence of one of the WHO-designated recurring translocations or inversions—that is, t(8;21), inv(16) or t(16;16), t(9;11), t(v;11)(v;q23.3), t(6;9), or inv(3) or t(3;3).
^These markers should not be used as an adverse prognostic marker if they co-occur with favorable-risk AML subtypes.

ITD in 60% of patients with *FLT3* mutations. *NPM1* mutations occur by themselves in 30% of cytogenetically normal AML and are associated with a good prognosis.

IDH1 mutations occur in 6% to 10% of relapsed/refractory (R/R) AML. *IDH2* mutations occur in 10% to 15% of R/R AML. These mutations result in the accumulation of the oncometabolite 2-hydroxygluterate. The prognostic relevance of these mutations is unclear and other co-occurring mutations affect patient prognosis.

Approximately one-third of patients with newly diagnosed AML have mutations in the fms-like tyrosine kinase 3 (*FLT3*) gene. Some 20% to 25% of patients with AML harbor the FLT3 internal tandem duplication (ITD) gene, which is associated with a more proliferative phenotype, increased blast percentage, a higher risk of relapse, and inferior OS compared with FLT3 wild-type disease after combination chemotherapy. Five percent to 10% of patients newly diagnosed AML have an FLT3–tyrosine kinase domain (TKD) mutation. The prognostic impact of FLT3-TKD mutations is currently unclear. The presence of a coexisting NPM1 mutation is associated with a decreased risk of relapse and improved survival in FLT3-ITD mutated AML and especially patients with a low FLT3-ITD allele burden. The allelic ratio of FLT3-ITD to WT-FLT3 strongly influences outcomes after induction chemotherapy that does not include an FLT3 inhibitor. A ratio of ≥ 0.5 is associated with a worse survival compared with a lower ratio.

Poor-Prognosis AML

TP53 mutations, although rare in AML, have gained importance because they have been found in 70% of AML cases with complex cytogenetic abnormalities and are an independent poor prognostic factor in this AML subset.[33,34] Half of AML cases have an abnormal karyotype divided between the poor-risk karyotypes and the favorable-risk CBF translocations and t(15; 17) of acute promyelocytic leukemia (APL). The group of patients with an abnormal karyotype includes patients with inv(3)(q21q26)/t(3;3)(q21;q26), *MLL* rearrangements other than t(9;11), −5, −7, del(5q), del(7q), abnormalities involving chromosome 17, and a complex karyotype. Patients with complex, monosomal karyotypes typically have the worst prognosis of all the karyotypes.[34,35]

CLINICAL PRESENTATION

Pathophysiologically, the leukemia stem cells give rise to progeny that do not differentiate and continue to proliferate in an uncontrolled fashion. The resulting clonal population of immature myeloid cells then outcompete and/or suppress normal hematopoietic cells in the bone marrow. In some patients, particularly those with myelomonocytic or monocytic leukemias, AML cells accumulate in extramedullary sites (termed "myeloid sarcomas" or "chloromas") such as lymph nodes, spleen, liver, skin (leukemia cutis), gums, or, in 1% to 3% of cases, the CNS.[32]

The signs and symptoms of AML result from decreased normal hematopoiesis and infiltration of healthy organs by leukemic blasts and include anemia and thrombocytopenia, and, consequently, fatigue, dyspnea, easy bruising, or overt bleeding. WBC count may be elevated, normal, or low, but most patients will have granulocytopenia, and one-third have signs of substantial or life-threatening infection.

DIAGNOSIS

Table 19-6 lists tests and procedures that are part of the routine workup of a patient with suspected AML. Examination of the peripheral blood and a bone marrow aspirate are part of the routine diagnostic workup of a patient with suspected AML.[34] A bone marrow trephine biopsy is not routinely required but should be obtained if the aspirate is dilute, hypocellular, or not aspirable. A lumbar puncture is required for patients with clinical symptoms suspicious for CNS involvement. Cytogenetic and molecular studies are essential for risk stratification. At a minimum, mutational testing for *c-KIT*, *FLT3*-ITD/*TKD*, *NPM1*, *CEBPA*, *IDH1*, *IDH2*, and *TP53* should be obtained. Multiplex gene panels and next-generation sequencing analysis should be used to obtain a more comprehensive prognostic assessment when possible.[30]

The 2016 revision of the WHO classification categorizes a myeloid neoplasm as AML if ≥ 20% blasts are present in the peripheral blood or bone marrow when the disease occurs de novo or evolves from a previously diagnosed MDS or MDS/MPN or a blast transformation from a previously diagnosed MPN, or if a myeloid sarcoma is present. Exceptions to this general rule include neoplasms with t(8;21) (q22;q22.1), inv(16)(p13.1q22) or t(16;16)(p13.1;q22), or APL that are considered AML regardless of the blast count (Table 19-7).

Morphology and Immunohistochemistry

AML cells are typically 12 to 20 μm in diameter and have discrete nuclear chromatin, multiple nucleoli, and azurophilic granules in the cytoplasm (Fig 19-2). Specific patterns of reactivity with immunohistochemical stains, particularly myeloperoxidase and nonspecific esterase, can be used to assign AML blasts to one (or more) cell lineage(s). Although the French-American-British Cooperative Group classified AML on the basis of morphology and immunohistochemistry,[36] cytochemical stains have largely been replaced by immunophenotypic analyses of AML cells.

Immunophenotype

Most cases of AML express antigens characteristic of neutrophilic or monocytic differentiation, including CD13, CD15, CD33, CD64, CD117, myeloperoxidase, and CD34.[37] Leukemias with monocytic features express CD14 together with other monocyte-associated antigens. Erythroid leukemias frequently express CD36, CD71, and CD235a (glycophorin A), whereas megakaryocytic leukemias express CD41 and CD61. In 10% to 20% of cases, the AML blasts also express antigens, which are usually restricted to B- or T-cell lineages, especially CD2, CD7, CD19, and CD56.

Treatment

Treatment of AML typically involves an induction chemotherapy phase and a postremission or consolidation phase. Age, comorbidities, performance status, organ function impairment, the

Table 19-6 **Tests and Procedures for Patients With Acute Myeloid Leukemia**[34]
Diagnostic tests
CBC count and differential count
Bone marrow aspirate
Bone marrow trephine biopsy[a]
Immunophenotyping
Genetic analyses
Cytogenetics[b]
Screening for gene mutations including[c]
NPM1, CEBPA, RUNX1, FLT3, TP53, ASXL1
Screening for gene rearrangements[d]
PML-RARA, CBFB-MYH11, RUNX1-RUNX1T1, BCR-ABL1, other fusion genes (if available)
Additional tests/procedures at diagnosis
Demographics and medical historye
Detailed family history[f]
Patient bleeding history[g]
Performance status (ECOG/WHO score)
Analysis of comorbidities
Biochemistry, coagulation tests, urine analysis[h]
Serum pregnancy test[i]
Information on oocyte and sperm cryopreservation[j]
Eligibility assessment for allogeneic HSCT (including HLA typing)[k]
Hepatitis A, B, C; HIV-1 testing
Chest radiograph, 12-lead electrocardiogram, and echocardiography or MUGA (on indication)
Lumbar puncture[l]
Biobanking[m]
Sensitive assessment of response by RT-qPCR or MFC[o]
RT-qPCR[o,p] for *NPM1* mutation, *CBFB-MYH11, RUNX1-RUNX1T1, BCR-ABL1*, other fusion genes (if available)[n]
MFC[p,q]

Abbreviations: CMV, cytomegalovirus; ECOG, Eastern Cooperative Oncology Group; HLA, human leukocyte antigen; HSCT, hematopoietic cell transplantation; MFC, multiparameter flow cytometry; MUGA, multigated acquisition; RT-qPCR, real-time quantitative polymerase chain reaction.

[a]In patients with a dry spinal tap (*punctio sicca*).

[b]Results from cytogenetics should be obtained preferably within 5 to 7 days. At least 20 bone marrow metaphases are needed to define a normal karyotype and recommended to describe an abnormal karyotype. Abnormal karyotypes may be diagnosed from blood specimens.

[c]Results from *NPM1* and *FLT3* mutational screening should be available within 48 to 72 hours (at least in patients eligible for intensive chemotherapy), and results from additional molecular genetics within the first treatment cycle. Screening for gene mutations is an evolving field of research; screening for single genes may be replaced by gene panel diagnostics.

[d]Screening for gene rearrangements should be performed if rapid information is needed for recommendation of suitable therapy, if chromosome morphology is of poor quality, or if there is typical morphology but the suspected cytogenetic abnormality is not present.

[e]Including race or ethnicity, prior exposure to toxic agents, prior malignancy, therapy for prior malignancy, information on smoking.

[f]Thorough family history needed to identify potential myeloid neoplasms with germline predisposition.

[g]History of bleeding episodes may inform cases of myeloid neoplasms with germline predisposition and preexisting platelet disorders.

[h]Biochemistry: levels of glucose, sodium, potassium, calcium, creatinine, aspartate amino transferase, alanine amino transferase, alkaline phosphatase, lactate dehydrogenase, bilirubin, urea, total protein, uric acid, total cholesterol, total triglycerides, and creatinine phosphokinase. Coagulation tests: prothrombin time; international normalized ratio, where indicated; activated partial thromboplastin time. Urine analysis: pH, and levels of glucose, erythrocytes, leukocytes, protein, and nitrite.

[i]In women with childbearing potential.

[j]Cryopreservation to be done in accordance with the wish of the patient.

[k]HLA typing and CMV testing should be performed in those patients eligible for allogeneic HSCT.

[l]Required in patients with clinical symptoms suspicious of CNS involvement; patient should be evaluated by imaging study for intracranial bleeding, leptomeningeal disease, and mass lesion; lumbar puncture considered optional in other settings (eg, high white blood cell count).

[m]Pretreatment leukemic bone marrow and blood sample; for further optional storing, see "Biobanking."

[n]Sensitive assessment of response can be performed at early time points, for example, following induction and consolidation courses to assess remission status and determine kinetics of disease response, and sequentially beyond consolidation to detect impending morphologic relapse. No generally applicable time points can be defined because kinetics of MRD response differs by treatment given, marker analyzed, and method used.

[o]Monitoring of response by RT-qPCR recommended in clinical trials and clinical practice.

[p]Sensitivity of response assessment varies by method used, and by marker tested; test used and sensitivity of the assay should always be reported; analyses should be done in experienced laboratories (centralized diagnostics).

[q]Increasing evidence that response assessment by MFC qualitatively provides a better remission status than morphologic assessment and is of high prognostic value.

Table 19-7 **Criteria for the Definition of Accelerated-Phase and Blast Phase Chronic Myeloid Leukemia[102]**

Disease Phase	Definition	
	ELN Criteria	**WHO Criteria**
Accelerated	Blasts in blood or marrow 15%-29%, or blasts plus promyelocytes in blood or marrow > 30%, with blasts < 30%; basophils in blood ≥ 20%; persistent thrombocytopenia (< 100,000/μL) unrelated to therapy; clonal chromosomal abnormalities on Ph-positive cells, major route,[a] on treatment	Blasts in blood or marrow 10%-19%; basophils in blood ≥ 20%; persistent thrombocytopenia (< 100,000/μL) unrelated to therapy; clonal chromosomal abnormalities on Ph-positive cells on treatment; thrombocytosis (> 1,000,000/μL) unresponsive to therapy; increasing spleen size and increasing WBC count unresponsive to therapy
Blast	Blasts in blood or marrow ≥ 30%; extramedullar blast proliferation, apart from spleen	Blasts in blood or marrow ≥ 20%; extramedullary blast proliferation, apart from spleen; large foci of clusters of blasts in the bone marrow biopsy

Abbreviations: ELN, European LeukemiaNet; Ph, Philadelphia chromosome.
[a]"Major route" abnormalities include trisomy 8, trisomy Ph (+der(22)t(9;22)(q34;q11)), isochromosome 17 (i17(q10)), trisomy 19, and ider(22)(q10)t(9;22)(q34;q11).

presence of preexisting myelodysplastic syndrome, and prior leukemogenic therapy typically influence the induction strategy.

In clinical practice, a physiologic age is the more important benchmark of overall fitness for induction than an absolute age cutoff, although age 60 years is often considered a differentiating point. Elderly patients who are unfit for standard induction therapy should consider a clinical trial their best option. Another available option is low-intensity chemotherapies such as hypomethylating agents (HMAs; ie, azactidine and decitabine), low-dose cytarabine, or supportive care.

Cytogenetics and molecular abnormalities are the most important prognosticators of overall response to therapy.[34,35] Failure to achieve remission after one cycle of induction therapy or a high tumor burden defined by a WBC count ≥ 40,000/μL are poor risk factors for attaining long-term remission.[35,38]

Initial Intensive Chemotherapeutic Approaches for Medically Fit Patients

The standard induction therapy uses an anthracycline for 3 days in combination with cytarabine for 7 days (known as 3+7 or 7+3) with a few recent modifications based on mutational or cellular marker expression. Many consensus panels also recommend enrolling a patient with AML who is 60 years old or younger in a clinical trial with curative intent.[34,35]

Daunorubicin at a dosage of 60 to 90 mg/m^2 or idarubicin at a dosage of 12 mg/m^2 for 3 days are the anthracyclines of choice in combination with 7 days of continuously infused cytarabine at a dosage of 100 to 200 mg/m^2 daily. Daunorubicin and idarubicin at these doses are comparable in terms of response to therapy. A phase III Eastern Cooperative Oncology Group (ECOG) trial demonstrated an improved complete response (CR) rate for daunorubicin at a dosage of 90 mg/m^2 daily for 3 days compared with 45 mg/m^2 for 3 days, with a survival benefit for patients with favorable and intermediate-risk karyotype (median OS, 34 *v* 21 months, respectively; *P* = .004) and for those < 50 years old (median OS, 34 *v* 19 months, respectively; *P* = .004). This OS benefit associated with a higher dose of daunorubicin was seen regardless of cytogenetic risk, including patients with *FLT3*-ITD, *DNMT3A*, and *NPM1* mutations. Patients aged 50 to 60 years with *FLT3*-ITD and *NPM1* mutations also had an improved OS with 90 mg/m^2/d dosage of daunorubicin.[39] In a randomized study based on a double-induction treatment strategy, however, no advantage was found for the 90 mg/m^2/d dosage of daunorubicin compared with 60 mg/m^2/d in the first treatment cycle except in patients with *FLT3*-ITD–mutated AML.[40]

Many experts recommend beginning a second cycle of induction in patients who still have > 5% blasts in their marrow 1 week after the last dose of chemotherapy. The role of double induction in improving OS in AML is still not obvious and more evidence from prospective studies is required in this regard. Patients with *FLT3*-mutated AML experience an improved OS when midostaurin is added to standard, front-line induction chemotherapy (Fig 19-3).

To improve results achieved with the 3+7 regimen, several newer agents were investigated and are approved by the FDA for the first-line treatment of AML. Midostaurin, a multikinase inhibitor with activity against mutant *FLT3*, improved OS compared with placebo (hazard ratio, 0.77; 95% CI, 0.63 to 0.95; *P* = .007).[41] The addition of midostaurin to 3+7 improved event-free survival and OS in a randomized trial for patients with AML who had *FLT3* mutations, leading to approval of midostaurin for this indication.

Gemtuzumab ozogamicin is approved for newly diagnosed CD33-positive AML in combination with daunorubicin and cytarabine on the basis of reduced relapse risk and improved OS.[42] These benefits seem to be restricted to patients with favorable and intermediate-risk disease (median event-free survival: 17.3 *v* 9.5 months for gemtuzumab and the standard chemotherapy arms, respectively; hazard ratio, 0.56; *P* < .001). Gemtuzumab is associated with increased risk of hepatotoxicity, including possible severe and fatal hepatic veno-occlusive disease.

In patients ages 60 to 75 years with untreated AML and a history of prior cytotoxic treatment, antecedent MDS, or chronic

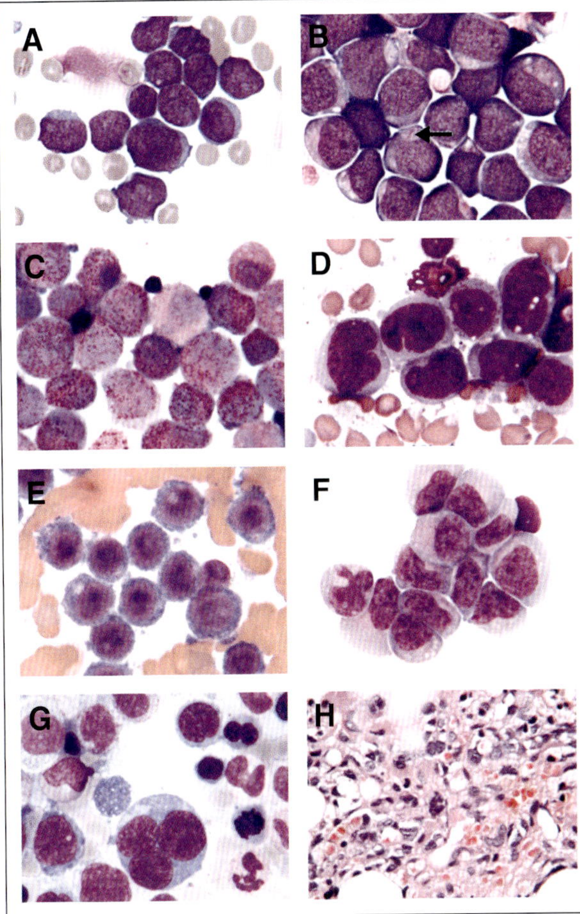

Fig. 19-2 The morphologic spectrum of the acute myeloid leukemias (AMLs).

AML with minimal maturation: The cells are myeloblasts with dispersed chromatin and variable amounts of agranular cytoplasm; some display medium-sized, poorly defined nucleoli. (B) Acute myeloblastic leukemia with maturation: Some of the blasts contain azurophilic granules, and there are promyelocytes. Note the Auer rod (arrow). (C) Acute promyelocyte leukemia: all of these cells are promyelocytes containing coarse cytoplasmic granules that sometimes obscure the nuclei. (D) Acute myelomonocytic leukemia: promonocytes with indented nuclei are present with myeloblasts; the dense nuclear staining is unusual. (E) Acute monoblastic leukemia: these characteristic monoblasts have round nuclei with delicate chromatin, and prominent nucleoli stain intensely with nonspecific esterase (not shown); cytoplasm is abundant. (F) Acute monocytic leukemia: most of the cells in this field are promonocytes; monoblasts and an abnormal monocyte are also present. (G) Acute erythroid leukemia: dysplastic multinucleated erythroid precursors with megaloblastoid nuclei are present. (H) Acute megakaryoblastic leukemia: in this marrow biopsy specimen, there are large and small blasts as well as atypical megakaryocytes.

myelomonocytic leukemia (with or without prior exposure to DNA methyltransferase inhibitors), CPX-351 (a liposomal formulation of cytarabine and daunorubicin coencapsulated at a fixed molar ratio [5:1] to maximize synergy between these two agents) at a dosage of cytarabine 100 mg/m^2 to daunorubicin 44 mg/m^2 on days 1, 3, and 5 significantly improved OS, event-free survival, and response rates without an increase in 60-day mortality rate or adverse events, compared with 3+7 therapy.[43]

Adding other chemotherapeutic agents such as thioguanine, topotecan, etoposide, and fludarabine to the induction therapy has not shown any advantage over the standard induction.[44]

Cladribine, a purine nucleoside analog added to the induction regimen at a dosage of 5 mg/m^2/d, has shown a higher CR rate than standard induction (63.5% *v* 47%; *P* = .0009). Patients with a higher WBC count and those with standard-risk disease have better outcomes. One study also demonstrated improved OS for a cladribine-containing induction regimen (24 *v* 14 months; *P* = .02).[45-47]

Patients with underlying poor cardiac function can be treated with cytarabine and non-anthracycline–based induction regimens.

Postremission Therapy

Results of multiple studies suggest high-dosage cytarabine (HiDAC) at 3 g/m^2 every 12 hours on days 1, 3, and 5 improves outcomes in patients < 60 years of age in comparison with standard-dosage cytarabine (SDAC; 100 mg/m^2 or 400 mg/m^2 by continuous infusion for 5 days)[48]. HiDAC carries an increased risk of chemical conjunctivitis (12.4%) compared with SDAC (0.5%). SDAC with anthracycline and midostaurin may also be considered for patients with *FLT3*-mutation–positive AML.[49] Most consensus panels recommend three to four cycles of HiDAC consolidation for patients aged < 60 years with favorable mutations or favorable-risk cytogenetics. Matched-sibling or alternate-donor allogeneic alloHSCT is recommended for patients with intermediate- or poor-risk cytogenetics and/or mutation.[34,35] Patients < 60 years of age with normal-cytogenetic AML have a comparable 5-year disease-free survival after four cycles of HiDAC (41%) or autologous HSCT (45%). There is currently no role for autologous HSCT for the intermediate- and the high-risk group outside of a clinical trial.[50]

Induction Regimens for Older or Medically Unfit Patients

Medically unfit patients with AML should be considered for clinical trials whenever possible. HMAs, such as azacitidine and decitabine, alone or in combination with venetoclax or glasdegib, can be used for the treatment of AML in older (> 65 years) or medically unfit patients. Several studies support the use of HMAs in this population.

In randomized studies, primarily older patients with AML assigned to receive azacitidine (75 mg/m^2/d for 7 days every 4 weeks) experienced a trend for improvement in OS compared with those assigned to conventional-care regimens (ie, supportive care only, low-dose cytarabine, or intensive chemotherapy), with benefits that appeared to extend across the entire risk spectrum of AML, including poor-risk karyotype.[51,52] A trend for superior survival was also found with decitabine in a similar trial that assigned patients with AML to decitabine (20 mg/m^2/d for 5 days every 4 weeks) or a choice of either supportive care only or low-dose cytarabine.[53] In another study, older patients treated with azacitidine with a monosomal karyotype (−5/5q, −7/7q, or 17p abnormalities) or a complex karyotype had a 31% to 46% reduced risk of death compared with conventional-care regimens.[33]

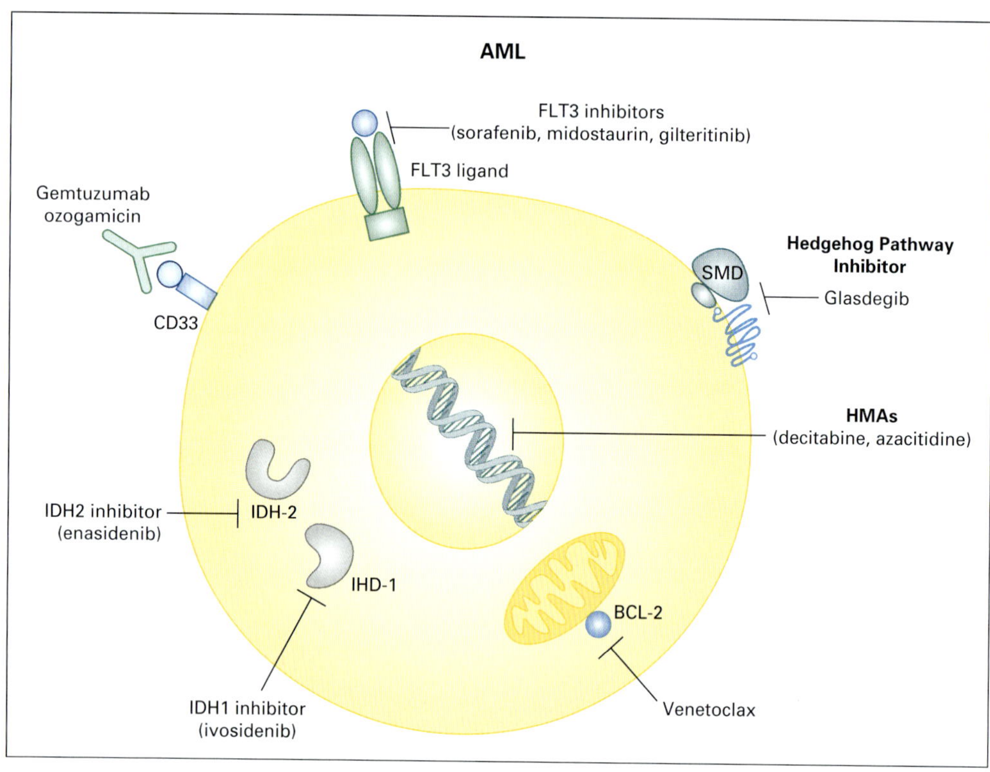

Fig. 19-3 US Food and Drug Administration–approved targeted therapies in acute myeloid leukemias and their sites of action.

Venetoclax in combination with HMAs or low-dose cytarabine has shown impressive activity in patients > 75 years old or unfit patients in two open-label, nonrandomized clinical trials. The response rate in combination with azacitidine was 37% in CR (95% CI, 26% to 50%), with time to median response of 5.5 months; in combination with decitabine was 54% (95% CI, 25% to 81%), with time to median response of 4.7 months; and in combination with low-dose cytarabine was 21% in CR (95% CI, 12% to 34%), with time to median response of 6 months.[54,55]

The combination of venetoclax and HMAs is gaining traction for use in treatment-naive patients that are unfit for induction therapy among other choices. Venetoclax can also cause tumor lysis syndrome (TLS), and appropriate preventive measures are required to avoid this complication. Venetoclax is metabolized by the CYP3A4 cytochrome system and its dose needs to be adjusted when given concurrently with common CYP3A4 inhibitors such as the antifungal agents posaconazole and fluconazole.[56] Research has suggested that a 10-day course of decitabine may be more favorable for patients with AML who have TP53 mutations and high-risk disease. This regimen continues to be investigated.[57-59]

Glasdegib, a hedgehog pathway inhibitor, is approved for treatment of AML in patients aged > 75 years in combination with low-dose cytarabine. Glasdegib is dosed at 100 mg orally daily in combination with cytarabine 20 mg subcutaneously twice daily on days 1 to 10 of a 28-day cycle. An OS benefit of 8.3 months was noted in comparison with 4.3 months for low-dose cytarabine alone.[60,61]

For patients who previously received an intensive induction regimen, a bone marrow biopsy should be performed at 4 to 6 weeks to assess for hematologic remission. For patients who previously received a lower intensity induction regimen such as HMAs, bone marrow should be performed at 8 to 12 weeks.[34,35]

Treatment of R/R or Persistent Disease

Patients with R/R AML may have new mutations at the time of relapse that are different from their original leukemia, and in such cases, this information should be used to guide additional therapy. Hence, genomic profiling should be repeated at the time of relapse. Purine analog (ie, fludarabine, cladribine, clofarabine)-containing regimens have resulted in remission rates of 30% to 45% in the R/R setting. These include regimens such as mitoxantrone, etoposide, and cytarabine,[62] fludarabine, cytarabine, and granulocyte-colony stimulating factor with or without idarubicin.[63,64] HiDAC can be administered in R/R disease if it has not been given previously. Clofarabine, in particular, has demonstrated improved OS in combination with cytarabine and against fludarabine as well, making it an appropriate purine nucleoside in the setting of R/R disease.[65,66]

IDH1 mutations occur in 6% to 10% of R/R AML cases. *IDH2* mutations occur in 10% to 15% of R/R AML. These mutations result in the accumulation of the oncometabolite 2-hydroxyglutarate. The *IDH1* inhibitor ivosidenib and the *IDH2* inhibitor enasidenib block the enzymatic activity of mutant *IDH1* and *IDH2*, respectively, lowering the levels of the oncometabolite 2-hydroxyglutarate. The *IDH1* inhibitor ivosidenib has demonstrated an overall response rate (ORR) of 41.6% at a dosage of 500 mg taken orally daily in R/R AML.[67] Enasidenib has demonstrated an ORR of 40.3% and OS of 9.3 months at a dosage of 100 mg taken orally daily. Both ivosidenib and enasidenib are associated with a differentiation syndrome that occurs in 10% to 14% of all patients and is clinically characterized by fever, dyspnea, pulmonary infiltrates, and hypoxia. Leukocytosis often accompanies differentiation syndrome. Early recognition is important because it can be fatal if untreated. Patients with a clinical suspicion for differentiation syndrome should be treated with systemic corticosteroids and close monitoring of hemodynamic status.[68,69]

Gemtuzumab ozogamicin is approved for the treatment of R/R AML as monotherapy administered as 6 mg/m^2 on day 1 and 3 mg/m^2 on day 8. Patients with no evidence of disease progression and no significant toxicities can continue receiving treatment of up to eight courses at a reduced dosage (2 mg/m^2 every 4 weeks). Another regimen is single-agent gemtuzumab ozogamicin at 3 mg/m^2 administered intravenously (IV) on days 1, 4, and 7.

Gilteritinib, a highly selective *FLT3* inhibitor, has been approved for R/R FLT3-ITD–positive AML at a dosage of 120 mg taken orally daily. A companion *FLT3*-mutation assay has also been approved. In an early-phase dose-escalation study, gilteritinib treatment resulted in a 40% ORR.[70] In the R/R setting, the CR plus complete response with partial recovery of blood cells rate was 21%, according to the prescribing information (ADMIRAL trial; unpublished data). Gilteritinib has activity against *FLT3*-TKD and non-ITD mutations as well.

Several novel agents considered to be epigenetic therapies (ie, guadecitabine), next-generation *FLT3* inhibitors (ie, quizartinib, crenolanib), and targeted immunotherapy directed toward AML-specific antigens (ie, CD123, CD33) are currently in late-phase clinical trials.[34]

HSCT for AML

AlloHSCT offers a strong antileukemic effect and continues to be the treatment of choice for all medically fit patients up to the age of 70 to 75 years except those with favorable cytogenetic- or molecular-risk profiles (ie, APL, CBF AML, double-allelic *CEPBA* mutation, or patients with *NPM1* mutation without *FLT3*/ITD who achieve an early first CR and have no evidence of MRD after induction), provided a human leukocyte antigen (HLA)-matched donor is available. If no HLA-matched donors are available, suitable alternative donor sources (eg, haploidentical donors, cord blood) are considered. For patients with intermediate-risk AML, the absolute benefit of alloHSCT in first CR is less marked than for patients with adverse-risk disease, and unresolved controversy remains as to whether equivalent survival may be achieved by delaying transplantation until after the first relapse.[35,71]

There continues to be a limited role of myeloablative regimens in the treatment of elderly patients with AML. Nonmyeloablative or reduced-intensity conditioning regimens have been developed to reduce the rate of nonrelapse mortality in older or less medically fit patients. Reduced-intensity conditioning in older patients has demonstrated survival benefit and improved relapse-free survival.[72-74] Data from one randomized trial show significantly higher rates of relapse and shorter relapse-free survival with reduced-intensity conditioning as compared with myeloablative conditioning.[75] Myeloablative conditioning, therefore, should be prioritized if the patient is considered a suitable candidate. For patients older than 40 years, the combination of busulfan plus fludarabine is associated with lower transplant-related mortality rates, but retained antileukemic effects, compared with busulfan plus cyclophosphamide.[76]

The low likelihood of response to salvage chemotherapy for patients with primary induction failure has led to attempts to use alloHSCT as first salvage therapy. Although the post-transplantation relapse rate is high, the 20% to 25% OS with alloHSCT for patients with primary induction failure is better than what would be expected with additional chemotherapy.[77]

MRD Monitoring

Monitoring MRD after standard therapy is now being incorporated into the treatment algorithm at several institutions in the United States. Currently, multiparameter flow cytometry and reverse transcriptase polymerase chain reaction (RT-PCR) are the two most commonly used methods to detect submicroscopic leukemic populations, the persistence of which after treatment is suggestive of a shorter time to relapse. Lack of standardization and harmonization of the various assays currently prevents the widespread implementation of MRD monitoring into clinical practice.[77,78]

Supportive Care During AML Therapy

Transfusions, tumor lysis syndrome (TLS) prophylaxis, growth factor support, anti-infective prophylaxis, and correction of coagulopathies are the crux of supportive care during AML therapy. Leukocyte-depleted and radiated blood products are preferred for all transplant-eligible candidates. Standard TLS prophylaxis administered during treatment includes hydration, diuresis, and treatment with allopurinol and/or rasburicase. Rasburicase is genetically engineered urate oxidase and should be strongly considered for TLS treatment and prophylaxis in the presence of a rapidly increasing blast count, high uric acid levels, and impaired renal function.

Monitoring for cerebellar and renal toxicity should be performed concurrently with HiDAC treatment. If signs of neurologic toxicity are detected, HiDAC should be discontinued and standard-dose cytarabine should only be used from that point in treatment onward.

Growth factors such as granulocyte-colony stimulating factor can decrease the duration of neutropenia and decrease the risk of life-threatening sepsis during treatment. Growth factors should be discontinued 1 week before a planned bone marrow biopsy.

Although CNS leukemia is rare in AML, patients with monocytic differentiation, biphenotypic leukemia, and WBC count > 40,000/μL should be screened for the presence of CNS leukemia with a lumbar puncture. Intrathecal chemotherapy should be incorporated into the treatment regimen if CNS leukemia is detected.[34,35,77,78]

Acute Promyelocytic Leukemia

APL is a distinct subtype of AML with unique clinical, morphologic, and cytogenetic features. In > 95% of the cases, APL has the characteristic t(15;17)(q24.1;q21.2) translocation. This translocation gives rise to a fusion product, PML/RARα, as a result of which an aberrant retinoic acid–receptor recruits corepressor complexes that cause a differentiation arrest of the myeloid cells at the promyelocyte stage.[79]

APL occurs most frequently in young, Hispanic, and obese patients. It has a distinct morphology characterized by abnormal granules and multiple Auer rods. Coagulopathy is a clinical hallmark of the disease and it presents as hypofibrinogenemia, decreased coagulation factors, increased fibrin degradation products, and increased platelet consumption manifesting as disseminated intravascular coagulation.

It is important to make an early diagnosis of APL and institute immediate treatment of the accompanying coagulopathy to reduce the risk of early death that accompanies the disease.[80-82] A unique feature of APL is its high sensitivity to treatment with all-trans retinoic acid (ATRA) and arsenic trioxide.[83] The robust activity of these agents led to studies combining them with conventional chemotherapy as initial therapy for APL. Randomized trials have demonstrated that the addition of ATRA to conventional chemotherapy improves CR rates to approximately 90% and, when initiated promptly in patients with suspected APL, decreases the incidence of substantial bleeding complications. Clinical trials conducted before the availability of ATRA demonstrated that APL is particularly sensitive to anthracycline therapy. Thus, substantial doses of anthracyclines were included during the consolidation treatment phase for APL. These trials also demonstrated a clear role for ATRA as maintenance therapy.

Results of a large randomized trial demonstrated that the use of arsenic trioxide during consolidation therapy further improves disease-free OS in both the low-risk group (defined as those with a WBC count < 10,000/mm^3) and in high-risk APL (WBC count > 10,000/mm^3).

With current therapies, survival at 3 years after diagnosis can be expected for > 85% of low-risk patients and for 75% of those with high-risk disease. Randomized studies have shown that patients with low-risk APL can be treated with ATRA and arsenic trioxide alone, with more sustained antileukemic efficacy and better survival than that seen with an ATRA plus chemotherapy-based regimen.[84,85] Maintenance therapy is not required after arsenic and ATRA therapy for low-risk APL.

When combined with at least one dose of gemtuzumab ozogamicin or an anthracycline during induction, ATRA and arsenic trioxide are also highly effective in high-risk APL.[86] A combination of ATRA and arsenic trioxide is preferred as consolidation therapy in APL with or without chemotherapy.[84,86] Some investigators recommend four to six doses of intrathecal chemotherapy be administered to high-risk patients during consolidation to decrease risk of CNS relapse.[87] A 1 to 2 year course of ATRA with mercaptopurine and methotrexate has been used as a maintenance therapy in high-risk APL, but it is not clear if this is required after ATRA and arsenic therapy. Molecular remission status is assessed during therapy and thereafter by RT-PCR monitoring for the PML-RARα transcript.

A small fraction of patients with APL morphology will have a different translocation, such as t(11;17), which is associated with a poor response to ATRA and arsenic trioxide.[88,89] During induction therapy with either ATRA or arsenic trioxide, it is important to monitor for the development of differentiation syndrome, which is manifested by fever, weight gain, respiratory distress, pulmonary infiltrates, episodic hypotension, and renal failure. This condition is thought to be related to the sudden maturation of promyeloblasts and usually responds to dexamethasone, which should be initiated immediately upon suspicion of this condition. Temporary discontinuation of ATRA or arsenic trioxide may be required for patients in very poor clinical condition as a result of severe renal or pulmonary impairment.[90]

Treatment with arsenic trioxide can be complicated by QT-interval prolongation and, rarely, by sudden death. Thus, before initiating treatment, any electrolyte imbalances should be corrected, especially hypomagnesemia and hypocalcemia, and other drugs that can prolong the QT interval should be discontinued.[84]

SECONDARY AML AND THERAPY-RELATED MDS/AML

Secondary AML and therapy-related MDS/AML arise in the setting of a prior hematologic malignancy as well as chemotherapy and radiation for the treatment of a previous malignancy or autoimmune disorder.[91] Prior exposure to alkylating agents predisposes to deletions in chromosomes 5 and 7. Disease arises typically 5 to 7 years after exposure.[92,93]

Topoisomerase II inhibitors can cause balanced translocations of *MLL* at chromosome 11q23 at a shorter latency period of 2 to 3 years.[93,94] Mutations in *TP53* are particularly common in therapy-related AML (21% to 38%) and are associated with a poor prognosis.[93] The presence of a mutation in *SRSF2*, *SF3B1*, *U2AF1*, *ZRSR2*, *ASXL1*, *EZH2*, *BCOR*, or *STAG2* is > 95% specific for the diagnosis of secondary AML.[95]

The outcomes with standard therapy are poor, with estimated median survival in the range of 8 to 16 months. AlloHSCT is currently the only curative option for therapy-related AML/MDS.[96-98]

KEY POINTS

- In 60% of AML cases, at least one clonal abnormality in chromosome number or structure can be found. These cytogenetic abnormalities, in combination with age and performance status, are the most important prognostic factors in AML and are indispensable in making therapeutic decisions.
- Genome-wide sequencing has identified > 50 genes that are recurrently mutated in AML. Of these, testing for mutations in *FLT3*, *NPM1*, *CEBPA*, *IDH1*, *IDH2*, and *TP53*, among others, is important in making treatment decisions for patients who enter first remission.
- On the basis of cytogenetic and molecular markers, AML can be divided into several categories with distinct disease risk.
- Standard induction therapy in AML involves the use of an anthracycline and cytarabine.

- All patients up to age 70 to 75 years who achieve a complete remission—except those with a favorable risk cytogenetic or molecular profile who achieve an early, first complete remission and have no evidence of measurable residual disease after induction—should be considered for alloHSCT, particularly if comorbidity scores are low and an HLA-matched donor is available.
- The prognosis is poor for patients with recurrent AML, and the likelihood of achieving second remission is predicted by the length of the first remission. Individuals who have remained in remission for > 1 year can be induced with the same chemotherapy given for first complete remission. Because of this poor outcome, transplantation should be considered for most patients with recurrent AML who are appropriate candidates.
- The suspicion of APL in a newly diagnosed patient with acute leukemia should trigger the immediate administration of ATRA to reduce the risk of early hemorrhagic death.
- Patients with APL should receive ATRA and arsenic trioxide as part of induction and/or consolidation therapy.

CHRONIC MYELOID LEUKEMIA

CML accounts for approximately 15% of all adult leukemias; median age of patients at presentation is 67 years.[99,100] The Philadelphia (Ph) chromosome, t(9,22)(q34;q11), which consists of a fusion of two genes—*BCR* (on chromosome 22) and *ABL1* (on chromosome 9)—results in the abnormal fusion protein BCR-ABL1, and this gives rise to a dysregulated tyrosine kinase (p210). Another fusion protein, p190, more common in the setting of Ph chromosome–positive (hereafter, Ph positive) ALL, is detected in 1% of patients with CML. This manifests clinically with uncontrolled production of granulocytes (ie, neutrophils, eosinophils, and basophils) in various states of maturation.[101]

CLINICAL PRESENTATION

CML has three different stages of presentation: the chronic phase, the accelerated phase, and the blast phase (blast crisis), with the disease presenting in the chronic phase > 85% of the time.

At the time of diagnosis, disease in > 90% of patients is in the chronic phase, and up to 50% of patients are diagnosed incidentally during routine blood testing. Untreated chronic-phase CML will progress to advanced-stage disease in 3 to 5 years.[102,103] Symptoms include fatigue, night sweats, malaise, weight loss, bone aches, and abdominal discomfort from splenomegaly. Patients typically have leukocytosis, thrombocytosis, and moderate anemia at the time of presentation. The marrow is virtually always hypercellular. The Ph chromosome is found in > 90% of cases. In the remaining cases, cryptic or complex translocations can be detected by fluorescent in situ hybridization (FISH) or PCR assays. Both WHO and European LeukemiaNet (ELN) have developed criteria to distinguish the chronic phase from the accelerated and blastic phases (Table 19-7).[102,104]

The accelerated phase is characterized by fever, night sweats, weight loss, bone pain, difficulty controlling blood counts, increased numbers of blasts, early myeloid cells in the marrow and peripheral blood, and, many times, evidence of karyotypic evolution. The most common cytogenetic changes associated with disease evolution are an additional Ph chromosome, trisomy 8, i(17q), and trisomy.

In > 60% of cases of blast crisis, the blasts are of myeloid lineage, as determined by morphology and cell-surface markers. In 25% to 30% of cases, the blasts are of lymphoid lineage, and in the remaining cases, blasts may be biphenotypic or undifferentiated. Determination of the blast lineage may be useful for selecting appropriate therapy.

The Sokal scoring system has been used to stratify risk for patients with CML into low-, intermediate- and high-risk groups for clinical trials evaluating the tyrosine kinase inhibitors (TKIs). The Sokal score is based on the patient's age, spleen size, platelet count, and percentage of blasts in the peripheral blood.[105]

TREATMENT

Oral, highly effective TKIs are now the first-line therapy for CML. Before the advent of TKIs, hydroxyurea, interferon-α with or without cytarabine, busulfan, and allogeneic stem cell transplant were used primarily in the management of CML. These therapies continue to be used in a limited manner. Response to therapy in CML is assessed by measuring the hematologic, cytogenetic, and molecular response to TKI treatment (Table 19-8).

First-Generation TKI Imatinib

The first-generation TKI imatinib can be used interchangeably with the second-generation TKIs dasatinib, nilotinib, and bosutinib for initiation of first-line therapy. The second-generation TKIs induce a deeper response more rapidly than imatinib in a higher proportion of patients. However, the proportion of patients achieving deep molecular remissions beyond 8 years with front-line imatinib continues to increase.[106-109] The ultimate confirmation of treatment efficacy is the ability to discontinue TKIs indefinitely without evidence of CML recurrence, which is referred to as treatment-free remission. The data are currently insufficient to recommend discontinuation of treatment outside of a clinical trial setting.[110]

At a dosage of 400 mg daily of imatinib, a complete cytogenetic response and major molecular response after 1 year have been achieved in 49% to 77% and 18% to 58% of patients, respectively. OS > 85% and progression-free survival (PFS) > 80% after 4 to 6 years have been observed in several large studies, with 60% to 80% of patients continuing to receive imatinib therapy after 3 to 5 years. A better early response can also be obtained with higher dosages of imatinib (600 to 800 mg/d).[104] Chronic fatigue, musculoskeletal pain, and muscle cramps are common adverse effects of imatinib that are associated with a decreased quality of life. Skin hypopigmentation,

Table 19-8 Criteria for Hematologic, Cytogenetic, and Molecular Response and Relapse[100]

Criteria
Complete Hematologic Response[241]
Complete normalization of peripheral blood counts with leukocyte count $< 10 \times 10^9$/L
Platelet count $< 450 \times 10^9$/L
No immature cells, such as myelocytes, promyelocytes, or blasts in peripheral blood
No signs and symptoms of disease with disappearance of palpable splenomegaly
Cytogenetic Response[a,280]
Complete cytogenetic response: No Ph-positive metaphases
Major cytogenetic response: 0%-35% Ph-positive metaphases
Partial cytogenetic response: 1%-35% Ph-positive metaphases
Minor cytogenetic response: > 35%-65% Ph-positive metaphases
Molecular Response[281,282]
Early molecular response: BCR-ABL1 (IS) ≤ 10% at 3 and 6 months
Major molecular response: BCR-ABL1 (IS) ≤ 0.1% or ≥ 3-log reduction in BCR-ABL1 mRNA from the standardized baseline, if qPCR (IS) is not available
Complete molecular response is variably described and is best defined by the assay's level of sensitivity (eg, MR4.5)
Relapse
Any sign of loss of response (defined as hematologic or cytogenetic relapse)
A 1-log increase in BCR-ABL1 transcript levels with loss of MMR should prompt bone marrow evaluation for loss of CCyR but is not itself defined as relapse (eg, hematologic or cytogenetic relapse)

Abbreviations: IS, international scale; MMR, major molecular response; qPCR, quantitative polymerase chain reaction.
[a]A minimum of 20 metaphases should be examined.

bone pain, diarrhea, peripheral edema, elevated lipase and alanine aminotransferase levels, and cytopenias are other reported adverse effects.[101,104]

The most common identifiable reasons for resistance include poor compliance with therapy, mutations in the BCR-ABL1 kinase domain that interfere with imatinib binding, *BCR-ABL1* amplification or overexpression, decreased drug bioavailability, or drug efflux. The ABL kinase domain mutation can be detected in samples collected before treatment, suggesting the delayed imatinib failure may reflect the considerable amount of time required for outgrowth of these selected clones. Not all mutations in *BCR-ABL1* have the same significance; mutations at *T315I* and those affecting the phosphate-binding loop are believed to confer the greatest degree of imatinib resistance, whereas others can be overcome by a dose increase or are functionally irrelevant.[104]

Second- and Third-Generation TKIs

Compared with imatinib, second-generation TKIs such as nilotinib, dasatinib, and bosutinib lead to higher complete cytogenetic response and major molecular response rates after at least 1 year and sometimes at later times, and may slightly reduce the rate of progression or failure, whereas no differences in OS have been documented. These drugs can also result in complete cytogenetic response rates in approximately 50% of patients whose disease is in the chronic phase and in whom resistance to imatinib develops; however, they are inactive against the *T315I* mutation.[104]

Ponatinib, a pan-TKI, is approved for the treatment of patients with T315I-positive CML and for adults for whom no other TKI is indicated. The adverse-effect profiles of these TKIs are similar to that for imatinib, although with notable distinctions. All second- and third-generation TKIs have cardiac toxicity, and some reports have highlighted vascular safety issues with these agents.

Dasatinib and, less so, bosutinib can cause pleural effusions. Dasatinib has also been associated with pulmonary hypertension and significant but reversible inhibition of platelet aggregation contributing to bleeding in some patients with accompanying thrombocytopenia.[111] Nilotinib has been associated with QT-interval prolongation and sudden death, increased serum glucose levels and worsened diabetic control, as well as peripheral arterial occlusive disease.[101,112,113] Importantly, vascular complications such as arterial and venous thrombosis and embolic events have occurred with nilotinib and ponatinib. Ischemic arterial occlusive events can occur in 25% to 30% of patients, or more, with ponatinib.[102,114]

The ELN and National Comprehensive Cancer Network (NCCN) guidelines currently recommend initial therapy of chronic-phase CML with imatinib (400 mg daily), nilotinib (300 mg twice daily), dasatinib (100 mg daily), or bosutinib

(400 mg daily). Although most patients will have an excellent response to initial TKI therapy, careful monitoring (via blood cell counts, routine cytogenetic analysis of bone marrow, as well as FISH and quantitative PCR analyses of peripheral blood or bone marrow) is critical for identifying failures and considering changing therapy.

Response to TKIs

The ELN has established milestones for response to TKIs as first-line therapy (Table 19-9).[104] Failure to achieve any of the goals of therapy at 3, 6, and 12 months or beyond is an indication to switch to a different treatment to limit the risk of progression and death. Definitions of expected responses to second-line therapy have also been developed, and they are relatively similar to those for first-line therapy. Failure to have adequate disease response to second-line therapy or losing response is an indication to proceed to alloHSCT. Patients with accelerated- or blast-phase CML can respond to TKIs, but responses are generally short lived, and the disease is relatively resistant to most types of therapy.

Hematopoietic Stem Cell Transplantation

AlloHSCT is now reserved for patients with CML with chronic-phase disease resistant to TKIs, those who have a *T315I* mutation (particularly if ponatinib therapy fails), or those who have disease progression.[103,115] Three-year survival rates can be as high as 90% and nonrelapse mortality rates lower than 10% when alloHSCT is used as second-line therapy after imatinib failure.[116] Patients with accelerated or blast-phase CML should undergo workup for alloHSCT rapidly because it is the only potentially curative therapy available to them. Results are somewhat better for patients whose disease is in the accelerated phase or blast crisis and that responds to TKIs by entering a second chronic phase prior to HSCT. Disease recurrence is now the most common cause of transplant failure in patients allografted for CML. Toxicity events from alloHSCT for CML have decreased over the past three decades mainly due to a decrease in the number of transplant-related deaths and, most notably, chronic graft-versus-host disease.[115]

KEY POINTS

- TKIs such as imatinib, nilotinib, dasatinib, and bosutinib are remarkably effective in newly diagnosed chronic-phase CML, leading to complete hematologic and cytogenetic responses for most patients with OS similar to age-matched control subjects. However, continued therapy and careful follow-up are necessary.
- Second-generation TKIs (ie, dasatinib, nilotinib, and bosutinib) result in quicker cytogenetic and molecular responses compared with imatinib, with no differences in OS.
- Patients with *T315I*-mutated CML may respond to ponatinib.
- Patients with accelerated or blast-phase CML can respond to TKIs, but responses are generally short lived, and the disease is relatively resistant to most types of therapy. AlloHSCT is potentially curative for these patients.

CLONAL HEMATOPOIESIS OF INDETERMINATE POTENTIAL

Clonal hematopoiesis of indeterminate potential (CHIP) is defined as the presence of a clonal blood cell population associated with a recognized hematologic neoplasm driver mutation at a variant allele frequency of > 2% in the absence of severe cytopenias or a WHO-defined disorder.[117] It is a common aging-associated biologic state that further predisposes to the development of cardiovascular disorders and hematologic malignancies such as MDS/AML. Although many CHIP-associated mutations are reported, *DNMT3A*, *TET2*, and *ASXL1* are the most commonly reported acquired variants, which account for > 50% of the cases. Clonal hematopoiesis that occurs after chemotherapy or radiation for a nonmyeloid malignancy is most often associated with

Table 19-9 European LeukemiaNet Definitions of Response to Tyrosine Kinase Inhibitors as First-Line Therapy[118]

Time	Optimal	Warning	Failure
Baseline	NA	High risk or CCA/Ph+, major route	NA
3 months	*BCR-ABL1* ≤ 10% and/or Ph+ ≤ 35%	*BCR-ABL1* > 10% and/or Ph+ 36%-95%	Non-CHR and/or Ph+ > 95%
6 months	*BCR-ABL1* < 1% and/or Ph+ 0	*BCR-ABL1* 1%-10% and/or Ph+ 1%-35%	*BCR-ABL1* < 10% and/or Ph+ > 35%
12 months	*BCR-ABL1* ≤ 0.1%	*BCR-ABL1* > 0.1%-1%	*BCR-ABL1* > 1% and/or Ph+ > 0
Then, and at any time	*BCR-ABL1* ≤ 0.1%	CCA/Ph− (−7, 7q−)	Loss of CHR; loss of CCyR; confirmed loss of MMR[a]; new mutations; CCA/Ph+

Abbreviations: CCA/Ph+, clonal chromosomal abnormalities in Ph-positive cells; CCyR, complete cytogenetic response; CHR, complete hematologic response; MMR, major molecular response; NA, not applicable.
[a]MMR: *BCR-ABL1* ≤ 0.1% or ≥ 3 log reduction of *BCR-ABL1*.

expansion of *TP53*-mutated clones.[30,118] CHIP-defining mutations confer a modest risk (0.5% to 1%) of increase in hematologic malignancies per year yet are associated with a 40% increased risk of cardiovascular events and deaths due to myocardial infarction and stroke. Experts currently do not recommend screening for CHIP, because evidence is lacking regarding the management of cardiovascular and hematologic neoplasm risk associated with CHIP.

Idiopathic cytopenia of undetermined significance is defined as single or multiple blood cytopenias that remain unexplained despite an appropriate evaluation including bone marrow examination. The condition excludes patients with a known clonal mutation.

Clonal cytopenia of undetermined significance is defined as the identification of a clonal mutation in a patient with one or more clinically meaningful unexplained cytopenias yet who does not meet WHO-defined criteria for a hematologic neoplasm.[119]

MYELODYSPLASTIC SYNDROMES

The myelodysplastic syndromes (MDSs) comprise a heterogeneous group of malignant HSC disorders characterized by disordered growth and differentiation of hematopoietic progenitors and a variable risk of transformation to AML.[120,121] MDS generally affects older individuals (median age at diagnosis, 65 to 70 years); only 10% of patients are younger than 50 years.[122]

PATHOGENESIS

MDS occurs as a result of sequential acquisition of somatic mutations in HSCs. Clonal mutations with higher allele frequencies are more likely to be present in the disease-initiating cells of MDS. CHIP, discussed in the previous section, is now considered to be an MDS precursor condition.

Typically, early driver mutations are in genes involved in RNA splicing and DNA methylation.[28] Links between cytogenetic abnormalities and MDS phenotype are now well established. For example, patients with deletions in 5q33 (ie, the 5q− syndrome) generally have severe macrocytic anemia, a normal or elevated platelet count, and a relatively low rate of progression to AML. Disease in these patients frequently responds to treatment with lenalidomide. *RPS14* and casein kinase 1A1 (*CK1α*) have been identified as likely candidate genes involved in the 5q− syndrome and response to lenalidomide.[123,124]

Sequencing studies have revealed a number of recurrent point mutations beyond those involving cytogenetic abnormalities. Among the most commonly mutated genes are *TET2*, *ASXL1*, *RUNX1*, *TP53*, *EZH2*, and *NRAS*. Several of these (*ASXL1*, *RUNX1*, *TP53*, and *EZH2*) are associated with shorter survival. *TET2*, *ASXL1*, and *EZH2* are involved with regulation of DNA methylation.[125] *SF3B1* encodes a core component of RNA splicing machinery and is frequently mutated in MDS cases with ring sideroblasts. These patients tend to have lower-stage disease and better prognosis overall.[126] The TGF-β superfamily plays a central role in the ineffective erythropoiesis of MDS. TGF-β ligands trigger receptor-mediated phosphorylation and activation of the inhibitory Smad 2/3 transcription factors, leading to suppression of terminal erythroid differentiation.[127]

CLINICAL PRESENTATION AND DIAGNOSIS

Clinical findings in MDS are nonspecific, are related to the reduction or dysfunction of blood cells present at diagnosis, and include fatigue, bleeding diathesis, and infections. Patients also often have immune disorders.

The diagnosis is based on the examination of the blood and the bone marrow, the latter of which classically shows peripheral cytopenias, a hypercellular marrow with dysplastic features, and in some cases, increased numbers of blasts.[122] WHO recognizes several categories of MDS, which are based primarily on the degree of dysplasia and blast percentages in peripheral blood and bone marrow (Table 19-10).[3]

Abnormal cytogenetics are present in 40% to 50% of cases and often demonstrate partial or complete loss or gain of chromosomes rather than balanced translocations (as seen in AML). The most frequent findings are del(5q), del(7), del (7q), +8, del(20q), or del(17p). Chromosomal abnormalities in MDS are of prognostic importance. Abnormalities of chromosomes 5 or 7 are associated with the shortest survival, whereas the longest survival is associated with a normal karyotype, −Y, del(11q), del(5q), or del(20q) as the sole abnormality.[122]

PROGNOSIS

The most important independent prognostic factors identified in MDS are percentage of bone marrow blasts, karyotype, and number of cytopenias.[122] These factors were used to develop the International Prognostic Scoring System (IPSS), which categorized patients with primary MDS into four risk groups with differing survival and risk of progression to AML.[128]

Findings from additional studies suggest that, stage for stage, the prognosis is worse for patients with therapy-related MDS than for patients with primary MDS. Several attempts have been made to refine prognostic scoring in MDS, with the most important systems being the WHO Prognostic Scoring System,[129] which is based on WHO classification, cytogenetics, and red cell transfusion need, and the revised IPSS (Table 19-11).[130]

TREATMENT

Disease Risk

The therapeutic strategy is based primarily on disease risk.[122] The main goals for patients with low- to intermediate-1–risk MDS are to reduce the consequences of cytopenias and improve quality of life, whereas for patients with intermediate-2 to high-risk disease, the focus is on disease modification with prevention of transformation into AML and prolongation of survival.

For low- to intermediate-1–risk disease or patients who are frail or elderly, supportive care with RBC and platelet transfusions as necessary is recommended. Lenalidomide, a 4-amino-glutarimide analog of thalidomide, has been approved for treatment of transfusion-dependent low- to intermediate-1–risk MDS associated with the 5q− syndrome and can lead to transfusion independence and cytogenetic response in many patients.[131]

Erythropoietin can improve the anemia associated with MDS in 20% of patients and is most effective in patients with low endogenous erythropoietin levels.[132] Addition of a myeloid

Table 19-10 2016 WHO Classification of MDS[3]

Disease	Dysplastic Lineages, Cytopenias, and RS[a]	BM and PB Blasts
MDS with single-lineage dysplasia	1 dysplastic lineage; 1-2 cytopenias; < 15%/ < 5% RSs	BM < 5%, PB < 1%, no Auer rods
MDS-RS	1-3 dysplastic lineages; 1-3 cytopenias; ≥ 15%/≥ 5% RSs[b]	BM < 5%, PB < 1%, no Auer rods
MRD-RS with single-lineage dysplasia		
MRD-RS with multilineage dysplasia		
MDS with multilineage dysplasia	2-3 dysplastic lineages; 1-3 cytopenias	BM < 5%, PB < 1%, no Auer rods
MDS with EB	0-3 dysplastic lineages; 1-3 cytopenias	EB-1: BM 5%-9% or PB 2%-4%, no Auer rods
MDS-EB-1		EB-2: BM 10%-19% or PB 5%-19%, no Auer rods
MDS-EB-2		
MDS with isolated del(5q)	1-3 dysplastic lineages; 1-2 cytopenias; no RSs	BM < 5%, PB < 1%,
		no Auer rods; del(5q) alone or with 1
		additional abnormality except −7 or del(7q)
MDS, unclassified	0-3 dysplastic lineages; 1-3 cytopenias[c]	BM < 5%, PB ≤ 1%, no Auer rods[d]
With 1% blood blasts		
With single-lineage dysplasia and pancytopenia		
Based on defining cytogenetic abnormality		
Provisional entity: refractory cytopenia of childhood	1-3 dysplastic lineages; 1-3 cytopenias; no RSs	BM < 5%, PB < 2%

Abbreviations: BM, bone marrow; EB, excess blast; MDS, myelodysplastic syndrome; PB, peripheral blood; RS, ring sideroblast.

[a]Cytopenias defined as hemoglobin concentration < 10 g/dL; platelet count < 100 × 10^9/L; and absolute neutrophil count < 1.8 × 10^9/L; peripheral-blood monocyte count must be < 1 × 10^9/L.

[b]If *SF3B1* mutation is present.

[c]If no dysplastic lineage, must have MDS-defining cytogenetic abnormality by conventional karyotyping.

[d]Cases with 1% PB blasts must be documented on at least two separate occasions.

growth factor may result in additional responses for 20% of the patients, with a median duration of response of 20-23 months. Myeloid growth factors, including granulocyte colony-stimulating factor and granulocyte-macrophage colony-stimulating factor, have poor responses in MDS and are currently not recommended as single agents.

Platelet counts have responded to the thrombopoietin mimetics romiplostim and eltrombopag, but concern regarding proliferation of leukemic blasts remain from earlier in vitro studies. Ongoing clinical trials with these agents will help further elucidate leukemic risk.[133,134] Patients with MDS who are receiving frequent RBC supportive transfusions are at risk for iron overload and end-organ (ie, heart, liver, and pancreas) complications. Iron overload is a contributing factor of early-stage mortality and morbidity in MDS.[135-137] The iron chelators deferoxamine and deferasirox are available to treat iron overload in MDS. Deferasirox has a black-box warning for fatal acute renal failure and hepatic failure.[138-140]

Luspatercept is a novel, recombinant fusion protein that contains the modified extracellular domain of the activin receptor IIB that blocks the TGF-β superfamily inhibitors of erythropoiesis.[127] A phase III randomized, double-blinded study comparing luspatercept with placebo in low- to intermediate-risk patients with MDS, anemia, ringed sideroblasts, and *SF3B1* mutations (90%) showed that patients treated with luspatercept had a significantly reduced transfusion burden compared with those treated with placebo (37.9% *v* 13.2%; *P* < .0001).[141] This agent is currently awaiting FDA approval.

Azacitidine and decitabine are both approved for treatment of MDS (azacitidine for all types of MDS; decitabine for intermediate 1–, intermediate 2–, and high-risk disease). Both are thought to have utility in MDS through their DNA demethylating activity, which leads to re-expression of key genes otherwise inactivated in MDS by hypermethylation.[142,143] The effects of azacitidine were demonstrated in a phase III trial in which researchers found improved OS compared with conventional care (ie, supportive care alone, low-dose cytarabine, or intensive chemotherapy, as selected by investigators before random assignment) for patients with intermediate-2– to high-risk disease.[144] Compared with best supportive care, treatment with decitabine was reported to significantly reduce the risk of AML transformation and to improve PFS in a randomized phase III trial in patients with intermediate-1–, intermediate-2–, and high-risk MDS, whereas OS was statistically nonsignificantly prolonged.[142] Neither azacitidine nor decitabine are curative. The presence

Table 19-11 **Revised International Prognostic Scoring System for Myelodysplastic Syndrome**[145]

IPSS-R	Score (no. of points)						
	0	0.5	1.0	1.5	2.0	3.0	4.0
Variable							
Cytogenetics[a]	Very good		Good		Intermediate	Poor	Very poor
Bone marrow blasts, %	≤ 2		> 2 to < 5		5-10	> 10	
Hemoglobin, g/dL	≥ 10		8 to < 10	< 8			
Platelets, cells/mL	≥ 100	50-100	< 50				
Absolute neutrophil count, cells/mL	≥ 0.8	< 0.8					
IPSS categories and outcomes	Very low	Low	Intermediate	High	Very high		
IPSS-R score	< 1.5	> 1.5-3.0	> 3-4.5	> 4.5-6	> 6		
Proportion of patients, %	19	38	20	13	10		
Median survival, years	8.8	5.3	3.0	1.6	0.8		
Time to 25% AML progression, years	> 14.5	10.8	3.2	1.4	0.7		

Abbreviations: AML, acute myeloid leukemia; IPSS, International Prognostic Scoring System; IPSS-R, revised International Prognostic Scoring System.
[a]Cytogenetic definitions: very good, -Y, del(11q); good, normal, del(5q), del(12p), del(20q), double including del(5q); intermediate, del(7q), +8, +19, i(17q), any other single or double independent clones; poor, −7, inv(3)t(3q)/del(3q), double including −7/del(7q), complex with three abnormalities; very poor, complex with at least three abnormalities.

of *TET2* mutations predicted better response to HMAs in some studies.[145]

Patients with MDS who express HLA-DR15, marrow hypoplasia, normal cytogenetics, low-risk disease and a paroxysmal nocturnal hemoglobinuria clone have shown enduring responses to anti-thymocyte globulin, cyclosporine, or the two agents in combination.[146-149]

Low-dose cytarabine has been studied as a treatment option for MDS, with responses seen in 10% to 20% of cases. Patients with MDS with excess blasts-1 or excess blasts-2 have, in some cases, been treated with AML-like induction chemotherapy. Although response rates are lower than the rates seen with de novo AML, CRs have been reported in 40% to 60% of patients in some studies,[122] but it is unknown whether this results in an overall improvement in survival.

Patients with intermediate- to high-risk MDS whose disease does not respond to HMAs have a poor prognosis (4 to 6 month OS) and investigational therapies should be promptly explored for this group of patients.

Hematopoietic Stem Cell Transplantation

AlloHSCT is currently the only curative therapy for MDS and can lead to long-term disease-free survival for 35% to 50% of patients, with many patients alive without evidence of disease for > 5 years after transplantation, and some for as long as 25 years.[122,150] Several mutations (*TP53*, *TET2*, and *DNMT3A*) have been associated with shorter survival after transplantation.[150] An important question is the appropriate timing of transplantation. Patients with early-stage MDS may live for a long time without any intervention, but after MDS evolves to AML, survival is short, and transplantation is less effective than if it had been performed earlier.

After an evidence-based review, an expert panel recommended transplantation for patients with an IPSS score of intermediate-2 or high risk and for selected patients with a low- or intermediate-1–risk IPSS score who have poor prognostic features not included in the IPSS (eg, older age, refractory cytopenias).[151] Similarly, a review focused on patients ages 60 to 70 years indicated that reduced-intensity alloHSCT offered an overall and quality-adjusted survival benefit for IPSS intermediate-2– to high-risk MDS.[152]

KEY POINTS

- CHIP is associated with increased risk of progression to hematologic neoplasia, cardiovascular death, and all-cause mortality. Experts recommend against screening for CHIP at this time.
- The important prognostic factors for patients with MDSs are percentage of marrow blasts, karyotype, number of peripheral cytopenias, and molecular mutations.
- The therapeutic strategy for MDS is based primarily on the disease risk, with the main goals of reducing consequences of cytopenias, improving quality of life for patients with lower-risk disease, prevention of transformation into AML,

and improvement of survival for patients with higher-risk disease.

- The del 5q− subtype responds to therapy with lenalidomide.
- AlloHSCT is the only curative treatment for high-risk MDS.

MYELOPROLIFERATIVE NEOPLASMS

A heterogeneous group of hematologic disorders is currently recognized by WHO as MPNs, myeloid or lymphoid neoplasms associated with eosinophilia and acquired mutations in growth factor receptors, and myeloid neoplasms with clinical, laboratory, and morphologic features that overlap MDS and MPN (Table 19-12).[3] This section focuses on the classic MPNs: PV, ET, and PMF.

PATHOGENESIS

MPNs are characterized by stem cell–derived clonal myeloproliferation that can evolve into AML or, in the case of PV and ET, myelofibrosis (secondary [post-PV/ET] myelofibrosis [MF]).[4] Over the past decade, multiple, recurrent, somatic mutations have been identified in these disorders. Most prominent among these are the mutually exclusive mutations in *JAK2* (primarily in exon 14; ie, V617F, and rarely in exon 12), calreticulin (*CALR*; primarily exon 9 deletions and insertions), and myeloproliferative leukemia virus oncogene (*MPL*; primarily exon 10 mutations).[4,153] *JAK2* mutations are found in almost 100% of PV cases, 50% to 60% of ET cases, and 55% to 65% of PMF cases; 20% to 25% of ET and PMF cases harbor *CALR* mutations, whereas MPL mutations are present in 3% to 4% of ET and 6% to 7% of PMF cases, respectively.[4] Increasingly, characteristic differences (eg, age at diagnosis, blood cell counts, risk of thrombosis) among these three mutations are recognized.[154] In approximately 10% to 15% of the patients with ET or PMF, neither a *JAK2*, *CALR*, nor *MPL* mutation is found (ie, "triple negative").[4]

In addition to these three genes, mutations in many other genes have been described, including in *LNK*, *CBL*, *DNMT3A*, *TET2*, *IDH1/2*, *EZH2*, and *ASXL1*. Several of these mutations constitutively activate cell-signaling pathways and lead to a clonal growth advantage. Other mutations affect genes involved in epigenetic regulation and are thought to cooperate with the first class of mutations. However, though activation of the JAK-STAT pathway is believed to be central for MPNs, the pathophysiologic role for many of the mutations found in these disorders has yet to be determined.[153] Similarly, not fully understood is why a single mutation such as *JAK2*-V617F can result in different, clinically distinct disorders, although differences in mutant allele burden, *STAT1* signaling, order of mutation acquisition, and clonal heterogeneity may play a role.[4,155]

Table 19-12 WHO Classification of Myeloproliferative Neoplasms, Myeloid Neoplasms Associated With Eosinophilia, and Myelodysplastic/Myeloproliferative Neoplasms[3]

Neoplasm	Classification
Myeloproliferative neoplasms	Chronic myeloid leukemia, *BCR-ABL1*-positive
	Chronic neutrophilic leukemia
	Polycythemia vera
	PMF
	PMF, prefibrotic/early stage
	PMF, overt fibrotic stage
	Essential thrombocytopenia
	Chronic eosinophilic leukemia, not otherwise specified
	MPN, unclassifiable
Mastocytosis	
Myeloid and lymphoid neoplasms associated with eosinophilia and abnormalities of *PDGFRA*, *PDGFRB*, or *FGFR1*, or with *PCM1-JAK2*	Myeloid/lymphoid neoplasms with *PDGFRA* rearrangement
	Myeloid/lymphoid neoplasms with *PDGFRB* rearrangement
	Myeloid and lymphoid neoplasms with *FGFR1* rearrangement
	Provisional entity: myeloid/lymphoid neoplasms with PCM1-JAK2
MDS/MPN	Chronic myelomonocytic leukemia
	Atypical chronic myeloid leukemia, *BCR-ABL1*-negative
	Juvenile myelomonocytic leukemia
	MDS/MPN with ring sideroblasts and thrombocytosis
	MDS/MPN, unclassifiable

Abbreviations: MDS, myelodysplastic; MPN, myeloproliferative neoplasm; PMF, primary myelofibrosis.

CLINICAL PRESENTATION AND DIAGNOSIS

Patients may have fatigue, constitutional symptoms (eg, fever, weight loss, night sweats), microvascular symptoms (eg, headaches, erythromelalgias), itching, bone pain, thromboses at unusual sites (eg, portal vein, hepatic vein), early satiety, and abdominal discomfort. Subsets of patients present with a thrombotic event or have a history of thrombosis.

On physical examination, palpable splenomegaly or hepatomegaly is common, and evidence for extramedullary hematopoiesis at other sites may be found. Peripheral-blood studies are noticeable for blood counts that exceed the upper limit of normal and changes consistent with hypermetabolism (eg, elevated lactate dehydrogenase [LDH] level and uric acid); leukoerythroblastic changes are characteristic of MR or PMF.[5,156] Secondary causes for erythrocytosis and thrombocytosis need to be excluded. Commonly used diagnostic criteria for PV, ET, and PMF are summarized in Table 19-13.[3]

Mutational screening is helpful to demonstrate the presence of clonal hematopoiesis. For example, with a *JAK2* mutation screening and a serum erythropoietin level, essentially all patients with PV will be identified. However, the presence of a mutation alone is not required for, nor is it proof of, an MPN diagnosis.[4]

A bone marrow examination is important for accurately diagnosing an MPN.[4] Characteristic findings enable distinguishing between PV (trilineage hematopoiesis with pleomorphic megakaryocytes), ET (megakaryocyte proliferation with large and mature morphology), and PMF (megakaryocyte proliferation and atypia, as well as reticulin and/or collagen fibrosis), and also help identify prefibrotic PMF (bone marrow morphology consistent with PMF but without fibrosis) or masked PV (bone marrow morphology consistent with PV but blood cell counts not meeting criteria for PV).[4,156]

PROGNOSTIC FACTORS

The median life expectancy varies considerably among patients with ET (20 years), PV (14 years), and PMF (6 years) because of varying risks for thrombosis, bleeding, and clonal evolution. The risk of leukemic transformation is substantially lower for PV or ET (at 20 years, < 10% for PV and < 5% for ET) than for PMF.[4] Once leukemic transformation has occurred, median survival is < 6 months.[157]

An increasing number of risk factors have been recognized for shorter survival in the various MPNs. The clinically most widely used ones are as follows:

- PV: advanced age, leukocytosis, thrombosis, and abnormal karyotype;
- ET: advanced age, leukocytosis, and thrombosis;
- PMF: age, anemia, leukocytosis, circulating blasts > 1%, constitutional symptoms, unfavorable karyotype, need for red cell transfusion, and thrombocytopenia. These eight factors are integrated in the Dynamic International Prognostic Scoring System (DIPSS)-plus score, which separates PMF into four risk groups (low, intermediate-1, intermediate-2, and high), with median survivals of 15.4, 6.5, 2.9, and 1.3 years, respectively.[158]

Table 19-13 2016 WHO Diagnostic Criteria for Polycythemia Vera, Essential Thrombocythemia, and Primary Myelofibrosis[3]

Diagnosis	Criteria Required for Diagnosis
Polycythemia vera (PV)	▪ Elevated hemoglobin concentration (men, > 16.5 g/dL; women, > 16.0 g/dL) or increased hematocrit (men, 49%; women, 48%) or increased red cell mass
	▪ BM hypercellularity, trilineage hematopoiesis with prominent erythroid, granulocytic, and megakaryocyte proliferation with pleomorphic, mature megakaryocytes
	▪ *JAK2V617F* or *JAK2* exon 12 mutation; if such a mutation is absent, diagnosis of PV is still possible if there is a subnormal erythropoietin level
Essential thrombocythemia (ET)	▪ Persistently elevated platelet count (≥ 450 × 10^9/L)
	▪ BM with predominant proliferation of enlarged, mature megakaryocytes with hyperlobulated nuclei
	▪ Not meeting diagnostic criteria for classic CML, PV, PMF, MDS, or other myeloid neoplasms
	▪ *JAK2V617*, *CALR*, or *MPL* mutation, or other clonal marker; if no clonal marker present, no evidence of reactive thrombocytosis
Primary myelofibrosis (PMF)	▪ Megakaryocyte proliferation and atypia. For pre-PMF: no reticulin fibrosis > grade 1, BM hypercellularity, granulocytic proliferation, often decreased erythropoiesis. For overt PMF: grade 2-3 reticulin and/or collagen fibrosis
	▪ Not meeting diagnostic criteria for classic CML, PV, ET, MDS, or other myeloid neoplasms
	▪ *JAK2V617*, *CALR*, or *MPL* mutation or other clonal marker; if no clonal marker present, no evidence of minor reactive BM reticulin fibrosis (for pre-PMF) or reactive myelofibrosis (for overt PMF)
	▪ ≥ 1 minor criterion: (1) anemia; (2) leukocytosis ≥ 11 × 10^9/L; (3) palpable splenomegaly; (4) LDH elevation; or (5), leukoerythroblastosis (for overt PMF only)

Abbreviations: BM, bone marrow; LDH, lactate dehydrogenase.

TREATMENT

The general goals of therapy for MPNs are to alleviate symptoms, prevent thrombosis or bleeding, minimize the risk of progression to MF (for PV and ET) and, particularly in MF, reduce the risk of leukemic transformation and improve survival rates.[4,156]

PV Therapy

For low-risk patients (younger than age 60 years, no thrombosis history), low-dose aspirin reduces the risk of thromboembolic events and treats microvascular symptoms.[4,156,159] Likewise, repeated phlebotomies to maintain a hematocrit of < 45% reduces cardiovascular deaths and major thrombosis. Attainment of a lower hematocrit value may be desirable in some cases and treatment should be individualized (eg, < 42% in female patients and those with progressive or residual vascular symptoms).[160]

High-risk patients (age ≥ 60 years and/or history of thrombosis) additionally require cytoreductive therapy to lower the risk of thrombotic complications. Other reasons to consider cytoreductive therapy would be symptomatic splenomegaly, constitutional symptoms, symptomatic thrombocytosis, leukocytosis, and poor compliance with or intolerance of phlebotomy. Hydroxyurea, titrated to keep the platelet count in the normal range, is usually considered the first-line treatment and is superior to anagrelide.

Second-line treatments for individuals whose disease is resistant to or who cannot tolerate hydroxyurea include interferon-α and busulfan (restricted to older patients, given its leukemogenic potential).[4,156,159] Interferon also may be considered first-line therapy for younger patients, especially in situations where hydroxyurea use needs to be deferred (eg, fertility preservation). In addition, the JAK inhibitor ruxolitinib is superior to standard therapy in controlling hematocrit, reducing spleen volume, and improving symptoms in patients with intolerance of, or resistance to, hydroxyurea.[161]

ET Therapy

For low-risk patients, aspirin is used to treat microvascular symptoms and may reduce the likelihood of vascular events in *JAK2*-mutated ET. Patients with *CALR* or *MPL* mutation and triple-negative ET have relatively lower thromboembolic risks, and antiplatelet therapy may not affect the risk of thrombosis. In high-risk patients (age ≥ 60 years or history of vascular complications), hydroxyurea or interferon-α (for younger patients in whom hydroxyurea needs to be deferred) reduces the thrombotic risk.[4,162] Debate remains about whether patients with extreme thrombocytosis (eg, platelet count > 1,000 to 1,500 × 10^9/L) without other risk factors should receive cytoreductive therapy.[163] Hydroxyurea and low-dose aspirin is superior to anagrelide and low-dose aspirin in the treatment of patients with ET with a high risk of vascular events, and is associated with a lower rate of arterial thrombosis.

PMF Therapy

For low or intermediate-1 DIPSS-plus risk, observation or hydroxyurea (for constitutional symptoms or symptomatic splenomegaly) may be most appropriate. Androgens, prednisone, danazol, immunomodulatory agents (eg, thalidomide or lenalidomide), or splenectomy may be useful for symptomatic anemia.

For intermediate-2 or high DIPSS-plus risk or genetically high-risk disease (ie, *CALR* mutation negative and *ASXL1* mutation positive), alloHSCT should be considered, because many patients will experience a durable remission after transplantation with matched-related or matched-unrelated donors.[4,156]

In randomized trials, ruxolitinib provided substantial clinical benefits relative to either standard therapy or placebo in IPSS intermediate-2 and high-risk myelofibrosis by reducing spleen size, ameliorating debilitating myelofibrosis-related symptoms, and, perhaps, improving OS.[164-166] However, ruxolitinib is not a specific inhibitor of the malignant clone and frequently results in myelosuppression, especially anemia and thrombocytopenia, as well as immunosuppression with risk of unusual infections.

Fedratinib, a JAK2 selective inhibitor, recently received FDA approval for the treatment of intermediate-2 or high-risk primary or secondary (post-ET, post-PV) MF. The JAKARTA study, a single-arm, open-label, nonrandomized, phase II study, evaluated oral fedratinib given daily at a dosage of 400 mg to patients with MF resistance to ruxolitinib or with intolerant primary or secondary intermediate-2 or high-risk MF. Of the 97 evaluable patients, 46 (55%; 95% CI, 44% to 66%) achieved the primary end point of a splenic response (≥ 35% reduction in splenic volume). The recommended dosage for treatment is 400 mg daily for those with a platelet count ≥ 50 × 10^9/L. Grade 3 to 4 anemia and thrombocytopenia were common and Wernicke encephalopathy was a rare and fatal complication of treatment. If Wernicke encephalopathy is suspected, treatment should be discontinued, and parenteral thiamine should be initiated.

Efforts are ongoing to develop new classes of drugs such as antianemia medications, antifibrotic agents, and telomerase inhibitors.[167]

MDS/MPN OVERLAP SYNDROMES.

MDS/MPN overlap syndromes are characterized by ineffective or dysplastic hematopoiesis of one or more myeloid lineages with concurrent proliferation (with or without dysplasia) of one or more myeloid lineages. This category encompasses several disease categories that include chronic myelomonocytic leukemia (CMML), juvenile myelomonocytic leukemia, MDS/MPN-ringed sideroblast and thrombocytosis (MDS/MPN-RS-T) and atypical (BCR/Abl1-negative) CML. Those cases that do not meet criteria for any of these diseases are classified as MDS/MPN unclassifiable.[168] Clinically, these diseases can present with cytopenias in one or more lineages or as a proliferative disease accompanied by splenomegaly, hepatosplenomegaly, and/or extramedullary hematopoiesis (skin, lymph nodes, liver, GI tract, or lungs). Patients with MDS/MPN-RS-T may present with thromboembolism.

Chronic myelomonocytic leukemia is characterized by persistent monocytosis of ≥ 3 months. The triad of *TET2*, *ASXL1*, and *SRSF2* mutations is highly specific for this disease. Those with increased blasts and adverse prognostic factors (*ASXL1* mutation) respond to treatment with HMAs (ie, azacitidine and decitabine), similar to MDS. Allogeneic stem cell transplantation is the only curative therapy available for this disease.

Patients with MDS/MPN-RS-T have ringed sideroblasts ≥ 15% and a persistently elevated platelet count (≥ 450 × 10^9/L). Classic hotspot mutations in *SF3B1* are found in > 80% of the cases. In addition, patients may also have mutations in *JAK2*, *CALR*, and *MPL*. The treatment is generally supportive with erythropoiesis-stimulating agents and transfusion support. Low-dose aspirin may be given to those patients with *JAK2* mutations and increased cardiovascular risk.[169,170]

KEY POINTS

- The treatment of PV, ET, and PMF is tailored to the likelihood of the development of venous or arterial thrombosis, bleeding, or evolution to AML—the major life-threatening and limiting complications of these MPNs.
- Besides alleviation of constitutional symptoms, the goal of treatment of MPNs is to reduce the risk of the development of these complications and to prolong survival.

BLASTIC PLASMACYTOID DENDRITIC NEOPLASM

Blastic plasmacytoid dendritic cell neoplasm (BPDCN) is a rare and aggressive hematopoietic neoplasm that originates from transformed plasmacytoid dendritic cells. It has a male predilection with 70 years being the median age of presentation. The disease most commonly presents with cutaneous tumors; other sites of involvement are the spleen, bone marrow, lymph nodes, and extramedullary organs. The overexpression of interleukin 3 receptor subunit α (*IL3RA* or *CD123*) occurs in almost all cases of BPDCN. The loss of multiple cell-cycle checkpoints leading to the altered G1/S transition appears to be substantial in the molecular pathogenesis of BPDCN. The disease has a dismal prognosis; median survival is < 2 years without treatment. Younger age (< 60 years) and early HSCT were predictive of superior outcomes.[171] Tagraxofusp-erzs, also known as SL-401, is an CD123-directed cytotoxin consisting of recombinant human IL-3 fused to a truncated diphtheria toxin. A recent, open-label, multicohort study led to the FDA approval of tagraxofusp-erzs for the treatment of BPDCN. Given at the higher dose of 12 μg/kg, the CR and clinical CR rate in previously untreated patients was 72% (95% CI, 53% to 87%). The median time to response was 43 days and the ORR of 90%. Of these patients 45% (n = 13 of 29) were bridged to HSCT while in CR. Among previously treated patients, the ORR was 67%; the median duration of response was 2.8 months with a median time to response of 24 days.[172] Hypoalbuminemia, transaminitis, and thrombocytopenia are common adverse effects of this treatment. Of patients that received the higher dose of tagraxofusp-erzs, 18% experienced a significant adverse effect of capillary leak syndrome, with most of the cases occurring within the first cycle of treatment. Management strategies for capillary leak syndrome included close monitoring of volume status, necessitating aggressive IV fluid resuscitation or diuresis; glucocorticoids; and IV albumin. Another treatment strategy currently being explored in BPDCN is BCL-2 inhibition. The antiapoptotic protein BCL-2 is overexpressed in BPDCN and preclinical and clinical studies have demonstrated sensitivity of the disease to the BCL-2 inhibitor venetoclax. There is an ongoing, early-phase clinical trial of venetoclax in BPDCN.[173,174]

ACUTE LYMPHOBLASTIC LEUKEMIA

ALL occurs in children and adults, but its incidence peaks between ages 2 and 5 years. Relative to childhood ALL, in which cure rates are > 80%, the prognosis of adult ALL is significantly worse, particularly in older individuals, with current 5-year relative survival rates of only 10% to 15%.[2] Numerous population-based studies in multiple countries have demonstrated improvements in survival over time in all age groups except patients older than 60 or 70 years.[175-177] These improvements have been attributed to the increasing use of pediatric-intensive regimens in young adults and greater use of alloHSCT in middle-aged and older adults.

PATHOGENESIS

ALL is a clonal disorder thought to arise from genetic lesions in hematopoietic progenitor cells committed to differentiate along the B-cell or T-cell pathway. The precise events that lead to ALL are unknown, and only a few cases are associated with genetic predispositions or exposure to exogenous factors such as radiation or chemotherapeutic agents.

CLINICAL PRESENTATION

Approximately 50% of patients with ALL present with enlarged lymph nodes, hepatomegaly, or splenomegaly. Bone pain is commonly reported by patients who have acute disease and patients who are younger. Approximately 5% of patients will have involvement of the CNS at the time of diagnosis; this is associated with a worse prognosis. T-cell ALL is commonly associated with male sex, a mediastinal mass, and disseminated lymph node involvement.

DIAGNOSIS

ALL can be categorized according to the following:

- morphology,
- histochemistry,
- cell-surface markers,
- cytogenetics, and
- molecular biology.

Morphology and Immunohistochemistry

The leukemia cells in ALL are typically smaller than AML blasts and are devoid of granules. The French-American-British Cooperative Group developed a morphology-based classification

(Fig 19-4),[178] which, although once widely used, has since been largely replaced by immunology and cytogenetic classification. ALL blasts are typically negative for myeloperoxidase and nonspecific esterase, whereas periodic acid-Schiff staining is more variable.

Immunophenotype

The majority of ALL is of precursor B-cell immunophenotype (B-ALL) with CD10, CD19, CD22, HLA-DR, and TDT.[179] Approximately 25% of ALL cases have a T-cell phenotype, and < 5% are of mature B-cell or Burkitt type (CD20, a surface immunoglobulin). In approximately 40% to 50% of adults, the leukemia expresses CD10 (the common ALL antigen). In approximately 10% of cases, B-ALL expresses cytoplasmic immunoglobulin but not surface immunoglobulin, whereas in 5% of cases, surface immunoglobulin is present (mature B-cell or Burkitt leukemia). A subset of B-ALLs expresses CD20, a marker that in some, but not all, studies performed without the addition of CD20 antibodies was associated with a worse outcome.[180] In 25% of ALL cases, a nondefinitive (ie, not myeloperoxidase) myeloid antigen can be detected. Although some studies suggest that such myeloid antigens are a negative prognostic factor, the bulk of evidence suggests no independent significance for their presence. As in AML, discordant combinations of antigens on leukemic blasts enable detection of small numbers of blasts in a morphologically normal marrow using multidimensional flow cytometry. A more sensitive method for the detection of small numbers of ALL blasts involves PCR-based detection of clonally rearranged B-cell immunoglobulin genes or T-cell receptor genes.[181] This technique requires the development of individualized patient-specific probes. More recently, a novel approach based on high-throughput sequencing has been developed; it is as sensitive as PCR-based detection, but it is much less labor intensive and more easily standardized.

In 2% to 5% of acute leukemias, definition of the disease as either myeloid or lymphoid is problematic, either because two or more distinct populations of cells exist in the same person (bilineage leukemias) or a single population coexpresses definitive myeloid and lymphoid markers (biphenotypic leukemias). The current WHO classification defines these diseases as mixed-phenotype acute leukemia.[3] Results of several studies suggest patients with this type of leukemia have a worse clinical outcome than those with either AML or ALL.[182]

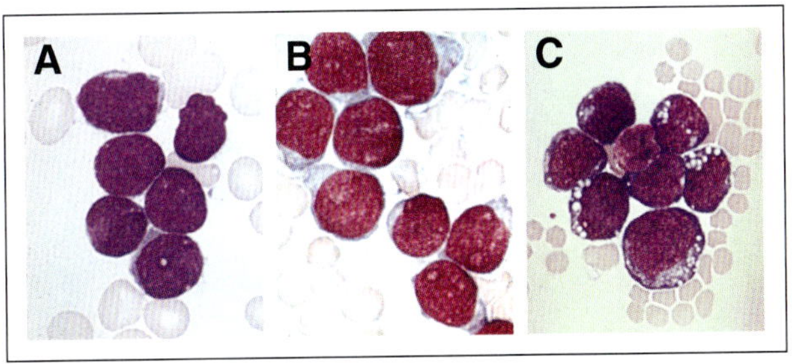

Fig. 19-4 Morphology of acute lymphoblastic leukemia (ALL) in adults.

(A) ALL childhood variant. The cells are small, homogeneous, with inconspicuous nucleoli (FAB-L1). (B) ALL adult variant. The cells are pleomorphic, with some cytoplasm and prominent nucleoli (FAB-L2). (C) Burkitt-like leukemia. The cells are homogeneous, with multiple nucleoli, deep blue cytoplasm, and sharply defined vacuoles (FAB-L3).

Cytogenetic and Molecular Abnormalities

Cytogenetic and molecular characteristics have important prognostic significance in ALL (Table 19-14; Fig 19-5).[183] In approximately 25% of cases, no cytogenetic abnormalities are found.[184] In approximately 10% of cases, an alteration in chromosome number (usually hyperdiploidy) is present without alteration in chromosome structure.[185] The most common translocation is the Ph chromosome, seen in 20% to 30% of adult ALL. The Ph chromosome results from a specific translocation, t(9;22)(q34.1;q11.2), which positions most of the *ABL1* proto-oncogene from chromosome 9 adjacent to the 5′ portion of the *BCR* gene on chromosome 22. The breakpoint on chromosome 9 is variable, whereas the breakpoints in the *BCR* gene on chromosome 22 occur within two regions: the major breakpoint cluster region (*M-bcr*) and the minor breakpoint cluster region (*m-bcr*). Rearrangements within the *M-bcr* are transcribed into a chimeric messenger RNA, which produces a hybrid 210-kd protein (p210BCR-ABL1), whereas breaks within the *m-bcr* express a chimeric messenger RNA that gives rise to a smaller 190-kd protein (p190BCR-ABL1). In CML, virtually all breakpoints are mapped to the *M-bcr* (CML-type Ph chromosome). Conversely, in ALL, breakpoints are found within both the *M-bcr* and *m-bcr*, and those within the *m-bcr* are termed the "ALL-type Ph chromosome."[186] The relative frequency of the two breakpoints in adult ALL has varied among studies, but overall, the two seem to be represented with equal frequency.[187] Ph-positive ALL with the CML-type of the *BCR-ABL1* translocation is not simply the lymphoid blast crisis phase of CML. Patients with this disease rarely have a long prediagnostic prodrome and do not routinely have marked splenomegaly. However, an underlying CML could potentially be recognized in the patients with p210-positive Ph-positive ALL once the ALL is in remission after initial induction (ie, the lymphoblasts are no longer detected by flow cytometry but the majority of the marrow cells still have evidence of BCR/ABL fusion by FISH or cytogenetics).

The other most common translocations seen in adult B-cell ALL are t(4;11)(q21;q23), which is seen in 7% of B-ALL, involves the *KMT2A* and *AF4* genes, and is associated with a poor prognosis; and the t(8;14)(q24.1;q32), which is seen in 2% to 4% of adult B-ALL, involves *c-MYC* and the immunoglobulin heavy chain, and is the translocation associated with Burkitt leukemia. T-cell ALLs (T-ALLs) often have translocations involving chromosomes 7 or 14 at T-cell receptor enhancer gene sites. The other most common cytogenetic changes seen in adult ALL involve del(9p), seen in 5% to 9% of cases; del(6q), seen in 5% to 7%; del(13q), seen in 3% to 5%, and the t(1;19)(q23;p13) involving the *TCF3* and *PBX1* genes, which has an improved prognosis with current ALL therapy. A newly described poor-risk entity found in 20% to 25% of adolescents and young and older adults is Ph-like ALL, which lacks the

Table 19-14 **WHO Classification of Myeloid Neoplasms and Acute Leukemia**
Acute Leukemias of Ambiguous Lineage
Acute undifferentiated leukemia
MPAL with t(9;22)(q34.1;q11.2); *BCR-ABL1*
MPAL with t(v;11q23.3); *KMT2A* rearranged
MPAL, B/myeloid, NOS
MPAL, T/myeloid, NOS
B-lymphoblastic leukemia/lymphoma
B-lymphoblastic leukemia/lymphoma, NOS
B-lymphoblastic leukemia/lymphoma with recurrent genetic abnormalities
B-lymphoblastic leukemia/lymphoma with t(9;22)(q34.1;q11.2);*BCR-ABL1*
B-lymphoblastic leukemia/lymphoma with t(v;11q23.3);*KMT2A* rearranged
B-lymphoblastic leukemia/lymphoma with t(12;21)(p13.2;q22.1); *ETV6-RUNX1*
B-lymphoblastic leukemia/lymphoma with hyperdiploidy
B-lymphoblastic leukemia/lymphoma with hypodiploidy
B-lymphoblastic leukemia/lymphoma with t(5;14)(q31.1;q32.3) *IL3-IGH*
B-lymphoblastic leukemia/lymphoma with t(1;19)(q23;p13.3);*TCF3-PBX1*
Provisional entity: B-lymphoblastic leukemia/lymphoma, BCR-ABL1–like
Provisional entity: B-lymphoblastic leukemia/lymphoma with iAMP21
T-lymphoblastic leukemia/lymphoma
Provisional entity: Early T-cell precursor lymphoblastic leukemia
Provisional entity: Natural killer cell lymphoblastic leukemia/lymphoma

Abbreviations: MPAL, mixed phenotype acute leukemia; NOS, not otherwise specified.

classic *BCR-ABL1* translocation but exhibits a gene expression profile that is similar to that of Ph-positive ALL.[188] Kinase-activating genetic rearrangements are characteristic of Ph-like ALL, including rearrangements of cytokine receptor–like factor 2 *(CRLF2)*, which are found in approximately 50% of all Ph-like ALL cases and are often associated with activating mutations in *JAK1/2*, but also include ABL class fusions in 10% among others.

An increasing number of genes in key signaling pathways (eg, regulation of lymphoid development, tumor suppression

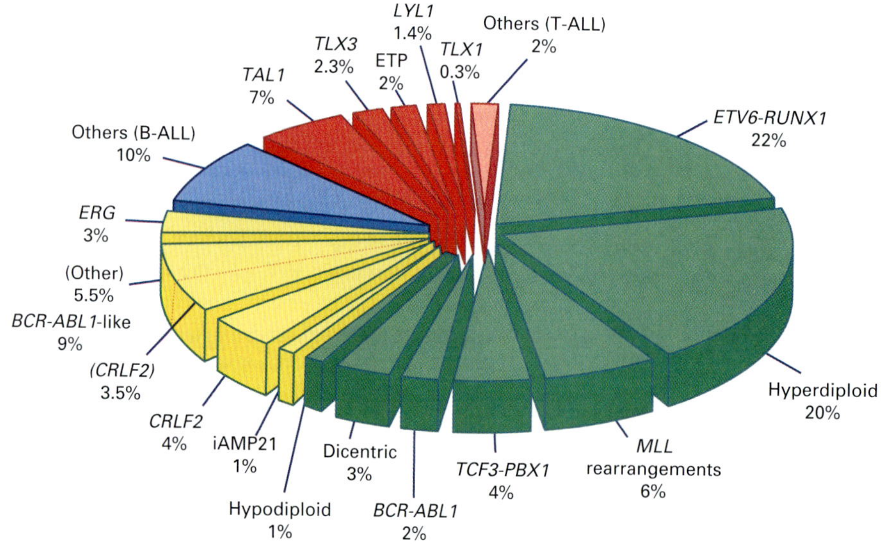

Fig. 19-5 Cytogenetic and molecular characteristics have important prognostic significance in acute lymphoblastic leukemia.

Abbreviation: T-ALL, T-cell acute lymphoblastic leukemia.

Reprinted from Seminars in Hematology, Vol. 50(4), Charles G. Mullighan, Genomic Characterization of Childhood Acute Lymphoblastic Leukemia, Pages No.314-324, Copyright (2013), with permission from Elsevier.

and cell cycle, cytokine receptors, lymphoid signaling, epigenetic modification) are recognized to be recurrently mutated in ALL.[189] Some of these are associated with a therapeutic response. For example, alterations in *IKAROS* gene family members are selectively found in different subtypes of high-risk ALL, such as Ph-positive ALL or Ph-like ALL, in which *IKZF1* mutations are a hallmark abnormality. T-ALL is characterized by activating mutations in *NOTCH1* (seen in > 50% of cases) and rearrangements of transcriptions factors *TLX1* (also known as *HOX11*), *TLX3* (*HOX11L2*), *LYL1*, *TAL1*, and *KMT2A*.[190]

PROGNOSTIC FACTORS

Pretreatment Factors

Various pretreatment characteristics have been shown to affect CR rates and survival, including increasing age, an elevated WBC count, CNS involvement, and, particularly, cytogenetic and molecular abnormalities (Table 19-15).

On the basis of such factors, investigators generally segregate ALL cases into standard risk and high risk. Although the exact schemas have inconsistencies, 5-year disease-free survival averages about 55% for standard-risk and 25% for high-risk patients.[191,192] With modern therapy, other factors, such as immunophenotypic characteristics of leukemic blasts (eg, expression of T-cell or myeloid antigens by ALL blasts), previously associated with a worse prognosis, have lost their independent prognostic importance.

Cytogenetic characteristics have important prognostic and therapeutic significance.[185] Between 10% and 20% of all cases of ALL are Ph positive (5% of childhood cases; 20% to 30% of adult cases), with an incidence that increases with age and can be seen in upward of 40% to 50% of patients older than 60 years, which may partially explain the importance of age as a prognostic variable. In studies conducted before the availability of imatinib, the likelihood of CR was somewhat lower for patients with Ph-positive ALL, and the probability of remaining in CR was much lower.

Studies designed to find molecular evidence of the *BCR-ABL1* rearrangement have shown that up to 10% of cases that are Ph negative or are inadequately assessed by cytogenetic analysis will have the *BCR-ABL1* rearrangement nonetheless; their prognosis seems to be the same as for patients who are Ph positive by cytogenetic analysis. Therefore, FISH and RT-PCR for the *BCR/ABL* fusion should be conducted at diagnosis for all patients with B-ALL. Although Ph-positive ALL has a poor prognosis when treated with conventional ALL therapy, results of trials that combined imatinib with standard induction are sufficiently encouraging to warrant inclusion of imatinib or other TKIs in the initial treatment of Ph-positive ALL.

The responsiveness of Ph-like ALL to TKIs remains undefined. Other cytogenetic abnormalities of adult ALL that carry a poor prognosis (both in terms of achieving a CR and remaining in CR) include t(4;11), t(8;14), low hypodiploidy/near triploidy, and having complex cytogenetics with five or more abnormalities. In contrast, adults with high hyperdiploidy or del(9p) seem to have a more favorable prognosis.[191-194] A higher risk of relapse is independently associated with *KMT2A* gene rearrangement, focal *IKZF1* gene deletion, or *TP53* mutations in B-ALL and no *NOTCH1/FBXW7* mutation and/or no *NRAS* or *KRAS* mutation and/or no *PTEN* gene alteration in T-ALL.[195,196]

Table 19-15 Prognostic Risk Factors in Acute Lymphoblastic Leukemia

Risk Factor
Pretreatment
Age
Leukocyte count
CNS involvement
Cytogenetic abnormalities
Molecular abnormalities
Posttreatment
Achievement of complete remission
Minimal residual disease state

Post-treatment Factors

Response to chemotherapy is a primary determinant of outcome in ALL. Several studies have shown that rapid clearance of blasts from the peripheral blood and bone marrow and a CR during the first chemotherapy course is associated with improved outcomes.[191,197] More recent focus has been on the use of MRD as a prognostic factor. Many studies have demonstrated that the presence of MRD after induction, after consolidation, or prior to HSCT can identify patients at high risk for disease recurrence.[181] These studies have provided the rationale to explore MRD-directed treatment interventions to optimize patient outcomes.

TREATMENT

Induction Chemotherapy

Standard induction therapy for adult ALL most commonly involves combination chemotherapy, including vincristine, prednisone, and an anthracycline. Asparaginase, an important component of pediatric ALL therapy, has been incorporated in the treatment of adult ALL in several prospective studies. With such regimens, 80% to 90% of patients achieve a first CR. Although a number of variations exist, no prospective, randomized trial has identified a clearly superior regimen.[191,192] A number of investigators have explored the use of hematopoietic growth factors immediately after induction chemotherapy. Similar to the findings for AML, the results of such studies demonstrate accelerated myeloid recovery and a decrease in the incidence of febrile neutropenia. In some trials, the CR rate was improved, but no findings have indicated an improvement in disease-free and OS.[198] For younger adults (< 60 years) with CD20-positive, Ph-negative B-ALL, adding the CD20 antibody rituximab to combination chemotherapy improves event-free survival.[199]

Postremission Therapy

If no additional therapy is administered after CR, the duration of remission is invariably short. Therapy after remission should include CNS prophylaxis, otherwise CNS disease will develop in at least 35% of adults. Patients with a high tumor burden at diagnosis, as evidenced by a high WBC count and elevated LDH levels, are at highest risk. With prophylaxis, the incidence of CNS leukemia as an isolated event is < 10%. Most trials have included several cycles of intensive consolidation therapy administered over several months after achievement of CR, as well as less intensive maintenance therapy administered over several years. Consolidation frequently includes combinations of high-dose methotrexate, cytarabine, cyclophosphamide, and an anthracycline, whereas maintenance usually comprises low-dose methotrexate, 6-mercaptopurine, vincristine, and prednisone.[191,192]

Some, but not all, data from randomized studies indicate that modification of postremission treatment intensity on the basis of MRD status can optimize treatment outcomes.[200-202] No single optimal regimen for CNS prophylaxis, consolidation therapy, and maintenance has been identified. Current trials are testing whether more-intensive regimens, such as those used in pediatric ALL, are tolerable and improve outcomes in adult ALL. Increasing evidence indicates such regimens are tolerated in patients younger than 40 years and appear to improve outcome.[203] One study suggested that patients up to age 55 years can also be considered for a pediatric-intensive regimen if the patients are fit and treated by experienced physicians.[204] With current regimens, approximately 35% to 40% of adult patients with ALL will remain alive and disease free at 5 years after diagnosis. With pediatric-inspired therapies, studies have shown 5-year survival rates of 67% to 78% in adolescents and younger adults (up to ages 18 to 30 years).[191,192]

Treatment of Persistent or Recurrent Disease

Patients whose disease does not go into CR or subsequently relapses have dismal outcomes, with long-term survival at 5 years generally not exceeding 10%. Therefore, the current strategy is to reduce tumor burdens (if possible) and then to proceed with alloHSCT. A variety of chemotherapeutic agents have been used in combinations similar to those used during induction such as (liposomal) vincristine, steroids, anthracyclines, asparaginase, methotrexate, and high-dose cytarabine. Newer drugs for R/R ALL include clofarabine, forodesine, rapamycin, and nelarabine, the latter of which can achieve CR rates of 30% or higher in patients with recurrent T-ALL but has significant neurotoxic effects.[191,192]

The bispecific, T-cell–engaging antibody blinatumomab, composed of the single-chain variable fragments of a CD19 and a CD3 antibody, has been approved by the FDA on the basis of the demonstration of a 40% to 45% remission rate as a single agent in relapsed or refractory B-ALL.[205] Unique toxicities include cytokine release syndrome and neurologic events. A randomized study reported higher remission rates and improved median OS (7.7 *v* 4.0 months) with blinatumomab compared with standard-of-care chemotherapy in adults with R/R B-ALL.[206]

A randomized study of the CD22 antibody–drug conjugate inotuzumab ozogamicin has demonstrated higher CR rates (80% *v* 30%) and longer PFS and OS, compared with standard-of-care chemotherapy in adults with R/R B-ALL. Inotuzumab ozogamicin is associated with sinusoidal obstruction syndrome (veno-occlusive disease) in approximately 10% of patients, mostly occurring among complete responders who went on to receive alloHSCT.[207]

Response rates approaching 100% have been reported with adoptive immunotherapies using T cells expressing chimeric antigen receptors (CARs) that recognize CD19 in small series of pediatric and adult relapsed ALL cases, even among patients in whom alloHSCT failed, but this approach is not yet widely available.[208] On the basis of early studies, tisagenlecleucel, a CAR T-cell therapy, is approved by the FDA for the treatment of B-ALL in patients up to 25 years of age whose disease has not responded to standard therapy or relapsed at least twice, making it the first gene therapy approved in the United States.[209,210] This type of immunotherapy shows promise in larger patient populations, although severe, potentially fatal, adverse effects, including cytokine release syndrome and neurologic toxicity, have been observed. Figure 19-6 is a schematic of various antibody-mediated immunotherapies that are currently available.

Hematopoietic Cell Transplantation

AlloHSCT is an important postremission treatment modality in ALL, but its curative potential must be balanced against transplant-related morbidity and mortality, late complications, and associated reductions in quality of life.[191] An evidence-based review of available trials led an expert panel to recommend the consideration of myeloablative alloHSCT for adults younger than 35 years with ALL in first CR after multiagent chemotherapy for all disease risk groups because of superior outcomes with regard to postremission chemotherapy.[211] However, although results obtained with transplantation have not yet been compared directly with pediatric-inspired chemotherapy regimens in younger adult patients with ALL, retrospective analyses suggest this chemotherapy approach may yield survival outcomes equal or superior to alloHSCT because of lower nonrelapse-associated mortality rate and no increased risk of relapse.[212] With increasing age, the survival advantage of alloHSCT diminishes because of increased rates of nonrelapse-associated mortality. In the absence of a suitable related or unrelated donor, cord blood can be considered as a stem cell source.

For patients in second or later CR, alloHSCT is recommended over chemotherapy. The superiority of any conditioning regimen is unclear, but some data suggest better outcomes with regimens that include total-body irradiation. More limited data suggest reduced-intensity conditioning may produce reasonable outcomes in patients thought to be unfit for myeloablative regimens.[211] Not surprisingly, the outcomes with HSCT depend largely on the disease status of the patient. If allogeneic transplantations are performed during the first CR, long-term survival rates range from approximately 40% to 60%. If such transplantations are performed in patients with disease resistant to conventional chemotherapy,

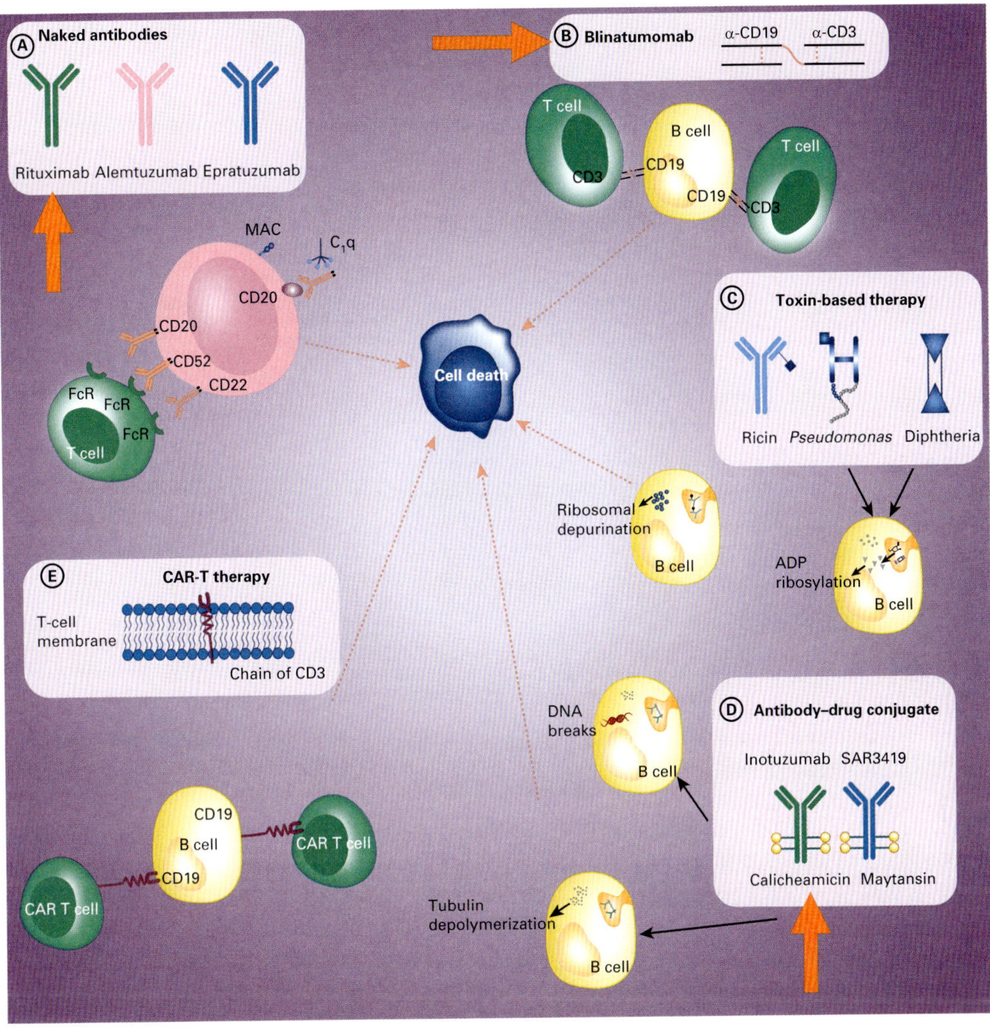

Mechanisms of action of monoclonal antibody conjugates

A. Naked (unconjugated) antibodies
B. Bi-specific T-cell-engaging antibody
C. Antibodies linked to toxins
D. Antibodies linked to drugs
E. Chimeric antigen receptor T cells

Fig. 19-6 Mechanisms of action of monoclonal antibody conjugates.

Abbreviation: CAR-T, chimeric antigen receptors T cell.

Permission to reuse given by Dr. Mark Liztow, from Parikh S, Litzow M. Philadelphia chromosome-negative acute lymphoblastic leukemia: therapies under development. Future Oncology *10:2201, 2014.*

long-term survival can be obtained in only 15% to 25% of patients.[211]

Efforts have been undertaken to use a risk-adapted approach to alloHSCT to spare patients transplant-related toxicities by allocating them to undergo chemotherapy if chemosensitivity was documented (eg, confirmed MRD-negative status after chemotherapy in standard-risk disease).[213] On the other hand, MRD persistence after induction and consolidation signals a high risk for subsequent relapse. MRD at the time of transplantation also indicates a higher risk of relapse, but outcomes are likely better than with chemotherapy alone. A recent study reported that for patients who were positive for MRD after chemotherapy, treatment with blinatumomab converted 78% to MRD negativity and patients who were MRD responders had improved relapse-free survival and OS compared with MRD nonresponders.[214] On the basis of this study, the FDA granted accelerated approval for use of blinatumomab in late March 2018 to treat adults and children with B-cell precursor ALL who are in remission but still have MRD.

SPECIAL TYPES OF ADULT ALL

Ph-Positive ALL

As noted, ALL associated with t(9;22) translocations has a poor prognosis when treated with conventional chemotherapy. However, the disease is sensitive to TKIs such as imatinib, dasatinib, nilotinib, or ponatinib. When combined with induction chemotherapy, CR rates have reached 90% to 100%, and OS appears to be improved. In younger adults, less-intensive chemotherapy combined with imatinib over the entire induction period is as effective as and less toxic than a more intensive regimen with imatinib given only over the first 2 weeks.[215]

AlloHSCT is still considered the best curative option, particularly for younger adults, but the degree of improvement in outcome over TKI-containing combination chemotherapy is unclear. One retrospective study of patients with Ph-positive ALL in first molecular remission after chemotherapy with TKI suggests that autologous HSCT, although associated with substantially higher post-transplantation relapse risk, may yield similar survival outcomes for matched-sibling and unrelated-donor alloHSCT.[216] If an MRD-negative remission is achieved early in Ph-positive ALL, chemotherapy combined with a TKI may provide an alternative treatment strategy, particularly if patients are thought to be at high risk for HSCT-related death.[217] Therapy with dasatinib and prednisone alone results in CRs in a high percentage of older patients with Ph-positive ALL without the need for concomitant chemotherapy, but disease in most patients ultimately relapses.[191]

The optimal TKI to use with induction chemotherapy remains unclear at this time, but high and improved response rates with ponatinib have been observed in retrospective studies compared with dasatinib. Concerns remain about the long-term vascular toxicity associated with ponatinib.[218,219]

Mature B-ALL

Mature B-ALL is grouped together with Burkitt lymphoma and is treated accordingly (see Chapter 20: Lymphomas).[191]

KEY POINTS

- Induction therapy in adult ALL should generally include vincristine, prednisone, an anthracycline, and asparaginase. With such regimens, complete remission can be achieved in 80% to 90% of patients. Consideration of a pediatric-inspired regimen should be given for all patients up to 40 years of age and possibly in selected patients up to 55 years of age.
- Patients with CD20-positive B-ALL should receive rituximab during induction and consolidation.
- Patients with Ph-positive ALL should receive a TKI in combination with chemotherapy.
- Blinatumomab can convert up to 80% of MRD-positive patients with B-cell ALL who are in remission to MRD negative and may also improve outcomes.
- Allogeneic transplantation is an important postremission treatment modality except perhaps in patients who have highly chemosensitive disease.
- Salvage treatment options for patients with R/R B-ALL include blinatumomab, inotuzumab ozogamicin, and tisagenlecleucel.

CHRONIC LYMPHOCYTIC LEUKEMIA

CLL is the most prevalent adult leukemia in western countries. The disease is more common in men than women (ratio, 1.7:1), with a steep age-specific incidence beginning approximately after age 40 years and peaking in the decade between ages 65 and 74 years. The incidence is higher in Jewish people of Russian or eastern European ancestry, but it is rare in Asian countries. There are no known risk factors for CLL; particularly, it is one of the few leukemias that does not seem to be associated with exposure to ionizing radiation, chemicals, or drugs, although data suggest a possible relationship with Agent Orange. However, a strong inherited component is well recognized, and genome-wide association studies have identified > 40 susceptibility loci.[220-222]

CLINICAL PRESENTATION

Most patients with CLL are asymptomatic at diagnosis, which is often made incidentally when lymphocytosis is noted during a routine evaluation. The findings on physical examination are normal for 20% to 30% of patients, whereas lymphadenopathy, hepatosplenomegaly, or both are observed in 40% to 50% of patients. However, as the disease progresses, generalized lymphadenopathy and splenomegaly become common features. Involvement of other organs is unusual and should suggest the possibility of transformation (ie, Richter syndrome [see the section Aggressive Transformation]) (Table 19-16).

Infections

Increased susceptibility to infections reflects quantitative and qualitative defects seen within the innate and adaptive immune response (eg, hypogammaglobulinemia, reduced levels of complement, impaired phagocytic killing of nonopsonized bacteria, reduction of functional impairment of T-cell subsets) that worsen with disease progression.[223] Historically, the most common pathogens have been those that require opsonization for bacteria killing, such as *Streptococcus pneumoniae, Staphylococcus aureus,* and *Haemophilus influenzae.* The increased use of immunosuppressive agents such as fludarabine, cladribine, pentostatin, and alemtuzumab has markedly increased

Table 19-16 Clinical Features of Chronic Lymphocytic Leukemia

Infections
Hypogammaglobulinemia
Reduced levels of complement
Impaired phagocytic killing of nonopsonized bacteria,
Reduction of functional impairment of T-cell subsets
Autoimmunity
Autoimmune hemolytic anemia
Immune thrombocytopenia
Pure red cell aplasia
Aggressive transformation
Richter transformation
Secondary malignant disease
Skin cancers (including melanomas)
Colon cancers
Lung cancers
Myeloid neoplasms

the number of infections with opportunistic organisms such as *Candida, Listeria, Pneumocystis jirovecii,* cytomegalovirus, *Aspergillus,* herpesviruses, and others. The prophylactic use of IV immunoglobulins or antimicrobial agents should be reserved for select patients with documented, repeated infections.

Autoimmunity

Autoimmune hemolytic anemia is noted in 10% to 15% of patients with CLL and has been associated with fludarabine treatment.[224] Many additional patients have a positive direct antiglobulin test but no clinical evidence of hemolysis. The frequency of immune thrombocytopenia seems to be approximately 2% to 15%. In most cases, these antibodies are polyclonal and not a product of the malignant B cells. Autoimmune anemia or thrombocytopenia generally responds to corticosteroids such as prednisone at a dosage of 60 to 100 mg/d, which may be tapered after 1 or 2 weeks with evidence of response. Patients who do not experience a disease response to corticosteroids may respond to high-dose IV immunoglobulins. Rituximab and alternative immunosuppressants such as cyclosporine or cyclophosphamide may also sometimes be useful.

Cytotoxic chemotherapy is an option for patients with highly refractory autoimmune hemolytic anemia. CLL-associated immune thrombocytopenia may respond to thrombopoietin receptor agonists such as romiplostim and eltrombopag. Splenectomy may be considered when systemic approaches fail. Radiation therapy to the spleen induces only transient responses.

Pure Red Cell Aplasia

Pure red cell aplasia is uncommon in CLL (< 1% of cases).[224,225] It is characterized by normochromic and normocytic anemia with an absolute reticulocyte count of < 10,000/mL and an absence or near absence of erythroblasts in the bone marrow; the WBC count, WBC differential count, and platelet counts are generally normal. Corticosteroids as well as cyclosporine and rituximab may be effective.[226]

Aggressive Transformation

Annually, in approximately 0.5% of patients with CLL, the disease will evolve into a more aggressive lymphoid malignant process termed Richter syndrome, which characteristically presents with increasing lymphadenopathy, hepatosplenomegaly, fever, abdominal pain, weight loss, progressive anemia, and thrombocytopenia with a rapid increase in the peripheral-blood lymphocyte count and an increased serum LDH level.[227]

This transformation is not clearly related to either the nature or extent of previous therapy. The WHO classification recognizes two distinct pathologic variants of Richter syndrome, namely the diffuse large B-cell lymphoma (DLBCL) variant and the Hodgkin lymphoma (HL) variant. Molecular lesions of tumor suppression *(TP53),* cell cycle *(CDKN2A),* and cell proliferation *(NOTCH1, MYC)* account for approximately 90% of cases of Richter syndrome. Approximately 80% of the variants (and 40% to 50% of the HL variants) are clonally related to the preceding CLL phase. In the other patients, analyses of immunoglobulin heavy-chain variable domain *(IGHV)*-D-J genes show different rearrangements compared with the paired CLL, indicating de novo lymphomas arising in a patient with CLL. The prognosis of the DLBCL variant is generally unfavorable but not uniform, with outcomes being better in patients with clonally unrelated Richter syndrome. Outcomes with the HL variant of Richter syndrome are better than with the DLBCL variant but not as good as with de novo HL.[227,228]

CLL also may evolve into prolymphocytic leukemia (PLL), which is associated with progressive anemia and thrombocytopenia, with ≥ 55% prolymphocytes in the peripheral blood. Clinical features include lymphadenopathy, hepatosplenomegaly, wasting syndrome, and increased resistance to therapy. Transformation to ALL, plasma cell leukemia, or multiple myeloma has also been noted anecdotally.

Secondary Malignant Diseases

Secondary malignant diseases occur with increased frequency in patients with CLL, related both to the immune defects of the disease and to the consequences of therapy. The most frequent tumors are skin cancers (including melanomas), colon cancers, lung cancers, and myeloid neoplasms.

DIAGNOSIS

Morphology

The diagnosis of CLL requires a sustained increase in mature-appearing B lymphocytes in the peripheral blood to > 5,000/mm^3; the presence of fewer B cells without palpable lymphadenopathy in an asymptomatic individual is called monoclonal B lymphocytosis. In CLL, it is not unusual to find a small percentage of larger atypical cells, cleaved cells, or prolymphocytes. The bone marrow usually is infiltrated by at least 30% lymphocytes. Although a bone marrow aspirate and biopsy specimen are not needed to make the diagnosis, they are useful to evaluate the etiology of cytopenias. Neither lymph node biopsy nor computed tomography scanning is needed in the initial evaluation and should be performed only if clinically indicated.[229,230]

Immunophenotype

The predominant cell population expresses B-cell markers (CD19, CD20, and CD23) and CD5, but not other pan–T-cell markers. The entity formerly described as T-cell CLL is now called T-cell prolymphocytic leukemia (T-PLL) and is not considered part of CLL. The B cells are monoclonal, as evidenced by the presence of either κ or λ light chains, and characteristically express surface immunoglobulin, CD79b, CD20, and CD22 with low density (as opposed to mantle cell lymphoma, which usually has higher expression of CD20 and surface immunoglobulin).[229] Distinguishing CLL from mantle cell lymphoma is essential, because both express CD5. CD23 is often helpful (often negative in mantle cell lymphoma), but absence of cyclin D1 expression is critical for differentiation and confirmation of CLL.

Cytogenetic and Molecular Abnormalities

Conventional banding techniques and FISH detect cytogenetic abnormalities in > 50% and > 80% of CLL cases, respectively.[231] The most common, either alone or in combination with other abnormalities, is deletion of 13q (55% of cases; Table 19-17).

Table 19-17 Cytogenetic and Molecular Abnormalities of Chronic Lymphocytic Leukemia

• Deletion of 13q14
• Deletion of 11q
• Trisomy 12
• Abnormalities of chromosome 17 (del17p with *TP53* gene disruption)
• *BCL-2* gene overexpression
• Immunoglobulin heavy chain variable domain mutations
• ZAP-70
• Recurrent mutations involving *TP53*, *NOTCH1*, *SF3B1*, and *BIRC3*

The disease course is more benign for patients with 13q14 abnormalities, and such patients often have a normal lifespan. Deletions of 11q are identified in 15% to 20% of cases and are associated with massive lymphadenopathy, often out of proportion to the increase in the peripheral-blood lymphocyte count. Trisomy 12 can be detected in 15% to 20% of cases. Structural abnormalities of chromosome 17 occur in ≥ 15% of patients when FISH testing is performed. 17p13 deletions lead to disruption of the *TP53* gene and are found more frequently in cases of atypical CLL, which is associated with a higher likelihood of Richter transformation, more prolymphocytes, advanced stage, resistance to chemotherapy, and a poor prognosis. More than one-third of patients have complex genetic abnormalities.

Translocations involving *BCL-2* [t(14;18)(q32;q21)] and *BCL-3* [t(14;19)(q32;q13.1)] have been detected in only 5% to 10% of cases, but overexpression of the *BCL-2* gene is present in > 70% of cases. The expression ratio of the antiapoptotic gene *BCL-2* to the proapoptotic gene *BAX* is increased in CLL cells, supporting the concept that CLL is more a disorder of prolonged cell survival than a hyperproliferative disease, although both factors probably contribute.

Lymphocytes from approximately half of patients with CLL are thought to develop from naïve B cells and have unmutated *IGHV*; the other half contain mutated *IGHV*, indicating their CLL cells derive from post–germinal-center B cells. *IGHV* mutation status does not change over the course of the disease. These two populations are characterized by markedly different clinical outcomes, with the survival significantly shorter for the group with unmutated *IGHV*. Other unfavorable molecular prognostic markers, such as positive ZAP-70,[232,233] positive CD38 expression, del(17p), and del(11q),[252] are also more commonly found in patients with unmutated *IGHV* than those with mutated *IGHV*. In practice, surface expression of ZAP-70 and CD38 can be assessed by flow cytometry using peripheral blood or bone marrow samples. Another flow cytometry–based prognostic marker more recently developed and validated in CLL is CD49d, which is associated with inferior survival when overexpressed.[235] Sequencing technologies have identified recurrent mutations in CLL involving *TP53, NOTCH1, SF3B1,* and *BIRC3*,[236,237] and are increasingly being used for risk prognostication. Among many mutations identified in CLL, *TP53* mutation is an inferior prognostic and predictive marker, as shown in multiple studies demonstrating inferior PFS and OS in this molecular subgroup after conventional chemoimmunotherapy. Because the presence of *TP53* mutation influences treatment decisions (ie, targeted agent *v* chemoimmunotherapy), the 2018 International Workshop for CLL Guideline strongly recommends testing for *TP53* mutation before treatment, alongside FISH and *IGHV* mutation status.

Cytogenetic and molecular markers in CLL can change over time, requiring reassessment if the tempo of disease seems to be changing.

PROGNOSTIC FACTORS

Several characteristics can stratify patients with CLL into groups according to different clinical outcomes that may require different therapeutic approaches. The five-stage Rai classification[238] is most commonly used in the United States (Table 19-18), and the three-stage Binet system[239] is most often applied in Europe (Table 19-19). The major difference between the two systems is that Rai stages 0 and I are mostly combined into Binet stage A, and Rai stages III and IV are combined into Binet stage C. Numerous new cytogenetic and molecular prognostic markers have been identified in recent years.[240] An internationally applicable prognostic index has been developed that is based on five independent prognostic factors, namely age, clinical stage, del(17p) and/or *TP53* mutation, unmutated *IGHV*,

Table 19-18 Rai Classification for Clinical Staging of Chronic Lymphocytic Leukemia[239]

Risk	Stage	Description	Median Survival (years)[a]
Low	0	Lymphocytosis in blood or bone marrow	> 12.5
Intermediate	I	Lymphadenopathy	8.5
	II	Splenomegaly and/or hepatomegaly with or without lymphadenopathy	6
High	III	Anemia (hemoglobin, < 11 g/dL)[b]	1.5
	IV	Thrombocytopenia (platelet count < 100,000/µL)[b]	1.5

[a]Of historical significance because outcomes are changing with newer therapies.
[b]Anemia and thrombocytopenia cannot be immune mediated.

Table 19-19 **Binet Classification for Clinical Staging of Chronic Lymphocytic Leukemia**[239]		
Stage	**Description**	**Median Survival (years)**[a]
A	< 2 node-bearing areas[b]	> 10
B	> 3 node-bearing areas	5
C	Anemia (< 10.0 g/dL) and/or thrombocytopenia (platelet count < 100,000/μL)	2

[a]Of historical significance because outcomes are changing with newer therapies.
[b]Five node-bearing areas are possible: cervical, axillary, inguinal-femoral, spleen, and liver.

and β_2-microglobulin), and separates patients with early-stage and from those with advanced-stage CLL into four different prognostic groups with substantially different 5-year OS (Table 19-20).[241]

TREATMENT

With the possible exception of alloHSCT, CLL is not curable with currently available therapies, and several randomized studies found no improvement in survival with early versus delayed treatment of patients with early-stage disease (Rai 0 to II or Binet A).[242] Therefore, asymptomatic patients with early-stage disease should be monitored, but they should not receive treatment unless enrolled in a clinical trial. Currently, indications to start therapy include evidence of progressive bone marrow failure (ie, anemia, thrombocytopenia not associated with autoimmune hemolytic anemia or ITP), massive, symptomatic or progressive splenomegaly, massive or progressive symptomatic lymphadenopathy, progressive lymphocytosis (with lymphocyte doubling time < 6 months), steroid-refractory autoimmune anemia or thrombocytopenia, and constitutional ("B") symptoms (ie, weight loss, night sweats, fevers).[243,244]

Initial Therapy

First-line chemoimmunotherapy prolongs survival in CLL as compared with chemotherapy alone.[245] The exact choice of therapy is generally based on the medical fitness of the patient and the presence or absence of del(17p)/*TP53* mutation.

Table 19-20 **International Prognostic Index for Chronic Lymphocytic Leukemia**[241]		
Score[a]	**Risk Level**	**5-Year Survival (%)**
0-1	Low	93
2-3	Intermediate	79
4-6	High	63
7-10	Very high	23

[a]The score comprises five independent prognostic factors: *TP53* gene mutation with a 17p deletion (4 points), unmutated immunoglobulin heavy-chain variable region (2 points), increasing β_2-microglobulin level > 3.5 mg/L (2 points), elevated clinical stage (Binet B/C or Rai I-IV; 1 point), and age > 65 years (1 point).

For younger, fit patients without del(17p)/*TP53* mutation, a chemoimmunotherapy regimen had been used in the past, most commonly with fludarabine, cyclophosphamide, and rituximab (FCR). More recently, three randomized phase III trials tested ibrutinib with or without an anti-CD20 monoclonal antibody in comparison with conventional chemoimmunotherapy in treatment-naïve CLL. The ECOG study (E1912) compared ibrutinib plus rituximab with FCR in younger treatment-naïve patients with CLL (age < 70 years).[246] The Alliance study was a three-arm trial comparing bendamustine plus rituximab (BR) with IR or ibrutinib alone in older treatment-naïve patients with CLL (age ≥ 65 years).[247] The ILLUMINATE trial compared IR with chlorambucil plus obinutuzumab in older treatment-naïve patients with CLL.[248] All three studies demonstrated superior PFS in ibrutinib-based arms compared with conventional chemoimmunotherapy. In the Alliance study, there was no PFS difference between two ibrutinib arms with or without rituximab, questioning the role of adding anti-CD20 monoclonal antibody during ibrutinib therapy. These results establish ibrutinib as effective first-line therapy for CLL regardless of age. Ibrutinib is currently approved as monotherapy for CLL and can be given as any line of therapy, including as a first-line treatment (Table 19-21).

Because ibrutinib is currently approved as indefinite therapy, not all patients may accept such a treatment approach because of concerns about cumulative toxicity and cost. In fact, with FCR, two studies demonstrated durable remission of up to 12 years in patients with mutated *IGHV* and without del(17p)/*TP53* mutations.[249,250] With patients who have the unmutated *VH* gene, more frequent relapses are seen and targeted therapy such as ibrutinib is an alternative strategy, with data from the recently reported E1912 trial showing an advantage for ibrutinib over FCR for patients with unmutated *IGHV*.[246]

For patients who are candidates for chemoimmunotherapy, acceptable alternatives to FCR include fludarabine and rituximab (FR), substituting pentostatin for fludarabine, and BR, among others. For patients with significant comorbidities or for those who are > 65 years, monotherapy with the oral Bruton tyrosine kinase (BTK) inhibitor ibrutinib has been approved on

Table 19-21 **Key Clinical Trials for Treatment of Newly Diagnosed Chronic Lymphocytic Leukemia in Adults**			
Trial	**Age (years)**	**Treatment**	**Outcome**
E1912	< 70	IR *v* FCR	IR improved PFS/OS
A0421202	> 65	BR *v* IR *v* I	IR or I improved PFS
RESONATE	> 65[a]	IO *v* CO	IO improved PFS

Abbreviations: BR, bendamustine and rituximab; CO, chlorambucil and obinutuzumab; FCR, fludarabine, cyclophosphamide and rituximab; I, ibrutinib; IO, ibrutinib and obinutuzumab; IR, ibrutinib and rituximab; OS, overall survival; PFS, progression-free survival.
[a]Or younger than 65 years with comorbidities.

the basis of results from a randomized trial showing longer PFS and OS, higher response rates, and improvement in hematologic variables as compared with chlorambucil.[251]

Patients with CLL with del(17p)/*TP53* mutation have more aggressive disease and generally poor outcomes with chemoimmunotherapy.[245] Ibrutinib is considered first-line therapy of CLL with del(17p)/*TP53* mutation even in young, fit patients.[230,245] Important adverse events associated with ibrutinib include bleeding and atrial fibrillation. Idelalisib, an oral phosphatidylinositide-3 kinase δ inhibitor, also is effective in CLL when used with rituximab in patients with comorbidities that precluded the use of intensive chemoimmunotherapy.[252] However, idelalisib has the potential for serious inflammatory complications that can manifest as severe diarrhea or transaminitis; therefore, it typically is not used in front-line therapy (Fig 19-7).

Patients with CLL who are treated with purine analogs become significantly immunosuppressed.[253] Thus, anti-infective prophylaxis for herpesvirus and *Pneumocystis jirovecii* is recommended. Other expected toxicities of most regimens include moderate myelosuppression. TLS occasionally occurs in patients treated for CLL, especially those with high WBC counts or bulky lymphadenopathy. This syndrome may be fatal and is not consistently preventable with the use of prophylactic allopurinol and/or hydration. Fludarabine may be associated with autoimmune hemolytic anemia and thrombocytopenia and should be stopped and switched to alternatives if such complications are seen. Despite the profound immunosuppression associated with single-agent fludarabine, the risk of secondary malignant disease does not seem to be increased with fludarabine alone, but there may be an increased incidence of myelodysplasia when fludarabine is combined with alkylating-agent therapy.[254]

Treatment of Relapsed or Refractory Disease

The management of relapsed CLL depends on several factors, including age, performance status, the presence of del(17p)/*TP53* mutation, previous therapy, response to and duration of therapy, and time from last therapy. With many potential treatments available, the exact sequence and timing of salvage therapies is being addressed in clinical trials. Current standard of care for R/R CLL includes ibrutinib monotherapy, idelalisib together with rituximab, venetoclax with or without rituximab, and duvelisib (currently approved as a third-line therapy).[255-257]

Ibrutinib has also been combined with other chemotherapeutics and has shown benefit, for example, when added to BR (Table 19-22).[258] More selective inhibitors of BTK (eg, acalabrutinib) are under clinical study[259] and may provide a better safety profile than ibrutinib. High response rates have been obtained with venetoclax, a BCL-2 inhibitor,[260] which is now approved for patients with R/R CLL. In a recently reported open-label, phase III trial, 389 patients were randomly assigned to receive venetoclax for up to 2 years in combination with rituximab (VR) for the first 6 months or BR for 6 months and showed a 2-year PFS advantage for VR at 85% versus 36% for BR.[261] Benefit was noted in all clinical and biologic subgroups including patients with 17p abnormalities. Clearance of MRD at

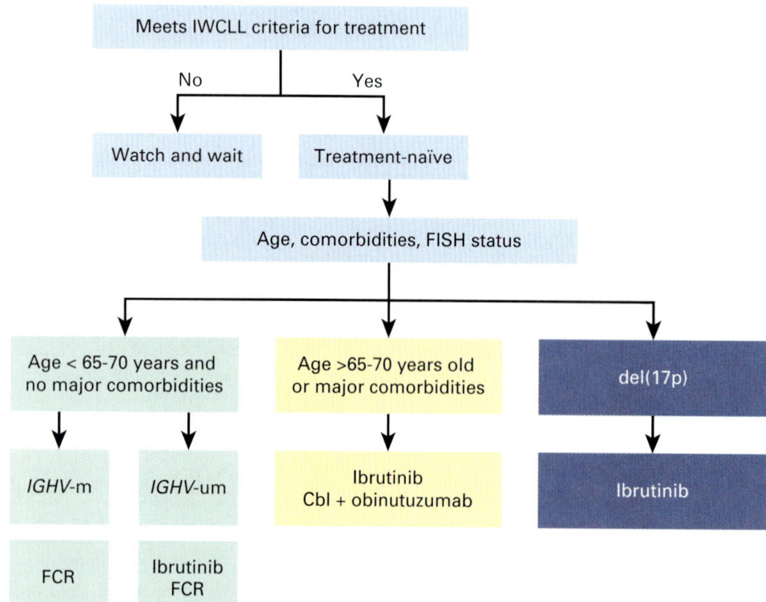

Fig. 19-7 Front-line therapy for CLL.

Abbreviations: Cbl, chlorambucil; CLL, chronic lymphocytic leukemia; FCR, fludarabine, cyclophosphamide, and rituximab; FISH, fluorescent in situ hybridization; IWCLL, International Workshop on Chronic Lymphocytic Leukemia.

Table 19-22 Comparison of Active Drugs for Chronic Lymphocytic Leukemia

Drug	Mechanism of Action	Indications	Dose	Toxicity
Ibrutinib	BTK inhibitor	CLL (alone or combination)	420 or 560 mg daily	Atrial arrhythmia, hypertension
		Mantle cell lymphoma		Bleeding
		Marginal zone lymphoma		PML
		Small lymphocytic lymphoma		Renal failure
		Waldenström macroglobulinemia		
Idelalisib	PI3 kinase inhibitor	CLL (alone or in combination)	150 mg twice daily	Diarrhea, erythroderma
		Follicular lymphoma		Hepatotoxicity, pneumonia
Venetoclax	BCL-2 inhibitor	CLL (alone or in combination)	400 mg daily (after ramp up)	TLS AIHA
		Small lymphocytic lymphoma		Pneumonia
		Acute myeloid leukemia		Sepsis

Abbreviations: AIHA, autoimmune hemolytic anemia; BCL-2, B-cell lymphoma 2; BTK, Bruton's tyrosine kinase; CLL, chronic lymphocytic leukemia; PI, phosphoinositide; PML, progressive multifocal leukoencephalopathy; TLS, tumor lysis syndrome.

9 months was significantly better for VR at 62% versus 13% for BR, and OS was improved with the VR group. Encouraging results have also been reported with CD19-targeted autologous T cells expressing CARs.[262] A proposed treatment approach to the management of R/R CLL and small lymphocytic lymphoma has recently been published (Fig 19-8).

Hematopoietic Stem Cell Transplantation

Given the advanced age of most patients with CLL, HSCT using high-dose preparative regimens has been limited to a minority of patients. The availability of reduced-intensity transplantation has widened the possible application of transplantation and enables long-term disease control and possible cure for a subset of patients.

For standard-risk CLL, alloHSCT should be considered in the absence of response or if disease progression occurs after treatment with B-cell receptor inhibitors. For high-risk CLL, alloHSCT is recommended after two lines of therapy have failed and shown an objective response to B-cell receptor inhibitors or to a clinical trial or after lack of response to or progression after treatment with B-cell receptor inhibitors.[263]

Supportive Measures

Splenectomy. Splenectomy may provide important palliation for patients with CLL for whom systemic treatment has failed and who have symptomatic splenomegaly or cytopenias that preclude chemotherapy. The procedure may also be considered for patients with autoimmune cytopenia whose disease does not respond to corticosteroids, IV immunoglobulins, or rituximab.

Leukapheresis. Leukapheresis results in only transient reductions in circulating lymphocytes and is not recommended for general practice. Patients with CLL rarely experience tumor-cell aggregates; therefore, regardless of the number of circulating cells, systemic treatment is usually sufficient.

Tumor Lysis Syndrome. Traditionally, in CLL, TLS has not been thought of as a major complication, because of lower proliferative potential of CLL cells and the generally slower response to chemotherapy. However, with the advent of novel targeted therapies to which CLL cells can be highly sensitive and in the context of patients with high tumor burdens with more rapid growth rates, TLS may pose a more significant risk with the potential to be fatal. This is best characterized with venetoclax, for which a 5-week ramp up in dosing is recommended with careful monitoring as an inpatient or outpatient to minimize the risk of TLS development.[264]

KEY POINTS

- Distinguishing CLL from other diseases, notably hairy cell leukemia or the leukemic phases of marginal zone lymphoma or mantle cell lymphoma, is based on the morphologic appearance of the cells and the distinct immunophenotype of the malignant cells.
- Survival for patients with CLL has improved over the past several years, and several novel, highly active agents have become available.
- Three randomized phase III trials testing ibrutinib with or without an anti-CD20 monoclonal antibody in comparison with conventional chemoimmunotherapy in treatment-naïve CLL demonstrated superior PFS in ibrutinib-based arms compared with conventional chemoimmunotherapy. These results establish ibrutinib as effective first-line therapy for CLL, regardless of patient age.
- In the R/R CLL setting, with many potential treatments available, the exact sequence and timing of salvage therapies are being addressed in clinical trials. Current

standards of care for R/R CLL include ibrutinib monotherapy, idelalisib together with rituximab, venetoclax with or without rituximab, and duvelisib (currently approved as a third-line therapy).

PROLYMPHOCYTIC LEUKEMIAS

B-cell prolymphocytic leukemia (B-PLL) and T-PLL are rare lymphoid neoplasms that occur predominantly in older adults; there is a slight male predominance.[265] At the time of presentation, the primary clinical features include rapidly increasing lymphocyte counts and splenomegaly. Lymphadenopathy, rashes, peripheral edema, and pleuroperitoneal effusions are relatively common in T-PLL but not B-PLL. The disease presents at an advanced stage for virtually all patients. B-PLL cells are large, with a round nucleus and a prominent nucleolus.

In de novo B-PLL, most of the peripheral blood mononuclear cells tend to be prolymphocytes; in the setting of an aggressive transformation from CLL, there is a dimorphic population in the peripheral blood. The immunophenotype is different from CLL. Cells in B-PLL are positive for CD19 and CD20 and strongly express CD22, surface immunoglobulins, CD79a, and FMC7. Most cases do not express CD5 or CD23. T-PLL typically expresses CD2, CD3, CD5, and CD7, with variable expression of CD4 and CD8. It does not express DNA nucleotidylexotransferase or CD1a. Common cytogenetic abnormalities include del(17p) in B-PLL and complex karyotypes typically involving chromosome 14 in T-PLL.

Patients with B-PLL generally receive the same regimens used to treat CLL, but response rates tend to be lower and response durations usually are shorter. For T-PLL, NCCN guidelines recommend alemtuzumab either as a single agent or combined with pentostatin or a combination of fludarabine, mitoxantrone, and cyclosphosphamide.[266] For relapsed T-PLL, responses with nelarabine and/or bendamustine have been observed.[267,268] Therapeutic activity of alemtuzumab and purine analogs tend to be transient in B- and T-PLLs. AlloHSCT should be considered in suitable patients in first remission.[265]

HAIRY CELL LEUKEMIA

Approximately 1,000 new cases of hairy cell leukemia occur each year in the United States, primarily in middle-aged individuals, with a 4:1 male predominance.[269]

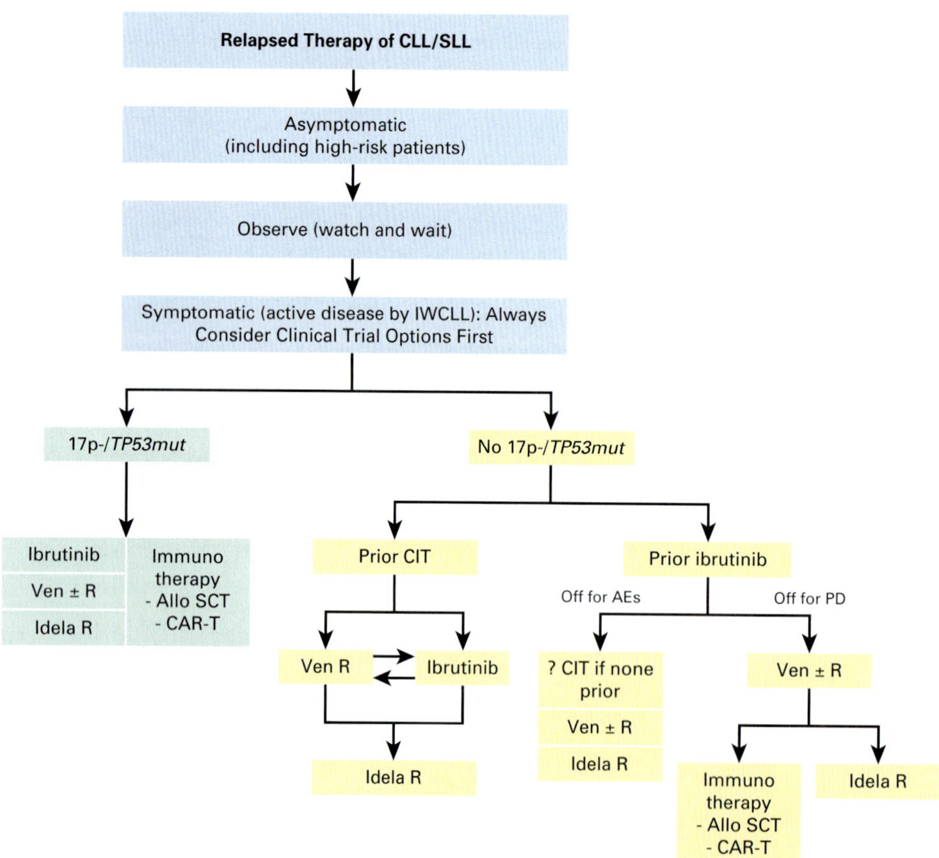

Fig. 19-8 Relapsed therapy of CLL and SLL.

Abbreviations: AE, adverse event; Allo, allogeneic; CAR-T, chimeric antigen receptor T cell; CIT, chemoimmunotherapy; CLL, chronic lymphocytic leukemia; Idela, idelalisib; IWCLL, International Workshop on Chronic Lymphocytic Leukemia; mut, mutation; PD, progressive disease; R, rituximab; SCT, stem cell transplantation; SLL, small lymphocytic lymphoma; Ven, venetoclax.

CLINICAL PRESENTATION AND DIAGNOSIS

Patients typically present with symptoms related to pancytopenia, including infections, weakness or fatigue, bleeding, or left upper quadrant abdominal pain related to splenomegaly. Besides cytopenias and splenomegaly, the most common sign is presence of circulating hairy cells. These cells generally have an eccentric, spongiform, kidney-shaped nucleus with characteristic filamentous cytoplasmic projections.

A bone marrow biopsy specimen is typically required to establish the diagnosis because an aspirate often cannot be obtained. The malignant cells in classic hairy cell leukemia are of B-cell origin, have no (or inconspicuous) nucleoli, and express CD19, CD20, CD123, and CD200, as well as the monocyte antigen CD11c and CD25, and VE1 (a BRAF V600E stain). The most specific marker is CD103. The cells stain positively with tartrate-resistant acid phosphatase. Mutations in *BRAF*, specifically V600E, have been found in virtually all cases of classic hairy cell leukemia.[270] *BRAF* V600E is thought of as a causal genetic event, leading to the constitutive activation of the RAF-MEK-ERK signaling pathway that represents the key event in the molecular pathogenesis of hairy cell leukemia.[271]

Hairy cell variant has a biology and clinical behavior that are distinct from that of classic hairy cell leukemia and often presents with significant leukocytosis. Cells are characterized by prominent nucleoli and lack of CD200 expression. They also typically do not express CD25 or CD123, and, molecularly, lack the *BRAF* V600E mutation.[272]

TREATMENT

Treatment is indicated in the setting of massive or progressive splenomegaly, worsening blood cell counts, recurrent infection, > 20,000 hairy cells/mm^3 of peripheral blood, or bulky lymphadenopathy. Historically, splenectomy was the standard treatment of hairy cell leukemia. This procedure improves symptoms related to splenomegaly and peripheral blood cell counts, often for prolonged periods, but it does not affect the disease itself. Splenectomy is now reserved for the rare occasion when a patient has disease that is refractory to treatment and has splenomegaly that is either symptomatic or is resulting in cytopenias.

Classic hairy cell leukemia typically follows an indolent disease course and is now highly controllable (Table 19-23). More than 80% of patients will experience a durable response to treatment with purine analogs (namely, cladribine or pentostatin) with or without an anti-CD20 antibody such as rituximab. The results with cladribine are equivalent to those with pentostatin. The shorter duration of treatment makes cladribine somewhat more attractive; in patients with renal impairment, purine analogs should be used with caution. Although interferon-α was the first systemic therapy to demonstrate activity in hairy cell leukemia, its current role is limited because the purine analogs are superior with regard to response duration, safety, and outcomes.

Ultimately, approximately 30% to 40% of patients will have a relapse. In many cases, relapse is characterized only by an increase in hairy cells in the bone marrow, with no indication for treatment. Patients who develop symptomatic disease or progressive cytopenia due to relapse will require retreatment. Selection of treatment at relapse is guided by duration of remission after initial therapy.[273] A second durable response is achieved for most patients. Treatment options at relapse include purine analog with or without anti-CD20 antibody; vemurafenib, an oral BRAF inhibitor[274]; anti-CD20 antibodies other than rituximab; an anti-CD22 immunotoxin (moxetumomab pasudotox)[275]; or a BTK inhibitor (ibrutinib).[269]

Table 19-23 Treatment of Hairy Cell Leukemia

Initial treatment
Cladribine or pentostatin ± rituximab
Relapse
Cladribine or pentostatin ± rituximab
Vemurafenib
Anti-CD20 antibodies other than rituximab
Moxetumomab pasudotox (anti-CD22 immunotoxin)
Ibrutinib

Variant hairy cell leukemia has a more aggressive disease course than does classic hairy cell leukemia, and treatment results with purine analog monotherapy are substantially inferior (ORR, < 50% *v* 75% to 100% for the classic version; CR rates, < 10% *v* > 50% to 70%), but addition of rituximab appears to improve outcomes.[272]

KEY POINTS

- Classic hairy cell leukemia is highly responsive to treatment with purine analogs (ie, cladribine or pentostatin) given alone or in combination with rituximab.
- Patients with relapsed or refractory disease who require treatment may respond to retreatment with purine analog–based therapy, anti-CD20 antibodies, anti-CD22 immunotoxin, a *BRAF* inhibitor, or ibrutinib.

CHRONIC T-CELL/NK-CELL LEUKEMIAS

Despite considerable effort, the classification of indolent T-cell leukemias remains ambiguous, with many uncommon and imperfectly defined categories.[276] Among the more common forms of chronic T-cell leukemia are T-PLL (see previous discussion), various subtypes of large granular lymphocytosis, adult T-cell leukemia/lymphoma, and NK-cell leukemia.

Large granular lymphocytoses can be divided into two major subsets: T-cell large granular lymphocytosis (CD3 positive, representing in vivo activated cytotoxic T cells), and NK-cell large granular lymphocytosis (CD3 negative). T-cell large granular lymphocytosis tends to occur in older persons, and most patients (60%) are symptomatic at diagnosis. Anemia and recurrent infections associated with neutropenia are common. The phenotype includes CD3, CD8, and CD57, with clonal rearrangement of T-cell receptor (*TCR*) gene. The NK-cell variety accounts for approximately 15% of large granular lymphocytoses and includes aggressive NK-cell leukemia and a more indolent NK-cell lymphocytosis. The cells are CD3 negative; positive for CD8, CD16, and CD56; and they may or may not be positive for CD57. *TCR* gene rearrangements are absent. For the indolent forms, a notable feature is the association with other diseases in up to 40% of cases, including rheumatoid arthritis and other hematologic disorders such as CLL, hairy cell leukemia, lymphoma, MDS, and monoclonal gammopathy of undetermined significance. With the indolent forms, standard treatment regimens vary and are not standardized. It is generally agreed that immunosuppressive therapy (ie, methotrexate, cyclophosphamide, cyclosporine) is the mainstay of initial treatment.[277] Patients affected by the aggressive form of the disease tend to be younger and do not have rheumatoid arthritis. Infiltration of the GI tract and bone marrow are common. Neutropenia is modest compared with the severity of anemia and thrombocytopenia. Patients often die as a result of multiorgan failure with a coagulopathy, generally within a few months of diagnosis, despite aggressive chemotherapy.

Approximately 5% of large granular lymphocytosis is a nonclonal expansion of CD3-positive large granular lymphocytosis that is generally unaccompanied by lymphadenopathy or hepatosplenomegaly. The features of the cells are positivity for CD3, CD16, and CD56, and negativity for CD4 and CD8. The disease is indolent, rarely requiring intervention unless accompanied by neutropenia. Prednisone and immunosuppressive agents have been used. It is not clear whether this disorder is actually neoplastic.

Adult T-cell leukemia/lymphoma is endemic in certain geographic areas including the southeastern portion of the United States, islands in southern Japan, the Caribbean basin including Jamaica and Trinidad, northeast Iran, western Africa, and Peru, and is linked to human T-cell lymphotropic virus type 1 infection. Four clinical variants of adult T-cell leukemia/lymphoma are (1) acute, (2) chronic, (3) smoldering, and (4) lymphomatous disease. The levels of serum calcium and LDH are prognostic for outcome. Patients with acute, lymphomatous, or unfavorable chronic types require multiagent chemotherapy with or without subsequent alloHSCT. The addition of the anti-CC4 antibody mogamulizumab to the multiagent chemotherapy improves the rate of CR and overall response and PFS.[278] For chronic or smoldering types, interferon-α and zidovudine or watchful waiting can be considered.[8] Antiviral therapy with zidovudine plus interferon-α has a controversial role; retrospective studies demonstrated OS benefit in patients with acute, chronic, and smoldering types, but not the lymphomatous type. Some 10% to 25% of patients present with CNS involvement at diagnosis or relapse[279]; therefore, patients with acute or aggressive presentations of the disease should be evaluated for CNS involvement and receive intrathecal chemotherapy for prophylaxis.

Acknowledgment

The following authors are acknowledged and graciously thanked for their contribution to prior versions of this chapter: Frederick R. Appelbaum, MD, FASCO; and Roland B. Walter, MD, PhD, MS.

Global Perspective: Leukemias

Itaru Matsumura, MD (Kindai University, Japan)

ETIOLOGY OF LEUKEMIA

The incidence of leukemias (including AML, ALL, CML, and CLL) is approximately 8.5 in 100,000 people per year in Japan, almost the same in the United States. At present, no reports indicate an apparent difference in biology of leukemias between the two countries. That is, the frequencies and types of main chromosomal abnormalities, including t(8;21)(q22;q22), t(15;17)(q22; q21), and inv(16); genetic abnormalities; and mutations of *FLT3*, *NPM1*, *DNMT3A*, *TET2*, *IDH1*, *IDH2*, and *TP53* are almost the same in Japan as those in the United States. However, the occurrences of leukemia subtypes in Japan are rather different from those in the United States. AML is the most common subtype of leukemia in Japan, accounting for 55% of leukemia cases. CLL is the most frequent type of leukemia in the United States; however, CLL is rare in Japan, accounting for only 8% of leukemia cases (Fig 19-9).

Most leukemias develop for unknown reasons, except secondary leukemia that develops after chemotherapy and/or radiation therapy for solid cancers. There is no difference in risk factors for AML between Japan and the United States. Recently, a concept of "leukemia predisposition" has been established, which means that a proportion of leukemias develop due to germline mutations in *RUNX1*, *CEBPA*, *GATA2*, *ANKRD26*, *ETV6*, *DDX41*, *TERC* or *TERT*, and *SRP72* genes. Because genetic screening covering these genes has not been applied in daily practice in Japan, a precise frequency of leukemias with the background of leukemia predisposition is unknown.

DIAGNOSIS AND CLASSIFICATION

The diagnosis of leukemia is based on morphologic and immunologic findings of peripheral blood and bone marrow samples. In addition, chromosomal analysis using bone marrow samples with G-banding technique is routinely conducted at the initial diagnosis. A multiplex chimeric mRNA screening is done in many institutions. On the basis of these findings, leukemia is classified according to WHO classification. The French-American-British classification is used for AML, as in the United States.

The screening of genetic abnormalities is not covered by the social insurance (universal national health insurance) in Japan. Therefore, these mutational analyses are mainly conducted in patients with leukemia for research purposes in academic university settings or in clinical trials.

Hematologic Malignancies Diagnosed in 2017 (from JSH Registry Data Presented at JSH 2018)

Diseases	< 20 Years	≥ 20 Years	Total
AML	258	3,042	3,300
ALL	512	640	1,152
CML	23	1,049	1,072
CLL	5	455	460
MPN	44	3,385	3,429
MDS	36	3,613	3,649
B-cell neoplasms	100	13,951	14,051
T-cell neoplasms	36	1,918	1,954
HD	32	695	727
MM	5	2,949	2,954

These registry data cover about half of cases in Japan

Incidence and frequencies of leukemias in Japan Registry data from Japanese Society of Hematology in 2017

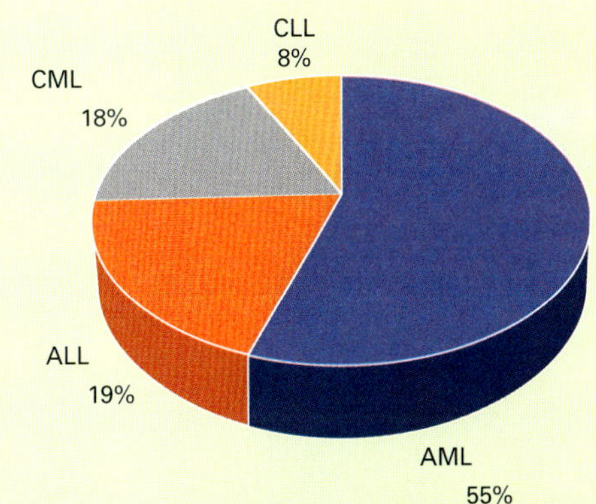

Fig. 19-9 Diagnosis and incidence of leukemias in Japan.

Abbreviations: ALL, acute lymphoblastic leukemia; AML, acute myeloid leukemia, CLL, chronic lymphocytic leukemia; CML, chronic myeloid leukemia; HD, Hodgkin lymphoma; JSH, Japanese Society of Hematology; MDS, myelodysplastic syndrome; MM, multiple myeloma; MPN, myeloproliferative neoplasm.

For acute leukemia, there is no difference in the timing of diagnosis and clinical symptoms of patients between Japan and in the United States. However, CML and CLL are likely to be diagnosed a little earlier in Japan than in the United States. For example, when we evaluate Sokal risk scores, which predict the risk of disease progression to accelerated phase or blastic crisis, in de novo CML at diagnosis, more patients are classified as a low-risk group (earlier stage of CML) in Japan than in the United States.

TREATMENT STRATEGIES AND JAPANESE GUIDELINES

The Japanese Society of Hematology has created and published a guideline for the treatment of hematologic malignancies in 2013, which was updated in 2018. As for leukemias including AML, ALL, CML, and CLL, there is no major difference in the treatment algorithms between Japan and the US NCCN guidelines, although some of the new drugs have not been approved in Japan. However, dosing schedules of some drugs are different from those used in the United States.

Treatment Strategies for AML, ALL, CML, CLL, AML

- Induction: Cytarabine plus an anthracycline (idarubicin or daunomycin) is used. The dosing schedule is different between Japan and the United States.
- Consolidation: High-dose cytarabine (three cycles (dose is different between Japan and the United States) or combination chemotherapies for four cycles (this option is not included in the United States))
- Postinduction: AlloHSCT at the first complete remission except AML subtypes with good prognosis such as t(8;21), inv(16), and t(15;17).
- ALL
  - Combinational chemotherapies with CNS prophylaxis
  - Pediatric protocol for patients in adolescents and young adults
  - Tyrosine kinase with combinational chemotherapies for Ph-positive ALL
- CML
  - De novo CML in chronic phase (CP): First-generation(1G) tyrosine kinase inhibitor (imatinib) or second-generation TKI (nilotinib or dasatinib)

Table 19-24 Clinical Staging of Chronic Lymphocytic Leukemia*

Classification and Stage	Description
Rai, stage	
0	Absolute lymphocytosis of > 10,000/μL in blood and ≥ 30% lymphocytes in bone marrow
I	Stage 0 plus enlarged lymph nodes
II	Stage 0 plus hepatomegaly or splenomegaly
III	Stage 0 plus anemia with hemoglobin level < 11 g/dL
IV	Stage 0 plus thrombocytopenia with platelet counts < 100,000/μL
Binet	
A	Absolute lymphocytosis of > 10,000/μL in blood and ≥ 30% lymphocytes in bone marrow
	Hemoglobin level ≥ 10 g/dL
	Platelets ≥ 100,000/μL
	Two or more involved sites[a]
B	As for stage A, but 3-5 involved sites
C	As for stage A or B, but hemoglobin level < 10 g/dL or platelets < 100,000/μL

[a]Sites considered: cervical, axillary, and inguinal lymph nodes; liver; and spleen.

- Resistance with or without point mutations in the *BCR-ABL* gene: Second-generation TKI (nilotinib, dasatinib, or bosutinib) or third-generation TKI ponatinib for *T315I*-mutation CML in accelerated phase; second-generation TKI for de novo cases; and alloHSCT if responses are not sufficient
- CML in blastic crisis: TKIs with combinational chemotherapies followed by alloHSCT

- CLL: Chemotherapy (eg, frudarabine) or molecular targeted therapies (eg, ibrutinib) for patients in advanced stages (stage C in Binet classification or stage 3/4 in Rai classification) (Table 19-24).

There is no apparent difference in the pharmacokinetics of leukemia drugs between Japanese and US patients. However, Japanese patients have a smaller body size compared with US patients; therefore, drug concentrations are like to be higher in Japanese patients when administered at the same dose for US patients, leading to higher efficacy, but more frequent adverse events.

20

LYMPHOMAS

Ariela Noy, MD

RECENT UPDATES

- Ibrutinib, a Bruton tyrosine kinase (BTK) inhibitor, received approval for any subtype of marginal zone lymphoma relapsing or refractory to any first-line therapy. (Noy A, *Blood* 2017)
- Copanlisib, a phosphatidylinositol 3-kinase (PI3K) inhibitor, received approval for the treatment of adult patients with relapsed follicular lymphoma (FL) who have received at least two prior systemic therapies. (Dreyling M, *Annals Onco* 2017)
- Acalabrutinib, a BTK inhibitor, received approval for treatment of mantle cell lymphoma after at least one prior therapy. (Wang M, *Leukemia* 2019)
- Obinutuzumab, an anti-CD20 monoclonal antibody, was approved in combination with first-line chemotherapy for FL. (Hiddemann W, *J Clin Oncol* 2019)
- Axicabtagene ciloleucel, an anti-CD19 chimeric antigen receptor T-cell (CAR-T) immunotherapy, was approved for relapsed or refractory large B-cell lymphoma. (Neelapu S, *N Eng J Med* 2017)
- Brentuximab vedotin, an anti-CD30 monoclonal antibody drug conjugate, was approved to treat adult patients with previously untreated stage III or IV classic Hodgkin lymphoma in combination with chemotherapy. (Connors JM, *N Eng J Med* 2018)
- Tisagenlecleucel, an anti-CD19 CAR-T immunotherapy, was approved for relapsed or refractory diffuse large B-cell lymphoma (DLBCL). (Schuster S, *N Eng J Med* 2019)
- Venetoclax, a BCL-2 inhibitor, received approval for use in patients with chronic lymphocytic leukemia (CLL) or small lymphocytic lymphoma (SLL), with or without 17p deletion, who have received at least one prior therapy. (Stilgenbauer S, *Lancet Onc* 2016; Coutre S, *Blood* 2018; Jones J, *Lancet Oncol* 2018)
- Pembrolizumab, an anti–PD-1 monoclonal antibody, was approved for the treatment of adult and pediatric patients with refractory, primary, mediastinal large B-cell lymphoma or who have relapsed after two or more prior lines of therapy. (Armand, *J Clin Oncol* 2019)
- Duvelisib, a PI3K inhibitor, received approval for use in adult patients with relapsed or refractory CLL or SLL after at least two prior therapies. In addition, duvelisib received accelerated approval for treatment of adult patients with relapsed or refractory FL after at least two prior systemic therapies. (O'Brien S, *Am J Hem* 2018)
- Brentuximab vedotin, an anti-CD30 monoclonal antibody drug conjugate, was approved for first-line therapy in combination with chemotherapy for peripheral T-cell lymphoma and anaplastic large-cell lymphoma. (Horwitz S, *Lancet* 2019)
- Polatuzumab vedotin-piiq, an antibody drug conjugate against CD79b, was approved for relapsed or refractory DLBCL, in combination with bendamustine and a rituximab product, after at least two prior therapies. (Sehn L, *J Clin Oncol* 2020)

OVERVIEW

Non-Hodgkin lymphomas (NHLs) are a heterogeneous group of malignancies derived from mature B, T, and natural killer (NK) cells; they encompass several broad categories and nearly 100 unique biologic subtypes (Fig 20-1). This chapter covers indolent B-cell lymphomas, aggressive B-cell lymphomas, and T-cell lymphomas (TCLs). In the United States, approximately 85% of NHLs are of B-cell origin, 10% to 15% are T-cell derived, and < 1% are NK cell malignancies.

Hodgkin lymphoma (HL), discussed in the final section of this chapter, is now understood to be a mature B-cell malignancy with a deregulated B-cell program. The initial diagnostic and staging considerations for NHLs and HL are similar and are discussed jointly. However, although biologically related, HL and NHLs have distinct historical and clinical approaches, and management is discussed separately. In this chapter, the term "lymphoma" is used whenever discussing issues pertinent to both NHLs and HL.

NON-HODGKIN LYMPHOMAS

EPIDEMIOLOGY AND ETIOLOGY

NHL is the sixth most common cause of cancer in men and the seventh most common cause in women. Annually, NHL accounts for approximately 80,000 new cases and 22,000 deaths.[1] The incidence of NHL has increased markedly in the past several decades, possibly because of the increasing exposure to carcinogens and the increasing prevalence of immunosuppressed individuals in the United States (including people with AIDS and those receiving immunosuppressive drug therapy). The greatest increases in incidence are in older individuals and in the number of cases of aggressive lymphomas. The median age of patients diagnosed with NHL varies by histologic subtype, although the incidence for most subtypes increases with age. With improved treatment, many patients can expect to be cured of lymphoma or to live with it for a prolonged time; an estimated 500,000 people are living with lymphoma. This is an important consideration when making treatment decisions, because survivors are at increased risk for late toxicity and organ damage related to treatment.

The etiology of NHL in most patients is unknown, beyond inherent genomic instability related to the B- and T-cell gene rearrangement process, but associations exist with lymphotropic organisms, innate or acquired immunodeficiency, environmental exposures, and, rarely, familial predisposition. Several viruses have been linked either directly or indirectly to specific lymphoma subtypes, including Epstein-Barr virus (EBV), hepatitis C, human herpesvirus 8, and HIV. Bacteria, such as *Helicobacter pylori* and *Chlamydia psittaci,* are the etiologic or contributory agents for extranodal gastric and orbital marginal-zone lymphomas, respectively. Autoimmune conditions and treatment of autoimmune conditions increase the risk of lymphoma. NHL was one of the earliest described AIDS-defining malignancies, but the spectrum of lymphomas in the era of antiretroviral therapy has evolved. Support for an environmental contribution to lymphoma risk comes from observations that NHL incidence increases in industrialized regions, and several pesticides and chemicals might contribute to lymphoma development.[2] Genetic predisposition plays a small role in lymphoma, and screening for mutations is largely unknown, but there are a number of ongoing studies are ongoing prompted by families in which multiple members have hematologic malignancies, including lymphoma.[3]

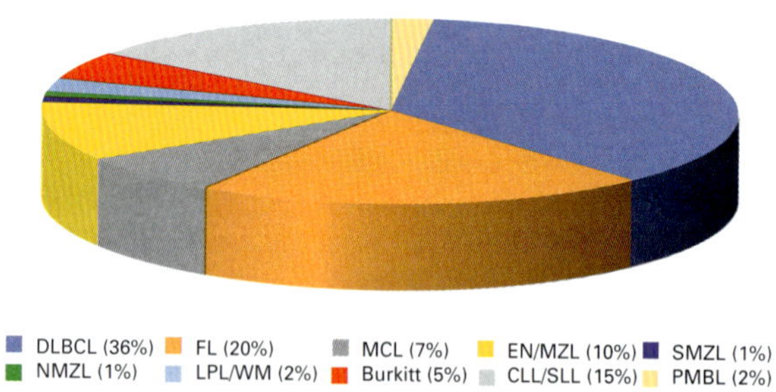

Fig. 20-1 Relative distribution of main non-Hodgkin lymphoma subtypes.

Frequencies are based on the WHO 2008 classification.

Abbreviations: CLL, chronic lymphocytic leukemia; DLBCL, diffuse large B-cell lymphoma; ENMZL, extranodal marginal zone lymphoma; FL, follicular lymphoma; LPL, lymphoplasmacytic lymphoma/; MCL, mantle cell lymphoma; NMZL, nodal marginal zone lymphoma; PMBL, primary mediastinal B-cell lymphoma; SLL, small lymphocytic lymphoma; SMZL, splenic marginal zone lymphoma; WM, Waldenström macroglobulinemia.

LYMPHOMA DIAGNOSIS AND CLASSIFICATION

Diagnosis

The clinical presentation of NHL is variable. Most patients with indolent disease present with incidentally noted, asymptomatic adenopathy or organomegaly or, occasionally, with peripheral-blood lymphocytosis detected during a routine examination. In contrast, patients with aggressive lymphomas often self-detect a rapidly growing lymph node, experience constitutional symptoms, or note pain associated with a site of disease. Symptoms may be related to compression of anatomic structures and include cough, jaundice, ureteral obstruction, and neurologic compromise. Constitutional symptoms may be the classic "B symptoms" (ie, unexplained fevers, night sweats, ≥ 10% unintentional weight loss) or may be generalized fatigue, asthenia, or weakness. Pruritus, a classic paraneoplastic phenomenon associated with HL, may also occur in other B-cell malignancies.

In terms of pathophysiology, B-cell NHL (B-NHL) develops at various points during normal B-cell ontogeny (Fig 20-2). The majority of B-cell lymphomas (BCLs) are thought to originate in the germinal center.[4] Because of their function in normal immunity, B cells are exposed to antigenic stimuli in the germinal center and undergo class-switch recombination and somatic hypermutation. These tremendous pressures and associated rapid proliferation likely increase adverse mutations and chromosomal errors, leading to malignancy.

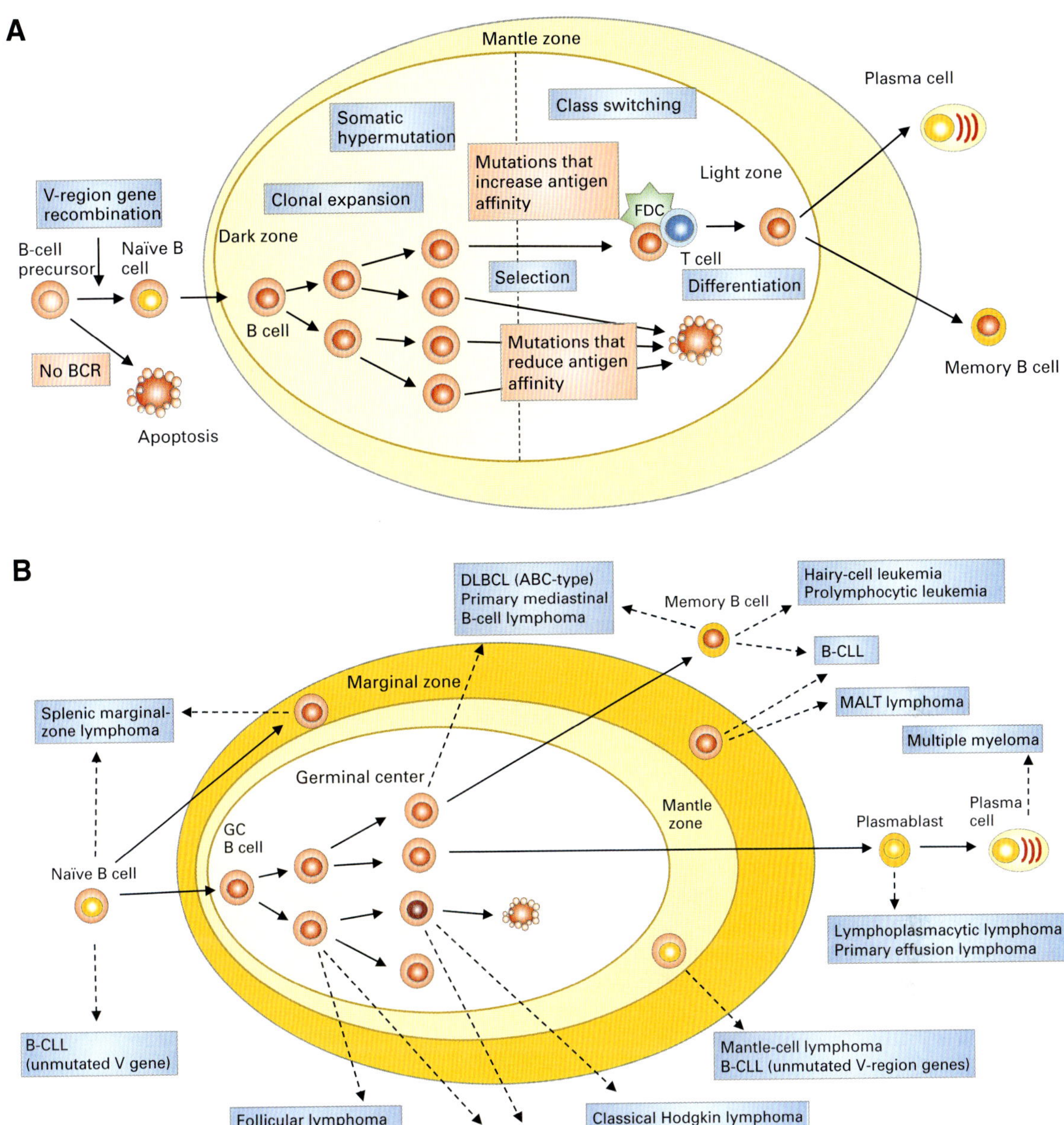

Fig. 20-2 Schematic representation of (A) normal B-cell development and (B) corresponding B-cell lymphomas.

Abbreviations: ABC, activated B cell; B-CLL, B-cell chronic lymphocytic leukemia; BCR, B-cell receptor; DLBCL, diffuse large B-cell lymphoma; FDC, follicular dendritic cell; GC, germinal center; MALT, mucosa-associated lymphoid tissue.

Classification

The WHO lymphoma classification, last published in 2008 and updated in 2016, is the gold standard for defining lymphoma subtypes.[4,5] Confirming a lymphoma diagnosis requires adequate tissue to perform histologic review, immunohistochemistry, and other essential tests based on subtype. An excisional biopsy (≥ 1 cm^3) provides the most tissue, but multiple core biopsies can suffice if a lymph node is difficult to access. Fine-needle aspiration is rarely sufficient for diagnostic and prognostic purposes.

A reasonably sized specimen allows the hematopathologist to identify whether a lymphoma has retained nodal architecture (ie, follicular lymphoma [FL]) or has a diffuse architecture (ie, diffuse large BCL [DLBCL], mantle cell lymphoma [MCL], small lymphocytic lymphoma [SLL], among others). Immunohistochemistry is an essential part of the diagnosis (Table 20-1) and is increasingly important for therapeutic purposes as well. For example, CD20 or CD30 positivity may support the use of specific agents. Cytogenetic analysis is also increasingly used in NHL; chromosomal rearrangements may be diagnostic or

Table 20-1 **Key Diagnostic Immunophenotypic and Cytogenetic Features of Non-Hodgkin Lymphomas**

Lymphoma Subtype	CD20	CD10	CD5	CD30	Other	Cytogenetics/FISH Results	Genes
DLBCL	+++	+/-	Rare	Rare		t(14;18) t(3;14) rare t(8;14) or t(8;22)	*BCL2 BCL6 MYC*
FL	+++	+	-	-		t(14;18)	*BCL2*
CLL/SLL	Dim	-	+	-	CD23 +		
MCL	+++	-	+	-	CD23-, Cyclin D1+, SOX11+	t(11;14)	*Cyclin D1*
MZL	+++	-	Rare	-		t(11;18) (ENMZL) trisomy 3, 18 (NMZL) del 7q (SMZL)	*API2-MALT*
LPL/WM	+++	-	Rare	-			*MYD88*
Burkitt lymphoma	+++	+	-	-	TdT-	t(8;14), t(8;22), t(2;8)	*MYC*
PMBL	+++	+/-	-	Occasional		t(16;X)	*CIITA*
Hairy cell leukemia	+++	-	-	-	CD11c+, CD25+, CD103+		
ALCL, ALK+	-	-	-	+++		t(2;5)	*ALK*
ALCL, ALK−	-	-	-	+++		t(6;7)	*DUSP22*
AITL	-	+/-	+/-	-	At least three T_{FH} markers: PD1, BCL6, CXCL13, ICOS, SAP, CCR5		*TET2, IDH2, DNMT3A, RHOA, ITK-SYK*
PTCL-NOS	-	+/-	+/-	-	Can have same immunophenotype as AITL; often with dropped CD3 or CD7		

Abbreviations: AITL, angioimmunoblastic T-cell lymphoma; ALCL, anaplastic large-cell lymphoma; CLL, chronic lymphocytic leukemia; DLBCL, diffuse large B-cell lymphoma; ENMZL, extranodal marginal zone lymphoma; FISH, fluorescence in situ hybridization FL, follicular lymphoma; MCL, mantle cell lymphoma; MZL, marginal zone lymphoma; NMZL, nodal marginal zone lymphoma; PMBL, primary mediastinal B-cell lymphoma; PTCL-NOS, peripheral T-cell lymphoma not otherwise specified; SLL, small lymphocytic lymphoma; SMZL, splenic marginal-zone lymphoma; T_{FH}, T-follicular helper cell.

supportive of a specific type of lymphoma. For example, the t(11;14) rearrangement at cyclin D1 is diagnostic for MCL. However, the t(14;18) rearrangement can be seen in both FL and more aggressive subtypes such as DLBCL or high-grade BCL. Some translocations are prognostic rather than diagnostic. For example, dual t(8;14) and t(14;18) rearrangements involving *MYC* and *BCL2* genes, respectively, in a high-grade B-cell neoplasm lead to an aggressive and chemoresistant phenotype termed "double-hit" lymphoma, which requires more intensive treatment.

STAGING AND INITIAL EVALUATION

The historical staging system for both HL and NHL is the Ann Arbor classification, Cottswold revision (Table 20-2).[6] Typical staging involves computed tomography (CT) scans of the chest, abdomen, and pelvis along with a bone marrow biopsy. With the advent of functional imaging via positron-emission tomography (PET), the Lugano classification was introduced and has several implications for the modern staging of lymphomas.[6] First, a staging bone marrow biopsy is no longer routinely required for the diagnosis of HL or DLBCL if PET/CT imaging has been performed. Second, PET/CT imaging should be used to assess response in fluorodeoxyglucose (FDG)-avid histologies; interpretation of PET scans should be via the 5-point scale,[7] also called the Deauville criteria (Table 20-3). Third, the suffix notations for absence (A) and presence (B) of B symptoms are required only for HL, although many practitioners continue to use these as a descriptive element for NHL.

Of note, and in stark contrast to many solid tumors, stage by itself rarely dictates treatment or prognosis. The purpose of staging is more descriptive for disease location (nodal *v* extranodal), extent (limited *v* advanced), and bulk (typically ≥ 10 cm). The specific subtype and its associated pathobiologic features are more important than precise stage in determining initial treatment. Clinicians group NHL

Table 20-2 Staging Systems for Lymphomas[6]

System and Stage	Involvement	Extranodal Status
Ann Arbor staging system[a]		
I	Involvement of a single lymph node region or lymphoid structure	
II	Involvement of two or more lymph node regions confined to one side of the diaphragm	
III	Involvement of two or more lymph node regions on both sides of the diaphragm	
IV	Disseminated involvement of a deep, visceral organ (eg, bone marrow, liver)	
Revised staging system for primary nodal lymphomas (Lugano Classification)[b]		
Limited	One node or a group of adjacent nodes. Two or more nodal groups on the same side of the diaphragm	Single extranodal lesions without nodal involvement
I		Stage I or II by nodal extent with limited contiguous extranodal
II		
II Bulky	II as above with "bulky" disease	Not applicable
Advanced	Nodes on both sides of the diaphragm; nodes above the diaphragm with spleen involvement. Additional noncontiguous, extralymphatic involvement	
III		Not applicable
IV		Not applicable

[a]The subscripts used for subtypes are A, absence of B symptoms; B, presence of at least one of the following: unexplained fevers, night sweats, unintentional weight loss > 10% of body weight; X, bulky disease ≥ 10 cm; E, primary extranodal involvement.
[b]Extent of disease is determined by positron emission tomography/computed tomography (CT) for avid lymphomas and CT for nonavid histologies. Tonsils, Waldeyer ring, and spleen are considered nodal tissue.

subtypes into indolent (slow-growing or low-grade), aggressive (fast-growing), and highly aggressive (very rapidly growing or high-grade) categories to facilitate clinical decision-making regarding therapy and to estimate disease behavior.

In addition to radiographic staging, a lumbar puncture should be performed in all patients with Burkitt lymphoma and should be considered for other high-grade lymphomas, typically in the setting of extranodal disease. A lumbar puncture detects occult CNS disease in high-risk patients, which requires CNS-directed therapy. A CNS-International Prognostic Index (IPI)[8] predicts patients with three or more of the following risk factors have > 10% risk of CNS recurrence after combination therapy with rituximab, cyclophosphamide, doxorubicin, vincristine, and prednisone (R-CHOP):

- kidney and/or adrenal gland involvement,
- age > 60 years,
- lactate dehydrogenase (LDH) level > normal,
- Eastern Cooperative Oncology Group (ECOG) performance status (PS) > 1,
- stage III/IV disease, or
- extranodal involvement > 1.

Other tests performed at the time of initial evaluation may include cardiac-function assessment (if treatment will include anthracyclines), pulmonary-function testing (if treatment will include bleomycin), and HIV, LDH, β_2-microglobulin, uric acid, CBC count, and hepatitis B and/or C testing. Testing for hepatitis B is required prior to use of rituximab and other anti-CD20 chemoimmunotherapy, because of the risk of viral reactivation and fatal hepatitis.

Table 20-3 Five-Point Scale (Deauville Criteria) for Positron Emission Tomography Assessment in Lymphoma[7]

Score	Positron Emission Tomography/Computed Tomography Scan Result
1	No uptake
2	Uptake equal to or below mediastinum
3	Uptake above mediastinum but equal to or below uptake in liver
4	Uptake moderately higher than in liver
5	Uptake markedly higher than in liver and/or new lesions
X	New areas of uptake unlikely to be related to lymphoma

Tests should include those for hepatitis B surface antigen and core antibody for patients without risk factors; patients with risk factors or a history of hepatitis B should be tested for e-antigen as well. Patients who are seropositive for hepatitis B surface antigen or hepatitis core antibody should receive prophylactic therapy, ideally for 12 months after therapy completion.[9,10] Note the stringency of these recommendations compared with other chemotherapies where treatment is often discretionary.

SURVIVORSHIP AND SURVEILLANCE

Improved diagnostic and staging methods, treatment options, and supportive care have all translated into tremendous survival benefits for patients with lymphomas. More than half a million people with lymphoma are either cured of their disease or living with chronic NHL in the United States. The success of initial treatment implies that survivorship is an important component of long-term management. The review of late effects of therapy is beyond the scope of this chapter, but several excellent reviews are available.[11,12]

Most patients with HL and the majority of those with DLBCL can expect to enter remission and be cured of their disease. The need to monitor patients for disease recurrence has historically been associated with routine radiographic imaging, often in asymptomatic patients. The risk of recurrence is highest in the first 2 years after initial therapy and then decreases. Relapses beyond 5 years are rare, and this is usually the point at which patients are considered cured. However, routine radiographic surveillance is no longer the standard of care, based largely on several retrospective analyses. Collectively, these studies found that recurrence was detected in only 2% to 5% of patients who were otherwise clinically and hematologically stable; furthermore, there was no difference in survival if relapse was detected radiographically or after the patient presented with signs or symptoms of disease recurrence.[13,14] Given the increased exposure to radiation and contrast dye, not to mention cost and patient inconvenience, routine surveillance scans after complete remission are no longer recommended in HL and in low-risk DLBCL, and beyond 2 years in higher-risk DLBCL. However, all patients should be followed clinically for disease monitoring.

KEY POINTS

- NHLs comprise a group of heterogeneous diseases that vary widely with respect to clinical presentation, therapy, and prognosis.
- Advances in the diagnosis and classification of these diseases are facilitated by immunophenotyping and by newer molecular and genetic approaches.
- Establishing a correct diagnosis at the time of initial presentation is critical to optimal management of NHL. Therefore, an adequately sized biopsy specimen is mandatory to permit rigorous classification. Fine-needle aspiration is virtually never adequate for establishing the initial subtype of NHL.
- Marked advances have been made in the treatment of these diseases in the past decade, largely because of the availability of monoclonal antibodies used either alone or in conjunction with chemotherapy.

INDOLENT NHL

Indolent lymphomas are characterized by slow growth, sometimes spanning decades, and by a waxing and waning course. They are incurable with standard approaches. The most common indolent lymphomas include FL, marginal zone lymphoma (MZL), lymphoplasmacytic lymphoma (LPL, which includes Waldenström macroglobulinemia), and SLL. The lifetime risk of transformation of an indolent NHL to an aggressive B-NHL is approximately 30%; the transformation rate is approximately 2% per year.

KEY POINTS

- Indolent NHLs usually grow very slowly and are also known as low-grade lymphomas. FL, MZL, LPL, and SLL are all indolent lymphomas.
- Transformation to a higher grade occurs at a rate of approximately 2% per year.

FOLLICULAR LYMPHOMA

EPIDEMIOLOGY

FL is the second most common type of lymphoma and represents the paradigm for indolent NHL. This disease is characterized by a follicular growth pattern seen in lymph node biopsy specimens, although diffuse areas also may be present and should be reported by the pathologist. The characteristic immunophenotype is CD20-positive, CD5-negative, CD23-negative, CD10-positive, and usually BCL6-positive. BCL2 is overexpressed in > 85% of patients, generally as a result of a t(14;18)(q32;q21) chromosome translocation, which can be detected by fluorescence in situ hybridization or standard cytogenetics.

Most patients with FL have an indolent course. The median life expectancy has increased over the past four decades and is approximately 12 to 15 years, based on SEER data. Single-center studies suggest life expectancy could be even longer; a Stanford analysis found survival after relapse of nearly 20 years.[15] However, not all patients will have a long survival, and identifying patients with more aggressive disease has proved to be challenging in the frontline setting.

STAGING AND PROGNOSIS

At diagnosis, several features help identify high- versus low-risk patients. First is histologic grade. FL is graded on the basis of the number of large cells (centroblasts) per high-powered field (Table 20-4).

Given a high degree of interobserver variability, grades 1 and 2 were collapsed into one category, now labeled FL1-2. FL3B is an aggressive lymphoma and is treated in the same way as DLBCL. FL3A is a rare subtype, often but not always indolent, and remains somewhat controversial.

Another tool for risk stratification at diagnosis is the Follicular Lymphoma International Prognostic Index (FLIPI), which includes five risk factors (RFs):

- more than four nodal sites,
- elevated LDH level,
- age > 60 years,
- stage 4 disease, and
- hemoglobin level < 12 g/dL.

A useful mnemonic is "NoLASH" (Table 20-5).[16] The FLIPI stratifies patients into three groups with differing 5-year overall survival (OS) rates:

- low risk (none to one RF; OS, 91%),
- intermediate risk (two RFs; OS, 78%), and
- high risk (three or more RFs; OS, 53%).

Although initially developed in the pre-rituximab era, FLIPI's use has been validated in modern clinical trials showing it provides important prognostic information.[17] The M7-FLIPI is a newly proposed prognostic index that incorporates PS, FLIPI score, and mutation status of seven key genes in FL pathogenesis.[18] The M7-FLIPI is in the process of being prospectively validated.

FLIPI scores provide prognostic information and help define both clinical trial populations and individual risk. However, these models do not direct the timing of treatment initiation. Even patients with high-risk FLIPI scores may not need immediate treatment, and the decision to offer therapy is based on the Groupe d'Etude des Lymphomes Folliculaires (GELF) criteria: involvement of three nodal sites > 3 cm, systemic symptoms, splenomegaly, cytopenias, pleural effusions or malignant ascites, any nodal or extranodal tumor mass > 7 cm, or impending organ dysfunction.[19] The general treatment approach to FL is shown in Fig 20-3.

Approximately 10% to 15% of patients with FL have stage I or nonbulky stage II disease at the time of initial presentation. Involved-field or extended-field radiation therapy produces a 10-year failure-free survival (FFS) rate of 50% to 60% and a median OS rate of 60% to 80%, and has traditionally been considered the standard of care. However, studies of observation alone in early-stage FL have shown similarly favorable outcomes.[20] Furthermore, one large observational study, the National LymphoCare Study,[21] showed that national guidelines endorsing radiotherapy alone for stage I FL were not followed by practicing clinicians in the majority of cases. Among 206 fully staged patients, all treatment approaches evaluated (observation alone, involved-field radiotherapy, rituximab, rituximab plus chemotherapy, and systemic therapy plus radiotherapy) resulted in excellent outcomes, though progression-free survival (PFS) was significantly better in patients treated with either rituximab plus chemotherapy or systemic therapy plus radiotherapy than with radiotherapy alone.

The remaining 85% to 90% of patients with follicular grade 1 or 2 NHL have advanced-stage disease (bulky stage II or stage III or IV) at the time of presentation. The OS reported for such patients was approximately 10 years from the time of diagnosis prior to the availability of antibody-containing regimens[22] and is now estimated to be > 15 years with the availability of monoclonal antibody–containing regimens. Despite this relatively long natural history, indolent lymphomas, including FL, are characterized by multiple recurrences and varied disease course. The initial treatment approach to advanced-stage FL depends on the patient's symptoms and assessment of tumor burden. Patients are categorized as having a low tumor burden or high tumor burden on the basis of the presence or absence of the GELF criteria discussed earlier. The key clinical questions in the initial management of FL are: (1) Does the patient need treatment? (2) Does the patient have low tumor burden or high tumor burden disease? (3) Is there a role for maintenance therapy?

Table 20-4 Grading of Follicular Lymphoma

Grade	No. of Centroblasts/hpf	Centrocyte Status
1	< 5	
2	5-15	
3a	> 15	Retained
3b	> 15	No longer present

Abbreviation: hpf, high-powered field.

KEY POINTS

- FL is the most common indolent lymphoma.
- Most patients with FL live for more than a decade.
- Prognostic scores using clinical risk factors can estimate OS.
- Defined treatment indications help guide when to treat patients versus actively surveil them without therapy.

MANAGEMENT OF DISEASE WITHOUT INDICATIONS FOR TREATMENT

It is important to understand that early therapeutic interventions do not prolong survival for patients with FL and no

Table 20-5 **Prognostic Indices for Non-Hodgkin Lymphomas**

Risk Factors	Risk Group	No. of Factors	Patient Distribution (%)	End Point, OS (%)
IPI for aggressive lymphoma[249]				
Age > 60 years				5-Year OS
PS > 1	Low	0-1	35	73
Serum LDH > ULN	Low intermediate	2	27	51
1 EN site	High intermediate	3	22	43
Stage III–IV	High	4-5	16	26
Age-adjusted IPI for aggressive lymphoma for patients ≤ 60[249]				
Age ≤ 60 years				5-Year OS
PS > 1	Low	0	22	83
Serum LDH > ULN	Low intermediate	1	32	69
1 EN site	High intermediate	2	32	46
Stage III–IV	High	3	14	32
IPI for patients treated with R-CHOP[250]				
Age > 60 years				3-Year OS
PS > 1	Low	0-1	52	91
Serum LDH > ULN	Low intermediate	2	21	81
1 EN site	High intermediate	3	17	65
Stage III–IV	High	4-5	10	59
R-IPI[94]				
Age > 60 years				4-Year OS
PS > 1	Very good	0	10	94
Serum LDH > ULN	Good	1, 2	45	79
1 EN site	Poor	3-5	45	55
Stage III–IV				
Stage-modified IPI for aggressive lymphoma[88]				
Age > 60 years				5-year OS
PS > 1		0-1	71	82
Serum LDH > ULN		2	22	71
Stage II		3	14	48
FLIPI[16]				
4 nodal sites				5-Year OS
Serum LDH > ULN	Low	0-1	36	91
Age > 60 years	Intermediate	2	37	78
Stage III-IV	High	3-5	27	36
Hemoglobin < 12 g/dL				
FLIPI-2[17]				
Age > 60 years				5-Year PFS
Serum β_2-microglobulin > ULN	Low	0	20	80
Hemoglobin < 12 g/dL	Intermediate	1,2	53	51

Table 20-5 continued

Risk Factors	Risk Group	No. of Factors	Patient Distribution (%)	End Point, OS (%)
Bone marrow involvement	High	3-5	27	19
Longest diameter of largest involved node > 6 cm				
MIPI[122]				
Age				5-Year OS
Performance status	Low	0-3	44	60
LDH:ULN	Intermediate	4, 5	35	45
WBC count	High	6-11	21	20
PIT[251]				
Age > 60 years				5-year OS
PS > 1	Group 1	0	20	62
Serum LDH > ULN	Group 2	1	33	53
Bone marrow involvement	Group 3	2	26	33
	Group 4	3-4	21	18

Abbreviations: EN, extranodal; FLIPI, Follicular Lymphoma International Prognostic Index; IPI, International Prognostic Index; LDH, lactate dehydrogenase; MIPI, Mantle Cell Lymphoma International Prognostic Index; OS, overall survival; PFS, progression-free survival; PIT, Prognostic Index for T-Cell Lymphoma; PS, performance status; R-CHOP, rituximab, cyclophosphamide, doxorubicin, vincristine, and prednisone; R-IPI, revised International Prognostic Index for Aggressive Lymphoma; ULN, upper limit of normal.

indications for treatment. Several prospective, phase III, randomized trials have compared observation against treatment with alkylating agents, interferon-α, or rituximab, and none has found a survival advantage. A three-armed international trial randomly assigned asymptomatic, patients with advanced-stage disease to either watchful waiting, rituximab 375 mg/m^2 weekly for 4 weeks (induction), or induction followed by 12 additional rituximab infusions every 8 weeks for 2 years (maintenance).[23] At 3 years, PFS in patients who did not need therapy was significantly higher in the maintenance group compared with the watchful waiting group (88% *v* 46%; $P < .0001$; (Fig 20-4). However, despite improved time to next

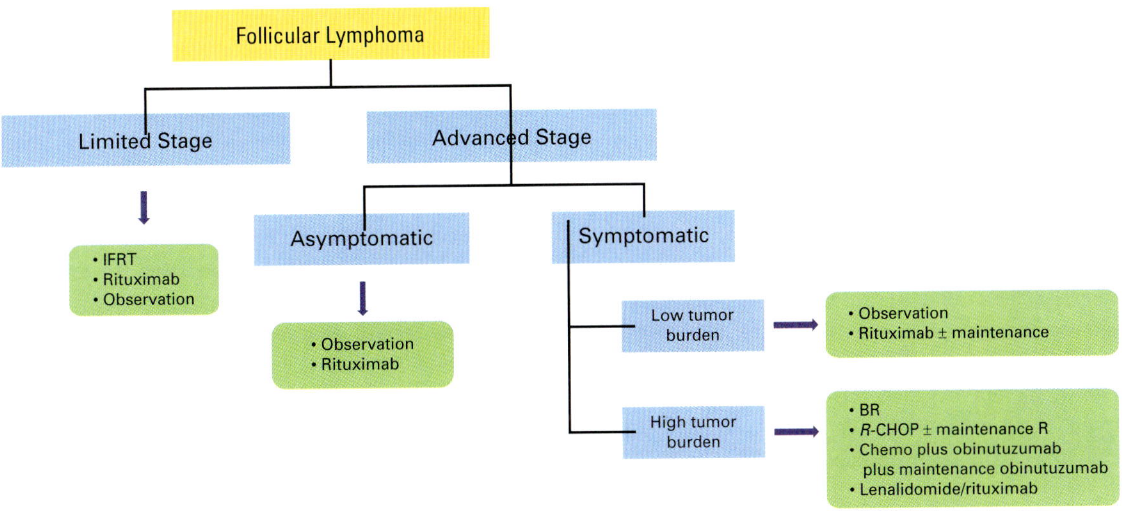

Fig. 20-3 Treatment algorithm for follicular non-Hodgkin lymphoma.

Abbreviations: Chemo, chemotherapy; IFRT, involved-field radiation therapy; R, rituximab; R-CHOP, rituximab, cyclophosphamide, doxorubicin, vincristine, and prednisone.

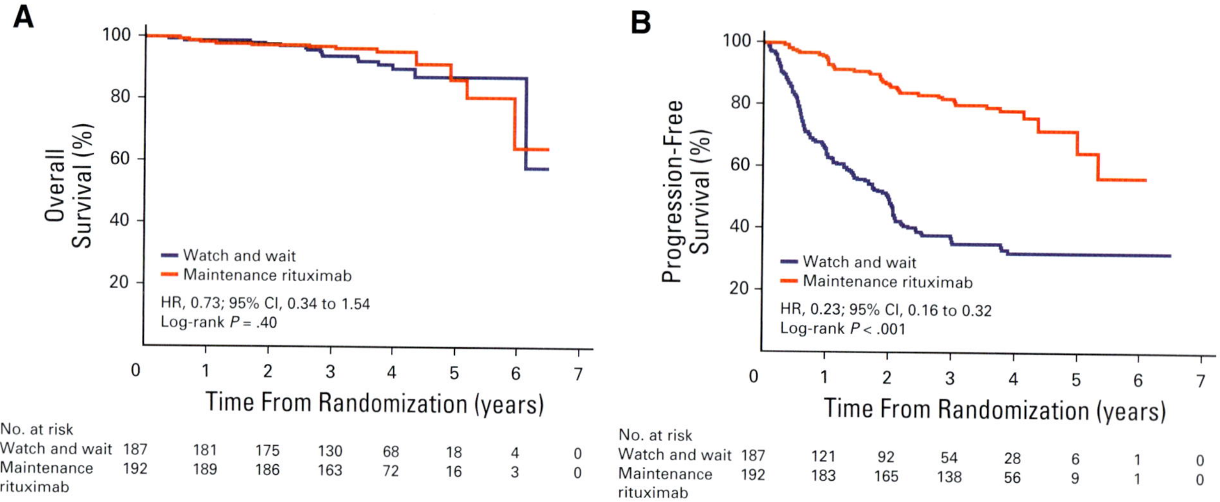

Fig. 20-4 Impact of rituximab treatment on asymptomatic patients with follicular lymphoma showing improved progression-free survival but no impact on overall survival.

Abbreviation: HR, hazard ratio.

treatment and improved PFS, there was no difference in OS. These data do not support the use of therapy by patients with asymptomatic disease outside the setting of a clinical trial.

MANAGEMENT OF DISEASE WITH INDICATIONS FOR TREATMENT

Patients with low tumor burden can be treated with single-agent anti-CD20 therapy. CD20 is a lineage-specific B-cell antigen that is first expressed during the pre–B-cell stage of development and persists on B cells until terminal plasma cell differentiation. Targeting CD20 has been extremely fruitful, with initial depletion of all mature B cells but eventual reconstitution of normal cells because the pluripotent stem cell does not express CD20 and thus remains intact. Rituximab, approved in 1997, has been extensively studied in CD20-positive B-cell malignancies. When rituximab is used as monotherapy in the initial treatment of patients with FL and low-grade NHL, the response rate ranges from 50% to 70%, with a median duration of response of 1.0 to 2.5 years.[24,25] Other anti-CD20–directed agents include radioimmunotherapy or second-generation monoclonal antibodies (namely, ofatumumab, obinutuzumab).

Patients with high tumor burden are treated with chemoimmunotherapy. The addition of rituximab to chemotherapy has clearly shown improved PFS, event-free survival (EFS), and even OS compared with chemotherapy induction alone.[26-29] The optimal chemotherapy regimen for the initial treatment of patients with FL is controversial. Two large phase III clinical trials compared combination therapy with rituximab, cyclophosphamide, vincristine, and prednisone (R-CVP), R-CHOP, and rituximab (R) plus fludarabine-containing regimens for treatment of grades 1 to 2 FL.[30,31] Both studies demonstrated superior PFS for patients treated with R-CHOP or *R*-fludarabine–based therapy compared with R-CVP, although OS did not differ among the three arms. Both studies also showed that regimens with fludarabine and rituximab had significantly more hematologic toxicity and a higher risk of secondary malignancies compared with R-CVP or R-CHOP, making fludarabine-based regimens less desirable than alkylator-based regimens. Some authorities believe these trials established R-CHOP as the preferred regimen for FL, but other lymphoma specialists are reluctant to use doxorubicin-containing regimens such as R-CHOP in patients with indolent lymphomas, because of the 1% to 2% risk of cardiomyopathy and the potential to reserve this regimen for subsequent transformation. Two subsequent trials compared bendamustine, a unique alkylating agent possessing a purine-like moiety, and rituximab against either R-CHOP or investigator's choice of R-CVP or R-CHOP.[32,33] These trials were designed as noninferiority trials, and outcomes seem similar overall. Consequently, bendamustine plus rituximab has become a preferred regimen because of the absence of treatment-induced alopecia, peripheral neuropathy, and steroid-associated toxicities observed with R-CVP and R-CHOP. None of these chemoimmunotherapy regimens improves OS, although R-CVP seems inferior, though less toxic, in nearly all settings, and fludarabine-based treatments have increased toxicity.

Recently, newer and second-generation anti-CD20 monoclonal antibodies have been tested. Obinutuzumab is a glycoengineered monoclonal antibody targeting CD20 with enhanced antibody-dependent, cell-mediated cytotoxicity compared with rituximab. The GALLIUM trial compared obinutuzumab plus chemotherapy versus rituximab plus chemotherapy in patients with treatment-naive FL and indolent lymphomas. The trial demonstrated a significant PFS but not OS advantage, albeit with increased toxicity, leading to US Food and Drug Administration (FDA) approval.[34]

In an effort to replace chemotherapy, the RELEVANCE trial was designed to show superiority of rituximab and lenalidomide in comparison with rituximab plus chemotherapy in previously untreated patients and was negative with equivalent 3-year PFS.[35] Overall, the toxicity was comparable between the arms and, with similar outcomes, some consider this an option free of cytotoxic therapy.

Maintenance Therapy

Maintenance strategies after induction to partial response (PR) or complete response (CR) have been examined in FL to delay or prevent disease relapse. Trials have shown improvement in PFS without improvement in OS. Thus, this remains an option for patients but is not mandatory. Completed trials include:

- ECOG 4402 in patients with FL who had low tumor burden: rituximab induction followed by surveillance or maintenance rituximab. This trial showed no improvement by maintenance in time to rituximab-refractory disease.[36]
- The PRIMA trial studied patients with FL who had high tumor burden.[31] Maintenance rituximab for 2 years improved PFS (75% *v* 58%, *P* = .0001) but did not affect OS, which was > 90% in both arms.
- The SAKK group found similar results in a randomized trial.[37]

An alternative to maintenance rituximab is consolidative radioimmunotherapy (RIT), which links yttrium-90 (^{90}Y) to an anti-CD20 monoclonal antibody (ibritumomab tiuxetan). With a median follow-up of 7.3 years, an update of the First-Line Indolent Trial showed that RIT consolidation after chemotherapy had a median time to next treatment of 8.1 years and a 3-year benefit in median PFS as compared with observation.[38] However, only a minority of patients were treated with rituximab-containing induction, making it difficult to interpret these results.

RELAPSED AND REFRACTORY FOLLICULAR AND LOW-GRADE LYMPHOMA

Although FL and other low-grade lymphomas have an indolent natural history, they are incurable malignancies and essentially all patients will experience relapse despite prolonged remissions. At the time of relapse, a similar approach of considering tumor burden and symptoms is applied, because not all patients with progression need immediate therapy.

There are limited prognostic tools at the time of relapse, but a pivotal study has allowed identification of a high-risk subgroup of patients. On the basis of observations that approximately 15% to 20% of unselected patients with FL experience disease relapse within 2 to 3 years after the end of treatment, the National Lymphocare Study sought to determine whether early relapse was associated with inferior survival.[39] Among 588 patients treated with R-CHOP, patients with progression of disease within 24 months (POD24) had a 5-year OS of only 50% (Fig 20-5). This is in stark contrast to patients without POD24, for whom 5-year survival was 90%. Clinical features associated with OS include POD24, age, and poor PS. The ability to identify a high-risk population in the setting of relapse has spawned a new generation of trials aiming to change these poor outcomes.

Symptomatic patients with progressive disease have a number of options without any evidence indicating a major survival advantage for any specific approach. The GADOLIN trial was a large phase III study comparing the second-generation anti-CD20 monoclonal antibody obinutuzumab plus bendamustine versus bendamustine alone in patients with relapsed indolent NHL.[40] Although the combined chemo-immunotherapy trial was superior in terms of PFS and OS, many have argued that the chemotherapy arm of bendamustine alone used a higher-than-usual dose and had no maintenance component, as well as no anti-CD20 monoclonal antibody. Furthermore, most patients in North America receive bendamustine as part of initial therapy, and the role of a second exposure to this agent is unclear. Targeted and/or biologic agents with promising activity include PI3 kinase inhibitors (namely, idelalisib, duvelisib, and copanlisib), lenalidomide, and venetoclax (ABT-199). Other approaches to relapsed or refractory disease include treatment with monoclonal antibodies, radioimmunotherapy, biologic therapies, and stem cell transplantation.

Monoclonal Antibodies

Rituximab, a chimeric monoclonal antibody targeting CD20, was initially approved in 1997 by the FDA.[41] Key points include:

- Four weekly infusions of rituximab at a dose of 375 mg/m^2.
- The response rate in FL was 46%, including a CR of 8% and a median time to progression (TTP) of approximately 1 year. The response rate was only 12% in SLL.
- Retreatment is possible with a second response of 40% in patients who have a relapse after an initial response to the antibody lasting at least 6 months.[42]
- Rituximab maintenance also prolongs remission durations in patients treated with a variety of chemotherapy regimens, and a meta-analysis suggested a survival advantage in the setting of relapse.[43]

Obinutuzumab, another anti-CD20 monoclonal antibody, is now approved for front-line combination chemoimmunotherapy and relapsed and refractory indolent NHL.

Radioimmunotherapy

Monoclonal antibodies labeled with isotopes, such as ^{131}I and ^{90}Y, are a treatment option. The FDA has approved Y-ibritumomab tiuxetan (anti-CD20) for the treatment of relapsed and refractory FL and low-grade NHL, transformed NHL, and disease that has not responded to rituximab, and as consolidation therapy for patients after initial chemotherapy. Response rates of > 80%, with a CR of 26%, were achieved for patients with relapsed and refractory indolent NHL; response rates were lower in rituximab-refractory populations.[44,45] In a randomized study, the rates of complete and overall response were higher with ^{90}Y–ibritumomab tiuxetan than with rituximab, but there was no difference in time to progression (TTP).[46]

Toxic effects associated with ^{90}Y–ibritumomab tiuxetan are primarily myelosuppression, with nadirs occurring 6 to 8 weeks

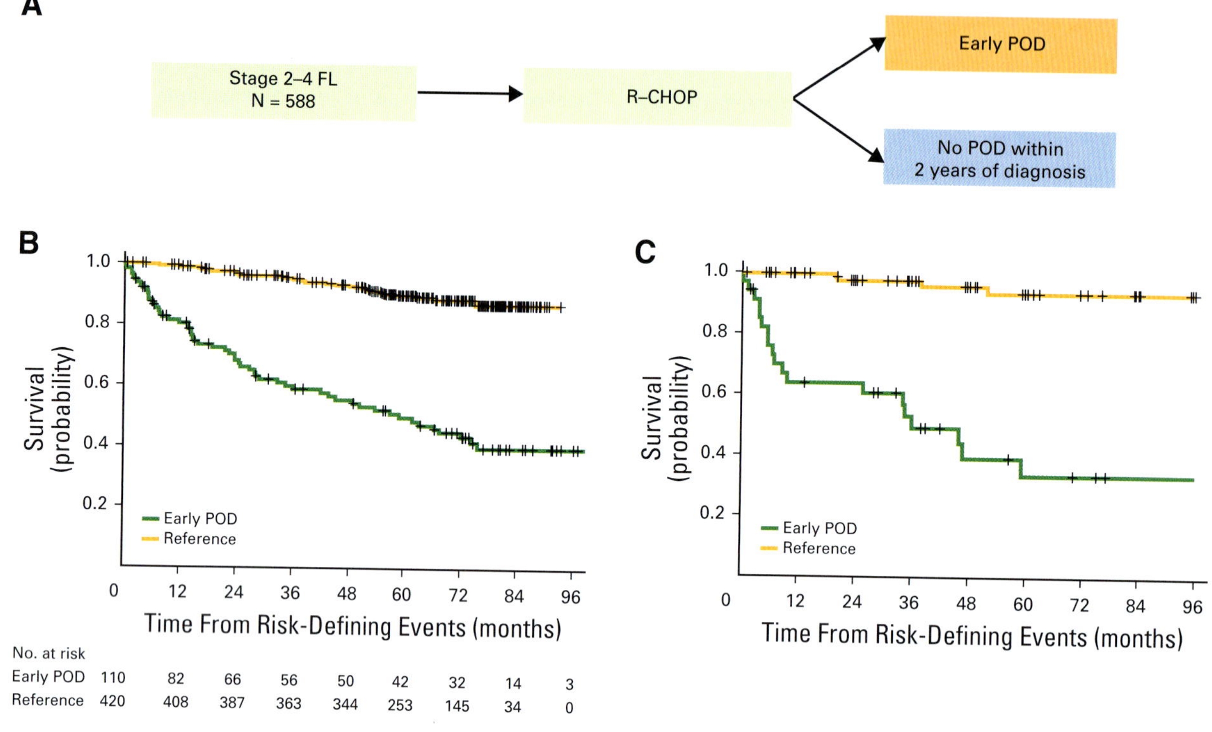

Fig. 20-5 Identification of a high-risk subgroup of follicular lymphoma (FL) based on early relapse after initial R-CHOP chemoimmunotherapy.

Abbreviations: POD, progression of disease; R-CHOP, rituximab, cyclophosphamide, doxorubicin, vincristine, and prednisone.

Reprinted with permission from Casulo C, Byrtek M, Dawson KL, et al. Early Relapse of Follicular Lymphoma After Rituximab Plus Cyclophosphamide, Doxorubicin, Vincristine, and Prednisone Defines Patients at High Risk for Death: An Analysis From the National LymphoCare Study [published correction appears in J Clin Oncol. 2016 Apr 20;34(12):1430]. J Clin Oncol. 2015;33(23):2516-2522.

after therapy. Patients with baseline thrombocytopenia or > 25% marrow involvement by B-NHL or < 10% normal cellularity should not receive RIT. Secondary acute myeloid leukemia (AML) and myelodysplastic syndrome may occur.

^{131}I-tositumomab (anti-CD20) was also approved by the FDA, with response rates for patients with relapsed or refractory FL or low-grade NHL of 50% to 80%, with a CR of approximately 30%, lasting a median of 9 months.[47] However, ^{131}I-tositumomab is no longer commercially available.

Other Biologic Therapies

Two oral phosphoinositide 3-kinase (PI3K) inhibitors (idelalisib and duvalisib) and one administered intravenously (copanalisib) are approved in the relapsed and refractory settings of FL. Response are in the 50% range and PFS in the 12-month range. Adverse events relate to the type of kinase inhibition.[48,49] Table 20-6 gives some examples. Although most of the toxic effects are early and reversible, some patients have a severe colitis that occurs after several months of therapy and requires treatment cessation.

Lenalidomide, an oral immunomodulatory agent, is active in relapsed FL, with approximately one-third of patients responding[50]; among responders, durability is long-lasting (> 16 months). When combined with rituximab, the response rate is 76% and CR rate is 39%.[51] A number of other agents are in development, including inhibitors of B-cell–receptor signaling spleen tyrosine kinase and inhibitors of BCL2. Venetoclax, a BCL-2 inhibitor, is approved in chronic lymphocytic leukemia (CLL) and SLL beyond first-line therapy or in those with a *p53* mutation conferring chemotherapy resistance. It is not approved for treatment of FL and appears to have only modest activity.

Stem Cell Transplantation and Cellular Therapies

Autologous hematopoietic cell transplantation (ASCT) may be useful for high-risk patients with early relapse. Results of

Table 20-6 Adverse Events Associated With Kinase Inhibitors

Kinase Inhibitor	PI3K Inhibition	GI (diarrhea, hepatitis)	Hypertension	Diabetes
Idelalisib	δ	++	+	+
Duvelisib	δ and γ	++	+	+
Copanalisib	pan	+	++	++

several studies suggest some of these patients may have prolonged benefit. This is weighed against the risk of secondary myelodysplasia and AML, which ranges from 7% to 19%. The availability of better front-line and more treatment options have made ASCT less attractive. Similarly, reduced-intensity allogeneic hematopoietic stem cell transplantation (RIC) has also shown a 4-year PFS of 76% in heavily pretreated patients. A National Clinical Trials Network prospective trial similarly found 3-year PFS and OS rates of 71% and 82%, respectively, with a nonrelapse mortality rate of 16%. RIC allogeneic transplantation is riskier and more morbid as compared with ASCT. Overall, the role of transplantation in FL has been controversial and the treatment is reserved for those with highest-risk disease in the rituximab era, particularly because targeted agents and less toxic therapies are in active development. Chimeric antigen receptor modified T-cells (CAR-Ts) are currently being evaluated in FL.

KEY POINTS

- Symptomatic patients with progressive FL or other low-grade lymphoma have a number of treatment options without any evidence indicating a major survival advantage for any specific approach.
- Traditional chemotherapies and immunotherapies alone or in combination are effective.
- Newer agents target specific molecules intrinsic to lymphoma cellular survival.

HISTOLOGIC TRANSFORMATION OF FL TO AGGRESSIVE LYMPHOMA

Approximately one-third of patients with FL undergo documented transformation to a more aggressive histology in their lifetime, typically to DLBCL. The annual rate of transformation is 2% to 3%; there is not a clear plateau in the rituximab era.[52] The pathogenesis and drivers of histologic transformation are complex and include cell cycle aberrations, increased genomic complexity, aberrant somatic hypermutation, and changes in the nodal microenvironment.[53] Although all low-grade lymphomas can transform, most literature focuses on FL.

Confirming a diagnosis of transformed FL can be difficult. The gold standard is a biopsy specimen of a lymph node showing an aggressive BCL that is clonally related to the FL. However, there is a high degree of sampling error because not all biopsy sites will show the histologic transformation. A PET scan is highly useful in this situation. Several studies have shown that higher standardized uptake values (> 13 to 17) have high positive predictive value and can be used to determine the biopsy site.[54,55] Clinical features associated with histologic transformation include rapid progression of nodal disease, increased LDH level, declining PS, hypercalcemia, new involvement in extranodal sites, and new-onset B symptoms.[52,56,57] If a biopsy procedure is not safe or feasible, clinical symptoms and supportive laboratory abnormalities can justify treatment of transformed disease.

Historical data show poor outcomes for transformed FL. However, this seems to be changing in the rituximab era,[58] although there is a paucity of clinical trials that focus specifically on transformed FL. If patients have not been treated already with anthracyclines, R-CHOP or a similar regimen is appropriate. Paradigms for therapy follow those of DLBCL generally and, when appropriate, include autologous transplant and CAR-Ts. In the pre-rituximab era, this would often be consolidated with ASCT, but this course is more controversial in modern times. If patients have already received anthracycline-based treatment, they should receive salvage chemotherapy followed by ASCT if physiologically eligible. Of note, in some patients, FL can transform in association with a new rearrangement of the *MYC* oncogene, usually with a t(8;14) acquisition. Because the vast majority of FL already has the t(14;18) rearrangement with BCL2 overexpression, this leads to a high-grade, double-hit phenotype (see discussion in section on Treatment of Newly Diagnosed Aggressive Lymphomas), and R-CHOP may be insufficient for disease control.

Unfortunately, many patients are elderly or frail at the time of transformation, and there are limited data to support a specific therapy. Radioimmunotherapy, which delivers targeted radioisotopes to CD20-positive disease, is one FDA-approved option. ^{131}I-tositumomab is no longer available, but ^{90}Y–ibritumomab tiuxetan offers a 1-week treatment with promising efficacy.[53]

KEY POINTS

- Asymptomatic patients with indolent NHL need not be treated at the time of diagnosis if they have low tumor burden. This is particularly true for elderly patients.
- Indications for initiation of therapy include the development of fever, drenching sweats, weight loss, threatened end-organ function, cytopenia secondary to lymphoma, bulky disease (GELF criteria), or steady or rapid progression of disease.
- Indolent lymphomas can be treated with a variety of options, including observation alone, single-agent anti-CD20 monoclonal antibody, and chemoimmunotherapy.
- Indolent lymphomas are typically associated with prolonged survival, though multiple relapses are common.
- Approximately 15% to 20% of patients with FL will experience disease progression or relapse within 24 months after undergoing chemoimmunotherapy. These patients have a significantly worse 5-year survival.[59]

MARGINAL ZONE LYMPHOMA

MZLs constitute 10% of B-NHLs and have an indolent course. SEER data show a 5-year survival rate of 88.7%, with a median OS of 12.6 years.[60] The three types of MZL have varying incidences, biology, and prognoses:

- extranodal marginal zone lymphoma (ENMZL; OS, 70%),
- splenic marginal zone lymphoma (SMZL; OS, 20%), and
- primary nodal MZL (OS, 10%).

ENMZL is further divided into gastric and nongastric types.

The clinical presentation depends on the site of involvement, but the most common site of disease is the GI tract, which accounts for almost two-thirds of all ENMZLs, and the stomach accounts for 30% to 50% of cases. Ocular adnexa, lung, thyroid gland, and skin are common nongastric sites.[61] Multifocal involvement of a single organ can be seen, and nodal and bone marrow involvement confer a worse prognosis.[62] The median age at presentation is 68 years, with a slight female preponderance. Most patients have limited-stage disease (stages IE-IIE); however, on complete staging, up to 25% of patients with gastric and 50% with nongastric ENMZL have disseminated disease.[63]

PATHOLOGY AND BIOLOGY

Histopathologically, centrocyte-like and monocytoid-like B cells clonally expand from the marginal zone with interfollicular expansion, occasional follicular colonization, and increased numbers of immunoblasts. These immunoblasts, which are larger than the other B cells, should not be confused with transformation to DLBCL unless they are forming sheets or large clusters. Secondary pathology review can be helpful to aid treatment decisions. The immunophenotype is that of a mature B cell (ie, CD20-positive, CD79a-positive, CD19-positive, immunoglobulin M [IgM]-positive, IgD-negative) but lacking CD5, CD10, CD23, BCL6, and cyclin D1.[4] Occasionally, CD5 can be positive and distinction from CLL or MCL must be done via other molecular or genetic testing. In addition, it can be difficult to distinguish MZL morphologically from LPL, which is also CD5 negative and CD10 negative; in these cases, *MYD88* mutation supports a diagnosis of LPL and is negative in MZL except sometimes in the splenic variant.[64] Given their extranodal homing, MZL cells can infiltrate epithelial structures, especially in the GI tract. This leads to the classic lymphoepithelial lesion.

A unique feature of MZL is the association with infectious agents and chronic antigenic stimulation. The concept of lymphoma as an antigen-driven disease is best described for gastric ENMZL, formerly called gastric mucosa-associated lymphoid tissue, in which *H. pylori* (HP) consistently irritates the mucosal T and B cells that line the stomach, causing them to proliferate.[65] At some point, the B cells become autoreactive and develop into an HP-dependent lymphoma. Gastric ENMZL can also be HP independent, often as a result of the t(11;18) rearrangement, which confers resistance to HP eradication. Other examples of chronic antigenic stimuli leading to MZL include *C. psittaci*, leading to ocular adnexal MZL; hepatitis C, leading to SMZL (treated successfully with elimination of hepatitis C); and *Borrelia burgdorferi*, leading to cutaneous MZL. Autoimmune conditions associated with MZL include Hashimoto thyroiditis, leading to thyroid MZL, and Sjögren disease, leading to salivary gland MZL.

GASTRIC AND NONGASTRIC EXTRANODAL MZL

The most common MZL is gastric ENMZL in association with HP. Patients typically present with nausea, abdominal discomfort, or GI bleeding. For stage IE disease, treatment is HP eradication with either triple therapy (proton-pump inhibitor plus two antimicrobials) or quadruple therapy (proton-pump inhibitor, bismuth, tetracycline, metronidazole) for 14 days, which results in nearly 80% HP eradication. HP-negative gastric ENMZL has a more aggressive course.[66]

Response assessment after HP eradication requires a repeated endoscopy, but this should not be done sooner than 3 months after therapy, because responses are often delayed. If a repeated endoscopy is normal but biopsy specimens show lymphoid aggregates, asymptomatic patients may be kept under observation. Surveillance can stop after two sequential negative endoscopies. Patients with HP-negative gastric ENMZL or with resistance to HP eradication should receive second-line options. Several retrospective series done primarily in the pre–rituximab era showed radiotherapy (26 to 40 Gy) to the stomach offers excellent local control and long-term survival of 10 to 15 years; relapses are rare and occur outside the initial treatment field.[67-69] In one study, rituximab monotherapy had an overall response rate (ORR) of 77% and CR of 46% in patients with resistant disease; with a median follow-up of 28 months, all 27 patients were alive, 54% of them were disease-free, and there was no difference in response based on t(11;18) status.[70] Radiation is preferred to rituximab in the National Comprehensive Cancer Network (NCCN) guidelines.

Systemic therapy for ENMZL is reserved for patients with symptomatic disease, with rituximab monotherapy being most commonly used. In a study of patients with gastric and nongastric ENMZL, the response rate was > 70%, but it was higher in treatment-naive patients (ORR, 87% *v* 45%; *P* = .03).[71] Although maintenance rituximab improved time to treatment failure (4.8 years *v* 1.4 years; *P* = .012) and time to first cytotoxic therapy, OS was not improved in another study.[31] One phase III trial compared chlorambucil monotherapy with rituximab monotherapy and with the combination; it was the largest prospective trial in ENMZL.[72] At a median follow-up of 7.4 years, combination chlorambucil and rituximab showed a significant 5-year EFS (68% *v* 50%; *P* = .0009) and PFS (72% *v* 57%) benefit compared with rituximab alone. Patients in all arms did well, with approximately a 90% 5-year survival. In 2017, ibrutinib monotherapy was approved for relapsed MZL on the basis of an ORR of 46% and good tolerability.[73] Other agents are also being tested, particularly because many underlying pathogenetic lesions in MZL are associated with constitutive activation of nuclear factor κ B (NF-κB) and aberrant B-cell receptor signaling.

SPLENIC MZL AND NODAL MZL

SMZL presents with symptomatic splenomegaly, lymphocytosis, and marrow infiltration. The clinical presentation is similar to CLL or hairy cell leukemia, which are the main differential diagnostic considerations. Flow cytometry of peripheral blood with the immunophenotype described earlier in this section on MZL is helpful. In addition, circulating villous lymphocytes with blunt projections at polar ends of the cell can be seen, and they have a different appearance than circulating hairy cells, which have more fine projections in a radial distribution. SMZL is sometimes associated with hepatitis C, and lymphoma regression has been reported with hepatitis C eradication.[74] However, most symptomatic patients will require lymphoma-specific treatment. Historically, splenectomy has provided good palliation of symptoms. More recently, rituximab monotherapy is also effective and spares the patient a surgical procedure.

Nodal MZL is an uncommon disease and may have a worse prognosis compared with other forms of MZL. This may be because it is at a more advanced stage at diagnosis. The treatment of NMZL follows the paradigm of FL, and few studies are dedicated to this specific subtype.

KEY POINTS

- Three types of MZL are EMZL, SMZL, and NMZL.
- MZLs are frequently antigen-driven diseases.
- Initial treatment of HP-associated gastric MZL consists of antimicrobial eradication.
- Gastric irradiation is the preferred treatment of gastric MZL persistent after HP eradication or independent of HP.
- Patients with any subtype of MZL in relapse or refractory to first-line therapy can be treated with the Bruton tyrosine kinase (BTK) inhibitor ibrutinib.

LYMPHOPLASMACYTIC LYMPHOMA/ WALDENSTRÖM MACROGLOBULINEMIA

LPL is an uncommon and incurable indolent BCL. The vast majority of LPLs produce an IgM paraprotein, designated Waldenström macroglobulinemia (WM). Because < 5% of cases produce IgG, IgA, or are nonsecretory, most studies pertain to WM.

LPL/WM is typically diagnosed because of the presence of cytopenias; the bone marrow is the major site of disease. Less commonly, patients may have adenopathy or organomegaly at the time of diagnosis. Slightly more men than women are afflicted, and the median age is in the 60s.[75] The diagnosis requires a bone marrow biopsy specimen that shows infiltration by small lymphocytes that are positive for CD19, CD20, CD22, CD25, and FMC7, and negative for CD10, CD23, and CD103.[4] Approximately 15% to 20% of patients have CD5 positivity, requiring further evaluation to distinguish LPL/WM from other lymphomas, such as MCL. It has been found that > 90% of WM harbor a point mutation in the *MYD88* gene (L265P),[64] aiding in diagnosis and differentiation from other lymphomas.

As with other indolent lymphomas, treatment of LPL/WM is indicated only if the patient has disease-related symptoms, cytopenias related to marrow infiltration, bulky disease, or IgM-related complications.[76] A number of other symptoms related to the paraprotein may prompt more urgent treatment, including hyperviscosity, cryoglobulinemia, and sensorimotor peripheral neuropathy.

First-line treatment options from the International Workshop on Waldenström Macroglobulinemia include rituximab monotherapy, chemoimmunotherapy, ibrutinib, or bortezomib-based treatment.[76] Several management aspects must be considered:

- An elevated paraprotein level alone is not an indication for therapy in asymptomatic patients.
- Rituximab monotherapy has been associated with a sudden increase in IgM levels, leading to symptomatic hyperviscosity.[77]
- Patients with symptomatic hyperviscosity and very high IgM levels should be considered for plasmapheresis as a bridge to more definitive treatment. Bortezomib is also an excellent option for rapid treatment of symptomatic hyperviscosity.

A number of new agents are in development for LPL/WM. Ibrutinib, an oral and irreversible BTK inhibitor, was approved in 2015 for both treatment-naive and relapsed disease. The pivotal study was a phase II trial of 63 patients with relapsed WM and in whom an ORR of 90% was observed[78]; of note, this response rate included both "partial" and "very good partial" responses, and there were no CRs. A *MYD88* mutation predicts response to ibrutinib; conversely, *CXCR4* mutations are associated with lower response rates. A second trial studying ibrutinib in patients with heavily pretreated, rituximab-refractory disease showed preserved a high response rate of 90% and PFS rate of 86% at 18 months.[79]

Although many patients with LPL/WM have initially responsive disease, relapse is inevitable, and most patients die of the disease. In selected patients, allogeneic, nonmyeloablative stem cell transplantation offers the chance for cure.

KEY POINTS

- LPL/WM are uncommon indolent lymphomas that usually produce a paraprotein.
- Greater than 90% of patients with LPL/WM have point mutations in *MYD88*, which can help distinguish this disease from other indolent lymphomas in histologically challenging cases.
- Rituximab monotherapy can lead to transient symptomatic hyperviscosity in patients with high IgM levels.
- Indications for treatment include hyperviscosity, cryoglobulinemia, peripheral neuropathy, cytopenias, and other symptoms.

SMALL LYMPHOCYTIC LYMPHOMA

SLL, the tissue counterpart of CLL, is characterized by an accumulation of small, mature-appearing lymphocytes in the blood, bone marrow, and lymph nodes. The classic immunophenotypic profile of CLL/SLL is expression of CD5, CD19, and CD23, with low-level expression of surface immunoglobulin and CD20. CLL and SLL are usually distinguished arbitrarily by a number of circulating clonal B cells > 5,000/mm^3 (CLL) or < 5,000/mm^3 (SLL). Thus, the diagnosis of SLL can be made in the absence of blood or bone marrow involvement. Although SLL often is included in clinical trials of FL and other low-grade NHLs, its biology and response to various therapies differ enough from those of the other indolent NHLs that it is better treated as CLL. The FDA has approved several new agents, including the BTK inhibitor ibrutinib, the BCL-2 inhibitor venetoclax, and the PI3K inhibitors idelalisib and duvelisib. A randomized study of rituximab ibrutinib versus rituximab, fludarabine, and cyclophosphamide demonstrated a PFS and OS advance for the ibrutinib-containing arm (see Chapter 19: Leukemias).[80]

AGGRESSIVE BCLS

Aggressive lymphomas are characterized by a rapid and usually symptomatic growth phase leading to clinical presentation. DLBCL is the prototype of aggressive B-NHL and constitutes 30% of all NHLs. Up to 40% of disease initially presents in extranodal locations, most commonly in the GI tract, but also with involvement of the CNS, genitourinary or reproductive tracts, lung, or other sites. Optimal diagnosis requires a tissue specimen sufficiently large to confirm histology and perform important prognostic and predictive tests; FNA is never appropriate as the sole means of diagnosis. The classic morphology is diffuse effacement of the normal lymph node architecture by intermediate-size to large cells expressing CD19, CD20, CD79a, and CD45. However, DLBCL is increasingly understood to be a heterogeneous disease with genetic, biologic, and clinical variants that have an important impact on clinical outcomes.

The early observation of heterogeneous outcomes prompted an evaluation for clinical features predictive of outcome. The IPI was a large analysis with multivariate testing of prognostic factors. Five features were most prognostic (Table 20-5) and stratify patients into four risk categories: age > 60 years, PS > 1, increased LDH level, more than one extranodal site, and stage III-IV disease. Efforts to improve on the original IPI include the R-IPI (revised IPI in the era of rituximab) and the NCCN IPI[81]; however, the original IPI continues to be the most widely used in clinical trials.

The genetic heterogeneity of DLBCL was first described > 15 years ago when gene expression profiling of 20,000 lymphoma-specific genes in frozen tumor specimens identified three unique patterns in otherwise clinically similar patients.[82] The patterns were named after normal B cells at similar stages of development and are referred to as the cell-of-origin (COO) model. DLBCL specimens genetically resembling normal germinal center B cells were called germinal center DLBCL (GCB-DLBCL), whereas those resembling activated B cells were called activated B-cell DLBCL (ABC-DLBCL). Despite similar clinical risk features, patients with ABC-DLBCL have an inferior survival compared with those with GCB-DLBCL treated with CHOP or R-CHOP (Fig 20-6).[83] GCB- and ABC-DLBCL have different spectrums of gene abnormalities, which may lead to specifically targeted therapies. Testing for COO is difficult in routine clinical practice because gene expression profiling requires frozen material and is not widely available. A number of immunohistochemical algorithms

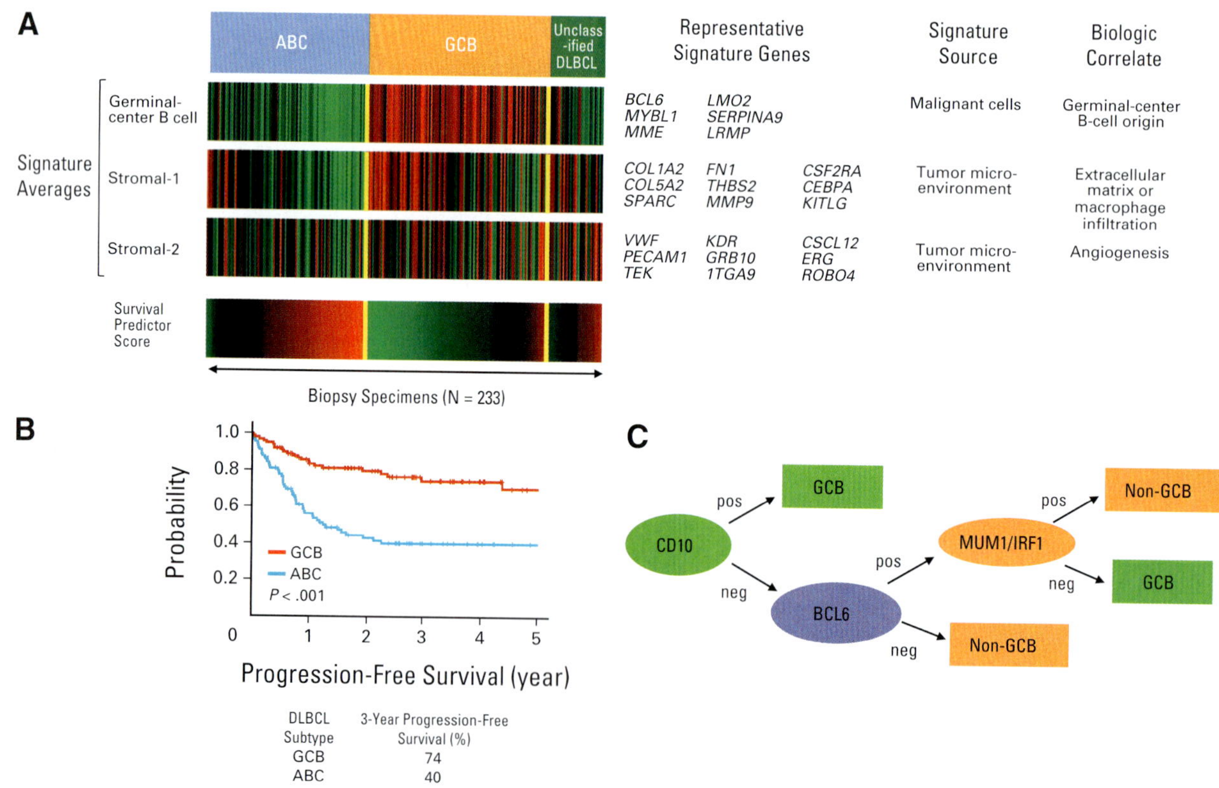

Fig. 20-6 Cell-of-origin (COO) model for DLBCL.

(A) Gene expression profiling heat map. (B) Survival outcomes by COO in patients treated with R-CHOP. (C) Hans algorithm for immunohistochemical determination of COO. See text for details.

Abbreviations: ABC, activated B cell; DLBCL, diffuse large B-cell lymphoma; GCB, germinal center B cell.

are used as a surrogate for COO, but there is an approximate 20% error rate. One of the more common algorithms is the Hans method, which stains for CD10, MUM1, and BCL6 to determine COO.[84] NanoString technology is promising and is being incorporated into prospective trials. Alternative molecular classification has emerged, but is not in routine clinical use.

MYC, a proto-oncogene and transcription factor classically rearranged in Burkitt lymphoma, is rearranged in up to 15% of cases of DLBCL. Because DLBCL is substantially more common than Burkitt lymphoma, many more patients with *MYC* rearrangements have DLBCL rather than Burkitt lymphoma in the United States. Of note, *MYC* rearrangement is *diagnostic* in Burkitt lymphoma but adversely *prognostic* in DLBCL, likely because of an entirely distinct set of target genes.[85] *MYC* activation delivers a potent proliferative signal. Although *MYC* rearrangement alone was initially thought to be a key adverse prognostic feature, it is more likely that the dual rearrangement of *MYC* with *BCL2* (or less commonly, *BCL6*), occurring in 5% to 7% of cases of DLBCL, is more clinically relevant. The combination of a strong growth signal (*MYC*) and a potent antiapoptotic factor (*BCL2*) leads to an entity dubbed double-hit lymphoma (DHL), a clinically aggressive phenotype with poor long-term survival after standard chemoimmunotherapy. Patients may also have *MYC*, *BCL2*, and *BCL6*—so-called triple-hit lymphoma—with the same pathobiology as DHL.

Complicating the picture further, both MYC and BCL2 proteins can be overexpressed either with or without the underlying respective chromosomal rearrangements in up to 30% of patients with DLBCL.[86,87] The double expression of MYC and BCL2 proteins has been acknowledged in the WHO 2016 Update in Classification of Lymphoid Malignancies as an adverse prognostic feature and is termed double-expressor lymphoma (DEL). When DEL occurs without underlying DHL, outcomes are still poor but not quite as dismal. As discussed later in this chapter, it is unknown precisely how these patients should be treated.

It is difficult to know which prognostic feature is most important, but clear overlaps exist among COO, DHL, DEL, and IPI. For example, patients with DHL almost always have a GCB-DLBCL phenotype, whereas most patients with DEL are older and have an ABC-DLBCL phenotype.[86,87]

KEY POINTS

- DLBCL is the most common and prototypical aggressive lymphoma.
- IPI remains the most commonly used prognostic tool.
- Molecular classifications, including the most commonly used COO, currently provide prognostic information but may also provide treatment strategies in the future.

TREATMENT OF NEWLY DIAGNOSED AGGRESSIVE LYMPHOMAS

Limited-Stage Disease

Approximately 20% of patients with DLBCL have limited disease (stage I or nonbulky stage II) at the time of presentation and have a superior prognosis compared with patients with advanced-stage disease. A stage-modified IPI was developed for risk stratification; it includes age > 60 years, stage II disease, increased LDH level, and PS > 1.[88]

A long-standing debate has been whether limited cycles (three or four) of R-CHOP are sufficient and whether radiation consolidation improves outcome. Early randomized trials did not include rituximab and did not include PET scanning to assess response. Modern single-arm studies have suggested this is a feasible approach. At the 2018 American Society of Hematology annual meeting, a randomized trial appeared to settle this in a subset of highly favorable patients who were < 60 years old, had low risk by age-adjusted IPI, and had nonbulky tumors (< 7.5 cm).[89] Patients were randomly assigned to receive six rounds of R-CHOP or four rounds of R-CHOP plus two rounds of rituximab at 21-day cycles. Radiotherapy was not administered except for prophylactic radiotherapy of the contralateral testis in patients with testicular lymphoma. The 3-year EFS was identical (89%) in both treatment arms. The 3-years OS was 99% in patients receiving the latter regimen and 98% in patients receiving the former regimen. These findings resolved the long-standing debate about cycles of R-CHOP treatment in this highly selective subset of DLBCL patients. Earlier trials did address a broader population of patients with early-stage disease, with somewhat less impressive results.

- The Southwest Oncology Group performed a pivotal trial in the pre-rituximab era comparing CHOP for three cycles plus involved-field radiation therapy (IFRT) with CHOP for eight cycles.[88] At 5 years, the combined-modality arm had improved survival, and this study thus influenced practice patterns. However, the advantage to combined-modality treatment disappears at 7 years, and very long-term follow-up of almost 20 years showed a pattern of continuous relapse in both arms, suggestive of a unique biology for limited-stage DLBCL.[90]
- In the rituximab era, results of the MabThera International Trial support R-CHOP for six cycles without radiation as an excellent option, with 6-year EFS and OS rates of 84% and 95%, respectively.[91] Preliminary results of a randomized trial show no advantage to radiation after four or six cycles of R-CHOP for patients in metabolic complete remission.[92]
- A large Canadian database analysis similarly found that radiation could be safely omitted for patients with a negative PET scan after three cycles.[93] PET-negative patients after three cycles of R-CHOP received a fourth cycle and had a 3-year TTP of 92%, compared with PET-positive patients, who had a 3-year TTP of 60% despite having undergone radiation therapy.

Thus, the routine use of radiation may not be required in limited-stage DLBCL and is definitively not needed in younger patients with highly favorable features. An important caveat to the discussion regarding limited-stage DLBCL is that none of these trials fully evaluated the impact of biology (ie, DHL, DEL, high-grade morphology) or specific extranodal sites (ie, primary breast). An extension to this latter point is that primary testicular lymphoma, which is often stage I-II, constitutes a distinct clinicopathologic subset of DLBCL and has its own treatment approach, including orchiectomy, contralateral testicular radiation, and CNS prophylaxis.

KEY POINTS

- Early-stage DLBCL is increasingly treated with immunochemotherapy alone without radiation, using PET scanning to tailor therapy.
- Patients < 60 years old, without IPI risk factors and with nonbulky tumors, should be treated with four cycles of R-CHOP alone.

Advanced-Stage Disease

In the early 2000s, rituximab added to CHOP chemotherapy demonstrated an advantage not only for PFS but also for OS of approximately 15% in younger and older patients.[59,91,94,95] Importantly, most studies have shown a plateau after 5 years, supporting the curative potential of treatment of DLBCL. However, not all patients are cured, and the preceding discussion highlights the clinical and biologic factors affecting curability. Attempts to improve on R-CHOP have taken several approaches, including dose-dense delivery, addition of etoposide or novel agents to an R-CHOP backbone, the use of consolidative stem cell transplantation, maintenance therapy, or delivery of treatment by infusion (see detailed review in Nowakowski et al[96]). None of these has proven beneficial in randomized trials. The standard of care is six cycles of R-CHOP; additional cycles show no added benefit.[97]

Patients with dual rearrangements of MYC and *BCL2* and/or *BCL6* (DHL), however, probably need augmented approaches. Large retrospective series have consistently shown < 20% long-term survival for DHL treated with R-CHOP.[87,98] Several retrospective reviews indicate more intensive regimens have better outcomes, and the largest multicenter analysis showed R-CHOP to be inferior to almost any other regimen, with a hazard ratio (HR) of 0.5.[99,100] Prospective data supporting the use of one regimen over another are limited, but a phase II trial spearheaded by the US National Cancer Institute (NCI) shows promising activity of the 5-day infused regimen of dose-adjusted etoposide, doxorubicin, vincristine, and cyclophosphamide (DA-EPOCH-R), although not all patients in this trial had true DHL.[101]

Primary Mediastinal BCL

Primary mediastinal BCL (PMBL) is a distinct, aggressive BCL derived from medullary thymic B cells and presents as a large and symptomatic mediastinal mass, often with superior vena cava syndrome and a predilection for extranodal organ involvement. The median age at onset is 30 years with a slight female predominance. Histopathology shows a diffuse infiltrate of large cells with CD20, CD79a, and PAX5, and usually positive for CD10, BCL6, and CD23.[4] CD30 can be expressed as well and is often weaker in intensity compared with HL. Of interest, there are significant similarities in gene expression between PMBL and classic HL, with deregulation of NF-κB, JAK2, and PDL1/PDL2.[102] Cases with intermediate histopathologic features between PMBL and HL are termed "gray-zone lymphomas", and these have a worse prognosis.[4,103]

The treatment of PMBL is controversial, and prospective data are limited. Prior to rituximab, several studies suggested improved outcomes with intensified treatments (ie, methotrexate with leucovorin rescue plus doxorubicin, cyclophosphamide, vincristine, prednisone, and bleomycin; etoposide with leucovorin rescue plus doxorubicin, cyclophosphamide, vincristine, prednisone, and bleomycin; combination prednisone, doxorubicin, cyclophosphamide, etoposide, cytarabine, bleomycin, vincristine, methotrexate, and leucovorin) compared with CHOP; many of these studies also included consolidative radiation. In the era of chemoimmunotherapy and functional imaging via PET, intensification still seems to have a role, although there is controversy over the ability to omit radiation. In a series of 58 patients, primary induction to R-CHOP was ineffective in 21% of patients with PMBL.[104] Long-term disease control with R-CHOP–like regimens was approximately 60% to 70%.[105] A prospective international trial of rituximab plus various chemotherapy backbones followed by radiation in the majority of patients showed 5-year PFS and OS rates > 90%, with the end-of-treatment PET being the most important discriminant of outcome.[106] Investigators at the NCI and Stanford tested DA-EPOCH-R as a means to obviate the need for radiation and reported a 5-year EFS rate of 93% with no relapses beyond 1 year.[107] An alternative radiation-sparing approach is to deliver intensified R-CHOP with ifosfamide, carboplatin, and etoposide (ICE) chemotherapy.[108] Given the mediastinal location, avoiding radiation is an appealing option.

Although the vast majority of patients will be cured with first- or second-line therapy, those with relapsed disease after two or more prior lines of therapy now have a new treatment option with the immune checkpoint inhibitor pembrolizumab.[109] At a median follow-up of 9.7 months, the ORR was 45% with a CR rate of 11% and a PR rate of 34%. Among the 24 responders, the median time to initial objective response was 2.8 (range, 2.1 to 8.5) months. The median duration of response was not reached (range, < 1.1 to < 19.2 months).

KEY POINTS

- Most patients with PMBL do well with chemoimmunotherapy (eg, R-CHOP) and radiation or approaches that eliminate radiation (eg, R-EPOCH or R-CHOP followed by ICE).
- The role of radiation remains a controversial issue.
- Pembrolizumab is now available in the relapsed setting.

Primary Testicular Lymphoma

Primary testicular lymphoma is usually an aggressive BCL limited to the testes. It is relatively rare and occurs in men in the sixth decade of life. Despite being localized (stage I-IIE) in most cases, outcomes are poor as compared with other early-stage DLBCLs. In particular, there is a high risk of CNS recurrence (up to 25%) and a continuous risk of relapse persisting even 10 years after diagnosis.[110] Treatment should include R-CHOP for six cycles, CNS prophylaxis, and radiation to the contralateral testis at the end of systemic therapy.[111]

CNS Prophylaxis

Aggressive BCLs can recur in the CNS, with an extremely high risk of fatal outcome within 1 year. CNS recurrence typically occurs early, within 6 to 12 months after initial treatment, and is often parenchymal. Fortunately, the overall risk of secondary CNS involvement in the rituximab era is low—approximately 3% to 5% in all patients with DLBCL. Defining patients with a higher risk of recurrence and delivering CNS prophylaxis is essential, but these areas remain incompletely outlined. Extranodal areas confer increased risk of CNS involvement, though not all anatomic areas confer the same risk. Marrow, paranasal sinuses, and breast involvement are examples of possible higher risk. One international collaboration evaluated 2,164 patients with aggressive BCLs and proposed a new CNS-IPI comprising kidney and/or adrenal gland involvement, age > 60 years, LDH level greater than normal, ECOG PS > 1, stage III-IV disease, or more than one extranodal site. Patients with high-risk disease had a 10% to 12% risk of CNS relapse. This study's results facilitate identification of patients who need prophylaxis.

Several management options for prophylaxis include intrathecal or systemic approaches. Prospective data are lacking to guide the best prophylactic regimen, but CNS prophylaxis can be with four to eight doses of intrathecal methotrexate and/or cytarabine, or systemic methotrexate (3 to 3.5 g/m^2) during the course of treatment.[112,113]

Relapsed or Refractory Disease

Despite improved cure rates with chemoimmunotherapy, approximately 30% to 40% of patients with DLBCL will have either primary refractory disease or will experience relapse after a prior response. The treatment approach to relapsed disease is based on the randomized Parma trial conducted > 20 years ago.[114] The trial randomly assigned 109 patients, who were < 60 years old and had relapsed aggressive BCLs, to either dexamethasone and cytarabine (ara-C)/platinum agent (DHAP) chemotherapy or autologous bone marrow transplant (ABMT). Patients undergoing transplantation had a superior EFS and OS rates of 46% versus 12% (P = .001) and 53% versus 32% (P = .038), respectively. However, several key caveats to this historic trial include that only chemosensitive patients were randomly assigned to one of the study arms, marrow involvement was excluded, and the study was conducted before the introduction of rituximab.

The modern role of ASCT for relapsed DLBCL is more debated. The CORAL trial randomly assigned patients with relapsed or refractory DLBCL after either CHOP or R-CHOP to one of two salvage regimens (rituximab plus ICE or rituximab plus DHAP [RDHAP]) before ASCT. Among 398 patients, the 3-year EFS rate was 31% overall, but it was 53% for those with chemosensitive disease who were undergoing transplantation. Patients relapsing within 12 months and having undergone prior R-CHOP therapy had a worse outcome, with 3-year PFS of 23%. RDHAP may have an advantage in germinal center phenotype DLBCL, but had more renal toxicity. A study from the National Cancer Institute of Canada showed similar results,[115] and many interpret the 30% EFS rate for all patients to suggest a limited role for ASCT at salvage. However, registry data and analysis of responding patients suggest chemosensitivity retains an important role, and patients able to proceed to transplantation have durable remissions of 40% to 50%.[116] Furthermore, patients unable to undergo ASCT have extremely poor outcomes, with a 3-year EFS rate of only 14%. Thus, although ASCT arguably benefits a smaller pool of patients with DLBCL in the rituximab era, some patients with chemosensitive disease continue to derive benefit.

Of note, none of the studies evaluating transplantation was powered to test the impact of adverse biologic features, and it is unclear whether poor outcomes are driven by patients with DEL, COO, or DHL. A two-institution analysis found that patients with DHL or DEL had worse outcomes with ASCT[117]; conversely, patients lacking these high-risk features had an excellent outcome with ASCT.

Despite the controversy over the benefit of ASCT for relapsed or refractory aggressive BCLs, it remains the standard of care in fit patients. Allogeneic transplant is rarely used due to its morbidity and uncertain benefit. Patients ineligible for transplantation or with recurrence despite transplantation have an abysmal survival of approximately 6 months.[96]

Two modified autologous CAR-Ts against the B-cell receptor antigen CD19 have been approved for relapsed disease after two prior lines of therapy. Axicabtagene ciloleucel demonstrated an ORR of 82% and a CR rate of 54%. Patients with CR appear to have sustained response; the OS rate at 18 months was 52%.[118] Tisagenlecleucel was the second CAR-T product approved after demonstrating an ORR of 54% and a CR rate of 32%. The median duration of response has not been reached in patients achieving CR.[119] Both treatments are associated with cytopenias and also neurologic toxicity including encephalopathy and cytokine-release syndrome, requiring careful monitoring and prompt intervention based on a defined clinical algorithm with specific interventions proportional to the severity of toxicity. The full impact of these very expensive treatment options is not known currently.

In June 2019, the FDA approved polatuzumab vedotin-piiq, an antibody drug conjugate against CD79b, for treatment of relapsed or refractory DLBCL, in combination with bendamustine and a rituximab product, after at least two prior therapies.[120] The payload is the small-molecule antimitotic agent monomethyl auristatin E (MMAE), similar to previously approved brentuximab vedotin for HL. The addition of this drug to bendamustine and rituximab alone in patients with at least one prior therapy improved response rates from 18% to 40%. Notably, the percentage of patients achieving at least a 12-month duration of response improved from 20% to 48%.

KEY POINTS

- Aggressive NHLs typically grow rapidly and nearly always require prompt initiation of therapy soon after the diagnosis is established to ameliorate symptoms, avert rapid progression of the disease, and optimize survival.
- Calculation of the IPI for a patient at the time of diagnosis with aggressive NHL permits estimation of projected survival on the basis of individual clinical characteristics.
- Multiagent chemoimmunotherapy regimens are the standard of care in the treatment of aggressive lymphomas.
- DLBCL is the most common aggressive NHL and is generally treated with R-CHOP, with a cure rate of approximately 60% to 70%. DLBCL is a heterogeneous disease with clinical and genomic variants.
- The presence of dual MYC and *BCL2* and/or *BCL6* rearrangements in aggressive BCLs is called "double-hit lymphoma" and has a poor prognosis with standard R-CHOP treatment.
- CNS prophylaxis is necessary for patients with DLBCL who present with high-risk features. (See separate sections for Burkitt lymphoma, lymphoblastic lymphoma, and Lymphomas Associated With Immunodeficiency).
- Fit patients with refractory or relapsed disease deemed chemosensitive undergo ASCT with curative intent unless the marrow remains contaminated by lymphoma.
- CAR-T directed against the B-cell receptor antigen CD19 represent a novel option for relapsed disease after two lines of prior therapy but are associated with neurotoxicity and cytokine-release syndrome, which must be carefully anticipated and managed.

MANTLE CELL LYMPHOMA

MCL is an uncommon subtype that occurs in approximately 3,000 to 5,000 patients per year in the United States. For unclear reasons, there is a strong predilection for male sex, with a 3:1 ratio. The median age at onset is 70 years. The malignant cells characteristically express CD20 and CD5, features shared with CLL. However, MCL does not express CD23 (a feature of CLL) or CD10 (found in most cases of FL). Diagnosis is confirmed by the presence of mature CD20-positive, CD5-positive B cells with cyclin D1 overexpression due to t(11;14)(q13;q32).[4]

Three clinicopathologic variants require different approaches: classic MCL, blastoid MCL, and indolent MCL. SOX11 is positive in classic and blastoid MCL but is frequently absent in indolent MCL, which presents with splenomegaly and lymphocytosis and has a better initial prognosis. Patients with indolent MCL can be safely observed in the absence of symptoms, although essentially all patients will eventually require treatment.[121] Most patients present with both adenopathy and extranodal involvement of the GI tract (lymphomatous polyposis) or with peripheral-blood lymphocytosis. The vast majority of patients have bone marrow involvement at diagnosis.

Prognosis in MCL is affected by clinical and biologic features. The Mantle Cell Lymphoma International Prognostic Index (MIPI) stratifies patients into low-, intermediate-, and high-risk groups on the basis of a calculation that involves age, PS, LDH level, and leukocyte count[122]; the MIPI has been validated in patients undergoing intensive chemoimmunotherapy and ASCT as well.[123] Gene expression profiling shows the proliferative index is a critical component of prognosis, and a new technique to identify the "proliferation signature" of 17 genes in paraffin-embedded tissue using NanoString platforms is promising; however, the tool is based on patients treated with R-CHOP.[124] For now, many trials describe proliferation via Ki67 immunohistochemical staining, with ≥ 30% being a high value with associated poor prognosis.[125]

Survival with MCL has substantially improved in the past decade, with many patients enjoying long disease-free survival (DFS). Because CHOP or R-CHOP showed high ORRs of 80% to 90% but only 14 to 21 months PFS,[126,127] other approaches emerged: consolidative high-dose chemotherapy (HDC) and autologous stem cell rescue for chemosensitive disease after initial induction. Today, there are two approaches to the initial treatment of MCL, primarily based on age (Fig 20-7). Younger and fit patients are offered intensive induction and ASCT, whereas older and unfit patients are offered less-intensive chemoimmunotherapy regimens. The designations *fit* and *unfit* are not clearly defined, but age is a frequent cut point in clinical trials.

The optimal induction strategy for an aggressive approach including transplantation remains unclear. Although R-CHOP has an ORR of 90%, cytarabine-containing regimens induce a higher rate of minimal residual disease (MRD) negativity (47% *v* 79%, $P < .0001$); MRD negativity is a potent prognostic factor for PFS and is independent of the MIPI score, induction regimen, and quality of remission.[128] Thus, inclusion of high-dose cytarabine is now part of several different pretransplant approaches. Other regimens are also being tested as induction prior to HDC or ASCT, including bendamustine plus rituximab, and bendamustine, rituximab, and cytarabine. ASCT in first remission offers impressive long-term disease control, with median OS and response duration exceeding 10 years, and a median EFS of > 7 years.[129] However, late relapses do occur; baseline MIPI and Ki67 being important prognostic factors. The addition of maintenance rituximab for 3 years improved PFS (82% *v* 65%; $P = .0005$), EFS (79% *v* 61; $P = .0012$) and OS (89% *v* 81%; $P = .0413$) in a study of patients undergoing ASCT.[130]

In addition to induction plus ASCT, the rituximab plus methotrexate and cytarabine alternating with cyclophosphamide, vincristine, doxorubicin, and dexamethasone (R-HCVAD; also called hyper-CVAD) regimen has been developed. Fifteen-year follow-up of the R-HCVAD regimen shows a median FFS and OS of 4.8 years and 10.7 years, respectively.[131] However, the

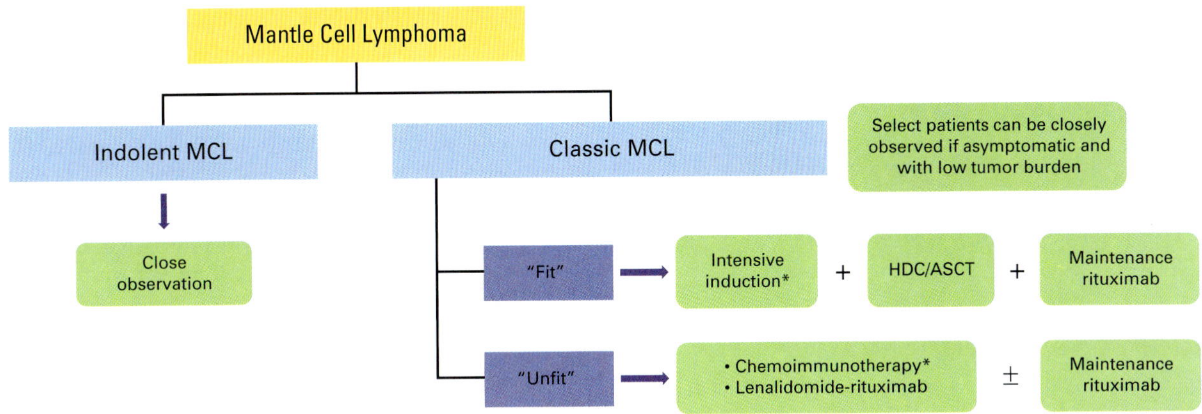

Fig. 20-7 Treatment algorithm for mantle cell lymphoma (MCL).

Chemoimmunotherapy includes bendamustine and rituximab, R-CHOP and R-CHP plus bortezomib, R-CHOP, and R-CHP plus bortezomib. Patients with blastoid MCL are treated similarly to fit patients with classic MCL.

Abbreviations: ASCT, autologous hematopoietic cell transplantation; HDC, high-dose chemotherapy; R-CHOP, rituximab, cyclophosphamide, doxorubicin, vincristine, and prednisone.

*Intensive induction is usually rituximab plus a cytarabine-containing regimen.

cumulative incidence of therapy-related myelodysplastic syndrome/AML is 6.2%, and the regimen is not well tolerated in patients older than 60 years.

For unfit patients, chemoimmunotherapy is the standard of care. As mentioned previously, R-CHOP has high initial response rates (80% to 90%), but CR rates (approximately 30%) and durable responses are limited. Results of a randomized phase III trial showed the addition of maintenance rituximab to R-CHOP reduced the risk of progression or death by 45%. Maintenance rituximab improved the OS rate to 87%, and this is an appropriate option for older patients. However, this trial was conducted before the introduction of bendamustine, a uniquely structured alkylating agent with activity in relapsed and refractory disease. Two prospective, randomized, noninferiority trials in frontline MCL showed less toxicity with bendamustine plus rituximab with preserved efficacy compared with R-CHOP or R-CVP.[32,33] Among 94 patients with MCL who were randomly assigned to one of these treatments and followed for 45 months, median PFS had not been reached for bendamustine plus rituximab, compared with 40.9 months for R-CHOP. Compared with R-CHOP, the added value of maintenance rituximab after treatment with bendamustine plus rituximab is not clear, and there is a high risk of increased myelosuppression and infection. For other first-line regimens in development, researchers are evaluating the roles of bortezomib, lower dose cytarabine, or lenalidomide.[132-134] The combination of lenalidomide and rituximab in this setting is promising, with an ORR > 90% and 2-year PFS of 85% in a small prospective trial; larger studies to confirm this activity are ongoing.

Given the efficacy of the oral BTK inhibitors in the relapsed refractory setting, current trials are exploring front-line approaches without consolidative autologous transplant.

Last, patients with *p53* mutations rarely respond to induction chemotherapy. A separate approach needs to be developed for these patients. This mutation correlates with Ki67 > 30%, blastoid morphology, and high-risk MIPI.[135]

KEY POINTS

- MCL is a heterogeneous disease. Those with an indolent variant can often forgo initial therapy, though most will need treatment eventually.
- Prognostic indices are available and are driven, in part, by the proliferation rate.
- Induction chemotherapy including high-dose cytarabine and high-dose autologous stem cell consolidation followed by rituximab maintenance is the standard of care for fit patients, but novel BTK inhibitors are being tested in combination with chemoimmunotherapy in the front-line setting to determine the feasibility of alternative approaches.

RELAPSED MCL

Disease-free survival curves in MCL do not have a plateau with current therapies, although the disease can remain in remission for a decade or more. At relapse, approaches include autologous or even allogeneic transplant in selected patients; however, newer agents assessed in phase II trials provide good disease control. These include bortezomib, lenalidomide, ibrutinib, acalabrutinib, and venetoclax alone or in combination with ibrutinib. Bortezomib and lenalidomide have responses in the 30% range lasting approximately 12 to 16 months.[136,137] The addition of rituximab to lenalidomide increases the ORR and CR rate.[138]

Oral inhibitors of BTK, ibrutinib, and acalabrutinib inhibit tonic B-cell receptor signaling and have the highest response rates in relapsed or refractory MCL. In one study, ibrutinib had an ORR of 68%, CR rate of 21%, and MRD of 17.5 months.[139] Acalabrutinib had an ORR of 81%, CR rate of 40%, and median duration of response had not been reached with 15.2 months of follow-up. The two drugs have not been compared directly, though acalabrutinib may be more selective with less atrial fibrillation.

KEY POINTS

- Relapsed MCL can be treated with a variety of strategies.
- BTK inhibitors are emerging as the most potent approach when transplantation is not being considered.
- Newer agents such as venetoclax are available for BTK-resistant MCL.

LYMPHOBLASTIC LYMPHOMA

Lymphoblastic lymphoma is an aggressive neoplasm that typically presents in young men (median age, 16 years) with mediastinal masses. The tumor exhibits an immature T-cell immunophenotype, with expression of CD7, cytoplasmic CD3, and TdT. Rearrangements of the T-cell receptor genes are virtually always present, and activating *Notch* mutations are present in the majority of cases. The clinical distinction between lymphoblastic lymphoma and T-cell acute lymphoblastic leukemia (T-ALL) is based on an arbitrary definition that assigns diagnosis as T-ALL if the bone marrow contains > 25% lymphoblasts, and lymphoblastic lymphoma if it contains < 25%. The presence of an elevated serum LDH level and bone marrow or CNS involvement confer an unfavorable prognosis.

Complete remission can be achieved in > 90% of patients treated with intensive, multiagent chemotherapy regimens, such as hyper-CVAD or a vincristine and prednisone backbone induction with additional agents.[140,141] Involvement of sanctuary sites such as the testes and CNS is common, mandating incorporation of intrathecal chemotherapy into treatment regimens. Patients with clinical evidence of initial testicular involvement that does not resolve after induction should be considered for testicular radiation. The role of mediastinal radiotherapy is controversial. Some series have suggested that intensive leukemia-type chemotherapy regimens produce long-term DFS rates of 73% to 90% in children and 45% to 72% in adults.[140] A role for high-dose therapy during first complete remission is under investigation for patients with high-risk disease.[142] Long-term survival rates are 63% for patients who undergo ASCT during first complete remission, 31% for patients who undergo transplantation during second complete remission, and only 15% for patients who undergo transplantation with resistant disease. The approach mirrors that of ALL; thus, please refer to Chapter 19: Leukemias.

KEY POINTS

- Lymphoblastic lymphoma is an aggressive lymphoma that expresses immature markers (ie, TdT) and is treated similarly to ALL.
- There is a high risk of CNS recurrence; therefore, CNS prophylaxis should be part of treatment of all patients.

BURKITT LYMPHOMA

Classic Burkitt lymphoma is a highly aggressive tumor characterized by an exceptionally high proliferation rate (Ki67 score of approximately 100%), a mature B-cell immunophenotype (monoclonal surface IgM, CD10, CD19, CD20, CD22, BCL6, CD38, and CD43 expression), and a histologic appearance demonstrating diffuse infiltration with a "starry sky" pattern of macrophages phagocytosing apoptotic tumor cells. All cases of classic Burkitt lymphoma possess a translocation of the *MYC* oncogene at band 8q24, most commonly associated with a t(8;14) translocation, although t(2;8) and t(8;22) translocations involving κ and λ loci, respectively, also occur. The three forms are endemic, sporadic, and HIV associated. The endemic version occurs in Africa, typically presenting as jaw tumors in children and is almost invariably associated with EBV. Sporadic cases occur elsewhere in the world, often presenting with ileocecal masses and associated with EBV in < 30% of cases. Burkitt lymphoma is about 10 times more common in those living with HIV/AIDS. High-risk features of Burkitt lymphomas include involvement of the CNS and/or bone marrow and a markedly elevated LDH level.

Burkitt lymphomas are characterized by a rapid growth rate, and treatment may be associated with a potentially fatal tumor-lysis syndrome, renal failure, hyperuricemia, and hyperkalemia. Biochemical abnormalities should be corrected rapidly before treatment, and patients should receive prophylactic rasburicase or xanthine oxidase inhibitors and hydration. Chemotherapy for Burkitt lymphoma has traditionally involved intensive therapy with regimens tested in phase II studies. These include R-HCVAD or cyclophosphamide plus vincristine, doxorubicin, and methotrexate alternating with ifosfamide plus etoposide and high-dose cytarabine (CODOX-M-IVAC), using treatment principles reminiscent of those used for ALL, including routine CNS prophylaxis.[143-145] The rate of CR with R-HCVAD or R-CODOX-M/IVAC is 85% to 95%, with 47% to 80% FFS at 5 years in various series, depending on patient-selection factors. The OS rate is 74% for adults treated with aggressive chemotherapy and CNS prophylaxis. R-CODOX-M/IVAC has been modified in some studies to reduce toxicity. Rituximab added to the French lymphome malin de Burkitt regimen improved the 3-year EFS rate from 62% to 75%.[146] See considerations for patients with HIV later in this chapter.

Investigators at the NCI have suggested that less intense regimens may also achieve excellent outcomes in Burkitt lymphoma. Dunleavy et al[147] treated 30 consecutive patients with infused EPOCH-R regimens, including 19 HIV-negative patients treated with DA-EPOCH-R and 11 HIV-positive patients treated with a short-course regimen incorporating a double dose of rituximab (SC-EPOCH-RR). The rates of freedom from progression of disease and OS were 95% and 100%, respectively, with DA-EPOCH-R and 100% and 90% with SC-EPOCH-RR. A larger multicenter trial, CTSU 9177, has been presented in abstract form showing EFS rates of 100% and 82% for low-risk and high-risk patients, respectively, including those with bone marrow, peripheral blood, or leptomeningeal involvement.[147] HIV did not affect survival. Patients with brain parenchymal disease were excluded from this trial.

Patients with Burkitt lymphoma who have a relapse after initial therapy are generally treated with aggressive salvage chemotherapy regimens followed by attempts at stem cell transplantation, but are rarely cured of their disease.

KEY POINTS

- Burkitt lymphoma is an aggressive lymphoma characterized by an *MYC* rearrangement, lack of *BCL2* expression, and an extremely high proliferation index.
- Treatment consists of intense regimens with CNS prophylaxis not evaluated in randomized trials.
- Cure rates are high overall with multiagent regimens that have not been compared in a randomized treatment.
- Rituximab improved EFS in one study.
- Patients with relapsed or primary refractory disease have few treatment options and are rarely cured.

PRIMARY CNS LYMPHOMA

Primary CNS lymphomas (PCNSLs) are uncommon de novo lymphomas limited to brain structures, including brain parenchyma, leptomeninges, eyes, or spinal cord. Intraocular involvement is seen in 10% to 20% of cases. These are usually aggressive BCLs, with DLBCL being the most common. PCNSL can occur in both immunocompromised (mostly HIV associated) and immunocompetent patients. Among immunocompetent patients, the median age is 60 years.

Patients typically present with symptoms related to mass effect or infiltration with neurologic compromise and symptoms. The diagnosis requires a tissue diagnosis, usually via a stereotactic biopsy. If possible, it is important to avoid steroids, which are lympholytic, prior to the biopsy because they can lead to a false-negative result or nondiagnostic biopsy with necrosis. If there is concern for irreversible neurologic compromise or impending herniation, avoiding steroids may not be possible. Histopathology shows a dense diffuse infiltrate of large B cells that are positive for CD20, CD19, and PAX5 and often of a nongerminal center phenotype with MUM1 positivity.[4] Diagnostic and staging evaluation should also include a lumbar puncture (if safe to perform); slit-lamp eye examination; CT scan of the chest, abdomen, and pelvis; bone marrow biopsy; and laboratory tests to exclude HIV. For men older than 60 years, a testicular examination and ultrasonography should also be performed.

Treatment of PCNSL has evolved. Whole-brain radiation (WBRT) alone was historically used, with no added benefit from regimens such as CHOP; despite high response rates, the 5-year OS rate was < 20%.[148] Moreover, leukoencephalopathy, particularly in patients older than 60 years, has led a number of investigators to seek chemotherapy-alone treatments and other groups to test lower doses of radiation. High-dose methotrexate (minimum dose, 3 g/m^2) with or without high-dose cytarabine produces superior results compared with radiotherapy alone, with a median survival of 51 months.[149-151] Despite controversy about the optimal dose and timing, WBRT is frequently relegated to the salvage setting.[152]

Radiation-sparing approaches include chemotherapy induction, high-dose methotrexate induction followed by either HDC and ASCT,[153-155] and or induction followed by chemotherapy consolidation.[156] Common induction regimens include methotrexate with temozolomide or rituximab with methotrexate, vincristine, and procarbazine. ASCT consolidation has impressive results, with > 90% survival at 2 years; however, this modality may be limited by age, comorbidities, and chemosensitivity. The addition of intravenous administration of rituximab, particularly in initial cycles of therapy, may also improve outcomes.[156]

The management options for relapsed or refractory PCNSL are limited overall, but several exciting agents and approaches are in development. If patients have not undergone prior HDC and ASCT, this may be an option if salvage regimens can be safely delivered and if there is chemosensitive disease.[157] WBRT is also used, either with or without preceding salvage chemotherapy. Temozolomide, ibrutinib, lenalidomide, and intraventricular rituximab are all in development with promising activity in salvage settings.

KEY POINTS

- Primary CNS lymphoma is a clinical variant of DLBCL that occurs exclusively in CNS structures, which may include the brain parenchyma, eyes, leptomeninges, and spinal cord.
- Treatment requires CNS-penetrating agents.
- Consolidation of initial remission can consist of chemotherapy, WBRT, or HDC with ASCT.

LYMPHOMAS ASSOCIATED WITH IMMUNODEFICIENCY

Acquired and iatrogenic immune suppression increase the risk of lymphomas. High-grade BCLs, often involving the CNS, were described early in the AIDS epidemic of the 1990s and were considered AIDS-defining illnesses. However, in the era of effective antiretroviral therapy (ART), the incidence of HIV-associated NHL has decreased by> 50%,[158] and the overall prognosis has improved substantially. AIDS-related lymphomas (ARLs) have significantly evolved with the advent and improvement of ART. Most ARLs in the pre-ART era were high-grade B-cell subtypes, often involving the CNS, and they were highly fatal. However, an analysis of 1,456 patients enrolled in clinical trials showed that survival in the contemporary era was approximately 70%.[159] Patients typically present with advanced-stage disease including extranodal and leptomeningeal disease. Of interest, the spectrum of ARL is influenced by baseline CD4 count and HIV viral load. Patients with HIV-associated HL and Burkitt lymphoma have higher CD4 counts and lower HIV RNA compared with other ARLs; in particular, patients with HIV-associated PCNSL have the lowest CD4 counts at diagnosis and thus HIV-associated PCNSL is exceedingly rare where ART is readily available.[160] Treatment of ARL generally follows treatment of non-HIV NHL, though DLBCL is typically treated with R-EPOCH, on the basis of results of phase II trials[161,162] and metanalyses.[163] Treatment of HIV-associated DLBCL can be delivered concurrently with ART as long as known drug interactions are eliminated in advance by selecting appropriate antivirals. Despite initial concern over increased infectious toxicity with the use of rituximab, a meta-analysis showed improved outcomes[159]; some studies avoid rituximab if the CD4 count at diagnosis is ≤ 50 cells/mm^3. The NCI has developed a PET-adapted approach to reduce the overall number of chemotherapy cycles (short-course DA-EPOCH-R) associated with a 5-year OS rate of 68% and acceptable toxicity, but it has not been replicated.[164]

Iatrogenic immunosuppression after solid organ transplantation or hematopoietic stem cell transplantation (HSCT) is associated with an increased risk of subsequent lymphomas, termed post-transplantation lymphoproliferative disorders (PTLDs). Iatrogenic T-cell suppression facilitates EBV-driven B-cell proliferation and consequent PTLD, particularly in cases diagnosed within the first year after transplantation. Thus, the vast majority of PTLDs are of B-cell origin, although other lymphomas can also occur. Risk factors for PTLD include recipient EBV-seronegative status, pediatric populations, coinfection with other viruses (eg, cytomegalovirus, hepatitis C, human herpesvirus 8) and the duration and intensity of immunosuppressive agents (reviewed by Dharnidharka et al[165]). There is significant interest in screening for PTLD with serial EBV viral load testing and implementing preventive antiviral prophylaxis in high-risk populations. Early PTLDs (< 1 to 2 years after transplantation) are EBV positive and may respond to reduced immunosuppression, whereas later PTLDs are more aggressive, less amenable to reduced immunosuppression, and EBV negative.

Confirming a diagnosis of PTLD requires a biopsy specimen. Histopathology can show "early lesions" (plasmacytic hyperplasia, infectious mononucleosis-like lesion), polymorphic PTLD, monomorphic PTLD (which includes DLBCL and Burkitt lymphoma), or classic HL-like PTLD.[4] A rising EBV titer and abrupt-onset adenopathy with constitutional symptoms increase the suspicion for PTLD. The general treatment approach to PTLD is prompt reduction of immunosuppression and rituximab therapy. Several phase II trials of rituximab monotherapy showed response rates of 40% to 60%.[166-168] The sequential addition of CHOP chemotherapy improved the response rate to 90%; however, treatment-related mortality was increased by approximately 10% in these fragile patients.[169]

Finally, autoimmune diseases (eg, rheumatoid arthritis, Sjögren disease, systemic lupus erythematosus) and treatment of autoimmune conditions have been associated with an increased risk of NHL.[170,171] Both the specific risk and NHL subtype is variable and may be up to six-fold higher compared with populations without autoimmune conditions.

KEY POINTS

- Immune suppression (either acquired, iatrogenic, or related to underlying autoimmunity) is associated with an increased risk of lymphoma.
- If possible, removing the cause of immune suppression can lead to lymphoma regression, particularly in early PTLD, leading to a stepwise approach. However, late PTLDs act like virulent lymphomas.
- In the era of effective ART, outcomes for HIV-associated lymphomas have dramatically improved. Drug-drug interactions between ART and chemotherapy must be avoided to prevent excess toxicity.

T- AND NK-CELL LYMPHOMAS

Lymphomas arising from mature NK and T cells (NK/TCL) make up 10% to 15% of NHL in the United States, but nearly 30% of NHL in Asian countries. The term *peripheral T-cell lymphoma* (PTCL) refers to a diverse group of post-thymic T-cell tumors that have a mature T-cell phenotype. Patients tend to have higher scores on the IPI, more B symptoms, advanced-stage disease, and higher serum microglobulin levels than comparable patients with DLBCL. Patients with PTCL generally have inferior treatment responses, a high rate of relapse, and few sustained remissions when treated with multiagent chemotherapy regimens such as CHOP. A prognostic index specific for PTCL (known as the PIT) includes patient age, LDH level, PS, and presence of bone marrow involvement.[172] Poor prognosis is also associated with *p53* expression, a high Ki67 proliferation index (> 25%), adverse chemokine expression patterns (CXCR3-positive/CCR4-negative), and expression of CD30 and CD56, BCL2, or BCLXL. A full exposition of the details of this diverse group of disorders is beyond the scope of this chapter, but an excellent review is available.[173]

NK/TCLs are diverse and individually relatively rare entities, with approximately 30 defined subtypes. The WHO divides them on the basis of the main site of clinical involvement: primary nodal, primary extranodal, leukemic, or cutaneous.[4] Until recently, few trials have been dedicated to NK/TCL, and most treatment paradigms are extrapolated from treatment of aggressive BCLs. Brief descriptions of the most common entities and general treatment principles follow.

PERIPHERAL T-CELL LYMPHOMA

Primary nodal TCLs are aggressive lymphomas and are also called PTCLs. The four major subtypes of PTCLs are:

- peripheral T-cell lymphoma not otherwise specified (PTCL-NOS)
- angioimmunoblastic T-cell lymphoma (AITL)
- ALK-positive anaplastic large-cell lymphoma (ALK+ ALCL)
- ALK-negative ALCL (ALK− ALCL).

PTCL-NOS is a provisional group encompassing mature aggressive TCLs not included in the other groups. A CD4-positive T-follicular helper cell (T_{FH}) has been identified as the malignant cell of origin in both AITL and in a subset of PTCL-NOS; this discovery may influence the next WHO classification.

General Approach to PTCL

Treatment of PTCL is challenging. CHOP is associated with ORRs of 60% to 70% but long-term disease control of only 25% to 30%,[174] and most of the benefit is in IPI low-risk groups. Despite being a weak regimen in PTCL, most trials test the addition of new agents to a CHOP backbone (ie, romidepsin plus CHOP, alemtuzumab plus CHOP). These have all been negative studies, with two exceptions. First, in a retrospective analysis of patients enrolled in sequential German trials, etoposide added to CHOP (CHOEP) improved PFS in a subset of patients; notably, CHOEP was too toxic for patients older than 60 years, most of the benefit was in ALCL histology, there was no OS difference, and this was not a prospective trial.[175] Second, replacing vincristine in CHOP with the antibody-drug conjugate brentuximab vedotin demonstrated dramatic improvement in PFS and improvement in OS in the Echelon-2 randomized phase III trial of 452 patients.[176] Brentuximab vedotin and chemotherapy yielded a PFS of 48 months compared with 21 months with CHOP alone. OS and ORRs were also significantly better in the brentuximab vedotin arm. Although seven subsets of PTCL were eligible for this trial and minimal CD30 positivity (the target of brentuximab vedotin) was required, 70% of the patients had ALCL. Those with ALCL were the one subset with proven superiority. The trial led to FDA approval for all CD30+ PTCL in this setting in November 2018.

Previously, results of nonrandomized trials suggested an advantage to consolidative ASCT with a 60% PFS rate. Similarly, registry studies also suggested an advantage to ASCT consolidation with a 5-year OS of 48% versus 26% in favor of patients undergoing consolidative ASCT.[177-179] ASCT is of less clear benefit for CD30+ PTCL if brentuximab combination is given first line, as it was in Echelon-2.[178] ASCT is also relatively ineffective in relapsed disease.[179]

Peripheral TCL Not Otherwise Specified

The most common PTCL is PTCL-NOS (25% to 30%), and this category is subject to revision as molecular distinctions are clarified. This disease is characterized by an aggressive growth phase with both nodal and extranodal involvement and frequent B symptoms. PTCL usually presents with paracortical or diffuse nodal infiltration of malignant lymphoid cells expressing T-cell markers, including CD2, CD3, T-cell receptor, and usually CD4. Proving clonality can be difficult because oligoclonal or small, clonal T-cell receptor populations can occur in nonmalignant tissue; however, a "dropped antigen" (ie, loss of a typical T-cell antigen) or downregulation of CD5 or CD7 is characteristic of neoplasia.[180] The median age of patients with PTCL is 60 years, with a male-to-female ratio of 1.9:1. The majority of patients present with advanced-stage disease (69%), and two-thirds of the patients have extranodal disease in addition to adenopathy. Results of nonrandomized trials suggest an advantage to consolidative ASCT with a 60% PFS rate. Patients with CD30+ PTCL-NOS can now be treated per ECHELON-2 (see previous section) with brentuximab vedotin substituted for vincristine in CHOP.

Angioimmunoblastic TCL

AITL accounts for 18% of TCLs worldwide and typically presents with generalized lymphadenopathy, fevers, weight loss, and rash, with autoimmune features including hypergammaglobulinemia and a positive Coombs test.[181] The disease is derived from T_{FH}, with malignant cells typically expressing CD10, BCL6, PD1, and CXCL13, in addition to typical T-cell markers (ie, CD2, CD3, CD5, and CD4). The disease course is typically complicated by serious and often fatal infections. EBV-associated BCL often develops during the course of treatment of AITL, apparently derived from EBV-infected B-cell blasts present in the tumor. An important discovery is the strong epigenetic signature associated with AITL; frequently mutated genes include *RHOA* (70%), *TET2* (82%), *IDH2* (30%), and *DNMT3A* (26%).[182,183] AITL was included in the Echelon-2 study noted in the two preceding sections.

Anaplastic Large-Cell Lymphoma

ALCL is a malignancy of large, pleomorphic, mature T lymphocytes that express the CD30 antigen (Ki-1) as well as T-cell surface markers such as CD2, CD4, and CD5. Curiously, the pan T-cell antigen CD3 is negative in > 75% of cases. There are two subtypes based on the presence or absence of nucleophosmin-ALK t(2;5) translocation: ALK+ and ALK− ALCL.[184] Patients with ALK+ ALCL are younger, with a median age at onset of 30 years, and the disease often occurs in pediatric populations. ALK− ALCL has a median age at onset of 55 years. ALCL is more common in men and is at advanced stage at presentation, with frequent extranodal involvement. ALK+ ALCL has a superior prognosis, with 5-year survival rates of 70% to 90% compared with only 40% to 60% for ALK− ALCL after CHOP or CHOP plus etoposide. However, a subset of patients with ALK− ALCL harboring a *DUSP22* translocation may have good outcomes on par with ALK+ ALCL.[185] ALCL was included in the ECHELON-2 trial for all ALK− patients and ALK+ patients with two negative IPI factors. Patients with relapsed disease may be treated with ALK inhibitors such as crizotinib or ceritinib (the latter is not FDA approved).

Relapsed or Refractory PTCL

Aggravating the poor results with first-line treatment is the inability to effectively salvage patients at relapse; population-based data have shown a median OS of < 6 months for patients who had relapsed.[186] This may be changing in the era of new agents. Four agents are approved for use in relapsed PTCL on the basis of results of large phase II trials: romidepsin, pralatrexate, brentuximab vedotin (for CD30-positive disease), and belinostat. Romidepsin and belinostat are histone deacetylase inhibitors and have response rates of 25% to 40%; despite a modest response rate, remissions can be durable. Brentuximab vedotin, an antibody-drug conjugate against CD30, is highly active with single-agent response rates of 85% (CR rates, > 50%) in relapsed or refractory ALCL and other CD30-positive TCL, but will be less useful in the relapsed and refractory setting if given first line.[187]

KEY POINTS

- PTCL treatment is evolving as previously younger patients were treated with induction and ASCT, largely on the basis of results of phase II and registry studies.
- Replacing vincristine in CHOP with the antibody-drug conjugate brentuximab vedotin demonstrated dramatic improvement in PFS and improvement in OS in the Echelon-2 randomized phase III trial of CD30+ PTCL, though the results are most applicable to CD30+ALCL.
- Multiple agents are available second line and beyond with no clear advantage of one over the other except for brentuximab vedotin for CD30+ PTCL, if the agent has not been previously used.

PRIMARY EXTRANODAL NK/TCL

Enteropathy-Associated TCL

Enteropathy-associated TCL (EATL) accounts for approximately 5% of TCLs and is more common in geographic areas with a higher incidence of celiac disease, including North America and Europe. Patients typically present with pain, weight loss, and bowel perforation.[188] Cases associated with celiac disease typically exhibit a pleomorphic histology and express CD3 and CD7, but not CD56, whereas patients without celiac disease often display a monomorphic histology and express CD56. Up to 70% of cases of EATL contain gains at chromosome 9q33-q34. Conventional therapy consists of CHOP, with a median OS of only 10 months in one international series of 62 patients and a median FFS of only 6 months.[188] The presence of clinical sprue and an adverse PIT score both predicted poor survival independently. One study suggested that outcomes with EATL may be improved by inducing remission with a novel regimen of ifosfamide plus etoposide and epirubicin alternating with intermediate-dose methotrexate followed by consolidation with ASCT.[189] This approach yielded a 5-year PFS rate of 52% and OS rate of 60% among 26 patients who underwent transplantation.

Extranodal NK/TCL

Extranodal NK/TCL is an angioinvasive, necrotizing lymphoma derived from cytotoxic NK or T cells that is almost invariably associated with EBV infection and typically presents in the nasal cavity, nasopharynx, or paranasal sinuses. It is divided into nasal and extranasal types and can affect skin, the GI tract, or testes. Nasal obstruction, bleeding, and ulceration are typical, hence the previous designation of this disease as "lethal midline granuloma." The malignant lymphoid cells of nasal NK/TCL typically express CD2, CD56, and cytoplasmic CD3ε (but not surface CD3), as well as cytotoxic molecules such as T-cell restricted intracellular antigen (TIA1), granzyme B, and perforin. The disease often presents at an early stage; radiotherapy is a critical therapeutic component of limited-stage disease, either preceding or concurrent with chemotherapy.[190] The disease is relatively resistant to CHOP-type chemotherapy but appears uniquely sensitive to asparaginase-containing regimens such as SMILE, which contains dexamethasone, methotrexate, ifosfamide, L-asparaginase, and etoposide.

Hepatosplenic γδ TCL

Hepatosplenic γδ TCL is a rare disease of young men derived from immature or nonactivated γδ T cells possessing an isochromosome 7q abnormality. This lymphoma typically infiltrates the liver, spleen, and marrow sinusoids, with minimal adenopathy. Patients often present with fever, chills, and other systemic symptoms. Cytopenias, especially thrombocytopenia, are typical and often accompanied by a fatal hemophagocytic syndrome. Outcome is poor regardless of management, though many authorities recommend aggressive chemotherapy followed by stem cell transplantation in first remission.

CUTANEOUS TCL

Cutaneous TCLs (CTCLs) are a heterogeneous group of lymphomas characterized by infiltration of the skin and other organs by malignant but mature T cells. In the WHO classification, these disorders are considered indolent T-cell malignancies. The most common type of CTCL is mycosis fungoides/Sezary syndrome (MF/SS), but other subtypes include primary cutaneous ALCL (not to be confused with systemic ALCL), subcutaneous panniculitis-like TCL, and many others.[4]

In most cases of mycosis fungoides, the diagnosis is made after a prolonged period of ill-defined skin disease or *para*-psoriasis. Subsequently, patches or plaques characteristic of mycosis fungoides develop. At the time of diagnosis, less than half of patients have limited plaques, one-third have extensive plaques, and 10% to 15% have generalized erythroderma. The spleen, liver, and lymph nodes also may be involved, especially in patients with advanced skin disease and circulating malignant cells. When the peripheral blood becomes extensively involved with the malignant T cells and erythroderma develops, the condition is called Sézary syndrome.

The treatment approach for MF/SS starts with a skin-directed approach, but may eventually require systemic agents.[191] Most patients with CTCLs initially are treated with topical measures, including corticosteroids, photochemotherapy with oral methoxypsoralen therapy followed by UV light, mechlorethamine, bexarotene, or electron-beam radiation (either localized or total skin). Systemic therapy is needed when these approaches fail or when major organ involvement, diffuse lymphadenopathy, or transformation to large-cell NHL develops. Treatment options for advanced CTCL include extracorporeal photopheresis, interferon-α, bexarotene, denileukin diftitox, liposomal doxorubicin, nucleoside analogs (eg, gemcitabine), alemtuzumab, or combination chemotherapy. Histone deacetylate inhibitors such as vorinostat and romidepsin have shown major activity in this condition, as has pralatrexate, and these drugs increasing are being used earlier in the disease course. Brentuximab vedotin is highly active if there is CD30 expression.[192] Patients with CTCL often die of infections, and as such, good skin care and oral antibiotics are important adjuncts to therapy. The only known curative therapy for mycosis fungoides is allogeneic stem cell transplantation, although this approach is appropriate for only a minority of patients.[193]

KEY POINTS

- TCLs are rare, heterogeneous, and aggressive diseases that are frequently chemoresistant.
- Initial treatment of PTCLs without CD30 expression consists of multiagent chemotherapy with CHOP or CHOEP for younger patients.
- Although registry data have suggested consolidative ASCT benefits fit chemosensitive patients, the ECHELON-2 trial has just shown a dramatic advantage of bentuximab vedotin substitution for vincristine in CHOP over CHOP alone.
- ALCL with ALK positivity and ALCL with ALK– and dusp22 mutation have a better prognosis.
- All patients with localized NK/TCL should have radiation therapy as part of their treatment, which improves OS.
- Mycosis fungoides is the most common type of CTCL and is an indolent disease in the majority of patients. Treatment is initially skin directed.
- Patients with relapsed or refractory PTCL have several treatment options with recently approved drugs, but treatment is typically palliative and the prognosis is relatively poor.

HODGKIN LYMPHOMA

EPIDEMIOLOGY AND ETIOLOGY

HL is a mature B-lymphoid neoplasm that annually is diagnosed in approximately 9,050 Americans and causes approximately 1,150 deaths. HL has a bimodal incidence distribution with respect to age at diagnosis, with an incidence peak in young adulthood and a second peak in the elderly. The etiology of HL is not known, although the likelihood of HL developing is increased three-fold for people with a history of clinical EBV (mononucleosis). HL nodes show evidence of EBV DNA in the genome of the Reed-Sternberg cell in 30% to 80% of cases. However, because many cases of HL are EBV negative, controversy remains as to causality. HIV infection and allogeneic bone marrow transplantation increase the risk of HL. In patients infected with HIV, HL tends to involve extranodal sites and to exhibit an aggressive clinical course, although the outcomes with chemotherapy are similar to the general population. Environmental exposures leading to increased risk have not been substantiated.

CLINICAL PRESENTATION AND CLASSIFICATION OF HL

HL typically presents with painless lymphadenopathy with or without splenomegaly, fevers, drenching night sweats, weight loss, and pruritus, or pain in a lymph node–bearing area that is associated with alcohol consumption. The diagnosis is best established by examination of an excisional lymph node biopsy specimen demonstrating large, atypical lymphocytes surrounded by a heterogeneous infiltrate of nonneoplastic inflammatory and accessory cells. The WHO classification of lymphomas distinguishes two major subtypes of HL: classic HL (cHL), which includes nodular sclerosis, mixed cellularity, lymphocyte-rich, and lymphocyte-depleted subtypes), and nodular lymphocyte-predominant HL.[4]

CLASSIC HL

cHL represents 95% of all cases of HL and is characterized pathologically by the presence of bizarre, monoclonal lymphoid cells that may be either mononuclear (Hodgkin cells) or multinucleated (Reed-Sternberg cells). The malignant Hodgkin and Reed–Sternberg (HRS) cells of cHL express CD15 and CD30 surface antigens but usually not typical B-cell markers, such as surface immunoglobulin, CD20, CD79a, or the common leukocyte antigen CD45.[3] The B-cell origin of HRS cells is nevertheless demonstrable by the expression of the B-cell–specific activator protein derived from the *PAX5* gene in 90% of cases.[4] Immunoglobulin genes are rearranged in 98% of HRS cells but are not transcribed, as a result of the absence of the transcription factor organic cation transporter 2 (Oct-2) and its coactivator B-cell–specific octamer-binding protein (BOB-1). The malignant (HRS) cells are typically surrounded by a heterogeneous infiltrate of reactive T and B lymphocytes, eosinophils, macrophages, fibroblasts, and variable amounts of collagen deposition (sclerosis). Chromosome 9p24.1 is frequently amplified in cHL, increasing the expression of the programmed cell death 1 (PD-1) ligands, PD-L1 and PD-L2, and promoting their induction through Janus kinase (JAK)–signal transducer and activator of transcription (STAT) signaling.[194]

Four discrete histologic subtypes of cHL are recognized by the WHO classification on the basis of the relative proportions of infiltrating small lymphocytes and of HRS cells and the amount of collagen (sclerosis) in the biopsy specimen: nodular-sclerosis subtype, mixed-cellularity HL, lymphocyte-rich cHL, and lymphocyte-depleted HL. All four subtypes of cHL are evaluated and treated similarly, lessening the importance of subclassification of cHL. Table 20-7 summarizes key points about the differences.

NODULAR LYMPHOCYTE-PREDOMINANT HL

Nodular lymphocyte-predominant HL (NLPHL) is a unique indolent B-cell neoplasm that is distinguished from cHL by histologic and immunophenotypic features, including the presence of large neoplastic cells known as "popcorn" or "lymphocytic and histiocytic" cells (L and H cells) residing in large nodular meshwork of follicular dendritic cell processes

Table 20-7 Subtypes of Classic Hodgkin Lymphoma

Subtype	Characteristic
Nodular sclerosis	• 60% of HL
	• Most common in women, adolescents, and young adults
	• Anterior mediastinal mass that may produce chest discomfort, dyspnea, or cough
Mixed cellularity	• 20% of HL
	• More common in men
	• More often advanced stage than nodular sclerosis
	• More common in HIV
	• EBV association is higher than nodular sclerosis
Lymphocyte-rich	• More commonly older men and presents at an early stage of disease
Lymphocyte-depleted	• 5% of HL
	• Older men

Abbreviation: EBV, Epstein-Barr virus; HL, Hodgkin lymphoma.

filled with nonneoplastic lymphocytes. In marked contrast to the HRS cells of cHL, the malignant L and H cells of NLPHL express typical B-cell surface antigens, including CD20 and CD79a, as well as the common leukocyte antigen CD45, but do not express CD15 or CD30.[195] Fifty percent of NLPHLs harbor *BCL6* rearrangements, in contrast to cHL, in which this is a rare occurrence.[196] NLPHL is responsible for approximately 5% of all cases of HL, typically affects men between ages 30 and 50 years, usually presents with localized lymphadenopathy (stages I to II), progresses slowly, and is associated with prolonged survival despite frequent relapses.

There is a spectrum of associated pathologic entities (reviewed in Savage et al[197]). Progressive transformation of germinal centers is a benign condition that may precede or occur simultaneously with NLPHL. In addition, up to 15% of patients with NLPHL can have a transformation to aggressive BCL, with advanced-stage and hepatosplenic involvement constituting important risk factors. NLPHL and the aggressive component are clonally related, which is frequently a T-cell–rich DLBCL and requires aggressive treatment.

STAGING AND INITIAL EVALUATION OF HL

Recommended diagnostic tests include a history; physical examination; excisional lymph node biopsy with specimen evaluation for histology and immunophenotype; CBC count with differential; a chemistry panel including liver-function tests, albumin and LDH levels; erythrocyte sedimentation rate; chest radiography; CT scan of the chest, abdomen, and pelvis; FDG-PET; and fertility counseling. Other tests useful in selected cases include pulmonary-function tests (prior to bleomycin therapy), determination of the cardiac ejection fraction (prior to anthracycline therapy), HIV testing, and, in selected cases, neck CT scans. Bone marrow biopsies are no longer routinely recommended for staging of HL, provided FDG-PET imaging is performed, because patients with early-stage disease rarely have bone marrow involvement in the absence of PET abnormalities, and those with advanced disease would not have their treatment changed on the basis of bone marrow biopsy findings.[6] After completion of the diagnostic workup, the extent of involvement with HL is designated using the Lugano staging criteria (Table 20-2).

The clinical approach to HL is based on the initial stage and prognostic factors into early stage (IA–IIA, with favorable or unfavorable features) or advanced stage (IIB, III, IV, or bulky disease). Prognostic factors for early-stage HL include a large mediastinal mass, elevated sedimentation rate, involvement of three or more nodal sites, extranodal disease, age > 50 years, or massive splenic disease.[198] Prognostic factors for advanced stage include age > 45 years, stage IV disease, male sex, leukocytosis (WBC count > 15,000/mL), lymphopenia (absolute lymphocyte count < 600/mL), low albumin level, or anemia (hemoglobin < 10.5 g/dL).[199] As will be discussed, metabolic response reflected by FDG-PET has emerged as one of the most important prognostic factors for survival, and it forms the rationale for response-adapted therapy.

KEY POINTS

- cHL consists of four subtypes but clinically is generally treated as one entity.
- NLPHL is a nonclassical HL. It is a unique indolent B-cell neoplasm that progresses slowly and is associated with prolonged survival despite frequent relapses.
- The clinical approach to HL is based on the initial stage and prognostic factors.

TREATMENT OF HL

A Historical Note

The treatment approach to cHL relies more heavily on stage and location than do other BCLs, partly because of long-standing observations of contiguous patterns of spread at presentation and when the disease recurs. Precise surgical and pathologic staging in the pre–PET era assessed the sites of known disease and determined the sites with the highest risk of recurrence. Thus, staging laparotomies, splenectomy, extensive lymph node dissection, and lymphangiography allowed the design of radiation fields such as mantle irradiation, inverted Y, para-aortic, extended-field radiation, and others. Although these techniques were highly effective in terms of disease control, morbidity and mortality from toxicity were excessive, and HL is a paradigm disease highlighting the dangers of late effects. Older studies showed that, although cure rates are high, HL survivors continue to experience an increased risk of death from second malignancies, cardiovascular compromise, and pulmonary disease from both chemotherapy and radiotherapy. The desire to optimize the risk-to-benefit ratio in this usually young group of patients is the overriding theme in clinical trial development, and very long-term follow up (> 10 years) is often needed to demonstrate the true impact of a therapeutic approach.

Early-Stage cHL

Patients with stage IA-IIA HL have an excellent expected outcome, with long-term survival exceeding 90% to 95%. The historic approach was radiotherapy alone, but the addition of combination treatment with doxorubicin, bleomycin, vinblastine, and dacarbazine (ABVD) chemotherapy allowed a reduction in field size and dose with an improved toxicity profile. In the pre-PET era, four cycles of ABVD plus 36 to 40 Gy involved-field radiation therapy (IFRT) achieved a 12-year OS rate of 94% in both favorable and unfavorable disease.[200] A subsequent German trial randomly assigned 1,370 patients with favorable prognostic factors to between two and four cycles of ABVD chemotherapy and 20 and 30 Gy IFRT in an effort to reduce both chemotherapy cycles and total radiation dose.[201] Response, PFS, and OS was equivalent among the four arms, and two cycles of ABVD plus 20 Gy IFRT is an appropriate means of limiting both chemotherapy and radiotherapy. Other studies have tested chemotherapy-only regimens. In general, omission of radiation therapy in nonbulky early-stage HL is associated with inferior disease control (EFS, PFS, local relapse) on the order of 3% to 7% (reviewed in Engert et al[201]); however, very long-term follow-up showed a 12-year OS rate of 94% among those receiving ABVD alone, setting up controversy over the role of combined-modality versus chemotherapy-alone approaches.[202]

Importantly, each of these trials was conducted prior to incorporation of PET and response-adapted approaches. Two randomized trials in favorable-risk (UK RAPID and EORTC H10F) and one in unfavorable-risk (EORTC H10U) patients[203,204] tested the omission of radiation therapy on the basis of a negative interim PET/CT, usually defined as a Deauville score < 2 after two cycles of chemotherapy. EORTC H10F favored a combined modality approach with respect to EFS; however, the 5-year OS rates were 96.7% versus 98.3% for ABVD plus INRT and ABVD-only arms, respectively.[203] Similar results were seen in the RAPID trial, which enrolled > 600 patients with stage IA-IIA HL. Patients with a negative PET scan after three cycles of ABVD (n = 426 patients; 74.6%) were randomly assigned to consolidative radiation versus no additional therapy.[204] The 3-year PFS was 94.6% versus 90.8% favoring radiotherapy, but with no difference in 3-year OS rates (97.1% *v* 99%; *P* = .27). Given the excellent outcomes, the RAPID (Randomised Phase III Trial to Determine the Role of FDG-PET Imaging in Clinical Stages IA/IIA Hodgkin's Disease) approach without radiotherapy is now integrated into NCCN guidelines. Of note, early-stage HL can be classified as favorable or unfavorable, but the various study groups and trials do not agree on the factors.

Advanced-Stage cHL

HL is highly curable with combination chemotherapy, even in advanced stages. Clinical trials have refined the optimal systemic therapy (excellent and detailed reviews by Johnson and McKenzie[205] and Lynch and Advani[206]), with important questions revolving around early and late toxicity, role of intensification, role of radiotherapy, and response-adapted treatment. Today, the approach is based on several principles and observations.

First, determining the true impact of a regimen may require prolonged follow-up. For example, ABVD became the North American treatment of choice based on 7- or 10-year FFS rates of 70% to 75%, coupled with an excellent toxicity profile.[207-209] The risk of secondary malignancies is extremely low, and fertility is preserved in most patients. More intense regimens, such as the escalated bleomycin, etoposide, doxorubicin, cyclophosphamide, vincristine, procarbazine, and prednisone (BEACOPP) regimen developed in Germany, offer improved disease control, but are associated with increased treatment-related mortality and significant infertility. An Italian intergroup study randomly assigned 331 patients with advanced-stage HL to ABVD or BEACOPP, and patients with residual or progressive disease were treated with a uniform salvage program.[209] There was more progression in the ABVD arm (45 *v* 20 patients), but the 7-year freedom from second progression and OS results were similar in the two groups. Overall, 70% of patients with advanced-stage HL are cured with ABVD, and it is difficult to determine who needs escalated BEACOPP as first-line therapy (based on baseline features).

Second, response-adapted therapy is an emerging component of treatment. A provocative and influential study of 205 patients showed a 2-year PFS rate of 95% versus 13% in patients with a negative versus positive PET after two cycles of chemotherapy ($P \leq .0001$).[210] Subsequent studies of PET have not recapitulated these massive differences, but it is clear that interim PET has an extremely high, negative predictive value. The use of consistent PET interpretation via the 5-point scale (Deauville criteria) is imperative in ensuring comparability between trials. The two approaches to integrate interim PET in the management of HL are:

(1) treatment intensification based on positive interim PET (eg, escalation from ABVD to BEACOPP) and
(2) treatment de-escalation based on negative interim PET (eg, de-escalation from BEACOPP to ABVD).[206]

The RATHL study used the latter concept to reduce bleomycin from ABVD, a known pulmonary toxin and the cause of pneumonitis and death, particularly in older individuals.[211] The RATHL study enrolled 1,214 patients with stage II bulky and advanced-stage HL; 84% achieved a PET-negative interim PET after two cycles of ABVD. These patients were randomly assigned to continue ABVD or to change to AVD for four additional cycles. With a median follow-up of 41 months, the 3-year PFS was 85.7% versus 84.4%, and 3-year OS rate was 97% in both arms. Thus, given increased toxicity from bleomycin, patients with a negative interim PET can safely have this agent omitted for cycles three to six.

When treating with ABVD, it is imperative to deliver treatment on time and without dose reduction to maximize efficacy. Although ABVD is associated with neutropenia, febrile neutropenia is very uncommon in this generally young and healthy population.[205] The use of routine growth factors is not recommended. There is controversy over the interaction between growth factors and bleomycin-induced lung injury, particularly in older patients.[212,213]

Brentuximab vedotin is an antibody drug conjugate against CD30 with a toxic payload of MMAE. It has extremely potent activity in the relapsed or refractory setting. A phase III study of AVD plus brentuximab vedotin showed a small modified PFS advantage over ABVD (82.1% vs 77.2%), albeit with increased toxicity and a requirement for hematopoietic growth factor support. Bleomycin and its associated toxicity was eliminated in this regimen.[214] The greatest advantage was seen in patients with stage IV disease. The combination is FDA approved.

Bulky HL

Up to 25% of patients with HL will have bulky disease, currently defined as a mass > 10 cm on CT scans or a mediastinal mass > 0.33 of the chest diameter on a chest radiograph at T5–T6. Bulky disease may or may not be symptomatic, and cough or chest pain are frequently associated symptoms. More abrupt symptoms, such as superior vena cava syndrome, are more likely to be from aggressive lymphomas involving the mediastinum such as primary mediastinal BCL. Bulky disease is connoted with the suffix or postscript "X" in the stage (eg, II_X or IIX). Bulk is a known adverse prognostic factor. The literature regarding bulky HL is confounded by the general inclusion of bulky disease in early-stage trials in Europe versus inclusion in advanced-stage trials in North America.

Treatment of bulky HL has traditionally been combined-modality therapy, but PET-directed omission of radiation is being evaluated. Given the primarily mediastinal location of bulky HL, radiation therapy is associated with secondary malignancies (especially medial breast cancer in young women), cardiovascular disease (which may be aggravated by concurrent use of anthracyclines), and pulmonary toxicity.

After six cycles of ABVD or Stanford V, 36 Gy consolidative radiation is associated with a 5-year FFS rate of > 80% in bulky HL.[215] Although retrospective data support the omission of radiation in patients with a negative PET scan, early results from prospective trials are more complex and controversial. A German trial (HD15) used PET-directed radiation in patients treated with escalated BEACOPP, and the researchers were able to reduce the use of radiation therapy to only 11% of patients[216]; extrapolation to ABVD is controversial. The RATHL trial mentioned in the previous section did not radiate the small subset of patients with stage II bulky disease. Overall, there is a strong move away from radiation for bulky mediastinal disease; several trials are expected to mature shortly.

Relapsed cHL

Although most patients with cHL are cured with initial treatment, approximately 10% to 20% (and up to 50% of high-risk patients) will have disease recurrence. The treatment approach at relapse is influenced by the time to relapse and the nature of the initial treatment, but generally consists of a multistep process of salvage chemotherapy, hematopoietic stem cell mobilization, HDC with autologous stem cell rescue, and consideration of consolidative brentuximab vedotin. In support of ASCT, two randomized trials showed superiority of HDC and ABMT over conventional chemotherapy.[217,218] The historic British National Lymphoma Investigation randomly assigned 20 patients apiece with nonresponding or relapsed disease to either mini-carmustine, etoposide, cytarabine and melphalan (BEAM) or BEAM (augmented doses of the same agents) followed by ABMT. The 3-year EFS was 53% versus 10% in favor of the transplantation group. A second trial, the German HD-R1 trial, randomized 161 patients to either dexa-BEAM or BEAM followed by ABMT and showed an improved freedom from treatment failure for HDC (55% *v* 34%, *P* = .019).[218] Of interest, neither of these trials was powered to determine a survival advantage for transplantation, but a meta-analysis confirmed the benefit of transplantation with mature follow-up, and ASCT is now the standard of care.[219]

The most important factors predicting outcome to salvage ASCT are time to relapse and chemosensitivity. The HD-R1 trial defined "early" and "late" relapse at 12 months and found limited benefit of transplantation for patients with early relapse.[218] Other trials confirm this observation, and patients with refractory disease or who have a relapse within 12 months derive less benefit from ASCT.[220-222] However, chemosensitivity to salvage regimens may supersede time to relapse, and achieving a PET-negative remission before ASCT affects outcome. Patients with a positive pre-ASCT PET had an EFS rate of 33% versus 77% (HR, 4.61; *P* = .00004) in a study, and PET negativity overcame other negative prognostic features.[223,224] Of note, different salvage regimens all have high activity, including ICE, DHAP, gemcitabine-containing regimens, and brentuximab vedotin alone or in combination, but have not been compared in randomized trials. An overarching principle is to achieve a PET-negative response before ASCT, even if that requires a second non–cross-resistant salvage therapy.[224]

Although transplantation is an active and appropriate treatment of relapsed HL, the long-term disease control rate is only 50% to 60% in randomized trials and registry analyses,[220,222,225] with relapses occurring mainly in the first 3 years after ASCT. The AETHERA trial randomly assigned 329 patients with high-risk relapsed or refractory HL to brentuximab vedotin consolidation therapy or observation. *High risk* was defined as primary refractory disease, relapse within 12 months, or extranodal disease. Brentuximab vedotin consolidation was associated with improved PFS (42.9 months *v* 24.1 months; HR, 0.57; $P = .0013$),[226] and this is now an approved indication. To date, there is no difference in OS.

Not all patients with relapsed HL need ASCT, and controversy exists with regard to the best approach for patients with limited relapse or those with minimal therapy in the first-line setting. In particular, patients with a late relapse and limited disease after chemotherapy may be treated with salvage radiation.[227]

The treatment options for multiply relapsed HL, either after ASCT or in patients who are ineligible for ASCT, have greatly expanded in the past several years. Allogeneic stem cell transplantation, usually with a reduced-intensity conditioning regimen, remains an important and effective option for eligible patients. However, two new treatments have significantly challenged the role and timing of allogeneic transplantation. First, the antibody-drug conjugate brentuximab vedotin has single-agent ORR and CR rates of 75% and 34%, respectively, with half of patients with CR remaining disease free at 5 years.[228] Brentuximab vedotin is administered at 1.8 mg/kg every 3 weeks and is well tolerated overall. The most common toxicity is sensory peripheral neuropathy, which occurs to some degree in most patients; > 80% of patients in the pivotal trial reported eventual resolution of symptoms. Clearly, brentuximab vedotin would be of limited value if already given in the first-line treatment. A second new option is checkpoint blockade. Amplification of 9p24 in HL leads to PD-L1 overexpression and activation of the JAK-STAT pathway, supporting the use of PD1/PD-L1 axis blockade. Nivolumab and pembrolizumab are both FDA approved in the following settings.[229]

- Nivolumab: HL relapsed or progressed after autologous HSCT or post-transplantation brentuximab vedotin or after three lines of prior therapy including autologous HSCT.
- Pembroluzumab: relapsed after three or more lines of prior therapy.

Therapy for NLPHL

The treatment of NLPHL has traditionally followed general guidelines for cHL, and the rarity of this disease precludes any randomized trials. However, the observation that NLPHL behaves more like an indolent lymphoma and has an overall good prognosis has raised controversy regarding optimal management to avoid overtreatment. This latter aspect is emphasized in very long-term follow-up showing that risk of death from toxicity was three-fold higher than risk of death from lymphoma in patients with early-stage disease.[230]

Early-stage disease is treated with either radiation alone or abbreviated chemotherapy plus radiation. Patients with stage IA disease with full excision may be observed. The choice of chemotherapy is controversial; most groups recommend ABVD for two to four cycles plus radiation, but retrospective data suggest alkylating agents are more effective, and CHOP or CVP can be used.[197,231,232] Survival after early-stage disease is excellent and approximates 90% with at least 10 years of follow-up. Patients with advanced-stage disease can be treated with six cycles of ABVD, CHOP, or CVP (reviewed in Savage et al[197]). Because NLPHL expresses CD20, the addition of rituximab to management strategies has been evaluated. As a single agent, rituximab has a response rate of 94% to 100% and may be palliative in relapsed settings.[233-235] R-CHOP appeared active in a small series of patients with no relapses at 42 months.[236] Patients with asymptomatic, relapsed disease may not need treatment, because prolonged survival is common. The major risk in NLPHL survivors appears to be transformation to DLBCL (or T-cell–rich DLBCL).

KEY POINTS

- HL comprises cHL (nodular sclerosis, mixed cellularity, lymphocyte-rich, lymphocyte-depleted) and NLPHL, each of which has a distinctive clinical presentation, treatment paradigm, and prognosis.
- cHL of any stage is curable in most afflicted patients.
- Combination chemotherapy with ABVD is the standard chemotherapy for cHL in North America.
- The number of courses of chemotherapy varies with the stage of the disease.
- Low-dose, IFRT is commonly administered after a short course of chemotherapy for the management of early-stage cHL, although the role of radiotherapy is undergoing reevaluation.
- PET-adapted therapy is now incorporated into treatment, although the ideal way to implement this is still being investigated.
- HL expresses CD30, which can be targeted by the antibody-drug conjugate brentuximab vedotin.
- Amplification of 9p24 is common in cHL and leads to overexpression of PDL-1, which is the basis for immune checkpoint inhibitors.
- Patients with relapsed or refractory HL can be treated with a variety of therapies with a goal of PET negativity prior to consolidative autologous transplantation in eligible patients.
- NLPHL is a type of HL that behaves similarly to indolent lymphomas and usually expresses CD20. There is a risk of transformation to DLBCL, usually a T-cell–rich variant DLBCL, which should be treated as any transformed aggressive BCL.

Acknowledgment

The following authors are acknowledged and graciously thanked for their contributions to prior versions of this chapter: Bruce D. Cheson, MD, FASCO; Oliver W. Press, MD, PhD; and Sonali Smith, MD, FASCO.

GLOBAL ONCOLOGY PERSPECTIVE: LYMPHOMAS

Kazuhito Yamamoto, MD, PhD (Aichi Cancer Center, Japan)

EPIDEMIOLOGY

Incidence of lymphoma is lower in East Asia, including Japan, than in Western countries, including the United States. According to the data from GLOBOCAN,[237] 1,715 and 28,008 new cases of HL and NHL, respectively, were diagnosed in Japan, whereas 9,295 and 73,253 were diagnosed in the United States. The age adjusted incidence rates of HL per 100,000 were 0.6 in Japan and 2.8 in the United States, and 7.9 and 14.7 for NHL, respectively.[238] Trends in incidence also differ significantly between Japan and the United States. Lymphoma incidence substantially increased in Japan,[238] but there was little change in incidence in the United States.[239] The increasing trend in lymphoma incidence in Japan may be explained by westernization of lifestyle and dietary habits.

The proportions of subtypes of malignant lymphoma differ between Japan and Western countries. Compared with the United States, Japan has higher rates of TCL and NK-cell lymphoma and lower rates of HL, FL, and CLL/SLL.

A low proportion of HL, which accounts for < 10% of lymphoma in Japan, is a common finding in Asian countries, compared with the high proportion (approximately 30%) in western countries.

DLBCL IS THE LARGEST SUBTYPE IN JAPAN AND THE UNITED STATES

FL is the most frequent subtype in Western countries, especially in the United States. In Japan and Asian countries, a lower proportion has been reported.[240,241] According to a recent report from Japan, however, FL accounted for 18.2% of lymphoma,[242] which is a relatively similar frequency to that of Western countries. The incidence of FL appears to be increasing, although responsible factors are unclear.[238] CLL and SLL show the largest difference in proportion between Japan (3.2%) and the United States (24.1%).[238]

The proportion of TCLs excluding human T-cell leukemia virus type 1 (HTLV-1) associated adult T-cell leukemia/lymphoma (ATL) was higher in Japan (9.8%) than in the United States (6.6%) due to both a higher incidence of some subtypes and a lower relative frequency of some BCL, such as FL. This difference becomes more profound when adding ATL to TCL (Japan,18.1%; United States, 6.8%).[238] For the major subtypes of nodal TCL, such as PTCL-NOS and AITL, the incidence is similar in Japan and in the United States. Only two subtypes, ATL and NK/TCL, nasal type, in Japan have a higher incidence than in the United States.

There is paucity of information on malignant lymphomas in sub-Saharan Africa, but it is estimated that 30,000 cases of NHL occur annually and up to 50% may be associated with AIDS. The incidence of NHL since the AIDS epidemic has increased by two- to three-fold in some countries and as much as 13-fold in others.[243-245]

Burkitt lymphoma, an aggressive BCL, is the commonest lymphoma in African children. According to GLOBOCAN 2018, 3,900 new cases were reported; two-thirds of cases were in male patients, and most (n = 3,175) in children younger than 14 years.

ETIOLOGY: DIFFERENCES IN LYMPHOMA PATHOGENESIS

Some viral infections such as HIV, HTLV-1 and EBV are associated with specific subtypes of ML. HIV infection significantly increases the risk of both NHL (77-fold) and HL (11-fold).[246] The prevalence of HIV in the United States is low among the general population (0.4% in 2008). The prevalence of HIV in Japan is extremely low (0.01% to 0.02%), indicating there is a large difference in the incidence of HIV-related lymphoma between the two countries.

In Japan, one of the main risk factors for TCL is HTLV-1 infection. HTLV-1 is the causative agent of ATL, is clonally integrated into the genome of T cells, and accelerates the transformation of the cell. In the endemic area of southwestern Japan, the seroprevalence of HTLV-1 is 8% to 10%. The cumulative lifetime risk for the development of ATL is 6.9% for seropositive men and 2.9% for seropositive women.[5]

EBV is involved in the pathogenesis of lymphoma. NK/TCL has higher prevalence rates in Asian countries, including Japan, and is closely related to EBV infection. There seems to be a difference in the immune response to EBV among Japanese.[247]

DIAGNOSIS AND CLINICAL PRESENTATION

There are no differences in the screening or early diagnosis of lymphoma or clinical presentation between Japan and the United States.

TREATMENT

Treatment algorithms or recommendations of the guideline of Japanese Society of Hematology are almost the same as those of NCCN, ASCO, and European Society for Medical Oncology (ESMO). Specific pharmacologic or pharmacogenetic differences related to chemotherapy or other treatments do not exist.

Treatment of lymphoma in sub-Saharan Africa follows NCCN, ESMO, and ASCO guidelines but remains a challenge due to lack of access to essential cancer medicines in most settings. There is no precise outcome research or cohort study on survival of lymphoma in Japan. Based on clinical trial data,[248] however, treatment outcome is almost the same as that in Western countries.

21

MULTIPLE MYELOMA

Sagar Lonial, MD, and Jonathan L. Kaufman, MD

Recent Updates

- Once-weekly carfilzomib dosing at 70 mg/m^2 was superior to the standard twice-weekly dosing at 27mg/m^2, with similar safety profile, in patients with multiple myeloma. (Moreau P, *Lancet* 2018)
- Denosumab was noninferior to zolendronic acid in preventing skeletal-related events, with a similar safely profile, in a randomized trial of patients with multiple myeloma (MM). (Raje N, *Lancet Oncol* 2018)
- In a randomized trial including nontransplant-eligible elderly patients with newly diagnosed MM, the combination of daratumumab with bortezomib (Velcade), melphalan, and prednisone (VMP) followed by daratumumab was superior to VMP without maintenance. (Mateos M-V, *N Engl J Med* 2018)
- In a randomized trial in including nontransplant-eligible patients with newly diagnosed MM, daratumumab, compared with lenalidomide and dexamethasone alone, demonstrated an improved progression-free survival (PFS). (Facon T, *N Engl J Med* 2019)
- Elotuzumab plus pomalidomide and dexamethasone were superior to pomalidomide and dexamethasone alone in terms of improved PFS without significant increase in adverse events in patients with MM. (Dimopoulos MA, *N Engl J Med* 2018)

OVERVIEW

Multiple myeloma (MM) is a plasma cell malignancy characterized by osteolytic bone lesions, anemia, hypercalcemia, and renal failure.[1,2] The disease is generally considered incurable, and the clinical course is typically characterized by remissions and relapses, with a decrease in the remission duration with each successive therapy.[3] The survival of patients with MM has improved, however, with the advent of biologic-based therapies. This improvement can be attributed to incorporation of drugs such as thalidomide, bortezomib, lenalidomide, carfilzomib,[4] pomalidomide,[5,6] and monoclonal antibodies[7] into the overall treatment strategy, as well as the use of autologous stem cell transplantation (ASCT) in selected patients and improvements in supportive care.

DISEASE DEFINITION

The definition of MM was updated by the International Myeloma Working Group in 2014.[8] The revised definition incorporates specific biomarkers associated with a high risk of progression to symptomatic disease and signs revealed by advanced imaging methods that aid diagnosing myeloma in patients who do not have standard features of end-organ damage. The new defining classification of MM results in patients with a higher risk of developing symptomatic disease being treated earlier. MM is currently determined by the following:

- the presence of ≥ 10% clonal plasma cells on bone marrow examination or biopsy-proven plasmacytoma, plus
- evidence of one or more of the following myeloma-defining events (MDEs):
  - evidence of hypercalcemia,
  - renal insufficiency,
  - anemia
  - bone lesions that can be attributed to the plasma cell proliferative disorder;
  - clonal bone marrow plasma cells ≥ 60%,
  - serum free light chain (FLC) ratio of ≥ 100, provided the involved FLC concentration is ≥ 100 mg/L, or
  - more than one focal lesion on magnetic resonance imaging (MRI).

Patients with MM must be differentiated from those with monoclonal gammopathy of undetermined significance (MGUS), smoldering multiple myeloma (SMM), and other related plasma cell disorders (Table 21-1).[8-14] Diagnostic criteria provided in Table 21-1 replace older criteria.[15,16]

MGUS is an asymptomatic, premalignant phase of MM.[17,18] The risk of progression of MGUS to myeloma or a related disorder is fixed at approximately 1% per year.[18] SMM is a more advanced, intermediate stage, defined by the presence of a serum monoclonal protein concentration greater than 3 g/dL or 10% to 60% clonal plasma cells in the marrow but without MDE or amyloidosis. SMM is a form of myeloma in which clonal expansion of disease is not yet associated with clinical manifestations and is at variable risk for progression, based on defined prognostic criteria.[19] In a study of 276 patients with SMM, the risk of progression to MM in the first 5 years after diagnosis was 10% per year, 3% per year over the next 5 years, and 1% per year thereafter.[20]

KEY POINTS

- The diagnosis of myeloma requires evidence of one or more MDEs: hypercalcemia, renal insufficiency, anemia, or bone lesions that can be attributed to the plasma cell proliferative disorder; clonal bone marrow plasma cells 60% or greater; serum FLC ratio > 100, provided the involved FLC level is > 100 mg/L; or more than one focal lesion on MRI.
- MGUS and SMM are asymptomatic plasma cell proliferative disorders that need to be distinguished from myeloma.

EPIDEMIOLOGY AND RISK FACTORS

MM accounts for 1% of all malignant disease and slightly > 10% of all hematologic malignancies. The annual incidence, age-adjusted to the 2000 US population, is 4.3 per 100,000.[21] In 2019, approximately 32,110 new cases are expected to occur in the United States, and 12,960 deaths are expected to be attributable to myeloma. There is a male-to-female predominance. Myeloma is twice as common in the black population as in the white population.[22] The median age of patients at diagnosis is approximately 65 years. There is no known etiology. Exposure to radiation, benzene, and other organic solvents, herbicides, and insecticides may play a role. There is an increased risk of MM in first-degree relatives.

PREVENTION

Prevention of myeloma is hampered by the low likelihood of progression in patients with the premalignant MGUS stage. If deaths due to unrelated competing causes are taken into account, myeloma will develop in only 10% of patients with MGUS. In SMM, the risk of progression in the first 5 years is considerably higher, at approximately 50%. Thus, preventive strategies for MM have focused on preventing progression in high-risk patients (≥ 10% bone marrow plasma cells and either a monoclonal protein level of ≥ 3 g/dL or the presence on an aberrant plasma cell immunophenotype in > 95% of clonal plasma cells plus reduction in the level of normal immunoglobulins) with newly diagnosed SMM. A randomized trial conducted by the Spanish Myeloma Group in patients with high-risk SMM found improved progression-free and overall survival (OS) with early use of lenalidomide plus dexamethasone versus observation.[23] The recently published Eastern Cooperative Oncology Group (ECOG) study confirmed this finding: high-risk patients with SMM had an improved progression-free survival (PFS) when lenalidomide was used to prevent progression to symptomatic myeloma compared with observation, which is the standard of care.[24]

KEY POINTS

- MM accounts for 1% of all cancers and approximately 10% of all hematologic cancers.
- Myeloma is twice as common in the black population as in the white population.
- Early intervention with lenalidomide has shown promise in the treatment of SMM and is now considered a standard option for high risk smoldering myeloma patients.

PATHOGENESIS

MM is almost always preceded by a premalignant phase, referred to as MGUS.[25] However, because MGUS is asymptomatic and can be detected only through specific laboratory testing, most patients diagnosed with MM do not have a history of MGUS. The pathogenesis of MM involves two initial steps:

1) development of the premalignant MGUS stage; and
2) progression of MGUS to symptomatic MM.

Table 21-1 Diagnostic Criteria for Plasma Cell Disorders

Disorder	Disease Definition	Reference
Non-IgM MGUS	All three criteria must be met:	Rajkumar et al[1]
	• Serum monoclonal protein (non-IgM type) < 3g/dL	
	• Clonal bone marrow plasma cells < 10%[a]	
	• Absence of end-organ damage, such as CRAB, that can be attributed to the plasma cell proliferative disorder	
Smoldering multiple myeloma	Both criteria must be met:	Rajkumar et al[1]
	• Serum monoclonal protein (IgG or IgA) ≥ 3g/dL, or urinary monoclonal protein ≥ 500 mg/24 h and/or clonal bone marrow plasma cells 10% to 60%	
	• Absence of MDEs or amyloidosis	
Multiple myeloma	Both criteria must be met:	Rajkumar et al[1]
	• Clonal bone marrow plasma cells > 10% or biopsy-proven bony or extramedullary plasmacytoma	
	• Any one or more of the following MDEs:	
	○ Evidence of end-organ damage that can be attributed to the underlying plasma cell proliferative disorder, specifically:	
	■ Hypercalcemia: serum calcium > 0.25 mmol/L (> 1 mg/dL) more than the upper limit of normal or > 2.75 mmol/L (> 11 mg/dL)	
	■ Renal insufficiency: creatinine clearance < 40 mL/min or serum creatinine > 1 77 µmol/L (> 2 mg/dL)	
	■ Anemia: hemoglobin value of > 2 g/dL below the lower limit of normal, or a hemoglobin value < 10 g/dL	
	■ Bone lesions: one or more osteolytic lesions on skeletal radiography, CT, or PET-CT	
	○ Clonal bone marrow plasma cell > 60%	
	○ Ratio of involved to uninvolved serum FLC ≥ 100 (involved FLC level must be ≥ 100 mg/L)	
	○ >One focal lesion ≥ 5 mm on MRI studies	
IgM MGUS	All three criteria must be met:	Rajkumar et al[1]
	• Serum IgM monoclonal protein < 3g/dL	
	• Bone marrow lymphoplasmacytic infiltration < 10%	
	• No evidence of anemia, constitutional symptoms, hyperviscosity, lymphadenopathy, or hepatosplenomegaly that can be attributed to the underlying lymphoproliferative disorder	
Smoldering Waldenström macroglobulinemia (also referred to as indolent or asymptomatic Waldenström macroglobulinemia)	Both criteria must be met:	Rajkumar et al[1]; Kyle et al[7]; Gobbi et al[12]; Baldini et al[9]; Owen et al[14]
	• Serum IgM monoclonal protein > 3g/dL and/or bone marrow lymphoplasmacytic infiltration ≥ 10%	
	• No evidence of anemia, constitutional symptoms, hyperviscosity, lymphadenopathy, or hepatosplenomegaly that can be attributed to the underlying lymphoproliferative disorder	
Waldenström macroglobulinemia	All criteria must be met:	Rajkumar et al[1]; Kyle et al[7]; Gobbi et al[12]; Baldini et al[9]; Owen et al[14]
	• IgM monoclonal gammopathy (regardless of the size of the M protein)	
	• > 10% bone marrow lymphoplasmacytic infiltration (usually intertrabecular) by small lymphocytes that exhibit plasmacytoid or plasma cell differentiation and a typical immunophenotype (eg, surface IgM+, CD5+, CD5−, CD10−, CD19+, CD20+, CD23−) that satisfactorily excludes other lymphoproliferative disorders, including chronic lymphocytic leukemia and mantle cell lymphoma	
	• Evidence of anemia, constitutional symptoms, hyperviscosity, lymphadenopathy, or hepatosplenomegaly that can be attributed to the underlying lymphoproliferative disorder	
Light-chain MGUS	All criteria must be met:	Rajkumar et al[1]
	• Abnormal FLC ratio (< 0.26 or > 1.65)	
	• Increased level of the appropriate involved light chain (increased κ FLC in patients with ratio > 1.65 and increased λ FLC in patients with ratio < 0.26)	
	• No immunoglobulin heavy-chain expression on immunofixation	
	• Absence of end-organ damage that can be attributed to the plasma cell proliferative disorder	
	• Clonal bone marrow plasma cells < 10%	
	• Urinary monoclonal protein < 500 mg/24 h	

Table 21-1 continued

Disorder	Disease Definition	Reference
Solitary plasmacytoma[b]	All four criteria must be met:	Rajkumar et al[1]
	• Biopsy-proven solitary lesion of bone or soft tissue with evidence of clonal plasma cells	
	• Normal bone marrow with no evidence of clonal plasma cells	
	• Normal skeletal survey and MRI (or CT scan) of spine and pelvis (except for the primary solitary lesion)	
	• Absence of end-organ damage such as CRAB that can be attributed to a lymphoplasma cell proliferative disorder	
Solitary plasmacytoma with minimal marrow involvement[a]	All four criteria must be met:	Rajkumar et al[1]
	• Biopsy-proven solitary lesion of bone or soft tissue with evidence of clonal plasma cells	
	• Clonal bone marrow plasma cells < 10%	
	• Normal skeletal survey and MRI (or CT scan) of spine and pelvis (except for the primary solitary lesion)	
	• Absence of end-organ damage such as CRAB that can be attributed to a lymphoplasma cell proliferative disorder	
Systemic AL amyloidosis[c]	All four criteria must be met:	Rajkumar et al[1]
	• Presence of an amyloid-related systemic syndrome (eg, renal, liver, heart, GI tract, or peripheral nerve involvement)	
	• Positive amyloid staining by Congo red in any tissue (eg, fat aspirate, bone marrow, organ biopsy specimen)	
	• Evidence that amyloid is light-chain related established by direct examination of the amyloid using MS-based proteomic analysis, or immunoelectron microscopy	
	• Evidence of a monoclonal plasma cell proliferative disorder (serum or urine M protein, abnormal FLC ratio, or clonal plasma cells in the bone marrow)	
POEMS syndrome[d]	All four criteria must be met:	Rajkumar et al[1]; Dispenzieri et al[11]; Dispenzieri[10]
	• Polyneuropathy	
	• Monoclonal plasma cell proliferative disorder (almost always λ)	
	• Any one of the following three other major criteria:	
	1. Sclerotic bone lesions	
	2. Castleman disease	
	3. Elevated levels of VEGF[e]	
	Any one of the following six minor criteria:	
	1. Organomegaly (splenomegaly, hepatomegaly, or lymphadenopathy)	
	2. Extravascular volume overload (edema, pleural effusion, or ascites)	
	3. Endocrinopathy (adrenal, thyroid, pituitary, gonadal, parathyroid, pancreatic)[f]	
	4. Skin changes (hyperpigmentation, hypertrichosis, glomeruloid hemangiomata, plethora, acrocyanosis, flushing, white nails)	
	5. Papilledema	
	6. Thrombocytosis or polycythemia	

Abbreviations: AL amyloidosis, light-chain amyloidosis; CRAB, hypercalcemia, renal insufficiency, anemia, and bone lesions; CT, computed tomography; FLC, free light chain; MDE, myeloma-defining event; MGUS, monoclonal gammopathy of undetermined significance; MRI, magnetic resonance imaging; MS, mass spectrometry; PET, positron-emission tomography; POEMS, polyneuropathy, organomegaly, endocrinopathy, M protein, and skin changes; VEGF, vascular endothelial growth factor.

[a]A bone marrow test can be deferred in patients with low-risk MGUS (IgG type, M protein < 15 g/L, normal FLC ratio) in whom there are no clinical features of myeloma.

[b]Solitary plasmacytoma with ≥ 10% clonal plasma cells is considered multiple myeloma.

[c]Approximately 2% to 3% of patients with AL amyloidosis will not meet the requirement for evidence of a monoclonal plasma cell disorder listed here; the diagnosis of AL amyloidosis must be made with caution in these patients. Patients with AL amyloidosis who also meet criteria for multiple myeloma are considered to have both diseases.

[d]Not every patient meeting the listed criteria will have POEMS syndrome; the features should have a temporal relationship to each other and no other attributable cause. Anemia and/or thrombocytopenia are distinctively unusual in this syndrome unless Castleman disease is present.

[e]The source data do not define an optimal cutoff value for considering elevated VEGF level as a major criterion. We suggest that VEGF measured in the serum or plasma should be at least three- to four-fold higher than the normal reference range for the laboratory that is doing the testing to be considered a major criterion

[f]To consider endocrinopathy as a minor criterion, an endocrine disorder other than diabetes or hypothyroidism is required, because these two disorders are common in the general population.

Reprinted from Rajkumar et al.[8] Used with permission from Elsevier, copyright 2014.

The evolution of a normal plasma cell to an MGUS clone is likely triggered by an abnormal response to antigenic stimulation. This results in the development of primary cytogenetic abnormalities in the affected plasma cells. In approximately 40% to 50% of MGUS cases, the primary cytogenetic abnormality is a reciprocal translocation involving the immunoglobulin heavy-chain (IgH) locus on chromosome 14q32 (IgH-translocated MGUS) and one of five recurrent partner chromosome loci: 11q13 (CCND1 [cyclin D1 gene]), 4p16.3 (*FGFR3* and *MMSET*), 6p21 (*CCND3* [cyclin D3 gene]), 16q23 (*c-Maf*), and 20q11

(*MAFB*) (Table 21-2).[26] In most of the remaining patients with MGUS, the primary abnormality is the development of trisomies of one or more of the odd-numbered chromosomes, often resulting in hyperdiploidy (referred to as hyperdiploid MGUS or IgH nontranslocated MGUS).[27] In a small proportion of cases, neither trisomies nor IgH translocations are found, and in some patients, both types of abnormalities are found in the same clone (Fig 21-1).

Once an MGUS clone is established, the second step of progression to MM follows a simple, random, two-hit genetic model of malignancy. Although several alterations, such as abnormalities involving the Myc family of oncogenes, *RAS* mutations, *p16* methylation, and *p53* mutations, have been associated with malignant transformation of MGUS to MM, the specific pathogenetic steps are unknown. Studies indicate there is significant clonal heterogeneity in myeloma, with different dominant clones emerging through the course of various treatments.[28]

Progression of MGUS to myeloma is typically accompanied by an increase in receptor activator of nuclear factor κ B ligand (RANKL) concentration, expression by osteoblasts, and a reduction in the level of the decoy receptor, osteoprotegerin (OPG).[29] This leads to an increased RANKL-to-OPG ratio, a key factor for osteoclast activation and subsequent bone resorption. Increased levels of macrophage inflammatory protein 1-α (MIP-1α), stromal-derived factor α (SDF-α), interleukin (IL)-3, IL-1β, and IL-6 may also play a role in osteoclast activation. At the same time, increased levels of IL-3, IL-7, and dickkopf 1 (DKK1) contribute to inhibition of osteoblast differentiation. This combination of osteoclast activation and osteoblast suppression leads to the pure osteolytic bone disease that is the hallmark of MM.

KEY POINTS

- Myeloma is preceded by a premalignant phase, clinically referred to as monoclonal gammopathy of undetermined significance.
- The two principal pathogenetic steps are (1) transition from normal plasma cell to MGUS, and (2) transition from MGUS to myeloma.
- The onset of MGUS is associated with IgH translocations in approximately 50% of cases and hyperdiploidy in the remaining 50% of cases.

CLINICAL PRESENTATION AND DIAGNOSIS

The most common presenting symptoms of MM are fatigue and bone pain.[30] Osteolytic bone lesions and/or compression fractures are hallmarks of the disease and can be detected on routine radiography, MRI, or computed tomography (CT) scans in approximately 70% of patients.[29] Anemia occurs in 70% of patients at diagnosis and is the primary cause of weakness and fatigue. Hypercalcemia is found in 15% of patients. Other symptoms may result from acute renal failure, radiculopathy, or infection.

When MM is suspected, patients should be tested for the presence of monoclonal (M) proteins by serum protein electrophoresis (SPEP), serum immunofixation (SIFE), urine protein electrophoresis (UPEP), urine immunofixation, and serum FLC assay. The serum FLC assay and urine studies help identify the subset of patients with MM who lack M protein heavy-chain expression (ie, light-chain MM). Only 82% of patients with MM

Table 21-2 Cytogenetic Categories of MGUS and MM[106]

Cytogenetic Type	Gene(s) Involved	Comment
I. Hyperdiploid MGUS or MM	Unknown; likely many	Characterized by trisomies of one or more odd-numbered chromosomes; in patients with myeloma, hyperdiploidy considered standard risk
II. IgH translocated (nonhyperdiploid) MGUS or MM		Reciprocal translocation involving the IgH gene on chromosome 14q32 and a variety of partner chromosomes
t(11;14)	*CCND1* (cyclin D1)	
t(4;14) MM	*FGFR3* and *MMSET*	
t(14;16) MM	*c-MAF*	Considered to indicate high-risk disease in setting of MM
t(6;14) MM	*CCND3* (cyclin D3)	
t(14;20) MM	*MAFB*	Considered to indicate high-risk disease in setting of MM
III. Unclassified MGUS or MM		

Abbreviations: IGH, immunoglobulin heavy-chain; MGUS, monoclonal gammopathy of undetermined significance; MM, multiple myeloma.
Permission to reuse given by S. V. Rajkumar.[106]

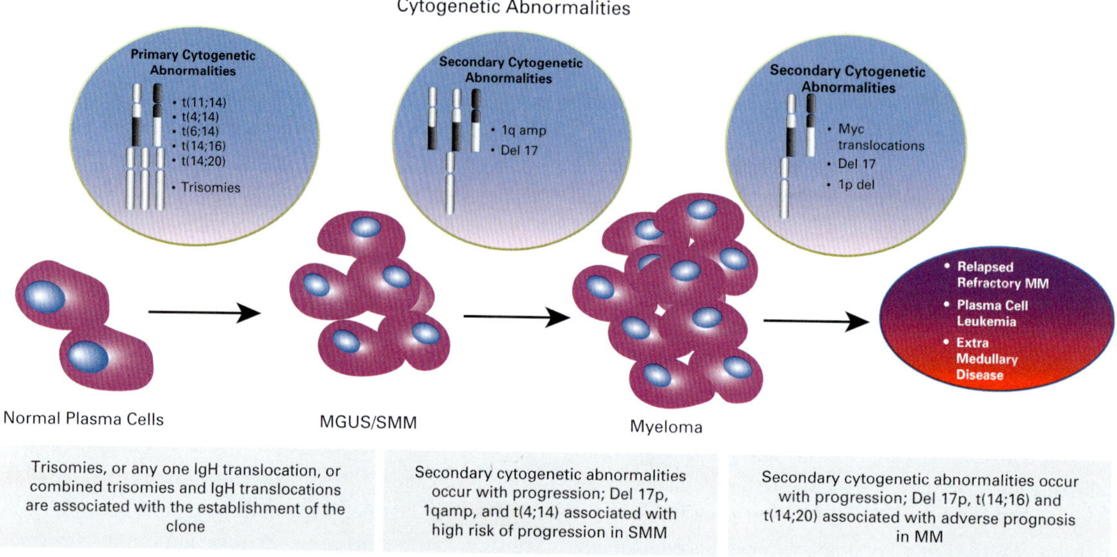
Cytogenetic Abnormalities
Primary Cytogenetic Abnormalities
• t(11;14)
• t(4;14)
• t(6;14)
• t(14;16)
• t(14;20)
• Trisomies
Secondary Cytogenetic Abnormalities
• 1q amp
• Del 17
Secondary Cytogenetic Abnormalities
• Myc translocations
• Del 17
• 1p del
• Relapsed Refractory MM
• Plasma Cell Leukemia
• Extra Medullary Disease
Normal Plasma Cells
MGUS/SMM
Myeloma
Trisomies, or any one IgH translocation, or combined trisomies and IgH translocations are associated with the establishment of the clone
Secondary cytogenetic abnormalities occur with progression; Del 17p, 1qamp, and t(4;14) associated with high risk of progression in SMM
Secondary cytogenetic abnormalities occur with progression; Del 17p, t(14;16) and t(14;20) associated with adverse prognosis in MM

Fig. 21-1 Cytogenetic abnormalities in multiple myeloma (MM).

Primary cytogenetic abnormalities occur early, when the normal plasma cell transitions to a clonal, premalignant stage. Most secondary cytogenetic abnormalities occur later in the disease course with malignant transformation or during progression of the malignancy. The effect of primary and secondary cytogenetic abnormalities on prognosis depends on the disease.[128]

Abbreviations: IgH, immunoglobulin heavy-chain; MGUS, monoclonal gammopathy of undetermined significance; SMM, smoldering multiple myeloma.

have an M protein that is detectable on SPEP, whereas SIFE will identify an M protein in 93% of patients.[30] Combining serum studies with either urine studies or the serum FLC assay will reveal an M protein in 97% to 98% of patients with MM.[30,31] Patients with serum M protein concentration < 1 g/dL and urine M protein of < 200 mg/d are considered to have oligosecretory myeloma. In addition, approximately 2% to 3% of patients with MM have true nonsecretory disease with no evidence of an M protein on serum or urine immunofixation; a subset of these patients who also have a normal serum FLC ratio are considered to have true nonsecretory myeloma.[31]

Other tests considered essential are CBC count, and serum creatinine, calcium, β-2 microglobulin, albumin, and lactate dehydrogenase (LDH) levels. A unilateral bone marrow aspiration and biopsy are needed for the diagnosis. The monotypic nature of marrow plasma cells must be established by an abnormal κ:λ ratio found on immunohistochemistry or flow cytometry. Myeloma cells typically stain positive for CD38, CD56, and CD138. Bone marrow plasma cells should also be studied with fluorescence in situ hybridization (FISH) and/or karyotyping to enable risk stratification (see section on Staging and Risk Stratification).[32] FISH studies do not require dividing cells; hence, they are considerably more informative in myeloma than conventional karyotyping, which requires the presence of metaphases.

Examination of all bones using whole-body, low-dose CT or positron-emission tomography (PET) is required to detect lytic bone lesions (Figs 21-2 and 21-3).[33] MRI and/or PET-CT or whole-body, low-dose CT imaging are required to differentiate SMM and solitary plasmacytoma from MM and are also useful in assessing extramedullary disease and also whenever there is a concern that the disease assessment may be inadequate with plain radiography and M protein assessments alone.

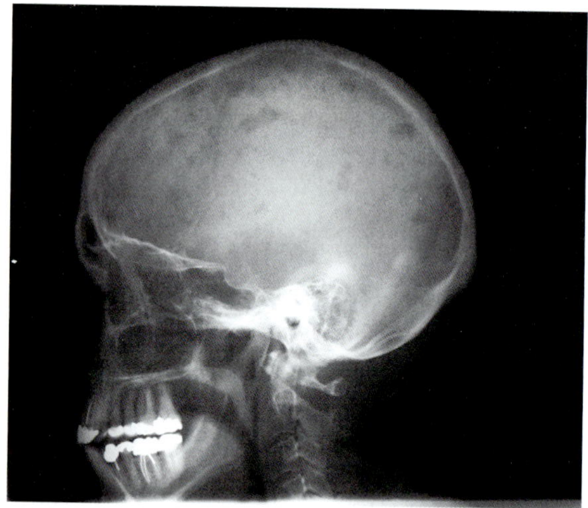

Fig. 21-2 Skull radiograph showing multiple osteolytic lesions.

DIFFERENTIAL DIAGNOSIS

Using the criteria listed in Table 21-1[6], myeloma should be differentiated from

- MGUS
- SMM
- solitary plasmacytoma
- Waldenström macroglobulinemia
- amyloid light-chain (AL) amyloidosis

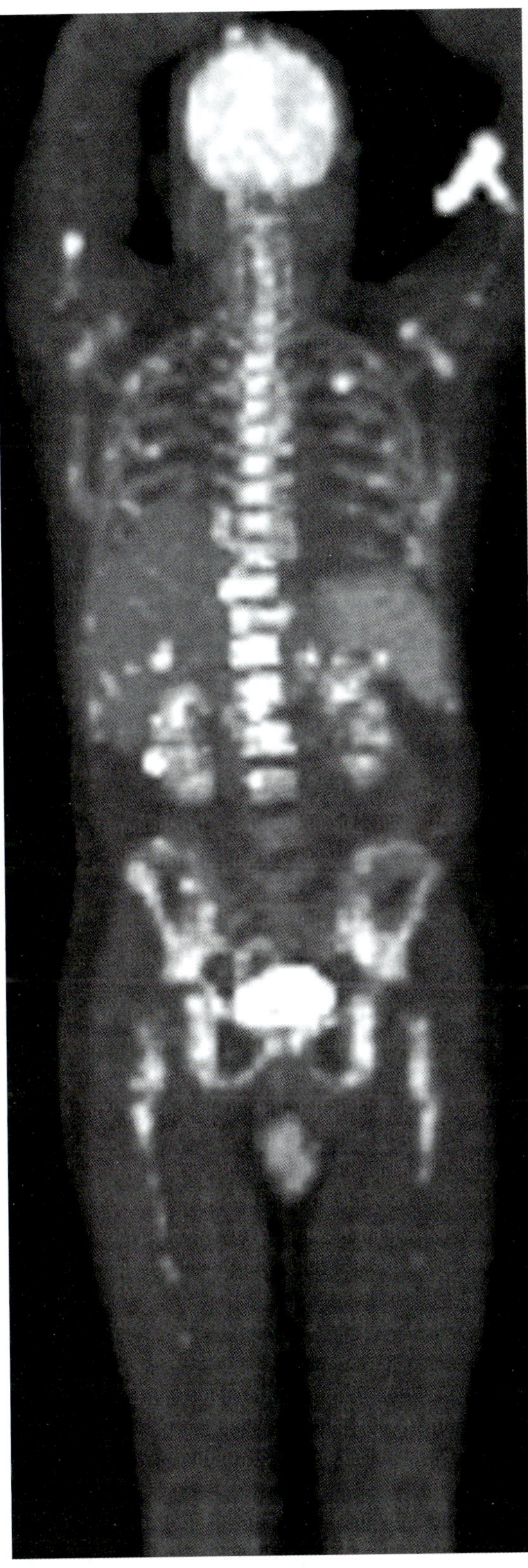

Fig. 21-3 Positron-emission tomography scan showing multiple bone lesions with increased uptake of fluorodeoxyglucose, consistent with active myeloma. There is also extramedullary involvement within the liver, gallbladder, kidney, and pancreas.

Note that patients with MGUS may have symptoms from unrelated conditions that need to be excluded (eg, kidney damage from diabetes or hypertension, hypercalcemia due to parathyroid disorder, or anemia related to other causes). To diagnose MM, the observed end-organ damage (ie, anemia, hypercalcemia, renal failure, or bone lesions) must be thought attributable to the underlying plasma cell disorder.

MONITORING

Once MM is diagnosed, patients require periodic measurements of CBCs, serum creatinine, serum calcium, and M protein levels by SPEP, SFLC, and UPEP to assess treatment response and to monitor for relapse. In patients with oligosecretory myeloma (serum M protein < 1 g/dL and urine M protein < 200 mg/24 hours) and in some patients with nonsecretory myeloma, the serum FLC assay can be used to monitor response to therapy, provided the FLC ratio is abnormal and the level of the involved FLC is ≥ 100 mg/L.[34] In patients with oligosecretory myeloma who have lower levels of FLC and in patients with true nonsecretory myeloma, monitoring is more difficult and requires periodic radiographic studies and bone marrow examinations. Serum and urine tests for monitoring are done monthly during active therapy and once every 3 to 4 months thereafter. Bone marrow studies are repeated if needed to confirm complete response or when clinically indicated to assess relapse. In patients who experience complete response, estimation of minimal residual disease (MRD) using next-generation flow cytometry, or next-generation sequencing provides important prognostic information; however, there are no data yet on using MRD results to guide therapy.[35,36] Response to therapy is assessed using the Revised International Myeloma Working Group uniform response criteria (Table 21-3).[37]

STAGING AND RISK STRATIFICATION

The two traditional methods of staging MM were the Durie-Salmon stage[38] and the International Staging System (ISS).[39] However these staging systems have many limitations, and they do not account for the considerable variation in outcome that is dictated by the underlying cytogenetics of the disease. Patients with del(17p), translocations t(14;16).t(14;20), t(4;14), and Gain (1q) are considered to have high-risk myeloma. Patients who do not have any of these abnormalities—typically those with trisomies or translocations t(11;14) and t(6;14)—are considered to have standard-risk myeloma.[32,40] The presence of concomitant trisomies may ameliorate the adverse prognosis associated with intermediate- and high-risk myeloma.

The Revised International Staging System (RISS) is the current recommended system for MM and incorporates important markers of disease biology, including standard ISS, FISH for high risk features, and LDH, a marker of increased proliferation, to provide a more accurate estimation of prognosis than did prior staging systems (Table 21-4).[41]

KEY POINTS

- The most common presenting symptoms of MM are fatigue and bone pain; other presenting features are hypercalcemia, infection, and acute renal failure.
- When MM is suspected, patients should be tested for the presence of M proteins by SPEP, SIFE, and the serum FLC assay.
- Bone imaging studies and a bone marrow biopsy are required if MM is suspected.
- Patients are staged using the RISS.
- Patients with 17p deletion and translocations t(14;16) and t(14;20) are considered to have high-risk myeloma. Patients with t(4;14) are considered at intermediate risk. Patients with trisomies or translocations t(11;14) and t(6;14) are considered to have standard-risk myeloma.
- The presence of concomitant trisomies ameliorates the adverse prognosis associated with intermediate- and high-risk myeloma.

THERAPEUTIC MANAGEMENT

Table 21-5 provides a list of the most commonly used treatment regimens in MM.[42-54] Table 21-6 provides the results of recent randomized trials with these regimens in MM.[42,47,48,51-59]

INITIAL THERAPY

The overall approach to therapy in patients with newly diagnosed MM is shown in Figure 21-4.[60] The most commonly used regimen in the United States for the treatment of newly diagnosed MM is bortezomib, lenalidomide, and dexamethasone (VRd). The combination of carfilzomib, lenalidomide, and dexamethasone is another initial option, particularly in the high-risk patient population.[61] Initial therapy for myeloma must take into account the eligibility of the patient for ASCT. In general, eligibility for stem cell transplantation is determined by age, performance status, and comorbidities. Age alone is not used in determining transplant eligibility. Patients who are not candidates for ASCT are treated with an induction regimen for 6 to 12 months, followed by lenalidomide, and dexamethasone.[47] Patients who are considered potential candidates for ASCT are first treated with three to four cycles of a triplet regimen, followed by stem cell harvest (Fig 21-4).[32] After stem cell harvest, most patients proceed to ASCT (the early ASCT approach), whereas some may choose to continue the initial treatment regimen and delay ASCT until relapse (the delayed ASCT approach). After initial treatment of transplant and nontransplant patients, ongoing therapy or maintenance is standard.

TREATMENT OF PATIENTS NOT CANDIDATES FOR ASCT

For patients who are not candidates for ASCT, melphalan-based regimens are no longer preferred as first-line therapy. In a randomized trial, lenalidomide and dexamethasone given until progression improved OS in comparison with melphalan, prednisone, and thalidomide (4-year survival rate, 59% and 51%, respectively), leading to the approval of lenalidomide, and dexamethasone as initial therapy for myeloma in the United States and several other countries.[58] In a more recent trial, PFS and OS were superior with VRd compared with lenalidomide, and dexamethasone.[47] The median PFS was 43 months versus 30 months (P = .0018); median OS was 75 months versus 64 months (P = .025). After the results of this trial, VRd is now considered the standard regimen for initial therapy in the United States, except in frail patients, for whom lenalidomide, and dexamethasone remains an option. Bortezomib, cyclophosphamide, and dexamethasone (VCd) and bortezomib, thalidomide, and dexamethasone (VTd) are alternatives to VRd in patients who lack access to lenalidomide and in patients who with acute renal failure due to light-chain cast nephropathy.[45,56] The risk of bortezomib-induced neuropathy can be greatly decreased by using a once-weekly schedule of bortezomib[59,62,63] and a subcutaneous route of administration.[64]

The specific regimen used for initial therapy varies across countries, depending on the availability of lenalidomide. In countries with access to lenalidomide, one reasonable treatment approach is VRd for 12 months followed by lenalidomide, and dexamethasone maintenance for fit patients with standard risk and VRd for 12 months followed by bortezomib-based maintenance for intermediate- and high-risk patients (Fig 21-4). Lenalidomide, and dexamethasone until progression is a reasonable option for frail, older patients and for patients aged ≥ 75 years. Daratumumab regimens have been studied in combination with standard regimens in nontransplant candidates. Daratumumab with VMP was compared with VMP alone. In the daratumumab arm, after the initial induction therapy, daratumumab was continued as a single agent. In this study, the daratumumab arm was associated with a significant improvement in PFS in the entire population. The OS was different between the two groups at the original analysis. In the subset of high-risk patients, there was no difference in PFS.[65] More recently, a combination of daratumumab, lenalidomide, and dexamethasone (DRd) was compared with lenalidomide, and dexamethasone in the same patient population. The PFS was superior for DRd compared with lenalidomide, and dexamethasone. No OS difference was demonstrated.[51] Both Dara VMP and DRd are approved by the US Food and Drug Administration (FDA) for this indication.

TREATMENT OF CANDIDATES FOR ASCT

The overall approach to the initial treatment of patients who are candidates for ASCT is shown in Figure 21-4. Three-drug combinations such as VRd; carfilzomib, lenalidomide, and dexamethasone (KRd); and VTd are the most common regimens used for induction therapy in patients eligible for ASCT.[47,56] VRd was associated with a higher response rate and a greater depth of response compared with lenalidomide, and dexamethasone in one randomized trial.[47] Although this trial was performed in the nontransplantation setting, the data are interpreted

Table 21-3 International Myeloma Working Group Criteria for Response Assessment, Including Criteria for MRD in Multiple Myeloma[37]

Criterion	Definition
Flow MRD-negative	Absence of phenotypically aberrant clonal plasma cells by NGF4 on bone marrow aspirates using the EuroFlow standard operation procedure for MRD detection in MM (or validated equivalent method) with a minimum sensitivity of ≥ 1 in 105 nucleated cells
Sequencing MRD-negative	Absence of clonal plasma cells by NGS on bone marrow aspirates in which presence of a clone is defined as < 2 identical sequencing reads obtained after DNA sequencing of bone marrow aspirates using the Lymphosight platform (or validated equivalent method) with a sensitivity of ≥ 1 in 105 nucleated cells
CR	Negative immunofixation on the serum AND urine AND disappearance of any soft-tissue plasmacytomas AND < 5% plasma cells in bone marrow aspiration
VGPR	Serum and urine M protein detectable by immunofixation but not on electrophoresis OR ≥ 90% reduction in serum M protein PLUS urine M-protein level < 100 mg/24 hour
PR	≥ 50% reduction of serum M protein PLUS reduction in 24-hour urinary M protein by ≥ 90% or to < 200 mg/24 h. If the serum and urine M protein are unmeasurable, a ≥ 50% decrease in the difference between involved and uninvolved FLC levels is required in place of the M-protein criteria
	If serum and urine M protein are unmeasurable, and serum FLC is also unmeasurable, ≥ 50% reduction in plasma cells is required in place of M protein, provided baseline bone marrow plasma cell ≥ 30%
	In addition to the above-listed criteria, if present at baseline, a ≥ 50% reduction in the size (SPD) of soft tissue plasmacytomas is also required
MR	≥ 25% but ≤ 49% reduction of serum M protein AND reduction in 24-h urine M protein by 50% to 89%
	In addition to the above-listed criteria, if present at baseline, a ≥ 50% reduction in the size (SPD) of soft tissue plasmacytomas is also required
SD	(Not recommended for use as an indicator of response; stability of disease is best described by providing the time-to-progression estimates)
	Not meeting criteria for CR, VGPR, PR, MR, or PD
PD[3,4]	Any one or more of the following:
	• Increase of 25% from lowest confirmed response value in one or more of the following:
	▪ Serum M protein (absolute increase must be ≥ 0.5 g/dL)
	▪ Serum M protein increase ≥ 1 g/dL, if the lowest M component was ≥ 5 g/dL
	▪ Urine M protein (absolute increase must be ≥ 200 mg/24 h)
	▪ In patients without measurable serum and urine M protein levels, the difference between involved and uninvolved FLC levels (absolute increase must be > 10 mg/dL)
	▪ In patients without measurable serum and urine M protein levels and without measurable involved FLC levels, bone marrow plasma cell percentage irrespective of baseline status (absolute percent increase must be > 10%)
	• Appearance of a new lesion(s), ≥ 50% increase from nadir in SPD of more than one lesion, or ≥ 50% increase in the greatest diameter of a lesion previously > 1 cm in short axis
	• ≥ 50% increase in circulating plasma cells (minimum of 200/mL) if this is the only measure of disease

NOTE. All response categories except MRD require two consecutive assessments to be made any time before the institution of any new therapy.
Abbreviations: CR, complete response; FLC, free light chain; MM, multiple myeloma; MR minimal response; MRD, minimal residual disease; NGF, next-generation flow cytometry; NGS, next-generation sequencing; PD, progressive disease; PR, partial response; SD, stable disease; SPD, sum of the products of the maximum perpendicular diameter; VGPR, very good partial response.

to apply to pretransplantation induction as well. Thus, VRd is the preferred induction regimen for the treatment of newly diagnosed MM in patients who are candidates for ASCT. However, VCd and VTd remain alternatives if there is lack of access to lenalidomide or in the setting of acute renal failure with light-chain cast nephropathy. In a randomized trial by the ECOG, lenalidomide plus low-dose dexamethasone (40 mg of dexamethasone once a week) was superior to lenalidomide plus high-dose dexamethasone (40 mg of dexamethasone on days 1 to 4, 9 to 12, and 17 to 20) in terms of OS.[42] On the basis of this trial, the use of high-dose dexamethasone is no longer recommended in newly diagnosed MM, and almost all new regimens including VRd and VCd use the once-weekly schedule of dexamethasone.

Stage	Frequency (% of patients)	5-Year Survival Rate (%)
Table 21-4 Revised International Staging System for Multiple Myeloma		
Stage I	28	82
• ISS stage I (serum albumin > 3.5 g/dL, serum β2-microglobulin < 3.5 mg/L) and		
• No high-risk cytogenetics		
• Normal LDH level		
Stage II	62	62
• Neither stage I nor III		
Stage III	10	40
• ISS stage III (serum β2-microglobulin > 5.5 mg/L) and		
• High-risk cytogenetics [t(4;14), t(14;16), or del(17p)] or elevated LDH level		

Abbreviations: ISS, International Staging System; LDH, lactate dehydrogenase. Derived from Palumbo et al.[41]

The use of lenalidomide for more than six cycles can impair collection of peripheral-blood stem cells in some patients when granulocyte colony-stimulating factor (G-CSF) alone is used for stem cell mobilization.[66] Stem cell mobilization in these patients is usually successful with a chemotherapy-containing mobilization regimen such as cyclophosphamide and G-CSF or, with the use of plerixafor, a CXCR4 inhibitor.

Phase II studies show the combination of KRd is highly active in newly diagnosed myeloma.[67] An ongoing randomized trial coordinated by ECOG is testing VRd versus KRd in newly diagnosed myeloma (ClinicalTrial.gov identifier: NCT01863550).

In patients with very aggressive disease (ie, plasma-cell leukemia or extramedullary disease), combination chemotherapy such as bortezomib, dexamethasone, and thalidomide (VDT) plus cisplatin, doxorubicin, cyclophosphamide, and etoposide (PACE) can be used as initial therapy to achieve rapid disease control.[68] Numerous other combinations have been developed, but randomized controlled trials have not shown a clear effect on long-term end points compared with the regimens just discussed.

KEY POINTS

- The preferred regimen for initial therapy of MM is the triplet regimen VRd. Studies comparing KRd and VRd are ongoing.
- VCd and VTd are alternatives, and they are preferred in the setting of acute renal failure with light-chain cast nephropathy.

AUTOLOGOUS STEM CELL TRANSPLANTATION

Although ASCT is not curative for MM, it prolongs median OS by approximately 12 months when compared with conventional chemotherapy.[69,70] The treatment-related mortality rate is very low (1% to 2%), and 40% to 50% of ASCTs can be done entirely on an outpatient basis.[71] Melphalan (at a dose of 200 mg/m^2) is used as the standard conditioning regimen, and trials are underway trying to improve the efficacy of the conditioning regimen. ASCT can be done immediately after initial therapy, or it can be delayed until first relapse. In either case, stem cells must be collected early in the disease course. A randomized trial that used VRd as initial therapy found PFS is superior with early ASCT (median, 50 months *v* 36 months; $P < .001$); OS is similar whether ASCT is performed early (after induction therapy) or late (at first relapse; 4-year OS rate, 83%). It is important to note that 79% of the patients with symptomatic relapse underwent ASCT as part of the treatment. Therefore, this was truly a study of early versus late transplant, not transplant versus no transplant. In general, on the basis of superior PFS, early ASCT is preferred. However, patient and physician preferences play an important role in deciding the timing of ASCT, especially in standard-risk patients. Although some earlier randomized trials showed a benefit with two ASCTs done back to back (tandem ASCT),[72,73] one randomized trial conducted in the United States found no benefit with tandem ASCT in the context of modern therapy.[74]

ALLOGENEIC STEM CELL TRANSPLANTATION

Allogeneic transplantation offers the potential benefit of a graft-versus-myeloma effect. However, conventional myeloablative allogeneic transplantation has a limited role in MM because of high treatment-related mortality rates. One study found a significant OS advantage with ASCT followed by nonmyeloablative allogeneic transplantation compared with ASCT alone.[75,76] However, other trials have not shown such a benefit.[77-81] Although safer, nonmyeloablative transplantation is associated with a greater risk of relapse and has not shown a consistent benefit compared with ASCT alone. Presently, allogeneic transplantation is generally not recommended for the treatment of MM outside of clinical trials.

MAINTENANCE THERAPY

Maintenance therapy with interferon-α, corticosteroids, and thalidomide results in a relatively modest benefit considering the high cost and toxicity of the regimen.[80] Three randomized studies have shown superior PFS with lenalidomide maintenance after ASCT.[81-83] In one trial, a significant OS benefit was found with lenalidomide maintenance therapy,[80] and this was confirmed on a subsequent meta-analysis of the three trials.[84] An increased risk of second cancers was seen in two randomized trials with lenalidomide maintenance (approximately 7% in the lenalidomide group compared with 3% in the placebo group; $P < .01$), and this needs to be discussed with the patient and monitored during follow-up (Table 21-7).[81,82] Lenalidomide maintenance is recommended for patients with standard-risk MM after ASCT. In high-risk patients, the benefit of

Table 21-5 Common Treatment Regimens in Multiple Myeloma

Regimen	Usual Dosing Schedule[a]
Lenalidomide and dexamethasone[42]	Lenalidomide 25 mg PO on days 1-21 every 28 days; dexamethasone 40 mg PO on days 1, 8, 15, and 22; repeated every 4 weeks
Pomalidomide and dexamethasone[43]	Pomalidomide 4 mg PO on days 1-21; dexamethasone 40 mg PO on days 1, 8, 15, and 22; repeated every 4 weeks
Bortezomib, thalidomide, and dexamethasone[b44]	Bortezomib 1.3 mg/m^2 SC on days 1, 8, 15, and 22; thalidomide 100-200 mg PO on days 1-21; dexamethasone 20 mg PO on day of and day after bortezomib (or 40 mg on days 1, 8, 15, and 22); repeated every 4 weeks for 4 cycles as pretransplantation induction therapy
Bortezomib, cyclophosphamide, and dexamethasone[b43]	Cyclophosphamide 300 mg/m^2 PO on days 1, 8, 15, and 22; bortezomib 1.3 mg/m^2 SC on days 1, 8, 15, and 22; dexamethasone 40 mg PO on days on days 1, 8, 15, and 22; repeated every 4 weeks
Bortezomib, lenalidomide, and dexamethasone[b47]	Bortezomib 1.3 mg/m^2 SC on days 1, 8, and 15; lenalidomide 25 mg PO on days 1-14; dexamethasone 20 mg PO on day of and day after bortezomib (or 40 mg on days 1, 8, 15, and 22); repeated every 3 weeks[c]
Carfilzomib, lenalidomide, and dexamethasone[48]	Carfilzomib 20 mg/m^2 (cycle 1) for dose 1, two if tolerated, then increase to 27 mg/m^2 on days 8, 9, 15, and 16 every 28 days, and 27 mg/ m^2 (subsequent cycles) IV on days 1, 2, 8, 9, 15, and 16; lenalidomide 25 mg PO on days 1-21; dexamethasone 20 mg PO on day of and day after carfilzomib (or 40 mg on days 1, 8, 15, and 22); repeated every 4 weeks
Carfilzomib, cyclophosphamide, and dexamethasone[d49]	Carfilzomib 20 mg/m^2 (cycle 1) and 36 mg/m^2 (subsequent cycles) IV on days 1, 2, 8, 9, 15, and 16; cyclophosphamide 300 mg/m^2 PO or IV on days 1, 8, and 15; dexamethasone 40 mg PO on days on days 1, 8, and 15; repeated every 4 weeks (not FDA approved or in the NCCN guidelines and may be denied by insurance)
Carfilzomib, pomalidomide, and dexamethasone[55]	Carfilzomib 20 mg/m^2 (cycle 1) and 27 mg/ m^2 (subsequent cycles) IV on days 1, 2, 8, 9, 15, and 16; pomalidomide 4 mg PO on days 1-21; dexamethasone 40 mg PO on days 1, 8, and 15; repeated every 4 weeks (not FDA approved or on the NCCN guidelines and may be denied by insurance)
Daratumumab, lenalidomide, and dexamethasone[51]	Daratumumab 16 mg/kg IV weekly for 8 weeks, then every 2 weeks for 4 months, and then once a month; lenalidomide 25 mg PO on days 1-21; dexamethasone 40 mg PO on days 1, 8, 15, and 22; lenalidomide, dexamethasone repeated on usual schedule every 4 weeks
Elotuzumab, lenalidomide, and dexamethasone[52]	Elotuzumab 10 mg/kg IV weekly for 8 weeks and then every 2 weeks; lenalidomide 25 mg PO on days 1-21; dexamethasone 40 mg PO on days 1, 8, 15, and 22; lenalidomide, dexamethasone repeated on usual schedule every 4 weeks
Ixazomib, lenalidomide, and dexamethasone[53]	Ixazomib 4 mg PO on days 1, 8, and 15; enalidomide 25 mg PO on days 1-21; dexamethasone 40 mg PO on days 1, 8, 15, and 22; repeated every 4 weeks
Daratumumab, bortezomib, and dexamethasone[b54]	Daratumumab 16 mg/kg IV weekly for 8 weeks, then every 2 weeks for 4 months, and then once a month; bortezomib 1.3 mg/m^2 SC on days 1, 8, 15, and 22; dexamethasone 20 mg PO on day of and day after bortezomib (or 40 mg on days 1, 8, 15, and 22; bortezomib and dexamethasone repeated on usual schedule every 4 weeks
Panobinostat and bortezomib[b60]	Panobinostat 20 mg PO three times a week for 2 weeks; bortezomib 1.3 mg/m^2 on days 1, 8, and 15; repeated every 3 weeks

Abbreviations: FDA, Food and Drug Administration; IV, intravenously; NCCN, National Comprehensive Cancer Network; PO, by mouth; SC, subcutaneously.
[a]All doses need to be adjusted for performance status, renal function, blood counts, and other toxic effects.
[b]Doses of dexamethasone and/or bortezomib were reduced on the basis of subsequent data showing lower toxicity and similar efficacy with reduced doses.
[c]Omit day 15 dose if counts are low or when the regimen is used as maintenance therapy; When used as maintenance therapy for high-risk patients, lenalidomide dose may be decreased to 10-15 mg/d, and delays can be instituted between cycles, as done in total therapy protocols.
[d]Dosing based on trial in patients with newly diagnosed disease. In relapsed patients, cycle 2 carfilzomib dose is 27 mg/m^2, consistent with approval summary.
Permission to reuse given by S. V. Rajkumar (Am J Hematol 91:720-734, 2016. PMID: 27291302).

lenalidomide maintenance was shown in the MRC XI trial. Patients with high-risk disease do benefit from lenalidomide maintenance compared with no maintenance, but the magnitude of that benefit is less.[85] Bortezomib maintenance (administered twice a month) after ASCT has also shown benefit and may be considered for patients with high- or intermediate-risk cytogenetics.[86] Ixazomib, an oral proteasome inhibitor, has recently been shown to improve PFS compared with placebo in the posttransplant setting. The PFS was improved from 21.3 months in the placebo group to 26.5 months in the ixaxomib group. At 31 months median follow-up, there is no difference in OS. In addition, the treatment was well tolerated

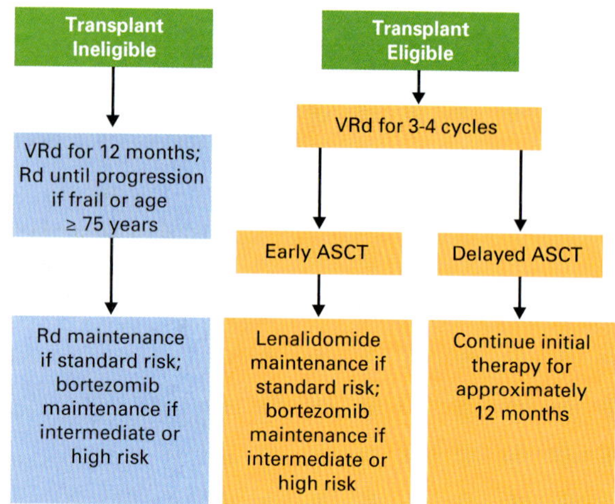

Fig. 21-4 Treatment approach for patients with newly diagnosed myeloma.

Abbreviations: ASCT, autologous stem-cell transplantation; CR, complete response; Rd, lenalidomide plus low-dose dexamethasone; VGPR, very good partial response; VRd, bortezomib, lenalidomide, and dexamethasone.

with no increase in second primary malignancies.[87] Ixazomib as a single agent as maintenance therapy is not FDA approved and its specific role as maintenance remains unclear.

KEY POINTS

- Patients considered potential candidates for ASCT are typically treated with three to four cycles of VRd (although other regimens such as VCd or VDT can also be used), followed by a stem cell harvest. After stem cell harvest, patients can either proceed to early ASCT or continue initial treatment regimen and delay ASCT until relapse.
- After ASCT, patients receive maintenance therapy with lenalidomide (standard risk) or bortezomib (high-risk).

TREATMENT OF RELAPSED DISEASE

Almost all patients with MM eventually experience relapse, and with each relapse, the remission duration decreases progressively.[88-90] In general, patients can be retreated with regimens that have been effective in the past if the initial remission duration was longer than 6 months. Alternatively, regimens that contain active drugs that the patient has not received before can also be tried (Table 21-5).

Panobinostat and elotuzumab lack single-agent activity in MM but provide clinical benefit in combination with other active agents; in contrast, the other drugs listed have a single-agent activity of approximately 25% in relapsed disease. In recent randomized trials, triplet combinations containing these new drugs improved response rates and prolonged PFS compared with backbone doublet regimens (Table 21-6). However, the newer triplet regimens have not been compared head-to-head in randomized trials, so the choice of a specific regimen at the time of relapse is based on many factors, such as response to prior therapy, aggressiveness of the relapse, patient characteristics, ease of use, and cost.

Based on the effect size seen in randomized trials, reasonable options for the treatment of first relapse are DRd for patients whose disease is not refractory to lenalidomide (defined as those who experience a relapse off-therapy or while receiving small doses of single-agent lenalidomide) and daratumumab, bortezomib, and dexamethasone for patients whose disease is refractory to lenalidomide.[91] Alternatives to the treatment of first and subsequent relapse include the regimens listed in Table 21-6. Carfilzomib once weekly was compared with twice weekly dosing in patients with relapsed disease. The median PFS was improved with the once weekly dosing at 11.2 months versus 7.6 months for the twice-weekly dosing. Toxicity was similar between the two arms. Combination studies in the upfront and relapsed setting have used the twice weekly dosing strategy and studies are ongoing to assess the optimal dose of weekly carfilzomib in multiple combinations.

Other combinations that have shown activity in phase II trials incorporate pomalidomide in place of lenalidomide and include regimens such as carfilzomib, pomalidomide, and dexamethasone and daratumumab, pomalidomide, and dexamethasone. The combination of elotuzumab, pomalidomide, and dexamethasone was compared with pomalidomide and dexamethasone in patients with relapsed and refractory disease. The three-drug combination had a superior PFS of 10.3 months compared with 4.7 months in the two-drug combination.

Patients with relapsed refractory myeloma should also be considered for clinical trials. Other investigational agents with single-agent activity in myeloma include marizomib and oprozomib (proteasome inhibitors), isatuximab (a monoclonal antibody to CD38), venetoclax (a Bcl-2 inhibitor), and selinexor (an XPO-1 inhibitor).[92] Cellular therapy using chimeric antigen receptor T cells and antibody-drug conjugates targeting the B-cell maturation antigen are also showing promise in clinical trials. Checkpoint inhibition remains investigational in myeloma. There is little single-agent activity and two trials in combination with lenalidomide and pomalidomide were ended early secondary to increased mortality rates.

In patients with extramedullary plasmacytomas or plasma cell leukemia, multidrug regimens such as VDT-PACE for 1 to 2 months may be used in an attempt to gain better disease control, but they are associated with greater toxicity. A second ASCT is feasible, although remission durations are approximately 50% of what was achieved with the first ASCT. Because there have been no randomized trials, a second ASCT is used in patients who have had a reasonable duration of remission with the first ASCT. Thus, patients who obtain a remission duration of longer than 36 months with maintenance therapy (or longer than 18 months without maintenance therapy) after the first ASCT are potential candidates for a second ASCT as salvage therapy.

KEY POINTS

- Several triplet combinations are effective for the treatment of relapsed myeloma.
- Daratumumab (targeting CD38) and elotuzumab (targeting SLAMF7) are the first monoclonal antibodies approved for the treatment of relapsed myeloma.

TREATMENT OF COMPLICATIONS AND PALLIATIVE CARE

TREATMENT OF DISEASE COMPLICATIONS

Patients with MM should receive bisphosphonates (pamidronate or zoledronic acid) once per month for 1 to 2 years to prevent bone disease.[92-95] In a randomized trial, OS was improved in MM with the use of zoledronic acid as prophylactic therapy.[96] Results of a more recent randomized trial suggest a reduced frequency of administration (once every 3 months) may be as effective as monthly administration.[97] Preliminary data

Table 21-6 Results of Selected Randomized Trials in Multiple Myeloma[1]

Myeloma Type and Reference	Regimen	No. of Patients	Overall Response Rate (%)	CR Plus VGPR (%)	Median PFS (months)	PFS *P*	OS[a]	OS *P*
Newly diagnosed myeloma								
Rajkumar et al.[42]	RD	223	81	50	19.1		75% at 3 years	
	Rd	222	70	40	25.3	.026	74% at 3 years	.47
Durie et al.[61]	Rd	261	72	32	31.0	.002	75 (median months)	.025
	VRd	264	82	43	43.0		64 (median months)	
Moreau et al.[56]	VCD	170	84	66	NA		NA	NA
	VTD	170	92	77	NA	NA	NA	
Attal et al.[57]	VRd	350	NA	46% CR	NR; 48% at 3 years		88% at 3 years	.25
	VRd-ASCT	350	NA	58% CR	NR; 61% at 3 years	< .001	88% at 3 years	
Relapsed myeloma								
Lonial et al.[52]	Rd	325	66	28	14.9		NA	NA
	ERd	321	79	33	19.4	< .001	NA	
Stewart et al.[48]	Rd	396	67	14	17.6		65% at 2 years	.04
	KRd	396	87	32	26.3	.0001	73% at 2 years	
Moreau et al.[53]	Rd	362	72	7	14.7		NA	NA
	IRd	360	78	12	20.6	.01	NA	
Dimopoulos et al.[51]	Rd	283	76	44	18.4	<.001	87% at 1 year	NS
	DRd	286	93	76	NR		92% at 1 year	
San-Miguel et al.[55]	Vd	381	55	6	8.1		30.4 (median months)	.26
	Pano-Vd	387	61	11	12.0	<.0001	33.7 (median months)	
Palumbo et al.[54]	Vd	247	63	29	7.2	<.001	70% at 1 year	.30
	DVd	251	83	59	NR		80% at 1 year	

Abbreviations: ASCT, autologous stem cell transplantation; CR, complete response; DRd, daratumumab, lenalidomide, dexamethasone; DVd, daratumumab, bortezomib, dexamethasone; ERd, elotuzumab, lenalidomide, dexamethasone; IRd, ixazomib, lenalidomide, dexamethasone; KRd, carfilzomib, lenalidomide, dexamethasone; NA, not available; NR, not reached; NS, not significant; OS, overall survival; Pano-Vd, panobinostat, bortezomib, dexamethasone; PFS, progression-free survival; Rd, lenalidomide plus low-dose dexamethasone; RD, lenalidomide plus high-dose dexamethasone; VCD, bortezomib, cyclophosphamide, dexamethasone; Vd, bortezomib, dexamethasone; VGPR, very good partial response; VRd, bortezomib, lenalidomide, dexamethasone; VTD, bortezomib, thalidomide, dexamethasone.

[a]Estimated from survival curves when not reported.

Permission to reuse given by S. V. Rajkumar.

Table 21-7 **Results of Randomized Phase III Trials of Lenalidomide Maintenance in Myeloma after Autologous Stem Cell Transplantation**

Reference	Regimen	No. of Patients	Median PFS (months)	PFS *P*	3-Year OS Rate (%)[a]	Median PS (months)	OS *P*	Second Cancer (%)[b]	Second Cancer Incidence *P*
McCarthy et al.[80]	Placebo;	229	27	< .001	80	NR	.03[c]	2.6	.008
	lenalidomide maintenance	231	46		88	NR		7.7	
Attal et al.[81]	Placebo;	307	23	< .001	84	NR	.70	3.0	.002
	lenalidomide maintenance	307	41		80	NR		7.5	

Abbreviations: NR, not reported; OS, overall survival; PFS, progression-free survival.

[a]Estimated from survival curves when not reported.

[b]Excludes nonmelanoma skin cancers.

[c]Derived from Cox proportional hazard models; it is not clear whether these were two-tailed or whether adjustment was made for covariates.

Permission to reuse given by S. V. Rajkumar (Rajkumar SV: Haematological cancer: Lenalidomide maintenance–perils of a premature denouement. Nat Rev Clin Oncol 9:372-374, 2012. PMID: 22665364).

suggest denosumab is also effective in the prevention of bone disease in MM and has shown a benefit in PFS compared with zoledronic acid in a randomized controlled trial. However, more data are needed to determine the optimal patient population that may benefit from this drug.[98] A large, blinded, randomized study demonstrated that denosumab was noninferior to zoledronic acid for the prevention of skeletal-related events. Adverse events were similar except there was more renal toxicity with zoledronic acid and more hypocalcemia with denosumab. Rates of osteonecrosis of the jaw were similar.[99] Calcium supplementation and daily vitamin D supplementation are needed for patients receiving bisphosphonates. Surgical fixation of fractures or impending fractures of long bones can be performed as needed. Palliative local radiation should be limited to patients with disabling pain that has not responded to analgesics and systemic therapy. Vertebroplasty and kyphoplasty may be useful to decrease pain.[100] Severe hypercalcemia can develop in some patients with MM. This is a medical emergency and requires treatment with hydration, corticosteroids, calcitonin, and either pamidronate (60 to 90 mg intravenously [IV] over 2 to 4 hours) or zoledronic acid (4 mg IV over 15 minutes).

Renal failure is common in MM and can be multifactorial. Volume depletion, nonsteroidal anti-inflammatory agents, infection, hypercalcemia, and radiographic contrast media may also contribute to renal failure. The most common cause of acute renal failure is light-chain cast nephropathy, which requires prompt therapy to lower serum light-chain levels. The role of plasmapheresis is controversial, but it may be incorporated in conjunction with VCd to treat patients with myeloma who have proven or suspected acute light-chain cast nephropathy with a goal of reducing the involved FLC level to < 500 mg/L.[101,102]

Other disease-related complications include anemia, infections, and hyperviscosity syndrome. Anemia usually improves with treatment of the underlying MM, but some patients may require transfusions or erythropoietin. IV gamma globulin is indicated only if patients have recurrent serious infections associated with severe hypogammaglobulinemia. Hyperviscosity syndrome manifests with symptoms such as epistaxis, mucosal bleeding, headache, and blurred vision. Hyperviscosity syndrome requires emergent plasmapheresis.

MANAGEMENT OF DRUG TOXICITY

The major adverse effects with thalidomide are sedation, constipation, and peripheral neuropathy. In contrast, the major adverse effects of lenalidomide are anemia, neutropenia, and thrombocytopenia. Both drugs cause fatigue. Because of the risk of teratogenicity, the use of any of the immunomodulatory agents (ie, thalidomide, lenalidomide, and pomalidomide) in pregnant patients is absolutely contraindicated. Furthermore, to prevent teratogenicity, there are strict requirements that must be met before these drugs can be prescribed. Patients receiving thalidomide, lenalidomide, and pomalidomide are also at significant risk of venous and arterial thrombotic events and require thromboprophylaxis with aspirin, low-molecular-weight heparin, or warfarin.[103,104] Thalidomide, lenalidomide, and pomalidomide can cause a skin rash that can be serious in a small proportion of patients. Medications such as sulfonamides and allopurinol may increase the risk and severity of skin toxicity and should be avoided if possible. Treatment with thalidomide, lenalidomide, and pomalidomide can lead to thyroiditis and subsequent hypothyroidism. Thyroid-function tests should be performed at baseline and every 3 to 4 months thereafter while a patient is receiving this therapy. Severe diarrhea can develop in approximately 10% to 15% of patients taking lenalidomide for a prolonged time. The treatment is cessation of therapy, standard antimotility agents, and a bile-acid sequestrant such as colestipol.

The major adverse effects of bortezomib are GI toxicity, thrombocytopenia, and neuropathy. The best way to reduce the risk of neuropathy is to use bortezomib in the once-weekly schedule instead of the twice-weekly schedule, and administer the medication subcutaneously instead of IV. Patients who are being treated with bortezomib (and other proteasome inhibitors) are at high risk for reactivation of herpes zoster, and routine prophylaxis with acyclovir is recommended. Neuropathy is less of a risk with ixazomib and carfilzomib compared with bortezomib. The main adverse effects of ixazomib are nausea and diarrhea. Major adverse effects of carfilzomib include fatigue, nausea, cytopenias, and shortness of breath.[105] Carfilzomib can also cause significant cardiac dysfunction in approximately 5% of patients; this must be considered carefully in the treatment of elderly patients.

The main adverse reactions with daratumumab and elotuzumab are infusion-related reactions, which are mostly seen with the first dose. With daratumumab, approximately 50% of patients may have a grade 3 or higher infusion reaction with the first dose; but this decreases to < 5% with subsequent doses. Montelukast should be given prior to the first dose of daratumumab to reduce infusion reactions.

Because steroids play a major role in the treatment of MM, patients often have major steroid-related adverse effects. These are best prevented by using the lowest possible dose of steroids. During the first few months of therapy, dexamethasone 40 mg once a week is sufficient.[42] Some patients require a lower dose even at the outset. After the first few months, an attempt should be made to rapidly reduce the dose of steroids. We typically recommend ongoing *Pneumocystis jirovecii* pneumonia prophylaxis for patients receiving chronic steroid treatment.

Bisphosphonate therapy is associated with a risk of osteonecrosis of the jaw, and dental hygiene should be assessed prior to initiation of bisphosphonate therapy. Other drug-induced complications include myelodysplastic syndrome and a risk of second primary malignancies.

KEY POINTS

- Patients with MM should receive bisphosphonates prophylactically to prevent skeletal-related events.
- Severe hypercalcemia is a medical emergency and requires treatment with hydration, corticosteroids, and IV administration of bisphosphonates.
- The most common cause of acute renal failure is light-chain cast nephropathy, which requires prompt therapy to lower serum light-chain levels.
- Patients receiving thalidomide, lenalidomide, and pomalidomide are at significant risk for venous and arterial thrombotic events and require routine thromboprophylaxis.
- The best way to reduce the risk of neuropathy is to use bortezomib in the once-weekly schedule instead of the twice-weekly schedule, and administer subcutaneously instead of IV.
- The standard dose of steroids to be used in myeloma therapy usually should not exceed dexamethasone 40 mg once per week (or equivalent) unless there is an emergent need.

RELATED DISORDERS

MONOCLONAL GAMMOPATHY OF UNDETERMINED SIGNIFICANCE

MGUS is a premalignant precursor of MM.[17,18] It is defined by a serum M protein concentration< 3 g/dL, < 10% clonal plasma cells in the bone marrow, and absence of lytic bone lesions, anemia, hypercalcemia, and renal insufficiency that can be attributed to a plasma cell disorder.[106] The three subtypes of MGUS are non-IgM MGUS, IgM MGUS, and light-chain MGUS (Table 21-1). MGUS is present in > 3% to 4% of the population older than age 50 years.[17] The risk of MGUS is significantly higher in the black population compared with the white population.[107,108] The risk of MGUS is also higher in first-degree relatives of patients with MGUS or MM[109] and in those exposed to certain pesticides.[110]

MGUS is asymptomatic, but in a small subset of patients, it may be associated with sensorimotor peripheral neuropathy (MGUS neuropathy), membranoproliferative glomerulonephritis, lichen myxedematosus (papular mucinosis, scleromyxedema), pyoderma gangrenosum, or necrobiotic xanthogranuloma. The main clinical significance of MGUS is its lifelong risk of transformation to MM or related malignancy at a rate of 1% per year.[18] The size and type of the M protein at diagnosis of MGUS and an abnormal serum FLC ratio are prognostic factors for progression (Table 21-8).[111] The baseline bone marrow evaluation can be deferred in patients with low-risk MGUS and patients with IgM MGUS who have a normal FLC ratio and no anemia, lymphadenopathy, or organomegaly.[112] Similarly, bone imaging at diagnosis can be deferred in patients with low-risk MGUS or IgM MGUS if there are no clinical concerns for MM or related disorder.

There is no treatment needed for MGUS. Patients with low-risk MGUS should be followed at 6 months and subsequently at the time of symptoms that may indicate progression. All other patients with MGUS should be followed at 6 months and, if stable, yearly thereafter.

SOLITARY PLASMACYTOMA

Solitary plasmacytoma is an early-stage plasma cell malignancy that is in between MGUS/SMM and MM along the spectrum of plasma cell disorders. It is defined by the presence of a single biopsy-proven plasmacytoma (bony or extramedullary) and a normal bone marrow examination.[106] An M protein may be present in serum or urine at diagnosis, but usually disappears with therapy. Treatment consists of radiation therapy (40 to 50 Gy) to the involved site. Patients with an apparent solitary plasmacytoma who have limited (< 10%) clonal marrow involvement are considered to

Table 21-8 **Risk-Stratification Model to Predict Progression of Monoclonal Gammopathy of Undetermined Significance to Myeloma or Related Disorders**[111]

Risk Group	No. of Patients	Relative Risk	Absolute Risk of Progression at 20 Years (%)	Absolute Risk of Progression at 20 Years Accounting for Death as a Competing Risk (%)
Low risk (serum M protein < 1.5 g/dL, IgG subtype, normal FLC ratio (0.26-1.65)	449	1	5	2
Low-intermediate risk (any one factor abnormal)	420	5.4	21	10
High-intermediate risk (any two factors abnormal)	226	10.1	37	18
High risk (all three factors abnormal)	53	20.8	58	27

Abbreviation: FLC, free light chain.
Permission to reuse given by S. V. Rajkumar.[111]

have solitary plasmacytoma with minimal marrow involvement (Table 21-1); these patients are also treated similarly to patients with solitary plasmacytoma. The risk of recurrence or progression to myeloma within 3 years is approximately 10% in patients with solitary plasmacytoma versus 20% to 60% in patients with solitary plasmacytoma and minimal marrow involvement.

PLASMA CELL LEUKEMIA

Plasma cell leukemia is an aggressive form of MM characterized by circulating clonal plasma cells in the peripheral blood and extramedullary disease. Treatment of plasma cell leukemia is unsatisfactory. Initial treatment with VRd or a multidrug regimen such as VDT-PACE for two to three cycles followed by ASCT and subsequent maintenance therapy is a reasonable strategy.

IMMUNOGLOBULIN AL AMYLOIDOSIS

Amyloid is a proteinaceous substance that consists of rigid, linear, nonbranching fibrils, 7.5 to 10 nm in width, aggregated in a beta-pleated sheet conformation.[113] It is detected on Congo red staining based on the classic apple-green birefringence. The several types of amyloidosis are classified on the basis of the major protein component of the amyloid. In AL amyloidosis, the fibrils consist of the variable portion of a monoclonal light chain. AL amyloidosis is an infrequent consequence of clonal plasma cell disorders and may be seen with MGUS, SMM, or MM (Table 21-1). All patients with a monoclonal gammopathy should be screened via standard laboratory evaluation and careful history and physical for evidence of amyloidosis if they have proteinuria, diastolic dysfunction, autonomic dysfunction, or neuropathy. It is a systemic disease that can affect numerous organs such as the tongue (macroglossia), heart, liver, kidney, peripheral nerves, and lungs. The standard treatment is a bortezomib-based regimen (eg, VCd) for approximately 1 year. Eligible patients can also be considered for ASCT.[114] To obtain an accurate diagnosis of AL amyloidosis in contrast to TTR or others, mass spectrometry is needed.

WALDENSTRÖM MACROGLOBULINEMIA

Waldenström macroglobulinemia is a malignancy of plasma cells that have not yet undergone switch recombination.[115] It might better be considered a lymphoproliferative disorder pathologically and clinically similar to low-grade lymphomas, in which an IgM paraprotein is present. The neoplastic cells in Waldenström macroglobulinemia secrete IgM M protein and have a morphologic appearance that is in between lymphocytes and true plasma cells, commonly referred to as "lymphoplasmacytic." The disease definition requires presence of an IgM M protein, ≥ 10% bone marrow involvement, and a typical immunophenotype (eg, surface IgM+, CD10−, CD19+, CD20+, CD23−) that would exclude other lymphoproliferative disorders (Table 21-1).[106] Most patients with Waldenström macroglobulinemia have a recurrent mutation of the *MYD88* gene (MYD88 L265P).[116] The main symptoms are weakness, fatigue, and hyperviscosity. Unlike in MM, lytic bone lesions are not seen. Indications for therapy include symptomatic anemia, hyperviscosity, organomegaly, or other cytopenias. Initial treatment is typically with ibrutinib,[116] bendamustine plus rituximab, or dexamethasone, rituximab, and cyclophosphamide.[117,118] In selected patients with limited disease, single-agent rituximab may be an option, but there is a risk of a tumor flare if single-agent rituximab is used, resulting in a rapid rise in IgM levels. Therefore, combination therapy is preferred for patients with high IgM monoclonal protein levels. Other active regimens for the treatment of Waldenström macroglobulinemia include bortezomib, rituximab, and dexamethasone; cladribine; or fludarabine alone or in combination with rituximab; and lenalidomide, and dexamethasone. Ibrutinib has shown remarkable activity in Waldenström macroglobulinemia and is rapidly becoming a preferred agent for the treatment of the disease.[119]

POEMS SYNDROME

This syndrome is characterized by polyneuropathy, organomegaly, endocrinopathy, M protein, and skin changes (POEMS).[120] Patients with POEMS syndrome usually have osteosclerotic bone lesions or Castleman disease (a rare polyclonal lymphoproliferative disorder). The major clinical problem in POEMS is a severe, chronic inflammatory-demyelinating polyneuropathy with predominantly motor features. Other abnormalities seen in POEMS syndrome are listed in Table 21-1. If the osteosclerotic lesions are in a limited area, radiation therapy is the treatment of choice. If there are widespread osteosclerotic lesions, treatment is similar to that for MM.

KEY POINTS

- MGUS can progress to myeloma or a related malignancy at a rate of 1% per year.
- The risk of progression to myeloma or related plasma cell disorder in SMM is 10-fold higher than with MGUS.
- Solitary plasmacytoma is defined by the presence of a single biopsy-proven plasmacytoma (bony or extramedullary) and a normal bone marrow.

examination. Treatment consists of radiation therapy (40 to 50 Gy) to the involved site.

- Plasma cell leukemia is an aggressive form of myeloma characterized by circulating clonal plasma cells in the peripheral blood and extramedullary disease.
- AL amyloidosis is a systemic plasma cell proliferative disorder that can affect numerous organs such as the kidney, heart, liver, GI system, and peripheral nerves.
- Waldenström macroglobulinemia is a malignancy of plasma cells that secrete IgM M protein and is treated with a combination of lymphoma and myeloma therapies.
- POEMS syndrome is a rare plasma cell disorder characterized by polyneuropathy, organomegaly, endocrinopathy, M protein, and skin changes.

Acknowledgment

The following authors are acknowledged and graciously thanked for their contribution to prior versions of this chapter: Bruce D. Cheson, MD, FASCO; Constantine S. Mitsiades, MD, PhD; Jacob Laubach, MD, MPP; Kenneth C. Anderson, MD, FASCO; Paul G. Richardson, MD; and S. Vincent Rajkumar, MD.

Global Perspective: Multiple Myeloma

María-Victoria Mateos, MD, PhD (University Hospital of Salamanca/IBSAL, Salamanca, Spain)

EPIDEMIOLOGY

MM usually affects the older patient population and the median age of patients is > 65 years; < 1% of cases are diagnosed in people younger than 35 years.

A systematic analysis of the global burden of MM revealed that in 2016, there were 138,509 incident cases, with an age-standardized incidence of 2.1 per 100,000 persons. MM was responsible for 98,437 deaths globally, with an age-standardized death rate of 1.5 per 100,000 persons. The three regions with the highest age-standardized incidence were Australasia (5.8), high-income North America (5.2), and Western Europe (4.6).

Of note, from 1990 to 2016, the rate of MM incidence increased by 126% and the largest increase was seen in middle-income countries and especially in East Asia (namely, China, North Korea, and Taiwan). The main reasons for the increase were a rise in age-specific incidence rates, aging population, and population growth. Moreover, epidemiologists believe there will be an increase in the number of diagnosed prevalent cases of MM in eight relevant countries, including the United States, France, Germany, Italy, Spain, the United Kingdom, Japan, and urban China.[121]

MM is slightly more common in men than in women and is twice as common in black people in the United States compared with white people. Recent studies have found significant and increasing racial disparities in OS and the limited access to novel therapies have been considered partly responsible for the lower survival in blacks. However, a recent study investigating the impact of racial disparities in outcome in a large series of US patients with MM with equal access to health care found, surprisingly, the survival for black patients with myeloma was longer than for whites, especially among those younger than 65 years, and equal for those older than 65 years. This finding raises an important question about race-related biologic and genomic differences in the disease process, which could influence the diagnostic, prevention, and therapeutic approaches.[122]

All MM proceeds from a premalignant stage called MGUS or SMM. MGUS is frequently detected in the population older than 50 years (3%) and the risk of progression to myeloma is uniform and low at a rate of 1% per year. The risk of progression to MM for patients with SMM is not uniform and the progression rate is 10% per year during the first 5 years, 3% per year during the following 5 years, and 1% later on. The diagnosis of both premalignant stages of MM is increasing because the detection is usually done in routine analysis, and more frequently is performed in middle- and high-income countries. Their identification implies a follow-up for patients with MGUS and those with SMM, especially those at low and intermediate risk of progression to MM, can result in early detection of any myeloma-defining event before overt symptoms are present. SMM at high risk of progression to MM benefits from early treatment as has been demonstrated in two phase III clinical trials with the immunomodulatory drug lenalidomide.[123]

RISK FACTORS AND PATHOPHYSIOLOGY

From the epidemiologic point of view, environmental risk factors have also been implicated in increasing MM risk, including obesity, immune dysfunction (including autoimmune disease, HIV, and transplantation), and agricultural or industrial exposure to chemicals, pesticides, or radiation. A key hypothesis addressed in numerous studies is that genetic variation governing individual response to environmental exposures may mediate some of the familial aggregation seen in MM. The descriptions of families with more than one case of MM support the suggestion that there is an underlying genetic predisposition with an increased relative risk (RR) of developing MM for first-degree relatives (RR, 2.1; 95% CI, 1.6 to 2.9) and of developing MGUS (RR, 2.1; 95% CI, 1.5 to 3.1).

Most patients with MM present in the clinic with common features like plasma-cell bone marrow infiltration, and M-component and myeloma-related symptoms; however, MM is not a single disease but multiple diseases. In 2011, the sequencing of the myeloma genome failed to identify a specific defect, although a wide range of molecular abnormalities was found. In addition, multiple different subclones are identified at diagnosis that can vary across the different stages of the disease and are influenced by the sensitivity or resistance to the different drugs. Mutations in myeloma are complex and the median missense mutational load is approximately 60 per patient. The myeloma genome has fewer mutations compared with those observed in other carcinogen-induced tumors such as melanoma and lung cancer.

Despite this complex heterogeneity, there is an accepted risk-stratification approach based first on the identification of important abnormalities by FISH, such as gain 1q, del 17p, and t(4;14), that, when combined with other markers, such as albumin, β2-microglobulin, and LDH, can be used as prognostic markers. Gene expression profile can also identify specific signatures predicting outcomes. However, the availability of all these assessments in routine practice is not uniform and is very limited in low-income countries.[124]

TREATMENT

The complexity observed in MM justifies, at least in part, the drug combinations used as part of MM treatment. The treatment of MM has changed dramatically in the past decade with the introduction of new drugs into therapeutic strategies in the frontline and relapsed settings. With the availability of at least six different classes of agents (ie, alkylators, steroids, proteasome inhibitors, immunomodulatory agents, histone deacetylase inhibitors, and monoclonal antibodies) that can be combined in doublet, triplet, or even quadruplet regimens and used together with high-dose therapy and ASCT, the choice of the optimal strategy at diagnosis and at relapse represents a challenge for physicians. Moreover, as a result of the development of new techniques, such as next-generation sequencing, next-generation flow cytometry, or PET-CT, MRD assessment is becoming widely available and might affect therapeutic algorithms in the near future. This is one of the reasons for the development of guidelines for helping physicians who treat patients with MM. There are two main international guidelines supported by the European Society for Medical Oncology (ESMO)[125] and the National Comprehensive Cancer Network (NCCN,)[126] and ASCO and Cancer Care Ontario have recently published evidence-based guideline recommendations.[127] All of them are not completely identical, but they are similar in principle.

Although these guidelines are evidence based and have the goal of harmonizing the treatment of patients with MM, the affordability of the different drug-based combinations and assessments differs worldwide and patients treated in low-resource settings are, unfortunately, receiving suboptimal combinations and are evaluated with obsolete techniques with an impact on outcome that would require a detailed analysis to consider crucial actions.

In developed countries, the approach to treat patients with newly diagnosed MM is homogeneous, and the first step is to identify if the patient is eligible for a transplantation. Whereas in Europe all patients younger than 65 years proceed to transplant after four to six induction cycles, in the US, the patient's preferences, as well as their biologic age, are mainly considered; as a result, the question of possibly deferring the transplant at relapse is a topic of debate. Patients receiving optimal induction regimens based on three-drug combinations plus a monoclonal antibody who achieve optimal responses can potentially proceed directly to maintenance and reserve the transplant for relapse, as suggested by early data. Duration of therapy is another topic of debate and future trials will answer this relevant question: Who needs continuous therapy, who does not, and if the former, when we should stop treatment. The approach to treat patients with disease relapse is challenging and prior therapies should be taken into consideration. Treatment is rapidly evolving, however, so updating the guidelines is mandatory when new combinations are available.

Cost and drug access, however, are crucial issues presently. Drugs approved by regulatory agencies in Europe, the United States, or Japan are not available in low-income regions of South America, Africa, or some countries in the Asia Pacific or European Union. Approval by regulatory agencies is not equivalent to reimbursement and full access, which means that ESMO, NCCN, or ASCO guidelines are useful but not universally applicable, so cost-effective approaches should be developed.

22

CELLULAR THERAPIES

Amrita Krishnan, MD, and Ryotaro Nakamura, MD

Recent Updates

- Ibrutinib was approved for the treatment of chronic graft-versus-host disease (GVHD) on the basis of phase II trial data. This is the first drug to be approved for GVHD in the United States. (Miklos D, *Blood* 2017)
- Letermovir for cytomegalovirus prophylaxis for seropositive recipients was approved on the basis of a phase III trial. (ClinicalTrials.gov identifier: NCT02137772). (Marty FM, *N Engl J Med* 2017)
- Post-transplant treatment with cyclophosphamide results in low rates of severe, acute GVHD or chronic GVHD after haploidentical allografting. (Luznik L, *Biol Blood Marrow Transplant* 2008)
- A study by the Center for International Blood and Marrow Transplant Research found low rates of GVHD with posttransplant treatment with cyclophosphamide and comparable overall survival to that from matched, unrelated donors for acute myeloid leukemia. (Ciurea SO, *Blood* 2015)
- On the basis of the results of a phase III trial, defibrotide was approved by the US Food and Drug Administration as treatment of severe sinusoidal obstruction syndrome (ClinicalTrials.gov identifier: NCT00358501). (Richardson PG, *Blood* 2016)

OVERVIEW

The term "bone marrow transplantation" was originally used to describe the process of transferring the lymphohematopoietic system from one individual to another. With the demonstration that peripheral blood and umbilical cord blood also are also sources of hematopoietic stem cells, the term "hematopoietic cell transplantation" (HCT) is now more appropriate. HCT can be used to replace an abnormal but nonmalignant hematopoietic system with one from a normal donor, as in the case of aplastic anemia. HCT is also used to treat a variety of malignancies, because it allows for the administration of higher doses of chemotherapy and radiotherapy than would otherwise be possible. In addition, in the setting of allogeneic HCT, it confers an immunologic graft-versus-tumor (GVT) effect. Worldwide, more than 1 million HCTs have been performed.[1] The frequency of HCT varies widely from country to country, with a close association of HCT rates with gross national income (GNI) per capita.[1] However, substantial differences exist among countries with similar GNI per capita with regard to HCT frequency, disease indication, and choice of donor. Racial disparities have also been observed.[2] This chapter focuses on general principles of HCT, including stem cell source, preparative regimens, and complications. The role of HCT in the treatment of specific diseases is discussed in greater detail in the chapters focused on those illnesses.

INDICATIONS

IMMUNODEFICIENCY STATES

Allogeneic HCT can successfully establish a normal immune system for patients with severe combined immunodeficiency disorders; it also can correct the abnormalities associated with Wiskott-Aldrich syndrome and other immunodeficiency states.[3,4]

NONMALIGNANT DISORDERS OF HEMATOPOIESIS

The most data about and the best outcomes of HCT for nonmalignant disorders of hematopoiesis are reported for severe aplastic anemia and thalassemia, with a growing experience for sickle cell anemia. Most patients with severe aplastic anemia (90%) can be cured with allogeneic HCT from a matched sibling[5]; results are slightly less favorable if a matched unrelated donor is used.[6] Allogeneic HCT cures 70% to 90% of patients with thalassemia major, with the best results seen among patients who received the transplant before the development of hepatomegaly or portal fibrosis.[7] Although data for sickle cell disease are more limited, current reports document 5-year survival and disease-free survival of 93% and 84%, respectively.[7-9] Cures also have been obtained for other nonmalignant disorders of hematopoiesis, including Fanconi anemia,[10-12] Blackfan-Diamond syndrome, chronic granulomatous disease,[13] Kostmann syndrome,[14] and leukocyte adhesion deficiency.[15] However, because allogeneic HCT still has significant and unpredictable complications, treatment recommendations should be based on identifying patients at high risk from their underlying diseases, for whom the risk of HCT is justified.

INBORN ERRORS OF METABOLISM

Allogeneic HCT can replace the abnormal enzyme systems and result in cure for patients with mucopolysaccharidosis and Gaucher disease.[16] Prior damage caused by the enzyme abnormality may not be reversible, arguing for early HCT for the more severe syndromes.

MALIGNANT DISEASES

The most frequent use of HCT has been for the treatment of malignant diseases. In the United States, the leading indications for allogeneic HCT are acute myeloid leukemia (AML; approximately 50%), followed by myelodysplasia (MDS) and acute lymphoblastic leukemia (ALL). HCT consistently achieves 5-year disease-free survival rates of 50% to 70% when performed for AML and ALL in first remission.[17] Meta-analyses of studies comparing the outcome of matched-sibling allogeneic HCT versus conventional chemotherapy for adult patients with these disorders show improved survival with HCT.[18-20] The advantages of HCT are most apparent for patients with higher-risk leukemia and less for those with lower-risk disease. If HCT is withheld until second remission, results are less favorable, with cure rates of 25% to 40%. Cure rates of 30% to 60% have been reported for patients with MDS who are treated with allogeneic HCT.[21] Because patients with early-stage MDS often live for long periods without treatment, HCT is generally reserved for patients with advanced-stage disease.[22,23] Although > 70% of patients with chronic myeloid leukemia (CML) in the chronic phase can be cured with allogeneic HCT, HCT is usually restricted to patients whose disease has progressed after initial therapy with a tyrosine kinase inhibitor (TKI)[24] or those with advanced states (ie, second chronic phase after blast crisis). Allogeneic HCT can reverse marrow fibrosis and cure patients with primary myelofibrosis.[25] Allogeneic HCT is also used in the treatment of patients with recurrent chronic lymphocytic leukemia and non-Hodgkin lymphoma (NHL) with marrow involvement[26] or those who relapsed after autologous HCT. It is used in a small fraction of patients with myeloma—results of studies of reduced intensity allogeneic transplant compared with autologous transplant have been conflicting.[27,28]

The leading indication for autologous HCT in the United States is multiple myeloma, followed by NHL and Hodgkin lymphoma. Prospective, randomized trials have shown that autologous HCT, when used as part of initial therapy, prolongs remission for patients with multiple myeloma, particularly when followed by lenalidomide maintenance therapy. This finding still holds true in the era of modern myeloma therapy.[29-31]

Autologous HCT is curative for 40% to 50% of patients with NHL or Hodgkin lymphoma that recurred after first-line therapy; these results are superior to what would be expected with additional chemotherapy.[32,33] Debate persists about the role of high-dose chemotherapy with autologous HCT as part of initial therapy for patients with high-risk NHL and mantle cell lymphoma.[34] It is also used for primary CNS lymphoma.[35] Furthermore, autologous HCT is used to treat chemosensitive solid tumors; the greatest experience is with testicular cancer and neuroblastoma.[36]

> **KEY POINTS**
>
> - All diseases of hematopoiesis, nonmalignant and malignant, are potentially curable with HCT.
> - HCT consistently achieves 5-year disease-free survival rates of 50% to 70% when performed for AML and ALL in first remission.
> - The leading indication for autologous HCT in the United States is multiple myeloma, followed by NHL and Hodgkin lymphoma.

SOURCES OF STEM CELLS

Hematopoietic stem cells used for HCT can be categorized according to the relationship between the donor and the recipient or according to anatomic source (Table 22-1). In the rare cases in which the patient has an identical (syngeneic) twin, HCT can be conducted without the risks of graft rejection or graft-versus-host disease (GVHD), because the individuals are genetically identical throughout the genome. However, these syngeneic HCTs confer fewer benefits of an immunologic effect, such that the risks of relapse of the underlying malignancy are higher.[37]

Table 22-1 Cell and Donor Sources for Autologous and Allogeneic Hematopoietic Cell Transplantation

Autologous	Allogeneic
Cell source	Cell source
Bone marrow	Bone marrow
Peripheral blood stem cells	Peripheral blood stem cells
	Donor source
	Sibling
	Matched related donor
	Matched unrelated donor
	Haploidentical donor
	Cord blood

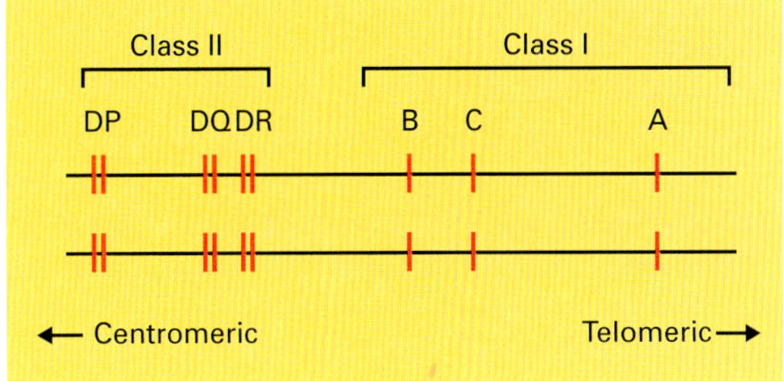

Fig. 22-1 Genes associated with human leukocyte antigen (HLA) typing.[38]

The genes encoding HLA class I *(HLA-A, HLA-B*, and *HLA-C)* and class II *(HLA-DP, HLA-DQ*, and *HLA-DR)* are located on chromosome 6, are tightly linked, codominantly expressed, and tend to be inherited as haplotypes with low recombination frequency. Thus, for any given patient, the likelihood that a full sibling will be HLA-matched with the patient is 25%.

ALLOGENEIC TRANSPLANTATION

When the marrow (hematopoietic progenitor cells) of a patient is clearly abnormal (eg, aplastic anemia, most cases of leukemia), allogeneic rather than autologous HCT is preferred. The best source of allogeneic hematopoietic stem cells is from an human leukocyte antigen (HLA)-identical sibling. HLA molecules display both exogenous peptides (eg, from an infecting organism) and endogenous peptides, presenting them to T cells to initiate an immune response. If two persons are HLA nonidentical, T cells from one person will react vigorously to the mismatched HLA molecules on the surface of cells from the second individual. The HLA molecules themselves are termed "major HLA determinants (major histocompatibility complex [MHC])." Even though nontwin siblings may be HLA matched, the endogenous peptides presented by the HLA molecules can differ on the basis of genetic polymorphisms in a wide range of genes between the HLA-matched siblings, resulting in T-cell responses against minor HLA determinants (minor histocompatibility antigens).

Sibling Donors

The genes encoding HLA class I *(HLA-A, HLA-B,* and *HLA-C)* and class II *(HLA-DP, HLA-DQ,* and *HLA-DR)* are located on chromosome 6, are tightly linked, codominantly expressed, and tend to be inherited as haplotypes with low recombination frequency (Fig 22-1).[38] Thus, for any given patient:

- the likelihood that a full sibling will be HLA matched with the patient is 25%;
- the likelihood of finding a matched sibling for a patient can be calculated by the formula $x = 1 - 0.75^n$, where x equals the probability of finding a matched sibling, and n equals the number of siblings; and
- given the size of families in the United States, the chance that a matched sibling can be identified for any patient is approximately 30%.

ABO Blood Groups

Because hematopoietic stem cells do not express ABO, HCT can be carried out across ABO blood group barriers by removing incompatible RBCs and/or isoagglutinins from the donor graft.[39] However, even with appropriate manipulation of the donor graft, a major ABO mismatch (eg, recipient O, donor A) can result in immediate or delayed hemolysis of donor RBCs or red cell aplasia by persistent recipient isohemagglutinins, and a minor mismatch (eg, recipient B, donor O) can result in immediate hemolysis of recipient RBCs by donor-derived isohemagglutinins in the graft or delayed hemolysis of recipient RBCs by newly generated isohemagglutinins from donor lymphocytes (ie, passenger lymphocytes).

Antigen-Mismatched Related Donors

Family members who are genotypically identical to the patient for one HLA haplotype and are either phenotypically identical or partially matched on the other HLA haplotype have been used as donors. Use of one-antigen–mismatched related donors results in a marginal increase in graft rejection, GVHD, and transplantation-related mortality.[40] If patients are undergoing HCT for leukemia that is in remission, this degree of mismatching appears to result in a slightly worse outcome. However, if patients are undergoing HCT for higher-risk leukemia, the increased GVT effect associated with a single mismatch appears to balance the negative effect.[41]

Historically, when conventional forms of GVHD prophylaxis were used, results using donors mismatched for two or three major HLA determinants resulted in high rates of graft rejection or GVHD. However, newer techniques, including the use of posttransplant high-dose cyclophosphamide, have been developed that allow the safe use of haploidentical donors who share one haplotype with the patient but are mismatched for two or more antigens on the nonshared haplotype.[42-44]

Unrelated Donors

Donors who are completely unrelated to the patient but are matched for *HLA-A, -B, -C,* and *DRB1* have been used in an increasing number of cases with improved results. Since the formation of the National Marrow Donor Program in 1986 and of other, international, registries, > 25 million healthy individuals have volunteered to serve as stem cell donors. The likelihood of finding a fully matched, available, unrelated donor varies among racial and ethnic groups, from 75% for whites of European decent to a low of 16% for blacks of South and Central American descent.[45]

When compared with the outcome of matched-sibling transplantation, transplants from unrelated donors matched with the patient at *HLA-A*, *-B*, *-C*, and *DRB1* (Fig 22-2) are associated with greater morbidity, mostly from GVHD, but survival at 3 to 5 years after HCT is similar.[46] A single-antigen mismatch is associated with more GVHD, higher rate of treatment-related mortality, and lower survival rate.[47] In a study of 3,857 HCTs from unrelated donors, which largely involved bone marrow as the source of stem cells, mismatches at *HLA-A* or *DRB1* were less well tolerated than mismatches at *HLA-B* or *HLA-C*. Mismatching at two loci was associated with greater risk.[48] Although HLA is the dominant factor affecting outcome, other donor factors, including age, sex, parity, and cytomegalovirus (CMV) serology, have a small but measurable impact.[49] If peripheral blood rather than marrow is the source of unrelated stem cells, mismatching for *HLA-C* appears to be less well tolerated.[50] It should be noted that these factors may be less relevant with the use of posttransplant cyclophosphamide.

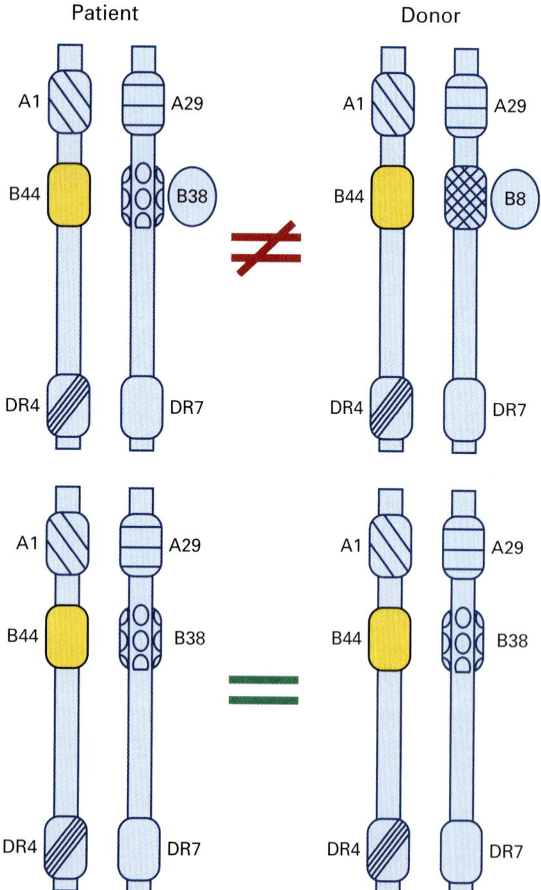

Fig. 22-2 **Graphical representation of a mechanism in which donor and recipient markers can mismatch (top) or match (bottom).**

It may be possible to identify "permissible" *HLA-C* mismatches with no greater risk than that seen with fully matched unrelated donors.[51] An approach that is intriguing but not widely applied is to use a form of MHC haplotype matching to map novel MHC-linked transplantation determinants.[52] More recently, mismatching at *HLA-DPB1* has been shown to increase the risk of transplant-related mortality, and methods to identify permissive *HLA-DPB1* mismatches have been developed.[53] Moreover, natural killer cells possess killer-cell immunoglobulin-like receptors (KIRs) that recognize epitopes shared by groups of HLA-class I alleles. Haploidentical HCT from KIR ligand–mismatched donors with activating KIRs leads to improved survival and reduced nonrelapse mortality.[54]

Umbilical Cord Blood

Umbilical cord blood also is rich in hematopoietic stem cells, and studies have shown that cord blood can serve as a source of stem cells for HCT. Because cord blood has relatively few mature T cells, the risk of GVHD with cord blood appears to be somewhat less than the risk associated with similarly matched marrow, although the risk of graft rejection or failure may be greater. Cord blood is sometimes used as a source of stem cells to treat family members suffering from hematologic disorders; survival is essentially equivalent to that seen after matched-sibling bone marrow HCT.[55] By far the most common use of cord blood has been in the treatment of unrelated recipients who lack matched related or unrelated donors. Because of the paucity of mature T cells in cord blood, matching criteria can be less stringent, allowing treatment of patients with one or two antigen mismatches.

In an analysis of 1,061 recipients of transplants from unrelated cord blood, the number of cells per kilogram infused had a considerable influence on the outcome, as did patient age and degree of match with donors, with improved survival associated with higher cell dose, younger patient age, and greater degree of matching.[56] Low cord-blood-cell dose increased the risk of graft failure, delayed hematopoietic engraftment, and delayed immune recovery, which previously limited cord-blood HCT to children and smaller adults.[57] Trials exploring the use of double-cord transplants (which provides a greater cord-blood-cell dose) demonstrated that even though only one cord ultimately engrafts, the use of two cords reduces the risk of graft failure and is associated with an enhanced GVT effect.[58,59] There does not appear to be an advantage to the use of two cords in cases in which a single cord provides a sufficient number of cells, at least in children and young adults.[60] Trials are ongoing using ex vivo expanded cord blood cells, and expansion techniques include using the aryl hydrocarbon–receptor antagonist StemRegenin-1 (SR-1), nicotinamide-based cultures, notch ligand–based cultures, and coculture with mesenchymal stem cells.[61]

Availability of Allogeneic Stem Cell Sources

With the availability of matched related, matched unrelated, single-antigen–mismatched related, haploidentical, and cord-blood donors, a source of allogeneic stem cells can be found for the vast majority of patients in need (Table 22-2). Although matched related donors are generally preferred, limited prospective randomized trials have compared alternative donors. This aspect is especially true in ethnic groups with limited availability of unrelated donors, whereas nearly all patients have an available haploidentical donor because all biologic parents and children of a patient are haploidentical. The major limitation is the presence of antidonor HLA antibodies, usually from women against paternal HLA antigens in their children, or due to exposures to multiple transfusions. Emerging data suggest relatively similar survival after matched unrelated, unrelated cord-blood, and haploidentical donor HCT.[44,62-65]

On average, the time between initiating the search for an alternative donor and performing the HCT is 3 to 4 months; however, in urgent circumstances, donors can be identified and grafts procured within 6 weeks. Although this time has shortened, one of the advantages of haploidentical HCT is the even shorter times required to evaluate the donor and procure the stem cells.

KEY POINTS

- Although GVHD after HCT is more common from matched unrelated donors than from matched siblings, survival rates appear similar.
- Methods have been developed that allow for the selection of "permissive" single-antigen–mismatched donors.
- HCT using either cord blood or haploidentical donors is feasible; consequently, an allogeneic donor can be found for most patients in need.
- Post-transplantation cyclophosphamide is well tolerated, allows wider use of haploidentical donors, and may replace calcineurin-based GVHD prevention.

AUTOLOGOUS TRANSPLANTATION

The use of a patient's own (ie, autologous) stem cells for HCT also is possible. The leading indication for autologous HCT is multiple myeloma[66]; this practice stems from work dating back to the 1980s that showed a response with high-dose melphalan.[67] Later trials in NHL demonstrated a superior progression-free survival (PFS) compared with traditional chemotherapy for relapsed NHL.[68] It is also used for relapsed Hodgkin lymphoma.[69] Autologous HCT also is sometimes used to treat malignancies of nonhematopoietic origin, including neuroblastoma and germ cell tumors. The technique also has been explored as a treatment option for patients with AML and ALL, using stem cells collected during remission. In the case of AML and ALL, a sufficient number of patients have received transplants with either allogeneic or autologous marrow to allow for comparisons of the two therapies. In general, autologous HCT is associated with fewer complications. GVHD does not occur, and the incidences of infectious complications, idiopathic pneumonia syndrome, and sinusoidal obstruction syndrome (SOS; formerly termed veno-occlusive hepatic disease) are lower. However, the risk of tumor recurrence is higher with autologous HCT, likely because of a lack of a GVT effect and because of tumor contamination of the reinfused stem cell product. Gene-marking studies have demonstrated that tumor cells within the transplanted marrow can contribute to relapse.[70] The use of autologous transplant in AML has declined and represents < 10% of autologous procedures in Europe and even less in the United States.[66] A large European retrospective analysis of 809 patients who underwent transplantation in first remission showed a 2-year leukemia-free survival of 51% and overall survival (OS) of 65%, in particular in patients with good cytogenetics, but its use is unlikely to increase in the United States.[71]

BONE MARROW

Because bone marrow is rich in hematopoietic stem cells, it was used first as the source of stem cells for HCT. Marrow for HCT usually is obtained through multiple aspirations from the posterior and sometimes from the anterior iliac crests. The marrow is heparinized and filtered through screens to remove osseous spicules and fat globules before either being infused into the patient or cryopreserved for later HCT. In some studies, the marrow has been treated before infusion or cryopreservation to test whether removal of T cells, or T-cell subsets, from allogeneic marrow can improve outcome by reducing GVHD, or whether tumor cells can be removed prior to autologous HCT.[72]

PERIPHERAL BLOOD

Hematopoietic stem cells circulate in the peripheral blood, albeit in small numbers. During recovery from drug-induced

Table 22-2 Probability of Finding an Allogeneic Donor for Hematopoietic Cell Transplantation

Race	Unrelated Donor (%)		Cord Blood (%)	Haploidentical (%)
	8/8 Matched	7/8 Matched		
White	70	90	> 95	> 95
Hispanic	35	75	95	> 95
Black	18	70	90	> 95

NOTE. Probability for matched sibling: 30%; for one-antigen–mismatched related donor: 3%.

cytopenias or after exposure to a hematopoietic growth factors, such as granulocyte-macrophage colony-stimulating factor or granulocyte colony-stimulating factor (G-CSF),[73] the number of hematopoietic progenitor cells in the peripheral blood increases considerably. With the use of these mobilizing techniques, followed by leukapheresis, it is possible to collect sufficient stem cells from the peripheral blood to permit successful HCT. Because peripheral blood has a higher proportion of T cells than does marrow, the first trials of peripheral-blood stem cell HCT were performed in the autologous setting, in which GVHD is not a concern. These studies demonstrated that such HCT is not only feasible but also results in faster engraftment than is seen with autologous marrow. When > 5.0 × 10^6 CD34+ cells/kg are infused, recovery to 0.5 × 10^3 granulocytes/mL and 20 × 10^3 platelets/mL is generally seen < 2 weeks after HCT. Because of the rapid engraftment, decreased costs, and improved safety associated with peripheral blood stem cell HCT, it has largely replaced marrow as the source of stem cells for autologous HCT.

Given the rapid recovery associated with the use of autologous peripheral-blood stem cells, pilot studies of allogeneic peripheral-blood stem cell HCT using HLA-identical sibling donors were performed.[74] The results of these studies demonstrated rapid engraftment without an increase in the incidence of acute GVHD. Randomized trials have confirmed these findings.[75] In most studies, the incidence of chronic GVHD associated with allogeneic peripheral-blood stem cell HCT is higher, but disease-free survival and OS rates appear to be improved, particularly for patients who received transplants for more advanced-stage disease.[76] In the unrelated-donor setting, a large randomized study comparing marrow with peripheral blood after myeloablative conditioning showed faster engraftment but more chronic GVHD with peripheral blood and equivalent OS. However, this trial was across hematologic malignancies, and limited data are available in the setting of reduced-intensity allogeneic transplantation.[77] A retrospective European study of peripheral-blood stem cell transplantation compared with bone marrow with reduced-intensity conditioning regimes for acute leukemia also showed an increase in chronic GVHD with peripheral stem cell transplant but better leukemia-free survival and OS.[78] Despite the need for a prospective randomized trial, generally the preference has still been to use peripheral-blood stem cells over bone marrow in the allogeneic setting.

Stromal cell–derived factor 1 (CXCL12) produced by marrow stromal cells is a key regulator of hematopoietic stem cell homing and retention in the marrow by interacting with the α-chemokine receptor CXCR4 found on stem cells. Plerixafor, an antagonist of CXCR4, results in mobilization of CD34+ cells into the peripheral blood. For patients with myeloma, a phase III trial of plerixafor in combination with G-CSF compared with G-CSF mobilization showed favorable safety and improved efficacy in the combination arm with respect to reaching target collection goals.[79] This outcome is especially important in myeloma, where general practice is to collect adequate stem cells for at least two transplants.[80] Comparisons to conventional chemotherapy mobilization have also suggested that the cost and complications of chemotherapy administration offset the costs of plerixafor.[81] Other cost-containment approaches include using plerixafor on demand if CD34+ stem cells numbers are suboptimal with G-CSF alone.[82]

The incidence of serious adverse events after bone marrow donation is 2.4% versus 0.6% after peripheral-blood stem cell donation. There is no evidence for an increased risk of cancer, autoimmune illness, or stroke in donors receiving G-CSF for stem cell mobilization.[83,84] Guidelines have been developed to determine medical suitability of unrelated adult donors and for the hematopoietic cell collection process.[85,86]

KEY POINTS

- In the matched unrelated-donor setting, a comparison of mobilized peripheral blood versus bone marrow after myeloablative conditioning showed faster engraftment but more chronic GVHD and equivalent survival with peripheral blood.
- Plerixafor, an antagonist of CXCR4, results in mobilization of CD34+ cells into the peripheral blood and has become a backbone of mobilization in autologous HCT, often replacing chemotherapy-based mobilization.
- Autologous HCT is safe and is associated with low transplant-related mortality rates, but relapse remains a concern. In lymphoma, consolidation strategies remain under investigation.

PREPARATIVE REGIMEN

The form of treatment administered to patients directly before HCT depends on the disease being treated, the source of the stem cells, and patient comorbidities. Patients with severe combined immunodeficiency diseases often require no preparative regimen before HCT because there is no abnormal cell population that must be eradicated and because their immune system is so severely compromised that the infused hematopoietic cells are rarely rejected if the donor is an HLA-matched sibling. In contrast, patients with aplastic anemia are sufficiently immunocompetent to reject allogeneic marrow if no pretransplant immunosuppression is given. Thus, high-dose cyclophosphamide alone or combined with antithymocyte globulin often is used as the preparative regimen for allogeneic HCT in aplastic anemia. When HCT is applied to the treatment of leukemia or other malignant diseases, the regimen must be myelosuppressive as well as immunosuppressive (in the setting of allogeneic HCT) and contribute to the eradication of the malignant disease. In the case of autologous HCT for lymphoma and myeloma, eradication of the malignant clone but not immunosuppression is the main goal of conditioning.

Although high-dose myeloablative preparative regimens were the initial approach to HCT for malignant diseases, the observation that some of the antitumor effects the may occur after allogeneic HCT are the result of a GVT response led to investigations of whether reduced-intensity regimens might be as effective and less toxic. Evidence for the existence of a GVT effect includes the finding that relapse rates after allogeneic marrow HCT are the lowest when acute and chronic GVHD develops, greater if no GVHD develops, and greater still if syngeneic or T-cell–depleted allogeneic marrow is used.[37,87] Additional evidence of a potent GVT effect comes from the use of viable donor lymphocyte infusions. The simple transfusion of as few as 1×10^7 viable donor lymphocytes per kilogram as treatment of patients whose disease relapsed after allogeneic HCT can result in complete remission for as many as 70% of patients with CML and for a smaller portion of patients with AML and MDS.[88]

Currently used preparative regimens for allogeneic HCT can be placed in three general categories. The myeloablative regimen causes irreversible marrow aplasia and requires replacement of the hematopoietic system; the nonmyeloablative regimen causes minimal marrow suppression, and reduced-intensity conditioning causes cytopenias of intermediate duration.[89] Compared with high-dose preparative regimens, nonmyeloablative and reduced-intensity regimens result in a shorter duration of pancytopenias with less or minimal mucositis, fewer bacterial infections, and a lower incidence of direct toxicities to the lung and liver.[90] Relapse rates are generally higher with reduced-dose regimens.[91] A prospective, randomized trial demonstrated increased relapse rates and diminished survival with the use of reduced-intensity conditioning compared with myeloablative conditioning in patients with AML and MDS.[92] Thus, reduced-intensity conditioning is generally restricted to older patients and those with significant comorbidities, whereas high-dose regimens are preferred for younger, fit patients. Patients who have relapsed after autologous transplant and are candidates for an allogeneic approach often receive reduced-intensity conditioning in an attempt to maximize efficacy but minimize organ toxicity. Suggested dose adjustments for patients with renal or hepatic impairment have been published.[93,94]

Several studies have compared outcomes from myeloablative regimens containing total body irradiation (TBI) with those from regimens consisting of only chemotherapy. One retrospective study did not find a significant difference between intravenous busulfan and cyclophosphamide and cyclophosphamide and TBI for patients with AML in remission.[95] However, a separate retrospective analysis of patients with AML in first remission revealed both less nonrelapse mortality and disease relapse with busulfan and cyclophosphamide over that of cyclophosphamide and TBI.[96] Moreover, a prospective analysis of patients with myeloid malignancies indicated superior survival with busulfan-based regimens without an increase in transplant-related mortality rate or relapse.[97] Comparison of reduced-intensity conditioning regimens has not been as extensive presently.

KEY POINTS

- The purpose of the preparative regimen used before autologous HCT is to help eliminate the underlying disease.
- The purpose of the preparative regimen in allogeneic HCT can be to eliminate the underlying disease and be sufficiently immunosuppressive to allow engraftment of donor cells, or, in the case of reduced-intensity or nonmyeloablative conditioning, it can be solely for sufficient immunosuppression.
- Evidence points to increased relapse rates and diminished survival with the use of reduced-intensity conditioning compared with myeloablative conditioning in patients with AML and MDS.

ENGRAFTMENT

After the administration of a myeloablative preparative regimen and the infusion of stem cells, a period of profound myelosuppression ensues. Within 1 to 2 weeks after HCT, the peripheral leukocyte count begins to increase, signifying engraftment. When stem cells are procured from marrow and no hematopoietic growth factors are used after HCT, the granulocyte count reaches $0.1 \times 10^3/\mu L$ by approximately day 16 and $0.5 \times 10^3/\mu L$ by day 25, and platelets reach $20 \times 10^3/L$ by day 19 (Fig 22-3, top). Administration of G-CSF can accelerate the recovery of peripheral granulocyte counts by as much as 1 week. Platelet-count recovery typically lags behind neutrophil engraftment, usually by several days, but possibly by several weeks for some patients.

When peripheral blood is the source of stem cells, engraftment is more rapid, with a granulocyte count of $0.5 \times 10^3/\mu L$ and a platelet count of $20 \times 10^3/\mu L$ achieved by day 12, on

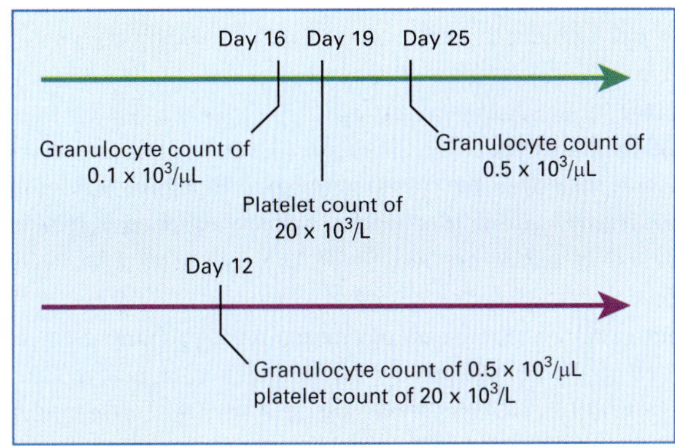

Fig. 22-3 Timeline of granulocyte and platelet count recovery after hematopoietic cell transplantation using (top) bone marrow and (bottom) peripheral blood stem cells.

average (Fig 22-3, bottom). Engraftment after cord-blood HCT is typically delayed by approximately 1 week compared with that after marrow HCT. Engraftment of allogeneic stem cells can be documented using fluorescence in situ hybridization of sex chromosomes if the donor and recipients are of opposite sexes, or DNA-based assays of short tandem repeat loci. With these techniques, the donor-versus-recipient origin of populations of cells can now be determined in virtually all cases.[98,99]

KEY POINT

- Using in situ hybridization with sex chromosome–specific probes or typing of the variable number of tandem repeat polymorphisms, the donor-versus-recipient origin of populations of cells can be determined in virtually all cases.

COMPLICATIONS OF MARROW TRANSPLANTATION

The nature and the degree of complications associated with HCT depend on the age and health of the patient, the specific preparative regimen used, and the source of stem cells. The frequency of complications is higher and the rate of survival is lower for patients with a Karnofsky performance score < 80% and for patients with significant comorbidities.[100] GVHD is normally seen only after allogeneic HCT, although it can rarely be a complication of autologous transplant, and subsequent infections related to the immunosuppression used to prevent or treat GVHD are leading causes of morbidity and mortality.[101] The extent of other specific organ toxicities depends largely on the specific preparative regimen used. Figure 22-4 illustrates the approximate timing of possible toxicities after allogeneic HCT using a typical intensive preparative regimen. HCT-specific scoring systems have been developed that can predict the overall likelihood of GVHD and overall mortality after allogeneic HCT. Such systems are useful in the selection of preparative regimens for individual patients, allowing those with few comorbidities to have the benefit of more intense regimens while selecting safer, less intense regimens for those with significant comorbidities.[102,103] The following sections discuss the major complications of HCT.

GRAFT FAILURE

In some instances, the transplanted graft functions briefly, but after a period of days or weeks, marrow function is lost and myeloid elements are absent on evaluation of marrow obtained by biopsy. In the setting of allogeneic HCT, failure of the graft usually is the result of residual host immune elements rejecting the donor marrow, a phenomenon termed graft rejection. After HCT involving an HLA-identical donor, graft rejection occurs most commonly when the patient has received multiple transfusions before HCT and little prior chemotherapy and when the preparative regimen is less immunosuppressive, such as with the use of cyclophosphamide monotherapy before HCT for aplastic anemia. In general, the greater the disparity in HLA antigens between donor and recipient, the higher the chance of rejection. In the setting of partially matched cord-blood HCT, in mismatched, unrelated-donor HCT[47] and in haploidentical HCT,[63] the presence of donor-specific anti-HLA antibodies in the patient prior to HCT, found in perhaps 10% of cases, predicts a high rate of graft rejection, so use of such cord units should be avoided.[104] Desensitization techniques can reduce these antibodies to levels permissible for donor engraftment.[105]

Also, because donor T cells react with and help eliminate host immunocompetent cells not eradicated by the preparative regimen, T-cell depletion of donor marrow prior to HCT can lead to persistence of host immunity, resulting in an increased chance of graft rejection.

Graft failure occurs rarely in recipients of autologous transplants. A single cause is often difficult to identify, but several have been implicated, including:

- prior exposure to stem cell poisons,
- marrow damage during in vitro processing and cryopreservation,
- drug toxicity after HCT, and
- viral infections.

Patients with graft failure—but not immunologically mediated graft rejection—sometimes have a response to treatment with a hematopoietic growth factor, such as G-CSF, with an increase in the granulocyte count that may be sustained even after discontinuation of the growth factor. If persistent host lymphocytes are detected, which documents graft rejection, a second marrow transplant after an immunosuppressive preparative regimen may be successful.[106]

GRAFT-VERSUS-HOST DISEASE

GVHD is a complication usually restricted to allogeneic transplants and is the result of a combination of factors originally ascribed only to allogeneic T cells, which are transfused with the graft, reacting against targets on the genetically different host.[107-109] Factors associated with an increased risk of moderate or severe acute GVHD include:

- HLA mismatching,
- older age of patient and donor,
- a multiparous woman as the donor, and
- exposure to more intensive conditioning regimens.

The evolution of clinical immunology has brought additional insight into the pathogenesis of GVHD and identified, in addition to the genetic component (ie, HLA compatibility), an immune biologic component including the intestinal epithelium and gut microbiome.[110] A National Institutes of Health (NIH) Consensus Report recognized two categories of GVHD, each with two subcategories (Table 22-3).[111] Acute GVHD usually develops 2 to 42 weeks after allogeneic HCT and typically presents with

Table 22-3 **Categories of Acute and Chronic GVHD**[111]			
Category	**Time of Symptoms After HCT**	**Presence of Acute GVHD Features**	**Presence of Chronic GVHD Features**
Acute GVHD			
Classic acute	≤ 100 days	Yes	No
Late-onset	> 100 days	Yes	No
Chronic GVHD			
Classic chronic	No time limit	No	Yes
Overlap	No time limit	Yes	Yes

Abbreviations: GVHD, graft-versus-host disease; HCT, hematopoietic cell transplantation.

an erythematous or maculopapular rash, nausea, vomiting, anorexia, diarrhea (sometimes profuse), ileus, or cholestatic jaundice. Sometimes the diagnosis can be less straightforward, and skin, liver, or GI biopsy specimens may be needed. In addition, a panel of plasma biomarkers including IL-2 receptor A, TNF receptor 1, IL-8, and hepatocyte growth factor are under study as diagnostic and prognostic tools.[112]

GHVD Prophylaxis

Immunosuppression remains the main prophylactic approach for GHVD, although there is no standard regimen. The most commonly used regimens to prevent GVHD include a combination of a calcineurin inhibitor (cyclosporine or tacrolimus) and an antimetabolite (methotrexate [MTX] or mycophenolate mofetil) or, more recently, the mTOR inhibitor sirolimus.[113] The addition of sirolimus to tacrolimus as an alternative to MTX or mycophenolate mofetil leads to earlier engraftment and less mucositis but also increases the incidence at which microangiopathy and sinusoidal obstructive syndrome occur. Three prospective, randomized trials reported that the addition of antilymphocyte globulin to standard prophylaxis led to a lower rate of acute and chronic GVHD without affecting OS. One study did show a reduction of chronic pulmonary dysfunction in patients receiving antithymocyte globulin (ATG) and a trend toward lower late nonrelapse mortality. However, there is no consensus on the dose (2.5 *v* 30 mg/kg) or type of ATG (thymoglobulin *v* Fresenius) to be used.[114] Although the European trials did not show a higher risk of relapse, the US prospective trial did.[115] Other approaches to preventing GVHD include the removal of T cells from the donor marrow, but this approach is not widely used, because of concerns of increased risk of relapse.[116,117] The use of posttransplant cyclophosphamide to target proliferating alloreactive T cells stimulated early after transplantation is gaining wider use. However, a recent large retrospective analysis by the Center for International Blood and Marrow Transplant Research (CIBMTR) demonstrated inferior outcomes with cyclosporine in combination with mycophenolate mofetil after HCT, in comparison with outcomes from combination tacrolimus and MTX and other regimens. Its original use was in haploidentical HCT but subsequently spread to HLA-matched and -mismatched HCT. Posttransplant cyclophosphamide can serve as the only GVHD prophylaxis after HLA-matched HCT and is associated with a similar incidence of acute GVHD and OS and reduced chronic GHVD rates compared with traditional calcineurin-based prophylaxis.[118,119]

Acute GVHD

With standard regimens, such as MTX plus tacrolimus, moderate, acute GVHD requiring therapy occurs in approximately 30% of patients who have undergone HCT from a matched-sibling donor. Acute GVHD usually is staged and graded using a modification of the original Seattle system (Tables 22-4 and 22-5).[120]

Standard treatment of acute GVHD is prednisone at a daily dose of 2 mg/kg, although a lower dose of 1 mg/kg may be used for grades 1 to 2 acute GVHD.[121] The optimal duration of steroid therapy is unknown but should be as limited as possible to avoid adverse effects of prolonged therapy. Management of patients with steroid-refractory acute GVHD, defined as failure

Table 22-4 **Clinical Staging of Acute Graft-Versus-Host Disease**[120]			
Clinical Stage	**Skin (Erythematous Rash)**	**Liver (Serum Bilirubin)**	**Gut (Diarrhea)**
1	25% of body surface	2-3 mg/dL	500-1,000 mL/d
2	25%-50% of body surface	3-6 mg/dL	1,000-1,500 mL/d
3	Generalized	6-15 mg/dL	> 1,500 mL/d
4	Desquamation and bullae	> 15 mg/dL	Pain or ileus

Table 22-5 **Clinical Grading of Acute Graft-Versus-Host Disease**[120]

Clinical Grade	Skin	Liver	Gut
I (Mild)	1 or 2	0	0
II (Moderate)	3	1	1
III (Severe)	1, 2, or 3	2 or 3	2, 3, or 4
IV (Life-threatening)	4	4	

to clinically respond to standard steroid therapy, remains a major challenge. These patients are often treated with secondary immunosuppressive or immunomodulatory agents such as basiliximab and antithymocyte globulin.[122] Recently, JAK inhibitors have shown promising results for steroid-refractory GVHD. A retrospective study of 95 patients with steroid-refractory GVHD from 19 transplant centers demonstrated an overall response rate of 81%.[123] In an effort to prognosticate acute GVHD at its onset and to better risk stratify treatments for GVHD patients, a scoring system (Ann Arber [AA] Score) based on three biomarkers (TNFR1, ST2, and REG3a) was developed and validated.[124] The GVHD biomarker-based classification (AA1-3), combined with a refined clinical risk score by one group,[125] is incorporated in a few therapeutic clinical trials for newly diagnosed acute GVHD (namely, ClinicalTrials.gov identifiers: NCT02806947 and NCT02133924).

Chronic GVHD

Chronic GVHD affects 20% to 40% of matched-sibling HCT recipients and resembles a collagen vascular disease involving skin, liver, eyes, mouth, upper respiratory tract, esophagus, and, less frequently, serosal surfaces, female genitalia, and fascia (Fig 22-5).[126] An NIH Consensus project developed a detailed staging system for chronic GVHD in which 12 organ systems are graded from 0 (no symptoms) to 3 (severe involvement), and these 12 scores are then combined into an NIH Global Severity Score of chronic GVHD, as shown in Table 22-6.[127]

Chronic GVHD is seen more frequently with HLA mismatching, with the use of peripheral-blood stem cells instead of marrow, among older patients and among patients who have had prior episodes of acute GVHD. If chronic GVHD develops while the calcineurin inhibitor is being tapered, increasing the inhibitor to therapeutic levels may be effective. Mild, chronic GVHD can sometimes be managed using local therapies alone (eg, topical steroids to the skin, cyclosporine eye drops). More severe disease is usually treated with prednisone alone or in combination with a calcineurin inhibitor, which can control chronic GVHD in 50% to 70% of cases. Randomized trials exploring alternative approaches to primary therapy have so far failed to identify a better approach.[109] Patients for whom primary treatment of chronic GVHD fails are sometimes treated with mycophenolate mofetil, sirolimus, extracorporeal photopheresis, rituximab, or low-dose interleukin-2. Ruxolitinib has also been used for chronic GVHD.[127-129] Because B and T cells play a role in the pathogenesis of chronic GVHD, the BTK inhibitor ibrutinib was studied and ultimately received US Food and Drug Administration (FDA) approval for chronic GVHD after failure of one or more lines of systemic therapy.[130] Eventually, immunosuppression can be tapered and discontinued in 80% to 90% of patients, but it may require many months to several years of immunosuppression before tolerance develops. The median duration of treatment is 2 to 3 years. Bacterial infection frequently occurs in patients with chronic GVHD, and prophylactic treatment with antibiotics should be administered while patients are receiving immunosuppressive therapy. A commonly used regimen includes trimethoprim and sulfamethoxazole plus penicillin, which provides protection against both *Pneumocystis jirovecii* and encapsulated organisms. Antifungal prophylaxis varies widely among centers but may include fluconazole, posaconazole, or voriconazole.

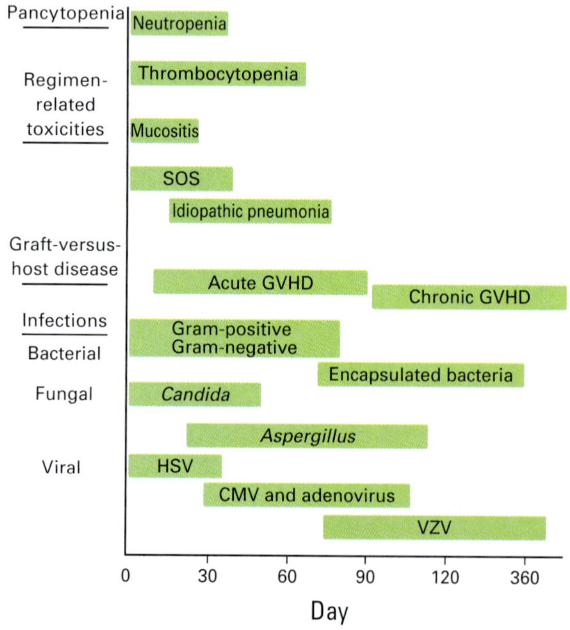

Fig. 22-4 The approximate timing of possible toxicities after allogeneic transplantation using a typical intensive preparative regimen.

Abbreviations: CMV, cytomegalovirus; GVHD, graft-versus-host disease; HSV, herpes simplex virus; SOS, sinusoidal obstruction syndrome; VZV, varicella zoster virus.

Autoimmune Disorders

After allogeneic HCT, an autoimmune disorder will develop in 3% to 5% of cases, most commonly autoimmune hemolytic anemia or idiopathic thrombocytopenia purpura. Unrelated

Table 22-6 **National Institutes of Health Global Severity of Chronic GVHD**[127]

Mild Chronic GVHD	Moderate Chronic GVHD	Severe Chronic GVHD
One or two organs involved with no more than a score of 1+	Three or more organs involved with no more than a score of 1	At least one organ with a score of 3
Lung score of 0	OR	OR
	At least one organ (not lung) with a score of 2	Lung score of 2 or 3
	OR	
	Lung score of 1	

Abbreviation: GVHD, graft-versus-host disease.

donor source and chronic GVHD are risk factors. Treatment is with cyclosporine, prednisone, or rituximab.[131]

KEY POINTS

- GVHD results from T cells in the donor graft reacting with allogeneic targets on the genetically different host.
- Biomarker approaches for diagnosis and risk stratification are under study.
- ATG reduces rates of acute and chronic GVHD.
- Ibrutinib may be used for chronic GVHD after failure of one prior therapy.

INFECTIOUS COMPLICATIONS

Infection is a major risk for nearly all transplant recipients. Recipients of autologous transplants are at risk for the early bacterial and fungal infections common to all patients with granulocytopenia. Recipients of allogeneic hematopoietic grafts, particularly patients in whom GVHD develops, also are at risk for late-onset bacterial, fungal, and viral diseases.

Bacterial and Fungal Infections

During the early neutropenic period after HCT, patients are likely to become febrile, and in approximately 50% of patients who are febrile neutropenic, a bacterial source can be identified. Before engraftment, fluoroquinolone is often administered if myeloablative conditioning regimens were used. After engraftment, antibiotic prophylaxis is typically discontinued, but patients remaining at risk for infection may receive antibiotics including penicillin and trimethoprim-sulfamethoxazole. Prophylaxis against fungal pathogens has been shown to reduce rates of fungal infection and improve OS.[132] Prophylaxis with fluconazole is generally recommended for patients at standard risk, whereas prophylaxis with a mold-active agent should be considered for patients with higher-risk disease, including patients with a prior fungal infection or recipients of a cord-blood or unrelated-donor transplant.[133] Although approaches vary, one standard approach is to continue fungal prophylaxis for 75 days after allogeneic HCT and until resolution of neutropenia after autologous HCT. Although having a prior invasive fungal infection increases transplant risk, with current methods of prophylaxis, it should not be considered a contraindication for HCT.[134] Patients who become or remain febrile despite treatment with broad-spectrum antibiotics and who have no obvious source of infection usually are treated with additional antifungal agents (eg, voriconazole, isavuconazole micafungin, or amphotericin lipid formulation, depending on the clinical situation). Recipients of cord-blood transplants sometime have "cord colitis," a syndrome of diarrhea responsive to metronidazole, alone or in combination with a fluoroquinolone.[135] Molecular studies suggest *Bradyrhizobium enterica* as the causative agent.[136]

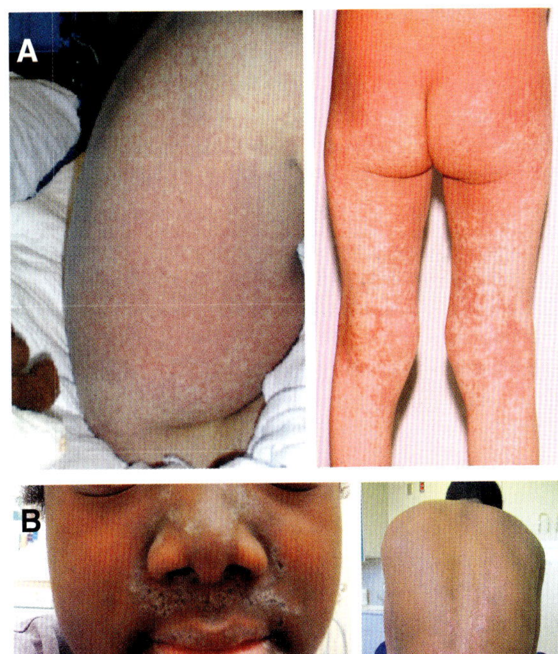

Fig. 22-5 Acute and chronic graft-versus-host disease of the skin.[126]

Acute GVHD classically develops within the first 3 months after allogeneic HCT and typically presents with (A) an erythematous or maculopapular rash. (B) Chronic GVHD develops sometime after the first 3 months, often presenting with cutaneous manifestations, including atrophic changes with depigmentation, lichen-planus–like lesions, and development of sclerotic features.

With current methods of supportive care, the risk of death as a result of infection during the early granulocytopenic period after HCT is < 3% for recipients of either allogeneic or autologous transplants. Protective environment rooms incorporate the use of high-efficiency particulate air filters with 99.97% efficiency for removing particles > 0.3 mm to minimize risk of infections from spores.

Herpes Simplex Infection

Herpes simplex infection, which can contribute to the severity of oral mucositis, can be prevented with the use of systemic acyclovir 250 mg/m^2 every 8 to 12 hours intravenously, beginning during conditioning and continuing for 1 month after HCT.[137] At many centers, acyclovir is continued for up to 1 year to prevent late infection or reactivation with varicella zoster virus (VZV) and often continued even longer in patients receiving immunosuppression therapy. The new zoster vaccine containing VZV glycoprotein E and the ASo1B adjuvant system was evaluated in a phase III trial that included patients who had an autologous transplant. It demonstrated favorable efficacy and safety. This finding led to the addition of this vaccine to the postautologous transplant immunization schedule. Its safety and efficacy in allogeneic transplant is still unknown.[138]

CMV Infection

In the past, symptomatic CMV infection, which typically involves either the GI tract or the lungs, occurred in approximately 25% of patients who received allogeneic transplants and led to death (typically from CMV pneumonia) in 10% to 15% of patients. The improvement in control and prevention of CMV in hematopoietic cell HCT has had one of the biggest impacts on improvement in OS. The initial approach was a preemptive strategy using bronchoscopy at day +35 in all allogeneic transplant recipients and treating patients positive for CMV with ganciclovir.[139] With the advent of more sensitive blood screening methods such as polymerase chain reaction, this approach was abandoned.

A randomized trial evaluated the prophylactic use of ganciclovir until day 100 after transplant and ultimately showed no difference in CMV disease by day 180 and similar OS. In addition, patients in the ganciclovir arm had a higher incidence of fungal and bacterial infections.[140] Hence, preemptive therapy using blood polymerase chain reaction monitoring is standard practice and not prophylactic therapy. However, even with this approach, early CMV reactivation remains associated with increased mortality.[141] Letermovir, an oral agent that inhibits CMV replication, was studied in a placebo-controlled trial in which fewer patients in the letermovir group had clinically significant CMV infection (37.5% *v* 60.6% in the control group). It was well tolerated and did not have the myelotoxic effects associated with ganciclovir; moreover, it offers a small survival advantage. Hence, the use of letermovir has been approved for prophylaxis in seropositive recipients after transplant until day 100. Extended use may also be considered in high-risk patients.[142]

Prophylactic ganciclovir generally is not recommended for patients who have an allogeneic transplant, except for cases in which T cells are removed from the stem cell inoculum. Foscarnet is effective for some patients in the context of ganciclovir resistance as well as for patients who cannot tolerate ganciclovir. Foscarnet, however, can be associated with severe electrolyte wasting and renal compromise.

Pneumonia

Pneumonia resulting from infection with *Pneumocystis jirovecii*, previously seen in 5%–10% of transplant recipients, can be prevented by treatment with oral trimethoprim/sulfamethoxazole for 1 week before HCT, with resumption of prophylaxis once the granulocyte count exceeds 0.5 × 10^3/μL. Treatment 2 days per week while patients are receiving immunosuppressive drugs after HCT usually is sufficient to prevent *Pneumocystis* disease. Allergic reactions to trimethoprim/sulfamethoxazole are common, and dapsone or atovaquone can serve as a substitute for trimethoprim/sulfamethoxazole.

Community-Acquired Viral Infections

Community-acquired viral infections, including respiratory syncytial virus (RSV), influenza virus, and parainfluenza virus, can cause lethal pneumonias in the transplant patient. Patients with upper respiratory symptoms before HCT should be screened by nasopharyngeal lavage for viral infections before proceeding to HCT. If RSV, influenza virus, or parainfluenza virus is found, HCT should be delayed. Ribavirin and anti-RSV antibody, although unproven, are used by some centers in treating established RSV infection in the transplant patient.

Vaccine-Preventable Disease

Antibody titers to vaccine-preventable diseases decline after allogeneic or autologous HCT if the recipient is not revaccinated. Therefore, posttransplantation revaccination against influenza, *Haemophilus influenzae*, meningococcus, pneumococcus, polio, diphtheria, tetanus, pertussis, hepatitis A and B, and human papillomavirus is generally recommended.[143] The choice of vaccine and schedule may vary depending on patient age, underlying diagnosis, and amount of continuing immunosuppression. Therefore, although several guidelines have been written, the decisions of who, when, and how to vaccinate should be made in consultation with infectious-disease experts and institutional transplant guidelines.[144]

KEY POINTS

- Fungal infections can be prevented and survival improved with the use of antifungal prophylaxis during the first few months after HCT.
- Letermovir prophylaxis can reduce the incidence of CMV infection.
- Patients should be screened for viral infections; a positive result may be cause for delaying HCT.
- Revaccination after HCT is generally recommended.

CHEMORADIOTHERAPY TOXICITIES

After most standard preparative regimens, immediate toxic effects, such as nausea, vomiting, fever, and mild skin erythema, are common. Unusual toxic effects associated with high-dose cyclophosphamide include hemorrhagic cystitis and, rarely, acute hemorrhagic carditis. Parotiditis commonly is seen among patients undergoing total-body irradiation therapy.

Oral mucositis requiring narcotic analgesia typically develops 5 to 7 days after HCT using high-dose preparative regimens. Patient-controlled analgesia provides the greatest patient satisfaction and results in lower cumulative doses of narcotics. Keratinocyte growth factor (palifermin) significantly shortens the duration of severe mucositis after high-dose autologous HCT regimens and is recommended for use in this setting.[145,146] However, palifermin is not currently indicated for patients with nonhematologic malignancies, it does not decrease mucositis when myelotoxic therapy is used, and it is not recommended for use with single-agent melphalan conditioning.

SOS can develop within 1 to 4 weeks after treatment with many high-dose preparative regimens as well as treatment with antibodies conjugated with calicheamicin (ie, inotuzumab ozogamicin, gemtuzumab ozogamicin), and its symptoms include weight gain, ascites, tender hepatomegaly, and jaundice. The overall incidence of SOS is approximately 5%, but the incidence and grade vary according to the preparative regimen. In general, the incidence is higher for patients with abnormal results of liver-function tests before HCT and for patients with an active infection at the time of HCT.[147] Defibrotide, a mixture of single-stranded oligonucleotides (not generally recognized as the dominant mechanism of action), has been approved by the FDA for treatment of SOS on the basis of retrospective, controlled trials.[148] Results of a randomized trial suggest defibrotide may also be effective if used prophylactically.[149] Prophylaxis with ursodeoxycholic acid may decrease the incidence of SOS, and randomized studies have shown decreased rates of acute GVHD and improved survival.[150]

Idiopathic pneumonia syndrome (IPS), which is thought to be a toxicity directly related to chemoradiotherapy, occurs 30 to 90 days after HCT in up to 5% of patients. As with other toxicities, the incidence of IPS depends, in part, on the preparative regimen, occurring more frequently after administration of regimens that include high doses of total-body irradiation. Preexisting lung disease, prior radiation therapy to the thorax, and older age also seem to be associated with an increased risk of IPS, whereas fractionated radiation instead of single-dose radiation appears to decrease this risk. The mortality rate associated with IPS is approximately 50%, and no available treatments are clearly effective, although early results with tumor necrosis factor blockade appear to be favorable.[151]

Two categories of chronic pulmonary dysfunction are seen among patients who survive longer than 3 months after allogeneic HCT: restrictive lung disease and obstructive lung disease. The most common cause of restrictive disease is cryptogenic organizing pneumonia, which is characterized by a dry cough, shortness of breath, fever, and radiographic findings showing a diffuse, fluffy infiltrate. Histology shows patchy fibrosis, granulation tissue within alveolar spaces and small airways, and absence of an infectious agent. The disease is quite responsive to corticosteroids and may reverse completely.[152] Bronchiolitis obliterans is an obstructive defect characterized by progressive dyspnea, nonproductive cough, and radiologic evidence of airway trapping.[153] Histology shows enhanced deposition of collagen and granulation tissue in and around bronchial structures and eventual obliteration of small airways.[152] The disease is the pulmonary manifestation of chronic GVHD. Management generally involves increasing immunosuppression. Preliminary results with a combination of fluticasone, azithromycin, and montelukast appear encouraging. However, more recent updates, such as the ALLOZITHRO study, suggest increased risk of hematologic malignancy relapse in the azithromycin arm, leading to an FDA alert against its use as prophylaxis against bronchiolitis obliterans.[154,155]

LATE EFFECTS AND LONG-TERM SURVIVORSHIP

The cumulative therapeutic exposure associated with HCT conditioning can injure normal tissue and result in premature onset of health conditions such as cardiac disease, secondary neoplasms, and musculoskeletal abnormalities. The 15-year cumulative incidence of chronic health conditions exceeds 40% in recipients of a hematopoietic cell transplant.[156-159]

Delayed complications attributable to the preparative regimen include decreased growth velocity in children and delayed development of secondary sexual characteristics. Most postpubescent women will experience ovarian failure, and few men regain spermatogenesis after HCT using high-dose preparative regimens. However, occasional patients will regain fertility after even myeloablative conditioning regimens, and patients should be counseled about this possibility.[108] Cataracts occur in as many as one-third of patients, with an increased risk among patients receiving high doses of total-body irradiation and patients requiring steroids for treatment of GVHD. Thyroid dysfunction, usually well compensated, also may occur. Patients treated with high-dose chemoradiotherapy and HCT are at an increased risk for the development of second cancers and posttransplantation lymphoproliferative disorders (PTLDs). The risk for Epstein-Barr virus–associated PTLD is highest for patients receiving T-cell–depleted allogeneic transplants and for patients who receive multiple cycles of highly immunosuppressive drugs to treat GVHD.[109] An increase in occurrence of solid tumors has been reported after HCT, with a 3% 10-year cumulative rate, which is two to three times the age-adjusted rate in the general population. A high incidence of MDS (nearly 10%) has been reported after autologous HCT for lymphoma, and an increased risk has been seen in patients treated with lenalidomide maintenance after autologous transplant for myeloma,[160,161] but whether MDS is a complication of HCT or is the long-term effect of chemotherapy used before HCT is unknown.[110]

There have been no randomized trials in this area, and most of the guidelines are developed by consensus.[162] In general, an approach based on patients' risk factors, which, in part, include the type of transplant and transplant conditioning, is recommended. In general, this situation necessitates increased awareness of risk, such as cardiovascular disease, which is one of the leading causes of nonrelapse mortality.[163] Monitoring for gonadal dysfunction and osteoporosis and screening for secondary neoplasms are also recommended.

KEY POINTS

- Common chemoradiotherapy toxicities include nausea, vomiting, fever, and mild skin erythema. High-dose regimens may lead to oral mucositis.
- SOS and IPS are serious potential complications requiring careful clinical management.
- Keratinocyte growth factor (palifermin) may significantly reduce the duration and severity of oral mucositis after intensive chemo- or radiotherapy.
- As survival improves for HCT recipients, additional attention should be paid to long-term complications, especially cardiovascular disease and endocrine effects.

RELAPSE AFTER TRANSPLANTATION

There is a substantial risk of recurrent malignant disease after HCT, particularly when HCT is performed after failure of conventional therapy rather than earlier in the course of the disease. The appropriate treatment of patients who do have a relapse after HCT depends on the disease and type of transplant. Patients whose disease recurs after autologous HCT may have a response to subsequent chemotherapy, and occasionally such responses are surprisingly complete and prolonged, particularly if the duration of remission after HCT was long. Newer agents such as targeted antibody therapy or checkpoint inhibitors can be used for relapses after autologous transplant and may induce responses that then serve as a bridge to allogeneic transplant.[164-166] In addition, reduced-intensity allogeneic HCT is tolerable for patients whose disease relapsed after an autologous HCT.[167]

On occasion, patients taking immunosuppressive drugs who have recurrent disease after allogeneic HCT will have a second complete remission after discontinuation of immunosuppressive therapy. Infusions of viable lymphocytes from the original stem cell donors (donor leukocyte infusion [DLI]) can result in complete remission for many patients. In a European study involving 135 patients, the rate of complete response was 70% for patients with chronic-phase CML, 12% for patients with advanced-phase CML, 29% for patients with AML or MDS, and 0% for patients with ALL.[88] Results of a small study suggest better OS with TKIs than with DLI, representing another option for CML relapse after allogeneic HCT.[168] Occasionally, patients with myeloma and NHL also have a response. Most experts recommend patients with recurrent acute leukemia undergo reinduction chemotherapy before DLI to decrease the leukemia cell burden and provide sufficient time for a graft-versus-leukemia (GVL) effect to develop. Some form of GVHD develops in approximately 60% of patients after infusion of donor lymphocytes; of those patients, 50% require therapy for GVHD and 15% experience life-threatening GVHD. In addition, marrow aplasia occurs in 35% of patients, and the overall mortality associated with infusion of donor lymphocytes is 20%. Limiting the dose of CD3+ lymphocytes to $< 10 \times 10^7$ can decrease the risk of GVHD and life-threatening complications without impairing the GVL effect.[169] Chimeric antigen receptor (CAR) CD19 is effective in the treatment of patients with ALL who have experienced a relapse after HCT (discussed in the next section).[170] Responses have also been seen after treatment with ipilimumab, but immune-mediated toxicity and GVHD flares were also seen.[171]

A number of patients have had a second allogeneic HCT as treatment of relapse after the first HCT. Such HCTs, if performed within 1 year of the original HCT, have been associated with a high risk of severe or fatal transplant-related toxicities, including SOS and idiopathic interstitial pneumonia. However, the results are more favorable when the second HCT is performed more than 1 year after the original HCT, with prolonged subsequent remissions reported for as many as 25% of patients.[167] Retrospective studies show similar outcomes whether the same donor is used as for the first HCT or a switch is made to a different donor.[172]

APPROACHES TO REDUCE RELAPSE AFTER TRANSPLANTATION

In general, HCT is delivered with a curative intent. However, relapse remains a leading cause of treatment failure after HCT, and the prognosis of hematologic malignancies that relapsed after HCT is extremely poor, particularly after allogeneic HCT. Therefore, there have been a number of approaches used to prevent posttransplant relapses, such as intensification of conditioning regimens, consolidation therapies, and maintenance therapies.

In an attempt to intensity conditioning regimens, CD20-targeting radioimmunotherapy (RIT) such as ^{131}I-tositumumab and ^{90}Y-ibritumomab has been used in combination with standard carmustine, etoposide, cytarabine, and melphalan (BEAM) or cyclophosphamide, carmustine, and etoposide regimens for NHL in phase I/II trials with promising results.[173-176] A large phase III trial comparing BEAM plus ^{131}I-tositumumab versus rituximab, however, showed no added benefit of ^{131}I-tositumumab in event-free survival or OS.[177] Novel conditioning therapies in allogeneic HCT have been evaluated in single-arm studies in allogeneic HCT, including incorporation of newer chemotherapeutic agents (ie, clofarabine, bendamustine),[178,179] CD45 targeting radioimmunotherapy,[180] and dose-intensified total-marrow irradiation.[181]

In multiple myeloma, consolidation therapy and maintenance therapy have been extensively studied, partly because of the limitation of single autologous HCT with a high rate of relapse. Nonmyeloablative allogeneic HCT as a consolidation therapy after standard autologous HCT was evaluated by a few groups with mixed results.[28,182,183] A recent, large clinical trial supported by the Blood and Marrow Transplant Clinical Trial Network (trial no. 0702) demonstrated that second autologous HCT (tandem auto) or a combination of lenalidomide, bortezomib, and dexamethasone consolidation was not associated with improved PFS or OS.[184] In myeloma, maintenance therapy after autologous HCT using lenalidomide improves PFS and OS and remains the standard therapy.[161,185] A phase III trial (SWOG1803) is currently evaluating daratumumab plus lenalidomide versus lenalidomide as postautologous HCT in patients with myeloma.

In lymphoma, the most commonly studied agent for post-HCT maintenance is rituximab. A phase III trial in recurrent large-cell lymphoma did not show an advantage in relapse-free survival or OS,[186] and a study in follicular lymphoma demonstrated an improvement in PFS without a difference in OS.[187] In mantle cell lymphoma, a randomized trial showed improved PFS and OS.[188] Brentuximab vedotin was evaluated in Hodgkin lymphoma after HCT, which demonstrated improved PFS with no increase in OS, leading to an FDA approval for this indication.[189] More recently, checkpoint inhibitors are being evaluated in this setting, with promising data.[190]

The role of maintenance therapy after allogeneic HCT has not been well defined. Low-dose 5-azacitidine, a hypomethylating agent, has been evaluated in a phase I trial as a maintenance therapy starting at 6 weeks after HCT, establishing an optimal dosing schedule with a promising 1-year OS rate of 77%.[191] Although TKIs have been widely used as maintenance after allogeneic HCT for Philadelphia chromosome–positive ALL, the associated data are largely from single-arm trials or retrospective registry data. An earlier study demonstrated the safety and feasibility of imatinib.[192] Large registry studies evaluating the efficacy of TKIs as maintenance therapy after allogeneic HCT showed conflicting results in that the cumulative incidence of relapse was not different between patients who received TKI and did not receive TKI in a CIBMTR study,[193] whereas an European Society for Blood and Marrow Program (EBMT) study showed an association between the use of TKIs and lower rates of relapse and improved leukemia-free survival and OS.[194] For AML with FMS-like tyrosine kinase 3 (*FLT3*)-internal tandem duplication, a number of *FLT3* TKIs are being evaluated as maintenance after allogeneic HCT, including sorafenib, quizartinib, and gilteritinib.[195-197] Checkpoint inhibitors are also being investigated as a potential maintenance therapy or preemptive therapy after allogeneic HCT,[198] with a potential risk for GVHD and immune-mediated toxicities.

KEY POINT

- Patients who experience a relapse after allogeneic HCT often respond to subsequent immunologic manipulation, including withdrawal of immunosuppression, donor lymphocyte infusions, and treatment with checkpoint inhibitors.

CAR T CELLS FOR HEMATOLOGIC MALIGNANCIES

CAR T-cell–directed therapy also falls under the same roof as HCT in that the intent is to use a cellular-based therapy to augment immune responses to treat hematologic malignancies. Indeed, one can consider the use of allogeneic donor lymphocytes infusions in relapsed leukemia as the first example of adoptive immune cell transfer.[199] Subsequently, gene transfer techniques allowed researchers to redirect the specificity of the T cells to specific antigens. The challenge with this approach is that, although adaptive immunity mediated by T and B lymphocytes is antigen specific, most of the tumor antigens are also self antigens expressed on normal tissues. Hence, natural immune responses have evolved to prevent autoimmunity. T-cell engineering to augment T-cell responses is a way to overcome this natural immune tolerance.

The foundation of CAR T-cell therapy (CAR-T) was "second-generation cells" that included both the T-cell activating domain and chimeric costimulatory receptors to enhance proliferation and expansion of the T cells. The first experience in hematologic malignancy was CD19 targeting for ALL. Subsequently, several trials have shown response rates of up to approximately 90% in adults and children with relapsed ALL.[200,201] Trials in chronic lymphocytic leukemia and NHL have also demonstrated responses including complete remissions in a substantial proportion of patients with lymphoma.[202,203] Subsequently, commercial CAR-T constructs, so-called living drugs, have been approved in the United States for relapsed and/or refractory ALL in patients up to age 25 years and in all patients with relapsed or refractory B-cell NHL after two prior lines of therapy.

The success of this approach in CD19-directed malignancies led to new constructs for other diseases such as a B-cell maturation antigen targeting approach for multiple myeloma. Although there is no FDA-approved CAR-T for myeloma yet, several phase I trials have shown response rates in the 80% range for heavily pretreated patients. However, durability of these responses seem less than that in NHL.[204]

The CAR-T products also bring unique toxicities, different from those from checkpoint inhibitors or other immune activators. B-cell aplasia was a predicted on-target effect of CD19-directed CAR-T, which, in turn, leads to long-term weaker humoral immunity. A effect seen across all CAR-T is a clinical syndrome dubbed cytokine-release syndrome (CRS), characterized by elevations in levels of serum cytokines (eg, IL6, interferon-γ) and clinically manifested as fevers, hypotension, and, in severe cases, capillary leakage and hypoxia. The FDA-approved tocilizumab is an anti-IL6 receptor antagonist for treatment of CAR-T–induced CRS.[205]

Immune effector cell–associated neurotoxicity syndrome (ICANS) is another unique complication of CAR-T across all targets. The early manifestations are usually tremor, dysgraphia, and mild expressive aphasia, especially with naming objects. There may also be decreased levels of consciousness that can be progressive from mild lethargy to complete obtundation.[206] Management includes diagnostic workup to rule out seizures and imaging of the brain to rule out cerebral edema. The use of levetiracetam, either prophylactically or after the onset of ICANS, and dexamethasone are recommended. Tocilizumab is not effective in the absence of CRS.

Last, prolonged cytopenias are common, likely related to ongoing CAR-T activity and direct immune effects to the bone marrow. This toxicity is managed with supportive care including growth factors, transfusions, and antibiotic and antiviral prophylaxis.

In short, CAR-T has opened a new set of options for patients with relapsed hematologic malignancies. They have unique toxicities; hence, it is important that oncologists gain awareness about the indications as well as the grading and management of these toxicities, because it is anticipated that this technology will be applied to more malignancies in the future.

Acknowledgment

The following author is acknowledged and graciously thanked for his contribution to prior versions of this chapter: Frederick R. Appelbaum, MD, FASCO. Dr. James Sanchez also is recognized for his editorial support in the preparation of the chapter.

Global Perspective: Cellular Therapies (Asia Perspective)

Li Mei Michelle Poon, MBBS, MRCP (National University Cancer Institute, Singapore)

Hematopoietic stem cell transplantation (HSCT) is a potentially curative treatment modality for a wide variety of malignant and nonmalignant disorders. Since the first transplant performed in the 1950s, there have been > 1 million transplants worldwide, with annual numbers of between 60,000 to 70,000 transplants and with increasing frequency over the years.[207,208] Over the past few decades, there has been significant progress in the field of transplantation, including improvements in supportive care, novel technologies allowing the increased use of alternative donor sources, and improvement in infrastructure.

HSCT trends and practices differ among countries and depend on disease prevalence and socioeconomic situations among the different regions. In the Asia-Pacific region, there appear to be vast differences among the countries in terms of economic and sociocultural background. Models of health care also vary markedly among the different countries. This has led to differing practices in HSCT in this region compared with the United States or Europe. Recognizing this, the Asia-Pacific Blood and Marrow Transplantation Group (APBMT) was established in 1990 to promote HSCT in the region. Since then, the group has gone on to include 21 countries or regions (Australia, Bangladesh, Cambodia, China, Hong Kong, India, Indonesia, Iran, Japan, Korea, Malaysia, Mongolia, Myanmar, New Zealand, Pakistan, the Philippines, Singapore, Sri Lanka, Taiwan, Thailand, and Vietnam). Through its registry and data center, the APBMT has been able to provide standardized HSCT activity data to the Worldwide Network for Blood and Marrow Transplantation (WBMT), allowing current perspective on transplant activity, trends and contemporary HSCT practices in the region.[209] This global perspective provides an overview of the current state of HSCT in the Asian region and explores the differences in donor selection, transplant procedures, and disease indications in the region compared with the United States.

ESTABLISHMENT OF HSCT PROGRAMS WITHIN ASIA

Setting up a specialized health care service such as HCT is often a labor- and resource-intensive endeavor. For HSCT programs, establishment and maintenance can be a challenge for some developing Asian countries due to the resources needed. Obstacles faced by these new transplant services include the limited training of staff, the cost of developing adequate hospital infrastructure and facilities, and the lack of standard procedures. The low per capita income for residents in these countries also limits the accessibility of HSCT to a selected proportion of patients. Through initiatives such as the publication of minimum requirements guidelines for safe and sustainable functioning of HSCT programs, mentoring schemes allowing trainees to be guided in more established centers within the region, and through regular educational programs and meetings, groups such as the APBMT and WBMT, among others, have helped increase the numbers of transplantation centers within the developing nations in Asia.[210] These efforts, as well as constant growth within established centers, have led to a marked increase in the number of HSCTs done in the Asia-Pacific region, with a survey by the APBMT in 2015 showing nearly a two-fold increase in HSCTs done within the region over the last decade (from an annual rate of approximately 7,000 transplants in 2005 to current rates of about approximately in 2015).[211] In addition, several studies from regional centers have shown that improvements in infrastructure and supportive and overall medical care have resulted in a significant improvement in survival over the last two to three decades.[212]

DIFFERENCES IN CLINICAL PRACTICES WITHIN HCT PROGRAMS

HCT is a complex treatment modality and is highly resource intensive. Clinical practices and trends of HCT are different among countries and reflect the differences in disease prevalence, infection epidemiology, HLA diversity, and cultural and economic situations in these countries.

PATIENT POPULATION INFECTION ISSUES

There are several infective complications that are more prevalent within the Asian population. This poses challenges unique to physicians practicing in this region compared with the United States. Among these, *Mycobacterium tuberculosis* (MTB), an aerobic, acid-fast, nonspore-forming nonmotile bacillus that can lead to pulmonary or extrapulmonary tuberculosis infections, is one of the organisms that has a higher rate of reactivation in an immunocompromised host. Of note, the incidence of MTB infection is extremely low in the United States (0.0014%), whereas it is much higher (4% to 9%) in endemic areas in Asia.[212] Therefore, doctors in the region must be cognizant of this potential infection and perform the appropriate investigations when evaluating these suspected cases. Similarly, viral infections such as chronic hepatitis B are endemic in Asia, and there are a significantly higher proportion of hepatitis B virus carriers in Asia compared with the United States.

DISEASE INDICATIONS

There are significant differences in the disease indications for HSCT, not just between Asia and United States, but also between the developing lower-income countries compared with the developed countries within the Asia region. There are several explanations for this. First, there are inherent differences in disease prevalence within countries in the Asian region, as well as compared with the United States. For example, thalassemia, a hemoglobinopathy, is common in south and southeast Asia but rare in northeast Asia and the United States, and a high proportion of HSCTs for this disorder was noted in countries in the former region compared with the latter.[209] The socioeconomic background for countries also affects the focus of their HSCT programs. Economically disadvantaged countries, for example, tend to focus on nonmalignant conditions associated with more favorable cost-benefit evaluations rather than malignant conditions that need expensive and intensive pretreatment and may be associated with poorer outcomes.[207]

DONOR SELECTION AND STEM CELL SOURCE:

Donors for allogeneic transplantation include matched, related donors, matched unrelated donors, mismatched unrelated donors (haploidentical transplantation), and cord-blood transplants. Choice of donor varies among the developing countries compared with the developed countries within Asia, and in the United States. Sociocultural aspects that affect family size, such as the one-child policy in China, may affect the availability of matched, related donors. For matched unrelated donors, the size of the donor pool and the activity of the donor program within each country are important. In Asian countries such as China and Japan, the inherently limited HLA diversities within the population and the establishment of robust marrow-donor programs have allowed for an increase in unrelated transplants in the last two decades.[213,214] Economic strengths of countries also impact on the donor selection. For example, matched unrelated-donors transplants are usually costlier than matched, related-donor transplants, because of the cost of donor selection, coordination and shipping of products; registry data from the Asia-Pacific region and Europe have confirmed the lower rates of unrelated HCTs countries with lower incomes.[209,215] Until recently, the use of alternative donor transplants such as haploidentical transplants was also limited to developed countries with robust economies, given the prohibitive costs of in vitro stem cell manipulations and the prolonged and costly supportive care needed. This has changed with the emerging technologies for haploidentical transplants, such as the posttransplant cyclophosphamide method pioneered at Johns Hopkins University, and the Beijing method, allowing for affordable, in vivo T-cell depletion.[208] A global survey done by the WBMT in 2012[207] showed an increase in the proportion of haploidentical transplants from 6% in 2006 to 10% in 2012 after the adoption of these new technologies.

QUALITY CONTROL WITHIN HCT PROGRAMS

Delineation of clear quality measures and consistent tracking of these parameters, as well as compliance with clear quality control principles, are essential requirements for HSCT centers seeking to improve their practices. Data reporting to registries such as the CIBMTR and the EBMT are some ways in which quality measures can be tracked. In addition, large professional societies such as the Joint Accreditation Committee-International Society for Cellular Therapy and European Society for Blood and Marrow Transplantation (JACIE) and the Foundation for the Accreditation of Cellular Therapy (FACT) have developed international standards providing guidance for practice by HSCT programs.

Recent data have also suggested that treatment in accredited centers results in superior relapse-free survival (HR, 0.85; 95% CI, 0.75 to 0.95) and OS (HR, 0.86; 95% CI, 0.76 to 0.98) in allogeneic transplant recipients.[216] As a result, these registries and practice standards have become an integral part of the quality program for many of the established HSCT programs worldwide. In the United States, for example, the reporting of outcome measures of every allogeneic HSCT is mandated by the Stem Cell Therapeutic and Research Act of 2005. In addition, FACT accreditation is embraced by the overwhelming majority of transplant programs and > 90% of HSCT programs in the United States are FACT accredited. In Asia, however, there has been a gradual recognition of the importance of these programs and increasing participation only in recent years. Currently, several Asian centers, including Hong Kong, Taiwan, Thailand, South Korea, Japan, China, and Singapore report to the CIBMTR. In addition, centers in Singapore have also participated in and attained JACIE and FACT accreditation, attesting to the increasing appreciation of the importance of these accreditation programs in improving treatment standards. The APBMT group has also tried to reach out to new and developing HSCT centers and, through support with surveys and data collection for the APMBT registry, help track quality outcomes and measures in the field.

In conclusion, HSCT remains a resource-intensive treatment modality and a challenge in Asia because of the high cost of establishment and maintenance. The development of large donor programs, establishment of the Asia-Pacific data registry, the establishment of mentoring programs between countries in the region and the embracement of new transplant technologies (eg, the use of novel methods for haploidentical transplants to overcome cost limitations) have enabled an increase in the numbers of HSCTs in the region over the past decade. Despite the differences in transplantation practices, the collaborative work between the APBMT with various partners under the auspices of the WBMT, and the gradual involvement of more established programs with internationally recognized quality management programs, will allow for continued improvement and excellence by Asian countries in the field of stem cell transplantation, stem cell donation, and cellular therapy.

INDEX

Note: Page numbers followed by f and t indicate figures and tables, respectively.

B

C

H

I

P

T

U